The Editor

NICHOLAS HALMI is University Lecturer in English Literature of the Romantic Period at the University of Oxford and Margaret Candfield Fellow of University College, Oxford. He is the author of *The Genealogy of the Romantic Symbol* (2007) and numerous articles on British and German Romanticism, editor of *Fearful Symmetry: A Study of William Blake* in the *Collected Works of Northrop Frye* (2004), co-editor (with Paul Magnuson and Raimonda Modiano) of the Norton Critical Edition of *Coleridge's Poetry and Prose* (2003), textual editor of the *Opus Maximum* in *The Collected Works of Samuel Taylor Coleridge* (2002), and an advisory editor of Oxford Scholarly Editions Online.

W. W. NORTON & COMPANY, INC.
Also Publishes

ENGLISH RENAISSANCE DRAMA: A NORTON ANTHOLOGY
edited by David Bevington et al.

THE NORTON ANTHOLOGY OF AFRICAN AMERICAN LITERATURE
edited by Henry Louis Gates Jr. and Nellie Y. McKay et al.

THE NORTON ANTHOLOGY OF AMERICAN LITERATURE
edited by Nina Baym and Robert Levine et al.

THE NORTON ANTHOLOGY OF CHILDREN'S LITERATURE
edited by Jack Zipes et al.

THE NORTON ANTHOLOGY OF DRAMA
edited by J. Ellen Gainor, Stanton B. Garner Jr., and Martin Puchner

THE NORTON ANTHOLOGY OF ENGLISH LITERATURE
edited by Stephen Greenblatt et al.

THE NORTON ANTHOLOGY OF LATINO LITERATURE
edited by Ilan Stavans et al.

THE NORTON ANTHOLOGY OF LITERATURE BY WOMEN
edited by Sandra M. Gilbert and Susan Gubar

THE NORTON ANTHOLOGY OF MODERN AND CONTEMPORARY POETRY
edited by Jahan Ramazani, Richard Ellmann, and Robert O'Clair

THE NORTON ANTHOLOGY OF POETRY
edited by Margaret Ferguson, Mary Jo Salter, and Jon Stallworthy

THE NORTON ANTHOLOGY OF SHORT FICTION
edited by R. V. Cassill and Richard Bausch

THE NORTON ANTHOLOGY OF THEORY AND CRITICISM
edited by Vincent B. Leitch et al.

THE NORTON ANTHOLOGY OF WORLD LITERATURE
edited by Martin Puchner et al.

THE NORTON FACSIMILE OF THE FIRST FOLIO OF SHAKESPEARE
prepared by Charlton Hinman

THE NORTON INTRODUCTION TO LITERATURE
edited by Kelly J. Mays

THE NORTON READER
edited by Linda H. Peterson and John C. Brereton et al.

THE NORTON SAMPLER
edited by Thomas Cooley

THE NORTON SHAKESPEARE, BASED ON THE OXFORD EDITION
edited by Stephen Greenblatt et al.

For a complete list of Norton Critical Editions, visit
wwnorton.com/college/English/nce

A NORTON CRITICAL EDITION

WORDSWORTH'S POETRY AND PROSE

AUTHORITATIVE TEXTS

CRITICISM

Selected and Edited by

NICHOLAS HALMI
UNIVERSITY OF OXFORD

Jeffry K. Subramanian

W · W · NORTON & COMPANY · *New York* · *London*

W. W. Norton & Company has been independent since its founding in 1923, when William Warder and Mary D. Herter Norton first published lectures delivered at the People's Institute, the adult education division of New York City's Cooper Union. The Nortons soon expanded their program beyond the Institute, publishing books by celebrated academics from America and abroad. By mid-century, the two major pillars of Norton's publishing program—trade books and college texts—were firmly established. In the 1950s, the Norton family transferred control of the company to its employees, and today—with a staff of four hundred and a comparable number of trade, college, and professional titles published each year—W. W. Norton & Company stands as the largest and oldest publishing house owned wholly by its employees.

Library of Congress Cataloging-in-Publication Data

Wordsworth, William, 1770–1850.
    [Works. Selections]
    Wordsworth's poetry and prose : authoritative texts, criticism / selected
and edited by Nicholas Halmi, University of Oxford.—First edition.
        pages cm. — (A Norton Critical Edition)
    Includes bibliographical references and index.
    ISBN 978-0-393-92478-7 (pbk.)
    I. Halmi, Nicholas, editor of compilation.   II. Title.
    PR5853.H35 2013
    821'.7–dc23

                                                        2013016702

W. W. Norton & Company, Inc., 500 Fifth Avenue,
New York, NY 10110
wwnorton.com

W. W. Norton & Company Ltd., Castle House,
75/76 Wells Street, London W1T 3QT

1 2 3 4 5 6 7 8 9 0

In Memory of Paul Magnuson

To Shanae,
A good friend. May you be inspired
by these poems. You are a smart woman.
Thank you for your help.
  From Jeff.

Contents

Criticism

CONTENTS

Illustrations

General Introduction

William Wordsworth is a poet of paradoxes. He insists on the centrality of marginal figures in society, on the universal significance of local attachments. While favoring "low and rustic" subjects, he makes exalted claims, in rhetoric self-consciously modeled on Milton's, for the vatic stance of the poet and the socially transformative power of poetry. Living for most of his life in relative isolation in his native Lake District, supported by his loving sister Dorothy and later his wife Mary, he takes a keen interest in contemporary society and politics, directly witnessing the immediate aftermath of the French Revolution and publicly addressing issues ranging from the conduct of the war against Napoleon to the building of railways in the Lake District. Politically radical in his youth, a frequenter of William Godwin's circle in 1795 and the object of government surveillance in 1797, he becomes increasingly conservative with age, accepting a government post in 1813 (as Distributor of Stamps for Westmorland) and canvassing for the Tory party in 1818. Declaring himself "a worshipper of Nature" in *Tintern Abbey* in 1798, he publishes a series of sonnets celebrating the Church of England in 1822. Refusing to court popularity with the reading public and derided by critics for much of his career, he is awarded an honorary doctorate by Oxford in 1839 and appointed Poet Laureate in 1843.

The diarist Henry Crabb Robinson was probably not exaggerating when he recorded the immensity of his friend's ambition: "Wordsworth, when he resolved to be a poet, feared competition only with Chaucer, Spenser, Shakespeare, and Milton" (*CRB*, 2:776). However immodest, his sense of himself as "a chosen Son" (*The Prelude* 3.82) might well seem to have been vindicated by his literary achievements. In the first edition of *Lyrical Ballads* (1798) he adapted the ballad as a vehicle for psychological exploration; in the second (1800) as well as in *The Ruined Cottage* he renovated two classical forms of pastoral poetry, the eclogue (dialogic) and the idyll (narrative), to engage with contemporary rural life. Publishing sonnets from the beginning (1787) to the end (1842) of his poetic career, he was one of the most prolific sonneteers in English literature and the most significant one since Milton, renewing the Petrarchan form of the sonnet while applying it to a wide variety of subjects. In poems of various genres drawing on his own travels, from *Descriptive Sketches* (1793) to *Memorials of a Tour of Italy, 1837* (1842), he combined aspects of the established genres of topographical poetry and travel narrative. In his odes he appropriated a form favored by eighteenth-century poets like Thomas Gray and William Collins and exploited its potential for representing contraries and uncertainties. Adopting the informal, associative structure of the blank-verse "conversation poem" developed by Samuel Taylor Coleridge,

Wordsworth invested it with epic length and grandeur in one the great intellectual and moral autobiographies of English literature, *The Prelude*. And not least, in his prose writings, particularly the Preface to *Lyrical Ballads* (1800 and 1802), he profoundly influenced the subsequent history of the lyric in English by outlining a subjectivist, expressivist poetics and by criticizing the canons of literary decorum that demanded a specialized diction of poetry.

At the same time, the poet who expressed "an invincible confidence that [his] writings * * * will co-operate with the benign tendencies in human nature and society; and that they will * * * be efficacious in making men wiser, better, and happier" (to Lady Beaumont, May 21, 1807: *WL*, 2:150) was perpetually dissatisfied with his poems, reluctant to publish them, and anxious about their reception. Probably no major Anglophone poet, excepting W. B. Yeats, revised his poems more frequently and extensively than did Wordsworth, both before and after publication, and sometimes (as with *Lyrical Ballads* and *Poems, in Two Volumes*) during the printing itself. In illustration of this process, which constitutes one side of Wordsworth's reception of his own work, some of the more important revisions to the first published versions of texts are presented in the footnotes of this Norton Critical Edition, while *The Ruined Cottage* (in its 1799 version) and the corresponding passages of book 1 of *The Excursion* (1814) are printed as parallel texts on facing pages. Some revisions, like those of *The Thorn*, were made in response to criticisms from friends or reviewers; but others, like those of *The Ruined Cottage*, are reflective of the poet's own conviction that imagination must learn "to ply her craft / By judgment steadied" (*The Prelude* 13.293–94). Although Wordsworth famously declared, in the Preface to *Lyrical Ballads* (1800), that "all good poetry is the spontaneous overflow of powerful feelings," the textual history of his poems reveals that their spontaneity was a carefully crafted appearance.

If Wordsworth was admittedly exaggerating when he claimed that he dreaded publishing "as much as death itself" (*WL*, 1:211), he was certainly prepared to withhold poems, including long and provisionally complete ones, from publication. Twentieth-century editors have reconstituted *The Ruined Cottage* (1798–99) from manuscripts and published it as an independent poem, but the author allowed it to appear before the public only as incorporated into *The Excursion*. Yet the fate of *The Ruined Cottage* is straightforward in comparison to that of the thirteen-book *Prelude* (1804–1805), a poem that the poet himself neither titled nor countenanced publishing except as "a sort of portico" to an even long and grander work, *The Recluse* (*WL*, 1:594), which in the event he never completed. What Wordsworth called the "Poem to Coleridge" was thus an epic both deferred and of deferral: deferred in that it was first published posthumously, and of deferral in that it originated in the poet's inability to make progress on *The Recluse* and did not, until the last years of his life, acquire an identity separate from that envisaged poem. Whereas *Paradise Lost* had sought, as Milton stated, to "justifie the wayes of God to men" (1.26), *The Prelude* sought, in effect, to justify the undertaking of *The Recluse* to Coleridge and to Wordsworth himself by reviewing his emotional, intellectual, and moral development. Whereas Milton's epic subject had been "long choosing, and beginning late" (*Paradise Lost* 9.26),

Wordsworth's—"Nature, Man, and Society" (WL, 1:212)—was chosen perhaps too rashly and too early. Not only was the subject so comprehensive that anything might fall within its scope, as Wordsworth conceded already in March 1798 (see the headnote to *The Excursion*), but its elaboration was dependent on continued intellectual companionship with Coleridge, with whom *The Recluse* was conceived in 1797–98, when both poets were living in Somerset.

To be sure, it was Wordsworth who emerged from the collaboration with Coleridge on *Lyrical Ballads* as the more self-confident poet, a fact attested by Coleridge's ready acceptance of the various indignities to which Wordsworth subjected him in preparing the second edition (1800): assigning *The Rime of the Ancient Mariner* a less prominent place than in the first edition, excluding *Christabel* from the collection, and declining to name Coleridge as a contributor (even as Wordsworth's own name now appeared on the title page). But where "the Task of his life" (WL, 1:576) was concerned, Wordsworth felt he could not proceed without the prodigiously learned Coleridge's assistance, which he sought explicitly in letters of March 19 and 29, 1804, after having completed the first five books of *The Prelude*: "I am very anxious to have your notes for the Recluse. I cannot say how much importance I attach to this, if it should please God that I survive you, I should reproach myself for ever in writing the work if I had neglected to procure this help" (WL, 1:452; see also 464). As the two poets became increasingly distant over the first decade of the nineteenth century, the likelihood that *The Recluse* would be realized in anything like the scope and form originally imagined began to recede, although Wordsworth was not willing to abandon the project, and indeed mentioned it publicly in the Preface to *The Excursion*.

This Norton Critical Edition seeks primarily to offer a view of Wordsworth's literary career as it unfolded before the eyes of his immediate contemporaries from 1798, when he and Coleridge published the first edition of *Lyrical Ballads* anonymously, to 1815, when he published his first collected edition, *Poems*. Limits of space have dictated the omission of his earliest published volumes, *An Evening Walk* (a 446-line poem in rhyming couplets evoking Lake District scenes) and *Descriptive Sketches* (an 813-line poem in rhyming couplets combining recollections of Wordsworth's Continental walking tour of 1790 with meditations on the French Revolution), both of 1793, and have restricted the presentation of his later career to a small number of poems. Works such as *The Ruined Cottage*, *Home at Grasmere* (1800, 1806), and the thirteen-book *Prelude*, now recognized as major poems in their own right but never published as such by Wordsworth, constitute a special editorial challenge. *The Ruined Cottage* is included along with its eventually published revision in *The Excursion* for illustrative reasons, as noted above. *Home at Grasmere* is omitted because the poet chose to leave it unpublished, apart from the concluding section that he extracted and printed with *The Excursion* as the Prospectus to *The Recluse*—which is included here in its published form of 1814. *The Prelude* is presented in its 1805 version, rather than the posthumously published one of 1850, because the existence of the former was publicly revealed in various ways—quoted from by Coleridge in his periodical *The Friend* (1809–10), referred to by Coleridge in *Biographia Literaria* (1817) and by Wordsworth himself in the Preface to *The Excursion*—and more importantly because the poem was read and annotated by the person to whom it was addressed, Coleridge, who in turn responded to it in *To a Gentleman*, a poem he published in 1817.

Wordsworth was understandably unwilling to publish so personal a poem as *The Prelude* in isolation from *The Recluse*, but he was also profoundly anxious about the reception of the poems he did publish. Despite his conviction that "every Author, as far as he is great and at the same time *original*, has the task of *creating* the taste by which he is to be enjoyed"—as he expressed it in the "Essay, supplementary to the Preface" in *Poems* (1815), repeating what he had written his friend Lady Beaumont eight years earlier (*WL*, 2:150)—Wordsworth did not trust the poems alone to accomplish that taste-making task. In advertisements, prefaces, notes, and other prose paratexts to his volumes of poetry, he sought by various means to win over reviewers and the reading public, or at least to forestall a negative response.

Thus, for example, in the Advertisement to the first edition of *Lyrical Ballads* he described his own contributions as "experiments," as if they were not to be considered full-fledged literary works, while in the Preface to the second edition (and more especially in the third edition) he simultaneously denigrated popular literary taste and conventional poetic diction and celebrated the poet as an agent of moral improvement. In the Preface to his 1815 volume Wordsworth elaborated a system of classifying his poems and a theoretical distinction between the faculties of imagination and fancy, while in the supplementary essay to that preface he nursed his long-standing grievance against the critic Francis Jeffrey's abusive reviews of his works. But the characteristic combination of defensiveness and belligerence in such prose statements, attacking those whose admiration Wordsworth desired, provoked critics and perhaps secured his poetry a less favorable reception during his lifetime than would otherwise have been the case. Coleridge, for one, suspected that the Preface to *Lyrical Ballads* was itself "the true origin of the unexampled opposition which Mr. Wordsworth's writings have been since doomed to encounter" (*NCC*, 408). Because Wordsworth's paratexts played an important role in shaping the contemporary (and later) perception of him and his poetic works, a generous selection of them is included in this edition: the Advertisement to *Lyrical Ballads* (1798), the Preface to *Lyrical Ballads* (1800, with the additions and alterations of 1802 distinguished typographically), the Preface and "Essay on Epitaphs" from *The Excursion*, and excerpts from the Preface and supplementary essay to *Poems* (1815). Other prose writings, such as *The Convention of Cintra* (1809) and *Letter to a Friend of Robert Burns* (1816), are cited in the headnotes and footnotes.

Wordsworth's poetic practice was shaped by his opposition to a contemporary literary scene in which, as he saw it, popular Gothic novels, melodramas, and overwrought poetry prized rhetorical extravagance and emotional stimuli for their own sake. His counterexample, which in his best and most distinctive poetry sought to reveal the extraordinariness of ordinary experiences and to foster imaginative sympathy among persons of disparate conditions, proceeded from his belief in the intimate relation between aesthetic and moral values. "Every great Poet is a Teacher: I wish either to be considered as a Teacher, or as nothing," Wordsworth confided to Sir George Beaumont in 1808 (*WL*, 2:195). While an instructional imperative may be most clearly evident in his prose writings, it is equally present in his poetry, in forms ranging from the psychologically subtle, as in *The Thorn*, to the politically explicit, as in the *Thanksgiving Ode* of 1816. What he hoped above all to teach was, as he stated to Coleridge in *The Prelude*, something of permanent value in "this time / Of dereliction and dismay" (2.446–47), an appreciation of the power and dignity of the human mind:

> what we have loved
> Others will love; and we may teach them how,
> Instruct them how the mind of Man becomes
> A thousand times more beautiful than the earth
> On which he dwells * * * (13.444–48)

The selection of poems in this Norton Critical Edition cannot do justice to the full length and breadth of Wordsworth's sixty-year poetic career, but it does seek to represent extensively the mature work of the years in which he struggled to find an appreciative readership—and in which he wrote most of the poems on which his subsequent reputation was to rest. His contributions to the first edition of *Lyrical Ballads* are included in their entirety, and the thirteen-book *Prelude* is presented in full, edited anew from the manuscript in Mary Wordsworth's hand (the rationale for the choice of manuscript being explained in the headnote to the poem). Generous selections from the poems added to the second edition of *Lyrical Ballads* and from *Poems, in Two Volumes* (1807) are also included. Poems are arranged according to the book in which they first appeared and the order in which they appeared within that book. The texts of poems published by Wordsworth follow the original editions (corrections from errata notices and other emendations being indicated in the footnotes). The headnotes to books up to and including *Thanksgiving Ode* describe each book's development, structure, circumstances of publication, and immediate biographical or historical context; give a brief account of each book's contemporary reception; and refer to relevant critical essays included in the section of Modern Criticism. Some readers will be surprised by the inclusion of the *Thanksgiving Ode*: but however limited its poetic appeal, it is an important statement of Wordsworth's political views in the immediate post–Napoleonic period, and its extreme rhetoric provoked vigorous responses from contemporary writers.

The small selections from the later poetry, written during the years in which Wordsworth consolidated his reputation, highlight thematically his responses to natural scenes and contemporary political events (particularly the Napoleonic wars) and his tributes to contemporaries (the abolitionist Thomas Clarkson, the painter Benjamin Robert Haydon, the poet James Hogg), and formally the sonnets and odes. Throughout this Norton Critical Edition the first footnote to each poem (or in the case of *Michael* and the Intimations Ode, the headnote) indicates the poem's date of composition and its classification in *Poems* (1815) or a later collected edition, and where relevant quotes Wordsworth's own commentary on the poem (in particular, from the notes he dictated to Isabella Fenwick in 1842–43). Other footnotes identify historical and literary references and gloss words with historically or regionally specific usages.

Within the limited space available, the Nineteenth-Century Responses selection represents both positive and negative reactions to Wordsworth's poetry by critics and other poets, while that of Modern Criticism illustrates differing approaches (including formalist, historicist, ecocritical, and feminist) to interpreting a sampling of the poems presented in this volume (e.g., *Goody Blake and Harry Gill, The Thorn, Tintern Abbey,* the "Lucy poems," *Michael, The Ruined Cottage,* the sonnets, several books of *The Prelude, Resolution and Independence,* and the Intimations Ode). Readers should note that some of the critical selections are shorter than the editor had intended owing to the high permissions fees demanded by publishers. The Biographical and Topographical Glossary gives basic biographical information about persons and places mentioned frequently in this Norton Critical Edition, and defines Northern English topographical terms (e.g., *fell* and *tarn*) used repeatedly in the poems. The Selected Bibliography lists primary and secondary texts, and full bibliographical information about works cited in brief form in the footnotes will be found either in the list of abbreviations or in the bibliography.

Textual Introduction

Works published by Wordsworth himself—both poetry and prose—are presented in this Norton Critical Edition under the headings and in the texts of their earliest published volumes. Where I have departed from this principle, as I have in printing the 1800 note to *The Thorn* immediately after the 1798 text of that poem and in printing a conflated version of the 1800 and 1802 Prefaces to *Lyrical Ballads*, I have explained the reasons for doing so in the relevant headnotes. *The Prelude* has been edited from the manuscript copied by Mary Wordsworth and known as MS B (DC MS 53), and both the rationale for following that manuscript and the principles of emending it are explained in the headnote to the poem.

Throughout the edition, I have retained the original spelling, capitalization, and punctuation of the printed source-texts, with the following exceptions:

1. Obvious printers' errors, as opposed to variant spellings permitted in Wordsworth's time, are corrected silently.

2. The long *s*, used occasionally in the 1798 edition of *Lyrical Ballads*, has been replaced with a short *s*, and large initial capitals with ordinary capital letters. Small capitals and italics are retained as they appear in the original editions.

3. In quotations extending across more than one line of verse, opening quotation marks are omitted from the beginnings of lines after the first. The exception to this principle is in quotations extending across more than one stanza: in these an opening quotation mark is repeated at the beginning of each stanza through which the quotation continues.

4. Terminal periods have been omitted in titles of poems, but otherwise the spelling and punctuation of titles in the source texts have been retained.

5. The possessive form of *it* has been regularized as *its*.

Acknowledgments

My first words of acknowledgment must be to Paul Magnuson, who collaborated with Raimonda Modiano and me on the Norton Critical Edition of *Coleridge's Poetry and Prose*. His editing of the poetry for that volume was my model for the present edition, which I gratefully dedicate to his memory.

A new editor of Wordsworth is fortunate in having such distinguished predecessors, and I owe an immense debt to the editors of the standard scholarly editions of Wordsworth's writings: the Cornell Wordsworth, begun and completed under the general editorship of the late Stephen Maxfield Parrish; the Oxford edition of *The Prose Works*, by W. J. B. Owen and Jane Worthington Smyser; and the Oxford edition of *The Letters of William and Dorothy Wordsworth*, by Chester L. Shaver, Mary Moorman, and Alan G. Hill. The Norton Critical Edition of *The Prelude: 1799, 1805, 1850*, edited by Jonathan Wordsworth, M. H. Abrams, and Stephen Gill, has been a constant reference and, as will be obvious to readers of that edition, the source of many of my notes on the thirteen-book *Prelude*. Mark Reed's two-volume *Chronology* of Wordsworth's life and works and Duncan Wu's two-volume catalogue of *Wordsworth's Reading* have also been essential companions. Wordsworth's notes to Isabella Fenwick have been reprinted from the e-book version of Jared Curtis's invaluable edition of *The Fenwick Notes of William Wordsworth*.

It is a pleasure to acknowledge support from the Royalty Research Fund of the University of Washington, without which I could not have begun this Norton Critical Edition, and from the John Fell Oxford University Press Research Fund, without which I might never have finished it. I must also thank the English Faculty of the University of Oxford and University College for research funding.

I am grateful for the assistance I have received from the staffs of the Bodleian Library, Oxford; the British Library, London; and the Wordsworth Trust Archive, Grasmere. Of the last I must particularly thank Jeff Cowton for assisting my transcription of manuscripts and Alex Black for arranging the photographs reproduced in this edition. The editor and publisher gratefully acknowledge permission from the Wordsworth Trust to publish the texts of manuscripts in its collection, and from Humanities Ebooks to quote extensively from Jared Curtis's edition of the Fenwick notes.

I especially thank Stephen Gill for kindly writing for this Norton Critical Edition his succinct, lucid overview of the textual complications of Wordsworth's poetry.

For advice on various aspects of this volume, I thank Marshall Brown, Jessica Burstein, Sally Bushell, Julia Carlson, Richard Dunn, Randall

McLeod, Charles Mahoney, Raimonda Modiano, Seamus Perry, Brian Reed, Matthew Scott, Heather Stansbury, and especially Ruth Abbott. My initial planning of the edition benefitted from suggestions made by my students at the University of Washington, and my annotation of *The Prelude* from suggestions made by my students at Stanford University in winter 2011: I thank both collectively.

I am particularly grateful to Jamie Baxendine, James Grande, Angela Sucich, and Julia Tejblum for research assistance; to Carol Bemis, my editor at W. W. Norton, for her forbearance, as well as to Rivka Genesen, Katharine Ings, and Thea Goodrich for preparing the manuscript for publication; to Claire Johnstone and Edward Sugden for assistance with proofreading; to Tiffany Stern and Laura Varnam, my colleagues at University College, for their support; and to Stephanie Dumke for saving me from numerous errors, not only scholarly.

Abbreviations

BL	Samuel Taylor Coleridge, *Biographia Literaria; or Biographical Sketches of My Literary Life and Opinions* (1817)
BL (CC)	Samuel Taylor Coleridge, *Biographia Literaria*, ed. James Engell and Walter Jackson Bate, vol. 7 (in 2 parts) of *The Collected Works of Samuel Taylor Coleridge* (Princeton, 1983)
Chrono: EY	Mark Reed, *Wordsworth: The Chronology of the Early Years, 1770–1799* (Cambridge, MA, 1967)
Chrono: MY	Mark Reed, *Wordsworth: The Chronology of the Middle Years, 1800–1815* (Cambridge, MA, 1975)
CH	*William Wordsworth: The Critical Heritage*, ed. Robert Woof, vol. 1 [all published] (London, 2001)
CL	*The Collected Letters of Samuel Taylor Coleridge*, ed. Earl Leslie Griggs, 6 vols. (Oxford, 1956–71)
CLL	*The Letters of Charles and Mary Anne Lamb*, ed. Edwin Marrs, Jr., 3 vols. (Ithaca, NY, 1975–78)
CN	*The Notebooks of Samuel Taylor Coleridge*, ed. Kathleen Coburn, 5 vols. in 10 (London, 1957–2002)
Cornell	George Harris Healey, *The Cornell Wordsworth Collection: A Catalogue of Books and Manuscripts Presented to the University by Mr. Victor Emanuel* (Ithaca, NY, 1957) (cited by item number)
CRB	*Henry Crabb Robinson on Books and Their Writers*, ed. Edith J. Morley, 3 vols. (London, 1938)
CW	The Cornell Wordsworth, gen. ed. Stephen Maxfield Parrish, 21 vols. (Ithaca, NY, 1975–2007) (see the Selected Bibliography for a list of volumes)
Doyle	William Doyle, *The Oxford History of the French Revolution* (Oxford, 1989)
DC	Dove Cottage (used to designate manuscripts held in the Wordsworth Trust Archive, Grasmere, e.g., DC MS 53)
DW	Dorothy Wordsworth (WW's sister; used in the notes)
DWJ	*The Journals of Dorothy Wordsworth*, ed. Ernest de Selincourt, 2 vols. (London, 1941)
Exc	William Wordsworth, *The Excursion* (1814)

Exc (CW)	William Wordsworth, *The Excursion*, ed. Sally Bushell, James Butler, and Michael Jaye (Ithaca, NY, 2007)
Friend	S. T. Coleridge, *The Friend*, ed. Barbara Rooke, 2 vols. (Princeton, 1969)
HCR	*The Correspondence of Henry Crabb Robinson with the Wordsworth Circle*, ed. E. J. Morley, 2 vols. (Oxford, 1927)
Gill	Stephen Gill, *William Wordsworth: A Life* (Oxford, 1989)
IF note	Commentary dictated by Wordsworth to Isabella Fenwick, 1842–43, and transcribed from her notes by Dora Wordsworth and Edward Qullinan; quoted from *The Fenwick Notes of William Wordsworth*, ed. Jared Curtis, 2nd ed. (e-book; Penrith, 2007)
Intimations Ode	William Wordsworth, *Ode [Intimations of Immortality from Recollections of Early Childhood]* (first published 1807)
LB	William Wordsworth and S. T. Coleridge, *Lyrical Ballads*
LB 1798	[William Wordsworth and S. T. Coleridge,] *Lyrical Ballads, with Other Poems* (London, 1798)
LB 1800	William Wordsworth [and S. T. Coleridge], *Lyrical Ballads, with Other Poems*, 2 vols. (London, 1800)
LB 1802	William Wordsworth [and S. T. Coleridge], *Lyrical Ballads, with Pastoral and Other Poems*, 2 vols. (London, 1802)
LB 1805	William Wordsworth [and S. T. Coleridge], *Lyrical Ballads, with Pastoral and Other Poems*, 2 vols. (London, 1805)
LB (CW)	William Wordsworth, *Lyrical Ballads, with Other Poems, 1797–1800*, ed. James Butler and Karen Green (Ithaca, NY, 1992)
LB (Mason)	[William Wordsworth and S. T. Coleridge,] *Lyrical Ballads*, ed. Michael Mason (Harlow, 1994)
McCracken	David McCracken, *Wordsworth and the Lake District: A Guide to the Poems and Their Places* (Oxford, 1984)
Moorman	Mary Moorman, *William Wordsworth: A Biography*, 2 vols. (Oxford, 1957–65)
MP 1820	*The Miscellaneous Poems of William Wordsworth*, 4 vols. (London, 1820)
MS, MSS	manuscript, manuscripts (used in the notes)
MW	Mary Wordsworth (WW's wife; used in the notes)
NCC	S. T. Coleridge, *Coleridge's Poetry and Prose*, ed. Nicholas Halmi, Paul Magnuson, and Raimonda Modiano (New York, 2003)

NCPrel	William Wordsworth, *The Prelude, 1799, 1805, 1850*, ed. Jonathan Wordsworth, M. H. Abrams, and Stephen Gill (New York, 1979)
OED	*Oxford English Dictionary, Second Edition on CD-ROM*, version 4.0 (Oxford, 2009)
OxPrel	William Wordsworth, *The Prelude or Growth of a Poet's Mind*, ed. Ernest de Selincourt and Helen Darbishire, 2nd ed. (Oxford, 1959)
P 1815	*Poems by William Wordsworth*, 2 vols. (London, 1815)
P2V	William Wordsworth, *Poems, in Two Volumes*, 2 vols. (London, 1807)
P2V (CW)	William Wordsworth, *Poems, in Two Volumes, and Other Poems, 1800–1807*, ed. Jared Curtis (Ithaca, NY, 1983)
PPrel	William Wordsworth, *The Prelude: The Four Texts (1798, 1799, 1805, 1850)*, ed. Jonathan Wordsworth (Harmondsworth, 1995)
Prel 1799	William Wordsworth, [*The Prelude*] (two-book version, completed in 1799)
Prel 1805	William Wordsworth, [*The Prelude*] (thirteen-book version, completed in 1805)
Prel 1805 (CW)	William Wordsworth, *The Thirteen-Book Prelude*, ed. Mark Reed, 2 vols. (Ithaca, NY, 1991)
Prel 1850	William Wordsworth, *The Prelude, or Growth of a Poet's Mind; An Autobiographical Poem* (fourteen-book version, completed in 1839 and published posthumously in 1850)
Prel 1850 (CW)	William Wordsworth, *The Fourteen-Book Prelude*, ed. W. J. B. Owen (Ithaca, NY, 1985)
The Prelude	William Wordsworth, [*The Prelude*] (13-book version, 1805), as printed in the present Norton Critical Edition (used in cross-references)
Prose	*The Prose Works of William Wordsworth*, ed. W. J. B. Owen and Jane Worthington Symser, 3 vols. (Oxford, 1974)
RC (CW)	William Wordsworth, *The Ruined Cottage and The Pedlar*, ed. James Butler (Ithaca, NY 1979)
Reading 1770–99	Duncan Wu, *Wordsworth's Reading 1770–1799* (Cambridge, 1993) (cited by entry number)
Reading 1800–15	Duncan Wu, *Wordsworth's Reading 1800–1815* (Cambridge, 1995) (cited by entry number)
Schneider	Ben Ross Schneider, Jr. *Wordsworth's Cambridge Education* (Cambridge, 1957)
STC	Samuel Taylor Coleridge (used in the notes)
Thompson	T. W. Thompson, *Wordsworth's Hawkshead*, ed. Robert Woof (London, 1970)

Tintern Abbey	William Wordsworth, *Lines written a few miles above Tintern Abbey, On revisiting the banks of the Wye during a tour, July 13, 1798* (first published in *LB 1798*)
WL	*The Letters of William and Dorothy Wordsworth*, rev. ed., ed. Chester L. Shaver, Mary Moorman, and Alan G. Hill, 8 vols. (Oxford, 1967–93)
WW	William Wordsworth (used in the notes)

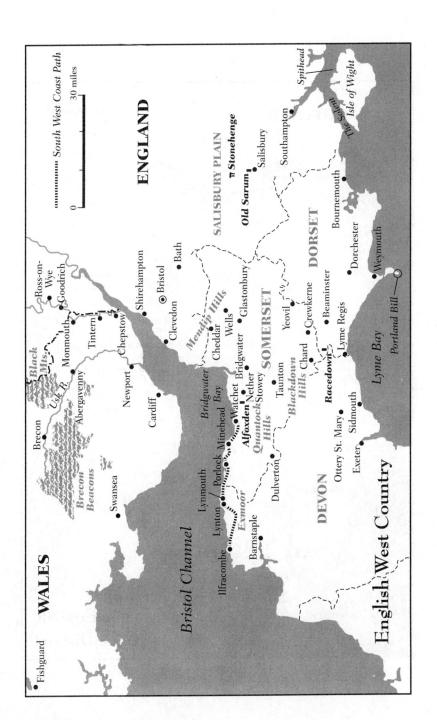

xxix

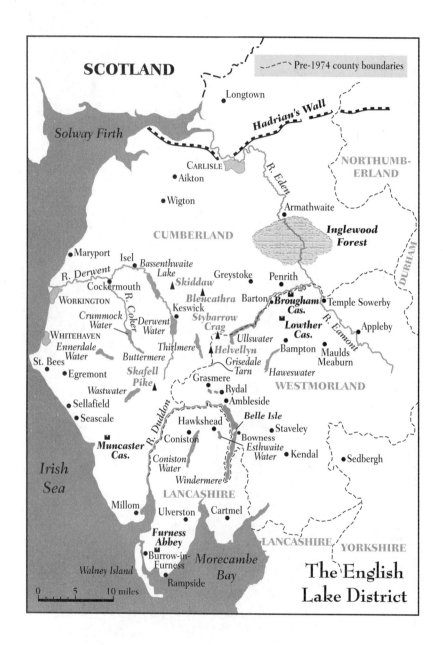

SCOTLAND

Pre-1974 county boundaries

Longtown

Hadrian's Wall

Solway Firth

CARLISLE
•Aikton

NORTHUMB-
ERLAND

•Wigton

CUMBERLAND

R. Eden

Armathwaite

*Inglewood
Forest*

DURHAM

•Maryport
Isel
R. Derwent
Cockermouth
WORKINGTON
Crummock
Water
WHITEHAVEN
Ennerdale
St. Bees Water
•Egremont
Wastwater
•Sellafield
•Seascale

*Bassenthwaite
Lake*
Greystoke
Penrith
▲*Skiddaw*
Keswick
Bleucathra
Barton
R. Coker
Derwent
Water
*Stybarrow
Crag*
Thirlmere
▲*Helvellyn*
Buttermere
*Skafell
Pike*▲
Grasmere
Rydal
•Ambleside

*Brougham
Cas.*
Temple Sowerby

*Lowther
Cas.*
Appleby

Ullswater
Bampton
Maulds
Meaburn

Grisedale
Tarn
Haweswater

WESTMORLAND

R. Eamont

*Irish
Sea*

*Muncaster
Cas.*

R. Duddon

Hawkshead
•Coniston
*Coniston
Water*
Windermere

Belle Isle
•Staveley
Bowness
*Esthwaite
Water* •Kendal
•Sedbergh

LANCASHIRE

Millom

Ulverston Cartmel

*Furness
Abbey*
•Burrow-in-
Furness
Walney Island
Rampside

*Morecambe
Bay*

LANCASHIRE YORKSHIRE

*The English
Lake District*

0   5   10 miles

WORDSWORTH'S POETRY AND PROSE

From LYRICAL BALLADS, WITH A FEW OTHER POEMS (1798)

Wordsworth and Coleridge first met in Bristol sometime between late August and late September 1795, and by the following May they had corresponded substantially and sympathetically enough for Coleridge to describe Wordsworth as a "very dear friend" (*CL*, 1:125). After a three-day visit to William and his sister Dorothy at Racedown, Dorset, in June 1797, Coleridge determined to relocate his friends in the vicinity of his own cottage in Nether Stowey, Somerset, and by July 7 it was arranged that the Wordsworths would rent Alfoxden House, about four miles from Nether Stowey, for a year. During that year, Coleridge "was with Wordsworth almost daily—& frequently for weeks at a time" (*CL*, 1:525). On a walking tour in early November 1797, Coleridge proposed to Wordsworth that they jointly compose a prose tale in three cantos on the death of Abel, modeled on the Swiss poet Solomon Gessner's prose epic on the same subject (*Der Tod Abels*, 1758; translated as *The Death of Abel*, 1761). Wordsworth, however, made no progress on his appointed canto, and Coleridge later conceded "the exceeding ridiculousness of the whole scheme" (*NCC*, 213; see also *The Prelude* 7.560). (For Coleridge's fragment, published in 1828 as *The Wanderings of Cain*, see *NCC*, 211–17.)

The failure of this first attempt at collaboration did not discourage the two poets from making a second attempt during another walking tour from November 12 to 20. They planned a ballad, *The Rime of the Ancient Mariner*, which they hoped to sell to the *Monthly Magazine* in order to defray the costs of their trip. But while Wordsworth suggested several crucial elements of the poem, he contributed no more than a few lines of poetry, whereas Coleridge composed some 300 by November 20 (*CL*, 1:357). "As we endeavoured to proceed conjointly," Wordsworth recalled over four decades later, "our respective manners proved so widely different that it would have been quite presumptuous in me to do anything but separate from an undertaking upon which I could only have been a clog" (IF note to *We are seven*). The first reference to the inclusion of *The Rime of the Ancient Mariner* in a jointly planned *volume* of poetry occurs in Dorothy Wordsworth's description, in a letter of November 20, 1797, of the poets' "employing themselves in laying the plan of a ballad, to be published with some pieces of William's" (*WL*, 1:194). Wordsworth himself recalled that the book was conceived once *The Rime of the Ancient Mariner* had become too long for publication in a magazine: "The Ancient Mariner grew & grew till it became too important for our first object which was limited to five pounds, and we began to talk of a volume, which was to consist as Mr. Coleridge has told the world, of Poems chiefly on supernatural subjects taken from common life but looked at, as much as might be, through an imaginative medium. Accordingly I wrote The Idiot Boy, Her Eyes are wild &c, We are Seven, The Thorn & some others" (IF note to *We are seven*).

What Coleridge had "told the world," in chapter 14 of his *Biographia Literaria* (1817), was more specifically of a division of labor in the compilation of *Lyrical Ballads*:

During the first year that Mr. Wordsworth and I were neighbours, our conversations turned frequently on the two cardinal points of poetry, the power of exciting the sympathy of the reader by a faithful adherence to the truth of nature, and the power of giving the interest of novelty by the modifying colours of imagination. * * * The thought suggested itself (to which us I do not recollect) that a series of poems might be composed of two sorts. In the one, the incidents and agents were to be, in part at least, supernatural; and the excellence aimed at was to consist in the interesting of the affections by the dramatic truth of such emotions, as would naturally accompany such situations, supposing them real. * * * For the second class, subjects were to be chosen from ordinary life; the characters and incidents were to be such, as will be found in every village and its vicinity, where there is a meditative and feeling mind to seek after them, or to notice them, when they present themselves.

In this idea originated the plan of the "Lyrical Ballads;" in which it was agreed, that my endeavours should be directed to persons and characters supernatural, or at least romantic * * *. Mr. Wordsworth, on the other hand, was to propose to himself as his object, to give the charm of novelty to things of every day, and to excite a feeling analogous to the supernatural, but awakening the mind's attention from the lethargy of custom, and directing it to the loveliness and the wonders of the world before us * * *. (NCC, 489–90)

Written more than fifteen years after the events to which it refers, Coleridge's account, though the fullest we possess and influential on later critical discussion of *Lyrical Ballads*, is too neatly schematic and overlooks the contingencies of the volume's compilation. In February 1798 the project was jeopardized when Coleridge, in desperate need of funds, offered *The Rime of the Ancient Mariner* to the Bristol publisher Joseph Cottle for inclusion in a new edition of his own poems (CL, 1:387). In early March the Wordsworths learned that their lease on Alfoxden House would not be renewed, and they formed with Coleridge the plan of going to Germany to spend two years learning the language (WL, 1:213, 220–21). On March 13, emphasizing that "money is necessary to our plan," Coleridge sent Cottle alternative proposals: either to publish a volume containing Coleridge's play *Osorio* and Wordsworth's play *The Borderers*, both of which had been rejected for performance by the London theaters to which had been sent in the autumn of 1797 (see WL, 1:192n, 194, 197), or to publish "Wordsworth's Salisbury Plain & Tale of a Woman [i.e., *The Ruined Cottage*] * * * with a few others which he will add & the notes"—the latter a book with no contribution from Coleridge himself (CL, 1:399–400).

Cottle was evidently unwilling to pay the sixty guineas demanded for the two tragedies, for in early April Coleridge withdrew that offer, "determined to procure the money some other way." But he left open the offer of a volume of Wordsworth's poems, if Cottle were willing to pay thirty guineas for it by the end of July (CL, 1:40–43). Between mid-March and late May Wordsworth seems to have composed at least eleven of the poems that would eventually be published in the first edition of *Lyrical Ballads* (*Chrono: EY*, 32–33; *LB* [CW], 10–12), and on May 9 he wrote cryptically to Cottle, "I have lately been busy about another plan which I do not wish to mention till I see you; let this be *very, very*, soon" (WL, 1:218). In the last week of May, Cottle visited the two poets at Alfoxden, and it was then that the contents and title of *Lyrical Ballads* were first discussed with him. The final form of the volume was settled subsequently in correspondence, Coleridge insisting on anonymous publication on the grounds that "Wordsworth's name is nothing—to a large number of persons mine *stinks*" (CL, 1:412). The volume was to begin with *The Rime of the Ancient Mariner* and include three additional poems by

Coleridge. Wordsworth contributed nineteen poems, the last to be composed, *Lines written a few miles above Tintern Abbey,* also concluding the volume. For all their variety in subject-matter, form, diction, and tone, Coleridge insisted to Cottle in May 1798 that the poems "are to a certain degree *one work,* in *kind tho' not in degree,* as an Ode is one work—& that our different poems are as stanzas, good relatively rather than absolutely:—Mark you, I say *in kind* tho' not in degree" (*CL,* 1:412).

Wordsworth was in Bristol for much of the summer of 1798 "to superintend the printing" (*WL,* 1:219), which was completed by late July. Shortly afterwards Coleridge's poem *The Nightingale* was substituted for his previously published *Lewti,* Wordsworth's Advertisement—which explained that the poems of *Lyrical* Ballads were to be considered experiments in the use of conversational language—was inserted between the title leaf and the table of contents, and a revised contents leaf was printed. Perhaps on account of financial difficulties, Cottle declined to publish the book despite having printed it; and, anticipating an agreement with T. N. Longman in London for its publication, he printed several copies (the "Bristol imprint," of which fourteen are known) with title pages listing himself as printer and Longman as publisher. In fact, however, Cottle and Longman could not agree on terms, and Wordsworth approached Joseph Johnson, who had published his *Evening Walk* and *Descriptive Sketches* in 1793. Johnson agreed to publish *Lyrical Ballads* (*WL,* 1:259), but Cottle, without Wordsworth's knowledge, sold the copyright to the firm J. & A. Arch in London (James Butler, "Wordsworth, Cottle, and the *Lyrical Ballads,*" 142–51). Writing from Germany on October 3, Wordsworth complained, "I do not yet know what is become of my poems, that is, who is their publisher" (*WL,* 1:232). The following day, the book was published in London, in an edition of 500 copies, with a new title page omitting Cottle's name and announcing Arch as the publisher (the "London imprint"). The authors were not identified. Although Cottle had agreed to pay Wordsworth thirty guineas upon completion of the printing, he in fact paid the less than a third of this amount before the poet's departure for Germany on September 16, 1798, and he paid the remainder only in July 1799 (*Chrono: EY,* 248 n. 44).

Contemporary reviews of the volume were mixed. The anonymous reviewers in the *Monthly Mirror* (October 1798), the *Analytical Review* (December 1798), and the *British Critic* (October 1799) praised Wordsworth's contributions (without recognizing his authorship) for their simplicity of diction and compared them favorably to the emotionally effusive poetry of the Della Cruscan movement (which had been fashionable in the 1780s) and to the stylistically ornate allegorical poetry of Erasmus Darwin (1731–1802). But the reviewer in the *New London Review* (January 1799) took issue with Wordsworth's "Advertisement" to the volume and condemned *Goody Blake and Harry Gill* on the grounds that "[t]he language of *conversation,* and that too of the *lower classes,* can never be considered as the language of *poetry*" (*CH,* 71). To Wordsworth's indignation (see *WL,* 1: 267–68), the unsigned review in the *Critical Review* (October 1798) by Robert Southey, who not only knew both authors but was Coleridge's brother-in-law (see Biographical and Topographical Glossary), condemned *The Rime of the Ancyent Marinere* and ridiculed *The Idiot Boy* at length while praising other poems very briefly and concluding that "the language of conversation * * * has been tried upon uninteresting subjects" (*CH,* 67). The most discerning and extensive review (in the *Monthly Review,* June 1799) was by the music historian Dr. Charles Burney, who commented on the poems individually and praised the volume as a whole for its "natural delineation of human passions," but also criticized as retrograde its stylistic imitations of the older ballads collected in Thomas Percy's popular *Reliques of Ancient English Poetry* (1765) (*CH,* 74–76).

The collection's title was somewhat paradoxical, *lyrical* implying short, private poems or songs, and *ballads* a more popular form of narrative poetry; and the contents were announced in Wordsworth's Advertisement as experiments. Yet most of the poems had precedents in style or subject-matter in the magazine poetry of the 1790s (see Robert Mayo, "The Contemporaneity of *Lyrical Ballads*"), and some (e.g., *The Thorn* and *The Idiot Boy*) are likely to have had specific literary models. "The style and versification are those of our antient ditties," Burney remarked, "but much polished, and more constantly excellent" (*CH*, 77). Overall, as Mary Jacobus observes, Wordsworth's "achievement is to adapt the ballad to portraying precisely those states and feelings least susceptible to narrative presentation. At the same time, he forces us to reassess the importance of the everyday" (*Tradition and Experiment*, 233). *Lines written a few miles above Tintern Abbey*, his most distinctive and personal contribution to the volume, and a major (if ambivalent) statement of his poetic vocation, adapts a form developed by Coleridge: the "conversation poem," in which the speaker addresses a silent but implicitly present auditor in conversational language (as in Coleridge's *The Nightingale; A Conversational Poem*, included in *LB 1798*), and in the end returns to the scene or imagery of the poem's beginning.

Modern criticism of the 1798 *Lyrical Ballads* has been extensive and richly diverse. In general, formalist approaches—concerned with poems' themes, literary contexts, and artistic distinctiveness—predominated until the early 1980s, while historicist approaches—concerned with the poems' relations to contemporary political and socioeconomic issues—predominated from the 1980s into the first decade of the twenty-first century. Of the criticism excerpted in the present Norton Critical Edition, Neil Fraistat's "The 'Field' of *Lyrical Ballads*" considers the collection's thematic coherence, while Mary Jacobus's *Tradition and Experiment in Wordsworth's "Lyrical Ballads" 1798* examines the poems' relations (in particular, those of *Goody Blake and Harry Gill* and *The Thorn*) to earlier ballads. James McKusick assesses the collection from an "ecocritical" perspective, noting the interactions between humans and nature in the various poems, while Nicholas Roe and Andrew Cooper address different aspects of *Tintern Abbey*. The formal qualities of several of the *Lyrical Ballads* are explored in Susan Wolfson's essay "Wordsworth's Craft."

The texts are printed from the London imprint of *LB 1798*, and in the same order as in that volume, incorporating the corrections from the printed errata list. For the reader's convenience, however, the note on *The Thorn* that Wordsworth added to *LB 1800* is printed immediately after that poem rather than with other texts from the 1800 edition. The notes indicate the classifications under which Wordsworth distributed the poems when he reprinted them in *P 1815*.

LYRICAL BALLADS,

WITH

A FEW OTHER POEMS.

LONDON:

PRINTED FOR J. & A. ARCH, GRACECHURCH-STREET.

1798.

ADVERTISEMENT†

It is the honourable characteristic of Poetry that its materials are to be found in every subject which can interest the human mind. The evidence of this fact is to be sought, not in the writings of Critics, but in those of Poets themselves.

The majority of the following poems are to be considered as experiments. They were written chiefly with a view to ascertain how far the language of conversation in the middle and lower classes of society is adapted to the purposes of poetic pleasure. Readers accustomed to the gaudiness and inane phraseology of many modern writers, if they persist in reading this book to its conclusion, will perhaps frequently have to struggle with feelings of strangeness and aukwardness: they will look round for poetry, and will be induced to enquire by what species of courtesy these attempts can be permitted to assume that title. It is desirable that such readers, for their own sakes, should not suffer the solitary word Poetry, a word of very disputed meaning, to stand in the way of their gratification; but that, while they are perusing this book, they should ask themselves if it contains a natural delineation of human passions, human characters, and human incidents; and if the answer be favorable to the author's wishes, that they should consent to be pleased in spite of that most dreadful enemy to our pleasures, our own pre-established codes of decision.

Readers of superior judgment may disapprove of the style in which many of these pieces are executed[;] it must be expected that many lines and phrases will not exactly suit their taste. It will perhaps appear to them, that wishing to avoid the prevalent fault of the day, the author has sometimes descended too low, and that many of his expressions are too familiar, and not of sufficient dignity. It is apprehended, that the more conversant the reader is with our elder writers, and with those in modern times who have been the most successful in painting manners and passions, the fewer complaints of this kind will he have to make.

An accurate taste in poetry, and in all the other arts, Sir Joshua Reynolds has observed, is an acquired talent, which can only be produced by severe thought, and a long continued intercourse with the best models of composition.[1] This is mentioned not with so ridiculous a purpose as to prevent the most inexperienced reader from judging for himself; but merely to temper the rashness of decision, and to suggest that if poetry be a subject on which much time has not been bestowed, the judgment may be erroneous, and that in many cases it necessarily will be so.

The tale of Goody Blake and Harry Gill is founded on a well-authenticated fact which happened in Warwickshire. Of the other poems in the collection, it may be proper to say that they are either absolute inventions of the

---

† This "Advertisement," added shortly after the printing of LB was finished (see the headnote), was replaced by the much longer Preface of LB 1800 and subsequent editions.
1. Reynolds makes comments along these lines in Discourses 1, 2, 7, and especially 12 of his Discourses on Art: "The habit of contemplating and brooding over the ideas of great geniusses, till you find yourself warmed by the contact, is the true method of forming an Artist-like mind" (The Works of Sir Joshua Reynolds [London, 1797], 1:258). Unlike WW, however, Reynolds (1723–1792), a successful portrait painter and the first president of the Royal Academy of Arts, assumed that poetry must use "a language in the highest degree artificial" (Discourse 13, Works, 1:276).

author, or facts which took place within his personal observation or that of his friends. The poem of the Thorn, as the reader will soon discover, is not supposed to be spoken in the author's own person: the character of the loquacious narrator will sufficiently shew itself in the course of the story.[2] The Rime of the Ancyent Marinere was professedly written in imitation of the *style*, as well as of the spirit of the elder poets;[3] but with a few exceptions, the Author believes that the language adopted in it has been equally intelligible for these three last centuries. The lines entitled Expostulation and Reply, and those which follow, arose out of conversation with a friend[4] who was somewhat unreasonably attached to modern books of moral philosophy.

LINES

LEFT UPON A SEAT IN

A YEW-TREE

WHICH STANDS NEAR THE LAKE OF ESTHWAITE,

ON A DESOLATE PART OF THE SHORE,

YET COMMANDING A BEAUTIFUL PROSPECT[†]

   —Nay, Traveller! rest. This lonely yew-tree stands
Far from all human dwelling: what if here
No sparkling rivulet spread the verdant herb;
What if these barren boughs the bee not loves;
5 Yet, if the wind breathe soft, the curling waves,
That break against the shore, shall lull thy mind
By one soft impulse saved from vacancy.

     —————————Who he was
That piled these stones, and with the mossy sod
10 First covered o'er, and taught this aged tree,
Now wild, to bend its arms in circling shade,
I well remember.—He was one who own'd

---

2. See *The Thorn*, below, for the note on the poem that WW added to *LB 1800*.
3. In 1817 STC published a revised and expanded version of the poem, with modernized spelling, under his own name in his collection *Sibylline Leaves*: see *NCC*, 54–99, for both versions.
4. Possibly William Hazlitt (see Biographical and Topographical Glossary).
† *P 1815*: Poems proceeding from Sentiment and Reflection. The tree was located on the eastern shore of Esthwaite Water, about two miles southeast of Hawkshead (McCracken, 225). IF note: "Composed in part at school in Hawkshead. * * * The spot was my favourite walk in the evenings during the latter part of my School-time. The individual whose habits are here given was a gentleman of the neighbourhood, a man of talent and learning who had been educated at one of our Universities, & returned to pass his time in seclusion on his own estate. He died a bachelor in middle age. Induced by the beauty of the prospect, he built a small summerhouse on the rocks above the peninsula on which the ferry-house stands. * * * So much used I to be delighted with the view from it, while a little boy, that some years before the first pleasure-house was built I led thither from Hawkshead a youngster about my own age, an Irish Boy who was a servant to an Itinerant Conjuror [i.e., magician]. My motive was to witness the pleasure I expected the boy would receive from the prospect of the islands below & the intermingling water. I was not disappointed; and I hope the fact, insignificant as it may seem to some, may be thought worthy of note by others who may cast their eye over these notes." WW's note suggests that composition began in 1786–87; the earliest surviving MS seems to date from 1797 (*Chrono: EY*, 192). The *gentleman of the neighbourhood* has been identified as the Rev. William Braithwaite, who was in fact still alive in 1798 (see line 43).

No common soul. In youth, by genius nurs'd,
And big with lofty views, he to the world
15 Went forth, pure in his heart,[1] against the taint
Of dissolute tongues, 'gainst jealousy, and hate,
And scorn, against all enemies prepared,
All but neglect:[2] and so, his spirit damped
At once, with rash disdain he turned away,
20 And with the food of pride sustained his soul
In solitude.—Stranger! these gloomy boughs
Had charms for him; and here he loved to sit,
His only visitants a straggling sheep,
The stone-chat, or the glancing sand-piper;[3]
25 And on these barren rocks, with juniper,
And heath, and thistle, thinly sprinkled o'er,
Fixing his downward eye, he many an hour
A morbid pleasure nourished, tracing here
An emblem of his own unfruitful life:
30 And lifting up his head, he then would gaze
On the more distant scene; how lovely 'tis
Thou seest, and he would gaze till it became
Far lovelier, and his heart could not sustain
The beauty still more beauteous. Nor, that time,[4]
35 Would he forget those beings, to whose minds,
Warm from the labours of benevolence,
The world, and man himself, appeared a scene
Of kindred loveliness: then he would sigh
With mournful joy, to think that others felt
40 What he must never feel: and so, lost man!
On visionary views would fancy feed,
Till his eye streamed with tears. In this deep vale
He died, this seat his only monument.

If thou be one whose heart the holy forms
45 Of young imagination have kept pure,
Stranger! henceforth be warned; and know, that pride,
Howe'er disguised in its own majesty,
Is littleness; that he, who feels contempt
For any living thing, hath faculties
50 Which he has never used; that thought with him
Is in its infancy. The man, whose eye
Is ever on himself, doth look on one,
The least of nature's works, one who might move
The wise man to that scorn which wisdom holds

1. *In youth . . . heart*: altered in *LB 1800* to "In youth by science nursed / And led by nature into a wild scene / Of lofty hopes, he to the world went forth / A favored being, knowing no desire / Which genius did not hallow."
2. In *LB 1800* WW ended the sentence with *neglect* and inserted these lines: "The world, for so it thought, / Owed him no service: he was like a plant / Fair to the sun, the darling of the winds, / But hung with fruit which no one, that passed by, / Regarded, and his spirit damped at once, / With indignation he did turn away."
3. In *P 1815* WW revised and expanded line 24 to "The stone-chat, or the sand-lark, restless Bird, / Piping along the margin of the lake," and in *MP 1820* he restored the 1798 version.
4. In *LB 1800* WW inserted the line "When Nature had subdued him to herself" after line 34.

55 Unlawful, ever. O, be wiser thou!
Instructed that true knowledge leads to love,
True dignity abides with him alone
Who, in the silent hour of inward thought,
Can still suspect, and still revere himself,
60 In lowliness of heart.[5]

THE
FEMALE VAGRANT[†]

By Derwent's side[1] my Father's cottage stood,
(The Woman thus her artless story told)
One field, a flock, and what the neighbouring flood
Supplied, to him were more than mines of gold.
5 Light was my sleep; my days in transport roll'd:
With thoughtless joy I stretch'd along the shore
My father's nets, or watched, when from the fold
High o'er the cliffs I led my fleecy store,
A dizzy depth below! his boat and twinkling oar.[2]

10 My father was a good and pious man,
An honest man by honest parents bred,
And I believe that, soon as I began
To lisp, he made me kneel beside my bed,
And in his hearing there my prayers I said:
15 And afterwards, by my good father taught,
I read, and loved the books in which I read;
For books in every neighbouring house I sought,
And nothing to my mind a sweeter pleasure brought.

5. Stephen Parrish has speculated, on the basis of verbal parallels to passages in STC's letters and poems, that STC had a role in the composition of lines 45–60 (Art of the Lyrical Ballads, 66–70).
† P 1815: Juvenile Pieces. The earliest surviving version of the poem was composed as part of Salisbury Plain (1793–94), but it was published first as a separate poem in LB 1798. It was later incorporated into Guilt and Sorrow (published in 1842), a revised version of Salisbury Plain (see The Salisbury Plain Poems [CW], 131–38, 139–46, and also the note on The Prelude 12.365). IF note: "° ° ° The chief incident of it, more particularly her description of her feelings on the Atlantic [from line 118] are taken from life." The IF note on Guilt and Sorrow is more expansive: "° ° ° All that relates to her sufferings as a Soldier's wife in America & her condition of mind during her voyage home were faithfully taken from the report made to me of her own case by a friend who had been subjected to the same trials & afflicted in the same way. ° ° ° It may be worth the while to remark that tho' the incidents of this attempt do only in a small degree produce each other & it deviates accordingly from the general rule by which narrative pieces ought to be governed, it is not therefore wanting in continuous hold upon the mind or in unity which is effected by the identity of moral interest that places the two personages upon the same footing in the reader's sympathies. ° ° °" Sending a revised and shortened version of the poem to an admirer of LB 1800, WW observed, "The diction of that Poem is often vicious, and the descriptions are often false, giving proofs of a mind inattentive to the true nature of the subject on which it was employed" (WL, 1:328). The poem is composed in Spenserian stanzas, of which the last lines are hexameter rather than pentameter.
1. The lake Derwent Water, immediately southwest of Keswick.
2. In LB 1800 WW altered lines 8–9 to "Saw on the distant lake his twinkling oar / Or watch'd his lazy boat still lessening more and more."

Can I forget what charms did once adorn
20 My garden, stored with pease, and mint, and thyme,
And rose and lilly[3] for the sabbath morn?
The sabbath bells, and their delightful chime;
The gambols and wild freaks[4] at shearing time;
My hen's rich nest through long grass scarce espied;
25 The cowslip-gathering at May's dewy prime;[5]
The swans, that, when I sought the water-side,
From far to meet me came, spreading their snowy pride.[6]

The staff I yet remember which upbore
The bending body of my active sire;
30 His seat beneath the honeyed sycamore
When the bees hummed, and chair by winter fire;
When market-morning came, the neat attire
With which, though bent on haste,[7] myself I deck'd;
My watchful dog, whose starts of furious ire,
35 When stranger passed, so often I have check'd;
The red-breast known for years, which at my casement peck'd.

The suns of twenty summers danced along,—
Ah! little marked, how fast they rolled away:
Then rose a mansion proud our woods among,
40 And cottage after cottage owned its sway,
No joy to see a neighbouring house, or stray
Through pastures not his own, the master took;
My Father dared his greedy wish gainsay;
He loved his old hereditary nook,
45 And ill could I the thought of such sad parting brook.

But, when he had refused the proffered gold,
To cruel injuries he became a prey,
Sore traversed[8] in whate'er he bought and sold:
His troubles grew upon him day by day,
50 Till all his substance fell into decay.
His little range of water was denied;[9]
All but the bed where his old body lay,
All, all was seized, and weeping, side by side,
We sought a home where we uninjured might abide.

---

3. The rose and lily are important symbols in Christian iconography, both associated particularly with the Virgin Mary, and the latter more generally with purity.
4. Dancing and games.
5. A wild plant with fragrant yellow flowers that blossom in spring.
6. In *LB 1802* WW omitted this stanza and the next.
7. An allusion (used also in *The Prelude* 1.391) to Milton, *Paradise Lost*, 12.1–2: "As one who on his journey bates [i.e., halts] at noon, / Though bent on speed."
8. Thwarted, opposed.
9. WW's note: "Several of the Lakes in the north of England are let out to different Fishermen, in parcels marked out by imaginary lines drawn from rock to rock." In *LB 1802* WW omitted the note and revised lines 51–53 to "They dealt most hardly with him, and he tried / To move their hearts—but it was vain—for they / Seized all he had; and, weeping side by side."

55 Can I forget that miserable hour,
     When from the last hill-top, my sire surveyed,
     Peering above the trees, the steeple tower,
     That on his marriage-day sweet music made?
     Till then he hoped his bones might there be laid,
60 Close by my mother in their native bowers:
     Bidding me trust in God, he stood and prayed,—
     I could not pray:—through tears that fell in showers,
     Glimmer'd our dear-loved home, alas! no longer ours!

     There was a youth whom I had loved so long,
65 That when I loved him not I cannot say.
     'Mid the green mountains many and many a song
     We two had sung, like little[1] birds in May.
     When we began to tire of childish play
     We seemed still more and more to prize each other:
70 We talked of marriage and our marriage day;
     And I in truth did love him like a brother,
     For never could I hope to meet with such another.

     His father said, that to a distant town
     He must repair, to ply the artist's[2] trade.
75 What tears of bitter grief till then unknown!
     What tender vows our last sad kiss delayed!
     To him we turned:—we had no other aid.
     Like one revived, upon his neck I wept,
     And her whom he had loved in joy, he said
80 He well could love in grief: his faith he kept;
     And in a quiet home once more my father slept.

     Four years each day with daily bread was blest,
     By constant toil and constant prayer supplied.
     Three lovely infants lay upon my breast;
85 And often, viewing their sweet smiles, I sighed,
     And knew not why. My happy father died
     When sad distress reduced the children's meal:
     Thrice happy! that from him the grave did hide
     The empty loom, cold hearth, and silent wheel,
90 And tears that flowed for ills which patience could not heal.

     'Twas a hard change, an evil time was come;
     We had no hope, and no relief could gain.
     But soon, with proud parade, the noisy drum
     Beat round, to sweep the streets of want and pain.
95 My husband's arms now only served to strain
     Me and his children hungering in his view:
     In such dismay my prayers and tears were vain:

1. Altered to "gladsome" in *LB 1800*.
2. Craftsman's, artisan's (an older meaning of *artist* still current in the nineteenth century).

To join those miserable men he flew;
And now to the sea-coast, with numbers more, we drew.

100 There foul neglect for months and months we bore,
Nor yet the crowded fleet its anchor stirred.
Green fields before us and our native shore,
By fever, from polluted air incurred,
Ravage was made, for which no knell was heard.
105 Fondly we wished, and wished away, nor knew,
'Mid that long sickness, and those hopes deferr'd,
That happier days we never more must view:
The parting signal[3] streamed, at last the land withdrew.

But from delay the summer calms were past.
110 On as we drove, the equinoctial deep
Ran mountains-high before the howling blast.[4]
We gazed with terror on the gloomy sleep
Of them that perished in the whirlwind's sweep,
Untaught that soon such anguish must ensue,
115 Our hopes such harvest of affliction reap,
That we the mercy of the waves should rue.
We reached the western world, a poor, devoted[5] crew.

Oh! dreadful price of being to resign
All that is dear *in* being! better far
120 In Want's most lonely cave till death to pine,
Unseen, unheard, unwatched by any star;
Or in the streets and walks where proud men are,
Better our dying bodies to obtrude,
Than dog-like, wading at the heels of war,
125 Protract a curst existence, with the brood
That lap (their very nourishment!) their brother's blood.[6]

The pains and plagues that on our heads came down,
Disease and famine, agony and fear,
In wood or wilderness, in camp or town,
130 It would thy brain unsettle even to hear.
All perished—all, in one remorseless year,
Husband and children! one by one, by sword
And ravenous plague, all perished: every tear
Dried up, despairing, desolate, on board
135 A British ship I waked, as from a trance restored.

Peaceful as some immeasurable plain
By the first beams of dawning light impress'd,
In the calm sunshine slept the glittering main.

---

3. A flag flown from a ship to signal its imminent departure.
4. The time of the autumnal equinox (September 22 or 23) is the peak of the storm season in the
Atlantic.
5. Doomed (a meaning of *devoted* attested from the seventeenth to nineteenth centuries).
6. In *LB 1802* WW omitted this stanza.

The very ocean has its hour of rest,
140 That comes not to the human mourner's breast.
Remote from man, and storms of mortal care,
A heavenly silence did the waves invest;[7]
I looked and looked along the silent air,
Until it seemed to bring a joy to my despair.

145 Ah! how unlike those late terrific sleeps!
And groans, that rage of racking famine spoke,
Where looks inhuman dwelt on festering heaps!
The breathing pestilence that rose like smoke!
The shriek that from the distant battle broke!
150 The mine's dire earthquake,[8] and the pallid host
Driven by the bomb's incessant thunder-stroke
To loathsome vaults, where heart-sick anguish toss'd,
Hope died, and fear itself in agony was lost!

Yet does that burst of woe congeal my frame,
155 When the dark streets appeared to heave and gape,
While like a sea the storming army came,
And Fire from Hell reared his gigantic shape,
And Murder, by the ghastly gleam, and Rape
Seized their joint prey, the mother and the child!
160 But from these crazing thoughts my brain, escape!
—For weeks the balmy air breathed soft and mild,[9]
And on the gliding vessel Heaven and Ocean smiled.

Some mighty gulph of separation past,
I seemed transported to another world:—
165 A thought resigned with pain, when from the mast
The impatient mariner the sail unfurl'd,
And whistling, called the wind that hardly curled
The silent sea. From the sweet thoughts of home,
And from all hope I was forever hurled.
170 For me—farthest from earthly port to roam
Was best, could I but shun the spot where man might come.

And oft, robb'd of my perfect mind, I thought
At last my feet a resting-place had found:
Here will I weep in peace, (so fancy wrought,)
175 Roaming the illimitable waters round;
Here watch, of every human friend disowned,
All day, my ready tomb the ocean-flood—

7. In *LB 1802* WW altered lines 140–42 to "I too was calm, though heavily distress'd! / Oh me, how quiet sky and ocean were! / My heart was healed within me, I was bless'd, / And looked, and looked along the silent air."
8. Explosive mines.
9. In *LB 1802* WW altered lines 154–61 to "At midnight once the storming Army came, / Yet do I see the miserable sight, / The Bayonet, the Soldier, and the Flame / They followed us and faced us in our flight; / When Rape and Murder by the ghastly light / Seized their joint prey, the Mother and the Child! / But I must leave these thoughts.—From night to night, / From day to day, the air breathed soft and mild."

To break my dream the vessel reached its bound:
And homeless near a thousand homes I stood,
180   And near a thousand tables pined, and wanted food.

By grief enfeebled was I turned adrift,
Helpless as sailor cast on desart rock;
Nor morsel to my mouth that day did lift,
Nor dared my hand at any door to knock.
185   I lay, where with his drowsy mates, the cock
From the cross timber of an out-house hung;
How dismal tolled, that night, the city clock!
At morn my sick heart hunger scarcely stung,
Nor to the beggar's language could I frame my tongue.

190   So passed another day, and so the third:
Then did I try, in vain, the crowd's resort,
In deep despair by frightful wishes stirr'd,
Near the sea-side I reached a ruined fort:
There, pains which nature could no more support,
195   With blindness linked, did on my vitals fall;
Dizzy my brain, with interruption short
Of hideous sense; I sunk, nor step could crawl,
And thence was borne away to neighbouring hospital.

Recovery came with food: but still, my brain
200   Was weak, nor of the past had memory.
I heard my neighbours, in their beds, complain
Of many things which never troubled me;
Of feet still bustling round with busy glee,
Of looks where common kindness had no part,
205   Of service done with careless cruelty,
Fretting the fever round the languid heart,
And groans, which, as they said, would make a dead man start.

These things just served to stir the torpid sense,
Nor pain nor pity in my bosom raised.
210   Memory, though slow, returned with strength; and thence
Dismissed, again on open day I gazed,
At houses, men, and common light, amazed.
The lanes I sought, and as the sun retired,
Came, where beneath the trees a faggot blazed;
215   The wild brood saw me weep, my fate enquired,
And gave me food, and rest, more welcome, more desired.

My heart is touched to think that men like these,
The rude earth's tenants, were my first relief:
How kindly did they paint their vagrant ease!
220   And their long holiday that feared not grief,
For all belonged to all, and each was chief.
No plough their sinews strained; on grating road

No wain[1] they drove, and yet, the yellow sheaf
In every vale for their delight was stowed:
225   For them, in nature's meads,[2] the milky udder flowed.

Semblance, with straw and panniered ass,[3] they made
Of potters wandering on from door to door:
But life of happier sort to me pourtrayed,
And other joys my fancy to allure;
230   The bag-pipe dinning on the midnight moor
In barn uplighted, and companions boon
Well met from far with revelry secure,
In depth of forest glade, when jocund June
Rolled fast along the sky his warm and genial moon.

235   But ill it suited me, in journey dark
O'er moor and mountain, midnight theft to hatch;
To charm the surly house-dog's faithful bark,
Or hang on tiptoe at the lifted latch;
The gloomy lantern, and the dim blue match,
240   The black disguise,[4] the warning whistle shrill,
And ear still busy on its nightly watch,
Were not for me, brought up in nothing ill;
Besides, on griefs so fresh my thoughts were brooding still.

What could I do, unaided and unblest?
245   Poor Father! gone was every friend of thine:
And kindred of dead husband are at best
Small help, and, after marriage such as mine,
With little kindness would to me incline.
Ill was I then for toil or service fit:
250   With tears whose course no effort could confine,
By high-way side forgetful would I sit
Whole hours, my idle arms in moping sorrow knit.

I lived upon the mercy of the fields,
And oft of cruelty the sky accused;
255   On hazard, or what general bounty yields,
Now coldly given, now utterly refused.
The fields I for my bed have often used:
But, what afflicts my peace with keenest ruth
Is, that I have my inner self abused,
260   Foregone the home delight of constant truth,
And clear and open soul, so prized in fearless youth.

---

1. A wagon drawn by horses or oxen and used for carrying heavy loads.
2. Meadows.
3. A donkey with a pair of large baskets (*panniers*) slung over its back.
4. A reference to the practice—made a felony by the "Black Act" of 1723—of poaching game with the face blackened as a disguise.

Three years a wanderer, often have I view'd,
In tears, the sun towards that country tend
Where my poor heart lost all its fortitude:
265 And now across this moor my steps I bend—
Oh! tell me whither——for no earthly friend
Have I.——She ceased, and weeping turned away,
As if because her tale was at an end
She wept;—because she had no more to say
270 Of that perpetual weight which on her spirit lay.

G O O D Y   B L A K E ,

AND

H A R R Y   G I L L ,

A TRUE STORY[†]

Oh! what's the matter? what's the matter?
What is't that ails young Harry Gill?
That evermore his teeth they chatter,
Chatter, chatter, chatter still.
5 Of waistcoats Harry has no lack,
Good duffle grey, and flannel fine;
He has a blanket on his back,
And coats enough to smother nine.

In March, December, and in July,
10 'Tis all the same with Harry Gill;
The neighbours tell, and tell you truly,
His teeth they chatter, chatter still.
At night, at morning, and at noon,
'Tis all the same with Harry Gill;
15 Beneath the sun, beneath the moon,
His teeth they chatter, chatter still.

Young Harry was a lusty drover,[1]
And who so stout of limb as he?
His cheeks were red as ruddy clover,
20 His voice was like the voice of three.
Auld[2] Goody Blake was old and poor,

---

† Composed probably in spring 1798 (*Chrono: EY*, 224). In the Advertisement and again in the
Preface to *LB 1800*, WW insisted on the factual basis of the poem's narrative. The IF note
identifies his source as Erasmus Darwin's *Zoönomia; or, The Laws of Organic Life* (2 vols.,
1794–96), a book he had requested from his publisher Joseph Cottle in March 1798 (*WL*,
1:198–99). Darwin recounts the newspaper story of a Warwickshire farmer who felt perpetu-
ally cold after being cursed by an old woman he caught stealing sticks from his hedges to use as
firewood. But unlike Darwin, who cites the story as an instance of insanity in which things
imagined are mistaken for realities, WW does not offer an explanation of Harry Gill's feeling.
In *P 1815* he included the ballad among the "Poems of the Imagination" and noted that, "as [it]
rather refer[s] to the imagination than [is] produced by it, [it] would not have been placed here
but to avoid a needless multiplication of the Classes" (1:316n.). See also p. 616 below.
1. One who leads livestock to market.
2. In *LB 1802* WW modernized the spelling to "Old."

Ill fed she was, and thinly clad;
And any man who pass'd her door,
Might see how poor a hut she had.

25 All day she spun in her poor dwelling,
And then her three hours' work at night!
Alas! 'twas hardly worth the telling,
It would not pay for candle-light.
—This woman dwelt in Dorsetshire,
30 Her hut was on a cold hill-side,
And in that country coals are dear,
For they come far by wind and tide.[3]

By the same fire to boil their pottage,[4]
Two poor old dames, as I have known,
35 Will often live in one small cottage,
But she, poor woman, dwelt alone.
'Twas well enough when summer came,
The long, warm, lightsome summer-day,
Then at her door the *canty*[5] dame
40 Would sit, as any linnet[6] gay.

But when the ice our streams did fetter,
Oh! then how her old bones would shake!
You would have said, if you had met her,
'Twas a hard time for Goody Blake.
45 Her evenings then were dull and dead;
Sad case it was, as you may think,
For very cold to go to bed,
And then for cold not sleep a wink.

Oh joy for her! when e'er in winter
50 The winds at night had made a rout,
And scatter'd many a lusty splinter,
And many a rotten bough about.
Yet never had she, well or sick,
As every man who knew her says,
55 A pile before-hand, wood or stick,
Enough to warm her for three days.

Now, when the frost was past enduring,
And made her poor old bones to ache,
Could any thing be more alluring,
60 Than an old hedge to Goody Blake?
And now and then, it must be said,

3. WW relocates the story from the original Warwickshire, close to major coal-producing areas, to Dorsetshire on the south coast of England, to which coal would have been transported by boat.
4. A thick soup made of boiled vegetables.
5. Cheerful, lively (a Scottish and northern English dialect word, not used in Dorsetshire, hence WW's italics).
6. A songbird of the finch family, formerly very common in Britain.

When her old bones were cold and chill,
She left her fire, or left her bed,
To seek the hedge of Harry Gill.

65 Now Harry he had long suspected
This trespass of old Goody Blake,
And vow'd that she should be detected,
And he on her would vengeance take.
And oft from his warm fire he'd go,
70 And to the fields his road would take,
And there, at night, in frost and snow,
He watch'd to seize old Goody Blake.

And once, behind a rick[7] of barley,
Thus looking out did Harry stand;
75 The moon was full and shining clearly,
And crisp with frost the stubble-land.
—He hears a noise—he's all awake—
Again?—on tip-toe down the hill
He softly creeps—'Tis Goody Blake,
80 She's at the hedge of Harry Gill.

Right glad was he when he beheld her:
Stick after stick did Goody pull,
He stood behind a bush of elder,
Till she had filled her apron full.
85 When with her load she turned about,
The bye-road back again to take,
He started forward with a shout,
And sprang upon poor Goody Blake.

And fiercely by the arm he took her,
90 And by the arm he held her fast,
And fiercely by the arm he shook her,
And cried, "I've caught you then at last!"
Then Goody, who had nothing said,
Her bundle from her lap let fall;
95 And kneeling on the sticks, she pray'd
To God that is the judge of all.

She pray'd, her wither'd hand uprearing,
While Harry held her by the arm—
"God! who art never out of hearing,
100 "O may he never more be warm!"
The cold, cold moon above her head,
Thus on her knees did Goody pray,
Young Harry heard what she had said,
And icy-cold he turned away.

7. A stack or pile.

105 He went complaining all the morrow
That he was cold and very chill:
His face was gloom, his heart was sorrow,
Alas! that day for Harry Gill!
That day he wore a riding-coat,
110 But not a whit the warmer he:
Another was on Thursday brought,
And ere the Sabbath he had three.

'Twas all in vain, a useless matter,
And blankets were about him pinn'd;
115 Yet still his jaws and teeth they clatter,
Like a loose casement in the wind.
And Harry's flesh it fell away;
And all who see him say 'tis plain,
That, live as long as live he may,
120 He never will be warm again.

No word to any man he utters,
A-bed or up, to young or old;
But ever to himself he mutters,
"Poor Harry Gill is very cold."
125 A-bed or up, by night or day;
His teeth they chatter, chatter still.
Now think, ye farmers all, I pray,
Of Goody Blake and Harry Gill.

LINES

WRITTEN AT A SMALL DISTANCE FROM MY HOUSE, AND SENT BY MY LITTLE BOY TO THE PERSON TO WHOM THEY ARE ADDRESSED[†]

It is the first mild day of March:
Each minute sweeter than before,
The red-breast sings from the tall larch[1]
That stands beside our door.

5 There is a blessing in the air,
Which seems a sense of joy to yield
To the bare trees, and mountains bare,
And grass in the green field.

---

† P 1815: Poems proceeding from Sentiment and Reflection. Composed probably between March 1 and 9, 1798 (*Chrono: EY*, 32). IF note: "Composed in front of Alfoxden House. My little boy messenger on this occasion was the son of Basil Montagu." At the time WW and DW were caring for Montagu's son (see Biographical and Topographical Glossary), also named Basil (not Edward, as in line 13 and in *Anecdote for Fathers* below).
1. A deciduous coniferous tree with needle-like leaves.

My Sister! ('tis a wish of mine)
10   Now that our morning meal is done,
Make haste, your morning task resign;
Come forth and feel the sun.

Edward will come with you, and pray,
Put on with speed your woodland dress,
15   And bring no book, for this one day
We'll give to idleness.

No joyless forms shall regulate
Our living Calendar:
We from to-day, my friend, will date
20   The opening of the year.

Love, now an universal birth,
From heart to heart is stealing,
From earth to man, from man to earth,
—It is the hour of feeling.

25   One moment now may give us more
Than fifty years of reason;[2]
Our minds shall drink at every pore
The spirit of the season.

Some silent laws our hearts may make,
30   Which they shall long obey;
We for the year to come may take
Our temper from to-day.

And from the blessed power that rolls
About, below, above;
35   We'll frame the measure of our souls,
They shall be tuned to love.

Then come, my sister! come, I pray,
With speed put on your woodland dress,
And bring no book; for this one day
40   We'll give to idleness.

2. In 1836, after DW had begun to show signs of dementia, WW altered this line to "Than years of toiling reason."

SIMON LEE,

THE OLD HUNTSMAN,

WITH AN INCIDENT IN WHICH HE WAS CONCERNED[†]

In the sweet shire of Cardigan,
Not far from pleasant Ivor-hall,
An old man dwells, a little man,
I've heard he once was tall.
5 Of years he has upon his back,
No doubt, a burthen weighty;
He says he is three score and ten,
But others say he's eighty.

A long blue livery-coat has he,
10 That's fair behind, and fair before;
Yet, meet him where you will, you see
At once that he is poor.
Full five and twenty years he lived
A running huntsman merry;
15 And, though he has but one eye left,
His cheek is like a cherry.

No man like him the horn could sound,
And no man was so full of glee;
To say the least, four counties round
20 Had heard of Simon Lee;
His master's dead, and no one now
Dwells in the hall of Ivor;
Men, dogs, and horses, all are dead;
He is the sole survivor.

25 His hunting feats have him bereft
Of his right eye, as you may see:
And then, what limbs those feats have left
To poor old Simon Lee!
He has no son, he has no child,
30 His wife, an aged woman,

---

† P 1815: Poems proceeding from Sentiment and Reflection. Composed probably between early
March and mid-May 1798 (*Chrono: EY*, 32), and heavily revised and reordered in later years.
Only the most significant revisions prior to 1820 are noted here. For the revisions from 1820
on, see *LB* (CW), 68–70. IF note: "This old man had been huntsman to the Squires of Alfox-
den, which, at the time we occupied it belonged to a minor. The old man's cottage stood upon
the common a little way from the entrance to Alfoxden Park. * * * It is unnecessary to add, the
fact was as mentioned in the poem, and I have, after an interval of 45 years, the image of the
old man as fresh before my eyes as if I had seen him yesterday." The huntsman was responsible
for the dogs during a hunt. WW transposes the setting from Somerset in southwestern England
to Cardiganshire, a coastal county in western Wales (a transposition discussed by David Simp-
son, *Wordsworth's Historical Imagination*, 149–59).

Lives with him, near the waterfall,
Upon the village common.[1]

And he is lean and he is sick,
His little body's half awry
35   His ancles they are swoln and thick;[2]
His legs are thin and dry.
When he was young he little knew
Of husbandry or tillage;
And now he's forced to work, though weak,
40   —The weakest in the village.

He all the country could outrun,
Could leave both man and horse behind;
And often, ere the race was done,
He reeled and was stone-blind.
45   And still there's something in the world
At which his heart rejoices;
For when the chiming hounds are out,
He dearly loves their voices!

Old Ruth works out of doors with him,
50   And does what Simon cannot do;
For she, not over stout of limb,
Is stouter of the two.
And though you with your utmost skill
From labour could not wean them,
55   Alas! 'tis very little, all
Which they can do between them.

Beside their moss-grown hut of clay,
Not twenty paces from the door,
A scrap of land they have, but they
60   Are poorest of the poor.
This scrap of land he from the heath
Enclosed when he was stronger;
But what avails the land to them,
Which they can till no longer?

65   Few months of life has he in store,
As he to you will tell,
For still, the more he works, the more
His poor old ancles swell.[3]
My gentle reader, I perceive
70   How patiently you've waited,

---

1. In *LB 1802* through *P 1815*, lines 25–48 (stanzas 4–6) were rearranged in the following order: lines 33–40, 41–48, and 25–32.
2. *little* (line 34): altered in *LB 1800* to "dwindled"; *ancles they*: altered in *P 1815* to "ancles, too." Swollen ankles are symptomatic of dropsy, an excess of watery fluids in bodily tissues or cavities.
3. *His poor old*: altered in *P 1815* to "Do his weak."

And I'm afraid that you expect
Some tale will be related.

O reader! had you in your mind
Such stores as silent thought[4] can bring,
75   O gentle reader! you would find
A tale in every thing.
What more I have to say is short,
I hope you'll kindly take it;
It is no tale; but should you think,
80   Perhaps a tale you'll make it.

One summer-day I chanced to see
This old man doing all he could
About[5] the root of an old tree,
A stump of rotten wood.
85   The mattock[6] totter'd in his hand;
So vain was his endeavour
That at the root of the old tree
He might have worked for ever.

"You're overtasked, good Simon Lee,
90   Give me your tool" to him I said;
And at the word right gladly he
Received my proffer'd aid.
I struck, and with a single blow
The tangled root I sever'd,
95   At which the poor old man so long
And vainly had endeavour'd.

The tears into his eyes were brought,
And thanks and praises seemed to run
So fast out of his heart, I thought
100   They never would have done.
—I've heard of hearts unkind, kind deeds
With coldness still returning.
Alas! the gratitude of men
Has oftener left me mourning.[7]

---

4. An allusion to Shakespeare's Sonnet 30, lines 1–2: "When to the sessions of sweet silent thought / I summon up remembrance of things past."
5. *About*: altered in *P 1815* to "To unearth."
6. A handtool with a chisel-like blade attached perpendicularly to the handle, used for loosening earth and digging up roots.
7. In *BL* STC quoted the last four lines of the poem as an example of a "characteristic excellence of Mr. W's works": "a correspondent weight and sanity of the Thoughts and Sentiments,—won, not from books; but—from the poet's own meditative observations. They are *fresh* and have the dew upon them" (NCC, 536–37).

ANECDOTE FOR FATHERS,

SHEWING HOW THE ART OF LYING MAY BE TAUGHT[†]

I have a boy of five years old,
His face is fair and fresh to see;
His limbs are cast in beauty's mould,
And dearly he loves me.

5   One morn we stroll'd on our dry walk,
Our quiet house all full in view,
And held such intermitted talk
As we are wont to do.

My thoughts on former pleasures ran;
10 I thought of Kilve's delightful shore,
My pleasant home, when spring began,
A long, long year before.

A day it was when I could bear
To think, and think, and think again;
15 With so much happiness to spare,
I could not feel a pain.

My boy was by my side, so slim
And graceful in his rustic dress!
And oftentimes I talked to him,
20 In very idleness.

The young lambs ran a pretty race;
The morning sun shone bright and warm;
"Klive," said I, "was a pleasant place,
And so is Liswyn farm."

25 "My little boy, which like you more,"
I said and took him by the arm—
"Our home by Kilve's delightful shore,
Or here at Liswyn farm?"

[†] *P 1815*: Poems referring to Childhood. Composed probably between early April and mid-May, 1798 (*Chrono: EY*, 32). IF note: "This was suggested in front of Alfoxden. The Boy was a son of my friend Basil Montagu, who had been two or three years under our care. The name of Kilve [line 10] is from a village on the Bristol Channel, about a mile from Alfoxden; and the name of Liswin Farm [line 24] was taken from a beautiful spot on the [River] Wye." In March 1796 WW had written in a letter that the boy "lies like a little devil" (*WL*, 1:168; *LB* [CW], 347). Llyswen was the name of the farm in the Wye Valley to which the radical orator John Thelwall (1764–1834) retired in 1797, and where WW, DW, and STC visited him in August 1798 (*WL*, 1:232, 7:249). In October 1826 WW informed an unidentified correspondent that his intention in the poem "was to point out the injurious effects of putting inconsiderate questions to Children" (*WL*, 4:486), and in 1845 he replaced the subtitle with a Latin epigraph from the third-century ecclesiastical historian Eusebius's *Praeparatio evangelica* 6.5: *Retine vim istam, falsa enim dicam si coges* (Restrain that vigor of yours, for if you compel me I shall tell lies).

"And tell me, had you rather be,"
30   I said and held him by the arm,
"At Kilve's smooth shore by the green sea,
Or here at Liswyn farm?"[1]

In careless mood he looked at me,
While still I held him by the arm,
35   And said, "At Kilve I'd rather be
Than here at Liswyn farm."

"Now, little Edward, say why so;
My little Edward, tell me why;"
"I cannot tell, I do not know."
40   "Why this is strange," said I.

"For, here are woods and green-hills warm;
There surely must some reason be
Why you would change sweet Liswyn farm
For Kilve by the green sea."

45   At this, my boy, so fair and slim,
Hung down his head, nor made reply;
And five times did I say to him,
"Why? Edward, tell me why?"[2]

His head he raised—there was in sight,
50   It caught his eye, he saw it plain—
Upon the house-top, glittering bright,
A broad and gilded vane.

Then did the boy his tongue unlock,
And thus to me he made reply;
55   "At Kilve there was no weather-cock,
"And that's the reason why."

Oh dearest, dearest boy! my heart
For better lore would seldom yearn,
Could I but teach the hundredth part
60   Of what from thee I learn.

---

1. The closing quotation marks, inserted here from *LB 1802*, are missing in *LB 1798* and *LB 1800*.
2. In *LB 1800* WW altered lines 45–48 to "At this my boy hung down his head, / He blush'd with shame nor made reply; / And five times to the child I said, / 'Why, Edward, tell me why?'"

WE ARE SEVEN[†]

A simple child, dear brother Jim,[1]
That lightly draws its breath,
And feels its life in every limb,
What should it know of death?

5   I met a little cottage girl,
She was eight years old, she said;
Her hair was thick with many a curl
That cluster'd round her head.

She had a rustic, woodland air,
10 And she was wildly clad;
Her eyes were fair, and very fair,
—Her beauty made me glad.

"Sisters and brothers, little maid,
How many may you be?"
15 "How many? seven in all," she said,
And wondering looked at me.

"And where are they, I pray you tell?"
She answered, "Seven are we,
And two of us at Conway[2] dwell,
20 And two are gone to sea.

---

† *P 1815:* Poems referring to Childhood. From the IF note: "Written at Alfoxden in the Spring of 1798, under circumstances somewhat remarkable. The little Girl who is the heroine I met within the area of Goodrich Castle [a ruined medieval castle in Herefordshire, on the English side of the River Wye] in the year 1793. * * * I composed it while walking in the grove of Alfoxden. My friends will not deem it too trifling to relate that while walking to and fro I composed the last stanza first, having begun with the last line. When it was all but finished, I came in and recited it to Mr. Coleridge and my Sister, and said, 'A prefatory Stanza must be added, and I should sit down to our little tea-meal with greater pleasure if my task was finished.' I mentioned in substance what I wished to be expressed, and Coleridge immediately threw off the stanza thus:

A little Child, dear brother Jem,—

I objected to the rhyme, dear brother Jem as being ludicrous, but we all enjoyed the joke of hitching in our friend James Tobin's name who was familiarly called Jem." The note proceeds to relate how Tobin (1767–1814), a friend of WW and STC from Bristol, entreated WW not to publish the poem because it would appear ridiculous; but it was published nonetheless (with *Jim* in line 1). In another section of the IF note omitted here, WW recalls the circumstances of his collaboration with STC on *LB:* see the headnote to *LB* in this Norton Critical Edition and in *NCC,* 54–57. In the Preface to *LB 1800* WW described the poem's purpose as to show "the perplexity and obscurity which in childhood attend our notion of death, or rather our utter inability to admit that notion." For STC's later critique of the poem in this connection, see the note to lines 120–23 of the Intimations Ode (p. 437 below). Alan Bewell (*Wordsworth and the Enlightenment,* 195–96) notes a thematic parallel to the poem in Jean-Jacques Rousseau's novel on childhood education, *Émile* (1762), which WW may have read in the 1790s or earlier (*Reading 1770–99,* no. 214).
1. In *P 1815* WW shortened this line to "——A simple child."
2. I.e., Conwy, a medieval walled town in northwest Wales.

"Two of us in the church-yard lie,
My sister and my brother,
And in the church-yard cottage, I
Dwell near them with my mother."

25 "You say that two at Conway dwell,
And two are gone to sea,
Yet you are seven; I pray you tell
Sweet Maid, how this may be?"

Then did the little Maid reply,
30 "Seven boys and girls are we;
Two of us in the church-yard lie,
Beneath the church-yard tree."

"You run about, my little maid,
Your limbs they are alive;
35 If two are in the church-yard laid,
Then ye are only five."

"Their graves are green, they may be seen,"
The little Maid replied,
"Twelve steps or more from my mother's door,
40 And they are side by side.

"My stockings there I often knit,
My 'kerchief there I hem;
And there upon the ground I sit—
I sit and sing to them.

45 "And often after sunset, Sir,
When it is light and fair,
I take my little porringer,[3]
And eat my supper there.

"The first that died was little Jane;
50 In bed she moaning lay,
Till God released her of her pain,
And then she went away.

"So in the church-yard she was laid,
And all the summer dry,
55 Together round her grave we played,
My brother John and I.

"And when the ground was white with snow,
And I could run and slide,

3. A small bowl for porridge or soup.

My brother John was forced to go,
60 And he lies by her side."

"How many are you then," said I,
"If they two are in Heaven?"
The little Maiden did reply,
"O Master! we are seven."

65 "But they are dead; those two are dead!
Their spirits are in heaven!"
'Twas throwing words away; for still
The little Maid would have her will,
And said, "Nay, we are seven!"

L I N E S
WRITTEN IN EARLY SPRING†

I heard a thousand blended notes,
While in a grove I sate reclined,
In that sweet mood when pleasant thoughts
Bring sad thoughts to the mind.

5 To her fair works did nature link
The human soul that through me ran;
And much it griev'd my heart to think
What man has made of man.

Through primrose-tufts, in that sweet bower,
10 The periwinkle trail'd its wreathes;
And 'tis my faith that every flower
Enjoys the air it breathes.

The birds around me hopp'd and play'd:
Their thoughts I cannot measure,
15 But the least motion which they made,
It seem'd a thrill of pleasure.

The budding twigs spread out their fan,
To catch the breezy air;

† *P 1815:* Poems proceeding from Sentiment and Reflection. Composed probably between early April and mid-May, 1798 (*Chrono: EY*, 32). IF note: "Actually composed while I was sitting by the side of the brook that runs from the *Comb* [valley], in which stands the village of Alford [actually Holford], through the grounds of Alfoxden. It was a chosen resort of mine. The brook fell down a sloping rock so as to make a waterfall considerable for that country, and, across the pool below, had fallen a tree, an ash if I remember rightly, from which rose perpendicularly boughs in search of the light intercepted by the deep shade above. The boughs bore leaves of green that for want of sunshine had faded into almost lily-white: and, from the underside of this natural sylvan bridge depended long & beautiful tresses of ivy which waved gently in the breeze that might poetically speaking be called the breath of the water in the brook." STC also described this scene in *This Lime Tree Bower My Prison* (1797), lines 10–19 (NCC, 137).

And I must think, do all I can,
20 That there was pleasure there.

If I these thoughts may not prevent,
If such be of my creed the plan,[1]
Have I not reason to lament
What man has made of man?

THE
T H O R N[†]

I.

There is a thorn; it looks so old,
In truth you'd find it hard to say,
How it could ever have been young,
It looks so old and grey.
5 Not higher than a two-years' child,
It stands erect this aged thorn;
No leaves it has, no thorny points;
It is a mass of knotted joints,
A wretched thing forlorn.
10 It stands erect, and like a stone
With lichens it is overgrown.

II.

Like rock or stone, it is o'ergrown
With lichens to the very top,
And hung with heavy tufts of moss,
15 A melancholy crop:
Up from the earth these mosses creep,
And this poor thorn they clasp it round
So close, you'd say that they were bent
With plain and manifest intent,
20 To drag it to the ground;
And all had joined in one endeavour
To bury this poor thorn for ever.

III.

High on a mountain's highest ridge,
Where oft the stormy winter gale
25 Cuts like a scythe, while through the clouds
It sweeps from vale to vale;
Not five yards from the mountain-path,
This thorn you on your left espy;
And to the left, three yards beyond,
30 You see a little muddy pond
Of water, never dry;
I've measured it from side to side:
'Tis three feet long, and two feet wide.[1]

IV.

And close beside this aged thorn,
35 There is a fresh and lovely sight,
A beauteous heap, a hill of moss,
Just half a foot in height.
All lovely colours there you see,
All colours that were ever seen,
40 And mossy network[2] too is there,
As if by hand of lady fair
The work had woven been,
And cups,[3] the darlings of the eye,
So deep is their vermilion dye.

V.

45 Ah me! what lovely tints are there!
Of olive-green and scarlet bright,
In spikes, in branches, and in stars,
Green, red, and pearly white.
This heap of earth o'ergrown with moss,
50 Which close beside the thorn you see,
So fresh in all its beauteous dyes,
Is like an infant's grave in size
As like as like can be:
But never, never any where,
55 An infant's grave was half so fair.

1. In *BL* STC commented that lines 32–33, 104–43, and 148–65 "are felt by many unprejudiced and unsophisticated hearts, as sudden and unpleasant sinkings from the height to which the poet had previously lifted them, and to which he again re-elevates both himself and his reader" (*NCC*, 501). His more general criticism that "it is not possible to imitate truly a dull and garrulous discourser, without repeating the effects of dulness and garrulity" echoed Robert Southey's complaint about the poem in his review of *LB 1798*: "The author should have recollected that he who personates tiresome loquacity, becomes tiresome himself" (*CH*, 66). When, in May 1815, Henry Crabb Robinson (see Biographical and Topographical Glossary) told WW he "dared not read them [lines 32–33] out in company," WW responded that "they ought to be liked" (*CRB*, 1:166). Nevertheless, in *MP 1820* WW revised the lines to "Though but of compass small and bare / To thirsty suns, and parching air."
2. In its literal sense, a netlike fabric.
3. Blossoms.

VI.

Now would you see this aged thorn,
This pond and beauteous hill of moss,
You must take care and chuse your time
The mountain when to cross.
60 For oft there sits, between the heap
That's like an infant's grave in size,
And that same pond of which I spoke,
A woman in a scarlet cloak,
And to herself she cries,
65 "Oh misery! oh misery!
Oh woe is me! oh misery!"

VII.[4]

At all times of the day and night
This wretched woman thither goes,
And she is known to every star,
70 And every wind that blows;
And there beside the thorn she sits
When the blue day-light's in the skies,
And when the whirlwind's on the hill,
Or frosty air is keen and still,
75 And to herself she cries,
"Oh misery! oh misery!
Oh woe is me! oh misery!"

VIII.

"Now wherefore thus, by day and night,
In rain, in tempest, and in snow,
80 Thus to the dreary mountain-top
Does this poor woman go?
And why sits she beside the thorn
When the blue day-light's in the sky,
Or when the whirlwind's on the hill,
85 Or frosty air is keen and still,
And wherefore does she cry?—
Oh wherefore? wherefore? tell me why
Does she repeat that doleful cry?"

IX.

I cannot tell; I wish I could;
90 For the true reason no one knows,
But if you'd gladly view the spot,
The spot to which she goes;

4. In *BL* STC quoted stanza 7 and asserted approvingly its nonconformity to WW's goal, stated in the Preface to *LB 1800*, of using "the real language of men": "I reflect with delight, how little a mere theory, though of his own workmanship, interferes with the processes of genuine imagination in a man of true poetic genius" (*NCC*, 506).

The heap that's like an infant's grave,
The pond—and thorn, so old and grey,
95 Pass by her door—'tis seldom shut—
And if you see her in her hut,
Then to the spot away!—
I never heard of such as dare
Approach the spot when she is there.

X.

100 "But wherefore to the mountain-top
Can this unhappy woman go,
Whatever star is in the skies,
Whatever wind may blow?"
Nay rack your brain—'tis all in vain,
105 I'll tell you every thing I know;
But to the thorn, and to the pond
Which is a little step beyond,
I wish that you would go:
Perhaps when you are at the place
110 You something of her tale may trace.

XI.

I'll give you the best help I can:
Before you up the mountain go,
Up to the dreary mountain-top,
I'll tell you all I know.[5]
115 'Tis now some two and twenty years,
Since she (her name is Martha Ray)[6]
Gave with a maiden's true good will
Her company to Stephen Hill;
And she was blithe and gay,
120 And she was happy, happy still
Whene'er she thought of Stephen Hill.[7]

XII.

And they had fix'd the wedding-day,
The morning that must wed them both;
But Stephen to another maid
125 Had sworn another oath;
And with this other maid to church

---

5. In *MP 1820* WW omitted lines 104–14 and formed a single stanza of lines 100–103 and 115–21.
6. WW's friend Basil Montagu (see Biographical and Topographical Glossary) was the illegitimate son of John Montagu, fourth Earl of Sandwich, and the singer Martha Ray, who had been murdered by a rejected suitor, James Hackman, in 1779. The murder was cited in Erasmus Darwin's *Zoönomia* (1794–96), WW's source for *Goody Blake and Harry Gill*, as an example of "the furious and melancholy insanity" of the spurned lover (*LB* [CW], 352). Basil Montagu Jr. accompanied WW and DW on their walk on the day that WW probably began the poem (*DWJ*, 1:13).
7. In *MP 1820* WW altered lines 120–21 to "While friends and kindred all approved / Of him whom tenderly she loved."

Unthinking Stephen went—
Poor Martha! on that woful day
A cruel, cruel fire, they say,
130 Into her bones was sent:
It dried her body like a cinder,
And almost turn'd her brain to tinder.[8]

XIII.

They say, full six months after this,
While yet the summer-leaves were green,
135 She to the mountain-top would go,
And there was often seen.
'Tis said, a child was in her womb,
As now to any eye was plain;[9]
She was with child, and she was mad,
140 Yet often she was sober sad
From her exceeding pain.
Oh me! ten thousand times I'd rather
That he had died, that cruel father![1]

XIV.

Sad case for such a brain to hold
145 Communion with a stirring child!
Sad case, as you may think, for one
Who had a brain so wild!
Last Christmas when we talked of this,
Old Farmer Simpson did maintain,
150 That in her womb the infant wrought[2]
About its mother's heart, and brought
Her senses back again:
And when at last her time drew near,
Her looks were calm, her senses clear.

XV.

155 No more I know, I wish I did,
And I would tell it all to you;
For what became of this poor child
There's none that ever knew:
And if a child was born or no,
160 There's no one that could ever tell;
And if 'twas born alive or dead,
There's no one knows, as I have said,

8. In *P 1815* WW altered lines 129–32 to "A pang of pitiless dismay / Into her soul was sent; / A Fire was kindled in her breast, / Which might not burn itself to rest."
9. In *MP 1820* WW altered lines 137–38 to "'Tis said, her lamentable state / Even to a careless eye was plain."
1. In *MP 1820* WW altered lines 142–43 to "O guilty Father,—would that death / Had saved him from that breach of faith!"
2. In *MP 1820* WW altered lines 149–50 to "And grey-haired Wilfred of the glen / Held that the unborn Infant wrought."

But some remember well,
That Martha Ray about this time
165 Would up the mountain often climb.

XVI.

And all that winter, when at night
The wind blew from the mountain-peak,
'Twas worth your while, though in the dark,
The church-yard path to seek:
170 For many a time and oft were heard
Cries coming from the mountain-head,
Some plainly living voices were,
And others, I've heard many swear,
Were voices of the dead:
175 I cannot think, whate'er they say,
They had to do with Martha Ray.

XVII.

But that she goes to this old thorn,
The thorn which I've described to you,
And there sits in a scarlet cloak,
180 I will be sworn is true.
For one day with my telescope,
To view the ocean wide and bright,
When to this country first I came,
Ere I had heard of Martha's name,
185 I climbed the mountain's height:
A storm came on, and I could see
No object higher than my knee.

XVIII.

'Twas mist and rain, and storm and rain,
No screen, no fence could I discover.
190 And then the wind! in faith, it was
A wind full ten times over.
I looked around, I thought I saw
A jutting crag, and off I ran,
Head-foremost, through the driving rain,
195 The shelter of the crag to gain,
And, as I am a man,
Instead of jutting crag, I found
A woman seated, on the ground.

XIX.

I did not speak—I saw her face,
200 Her face it was enough for me;
I turned about and heard her cry,
"O misery! O misery!"

And there she sits, until the moon
Through half the clear blue sky will go,
205 And when the little breezes make
The waters of the pond to shake,
As all the country know,
She shudders and yon hear her cry,
"Oh misery! oh misery!

XX.

210 "But what's the thorn? and what's the pond?
And what's the hill of moss to her?
And what's the creeping breeze that comes
The little pond to stir?"
I cannot tell; but some will say
215 She hanged her baby on the tree,
Some say she drowned it in the pond,
Which is a little step beyond,
But all and each agree,
The little babe was buried there,
220 Beneath that hill of moss so fair.

XXI.

I've heard the scarlet moss is red[3]
With drops of that poor infant's blood;
But kill a new-born infant thus!
I do not think she could.
225 Some say, if to the pond you go,
And fix on it a steady view,
The shadow of a babe you trace,
A baby and a baby's face,
And that it looks at you;
230 Whene'er you look on it, 'tis plain
The baby looks at you again.

XXII.

And some had sworn an oath that she
Should be to public justice brought;
And for the little infant's bones
235 With spades they would have sought.
But then the beauteous hill of moss
Before their eyes began to stir;
And for full fifty yards around,
The grass it shook upon the ground;
240 But all do still aver
The little babe is buried there,
Beneath that hill of moss so fair.

---

3. In *LB 1800* WW altered line 221 to "I've heard, the moss is spotted red."

XXIII.

I cannot tell how this may be,
But plain it is, the thorn is bound
With heavy tufts of moss, that strive
To drag it to the ground.
And this I know, full many a time,
When she was on the mountain high,
By day, and in the silent night,
When all the stars shone clear and bright,
That I have heard her cry,
"Oh misery! oh misery!
O woe is me! oh misery!"

Note to *The Thorn* (1800)[†]

This Poem ought to have been preceded by an introductory Poem, which
I have been prevented from writing by never having felt myself in a mood
when it was probable that I should write it well.—The character which I
have here introduced speaking is sufficiently common. The Reader will
perhaps have a general notion of it, if he has ever known a man, a Cap-
tain of a small trading vessel for example, who being past the middle age
of life, had retired upon an annuity or small independent income to some
village or country town of which he was not a native, or in which he had
not been accustomed to live.[1] Such men having little to do become credu-
lous and talkative from indolence; and from the same cause, and other
predisposing causes by which it is probable that such men may have been
affected, they are prone to superstition. On which account it appeared to
me proper to select a character like this to exhibit some of the general laws
by which superstition acts upon the mind. Superstitious men are almost
always men of slow faculties and deep feelings; their minds are not loose
but adhesive; they have a reasonable share of imagination, by which word
I mean the faculty which produces impressive effects out of simple ele-
ments; but they are utterly destitute of fancy, the power by which pleasure
and surprise are excited by sudden varieties of situation and by accumu-
lated imagery.[2]

　　It was my wish in this poem to shew the manner in which such men
cleave to the same ideas; and to follow the turns of passion, always differ-
ent, yet not palpably different, by which their conversation is swayed. I had
two objects to attain; first, to represent a picture which should not be

† This note was not present in *LB 1798* but was added to *LB 1800* and retained in the editions of
　1802 and 1805. WW did not, however, reprint the note when he included *The Thorn* in *P 1815*
　and later editions of his poetry.
1. This sentence conjuring up the poem's speaker was ridiculed by Francis Jeffrey in a review of
　George Crabbe's *Poems* in the *Edinburgh Review*, April 1808 (*CH*, 228–29); quoted disapprov-
　ingly by STC in *BL* (*NCC*, 501–502); and parodied by Lord Byron in the manuscript preface
　(which he never published) to the first canto of *Don Juan* (*Complete Poetical Works*, ed. Jerome
　McGann [Oxford, 1980–93], 5:81–84).
2. WW adopts a similar conception of imagination in *The Prelude* 13.98–99, and a similar con-
　ception of fancy in his Preface to *P 1815* (pp. 516–18 below). But his later distinction between
　imagination and fancy, which assumes the superiority of the former, is based on a different
　conception of imagination: see *The Prelude* 8.583–86 and 13.289–94, and the Preface to
　P 1815.

unimpressive yet consistent with the character that should describe it, secondly, while I adhered to the style in which such persons describe, to take care that words, which in their minds are impregnated with passion, should likewise convey passion to Readers who are not accustomed to sympathize with men feeling in that manner or using such language. It seemed to me that this might be done by calling in the assistance of Lyrical and rapid Metre. It was necessary that the Poem, to be natural, should in reality move slowly; yet I hoped, that, by the aid of the metre, to those who should at all enter into the spirit of the Poem, it would appear to move quickly. The Reader will have the kindness to excuse this note as I am sensible that an introductory Poem is necessary to give this Poem its full effect.

Upon this occasion I will request permission to add a few words closely connected with The Thorn and many other Poems to these Volumes.[3] There is numerous class of readers who imagine that the same words cannot be repeated without tautology: this is a great error: virtual tautology is much oftener produced by using different words when the meaning is exactly the same. Words, a Poet's words more particularly, ought to be weighed in the balance of feeling and not measured by the space which they occupy upon paper. For the Reader cannot be too often reminded that Poetry is passion: it is the history or science of feelings: now every man must know that an attempt is rarely made to communicate impassioned feelings without something of an accompanying consciousness of the inadequateness of our own powers, or the deficiencies of language. During such efforts there will be a craving in the mind, and as long as it is unsatisfied the Speaker will cling to the same words, or words of the same character. There are also various other reasons why repetition and apparent tautology are frequently beauties of the highest kind. Among the chief of these reasons is the interest which the mind attaches to words, not only as symbols of the passion, but as *things,* active and efficient, which are of themselves part of the passion. And further, from a spirit of fondness, exultation, and gratitude, the mind luxuriates in the repetition of words which appear successfully to communicate its feelings. The truth of these remarks might be shewn by innumerable passages from the Bible and from the impassioned poetry of every nation.

"Awake, awake Deborah: awake, awake, utter a song:
Arise Barak, and lead thy captivity captive, thou Son of Abinoam.
At her feet he bowed, he fell, he lay down: at her feet he bowed, he fell; where he bowed there he fell down dead.
Why is his Chariot so long in coming? Why tarry the Wheels of his Chariot?"—Judges, Chap. 5th. Verses 12th, 27th, and part of 28th.—See also the whole of that tumultuous and wonderful Poem.[4]

3. *LB 1800* was published in two volumes, this note appearing at the end of vol. 1.
4. Although WW follows the King James translation, these passages from Judges may have been suggested to him by Robert Lowth's *Lectures on the Sacred Poesy of the Hebrews,* trans. G. Gregory (London, 1787), 1:291–93, in which they are praised for "the utmost elegance in the repetitions" (*LB* [Mason], 39). Making a similar point about the connection between passion and verbal repetition, STC cited WW's quotation from Judges approvingly in *BL* (NCC, 505).

THE

LAST OF THE FLOCK[†]

In distant countries I have been,
And yet I have not often seen
A healthy man, a man full grown,
Weep in the public roads alone.
5 But such a one, on English ground,
And in the broad high-way, I met;
Along the broad high-way he came,
His cheeks with tears were wet.
Sturdy he seemed, though he was sad;
10 And in his arms a lamb he had.

He saw me, and he turned aside,
As if he wished himself to hide:
Then with his coat he made essay
To wipe those briny tears away.
15 I follow'd him, and said, "My friend
"What ails you? wherefore weep you so?"
—"Shame on me, Sir! this lusty lamb,
He makes my tears to flow.
To-day I fetched him from the rock;
20 He is the last of all my flock.

When I was young, a single man,
And after youthful follies ran,
Though little given to care and thought,
Yet, so it was, a ewe I bought;
25 And other sheep from her I raised,
As healthy sheep as you might see,
And then I married, and was rich
As I could wish to be;
Of sheep I number'd a full score,
30 And every year encreas'd my store.

Year after year my stock it grew,
And from this one, this single ewe,
Full fifty comely sheep I raised,
As sweet a flock as ever grazed!
35 Upon the mountain did they feed;

† P 1815: Poems founded on the Affections. Composed probably between early March and mid-May 1798 (*Chrono: EY*, 32). IF note: "Produced at the same time, & for the same purpose [as *The Complaint of a Forsaken Indian Woman*]. The incident occurred in the village of Holford, close by Alfoxden." In 1836, answering a question about the origin of line 4, WW explained, "I never in my whole life saw a man weep *alone* in the roads; but a friend of mine *did* see this poor man weeping *alone*, with the Lamb, the last of his flock, in his arms" (*WL*, 6:292). Assuming that the poem, because it represents rural poverty, must have been intended as a political protest, one of the reviewers of *LB 1798*, Charles Burney, was puzzled that "No oppression is pointed out; nor are any means suggested for his relief" (*CH*, 76). Other critics maintain that the poem criticizes William Godwin's denunciation of property itself in *Political Justice* (1793), bk. 8, chap. 2 (*LB* [CW], 353).

They throve, and we at home did thrive.
—This lusty lamb of all my store
Is all that is alive:
And now I care not if we die,
40 And perish all of poverty.

Ten[1] children, Sir! had I to feed,
Hard labour in a time of need!
My pride was tamed, and in our grief,
I of the parish ask'd relief.
45 They said I was a wealthy man;
My sheep upon the mountain fed,
And it was fit that thence I took
Whereof to buy us bread:"
"Do this; how can we give to you,"
50 They cried, "what to the poor is due?"

I sold a sheep as they had said,
And bought my little children bread,
And they were healthy with their food;
For me it never did me good.
55 A woeful time it was for me,
To see the end of all my gains,
The pretty flock which I had reared
With all my care and pains,
To see it melt like snow away!
60 For me it was a woeful day.

Another still! and still another!
A little lamb, and then its mother!
It was a vein that never stopp'd,
Like blood-drops from my heart they dropp'd.
65 Till thirty were not left alive
They dwindled, dwindled, one by one,
And I may say that many a time
I wished they all were gone:
They dwindled one by one away;
70 For me it was a woeful day.

To wicked deeds I was inclined,
And wicked fancies cross'd my mind,
And every man I chanc'd to see,
I thought he knew some ill of me.
75 No peace, no comfort could I find,
No ease, within doors or without,
And crazily, and wearily,
I went my work about.
Oft-times I thought to run away;
80 For me it was a woeful day.

1. Altered to "six" in *LB 1800* and in a separate printing of the poem in *The Courier*, April 9, 1800.

Sir! 'twas a precious flock to me,
As dear as my own children be;
For daily with my growing store
I loved my children more and more.
85 Alas! it was an evil time;
God cursed me in my sore distress,
I prayed, yet every day I thought
I loved my children less;
And every week, and every day,
90 My flock, it seemed to melt away.

They dwindled, Sir, sad sight to see!
From ten to five, from five to three,
A lamb, a weather,[2] and a ewe;
And then at last, from three to two;
95 And of my fifty, yesterday
I had but only one,
And here it lies upon my arm,
Alas! and I have none;
To-day I fetched it from the rock;
100 It is the last of all my flock."

THE

MAD MOTHER[†]

Her eyes are wild, her head is bare,
The sun has burnt her coal-black hair,
Her eye-brows have a rusty stain,
And she came far from over the main.[1]
5 She has a baby on her arm,
Or else she were alone;
And underneath the hay-stack warm,
And on the green-wood stone,
She talked and sung the woods among;
10 And it was in the English tongue.[2]

"Sweet babe! they say that I am mad,
But nay, my heart is far too glad;

---

2. A now-obsolete spelling of *wether*, meaning a castrated ram.
† P 1815: Poems founded on the Affections. Composed probably between early March and mid-May 1798 (*Chrono: EY*, 32). IF note: "The subject was reported to me by a Lady of Bristol who had seen the poor creature." However, *LB* (Mason) notes WW's probable indebtedness to two ballads, *The Mother's Lullaby* (printed in Joseph Ritson's *Ancient Songs* [1792]) and more particularly *Lady Anne Bothwell's Lament* (printed in Thomas Percy's *Reliques of Ancient English Poetry* [1765] and reprinted by Mason, 386–87). In *P 1815* WW omitted the title, and the poem was more commonly known thereafter as *Her eyes are wild*.
1. I.e., "main sea," meaning open sea (a poetic usage).
2. Responding in September 1836 to the poet John Kenyon's objection that line 10 was superfluous, WW explained that although "she came from far, English was [the mother's] native tongue—which shows her either to have been of these Islands, or a North American. On the latter supposition, while the distance removes her from us, the fact of her speaking our language brings us at once into close sympathy with her" (*WL*, 6:293).

And I am happy when I sing
Full many a sad and doleful thing:
15 Then, lovely baby, do not fear!
I pray thee have no fear of me,
But, safe as in a cradle, here
My lovely baby! thou shalt be,
To thee I know too much I owe;
20 I cannot work thee any woe.

A fire was once within my brain;
And in my head a dull, dull pain;
And fiendish faces one, two, three,
Hung at my breasts, and pulled at me.
25 But then there came a sight of joy;
It came at once to do me good;
I waked, and saw my little boy,
My little boy of flesh and blood;
Oh joy for me that sight to see!
30 For he was here, and only he.

Suck, little babe, oh suck again!
It cools my blood; it cools my brain;
Thy lips I feel them, baby! they
Draw from my heart the pain away.
35 Oh! press me with thy little hand;
It loosens something at my chest;
About that tight and deadly band
I feel thy little fingers press'd.
The breeze I see is in the tree;
40 It comes to cool my babe and me.[3]

Oh! love me, love me, little boy!
Thou art thy mother's only joy;
And do not dread the waves below,
When o'er the sea-rock's edge we go;
45 The high crag cannot work me harm,
Nor leaping torrents when they howl;
The babe I carry on my arm,
He saves for me my precious soul;
Then happy lie, for blest am I;
50 Without me my sweet babe would die.

Then do not fear, my boy! for thee
Bold as a lion I will be;

3. In chap. 22 of BL, STC quoted lines 31–40 and 61–70, praising them "for their pathos, and the former for the fine transition in the two concluding lines of the stanza, so expressive of the deranged state, in which from the increased sensibility the sufferer's attention is abruptly drawn off by every trifle, and in the same instant plucked back up again by the one despotic thought, and bringing home with it, by the blending, *fusing* power of the Imagination and Passion, the alien object to which it had been so abruptly diverted, no longer an alien but an ally and an inmate" (NCC, 540–41).

And I will always be thy guide,
Through hollow[4] snows and rivers wide.
55   I'll build an Indian bower; I know
The leaves that make the softest bed:
And if from me thou wilt not go,
But still be true 'till I am dead,
My pretty thing! then thou shalt sing,
60   As merry as the birds in spring.

Thy father cares not for my breast,
'Tis thine, sweet baby, there to rest:
'Tis all thine own! and if its hue
Be changed, that was so fair to view,
65   'Tis fair enough for thee, my dove!
My beauty, little child, is flown;
But thou wilt live with me in love,
And what if my poor cheek be brown?
'Tis well for me; thou canst not see
70   How pale and wan it else would be.

Dread not their taunts, my little life!
I am thy father's wedded wife;
And underneath the spreading tree
We two will live in honesty.
75   If his sweet boy he could forsake,
With me he never would have stay'd:
From him no harm my babe can take,
But he, poor man! is wretched made,
And every day we two will pray
80   For him that's gone and far away.

I'll teach my boy the sweetest things;
I'll teach him how the owlet sings.
My little babe! thy lips are still,
And thou hast almost suck'd thy fill.
85   —Where art thou gone my own dear child?
What wicked looks are those I see?
Alas! alas! that look so wild,
It never, never came from me:
If thou art mad, my pretty lad,
90   Then I must be for ever sad.

Oh! smile on me, my little lamb!
For I thy own dear mother am.
My love for thee has well been tried:
I've sought thy father far and wide.
95   I know the poisons of the shade,
I know the earth-nuts[5] fit for food;

4. Not solid.
5. The roundish tubers of various plants, also called "pig-nuts" and "earth-chestnuts."

Then, pretty dear, be not afraid;
We'll find thy father in the wood.
Now laugh and be gay, to the woods away!
100 And there, my babe; we'll live for aye.

THE

I D I O T   B O Y †

'Tis eight o'clock,—a clear March night,
The moon is up—the sky is blue,
The owlet in the moonlight air,
He shouts from nobody knows where;
5 He lengthens out his lonely shout,
Halloo! halloo! a long halloo!¹

—Why bustle thus about your door,
What means this bustle, Betty Foy?
Why are you in this mighty fret?
10 And why on horseback have you set
Him whom you love, your idiot boy?

Beneath the moon that shines so bright,
Till she is tired, let Betty Foy
With girt and stirrup fiddle-faddle;²
15 But wherefore set upon a saddle
Him whom she loves, her idiot boy?

There's scarce a soul that's out of bed;
Good Betty! put him down again;

† P 1815: Poems founded on the Affections. Composed between early March and mid-May, 1798 (*Chrono: EY*, 32). The word *idiot* is used in this poem in the older sense of "one congenitally deficient in reasoning powers" (*OED*). IF note: "The last stanza * * * was the foundation of the whole. The words were reported to me by my dear friend Thomas Poole; but I have since heard the same repeated of other Idiots. Let me add that this long poem was composed in the Groves of Alfoxden almost extempore; not a word, I believe, being corrected, though one stanza was omitted. I mention this in gratitude to those happy moments, for, in truth, I never wrote anything with so much glee." (Poole [1765–1837], a tanner and philanthropist known for his democratic views, was a neighbor and friend of STC in Nether Stowey.) In his review of *LB 1798* in the *Critical Review*, October 1798, Robert Southey (see Biographical and Topographical Glossary) judged the poem's subject matter particularly harshly: "No tale less deserved the labour that appears to have been bestowed upon this. It resembles a Flemish painting in the worthlessness of its design and the excellence of its execution" (*CH*, 66). Responding in June 1802 to a letter about *LB* from John Wilson, an undergraduate at Glasgow University, WW defended the poem at length, explaining that "the loathing and disgust which many people feel at the sight of an Idiot, is a feeling which, though having som[e] foundation in human nature is not necessarily attached to it in any * * * degree, but is owing, in a great measure to a false delicacy, and * * * a certain want of comprehensiveness of think[ing] and feeling. * * * I have often applied to Idiots, in my own mind, that sublime expression of scripture that, "*their life is hidden with God*" [misquoting Ephesians 3:9 or Colossians 3:3]. * * * I have often looked upon the conduct of fathers and mothers of the lower classes of society towards Idiots as the great triumph of the human heart" (*WL*, 1:356–57). On the poem's generic antecedents, see Mary Jacobus, *Tradition and Experiment*, 250–61.
1. Jacobus observes that this stanza "teasingly echoes the exclamatory refrains" of William Taylor's well-known translation (1796) of the German poet Gottfried Bürger's ballad *Lenore* (1774): "The moon is bryghte, and blue the nyghte" and "Halloo! Halloo! away they goe" (*Tradition and Experiment*, 250; and see 276–83 for the complete translation).
2. To fuss over trifles; *girt*: a girth, the leather strap placed around a horse's body to secure the saddle.

His lips with joy they burr at you,
20   But, Betty! what has he to do
With stirrup, saddle, or with rein?

The world will say 'tis very idle,
Bethink you of the time of night;
There's not a mother, no not one,
25   But when she hears what you have done,
Oh! Betty she'll be in a fright.

But Betty's bent on her intent,
For her good neighbour, Susan Gale,
Old Susan, she who dwells alone,
30   Is sick, and makes a piteous moan,
As if her very life would fail.

There's not a house within a mile,
No hand to help them in distress:
Old Susan lies a bed in pain,
35   And sorely puzzled are the twain,
For what she ails they cannot guess.

And Betty's husband's at the wood,
Where by the week he doth abide,
A woodman in the distant vale;
40   There's none to help poor Susan Gale,
What must be done? what will betide?

And Betty from the lane has fetched
Her pony, that is mild and good,
Whether he be in joy or pain,
45   Feeding at will along the lane,
Or bringing faggots³ from the wood.

And he is all in travelling trim,
And by the moonlight, Betty Foy
Has up upon the saddle set,
50   The like was never heard of yet,
Him whom she loves, her idiot boy.

And he must post without delay
Across the bridge that's in the dale,
And by the church, and o'er the down,
55   To bring a doctor from the town,
Or she will die, old Susan Gale.

There is no need of boot or spur,
There is no need of whip or wand,
For Johnny has his holly-bough,

3. Bundles of twigs (for use as fuel).

60   And with a hurly-burly[4] now
      He shakes the green bough in his hand.

      And Betty o'er and o'er has told
      The boy who is her best delight,
      Both what to follow, what to shun,
65   What do, and what to leave undone,
      How turn to left, and how to right.

      And Betty's most especial charge,
      Was, "Johnny! Johnny! mind that you
      Come home again, nor stop at all,
70   Come home again, whate'er befal,
      My Johnny do, I pray you do."

      To this did Johnny answer make,
      Both with his head, and with his hand,
      And proudly shook the bridle too,
75   And then! his words were not a few,
      Which Betty well could understand.

      And now that Johnny is just going,
      Though Betty's in a mighty flurry,
      She gently pats the pony's side,
80   On which her idiot boy must ride,
      And seems no longer in a hurry.

      But when the pony moved his legs,
      Oh! then for the poor idiot boy!
      For joy he cannot hold the bridle,
85   For joy his head and heels are idle,
      He's idle all for very joy.

      And while the pony moves his legs,
      In Johnny's left-hand you may see,
      The green bough's motionless and dead;
90   The moon that shines above his head
      Is not more still and mute than he.

      His heart it was so full of glee,
      That till full fifty yards were gone,
      He quite forgot his holly whip,
95   And all his skill in horsemanship,
      Oh! happy, happy, happy John.

      And Betty's standing at the door,
      And Betty's face with joy o'erflows,
      Proud of herself, and proud of him,

4. Commotion.

100　She sees him in his travelling trim;
　　　How quietly her Johnny goes.

　　　The silence of her idiot boy,
　　　What hopes it sends to Betty's heart!
　　　He's at the guide-post—he turns right,
105　She watches till he's out of sight,
　　　And Betty will not then depart.

　　　Burr, burr—now Johnny's lips they burr,[5]
　　　As loud as any mill, or near it,
　　　Meek as a lamb the pony moves,
110　And Johnny makes the noise he loves,
　　　And Betty listens, glad to hear it.

　　　Away she hies to Susan Gale:
　　　And Johnny's in a merry tune,[6]
　　　The owlets hoot, the owlets curr,[7]
115　And Johnny's lips they burr, burr, burr,
　　　And on he goes beneath the moon.

　　　His steed and he right well agree,
　　　For of this pony there's a rumour,
　　　That should he lose his eyes and ears,
120　And should he live a thousand years,
　　　He never will be out of humour.

　　　But then he is a horse that thinks!
　　　And when he thinks his pace is slack;
　　　Now, though he knows poor Johnny well,
125　Yet for his life he cannot tell
　　　What he has got upon his back.[8]

　　　So through the moonlight lanes they go,
　　　And far into the moonlight dale,
　　　And by the church, and o'er the down,
130　To bring a doctor from the town,
　　　To comfort poor old Susan Gale,

　　　And Betty, now at Susan's side,
　　　Is in the middle of her story,
　　　What comfort Johnny soon will bring,
135　With many a most diverting thing,
　　　Of Johnny's wit and Johnny's glory.

5. Make a whirring noise.
6. Mood, humor.
7. Make a low murmuring sound.
8. *LB* (Mason) notes a parallel to William Cowper's *Diverting History of John Gilpin* (1782), lines 95–96, also referring to a horse: "What thing upon his back had got, / Did wonder more and more."

And Betty's still at Susan's side:
By this time she's not quite so flurried;
Demure with porringer and plate
140   She sits, as if in Susan's fate
Her life and soul were buried.

But Betty, poor good woman! she,
You plainly in her face may read it,
Could lend out of that moment's store
145   Five years of happiness or more,
To any that might need it.

But yet I guess that now and then
With Betty all was not so well,
And to the road she turns her ears,
150   And thence full many a sound she hears,
Which she to Susan will not tell.

Poor Susan moans, poor Susan groans,
"As sure as there's a moon in heaven,"
Cries Betty, "he'll be back again;
155   They'll both be here, 'tis almost ten,
They'll both be here before eleven."

Poor Susan moans, poor Susan groans,
The clock gives warning for eleven;
'Tis on the stroke—"If Johnny's near,"
160   Quoth Betty "he will soon be here,
As sure as there's a moon in heaven."

The clock is on the stroke of twelve,
And Johnny is not yet in sight,
The moon's in heaven, as Betty sees,
165   But Betty is not quite at ease;
And Susan has a dreadful night.

And Betty, half an hour ago,
On Johnny vile reflections cast;
"A little idle sauntering thing!"
170   With other names, an endless string,
But now that time is gone and past.

And Betty's drooping at the heart,
That happy time all past and gone,
"How can it be he is so late?
175   The doctor he has made him wait,
Susan! they'll both be here anon."

And Susan's growing worse and worse,
And Betty's in a sad quandary;
And then there's nobody to say

180 If she must go or she must stay:
—She's in a sad quandary.

The clock is on the stroke of one;
But neither Doctor nor his guide
Appear along the moonlight road,
185 There's neither horse nor man abroad,
And Betty's still at Susan's side.

And Susan she begins to fear
Of sad mischances not a few,
That Johnny may perhaps be drown'd,
190 Or lost perhaps, and never found;
Which they must both for ever rue.

She prefaced half a hint of this
With, "God forbid it should be true!"
At the first word that Susan said
195 Cried Betty, rising from the bed,
"Susan, I'd gladly stay with you.

"I must be gone, I must away,
Consider, Johnny's but half-wise;
Susan, we must take care of him,
200 If he is hurt in life or limb"—
"Oh God forbid!" poor Susan cries.

"What can I do?" says Betty, going,
"What can I do to ease your pain?
Good Susan tell me, and I'll stay;
205 I fear you're in a dreadful way,
But I shall soon be back again."

"Good Betty go, good Betty go,
There's nothing that can ease my pain."
Then off she hies, but with a prayer
210 That God poor Susan's life would spare,
Till she comes back again.

So, through the moonlight lane she goes,
And far into the moonlight dale;
And how she ran, and how she walked,
215 And all that to herself she talked,
Would surely be a tedious tale.

In high and low, above, below,
In great and small, in round and square,
In tree and tower was Johnny seen,
220 In bush and brake,[9] in black and green,
'Twas Johnny, Johnny, every where.

9. A thicket.

She's past the bridge that's in the dale,
And now the thought torments her sore,
Johnny perhaps his horse forsook,
225   To hunt the moon that's in the brook,
And never will be heard of more.

And now she's high upon the down,
Alone amid a prospect wide;
There's neither Johnny nor his horse,
230   Among the fern or in the gorse;[1]
There's neither doctor nor his guide.

"Oh saints! what is become of him?
Perhaps he's climbed into an oak,
Where he will stay till he is dead;
235   Or sadly he has been misled,
And joined the wandering gypsey-folk.

"Or him that wicked pony's carried
To the dark cave, the goblins'[2] hall,
Or in the castle he's pursuing,
240   Among the ghosts, his own undoing;
Or playing with the waterfall."

At poor old Susan then she railed,
While to the town she posts away;
"If Susan had not been so ill,
245   Alas! I should have had him still,
My Johnny, till my dying day."

Poor Betty! in this sad distemper,
The doctor's self would hardly spare,
Unworthy things she talked and wild,
250   Even he, of cattle[3] the most mild,
The pony had his share,

And now she's got into the town,
And to the doctor's door she hies;
'Tis silence all on every side;
255   The town so long, the town so wide,
Is silent as the skies.

And now she's at the doctor's door,
She lifts the knocker, rap, rap, rap,
The doctor at the casement shews,
260   His glimmering eyes that peep and doze;
And one hand rubs his old night-cap.

1. A prickly evergreen shrub.
2. Altered in *LB 1802* to "goblin's."
3. Horses (an application of the word *cattle* attested into the late nineteenth century).

"Oh Doctor! Doctor! where's my Johnny?"
"I'm here, what is't you want with me?"
"Oh Sir! you know I'm Betty Foy,
265 And I have lost my poor dear boy,
You know him—him you often see;

"He's not so wise as some folks be."
"The devil take his wisdom!" said
The Doctor, looking somewhat grim,
270 "What, woman! should I know of him?"
And, grumbling, he went back to bed.

"O woe is me! O woe is me!
Here will I die; here will I die;
I thought to find my Johnny here,
275 But he is neither far nor near,
Oh! what a wretched mother I!"

She stops, she stands, she looks about,
Which way to turn she cannot tell.
Poor Betty! it would ease her pain
280 If she had heart to knock again;
—The clock strikes three—a dismal knell!

Then up along the town she hies,
No wonder if her senses fail,
This piteous news so much it shock'd her,
285 She quite forgot to send the Doctor,
To comfort poor old Susan Gale.

And now she's high upon the down,
And she can see a mile of road,
"Oh cruel! I'm almost three-score;
290 Such night as this was ne'er before,
There's not a single soul abroad."

She listens, but she cannot hear
The foot of horse, the voice of man;
The streams with softest sound are flowing,
295 The grass you almost hear it growing,
You hear it now if e'er you can.

The owlets through the long blue night
Are shouting to each other still:
Fond lovers, yet not quite hob nob,[4]
300 They lengthen out the tremulous sob,
That echoes far from hill to hill.

4. On friendly terms, in cheerful fellowship.

Poor Betty now has lost all hope,
Her thoughts are bent on deadly sin;
A green-grown pond[5] she just has pass'd,
305 And from the brink she hurries fast,
Lest she should drown herself therein.

And now she sits her down and weeps;
Such tears she never shed before;
"Oh dear, dear pony! my sweet joy!
310 Oh carry back my idiot boy!
And we will ne'er o'erload thee more."

A thought is come into her head;
"The pony he is mild and good,
And we have always used him well;
315 Perhaps he's gone along the dell,
And carried Johnny to the wood."

Then up she springs as if on wings;
She thinks no more of deadly sin;
If Betty fifty ponds should see,
320 The last of all her thoughts would be,
To drown herself therein.

Oh reader! now that I might tell
What Johnny and his horse are doing!
What they've been doing all this time,
325 Oh could I put it into rhyme,
A most delightful tale pursuing!

Perhaps, and no unlikely thought!
He with his pony now doth roam
The cliffs and peaks so high that are,
330 To lay his hands upon a star,
And in his pocket bring it home.

Perhaps he's turned himself about,
His face unto his horse's tail,
And still and mute, in wonder lost,
335 All like a silent horseman-ghost,
He travels on along the vale.

And now, perhaps, he's hunting sheep,
A fierce and dreadful hunter he!
Yon valley, that's so trim and green,
340 In five months' time, should he be seen,
A desart wilderness will be.

5. A pond covered with algae.

Perhaps, with head and heels on fire,
And like the very soul of evil,
He's galloping away, away,
345 And so he'll gallop on for aye,
The bane of all that dread the devil.

I to the muses have been bound,
These fourteen years, by strong indentures;[6]
Oh gentle muses! let me tell
350 But half of what to him befel,
For sure he met with strange adventures.

Oh gentle muses! is this kind?
Why will ye thus my suit repel?
Why of your further aid bereave me?
355 And can ye thus unfriended leave me?
Ye muses! whom I love so well.

Who's yon, that, near the waterfall,
Which thunders down with headlong force,
Beneath the moon, yet shining fair,
360 As careless as if nothing were,
Sits upright on a feeding horse?

Unto his horse, that's feeding free,
He seems, I think, the rein to give;
Of moon or stars he takes no heed;
365 Of such we in romances read,
—'Tis Johnny! Johnny! as I live.

And that's the very pony too.
Where is she, where is Betty Foy?
She hardly can sustain her fears;
370 The roaring water-fall she hears,
And cannot find her idiot boy.

Your pony's worth his weight in gold,
Then calm your terrors, Betty Foy!
She's coming from among the trees,
375 And now, all full in view, she sees
Him whom she loves, her idiot boy.

And Betty sees the pony too:
Why stand you thus Good Betty Foy?
It is no goblin, 'tis no ghost,
380 'Tis he whom you so long have lost,
He whom you love, your idiot boy.

---

6. A figurative use of the term for the contract binding an apprentice to the master who is to teach him a trade.

She looks again—her arms are up—
She screams—she cannot move for joy;
She darts as with a torrent's force,
385 She almost has o'erturned the horse,
And fast she holds her idiot boy.

And Johnny burrs and laughs aloud,
Whether in cunning or in joy,
I cannot tell; but while he laughs,
390 Betty a drunken pleasure quaffs,
To hear again her idiot boy.

And now she's at the pony's tail,
And now she's at the pony's head,
On that side now, and now on this,
395 And almost stifled with her bliss,
A few sad tears does Betty shed.

She kisses o'er and o'er again,
Him whom she loves, her idiot boy,
She's happy here, she's happy there,
400 She is uneasy every where;
Her limbs are all alive with joy.

She pats the pony, where or when
She knows not, happy Betty Foy!
The little pony glad may be,
405 But he is milder far than she,
You hardly can perceive his joy.

"Oh! Johnny, never mind the Doctor;
"You've done your best, and that is all."
She took the reins, when this was said,
410 And gently turned the pony's head
From the loud water-fall.

By this the stars were almost gone,
The moon was setting on the hill,
So pale you scarcely looked at her:
415 The little birds began to stir,
Though yet their tongues were still.

The pony, Betty, and her boy,
Wind slowly through the woody dale:
And who is she, be-times abroad,
420 That hobbles up the steep rough road?
Who is it, but old Susan Gale?

Long Susan lay deep lost in thought,
And many dreadful fears beset her,
Both for her messenger and nurse;

425 And as her mind grew worse and worse,
      Her body it grew better.

      She turned, she toss'd herself in bed,
      On all sides doubts and terrors met her;
      Point after point did she discuss;
430 And while her mind was fighting thus,
      Her body still grew better.

      "Alas! what is become of them?
      These fears can never be endured,
      I'll to the wood."—The word scarce said,
435 Did Susan rise up from her bed,
      As if by magic cured.

      Away she posts up hill and down,
      And to the wood at length is come,
      She spies her friends, she shouts a greeting;
440 Oh me! it is a merry meeting,
      As ever was in Christendom.

      The owls have hardly sung their last,
      While our four travellers homeward wend;
      The owls have hooted all night long,
445 And with the owls began my song,
      And with the owls must end.

      For while they all were travelling home,
      Cried Betty, "Tell us Johnny, do,
      Where all this long night you have been,
450 What you have heard, what you have seen,
      And Johnny, mind you tell us true."

      Now Johnny all night long had heard
      The owls in tuneful concert strive;
      No doubt too he the moon had seen;
455 For in the moonlight he had been
      From eight o'clock till five.

      And thus to Betty's question, he
      Made answer, like a traveller bold,
      (His very words I give to you,)
460 "The cocks did crow to-whoo, to-whoo,
      And the sun did shine so cold."
      —Thus answered Johnny in his glory,
      And that was all his travel's story.

LINES

WRITTEN NEAR RICHMOND, UPON THE THAMES,

AT EVENING†

How rich the wave, in front, imprest
With evening-twilight's summer hues,
While, facing thus the crimson west,
The boat her silent path pursues!
5 And see how dark the backward stream!¹
A little moment past, so smiling!
And still, perhaps, with faithless gleam,
Some other loiterer beguiling.

Such views the youthful bard allure,
10 But, heedless of the following gloom,
He deems their colours shall endure
'Till peace go with him to the tomb.
—And let him nurse his fond deceit,
And what if he must die in sorrow!
15 Who would not cherish dreams so sweet,
Though grief and pain may come to-morrow?

Glide gently, thus for ever glide,
O Thames! that other bards may see,
As lovely visions by thy side
20 As now, fair river! come to me.
Oh glide, fair stream! for ever so;
Thy quiet soul on all bestowing,
'Till all our minds for ever flow,
As thy deep waters now are flowing.²

25 Vain thought! yet be as now thou art,
That in thy waters may be seen
The image of a poet's heart,

† Begun possibly as early as 1788; completed by March 29, 1797 (*Chrono: EY*, 22, 195, 305–306).
Formerly a suburb and now administratively a part of London, Richmond is a town on the River
Thames nine miles southwest of the city center. In *LB 1800* WW divided the poem into two
poems, printing lines 1–16 under the title *Lines written when sailing in a Boat at Evening* and
the remainder under the title *Lines written near Richmond, upon the Thames* (the latter title
altered in *LB 1802* to *Remembrance of Collins, Written upon the Thames, near Richmond*).
WW maintained this division in subsequent editions of *LB* and his collected poems, and in *P
1815* he classed both as "Poems proceeding from Sentiment and Reflection." In his IF note on
Lines written when sailing, WW dated the poem 1789 and commented, "This title is scarcely
correct. It was during a solitary walk on the banks of the Cam [in Cambridge] that I was first
struck with this appearance, & applied it to my own feelings in the manner here expressed,
changing the scene to the Thames, near Windsor. This, and the three stanzas of the following
poem * * * formed one piece; but on the recommendation of Coleridge, the last three stanzas
were separated from the other."
1. As *LB* (Mason) notes, a probable allusion to Shakespeare, *The Tempest* 1.2.49–50: "What seest
thou else / In the dark backward and abysm of time?"
2. This stanza alludes to the apostrophe to the Thames, well known to WW's contemporaries, in
Sir John Denham's *Cooper's Hill* (1642), lines 189–92: "O could I flow like thee! and make thy
stream / My great example, as it is my theme! / Though deep, yet clear, though gentle, yet not
dull, / Strong without rage, without o'erflowing full."

How bright, how solemn, how serene!
Such heart[3] did once the poet bless,
30   Who, pouring here a *later*[4] ditty,
Could find no refuge from distress,
But in the milder grief of pity.

Remembrance! as we glide[5] along,
For him suspend the dashing oar,
35   And pray that never child of Song
May know his freezing[6] sorrows more.
How calm! how still! the only sound,
The dripping of the oar suspended!
—The evening darkness gathers round
40   By virtue's holiest powers attended.

EXPOSTULATION

AND

R E P L Y[†]

"Why William, on that old grey stone,
Thus for the length of half a day,
Why William, sit you thus alone,
And dream your time away?

5   "Where are your books? that light bequeath'd
To beings else forlorn and blind!
Up! Up! and drink the spirit breath'd
From dead men to their kind.

---

3. Replaced with "as" in *LB 1800*.
4. WW's note in *LB 1798* (reprinted with *Lines written near Richmond, upon the Thames* in *LB 1800* and thereafter): "Collins's Ode on the Death of Thomson, the last written, I believe, of the poems which were also published during his life-time. This Ode is also alluded to in the next stanza." Lines 31–32 allude to lines 21–23 of William Collins's *Ode Occasioned by the Death of Mr. Thomson* (1749), an elegy on the poet James Thomson (1700–1748): "But thou, who own'st that earthy bed, / Ah! what will every dirge avail? / Or tears, which Love and Pity shed / That mourn beneath the gliding sail!" WW assumes that Collins's own depression was expressed in the ode. To which of Collins's poems WW refers in line 29 is not certain, but the *Ode on the Poetical Character* and *Ode to Simplicity* (both 1746) are possibilities.
5. Replaced with "float" in *LB 1800*. Lines 33–34 allude to lines 13–16 of Collins's ode on Thomson: "Remembrance oft shall haunt the shore / When Thames in summer wreaths is dressed, / And oft suspend the dashing oar / To bid his gentle spirit rest."
6. Altered to "that Poet's" in *LB 1802*.
† P 1815: Poems proceeding from Sentiment and Reflection. The advertisement to *LB 1798* (see above) explains that this poem and the following one "arose out of conversation with a friend who was somewhat unreasonably attached to modern books of moral philosophy." Assuming that this conversation was with William Hazlitt on May 23, 1798, Reed assigns the two poems' composition to that day or shortly after (*Chrono: EY*, 33, 238). In 1823 Hazlitt recalled the conversation as "a metaphysical argument * * * in which we neither of us succeeded in making ourselves perfectly clear and intelligible" ("My First Acquaintance with Poets," in *Selected Writings*, ed. Duncan Wu [London, 1998], 9:106). IF note: "This poem is a great favourite among the Quakers, as I have learnt on many occasions. It was composed in front of the house at Alfoxden, in the Spring of 1798." The reference to *Esthwaite Lake* in line 13, however, establishes the poem's setting as the Lake District. Stephen Parrish, *The Art of the Lyrical Ballads*, 126, suggests Robert Burns's *Epistle to J. L[aiprik], An Old Scotch Ballad* (1768), in which the speaker commends the observation of nature over book learning, as a model for WW's poem.

"You look round on your mother earth,
10   As if she for no purpose bore you;
As if you were her first-born birth,
And none had lived before you!"

One morning thus, by Esthwaite lake,
When life was sweet I knew not why,
15   To me my good friend Matthew spake,
And thus I made reply.

"The eye it cannot chuse but see,
We cannot bid the ear be still;
Our bodies feel, where'er they be,
20   Against, or with our will.

"Nor less I deem that there are powers,
Which of themselves our minds impress,
That we can feed this mind of ours,
In a wise passiveness.

25   "Think you, mid all this mighty sum
Of things for ever speaking,
That nothing of itself will come,
But we must still be seeking?

"—Then ask not wherefore, here, alone,
30   Conversing as I may,
I sit upon this old grey stone,
And dream my time away."

THE TABLES TURNED;

AN EVENING SCENE, ON THE SAME SUBJECT[†]

Up! up! my friend, and clear your looks,
Why all this toil and trouble?
Up! up! my friend, and quit your books,
Or surely you'll grow double.[1]

5   The sun above the mountain's head,
A freshening lustre mellow,
Through all the long green fields has spread,
His first sweet evening yellow.

---

† P 1815: Poems proceeding from Sentiment and Reflection. IF note: "Composed at the same time [as *Expostulation and Reply*]." On the date of composition, see the note on the preceding poem.
1. I.e., become permanently stooped.

    Books! 'tis a dull and endless strife,
10 Come, hear the woodland linnet,[2]
    How sweet his music; on my life
    There's more of wisdom in it.

    And hark! how blithe the throstle[3] sings!
    And he[4] is no mean preacher;
15 Come forth into the light of things,
    Let Nature be your teacher.

    She has a world of ready wealth,
    Our minds and hearts to bless—
    Spontaneous wisdom breathed by health,
20 Truth breathed by chearfulness.

    One impulse from a vernal wood
    May teach you more of man;
    Of moral evil and of good,
    Than all the sages can.

25 Sweet is the lore which nature brings;
    Our meddling intellect
    Mishapes the beauteous forms of things;
    —We murder to dissect.

    Enough of science and of art;
30 Close up these barren leaves;
    Come forth, and bring with you a heart
    That watches and receives.

OLD MAN TRAVELLING;

ANIMAL TRANQUILLITY AND DECAY,

A SKETCH[†]

            The little hedge-row birds,
    That peck along the road, regard him not.
    He travels on, and in his face, his step,
    His gait, is one expression; every limb,
5   His look and bending figure, all bespeak
    A man who does not move with pain, but moves

---

2. A songbird common in England. It normally nests in thick bushes in open land rather than in woodlands.
3. The thrush, another songbird common in England.
4. In *P 1815* WW altered the beginning of line 14 to "He, too."
† *P 1815*: Poems referring to the Period of Old Age. Composed between the second half of 1796 and early June 1797 as part of *Description of a Beggar*, which also contributed to *The Old Cumberland Beggar* (Chrono: EY, 27, 342–43). In his IF note WW recalled that "these verses were an overflowing from the old Cumberland Beggar." In the Preface to *LB 1800* he numbered this poem among those in which he had sought "to sketch characters under the influence of less impassioned feelings, * * * characters of which the elements are simple, belonging rather to nature than to manners * * *." From *LB 1800* on he omitted *Old Man travelling* from the title.

With thought—He is insensibly subdued
To settled quiet: he is one by whom
All effort seems forgotten, one to whom
10 Long patience has[1] such mild composure given,
That patience now doth seem a thing, of which
He hath no need.   He is by nature led
To peace so perfect, that the young behold
With envy, what the old man hardly feels.
15 —I asked him whither he was bound, and what
The object of his journey; he replied
"Sir! I am going many miles to take
A last leave of my son, a mariner,
Who from a sea-fight has been brought to Falmouth,[2]
20 And there is dying in an hospital."[3]

THE COMPLAINT
OF A FORSAKEN
INDIAN WOMAN[†]

[When a Northern Indian, from sickness, is unable to continue his journey
with his companions; he is left behind, covered over with Deer-skins, and is
supplied with water, food, and fuel if the situation of the place will afford it. He
is informed of the track which his companions intend to pursue, and if he is
unable to follow, or overtake them, he perishes alone in the Desart; unless he
should have the good fortune to fall in with some other Tribes of Indians. It is
unnecessary to add that the females are equally, or still more, exposed to the
same fate. See that very interesting work, Hearne's Journey from Hudson's Bay
to the Northern Ocean.[1] When the Northern Lights, as the same writer informs
us, vary their position in the air, they make a rustling and a crackling noise.
This circumstance is alluded to in the first stanza of the following poem.]

1. Altered to "hath" in LB 1805.
2. A port town in Cornwall, southwest England, with the third-deepest natural harbor in the
world.
3. Reviewing LB 1798 in 1799, Charles Burney interpreted lines 16–20 disapprovingly as intimat-
ing WW's opposition to Britain's war with France, which had begun in 1793 (CH, 77). In LB
1800 to LB 1805 WW altered these lines to make them spoken by the narrator rather than by
the old man: thus he omitted the quotation marks, replaced Sir! I am (line 17) with "That he
was," my (line 18) with "his," has (line 19) with "had," and is (line 20) with "was." In P 1815
WW omitted lines 15–20 altogether. LB (CW), 356, notes their similarity to lines 18–21 of
Robert Southey's The Sailor's Mother (1798): "Sir, I am going / To see my son at Plymouth, sadly
hurt / In the late action, and in the hospital / Dying, I fear me now."
† P 1815: Poems founded on the Affections. Composed probably between early March and mid-
May 1798 (Chrono: EY, 32). IF note: "Written at Alfoxden, in 1798, when I read Hearne's
Journey with deep interest. It was composed for the volume of Lyrical Ballads." On Hearne see
the next note. In the Preface to LB 1800 WW described the poem as "accompanying the last
struggles of a human being at the approach of death, cleaving in solitude to life and society."
The headnote to the poem is by WW.
1. Samuel Hearne, A Journey from the Prince of Wales's Fort in Hudson's Bay, to the Northern
Ocean (London, 1795), 202–203, recalls an ill Chipewyan woman left behind by the other
members of her traveling party (which included Hearne himself): "The poor woman * * * came
up with us three several times, after having been left in the manner described. At length, poor
creature! she dropt behind, and no one attempted to go back in search of her." WW may have
been introduced to this book by STC, who had borrowed it from the Bristol Library in 1795
(Reading 1770–99, no. 127).

THE COMPLAINT, &c.

Before I see another day,
Oh let my body die away!
In sleep I heard the northern gleams;
The stars they were among my dreams;
In sleep did I behold the skies,
I saw the crackling flashes drive;
And yet they are upon my eyes,
And yet I am alive.
Before I see another day,
Oh let my body die away!

My fire is dead: it knew no pain;
Yet is it dead, and I remain.
All stiff with ice the ashes lie;
And they are dead, and I will die.
When I was well, I wished to live,
For clothes, for warmth, for food, and fire;
But they to me no joy can give,
No pleasure now, and no desire.
Then here contented will I lie;
Alone I cannot fear to die.

Alas! you might have dragged me on
Another day, a single one!
Too soon despair o'er me prevailed;
Too soon my heartless spirit failed;[2]
When you were gone my limbs were stronger,
And Oh how grievously I rue,
That, afterwards, a little longer,
My friends, I did not follow you!
For strong and without pain I lay,
My friends, when you were gone away.

My child! they gave thee to another,
A woman who was not thy mother.
When from my arms my babe they took,
On me how strangely did he look!
Through his whole body something ran,
A most strange something[3] did I see;
—As if he strove to be a man,
That he might pull the sledge for me.
And then he stretched his arms, how wild!
Oh mercy! like a little[4] child.

2. In *P 1815* WW altered lines 23–24 to "Too soon I yielded to despair; / Why did ye listen to my prayer?" Throughout the poem in *P 1815* he substituted "ye" and "Ye" for *you* and *You* respectively.
3. Altered in *P 1815* to "working."
4. Altered in *P 1815* to "helpless."

My little joy! my little pride!
In two days more I must have died.
Then do not weep and grieve for me;
I feel I must have died with thee.
45 Oh wind that o'er my head art flying,
The way my friends their course did bend,
I should not feel the pain of dying,
Could I with thee a message send.
Too soon, my friends, you went away;
50 For I had many things to say.

I'll follow you across the snow,
You travel heavily and slow:
In spite of all my weary pain,
I'll look upon your tents again.
55 My fire is dead, and snowy white
The water which beside it stood;
The wolf has come to me to-night,
And he has stolen away my food.
For ever left alone am I,
60 Then wherefore should I fear to die?

My journey will be shortly run,
I shall not see another sun,
I cannot lift my limbs to know
If they have any life or no.
65 My poor forsaken child! if I
For once could[5] have thee close to me,
With happy heart I then would die,
And my last thoughts would happy be.
I feel my body die away,
70 I shall not see another day.[6]

THE CONVICT[†]

The glory of evening was spread through the west;
  —On the slope of a mountain I stood,
While the joy that precedes the calm season of rest
Rang loud through the meadow and wood.

---

5. Altered to "should" in *LB 1800* and the two subsequent editions.
6. In *P 1815* WW omitted the last stanza altogether.
† Composed probably between March 21 and early October 1796 (*Chrono: EY*, 26, 344–45). First published in the *Morning Post*, December 14, 1797, under the pseudonym Mortimer (the name of a character in WW's play *The Borderers*). Stephen Parrish, *The Art of the Lyrical Ballads*, 192–95, conjectures, on the basis of divergences between the MSS and the published versions, that STC revised the poem for the *Morning Post* and that WW himself revised it further for *LB 1798*. WW never reprinted the poem after *LB 1798*, and there is no IF note about it. Jacobus, *Tradition and Experiment*, 186, argues that the poem was inspired by the condemnation of the prison system in William Godwin's novel *Caleb Williams* (1794), while *LB* (CW), 357, proposes lines 79–88 of Robert Burns's poem *A Winter Night* (1786) as a possible source. The meter, with its high proportion of anapests (two unstressed syllables followed by a stressed syllable), is unusual for WW.

5 "And must we then part from a dwelling so fair?"
    In the pain of my spirit I said,
  And with a deep sadness I turned, to repair
    To the cell where the convict is laid.

  The thick-ribbed walls that overshadow the gate
10   Resound; and the dungeons unfold:
  I pause; and at length, through the glimmering grate,
    That outcast of pity behold.

  His black matted head on his shoulder is bent,
    And deep is the sigh of his breath,
15 And with stedfast dejection his eyes are intent
    On the fetters that link him to death.

  'Tis sorrow enough on that visage to gaze,
    That body dismiss'd from his care;
  Yet my fancy has pierced to his heart, and pourtrays
20   More terrible images there.

  His bones are consumed, and his life-blood is dried,
    With wishes the past to undo;
  And his crime, through the pains that overwhelm him, descried,
    Still blackens and grows on his view.

25 When from the dark synod,[1] or blood-reeking field,
    To his chamber the monarch is led,
  All soothers of sense their soft virtue shall yield,
    And quietness pillow his head.

  But if grief, self-consumed, in oblivion would doze,
30   And conscience her tortures appease,
  'Mid tumult and uproar this man must repose;
    In the comfortless vault of disease.

  When his fetters at night have so press'd on his limbs,
    That the weight can no longer be borne,
35 If, while a half-slumber his memory bedims,
    The wretch on his pallet should turn,

  While the jail-mastiff howls at the dull clanking chain,
    From the roots of his hair there shall start
  A thousand sharp punctures of cold-sweating pain,
40   And terror shall leap at his heart.

  But now he half-raises his deep-sunken eye,
    And the motion unsettles a tear;
  The silence of sorrow it seems to supply,
    And asks of me why I am here.

1. Assembly, council.

45 "Poor victim! no idle intruder has stood
    With o'erweening complacence our state to compare,
    But one, whose first wish is the wish to be good,
    Is come as a brother thy sorrows to share.

    "At thy name though compassion her nature resign,
50   Though in virtue's proud mouth thy report be a stain,
    My care, if the arm of the mighty were mine,
    Would plant thee[2] where yet thou might'st blossom again."

LINES

WRITTEN A FEW MILES ABOVE

TINTERN ABBEY,

On revisiting the banks of the WYE during

a tour,

July 13, 1798[†]

Five years have passed; five summers, with the length
Of five long winters! and again I hear
These waters, rolling from their mountain-springs
With a sweet inland murmur.[1]—Once again

2. I.e., would deport the convict (a practice known as "penal transportation") rather than imprison him. From 1717 to 1775 the North American and West Indian colonies were the primary recipients of transported English convicts, and from 1788 to 1868 (when the practice was stopped) Australia was the primary recipient. The *Morning Post* version of the poem ended with an additional stanza: "Vain wish! Yet misdeem not that vainly I grieve— / When vengeance has quitted her grasp on thy frame, / My pity thy children and wife shall reprieve / From the dangers that wait round the dwellings of shame."

† *P 1815*: Poems of the Imagination. Composed during a walking tour in the Wye River valley in Wales, probably between July 10 or 11 and July 13, 1798 (*Chrono: EY*, 33, 243). The prominence of the date in the title has encouraged speculation about its significance: while it may in fact have been the date on which WW finished composing the poem, it was also the eighth anniversary of his first arrival in France with Robert Jones (see *The Prelude* 6.355–57), the fifth anniversary of the murder of the French Revolutionary figure Jean-Paul Marat, and the day before the ninth anniversary of the storming of the Bastille (J. R. Watson, "A Note on the Date in the Title of 'Tintern Abbey,'" *Wordsworth Circle* 10 [1979]: 379–80). IF note: "No poem was composed under circumstances more pleasant for me to remember than this: I began it upon leaving Tintern, after crossing the Wye, and concluded it just as I was entering Bristol in the evening, after a ramble of 4 or 5 days, with my sister. Not a line of it was altered, and not any part of it written down till I reached Bristol. It was published almost immediately after in the little volume of which so much has been said in these notes (The Lyrical Ballads, as first published at Bristol by Cottle)." In a note intended apparently for his nephew, WW described his itinerary, which began and ended in Bristol: "We crossed the Severn [River] Ferry, and walked ten miles further to Tintern Abbey, a very beautiful ruin on the Wye. The next morning we walked along the river through Monmouth to Goodrich Castle, there slept, and returned the next day to Tintern, thence to Chepstow, and from Chepstow back again in a boat to Tintern, where we slept, and thence back in a small vessel to Bristol" (quoted in Moorman, 1:401). The thirteenth-century abbey, left to decay after its dissolution in 1537, had become a tourist attraction in the mid-eighteenth century. In *LB 1800* WW included the following note on the poem at the end of vol. 1: "I have not ventured to call this Poem an Ode; but it was written with a hope that in the transitions, and the impassioned music of the versification would be found the principal requisites of that species of composition." On the poem's political contexts and implications, see Nicholas Roe's "The Politics of 'Tintern Abbey'" (pp. 636–41 below); on WW's meditation on writing and the role of DW in the poem, see the excerpt from Andrew Cooper's *Doubt and Identity in Romantic Poetry* (pp. 641–44 below).

1. WW's note: "The river is not affected by the tides a few miles above Tintern." The tidal effect stops between the two bridges on which WW and DW could have crossed the Wye, about three miles north of Tintern. WW had first visited the Wye valley alone in the summer (perhaps early August) of 1793 (*Chrono: EY*, 145).

5   Do I behold these steep and lofty cliffs,
    Which on a wild secluded scene impress
    Thoughts of more deep seclusion; and connect
    The landscape with the quiet of the sky.[2]
    The day is come when I again repose
10 Here, under this dark sycamore, and view
    These plots of cottage-ground, these orchard-tufts,[3]
    Which, at this season, with their unripe fruits,
    Among the woods and copses lose themselves,
    Nor, with their green and simple hue, disturb
15 The wild green landscape. Once again I see
    These hedge-rows, hardly hedge-rows, little lines
    Of sportive wood run wild; these pastoral farms
    Green to the very door; and wreathes of smoke
    Sent up, in silence, from among the trees,[4]
20 With some uncertain notice, as might seem,
    Of vagrant dwellers in the houseless woods,
    Or of some hermit's cave, where by his fire
    The hermit sits alone.

                        Though absent long,
    These forms of beauty have not been to me,
25 As is a landscape to a blind man's eye:[5]
    But oft, in lonely rooms, and mid the din
    Of towns and cities, I have owed to them,
    In hours of weariness, sensations sweet,
    Felt in the blood, and felt along the heart,
30 And passing even into my purer mind
    With tranquil restoration:—feelings too
    Of unremembered pleasure; such, perhaps,
    As may have had no trivial influence
    On that best portion of a good man's life;[6]
35 His little, nameless, unremembered acts
    Of kindness and of love. Nor less, I trust,

2. Moorman, 1:402, notes that lines 8–19 are indebted to a passage in a guide book that WW and DW may have taken with them on their tour, William Gilpin's *Observations on the River Wye, and Several Parts of South Wales, &c., Relative Chiefly to Picturesque Beauty,* 2nd ed. (London, 1789), 22–23 (*Reading* 1770–99, no. 116.vii): "Many of the furnaces, on the banks of the river, consume charcoal, which is manufactured on the spot; and the smoke, which is frequently seen issuing from the sides of the hills; and spreading its thin veil over a part of them, beautifully breaks their lines, and unites them with the sky." The furnaces, to which WW does not refer, were the forges of the area's iron industry.
3. Small groups of trees.
4. LB 1798 mistakenly printed an additional line after line 19 ("And the low copses—coming from the trees"), but the mistake was noticed in time to be included in the errata list at the end of the volume.
5. In his "Essay, Supplementary to the Preface" in *P 1815*, while denigrating the descriptive powers of the poets John Dryden and Alexander Pope, WW remarked, "A blind man, in the habit of attending accurately to descriptions casually dropped from the lips of those around him, might easily depict these appearances with more truth" (*Prose*, 3:73).
6. As *LB* (CW) notes, WW is perhaps recalling in this line a passage from Milton's preface to his *Judgment of Martin Bucer concerning Divorce* (1644): "wherby good men in the best portion of their lives, and in that ordinance of God which entitles them from the beginning to most just and requisite contentments, are compell'd to civil indignities" (*Complete Prose Works,* ed. Ernest Sirluck et al. [New Haven, 1953–79], 2:438–89). That WW intended a direct allusion, however, is less likely.

To them I may have owed another gift,
Of aspect more sublime; that blessed mood,
In which the burthen[7] of the mystery,
40 In which the heavy and the weary weight
Of all this unintelligible world
Is lighten'd:—that serene and blessed mood,
In which the affections gently lead us on,
Until, the breath of this corporeal frame,
45 And even the motion of our human blood
Almost suspended, we are laid asleep
In body, and become a living soul:
While with an eye made quiet by the power
Of harmony, and the deep power of joy,
50 We see into the life of things.[8]

              If this[9]
Be but a vain belief, yet, oh! how oft,
In darkness, and amid the many shapes
Of joyless day-light; when the fretful stir
Unprofitable, and the fever of the world,[1]
55 Have hung upon the beatings of my heart,
How oft, in spirit, have I turned to thee
O sylvan[2] Wye! Thou wanderer through the woods,
How often has my spirit turned to thee![3]

And now, with gleams of half-extinguish'd thought,
60 With many recognitions dim and faint,
And somewhat of a sad perplexity,
The picture of the mind revives again:
While here I stand, not only with the sense
Of present pleasure, but with pleasing thoughts
65 That in this moment there is life and food
For future years. And so I dare to hope
Though changed, no doubt, from what I was, when first
I came among these hills; when like a roe
I bounded o'er the mountains, by the sides
70 Of the deep rivers, and the lonely streams,
Wherever nature led;[4] more like a man
Flying from something that he dreads, than one
Who sought the thing he loved. For nature then

7. Burden (a variant spelling still common in WW's time).
8. The *serene and blessed mood* described in lines 42–50 is comparable to the *holy calm* described in *The Prelude* 2.367–71.
9. The referent of *this* is presumably the belief expressed in lines 36–50 that WW may have owed his *blessed mood* to the memory of his first visit to the Wye valley.
1. A possible echo of Shakespeare's *Hamlet* 1.2.133–34: "How * * * unprofitable / Seem to me all the uses of this world."
2. Forested.
3. Lucy Newlyn, *Coleridge, Wordsworth, and the Language of Allusion*, 35, observes an allusion in lines 50–58 to STC's *Frost at Midnight* (1798), lines 28–31: "How often in my early school-boy days, / With most believing superstitious wish / Presageful have I gaz'd upon the bars, / To watch the *stranger* there!" (NCC, 120–21).
4. WW recalls this period of his life in similar terms in *The Prelude* 11.186–94 and 13.236–40.

(The coarser pleasures of my boyish days,
75 And their glad animal movements all gone by,)[5]
To me was all in all.—I cannot paint
What then I was. The sounding cataract
Haunted me like a passion:[6] the tall rock,
The mountain, and the deep and gloomy wood,
80 Their colours and their forms, were then to me
An appetite: a feeling and a love,
That had no need of a remoter charm,
By thought supplied, or any interest
Unborrowed from the eye.—That time is past,
85 And all its aching joys are now no more,
And all its dizzy raptures. Not for this
Faint I, nor mourn nor murmur: other gifts
Have followed, for such loss, I would believe,
Abundant recompence. For I have learned
90 To look on nature, not as in the hour
Of thoughtless youth, but hearing oftentimes
The still, sad music of humanity,
Not harsh nor grating, though of ample power
To chasten and subdue. And I have felt
95 A presence that disturbs me with the joy
Of elevated thoughts; a sense sublime
Of something far more deeply interfused,
Whose dwelling is the light of setting suns,
And the round ocean, and the living air,
100 And the blue sky, and in the mind of man,
A motion and a spirit, that impels
All thinking things, all objects of all thought,
And rolls through all things.[7] Therefore am I still
A lover of the meadows and the woods,
105 And mountains; and of all that we behold
From this green earth; of all the mighty world
Of eye and ear, both what they half-create,[8]
And what perceive; well pleased to recognize
In nature and the language of the sense,
110 The anchor of my purest thoughts, the nurse,

5. The parenthesis clarifies that *then* in line 73 refers to the time of WW's first visit to the Wye valley, not to his *boyish days*. Compare *The Prelude* 8.476–85.
6. Possibly an allusion to lines 31–38 of *Frost at Midnight*, in which STC recalls that the church-bells of his birthplace "haunted [him] / With a wild pleasure" (NCC, 121).
7. James Averill, "Wordsworth and Natural Science," 238–40, suggests that lines 94–104 may be indebted to Virgil's *Aeneid* 6.724–27, quoted and translated by Erasmus Darwin on the title page of vol. 1 of his *Zoönomia; or, The Laws of Organic Life* (1794), a book WW had borrowed from Joseph Cottle in March 1798 (*Reading 1770–99*, no. 74.v): "Earth, on whose lap a thousand nations tread, / And Ocean, brooding his prolific bed, / Night's changeful orb, blue pole, and silvery zones, / Where other worlds encircle other suns, / One Mind inhabits, one diffusive Soul / Wields the large limbs, and mingles with the whole." Another possible source is STC's *Religious Musings* (1796), lines 423–25: "And ye [Spirits] of plastic power, that interfus'd / Roll thro' the grosser and material mass / In organizing surge!" (NCC, 34).
8. WW's note: "This line has a close resemblance to an admirable line of Young, the exact expression of which I cannot recollect." WW refers to Edward Young's *Night Thoughts* (1742–45) 6.427: "And half create the wondrous World, they see."

The guide, the guardian of my heart, and soul
Of all my moral being.[9]

               Nor, perchance,
If I were not thus taught, should I the more
Suffer my genial spirits to decay:
115 For thou art with me,[1] here, upon the banks
Of this fair river; thou, my dearest Friend,
My dear, dear Friend, and in thy voice I catch
The language of my former heart, and read
My former pleasures in the shooting lights
120 Of thy wild eyes. Oh! yet a little while
May I behold in thee what I was once,
My dear, dear Sister! And this prayer I make,
Knowing that Nature never did betray
The heart that loved her;[2] 'tis her privilege,
125 Through all the years of this our life, to lead
From joy to joy: for she can so inform
The mind that is within us, so impress
With quietness and beauty, and so feed
With lofty thoughts, that neither evil tongues,[3]
130 Rash judgments, nor the sneers of selfish men,
Nor greetings where no kindness is, nor all
The dreary intercourse of daily life,
Shall e'er prevail against us,[4] or disturb
Our chearful faith that all which we behold
135 Is full of blessings. Therefore let the moon
Shine on thee in thy solitary walk;
And let the misty mountain winds be free
To blow against thee: and in after years,
When these wild ecstasies shall be matured
140 Into a sober pleasure, when thy mind
Shall be a mansion for all lovely forms,
Thy memory be as a dwelling-place
For all sweet sounds and harmonies; Oh! then,
If solitude, or fear, or pain, or grief,
145 Should be thy portion, with what healing thoughts
Of tender joy wilt thou remember me,

9. Possibly an echo of Mark Akenside's *Pleasures of Imagination* (1744) 1.21–23: "with thee [Harmony] comes / The guide, the guardian of their lovely sports, / Majestic Truth."
1. An echo of Psalm 23.4: "Yea, though I walk through the valley of the shadow of death, I will fear no evil: for thou art with me; thy rod and thy staff they comfort me." *Genial spirits*: a phrase WW possibly recalls from Milton's *Samson Agonistes* (1671), lines 594–96: "So much I feel my genial spirits droop, / My hopes fall flat, nature within me seems / In all her functions weary of her self." Several senses of *genial* may be relevant here: "sympathetically cheerful," "enlivening," and the older "pertaining to 'genius' or natural disposition" (*OED*).
2. An allusion to STC's *This Lime Tree Bower My Prison* (1800), lines 60–61: "Henceforth I shall know / That Nature ne'er deserts the wise and pure."
3. An allusion to Milton's reference to himself in *Paradise Lost* 7.24–26: "More safe I Sing with mortal voice, unchang'd / To hoarce or mute, though fall'n on evil dayes, / On evil dayes though fall'n, and evil tongues."
4. An allusion to Christ's words to Peter in Matthew 16.18: "And I say also unto thee, that thou art Peter, and upon this rock I will build my church; and the gates of hell shall not prevail against it."

And these my exhortations! Nor, perchance,
If I should be, where I no more can hear
Thy voice, nor catch from thy wild eyes these gleams
150   Of past existence, wilt thou then forget
That on the banks of this delightful stream
We stood together; and that I, so long
A worshipper of Nature,[5] hither came,
Unwearied in that service: rather say
155   With warmer love, oh! with far deeper zeal
Of holier love. Nor wilt thou then forget,
That after many wanderings, many years
Of absence, these steep woods and lofty cliffs,
And this green pastoral landscape, were to me
160   More dear, both for themselves, and for thy sake.

E N D.

5. In January 1815, defending himself against an accusation of "not distinguishing between nature as the work of God and God himself," WW described the phrase *worshipper of Nature* as "a passionate expression uttered incautiously in the Poem upon the Wye" (*WL*, 3:188). But he did not alter the phrase.

From LYRICAL BALLADS, WITH OTHER POEMS (1800)

In the spring of 1800 Wordsworth was contemplating a new edition of *Lyrical Ballads*, to include poems he had written in Germany in the winter of 1798–99 and since settling in Grasmere in December 1799, the latter set mostly in the Lake District and often, as Wordsworth later told Henry Crabb Robinson, "founded on some incident that he had witnessed or had heard of" (*CRB*, 1:190). On April 10, 1800, near the beginning of a month-long visit to Dove Cottage, Coleridge reported to Robert Southey that "Wordsworth publishes a second Volume of Lyrical Ballads, & Pastorals" (*CL*, 1:585). Evidently Coleridge, acting as Wordsworth's agent, interested the publisher T. N. Longman in the project, notwithstanding that in 1799 the same firm had "reckoned *as nothing*" the copyright of the first edition (Joseph Cottle, *Reminiscences of Samuel Taylor Coleridge and Robert Southey* [London, 1847], 259). Longman may also have been encouraged by the sales of the 1798 volume after favorable reviews of it appeared in the *British Critic* (October 1799) and the *Antijacobin Review* (April 1800) (*LB* [CW], 23–24; *CH*, 78–81, 84). By June 10 Wordsworth could inform his brother Richard that "[t]he first edition of the Lyrical Ballads is sold off" and Longman would offer him £80 for the right of publishing a new edition. Mindful of his financial interests, Wordsworth added, "I think I shall accept the offer as if the books sell quickly I shall soon have the right of going to market with them again when their merit will be known, and if they do not sell tolerably, Longman will have given enough for them" (*WL*, 1:283). The new edition, with Wordsworth's name (but not Coleridge's) on the title pages, would consist of two volumes, the first reprinting the poems of the 1798 volume, and the second containing poems composed subsequently. Biggs and Cottle, the Bristol firm that had printed the first edition, was again engaged to print the second.

Returning to Grasmere on June 29, 1800, after several weeks in Bristol, Coleridge joined William and Dorothy in preparing the new edition. In July Coleridge sent Biggs and Cottle detailed instructions for the printing of volume 1 (*LB* [CW], 729–34). Convinced that "the strange words and oddity" of *The Rime of the Ancyent Marinere* had hampered the reception of *Lyrical Ballads*, Wordsworth had told Joseph Cottle in June 1799 that he wanted to replace Coleridge's poem with poems "more likely to suit the common taste" in the event of a second edition (*WL*, 1:264). But thirteen months later, probably because two volumes now had to be filled, the *Rime* was retained, although relocated, according to instructions sent by Coleridge himself, from first to penultimate place in the volume—just before *Tintern Abbey*—and with its archaic spellings modernized (*CL*, 1:593, 598–602). On ca. October 1, however, Wordsworth sent the printer the text of a note (which Coleridge is unlikely to have seen before it was in print) in which he at once claimed credit for reprinting the poem and enumerated its "great defects": "I cannot refuse myself the gratification of informing such Readers as may have been pleased with this poem * * * that they owe their pleasure in some sort to me;

71

as the Author was himself very desirous that it should be suppressed" (see *CL*, 1:602n, and *LB* [CW], 791, for the full text). This graceless note, which Charles Lamb criticized (*CLL*, 1:266), was omitted from the 1802 and 1805 editions of *Lyrical Ballads*. The other substantive changes to the "second edition" of the 1798 *Lyrical Ballads* were the replacement of Wordsworth's *The Convict* with Coleridge's *Love* (*CL*, 1:594–97), and the division of *Lines written near Richmond* into two poems, *Lines written when sailing in a Boat at evening* and *Lines written near Richmond, upon the Thames*.

Copy and instructions for volume 2 were sent to the printer between late July and December 18, 1800 (*LB* [CW], 729–34; *WL*, 1:290–93, 302–309), and they reflected Wordsworth's meticulous concern with the physical presentation of his poetry, including the typography and spacing between stanzas. Because neither Wordsworth nor Coleridge was in Bristol to supervise the printing directly, they enlisted the chemist Humphry Davy (whom Coleridge had met the year before) to correct the punctuation of the manuscripts and the printer's proofs (*WL*, 1: 289–90). But the printing was greatly complicated by the protracted submission of the manuscripts, the unreliability of the postal service, Davy's illness for much of the autumn, Wordsworth's revisions of poems and reordering of the volume after printing had begun, his request (refused by Longman) to change the title to *Poems in two Volumes* (*WL*, 1:303), and the probability that neither he nor Coleridge saw more than a few proofsheets (see *LB* [CW], 124–26). While Coleridge's expected contributions to the "Poems on the Naming of Places" never materialized (*WL*, 1:304–305; *DWJ*, 1:67, 69), part of his long poem *Christabel*, which was to have concluded volume 2, was certainly sent to the printer before September 15 (*WL*, 1:302). But on October 6 Wordsworth decided that the yet-unfinished poem was stylistically inappropriate for the volume, as Coleridge reported to Davy on October 9 (*CL*, 1:631) and Wordsworth himself explained to Longman on December 18: "upon mature deliberation I found that the Style of this Poem was so discordant with my own that it could not be printed along with my poems with any propriety. I had some other poems by me of my own which would have been sufficient for our purpose but some of them being connected with political subjects I judged that they would be injurious to the sale of the Work" (*WL*, 1:309).

From October to mid-December Wordsworth worked with difficulty on *Michael*, his replacement for *Christabel*, sending the manuscript to the printer on December 18 and assuring the publisher that his poem "will be highly serviceable to the Sale" of the edition (*WL*, 1:309). This substitution necessitated the cancelation of the already-printed first leaf of the Preface, in which Wordsworth had referred to *Christabel*, and delayed publication of the edition until ca. January 25, 1801, although the date 1800 still appeared on the title pages (*LB* [CW], 29–31). The print run was 750 copies of volume 1, designated the "Second Edition," and 1000 copies of volume 2; each volume was priced at five shillings (Owen, "Costs, Sales and Profits," 94). Volume 2, containing 41 poems, begins with *Hart-leap Well*, ends with *Michael* (and its note), and includes five poems subtitled *A Pastoral* (three of which, *The Brothers*, *The Idle Shepherd-Boys* and *Michael*, are reprinted in the present selection), a section of five "Poems on the Naming of Places," and several of the lyrics commonly grouped as the "Lucy Poems" (on which see the first note to *Strange fits of passion I have known*). The defiant Latin epigraph printed on the title pages *Quam nihil ad genium, Papiniane, tuum!* may be paraphrased, "How worthless these poems will seem according to your temperament, Papinianus." The source was probably John Selden's "From the Author of the Illustrations," a preface to Michael Drayton's *Poly-Olbion* (1612–22), as reprinted in Robert Anderson's *Works of the British Poets* (London, 1792–95), 3:238 (see the long note in *LB* [CW], 377–78). Although the Roman jurist Papinianus (d. 212) was a historical figure, Wordsworth and Coleridge may have thought of his name as alluding slyly to the eighteenth-century poet Alexander Pope, if Papinianus is taken as a derivative of *papa* (Latin for "pope" as well as "father"): hence "disciple of Pope." As in *LB 1798*, Coleridge was not named as a contributor.

Once the expanded edition of *Lyrical Ballads* was published, Wordsworth took equal pains to promote it and to correct the numerous printing errors, especially in volume 2, the most egregious of which was the omission of lines 212–16 of *Michael* (see the headnote to that poem). On April 9, 1801, he advised his friend Thomas Poole that "half a sheet" with corrections was available from Longman (*WL*, 1:323), and between summer 1801 and April 1802—anticipating another edition, which was published in June 1802—William and Dorothy wrote corrections and revisions into two copies of the 1800 edition sent to them by the publisher (*LB* [CW], 32). Already on December 18, 1800, Wordsworth, at Coleridge's suggestion, had advised Longman, "The Lyrical Ballads are written upon a theory professedly new, and on principles which many persons will be unwilling to admit. I think therefore there would be propriety in your sending a few copies to the amount of half a dozen to persons of eminence either in Letters or in the state" (*WL*, 1:310; compare *CL*, 1:654). In mid-January Coleridge dictated several such letters—to Georgina Cavendish, Duchess of Devonshire (1759–1806), a Whig socialite; to the Anglo-Irish actress Dorothea Jordan (1761–1816); to William Wilberforce (1759–1833), parliamentary leader of the abolitionist movement; to the well-connected parliamentarian Sir James Bland Burges (1752–1824); to John Taylor, editor and co-owner of the *Sun* newspaper (1755–1832); and possibly to the prominent poet Anna Letitia Barbauld (1743–1825) (*WL*, 1:325 and n. 1, 337, 683–85)—while Wordsworth himself wrote on January 14 to Charles James Fox (1749–1806), parliamentary leader of the Whig opposition to William Pitt's government. Lamenting the "rapid decay of the domestic affections among the lower orders of society" as a consequence of industrialization, the increasing disparity between incomes and living costs, and the dissolution of small inherited estates, Wordsworth recommended *The Brothers* and *Michael* in particular to Fox as "faithful copies from nature," capable of exciting "profitable sympathies in many kind and good hearts" (*WL*, 1:312–15). Despite what he had told Longman in December about excluding poems on "political subjects" from *Lyrical Ballads*, Wordsworth obviously conceived at least the second volume, with its representations of rural life, as vitally engaged with the nation's social and political concerns. (Replying on May 25, 1801, Fox stated his preference from some of the original *Lyrical Ballads* in volume 1, and confessed that, with respect to *The Brothers* and *Michael*, "I am no great friend to blank verse for subjects which are to be treated of with simplicity" [*CH*, 106].)

If Wordsworth was disappointed by the lack of enthusiastic responses from the "persons of eminence" to whom he had sent copies, he could still boast to his brother Richard on June 23, 1801, that he had received "high encomiums on the poems from the most respectable quarters" and that the edition had already been "sold to within 130 copies" (*WL*, 1:337). Favorable reviews appeared in the *British Critic* and the *Monthly Mirror* between February and June 1801 (*CH*, 138–45), and in the next two years Wordsworth received effusive fan letters from two undergraduate readers of *Lyrical Ballads*, the seventeen-year-old John Wilson (*CH*, 108–14) and the eighteen-year-old Thomas De Quincey (*CH*, 122), who in 1807 would meet and befriend the Wordsworths (see Biographical and Typographical Glossary). Harsh criticism, however, was to follow the publication of the 1802 edition of *Lyrical*

Ballads, when Francis Jeffrey, in the inaugural issue of the *Edinburgh Review*, began his long campaign against Wordsworth and the "Lake School" of poetry by condemning the principles elaborated in the Preface to *Lyrical Ballads* (*CH*, 153–59)—a campaign that would finally provoke Wordsworth to his thinly veiled counterattack in the Preface to the 1815 *Poems*. Eventually to become one of the most famous and influential manifestos in English literature (supplying such phrases as "the spontaneous overflow of powerful feelings" and "emotion recollected in tranquillity"), Wordsworth's Preface, especially as expanded in 1802, conceives the poet as a prophetic figure who promotes social cohesion by cultivating readers' imaginative sympathy with others unlike themselves; but it does so in defiance and hope against a perceived degradation of public taste. While defining a subjectivist, expressivist poetics that continues to condition poets' and critics' understanding of the lyric, the Preface simultaneously affirms a standard of verisimilitude premised on an older conception of poetry as imitative of external reality. And Wordsworth's rejection of a distinctly poetic rhetoric, though not entirely applicable to the *Lyrical Ballads* themselves (as has often been noted), was affirmed by many later poets, particularly in the twentieth century. (The Preface is analysed most fully by W. J. B. Owen, *Wordsworth as Critic*, chaps. 1–5.)

Modern criticism has tended to focus on the Preface, individual poems (especially *Michael*), or groups of poems (the "Lucy poems," the pastorals) in the 1800 *Lyrical Ballads* rather than on the collection as a whole (or more precisely, the two collections yoked by a single title). But important exceptions to this tendency are the essays assembled by Nicola Trott and Seamus Perry in *1800: The New Lyrical Ballads*, and Kenneth Johnston's *The Hidden Wordsworth*, chap. 30. As Johnston observes (725), whereas solitary outcasts are characteristic of the 1798 edition, threatened relationships and communities form the subject matter of much of volume 2 of the 1800 edition. Among the critical selections in the present volume that address writings first published in *LB 1800* are the essays by Susan Wolfson (Preface, *Michael*, *Strange fits of passion*), Lucy Newlyn (Preface), Mark Jones ("Lucy poems"), and Thomas Pfau (*Michael*).

LB 1800 is "bibliographically the most complex of all Wordsworth's books and appears in a number of different states" (*Cornell*, no. 6). Most recorded copies have a cancel leaf in the Preface (mentioned above), the incomplete text of *Michael*, and a three-item errata list at the end of volume 2. At some point, probably after most of the edition had been sold, the printer responded to Wordsworth's corrections of volume 2 by replacing pages 209–12 with three new leaves (paginated 209–10, *209–*210, 211–12) with the missing 15 lines of *Michael*, and replacing the original errata list with one of 27 items (*Cornell*, nos. 6, 11; *LB* [*CW*], 125–27). This Norton Critical Edition incorporates corrections from the second errata list (as signaled in the notes) and includes lines 202–16 of *Michael* from the cancel leaves found in seven located copies of *LB 1800* (see *LB* [*CW*], 126 n. 8). The classification of the poems in *P 1815* is indicated in the notes. The Preface, owing to its expansion in *LB 1802*, calls for special treatment: the text presented here follows the 1800 version (including the cancel leaf), but inserts the substantive alterations and additions of 1802 within square brackets and in a different typeface, preceded in each instance by the editor's indication in italics of their relation to the text of 1800. Thus both the 1800 and the more familiar 1802 version can be read while remaining distinguishable from one another.

LYRICAL BALLADS,

WITH

OTHER POEMS.

IN TWO VOLUMES.

By W. WORDSWORTH.

Quam nihil ad genium, Papiniane, tuum!

VOL. I.

SECOND EDITION.

LONDON:

PRINTED FOR T. N. LONGMAN AND O. REES, PATERNOSTER-ROW,

BY BIGGS AND CO. BRISTOL.

1800.

Preface[†]

The First Volume[1] of these Poems has already been submitted to general perusal. It was published, as an experiment which, I hoped, might be of some use to ascertain, how far, by fitting to metrical arrangement a selection of the real language of men in a state of vivid sensation, that sort of pleasure and that quantity of pleasure may be imparted, which a Poet may rationally endeavour to impart.

I had formed no very inaccurate estimate of the probable effect of those Poems: I flattered myself that they who should be pleased with them would read them with more than common pleasure: and on the other hand I was well aware that by those who should dislike them they would be read with more than common dislike. The result has differed from my expectation in this only, that I have pleased a greater number, than I ventured to hope I should please.

For the sake of variety and from a consciousness of my own weakness I was induced to request the assistance of a Friend, who furnished me with the Poems of the ANCIENT MARINER, the FOSTER-MOTHER'S TALE, the NIGHTINGALE, the DUNGEON, and the Poem entitled LOVE.[2] I should not, however, have requested this assistance, had I not believed that the poems of my Friend would in a great measure have the same tendency as my own, and that, though there would be found a difference, there would be found no discordance in the colours of our style; as our opinions on the subject of poetry do almost entirely coincide.

Several of my Friends are anxious for the success of these Poems from a belief, that if the views, with which they were composed, were indeed realized, a class of Poetry would be produced, well adapted to interest mankind permanently, and not unimportant in the multiplicity and in the quality of its moral relations: and on this account they have advised me to prefix a systematic defence of the theory, upon which the poems were written.[3] But I was unwilling to undertake the task, because I knew

[†] As indicated in the headnote, the text of the Preface as printed here follows that of *LB 1800*, while substantive alterations and additions introduced in *LB 1802* are printed within square brackets and in a different typeface, prefaced by the editor's indication in italics of their relation to the text of 1800. WW reprinted the 1802 version (with minor changes) and its Appendix (see p. 157 below) in *LB 1805* and, at the conclusion of his shorter poems, in collected editions from *P 1815* to the *Poetical Works* of 1850.

1. I.e., *LB 1798*. The poetic contents of the first volume of *LB 1800* were nearly the same as, though differently ordered than, in *LB 1798*, except that STC's *Love* replaced WW's *The Convict*. In the succeeding sentence WW recalls the wording of his Advertisement to *LB 1798*.

2. Since the Preface to *LB 1800* was printed before WW decided to not to include STC's uncompleted *Christabel* in the collection, this passage originally read, "I have again requested the assistance of a Friend who contributed largely to the first volume, and who has now furnished me with the Poem of Christabel, without which I should not yet have ventured to present a second volume to the public." In a footnote to the sentence WW listed STC's five other contributions. On October 6/7, 1800, he sent the publishers a substitute sentence incorporating the footnote and omitting reference to *Christabel* (*WL*, 1:304–305), and on December 18 a revision of that sentence (*WL*, 1:307); the latter was printed on a cancel leaf that appears in most copies of *LB 1800*, although at least three copies with the original leaf survive (*Cornell*, no. 6; *Prose*, 1:115, 118n., 120n., 167). In *LB 1802* WW omitted *The Dungeon* and the reference to it in the Preface.

3. In letters of July 1802 STC told the poets William Sotheby and Robert Southey that the Preface had emerged from "the heads of our mutual Conversations &c—& the f[irst pass]ages were indeed partly taken from notes of mine" (*CL*, 2:811), and that it was "half a child of my own Brain" (*CL*, 2:830). In December 1839 WW himself affirmed, in a note to his friend Barron Field, "I never cared a straw about the theory—& the Preface was written at the request of Mr Coleridge out of sheer good nature—I recollect the very spot, a deserted Quarry in the Vale of Grasmere where he pressed the thing upon me, & but for that it would never have been thought of" (*Barron Field's Memoirs of Wordsworth*, ed. Geoffrey Little [Sydney, 1975], 62 n. 101; see also *WL*, 6:508–509).

that on this occasion the Reader would look coldly upon my arguments, since I might be suspected of having been principally influenced by the selfish and foolish hope of *reasoning* him into an approbation of these particular Poems: and I was still more unwilling to undertake the task, because adequately to display my opinions and fully to enforce my arguments would require a space wholly disproportionate to the nature of a preface. For to treat the subject with the clearness and coherence, of which I believe it susceptible, it would be necessary to give a full account of the present state of the public taste in this country, and to determine how far this taste is healthy or depraved; which again could not be determined, without pointing out, in what manner language and the human mind act and react on each other, and without retracing the revolutions not of literature alone but likewise of society itself. I have therefore altogether declined to enter regularly upon this defence; yet I am sensible, that there would be some impropriety in abruptly obtruding upon the Public, without a few words of introduction, Poems so materially different from those, upon which general approbation is at present bestowed.[4]

It is supposed, that by the act of writing in verse an Author makes a formal engagement that he will gratify certain known habits of association, that he not only thus apprizes the Reader that certain classes of ideas and expressions will be found in his book, but that others will be carefully excluded. This exponent or symbol held forth by metrical language must in different æras of literature have excited very different expectations: for example, in the age of Catullus, Terence and Lucretius, and that of Statius or Claudian,[5] and in our own country, in the age of Shakespeare and Beaumont and Fletcher, and that of Donne and Cowley, or Dryden, or Pope.[6] I will not take upon me to determine the exact import of the promise which by the act of writing in verse an Author in the present day makes to his Reader; but I am certain it will appear to many persons that I have not fulfilled the terms of an engagement thus voluntarily contracted. [*LB 1802 inserts:* **They who have been accustomed to the gaudiness and inane phraseology of many modern writers, if they persist in reading this book to its conclusion, will, no doubt, frequently have to struggle with feelings of strangeness and aukwardness: they will look round for poetry, and will be induced to inquire by what species of courtesy these attempts can be permitted to assume that title.**][7] I hope therefore the Reader will not censure me, if I attempt to state what I have proposed to myself to perform, and also, (as far as the limits of a preface will permit) to explain some of the chief reasons which have determined me in the choice of my

---

4. WW exaggerates: in fact poetry published in the 1790s, especially in magazines, offered precedents in subject-matter and even in style for the poems of *LB*, with the exception of STC's *Rime of the Ancyent Marinere* (see Robert Mayo, "The Contemporaneity of the *Lyrical Ballads*").
5. WW treats the chronology of these Roman writers casually: the comic playwright Terence (d. 159 B.C.E.) lived a century earlier than the philosophical poet Lucretius (ca. 95–ca. 55 B.C.E.) and the lyric poet Catullus (ca. 85–ca. 54 B.C.E.), and Statius (ca. 45/50–96 B.C.E.), an epic and lyric poet, three centuries earlier than Claudian (ca. 370–ca. 404 C.E.), a poet known for his panegyrics and invectives.
6. Alexander Pope (1688–1744), the most prominent poet of the early eighteenth century; Francis Beaumont (1584–1616) and John Fletcher (1579–1625), dramatists of Shakespeare's time who co-wrote some fifteen plays; John Donne (1572–1631) and Abraham Cowley (1618–1667), both "metaphysical" poets, although their lives overlapped by only thirteen years; John Dryden (1631–1700), poet and playwright, England's first official Poet Laureate.
7. The insertion is repeated from the Advertisement to *LB* 1798.

purpose: that at least he may be spared any unpleasant feeling of disappointment, and that I myself may be protected from the most dishonorable accusation which can be brought against an Author, namely, that of an indolence which prevents him from endeavouring to ascertain what is his duty, or, when his duty is ascertained prevents him from performing it.

The principal object then which I proposed to myself in these Poems was to make the incidents of common life interesting [*LB 1802 alters* "*to make . . . interesting*" *to:* **to chuse incidents and situations from common life, and to relate or describe them, throughout, as far as was possible, in a selection of language really used by men; and, at the same time, to throw over them a certain colouring of imagination, whereby ordinary things should be presented to the mind in an unusual way; and, further, and above all, to make these incidents and situations interesting**] by tracing in them, truly though not ostentatiously, the primary laws of our nature: chiefly as far as regards the manner in which we associate ideas[8] in a state of excitement. Low and rustic life was generally chosen because in that situation the essential passions of the heart find a better soil in which they can attain their maturity, are less under restraint, and speak a plainer and more emphatic language; because in that situation our elementary feelings exist in a state of greater simplicity and consequently may be more accurately contemplated and more forcibly communicated; because the manners[9] of rural life germinate from those elementary feelings; and from the necessary character of rural occupations are more easily comprehended; and are more durable; and lastly, because in that situation the passions of men are incorporated[1] with the beautiful and permanent forms of nature. The language too of these men is adopted (purified indeed from what appear to be its real defects, from all lasting and rational causes of dislike or disgust) because such men hourly communicate with the best objects from which the best part of language is originally derived;[2] and because, from their rank in society and the sameness and narrow circle of their intercourse, being less under the action of social

---

8. WW alludes to the associationist philosophy of David Hartley (1705–1757), whose *Observations on Man* (1749; *Reading 1770–99*, no. 125) sought to establish the principles by which ideas are formed out of sense-data and other ideas.
9. "The modes of life, customary rules of behaviour, conditions of society, prevailing in a people" (*OED*). WW's use of the word here recalls that in remark of February 1799 to STC about Bürger: "I do not so ardently desire character in poems like Burger's, as manners, not transitory manners reflecting the wearisome unintelligible obliquities of city-life, but manners connected with the permanent objects of nature and partaking of the simplicity of those objects" (*WL*, 1:255).
1. Associated, connected. As *Prose*, 1:167–68, notes, WW's vindication of rural life has parallels in eighteenth-century "primitivist" aesthetics, such as James Beattie's *Dissertations Moral and Critical* (London, 1783), 191–92: "to be gratified with accurate representations of human manners, especially in that primitive simplicity, in which they give a full display of the character * * * is surely natural to any reasonable being, who has leisure to attend to these things."
2. WW follows the rhetorician Hugh Blair's argument, in the 38th of his *Lectures on Rhetoric and Belles Lettres* (1783; *Reading 1770–99*, no. 29), that primitive language consists in emotional effusions prompted by immediate objects or events. In *BL* STC objected, first, "that in the most interesting of the poems, in which the author is more or less dramatic, as the 'Brothers,' 'Michael,' 'Ruth,' the 'Mad Mother,' &c. the persons introduced are by no means taken *from low or rustic life* in the common acceptation of those words; and * * * that the sentiments and language * * * are attributable to causes and circumstances not necessarily connected with 'their occupations and abode'"; and second, "that a rustic's language, purified from all provincialism and grossness, and so far reconstructed as to be made consistent with the rules of grammar * * * will not differ from the language of any other man, except as far as the notions, which the rustic has to convey, are fewer and more indiscriminate" (*NCC*, 497, 502).

vanity they convey their feelings and notions in simple and unelaborated expressions. Accordingly such a language arising out of repeated experience and regular feelings is a more permanent and a far more philosophical[3] language than that which is frequently substituted for it by Poets, who think that they are conferring honour upon themselves and their art in proportion as they separate themselves from the sympathies of men, and indulge in arbitrary and capricious habits of expression in order to furnish food for fickle tastes and fickle appetites of their own creation.[4]

I cannot be insensible of the present outcry against the triviality and meanness both of thought and language, which some of my contemporaries have occasionally introduced into their metrical compositions; and I acknowledge that this defect where it exists, is more dishonorable to the Writer's own character than false refinement or arbitrary innovation, though I should contend at the same time that it is far less pernicious in the sum of its consequences. From such verses the Poems in these volumes will be found distinguished at least by one mark of difference, that each of them has a worthy *purpose*. Not that I mean to say, that I always began to write with a distinct purpose formally conceived; but I believe that my habits of meditation have so formed my feelings, as that my descriptions of such objects as strongly excite those feelings, will be found to carry along with them a *purpose*. If in this opinion I am mistaken I can have little right to the name of a Poet. For all good poetry is the spontaneous overflow of powerful feelings; but though this be true, Poems to which any value can be attached, were never produced on any variety of subjects but by a man who being possessed of more than usual organic sensibility[5] had also thought long and deeply. For our continued influxes of feeling are modified and directed by our thoughts, which are indeed the representatives of all our past feelings; and as by contemplating the relation of these general representatives to each other, we discover what is really important to men, so by the repetition and continuance of this act feelings connected with important subjects will be nourished [*LB 1802 alters phrase after "feelings" to:* **will be connected with important subjects**], till at length, if we be originally possessed of much organic sensibility, such habits of mind will be produced that by obeying blindly and mechanically the impulses of those habits we shall describe objects and utter sentiments of such a nature and in such connection with each other, that the understanding of the being to whom we address ourselves, if he be in a healthful state of association, must necessarily be in some degree enlightened, his taste exalted [*LB 1802 omits "his taste exalted"*], and his affections ameliorated.

I have said that each of these poems has a purpose. I have also informed my Reader what this purpose will be found principally to be: namely to illustrate the manner in which our feelings and ideas are associated in a state of excitement. But speaking in less general language, it is to follow the fluxes and refluxes of the mind when agitated by the great and simple

---

3. I.e., precise, accurate.
4. WW's note: "It is worth while here to observe that the affecting parts of Chaucer are almost always expressed in language pure and universally intelligible even to this day."
5. WW seems to mean a sensitivity derived from or relating to the individual's essentially human characteristics, the word *organic* apparently used in *OED* sense 5a: "Belonging to or inherent in the organization or constitution (bodily or mental) of a living being; constitutional; fundamental."

affections of our nature. This object I have endeavoured in these short essays to attain by various means; by tracing the maternal passion through many of its more subtle windings, as in the poems of the IDIOT BOY and the MAD MOTHER; by accompanying the last struggles of a human being at the approach of death, cleaving in solitude to life and society, as in the Poem of the FORSAKEN INDIAN; by shewing, as in the Stanzas entitled WE ARE SEVEN, the perplexity and obscurity which in childhood attend our notion of death, or rather our utter inability to admit that notion; or by displaying the strength of fraternal, or to speak more philosophically, of moral attachment when early associated with the great and beautiful objects of nature, as in THE BROTHERS; or, as in the Incident of SIMON LEE, by placing my Reader in the way of receiving from ordinary moral sensations another and more salutary impression than we are accustomed to receive from them. It has also been part of my general purpose to attempt to sketch characters under the influence of less impassioned feelings, as in the [LB 1802 *inserts here:* TWO APRIL MORNINGS, THE FOUNTAIN,] OLD MAN TRAVELLING, THE TWO THIEVES, &c. characters of which the elements are simple, belonging rather to nature[6] than to manners, such as exist now and will probably always exist, and which from their constitution may be distinctly and profitably contemplated. I will not abuse the indulgence of my Reader by dwelling longer upon this subject; but it is proper that I should mention one other circumstance which distinguishes these Poems from the popular Poetry of the day; it is this, that the feeling therein developed gives importance to the action and situation and not the action and situation to the feeling. My meaning will be rendered perfectly intelligible by referring my Reader to the Poems entitled POOR SUSAN and the CHILDLESS FATHER, particularly to the last Stanza of the latter Poem.

I will not suffer a sense of false modesty to prevent me from asserting, that I point my Reader's attention to this mark of distinction far less for the sake of these particular Poems than from the general importance of the subject. The subject is indeed important! For the human mind is capable of excitement without the application of gross and violent stimulants; and he must have a very faint perception of its beauty and dignity who does not know this, and who does not further know that one being is elevated above another in proportion as he possesses this capability.[7] It has therefore appeared to me that to endeavour to produce or enlarge this capability is one of the best services in which, at any period, a Writer can be engaged; but this service, excellent at all times, is especially so at the present day. For a multitude of causes unknown to former times are now acting with a combined force to blunt the discriminating powers of the mind, and unfitting it for all voluntary exertion to reduce it to a state of almost savage torpor. The most effective of these causes are the great national events which are daily taking place, and the encreasing accumulation of men in cities, where the uniformity of their occupations

---

6. "The general inherent character or disposition of mankind" (*OED* sense 2b). The contrast with *manners* seems to imply that the characters are to be understood as typical rather than highly individualized.

7. A point WW repeated in *The Prelude* 13.90–102: "higher minds * * * build up greatest things / From least suggestions, * * * They need not extraordinary calls / To rouze them." See also his definition of imagination in the Note to *The Thorn*.

produces a craving for extraordinary incident which the rapid communi-
cation[8] of intelligence hourly gratifies. To this tendency of life and man-
ners the literature and theatrical exhibitions of the country have conformed
themselves. The invaluable works of our elder writers, I had almost said the
works of Shakespear and Milton, are driven into neglect by frantic novels,
sickly and stupid German Tragedies, and deluges of idle and extravagant
stories in verse.[9]—When I think upon this degrading thirst after outra-
geous stimulation I am almost ashamed to have spoken of the feeble effort
with which I have endeavoured to counteract it; and reflecting upon the
magnitude of the general evil, I should be oppressed with no dishonorable
melancholy, had I not a deep impression of certain inherent and inde-
structible qualities of the human mind, and likewise of certain powers in
the great and permanent objects that act upon it which are equally inher-
ent and indestructible; and did I not further add to this impression a belief
that the time is approaching when the evil will be systematically opposed
by men of greater powers and with far more distinguished success.

Having dwelt thus long on the subjects and aim of these Poems, I shall
request the Reader's permission to apprize him of a few circumstances
relating to their *style*, in order, among other reasons, that I may not be
censured for not having performed what I never attempted. Except in a
very few instances the Reader will find no personifications of abstract
ideas in these volumes, not that I mean to censure such personifications:
they may be well fitted for certain sorts of composition, but in these Poems
I propose to myself to imitate, and, as far as is possible, to adopt the very
language of men, and I do not find that such personifications make any
regular or natural part of that language. I wish to keep my Reader in the
company of flesh and blood, persuaded that by so doing I shall interest
him. Not but that I believe that others who pursue a different track may
interest him likewise: [*LB 1802 replaces "Except in . . . him likewise" with:*
**The Reader will find that personifications of abstract ideas rarely
occur in these volumes; and, I hope, are utterly rejected as an ordi-
nary device to elevate the style, and raise it above prose.[1] I have
proposed to myself to imitate, and, as far as is possible, to adopt
the very language of men; and assuredly such personifications**

8. WW probably means the mail-coach, a service introduced in 1784; *great national events*:
doubtless a reference to the consequences of the French Revolution, including the war between
France and Britain, which had begun in 1793; *accumulation of men in cities*: During the eigh-
teenth century the proportion of the English population living in cities grew from ca. 20 per-
cent to ca. 30 percent, London's population increasing by 45 percent and other cities' (e.g.,
Birmingham and Manchester) by even higher rates (Paul Langford, *A Polite and Commercial
People: England 1727–1783* [Oxford, 1989], 417–18).
9. WW may mean the ballads—filled with terrifying and supernatural events—of Gottfried
August Bürger (1747–1794), which in translation enjoyed immense popularity in England in
the 1790s (see Geoffrey Hartman, *The Unremarkable Wordsworth*, 53–57). WW had acquired
a German edition of Bürger's works in Hamburg on October 1, 1798, and reported to STC a
month or two later, "Bürger is one of those authors whose book I like to have in my hand, but
when I have laid the book down I do not think about him. I remember a hurry of pleasure, but
I have few distinct forms that people my mind, nor any recollection of delicate or minute feel-
ings which he has either communicated to me or taught me to recognise" (*WL*, 1:234; *Reading
1770–99*, no. 40.iii). *frantic novels*: presumably Gothic novels; *German tragedies*: WW evi-
dently refers to the popular English adaptations of melodramas, not limited to tragedies, by
August von Kotzebue (1761–1819), such as *Lover's Vows* (1798), *The Stranger* (1798), *Pizarro*
(1799), *False Shame* (1799), and *Self Immolation* (1799).
1. As *Prose*, 1:172, comments, WW's rejection of personification may be directed against Erasmus
Darwin's identification of it, in the first prose interlude to his allegorical poem *The Loves of the
Plants*, as a distinguishing feature of poetry generally in contrast to prose (*The Botanic Garden*
[London, 1789–90], 2:43–44).

do not make any natural or regular part of that language. They are, indeed, a figure of speech occasionally prompted by passion, and I have made use of them as such; but I have endeavoured utterly to reject them as a mechanical device of style, or as a family language which Writers in metre seem to lay claim to by prescription. I have wished to keep my Reader in the company of flesh and blood, persuaded that by so doing I shall interest him. I am, however, well aware that others who pursue a different track may interest him likewise;] I do not interfere with their claim, I only wish to prefer a different claim of my own. There will also be found in these volumes little of what is usually called poetic diction;[2] I have taken as much pains to avoid it as others ordinarily take to produce it; this I have done for the reason already alleged, to bring my language near to the language of men, and further, because the pleasure which I have proposed to myself to impart is of a kind very different from that which is supposed by many persons to be the proper object of poetry. I do not know how without being culpably particular I can give my Reader a more exact notion of the style in which I wished these poems to be written than by informing him that I have at all times endeavoured to look steadily at my subject, consequently I hope it will be found that there is in these Poems little falsehood of description, and that my ideas are expressed in language fitted to their respective importance. Something I must have gained by this practice, as it is friendly to one property of all good poetry, namely good sense; but it has necessarily cut me off from a large portion of phrases and figures of speech which from father to son have long been regarded as the common inheritance of Poets. I have also thought it expedient to restrict myself still further, having abstained from the use of many expressions, in themselves proper and beautiful, but which have been foolishly repeated by bad Poets till such feelings of disgust are connected with them as it is scarcely possible by any art of association to overpower.

If in a Poem there should be found a series of lines, or even a single line, in which the language, though naturally arranged and according to the strict laws of metre, does not differ from that of prose, there is a numerous class of critics who, when they stumble upon these prosaisms as they call them, imagine that they have made a notable discovery, and exult over the Poet as over a man ignorant of his own profession. Now these men would establish a canon of criticism which the Reader will conclude he must utterly reject if he wishes to be pleased with these volumes. And it would be a most easy task to prove to him that not only the language of a large portion of every good poem, even of the most elevated character, must necessarily, except with reference to the metre, in no respect differ from that of good prose, but likewise that some of the most interesting parts of the best poems will be found to be strictly the language of prose when prose is well written.[3]

---

2. See also WW's Appendix to *LB 1802* (p. 157 below).
3. *Prose*, 1:173, suggests that WW's argument here derives from the essay (possibly by William Enfield) "Is Verse Essential to Poetry?" in the *Monthly Magazine* 2 (1796): 455: "It will be admitted, that metaphorical language, being more impressive than general terms, is best suited to poetry. That excited state of mind, which poetry supposes, naturally prompts a figurative style. But the language of fancy, sentiment, and passion is not peculiar to verse. Whatever is the natural or proper expression of any conception or feeling in metre or rhyme, is its natural or proper expression in prose."

The truth of this assertion might be demonstrated by innumerable passages from almost all the poetical writings, even of Milton himself. I have not space for much quotation; but, to illustrate the subject in a general manner, I will here adduce a short composition of Gray,[4] who was at the head of those who by their reasonings have attempted to widen the space of separation betwixt Prose and Metrical composition, and was more than any other man curiously elaborate in the structure of his own poetic diction.

> In vain to me the smiling mornings shine,
> And reddening Phœbus[5] lifts his golden fire:
> The birds in vain their amorous descant join,
> Or chearful fields resume their green attire:
> These ears alas! for other notes repine;
> *A different object do these eyes require;*
> *My lonely anguish melts no heart but mine;*
> *And in my breast the imperfect joys expire;*
> Yet Morning smiles the busy race to cheer,
> And new-born pleasure brings to happier men;
> The fields to all their wonted tribute bear;
> To warm their little loves the birds complain.
> *I fruitless mourn to him that cannot hear*
> *And weep the more because I weep in vain.*

It will easily by perceived that the only part of this Sonnet which is of any value is the lines printed in Italics: it is equally obvious that except in the rhyme, and in the use of the single word "fruitless" for fruitlessly, which is so far a defect, the language of these lines does in no respect differ from that of prose.

Is there then, it will be asked, no essential difference between the language of prose and metrical composition? I answer that there neither is nor can be any essential difference [LB 1802 replaces "Is there . . . essential difference" with: **By the foregoing quotation I have shewn that the language of Prose may yet be well adapted to Poetry; and I have previously asserted that a large portion of the language of every good poem can in no respect differ from that of good Prose. I will go further. I do not doubt that it may be safely affirmed, that there neither is, nor can be, any essential difference between the language of prose and metrical composition**]. We are fond of tracing the resemblance between Poetry and Painting, and, accordingly, we call them Sisters:[6] but where shall we find bonds of connection sufficiently strict to typify the affinity betwixt metrical and prose composition? They both speak by and to the same organs; the bodies in which both of

---

4. *Sonnet on the Death of Mr. Richard West* by Thomas Gray (1716–1771). The *reasonings* to which WW refers in the next clause may be Gray's dictum, in a letter of April 1742 to West, that "the language of the age is never the language of poetry" (*The Poems of Mr. Gray* [London, 1775], 139).
5. I.e., Apollo, Greek and Roman god of music, poetry, prophecy, medicine, and the sun.
6. WW refers to a critical tradition deriving from Horace's formula *ut pictura poesis* [a poem is like a painting] (*Ars poetica*, line 361) and represented by, e.g., the painter Sir Joshua Reynolds (1723–1792), who designated painting "a sister of poetry" in the third of his *Discourses on Art* (*Works* [London, 1797], 1:47; see also Discourse 13, *Works*, 1:276–77).

them are clothed may be said to be of the same substance, their affections are kindred and almost identical, not necessarily differing even in degree;[7] Poetry sheds no tears "such as Angels weep," but natural and human tears; she can boast of no celestial Ichor[8] that distinguishes her vital juices from those of prose; the same human blood circulates through the veins of them both.

If it be affirmed that rhyme and metrical arrangement of themselves constitute a distinction which overturns what I have been saying on the strict affinity of metrical language with that of prose, and paves the way for other [*LB 1802 inserts after "other"*: **artificial**] distinctions which the mind voluntarily admits, I answer that [*LB 1802 inserts here*: **the language of such Poetry as I am recommending is, as far as is possible, a selection of the language really spoken by men; that this selection, wherever it is made with true taste and feeling, will of itself form a distinction far greater than would at first be imagined, and will entirely separate the composition from the vulgarity and meanness of ordinary life; and, if metre be superadded thereto, I believe that a dissimilitude will be produced altogether sufficient for the gratification of a rational mind. What other distinction would we have? Whence is it to come? And where is it to exist? Not, surely, where the Poet speaks through the mouths of his characters: it cannot be necessary here, either for elevation of style, or any of its supposed ornaments: for, if the Poet's subject be judiciously chosen, it will naturally, and upon fit occasion, lead him to passions the language of which, if selected truly and judiciously, must necessarily be dignified and variegated, and alive with metaphors and figures.[9] I forbear to speak of an incongruity which would shock the intelligent Reader, should the Poet interweave any foreign splendour of his own with that which the passion naturally suggests: it is sufficient to say that such addition is unnecessary. And, surely, it is more probable that those passages, which with propriety abound with metaphors and figures, will have their due effect, if, upon other occasions where the passions are of a milder character, the style also be subdued and temperate.**

But, as the pleasure which I hope to give by the Poems I now present to the Reader must depend entirely on just notions upon this subject, and, as it is in itself of the highest importance to our taste and moral feelings, I cannot content myself with these detached remarks. And if, in what I am about to say, it shall appear to some that my labour is unnecessary, and that I am like a man

---

7. WW's note: "I here use the word "Poetry" (though against my own judgment) as opposed to the word Prose, and synonymous with metrical composition. But much confusion has been introduced into criticism by this contradistinction of Poetry and Prose, instead of the more philosophical one of Poetry and [*LB 1802 inserts here*: **Matter of fact, or**] Science. The only strict antithesis to Prose is Metre" [*WW's note in LB 1802 is extended as follows after "Metre"*: **nor is this, in truth, a *strict* antithesis; because lines and passages of metre so naturally occur in writing prose, that it would be scarcely possible to avoid them, even were it desirable**].
8. In Greek mythology, the fluid that flows instead of blood through the veins of the gods; *"such as Angels weep"*: from Milton, *Paradise Lost* 1.620.
9. The association of figurative language with passion was widely held in eighteenth-century aesthetics, by Blair and others (see *Prose*, 1:174–75, for examples). WW's argument was repeated by STC in a letter of 1802: "every phrase, every metaphor, every personification, should have its justifying cause in some *passion* whether of the Poet's mind, or of the Characters described by the poet" (*CL*, 2:812).

fighting a battle without enemies, I would remind such persons, that, whatever may be the language outwardly holden by men, a practical faith in the opinions which I am wishing to establish is almost unknown. If my conclusions are admitted, and carried as far as they must be carried if admitted at all, our judgments concerning the works of the greatest Poets both ancient and modern will be far different from what they are at present, both when we praise, and when we censure: and our moral feelings influencing, and influenced by these judgments will, I believe, be corrected and purified.

Taking up the subject, then, upon general grounds, I ask what is meant by the word Poet? What is a Poet? To whom does he address himself? And what language is to be expected from him?[1] He is a man speaking to men: a man, it is true, endued with more lively sensibility, more enthusiasm and tenderness, who has a greater knowledge of human nature, and a more comprehensive[2] soul, than are supposed to be common among mankind; a man pleased with his own passions and volitions, and who rejoices more than other men in the spirit of life that is in him; delighting to contemplate similar volitions and passions as manifested in the goings-on of the Universe, and habitually impelled to create them where he does not find them. To these qualities he has added a disposition to be affected more than other men by absent things as if they were present;[3] an ability of conjuring up in himself passions, which are indeed far from being the same as those produced by real events, yet (especially in those parts of the general sympathy which are pleasing and delightful) do more nearly resemble the passions produced by real events, than any thing which, from the motions of their own minds merely, other men are accustomed to feel in themselves; whence, and from practice, he has acquired a greater readiness and power in expressing what he thinks and feels, and especially those thoughts and feelings which, by his own choice, or from the structure of his own mind, arise in him without immediate external excitement.

But, whatever portion of this faculty we may suppose even the greatest Poet to possess, there cannot be a doubt but that the language which it will suggest to him, must, in liveliness and truth, fall far short of that which is uttered by men in real life, under the actual pressure of those passions, certain shadows of which the Poet thus produces, or feels to be produced, in himself.[4]

1. WW's formulation of these questions may derive from Hugh Blair's *Lectures on Rhetoric and Belles Lettres*, lect. 38: "Our first enquiry must be, what is Poetry? and wherein does it differ from prose?" (2:311).
2. "Embracing many things, broad in mental grasp, sympathies, or the like" (*OED* sense 2b).
3. WW recalls the *Institutio oratoria* [*The Orator's Education*] 6.2.29, in which the Roman rhetorician Quintilian (b. ca. 35 C.E.) teaches that those who have cultivated their *phantasia* (imagination)—i.e., the faculty by which absent things are presented to the mind as if they were physically present and actually visible—have the greatest capacity for conveying emotion. WW may have read Quintilitan at Hawkshead Grammar School, and he acquired two copies of the *Institutio* (*Reading 1770–99*, no. 203).
4. In July 1802 STC expressed to William Sotheby his disagreement with WW's qualification of the poet's ability to represent passionate expression: "But *metre itself* implies a *passion*, i.e. a state of excitement, both in the Poet's mind, & is expected in that of the Reader—and tho' I stated this to Wordsworth, & he has in some way stated it in his preface, yet he has [not] done justice to it, nor has in my opinion sufficiently answered it. * * * Indeed, we have lately had

However exalted a notion we would wish to cherish of the character of a Poet, it is obvious, that, while he describes and imitates passions, his situation is altogether slavish and mechanical, compared with the freedom and power of real and substantial action and suffering. So that it will be the wish of the Poet to bring his feelings near to those of the persons whose feelings he describes, nay, for short spaces of time perhaps, to let himself slip into an entire delusion, and even confound and identify his own feelings with theirs; modifying only the language which is thus suggested to him, by a consideration that he describes for a particular purpose, that of giving pleasure.[5] Here, then, he will apply the principle on which I have so much insisted, namely, that of selection; on this he will depend for removing what would otherwise be painful or disgusting in the passion; he will feel that there is no necessity to trick out or to elevate nature: and, the more industriously he applies this principle, the deeper will be his faith that no words, which his fancy or imagination can suggest, will be to be compared with those which are the emanations of reality and truth.

But it may be said by those who do not object to the general spirit of these remarks, that, as it is impossible for the Poet to produce upon all occasions language as exquisitely fitted for the passion as that which the real passion itself suggests, it is proper that he should consider himself as in the situation of a translator, who deems himself justified when he substitutes excellences of another kind for those which are unattainable by him; and endeavours occasionally to surpass his original, in order to make some amends for the general inferiority to which he feels that he must submit. But this would be to encourage idleness and unmanly despair. Further, it is the language of men who speak of what they do not understand; who talk of Poetry as of a matter of amusement and idle pleasure; who will converse with us as gravely about a *taste* for Poetry, as they express it, as if it were a thing as indifferent as a taste for Rope-dancing, or Frontiniac or Sherry.[6] Aristotle, I have been told, hath said, that Poetry is the most philosophic of all writing:[7] it is so: its object is truth, not individual and local, but general, and opera-

---

some controversy on this subject—& we begin to suspect * * * a *radical* Difference [in our] opinions" (*CL*, 2:812; see also 830). In *BL* he articulated this difference publicly: "the very *act* of poetic composition *itself* is, and is *allowed* to imply and to produce, an unusual state of excitement, which of course justifies and demands a correspondent difference of language, as truly * * * as the excitement of love, fear, rage, or jealousy" (*NCC*, 512–13).

5. *Prose*, 1:176, notes a parallel to a passage in Quintilian 10.7.15 (in translation, "It is passion and power of mind that make us eloquent") which WW quoted when sending a copy of *LB 1800* to Charles James Fox (see the headnote) and added to the half-title page of *LB 1802* and *LB 1805*.
6. The English name of a fortified wine made from white grapes grown near Jerez in the Cádiz province of southwestern Spain; *Rope-dancing*: acrobatics performed on a tight-rope; *Frontiniac*: the English name of a white Muscat wine produced in Frontignan on the south coast of France.
7. In fact Aristotle asserts that poetry is "more philosophical and more elevated" than historical writing because poetry conveys the universal and history the particular (*Poetics* 1451b5–7). *Prose*, 1:179, speculates that Coleridge—who was to misrepresent Aristotle similarly in *BL* (*NCC*, 499, 527)—supplied the reference to WW. That art should represent general truths was in the eighteenth century a widely held view, which WW would have encountered in chapter 10 of Samuel Johnson's *History of Rasselas, Prince of Abissinia* (1759) and Reynolds's third *Discourse* (1771). WW distinguishes poetry and history again in *The Prelude* 11.91–92.

tive; not standing upon external testimony, but carried alive into the heart by passion; truth which is its own testimony, which gives strength and divinity to the tribunal to which it appeals, and receives them from the same tribunal. Poetry is the image of man and nature. The obstacles which stand in the way of the fidelity of the Biographer and Historian, and of their consequent utility, are incalculably greater than those which are to be encountered by the Poet who has an adequate notion of the dignity of his art. The Poet writes under one restriction only, namely, that of the necessity of giving immediate pleasure to a human Being possessed of that information which may be expected from him, not as a lawyer, a physician, a mariner, an astronomer or a natural philosopher, but as a Man. Except this one restriction, there is no object standing between the Poet and the image of things; between this, and the Biographer and Historian there are a thousand.

Nor let this necessity of producing immediate pleasure be considered as a degradation of the Poet's art. It is far otherwise. It is an acknowledgment of the beauty of the universe, an acknowledgment the more sincere because it is not formal, but indirect; it is a task light and easy to him who looks at the world in the spirit of love: further, it is a homage paid to the native and naked dignity of man, to the grand elementary principle of pleasure, by which he knows, and feels, and lives, and moves. We have no sympathy but what is propagated by pleasure: I would not be misunderstood; but wherever we sympathize with pain it will be found that the sympathy is produced and carried on by subtle combinations with pleasure. We have no knowledge, that is, no general principles drawn from the contemplation of particular facts, but what has been built up by pleasure, and exists in us by pleasure alone. The Man of Science, the Chemist and Mathematician, whatever difficulties and disgusts they may have had to struggle with, know and feel this. However painful may be the objects with which the Anatomist's knowledge is connected, he feels that his knowledge is pleasure; and where he has no pleasure he has no knowledge. What then does the Poet? He considers man and the objects that surround him as acting and re-acting upon each other, so as to produce an infinite complexity of pain and pleasure; he considers man in his own nature and in his ordinary life as contemplating this with a certain quantity of immediate knowledge, with certain convictions, intuitions, and deductions which by habit become of the nature of intuitions; he considers him as looking upon this complex scene of ideas and sensations, and finding every where objects that immediately excite in him sympathies which, from the necessities of his nature, are accompanied by an overbalance of enjoyment.

To this knowledge which all men carry about with them, and to these sympathies in which without any other discipline than that of our daily life we are fitted to take delight, the Poet principally directs his attention. He considers man and nature as essentially adapted to each other, and the mind of man as naturally the mirror of the fairest and most interesting qualities of nature. And thus the Poet, prompted by this feeling of pleasure which accompanies him through the whole course of his studies, converses with general nature with affections akin to those, which, through labour and length of time, the Man of Science has raised up in himself, by conversing with those particular parts of nature which are the objects of his studies. The knowledge both of the Poet and the Man of Science is pleasure; but the knowledge of the one cleaves to us as a necessary part of our existence, our natural and unalienable inheritance; the other is a personal and individual acquisition, slow to come to us, and by no habitual and direct sympathy connecting us with our fellow-beings. The Man of Science seeks truth as a remote and unknown benefactor; he cherishes and loves it in his solitude: the Poet, singing a song in which all human beings join with him, rejoices in the presence of truth as our visible friend and hourly companion. Poetry is the breath and finer spirit of all knowledge; it is the impassioned expression which is in the countenance of all Science. Emphatically may it be said of the Poet, as Shakespeare hath said of man, "that he looks before and after."[8] He is the rock of defence of human nature; an upholder and preserver, carrying every where with him relationship and love. In spite of difference of soil and climate, of language and manners, of laws and customs, in spite of things silently gone out of mind and things violently destroyed, the Poet binds together by passion and knowledge the vast empire of human society, as it is spread over the whole earth, and over all time. The objects of the Poet's thoughts are every where; though the eyes and senses of man are, it is true, his favorite guides, yet he will follow wheresoever he can find an atmosphere of sensation in which to move his wings. Poetry is the first and last of all knowledge—it is as immortal as the heart of man. If the labours of men of Science should ever create any material revolution, direct or indirect, in our condition, and in the impressions which we habitually receive, the Poet will sleep then no more than at present, but he will be ready to follow the steps of the man of Science, not only in those general indirect effects, but he will be at his side, carrying sensation into the midst of the objects of the Science itself. The remotest discoveries of the Chemist, the Botanist, or Mineralogist, will be as proper objects of the Poet's art as any upon which it can be employed, if the time should ever come when these things shall be familiar to us, and the relations under which they are contemplated by the followers of these respective Sciences shall be manifestly and palpably material to us as enjoying and suffering beings. If the time should ever come when what is now called Science, thus famil-

8. *Hamlet* 4.4.37: "Looking before and after." WW may have elaborated the complementary relationship between the poet and the scientist in response to the chemist Humphry Davy, who in a public lecture of January 21, 1802 (attended by STC), had proposed, echoing some of WW's own phraseology from the Preface to *LB 1800*, that science "must always be more or less connected with the love of the beautiful and sublime" and "may become a source of consolation and of happiness" (Roger Sharrock, "The Chemist and the Poet"). On Davy's role in the publication of *LB 1800*, see the headnote.

iarized to men, shall be ready to put on, as it were, a form of flesh and blood, the Poet will lend his divine spirit to aid the transfiguration, and will welcome the Being thus produced, as a dear and genuine inmate of the household of man.—It is not, then, to be supposed that any one, who holds that sublime notion of Poetry which I have attempted to convey, will break in upon the sanctity and truth of his pictures by transitory and accidental ornaments, and endeavour to excite admiration of himself by arts, the necessity of which must manifestly depend upon the assumed meanness of his subject.

What I have thus far said applies to Poetry in general; but especially to those parts of composition where the Poet speaks through the mouths of his characters; and upon this point it appears to have such weight that I will conclude, there are few persons, of good sense, who would not allow that the dramatic parts of composition are defective, in proportion as they deviate from the real language of nature, and are coloured by a diction of the Poet's own, either peculiar to him as an individual Poet, or belonging simply to Poets in general, to a body of men who, from the circumstance of their compositions being in metre, it is expected will employ a particular language.

It is not, then, in the dramatic parts of composition that we look for this distinction of language; but still it may be proper and necessary where the Poet speaks to us in his own person and character. To this I answer by referring my Reader to the description which I have before given of a Poet. Among the qualities which I have enumerated as principally conducing to form a Poet, is implied nothing differing in kind from other men, but only in degree. The sum of what I have there said is, that the Poet is chiefly distinguished from other men by a greater promptness to think and feel without immediate external excitement, and a greater power in expressing such thoughts and feelings as are produced in him in that manner. But these passions and thoughts and feelings are the general passions and thoughts and feelings of men. And with what are they connected? Undoubtedly with our moral sentiments and animal sensations, and with the causes which excite these; with the operations of the elements and the appearances of the visible universe; with storm and sun-shine, with the revolutions of the seasons, with cold and heat, with loss of friends and kindred, with injuries and resentments, gratitude and hope, with fear and sorrow. These, and the like, are the sensations and objects which the Poet describes, as they are the sensations of other men, and the objects which interest them. The Poet thinks and feels in the spirit of the passions of men. How, then, can his language differ in any material degree from that of all other men who feel vividly and see clearly? It might be *proved* that it is impossible. But supposing that this were not the case, the Poet might then be allowed to use a peculiar language, when expressing his feelings for his own gratification, or that of men like himself. But Poets do not write for Poets alone, but for men. Unless therefore we are advocates for that admiration

which depends upon ignorance, and that pleasure which arises from hearing what we do not understand, the Poet must descend from this supposed height, and, in order to excite rational sympathy, he must express himself as other men express themselves. To this it may be added, that while he is only selecting from the real language of men, or, which amounts to the same thing, composing accurately in the spirit of such selection, he is treading upon safe ground, and we know what we are to expect from him. Our feelings are the same with respect to metre; for, as it may be proper to remind the Reader,] the distinction of rhyme and metre is regular and uniform, and not, like that which is produced by what is usually called poetic diction, arbitrary and subject to infinite caprices upon which no calculation whatever can be made. In the one case the Reader is utterly at the mercy of the Poet respecting what imagery or diction he may choose to connect with the passion, whereas in the other the metre obeys certain[9] laws, to which the Poet and Reader both willingly submit because they are certain, and because no interference is made by them with the passion but such as the concurring testimony of ages has shewn to heighten and improve the pleasure which co-exists with it.

It will now be proper to answer an obvious question, namely, why, professing these opinions have I written in verse? To this in the first place I reply, [LB 1802 *replaces "To this . . . I reply" with:* **To this, in addition to such answer as is included in what I have already said, I reply in the first place,**] because, however I may have restricted myself, there is still left open to me what confessedly constitutes the most valuable object of all writing whether in prose or verse, the great and universal passions of men, the most general and interesting of their occupations, and the entire world of nature, from which I am at liberty to supply myself with endless combinations of forms and imagery. Now, granting for a moment that whatever is interesting in these objects may be as vividly described in prose, why am I to be condemned if to such description I have endeavoured to superadd the charm which by the consent of all nations is acknowledged to exist in metrical language? To this it will be answered [LB 1802 *replaces "To this . . . be answered" with:* **To this, by such as are unconvinced by what I have already said, it may be answered**], that a very small part of the pleasure given by Poetry depends upon the metre, and that it is injudicious to write in metre unless it be accompanied with the other artificial distinctions of style with which metre is usually accompanied, and that by such deviation more will be lost from the shock which will be thereby given to the Reader's associations than will be counterbalanced by any pleasure which he can derive from the general power of numbers.[1] In answer to those who thus contend for the necessity of accompanying metre with certain appropriate colours of style in order to the accomplishment of its appropriate end, and who also, in my opinion, greatly under-rate the power of metre in itself, it might perhaps be almost sufficient to observe that poems are extant, written upon more humble subjects, and in a more naked and simple style than

9. I.e., fixed.
1. Metrical feet, poetic rhythm.

what I have aimed at [*LB 1802 replaces "it might perhaps . . . aimed at" with:* **it might perhaps, as far as relates to these Poems, have been almost sufficient to observe, that poems are extant, written upon more humble subjects, and in a more naked and simple style than I have aimed at**], which poems have continued to give pleasure from generation to generation. Now, if nakedness and simplicity be a defect, the fact here mentioned affords a strong presumption that poems somewhat less naked and simple are capable of affording pleasure at the present day; and all that I am now attempting is to [*LB 1802 replaces "and all . . . is to" with:* **and, what I wished *chiefly* to attempt, at present, was to**] justify myself for having written under the impression of this belief.

But I might point out various causes why, when the style is manly, and the subject of some importance, words metrically arranged will long continue to impart such a pleasure to mankind as he who is sensible of the extent of that pleasure will be desirous to impart. The end of Poetry is to produce excitement in coexistence with an overbalance of pleasure. Now, by the supposition, excitement is an unusual and irregular state of the mind; ideas and feelings do not in that state succeed each other in accustomed order. But if the words by which this excitement is produced are in themselves powerful, or the images and feelings have an undue proportion of pain connected with them, there is some danger that the excitement may be carried beyond its proper bounds. Now the co-presence of something regular, something to which the mind has been accustomed when in an unexcited or a less excited state, cannot but have great efficacy in tempering and restraining the passion by an intertexture of ordinary feeling [*LB 1802 inserts a comma after "feeling" and adds:* **and of feeling not strictly and necessarily connected with the passion. This is unquestionably true, and hence, though the opinion will at first appear paradoxical, from the tendency of metre to divest language in a certain degree of its reality, and thus to throw a sort of half consciousness of unsubstantial existence over the whole composition, there can be little doubt but that more pathetic situations and sentiments, that is, those which have a greater proportion of pain connected with them, may be endured in metrical composition, especially in rhyme, than in prose. The metre of the old Ballads is very artless; yet they contain many passages which would illustrate this opinion, and, I hope, if the following Poems be attentively perused, similar instances will be found in them**]. This may be illustrated [*LB 1802 changes "This may be illustrated" to:* **This opinion may be further illustrated**] by appealing to the Reader's own experience of the reluctance with which he comes to the re-perusal of the distressful parts of Clarissa Harlowe, or the Gamester.[2] While Shakespeare's writings, in the most pathetic scenes, never act upon us as pathetic beyond the bounds of pleasure—an effect which is in a great degree to be ascribed [*LB 1802 replaces "an effect . . . be ascribed" with:* **an effect which, in a much greater degree than might at first be imagined, is to be ascribed**] to small, but continual and regular

---

2. A popular domestic tragedy by the dramatist Edward Moore (1712–1757), first performed in 1753; *Clarissa Harlowe:* Samuel Richardson's epistolary novel *Clarissa, or the History of a Young Lady* (1748), in which the heroine is abducted, eventually drugged and raped, and dies.

impulses of pleasurable surprise from the metrical arrangement.—On the other hand (what it must be allowed will much more frequently happen) if the Poet's words should be incommensurate with the passion, and inadequate to raise the Reader to a height of desirable excitement, then, (unless the Poet's choice of his metre has been grossly injudicious) in the feelings of pleasure which the Reader has been accustomed to connect with metre in general, and in the feeling, whether chearful or melancholy, which he has been accustomed to connect with that particular movement of metre, there will be found something which will greatly contribute to impart passion to the words, and to effect the complex end which the Poet proposes to himself.

If I had undertaken a systematic defence of the theory upon which these poems are written, it would have been my duty to develope the various causes upon which the pleasure received from metrical language depends. Among the chief of these causes is to be reckoned a principle which must be well known to those who have made any of the Arts the object of accurate reflection; I mean the pleasure which the mind derives from the perception of similitude in dissimilitude.[3] This principle is the great spring of the activity of our minds and their chief feeder. From this principle the direction of the sexual appetite, and all the passions connected with it take their origin: It is the life of our ordinary conversation; and upon the accuracy with which similitude in dissimilitude, and dissimilitude in similitude are perceived, depend our taste and our moral feelings. It would not have been a useless employment to have applied this principle to the consideration of metre, and to have shewn that metre is hence enabled to afford much pleasure, and to have pointed out in what manner that pleasure is produced. But my limits will not permit me to enter upon this subject, and I must content myself with a general summary.

I have said that Poetry is the spontaneous overflow of powerful feelings: it takes its origin from emotion recollected in tranquillity: the emotion is contemplated till by a species of reaction the tranquillity gradually disappears, and an emotion, similar [*LB 1802 replaces "similar" with:* **kindred**] to that which was before the subject of contemplation, is gradually produced, and does itself actually exist in the mind. In this mood successful composition generally begins, and in a mood similar to this it is carried on; but the emotion, of whatever kind and in whatever degree, from various causes is qualified by various pleasures, so that in describing any passions whatsoever, which are voluntarily described, the mind will upon the whole be in a state of enjoyment. Now if Nature be thus cautious in preserving in a state of enjoyment a being thus employed, the Poet ought to profit by the lesson thus held forth to him, and ought especially to take care, that whatever passions he communicates to his Reader, those passions, if his Reader's mind be sound and vigorous, should always be accompanied with an overbalance of pleasure. Now the music of harmonious metrical language, the sense of difficulty overcome, and the blind association of pleasure which has been previously received from

---

3. Another commonplace of eighteenth-century aesthetics: see *Prose*, 1:184, for instances. In *BL* STC insisted that poetic images offer "proofs of original genius" only "when they have the effect of reducing multitude to unity" (*BL* [CC], 2:23).

works of rhyme or metre of the same or similar construction, [*LB 1802 inserts after "construction,"*: **an indistinct perception perpetually renewed of language closely resembling that of real life, and yet, in the circumstance of metre, differing from it so widely,**] all these imperceptibly make up a complex feeling of delight, which is of the most important use in tempering the painful feeling which will always be found intermingled with powerful descriptions of the deeper passions. This effect is always produced in pathetic and impassioned poetry; while in lighter compositions the ease and gracefulness with which the Poet manages his numbers are themselves confessedly a principal source of the gratification of the Reader. I might perhaps include all which it is *necessary* to say upon this subject by affirming what few persons will deny, that of two descriptions either of passions, manners, or characters, each of them equally well executed, the one in prose and the other in verse, the verse will be read a hundred times where the prose is read once. We see that Pope by the power of verse alone, has contrived to render the plainest common sense interesting, and even frequently to invest it with the appearance of passion. In consequence of these convictions I related in metre the Tale of Goody Blake and Harry Gill, which is one of the rudest of this collection. I wished to draw attention to the truth that the power of the human imagination is sufficient to produce such changes even in our physical nature as might almost appear miraculous. The truth is an important one; the fact (for it is a *fact*) is a valuable illustration of it. And I have the satisfaction of knowing that it has been communicated to many hundreds of people who would never have heard of it, had it not been narrated as a Ballad, and in a more impressive metre than is usual in Ballads.

Having thus adverted to [*LB 1802 replaces "adverted to" with:* **explained**] a few of the reasons why I have written in verse, and why I have chosen subjects from common life, and endeavoured to bring my language near to the real language of men, if I have been too minute in pleading my own cause, I have at the same time been treating a subject of general interest; and it is for this reason that I request the Reader's permission to add a few words with reference solely to these particular poems, and to some defects which will probably be found in them. I am sensible that my associations must have sometimes been particular instead of general, and that, consequently, giving to things a false importance, sometimes from diseased impulses I may have written upon unworthy subjects; but I am less apprehensive on this account, than that my language may frequently have suffered from those arbitrary connections of feelings and ideas with particular words [*LB 1802 inserts after "words"*: **and phrases**], from which no man can altogether protect himself. Hence I have no doubt that in some instances feelings even of the ludicrous may be given to my Readers by expressions which appeared to me tender and pathetic. Such faulty expressions, were I convinced they were faulty at present, and that they must necessarily continue to be so, I would willingly take all reasonable pains to correct. But it is dangerous to make these alterations on the simple authority of a few individuals, or even of certain classes of men; for where the understanding of an Author is not convinced, or his feelings altered, this cannot be done without great injury to himself: for his own feelings are his stay and support, and if he sets them aside in one instance, he may be induced to repeat this act till his mind loses all confidence in itself and becomes utterly debilitated. To this it may be added, that the Reader ought never to forget that he is himself exposed to the same errors as the Poet, and perhaps in a much greater degree: for there can be no presumption in saying that it is not probable he will be so well acquainted with the various stages of meaning through which words have passed, or with the fickleness or stability of the relations of particular ideas to each other; and above all, since he is so much less interested in the subject, he may decide lightly and carelessly.

Long as I have detained my Reader, I hope he will permit me to caution him against a mode of false criticism which has been applied to Poetry in which the language closely resembles that of life and nature. Such verses have been triumphed over in parodies of which Dr. Johnson's Stanza is a fair specimen.

> I put my hat upon my head,
> And walk'd into the Strand,
> And there I met another man
> Whose hat was in his hand.[4]

Immediately under these lines I will place one of the most justly admired stanzas of the "Babes in the Wood."

> These pretty Babes with hand in hand
> Went wandering up and down;
> But never more they saw the Man
> Approaching from the Town.

In both of these stanzas the words, and the order of the words, in no respect differ from the most unimpassioned conversation. There are words in both, for example, "the Strand," and "the Town," connected with none but the most familiar ideas; yet the one stanza we admit as admirable, and the other as a fair example of the superlatively contemptible. Whence arises this difference? Not from the metre, not from the language, not from the order of the words; but the *matter* expressed in Dr. Johnson's stanza is contemptible. The proper method of treating trivial and simple verses to which Dr. Johnson's stanza would be a fair parallelism is not to say this is a bad kind of poetry, or this is not poetry, but this wants sense; it is neither interesting in itself, nor can *lead* to any thing interesting; the images neither originate in that sane state of feeling which arises out of thought, nor can excite thought or feeling in the Reader. This is the only sensible manner of dealing with such verses: Why trouble yourself about the species till you have previously decided upon the genus? Why take pains to prove that an Ape is not a Newton when it is self-evident that he is not a man.[5]

---

4. Samuel Johnson's quatrain, published in the *London Magazine* of April 1785, was a parody of *The Hermit of Warkworth* (1771), a ballad composed by the antiquarian and bishop Thomas Percy (1729–1811), whose *Reliques of Ancient English Poetry* (1765), a collection of older and original ballads, greatly fostered eighteenth-century interest in the ballad form. WW proceeds to quote a variant form of one stanza from a ballad included in the *Reliques* under the title *The Children in the Wood* but better known as *The Babes in the Wood*.
5. An allusion to Alexander Pope's *Essay on Man* (1734) 2.31–34: "Superior being, when of late they saw / A mortal Man unfold all Nature's law, / Admir'd such wisdom in an earthly shape, / And shew'd a NEWTON as we shew an Ape." *Newton*: the physicist and mathematician Sir Isaac Newton (1642–1727).

I have one request to make of my Reader, which is, that in judging these Poems he would decide by his own feelings genuinely, and not by reflection upon what will probably be the judgment of others. How common is it to hear a person say, "I myself do not object to this style of composition or this or that expression, but to such and such classes of people it will appear mean or ludicrous." This mode of criticism so destructive of all sound unadulterated judgment is almost universal: I have therefore to request that the Reader would abide independently by his own feelings, and that if he finds himself affected he would not suffer such conjectures to interfere with his pleasure.

If an Author by any single composition has impressed us with respect for his talents, it is useful to consider this as affording a presumption, that, on other occasions where we have been displeased, he nevertheless may not have written ill or absurdly; and, further, to give him so much credit for this one composition as may induce us to review what has displeased us with more care than we should otherwise have bestowed upon it. This is not only an act of justice, but in our decisions upon poetry especially, may conduce in a high degree to the improvement of our own taste: for an *accurate* taste in Poetry and in all the other arts, as Sir Joshua Reynolds has observed, is an *acquired* talent, which can only be produced by thought and a long continued intercourse with the best models of composition.[6] This is mentioned not with so ridiculous a purpose as to prevent the most inexperienced Reader from judging for himself, (I have already said that I wish him to judge for himself;) but merely to temper the rashness of decision, and to suggest that if Poetry be a subject on which much time has not been bestowed, the judgment may be erroneous, and that in many cases it necessarily will be so.

I know that nothing would have so effectually contributed to further the end which I have in view as to have shewn of what kind the pleasure is, and how the pleasure is produced which is confessedly produced by metrical composition essentially different from what I have here endeavoured to recommend; for the Reader will say that he has been pleased by such composition and what can I do more for him? The power of any art is limited and he will suspect that if I propose to furnish him with new friends it is only upon condition of his abandoning his old friends. Besides, as I have said, the Reader is himself conscious of the pleasure which he has received from such composition, composition to which he has peculiarly attached the endearing name of Poetry; and all men feel an habitual gratitude, and something of an honorable bigotry for the objects which have long continued to please them: we not only wish to be pleased, but to be pleased in that particular way in which we have been accustomed to be pleased. There is a host of arguments in these feelings; and I should be the less able to combat them successfully, as I am willing to allow, that, in order entirely to enjoy the Poetry which I am recommending, it would be necessary to give up much of what is ordinarily enjoyed. But would my limits have permitted me to point out how this pleasure is produced, I might have removed many obstacles, and assisted my Reader in perceiving that the powers of language are not so limited as

6. See n. 1 to the Advertisement to *LB 1798*, from which WW repeats this reference to Reynolds (p. 8).

he may suppose; and that it is possible that poetry may give other enjoyments, of a purer, more lasting, and more exquisite nature. But this part of my subject I have been obliged altogether to omit: [*LB 1802 replaces* "*But this . . . to omit:*" *with:* **This part of my subject I have not altogether neglected;**] as it has been less my present aim to prove that the interest excited by some other kinds of poetry is less vivid, and less worthy of the nobler powers of the mind, than to offer reasons for presuming, that, if the object which I have proposed to myself were adequately attained, a species of poetry would be produced, which is genuine poetry; in its nature well adapted to interest mankind permanently, and likewise important in the multiplicity and quality of its moral relations.

From what has been said, and from a perusal of the Poems, the Reader will be able clearly to perceive the object which I have proposed to myself: he will determine how far I have attained this object; and, what is a much more important question, whether it be worth attaining; and upon the decision of these two questions will rest my claim to the approbation of the public.

HART-LEAP WELL[†]

Hart-Leap Well is a small spring of water, about five miles from Richmond in Yorkshire, and near the side of the road which leads from Richmond to Askrigg.[1] *Its name is derived from a remarkable chace, the memory of which is preserved by the monuments spoken of in the second Part of the following Poem, which monuments do now exist as I have there described them.*

The Knight had ridden down from Wensley[2] moor
With the slow motion of a summer's cloud;   good
He turn'd aside towards a Vassal's[3] door,
And, "Bring another Horse!" he cried aloud.

5   "Another Horse!"—That shout the Vassal heard,
And saddled his best steed, a comely Grey;
Sir Walter mounted him; he was the third
Which he had mounted on that glorious day.

† P 1815: Poems of the Imagination. IF note: "The first eight stanzas were composed extempore one winter evening in the cottage; when, after having tired and disgusted myself with labouring at an awkward passage in "The Brothers," I started with a sudden impulse to this to get rid of the other, and finished it in a day or two. My Sister and I had past the place a few weeks before in our wild winter journey from Sockburn [a village in County Durham, northeast England] on the banks of the [River] Tees to Grasmere. A peasant whom we met near the spot told us the story so far as concerned the name of the well, and the hart; and pointed out the stones. Both the stones and the well are objects that may easily be missed: the tradition by this time may be extinct in the neighbourhood: the man who related it to us was very old." The journey occurred between December 17 and 20, 1799 (*Chrono: EY*, 282–83; *WL*, 1:277–80). The poem's primary literary model (on which see Geoffrey Hartman, *The Unremarkable Wordsworth*, 53–57) was evidently Gottfried August Bürger's ballad *Der wilde Jäger* (1786), which WW might have read in the original German (*Reading 1770–99*, no. 40.iii) or in Walter Scott's adaptations, *The Chace* (1796) and *The Wild Huntsman* (1797). But WW dispenses with the supernaturalism of Bürger's ballad, in which the hunter is suddenly struck dead and condemned by God to eternal punishment for having broken the Sabbath and pursued the deer he was chasing into a hermit's sanctuary.
1. A small village in the Yorkshire Dales, ca. eighteen miles southwest of Richmond, a market town in North Yorkshire.
2. A small village on the River Ure in North Yorkshire, ca. ten miles southwest of Richmond.
3. In the feudal systems of medieval Europe, a person granted land or some other benefit by a lord in exchange for allegiance and service or the provision of part of the harvest to the lord.

Joy sparkled in the prancing Courser's eyes;
10 The horse and horseman are a happy pair;
But, though Sir Walter like a falcon flies,
There is a doleful silence in the air.

A rout this morning left Sir Walter's Hall,
That as they gallop'd made the echoes roar;
15 But horse and man are vanish'd, one and all;
Such race, I think, was never seen before.

Sir Waiter, restless as a veering wind,
Calls to the few tired dogs that yet remain:
Brach, Swift and Music, noblest of their kind,
20 Follow, and up the weary mountain strain.

The Knight halloo'd, he chid and cheer'd them on
With suppliant gestures and upbraidings stern;
But breath and eye-sight fail, and, one by one,
The dogs are stretch'd among the mountain fern.

25 Where is the throng, the tumult of the chace?
The bugles that so joyfully were blown?
—This race it looks not like an earthly race;
Sir Walter and the Hart are left alone.

The poor Hart toils along the mountain side;
30 I will not stop to tell how far he fled,
Nor will I mention by what death he died;
But now the Knight beholds him lying dead.

Dismounting then, he lean'd against a thorn;
He had no follower, dog, nor man, nor boy:
35 He neither smack'd his whip, nor blew his horn,
But gaz'd upon the spoil with silent joy.

Close to the thorn on which Sir Walter lean'd,
Stood his dumb partner in this glorious act;
Weak as a lamb the hour that it is yean'd,[4]
40 And foaming like a mountain cataract. — good metaphor

Upon his side the Hart was lying stretch'd:
His nose half-touch'd a spring beneath a hill,
And with the last deep groan his breath had fetch'd
The waters of the spring were trembling still.

45 And now, too happy for repose or rest,
Was never man in such a joyful case,
Sir Walter walk'd all round, north, south and west,
And gaz'd, and gaz'd upon that darling place.

4. Born.

And turning up the hill, it was at least
50   Nine roods⁵ of sheer ascent, Sir Walter found
Three several marks which with his hoofs the beast
Had left imprinted on the verdant ground.

Sir Walter wiped his face, and cried, "Till now
Such sight was never seen by living eyes:
55   Three leaps have borne him from this lofty brow,
Down to the very fountain where he lies.

I'll build a Pleasure-house upon this spot,
And a small Arbour, made for rural joy;
'Twill be the traveller's shed, the pilgrim's cot,
60   A place of love for damsels that are coy.

A cunning Artist will I have to frame
A bason for that fountain in the dell;
And they, who do make mention of the same,
From this day forth, shall call it Hart-leap Well.

65   And, gallant brute! to make thy praises known,
Another monument shall here be rais'd;
Three several pillars, each a rough hewn stone,
And planted where thy hoofs the turf have graz'd.

And in the summer-time when days are long,
70   I will come hither with my paramour,
And with the dancers, and the minstrel's song,
We will make merry in that pleasant bower.

Till the foundations of the mountains fail
My mansion with its arbour shall endure,
75   —The joy of them who till the fields of Swale,
And them who dwell among the woods of Ure."⁶

Then home he went, and left the Hart, stone-dead,
With breathless nostrils stretch'd above the spring.
And soon the Knight perform'd what he had said,
80   The fame whereof through many a land did ring.

Ere thrice the moon into her port had steer'd,
A cup of stone receiv'd the living well;
Three pillars of rude stone Sir Walter rear'd,
And built a house of pleasure in the dell.

85   And near the fountain, flowers of stature tall
With trailing plants and trees were intertwin'd,

5. Ca. sixty-three yards (the rood being an older unit of measure in England, not fixed but typically between six and eight yards).
6. The River Swale flows southeast through North Yorkshire past Richmond before joining the River Ure ca. ten miles northwest of the city of York.

Which soon composed a little sylvan hall,
A leafy shelter from the sun and wind.

And thither, when the summer days were long,
90 Sir Walter journey'd with his paramour;
And with the dancers and the minstrel's song
Made merriment within that pleasant bower.

The Knight, Sir Walter, died in course of time,
And his bones lie in his paternal vale.—
95 But there is matter for a second rhyme,
And I to this would add another tale.

PART SECOND

The moving accident[7] is not my trade.
To freeze[8] the blood I have no ready arts;
'Tis my delight, alone in summer shade,
100 To pipe a simple song to thinking hearts. *excellent.*

As I from Hawes[9] to Richmond did repair,
It chanc'd that I saw standing in a dell
Three aspins at three corners of a square,
And one, not four yards distant, near a well.

105 What this imported I could ill divine,
And, pulling now the rein my horse to stop,
I saw three pillars standing in a line,
The last stone pillar on a dark hill-top.

The trees were grey, with neither arms nor head;
110 Half-wasted the square mound of tawny green;
So that you just might say, as then I said,
"Here in old time the hand of man has been."

I look'd upon the hills both far and near;
More doleful place did never eye survey;
115 It seem'd as if the spring-time came not here,
And Nature here were willing to decay.

I stood in various thoughts and fancies lost,
When one who was in Shepherd's garb attir'd,
Came up the hollow. Him did I accost,
120 And what this place might be I then inquir'd.

---

7. A phrase from Shakespeare, *Othello* 1.3.135: "Of moving accidents by flood and field."
8. Replaces the original reading "curl" in accordance with the second errata list (which itself mistakes "curb" for "curl" as the word to be replaced). The corrected reading perhaps alludes to *Hamlet* 1.5.15–16: "I could a tale unfold whose lightest word / Would harrow up thy soul, freeze thy young blood." In lines 102–103 WW introduces the retrospective second part by distancing himself self-consciously from the kind of poetry represented by Bürger.
9. A small market town on the River Ure in North Yorkshire, ca. five miles west of Askrigg.

The Shepherd stopp'd, and that same story told
Which in my former rhyme I have rehears'd.
"A jolly place," said he, "in times of old,
But something ails it now; the spot is curs'd.

125   You see these lifeless stumps of aspin wood,
Some say that they are beeches, others elms,
These were the Bower; and here a Mansion stood,
The finest palace of a hundred realms.

The arbour does its own condition tell,
130   You see the stones, the fountain, and the stream,
But as to the great Lodge, you might as well
Hunt half a day for a forgotten dream.

There's neither dog nor heifer, horse nor sheep,
Will wet his lips within that cup of stone;
135   And, oftentimes, when all are fast asleep,
This water doth send forth a dolorous groan.

Some say that here a murder has been done,
And blood cries out for blood: but, for my part,
I've guess'd, when I've been sitting in the sun,
140   That it was all for that unhappy Hart.

What thoughts must through the creature's brain have pass'd!
From the stone on the summit of[1] the steep
Are but three bounds, and look, Sir, at this last!
O Master! it has been a cruel leap.

145   For thirteen hours he ran a desperate race;
And in my simple mind we cannot tell
What cause the Hart might have to love this place,
And come and make his death-bed near the well.

Here on the grass perhaps asleep he sank,
150   Lull'd by this fountain in the summer-tide;
This water was perhaps the first he drank
When he had wander'd from his mother's side.

In April here beneath the scented thorn
He heard the birds their morning carols sing,
155   And he, perhaps, for aught we know, was born
Not half a furlong from that self-same spring.

But now here's neither grass nor pleasant shade;
The sun on drearier hollow never shone:

---

1. Corrected according to the second errata list from the original reading, "To this place from the
stone upon."

So will it be, as I have often said,
160 Till trees, and stones, and fountain all are gone."

"Grey-headed Shepherd, thou hast spoken well;
Small difference lies between thy creed and mine; *good*
This beast not unobserv'd by Nature fell,
His death was mourn'd by sympathy divine. *good*

165 The Being, that is in the clouds and air,
That is in the green leaves among the groves, *Holy Ghost*
Maintains a deep and reverential care
For them the quiet creatures whom he loves.

The Pleasure-house is dust:—behind, before,
170 This is no common waste, no common gloom;
But Nature, in due course of time, once more
Nature Shall here put on her beauty and her bloom.

She leaves these objects to a slow decay
That what we are, and have been, may be known;
175 But, at the coming of the milder day,
These monuments shall all be overgrown.

One lesson, Shepherd, let us two divide,
Taught both by what she shews, and what conceals, *Nature*
Never to blend our pleasure or our pride
180 With sorrow of the meanest thing that feels.
good *didactic*

THE

BROTHERS,

A PASTORAL POEM[†]

These Tourists, Heaven preserve us! needs must live
A profitable life: some glance along,
Rapid and gay, as if the earth were air,
And they were butterflies to wheel about
5 Long as their summer lasted; some, as wise,

† P 1815: Poems founded on the Affections. IF note: "This poem was composed in a grove at the north-eastern end of Grasmere Lake, which grove was in a great measure destroyed by turning the high road along the side of the water. The few trees that are left were spared at my intercession. The poem arose out of the fact mentioned to me at Ennerdale that a shepherd had fallen asleep upon the top of the rock called The Pillar, and perished as here described, his staff being left midway on the rock." During their walking tour of the Lake District in autumn 1799, WW and STC probably visited Ennerdale (the westernmost lake in the Lake District) on November 12 (*Chrono: EY*, 279) and heard the stories of James Bowman, who had died after breaking a leg near Scale Force (the highest waterfall in the Lake District), and his son, who had fallen off a cliff while sleep-walking (*WL*, 1:277; *CN*, 1:540). Sending *LB 1800* to Charles James Fox (see headnote), WW specified this poem and *Michael* as representing the "domestic affections" of "small independent *proprietors* of land * * * men of respectable education who daily labour on their own little properties" (*WL*, 1:314). WW's note: "This Poem was intended to be the concluding poem of a series of pastorals, the scene of which was laid among the mountains of Cumberland and Westmoreland. I mention this to apologise for the abruptness with which the poem begins."

Upon the forehead of a jutting crag
Sit perch'd with book and pencil on their knee,
And look and scribble, scribble on and look,
Until a man might travel twelve stout miles,[1]
10   Or reap an acre of his neighbour's corn.
But, for that moping son of Idleness
Why can he terry *yonder?*—In our church-yard
Is neither epitaph nor monument,
Tomb-stone nor name, only the turf we tread,
15   And a few natural graves. To Jane, his Wife,
Thus spake the homely Priest of Ennerdale.[2]
It was a July evening, and he sate
Upon the long stone-seat beneath the eaves
Of his old cottage, as it chanced that day,
20   Employ'd in winter's work. Upon the stone
His Wife sate near him, teasing matted wool,
While, from the twin cards tooth'd with glittering wire,
He fed the spindle of his youngest child,
Who turn'd her large round wheel in the open air
25   With back and forward steps. Towards the field
In which the parish chapel stood alone,
Girt round with a bare ring of mossy wall,
While half an hour went by, the Priest had sent
Many a long look of wonder, and at last,
30   Risen from his seat, beside the snow-white ridge
Of carded wool[3] which the old Man had piled
He laid his implements with gentle care,
Each in the other lock'd; and, down the path
Which from his cottage to the church-yard led,
35   He took his way, impatient to accost
The Stranger, whom he saw still lingering there.

'Twas one well known to him in former days,
A Shepherd-lad; who ere his thirteenth year
Had chang'd his calling,[4] with the mariners
40   A fellow-mariner, and so had fared
Through twenty seasons; but he had been rear'd
Among the mountains, and he in his heart
Was half a Shepherd on the stormy seas.
Oft in the piping shrouds had Leonard heard
45   The tones of waterfalls, and inland sounds
Of caves and trees; and when the regular wind
Between the tropics fill'd the steady sail
And blew with the same breath through days and weeks,

1. I.e., old English miles of 2428 yards each (as opposed to "statute miles" of 1760 yards each), hence a total distance 29,136 yards or 87,408 feet.
2. As an Anglican priest, he is permitted to marry.
3. Wool prepared for spinning by being combed and straightened out with cards by the process described in lines 20–22.
4. *LB* (CW) suggests that WW's description of Leonard's maritime career derives from the experiences of his brother John (see Biographical and Topographical Glossary), who accompanied him and STC on part of their 1799 walking tour.

Lengthening invisibly its weary line
50 Along the cloudless main, he, in those hours
Of tiresome indolence would often hang
Over the vessel's side, and gaze and gaze,
And, while the broad green wave and sparkling foam
Flash'd round him images and hues, that wrought
55 In union with the employment of his heart,
He, thus by feverish passion overcome,
Even with the organs of his bodily eye,
Below him, in the bosom of the deep
Saw mountains, saw the forms of sheep that graz'd
60 On verdant hills, with dwellings among trees,
And Shepherds clad in the same country grey
Which he himself had worn.[5]
       And now at length,
From perils manifold, with some small wealth
Acquir'd by traffic in the Indian Isles,
65 To his paternal home he is return'd,
With a determin'd purpose to resume
The life which he liv'd there, both for the sake
Of many darling pleasures, and the love
Which to an only brother he has borne
70 In all his hardships, since that happy time
When, whether it blew foul or fair, they two
Were brother Shepherds on their native hills.
—They were the last of all their race;[6] and now,
When Leonard had approach'd his home, his heart
75 Fail'd in him, and, not venturing to inquire
Tidings of one whom he so dearly lov'd,
Towards the church-yard he had turn'd aside,
That, as he knew in what particular spot
His family were laid, he thence might learn
80 If still his Brother liv'd, or to the file
Another grave was added.—He had found
Another grave, near which a full half hour
He had remain'd, but, as he gaz'd, there grew
Such a confusion in his memory,
85 That he began to doubt, and he had hopes
That he had seen this heap of turf before,
That it was not another grave, but one,
He had forgotten. He had lost his path,
As up the vale he came that afternoon,
90 Through fields which once had been well known to him.

---

5. WW's note: "This description of the Calenture is sketched from an imperfect recollection of an admirable one in prose, by Mr. Gilbert, Author of the Hurricane." The specific sense of *calenture* that WW uses is defined by the *OED* as a "disease incident to sailors within the tropics, characterized by delirium in which the patient, it is said, fancies the sea to be green fields, and desires to leap into it." In 1839 WW reported that he had "often conversed with" William Gilbert (?1760–?1825), author of the poem *The Hurricane: A Theosophical and Western Eclogue* (1796), in Bristol between 1795 and 1798 and had "admired his genius though he was in fact insane" (*WL*, 6:726). Gilbert's description of calenture is lost.
6. Family.

And Oh! what joy the recollection now
Sent to his heart! he lifted up his eyes,
And looking round he thought that he perceiv'd
Strange alteration wrought on every side
95   Among the woods and fields, and that the rocks,
And the eternal hills, themselves were chang'd.

    By this the Priest who down the field had come
Unseen by Leonard, at the church-yard gate
Stopp'd short, and thence, at leisure, limb by limb
100 He scann'd him with a gay complacency.[7]
Aye, thought the Vicar, smiling to himself,
'Tis one of those who needs must leave the path
Of the world's business, to go wild alone:
His arms have a perpetual holiday,
105 The happy man will creep about the fields
Following his fancies by the hour, to bring
Tears down his cheek, or solitary smiles
Into his face, until the setting sun
Write Fool upon his forehead. Planted thus
110 Beneath a shed that overarch'd the gate
Of this rude church-yard, till the stars appear'd
The good man might have commun'd with himself
But that the Stranger, who had left the grave,
Approach'd; he recogniz'd the Priest at once,
115 And after greetings interchang'd, and given
By Leonard to the Vicar as to one
Unknown to him, this dialogue ensued.

LEONARD.

You live, Sir, in these dales, a quiet life:
Your years make up one peaceful family;
120 And who would grieve and fret, if, welcome come
And welcome gone, they are so like each other,
They cannot be remember'd. Scarce a funeral
Comes to this church-yard once in eighteen months;
And yet, some changes must take place among you,
125 And you, who dwell here, even among these rocks
Can trace the finger of mortality,
And see, that with our threescore years and ten
We are not all that perish.——I remember,
For many years ago I pass'd this road,
130 There was a foot-way all along the fields
By the brook-side—'tis gone—and that dark cleft!
To me it does not seem to wear the face
Which then it had.

7. *LB* (CW) notes an echo in lines 99–100 of Shakespeare, *Troilus and Cressida* 4.5.238–39: "I will the second time, / As I would buy thee, view thee limb by limb."

PRIEST.

      Why, Sir, for aught I know,
That chasm is much the same—

LEONARD.

           But, surely, yonder—

PRIEST.

135 Aye, there indeed, your memory is a friend
That does not play you false.—On that tall pike,
(It is the loneliest place of all these hills)
There were two Springs[8] which bubbled side by side,
As if they had been made that they might be
140 Companions for each other: ten years back,
Close to those brother fountains, the huge crag
Was rent with lightning—one is dead and gone,
The other, left behind, is flowing still——
For accidents and changes such as these,
145 Why we have store of them! a water spout
Will bring down half a mountain; what a feast
For folks that wander up and down like you,
To see an acre's breadth of that wide cliff
One roaring cataract—a sharp May storm
150 Will come with loads of January snow,
And in one night send twenty score of sheep
To feed the ravens, or a Shepherd dies
By some untoward death among the rocks:
The ice breaks up and sweeps away a bridge—
155 A wood is fell'd:—and then for our own homes!
A child is born or christen'd, a field plough'd,
A daughter sent to service, a web spun,
The old house-clock is deck'd with a new face;
And hence, so far from wanting facts or dates
160 To chronicle the time, we all have here
A pair of diaries, one serving, Sir,
For the whole dale, and one for each fire-side,
Your's was a stranger's judgment: for historians
Commend me to these vallies.

LEONARD.

           Yet your church-yard
165 Seems, if such freedom may be used with you,
To say that you are heedless of the past.

---

8. WW's note: "The impressive circumstance here described, actually took place some years ago in this country, upon an eminence called Kidstow [i.e., Kidsty] Pike, one of the highest of the mountains [2,559 feet] that surround Hawes-water. The summit of the pike was stricken by lightning; and every trace of one of the fountains disappeared, while the other continued to flow as before."

An Orphan could not find his mother's grave.[9]
Here's neither head nor foot-stone, plate of brass,
Cross-bones or skull, type of our earthly state
170   Or emblem of our hopes: the dead man's home
Is but a fellow to that pasture field.

PRIEST.

Why there, Sir, is a thought that's new to me.
The Stone-cutters, 'tis true, might beg their bread
If every English church-yard were like ours:
175   Yet your conclusion wanders from the truth.
We have no need of names and epitaphs,
We talk about the dead by our fire-sides.
And then for our immortal part, *we* want
No symbols, Sir, to tell us that plain tale:
180   The thought of death[1] sits easy on the man
Who has been born and dies among the mountains.

LEONARD.

Your dalesmen, then, do in each other's thoughts
Possess a kind of second life: no doubt
You, Sir, could help me to the history
185   Of half these Graves?

PRIEST.

                                     For eight-score winters past[2]
With what I've witness'd, and with what I've heard,
Perhaps I might, and, on a winter's evening,
If you were seated at my chimney's nook
By turning o'er these hillocks one by one,
190   We two could travel, Sir, through a strange round,
Yet all in the broad high-way of the world.
Now there's a grave—your foot is half upon it,
It looks just like the rest, and yet that man
Died broken-hearted.

LEONARD.

                              'Tis a common case,
195   We'll take another: who is he that lies
Beneath yon ridge, the last of those three graves;—
It touches on that piece of native rock
Left in the church-yard wall.

9. This line is supplied from the second errata list to *LB 1800*.
1. WW's note: "There is not any-thing more worthy of remark in the manners of the inhabitants
   of these mountains, than the tranquility, I might say the indifference, with which they think
   and talk upon the subject of death. Some of the country church-yards, as here described, do
   not contain a single tombstone, and most of them have a very small number."
2. This half-line is supplied from the second errata list to *LB 1800*.

PRIEST.

                 That's Walter Ewbank.
He had as white a head and fresh a cheek
200 As ever were produc'd by youth and age
Engendering in the blood of hale fourscore.
For five long generations had the heart
Of Walter's forefathers o'erflow'd the bounds
Of their inheritance, that single cottage,
205 You see it yonder, and those few green fields.
They toil'd and wrought, and still, from sire to son,
Each struggled, and each yielded as before
A little—yet a little—and old Walter,
They left to him the family heart, and land
210 With other burthens than the crop it bore.
Year after year the old man still preserv'd
A chearful mind, and buffeted with bond,
Interest and mortgages; at last he sank,
And went into his grave before his time.
215 Poor Walter! whether it was care that spurr'd him
God only knows, but to the very last
He had the lightest foot in Ennerdale:
His pace was never that of an old man:
I almost see him tripping down the path
220 With his two Grandsons after him—but you,
Unless our Landlord be your host to-night,
Have far to travel, and in these rough paths
Even in the longest day of midsummer—

LEONARD.

But these two Orphans!

PRIEST.

               Orphans! such they were—
225 Yet not while Walter liv'd—for, though their Parents
Lay buried side by side as now they lie,
The old Man was a father to the boys,
Two fathers in one father: and if tears
Shed, when he talk'd of them where they were not,
230 And hauntings from the infirmity of love,
Are aught of what makes up a mother's heart,
This old Man in the day of his old age
Was half a mother to them.—If you weep, Sir,
To hear a stranger talking about strangers,
235 Heaven bless you when you are among your kindred!
Aye. You may turn that way—it is a grave
Which will bear looking at.

LEONARD.

These Boys I hope
They lov'd this good old Man—

PRIEST.

                              They did—and truly,
But that was what we almost overlook'd,
240 They were such darlings of each other. For
Though from their cradles they had liv'd with Walter,
The only kinsman near them in the house,
Yet he being old, they had much love to spare,
And it all went into each other's hearts.
245 Leonard, the elder by just eighteen months,
Was two years taller: 'twas a joy to see,
To hear, to meet them! from their house the School
Was distant three short miles, and in the time
Of storm and thaw, when every water-course
250 And unbridg'd stream, such as you may have notic'd
Crossing our roads at every hundred steps,
Was swoln into a noisy rivulet,
Would Leonard then, when elder boys perhaps
Remain'd at home, go staggering through the fords
255 Bearing his Brother on his back.—I've seen him,
On windy days, in one of those stray brooks,
Aye, more than once I've seen him mid-leg deep,
Their two books lying both on a dry stone
Upon the hither side:—and once I said,
260 As I remember, looking round these rocks
And hills on which we all of us were born,
That God who made the great book of the world
Would bless such piety—

LEONARD.

                              It may be then—

PRIEST.

Never did worthier lads break English bread:
265 The finest Sunday that the Autumn saw,
With all its mealy clusters of ripe nuts,
Could never keep these boys away from church,
Or tempt them to an hour of sabbath breach.
Leonard and James! I warrant, every corner
270 Among these rooks and every hollow place
Where foot could come, to one or both of them
Was known as well as to the flowers that grow there.
Like roe-bucks they went bounding o'er the hills:
They play'd like two young ravens on the crags:[3]

3. Lines 273–74 recall *Tintern Abbey*, lines 68–69: "when like a roe / I bounded o'er the mountains."

275 Then they could write, aye and speak too, as well
     As many of their betters—and for Leonard!
     The very night before he went away,
     In my own house I put into his hand
     A Bible, and I'd wager twenty pounds,
280 That, if he is alive, he has it yet.

LEONARD.

     It seems, these Brothers have not liv'd to be
     A comfort to each other.—

PRIEST.

                    That they might
     Live to that end, is what both old and young
     In this our valley all of us have wish'd,
285 And what, for my part, I have often pray'd:
     But Leonard—

LEONARD.

          Then James still is left among you—

PRIEST.

     'Tis of the elder Brother I am speaking:
     They had an Uncle, he was at that time
     A thriving man, and traffick'd on the seas:
290 And, but for this same Uncle, to this hour
     Leonard had never handled rope or shroud.
     For the Boy lov'd the life which we lead here;
     And, though a very Stripling, twelve years old;
     His soul was knit to this his native soil.
295 But, as I said, old Walter was too weak
     To strive with such a torrent; when he died,
     The estate and house were sold, and all their sheep,
     A pretty flock, and which, for aught I know,
     Had clothed the Ewbanks for a thousand years.
300 Well—all was gone, and they were destitute.
     And Leonard, chiefly for his brother's sake,
     Resolv'd to try his fortune on the seas.
     'Tis now twelve years since we had tidings from him.
     If there was one among us who had heard
305 That Leonard Ewbank was come home again,
     From the great Gavel,[4] down by Leeza's Banks,
     And down the Enna, far as Egremont,

---

4. WW's note: "The great Gavel [a northern English variant of "gable"], so called I imagine, from
its resemblance to the Gable end of a house, is one of the highest of the Cumberland moun-
tains [2,949 feet]. It stands at the head of the several vales of Ennerdale, Wastdale, and Bor-
rowdale. The Leesa is a River which follows into the Lake of Ennerdale: on issuing from the
Lake, it changes its name, and is called the Enf, Eyne, or Enna. It falls into the sea a little
below Egremont."

The day would be a very festival,
And those two bells of ours, which there you see
310 Hanging in the open air—but, O good Sir!
This is sad talk—they'll never sound for him
Living or dead—When last we heard of him
He was in slavery among the Moors
Upon the Barbary Coast—'Twas not a little
315 That would bring down his spirit, and, no doubt,
Before it ended in his death, the Lad
Was sadly cross'd—Poor Leonard! when we parted,
He took me by the hand and said to me,
If ever the day came when he was rich,
320 He would return, and on his Father's Land
He would grow old among us.

LEONARD.

                    If that day
Should come, 'twould needs be a glad day for him;
He would himself, no doubt, be happy then
As any that should meet him—

PRIEST.

                    Happy, Sir—

LEONARD.

325 You said his kindred all were in their graves,
And that he had one Brother—

PRIEST.

                    That is but
A fellow tale of sorrow. From his youth
James, though not sickly, yet was delicate,
And Leonard being always by his side
330 Had done so many offices about him,
That, though he was not of a timid nature,
Yet still the spirit of a mountain boy
In him was somewhat check'd, and when his Brother
Was gone to sea and he was left alone
335 The little colour that he had was soon
Stolen from his cheek, he droop'd, and pin'd and pin'd:

LEONARD.

But these are all the graves of full grown men!

PRIEST.

Aye, Sir, that pass'd away: we took him to us.
He was the child of all the dale—he liv'd

340   Three months with one, and six months with another:[5]
      And wanted neither food, nor clothes, nor love,
      And many, many happy days were his.
      But, whether blithe or sad, 'tis my belief
      His absent Brother still was at his heart.
345   And, when he liv'd beneath our roof, we found
      (A practice till this time unknown to him)
      That often, rising from his bed at night,
      He in his sleep would walk about, and sleeping
      He sought his Brother Leonard—You are mov'd!
350   Forgive me, Sir: before I spoke to you,
      I judg'd you most unkindly.

LEONARD.

                              But this youth,
      How did he die at last?

PRIEST.

                        One sweet May morning,
      It will be twelve years since, when Spring returns,
      He had gone forth among the new-dropp'd lambs,
355   With two or three companions whom it chanc'd
      Some further business summon'd to a house
      Which stands at the Dale-head. James, tir'd perhaps,
      Or from some other cause remain'd behind.
      You see yon precipice—it almost looks
360   Like some vast building made of many crags,
      And in the midst is one particular rock
      That rises like a column from the vale,
      Whence by our Shepherds it is call'd, the Pillar.[6]
      James pointed to its summit, over which
365   They all had purpos'd to return together,
      And told them that he there would wait for them:
      They parted, and his comrades pass'd that way
      Some two hours after, but they did not find him
      At the appointed place, a circumstance
370   Of which they took no heed: but one of them,
      Going by chance, at night, into the house[7]
      Which at this time was James's home, there learn'd

---

5. James (like Richard Bateman in *Michael*, lines 269–70) is a "parish-boy," maintained finan-
cially by the local parish while assigned (like a foster-child) to live with different families for
set periods.
6. Pillar Rock is a spur on the mountain Pillar (2,927 feet), ca. two miles southeast of Ennerdale
Water. *LB* (CW) notes WW's poetic license in locating the story on Pillar Rock, which in fact
was first climbed only in 1826. For the origin of James's story, see the source note to this poem.
7. The readings *James pointed* (line 364) and *And told* (line 366) are supplied from the second
errata notice, replacing the original "James, pointing" and "Inform'd." In *BL* (CC), 2:80, STC
objected to the syntax of the phrase *a circumstance / Of which they took no heed*, and in *MP
1820*, doubtless in response to STC's criticism, WW revised lines 364–71 substantially: "Upon
its aëry summit crowned with heath, / The Loiterer, not unnoticed by his Comrades, / Lay
stretched at ease; but, passing by the place / On their return, they found that he was gone. /
From this no ill was feared; but one of them, / Entering by chance, at even-tide, the house."

That nobody had seen him all that day:
The morning came, and still, he was unheard of:
375 The neighbours were alarm'd, and to the Brook
Some went, and some towards the Lake; ere noon
They found him at the foot of that same Rock
Dead, and with mangled limbs. The third day after
I buried him, poor Lad, and there he lies.

LEONARD.

380 And that then *is* his grave!—Before his death
You said that he saw many happy years?

PRIEST.

Aye, that he did—

LEONARD.

And all went well with him—

PRIEST.

If he had one, the Lad had twenty homes.

LEONARD.

And you believe then, that his mind was easy—

PRIEST.

385 Yes, long before he died, he found that time
Is a true friend to sorrow, and unless
His thoughts were turn'd on Leonard's luckless fortune,
He talk'd about him with a chearful love.

LEONARD.

He could not come to an unhallow'd end![8]

PRIEST.

390 Nay, God forbid! You recollect I mention'd
A habit which disquietude and grief
Had brought upon him, and we all conjectur'd
That, as the day was warm, he had lain down
Upon the grass, and, waiting for his comrades
395 He there had fallen asleep, that in his sleep
He to the margin of the precipice
Had walk'd, and from the summit had fallen head-long,
And so no doubt he perish'd: at the time,
We guess, that in his hands he must have had
400 His Shepherd's staff; for midway in the cliff

---

8. Unholy or impious, i.e., suicide.

It had been caught, and there for many years
It hung—and moulder'd there.
                                    The Priest here ended—
The Stranger would have thank'd him, but he felt
Tears rushing in; both left the spot in silence,
405 And Leonard, when they reach'd the church-yard gate,
As the Priest lifted up the latch, turn'd round,
And, looking at the grave, he said, "My Brother."
The Vicar did not hear the words: and now,
Pointing towards the Cottage, he entreated
410 That Leonard would partake his homely fare:
The other thank'd him with a fervent voice,
But added, that, the evening being calm,
He would pursue his journey. So they parted.

It was not long ere Leonard reach'd a grove
415 That overhung the road: he there stopp'd short,
And, sitting down beneath the trees, review'd
All that the Priest had said: his early years
Were with him in his heart: his cherish'd hopes,
And thoughts which had been his an hour before,
420 All press'd on him with such a weight, that now,
This vale, where he had been so happy, seem'd
A place in which he could not bear to live:
So he relinquish'd all his purposes.
He travell'd on to Egremont; and thence,
425 That night, address'd a letter to the Priest
Reminding him of what had pass'd between them.
And adding, with a hope to be forgiven,
That it was from the weakness of his heart,
He had not dared to tell him, who he was.

430 This done, he went on shipboard, and is now
A Seaman, a grey headed Mariner.

Strange fits of passion I have known[†]

Strange fits of passion I have known,
And I will dare to tell,

† P 1815: Poems founded on the Affections. The evidence of DC MS 15 suggests that this poem and the next two were composed between October 6 and December 28, 1798, when WW and DW were in Goslar (LB [CW], 383, 719; Chrono: EY, 35). In a letter of December 1798 (WL, 1:235–43), WW and DW sent STC fair copies of Strange fits and Song with significant variants, noted below, from the versions subsequently published. These two poems, A slumber, and Three years she grew are commonly classified among the so-called "Lucy poems," although WW himself never designated such a group and critics debate which poems should be included in it. For discussion of the issue, see the selection from Mark Jones reprinted in this edition (pp. 644–53); for an influential analysis of the group, see Geoffrey Hartman, Wordsworth's Poetry, 157–62. Among WW's published poems, the name Lucy appears in Strange fits, She dwelt, Lucy Gray, and Three years she grew in LB 1800 and Among all lovely things and I travell'd among unknown Men in P2V (but not in A slumber). Much profitless effort (summarized in LB [CW],

But in the lover's ear alone,
What once to me befel.[1]

5 When she I lov'd, was strong and gay
And like a rose in June,
I to her cottage bent my way,
Beneath the evening moon.

Upon the moon I fix'd my eye,
10 All over the wide lea;[2]
My horse trudg'd on, and we drew nigh
Those paths so dear to me.

And now we reach'd the orchard plot,
And, as we climb'd the hill,
15 Towards the roof of Lucy's cot[3]
The moon descended still.

In one of those sweet dreams I slept,
Kind Nature's gentlest boon!
And, all the while, my eyes I kept
20 On the descending moon.

My horse mov'd on; hoof after hoof
He rais'd and never stopp'd:
When down behind the cottage roof
At once the planet dropp'd.

25 What fond and wayward thoughts will slide
Into a Lover's head—
"O mercy!" to myself I cried,
"If Lucy should be dead!"[4]

SONG[†]

She dwelt among th' untrodden ways
Beside the springs of Dove,[1]

---

383) has been spent on identifying Lucy and interpreting the poems biographically, beginning
with STC, who wrote in April 1799 of *A slumber,* "Wordsworth transmitted to me a sublime
Epitaph / whether it had any reality, I cannot say.—Most probably, in some gloomier moment
he had fancied the moment in which his Sister might die" (*CL*, 1:479).
1. The version of the poem sent to STC did not include this stanza.
2. A tract of open ground (a word used chiefly in poetry).
3. Cottage.
4. The version of the poem sent to STC included an additional stanza that was omitted from all
published versions: "I told her this; her laughter light / Is ringing in my ears; / And when I think
upon that night / My eyes are dim with tears" (*WL*, 1:238).
† *P 1815*: Poems founded on the Affections. The version of the poem sent to STC (see the first
note on *Strange fits*) included an initial stanza that was omitted from all published versions:
"My hope was one, from cities far, / Nursed on a lonesome heath; / Her lips are red as roses are,
/ Her hair a woodbine wreath" (*WL*, 1:236; *LB* [CW], 295).
1. There are several English rivers of this name, the largest flowing through the Peak District of
the English Midlands and forming the boundary between Derbyshire and Staffordshire.

A Maid whom there were none to praise
And very few to love.

5   A Violet by a mossy stone
Half-hidden from the Eye!
—Fair, as a star when only one
Is shining in the sky![2]

She *liv'd* unknown, and few could know
10   When Lucy ceas'd to be;
But she is in her Grave, and Oh!
The difference to me.[3]

A slumber did my spirit seal[†]

A slumber did my spirit seal,
I had no human fears:
She seem'd a thing that could not feel
The touch of earthly years.

5   No motion has she now, no force
She neither hears nor sees
Roll'd round in earth's diurnal course
With rocks and stones and trees!

LUCY GRAY[†]

Oft had I heard of Lucy Gray,
And when I cross'd the Wild,[1]

2. Venus, after the moon the brightest celestial object in the night sky, at its maximum brightness just before sunrise and just after sunset.
3. In *LB 1800* WW condensed into one stanza what had been two stanzas in the version sent to STC: "And she was graceful as the broom / That flowers by Carron's side; / But slow distemper checked her bloom, / And on the Heath she died. // Long time before her head lay low / Dead to the world was she: / But now she's in her grave, and Oh! / The difference to me!" (*WL*, 1:237; *LB* [CW], 295). *Carron:* a Scottish river.
† *P 1815:* Poems of the Imagination.
† *P 1815:* Poems referring to Childhood. *P 1815* and *MP 1820* included an illustration of the poem, engraved by J. C. Bromley after a painting by Sir George Beaumont (see Biographical and Topographical Glossary). IF note: "Written at Goslar in Germany in 1799 [actually between October 6, 1798, and February 23, 1799 (*Chrono: EY*, 34)]. It was founded on a circumstance told me by my Sister, of a little girl, who not far from Halifax in Yorkshire was bewildered in a snow-storm. Her footsteps were traced by her parents to the middle of the lock of a canal, and no other vestige of her, backward or forward, could be traced. The body however was found in the canal. The way in which the incident was treated & the spiritualizing of the character might furnish hints for contrasting the imaginative influences which I have endeavoured to throw over common life with Crabbe's matter of fact style of treating subjects of the same kind. This is not spoken to his disparagement; far from it; but to direct the attention of thoughtful readers into whose hands these notes may fall to a comparison that may both enlarge the circle of their sensibilities and tend to produce in them a catholic judgement." WW refers to the poet George Crabbe (1754–1832), best known for his long poems *The Village* (1783) and *The Borough* (1810), which portray provincial life unsentimentally.
1. There are two distinct states of the first two stanzas: in some copies of *LB 1800* line 1 begins "Oft had I" and line 6 concludes "wide Moor"; in others line 1 begins "Oft I had" and line 6 concludes "wild Moor" (*LB* [CW], 170; *Cornell*, nos. 6–11; J. E. Wells, "*Lyrical Ballads*, 1800: Cancel Leaves," *PMLA* 53 [1932]: 214–15). This Norton Critical Edition adopts the former

I chanc'd to see at break of day
The solitary Child.

5 No Mate, no comrade Lucy knew;
She dwelt on a wide Moor,
The sweetest Thing that ever grew
Beside a human door!

You yet may spy the Fawn at play,
10 The Hare upon the Green;
But the sweet face of Lucy Gray
Will never more be seen.

"To-night will be a stormy night,
You to the Town must go,
15 And take a lantern, Child, to light
Your Mother thro' the snow."

"That, Father! will I gladly do;
'Tis scarcely afternoon—
The Minster-clock has just struck two,
20 And yonder is the Moon."[2]

At this the Father rais'd his hook
And snapp'd a faggot-band;[3]
He plied his work, and Lucy took
The lantern in her hand.

25 Not blither is the mountain roe,
With many a wanton stroke
Her feet disperse the powd'ry snow
That rises up like smoke.

The storm came on before its time,
30 She wander'd up and down,
And many a hill did Lucy climb
But never reach'd the Town.[4]

The wretched Parents all that night
Went shouting far and wide;

---

variant, which accords with the fair copy MS (in STC's hand) sent to the printer on August 7, 1800 (*LB* [CW], 170, 730–31; *WL*, 1:291). In *LB 1802* WW corrected "wild" to "wide," but let stand "Oft I had," which remained the reading in all subsequent lifetime editions.
2. In September 1816 WW's friend Henry Crabb Robinson recorded the poet as telling him that "*Lucy Gray,* that tender and pathetic narrative of a child mysteriously lost on a common, was occasioned by the death of a child who fell ill into the lock of a canal. He removed from his poem all that pertained to art, and it being his object to exhibit poetically entire *solitude,* he represents his child as observing the day-*moon* which no town or village girl would ever notice" (*CRB,* 1:190). *Minster-clock*: the clock on a monastery church or, more generally, any large church.
3. The binding around a small bundle of sticks or branches to be used for fuel.
4. Lines 30–32 echo the "justly admired" stanza that WW quoted in the Preface from the ballad *The Babes in the Wood* (see p. 94 above).

35 But there was neither sound nor sight
To serve them for a guide.

At day-break on a hill they stood
That overlook'd the Moor;
And thence they saw the Bridge of Wood
40 A furlong from their door.

And now they homeward turn'd, and cry'd
"In Heaven we all shall meet!"
When in the snow the Mother spied.
The print of Lucy's feet.

45 Then downward from the steep hill's edge
They track'd the footmarks small;
And through the broken hawthorn-hedge,
And by the long stone-well;

And then an open field they cross'd,
50 The marks were still the same;
They track'd them on, nor ever lost,
And to the Bridge they came.

They follow'd from the snowy bank
The footmarks, one by one,
55 Into the middle of the plank,
And further there were none.

Yet some maintain that to this day
She is a living Child,
That you may see sweet Lucy Gray
60 Upon the lonesome Wild.

O'er rough and smooth she trips along,
And never looks behind;
And sings a solitary song
That whistles in the wind.

The IDLE SHEPHERD BOYS,

OR

DUNGEON-GILL FORCE,

A PASTORAL[†]

I.

The valley rings with mirth and joy,
Among the hills the Echoes play
A never, never ending song
To welcome in the May.
5   The Magpie chatters with delight;
The mountain Raven's youngling Brood
Have left the Mother and the Nest,
And they go rambling east and west
In search of their own food,
10 Or thro' the glittering Vapors dart
In very wantonness of Heart.

II.

Beneath a rock, upon the grass,
Two Boys are sitting in the sun;
It seems they have no work to do
15 Or that their work is done.
On pipes of sycamore they play
The fragments of a Christmas Hymn,
Or with that plant which in our dale
We call Stag-horn, or Fox's Tail
20 Their rusty[1] Hats they trim:
And thus as happy as the Day,
Those Shepherds wear the time away.

III.

Along the river's stony marge[2]
The sand-lark chaunts a joyous song;

---

† P 1815: Poems referring to Childhood. Composed by July 29, 1800 (*Chrono: MY*, 19). WW's note on the title: "Gill in the dialect of Cumberland and Westmoreland is a short and for the most part a steep narrow valley, with a stream running through it. Force is the word universally employed in these dialects for Waterfall." Dungeon Ghyll Force is ca. three miles southwest of Grasmere.

1. Rustic. *Stag-horn*: a kind of moss with stems of many branches, densely covered with short, spirally arranged leaves. From the IF note: "I will only add a little monitory anecdote concerning this subject. When Coleridge & Southey were walking together upon the Fells, Southey observed that, if I wished to be considered a faithful painter of rural manners, I ought not to have said that my Shepherd-Boys trimmed their rushen [i.e., made of rushes] hats as described in the poem. Just as the words had past his lips two boys appeared with the very plant entwined round their hats. I have often wondered that Southey, who rambled so much about the mountains, should have fallen into this mistake, & I record it as a warning for others who with far less opportunity than my dear friend had of knowing what things are, and far less sagacity, give way to presumptuous criticism, from which he was free, though in this matter mistaken."

2. Shore.

25 The thrush is busy in the Wood,
    And carols loud and strong.
    A thousand lambs are on the rocks,
    All newly born! both earth and sky
    Keep jubilee, and more than all,
30 Those Boys with their green Coronal,[3]
    They never hear the cry,
    That plaintive cry! which up the hill
    Comes from the depth of Dungeon-Gill.

IV.

    Said Walter, leaping from the ground,
35 "Down to the stump of yon old yew
    I'll run with you a race."—No more—
    Away the Shepherds flew:
    They leapt, they ran, and when they came
    Right opposite to Dungeon-Gill,
40 Seeing, that he should lose the prize,
    "Stop!" to his comrade Walter cries—
    James stopp'd with no good will:
    Said Walter then, "Your task is here,
    'Twill keep you working half a year.

V.

45 Till you have cross'd where I shall cross,
    Say that you'll neither sleep nor eat."
    James proudly took him at his word,
    But did not like the feat.
    It was a spot, which you may see
50 If ever you to Langdale[4] go:
    Into a chasm a mighty Block
    Hath fallen, and made a bridge of rock;
    The gulph is deep below,
    And in a bason black and small
55 Receives a lofty Waterfall.

VI.

    With staff in hand across the cleft
    The Challenger began his march;
    And now, all eyes and feet, hath gain'd
    The middle of the arch.
60 When list! he hears a piteous moan—
    Again! his heart within him dies—
    His pulse is stopp'd, his breath is lost,
    He totters, pale as any ghost,

3. Garland, here referring figuratively to the boys' hats. WW uses similar phrasing in the Intimations Ode, lines 36–40.
4. Great Langdale, a valley southwest of Grasmere, bordered on the north by the Langdale Pikes. Dungeon Ghyll, where the waterfall is located, is a ravine on the north side of the valley.

And, looking down, he spies
65 A Lamb, that in the pool is pent
Within that black and frightful rent.

VII.

The Lamb had slipped into the stream,
And safe without a bruise or wound
The Cataract had borne him down
70 Into the gulph profound.
His dam had seen him when he fell,
She saw him down the torrent borne;
And while with all a mother's love
She from the lofty rocks above
75 Sent forth a cry forlorn,
The Lamb, still swimming round and round
Made answer to that plaintive sound.

VIII.

When he had learnt, what thing it was,
That sent this rueful cry; I ween,
80 The Boy recover'd heart, and told
The sight which he had seen.
Both gladly now deferr'd their task;
Nor was there wanting other aid—
A Poet, one who loves the brooks
85 Far better than the sages' books,
By chance had thither stray'd;
And there the helpless Lamb he found
By those huge rocks encompass'd round.

IX.

He drew it gently from the pool,
90 And brought it forth into the light:
The Shepherds met him with his charge
An unexpected sight!
Into their arms the Lamb they took,
Said they, "He's neither maim'd nor scarr'd"—
95 Then up the steep ascent they hied[5]
And placed him at his Mother's side;
And gently did the Bard
Those idle Shepherd-boys upbraid,
And bade them better mind their trade.

5. Hastened.

'Tis said, that some have died for love[†]

'Tis said, that some have died for love:
And here and there a church-yard grave is found
In the cold North's unhallow'd ground,
Because the wretched man himself had slain,
5   His love was such a grievous pain.
And there is one whom I five years have known;
He dwells alone
Upon Helvellyn's[1] side.
He loved——The pretty Barbara died,
10 And thus he makes his moan:
Three years had Barbara in her grave been laid
When thus his moan he made.

Oh! move thou Cottage from behind that oak
Or let the aged tree uprooted lie,
15 That in some other way yon smoke
May mount into the sky!
The clouds pass on; they from the Heavens depart:
I look—the sky is empty space;
I know not what I trace;
20 But when I cease to look, my hand is on my heart.

O! what a weight is in these shades! Ye leaves,
When will that dying murmur be suppress'd?
Your sound my heart of peace bereaves,
It robs my heart of rest.
25 Thou Thrush, that singest loud and loud and free,
Into yon row of willows flit,
Upon that alder sit;
Or sing another song, or chuse another tree![2]

Roll back, sweet rill! back to thy mountain bounds,
30 And there for ever be thy waters chain'd!
For thou dost haunt the air with sounds
That cannot be sustain'd;
If still beneath that pine-tree's ragged bough
Headlong yon waterfall must come,

---

† P 1815: Poems founded on the Affections. Evidence in the MSS suggests that WW may have begun composing this poem in Goslar, adding the first and last stanzas later (LB [CW], 386). The first ten lines of the rhymed first stanza and the concluding unrhymed eight-line stanza form a narrative frame for the lament of the *wretched man* (line 4) in lines 10–11 and the following four rhymed eight-line stanzas.

1. See Biographical and Topographical Glossary.

2. WW's friend Barron Fields noted the similarity of this stanza to Robert Burns's *The Banks o' Doon* (1798), lines 1–4: "Ye banks and braes [hillsides] o' bonnie Doon [a Scottish river], / How can ye bloom sae [so] fresh and fair; / How can ye chant, ye little birds, / And I sae weary, fu' o' care!" (LB [CW], 386). Although WW was probably reading Burns (see Biographical and Topographical Glossary) in 1797–99 (*Reading 1770–99*, no. 42), there is no direct evidence of his familiarity with this poem.

35 Oh let it then be dumb!—
Be any thing, sweet rill, but that which thou art now.

Thou Eglantine[3] whose arch so proudly towers
(Even like a rainbow spanning half the vale)
Thou one fair shrub, oh! shed thy flowers,
40 And stir not in the gale.
For thus to see thee nodding in the air,
To see thy arch thus stretch and bend,
Thus rise and thus descend,
Disturbs me, till the sight is more than I can bear.

45 The man who makes this feverish complaint
Is one of giant stature, who could dance
Equipp'd from head to foot in iron mail.
Ah gentle Love! if ever thought was thine
To store up kindred hours for me, thy face
50 Turn from me, gentle Love, nor let me walk
Within the sound of Emma's voice,[4] or know
Such happiness as I have known to-day.

To a SEXTON[†]

Let thy wheel-barrow alone.
Wherefore, Sexton, piling still
In thy bone-house[1] bone on bone?
'Tis already like a hill
5 In a field of battle made,
Where three thousand skulls are laid.
——These died in peace each with the other,
Father, Sister, Friend, and Brother.

Mark the spot to which I point!
10 From this platform eight feet square
Take not even a finger-joint:
Andrew's whole fire-side[2] is there.
Here, alone, before thine eyes,
Simon's sickly Daughter lies
15 From weakness, now, and pain defended,
Whom he twenty winters tended.

---

3. Sweet-briar, a wild rose.
4. Donald Reiman suggests that Emma stands for DW (*TLS*, September 13, 1974: 799–800). The name was inserted in the printer's copy of the poem, probably between August 8 and 13, 1800 (*LB* [CW], 386).
† *P 1815*: Poems of the Fancy. Composed probably in Goslar between October 6, 1798, and February 23, 1799 (*Chrono: EY*, 34). *Sexton*: traditionally, a church officer responsible for cleaning a church, ringing its bells, and digging graves.
1. A charnel-house or ossuary, used for containing disinterred human skeletons, especially in places where burial space is scarce.
2. I.e., family.

Look but at the gardener's pride,
How he glories, when he sees
Roses, lilies, side by side,
20   Violets in families.
By the heart of Man, his tears,
By his hopes and by his fears,
Thou, old Grey-beard! art the Warden
Of a far superior garden.

25   Thus then, each to other dear,
Let them all in quiet lie,
Andrew there and Susan here,
Neighbours in mortality.
And should I live through sun and rain
30   Seven widow'd years without my Jane,
O Sexton, do not then remove her,
Let one grave hold the Lov'd and Lover!

The TWO THIEVES,

Or the last Stage of AVARICE†

Oh now that the genius of Bewick were mine
And the skill which he learn'd on the Banks of the Tyne;[1]
Then the Muses might deal with me just as they chose
For I'd take my last leave both of verse and of prose.

5   What feats would I work with my magical hand!
Book-learning and books should be banish'd the land
And for hunger and thirst and such troublesome calls
Every ale-house should then have a feast[2] on its walls.

The Traveller would hang his wet clothes on a chair,
10   Let them smoke, let them burn, not a straw would he care,
For the Prodigal Son, Joseph's Dream[3] and his Sheaves,
Oh what would they be to my tale of two Thieves!

† P 1815: Poems referring to Old Age. IF note: "This is described from the life as I was in the habit
of observing when a boy at Hawkeshead school. Daniel was more than 80 years older than myself
when he was daily, thus occupied, under my notice, no book could have so early taught me to
think of the changes to which human life is subject, & while looking at him I could not but say to
myself we may, any of us I, or the happiest of my play mates, live to become still more the object
of pity than this old man, this half-doating pilferer." Thompson, 192–93, identifies the old man as
Daniel Mackreth (1693–1788), a Hawkshead shoemaker, and his grandson as William (b. 1775).
1. Thomas Bewick (1753–1828), English engraver born near Newcastle-upon-Tyne and best
known for his wood engravings of animals in *A General History of Quadrupeds* (1790) and *History of British Birds* (1797–1804). In a version of the poem copied by DW in 1800 (DC MS 29),
WW compared Bewick favorably to the painter Sir Joshua Reynolds (on whom see n. 1 to the
Advertisement of *LB 1798*, p. 8): "Oh! now that the box-wood and graver were mine / Of the
Poet who lives on the banks of the Tyne! / Who has plied his rude tools with more fortunate toil
/ Than Reynolds e'er brought to his canvass and oil. // Then, Books and Book-learning! I'd ring
out your knell! / The Vicar should scarce know an A from an L" (*LB* [CW], 186). *Then* (line 3):
corrected in the second errata list from "When."
2. I.e., a feast for the eyes in the form of prints hung on the walls.
3. In Genesis 37.5–8, Joseph enrages his brothers (who later sell him into slavery) by recounting a
dream in which, after he and his brothers have bound grain into sheaves, their sheaves bow to
his, signifying the brothers' future submission to him. *Prodigal Son*: the parable told in Luke 15.

Little Dan is unbreech'd,[4] he is three birth-days old,
His Grandsire that age more than thirty times told,
15 There are[5] ninety good seasons of fair and foul weather
Between them, and both go a stealing together.

With chips is the Carpenter strewing his floor?
Is a cart-load of peats at an old Woman's door?
Old Daniel his hand to the treasure will slide,
20 And his Grandson's as busy at work by his side.

Old Daniel begins, he stops short and his eye
Through the lost look of dotage is cunning and sly.
'Tis a look which at this time is hardly his own,
But tells a plain tale of the days that are flown.

25 Dan once had a heart which was mov'd by the wires[6]
Of manifold pleasures and many desires:
And what if he cherish'd his purse? 'Twas no more
Than treading a path trod by thousands before.

'Twas a path trod by thousands, but Daniel is one
30 Who went something farther than others have gone;
And now with old Daniel you see how it fares
You see to what end he has brought his grey hairs.

The pair sally forth hand in hand; ere the sun
Has peer'd o'er the beeches their work is begun:
35 And yet into whatever sin they may fall,
This Child but half knows it and that not at all.

They hunt through the street with deliberate tread,
And each in his turn is both leader and led;
And wherever they carry their plots and their wiles,
40 Every face in the village is dimpled with smiles.

Neither check'd by the rich nor the needy they roam,
For grey-headed Dan has a daughter at home;
Who will gladly repair all the damage that's done,
And three, were it ask'd, would be render'd for one.

45 Old Man! whom so oft I with pity have ey'd,
I love thee and love the sweet boy at thy side:
Long yet may'st thou live, for a teacher we see
That lifts up the veil of our nature in thee.

---

4. Not yet dressed in breeches (short trousers).
5. Corrected in the second errata list from "There's."
6. As if he were a puppet.

LINES WRITTEN ON A TABLET
IN A SCHOOL†

*In the School of ———— is a tablet on which are inscribed, in gilt letters, the
names of the several persons who have been Schoolmasters there since the
foundation of the School, with the time at which they entered upon and quitted
their office. Opposite one of those names the Author wrote the following lines.*

If Nature, for a favorite Child
In thee hath temper'd so her clay,
That every hour thy heart runs wild
Yet never once doth go astray,

5 Read o'er these lines; and then review
This tablet, that thus humbly rears
In such diversity of hue
Its history of two hundred years.

—When through this little wreck of fame,
10 Cypher and syllable, thine eye
Has travell'd down to Matthew's name,
Pause with no common sympathy.

And if a sleeping tear should wake
Then be it neither check'd nor stay'd:
15 For Matthew a request I make
Which for himself he had not made.

Poor Matthew, all his frolics o'er,
Is silent as a standing pool,
Far from the chimney's merry roar,
20 And murmur of the village school.

The sighs which Matthew heav'd were sighs
Of one tir'd out with fun and madness;
The tears which came to Matthew's eyes
Were tears of light, the oil of gladness.[1]

† *P 1815*: Poems proceeding from Sentiment and Reflection. Composed probably in Goslar
between October 6, 1798, and February 23, 1799 (*Chrono: EY*, 34). The title is given in the
table of contents in *LB 1800* but not printed above the poem itself. In 1831 WW changed the
title to *Matthew, or the Schoolmaster* (later shortened to *Matthew*). IF note: "Such a tablet as is
here spoken of continued to be preserved in Hawkshead School, though the inscriptions were
not brought down to our time. This and other poems connected with Matthew would not gain
by a literal detail of facts. Like the Wanderer in the Excursion, this Schoolmaster was made up
of several both of his class & men of other occupations. I do not ask pardon for what there is of
untruth in such verses, considered strictly as matters of fact. It is enough, if, being true & con-
sistent in spirit, they move & teach in a manner not unworthy of a poet's calling." WW made a
similar comment about the figure of Matthew in a letter of March 27, 1843, to Henry Reed, the
editor of the first American edition of WW's collected poems (*WL*, 7:416). Thompson, 151–66,
suggests possible models for Matthew in this poem and the next two among people in Hawks-
head whom WW would have encountered as a schoolboy.
1. A phrase from Hebrews 1.9: "Thou hast loved righteousness, and hated iniquity; therefore
God, even thy God, hath anointed thee with the oil of gladness above thy fellows."

25 Yet sometimes when the secret cup
Of still and serious thought went round
It seem'd as if he drank it up,
He felt with spirit so profound.

—Thou soul of God's best earthly mould,
30 Thou happy soul, and can it be
That these two words of glittering gold
Are all that must remain of thee?

THE

Two APRIL MORNINGS†

We walk'd along, while bright and red
Uprose the morning sun,
And Matthew stopp'd, he look'd, and said,
"The will of God be done!"

5 A village Schoolmaster was he,
With hair of glittering grey;
As blithe a man as you could see
On a spring holiday.

And on that morning, through the grass,
10 And by the steaming rills,
We travell'd merrily to pass
A day among the hills.

"Our work," said I, "was well begun;
Then, from thy breast what thought,
15 Beneath so beautiful a sun,
So sad a sigh has brought?"

A second time did Matthew stop,
And fixing still his eye
Upon the eastern mountain-top
20 To me he made reply.

Yon cloud with that long purple cleft
Brings fresh into my mind
A day like this which I have left
Full thirty years behind.

25 And on that slope of springing corn
The self-same crimson hue
Fell from the sky that April morn,
The same which now I view!

† *P 1815*: Poems proceeding from Sentiment and Reflection. Composed probably in Goslar between October 6, 1798, and February 23, 1799 (*Chrono: EY*, 34).

With rod and line my silent sport
30   I plied by Derwent's wave,[1]
And, coming to the church, stopp'd short
Beside my Daughter's grave.

Nine summers had she scarcely seen
The pride of all the vale;
35   And then she sang!—she would have been
A very nightingale.

Six feet in earth my Emma lay,
And yet I lov'd her more,
For so it seem'd, than till that day
40   I e'er had lov'd before.

And, turning from her grave, I met
Beside the church-yard Yew
A blooming Girl, whose hair was wet
With points of morning dew.

45   A basket on her head she bare,
Her brow was smooth and white,
To see a Child so very fair,
It was a pure delight!

No fountain from its rocky cave
50   E'er tripp'd with foot so free,
She seem'd as happy as a wave[2]
That dances on the sea.

There came from me a sigh of pain
Which I could ill confine;
55   I look'd at her and look'd again;
—And did not wish her mine.

Matthew is in his grave, yet now
Methinks I see him stand,
As at that moment, with his bough
60   Of wilding[3] in his hand.

---

1. The River Derwent, which flows through Cockermouth, WW's birthplace.
2. Possibly an echo of Shakespeare, *The Winter's Tale* 1.4.140–41: "When you do dance, I wish you / A wave o' th' sea."
3. A wild apple or crab-apple tree.

The FOUNTAIN,

A Conversation[†]

We talk'd with open heart, and tongue
Affectionate and true,
A pair of Friends, though I was young,
And Matthew seventy-two.

5 We lay beneath a spreading oak,
Beside a mossy seat,
And from the turf a fountain broke,
And gurgled at our feet.

Now, Matthew, let us try to match
10 This water's pleasant tune
With some old Border-song, or catch[1]
That suits a summer's noon.

Or of the Church-clock and the chimes
Sing here beneath the shade,
15 That half-mad thing of witty rhymes[2]
Which you last April made!

In silence Matthew lay, and eyed
The spring beneath the tree;
And thus the dear old Man replied,
20 The grey-hair'd Man of glee.

"Down to the vale this water steers,
How merrily it goes!
'Twill murmur on a thousand years,
And flow as now it flows.

25 And here, on this delightful day,
I cannot chuse but think
How oft, a vigorous Man, I lay
Beside this Fountain's brink.

My eyes are dim with childish tears,
30 My heart is idly stirr'd,
For the same sound is in my ears,
Which in those days I heard.

† P 1815: Poems proceeding from Sentiment and Reflection. Composed probably in Goslar
between October 6, 1798, and February 23, 1799 (*Chrono: EY*, 34).
1. "A short composition for three or more voices, which sing the same melody, the second singer
beginning the first line as the first goes on to the second line, and so with each successive
singer" (*OED*). *Border-song*: a song from the border region between Scotland and England.
2. Thompson, 172–75, records that the unreliable clock of St. Michael's Church in Hawkshead
was the subject of rhymes by one of the possible models for Matthew, Thomas Cowperthwaite
(1709–1782), an ironmonger.

Thus fares it still in our decay:
And yet the wiser mind
35 Mourns less for what age takes away
Than what it leaves behind.

The blackbird in the summer trees,
The lark upon the hill,
Let loose their carols when they please,
40 Are quiet when they will.

With Nature never do *they* wage
A foolish strife; they see
A happy youth, and their old age
Is beautiful and free:

45 But we are press'd by heavy laws,
And often, glad no more,
We wear a face of joy, because
We have been glad of yore.

If there is one who need bemoan
50 His kindred laid in earth,
The houshold hearts that were his own,
It is the man of mirth.

My days, my Friend, are almost gone,
My life has been approv'd,
55 And many love me, but by none
Am I enough belov'd."

"Now both himself and me he wrongs,
The man who thus complains!
I live and sing my idle songs
60 Upon these happy plains,

And, Matthew, for thy Children dead
I'll be a son to thee!"
At this he grasp'd his hands, and said,
"Alas! that cannot be."

65 We rose up from the fountain-side,
And down the smooth descent
Of the green sheep-track did we glide,
And through the wood we went,

And, ere we came to Leonard's Rock,
70 He sang those witty rhymes
About the crazy old church-clock
And the bewilder'd chimes.

NUTTING†

——————— It seems a day,
I speak of one from many singled out,[1]
One of those heavenly days which cannot die,
When forth I sallied from our cottage-door,[2]
5   And with a wallet o'er my shoulder slung,
A nutting crook in hand, I turn'd my steps
Towards the distant woods, a Figure quaint,
Trick'd out in proud disguise of Beggar's weeds[3]
Put on for the occasion, by advice
10 And exhortation of my frugal Dame.[4]
Motley accoutrement! of power to smile
At thorns, and brakes, and brambles, and, in truth,
More ragged than need was. Among the woods,
And o'er the pathless rocks, I forc'd my way
15 Until, at length, I came to one dear nook
Unvisited, where not a broken bough
Droop'd with its wither'd leaves, ungracious sign
Of devastation, but the hazels rose
Tall and erect, with milk-white clusters hung,
20 A virgin scene!—A little while I stood,
Breathing with such suppression of the heart
As joy delights in; and with wise restraint
Voluptuous, fearless of a rival, eyed
The banquet, or beneath the trees I sate
25 Among the flowers, and with the flowers I play'd;
A temper known to those, who, after long
And weary expectation, have been bless'd

† P 1815: Poems of the Imagination. Composed probably between October 6 and December 28, 1798 (*Chrono: EY*, 35). IF note: "Written in Germany, intended as part of a poem on my own life, but struck out as not being wanted there. Like most of my schoolfellows I was an impassioned nutter. For this pleasure the Vale of Esthwaite abounding in coppice-wood, furnished a very wide range. These verses arose out of the remembrance of feelings I had often had when a boy, and particularly in the extensive woods that still stretch from the side of Esthwaite Lake towards Graythwaite, the seat of the ancient family of Sandys." Graythwaite Wood extends from the south side of Esthwaite Water, while Graythwaite Hall is located two-and-a-half miles south of the lake.
    The history of the poem's composition is complex (for full accounts see *Chrono: EY*, 331–32; and *LB* [CW], 218, 391–92), but it seems that WW very quickly began to conceive it as separate from the other autobiographical materials he was composing, which went into *Prel 1799*. On December 21 or 28, 1798, DW sent STC a draft, describing it as "the conclusion of a poem of which the beginning is not written" (*WL*, 1:238, 241–42; *Chrono: EY*, 259 and n. 2). This introduction (addressed to "my beloved Maid"—i.e., DW—and incorporating material later adapted for *The Prelude* 11.214–21) was composed probably between December 21, 1798, and late April 1799, and the long version of the poem (in 99 lines, printed in *LB* [CW], 302–305) was certainly completed by June 5, 1800. It could not have satisfied WW, however, because he published *Nutting* without the introduction in *LB 1800* and later extracted part of the introduction as a separate poem, *Travelling* (see *LB* [CW], 307), itself revised and published as *To the Same* [*Lycoris*] (see *Poems, 1807–1820* [CW], 251–55).
1. This line is inserted from the second errata list.
2. WW's note: "The house at which I boarded during the time I was at School [in Hawkshead]."
3. Clothes; *nutting crook* (line 6): a hooked stick used to shake the branches and make the nuts fall.
4. Ann Tyson, with whom WW boarded (see Biographical and Topographical Glossary under "Hawkshead" and *The Prelude* 4.16–67).

With sudden happiness beyond all hope.—
—Perhaps it was a bower beneath whose leaves
30   The violets of five seasons re-appear
And fade, unseen by any human eye,
Where fairy water-breaks do murmur on[5]
For ever, and I saw the sparkling foam,
And with my cheek on one of those green stones
35   That, fleec'd with moss, beneath the shady trees,
Lay round me scatter'd like a flock of sheep,
I heard the murmur and the murmuring sound,
In that sweet mood when pleasure loves to pay
Tribute to ease, and, of its joy secure
40   The heart luxuriates with indifferent things,
Wasting its kindliness on stocks[6] and stones,
And on the vacant air. Then up I rose,
And dragg'd to earth both branch and bough, with crash
And merciless ravage; and the shady nook
45   Of hazels, and the green and mossy bower
Deform'd and sullied, patiently gave up
Their quiet being: and unless I now
Confound my present feelings with the past,
Even then, when from the bower I turn'd away,
50   Exulting, rich beyond the wealth of kings
I felt a sense of pain when I beheld
The silent trees and the intruding sky.—

Then, dearest Maiden! move along these shades
In gentleness of heart with gentle hand
55   Touch,——for there is a Spirit in the woods.

Three years she grew in sun and shower[†]

Three years she grew in sun and shower,
Then Nature said, "A lovelier flower
On earth was never sown;
This Child I to myself will take,
5   She shall be mine, and I will make
A Lady of my own.

Myself will to my darling be
Both law and impulse, and with me

5. I.e., sounding like small rapids in a stream.
6. Stumps.
† *P 1815*: Poems of the Imagination. Composed probably between October 6 and December 28, 1798, but possibly between February 23 and 27, 1799 (*LB* [CW], 221). In the IF note WW claimed to have composed the poem "in the Hartz Forest" outside Goslar. Commonly classed among the "Lucy poems" (see the source note to *Strange fits of passion*, p. 113), the poem was printed with the running head "Lucy" in WW's collections from 1820 to 1843.

The Girl in rock and plain,
10   In earth and heaven, in glade and bower,
Shall feel an overseeing power
To kindle or restrain.

She shall be sportive as the fawn
That wild with glee across the lawn
15   Or up the mountain springs,
And hers shall be the breathing balm,
And hers the silence and the calm
Of mute insensate things.

The floating clouds their state shall lend
20   To her, for her the willow bend,
Nor shall she fail to see
Even in the motions of the storm
Grace that shall mould the maiden's form[1]
By silent sympathy.

25   The stars of midnight shall be dear
To her, and she shall lean her ear
In many a secret place
Where rivulets dance their wayward round,
And beauty born of murmuring sound
30   Shall pass into her face.

And vital feelings of delight
Shall rear her form to stately height,
Her virgin bosom swell,
Such thoughts to Lucy I will give
35   While she and I together live
Here in this happy dell.

Thus Nature spake—The work was done—
How soon my Lucy's race was run!
She died and left to me
40   This heath, this calm and quiet scene,
The memory of what has been,
And never more will be.

---

1. This line appears in the second errata list as a replacement for the one originally printed: "A beauty that shall mould her form."

The OLD CUMBERLAND BEGGAR,

A DESCRIPTION†

The class of Beggars to which the old man here described belongs, will probably soon be extinct. It consisted of poor, and, mostly, old and infirm persons, who confined themselves to a stated round in their neighbourhood, and had certain fixed days, on which, at different houses, they regularly received charity; sometimes in money, but mostly in provisions.

I saw an aged Beggar in my walk,
And he was seated by the highway side
On a low structure of rude masonry
Built at the foot of a huge hill, that they
5 Who lead their horses down the steep rough road
May thence remount at ease. The aged man
Had placed his staff across the broad smooth stone
That overlays the pile, and from a bag
All white with flour the dole¹ of village dames,
10 He drew his scraps and fragments, one by one,
And scann'd them with a fix'd and serious look
Of idle computation. In the sun,
Upon the second step of that small pile,
Surrounded by those wild unpeopled hills,
15 He sate, and eat his food in solitude;
And ever, scatter'd from his palsied hand,
That still attempting to prevent the waste,
Was baffled still, the crumbs in little showers
Fell on the ground, and the small mountain birds,
20 Not venturing yet to peck their destin'd meal,
Approached within the length of half his staff.

Him from my childhood have I known, and then
He was so old, he seems not older now;

† P 1815: Poems referring to Old Age. Begun as *Description of a Beggar* (in *LB* [CW], 273–77) between mid-1796 and June 1797, separated as an independent poem between January 25 and March 5, 1798, and revised into its published form between April 1799 and October 10, 1800 (*Chrono: EY*, 27, 342–33). IF note: "Observed & with great benefit to my own heart when I was a child—written at Race Down & Alfoxden in my 23d. [presumably a mistake for 28th] year. The political economists were about that time beginning their war upon mendicity [i.e., begging] in all its forms & by implication, if not directly, on Alms-giving also. This heartless process has been carried as far as it can go by the amended poor-law bill, tho' the inhumanity that prevails in this measure is somewhat disguised by the profession that one of its objects is to throw the poor upon the voluntary donations of their neighbours, that is, if rightly interpreted, to force them into a condition between relief in the union poor House & Alms robbed of their Christian grace & spirit, as being *forced* rather from the benevolent than given by them, while the avaricious & selfish, & all in fact but the humane & charitable, are at liberty to keep all they possess from their distressed brethren." The poem (of which lines 67–73 are addressed directly to contemporary politicians) is WW's intervention in a public debate, conducted in parliament and the press in the late 1790s, about how best to address the growth of severe poverty resulting from wartime economic deprivation and bad harvests in 1794–95 (Gill, 140–41). On the poor law see n. 8. A possible literary model for the poem is Crabbe's *The Village* (see the source note on *Lucy Gray*, p. 115), from which WW read, as excerpted in the *Annual Register* in 1783, descriptions of a workhouse and a pauper's death (Moorman, 1:55; *Reading 1770–99*, no. 68). Charles Lamb objected in January 1801 that "the instructions conveyed in [the poem] are too direct and like a lecture" (*CLL*, 1:265), but WW did not subsequently alter this directness.
1. Gift (given as charity).

He travels on, a solitary man,
25 So helpless in appearance, that for him
The sauntering horseman-traveller does not throw
With careless hand his alms upon the ground,
But stops, that he may safely lodge the coin
Within the old Man's hat; nor quits him so,
30 But still when he has given his horse the rein
Towards the aged Beggar turns a look,
Sidelong and half-reverted. She who tends
The toll-gate, when in summer at her door
She turns her wheel, if on the road she sees
35 The aged Beggar coming, quits her work,
And lifts the latch for him that he may pass.[2]
The Post-boy when his rattling wheels o'ertake
The aged Beggar, in the woody lane,
Shouts to him from behind, and, if perchance
40 The old Man does not change his course, the Boy
Turns with less noisy wheels to the road-side,
And passes gently by, without a curse
Upon his lips, or anger at his heart.
He travels on, a solitary Man,
45 His age has no companion. On the ground
His eyes are turn'd, and, as he moves along,
They move along the ground; and evermore,
Instead of common and habitual sight
Of fields with rural works, of hill and dale,
50 And the blue sky, one little span of earth
Is all his prospect.[3] Thus, from day to day,
Bowbent, his eyes for ever on the ground,
He plies his weary journey, seeing still,
And never knowing that he sees, some straw,
55 Some scatter'd leaf, or marks which, in one track,
The nails of cart or chariot wheel have left
Impress'd on the white road, in the same line,
At distance still the same. Poor Traveller!
His staff trails with him, scarcely do his feet
60 Disturb the summer dust, he is so still
In look and motion that the cottage curs,[4]
Ere he have pass'd the door, will turn away
Weary of barking at him. Boys and girls,
The vacant and the busy, maids and youths,
65 And urchins newly breech'd all pass him by:
Him even the slow-pac'd waggon leaves behind.

But deem not this man useless.——Statesmen! ye
Who are so restless in your wisdom, ye

2. I.e., pass without having to pay the toll. From the seventeenth to the late nineteenth century, tolls were collected on the principal roads of Britain to fund their upkeep.
3. An echo of Milton, *Paradise Lost* 6.640–41: "For Earth hath this variety from Heav'n / Of pleasure situate in Hill and Dale."
4. Probably an echo of James Beattie, *The Minstrel* (1771) 1.41: "The cottage-curs at early pilgrim bark" (*LB* [CW], 395).

Who have a broom still ready in your hands
70   To rid the world of nuisances; ye proud,
Heart-swoln, while in your pride ye contemplate
Your talents, power, and wisdom, deem him not
A burthen of the earth. 'Tis Nature's law
That none, the meanest of created things,
75   Of forms created the most vile and brute,
The dullest or most noxious, should exist
Divorced from good, a spirit and pulse of good,
A life and soul to every mode of being
Inseparably link'd. While thus he creeps
80   From door to door, the Villagers in him
Behold a record which together binds
Past deeds and offices of charity
Else unremember'd, and so keeps alive
The kindly mood in hearts which lapse of years,
85   And that half-wisdom half-experience gives
Make slow to feel, and by sure steps resign
To selfishness and cold oblivous cares.
Among the farms and solitary huts
Hamlets, and thinly-scattered villages,
90   Where'er the aged Beggar takes his rounds,
The mild necessity of use compels
To acts of love; and habit does the work
Of reason, yet prepares that after joy
Which reason cherishes. And thus the soul,
95   By that sweet taste of pleasure unpursu'd
Doth find itself insensibly dispos'd
To virtue and true goodness. Some there are,
By their good works exalted, lofty minds
And meditative, authors of delight
100   And happiness, which to the end of time
Will live, and spread, and kindle; minds like these,
In childhood, from this solitary being,
This helpless wanderer, have perchance receiv'd,
(A thing more precious far than all that books
105   Or the solicitudes of love can do!)
That first mild touch of sympathy and thought,
In which they found their kindred with a world
Where want and sorrow were. The easy man
Who sits at his own door, and like the pear
110   Which overhangs his head from the green wall,
Feeds in the sunshine; the robust and young,
The prosperous and unthinking, they who live
Shelter'd, and flourish in a little grove
Of their own kindred, all behold in him
115   A silent monitor, which on their minds
Must needs impress a transitory thought
Of self-congratulation, to the heart
Of each recalling his peculiar boons,
His charters and exemptions; and perchance,

120   Though he to no one give the fortitude
      And circumspection needful to preserve
      His present blessings, and to husband up
      The respite of the season, he, at least,
      And 'tis no vulgar service, makes them felt.

125   Yet further.——Many, I believe, there are
      Who live a life of virtuous decency,
      Men who can hear the Decalogue⁵ and feel
      No self-reproach, who of the moral law
      Establish'd in the land where they abide
130   Are strict observers, and not negligent,
      Meanwhile, in any tenderness of heart
      Or act of love to those with whom they dwell,
      Their kindred, and the children of their blood.
      Praise be to such, and to their slumbers peace!
135   —But of the poor man ask, the abject poor,
      Go and demand of him, if there be here,
      In this cold abstinence from evil deeds,
      And these inevitable charities,
      Wherewith to satisfy the human soul.
140   No—man is dear to man: the poorest poor
      Long for some moments in a weary life
      When they can know and feel that they have been
      Themselves the fathers and the dealers out
      Of some small blessings, have been kind to such
145   As needed kindness, for this single cause,
      That we have all of us one human heart.
      —Such pleasure is to one kind Being known
      My Neighbour, when with punctual care, each week
      Duly as Friday comes, though press'd herself
150   By her own wants, she from her chest of meal
      Takes one unsparing handful for the scrip⁶
      Of this old Mendicant, and, from her door
      Returning with exhilarated heart,
      Sits by her fire and builds her hope in heav'n.

155   Then let him pass, a blessing on his head!
      And while, in that vast solitude to which
      The tide of things has led him, he appears
      To breathe and live but for himself alone,
      Unblam'd, uninjur'd, let him bear about
160   The good which the benignant law of heaven
      Has hung around him, and, while life is his,
      Still let him prompt the unletter'd Villagers
      To tender offices and pensive thoughts.
      Then let him pass, a blessing on his head!

5. The Ten Commandments.
6. A satchel carried by a beggar or pilgrim (a now-archaic word).

165 And, long as he can wander, let him breathe
The freshness of the vallies, let his blood
Struggle with frosty air and winter snows,
And let the charter'd[7] wind that sweeps the heath
Beat his grey locks against his wither'd face.
170 Reverence the hope whose vital anxiousness
Gives the last human interest to his heart.
May never House,[8] misnamed of industry,
Make him a captive; for that pent-up din,
Those life-consuming sounds that clog the air,
175 Be his the natural silence of old age.
Let him be free of mountain solitudes,
And have around him, whether heard or not,
The pleasant melody of woodland birds.
Few are his pleasures; if his eyes, which now
180 Have been so long familiar with the earth,
No more behold the horizontal sun
Rising or setting, let the light at least
Find a free entrance to their languid orbs.
And let him, *where* and *when* he will, sit down
185 Beneath the trees, or by the grassy bank
Of high-way side, and with the little birds
Share his chance-gather'd meal, and, finally,
As in the eye of Nature he has liv'd,
So in the eye of Nature let him die.

A POET's EPITAPH[†]

Art thou a Statesman, in the van
Of public business train'd and bred,
—First learn to love one living man;
Then may'st thou think upon the dead.

5 A Lawyer art thou?—draw not nigh;
Go, carry to some other place

---

7. Unrestrained (a figurative usage apparently derived from the usual figurative meaning of *chartered* in WW's time, "privileged," hence contrasting with the beggar).

8. A workhouse, an institution created by parishes (under the provisions of the Workhouse Test Act of 1723) for housing the poor and providing work for the able-bodied among them. The Relief of the Poor Act (Gilbert's Act) of 1782 permitted, as alternatives to the workhouse, various forms of "outdoor" relief, e.g., money or food given to people in their own homes and subsidies for apprenticing pauper children and temporarily employing unemployed adults (see Thompson, 274–83, for the situation in Hawkshead during WW's schooldays). The Poor Law Amendment Act (New Poor Law) of 1834, which WW condemns in his IF note (see source note), restricted outdoor relief to children and the infirm and compelled the able-bodied poor to reside in workhouses in order to receive public assistance.

† P 1815: Poems proceeding from Sentiment and Reflection. Composed probably between October 6, 1798, and February 23, 1799 (*Chrono: EY*, 34). In his IF note to another poem, *Lines written in Germany*, WW recorded that he had composed the *Epitaph* during walks on the ramparts of the medieval walls of Goslar. Parrish, *The Art of the Lyrical Ballads*, proposes that Robert Burns's elegy *A Bard's Epitaph* (1786) may have been a model for the poem.

The hardness of thy coward eye,
The falshood of thy sallow face.[1]

Art thou a man of purple cheer?
10 A rosy man, right plump to see?
Approach; yet Doctor, not too near:
This grave no cushion[2] is for thee.

Art thou a man of gallant pride,
A Soldier, and no man of chaff?
15 Welcome!—but lay thy sword aside,
And lean upon a Peasant's staff.

Physician art thou? One, all eyes,
Philosopher![3] a fingering slave,
One that would peep and botanize
20 Upon his mother's grave?

Wrapp'd closely in thy sensual fleece
O turn aside, and take, I pray,
That he below may rest in peace,
Thy pin-point of a soul away![4]

25 —A Moralist[5] perchance appears;
Led, Heaven knows how! to this poor sod:
And He has neither eyes nor ears;
Himself his world, and his own God;

One to whose smooth-rubb'd soul can cling
30 Nor form nor feeling great nor small,
A reasoning, self-sufficing thing,
An intellectual All in All!

Shut close the door! press down the latch:
Sleep in thy intellectual crust,
35 Nor lose ten tickings of thy watch,
Near this unprofitable dust.

But who is He with modest looks,
And clad in homely russet brown?[6]

1. In MP 1820 WW revised lines 7–8 to "The keenness of that practised eye, / The hardness of that sallow face." LB (CW) speculates that WW was responding to Charles Lamb's objection of January 30, 1801, to "the vulgar satire upon parson and lawyers in the beginning" (CLL, 1:265).
2. Pulpit; Doctor: of divinity.
3. I.e., natural philosopher, scientist. Averill, "Wordsworth and Natural Science," 245–46, suggests that in this stanza WW may have been satirizing the physician, scientist, and poet Erasmus Darwin (1731–1802), whose treatise Zoonomia; or, the Laws of Organic Life (1794–96) he had read in 1798 (Reading 1770–99, no. 74.v; WL, 1:214–15, 218). Compare The Tables Turned, lines 25–28 (p. 59 above).
4. In P 1815 WW altered line 24 (in which Lamb had criticized the word pin-point) to "That abject thing, thy soul, away!"
5. I.e., a moral philosopher.
6. Possibly an echo of James Thomson's The Castle of Indolence: an Allegorical Poem (1748) 2.33, in which the Bard is also clothed "In Russet brown."

He murmurs near the running brooks
40   A music sweeter than their own.

He is retired as noontide dew,
Or fountain in a noonday grove;
And you must love him, ere to you
He will seem worthy of your love.

45   The outward shews of sky and earth,
Of hill and valley he has view'd;
And impulses of deeper birth
Have come to him in solitude.

In common things that round us lie
50   Some random truths he can impart
The harvest of a quiet eye
That broods and sleeps on his own heart.

But he is weak, both man and boy,
Hath been an idler in the land;
55   Contented if he might enjoy
The things which others understand.

—Come hither in thy hour of strength,
Come, weak as is a breaking wave!
Here stretch thy body at full length;
60   Or build thy house upon this grave.—[7]

From POEMS ON THE NAMING OF PLACES[†]

ADVERTISEMENT

By Persons resident in the country and attached to rural objects, many places will be found unnamed or of unknown names, where little Incidents will have occurred, or feelings been experienced, which will have given to such places a private and peculiar interest. From a wish to give some sort of record to such Incidents or renew the gratification of such Feelings, Names have been given to Places by the Author and some of his Friends, and the following Poems written in consequence.

7. T. E. Casson ("Wordsworth and Theocritus," *Times Literary Supplement*, September 11, 1937: 656) notes the parallel between this stanza and the *Epitaph on the Poet Hipponax* by the Sicilian Greek poet Theocritus (early third century B.C.E.). On February 27, 1799, WW wrote STC that he had read Theocritus's works only "in a most villainous translation" (*WL*, 1:255). This is likely to have been Richard Polwhele's *The Idyllia, Epigrams, and Fragments, of Theocritus, Bion, and Moschus* (Exeter, 1786), in which the epigram is numbered 21 (not 19 as in other editions): "The Poet HIPPONAX lies here: / If bad, O come not, come not near! / But, if you're good, here sit at Ease— / And sleep, O Stranger, if you please!" (228).
† WW grouped five poems (*It was an April morning*, *To Joanna*, *There is an Eminence*, *A narrow girdle of rough stones*, and *To M. H.*) under this heading, which he later used as one of the classifications of his poems in *P 1815*, adding *When, to the attractions of the busy World* (composed in 1802) to the original five. In *LB 1800* to *LB 1805*, the poems were printed, in accordance with instructions transmitted by STC to the printer, after their own title page and Advertisement (*WL*, 1:305–306; *CL*, 1:637).

II.

To JOANNA[†]

Amid the smoke of cities did you pass
Your time of early youth, and there you learn'd,
From years of quiet industry, to love
The living Beings by your own fire-side,
5   With such a strong devotion, that your heart
Is slow towards the sympathies of them
Who look upon the hills with tenderness,
And make dear friendships with the streams and groves.
Yet we who are transgressors in this kind,
10 Dwelling retired in our simplicity
Among the woods and fields, we love you well,
Joanna! and I guess, since you have been
So distant from us now for two long years,
That you will gladly listen to discourse
15 However trivial, if you thence are taught
That they, with whom you once were happy, talk
Familiarly of you and of old times.

While I was seated, now some ten days past,
Beneath those lofty firs, that overtop
20 Their ancient neighbour, the old Steeple tower,
The Vicar from his gloomy house hard by
Came forth to greet me, and when he had ask'd,
"How fares Joanna, that wild-hearted Maid!
And when will she return to us?" he paus'd,
25 And after short exchange of village news,
He with grave looks demanded, for what cause,
Reviving obsolete Idolatry,

† The poem was composed in Grasmere probably by August 23, 1800, WW's topographical notes probably sometime between August 23 and October 15 (*Chrono: MY*, 20). The Joanna of the title is Mary Hutchinson's sister Joanna (1780–1843), but she is presented imaginatively in the poem: in fact she was not raised *Amid the smoke of cities* (line 1), and the poem's chronology "fits neither WW's 1799 arrival in Grasmere nor his recent contacts with Joanna Hutchinson" (*LB* [CW], 398). Probably shortly after the poem's composition, WW provided a commentary that DW transcribed into DC MS 33 (reprinted here from *LB* [CW], 398): "The poem supposes that at the Rock something had taken place in my mind either then, or afterwards in thinking upon what then took place which if related will cause the Vicar to smile. For something like this you are prepared by the phrase 'Now by those dear immunities &c.['] [line 32] I begin to relate the story, meaning in a certain degree to divert or partly play upon the Vicar. I begin,—my mind partly forgets its purpose being softened by the images of beauty in the description of the rock, & the delicious morning & when I come up to the 2 lines 'The Rock like something &c' [lines 54–55] I am caught in the Trap of my own imagination. I entirely lose sight of my first purpose. I take fire in the lines [56–57] 'That ancient woman.' I go on in that strain of fancy 'Old Skiddaw' & terminate the description in tumult 'And Kirkstone' &c [line 65], describing what for a moment I believed either actually took place at the time, or when I have been reflecting on what did take place, I have had a temporary belief in some fit of imagination, did really or might have taken place. When the description is closed, or perhaps partly before I waken from the dream, & see that the Vicar thinks I have been extravagating, as I intended he should, I then tell the story as it happened really; & as the recollection of it exists permanently & regularly in my mind, mingling allusions suffused with humour, partly to the trance in which I have been, & partly to the trick I have been playing upon the Vicar. The poem then concludes in a strain of deep tenderness."

I like a Runic Priest,[1] in characters
Of formidable size, had chisel'd out
30   Some uncouth name upon the native rock,
Above the Rotha, by the forest side.
—Now, by those dear immunities of heart
Engender'd betwixt malice and true love,
I was not loth to be so catechiz'd,
35   And this was my reply.—"As it befel,
One summer morning we had walk'd abroad
At break of day, Joanna and myself.
—'Twas that delightful season, when the broom,
Full flower'd, and visible on every steep,
40   Along the copses runs in veins of gold.
Our pathway led us on to Rotha's banks,[2]
And when we came in front of that tall rock
Which looks towards the East, I there stopp'd short,
And trac'd the lofty barrier with my eye
45   From base to summit; such delight I found
To note in shrub and tree, in stone and flower,
That intermixture of delicious hues,
Along so vast a surface, all at once,
In one impression, by connecting force
50   Of their own beauty, imag'd in the heart.
—When I had gaz'd perhaps two minutes' space,
Joanna, looking in my eyes, beheld
That ravishment of mine, and laugh'd aloud.
The rock, like something starting from a sleep,
55   Took up the Lady's voice, and laugh'd again:[3]
That ancient Woman seated on Helm-crag
Was ready with her cavern; Hammar-Scar,
And the tall Steep of Silver-How sent forth
A noise of laughter; southern Loughrigg heard,
60   And Fairfied answer'd with a mountain tone:
Helvellyn far into the clear blue sky
Carried the Lady's voice,—old Skiddaw blew
His speaking trumpet;—back out of the clouds
Of Glaramara southward came the voice;
65   And Kirkstone toss'd it from his misty head.
Now whether, (said I to our cordial Friend

1. WW's note (printed after the poem in *LB 1800*): "In Cumberland and Westmoreland are several Inscriptions upon the native rock which from the wasting of time and the rudeness of the Workmanship had been mistaken for Runic. They are without doubt Roman."
2. WW's note (printed after the poem in *LB 1800*): "The Rotha, mentioned in this poem, is the River which flowing through the Lakes of Grasmere and Rydole falls into Wyndermere. On Helm-Crag [see line 56], that impressive single Mountain at the head of the Vale of Grasmere, is a Rock which from the most points of view bears a striking resemblance to an Old Woman cowering. Close by this rock is one of those Fissures or Caverns, which in the language of the country are called Dungeons. The other Mountains either immediately surround the Vale of Grasmere, or belong to the same Cluster."
3. In his IF note WW remarked, "The effect of her laugh is an extravagance; though the effect of the reverberation of voices in some parts of these mountains is very striking." In *BL* STC identified the description of Joanna's laugh as a "noble imitation * * * (if it was not rather a coincidence)" of Michael Drayton's *Poly-Olbion* (1613), Song 30, lines 155–64 (*NCC*, 521).

Who in the hey-day of astonishment
Smil'd in my face) this were in simple truth
A work accomplish'd by the brotherhood
70 Of ancient mountains, or my ear was touch'd
With dreams and visionary impulses,
Is not for me to tell; but sure I am
That there was a loud uproar in the hills.
And, while we both were listening, to my side
75 The fair Joanna drew, is if she wish'd
To shelter from some object of her fear.
—And hence, long afterwards, when eighteen moons
Were wasted, as I chanc'd to walk alone
Beneath this rock, at sun-rise, on a calm
80 And silent morning, I sate down, and there,
In memory of affections old and true,
I chissel'd out in those rude characters
Joanna's name upon the living[4] stone.
And I, and all who dwell by my fire-side
85 Have call'd the lovely rock, Joanna's Rock."

IV.[†]

A narrow girdle of rough stones and crags,
A rude and natural causeway, interpos'd
Between the water and a winding slope
Of copse and thicket, leaves the eastern shore
5 Of Grasmere safe in its own privacy.
And there, myself and two beloved Friends,
One calm September morning, ere the mist
Had altogether yielded to the sun,
Saunter'd on this retir'd and difficult way.
10 ——Ill suits the road with one in haste, but we
Play'd with our time; and, as we stroll'd along,
It was our occupation to observe
Such objects as the waves had toss'd ashore,
Feather, or leaf, or weed, or wither'd bough,
15 Each on the other heap'd along the line
Of the dry wreck.[1] And in our vacant mood,
Not seldom did we stop to watch some tuft
Of dandelion seed or thistle's beard,
Which, seeming lifeless half, and half impell'd

---

4. I.e., native.
† Composed probably between July 23 and November 6, 1800, and in part on October 10 (*Chrono: MY*, 19). In her journal DW called the poem *Point Rash Judgment* (*DWJ*, 1:71) but WW never published it under that title. IF note: "The character of the eastern shore of Grasmere Lake is quite changed since these verses were written, by the public road being carried along its side. The friends spoken of [in line 6] were Coleridge and my Sister, & the fact occurred strictly as recorded." The poem is likely to have been based at least partly on an encounter recorded by STC ca. July 23, 1800 (when he was visiting WW and DW in Grasmere): "Poor fellow at a distance idle? in this haytime when wages are so high? Come near—thin, pale, can scarce speak—or throw out his fishing rod" (CN, 1:671). On the topographical details in the poem, see McCracken, 101–102, 234–35.
1. I.e., wrack, debris washed ashore from the lake (a northern English dialect usage).

20 By some internal feeling, skimm'd along
     Close to the surface of the lake that lay
     Asleep in a dead calm, ran closely on
     Along the dead calm lake, now here, now there,
     In all its sportive wanderings all the while
25 Making report of an invisible breeze
     That was its wings, its chariot, and its horse,
     Its very playmate, and its moving soul.[2]
     ——And often, trifling with a privilege
     Alike indulg'd to all, we paus'd, one now,
30 And now the other, to point out, perchance
     To pluck, some flower or water-weed, too fair
     Either to be divided from the place
     On which it grew, or to be left alone
     To its own beauty. Many such there are,
35 Fair ferns and flowers, and chiefly that tall plant
     So stately, of the Queen Osmunda nam'd,[3]
     Plant lovelier in its own retir'd abode
     On Grasmere's beach, than Naid by the side
     Of Grecian brook, or Lady of the Mere[4]
40 Sole-sitting by the shores of old Romance.
     ——So fared we that sweet morning: from the fields
     Meanwhile, a noise was heard, the busy mirth
     Of Reapers, Men and Women, Boys and Girls.
     Delighted much to listen to those sounds,
45 And in the fashion which I have describ'd,
     Feeding unthinking fancies, we advanc'd
     Along the indented shore; when suddenly,
     Through a thin veil of glittering haze, we saw
     Before us on a point of jutting land
50 The tall and upright figure of a Man
     Attir'd in peasant's garb, who stood alone
     Angling beside the margin of the lake.
     That way we turn'd our steps; nor was it long,
     Ere making ready comments on the sight
55 Which then we saw, with one and the same voice
     We all cried out, that he must be indeed
     An idle man, who thus could lose a day
     Of the mid harvest, when the labourer's hire
     Is ample, and some little might be stor'd
60 Wherewith to chear him in the winter time.
     Thus talking of that Peasant we approach'd
     Close to the spot where with his rod and line
     He stood alone; whereat he turn'd his head
     To greet us—and we saw a man worn down

---

2. *LB* (CW) notes a similar observation to lines 17–27 made by STC in Grasmere on September 1, 1800: "the beards of Thistle & dandelions flying above the lonely mountains like life, & I saw them thro' the Trees skimming the lake like Swallows" (*CN*, 1:799).
3. A large fern, also called the Old World royal fern.
4. The supernatural Lady of the Lake in Arthurian legends; *Naid*: i.e., Naiad, in Greek mythology a nymph and tutelary spirit of a spring, river, or lake.

65 By sickness, gaunt and lean, with sunken cheeks
   And wasted limbs, his legs so long and lean
   That for my single self I look'd at them,
   Forgetful of the body they sustain'd.—
   Too weak to labour in the harvest field,
70 The man was using his best skill to gain
   A pittance from the dead unfeeling lake
   That knew not of his wants. I will not say
   What thoughts immediately were ours, nor how
   The happy idleness of that sweet morn,
75 With all its lovely images, was chang'd
   To serious musing and to self-reproach.
   Nor did we fail to see within ourselves
   What need there is to be reserv'd in speech,
   And temper all our thoughts with charity.
80 —Therefore, unwilling to forget that day,
   My Friend, Myself, and She who then receiv'd
   The same admonishment, have call'd the place
   By a memorial name, uncouth indeed
   As e'er by Mariner was giv'n to Bay
85 Or Foreland on a new-discover'd coast,
   And, POINT RASH-JUDGMENT is the Name it bears.[5]

Michael, A Pastoral Poem

After Wordsworth decided on October 6, 1800, "not to print [Coleridge's unfinished] Christabel with the L.B." (*DWJ*, 1:64), he had to supply material to fill an equivalent amount of space in the second volume of *LB 1800*. The result was *Michael*, which he may have begun before October 11, when he and Dorothy "walked up Greenhead Gill [a stream ca. one mile northeast of Dove Cottage] in search of a sheepfold" and found one in ruinous condition, "built nearly in the form of a heart unequally divided" (*DWJ*, 1:65–66). (For Wordsworth's own description of a sheepfold, see the note on line 334.) On December 31, 1803, Coleridge recorded that while "sitting on the very Sheepfold dear William read to me his divine Poem, Michael" (*CN*, 1:1782), though whether it was the same one that William and Dorothy had encountered three years earlier is unknown.

Composition of the poem continued into December 1800, as Dorothy's journal records, and it may have been the poem she meant when she noted on December 9, "Wm. finished his poem to-day" (*DWJ*, 1:76). He composed much more than he finally included in the poem, however, and some of this additional material (transcribed in *LB* [CW], 325–38, 604–709) was later revised and incorporated into *The Prelude* 7.701–705, 8.222–311, and 12.185–204. On December 18 Wordsworth sent the printer in Bristol the manuscript of *Michael* and a separate letter of instructions: "If it be sufficient to fill the volume to 206 pages or upwards, printing it at 18 lines, or never more than 19 in a page as was done in the first edition of Lyrical Ballads you will print this poem immediately after the Poems on the *Naming of places* and consider it as, (with the two or three Notes adjoined) finishing the work" (*WL*, 1:307). In fact the poem, preceded by its own title page, did conclude the volume; but lines 202–16 were omitted, and the lower half of page 210 was left blank, "[b]y a shameful negligence of the printer," as Wordsworth subsequently com-

5. McCracken, 235, identifies the spot roughly in the middle of Grasmere's eastern shore, a few hundred yards south of Dove Cottage.

plained to his friend Thomas Poole, for whom Dorothy copied out the lines
(*WL*, 1:322). Most of the edition seems to have been sold with this error
uncorrected, but the Cornell Wordsworth editors have located nine corrected
copies: two with a printed slip containing the omitted lines, tipped in between
pages 210 and 211; and seven with three cancel (replacement) leaves supply-
ing the missing lines and adjacent text (*LB* [CW], 125–26; see also *Cornell*,
nos. 6 and 11). These lines are included in the present text. In *P 1815* the
poem was classified under "Poems founded on the Affections."

Wordsworth told Isabella Fenwick that the poem was "[w]ritten about the
same time as 'The Brothers.' The Sheepfold, on which so much of the poem
turns, remains, or rather the ruins of it. The character & circumstances of
Luke were taken from a family to whom had belonged, many years before,
the house we lived in at Town-End [i.e., Dove Cottage], along with some
fields and woodlands on the eastern shore of Grasmere. The name of the
Evening Star was not in fact given to this house but to another on the same
side of the valley more to the north." Wordsworth drew attention to the social
conditions described in the poem in his letter of January 14, 1801, to the
Whig leader, Charles James Fox (for which see the headnote to *LB 1800*),
and in a letter of April 9, 1801, to his friend Thomas Poole: "I have attempted
to give picture of a man, of strong mind and lively sensibility, agitated by two
of the most powerful affections of the human heart; the parental affection,
and the love of property, *landed* property, including the feelings of inheri-
tance, home, and persona; and family independence. The Poem has, I know,
drawn tears from the eyes of more than one, persons well acquainted with
the manners of the 'Statesmen, as they are called, of this country; and, more-
over, persons who never wept, in reading verse, before" (*WL*, 1:322).

For possible biographical sources of the story of Michael, see *LB* (CW), 400–
401; on the economic and political context, see David Simpson, *Wordsworth's
Historical Imagination*, 141–49; on the Biblical allusions, see Randel Helms,
"On the Genesis of Wordsworth's *Michael*," *English Language Notes* 15 (1977):
38–43. Interpreting the poem through its parallels with the story of Abraham's
near-sacrifice of his son Isaac (Genesis 22), Marjorie Levinson argues that
Michael treats his son as an object of economic exchange (*Wordsworth's Great
Period Poems*, 58–79), while Thomas Pfau (see below, pp. 653–61) and Fiona
Stafford ("Plain Living and Ungarnish'd Stories") relate the economic condi-
tions described in the poem to the genre of the pastoral ballad.

MICHAEL,

A PASTORAL POEM

If from the public way you turn your steps
Up the tumultuous brook of Green-head Gill,
You will suppose that with an upright path
Your feet must struggle; in such bold ascent
5   The pastoral Mountains front you, face to face.
But, courage! for beside that boisterous Brook
The mountains have all open'd out themselves,
And made a hidden valley of their own.
No habitation there is seen; but such
10   As journey thither find themselves alone
With a few sheep, with rocks and stones, and kites[1]

1. Long-winged birds of prey. *LB* (CW) notes the similarity of WW's phrasing in lines 10–12 to
DW's account of their walk to the sheepfold on October 11, 1800 (see the headnote): "kites

That overhead are sailing in the sky.
It is in truth an utter solitude,
Nor should I have made mention of this Dell
15 But for one object which you might pass by,
Might see and notice not. Beside the brook
There is a straggling heap of unhewn stones!
And to that place a story appertains,
Which, though it be ungarnish'd with events,
20 Is not unfit, I deem, for the fire-side,
Or for the summer shade. It was the first,
The earliest of those tales that spake to me
Of Shepherds, dwellers in the vallies, men
Whom I already lov'd, not verily
25 For their own sakes, but for the fields and hills
Where was their occupation and abode.
And hence this Tale, while I was yet a boy
Careless of books, yet having felt the power
Of Nature, by the gentle agency
30 Of natural objects led me on to feel
For passions that were not my own, and think
At random and imperfectly indeed
On man; the heart of man and human life.[2]
Therefore, although it be a history
35 Homely and rude,[3] I will relate the same
For the delight of a few natural hearts,
And with yet fonder feeling, for the sake
Of youthful Poets, who among these Hills
Will be my second self when I am gone.

40 Upon the Forest-side in Grasmere Vale[4]
There dwelt a Shepherd, Michael was his name,
An old man, stout of heart, and strong of limb.
His bodily frame had been from youth to age
Of an unusual strength: his mind was keen
45 Intense and frugal, apt for all affairs,
And in his Shepherd's calling he was prompt
And watchful more than ordinary men.
Hence he had learn'd the meaning of all winds,
Of blasts of every tone, and often-times[5]
50 When others heeded not, He heard the South
Make subterraneous music, like the noise

sailing in the sky above our heads; sheep bleating and in lines and chains and patterns scattered over the mountains" (*DWJ*, 1:66).
2. Compare WW's explanation (in a letter of March 6, 1798, to James Tobin) of his aim in *The Recluse* "to give pictures of Nature, Man, and Society" (*WL*, 1:212), and the verse Prospectus published in the Preface to *The Excursion* (p. 444 below).
3. Unrefined, unsophisticated.
4. I.e., the side of Grasmere Vale lying south of Greenhead Gill, between the stream and Town End (where Dove Cottage is located). A house in the area is still called Forest Side (McCracken, 39, 208).
5. In lines 48–49 WW echoes the advice given to shepherds in Virgil's *Georgics* 1.51–52: "ventos et varium caeli praediscere morem cura sit" [let it be our concern to learn the winds and various moods of the sky] (*LB* [CW], 402).

Of Bagpipers on distant Highland hills;
The Shepherd, at such warning, of his flock
Bethought him, and he to himself would say
55 The winds are now devising work for me!
And truly at all times the storm, that drives
The Traveller to a shelter, summon'd him
Up to the mountains: he had been alone
Amid the heart of many thousand mists
60 That came to him and left him on the heights.
So liv'd he till his eightieth year was pass'd.

And grossly that man errs, who should suppose
That the green Valleys, and the Streams and Rocks
Were things indifferent to the Shepherd's thoughts.
65 Fields, where with chearful spirits he had breath'd
The common air; the hills, which he so oft
Had climb'd with vigorous steps; which had impress'd
So many incidents upon his mind
Of hardship, skill or courage, joy or fear;
70 Which like a book preserv'd the memory
Of the dumb animals, whom he had sav'd,
Had fed or shelter'd, linking to such acts,
So grateful in themselves, the certainty
Of honorable gains; these fields, these hills
75 Which were his living Being, even more
Than his own Blood—what could they less? had laid
Strong hold on his affections, were to him
A pleasurable feeling of blind love,
The pleasure which there is in life itself.

80 He had not passed his days in singleness.
He had a Wife, a comely Matron, old
Though younger than himself full twenty years.
She was a woman of a stirring life
Whose heart was in her house: two wheels she had
85 Of antique form, this large for spinning wool,
That small for flax, and if one wheel had rest,
It was because the other was at work.[6]
The Pair had but one Inmate in their house,
An only Child, who had been born to them
90 When Michael telling o'er his years began
To deem that he was old, in Shepherd's phrase,
With one foot in the grave.[7] This only son,

6. Later, in his *Description of the Scenery of the Lakes in the North of England* (London, 1822), originally published anonymously as the introduction to Joseph Wilkinson's *Select Views of Cumberland, Westmoreland, and Lancashire* (1810), WW observed, "The family of each man, whether *estatesman* or farmer, formerly has a twofold support; first, the produce of his lands and flocks; and, secondly, the profit drawn from the employment of the women and children, as manufacturers; spinning their own wool in their own houses (work chiefly done in the winter season) and carrying it to market for sale. * * * But, by the invention and universal application of machinery, this second resource has been cut off" (99).
7. Levinson, *Wordsworth's Great Period Poems*, 69–70, notes the parallel between Luke and Isaac, who is born when Abraham is "in his old age" (Genesis 21.2).

With two brave sheep dogs tried in many a storm,
The one of an inestimable worth,
95   Made all their Household. I may truly say,
That they were as a proverb in the vale
For endless industry. When day was gone,
And from their occupations out of doors
The Son and Father were come home, even then
100   Their labour did not cease, unless when all.
Turn'd to their cleanly supper-board, and there
Each with a mess of pottage[8] and skimm'd milk,
Sate round their basket pil'd with oaten cakes,
And their plain home-made cheese. Yet when their meal
105   Was ended, LUKE (for so the Son was nam'd)
And his old Father, both betook themselves
To such convenient work, as might employ
Their hands by the fire-side; perhaps to card
Wool[9] for the House-wife's spindle, or repair
110   Some injury done to sickle, flail, or scythe,
Or other implement of house or field.

Down from the cieling by the chimney's edge,
Which in our ancient uncouth country style
Did with a huge projection overbrow
115   Large space beneath, as duly as the light
Of day grew dim, the House-wife hung a lamp;
An aged utensil, which had perform'd
Service beyond all others of its kind.
Early at evening did it burn and late,
120   Surviving Comrade of uncounted Hours
Which going by from year to year had found
And left the Couple neither gay perhaps
Nor chearful, yet with objects and with hopes
Living a life of eager industry.
125   And now, when LUKE was in his eighteenth year,
There by the light of this old lamp they sate,
Father and Son, while late into the night
The House-wife plied her own peculiar work,
Making the cottage thro' the silent hours
130   Murmur as with the sound of summer flies.
Not with a waste of words, but for the sake
Of pleasure, which I know that I shall give
To many living now, I of this Lamp
Speak thus minutely: for there are no few
135   Whose memories will bear witness to my tale.
The Light was famous in its neighbourhood,
And was a public Symbol of the life,

---

8. A soup made of boiled vegetables, but more importantly the phrase alludes to Genesis 25.29–34, in which Esau, in extreme hunger, sells his birthright to his brother Jacob for a mess of pottage.
9. See note on *The Brothers*, line 31.

The thrifty Pair had liv'd. For, as it chanc'd,
Their Cottage on a plot of rising ground
140 Stood single, with large prospect North and South,
High into Easedale, up to Dunmal-Raise,
And Westward to the village near the Lake.
And from this constant light so regular
And so far seen, the House itself by all
145 Who dwelt within the limits of the vale,
Both old and young, was nam'd The Evening Star.[1]

Thus living on through such a length of years,
The Shepherd, if he lov'd himself, must needs
Have lov'd his Help-mate; but to Michael's heart
150 This Son of his old age[2] was yet more dear—
Effect which might perhaps have been produc'd
By that instinctive tenderness, the same
Blind Spirit, which is in the blood of all,
Or that a child, more than all other gifts,
155 Brings hope with it, and forward-looking thoughts,
And stirrings of inquietude, when they
By tendency of nature needs must fail.
From such, and other causes, to the thoughts
Of the old Man his only Son was now
160 The dearest object that he knew on earth.
Exceeding was the love he bare to him,
His Heart and his Heart's joy! For oftentimes
Old Michael, while he[3] was a babe in arms,
Had done him female service, not alone
165 For dalliance and delight, as is the use
Of Fathers, but with patient mind enforc'd
To acts of tenderness; and he had rock'd
His cradle with a woman's gentle hand.

And in a later time, ere yet the Boy
170 Had put on Boy's attire, did Michael love,
Albeit of a stern unbending mind,
To have the young one in his sight, when he
Had work by his own door, or when he sate
With sheep before him on his Shepherd's stool,
175 Beneath that large old Oak, which near their door
Stood, and from its enormous breadth of shade
Chosen for the Shearer's covert from the sun,
Thence in our rustic dialect was call'd
The CLIPPING TREE,[4] a name which yet it bears.
180 There, while they two were sitting in the shade,

1. McCracken, 39, identifies possible locations of Michael's cottage from the indication given in WW's IF note (quoted in the headnote). *Easedale* (line 141): a hilly area a mile northwest of Grasmere; *Dunmal-Raise* (or Dunmail Raise): a hill two miles north of the village.
2. WW appropriates the description of Jacob's favorite son, Joseph, from Genesis 37.3.
3. I.e., Luke.
4. WW's note: "Clipping is the word used in the North of England for shearing."

With others round them, earnest all and blithe,
Would Michael exercise his heart with looks
Of fond correction and reproof bestow'd
Upon the child, if he disturb'd the sheep
185 By catching at their legs, or with his shouts
Scar'd them, while they lay still beneath the shears.

And when by Heaven's good grace the Boy grew up
A healthy Lad, and carried in his cheek
Two steady roses that were five years old,
190 Then Michael from a winter coppice cut
With his own hand a sapling, which he hoop'd
With iron, making it throughout in all
Due requisites a perfect Shepherd's Staff,
And gave it to the Boy; wherewith equipp'd
195 He as a Watchman oftentimes was plac'd
At gate or gap, to stem or turn the flock,
And to his office prematurely call'd
There stood the urchin, as you will divine,
Something between a hindrance and a help,
200 And for this cause not always, I believe,
Receiving from his Father hire[5] of praise,
Though nought was left undone, which staff or voice,
Or looks, or threatening gestures could perform.
    But soon as Luke, full ten years old, could stand
205 Against the mountain blasts, and to the heights,
Not fearing toil, nor length of weary ways,
He with his Father daily went, and they
Were as companions, why should I relate
That objects which the Shepherd lov'd before
210 Were dearer now? that from the Boy there came
Feelings and emanations, things which were
Light to the sun and music to the wind;
And that the Old Man's heart seem'd born again.
    Thus in his Father's sight the Boy grew up:
215 And now when he had reach'd his eighteenth year,
He was his comfort and his daily hope.

While this good household thus were living on
From day to day, to Michael's ear there came
Distressful tidings. Long before the time
220 Of which I speak, the Shepherd had been bound
In surety for his Brother's Son,[6] a man
Of an industrious life, and ample means,
But unforeseen misfortunes suddenly
Had press'd upon him, and old Michael now
225 Was summon'd to discharge the forfeiture,

---

5. Reward.
6. I.e., Michael is required by the terms of a surety bond to meet his nephew's financial obligations to
    a third party (not identified in the poem) if, as has now happened, his nephew is unable to do so.

A grievous penalty, but little less
Than half his substance. This un-look'd for claim
At the first hearing, for a moment took
More hope out of his life than he supposed
230 That any old man ever could have lost.
As soon as he had gather'd so much strength
That he could look his trouble in the face,
It seem'd that his sole refuge was to sell
A portion of his patrimonial fields.[7]
235 Such was his first resolve; he thought again,
And his heart fail'd him. "Isabel," said he,
Two evenings after he had heard the news,
"I have been toiling more than seventy years,
And in the open sun-shine of God's love
240 Have we all liv'd, yet if these fields of ours
Should pass into a Stranger's hand, I think
That I could not lie quiet in my grave.
Our lot is a hard lot; the Sun itself
Has scarcely been more diligent than I,
245 And I have liv'd to be a fool at last
To my own family. An evil Man
That was, and made an evil choice, if he
Were false to us; and if he were not false,
There are ten thousand to whom loss like this
250 Had been no sorrow. I forgive him—but
'Twere better to be dumb than to talk thus.
When I began, my purpose was to speak
Of remedies and of a chearful hope.
Our Luke shall leave us, Isabel; the land
255 Shall not go from us, and it shall be free,[8]
He shall possess it, free as is the wind
That passes over it. We have, thou knowest,
Another Kinsman, he will be our friend
In this distress. He is a prosperous man,
260 Thriving in trade, and Luke to him shall go,
And with his Kinsman's help and his own thrift,
He quickly will repair this loss, and then
May come again to us. If here he stay,
What can be done? Where every one is poor
265 What can be gain'd?" At this, the old man paus'd,
And Isabel sate silent, for her mind
Was busy, looking back into past times.
There's Richard Bateman, thought she to herself,
He was a parish-boy[9]—at the church-door

7. This phrase seems to imply (as do lines 255–56) that Michael is a freeholder, owning his land
outright, rather than (as were the majority of "statesmen") a copyholder, holding an inheritable
tenancy of a property. A legacy of feudalism, copyholds were gradually abolished by the begin-
ning of the twentieth century.
8. I.e., Michael is resolved neither to sell the land nor to mortgage it, so that Luke will inherit it
free, in contrast to Michael himself (see lines 384–86).
9. See note on The Brothers, line 340. WW's note (printed after the poem in LB 1800): "'There's
Richard Bateman,' &c. The story alluded to here is well known in the country. The chapel is called

270 They made a gathering for him, shillings, pence,
     And halfpennies, wherewith the Neighbours bought
     A Basket, which they fill'd with Pedlar's wares,
     And with this Basket on his arm, the Lad
     Went up to London, found a Master there,
275 Who out of many chose the trusty Boy
     To go and overlook his merchandise
     Beyond the seas, where he grew wond'rous rich,
     And left estates and monies to the poor,
     And at his birth-place built a Chapel, floor'd
280 With Marble, which he sent from foreign lands.
     These thoughts, and many others of like sort,
     Pass'd quickly thro' the mind of Isabel,
     And her face brighten'd. The Old Man was glad,
     And thus resum'd. "Well! Isabel, this scheme
285 These two days has been meat and drink to me.
     Far more than we have lost is left us yet.
     —We have enough—I wish indeed that I
     Were younger, but this hope is a good hope.
     —Make ready Luke's best garments, of the best
290 Buy for him more, and let us send him forth
     To-morrow, or the next day, or to-night:
     —If he could go, the Boy should go to-night."[1]

     Here Michael ceas'd, and to the fields went forth
     With a light heart. The House-wife for five days
295 Was restless morn and night, and all day long
     Wrought on with her best fingers to prepare
     Things needful for the journey of her Son.
     But Isabel was glad when Sunday came
     To stop her in her work; for, when she lay
300 By Michael's side, she for the two last nights
     Heard him, how he was troubled in his sleep:
     And when they rose at morning she could see
     That all his hopes were gone. That day at noon
     She said to Luke, while they two by themselves
305 Were sitting at the door, "Thou must not go,
     We have no other Child but thee to lose,
     None to remember—do not go away,
     For if thou leave thy Father he will die."[2]
     The Lad made answer with a jocund voice,
310 And Isabel, when she had told her fears,
     Recover'd heart. That evening her best fare

Ings Chapel; and is on the right hand side of the road leading from Kendal to Ambleside." Lines
269–80 recount the story of Robert (not Richard) Bateman, a native of the area who became a
wealthy merchant and in the 1740s funded the rebuilding of St. Anne's Church in Ings, a village
two miles northwest of Kendal, with a floor of Italian marble (see Thompson, 311). WW, MW, and
DW visited the church on October 4, 1802 (DWJ, 1:183, DW also calling Bateman Richard).
1. Compare Genesis 44.11–14, in which the famished Jacob sends his sons Judah and Benjamin
with presents and money to Egypt to buy corn from their spurned brother Joseph.
2. This line echoes Judah's words to Joseph's steward concerning Benjamin, "The lad cannot
leave his father: for if he should leave his father, his father would die" (Genesis 44.22).

Did she bring forth, and all together sate
Like happy people round a Christmas fire.

Next morning Isabel resum'd her work,
315 And all the ensuing week the house appear'd
As cheerful as a grove in Spring: at length
The expected letter from their Kinsman came,
With kind assurances that he would do
His utmost for the welfare of the Boy,
320 To which requests were added that forthwith
He might be sent to him. Ten times or more
The letter was read over; Isabel
Went forth to shew it to the neighbours round:
Nor was there at that time on English Land
325 A prouder heart than Luke's. When Isabel
Had to her house return'd, the Old Man said,
"He shall depart to-morrow." To this word
The House-wife answered, talking much of things
Which, if at such short notice he should go,
330 Would surely be forgotten. But at length
She gave consent, and Michael was at ease.

Near the tumultuous brook of Green-head Gill,
In that deep Valley, Michael had design'd
To build a Sheep-fold,³ and, before he heard
335 The tidings of his melancholy loss,
For this same purpose he had gathered up
A heap of stones, which close to the brook side
Lay thrown together, ready for the work.
With Luke that evening thitherward he walk'd;
340 And soon as they had reach'd the place he stopp'd,
And thus the Old Man spake to him. "My Son,
To-morrow thou wilt leave me; with full heart
I look upon thee, for thou art the same
That wert a promise to me ere thy birth,
345 And all thy life hast been my daily joy.
I will relate to thee some little part
Of our two histories; 'twill do thee good
When thou art from me, even if I should speak
Of things thou canst not know of.——After thou
350 First cam'st into the world, as it befalls
To new-born infants, thou didst sleep away
Two days, and blessings from thy Father's tongue
Then fell upon thee. Day by day pass'd on,
And still I lov'd thee with encreasing love.
355 Never to living ear came sweeter sounds

---

3. WW's note (printed after the poem in *LB 1800*): "'——had design'd to build a sheep-fold.' &c. It
may be proper to inform some readers, that a sheep-fold in these mountains is an unroofed building
of stone walls, with different divisions. It is generally placed by the side of a brook, for the conve-
nience of washing the sheep; but it is also useful as a shelter for them, and as a place to drive them
into, to enable the shepherds conveniently to single out one or more for any particular purpose."

Than when I heard thee by our own fire-side
First uttering without words a natural tune,
When thou, a feeding babe, didst in thy joy
Sing at thy Mother's breast. Month follow'd month,
360 And in the open fields my life was pass'd
And in the mountains, else I think that thou
Hadst been brought up upon thy father's knees.
—But we were playmates, Luke; among these hills,
As well thou know'st, in us the old and young
365 Have play'd together, nor with me didst thou
Lack any pleasure which a boy can know."
Luke had a manly heart; but at these words
He sobb'd aloud; the Old Man grasp'd his hand,
And said, "Nay do not take it so—I see
370 That these are things of which I need not speak.
—Even to the utmost I have been to thee
A kind and a good Father: and herein
I but repay a gift which I myself
Receiv'd at others' hands, for, though now old
375 Beyond the common life of man, I still
Remember them who lov'd me in my youth.
Both of them sleep together: here they liv'd
As all their Forefathers had done, and when
At length their time was come, they were not loth
380 To give their bodies to the family mold.
I wish'd that thou should'st live the life they liv'd.
But 'tis a long time to look back, my Son,
And see so little gain from sixty years.
These fields were burthen'd when they came to me;
385 'Till I was forty years of age, not more
Than half of my inheritance was mine.[4]
I toil'd and toil'd; God bless'd me in my work,
And 'till these three weeks past the land was free.
—It looks as if it never could endure
390 Another Master. Heaven forgive me, Luke,
If I judge ill for thee, but it seems good
That thou should'st go." At this the Old Man paus'd,
Then, pointing to the Stones near which they stood,
Thus, after a short silence, he resum'd:
395 "This was a work for us, and now, my Son,
It is a work for me. But, lay one Stone—
Here, lay it for me, Luke, with thine own hands.
I for the purpose brought thee to this place.
Nay, Boy, be of good hope:—we both may live
400 To see a better day. At eighty-four
I still am strong and stout;—do thou thy part,
I will do mine.—I will begin again
With many tasks that were resign'd to thee;
Up to the heights, and in among the storms,

4. I.e., when Michael inherited the land, it was heavily mortgaged.

405 Will I without thee go again, and do
All works which I was wont to do alone,
Before I knew thy face.——Heaven bless thee, Boy!
Thy heart these two weeks has been beating fast
With many hopes—it should be so—yes—yes—
410 I knew that thou could'st never have a wish
To leave me, Luke, thou hast been bound to me
Only by links of love, when thou art gone
What will be left to us!—But, I forget
My purposes. Lay now the corner-stone,
415 As I requested, and hereafter, Luke,
When thou art gone away, should evil men
Be thy companions, let this Sheep-fold be
Thy anchor and thy shield; amid all fear
And all temptation, let it be to thee
420 An emblem of the life thy Fathers liv'd,
Who, being innocent, did for that cause
Bestir them in good deeds. Now, fare thee well—
When thou return'st, thou in this place wilt see
A work which is not here, a covenant[5]
425 'Twill be between us——but whatever fate
Befall thee, I shall love thee to the last,
And bear thy memory with me to the grave."[6]

The Shepherd ended here; and Luke stoop'd down,
And as his Father had requested, laid
430 The first stone of the Sheep-fold; at the sight
The Old Man's grief broke from him, to his heart
He press'd his Son, he kissed him and wept;
And to the House together they return'd.

Next morning, as had been resolv'd, the Boy
435 Began his journey, and when he had reach'd
The public Way, he put on a bold face;
And all the Neighbours as he pass'd their doors
Came forth, with wishes and with farewell pray'rs,
That follow'd him 'till he was out of sight.
440 A good report did from their Kinsman come,
Of Luke and his well-doing; and the Boy
Wrote loving letters, full of wond'rous news,
Which, as the House-wife phrased it, were throughout
The prettiest letters that were ever seen.
445 Both parents read them with rejoicing hearts.
So, many months pass'd on: and once again
The Shepherd went about his daily work
With confident and cheerful thoughts; and now
Sometimes when he could find a leisure hour

---

5. This scene recalls Genesis 31.43–55, in which Jacob and his father-in-law Laban assemble a
pile of stones in witness of their covenant (not to encroach on each other's territory).
6. An echo of Jacob's mourning for Joseph: "For I will go down into the grave unto my son mourn-
ing" (Genesis 37.35).

450 He to that valley took his way, and there
Wrought at the Sheep-fold. Meantime Luke began
To slacken in his duty, and at length
He in the dissolute city gave himself
To evil courses: ignominy and shame
455 Fell on him, so that he was driven at last
To seek a hiding-place beyond the seas.

There is a comfort in the strength of love;
'Twill make a thing endurable, which else
Would break the heart:—Old Michael found it so.
460 I have convers'd with more than one who well
Remember the Old Man, and what he was
Years after he had heard this heavy news.
His bodily frame had been from youth to age
Of an unusual strength. Among the rocks
465 He went, and still look'd up upon the sun,
And listen'd to the wind; and as before
Perform'd all kinds of labour for his Sheep,
And for the land his small inheritance.[7]
And to that hollow Dell from time to time
470 Did he repair, to build the Fold of which
His flock had need. 'Tis not forgotten yet
The pity which was then in every heart
For the Old Man—and 'tis believ'd by all
That many and many a day he thither went,
475 And never lifted up a single stone.
There, by the Sheep-fold, sometimes was he seen
Sitting alone, with that his faithful Dog,
Then old, beside him, lying at his feet.
The length of full seven years from time to time
480 He at the building of this Sheep-fold wrought,
And left the work unfinished when he died.

Three years, or little more, did Isabel,
Survive her Husband: at her death the estate
Was sold, and went into a Stranger's hand.
485 The Cottage which was nam'd The Evening Star
Is gone, the ploughshare has been through the ground
On which it stood; great changes have been wrought
In all the neighbourhood, yet the Oak is left
That grew beside their Door; and the remains
490 Of the unfinished Sheep-fold may be seen
Beside the boisterous brook of Green-head Gill.

7. This line and lines 483–84 establish that Michael did not lose all of his land after Luke's enforced departure, but they do not clarify if he had to sell or mortgage any *part* of the estate.

From LYRICAL BALLADS WITH PASTORAL AND OTHER POEMS (1802)

Appendix

See Preface, page [82].—"by what is usually called Poetic Diction."[†]

As perhaps I have no right to expect from a Reader of an Introduction to a volume of Poems that attentive perusal without which it is impossible, imperfectly as I have been compelled to express my meaning, that what I have said in the Preface should throughout be fully understood, I am the more anxious to give an exact notion of the sense in which I use the phrase *poetic diction*; and for this purpose I will here add a few words concerning the origin of the phraseology which I have condemned under that name.——The earliest Poets of all nations generally wrote from passion excited by real events; they wrote naturally, and as men: feeling powerfully as they did, their language was daring, and figurative. In succeeding times, Poets, and men ambitious of the fame of Poets, perceiving the influence of such language, and desirous of producing the same effect, without having the same animating passion, set themselves to a mechanical adoption of those figures of speech, and made use of them, sometimes with propriety, but much more frequently applied them to feelings and ideas with which they had no natural connection whatsoever. A language was thus insensibly produced, differing materially from the real language of men in *any situation*. The Reader or Hearer of this distorted language found himself in a perturbed and unusual state of mind: when affected by the genuine language of passion he had been in a perturbed and unusual state of mind also: in both cases he was willing that his common judgment and understanding should be laid asleep, and he had no instinctive and infallible perception of the true to make him reject the false; the one served as a passport for the other. The agitation and confusion of mind were in both cases delightful, and no wonder if he confounded the one with the other, and believed them both to be produced by the same, or similar causes. Besides, the Poet spake to him in the character of a man to be looked up to, a man of genius and authority. Thus, and from a variety of other causes, this distorted language was received with admiration; and Poets, it is probable, who had before contented themselves for the most part with misapplying only expressions which at first had been dictated by real passion, carried the abuse still further, and introduced

---

[†] This appendix, an elaboration of the idea of poetic diction discussed in the Preface to *LB 1800*, was first published at the end of volume 2 of *LB 1802* and reprinted in *LB 1805* as well as in WW's collected editions from *P 1815* to the *Poetical Works* of 1850.

phrases composed apparently in the spirit of the original figurative language of passion, yet altogether of their own invention, and distinguished by various degrees of wanton deviation from good sense and nature.

It is indeed true that the language of the earliest Poets was felt to differ materially from ordinary language, because it was the language of extraordinary occasions; but it was really spoken by men, language which the Poet himself had uttered when he had been affected by the events which he described, or which he had heard uttered by those around him. To this language it is probable that metre of some sort or other was early superadded. This separated the genuine language of Poetry still further from common life, so that whoever read or heard the poems of these earliest Poets felt himself moved in a way in which he had not been accustomed to be moved in real life, and by causes manifestly different from those which acted upon him in real life. This was the great temptation to all the corruptions which have followed: under the protection of this feeling succeeding Poets constructed a phraseology which had one thing, it is true, in common with the genuine language of poetry, namely, that it was not heard in ordinary conversation; that it was unusual. But the first Poets, as I have said, spake a language which though unusual, was still the language of men. This circumstance, however, was disregarded by their successors; they found that they could please by easier means: they became proud of a language which they themselves had invented, and which was uttered only by themselves; and, with the spirit of a fraternity, they arrogated it to themselves as their own. In process of time metre became a symbol or promise of this unusual language, and whoever took upon him to write in metre, according as he possessed more or less of true poetic genius, introduced less or more of this adulterated phraseology into his compositions, and the true and the false became so inseparably interwoven that the taste of men was gradually perverted; and this language was received as a natural language; and, at length, by the influence of books upon men, did to a certain degree really become so. Abuses of this kind were imported from one nation to another, and with the progress of refinement this diction became daily more and more corrupt, thrusting out of sight the plain humanities of nature by a motley masquerade of tricks, quaintnesses, hieroglyphics, and enigmas.

It would be highly interesting to point out the causes of the pleasure given by this extravagant and absurd language; but this is not the place; it depends upon a great variety of causes, but upon none perhaps more than its influence in impressing a notion of the peculiarity and exaltation of the Poet's character, and in flattering the Reader's self-love by bringing him nearer to a sympathy with that character; an effect which is accomplished by unsettling ordinary habits of thinking, and thus assisting the Reader to approach to that perturbed and dizzy state of mind in which if he does not find himself, he imagines that he is *balked* of a peculiar enjoyment which poetry can, and ought to bestow.

The sonnet which I have quoted from Gray, in the Preface,[1] except the lines printed in Italics, consists of little else but this diction, though not of the worst kind; and indeed, if I may be permitted to say so, it is far too common in the best writers, both antient and modern. Perhaps I

---

1. Thomas Gray's *Sonnet on the Death of Mr. Richard West*: see p. 83 above.

can in no way, by positive example, more easily give my Reader a notion of what I mean by the phrase *poetic diction* than by referring him to a comparison between the metrical paraphrases which we have of passages in the old and new Testament, and those passages as they exist in our common Translation. See Pope's "Messiah" throughout, Prior's "Did sweeter sounds adorn my flowing tongue," &c. &c. "Though I speak with the tongues of men and of angels," &c. &c. See 1st Corinthians Chapter 13th.[2] By way of immediate example, take the following of Dr. Johnson.

> Turn on the prudent Ant thy heedless eyes,
> Observe her labours, Sluggard, and be wise;
> No stern command, no monitory voice,
> Prescribes her duties, or directs her choice;
> Yet timely provident she hastes away,
> To snatch the blessings of a plenteous day;
> When fruitful Summer loads the teeming plain,
> She crops the harvest and she stores the grain.
> How long shall sloth usurp thy useless hours,
> Unnerve thy vigour, and enchain thy powers?
> While artful shades thy downy couch enclose,
> And soft solicitation courts repose,
> Amidst the drowsy charms of dull delight,
> Year chases year with unremitted flight,
> Till want now following, fraudulent and slow,
> Shall spring to seize thee, like an ambushed foe.[3]

From this hubbub of words pass to the original. "Go to the Ant, thou Sluggard, consider her ways, and be wise: which having no guide, overseer, or ruler, provideth her meat in the summer, and gathereth her food in the harvest. How long wilt thou sleep, O Sluggard? when wilt thou arise out of thy sleep? Yet a little sleep, a little slumber, a little folding of the hands to sleep. So shall thy poverty come as one that travaileth, and thy want as an armed man." Proverbs, chap. 6.

One more quotation and I have done. It is from Cowper's verses supposed to be written by Alexander Selkirk.

> Religion! What treasure untold
> Resides in that heavenly word!
> More precious than silver and gold,
> Or all that this earth can afford.
> But the sound of the church-going bell
> These valleys and rocks never heard
> Ne'er sigh'd at the sound of a knell,
> Or smiled when a sabbath appear'd.

2. WW refers to Alexander Pope's *Messiah, A Sacred Eclogue* (1712), an imitation of Virgil's fourth *Eclogue* that substitutes prophecies from the Book of Isaiah for Virgil's own prediction of the birth of an infant whose lifetime would witness the restoration of the golden age associated in Greek and Roman myth with the god Saturn. WW's quotations contrast the first line of Matthew Prior's *Charity: A Paraphrase on the Thirteenth Chapter of the First Epistle to the Corinthians* (1704), a poem in heroic couplets, and its source in 1 Corinthians 13.1.
3. Samuel Johnson, *The Ant* (originally published in 1766, though WW reprints the version in Johnson's *Works* [London, 1787], 11:372), a paraphrase of Proverbs 6.6–11, which WW proceeds to quote from the King James Bible.

> Ye winds, that have made me your sport,
> Convey to this desolate shore
> Some cordial endearing report
> Of a land I must visit no more.
> My Friends, do they now and then send
> A wish or a thought after me?
> O tell me I yet have a friend
> Though a friend I am never to see.[4]

I have quoted this passage as an instance of three different styles of composition. The first four lines are poorly expressed; some Critics would call the language prosaic; the fact is, it would be bad prose, so bad, that it is scarcely worse in metre. The epithet "church-going" applied to a bell, and that by so chaste a writer as Cowper, is an instance of the strange abuses which Poets have introduced into their language till they and their Readers take them as matters of course, if they do not single them out expressly as objects of admiration. The two lines "Ne'er sigh'd at the sound," &c. are, in my opinion, an instance of the language of passion wrested from its proper use, and, from the mere circumstance of the composition being in metre, applied upon an occasion that does not justify such violent expressions, and I should condemn the passage, though perhaps few Readers will agree with me, as vicious poetic diction. The last stanza is throughout admirably expressed: it would be equally good whether in prose or verse, except that the Reader has an exquisite pleasure in seeing such natural language so naturally connected with metre. The beauty of this stanza tempts me here to add a sentiment which ought to be the pervading spirit of a system, detached parts of which have been imperfectly explained in the Preface, namely, that in proportion as ideas and feelings are valuable, whether the composition be in prose or in verse, they require and exact one and the same language.

---

4. William Cowper, *Verses, Supposed to Be Written by Alexander Selkirk, during his Solitary Abode in the Island of Juan Fernandez* (1782), lines 25–40. Selkirk (1676–1721) was a Scottish sailor whose four years marooned in the Juan Fernández Islands off Chile may have been an inspiration for Daniel Defoe's novel *Robinson Crusoe* (1719).

THE PRELUDE (1805)

Although generally regarded as Wordsworth's masterpiece, and one of the great long poems in English literature, *The Prelude* was not originally conceived as an independent poem, was not published (apart from isolated sections listed in *Chrono: MY*, 15) in Wordsworth's lifetime, exists in multiple states, and is to an extent a creation of its editors—not least in its title, which was given to the poem after the poet's death.

Distinct from but closely related to the project of *The Recluse*, which Wordsworth first mentioned in March 1798 as "a poem in which I contrive to give most of the knowledge of which I am possessed" (*WL*, 1:212; see also the headnote to *The Excursion*), *The Prelude* originated—evidently out of his frustration at not making progress with *The Recluse*—in some disconnected passages of autobiographical blank verse that Wordsworth composed in Germany in autumn 1798 (transcribed in *The Prelude 1798–1799* [*CW*], 124–30). These passages include lines later incorporated into the "glad preamble" of *Prel 1805* (see note on 1.5) and memories of childhood that also found their way into *Prel 1805* (e.g., the boat-stealing episode of 1.375–430, the skating scene of 1.455–93, and the boy of Winander of 5.389–413, the first two of which Dorothy copied out and sent to Coleridge in late December 1798 [*WL*, 1:239–41]). The longest passage, of 149 lines beginning with a self-questioning apostrophe to the River Derwent, "was it for this / That one, the fairest of all rivers, / Loved to blend his murmurs with my nurse's song" (compare *Prel 1805* 1.274–88), became the basis of part 1 of a two-part poem, addressed to Coleridge, that Wordsworth composed in 1799. The addressee must have received no more than a hint of the poem, however, when he wrote to Wordsworth on October 12, "O let it be the tail-piece of 'The Recluse'! for of nothing but 'The Recluse' can I hear patiently. That it is to be addressed to me makes me more desirous that it should not be a poem of itself" (*CL*, 1:538).

Notwithstanding Coleridge's wish, Wordsworth was already composing the second part of the unnamed poem while he and Dorothy stayed with the Hutchinsons in Sockburn, County Durham (ca. early May–December 17, 1799). By the end of the year Dorothy Wordsworth and Mary Hutchinson made fair copies of both parts. These manuscripts, centered on "spots of time" from Wordsworth's childhood and youth (compare *The Prelude* 11.256–75)—episodes that he subsequently recognized as having been decisive in his emotional, moral, and intellectual development, but also of broader import (see Jonathan Bishop, "Wordsworth and the Spots of Time")—are versions of what Jonathan Wordsworth and Stephen Gill first identified and published (in 1974) as a distinct state of the poem, now known as the two-part or 1799 *Prelude* (see *NCPrel*, 1–27, or *Prelude, 1798–1799* [*CW*], 43–67, for the text). As it stood, the poem was, as Stephen Parrish describes it, "a record of the growth of his poetic sensibility under the ministering powers of nature" (*Prelude, 1798–1799* [*CW*], 36).

On January 4, 1804, Wordsworth read to Coleridge "the second Part of his divine Self-biography" (*CN*, 1:1801). By that time—probably between April 1801 and late 1803 (*Chrono: MY*, 11–12)—he had begun desultorily revising *Prel 1799* and adding material, bringing the account of his intellectual development up to his undergraduate years (in what would become book 3 of *Prel*

1805). Knowing that Coleridge planned to go abroad in the spring for the sake of his health, Wordsworth worked rapidly between ca. January 14 and early March 1804 on what he now conceived as a five-book poem (drafts preserved in DC MSS 43 and 38)—but as he was finishing he decided to extend the poem, and reworked books 1–5 into what became their *Prel 1805* form, a copy of which was prepared by March 18, 1804, for Coleridge to take to Malta (MS M=DC MS 44). In April and May Wordsworth drafted materials for book 7 and parts of books 6 and 8, and in October resumed work planning and drafting books 8–13 (*Chrono: MY*, 12–15). Unable, after the drowning of his brother John, to make any progress on the poem from mid-February to mid-April 1805, Wordsworth completed it ca. May 20, and fair copies were written out by Dorothy between November 1805 and February 1806 (MS A=DC MS 52) and by Mary (now William's wife) between December and February (MS B=DC MS 53), the latter with an ornamental title page (see illustration on p. 166) probably by Mary's brother George Hutchinson (*Prel 1805* [CW], 2:1004n). The "title" was *Poem Title not yet fixed upon by William Wordsworth Addressed to S. T. Coleridge*. In early January 1807 Wordsworth read the entire poem to Coleridge (see source note on Coleridge's *To W. Wordsworth* in Nineteenth-Century Responses, p. 557 below), and thereafter lent him MS B, which Coleridge annotated at the end of book 6. This state of the poem, in thirteen books and including accounts of Wordsworth's Continental excursion of 1790 (book 6) and residence in France in 1791–92 (books 9–10), was first published by Ernest de Selincourt in 1926 and is now known as the thirteen-book or 1805 *Prelude*.

If the central theme of *Prel 1799* was the formative power of nature on the young Wordsworth's sensibilities and moral development, the expanded poem—in which M. H. Abrams sees a secular parallel to Christian crisis-autobiographies—relates this aspect of his education to his subsequent encounters with human society in grammar school, in university, in London, and in Revolutionary France, and to his recognition (expressed especially in books 6 and 13) of the powers of the imagination. The narrative is at once retrospective, recounting formative experiences of his childhood and youth, and teleological, asserting that those experiences had destined Wordsworth to become a poet of "lasting inspiration, sanctified / By reason and by truth" (13.443–44). Because, however, the definitive manifestation of his powers as poet and teacher of humanity was to be *The Recluse*, a philosophical poem on nothing less than "Nature, Man, and Society" (see the headnote to *The Excursion*), Wordsworth remained ambivalent about the status of the autobiographical poem he referred to only as the "Poem to Coleridge" or the poem "on the growth of [his] own mind" (*WL*, 1:518). While revealing its existence first to friends—and later, in the Preface to *The Excursion* (1814), to the public (see p. 443 below)—he withheld the text itself, insisting to Thomas De Quincey in March 1804 (*WL*, 1:454) and Richard Sharp the following month that it could not be published "till another work [*The Recluse*] has been written and published, of sufficient importance to justify me in giving my own history to the world" (*WL*, 1:470), and to Sir George Beaumont in May 1805 that it was "a thing unprecedented in Literary history that a man should talk so much about himself" (*WL*, 1:586). Even if he declared the subject of "my own heart * * * and my youthful mind" to be "in truth heroic argument / And genuine prowess" (3.176–77, 182–83)—one of many allusions to *Paradise Lost*, the verse form of which Wordsworth also appropriated—he seems to have thought of the poem less as an epic, despite its eventual length, than as an extended and essentially private conversation poem addressed to Coleridge and seeking to justify Coleridge's faith in his ability to produce a poem with a genuine epic subject, *The Recluse*. Modern criticism has been more willing than Wordsworth himself was to accept *The Prelude* as the substitute for the uncompleted *Recluse* project.

The post-1805 development of the *Poem Title not yet fixed upon* may be summarized more briefly. Between late 1818 and early 1820 Wordsworth revised it extensively (for this text, of which an incomplete fair copy survives, see *Prel 1805* [CW], 2:5–231), and in 1831–32 he again revised it extensively, dividing book 10 into two books while reducing the overall number of lines in the poem (for Mary's fair copy, MS D=DC MS 124, see *Prel 1850* [CW]). In spring 1839, accepting that he would never complete *The Recluse* and intending that his autobiographical poem should be published posthumously as an independent work, Wordsworth revised it for the last time; and his daughter Dora copied this version (carelessly) into notebooks known collectively as MS E or DC MS 145. Edited by Wordsworth's nephew Christopher with changes imposed by the executors (see *NCPrel*, 526), MS E provided the copytext for the first edition of the poem, published by the firm of Edward Moxon in July 1850, three months after the poet's death. Only as published did the poem acquire a proper title, though it was chosen by Mary Wordsworth and the executors: *The Prelude, or Growth of a Poet's Mind; An Autobiographical Poem*. In all three of the versions that are currently accepted as textually distinct—in two parts, thirteen books, and fourteen books—the poem is now universally known as *The Prelude*.

Three points about *The Prelude* must be emphasized. First, although it is autobiographical in content, the narrative is neither chronologically linear nor strictly factual: it offers an *interpretation*, not a transcript, of Wordsworth's experiences, and selected ones at that. In book 9, for example, Wordsworth includes the excursive story of the doomed French lovers Vaudracour and Julia, but passes over in silence his own relationship with Annette Vallon in France in 1792 (see Biographical and Topographical Glossary and the note to 9.551): dictating lines on that subject, after he had married Mary Hutchinson in 1802, would doubtless have been awkward, and its eventual appearance in print would have caused scandal. The following chart indicates the complex relation between the poem's structure and the chronology of the events it recounts:

TITLE OF BOOK	PRINCIPAL BIOGRAPHICAL REFERENCES WITH DATES (SOMETIMES SPECULATIVE)
1: "Introduction— Childhood and School-time"	Decision to move to Grasmere (1799); theme of his "philosophic song" (1799–1804); early childhood in Cockermouth (1770–79); schooldays in Hawkshead (1779–ca. 1787)
2: "School-time (Continued)"	Schooldays in Hawkshead (1779–87) and return visit (1799)
3: "Residence at Cambridge"	Undergraduate years at St. John's College, Cambridge (1787–91)
4: "Summer vacation"	Summer vacation in Lake District, encounter with discharged soldier (1788)
5: "Books"	Mother's death (March 1778); first arrival at Hawkshead (May 1779); sight of drowned man (June 1799); friendship with John Fleming at Hawkshead (ca. 1783)

6: "Cambridge and the Alps"	Winter at Cambridge (1788–89); decision not to study for honors degree (late 1789); plan of *The Recluse* (34th birthday, April 7, 1804); Coleridge's departure for Malta (April 1804); departure from Cambridge (January 1791); summer walking tour with Robert Jones (July–October 1790)
7: "Residence in London"	Composition of "glad preamble" (November 1799); decision to expand *Prelude* from 5 books, copying of books 1–5 for Coleridge (March 1804); departure from Cambridge (January 1791); residence in London (conflating three periods, early 1791, ca. December 1792–mid 1793, ca. February–August 1795); visit to imprisoned John Hatfield (August 16, 1803); first visit to southern England (Cambridge, October 1787); visit to Bartholomew Fair (September 7, 1802)
8: "Retrospect: Love of Nature Leading to Love of Mankind"	Ann Tyson's story (between 1779 and 1787); sojourn with Dorothy in Goslar (October 6, 1798–ca. February 23, 1799); visit with brother John to Den of Yordas, Yorkshire (between May 19 and June 5, 1800)
9: "Residence in France"	Sojourn in London (January–May 1791); voyage to Paris, then Orléans (late November–December 6, 1791); friendship with Michel Beaupuy in Blois (February–September or October 1792)
10: "Residence in France and French Revolution"	Return to Paris, witnessing of political turmoil (October–November 1792); return to England in financial straits (late November or early December 1792); French declaration of war against England and subsequent Terror in France (February 1, 1793, and July 1793–July 1794); visit to Arras with Robert Jones (July 16, 1790); visit to cousins in Rampside (report of Robespierre's execution, ca. August 16, 1794); first poems (September or October 1784); deepening interest in politics under Beaupuy's tutelage (early 1792); first acquaintance with Coleridge, residence with Dorothy in Racedown, Dorset (September 1795–July 1797); Coleridge's sojourn in Sicily (August–September 1804)
11: "Imagination, How Impaired and Restored"	Moral crisis (spring 1796); love for Mary Hutchinson (1802); sight of gibbet (ca. 1775); summer with Dorothy and Mary (1787); father's illness and death (December 1783)
12: "Same Subject (Continued)"	Recovery from moral crisis (?summer–autumn 1796); solitary walking tour of Salisbury Plain (July or August 1793)

| 13: "Conclusion" | Ascent of Mt. Snowden with Robert Jones (summer 1791); residence with Dorothy in Racedown and Alfoxden (spring 1796–July 1798); Raisley Calvert's death and monetary legacy (January 1795); collaboration with Coleridge on *Lyrical Ballads* in Somerset (winter–summer 1798) |

Second, the public reception of *The Prelude* was confined almost entirely to the second half of the nineteenth century and later. With the notable exceptions of Coleridge and De Quincey, the poem lacked readers among Romantic-era writers. Published with an editorial note specifying its dates of composition as 1799–1805 (without reference to the later revisions), and taking the French Revolution as a central point of historical reference, the poem must have seemed anachronistic to Victorian readers, although it was respectfully reviewed and the 2000 copies of the first edition were sold within a year (see *NCPrel*, 547–59; Stephen Gill, *The Prelude*, 94–95). Moreover, Matthew Arnold's stated preference for Wordsworth's lyric poems (see Nineteenth-Century Responses, p. 575 below) may have, owing to Arnold's cultural authority, discouraged serious critical (as opposed to biographical) interest in *The Prelude* until the twentieth century, after de Selincourt's edition of 1926 (revised by Helen Darbishire in 1959) made the 1805 version available and revealed the poem's immense textual complexity. Of the critics whose discussions of *The Prelude* are excerpted here in Modern Criticism, Susan Wolfson addresses Wordsworth's use of blank verse, M. H. Abrams the poem's overall narrative and conceptual structure, Paul de Man an anxiously self-questioning tendency in Wordsworth's rhetoric, Alan Liu the repression of historical consciousness by the exaltation of nature in book 6, and Simon Jarvis Wordsworth's difficulty in representing his experience of London in books 7 and 8.

Third, there is no "definitive" textual state of *The Prelude*. The two faircopies of *Prel 1799* (MSS U and V) are not identical, and both contain Wordsworth's post-1799 revisions. The two faircopies of *Prel 1805* (MSS A and B) are also not identical, and both contain revisions (themselves not identical) of 1818–20. The first edition, although reflecting Wordsworth's final revisions, was set from an inaccurately copied manuscript (MS E) and included emendations not authorized by the poet himself, while the two faircopies of *Prel 1850* (MSS D and E) are separated by seven years and differ significantly from each other. Thus editors who wish to recover a particular version of *The Prelude* from the manuscripts, as opposed to merely reprinting the first printed edition, must construct a text, reconciling divergent readings (or privileging one over another) and ignoring later revisions. For the reason noted above, *The Prelude* presents a particular challenge for an edition that presents texts in the versions first received by the poet's contemporaries. Since the 1970s a critical consensus has emerged in favor of *Prel 1805* as the most artistically accomplished and ideologically palatable of the three canonical versions of the poem (although Donald Reiman in "The Cornell Wordsworth and the Norton *Prelude*" has defended *Prel 1850* against its detractors). The present edition offers the 1805–06 version of the "Poem to Coleridge" because it was the version read by Coleridge himself.

All previous critical editions of *Prel 1805* are based on MS A (although inevitably with occasional readings supplied from the more complete MS B), as it was written first and was more thoroughly revised by Wordsworth himself, and therefore likely to be "the more consistently reliable index of his preferences" than MS B (*Prel 1805* [CW], 1:61–62). The text in this Norton Critical Edition, in contrast, is based on MS B, the one that Coleridge actually

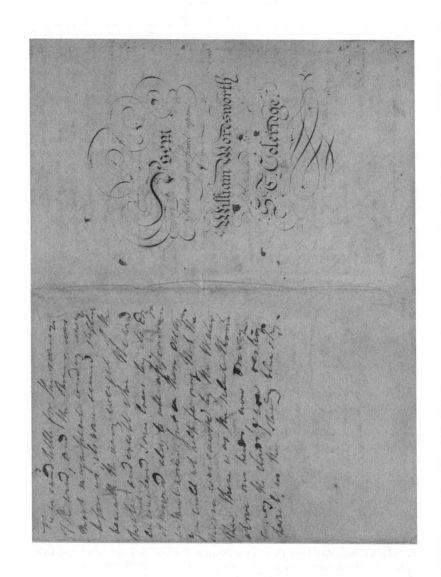

read and annotated in early 1807. But because, especially in an edition meant for classroom use, the generally light and sometimes misleading punctuation of the manuscript would undoubtedly create obstacles to comprehension of the poem's content, punctuation has been supplied, where the editor thought it warranted, from MS A (most frequently) or editorially. (All "reading texts" of the poem, as in *NCPrel* and CW, supplement the original punctuation.) Although exigencies of space preclude inclusion of a complete list of such emendations, all those *not* taken from MS A are listed at the end of the poem, so that changes without manuscript authorization will be recognizable. The spelling in the manuscript is preserved—with two important exceptions—and readers will observe Mary Wordsworth's tendency, characteristic of the period, to capitalize many common nouns. The exceptions are the consistent expansion of ampersands to *and*, and of the preterite verb ending *'d* to *ed* (voiced syllables being indicated as *èd*). The rationale for the latter emendation is that both MSS A and B are inconsistent in their practice (e.g., 6.244: *Exposed* in A, *Expos'd* in B; 9.837: *Arriv'd* in A, *Arrived* in B; 12.78: *perceiv'd* in A, *perceived* in B) and that the choice between *'d* and *ed* appears to have been neither authorial nor of significance to Mary or Dorothy. Overall, however, editorial intervention in the present text is much lighter than in *NCPrel*.

Poem
Title not yet fixed upon
by
William Wordsworth
Addressed to S. T. Coleridge†

Book First

INTRODUCTION, CHILDHOOD & SCHOOL TIME

Oh there is blessing in this gentle breeze
That blows from the green fields and from the clouds
And from the sky: it beats against my cheek
And seems half conscious of the joy it gives.
5 O welcome Messenger! O welcome Friend[1]
A Captive greets thee, coming from a house
Of bondage, from yon City's walls set free,
A prison where he hath been long immured.[2]
Now I am free, enfranchised and at large,
10 May fix my habitation where I will.
What dwelling shall receive me? In what Vale

† Reprinted by permission of the Wordsworth Trust.
1. STC. WW probably began composing lines 1–54, which he called the "glad preamble" (7.1–4), on November, 18, 1799, the date he determined to reside in Grasmere with DW, and he added them to *The Prelude* in January 1804 (John Alban Finch, "Wordsworth's Two-Handed Engine").
2. An echo of Exodus 3.14: "the Lord had brought us out from Egypt, from the home of bondage." WW had lived in London, a city he found uncongenial, in February–August 1795, and in the German town of Goslar, whose "melancholy Walls" he mentions in 8.348, in October 1798–February 1799. But he is probably also alluding, as at 2.466–67, to STC's description in *Frost at Midnight* (1798) of his own childhood "In the great city, pent mid cloisters dim" (line 57).

Shall be my harbour? Underneath what grove
Shall I take up my home, and what sweet stream
Shall with its murmur lull me to my rest?
15 The earth is all before me: with a heart
Joyous, nor scared at its own liberty
I look about, and should the guide I chuse
Be nothing better than a wandering cloud
I cannot miss my way.[3] I breathe again;
20 Trances of thought and mountings of the mind
Come fast upon me: it is shaken off,
As by miraculous gift 'tis shaken off,
That burthen of my own unnatural self,
The heavy weight of many a weary day
25 Not mine, and such as were not made for me.[4]
Long months of peace (if such bold word accord
With any promises of human life)
Long months of ease and undisturbed delight
Are mine in prospect: whither shall I turn
30 By road or pathway or through open field
Or shall a twig or any floating thing
Upon the river point me out my course?
            Enough that I am free; for months to come
May dedicate myself to chosen tasks;[5]
35 May quit the tiresome sea, and dwell on shore,
If not a settler on the soil, at least
To drink wild water, and to pluck green herbs
And gather fruits fresh from their native bough.
Nay more, if I may trust myself, this hour
40 Hath brought a gift that consecrates my joy;
For I, methought, while the sweet breath of Heaven
Was blowing on my body felt within
A corresponding mild creative breeze,
A vital breeze which travelled gently on
45 O'er things which it had made, and is become
A tempest, a redundant[6] energy
Vexing its own creation. 'Tis a power
That does not come unrecognised, a storm,
Which breaking up a long continued frost
50 Brings with it vernal promises, the hope
Of active days, of dignity and thought,
Of prowess in an honourable field,
Pure passions, virtue, knowledge and delight,
The holy life of music and of verse.[7]

---

3. An allusion to the last lines of *Paradise Lost* 12.646–49: "The World was all before them, where
to choose / Thir place of rest, and Providence thir guide: / They hand in hand with wandring
steps and slow / Through Eden took thir solitarie way." The *wandering cloud* may also allude to
the pillar of cloud in which, in Exodus 13:21–22, the Lord guides the Israelites out of Egypt.
4. Cf. *Tintern Abbey*, lines 41–43: "the heavy and the weary weight / Of all this unintelligible
world / Is lighten'd."
5. MS M reads, "Enough that I am free, embrace to day / An uncontroul'd enfranchisement; for
months / To come may live a life of chosen tasks" (*Prel 1805* [CW], 1:1256).
6. Excessive, exuberant.
7. A reference to *The Recluse*, which WW had planned in 1798 but deferred writing.

55   Thus far, O Friend! did I, not used to make
        A present joy the matter of my Song,
        Pour out, that day, my soul in measured strains,
        Even in the very words which I have here
        Recorded: to the open fields I told
60   A prophecy: poetic numbers came
        Spontaneously, and clothed in priestly robes
        My spirit, thus singled out, as it might seem
        For holy services: great hopes were mine;
        My own voice cheared me, and, far more, the mind's
65   Internal echo of the imperfect sound:
        To both I listened, drawing from them both
        A chearful confidence in things to come.
                Whereat being not unwilling now to give
        A respite to this passion, I paced on
70   Gently, with careless steps, and came erelong
        To a green shady place where down I sate
        Beneath a tree, slackening my thoughts by choice
        And settling into gentler happiness.
        'Twas Autumn, and a calm and placid day,
75   With warmth as much as needed, from a sun
        Two hours declined towards the west, a day
        With silver clouds, and sunshine on the grass
        And, in the sheltered grove where I was couched,
        A perfect stillness. On the ground I lay
80   Passing through many thoughts, yet mainly such
        As to myself pertained. I made a choice
        Of one sweet Vale whither my steps should turn
        And saw, methought, the very house[8] and fields
        Present before my eyes: nor did I fail
85   To add, meanwhile, assurance of some work
        Of glory, there forthwith to be begun,
        Perhaps, too, there performed. Thus long I lay
        Cheared by the genial pillow of the earth
        Beneath my head, soothed by a sense of touch
90   From the warm ground, that balanced me [else lost][9]
        Entirely, seeing nought, nought hearing, save
        When here and there, about the grove of Oaks
        Where was my bed, an acorn from the trees
        Fell audibly, and with a startling sound.
95   Thus occupied in mind I lingered here
        Contented, nor rose up until the sun
        Had almost touched the horizon, bidding then
        A farewell to the City left behind,[1]
        Even on the strong temptation of that hour
100   And with its chance equipment, I resolved
        To journey towards the Vale which I had chosen.

8. Dove Cottage; *Vale*: Grasmere, to which WW and DW had moved in December 1799.
9. A later insertion, possibly from the 1818–20 revision. MS M reads "though lost."
1. Probably a reference to Goslar, Germany, where WW had spent the winter of 1798–99 with
   DW and composed *Prel 1799*. See also 8.345–53.

It was a splendid evening: and my soul
Did once again make trial of her strength
Restored to her afresh, nor did she want
105 Eolian[2] visitations; but the harp
Was soon defrauded; and the banded host
Of harmony dispersed in straggling sounds
And lastly utter silence. "Be it so,
It is an injury," said I, "to this day
110 To think of any thing but present joy."
So like a Peasant I pursued my road
Beneath the evening sun; nor had one wish
Again to bend the sabbath of that time
To a servile yoke.[3] What need of many words?
115 A pleasant loitering journey, through two days
Continued, brought me to my hermitage.[4]
            I spare to speak, my Friend, of what ensued,
The admiration and the love, the life
In common things, the endless store of things
120 Rare, or at least so seeming, every day
Found all about me in one neighbourhood,
The self-congratulation,[5] the complete
Composure, and the happiness entire.
But speedily a longing in me rose
125 To brace myself to some determined aim,
Reading or thinking, either to lay up
New stores, or rescue from decay the old
By timely interference, I had hopes
Still higher, that I might with outward life
130 Endue and station in a visible home
Some portion of those phantoms of conceit[6]
That had been floating loose about so long,
And to such Beings temperately deal forth
The many feelings that oppressed my heart.
135 But I have been discouraged: gleams of light
Flash often from the East, then disappear
And mock me with a sky that ripens not
Into a steady morning: if my mind,
Remembering the sweet promise of the past,
140 Would gladly grapple with some noble theme,
Vain is her wish; where'er she turns she finds

2. Wind-borne (from Aeolus, Greek god of wind). The eolian harp, a stringed instrument that produces sounds when the wind blows over it, became in Romantic poetry a symbol of the inspired mind. STC's *Effusion XXXV* [*The Eolian Harp*] and *Dejection: An Ode* include notable uses of the image.
3. A phrase from Milton, *Paradise Regained* 4.102.
4. After arranging to rent Dove Cottage, WW and DW left Sockburn-on-Tees in northeastern England, where they had been living with the Hutchinsons for seven months, on December 17, 1799, and arrived at Dove Cottage probably on December 20. In *Prel 1850* WW changed "two days" to "three days."
5. Rejoicing (a sense of *congratulation* current until the end of the nineteenth century).
6. At an indeterminable stage WW inserted the line "For discipline and honour, a fair troop" after line 130 and altered line 131 to "Secluded from those phantoms of conceit," and then further revised these lines to "For permanent communion a fair band / Selected from those phantom[s of conceit]."

Impediments from day to day renewed.
　　　　And now it would content me to yield up
Those lofty hopes a while for present gifts
145 Of humbler industry.[7] But, O dear Friend!
The Poet, gentle creature as he is,
Hath, like the Lover, his unruly times;
His fits when he is neither sick nor well,
Though no distress be near him but his own
150 Unmanageable thoughts. The mind itself,
The meditative mind, best pleased, perhaps,
While she, as duteous as the mother dove,
Sits brooding,[8] lives not always to that end;
But hath less quiet instincts, goadings on
155 That drive her, as in trouble through the groves.
With me is now such passion, which I blame
No otherwise than as it lasts too long.
　　　　When, as becomes a Man who would prepare
For such a glorious work, I through myself
160 Make rigorous inquisition, the report
Is often chearing, for I neither seem
To lack that first great gift! the vital soul,
Nor general truths which are themselves species[9]
Of Elements and Agents, Under-powers,
165 Subordinate helpers of the living mind.
Nor am I naked in external things,
Forms, images;[1] nor numerous other aids
Of less regard, though won perhaps with toil,
And needful to build up a Poet's praise.
170 Time, place, and manners; these I seek, and these
I find in plenteous store; but no where such
As may be singled out with steady choice;
No little band of yet remembered names
Whom I, in perfect confidence, might hope
175 To summon back from lonesome banishment
And make them inmates in the hearts of men
Now living, or to live in times to come.
Sometimes, mistaking vainly, as I fear,
Proud spring-tide swellings for a regular sea
180 I settle on some British theme, some old
Romantic tale, by Milton left unsung,[2]
More often, resting at some gentle place
Within the groves of Chivalry, I pipe
Among the Shepherds, with reposing Knights
185 Sit by a Fountain-side, and hear their tales

7. I.e., lyric and shorter narrative poems.
8. An allusion to the muse invoked in *Paradise Lost* 1.19–22: "Thou from the first / Wast present, and with mighty wings outspread / Dove-like satst brooding on the vast Abyss / And mad'st it pregnant." Milton, however, was referring not to the mind but to the Holy Spirit.
9. Substituted in MS B for the original reading "a sort," presumably to conform to the plural nouns.
1. Mental representations of external objects or scenes.
2. A reference to Milton's decision, recorded in *Paradise Lost* 9.25–41, not to write a romance epic about knights in battles or tournaments.

[Of hard adventure brought to happy end
And recompensed by faithful Lady's love].[3]
Sometimes, more sternly moved, I would relate
How vanquished Mithridates northward passed,
190 And, hidden in the cloud of years, became
That Odin, Father of the Race by whom
Perished the Roman Empire:[4] how the Friends
And Followers of Sertorius, out of Spain
Flying, found shelter in the Fortunate isles;[5]
195 And left their usages, their arts, and laws
To disappear by a slow gradual death;
To dwindle and to perish one by one
Starved in those narrow bounds: but not the Soul
Of Liberty, which fifteen hundred years
200 Survived, and when the European came
With skill and power that could not be withstood,
Did like a pestilence maintain its hold,
And wasted down by glorious death that Race
Of natural Heroes. Or I would record
205 How in tyrannic times some unknown Man,
Unheard of in the Chronicles of Kings,
Suffered in silence for the love of truth:
How that one Frenchman[6] through continued force
Of meditation on the inhuman deeds
210 Of the first Conquerors of the Indian Isles,
Went single in his ministry across
The Ocean, not to comfort the Oppressed,
But, like a thirsty wind, to roam about,
Withering the Oppresser: how Gustavus[7] found
215 Help at his need in Dalecarlia's Mines;
How Wallace fought for Scotland, left the name
Of Wallace to be found like a wild flower,
All over his dear Country, left the deeds
Of Wallace,[8] like a Family of Ghosts
220 To people the steep rocks and river banks,

3. Lines 186–87, which do not appear in MS A, were inserted into MS B in pencil at an indeter-
minable date. WW elaborates on the traditional themes of medieval romance narratives before
turning to figures associated in one way or another with liberty.
4. In Norse mythology Odin is the god of war and wisdom; but in a legend that WW may have
encountered in Edward Gibbons's *Decline and Fall of the Roman Empire* (1776–88), chap. 10,
or Paul-Henri Mallet's *Northern Antiquities* (1770), chap. 4 (*Reading 1800–15*, nos. 176 and
267), Odin is identified as a tribal leader from the Black Sea region who after Mithridates's
defeat led the Goths to the safety of Sweden to plot eventual revenge against the Romans.
Mithridates: king of Pontus (120–63 B.C.E.) in Asia Minor and a formidable enemy of the
Roman Republic until his defeat by the Roman general Pompey the Great in 66 B.C.E.
5. Sertorius (ca. 123–73 B.C.E.), Roman military commander in Spain whose followers, according
to legend, fled after his assassination to the Canary Islands (*Fortunate Isles*), where they flour-
ished until the islands were colonized by the Spanish in the fifteenth century.
6. WW's note in *Prel 1850*: "Dominique de Gourgues, a French gentleman who went in 1568 to
Florida to avenge the massacre of the French by the Spaniards there." Settled in 1564 by
French Protestants, Fort Caroline (now Jacksonville) was captured in 1565 by Spanish forces
and then recaptured by French forces under de Gourgues (ca. 1530–1593).
7. Gustavus Vasa (1496–1560) raised an army in the Swedish mining district of Dalarna (*Dalecarlia*,
line 215) and led a successful rebellion against Danish rule in 1521–23, after which he was made
king of Sweden. In 1798 WW had read Henry Brooke's 1739 verse tragedy about Vasa (*WL*, 1:210).
8. Sir William Wallace (ca. 1270–1305), Scottish knight and patriot, captured by English forces
near Glasgow and executed in London. During a walking tour of Scotland with WW in

Her natural sanctuaries, with a local soul
Of independence and stern liberty.
Sometimes it suits me better to shape out
Some Tale from my own heart, more near akin
225 To my own passions and habitual thoughts,
Some variegated story, in the main
Lofty, with interchange of gentler things;
But deadening admonitions will succeed,
And the whole beauteous Fabric seems to lack
230 Foundation, and withal, appears throughout
Shadowy and unsubstantial. Then, last wish,
My last and favourite aspiration! then
I yearn towards some philosophic Song
Of Truth that cherishes[9] our daily life;
235 With meditations passionate from deep
Recesses in man's heart, immortal verse
Thoughtfully fitted to the Orphean lyre;[1]
But from this awful burthen I full soon
Take refuge, and beguile myself with trust
240 That mellower years will bring a riper mind
And clearer insight. Thus from day to day
I live a mockery of the brotherhood
Of vice and virtue, with no skill to part
Vague longing that is bred by want of power
245 From paramount impulse not to be withstood,
A timorous capacity from prudence;
From circumspection, infinite delay.
Humility and modest awe themselves
Betray me, serving often for a cloak
250 To a more subtile selfishness, that now
Doth lock my functions up in blank reserve,[2]
Now dupes me by an over anxious eye
That with a false activity beats off
Simplicity and self-presented truth
255 —Ah! better far than this, to stray about
Voluptuously through fields and rural walks,
And ask no record of the hours given up
To vacant musing, unreproved neglect
Of all things, and deliberate holiday:
260 Far better never to have heard the name
Of zeal and just ambition than to live
Thus baffled by a mind that every hour

August–September 1803, DW had observed numerous memorials to Wallace (*DWJ*, 1:228).
WW later used lines 216–22 as the epigraph to *Composed at Cora Linn* (p. 541 below).
9. Cheers, encourages.
1. A reference to the project of writing the central, philosophical section of *The Recluse*, about
which WW urgently sought STC's advice in March 1804 (*WL*, 1:452, 464). *Immortal verse . . .
Orphean lyre*: WW adopts phrases from Milton's *L'Allegro*, line 137, and *Paradise Lost* 3.17. In
Greek myth Orpheus is a poet and musician of such skill that he can spellbind wild animals.
2. Fruitless inactivity. *Prel 1850* (CW) notes a possible recollection of Alexander Pope, *The First
Epistle of the First Book of Horace Imitated* (1738), lines 39–42: "So slow th'unprofitable
Moments roll, / That lock up all the Functions of my soul; / That keep me from Myself; and still
delay / Life's instant business to a future day."

Turns recreant to her task, takes heart again,
Then feels immediately some hollow thought
265 Hang like an interdict[3] upon her hopes.
This is my lot; for either still I find
Some imperfection in the chosen theme,
Or see of absolute accomplishment
Much wanting, so much wanting in myself,
270 That I recoil and droop, and seek repose
In indolence from vain perplexity,
Unprofitably travelling towards the grave,
Like a false Steward who hath much received
And renders nothing back.[4]—Was it for this
275 That one, the fairest of all Rivers, loved
To blend his murmurs with my Nurse's song
And from his alder shades and rocky falls,
And from his fords and shallows, sent a voice
That flowed along my dreams?[5] For this didst Thou,
280 O Derwent! travelling over the green Plains
Near my sweet Birth-place,[6] didst thou, beauteous Stream,
Make ceaseless music through the night and day,
Which with its steady cadence tempering
Our human waywardness, composed my thoughts
285 To more than infant softness, giving me,
Among the fretful dwellings of mankind,
A knowledge, a dim earnest of the calm
Which Nature breathes among the hills and groves.
    When having left his Mountains, to the Towers
290 Of Cockermouth that beauteous River came,
Behind my Father's House he passed, close by,
Along the margin of our Terrace walk.
He was a Playmate whom we dearly loved.
Oh! many a time have I, a five years' Child,
295 A naked Boy, in one delightful Rill,
A little Mill-race severed from his stream,
Made one long bathing of a summer's day,
Basked in the sun, and plunged, and basked again,
Alternate all a summer's day, or coursed
300 Over the sandy fields, leaping through groves
Of yellow grunsel, or when crag and hill,
The woods, and distant Skiddaw's[7] lofty height,
Were bronzed with a deep radiance, stood alone
Beneath the sky, as if I had been born

3. Prohibition.
4. A reference to the parable of the servant who is rebuked for burying rather than investing the silver pieces his master gives him (Matthew 25.14–30).
5. *Prel 1799* had begun with this question. The river, identified in line 280, is the Derwent, which flows behind the house in Cockermouth in which WW was born and spent his early childhood. For further instances of the use of a river as a figure for WW's moral and intellectual development, see the note on 13.184.
6. *Birth-place*: a quotation from STC's *Frost at Midnight*, line 33, which WW later enclosed in quotation marks.
7. The fourth highest mountain in the Lake District (3,053 feet), Skiddaw is located nine miles east of Cockermouth; *grunsel*: changed in *Prel 1850* to "ragwort," i.e., ragweed.

305   On Indian Plains,[8] and from my Mother's hut
      Had run abroad in wantonness, to sport,
      A naked Savage, in the thunder shower.
            Fair seed-time had my soul, and I grew up
      Fostered alike by beauty and by fear;
310   Much favored in my birth-place, and no less
      In that beloved Vale[9] to which, erelong,
      I was transplanted. Well I call to mind,
      ('Twas at an early age, ere I had seen
      Nine summers) when upon the mountain slope
315   The frost and breath of frosty wind had snapped
      The last autumnal crocus, 'twas my joy
      To wander half the night among the Cliffs
      And the smooth Hollows, where the woodcocks ran
      Along the open turf. In thought and wish,
320   That time, my shoulder all with springes hung,
      I was a fell[1] destroyer. On the heights
      Scudding away from snare to snare, I plied
      My anxious visitation, hurrying on,
      Still hurrying, hurrying onward. Moon and stars
325   Were shining o'er my head; I was alone
      And seemed to be a trouble to the peace
      That was among them. Sometimes it befel
      In these night-wanderings, that a strong desire
      O'erpowered my better reason, and the Bird
330   Which was the captive of another's toils[2]
      Became my prey; and when the deed was done,
      I heard among the solitary hills
      Low breathings, coming after me, and sounds
      Of undistinguishable motion, steps
335   Almost as silent as the turf they trod.
            Nor less in spring-time when [on][3] southern banks
      The shining sun had from her knot of leaves
      Decoyed the primrose-flower, and when the Vales
      And woods were warm, was I a plunderer then
340   In the high places, on the lonesome peaks
      Where'er, among the mountains and the winds,
      The Mother Bird had built her lodge. Though mean
      My object, and inglorious, yet the end
      Was not ignoble.[4] Oh! when I have hung
345   Above the Raven's nest, by knots of grass
      And half-inch fissures in the slippery rock
      But ill sustained, and almost, as it seemed,
      Suspended by the blast which blew amain,

8. Plains of North America (a reference to American Indians); *as* (line 304): as if.
9. Esthwaite Vale in the southern Lake District, location of Hawkshead, where WW attended the Grammar School from 1779 to 1787 (see Biographical and Topographical Glossary).
1. Fierce; *springes*: snares for catching small game.
2. WW exploits two meanings of *toils*: "exertions" and "snares" (the second now obsolete).
3. Omitted in MS B (where a word has been erased and its space left blank), though present in MS A.
4. "Ravens are a danger to lambs; the boy's 'inglorious' purpose was to claim the bounty paid by the parish to those who destroyed their nests" (*PPrel*). See also 8.397–402.

Shouldering the naked crag; oh! at that time,
350 While on the perilous ridge I hung alone,
With what strange utterance did the loud dry wind
Blow through my ears! the sky seemed not a sky
Of earth, and with what motion moved the clouds!
        The mind of man is framed even like the breath
355 And harmony of music. There is a dark
Invisible workmanship that reconciles
Discordant elements, and makes them move
In one society. Ah me! that all
The terrors, all the early miseries,
360 Regrets, vexations, lassitudes, that all
The thoughts and feelings which have been infused
Into my mind should ever have made up
The calm existence that is mine when I
Am worthy of myself. Praise to the end!
365 Thanks likewise for the means. But I believe
That Nature, oftentimes, when she would frame
A favored Being, from his earliest dawn
Of infancy doth open out the clouds,
As at the touch of lightening,[5] seeking him
370 With gentlest visitation: not the less,
Though haply aiming at the self-same end,
Does it delight her sometimes to employ
Severer interventions,[6] ministry
More palpable, and so she dealt with me.
375   One evening (surely I was led by her)
I went alone into a Shepherd's Boat,
A Skiff that to a Willow-tree was tied,
Within a rocky Cove, its usual home.
'Twas by the shores [of] Patterdale,[7] a Vale
380 Wherein I was a Stranger, thither come,
A School-boy Traveller, at the Holidays.
Forth rambled from the Village-Inn alone
No sooner had I sight of this small Skiff,
Discovered thus by unexpected chance,
385 Than I unloosed her tether, and embarked.
The moon was up, the Lake was shining clear
Among the hoary mountains: from the shore
I pushed, and struck the oars, and struck again
In cadence, and my little Boat moved on
390 Even like a Man who walks with stately step
Though bent on speed.[8] It was an act of stealth
And troubled pleasure: nor without the voice
Of mountain-echoes did my Boat move on,

5. Lightning.
6. Severer, for example, than the "secret ministry of cold" in STC's *Frost at Midnight* (1798), line 77, a passage WW is likely to have had in mind.
7. At the southern end of the lake Ullswater in the northeastern Lake District. The preposition *of* (line 379) is present in MS A.
8. An allusion (as in *The Female Vagrant*, line 33) to *Paradise Lost* 12.1–2: "As one who in his journey bates [halts] at Noon, / Though bent on speed."

Leaving behind her still on either side
395   Small circles glittering idly in the moon
Until they melted all into one track
Of sparkling light.⁹ A rocky steep uprose
Above the Cavern of the Willow-tree,
And now as suited one who proudly rowed
400   With his best skill, I fixed a steady view
Upon the top of that same craggy ridge,
The bound of the horizon; for behind
Was nothing but the stars and the grey sky.
She was an elfin Pinnace;¹ lustily
405   I dipped my oars into the silent Lake,
And, as I rose upon the stroke, my Boat
Went heaving through the water, like a Swan,
When from behind that craggy Steep, till then
The bound of the horizon, a huge Cliff,
410   [As if with voluntary power instinct,
Upreared its head: I struck, and struck again,
And, growing still in stature, the huge Cliff]²
Rose up between me and the stars, and still,
With measured motion, like a living thing,
415   Strode after me. With trembling hands I turned,
And through the silent water stole my way
Back to the Cavern of the Willow-tree.
There in her mooring-place, I left my Bark
And through the meadows went with grave³
420   And serious thoughts: and after I had seen
That spectacle, for many days my brain
Worked with a dim and undetermined sense
Of unknown modes of being: in my thoughts
There was a darkness, call it solitude,
425   Or blank desertion, no familiar shapes
Of hourly objects, images of trees,
Of sea, or sky, no colours of green fields;
But huge and mighty Forms that do not live
Like living men moved slowly through my mind
430   By day and were the trouble of my dreams.
Wisdom and Spirit of the Universe!⁴

9. Probably an allusion to the "tracks of shining white" made by the water snakes in STC's *Rime of the Ancient Mariner* (1798), line 265 (*NCPrel*).
1. A small boat.
2. These lines are present in MS A and omitted in MS B, presumably accidentally. The *huge Cliff* may have been Black Crag (2,716 feet high, west of Ullswater), which would appear from behind Stybarrow Crag (a cliff bordering the lake) as one rowed away from the shore; or it may have been Place Fell (2,156 feet, east of the lake).
3. WW later inserted "homeward" before "went" in MS A to make this line pentameter.
4. Lines 431–92 were published under the title *Growth of Genius from the Influences of Natural Objects, on the Imagination in Boyhood, and Early Youth* in STC's periodical *The Friend*, no. 19 (December 28, 1809), and reprinted by WW under the title *Influence of Natural Objects in calling forth and strengthening the Imagination in Boyhood and early Youth; From an unpublished Poem* in *P 1815*. In an introductory note STC described the lines as having been "extracted, with the Author's permission, from an unpublished Poem on the growth and revolutions of an individual mind, by WORDSWORTH" (*Friend*, 2:258–59). STC concluded his introductory note by quoting a variant of lines 37–39 of his poem *To W. Wordsworth* (reprinted below in Nineteenth-Century Responses).

Thou Soul that art the Eternity of Thought!
And giv'st to forms and images a breath
And everlasting motion! not in vain,
435   By day or star-light thus from my first dawn
Of Childhood didst Thou intertwine for me
The passions that build up our human Soul,
Not with the mean and vulgar works of Man,
But with high objects, with enduring things,
440   With life and nature, purifying thus
The elements of feeling and of thought,
And sanctifying by such discipline
Both pain and fear, until we recognise
A grandeur in the beatings of the heart.
445   Nor was this fellowship vouchsafed to me
With stinted kindness. In November days
When vapours, rolling down the valleys, made
A lonely scene more lonesome; among woods
At noon, and 'mid the calm of summer nights,
450   When by the margin of the trembling Lake,
Beneath the gloomy hills I homeward went
In solitude, such intercourse was mine;
'Twas mine among the fields both day and night,
And by the waters all the summer long.
455   —And in the frosty season, when the sun
Was set, and, visible for many a mile,
The cottage windows through the twilight blazed,
I heeded not the summons:—happy time
It was indeed for all of us, to me
460   It was a time of rapture: clear and loud
The village clock tolled six; I wheeled about,
Proud and exalting, like an untired horse,
That cares not for its home.—All shod with steel
We hissed along the polished ice, in games
465   Confederate, imitative of the chace,
And woodland pleasures, the resounding horn,
The Pack loud bellowing, and the hunted hare.
So through the darkness and the cold we flew
And not a voice was idle: with the din,
470   Meanwhile, the precipices rang aloud,
The leafless trees, and every icy crag
Tinkled like iron, while the distant hills
Into the tumult sent an alien sound
Of melancholy, not unnoticed, while the stars,[5]
475   Eastward, were sparkling clear, and in the west
The orange sky of evening died away.
          Not seldom from the uproar I retired
Into a silent bay, or sportively
Glanced sideway, leaving the tumultuous throng,

5. An hexameter line.

480 To cut across the image of a star
That gleamed upon the ice; and oftentimes,
When we had given our bodies to the wind,
And all the shadowy banks on either side,
Came sweeping through the darkness, spinning still,
485 The rapid line of motion; then at once
Have I, reclining back upon my heels,
Stopped short, yet still the solitary Cliffs
Wheeled by me, even as if the earth had rolled
With visible motion her diurnal⁶ round;
490 Behind me did they stretch in solemn train
Feebler and feebler, and I stood and watched
Till all was tranquil as [a summer sea.]⁷
      Ye Presences of Nature, in the sky
Or on the earth! Ye Visions of the hills!
495 And Souls of lonely places! can I think
A vulgar hope was yours when Ye employed
Such ministry, when Ye through many a year
Haunting me thus among my boyish sports,
On caves and trees, upon the woods and hills,
500 Impressed upon all forms the characters⁸
Of danger or desire, and thus did make
The surface of the universal earth
With triumph, and delight, and hope, and fear
Work like a sea.
            Not uselessly employed,
505 I might pursue this theme through every change
Of exercise and play, to which the year
Did summon us in its delightful round.
—We were a noisy crew; the sun in heaven
Beheld not Vales more beautiful than ours
510 Nor saw a Race, in happiness and joy
More worthy of the fields where they were sown.
I would record with no reluctant voice
The woods of autumn and their hazel bowers
With milk-white clusters hung;⁹ the rod and line,
515 True symbol of the foolishness of hope
Which with its strong enchantment led us on
By rocks and pools, shut out from every star
All the green summer, to forlorn cascades
Among the windings of the mountain-brooks.
—Unfading recollections! at this hour
520 The heart is almost mine with which I felt,
From some hill-top, on sunny afternoons

6. Daily. WW's use of the word here recalls his own *A slumber did my spirit seal*, lines 7–8 ("Roll'd round in earth's diurnal course / With rocks and stones and trees") as well as *Paradise Lost* 7.22–23 ("Within the visible Diurnal Sphere; / Standing on Earth").
7. This line was originally left unfinished in MSS B and A. In MS M, *The Friend*, and later reprintings during WW's lifetime, the line ends "a summer sea"; but in the 1830s a revised ending, "a dreamless sleep," was inserted into MS A.
8. Marks, signs (as also at 6.570).
9. *NCPrel* suggests a reference to *Nutting*, which WW had composed in November–December 1798.

The Kite high up among the fleecy clouds
Pull at its chain¹ like an impatient Courser,
Or, from the meadows sent on gusty days
525 Beheld her breast the wind, then suddenly
Dashed headlong;—and rejected by the storm.
        Ye lowly Cottages in which we dwelt,
A ministration of your own was yours,
A sanctity, a safeguard, and a love!
530 Can I forget you, being as ye were
So beautiful among the pleasant fields
In which ye stood? Or can I here forget
The plain and seemly countenance with which
Ye dealt out your plain comforts? Yet had ye
535 Delights and exultations of your own.
Eager and never weary, we pursued
Our home amusements by the warm peat-fire
At evening; when with pencil and with slate,
In square divisions parcelled out, and all
540 With crosses and with cyphers scribbled o'er,²
We schemed and puzzled, head opposed to head,
In strife too humble to be named in verse.
Or round the naked Table, snow-white deal,
Cherry or maple, sate in close array
545 And to the combat, Lu or Whist, led on
A thick ribbed³ army, not as in the world
Neglected and ungratefully thrown by
Even for the very service they had wrought,
But husbanded through many a long campaign.
550 Uncouth assemblage was it where no few
Had changed their functions, some, plebean cards,⁴
Which Fate beyond the promise of their birth
Had glorified, and called to represent
The persons of departed Potentates.
555 Oh! with what echoes on [the]⁵ board they fell
Ironic Diamonds; Clubs, Hearts, Diamonds, Spades,
A congregation piteously akin.
Cheap matter did they give to boyish wit,
Those sooty Knaves, precipitated down
560 With scoffs and taunts, like Vulcan out of Heaven.
The paramount Ace, a moon in her eclipse,
Queens, gleaming through their splendor's last decay,
And Monarchs, surly at the wrongs sustained

1. Thus in MSS B and M; "reins" in MS A.
2. A mock-heroic description of tic-tac-toe (called noughts-and-crosses in Britain), adapting Milton's line "With Centric and Eccentric scribl'd o'er" (*Paradise Lost* 8.83).
3. "Refers probably to the thickening of the cards' edges through use" (*NCPrel*); *Lu*: a card game requiring three or more players. The mock-heroic description of the card game recalls those in William Cowper's *The Task* (1785) 4.214–19, and more particularly Alexander Pope's *The Rape of the Lock* (1714), canto 3. Lines 546–48 refer obliquely to the discharged soldier of whom WW writes in 4.363–503.
4. The numbered cards, as opposed to the court cards. *NCPrel* notes the borrowing from *The Rape of the Lock* 3.54: "Gain'd but one Trump and one Plebeian Card."
5. MS B reads "they," an error for "the," the reading in MS A.

By royal visages. Meanwhile abroad
565 The heavy rain was falling, or the frost
Raged bitterly with kean and silent tooth,
And, interrupting the impassioned game,
From Esthwaite's neighbouring Lake the splitting ice,
While it sank down towards the water, sent,
570 Among the meadows and the hills, its long
And dismal yellings, like the noise of Wolves
When they are howling round the Bothnic Main.[6]
         Nor sedulous[7] as I have been to trace
How Nature by extrinsic passion
575 Peopled my mind with beauteous forms or grand,[8]
And made me love them, may I well forget
How other pleasures have been mine, and joys
Of subtler origin; how I have felt
Not seldom, even in that tempestuous time,
580 Those hallowed and pure motions of the sense
Which seem in their simplicity, to own
An intellectual charm, that calm delight
Which, if I err not, surely must belong
To those first-born[9] affinities that fit
585 Our new existence to existing things
And, in our dawn of being, constitute
The bond of union betwixt life and joy.
         Yes, I remember, when the changeful earth,
And twice five seasons on my mind had stamped
590 The faces of the moving year, even then,
A Child, I held unconscious intercourse
With the eternal Beauty, drinking in
A pure organic pleasure from the lines
Of curling mist, or from the level plain
595 Of waters coloured by the steady clouds.
         The Sands of Westmorland, the Creeks and Bays
Of Cumbria's rocky limits, they can tell
How when the Sea threw off his evening shade
And to the Shepherd's huts[1] beneath the crags
600 Did send sweet notice of the rising moon,
How I have stood to fancies such as these,
Engrafted in the tenderness of thought,
A stranger, linking with the spectacle

6. The Baltic region. The following revised and expanded version of lines 568–71, of uncertain date, is inserted into the margins in MS B: "From Esthwaite's Lake the splitting ice sent forth, / Among the meadows and the hills, a long / And dismal outcry like the noise of wolves / Howling in troops along the Bothnic main / And sometimes not unlike the sound that issues / From out the deep chest of a lonely Bull / By no apparent enmity provoke / To bend his head and mutter with a voice / Sullenly answered by the hollow ground. / So growled the frozen element, or yelled / Startling the valley and our bright fire side." In 1818–20WW abandoned most of this revision (Prel 1805 [CW], 2:29).
7. Diligent. An allusion to Milton's justification of his epic subject in Paradise Lost 9.27–29: "Not sedulous by Nature to indite / Warrs, hitherto the onely Argument / Heroic deem'd."
8. I.e., how WW's mind during his childhood was filled involuntarily and unconsciously with images supplied by nature.
9. Innate.
1. Changed in Prel 1850 to "hut."

No conscious memory of a kindred sight,
605 And bringing with me no peculiar sense
Of quietness or peace, yet I have stood,
Even while mine eye has moved o'er three long leagues
Of shining water, gathering, as it seemed,
Through every hair-breadth of that field of light,
610 New pleasure, like a bee among the flowers.
            Thus often in those fits of vulgar joy[2]
Which through all seasons, on a Child's pursuits
Are prompt attendants, mid that giddy bliss
Which, like a tempest, works along the blood
615 And is forgotten; even then I felt[3]
Gleams like the flashing of a shield: the earth
And common face of Nature spake to me
Rememberable things: somethings, 'tis true,
By chance collisions, and quaint accidents
620 Like those ill-sorted unions, work supposed
Of evil-minded fairies, yet not vain,
Nor profitless, if haply they impressed
Collateral objects and appearances,
Albeit lifeless then, and doomed to sleep
625 Until maturer seasons called them forth
To impregnate and to elevate the mind.
—And if the vulgar joy by its own weight
Wearied itself out of the memory
The scenes which were a witness of that joy
630 Remained, in their substantial lineaments
Depicted on the brain, and to the eye
Were visible, a daily sight: and thus,
By the impressive discipline of fear,
By pleasure, and repeated happiness,
635 So frequently repeated, and by force
Of obscure feelings representative
Of joys that were forgotten, these same scenes,
So beauteous and majestic in themselves,
Though yet the day was distant, did at length
640 Become habitually dear; and all
Their hues and forms were by invisible links
Allied to the affections.
                    I began
My Story early, feeling as I fear,
The weakness of a human love, for days
645 Disowned by memory, ere the birth of Spring
Planting my snow-drops among the winter snows.
Nor will it seem to thee, my Friend! so prompt
In sympathy, that I have lengthened out
With fond and feeble tongue a tedious tale.
650 Meanwhile, my hope has been that I might fetch

2. An unreflective, nonintellectual pleasure, like the "coarser pleasures of my boyish days" described in *Tintern Abbey*, lines 64–72.
3. In MS B this line ends "gleams," an accidental anticipation of the beginning of the following line.

Invigorating thoughts from former years,
[Might fix the wavering balance of my mind,]⁴
And haply meet reproaches too, whose power
May spur me on, in manhood now mature
655 To honourable toil.⁵ Yet should these hopes
Be vain, and thus should neither I be taught
To understand myself, nor Thou to know
With better knowledge, how the heart was framed
Of him Thou loves't, need I dread from Thee
660 Harsh judgements, if I am so loth to quit
Those recollected hours that have the charm
Of visionary things, and lovely forms,
And sweet sensations that throw back our life
And almost make our Infancy itself
665 A visible scene on which the sun is shining.
        One end hereby at least hath been attained,
My mind hath been revived, and if this mood
Desert me not, I will forthwith bring down,
Through later years, the story of my life.
670 The road lies plain before me; 'tis a theme
Single, and of determined bounds; and hence
I chuse it rather, at this time, than work
Of ampler, or more varied argument,
[Where I might be discomfited, or lost
675 And certain hopes are with me that to thee
This labour will be welcome, honored Friend.]⁶

Book Second

SCHOOL TIME CONTINUED

Thus far, O Friend! have we, though leaving much
Unvisited, endeavoured to retrace
My life through its first years, and measured back
The way I travelled when I first began
5 To love the woods and fields: the passion yet
Was in its birth, sustained as might befal,
By nourishment that came unsought; for still,
From week to week, from month to month, we lived
A round of tumult: duly were our games
10 Prolonged in summer till the day-light failed;
No chair remained before the doors, the bench
And threshold steps were empty; fast asleep
The Labourer, and the old Man who had sate,
A later lingerer, yet the revelry

4. This line, supplied from MS A, was omitted in MS B, perhaps inadvertently.
5. I.e., writing the central section of *The Recluse*, as STC hoped WW would do. These lines were composed in February 1799.
6. The fair copy ends with line 673, but the terminal punctuation—a semicolon, changed in this edition to a comma as in MS A—implies that further lines were to be added. Lines 674–76 were inserted in the lower margin, possibly though not certainly during the 1818–20 revisions. The rest of this paragraph was composed in January 1804 and announces WW's intention to expand *The Prelude* rather than proceed with *The Recluse*.

15   Continued, and the loud uproar: at last,
     When all the ground was dark, and the huge clouds
     Were edged with twinkling stars, to bed we went
     With weary joints, and with a beating mind.[1]
     Ah! is there one who ever has been young
20   And needs a monitory voice to tame
     The pride of virtue, and of intellect?[2]
     And is there one, the wisest and the best
     Of all mankind, who does not sometimes wish
     For things which cannot be, who should not give,
25   If so he might, to duty and to truth
     The eagerness of infantine desire?
     A tranquillizing spirit presses now
     On my corporeal frame:[3] so wide appears
     The vacancy between me and those days,
30   Which yet have such self-presence in my mind
     That, sometimes, when I think of them I seem
     Two consciousnesses, conscious of myself
     And of some other Being. A grey stone
     Of native rock, left midway in the Square
35   Of our small market Village, was the home
     And centre of these joys, and when, returned
     After long absence,[4] thither I repaired
     I found that it was split, and gone to build
     A smart Assembly-room that perked and flared
40   With wash and rough cast, elbowing the ground
     Which had been ours.[5] But let the fiddle scream
     And be happy! yet, my Friends, I know
     That more than one of you will think, with me,
     Of those soft starry nights, and that old Dame
45   From whom the Stone was named who there had sate
     And watched her Table with its huxter's[6] wares
     Assiduous, through the length of sixty years.
     —We ran a boisterous race; the year span round
     With giddy motion. But the time approached
50   That brought with it a regular desire
     For calmer pleasures, when the beauteous forms
     Of Nature were collaterally attached

1. Perhaps a recollection of Prospero in Shakespeare's *Tempest* 4.1.162–63: "A turn or two I'll walk / To still my beating brain."
2. An obscure sentence that has been paraphrased variously. *NCPrel* suggests, "Can anyone who remembers the vitality of youth need to be warned not to overrate the qualities of age?" *Prel 1805* (CW) suggests, more precisely, "Can anyone who has had the experience of youth really require any further warning against moral and intellectual pride?"
3. Body. WW had used the phrase earlier in *Tintern Abbey*, line 45: "the breath of this corporeal frame."
4. WW returned to Hawkshead on November 2, 1799, during a walking tour with his brother John and STC, ten years after his last visit (*Chrono: EY*, 95, 276). On November 8 he remarked to DW on the "great change amongst the People since we were last there" (*WL*, 1:271).
5. The Hawkshead Town Hall, built in 1790; *wash and rough cast*: whitewash and stucco. As he elaborated in his *Description of the Scenery of the Lakes in the North of England* (1822), WW considered whitewashed buildings generally out of place in the Lake District (*Prose*, 2:215–17).
6. An archaic spelling of *huckster*, used here nonpejoratively in the sense of a "retailer of small goods, in a petty shop or booth, or at a stall" (*OED*); *old Dame*: identified as Nanny Holme, the stone in the Market Square having been known as Nanny's Stone (Thompson, 251–56).

And every boyish sport, less grateful[7] else,
And languidly pursued.
55   When summer came
It was the pastime of our afternoons
To beat along the Plain of Windermere
With rival oars, and the selected bourne[8]
Was now an Island, musical with birds
60 That sang for ever; now a Sister Isle,
Beneath the oak's umbrageous covert, sown
With lillies of the valley, like a field;
And now a third small Island where remained
An old stone Tablet, and a mouldered Cave,
65 A Hermit's history.[9] In such a race,
So ended, disappointment could be none,
Uneasiness, or pain, or jealousy;
We rested in the shade, all pleased alike,
Conquered and Conqueror. Thus the strength,[1]
70 And the vain-glory of superior skill
Were interfused with objects which subdued
And tempered them, and gradually produced
A quiet independence of the heart.
And to my Friend, who knows me, I may add,
75 Unapprehensive of reproof, that hence
Ensued a diffidence and modesty,
And I was taught to feel, perhaps too much,
The self-sufficing power of solitude.
     No delicate viands sapped our bodily strength;
80 More than we wished we knew the blessing then
Of vigorous hunger, for our daily meals
Were frugal, Sabine fare![2] and then, exclude
A little weekly stipend, and we lived
Through three divisions of the quartered year
85 In pennyless poverty. But now, to School
Returned from the half-yearly holidays,
We came with purses more profusely filled,[3]
Allowance which abundantly sufficed
To gratify the palate with repasts
90 More costly than the Dame of whom I spake,
That ancient Woman, and her board supplied.
Hence inroads into distant Vales, and long
Excursions far away among the hills,
Hence rustic dinners on the cool green ground,

7. Pleasing. Activities once enjoyed solely for their own sake would have become less enjoyable, as the boys aged, without the *collateral* pleasures offered by nature's beauty.
8. Destination; *Plain*: the surface of the water on Lake Windermere, two miles east of Hawkshead.
9. Islands in Windermere: the first two may have been Lilies of the Valley East and West, as they are now called; the third, as WW's revision in *Prel 1850* clarified ("where survived * * * the ruins of a shrine / Once to our Lady dedicate"), was Ladyholme, on which a chapel dedicated to the Virgin Mary had once stood (see *Prel 1850* [CW], 48).
1. Altered in pencil at an indeterminable date to "the pride of strength" (as in MS A).
2. Alluding to the frugal way of life led by the Roman poet Horace (65–8 B.C.E.) on his farm in the Sabine region of central Italy (*Odes* 2.18).
3. In January 1787 WW returned to school from the Christmas holiday with a guinea, or 42 times his regular weekly allowance of sixpence (Thompson, 98, 372).

95   Or in the woods, or near a river side,
      Or by some shady fountain, while soft airs
      Among the leaves were stirring, and the sun,
      Unfelt, shone sweetly round us in our joy.
            Nor is my aim neglected, if I tell
100   How twice in the long length of those half-years
      We from our funds, perhaps, with bolder hand
      Drew largely, anxious for one day, at least,
      To feel the motion of the galloping Steed;
      And with the good old Innkeeper, in truth,
105   On such occasion sometimes we employed
      Sly subterfuge; for the intended bound
      Of the day's journey was too distant far
      For any cautious man, a Structure famed
      Beyond its neighbourhood, the antique Walls
110   Of that large Abbey, which within the Vale
      Of Nightshade to St Mary's honour built
      Stands yet, a mouldering Pile, with fractured Arch,
      Belfrey, and Images, and living Trees,
      A holy Scene!⁴ along the smooth green turf
115   Our Horses grazed: to more than inland peace
      Left by the Sea-wind passing overhead
      (Though wind of roughest temper) trees and towr's
      May in the Valley oftentimes be seen,
      Both silent and both motionless alike,
120   Such is the shelter that is there, and such
      The safeguard for repose and quietness.
            Our Steeds remounted, and the summons giv'n,
      With whip and spur we by the Chauntry flew
      In uncouth race and left the cross-legged Knight,
125   And the Stone-Abbot,⁵ and that single Wren
      Which one day sang so sweetly in the Nave
      Of the old Church, that, though from recent showr's
      The earth was comfortless, and touched by faint
      Internal breezes, sobbings of the place,
130   And respirations, from the roofless walls
      The shuddering ivy dripped large drops, yet still,
      So sweetly 'mid the gloom the invisible Bird
      Sang to itself, that there I could have made
      My dwelling-place, and lived for ever there
135   To hear such music. Through the walls we flew
      And down the Valley, and a circuit made
      In wantonness of heart, through rough and smooth
      We scampered homeward. Oh! ye Rocks and Streams,
      And that still spirit of the evening air,

4. Built in the twelfth century, Furness Abbey, near Barrow-in-Furness, twenty miles southwest
   of Hawkshead and one mile from the Irish Sea, had fallen into ruin after its dissolution by
   Henry VIII in 1536.
5. A stone effigy, as is *the cross-legged Knight,* which is now in the abbey museum. WW refers to
   the effigy again in 10.560–66. *Chauntry:* chantry, a chapel endowed for the singing of Masses
   for the dead.

140 Even in this joyous time I sometimes felt
     Your presence, when with slackened step we breathed
     Along the sides of the steep hills, or when,
     Lighted by gleams of moonlight from the sea,
     We beat with thundering hoofs the level sand.[6]
145   Upon the Eastern Shore of Windermere,
     Above the crescent of a pleasant Bay,
     There was an Inn, no homely-featured Shed,
     Brother of the surrounding Cottages,
     But twas a splendid place, the door beset
150 With Chaises, Grooms, and Liveries, and within
     Decanters, Glasses and the blood-red Wine.[7]
     In ancient times, or ere the Hall was built
     On the large Island,[8] had this Dwelling been
     More worthy of a Poet's love, a Hut
155 Proud of its one bright fire, and sycamore shade.
     But though the rhymes were gone, which once inscribed
     The threshold, and large golden characters
     On the blue-frosted Sign-board had usurped
     The place of the old Lion, in contempt
160 And mockery of the rustic Painter's hand,
     Yet to this hour this spot to me is dear
     With all its foolish pomp. The garden lay
     Upon a slope surmounted by the plain
     Of a small Bowling-green; beneath us stood
165 A grove, with gleams of water through the trees
     And over the tree tops; nor did we want
     Refreshment, strawberries and mellow cream.
     And there, through half an afternoon, we played
     On the smooth platform, and the shouts we sent
170 Made all the mountains ring. But ere the fall
     Of night, when in our pinnace we returned
     Over the dusky Lake, and to the beach
     Of some small Island steered our course with one,
     The Minstrel of our troop, and left him there,
175 And rowed off gently, while he blew his flute
     Alone upon the rock,[9] Oh! then the calm
     And dead still water lay upon my mind
     Even with a weight of pleasure, and the sky
     Never before so beautiful, sank down
180 Into my heart, and held me like a dream.
             Thus daily were my sympathies enlarged,
     And thus the common range of visible things
     Grew dear to me: already I began

6. The boys' circuitous route back to Hawkshead takes them from Rampside to Greenodd along
   the Leven Sands on the eastern shore of the Barrow Peninsula, and from there inland up the
   eastern side of Windermere.
7. *Blood-red Wine*: a phrase from *The Ballad of Sir Patrick Spens*, line 2. *Inn*: the White Lion in
   Bowness; *Liveries*: uniformed servants.
8. The round Curwen house, built in the 1770s on Belle Isle, the largest island in Windermere.
9. Thompson, 79, identifies the flautist as WW's friend Robert Greenwood, who was to become a
   fellow of Trinity College, Cambridge, in 1792.

To love the sun, a Boy I loved the sun,
185 Not as I since have loved him, as a pledge
And surety of our earthly life, a light
Which while we view, we feel we are alive;
But for this cause, that I had seen him lay
His beauty on the morning hills, had seen
190 The western mountain touch his setting orb,
In many a thoughtless hour, when, from excess
Of happiness, my blood appeared to flow
With its own pleasure, and I breathed with joy.
And from like feelings, humble though intense,
195 To patriotic and domestic love
Analogous, the moon to me was dear;
For I would dream away my purposes,
Standing to look upon her while she hung
Midway between the hills, as if she knew
200 No other region; but belonged to thee,
Yea, appertained by a peculiar right
To thee and thy grey huts,[1] my darling Vale!
        Those incidental charms which first attached
My heart to rural objects, day by day
205 Grew weaker, and I hasten on to tell
How Nature, intervenient[2] till this time,
And secondary, now at length was sought
For her own sake. But who shall parcel out
His intellect by geometric rules,
210 Split like a Province, into round and square?[3]
Who knows the individual hour in which
His habits were first sown, even as a seed,
Who that shall point, as with a wand, and say,
"This portion of the river of my mind
215 Came from yon fountain?"[4] Thou, my Friend! art one
More deeply read in thy own thoughts; to thee
Science appears but, what in truth she is,
Not as our glory and our absolute boast,
But as a succedaneum,[5] and a prop
220 To our infirmity. Thou art no slave
Of that false secondary power, by which,
In weakness, we create distinctions, then
Deem that our puny boundaries are things
Which we perceive, and not which we have made.
225 To Thee, unblinded by these outward shows

1. Cottages built of the local slate.
2. Literally "coming between." Until now nature had imposed itself on WW's consciousness only amidst other experiences and concerns.
3. In this critique of analytic reason WW may have in mind associationist philosophers like David Hartley, whose *Observations on Man* (1749) offers a physiological explanation of the formation and association of ideas, or less likely the Dutch philosopher Benedictus de Spinoza, whose *Ethics, Demonstrated in Geometric Order* (1677) includes an account of human thought and feeling.
4. The river is a recurrent metaphor for the mind in *The Prelude*: see also 3.10–12 and 13.172–84.
5. WW seems to use the word in the attested but incorrect sense of "remedy" rather than in the correct sense of "substitute."

The unity of all has been revealed
And Thou wilt doubt with me, less aptly skilled
Than many are to class the cabinet
Of their sensations,[6] and in voluable phrase,
230 Run through the history and birth of each,
As of a single independent thing.
Hard task to analyse a soul,[7] in which,
Not only general habits and desires,
But each most obvious and particular thought,
235 Not in a mystical and idle sense,
But in the words of reason deeply weighed,
Hath no beginning.   Blessed[8] the infant Babe,
(For with my best conjectures I would trace
The progress of our being) blest the Babe,
240 Nursed in his Mother's arms, the Babe who sleeps
Upon his Mother's breast, who, when his soul
Claims manifest kindred with an earthly soul,
Doth gather passion from his Mother's eye!
Such feelings pass into his torpid life
245 Like an awakening breeze, and hence his mind
Even [in the first trial of its powers][9]
Is prompt and watchful, eager to combine
In one appearance, all the elements
And parts of the same object, else detached
250 And loth to coalesce. Thus day by day,
Subjected to the discipline of love,
His organs and recipient faculties
Are quickened, are more vigorous, his mind spreads,
Tenacious of the forms[1] which it receives.
255 In one beloved Presence, nay and more,
In that most apprehensive habitude[2]
And those sensations which have been derived
From this beloved Presence, there exists
A virtue which irradiates and exalts
260 All objects through all intercourse of sense.[3]
No outcast he, bewildered and depressed:
Along his Infant veins are interfused
The gravitation and the filial bond

6. I.e., to classify feelings as if they were specimens in a scientific display case. WW's address to STC in this sentence recalls lines 65–67 of Frost at Midnight, in which STC had described nature as "that eternal language, which thy God / Utters, who from eternity doth teach / Himself in all, and all things in himself."
7. In Paradise Lost 5.564, Raphael refers to narrating the war in heaven as a "Sad task and hard." Commentators note that by means of this allusion, WW implicitly claims epic status for his own subject.
8. Pronounced as one syllable.
9. This line, left blank after Even in MSS B and A, is supplied from MS M (Prel 1805 [CW], 2:525).
1. Visual images.
2. In that relationship (habitude) most conducive to perception and thought (most apprehensive).
3. In effect WW here revises Tintern Abbey, lines 93–103, in which he attributed to an unspecific "presence" his sense of "A motion and a spirit that impels / All thinking things, all objects of all thought, / And rolls through all things." The verb interfused in line 262 is also used in Tintern Abbey, line 96.

Of nature, that connect him with the world.[4]
265 Emphatically such a Being lives,
An inmate of this *active* universe;
From nature largely he receives; nor so
Is satisfied, but largely gives again,
For feeling has to him imparted strength,
270 And powerful in all sentiments of grief,
Of exultation, fear and joy, his mind,
Even as an agent of the one great mind,
Creates, creator and receiver both,
Working but in alliance with the works
275 Which it beholds.[5]—Such verily is the first
Poetic spirit of our human life;
By uniform controul of after years
In most abated and suppressed, in some,
Through every change of growth or of decay
Pre-eminent till death.
280   From early days,
Beginning not long after that first time
In which, a Babe, by intercourse of touch,
I held mute dialogues with my Mother's heart,
I have endeavoured to display the means
285 Whereby the infant sensibility,
Great birth-right of our Being, was in me
Augmented and sustained. Yet is a path
More difficult before me, and I fear
That in its broken windings we shall need
290 The Chamois'[6] sinews, and the Eagle's wing:
For now a trouble came into my mind
From unknown causes. I was left alone,
Seeking the visible world, nor knowing why.
The props[7] of my affection were removed,
295 And yet the building stood as if sustained
By its own spirit. All that I beheld
Was dear to me, and from this cause it came,
That now to Nature's finer influxes[8]
My mind lay open, to that more exact
300 And intimate communion which our hearts
Maintain with the minuter properties
Of objects which already are beloved,
And of those only. Many are the joys
Of youth; but Oh! what happiness to live
305 When every hour brings palpable access

4. I.e., the infant's ability to form bonds with the external world is innate and strengthened through its bonds with its mother.
5. In *Tintern Abbey* too WW affirmed an active aspect of sense perception: "the mighty world / Of eye and ear, both what they half-create / And what perceive" (lines 105–107). See also WW's assertion, in 13.66–96 below, that the individual imagination, with its receptive and transformative powers, mirrors "a mighty Mind * * * that feeds upon infinity" (13.69–70).
6. A goatlike antelope found in the Alps.
7. Such as the *incidental charms* mentioned in line 203. See also 3.230–32 and 7.493.
8. Influences.

Of knowledge, when all knowledge is delight,
And sorrow is not there. The seasons came,
And every season to my notice brought
A store of transitory qualities
310 Which, but for this most watchful power of love
Had been neglected,[9] left a register
Of permanent relations, else unknown,
Hence life, and change and beauty, solitude
More active, even, than "best society,"[1]
315 Society made sweet as solitude
By silent inobtrusive sympathies,
And gentle agitations of the mind[2]
From manifold distinctions, difference
Perceived in[3] things where to the common eye
320 No difference is, and hence, from the same source
Sublimer joy: for I would walk alone
In storm and tempest, and in star-light nights,
Beneath the quiet Heavens, and at that time,
Have felt whate'er there is of power in sound
325 To breathe an elevated mood, by form
Or image unprofaned: and I would stand
Beneath some rock, listening to sounds that are
The ghostly language of the ancient earth,
Or make their dim abode in distant winds.
330 Thence did I drink the visionary power.
I deem not profitless those fleeting moods
Of shadowy exultation: not for this,
That they are kindred to our purer mind
And intellectual life; but that the soul,
335 Remembering how she felt, but what she felt
Remembering not, retains an obscure[4] sense
Of possible sublimity, to which,
With growing faculties she doth aspire,
With faculties still growing, feeling still
340 That whatsoever point they gain, they still
Have something to pursue.[5]
                              And not alone
In grandeur and in tumult, but no less
In tranquil scenes, that universal power
And fitness in the latent qualities
345 And essences of things, by which the mind

9. I.e., would have *been neglected* except for *this most watchful power of love.*
1. A quotation from *Paradise Lost* 9.249: "For solitude som[e]times is best societie."
2. MS B has a period after this word, so that line 318 begins a new sentence. The text here is emended in accordance with the reading in MS A, which has no punctuation after *mind.* *Gentle agitations*: As NCPrel notes, this phrase does not depend on *by* in line 316, but rather is the last item in the list that follows *Hence* in line 313.
3. MS B has "it," presumably in error for "in," the reading in MS A.
4. Stressed on the first syllable.
5. Lines 322–41 were originally composed in ca. March 1798 as part of a fragment connected with *The Pedlar*, and then used in *Prel 1799* 2.352–71 (see *The Ruined Cottage and the Pedlar* [CW], 371–72, and *The Prelude 1798–1799* [CW], 63, 159, for the earlier versions of the lines). WW also drew on this fragment for *Prel 1805* 7.722–30.

Is moved with feelings of delight, to me
Came strengthened with a supperadded soul,
A virtue not its own. My morning walks
Were early; oft before the hours of School
350 I travelled round our little Lake, five miles
Of pleasant wandering, happy time! more dear
For this, that one was by my side, a Friend
Then passionately loved:[6] with heart how full
Will he peruse these lines, this page, perhaps
355 A blank to other Men! for many years
Have since flowed in between us; and our minds,
Both silent to each other, at this time
We live as if those hours had never been.
Nor seldom did I lift our cottage latch
360 Far earlier, and before the vernal thrush
Was audible, among the hills I sate
Alone, upon some jutting eminence[7]
At the first hour of morning, when the Vale
Lay quiet in an utter solitude.
365 How shall I trace the history, where seek
The origin of what I then have felt?
Oft in those moments such a holy calm
Did overspread my soul, that I forgot
That I had bodily eyes, and what I saw
370 Appeared like something in myself, a dream,
A prospect in my mind.
                 'Twere long to tell
What spring and autumn, what the winter snows,
And what the summer shade, what day and night,
The evening and the morning, what my dreams
375 And what my wakeing thoughts supplied, to nurse
That spirit of religious love in which
I walked with Nature. But let this, at least
Be not forgotten, that I still retained
My first creative sensibility,
380 That by the regular action of the world
My soul was unsubdued. A plastic power
Abode with me, a forming hand,[8] at times
Rebellious, acting in a devious mood,
A local spirit of his own, at war
385 With general tendency, but for the most
Subservient strictly to the external things
With which it communed. An auxiliar light
Came from my mind which on the setting sun

6. John Fleming, who went to Cambridge in 1785 and became a clergyman. WW had celebrated their friendship in a poem he composed in Hawkshead and never published, *The Vale of Esthwaite* (Thompson, 104–105, 117). *Hours of School*: the school day at Hawkshead began between 6:00 and 6:30 a.m. in summer and an hour later in winter; *little Lake*: Esthwaite Water.
7. NCPrel notes a recollection of James Thomson's *Seasons* (1730), bk. 2 (*Summer*), line 942: "Sad on the jutting Eminence he sits."
8. Recalling *Paradise Lost* 8.472: "Under his [God's] forming hands a Creature [Eve] grew"; *plastic*: formative.

Bestowed new splendor, the melodious birds,
390 The gentle breezes, fountains that ran on,
Murmuring so sweetly in themselves, obeyed
A like dominion; and the midnight storm
Grew darker in the presence of my eye.
Hence my obeisance, my devotion hence,
And *hence* my transport.[9]
395   Nor should this, perchance,
Pass unrecorded, that I still had loved
The exercise and produce of a toil
Than analytic industry to me
More pleasing, and whose character, I deem,
400 Is more poetic, as resembling more
Creative agency. I mean to speak
Of that interminable building reared
By observation of affinities
In objects where no brotherhood exists
405 To common minds. My seventeenth year was come
And whether from this habit rooted now
So deeply in my mind, or from excess
Of the great social principle of life,
Coercing all things into sympathy,
410 To unorganic natures I transferred
My own enjoyments, or, the power of truth
Coming in revelation, I conversed
With things that really are, I at this time
Saw blessings spread around me like a sea.
415 Thus did my days pass on, and now at length,
From Nature and her overwhelming soul
I had received so much that all my thoughts
Were steeped in feeling; I was only then
Contented when with bliss ineffable
420 I felt the sentiment of Being spread
O'er all that moves, and all that seemeth still,
O'er all that, lost beyond the reach of thought
And human knowledge, to the human eye
Invisible, yet liveth to the heart,
425 O'er all that leaps, and runs, and shouts, and sings,
Or beats the gladsome air, o'er all that glides
Beneath the wave, yea in the wave itself
And mighty depth of waters. Wonder not
If such my transports were; for in all things
430 I saw one life, and felt that it was joy.[1]
One song they sang and it was audible,
Most audible then when the fleshly ear,
O'ercome by grosser prelude of that strain,

9. I.e., WW's increased devotion to nature followed from its subordination to the creative powers
   of his mind.
1. An insight like that described in *Tintern Abbey*, lines 93–103.

Forgot its functions, and slept undisturbed.
435   If this be error,[2] and another faith
Find easier access to the pious mind,
Yet were I grossly destitute of all
Those human sentiments that make this earth
So dear, if I should fail, with grateful voice
440 To speak of you, ye Mountains! and ye Lakes,
And sounding Cataracts! Ye Mists and Winds
That dwell among the Hills where I was born.
If in my Youth, I have been pure in heart,
If, mingling with the world, I am content
445 With my own modest pleasures, and have lived,
With God and Nature communing, removed
From little enmities and low desires,
The gift is Yours: if in these times of fear,
This melancholy waste of hopes o'erthrown,
450 If, mid indifference and apathy
And wicked exultation, when good Men,
On every side, fall off we know not how,
To selfishness,[3] disguised in gentle names
Of peace, and quiet, and domestic love,
455 Yet mingled, not unwillingly, with sneers
On visionary minds: if in this time
Of dereliction and dismay, I yet
Despair not of our Nature, but retain
A more than Roman confidence, a faith
460 That fails not, in all sorrow my support,
The blessing of my life, the gift is yours,
Ye Mountains! thine, O Nature! Thou hast fed
My lofty speculations; and in Thee
For this uneasy heart of ours, I find
465 A never-failing principle of joy,
And purest passion.
                    Thou, my Friend! wert reared
In the great City, mid far other scenes;[4]
But we, by different roads at length, have gained
The self-same bourne. And for this cause to Thee
470 I speak, unapprehensive of contempt,
The insinuated scoff of coward tongues,
And all that silent language which so oft
In conversation betwixt man and man
Blots from the human countenance all trace
475 Of beauty and of love. For Thou hast sought
The truth in solitude, and Thou art one,

---

2. A phrase from Shakespeare's Sonnet 116, line 13, but also recalling *Tintern Abbey*, lines 49–
50: "If this / Be but a vain belief * * *."
3. A possible adaptation of the opening lines of Samuel Butler's *Hudibras* (1662–77): "When civil
Fury first grew high, / And men fell out they knew not why." More generally, WW's phraseology
in lines 448–52 recalls STC's in *Fears in Solitude* (1798) and in a letter of September 1799 to
WW, urging him to compose *The Recluse* (CL 1:527).
4. A quotation of STC's *Frost at Midnight* (1798), lines 56–57: "For I was rear'd / In the great city,
pent mid cloisters dim."

The most intense of Nature's worshippers,
In many things my Brother, chiefly here,
In this my deep devotion.
                                    Fare Thee well!
480 Health and the quiet of a healthful mind
Attend Thee! seeking oft the haunts of Men,
And yet more often living with Thyself,
And for Thyself, so haply shall thy days
Be many, and a blessing to mankind.

Book Third

RESIDENCE AT CAMBRIDGE

It was a dreary morning when the Chaise
Rolled over the flat plains of Huntingdon
And through the open windows first I saw
The long-backed Chapel of King's College rear
5 His pinnacles above the dusky groves.[1]
        Soon afterwards we espied upon the road
A Student clothed in Gown and tasseled Cap;
He passed, nor was I master of my eyes
'Till he was left a hundred yards behind.
10 The place as we approached seemed more and more
To have an eddy's force and sucked us in
More eagerly at every step we took.
Onward we drove beneath the Castle, down
By Magdalene Bridge we went and crossed the Cam
15 And at the Hoop we landed, famous Inn!
        My spirit was up, my thoughts were full of hope,
Some Friends I had, Acquaintances who there
Seemed Friends, poor simple School-boys now hung round
With honour and importance;[2] in a world
20 Of welcome faces up and down I roved;
Questions, directions, counsel and advice
Flowed in upon me from all sides, fresh day
Of pride and pleasure! to myself I seemed
A man of business and expence, and went
25 From Shop to Shop about my own affairs,
To Tutors or to Tailors, as befel,
From Street to Street with loose and careless heart.
        I was the Dreamer, they the Dream; I roamed
Delighted, through the motley spectacle;
30 Gowns grave or gaudy, Doctors, Students, Streets,
Lamps, Gateways, Flocks of Churches, Courts and Towers.[3]

1. WW was admitted to St. John's College, Cambridge, on July 5, 1787, and in October he traveled
   to the city—his first trip outside the Lake District—with his cousin John Myers, who had also
   been admitted to St. John's. They arrived probably on October 30, the coach stopping at the
   Hoop Inn (line 15), close to their college (*Chrono: EY*, 75–76).
2. During WW's time at Cambridge, six former pupils of the Hawkshead Grammar School,
   including John Fleming (see note to 2.353), achieved high academic honors (Schneider, 5).
3. Evidently following the revision made in MS A, MW wrote the alternatives "Groves" and
   "Cloisters" above the first two words of line 31, but without canceling the original reading.
   Courts: quadrangles (a usage peculiar to Cambridge).

Strange transformation for a mountain Youth,
A northern Villager! As if by word
Of magic, or some Fairy's power, at once
35 Behold me rich in monies, and attired
In splendid clothes, with hose of silk, and hair
Glittering like rimy[4] trees when frost is keen.
My lordly Dressing-gown I pass it by,
With other signs of manhood which supplied
40 The lack of beard.—The weeks went roundly on,
With invitations, suppers, wine and fruit,
Smooth housekeeping within, and all without
Liberal and suiting Gentleman's array!
The Evangelist, St. John, my Patron was.[5]
45 Three gloomy Courts are his; and in the first
Was my abiding-place, a nook obscure!
Right underneath, the College Kitchens made
A humming sound, less tuneable than bees,
But hardly less industrious; with shrill notes
50 Of sharp command and scolding intermixed.[6]
Near me was Trinity's loquacious Clock,
Who never let the Quarters, night or day,
Slip by him unproclaimed, and told the hours
Twice over with a male and female voice.[7]
55 Her pealing Organ was my neighbour, too,
And, from my Bed-room, I in moonlight nights
Could see, right opposite, a few yards off,
The Antichapel, where the Statue stood
Of Newton, with his Prism and silent Face.
60   Of College labours, of the Lecturer's Room,
All studded round, as thick as chairs could stand
With loyal Students, faithful to their books,
Half-and-half Idlers, hardy Recusants,[8]
And honest Dunces;—of important Days,
65 Examinations, when the Man was weighed
As in the balance![9]—of excessive hopes,
Tremblings withal, and commendable fears,
Small jealousies, and triumphs good or bad

4. Frosty, covered with hoar frost. WW refers to the fashion, which he adopted, of using white hair powder. DW commented after visiting her brother in Cambridge in December 1788, "I could scarcely help imagining myself in a different country when I was walking in the college courts and groves; it looked so odd to see smart powdered heads with black caps like helmets * * * and gowns, something like those that clergymen wear" (WL, 1:19).
5. St. John's College, Cambridge, is dedicated to St. John the Evangelist.
6. WW's rooms above the kitchens reflected his lowly social status as a "sizar," an undergraduate who received financial assistance from his college to enable him to study there. Although by WW's time sizars were no longer required to act as servants to the college fellows and wealthy students, they still wore distinctive gowns and were given inferior quarters and food (Schneider, 42).
7. The clock of the neighboring Trinity College chapel sounds the hours with two bells, the second of a higher pitch than the first. Inside the chapel is a celebrated statue, sculpted in 1755 by Louis François Roubiliac, of Sir Isaac Newton holding a prism (lines 58–59). Newton had been a sizar at Trinity before becoming a fellow.
8. Those who refused to study. Historically, the term recusants was applied to those, especially Roman Catholics, who declined to attend services of the Church of England (and hence would not have been permitted to receive a degree from Cambridge or Oxford).
9. "Thou art weighed in the balances, and art found wanting" (Daniel 5.27). WW also puns on the derivation of examination from the Latin examen, "a balance" (NCPrel).

I make short mention; things they were which then
70 I did not love, nor do I love them now.
Such glory was but little sought by me
And little won. But it is right to say
That even so early, from the first crude days
Of settling-time in this my new abode,
75 Not seldom I had melancholy thoughts,
From personal and family regards,
Wishing to hope without a hope, some fears
About my future worldly maintenance,[1]
And, more than all, a strangeness in my mind,
80 A feeling that I was not for that hour,
Nor for that place. But wherefore be cast down?[2]
Why should I grieve? I was a chosen Son.[3]
For hither I had come with holy powers
And faculties, whether to work or feel:
85 To apprehend all passions and all moods
Which time, and place, and season do impress
Upon the visible universe, and work
Like changes there by force of my own mind.
I was a Freeman: in the purest sense
90 Was free, and to majestic ends was strong.
I do not speak of knowledge, moral truth,
Or understanding: 'twas enough for me
To know that I was otherwise endowed.
When the first glitter of the shew was past,
95 And the first dazzle of the taper-light,
As if with a rebound, my mind returned
Into its former self. Oft did I leave
My comrades and the crowd, buildings and groves,
And walked along the fields, the level fields,
100 With Heaven's blue concave reared above my head.
And now it was, that from such change entire
And this first absence from those shapes sublime
Wherewith I had been conversant, my mind
Seemed busier in itself than heretofore;
105 At least, I more directly recognised
My powers and habits; let me dare to speak
A higher language, say that now I felt
The strength and consolation that were mine.
As if awakened, summoned, rouzed, constrained,
110 I looked for universal things, perused
The common countenance of earth and heaven,
And, turning the mind in upon itself,

1. A reference to the expectation of WW's relatives that he would qualify for a fellowship at St. John's and thereafter take holy orders (Schneider, 7–9).
2. "Why art thou cast down, O my soul? and why art thou disquieted within me?" (Psalms 42.11 and 43.5).
3. Compare 4.341–45, where WW describes his feeling of being a "dedicated Spirit." In *Prel 1850* he replaced this reference to being a *chosen Son* with a parenthesis: "For (not to speak of Reason and her pure / Reflective acts to fix the moral law / Deep in the conscience; nor of Christian Hope / Bowing her head before her Sister Faith / As one far mightier), hither I had come * * *" (*Prel 1850* [CW], 63).

Pored, watched, expected, listened; spread my thoughts,
And spread them with a wider creeping; felt
115   Incumbences more awful,[4] visitings
Of the Upholder, of the tranquil Soul,
Which underneath all passion lives secure,
A steadfast life.[5] But peace! it is enough
To notice that I was ascending now
120   To such community with highest truth.
            A track pursuing not untrod before,
From deep analogies by thought supplied,
Or consciousnesses not to be subdued,
To every natural form, rock, fruit, or flower,
125   Even the loose stones that cover the high-way,
I gave a mortal life, I saw them feel,
Or linked them to some feeling: the great mass
Lay bedded in a quickening soil,[6] and all
That I beheld respired[7] with inward meaning.
130   Thus much for the one Presence, and the Life
Of the great whole: suffice it here to add
That, whatsoe'er of Terror or of Love,
Or Beauty, Nature's daily face put on
From transitory passion, unto this
135   I was as wakeful even as waters are
To the sky's motion; in a kindred sense[8]
Of passion was obedient as a lute
That waits upon the touches of the wind.
So it was with me in my solitude,
140   So, often among multitudes of men.
Unknown, unthought of, yet I was most rich,
I had a world about me; 'twas my own,
I made it; for it only lived to me,
And to the God who looked into my mind.
145   Such sympathies would sometimes shew themselves
By outward gestures and by visible looks.
Some called it madness: such, indeed, it was,
If child-like fruitfulness in passing joy,
If steady moods of thoughtfulness, matured
150   To inspiration, sort with such a name;
If prophesy be madness; if things viewed
By Poets of old time, and higher up[9]
By the first men, earth's first inhabitants,

4. Awe-inspiring; *Incumbences* (revised from "Incumbencies"): broodings (a rare usage).
5. Compare WW's reference to the men "Who are their own upholders, / To themselves encouragement" in 12.261–62.
6. Life-giving soil: a reading unique to MS B and evidently a revision of "soul," the reading in MSS M and A. In MS A "ground" was proposed but rejected as an alternative (*Prel 1805* [CW], 2:546), and "soul" was retained in *Prel 1850*. The sense is of the physical world being nourished by a vital force or spirit.
7. Breathed. See also line 188 below and compare WW's reference to feeling "the pulse of Being everywhere" in 8.624–31.
8. At some stage lines 135–36 were revised to "I was more sensible than waters are / To the sky's motion; in a kindred tone," but this revision was not made in MS A or incorporated into later versions of the poem.
9. Further back in time (a now-obsolete sense of *higher*).

May in these tutored days no more be seen
155 With undisordered sight: but leaving this
It was no madness: for I had an eye
Which, in my strongest workings, evermore
Was looking for the shades of difference
As they lie hid in all exterior forms
160 Near or remote, minute or vast, an eye
Which from a stone, a tree, a withered leaf
To the broad ocean and the azure heavens
Spangled with kindred multitudes of stars,
Could find no surface where its power might sleep,
165 Which spake perpetual logic to my soul,
And by an unrelenting agency
Did bind my feelings, even as in a chain.
          And here, O Friend! have I retraced my life
Up to an eminence, and told a tale
170 Of matters which, not falsely, I may call
The glory of my Youth. Of Genius, Power,
Creation, and Divinity itself
I have been speaking, for my theme has been
What passed within me. Not of outward things
175 Done visibly for other minds, words, signs,
Symbols, or actions; but of my own heart
Have I been speaking, and my youthful mind.
O Heavens! how awful is the might of Souls
And what they do within themselves, while yet
180 The yoke of earth is new to them, the world
Nothing but a wild field where they were sown.
This is in truth heroic argument,
And genuine prowess;[1] which I wished to touch
With hand however weak; but in the main
185 It lies far hidden from the reach of words.
Points have we all of us within our souls,
Where all stand single; this I feel, and make
Breathings for incommunicable powers.
Yet each man is a memory to himself:
190 And, therefore, now that I must quit this theme,
I am not heartless;[2] for there's not a man
That lives who hath not had his god-like hours,
And knows not what majestic sway we have,
As natural beings, in the strength of nature.
195   Enough: for now into a populous Plain
We must descend.—A Traveller I am
And all my Tale is of myself; even so,
So be it, if the pure in heart delight
To follow me; and Thou, O honored Friend!
200 Who in my thoughts art ever at my side,

---

1. An allusion to Milton's defense of his subject in *Paradise Lost* 9.13–14: "argument / Not less but
   more Heroic" than the battles narrated by Homer and Virgil.
2. Disheartened, dejected.

Uphold, as heretofore, my fainting steps.[3]
          It hath been told already how my sight
Was dazzled by the novel shew, and how,
Erelong I did into myself return.
205 So did it seem, and so, in truth, it was.
Yet this was but short-lived: thereafter came
Observance less devout. I had made a change
In climate; and my nature's outward coat
Changed also, slowly and insensibly.
210 To the deep quiet and majestic thoughts
Of loneliness succeeded empty noise
And superficial pastimes: now and then,
Forced labour; and, more frequently, forced hopes;
And worse than all, a treasonable growth
215 Of indecisive judgements that impaired
And shook the mind's simplicity. And yet
This was a gladsome time. Could I behold,
Who less insensible than sodden clay
On a sea River's bed at ebb of tide,
220 Could have beheld with undelighted heart
So many happy Youths, so wide and fair
A congregation, in its budding time
Of health, and hope, and beauty; all at once
So many divers samples of the growth
225 Of life's sweet season, could have seen unmoved
That miscellaneous garland of wild flowers
Upon the matron temples of a Place
So famous through the world?[4] To me, at least,
It was a goodly prospect; for, through youth,
230 Though I had been trained up to stand unpropped,[5]
And independent musings pleased me so
That spells seemed on me when I was alone,
Yet I could only cleave to solitude
In lonesome places; if a throng was near
235 That way I leaned by nature; for my heart
Was social, and loved idleness and joy.[6]
          Not seeking those who might participate[7]
My deeper pleasures, (nay I had not once,
Though not unused to mutter lonesome songs,
240 Even with myself divided such delight,
Or looked that way for aught that might be cloathed
In human language) easily I passed
From the remembrances of better things,
And slipped into the week-day works of youth,

3. "Secret refreshings, that repair his strength, / And fainting steps uphold" (Milton, *Samson Agonistes*, lines 665–66).
4. Undergraduates are the *flowers* that Cambridge University, the *matron* (i.e., *alma mater*), wears as a garland.
5. See 2.294–96.
6. NCPrel cites as corroboration of WW's sociability a letter of November 1794, written from the Lake District to a friend in London: "I begin to wish much to be in town; cataracts and mountains, are good occasional society, but they will not do for constant companions" (WL, 1:136).
7. Share.

245 Unburthened, unalarmed, and unprofaned.
    Caverns there were within my mind, which sun
    Could never penetrate, yet did there not
    Want store of leafy arbours where the light
    Might enter in at will. Companionships,
250 Friendships, acquaintances, were welcome;
    We sauntered, played, we rioted,[8] we talked
    Unprofitable talk at morning hours,
    Drifted about along the streets and walks,
    Read lazily in lazy books, went forth
255 To gallop through the country in blind zeal
    Of senseless horsemanship; or on the breast
    Of Cam[9] sailed boisterously; and let the stars
    Come out, perhaps, without one quiet thought.
        Such was the tenor of the opening act[1]
260 In this new life. Imagination slept,
    And yet not utterly: I could not print
    Ground, where the grass had yielded to the steps
    Of generations of illustrious Men
    Unmoved: I could not always lightly pass
265 Through the same Gateways: sleep where they had slept,
    Wake where they waked, range that enclosure old,
    That garden of great intellects undisturbed.
    Place also by the side of this dark sense
    Of nobler feeling, that those spiritual Men,
270 Even the great Newton's own etherial Self
    Seemed humbled in these precincts; thence to be
    The more beloved; invested here with tasks
    Of life's plain business, as a daily garb;
    Dictators at the Plough, a change that left
275 All genuine admiration unimpaired.[2]
    —Beside the pleasant Mills of Trompington
    I laughed with Chaucer, in the hawthorn shade
    Heard him, while birds were warbling, tell his tales
    Of amorous passion.[3] And that gentle Bard,
280 Chosen by the Muses for their Page of State,
    Sweet Spencer, moving through his clouded heaven
    With the moon's beauty, and the moon's soft pace;
    I called him Brother, Englishman, and Friend.[4]

8. In the sense of living "in a wanton, dissipated, or unrestrained manner" (OED).
9. The River Cam in Cambridge.
1. Altered in Prel 1850 to "second act" to reflect that WW's phase of social activity at Cambridge had followed an initial phase of isolation.
2. Lines 274–75 are bracketed in ink, possibly in STC's hand, with the comment "perhaps better out," and there is another bracket in ink in the margin of line 279. Dictators at the Plough: an allusion to Cincinnatus, who according to legend was summoned from ploughing in 458 B.C.E. to become the Roman dictator and, after leading the army to victory, returned to his farm. Like Cincinnatus on his farm, Britain's intellectual élite seem humbled while going about their daily business at Cambridge.
3. Chaucer's Reeve's Tale, which concerns two Cambridge undergraduates who are cheated by a miller and avenge themselves by sleeping with his wife and daughter, is set in the village of Trumpington just south of Cambridge.
4. Edmund Spenser, who had been a sizar at Cambridge in 1569–74, described his Faerie Queene (1590–96), an allegorical epic glorifying Elizabeth I, as a "darke conceit * * * clowdily enwrapped in Allegorical devises."

Yea, our blind Poet, who, in his later days,
285   Stood almost single, uttering odious truth,
Darkness before, and danger's voice behind;[5]
Soul awful! if the earth hath ever lodged
An awful Soul, I seemed to see him here
Familiarly, and in his Scholar's dress
290   Bounding before me, yet a stripling Youth,
A Boy, no better, with his rosy cheeks
Angelical, keen eye, courageous look,
And conscious step of purity and pride.[6]
        Among the band of my Compeers was one,
295   My Class-fellow at School, whose chance it was
To lodge in the Apartments which had been,
Time out of mind[7] honoured by Milton's name,
The very shell of the abode
Which he had tenanted.[8] O temperate Bard!
300   One afternoon, the first time I set foot
In this thy innocent Nest and Oratory,
Seated with others in a festive ring
Of common-place convention,[9] I to thee
Poured out libations, to thy memory drank,
305   Within my private thoughts, till my brain reeled;
Never so clouded by the fumes of wine
Before that hour or since. Thence forth I ran,
From that assembly, through a length of streets
Ran, Ostrich-like, to reach our Chapel Door
310   In not a desperate or opprobrious time,
Albeit long after the importunate Bell
Had stopped, with wearisome Cassandra[1] voice
No longer haunting the dark winter night.
Call back, O Friend! a moment to thy mind
315   The place itself and fashion of the rites.
Up-shouldering in a dislocated lump,
With shallow, ostentatious carelessness,
My Surplice, gloried in, and yet despised,
I clove in pride through the inferior throng
320   Of the plain Burghers, who in audience stood
On the last skirts of their permitted ground
Beneath the pealing Organ.[2] Empty thoughts!

5. Milton, whose republicanism (and consequent isolation after the restoration of Charles II in 1660) WW emphasizes. Line 286 alludes to Milton's self-description in *Paradise Lost* 7.27–28: "In darkness, and with dangers compast round, / And solitude."
6. While a student at Cambridge in 1625–32, Milton was nicknamed "the lady of Christ's College" on account of his fair complexion and fastidious manners.
7. From time immemorial.
8. Edward Birkett, an undergraduate at Christ's College, had been a pupil at Hawkshead and was a friend of both WW and his brother Christopher.
9. Meeting, gathering. Afternoon wine parties were a regular feature of undergraduate life at Cambridge. *Oratory*: shrine.
1. In Greek mythology, a Trojan princess whose prophecy of the destruction of Troy went unheeded. *Ostrich-like*: holding his academic gown up in order to run faster (because undergraduates were required to attend twice-daily services in their college chapels, and fined if they failed to do so); *opprobrious*: shameful (i.e., shamefully late).
2. Arriving late, WW passes through the area of the chapel in which townspeople were permitted into the area reserved for college members, his *surplice*, a white linen tunic that fellows and

I am ashamed of them: and that great Bard
And Thou, O Friend! who in thy ample mind
325 Hast stationed me for reverence and love,
Ye will forgive the weakness of that hour
In some of its unworthy vanities,
Brother of many more.
                         In this mixed sort
The months passed on, remissly, not given up
330 To wilful alienation from the right,
Or walks of open scandal; but in vague
And loose indifference, easy likings, aims
Of a low pitch; duty and zeal dismissed,
Yet nature, or a happy course of things
335 Not doing in their stead the needful work.
The memory languidly revolved, the heart
Reposed in noontide rest; the inner pulse
Of contemplation almost failed to beat.
Rotted as if by a charm, my life became
340 A floating island, an amphibious thing
Unsound, of spungy texture, yet withal,
Not wanting³ a fair face of water weeds
And pleasant flowers.—The thirst of living praise,
A reverence for the glorious Dead, the sight
345 Of those long Vistos,⁴ Catacombs in which
Perennial minds lie visibly entombed,
Have often stirred the heart of Youth, and bred
A fervent love of rigorous discipline.
Alas! such high commission touched not me;⁵
350 No look was in these walls to put to shame
My easy spirits, and discountenance
Their light composure, far less to instil
A calm resolve of mind, firmly addressed
To puissant⁶ efforts. Nor was this the blame
355 Of others but my own. I should, in truth,
As far as doth concern my single self
Misdeem most widely, lodging it elsewhere.
For I, bred up in Nature's lap, was even
As a spoiled Child; and rambling like the wind
360 As I had done in daily intercourse
With those delicious rivers, solemn heights,
And mountains, ranging like a fowl of the air,
I was ill tutored for captivity,

students were required to wear during services, signaling his distinction from the *plain Burghers*.
3. Lacking. NCPrel identifies the source of this peculiar image as a phenomenon that WW described in his *Guide to the Lakes*: "there occasionally appears above the surface of Derwentwater, and always in the same place, a considerable tract of spongy ground covered with aquatic plants, which is called the Floating * * * Island" (*Prose*, 2:184).
4. An alternative spelling of *vistas* (seventeenth to nineteenth centuries).
5. WW contrasts himself with the sort of student satirized in Samuel Johnson's *Vanity of Human Wishes* (1749), lines 135–38: "When first the college rolls receive his name, / The young enthusiast quits his ease for fame; / Through all his veins the fever of renown / Spreads from the strong contagion of the gown."
6. Powerful.

To quit my pleasure, and from month to month
365 Take up a station calmly on the perch
Of sedentary peace. Those lovely forms
Had also left less space within my mind,
Which, wrought upon instinctively, had found
A freshness in those objects of its love,
370 A winning power, beyond all other power.
Not that I slighted Books; that were to lack
All sense; but other passions had been mine
More fervent, making me less prompt, perhaps,
To in-door study than was wise or well
375 Or suited to my years:[7] yet I could shape
The image of a Place which, soothed and lulled
As I had been, trained up in paradise
Among sweet garlands and delightful sounds,
Accustomed in my loneliness to walk
380 With Nature magisterially, yet I,
Methinks, could shape the image of a Place
Which with its aspect should have bent me down
To instantaneous service, should at once
Have made me pay to science and to arts
385 And written Lore, acknowledged my liege Lord,
A homage, frankly offered up, like that
Which I had paid to Nature. Toil and pains
In this recess which I have bodied forth
Should spread from heart to heart;[8] and stately groves,
390 Majestic edifices, should not want
A corresponding dignity within.
The congregating temper[9] which pervades
Our unripe years, not wasted, should be made
To minister to works of high attempt,
395 Which the enthusiast would perform with love;
Youth should be awed, possessed, as with a sense
Religious, of what holy joy there is
In knowledge, if it be sincerely sought
For its own sake, in glory and in praise,
400 If but by labour won, and to endure.
The passing Day[1] should learn to put aside
Her trappings here, should strip them off, abashed
Before antiquity, and stedfast truth,
And strong book-mindedness; and over all

---

7. In June 1791 DW reported that "William * * * lost the chance, indeed the certainty of a fellow-ship by not combatting his inclinations, he gave way to his natural dislike of studies as dry as many parts of the mathematics, consequently could not succeed at Cambridge. He reads Ital-ian, Spanish, French, Greek and Latin, and English, but never opens a mathematical book" (*WL*, 1:52). Though he had been well prepared in mathematics at Hawkshead, after his fresh-man year at Cambridge WW did not take any examinations in the subject, as he would have needed to do to receive honors or a fellowship (Moorman, 1:97–99).
8. "And as imagination bodies forth / The forms of things unknown, the poet's pen / Turns them to shapes" (Shakespeare, *A Midsummer Night's Dream* 5.1.14–16). WW imagines the work he might have done in an ideal academic environment.
9. Sociability.
1. The present.

405   Should be a healthy, sound simplicity,
      A seemly plainness,[2] name it as you will,
      Republican or pious.
                        If these thoughts
      Be a gratuitous emblazonry
      That does but mock this recreant[3] age, at least
410   Let Folly and False-seeming, we might say,
      Be free to affect whatever formal gait
      Of moral or scholastic discipline
      Shall raise them highest in their own esteem;
      Let them parade among the Schools at will;
415   But spare the House of God.[4] Was ever known
      The witless Shepherd who would drive his Flock
      With serious repetition to a pool
      Of which 'tis plain to sight they never taste?
      A weight must surely hang on days, begun
420   And ended with worst mockery: be wise,
      Ye Presidents and Deans, and to your Bells
      Give seasonable rest; for 'tis a sound
      Hollow as ever vexed the tranquil air;
      And your officious doings bring disgrace
425   On the plain Steeples of our English Church
      Whose worship 'mid remotest Village trees
      Suffers for this.[5] Even Science, too, at hand,
      In daily sight of such irreverence,
      Is smitten thence with an unnatural taint,
430   Loses her just authority, falls beneath
      Collateral suspicion, else unknown.[6]
      This obvious truth did not escape me then,
      Unthinking as I was, and I confess
      That, having in my native hills given loose
435   To a School-boy's dreaming, I had raised a pile[7]
      Upon the basis of the coming time,
      Which now before me melted fast away,
      Which could not live, scarcely had life enough
      To mock the Builder. Oh! what joy it were
440   To see a Sanctuary for our Country's Youth,
      With such a spirit in it as might be
      Protection for itself, a Virgin grove
      Primæval in its purity and depth;
      Where, though the shades were filled with chearfulness,
445   Nor indigent of songs, warbled from crowds
      In under-coverts, yet the countenance

2. Like that of the Roman Republic or of early Christianity.
3. Cowardly, apostate (the latter in the more specifically religious sense of the word).
4. In lines 415–31 WW condemns the requirement that students attend chapel (a requirement
   that his brother Christopher, in contrast, was to uphold after becoming master of Trinity Col-
   lege, Cambridge, in 1820).
5. I.e., college fellows who resign their fellowship (as they were required to do if they married)
   and become parish priests foster the same contempt for the Church among their parishioners
   that mandatory chapel fosters among college students.
6. A decline in respect for science (or knowledge more generally) follows that for religion.
7. I.e., of expectations.

Of the whole place should wear a stamp of awe:
A habitation sober and demure
For ruminating creatures, a domain
450 For quiet things to wander in, a haunt
In which the Heron might delight to feed
By the shy rivers, and the Pelican
Upon the cypress spire, a lonely thought,
Might sit and sun himself.[8] Alas! alas!
455 In vain for such solemnity we look;
Our eyes are crossed by Butterflies, our ears
Hear chattering Popinjays; the inner heart
Is trivial, and the impresses without
Are of a gaudy region.[9]
                              Different sight
460 Those venerable Doctors saw of old
When all who dwelt within these famous Walls
Led in abstemiousness a studious life,
When, in forlorn and naked chambers cooped
And crowded, o'er their ponderous Books they sate,
465 Like caterpillars eating out their way,
In silence, or with keen devouring noise
Not to be tracked or fathered.[1] Princes then
At matins froze, and couched at curfew-time,[2]
Trained up, through piety and zeal, to prize
470 Spare diet, patient labour, and plain weeds:[3]
O Seat of Arts! renowned throughout the world,
Far different service in those homely days
The Nurslings of the Muses underwent
From their first childhood; in that glorious time,
475 When Learning, like a Stranger come from far,
Standing through Christian Lands her Trumpet rouzed
The Peasant and the King; when Boys and Youths,
The growth of ragged villages and huts,
Forsook their homes; and, errant in the quest
480 Of Patron, famous School, or friendly Nook
Where, pensioned, they in shelter might sit down,
From Town to Town, and through wide-scattered Realms,
Journeyed, with their huge Folios in their hand,
And often, starting from some covert place,
485 Saluted the chance comer in the road,
Crying, "an obolus,[4] a penny give
To a poor Scholar": when illustrious Men,

---

8. NCPrel notes that WW found this image of the pelican in William Bartram's *Travels through North and South Carolina* (2nd ed., 1794; *Reading 1770–99*, no. 19), which was also a source for imagery in *Ruth* and in STC's *Kubla Khan*.
9. The external world creates impressions of gaudiness. *Popinjays*: parrots (and in a figurative sense, superficial, vain people).
1. Traced to a source; see also "unfathered vapour" (i.e., imagination) at 6.527 below.
2. Went to bed when the college gates were closed for the night; *matins*: morning prayers.
3. Garments.
4. In usual English usage, a halfpenny. But WW alludes, as he acknowledged to STC (*WL*, 1:465), to the legend that the disgraced Byzantine general Belisarius (sixth century) was reduced to begging, "*Date obolum Belisario*" [Give a coin to Belisarius].

Lovers of truth, by penury constrained,
Bucer, Erasmus, or Melancthon read
490 Before the doors and windows of their Cells
By moonshine, through mere lack of taper light.[5]
       But peace to vain regrets! we see but darkly
Even when we look behind us;[6] and best things
Are not so pure by nature that they needs
495 Must keep to all, as fondly all believe,
Their highest promise. If the Mariner,
When at reluctant distance he hath passed
Some fair enticing Island, did but know
What fate might have been his, could he have brought
500 His Bark to land upon the wished-for spot,
Good cause full often would he have to bless
The belt of churlish Surf that scared him thence,
Or haste of the inexorable wind.
For me, I grieve not; happy is the Man
505 Who only misses what I missed, who falls
No lower than I fell.
              I did not love,
As hath been noticed heretofore, the guise
Of our scholastic studies, could have wished
The river to have had an ampler range,
510 And freer pace; but this I tax[7] not; far,
Far more I grieved to see among the Band
Of those who in the field of contest stood
As combatants, passions that did to me
Seem low and mean; from ignorance of mine,
515 In part, and want of just forbearance, yet
My wiser mind grieves now for what I saw.
Willingly did I part from these, and turn
Out of their track, to travel with the shoal[8]
Of more unthinking Natures, easy Minds
520 And pillowy, and not wanting love that makes
The day pass lightly on, when foresight sleeps,
And wisdom, and the pledges interchanged
With our own inner being are forgot.
       To Books, our daily fare prescribed, I turned
525 With sickly appetite, and when I went,
At other times, in quest of my own food,
I chaced not steadily the manly deer,
But laid me down to any casual feast
Of wild-wood-honey; or, with truant eyes
530 Unruly, peeped about for vagrant fruit.
       And as for what pertains to human life,

5. Three famous scholars associated with the Reformation: Martin Bucer (1491–1551), a German
   theologian and in his last years professor of divinity at Cambridge; Desiderius Erasmus (ca.
   1466–1536), a Dutch humanist and the first teacher of Greek at Cambridge; and Philipp Mel-
   anchthon (1497–1560), a German theologian and classicist.
6. "For now we see through a glass, darkly; but then face to face" (1 Corinthians 13.12).
7. Blame.
8. Crowd.

The deeper passions working round me here,
Whether of envy, jealousy, pride, shame,
Ambition, emulation, fear, or hope,
535 Or those of dissolute pleasure, were by me
Unshared, and only now and then observed,
So little was their hold upon my being,
As outward things that might administer
To knowledge or instruction. Hushed, meanwhile,
540 Was the under soul, locked up in such a calm
That not a leaf of the great nature stirred.[9]
        Yet was this deep vacation not given up
To utter waste. Hitherto I had stood
In my own mind remote from human life,
545 At least from what we commonly so name,
Even as a shepherd on a promontory,
Who, lacking occupation, looks far forth
Into the endless sea, and rather makes
Than finds what he beholds.[1] And sure it is
550 That this first transit from the smooth delights,
And wild outlandish walks of simple youth,
To something that resembled an approach
Towards mortal business, to a privileged world
Within a world, a midway residence
555 With all its intervenient imagery,
Did better suit my visionary mind,
Far better, than to have been bolted forth,[2]
Thrust out abruptly into Fortune's way,
Among the conflicts of substantial life,
560 By a more just gradation did lead on
To higher things, more naturally matured,
For permanent possession, better fruits
Whether of truth or virtue to ensue.[3]
        In playful zest of fancy did we note,
565 (How could we less?) the manners and the ways
Of those who in the livery were arrayed
Of good or evil fame; of those with whom
By frame of academic discipline
Perforce we were connected, men whose sway
570 And whose authority of Office served
To set our minds on edge, and did no more.
Nor wanted we rich pastime of this kind,
Found every where; but chiefly in the ring

9. In his 1818–20 revisions WW omitted lines 524–41. In line 542 he refers ironically to his time at Cambridge as a *vacation*.
1. NCPrel notes WW's allusion to the isolated, bookish Scottish shepherd in James Thomson's *Castle of Indolence* (1748) 1.30, who imagines he sees "A vast assembly moving to and fro" while Apollo dips his chariot in the sea.
2. Forced out into the world, as a hunted animal is driven out from its cover.
3. This long and grammatically ambiguous sentence summarizes WW's development from his *simple youth* in the Lake District to his *midway residence* at Cambridge, which as a *just gradation* between childhood and adulthood led him to *higher things, more naturally matured* than he could have achieved if he had been forced to assume adult responsibilities (*the conflicts of substantial life*) sooner.

Of the grave Elders, Men unscoured, grotesque
575 In character, tricked out like aged trees
Which, through the lapse of their infirmity,
Give ready place to any random seed
That chuses to be reared upon their trunks.
        Here, on my view, confronting as it were
580 Those Shepherd Swains whom I had lately left,
Did flash a different image of old age,
How different! yet both, withal, alike
A Book of rudiments for the unpractised sight,
Objects embossed![4] and which with sedulous care
585 Nature holds up before the eye of Youth
In her great School: with further view, perhaps,
To enter early on her tender scheme
Of teaching comprehension with delight,
And mingling playful with pathetic thoughts.
590   The surfaces of artificial life
And manners freely spun, the delicate race
Of colours, lurking, gleaming up and down
Through that state arras,[5] woven with silk and gold,
This wily interchange of snakey hues,
595 Willingly and unwillingly revealed
I had not learned to watch, and at this time
Perhaps, had such been in my daily sight
I might have been indifferent thereto
As Hermits are to tales of distant things.
600 Hence for these rarities elaborate
Having no relish yet, I was content
With more homely produce, rudely piled
In this our coarser warehouse. At this day
I smile in many a mountain solitude
605 At passages and fragments that remain[6]
Of that inferior exhibition, played
By wooden images, a theatre
For Wake or Fair.[7] And oftentimes do flit
Remembrances before me of old Men,
610 Old Humourists,[8] who have been long in their graves
And, having almost in my mind put off
Their human names, have into Phantoms passed,
Of texture midway betwixt life and books.
        I play the Loiterer: 'tis enough to note
615 That here, in dwarf proportions, were expressed
The limbs of the great world, its goings on
Collaterally pourtrayed, as in mock fight,

4. "Standing out in relief" (OED); *rudiments*: "those points which are first taught to, or acquired
by, one commencing the study or practice of a branch of knowledge" (OED).
5. Tapestry. WW's imagery through line 596 recalls that in Spenser's *Faerie Queene* 3.11.28.
6. A blank line was left after line 605 in MSS B and A, and not until 1831–32 was the line "Of
unlimited Comedy, quaint scenes" inserted into the equivalent location in a later manuscript
(*Prel 1805* [CW], 2:60).
7. "The local annual festival of an English (now chiefly rural) parish," characterized by "village
sports, dancing, and other amusements" (OED).
8. In the now-obsolete sense of eccentrics, persons "subject to 'humours' or fancies" (OED).

A Tournament of blows, some hardly[9] dealt,
Though short of mortal Combat. And whate'er
620   Might of this pageant be supposed to hit
A simple Rustic's notice, this way less,
More that way, was not wasted upon me.
—And yet this Spectacle may well demand
A more substantial name, no mimic shew,
625   Itself a living part of a live whole,
A creek of the vast sea. For all Degrees
And Shapes of spurious fame, and short-lived praise
Here sate in state, and fed with daily alms
Retainers won away from solid good;
630   And here was Labour, his own Bond-slave, Hope
That never set the pains against the prize,
Idleness, halting with his weary clog,
And poor misguided Shame, and witless Fear,
And simple Pleasure foraging for Death,
635   Honour misplaced, and Dignity astray;
Feuds, Factions, Flatteries, Enmity and Guile;
Murmuring Submission and bald[1] Government;
The Idol weak as the Idolater,
And Decency and Custom starving Truth;
640   And blind Authority, beating with his Staff
The Child that might have led him; Emptiness
Followed as of good omen; and meek Worth
Left to itself, unheard-of, and unknown.[2]
Of these and other kindred notices
645   I cannot say what portion is in truth
The naked recollection of that time
And what may rather have been called to life
By after meditation. But delight
That, in an easy temper lulled asleep,
650   Is still with innocence its own reward,
This surely was not wanting. Carelessly
I gazed, roving as through a Cabinet[3]
Or wide Museum (thronged with fishes, gems,
Birds, crocodiles, shells,) where little can be seen,
655   Well understood, or naturally endeared,
Yet still does every step bring something forth
That quickens, pleases, stings; and here and there
A casual rarity is singled out,
And has its brief perusal, then gives way
660   To others, all supplanted in their turn.
Meanwhile, amid this gaudy Congress,[4] framed
Of things, by nature, most unneighbourly,

---

9. Forcefully.
1. Graceless, unsubtle.
2. *Prel 1805* (CW) notes that this passage of personifications, unusual for *The Prelude*, draws on
   the allegory of the scholar Discipline in William Cowper's *The Task* (1785) 2.699–750, as well
   as on Shakespeare's Sonnet 66 ("Tired with all these for restful death I cry").
3. A display case, as at 2.228.
4. Assembly, society (of Cambridge).

The head turns round, and cannot right itself;
And, though an aching and a barren sense
665 Of gay confusion still be uppermost,
With few wise longings and but little love,
Yet something to the memory sticks at last,
Whence profit may be drawn in times to come.
      Thus, in submissive idleness,[5] my Friend,
670 The labouring time of Autumn, Winter, Spring,
Nine months, rolled pleasingly away; the tenth
Returned me to my native hills again.[6]

Book Fourth

SUMMER VACATION

A pleasant sight it was when, having clomb[1]
The Heights of Kendal, and that dreary Moor
Was crossed, at length as from a rampart's edge
I overlooked the bed of Windermere.
5 I bounded down the hill, shouting amain
A lusty summons to the farther shore
For the old Ferryman, and when he came
I did not step into the well-known Boat
Without a cordial welcome. Thence right forth
10 I took my way, now drawing towards home,
To that sweet Valley[2] where I had been reared.
'Twas but a short hour's walk ere, veering round,
I saw the snow-white Church upon its hill
Sit like a thronèd Lady, sending out
15 A gracious look all over its domain.[3]
Glad greetings had I and some tears perhaps
From my old Dame, so motherly and good
While she perused me with a Parent's pride.[4]
The thoughts of gratitude shall fall like dew
20 Upon thy grave, good Creature! while my heart
Can beat I never will forget thy name.
Heaven's blessing be upon thee where thou liest,
After thy innocent and busy stir
In narrow cares, thy little daily growth
25 Of calm enjoyments, after eighty years,
And more than eighty, of untroubled life
Childless, yet by the Strangers to thy blood

5. An ironic revision, which STC would have recognized, of Horace's phrase *strenua inertia* ("busy idleness") in *Epistles* 1.11.28.
6. An allusion, doubtless ironic, to Milton's invocation of his muse after his narration of the battle in Heaven: "Into the Heav'n of Heav'ns I have presum'd, / An Earthlie Guest ° ° ° / With like safetie guided down / Return me to my Native Element" (*Paradise Lost* 7.13–16).
1. Climbed (a now-archaic form of the past participle). In lines 1–4 WW refers to the summer of 1788, when he had traveled by coach from Cambridge to Kendal, then walked ten miles north-west to the Windermere ferry via Cleabarrow, a 550-foot-high ridge affording a view of the lake.
2. The Vale of Esthwaite; *home*: Hawkshead, where WW had attended school.
3. St. Michael's Church, Hawkshead, is located atop a hill, just above the level of the roofs of other buildings in the village.
4. Ann Tyson, WW's former landlady, who died in 1796, aged eighty-three (her death is alluded to in line 20).

Honoured with little less than filial love.
Great joy was mine to see thee once again,
30   Thee and thy dwelling; and a throng of things
About its narrow precincts, all beloved,
And many of them seeming yet my own.
Why should I speak of what a thousand hearts
Have felt, and every man alive can guess?
35   The rooms, the court, the garden were not left
Long unsaluted, and the spreading Pine
And broad stone Table underneath its boughs,
Our summer seat in many a festive hour;
And that unruly Child of mountain birth,
40   The froward[5] Brook, which soon as he was boxed
Within our Garden, found himself at once,
As if by trick insidious and unkind,
Stripped of his voice, and left to dimple down,
Without an effort, and without a will,
45   A channel paved[6] by the hand of man.
I looked at him, and smiled, and smiled again,
And in the press of twenty thousand thoughts,
"Ha," quoth I, "pretty Prisoner, are you there?"
And now, reviewing soberly that hour,
50   I marvel that a fancy did not flash
Upon me, and a strong desire, straitway,
At sight of such an emblem, that shewed forth
So aptly my late course of even days
And all their smooth enthralment,[7] to pen down
55   A satire on myself. My aged Dame
Was with me at my side; She guided me;
I willing, nay—nay—wishing to be led.
—The face of every neighbour whom I met
Was as a volume to me.[8] Some I hailed
60   Far off, upon the road, or at their work,
Unceremonious greetings, interchanged
With half the length of a long field between.
Among my School-fellows I scattered round
A salutation that was more constrained,
65   Though earnest, doubtless with a little pride,
But with more shame, for my habiliments,[9]
The transformation, and the gay attire.
         Delighted did I take my place again
At our domestic Table; and, dear Friend![1]
70   Relating simply, as my wish hath been,
A Poet's History, can I leave untold

5. Ungovernable.
6. Pronounced as two syllables.
7. I.e., WW's first year at Cambridge.
8. Compare WW's description of London as a place in which "the face of every one / That passes by me is a mystery" (7.597–98).
9. Clothes.
1. The remainder of this sentence is an extended rhetorical question, although it lacks a question mark in the manuscript.

The joy with which I laid me down at night
In my accustomed Bed, more welcome now,
Perhaps, than if it had been more desired,
75 Or been more often thought of with regret:
That Bed whence I had heard the roaring wind
And clamorous rain,[2] that Bed where I, so oft,
Had lain awake, on breezy nights, to watch
The moon in splendour couched among the leaves
80 Of a tall Ash, that near our Cottage stood,
Had watched her with fixed eyes, while to and fro,
In the dark summit of the moving Tree,
She rocked with every impulse of the wind.
      Among the faces which it pleased me well
85 To see again, was one, by ancient right
Our Inmate, a rough Terrier of the hills,
By birth and call of Nature pre-ordained
To hunt the badger, and unearth the fox,
Among the impervious crags, but, having been
90 From youth our own adopted, he had passed
Into a gentler service. And when first
The boyish spirit flagged, and day by day
Along my veins I kindled with the stir,
The fermentation, and the vernal heat
95 Of Poesy, affecting private shades[3]
Like a sick lover, then this Dog was used
To watch me, an attendant and a friend
Obsequious[4] to my steps, early and late,
Though often of such dilatory walk
100 Tired and uneasy at the halts I made.
A hundred times, when in these wanderings
I have been busy with the toil of verse,
Great pains and little progress, and at once
Some fair enchanting Image in my mind
105 Rose up, full formed like Venus from the sea,
Have I sprung forth towards him, and let loose
My hand upon his back with stormy joy,
Caressing him again, and yet again.[5]
And when in the public roads at eventide
110 I sauntered, like a river murmuring
And talking to itself, at such a season
It was his custom to jog on before;
But duly, whensoever he had met
A passenger[6] approaching, would he turn
115 To give me timely voice, and straitway,

2. An image repeated in 7.487–88.
3. Assuming imaginary personae.
4. Compliant, obedient (an older sense of *obsequious*).
5. Lines 101–8 are a revision of WW's youthful poem *The Dog: An Idyllium*, composed in 1786–
   87. *Venus* (line 105): Roman name for Aphrodite, Greek goddess of love, who according to
   Hesiod's *Theogony* (ca. 700 B.C.E.), lines 188–206, rose from the foam of the sea surrounding
   the severed genitals of Uranus, god of the heavens.
6. Traveler (a now-obsolete sense of *passenger*).

Punctual to such admonishment I hushed
My voice, composed my gait, and shaped myself
To give and take a greeting that might save
My name from piteous rumours, such as wait
120 On men suspected to be crazed in brain.
          Those walks well worthy to be prized and loved,
Regretted! that word, too, was on my tongue,
But they were richly laden with all good,
And cannot be remembered but with thanks
125 And gratitude, and perfect joy of heart.
Those walks did now like a returning spring
Come back on me again. When first I made
Once more the circuit of our little Lake
If ever happiness hath lodged with Man,
130 That day consummate[7] happiness was mine,
Wide-spreading, steady, calm, contemplative.
The sun was set, or setting, when I left
Our cottage door, and evening soon brought on
A sober hour, not winning or serene,
135 For cold and raw the air was, and untuned.
But as a face we love is sweetest then
When sorrow damps it, or, whatever look
It chance to wear is sweetest if the heart
Have fulness in itself, even so with me
140 It fared that evening. Gently did my soul
Put off her veil, and, self-transmuted, stood
Naked as in the presence of her God.[8]
As on I walked a comfort seemed to touch
A heart that had not been disconsolate,
145 Strength came where weakness was not known to be,
At least not felt, and restoration came,
Like an intruder, knocking at the door
Of unacknowledged weakness. I took
The balance in my hand, and weighed myself.
150 Of that external scene which round me lay,[9]
I saw but little, and thereat was pleased;
Little did I remember, and even this
Still pleased me more; but I had hopes and peace
And swellings of the spirits, was wrapped and soothed;
155 Conversed with promises; had glimmering views
How Life pervades the undecaying mind,
How the immortal Soul with Godlike power
Informs, creates, and thaws the deepest sleep

7. Stressed on the second syllable.
8. An allusion to Exodus 34.34: after descending from Mt. Sinai, Moses' face shone so brightly that he veiled it when speaking to the Israelites, but he removed the veil when speaking to God.
9. Not present in MS A, line 150 was introduced into MS B and retained in *Prel 1850*. The passage is ambiguous if *that external scene* is assumed (as in *NCPrel*) to refer to WW himself as he contemplates himself metaphorically in the *balance* (line 149). But WW's revision in *Prel 1850*, inserting a dash at the beginning of the equivalent to line 150, suggests that he intended *that external scene* to be understood solely as the object of *I saw*, without reference to lines 148–49 (see *Prel 1850* [CW], 83). *Prel 1805* (CW) suggests that *weakness* in line 148 is an error for "weariness," the reading adopted in 1818–20 and retained thereafter.

That time can lay upon her; how on earth,
160 Man, if he do but live within the light
Of high endeavour, daily spreads abroad
His being with a strength that cannot fail.
Nor was there want of milder thoughts, of love
Of innocence, and holiday repose;[1]
165 And more than pastoral quiet, in the heart
Of amplest projects; and a peaceful end
At last, or glorious, by endurance won.
Thus musing in a wood I sate me down,
[Alone][2] continuing there to muse: meanwhile,
170 The mountain heights were slowly overspread
With darkness, and before a rippling breeze
The long Lake lengthened out its hoary line:
And in the sheltered coppice[3] where I sate,
Around me, from among the hazel leaves,
175 Now here, now there, stirred by the straggling wind
Came intermittingly a breath-like sound,
A respiration short and quick, which oft,
Yea, might I say, again and yet again,
Mistaking for the panting of my Dog,
180 The off and on Companion of my walk,
I turned my head, to look if he were there.
      A freshness also found I at this time
In human Life, the life, I mean, of those
Whose occupations really I loved.
185 The prospect[4] often touched me with surprize,
Crowded and full, and changed, as seemed to me,
Even as a garden in the heat of spring,
After an eight days' absence. For (to omit
The things which were the same, and yet appeared
190 So different) amid this solitude,
The little Vale where was my chief abode,
'Twas not indifferent to a youthful mind
To note, perhaps, some sheltered Seat, in which
An old Man had been used to sun himself,
195 Now empty; pale-faced Babes whom I had left
In arms, known children of the neighbourhood,
Now rosy prattlers, tottering up and down;
And growing Girls, whose beauty, filched away
With all its pleasant promises, was gone
200 To deck some slighted Play-mate's homely cheek.[5]
      Yes, I had something of another eye,

1. Interpreting *love, innocence,* and *holiday repose* as distinct items in WW's list, NCPrel and the "reading text" of *Prel 1805* (CW) emend the text by inserting a comma after *love.* Yet both MSS B and A read love / Of innocence, and this reading was retained in MS D of the 1830s (see *Prel 1850* [CW], 552–53).
2. Inserted at the beginning of this hypometric line in MSS B and A, probably during the 1818–20 revisions, but repeating the insertion made earlier in MS M (*Prel 1805* [CW], 1:1269).
3. A small wood or thicket of small trees or shrubs.
4. Of human occupations.
5. An allusion to Milton's *Lycidas* (1637), line 65: "To tend the homely slighted Shepherds trade." Milton was contrasting the rigors of poetic composition with sensual indulgences.

And often, looking round, was moved to smiles,
Such as a delicate work of humour breeds.
I read, without design,[6] the opinions, thoughts
205   Of those plain-living People, in a sense
Of love and knowledge: with another eye
I saw the quiet Woodman in the Woods,
The Shepherd on the Hills. With new delight,
This chiefly, did I view my grey-haired Dame,[7]
210   Saw her go forth to Church, or other work
Of state, equipped in monumental trim,
Short Velvet Cloak (her Bonnet of the like),
A Mantle such as Spanish Cavaliers[8]
Wore in old time. Her smooth domestic life,
215   Affectionate, without uneasiness,
Her talk, her business[9] pleased me, and no less
Her clear, though shallow stream of piety,
That ran on Sabbath days a fresher course.
With thoughts unfelt till now I saw her read
220   Her Bible on the Sunday afternoons;
And loved the Book, when she had dropped asleep,
And made a pillow of it for her head.
        Nor less do I remember to have felt
Distinctly manifested at this time
225   A dawning, even as of another sense,
A human-heartedness about love
For objects, hitherto the gladsome air
Of my own private being, and no more;
Which I had loved, even as a blessed Spirit,
230   Or Angel, if he were to dwell on earth,
Might love in individual happiness.
But now there opened on me other thoughts,
Of change, congratulation, and regret,
A new-born feeling. It spread far and wide;
235   The trees, the mountains shared it, and the brooks;
The stars of Heaven, now seen in their old haunts,
White Sirius, glittering o'er the southern crags,
Orion with his belt, and those fair Seven,
Acquaintances of every little Child,
240   And Jupiter,[1] my own belovèd Star.
Whatever shadings of mortality
Had fallen upon these objects heretofore
Were different in kind; not tender: strong,
Deep, gloomy were they, and severe, the scatterings
245   Of Childhood; and moreover had given way,
In later Youth, to beauty, and to love

6. Without an ulterior motive.
7. Ann Tyson.
8. Knights.
9. I.e., busy-ness.
1. In astrology, the planet under which WW was born on April 7, 1770; *fair Seven*: the Pleiades or Seven Sisters, a cluster of stars in the constellation Taurus.

Enthusiastic, to delight and joy.
　　　As one who hangs down-bending from the side
　　　Of a slow-moving Boat, upon the breast
250　Of a still water, solacing himself
　　　With such discoveries as his eye can make,
　　　Beneath him, in the bottoms of the deeps,
　　　Sees many beauteous sights, weeds, fishes, flowers,
　　　Grots, pebbles, roots of trees, and fancies more;
255　Yet often is perplexed, and cannot part
　　　The shadow from the substance, rocks and sky,
　　　Mountains and clouds, from that which is indeed
　　　The region, and the things which there abide
　　　In their true dwelling; now is crossed by gleam
260　Of his own image, by a sunbeam now
　　　And motions that are sent he knows not whence,
　　　Impediments that make his task more sweet.
　　　—Such pleasant office have we long pursued
　　　Incumbent on the surface of past time
265　With like success: nor have we often looked
　　　On more alluring shows (to me at least)
　　　More soft, or less ambiguously descried,
　　　Than those which now we have been passing by,
　　　And where we still are lingering.[2] Yet, in spite
270　Of all these new employments of the mind
　　　There was an inner falling-off; I loved,
　　　Loved deeply, all that I had loved before,
　　　More deeply, even than ever: but a swarm
　　　Of heady thoughts, jostling each other, gawds,[3]
275　And feast, and dance, and public revelry,
　　　And sports, and games, (less pleasing in themselves
　　　Than as they were a badge, glossy and fresh
　　　Of manliness and freedom) these did now
　　　Seduce me from the firm habitual quest
280　Of feeding pleasures,[4] from that eager zeal,
　　　Those yearnings which had every day been mine,
　　　A wild unworldly-minded Youth, given up
　　　To Nature and to Books, or, at the most,
　　　From time to time by inclination shipped,
285　One among many, in societies,
　　　That were, or seemed, as simple as myself.
　　　But now was come a change; it would demand
　　　Some skill, and longer time than may be spared,
　　　To paint even to myself these vanities,
290　And how they wrought. But sure it is, that now
　　　Contagious air did oft environ me,
　　　Unknown among these haunts of former days.

2. Lines 248–69 form the first of two extended similes referring to water; the second, at 9.1–9, also compares the course of WW's narrative to a river. A similar scenario of doubling appears in lines 50–62 of The Brothers (p. 103 above).
3. Gauds, i.e., idle pastimes.
4. Pleasures that nourish the mind.

The very garments that I wore appeared
To prey upon my strength, and stopped the course
295   And quiet stream of self-forgetfulness.
Something there was about me that perplexed
The authentic sight of reason, pressed too closely
On that religious dignity of mind,
That is the very faculty of truth,[5]
300   Which wanting, either from the very first,
A function never lighted up, or else
Extinguished, Man, a creature great and good,
Seems but a pageant play-thing with wild claws,[6]
And this great frame of breathing elements
A senseless Idol.
305   This vague heartless[7] chace
Of trivial pleasures was a poor exchange
For Books and Nature at that early age.
'Tis true some casual knowledge might be gained
Of character or life; but at that time
310   Of manners put to School[8] I took small note,
And all my deeper passions lay elsewhere.
Far better had it been to exalt the mind
By solitary study, to uphold
Intense desire by thought and quietness.
315   And yet in chastisement of these regrets
The memory of one particular hour
Doth here rise up against me. In a throng,
A festal Company of Maids and Youths,
Old Men and Matrons staid, promiscuous rout,[9]
320   A medley of all tempers,[1] I had passed
That night in dancing, gaiety and mirth,
With din of instruments and shuffling feet,
And glancing forms and tapers glittering
And unaimed prattle flying up and down,
325   Spirits upon the stretch and here and there
Slight shocks of young love-liking interspersed,
That mounted up like joy into the head
And tingled through the veins. Ere we retired
The Cock had crowed, the sky was bright with day.
330   Two miles I had to walk along the fields
Before I reached my home. Magnificent

5. NCPrel compares STC's later definition of reason in The Friend (1818) as "the mind's eye," "an organ bearing the same relation to spiritual objects, the Universal, the Eternal, and the Necessary, as the [physical] eye bears to material and contingent phænomena" (NCC, 556, 555).
6. Lines 302–303 gave WW some difficulty, and he attempted various revisions in 1818–20, such as substituting "vile" for "wild," before finally abandoning the lines altogether for Prel 1850. W. J. B. Owen notes a specific reference here to a lifesize model, once displayed at the East India Company (and now at the Victoria and Albert Museum) in London, of a tiger attacking a man ("Tipu's Tiger," Notes & Queries 115 [1970]: 379–80).
7. Discouraging, unfruitful.
8. The observation of human behavior.
9. Mixed company. The phrase is Miltonic: see Paradise Lost 1.380 ("the promiscuous croud stood yet aloof") and 7.34 ("that wilde Rout that tore the Thracian Bard," referring to the tearing of Orpheus to pieces by worshippers of Bacchus). festal: joyous, merry-making.
1. Temperaments.

The Morning was, a memorable pomp,
More glorious than I ever had beheld
The Sea was laughing at a distance; all
335   The solid Mountains were as bright as clouds,
Grain-tinctured, drenched in empyrean[2] light;
And in the meadows and the lower grounds
Was all the sweetness of a common dawn,
Dews, vapours, and the melody of birds,[3]
340   And Labourers going forth into the fields.
—Ah! need I say, dear Friend,[4] that to the brim
My heart was full; I made no vows, but vows
Were then made for me, bond unknown to me
Was given, that I should be, else sinning greatly,
345   A dedicated Spirit.[5] On I walked
In blessedness which even yet remains.
          Strange rendezvous my mind was at that time,
A party-coloured show of grave and gay,
Solid and light, short-sighted and profound
350   Of inconsiderate habits and sedate,
Consorting in one mansion unreproved.
I knew the worth of that which I possessed,
Though slighted and misused. Besides in truth
That summer, swarming as it did with thoughts
355   Transient and loose, yet wanted not a store
Of primitive hours,[6] when by these hindrances
Unthwarted, I experienced in myself
Conformity as just as that of old
To the end and written spirit of God's works,
360   Whether held forth in Nature or in Man.
          From many wanderings that have left behind
Remembrances not lifeless, I will here
Single out one, then pass to other themes.[7]
—A favorite pleasure hath it been with me
365   From time of earliest youth, to walk alone
Along the public Way, when, for the night
Deserted, in its silence it assumes
A character of deeper quietness
Than pathless solitudes. At such an hour
370   Once, ere those summer months were passed away
I slowly mounted up a steep ascent
Where the road's watry surface, to the ridge

2. Heavenly (in classical cosmology, the highest heaven and sphere of pure fire; in Christian cosmology, the abode of God and the angels). Grain-tinctured: scarlet or crimson colored, from the phrase dyed in grain (meaning fast-dyed, especially scarlet or crimson), but also recalling Milton's description of Raphael's wings as "Skie-tinctur'd grain" (Paradise Lost 5.285).
3. NCPrel notes an echo of Paradise Lost 8.526–28: "These delicacies / I mean of Taste, Sight, Smell, Herbs, and Flours, / Walks, and the melodie of Birds."
4. Coleridge.
5. Compare 3.82, where WW elaborates on his sense of being "a chosen Son."
6. The memory of times when his thoughts were less troubled.
7. The account that follows (lines 364–505) of WW's encounter with a discharged soldier on the road from the Windermere ferry dock to Hawkshead was originally composed as an independent poem in early 1798 (see LB [CW], 279–82, for the text) and incorporated into The Prelude in February 1804.

Of that sharp rising glittered in the moon,
And seemed before my eyes another stream
375 Creeping with silent lapse[8] to join the brook
That murmured in the Valley. On I went
Tranquil, receiving in my own despite
Amusement, as I slowly passed along
From such near objects as from time to time
380 Perforce intruded on the listless sense
Quiescent, and disposed to sympathy
With an exhausted mind, worn out by toil,
And all unworthy of the deeper joy
Which waits on distant prospect, cliff or sea,
385 The dark blue vault, and universe of stars.
Thus did I steal along that silent road,
My body from the stillness drinking in
A restoration like the calm of sleep
But sweeter far. Above, before, behind,
390 Around me, all was peace and solitude,
I looked not round, nor did the solitude
Speak to my eye; but it was heard and felt.
O happy state! what beauteous pictures now
Rose in harmonious imagery—they rose
395 As from some distant region of my soul
And came along like dreams; yet such as left
Obscurely mingled with their passing forms
A consciousness of animal delight,
A self-possession felt in every pause
400 And every gentle movement of my frame.
While thus I wandered, step by step led on[9]
It chanced a sudden turning of the road
Presented to my view an uncouth shape[1]
So near, that slipping back into the shade
405 Of a thick hawthorn, I could mark him well,
Myself unseen. He was of stature tall,
A foot above Man's common measure tall,
Stiff in his form and upright, lank and lean,
A man more meagre, as it seemed to be,
410 Was never seen abroad by night or day.[2]
His arms were long, and bare his hands, his mouth
Shewed ghastly[3] in the moonlight, from behind

8. Flow (an echo of *Paradise Lost* 8.263: "And liquid Lapse of murmuring Streams"); *steep ascent* (line 371): identifiable as Briers Brow, a hill overlooking the Windermere ferry on the west side of the lake, three miles southeast of Hawkshead; *glittered in the moon* (line 373): WW appropriates for the Lake District an observation DW had made in Alfoxden, Somerset, on the moonlit evening of January 31, 1798: "The road to the village of Holford glittered like another stream" (*DWJ*, 1:5).
9. A quotation from Milton's *Paradise Regained* 1.192, referring to the beginning of Christ's forty days in the wilderness: "Thought following thought, and step by step led on."
1. Recalling the "execrable shape" of Death in *Paradise Lost* 2.681 (Newlyn, *Coleridge, Wordsworth, and the Language of Allusion*, 30).
2. WW here shortens his description of the man from the original version in *The Discharged Soldier*, lines 41–47: "[He was in stature tall,] / A foot above man's common measure tall, / And lank, and upright. There was in his form / A meagre stiffness. You might almost think / That his bones wounded him. His legs were long, / So long and shapeless that I looked at them / Forgetful of the body they sustained" (*LB* [CW], 278–79).
3. Ghostly.

A mile-stone propped him, and his figure seemed
Half-sitting, and half-standing. I could mark
415 That he was clad in military garb,
Though faded, yet entire.[4] He was alone,
Had no attendant, neither dog, nor staff,
Nor knapsack, in his very dress appeared
A desolation, a simplicity,
420 That seemed akin to solitude. Long time
Did I peruse him with a mingled sense
Of fear and sorrow. From his lips, meanwhile,
There issued murmuring sounds, as if of pain
Or of uneasy thought, yet still his form
425 Kept the same steadiness, and at his feet
His shadow lay and moved not. In a Glen
Hard by, a Village stood, whose roofs and doors
Were visible among the scattered trees,
Scarce distant from the spot an arrow's flight;
430 I wished to see him move, but he remained
Fixed to his place, and still from time to time
Sent forth a murmuring voice of dead complaint,
Groans scarcely audible. Without self-blame
I had not thus prolonged my watch, and now
435 Subduing my heart's specious cowardise,[5]
I left the shady nook where I had stood
And hailed him. Slowly from his resting-place
He rose, and with a lean and wasted arm
In measured gesture lifted to his head
440 Returned my salutation, then resumed
His station as before, and when erelong
I asked his history, he in reply
Was neither slow nor eager, but unmoved,
And with a quiet uncomplaining voice,
445 A stately air of mild indifference,
He told in few simple words a Soldier's Tale;
That in the Tropic Islands[6] he had served,
Whence he had landed, scarcely ten days past,
That on his landing he had been dismissed,
450 And now was travelling to his native home.
At this, I turned and looked towards the Village
But all were gone to rest, the fires all out,
And every silent window to the moon
Shone with a yellow glitter. "No one there,"
455 Said I, "is waking; we must measure back
The way which we have come; behind yon wood

---

4. WW here omits a sentence from *The Discharged Soldier*, lines 55–60: "His face was turn'd /
Towards the road, yet not as if he sought / For any living object,—he appeared / Forlorn and
desolate, a man cut off / From all his kind, and more than half detached / From his own nature"
(*LB* [CW], 279).
5. I.e., WW was not willing to admit to himself his fearfulness. This spelling of *cowardice* was
accepted in the eighteenth century.
6. The West Indies, where nearly one-quarter of British battalions were stationed during the eigh-
teenth century.

A Labourer dwells, and take it on my word
He will not murmur should we break rest,
And with a ready heart will give you food
460 And lodging for the night." At this he stooped
And from the ground took up an oaken staff
By me yet unobserved, a Traveller's staff
Which I suppose from his slack hand had dropped
And lain till now neglected in the grass.
465   Towards the Cottage without more delay
We shaped our course, as it appeared to me
He travelled without pain, and I beheld
With ill-suppressed astonishment his tall
And ghastly figure moving at my side;
470 Nor while we journeyed thus, could I forbear
To question him of what he had endured
From hardship, battle or the pestilence.
He all the while was in demeanor calm,
Concise in answer: solemn and sublime
475 He might have seemed but that in all he said
There was a strange half-absence, and a tone
Of weakness and indifference, as of one
Rememb'ring the importance of his theme
But feeling it no longer. We advanced
480 Slowly, and, ere we to the wood were come,
Discourse had ceased. Together on we passed,
In silence, through the shades gloomy and dark;
Then turning up along an open field
We gained the Cottage. At the door I knocked,
485 Calling aloud, "my Friend, here is a Man
By sickness overcome; beneath your roof
This night let him find rest, and give him food,
If food he need, for he is faint and tired."
Assured that now my Comrade would repose
490 In comfort, I entreated that henceforth
He would not linger in the public ways
But ask for timely furtherance and help
Such as his state required.—At this reproof,[7]
With the same ghastly mildness in his look,
495 He said, "my trust is in the God of Heaven
And in the eye of him that passes me."
        The Cottage door was speedily unlocked,
And now the Soldier touched his hat again
With his lean hand, and in a voice that seemed
500 To speak with a reviving interest,
'Till then unfelt, he thanked me; I returned
The blessing of the poor unhappy Man,
And so we parted. Back I cast a look,

---

7. This *reproof* was expressed more bluntly in *The Discharged Soldier*, lines 157–60: "* * * But at the door of cottage or of inn / Demand the succor which his state required, / And told him feeble as he was, 'twere fit / He asked relief or alms" (*LB* [CW], 282), *relief* being poor relief, i.e., assistance provided by parishes to the poor.

And lingered near the door a little space,
505 Then sought with quiet heart my distant home.

Book Fifth

BOOKS

Even in the steadiest mood of reason, when
All sorrow for thy transitory pains
Goes out, it grieves me for thy state, O Man,
Thou paramount Creature! and thy race, while Ye
5 Shall sojourn on this planet; not for woes
Which thou endur'st; that weight, albeit huge,
I charm away; for those palms[1] atchieved
Through length of time, by study and hard thought,
The honours of thy high endowments, there
10 My sadness finds its fuel. Hitherto,
In progress through this Verse, my mind hath looked
Upon the speaking face of earth and heaven
As her prime Teacher, intercourse with Man
Established by the sovereign Intellect,
15 Who through that bodily Image[2] hath diffused
A soul divine which we participate,
A deathless Spirit. Thou also, Man, hast wrought,
For commerce of thy nature with itself,
Things worthy of unconquerable life;[3]
20 And yet we feel, we cannot chuse but feel
That these must perish. Tremblings of the heart
It gives, to think that the immortal being
No more shall need such garments;[4] and yet Man,
As long as he shall be the Child of Earth,
25 Might almost "weep to have" what he may lose,
Nor be himself extinguished; but survive
Abject, depressed, forlorn, disconsolate.[5]
A thought is with me sometimes, and I say,
Should earth by inward throes be wrenched throughout
30 Or fire be sent from far, to wither all
Her pleasant habitations, and dry up
Old Ocean in his bed, left singed and bare,
Yet would the living Presence[6] still subsist
Victorious; and composure would ensue,

1. Honors, triumphs (from the ancient Roman custom of awarding victors in contests the branch of a palm tree); *charm away*: pass over (as if to dispel by magic).
2. Visible nature, *the speaking face of earth and heaven* (line 12). In *Prel 1850* WW revised line 16, eliminating the reference to human participation in the *soul divine* and instead emphasizing the distance between humanity and the *sovereign Intellect*: "As might appear to the eye of fleeting Time" (*Prel 1850* [CW], 93).
3. Just as the *sovereign Intellect* communicates to humanity through natural phenomena, so humanity communicates with itself through works of immortal greatness.
4. The *Things* of line 19. That is, mortal man's greatest achievements are irrelevant to his *immortal being*.
5. The quotation is from Shakespeare, Sonnet 64, lines 13–14: "This thought is as a death, which cannot choose / But weep to have that which it fears to lose." WW seems to mean that man can regret possessing what he may later be forced to live unhappily without.
6. Of the *soul divine* (line 16), presumably.

35   And kindlings like the morning, presage sure,
      Though slow, perhaps, of a returning day.
      But all the meditations of mankind,
      Yea, all the adamantine holds[7] of truth,
      By reason built, or passion, which itself
40   Is highest reason in a soul sublime;
      The consecrated works of Bard or Sage,
      Sensuous or intellectual; wrought by Men,
      Twin labourers, and heirs of the same hopes,
      Where would they be? Oh! why hath not the mind
45   Some element to stamp her image on
      In nature somewhat nearer to her own?
      Why, gifted with such powers to send abroad
      Her spirit, must it lodge in shrines so frail?[8]
              One day, when in the hearing of a Friend[9]
50   I had given utterance to thoughts like these,
      He answered with a smile, that in plain truth
      'Twas going far to seek disquietude;
      But, on the front of his reproof, confessed
      That he, at sundry seasons, had himself
55   Yielded to kindred hauntings.—And forthwith,
      Added, that once upon a summer's noon,
      While he was sitting in a rocky cave
      By the Sea-side, perusing, as it chanced,
      The famous History of the Errant Knight,
60   Recorded by Cervantes,[1] these same thoughts
      Came to him; and to height unusual rose
      While listlessly he sate, and having closed
      The Book, had turned his eyes towards the Sea.
      On Poetry and geometric Truth,
65   The knowledge that endures, upon these two,
      And their high privilege of lasting life,
      Exempt from all internal injury,
      He mused; upon these chiefly: and at length,
      His senses yielding to the sultry air,
70   Sleep seized him, and he passed into a dream.[2]

7. Impregnable fortresses. In 13.166–70 WW describes imagination as "reason in her most exalted mood."
8. That is, why must works of art and science (*works of Bard or Sage*, line 41) take material forms less permanent than the minds that create them?
9. Probably STC, if indeed the episode is not wholly fictional. In *Prel 1850* WW presented the dream that follows as his own experience rather than his friend's.
1. Miguel de Cervantes's satirical romance *Don Quixote* (1605–15), which WW himself had read as a child (*Prose*, 3:372).
2. Jane Worthington Smyser, "Wordsworth's Dream of Poetry and Science," *PMLA* 71 (1956): 269–75, identified the source of the dream narrative of lines 71–139 as Adrien Baillet's *Vie de Descartes* (1691). WW adapts Baillet's account of the third of three dreams experienced by the French philosopher René Descartes (1596–1650) on November 10, 1619. In the dream, Descartes notices a dictionary and an anthology of Latin poetry on his desk, and opens the latter to a poem by the fourth-century writer Ausonius, *Quod vitae sectabor iter?* [*What way in life shall I follow?*]. An unknown man appears with Ausonius's poem *Est et non* [*It is and it is not*], which Descartes recognizes and tries unsuccessfully to find in the anthology, whereupon both the man and the books vanish. While still dreaming, Descartes interprets the dictionary as representing all the sciences and the anthology as the union of philosophy and wisdom, and after waking he interprets the poems as pertaining to his own choice of philosophical study. (Baillet's account is reprinted in *Oeuvres de Descartes*, ed. Charles Adam and Paul Tannéry, 2nd ed. [Paris, 1964–76], 10:180–85.)

He saw before him an Arabian Waste,
A Desert; and he fancied that himself
Was sitting there in the wide wilderness,
Alone upon the Sands. Distress of mind
75 Was growing in him when, behold! at once
To his great joy, a Man was at his side[3]
Upon a Dromedary mounted high.
He seemed an Arab of the Bedouin Tribes,
A lance he bore;[4] and underneath one arm
80 A Stone, and in the opposite hand, a Shell
Of a surpassing brightness. Much rejoiced
The dreaming Man that he should have a Guide
To lead him through the Desert; and he thought
While questioning himself what this strange freight
85 (Which the New-comer carried through the Waste)
Could mean, the Arab told him that the Stone,
To give it in the language of the Dream,
Was Euclid's Elements,[5] "and this," said he,
"This other," pointing to the Shell, "this Book
90 Is something of more worth." And at the word,
The Stranger, said my Friend, continuing,
Stretched forth the Shell towards me, with command
That I should hold it to my ear: I did so,
And heard that instant in an unknown Tongue,
95 Which yet I understood, articulate sounds,
A loud prophetic blast of harmony,
An Ode,[6] in passion uttered, which foretold
Destruction to the Children of the Earth,
By Deluge now at hand. No sooner ceased
100 The Song, but with calm look the Arab said
That all was true; that it was even so
As had been spoken; and that he himself
Was going then to bury those two Books,
The one that held acquaintance with the stars,
105 And wedded man to man, by purest bond
Of nature, undisturbed by space or time;

3. In *Prel 1850* WW altered line 76 to read "Close at my side, an uncouth Shape appeared" (*Prel 1850* [CW], 95), thereby suggesting a parallel between the Arab in the dream and the "uncouth shape" of the discharged soldier in 4.403.
4. The man in the dream bears a resemblance—made explicit in lines 123–24 below—to Don Quixote, who, mistaking windmills for giants, charges at them with his lance (*Don Quixote*, pt. 1, bk. 1, chap. 8). Glen Most, "Wordsworth's 'Dream of the Arab' and Cervantes," *English Language Notes* 22.3 (March 1985): 52–58, notes further connections: after the windmills episode Don Quixote encounters two monks (whom he mistakes for magicians) riding dromedaries, and the continuation of his narrative (in pt. 1, bk. 2, chap. 1) is said to be recorded in an Arabic manuscript. Kelly Grovier, "Dream Walker: A Wordsworth Mystery Solved," *Romanticism* 13 (2007): 156–63, claims that the dream narrative is a "coded tribute" to John "Walking" Stewart (1747–1822), who was reputed to have spent thirty years traveling by foot across Europe, the Middle East, India, and elsewhere, and may have met WW in Paris in 1792. Another dromedary appears in 7.193.
5. Composed by the Greek mathematician Euclid (third century B.C.E.), the *Elements* remained the standard textbook of mathematics for two millennia and was assigned reading for WW at both Hawkshead and Cambridge (*Reading 1770–99*, no. 96). A book of geometry also appears in 6.165–74.
6. Historically, "a poem intended to be sung" (*OED*). In *LB 1800* WW identified the "impassioned music of the versification" in *Tintern Abbey* with the ode form (see p. 65 above).

Th'other that was a God, yea many Gods,
Had voices more than all the winds, and was
A joy, a consolation, and a hope.
110 My Friend continued, "strange as it may seem,
I wondered not, although I plainly saw
The one to be a Stone, th' other a Shell,
Nor doubted once but that they both were Books,
Having a perfect faith in all that passed,
115 A wish was now engendered in my fear
To cleave unto[7] this Man, and I begged leave
To share his errand with him. On he passed,
Not heeding me; I followed, and took note
That he looked often backward with wild look,
120 Grasping his twofold treasure to his side.
—Upon a Dromedary, Lance in rest
He rode, I keeping pace with him, and now
I fancied that he was the very Knight
Whose Tale Cervantes tells, yet not the Knight,
125 But was an Arab of the Desart too;
Of these was neither, and was both at once.
His countenance, meanwhile, grew more disturbed,
And, looking backwards when he looked, I saw
A glittering light, and asked him whence it came,
130 "It is," said he, "the waters of the deep
Gathering upon us"; quickening then his pace,
He left me; I called after him aloud,
He heeded not; but with his twofold charge
Beneath his arm, before me full in view
135 I saw him riding o'er the Desart Sands,
With the fleet waters of the drowning world
In chace of him, whereat I waked in terror
And saw the Sea before me; and the Book
In which I had been reading at my side.
140   Full often taking from the world of sleep
This Arab Phantom which my Friend beheld,
This Semi-Quixote, I to him have given
A substance, fancied him a living Man,
A gentler Dweller in the Desart, crazed
145 By love, and feeling, and internal thought,
Protracted among endless solitudes;
Have shaped him in the oppression of his brain,
Wandering upon this quest, and thus equipped.
And I have scarcely pitied him, have felt
150 A reverence for a Being thus employed;
And thought that in the blind and awful lair
Of such a madness reason did lie couched.
Enow[8] there are on earth to take in charge
Their Wives, their Children, and their virgin Loves,

7. Cling to.
8. Enough (an archaic plural form).

155 Or whatsoever else the heart holds dear;
     Enow to think of these; yea, will I say,
     In sober contemplation of the approach
     Of such great overthrow made manifest
     By certain evidence, that I, methinks,
160 Could share that Maniac's anxiousness, could go
     Upon like errand. Oftentimes, at least,
     Me hath some deep entrancement half-possessed,
     When I have held a Volume in my hand,
     Poor earthly casket of immortal Verse!
165 Shakespear, or Milton, Labourers divine!
              Mighty indeed, supreme must be the power
     Of living Nature which could thus so long
     Detain me from the best of other thoughts.
     Even in the lisping time of Infancy,
170 And later down, in prattling Childhood, even
     While I was travelling back among those days,
     How could I ever play an ingrate's part?[9]
     Once more should I have made those bowers resound,
     And intermingled strains of thankfulness
175 With their own thoughtless melodies; at least,
     It might have well beseemed me to repeat
     Some simply-fashioned tale; to tell again,
     In slender accents[1] of sweet Verse, some tale
     That did bewitch me then, and soothes me now.
180 O Friend! O Poet! Brother of my soul,[2]
     Think not that I could ever pass along
     Untouched by these remembrances; no, no,
     But I was hurried forward by a stream,
     And could not stop. Yet wherefore should I speak,
185 Why call upon a few weak words to say
     What is already written in the hearts
     Of all that breathe! what in the path of all
     Drops daily from the tongue of every Child,
     Wherever Man is found. The trickling tear
190 Upon the cheek of listening Infancy
     Tells it, and the insuperable look
     That drinks as if it never could be full.
              That portion of my Story I shall leave
     There registered; whatever else there be
195 Of power or pleasure sown or fostered thus,
     Peculiar to myself, let that remain
     Where it lies hidden in its endless home
     Among the depths of time. And yet it seems

9. Be ungrateful; *travelling back:* in memory, through the process of composing this poem.
1. Soft notes (a usage of *slender* attested only from the late eighteenth century). *OxPrel* quotes
   from Christopher Wordsworth's *Memoirs* WW's remark of 1847 that "my earliest days at school
   * * * were very happy ones, chiefly because I was left at liberty * * * to read whatever books I
   liked. For example, I read all Fielding's works, *Don Quixote*, [Alain-René Lesage's novel] *Gil
   Blas*, and any part of Swift that I liked" (1:10). See also lines 364–69 and 482–500 below.
2. WW's echoes STC's apostrophe to him in the first published version of *Dejection: An Ode*, lines
   137–38, in the *Morning Post*, October 4, 1802: "O lofty Poet, full of light and love, / Brother
   and Friend of my devoutest choice."

That here, in memory of all Books which lay
200   Their sure foundations in the heart of Man;
Whether by native prose or numerous verse:[3]
That in the name of all inspired Souls,
From Homer, the great Thunderer; from the voice
Which roars along the bed of Jewish Song;
205   And that more varied and elaborate,
Those trumpet tones of harmony that shake
Our Shores in England;[4] from those loftiest notes
Down to the low and wren-like warblings, made
For Cottagers, and Spinners at the wheel,
210   And weary Travellers, when they rest themselves
By the highways and hedges; ballad tunes,
Food for the hungry ears of little Ones,
And of old Men who have survived their joy.
It seemeth, in behalf of these, the works
215   And of the Men who framed them, whether known,
Or sleeping nameless in their scattered graves,
That I should here assert their rights, attest
Their honours; and should, once for all, pronounce
Their benedictions; speak of them as Powers
220   For ever to be hallowed; only less,
For what we may become, and what we need,
Than Nature's self, which is the breath of God.[5]
          Rarely, and with reluctance, would I stoop
To transitory themes; yet I rejoice
225   And by these thoughts admonished, must speak out
Thanksgivings from my heart, that I was reared
Safe from an evil which these days have laid
Upon the Children of the Land, a pest
That might have dried me up, body and soul.[6]
230   This verse is dedicate to Nature's self,
And things that teach as Nature teaches, then
Oh! where had been the Man, the Poet where?
Where had we been, we two, beloved Friend,
If we, in lieu of wandering as we did
235   Through heights and hollows, and bye spots of tales
Rich with indigenous produce, open ground
Of fancy, happy pastures ranged at will;
Had been attended, followed, watched and noosed,[7]
Each in his several[8] melancholy walk

---

3. The phrase *prose or numerous verse* is from *Paradise Lost* 5.150; *native*: plain, not artificial; *numerous*: harmonious (a sense attested from the late sixteenth to early nineteenth century).
4. Milton, who drew on both the classical epic tradition (*Homer*, one of whose epithets for Zeus is *Thunderer*) and the Hebrew Bible (*Jewish Song*). WW again refers to Milton's poetry as a *trumpet* in *Scorn not the sonnet*, line 13.
5. In 12.309–12 WW expresses the hope that his own poetry "might become / A power like one of Nature's."
6. As *NCPrel* notes, the *evil* alluded to is the appearance of numerous educational theories in England after the publication of Jean-Jacques Rousseau's widely read novel about childhood education, *Émile* (1762).
7. Restricted or constrained, like livestock fitted with halters.
8. Individual, separate.

240 Stringed like a poor Man's Heifer, at its feed
     Led through the lanes in forlorn servitude;
     Or rather, like a stallèd Ox shut out
     From touch of growing grass, that may not taste
     A flower till it have yielded up its sweets,
245 A prelibation[9] to the Mower's scythe.
          Behold the Parent Hen amid her brood,
     Though fledged and feathered, and well pleased to part,
     And straggle from her presence, still a Brood;
     And she herself from the maternal bond
250 Still undischarged; yet doth she little more
     Than move with them in tenderness and love,
     A centre of the circle which they make;
     And now and then, alike from need of theirs
     And call of her own natural appetites,
255 She scratches, ransacks up the earth for food
     Which they partake at pleasure. Early died
     My honoured Mother, she who was the heart
     And hinge[1] of all our learnings and our loves;
     She left us destitute, and as we might
260 Trooping together. Little suits it me
     To break upon the sabbath of her rest
     With any thought that looks at other's blame,
     Nor would I praise her but in perfect love.
     Hence I am checked.[2] But I will boldly say,
265 In gratitude, and for the sake of truth,
     Unheard by her, that she, not falsely taught,
     Fetching her goodness rather from times past
     Than shaping novelties from those to come,
     Had no presumption, no such jealousy;
270 Nor did by habit of her thoughts mistrust
     Our Nature; but had virtual[3] faith that He
     Who fills the Mother's breasts with innocent milk,
     Doth also for our nobler part provide,
     Under his great correction and controul,
275 As innocent instincts, and as innocent food.
     This was her creed; and therefore she was pure
     From feverish dread of error or[4] mishap
     And evil, overweeningly so called;

9. A foretaste. To paraphrase the simile, the ox is not let out to graze until after the first crop of
   hay has been cut, as if the hay were an offering to the mower. WW "has in mind the reduction
   of literature to edifying tales such as those of Thomas Day's *Sandford and Merton* (1783–89)
   and Maria Edgeworth's *Parent's Assistant* (1796–1801)" (*NCPrel*). PPrel notes an ironic echo of
   Cowper's *The Task* 5.573–74: "of his fruits he [God] sends / Large prelibation oft to saints
   below."
1. Prop, pivot. WW's mother, Ann, died in March 1778, about a month before his eighth
   birthday.
2. That is, WW hesitates to praise his mother at the expense of the relatives who took over
   responsibility for him. He probably alludes in particular to his maternal grandparents, with
   whom he and his siblings lived unhappily in Penrith in the months following their mother's
   death. In June 1778 DW went to live with cousins in Halifax, Yorkshire, where she remained
   until 1787, and in May 1779 WW and his brother Richard departed for Hawkshead.
3. Potent, powerful (a now-obsolete sense).
4. Thus in MS B, but possibly an error for "and," the reading in MS A.

Was not puffed up by false unnatural hopes;
280 Nor selfish with unnecessary cares;
Nor with impatience from the season asked
More than its timely produce, rather loved
The hours for what they are, than from regards
Glanced on their promises in restless pride.[5]
285 Such was she; not from faculties more strong
Than others have, but from the times, perhaps,
And spot in which she lived; and through a grace
Of modest meekness, simple-mindedness,
A heart that found benignity and hope,
Being itself benign.
290   My drift hath scarcely,
I fear, been obvious; for I have recoiled
From shewing it as it is, the monster birth
Engendered by these too industrious times.[6]
Let few words paint it: 'tis a Child, no Child,
295 But a dwarf Man; in knowledge, virtue, skill,
In what he is not, and in what he is,
The noontide shadow of a Man complete,
A worshipper of worldly seemliness,
Not quarrelsome; for that were far beneath
300 His dignity: with gifts he bubbles o'er
As generous as a fountain: selfishness
May not come near him, gluttony or pride;
The wandering Beggars propagate his name,
Dumb creatures find him tender as a Nun.[7]
305 Yet deem him not for this a naked dish
Of goodness merely, he is garnished out.[8]
Arch are his notices, and nice his sense
Of the ridiculous; deceit and guile,
Meanness and falsehood he detects, can treat
310 With apt and graceful laughter; nor is blind
To the broad follies of the licenced[9] world,
Though shrewd, yet innocent himself withal

5. That is, WW's mother accepted life as it was, without demanding *in restless pride* whether it had fulfilled her expectations (*promises*).
6. Composed in February 1804 as a contrast to the portrait of the boy of Winander (lines 389–422 below), the depiction of the infant prodigy of learning in lines 294–369 satirizes the effects of what WW considered an overemphasis on book-learning in contemporary childhood education. In a note on this passage in *OxPrel*, de Selincourt points out that WW was also critical, however, of Rousseau, who, while devaluing book-learning—in particular, imaginative tales of the sort that WW himself had enjoyed as a child (see lines 166–222 above and 364–69 below)—still did not trust children to learn from nature without close adult supervision. In a letter of March 19, 1797, DW described the educational "system" she and WW had adopted while caring for the young Basil Montagu in 1796–97: "We teach him nothing at present but what he learns from the evidence of the senses. He has an insatiable curiosity which we are always careful to satisfy to the best of our ability. It is direct to everything he sees, the sky, the fields, trees, shrubs, corn, the making of tools, carts, &c &c &c. He knows his letters, but we have not attempted any further step in the path of *book learning*" (*WL*, 1:180).
7. WW's prodigy may have been modeled after the precociously accomplished protagonist of Day's *Sandford and Merton*, Harry Sandford, who is "brave, generous to beggars, kind to animals" (*OxPrel*).
8. Adorned, embellished (with the worldly elegance and wisdom described in lines 307–12).
9. Unrestrained, privileged.

And can read[1] lectures upon innocence.
He is fenced round, nay armed for aught we know
315 In panoply[2] complete, and fear itself,
Natural, or supernatural, alike,
Unless it leap upon him in a dream,
Touches him not.[3] Briefly, the moral part
Is perfect, and in learning and in books
320 He is a prodigy. His discourse moves slow,
Massy and ponderous as a prison door,
Tremendously embossed with terms of art,[4]
Rank growth of propositions overruns
The Stripling's brain; the path in which he treads
325 Is choked with grammers; cushion of Divine
Was never such a type of thought profound
As is the pillow where he rests his head.[5]
The Ensigns of the Empire which he holds,
The globe and septre[6] of his royalties
330 Are telescopes, and crucibles, and maps.
Ships he can guide across the pathless Sea,
And tell you all their cunning:[7] he can read
The inside of the earth, and spell[8] the stars.
He knows the policies of foreign Lands,
335 Can string you names of districts, cities, towns,
The whole world over, tight as beads of dew
Upon a gossamer thread; he sifts, he weighs,
Takes nothing upon trust; his Teachers stare,
The Country People pray for God's good grace,
340 And tremble at his deep experiments.[9]
All things are put to question; he must live
Knowing that he grows wiser every day
Or else not live at all; and seeing, too,
Each little drop of wisdom as it falls
345 Into the dimpling cistern[1] of his heart.
Meanwhile, old Grandame Earth is grieved to find
The playthings which her love has designed for him
Unthought of:[2] in their woodland beds the flowers

1. Recite.
2. A complete suit of armor.
3. In contrast to WW, whose own moral development was "Fostered alike by beauty and by fear" (1.309). The prodigy's indifference to nature is stated in lines 346–49 below.
4. Technical terminology, learned discourse.
5. A rather obscure metaphor perhaps suggested by Cowper's The Task 4.596–98, in which the complacent parson "lays / His rev'rence and his worship both to rest / On the same cushion of habitual sloth": the pillow on which the prodigy sleeps is a better symbol (type) of profound thought than the cushion on which a parson (Divine) rests his Bible in the pulpit (PPrel).
6. An archaic spelling. The prodigy's scientific instruments (line 330) are symbols of his learning, just as the orb and scepter are the traditional symbols of a monarch's authority.
7. Skill, knowledge. Harry Sanford, when lost, finds his way home by the polestar (OxPrel).
8. Contemplate or study (a poetic usage, as in Milton's Il Penseroso [1645], lines 170–71: "Where I may sit and rightly spell / Of every Star that Heav'n doth shew").
9. In fear that the prodigy is seeking forbidden knowledge. In Shakespeare's 1 Henry IV, the magician Glyndwr refers to his "deep experiments" (3.1.47).
1. Figuratively, a rain barrel in which the water is rippling (dimpling).
2. NCPrel notes WW's conflation of the phrases "old beldam earth" and "our grandam earth" (both meaning Grandmother Earth) from 1 Henry IV 3.1.30 and 32, and the contrast here to the Intimations Ode, lines 77–84, in which nature's sensuous pleasures make the child forget the preexistence of its own soul.

Weep, and the river sides are all forlorn.
350   Now this is hollow, 'tis a life of lies
From the beginning, and in lies must end.
Forth bring him to the air of Common sense,
And fresh and shewy as it is, the Corps[3]
Slips from us into powder. Vanity,
355 That is his soul, there lives he, and there moves;[4]
It is the soul of every thing he seeks;
That gone, nothing is left which he can love:
Nay, if a thought of purer birth should rise
To carry him towards a better clime,
360 Some busy helper still is on the watch
To drive him back, and pound him like a Stray
Within the pinfold of his own conceit;[5]
Which is his home, his natural dwelling-place.
Oh! give us once again the Wishing-cap
365 Of Fortunatus, and the invisible Coat
Of Jack the Giant-killer, Robin Hood,
And Sabra[6] in the Forest with Saint George:
The Child whose love is here, at least doth reap
One precious gain, that he forgets himself.
370   These mighty workmen of our later age
Who with a broad highway have overbridged
The froward[7] chaos of futurity,
Tamed to their bidding, they who have the art
To manage books and things, and make them work
375 Gently on infant minds, as does the sun
Upon a flower; the Tutors of our Youth,
The Guides, the Wardens of our faculties,
And Stewards of our labour, watchful Men
And skillful in the usury of time,
380 Sages, who in their prescience would controul
All accidents, and to the very road
Which they have fashioned would confine us down
Like engines,[8] when will they be taught

3. Body, corpse (an older spelling).
4. An ironic allusion to Acts 17.28: "In him [Christ] we live, and move, and have our being."
5. If the prodigy begins to think of something beyond his own accomplishments, one of his teachers (*Some busy helper*) will always (*still*) be sure to impound (*pound*) him like a stray animal in the enclosure (*pinfold*) formed by the prodigy's favorable estimation of his own intellect (*conceit*). In other words, teachers discourage the prodigy's intellectual development by reinforcing his vanity.
6. In medieval legend, the princess rescued by St. George from the dragon who is terrorizing her city; *Fortunatus*: in a widely translated and adapted German folk tale (first printed in 1509), a beggar who receives an inexhaustible purse from Fortune and steals a *Wishing-cap* that makes its wearer invisible and transports him instantly to wherever he pleases; *Jack the Giant-killer*: English nursery tale about Jack, a farmer's son who rids the country of giants with the aid of a coat that makes him invisible, shoes that give him exceptional speed, and a magic sword; *Robin Hood*: the legendary medieval English outlaw to whom much popular literature was devoted.
7. Perverse. The *workmen* (i.e., devisers of educational systems) are implicitly compared to Milton's Sin and Death, who build a bridge across Chaos from Hell to the created world (*Paradise Lost* 10.282–305).
8. Lines 381–82 as printed here follow the revision made in MW's hand, evidently at an early stage, in accordance with the revision of the same lines in MS A. As originally written in both MSS A and B, line 381 is hypermetrical: "All accidents and to the very road which they / Have fashion'd would confine us down" (*Prel 1805* [CW], 2:621).

That in the unreasoning progress of the world
385 A wiser Spirit is at work for us,
A better eye than theirs, most prodigal
Of blessings, and most studious of our good
Even in what seem our most unfruitful hours.
There was a Boy, ye knew him well, ye Cliffs
390 And Islands of Winander![9] many a time
At Evening, when the Stars had just begun
To move along the edges of the hills,
Rising or setting, would he stand alone,
Beneath the trees, or by the glimmering Lake,
395 And there, with fingers interwoven, both hands
Pressed closely, palm to palm, and to his mouth
Uplifted, he, as through an instrument,
Blew mimic hootings to the silent Owls
That they might answer him.—And they would shout
400 Across the watry Vale, and shout again,
Responsive to his call, with quivering peals,
And long halloos, and screams, and echoes loud
Redoubled and redoubled, a concourse wild
Of mirth and jocund din! And when it chanced
405 That pauses of deep silence mocked his skill,
Then, sometimes in that silence, while he hung
Listening, a gentle shock of mild surprize
Has carried far into his heart the voice
Of mountain torrents, or the visible scene
410 Would enter unawares into his mind
With all its solemn imagery, its rocks,
Its woods, and that uncertain Heav'n received
Into the bosom of the steady Lake.[1]
This Boy was taken from his Mates, and died
415 In childhood, ere he was full ten years old.
—Fair are the woods, and beauteous is the Spot,
The Vale where he was born: the Church-yard hangs
Upon a Slope above the Village School,
And there along that bank, when I have passed

9. An older name of Windermere. The earliest version of this passage on the boy of Winander, corresponding to lines 389–413 here but with a first-person narration, was composed in Goslar in autumn 1798 along with book 1 of *Prel 1799* (see *NCPrel*, 492, for the text). A revised, third-person version with seven additional lines, corresponding to but differently ordered from lines 414–22 here, was published as an untitled independent poem in *LB 1800* and reprinted in *P 1815* (see *LB* [CW], 139–41). WW commented on the poem in the preface to *P 1815*: "Guided by one of my own primary consciousnesses, I have represented a commutation and transfer of internal feelings, co-operating with external accidents, to plant, for immortality, images of sound and sight, in the celestial soil of the Imagination. The Boy, there introduced, is listening, with something of a feverish and restless anxiety, for the recurrence of the riotous sounds which he had previously excited; and, at the moment when the intenseness of his mind is beginning to remit, he is surprised into a perception of the solemn and tranquillizing images which the Poem describes" (*Prose*, 3:35n).
1. After being sent the original version of *There was a boy*, STC wrote WW on December 10, 1798, "I observed, I remember, that the 'fingers woven,' &c. [see line 395 here], only puzzled me; and though I liked the twelve or fourteen first lines very well, yet I like the remainder much better. Well, now I have read them again, they are very beautiful, and leave an affecting impression. That 'Uncertain heaven received / Into the bosom of the steady lake,' I should have recognised any where; and had I met these lines running wild in the deserts of Arabia, I should have instantly screamed out 'Wordsworth!'" (*CL*, 1:452–53).

420 At evening, I believe that oftentimes
A full half-hour together I have stood
Mute—looking at the grave in which he lies.[2]
    Even now, methinks, I have before my sight
That self-same Village Church, I see her sit,
425 The thronèd Lady spoken of erewhile,[3]
On her green hill; forgetful of this Boy
Who slumbers at her feet; forgetful, too,
Of all her silent neighbourhood of graves,
And listening only to the gladsome sounds
430 That, from the rural School ascending, play
Beneath her and about her. May she long
Behold a race of Young ones like to those
With whom I herded! (easily, indeed,
We might have fed upon a fatter soil
435 Of Arts and Letters, but be that forgiven,)[4]
A race of real Children, not too wise,
Too learned, or too good: but wanton, fresh,
And bandied up and down by love and hate,
Fierce, moody, patient, venturous, modest, shy;
440 Mad at their sports like withered leaves in winds;
Though doing wrong, and suffering, and full oft
Bending beneath our life's mysterious weight
Of pain and fear; yet still, in happiness
Not yielding to the happiest upon earth.
445 Simplicity in habit, truth in speech,
Be these the daily strengtheners of their minds!
May books and nature be their early joy!
And knowledge, rightly honoured with that name,
Knowledge not purchased with the loss of power.
450   Well do I call to mind the very week,[5]
When I was first entrusted to the care
Of that sweet Valley, when its paths, its shores,
And brooks, were like a dream of novelty
To my half infant thoughts; that very week
455 While I was roving up and down alone,
Seeking I knew not what, I chanced to cross
One of those open fields, which, shaped like ears,
Make green peninsulas on Esthwaite's Lake.
Twilight was coming on; yet through the gloom,
460 I saw distinctly on the opposite Shore
A heap of garments, left, as I supposed,

2. According to Thompson, 56, WW informed a cousin that the grave was that of a Hawkshead
   classmate, John Tyson, who is recorded as having died on August 25, 1782, and been buried
   two days later.
3. St. Michael's, Hawkshead, referred to in 4.13–15.
4. At Hawkshead WW would have received extensive instruction not only in mathematics (for
   which his school was renowned) but, as at all schools preparing boys for university, in Latin
   and Greek literature (see *Reading 1770–1799*, Appendix 2, for a conjectural reconstruction of
   the school's classical syllabus). Although English literature would not have been officially
   included in the curriculum, WW was encouraged by his schoolmaster to read books of English
   poetry in the school library (*Reading 1770–1799*, 163; Schneider, 76–79).
5. In May 1779.

By one who there was bathing: long I watched,
But no one owned them: meanwhile the calm Lake
Grew dark, with all the shadows on its breast,
465 And now and then, a fish upleaping snapped
The breathless stillness. The succeeding day,
(Those unclaimed garments telling a plain Tale)
Went there a Company, and in their Boat,
Sounded with grappling irons and long poles.
470 At length, the dead Man, 'mid that beauteous scene
Of trees, and hills, and water, bolt upright
Rose with his ghastly face: a spectre-shape
Of terror even! and yet no vulgar fear,
Young as I was, a Child not nine years old,
475 Possessed me; for my inner eye had seen
Such sights before, among the shining streams
Of Fairy Land, the Forests of Romance.[6]
Thence came a Spirit hallowing what I saw
With decoration, and ideal grace,
480 A dignity, a smoothness, like the works
Of Grecian Art, and purest Poesy.
        I had a precious treasure at that time,
A little, yellow canvas-covered Book,
A slender abstract of the Arabian Tales;[7]
485 And when I learned, as now I first did learn,
From my Companions in this new abode,
That this dear prize of mine was but a block
Hewn from a mighty quarry; in a word,
That there were four large Volumes, laden all
490 With kindred matter, 'twas in truth to me
A promise scarcely earthly. Instantly
I made a league, a covenant, with a Friend
Of my own age, that we should lay aside
The monies we possessed, and hoard up more,
495 Till our joint savings had amassed enough
To make this book our own. Through several months
Religiously[8] did we preserve that vow,
And spite of all temptation, hoarded up
And hoarded up; but firmness failed at length,
500 Nor were we ever masters of our wish.
        And, afterwards, when to my Father's House
Returning at the holidays, I found
That golden store of books which I had left,

6. I.e., in his childhood reading. James Jackson, a schoolmaster in the village of Sawrey, drowned
  on June 18, 1779, while swimming in Esthwaite Water. Lines 450–72 were originally composed
  as part of the sequence of "spots of time" in *Prel 1799* 1.258–74 (*NCPrel*, 7–8).
7. *The Arabian Nights Entertainments*, better known as *The Thousand and One Nights*, an Ara-
  bic collection of stories from Persian and other sources. Translated into French and then
  English in the early eighteenth century, the collection was popular children's reading in
  WW's time and afterwards. The *four large Volumes* mentioned in line 489 are probably of the
  anonymous English translation of 1777 (*Reading 1770–1799*, no. 11). STC recalled in 1797
  that his childhood obsession with the book had prompted his father to burn the family copy
  (*NCC*, 619).
8. Scrupulously.

Open to my enjoyment, once again
505   What heart was mine! Full often through the course
Of those glad respites, in the summer time,
When, armed with rod and line we went abroad,
For a whole day together I have lain
Down by thy side, O Derwent! murmuring Stream,
510   On the hot stones and in the glaring sun,
And there have read, devouring as I read,
Defrauding the day's glory, desperate,
'Till, with a sudden bound of smart reproach,
Such as an Idler deals with, in his shame,
515   I to my sport betook myself again.
         A gracious Spirit o'er this earth presides,
And o'er the heart of Man: invisibly
It comes, directing those to works of love,
Who care not, know not, think not what they do;
520   The Tales that charm away the wakeful night
In Araby; Romances, Legends, penned,
For solace, by the light of monkish Lamps;
Fictions for Ladies, of their Love, devised
By youthful Squires; adventures endless, spun
525   By the dismantled[9] Warrior in old age,
Out of the bowels of those very thoughts
In which his youth did first extravagate,[1]
These spread like day, and something in the shape
Of these, will live till Man shall be no more.
530   Dumb yearnings, hidden appetites are ours,
And they must have their food; our childhood sits,
Our simple childhood sits upon a throne
That hath more power than all the elements.[2]
I guess not what this tells of Being past,
535   Nor what it augurs of the life to come;[3]
But so it is, and in that dubious hour,
That twilight when we first begin to see
This dawning earth, to recognise, expect;
And, in the long probation that ensues,
540   The time of trial, ere we learn to live
In reconcilement with our stinted powers,
To endure this state of meagre vassalage;
Unwilling to forego, confess, submit,
Uneasy and unsettled; yokefellows
545   To custom, mettlesome, and not yet tamed
And humbled down, Oh then we feel, we feel,
We know when we have friends—Ye dreamers, then,
Forgers of lawless[4] Tales! we bless you then,

---

9. No longer wearing a *mantle*, the covering (cloak, armor, etc.) he would have worn as an active soldier.
1. Wander, roam freely (in a figurative sense).
2. Of nature.
3. I.e., WW declines (here) to speculate on what childhood imaginative power implies about the existence of the soul before birth (*Being past*) or after death (*life to come*).
4. Fantastic, improbable.

Imposters, drivellers, dotards, as the ape[5]
550 Philosophy will call you; then we feel
With what, and how great might ye are in league,
Who make our wish our power, our thought a deed,
An empire, a possession; Ye whom Time,
And Seasons serve, all Faculties; to whom
555 Earth crouches, th'elements are Potter's clay,
Space like a Heaven filled up with Northern lights,[6]
Here, nowhere, there, and everywhere at once.
            It might demand a more impassioned strain
To tell of later pleasures linked to these,[7]
560 A tract of the same isthmus which we cross
In progress from our native continent
To earth and human life.[8] I mean to speak
Of that delightful time of growing Youth
When cravings for the marvellous relent,
565 And we begin to love what we have seen;
And sober truth, experience, sympathy
Take stronger hold of us; and words themselves
Move us with conscious pleasure.
                            I am sad
At thought of raptures, now for ever flown,
570 Even unto tears, I sometimes could be sad
To think of, to read over, many a page,
Poems, withal of name, which at that time
Did never fail to entrance me, and are now
Dead in my eyes, as is a theatre
575 Fresh emptied of Spectators.[9] Thirteen years,
Or haply less, I might have seen, when first
My ears began to open to the charm
Of words in tuneful order, found them sweet
For their own sakes, a passion and a power,
580 And phrases pleased me, chosen for delight,
For pomp or love. Oft in the public roads,
Yet unfrequented, while the morning light
Was yellowing the hill tops, with that dear Friend,
The same whom I have mentioned heretofore,[1]
585 I went abroad, and for the better part
Of two delightful hours we strolled along
By the still borders of the misty Lake,
Repeating favorite Verses with one voice,

5. Fool (a figurative sense current through the eighteenth century).
6. The aurora borealis; *elements*: the four elements of which the world was traditionally thought to be composed: earth, air, water, and fire.
7. Presumably a reference to the projected (but never completed) *Recluse*.
8. The soul's passage from its preexistent, immortal state (*our native continent*) into mortal life. WW's use of the word *isthmus* (literally a narrow piece of land surrounded by water and connecting two larger pieces of land, or a narrow piece of a bodily organ connecting two larger parts) recalls Alexander Pope's *Essay on Man* (1733–34) 2.3.3–7: "Placed on this isthmus of a middle state, / A being darkly wise, and rudely great: / With too much knowledge for the Sceptic side, / With too much weakness for the Stoic's pride, / He [man] hangs between * * *."
9. Stressed on the second syllable.
1. John Fleming, mentioned in 2.352–53.

Or conning[2] more, as happy as the birds
590 That round us chaunted. Well might we be glad,
Lifted above the ground by airy fancies
More bright than madness or the dreams of wine,
And, though full oft the objects of our love
Were false, and in their splendor overwrought,[3]
595 Yet, surely, at such time no vulgar power
Was working in us, nothing less, in truth,
Than that most noble attribute of Man,
Though yet untutored, and inordinate,[4]
That wish for something loftier, more adorned
600 Than is the common aspect, daily garb
Of human life. What wonder, then, if sounds
Of exultation echoed through the groves;
For images, and sentiments, and words,
And every thing with which we had to do
605 In that delicious world of poesy,
Kept holiday, a never ending show,
With music, incense, festival and flowers!
        Here must I pause: this only will I add
From heart-experience, and in humblest sense
610 Of modesty, that he, who, in his youth
A wanderer among the woods and fields,
With living Nature hath been intimate,
Not only in that raw unpractised time
Is stirred to ecstasy, as others are,
615 By glittering Verse; but he doth furthermore,
In measure only dealt out to himself,
Receive enduring touches of deep joy
From the great Nature that exists in works
Of mighty Poets. Visionary Power
620 Attends upon the motions of the winds
Embodied in the mystery of the words.
There darkness makes abode, and all the host
Of shadowy things do work their changes there,
As in a mansion like their proper home:
625 Even forms and substances are circumfused[5]
By that transparent veil with light divine,
And, through the turnings intricate of Verse,
Present themselves as objects recognised,
In flashes, and with a glory scarce their own.
630   Thus far a scanty record is deduced

2. Learning by heart.
3. According to Thomas De Quincey in "Lake Reminiscences: William Wordsworth" (1839), WW refers here to the poetry of Oliver Goldsmith (?1728–1774) and Thomas Gray (1716–1771): "At another period of the year, when the golden summer allowed the students a long season of early play before the studies of the day began, he describes himself as roaming, hand-in-hand, with one voice, the verses of Goldsmith and of Gray—verses which, at the time of recording the fact, he had come to look upon as either in parts false in the principles of their composition, or, at any rate, as wofully below the tone of high poetic passion" (*Works*, gen. ed. Grevel Lindop [London, 2000–2003], 11:79). See the Preface to *LB 1800* for WW's criticism of Gray's diction.
4. Disordered.
5. Surrounded, enveloped.

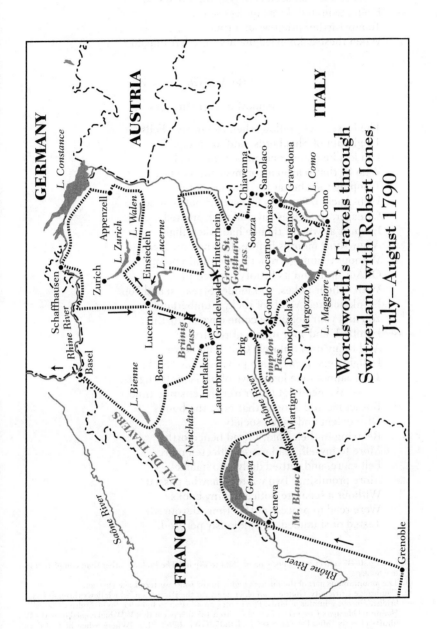

Wordsworth's Travels through
Switzerland with Robert Jones,
July–August 1790

GERMANY

L. Constance

AUSTRIA

Schaffhausen

Rhine River

Basel

Zurich

Appenzell

L. Zurich

L. Walen

Einsiedeln

Lucerne

L. Lucerne

Brünig
Pass

Grindelwald

Hinterrhein

Great St.
Gotthard
Pass

ITALY

Chiavenna

Samolaco

Gravedona

L. Como

Soazza

Locarno

Domaso

Lugano

Como

Gondo

Mergozzo

L. Maggiore

Domodossola

Simplon
Pass

Brig

Martigny

Rhône River

VAL DE TRAVERS

L. Bienne

L. Neuchâtel

Berne

Interlaken

Lauterbrunnen

Saône River

FRANCE

L. Geneva

Geneva

Mt. Blanc

Rhône River

Grenoble

Of what I owed to Books in early life;
Their later influence yet remains untold.
But as this work was taking in my thoughts
Proportions that seemed larger than had first
635 Been meditated, I was indisposed
To any further progress at a time
When these acknowledgments were left unpaid.[6]

Book Sixth

CAMBRIDGE AND THE ALPS

The leaves were yellow when to Furness Fells,[1]
The haunt of Shepherds, and to cottage life
I bade adieu, and, one among the Flock
Who by that season are convened, like birds
5   Trooping together at the Fowler's lure
Went back to Granta's Cloisters,[2] not so fond
Or eager, though as gay and undepressed
In spirit as when I thence had taken flight
A few short months before. I turned my face
10   Without repining, from the mountain pomp
Of Autumn, and its beauty entered in
With calmer Lakes, and louder Streams: and You,
Frank-hearted Maids of rocky Cumberland,
You and your not unwelcome days of mirth
15   I quitted, and your nights of revelry,
And in my own unlovely Cell[3] sate down
In lightsome mood, such privilege has Youth,
That cannot take long leave of pleasant thoughts.
            We need not linger o'er the ensuing time,
20   But let me add at once that now, the bonds
Of indolent and vague society
Relaxing in their hold, I lived henceforth
More to myself, read more, reflected more,
Felt more, and settled daily into habits
25   More promising. Two winters may be passed
Without a separate notice:[4] many books
Were read in process of this time, devoured,
Tasted or skimmed, or studiously perused,[5]

---

6. Lines 630–37 reflect WW's decision of 1804 to expand *The Prelude* rather than complete it in
five books.
1. The mountainous part of the Furness region in the southwestern Lake District.
2. Cambridge University. *Granta* is an older name for the River Cam, which flows through Cam-
bridge. *Fowler*: a hunter of birds. PPrel notes an allusion to lines 95–96 of Andrew Marvell's
Horation Ode upon Cromwell's Return (written 1650), a poem that WW had copied into MS W
(drafts of early 1804, for which see *Prel 1805* [CW], 2:262–313): "Where, when he first does
lure, / The falc'ner has her sure."
3. WW's rooms above the kitchens of St. John's College (on which see the note at 3.50).
4. The winters of 1788–89 and 1789–90.
5. WW's phrasing recalls Francis Bacon's "Of Studies" (1597): "Some *Bookes* are to be tasted,
Others to be Swallowed, and Some Few to be Chewed and Digested."

Yet with no settled plan. I was detached
30 Internally from academic cares,
From every hope of prowess and reward,
And wished to be a lodger in that house
Of Letters,[6] and no more: and should have been
Even such, but for some personal concerns
35 That hung about me in my own despite
Perpetually, no heavy weight, but still
A baffling and a hindrance, a controul
Which made the thought of planning for myself
A course of independent study seem
40 An act of disobedience towards them
Who loved me, proud rebellion and unkind.[7]
This bastard virtue, rather let it have
A name it more deserves, this cowardice
Gave treacherous sanction to that overlove
45 Of freedom planted in me from the very first
And indolence, by force of which I turned
From regulations even of my own,
As from restraints and bonds. And who can tell,
Who knows, what thus may have been gained, both then
50 And at a later season, or preserved;
What love of nature, what original strength
Of contemplation, what intuitive truths
The deepest and the best, and what research
Unbiassed, unbewildered, and unawed?
55   The Poet's soul was with me at this time,
Sweet meditations, the still overflow
Of happiness and truth. A thousand hopes
Were mine, a thousand tender dreams, of which
No few have since been realized, and some
60 Do yet remain hopes for my future life.[8]
Four years and thirty, told this very week
Have I been now a sojourner on earth,
And yet the morning gladness is not gone
Which then was in my mind.[9] Those were the days
65 Which also first encouraged me to trust
With firmness, hitherto but lightly touched
With such a daring thought, that I might leave
Some monument behind me which pure hearts

6. I.e., to be a writer.
7. By the end of 1789 WW had decided, contrary to his relatives' wishes, not to study for an honors degree, which he would have needed to secure a college fellowship. But he also did not systematically pursue an independent course of study, he proceeds to explain (lines 42–47), as much because of his own *indolence* as because of his fear (*cowardice*) of offending his relatives. See the note on 3.375 for DW's account of her brother's reading at Cambridge.
8. WW alludes to his plan to write the philosophical section of *The Recluse*, postponed by March 1804 in favor of expanding *The Prelude*. By this time WW had published *An Evening Walk* and *Descriptive Sketches* (both in 1793) and three editions of *Lyrical Ballads* (1798, 1800, 1802), and composed much more poetry that was still unpublished. See also 13.273–78.
9. WW's thirty-fourth birthday was Thursday, April 7, 1804. He had started composing book 6 at the end of March and was to complete it by April 29.

Should reverence.[1] The instinctive humbleness
70 Upheld even by the very name and thought
Of printed books and authorship, began
To melt away, and further, the dread awe
Of mighty names was softened down, and seemed
Approachable, admitting fellowship
75 Of modest sympathy. Such aspect now,
Though not familiarly, my mind put on;
I loved, and I enjoyed, that was my chief
And ruling business, happy in the strength
And loveliness of imagery and thought.
80 All winter long, whenever free to take
My choice, did I at nights frequent our Groves
And tributary walks,[2] the last, and oft,
The only one who had been lingering there
Through hours of silence, till the Porter's Bell,
85 A punctual follower on the stroke of nine,
Rang with its blunt unceremonious voice,
Inexorable summons.[3] Lofty Elms,
Inviting shades of opportune recess
Did give composure to a neighborhood
90 Unpeaceful in itself. A single Tree
There was, no doubt yet standing there, an Ash
With sinuous trunk, boughs exquisitely wreathed;
Up from the ground and almost to the top
The trunk and master-branches, every where
95 Were green with ivy; and the lightsome twigs
And outer spray profusely tipped with seeds
That hung in yellow tassels and festoons,
Moving or still, a favourite trimmed out
By Winter for himself, as if in pride,
100 And with outlandish grace.[4] Oft have I stood
Foot-bound, uplooking at this lovely Tree
Beneath a frosty moon. The hemisphere
Of magic fiction verse of mine perhaps
May never tread;[5] but scarcely Spenser's self
105 Could have more tranquil visions in his youth,
More bright appearances could scarcely see
Of human Forms and super-human Powers

1. Possibly a recollection of Milton's reference, in the preface to book 2 of *The Reason of Church-Government* (1641), to his desire to write an epic poem: "an inward prompting which now grew daily upon me, that by labour and intent study * * * joyn'd with the strong propensity of nature, I might perhaps leave something so written to aftertimes, as they should not willingly let it die." See also 12.309–12. In April 1814 WW quoted the last phrase of Milton's sentence with reference to *The Recluse* and called Milton his "great Predecessor" (*WL*, 3:146).
2. The college gardens along the River Cam.
3. The bell signaled the hour when the college gates were closed for the night and the students were expected to be back in their rooms.
4. WW's description of the ash may be indebted to Erasmus Darwin's description of an elm in *The Economy of Vegetation: A Poem* (1791) 4.541–44: "Round her tall Elm with dewy fingers twine / The gadding tendrils of the adventurous Vine; / From arm to arm in gay festoons suspend / Her fragrant flowers, her graceful foliage bend."
5. An allusion to the planning of *LB*, in which it was agreed that STC, as he recalled later in *BL*, would write about supernatural "incidents and agents," whereas WW himself would address "the loveliness and the wonders of the world before us" (*NCC*, 490).

Than I beheld, standing on winter nights,
Alone, beneath this fairy work of earth.
110 'Twould be a waste of labour to detail
The rambling studies of a truant Youth,
Which further may be easily divined,
What, and what kind they were. My inner knowledge
(This barely will I note) was oft in depth
115 And delicacy like another mind
Sequestered from my outward taste in books,
And yet the books which then I loved the most
Are dearest to me now: for, being versed
In living Nature, I had there a guide
120 Which opened frequently my eyes, else shut,
A standard which was usefully applied,
Even when unconsciously, to other things
Which less I understood. In general terms,
I was a better judge of thoughts than words,
125 Misled as to these latter, not alone
By common inexperience of youth
But by the trade in classic niceties,
Delusion to young Scholars incident,[6]
And old ones also, by that overprized
130 And dangerous craft of picking phrases out
From languages that want the living voice
To make of them a nature to the heart,
To tell us what is passion, what is truth,
What reason, what simplicity and sense.[7]
135   Yet must I not entirely overlook
The pleasure gathered from the elements
Of geometric science. I had stepped
In these inquiries but a little way,
No farther than the threshold: with regret
140 Sincere I mention this; but there I found
Enough to exalt, to chear me and compose.
With Indian[8] awe and wonder, ignorance
Which even was cherished, did I meditate
Upon the alliance of those simple, pure
145 Proportions and relations with the frame
And laws of Nature, how they could become
Herein a leader to the human mind,
And made endeavours frequent to detect
The process by dark guesses of my own.
150 Yet from this source more frequently I drew
A pleasure calm and deeper, a still sense
Of permanent and universal sway

6. Likely to befall (a now-obsolete meaning of the adjective). *NCPrel* detects a facetious allusion to Shakespeare, *The Winter's Tale* 4.4.124–25: "a malady / Most incident to maids."
7. WW is evidently referring to the practice, common in British classical education of the time (and later), of having schoolboys compose verses in Latin. In chap. 1 of *BL*, STC recalled a conversation with WW about the injurious influence on eighteenth-century English poetry of this practice, which STC characterized as "translations of prose thoughts into poetic language" (NCC, 387–88).
8. American Indian (as in line 451 below and in 1.305).

And paramount endowment in the mind,
An image not unworthy of the one
155 Surpassing life which out of space and time,
Nor touched by welterings of passion, is
And hath the name of God. Transcendant peace
And silence did await upon these thoughts
That were a frequent comfort to my youth.
160 And as I have read of one by shipwreck thrown
With fellow Sufferers whom the waves had spared
Upon a region uninhabited
An island of the Deep, who having brought
To land a single Volume and no more,
165 A Treatise of Geometry,[9] was used,
Although of food and clothing destitute,
And beyond common wretchedness depressed,
To part from company and take this book
(Then first a self-taught pupil in those truths)
170 To spots remote and corners of the Isle
By the sea-side, and draw his diagrams
With a long stick upon the sand, and thus
Did oft beguile his sorrow, and almost
Forget his feeling;[1] even so, if things
175 Producing like effect from outward cause
So different, may rightly be compared,
So was it with me then, and so will be
With Poets ever. Mighty is the charm
Of those abstractions to a mind beset
180 With images, and haunted by itself
And specially delightful unto me
Was that clear Synthesis built up aloft
So gracefully, even then when it appeared
No more than as a plaything or a toy
185 Embodied to the sense, not what it is
In verity, an independent world
Created out of pure Intelligence.
          Such dispositions then were mine, almost
Through grace of Heaven and inborn tenderness.[2]
190 And not to leave the picture of that time
Imperfect, with these habits I must rank
A melancholy from humours of the blood[3]
In part, and partly taken up, that loved
A pensive sky, sad days, and piping winds,[4]

---

9. Compare the reference to "Poetry and geometric Truth, / The knowledge that endures," in 5.64–65.
1. In lines 160–74 WW draws closely on a passage copied out in 1798–99 by DW from John Newton's *Authentic Narrative* (1764; *Reading 1770–1799*, no. 188). Author of the hymn *Amazing Grace*, Newton (1725–1807) became a curate, abolitionist, and friend of the poet William Cowper after a maritime career in the slave trade.
2. Sensitivity to impressions.
3. Next to this line in the manuscript STC has written, without further comment, "14," i.e., line 14 of the page.
4. A possible recollection of Milton's *Il Penseroso*, line 126: "While rocking Winds are Piping loud" (*OxPrel*).

195 The twilight more than dawn, Autumn than Spring,
  A treasured and luxurious gloom, of choice
  And inclination mainly, and the mere
  Redundancy of Youth's contentedness.
  Add unto this a multitude of hours
200 Pilfered away by what the Bard who sang
  Of the Enchanter Indolence hath called
  "Good-natured lounging,"[5] and behold a map
  Of my Collegiate life, far less intense
  Than Duty called for, or without regard
205 To Duty, might have sprung up of itself
  By change of accident, or even, to speak
  Without unkindness, in another place.
    In summer among distant nooks I roved,
  Dove-dale,[6] or Yorkshire Dales, or through bye-tracts
210 Of my own native region, and was blest
  Between those sundry wanderings with a joy
  Above all joys, that seemed another morn
  Risen on mid noon,[7] the presence, Friend, I mean
  Of that sole Sister, she who hath been long
215 Thy Treasure also, thy true Friend and mine,
  Now, after separation desolate
  Restored to me, such absence that she seemed
  A gift[8] then first bestowed. The gentle Banks
  Of Emont, hitherto unnamed in Song,
220 And that monastic Castle, on a Flat
  Low-standing by the margin of the Stream,
  A Mansion not unvisited of old
  By Sydney, where, in sight of our Helvellyn,
  Some snatches he might pen, for aught we know,
225 Of his Arcadia, by fraternal love
  Inspired; that River and that mouldering Dome[9]
  Have seen us sit in many a summer hour,
  My sister and myself, when having climbed
  In danger through some window's open space,
230 We looked abroad, or on the Turret's head
  Lay listening to the wild flowers and the grass,
  As they gave out their whispers to the wind.
  Another Maid there was,[1] who also breathed
  A gladness o'er that season, then to me

---

5. James Thomson, *The Castle of Indolence* (1748) 1.15–16: "Here nought but candour reigns, indulgent ease, / Good-natured lounging, sauntering up and down."
6. Dovedale, a scenic valley traversed by the River Dove in Derbyshire in the English Midlands.
7. *Seemed . . . noon*: a quotation from *Paradise Lost* 5.310–11, in which Adam describes to Eve the approaching archangel Raphael.
8. NCPrel notes that WW, like STC in a letter of July 1803 (CL, 2:958), puns on Dorothy's name, which means "gift of God." *Now*: summer 1787, when WW was first reunited with DW, who had been living with cousins in Halifax since the death of their mother nine years earlier.
9. Stately building (a poetic usage); *Castle* (line 220): WW refers to Brougham Castle, a medieval castle (though not part of a *monastic* foundation) situated in a low-lying area (*Flat*) at the confluence of the Rivers Eamont and Lowther, two miles southeast of Penrith. Sir Philip Sidney wrote his prose romance *Arcadia* (1581) for his sister, but did not in fact visit Brougham Castle. *Helvellyn*: see Biographical and Topographical Glossary.
1. DW's friend Mary Hutchinson, whom WW would marry in October 1802. See also 11.199–201.

235   By her exulting outside look of youth
And placid under countenance first endeared,
That other Spirit, Coleridge, who is now
So near to us,[2] that meek confiding heart
So reverenced by us both. O'er paths and fields
240   In all that neighbourhood, through narrow lanes
Of eglantine; and through the shady woods,
And o'er the Border Beacon,[3] and the Waste
Of naked Pools and common Crags that lay
Exposed on the bare Fell, was scattered love,
245   A spirit of pleasure and youth's golden gleam.
O Friend! we had not seen thee at that time;
And yet a power is on me and a strong
Confusion, and I seem to plant Thee there.[4]
Far art Thou wandered now in search of health,
250   And milder breezes, melancholy lot![5]
But Thou art with us, with us in the past,
The present, with us in the times to come:
There is no grief, no sorrow, no despair,
No languor, no dejection, no dismay,
255   No absence scarcely can there be for those
Who love as we do. Speed Thee well![6] divide
Thy pleasure with us, thy returning strength,
Receive it daily as a joy of ours;
Share with us thy fresh spirits, whether gift
260   Of gales Etesian,[7] or of loving thoughts.
      I, too, have been a Wanderer: but alas!
How different is the fate of different Men!
Though Twins almost in genius and in mind.
Unknown unto each other, yea, and breathing
265   As if in different elements, we were framed
To bend at last to the same discipline,
Predestined, if two Beings ever were,
To seek the same delights, and have one health,
One happiness. Throughout this narrative,
270   Else sooner ended, I have known full well
For whom I thus record the birth and growth
Of gentleness, simplicity, and truth,
And joyous loves that hallow innocent days
Of peace and self-command. Of Rivers, Fields,
275   And Groves, I speak to Thee, my Friend, to Thee

2. In spirit, that is, rather than physically: see note to line 250.
3. A stone signal beacon built in 1719 on Beacon Hill, overlooking the town of Penrith. WW mentions the beacon again in 11.305, and repeats line 245 in 11.323.
4. I.e., in the summer of 1787. In fact WW and STC first met in Bristol in August or September 1795, but did not become close friends until June 1797, when STC also met DW for the first time.
5. These lines were composed after March 22, 1804, the date WW thought STC had sailed to the Mediterranean island of Malta, then a British colony, in the hope of recovering his health and overcoming his dependency on opium (he was actually in London, and sailed only on April 9). STC took with him a hastily prepared copy (MS M) of the first five books of The Prelude, but he would not have heard or read these lines addressed to him until his visit to the Wordsworths in December 1806. See also 10.977–87.
6. WW puns on the name of the ship on which STC was to sail, the Speedwell (NCPrel).
7. Summer winds in the Mediterranean.

Who, yet a liveried School Boy, in the depths
Of the huge City, on the leaded roof
Of that wide Edifice, thy Home and School,
Wast used to lie and gaze upon the clouds
280 Moving in Heaven; or, haply tired of this,
To shut thine eyes, and by internal light
See trees and meadows, and thy native Stream
Far distant, thus beheld from year to year
Of thy long exile.[8] Nor could I forget
285 In this late portion of my argument
That scarcely had I finally resigned
My rights among those academic Bowers
When Thou wert thither guided.[9] From the heart
Of London, and from Cloisters there Thou camest[1]
290 And didst sit down in temperance and peace,
A rigorous Student. What a stormy course
Then followed: oh! it is a pang that calls
For utterance, to think how small a change
Of circumstances might to Thee have spared
295 A world of pain, ripened ten-thousand hopes
For ever withered.[2] Through this retrospect
Of my own College life I still[3] have had
Thy after sojourn in the self-same place
Present before my eyes: I have played with times
300 (I speak of private business of the thought),
And accidents, as children do with cards,
Or as a Man, who, when his house is built,
A frame locked up in wood and stone, doth still
In impotence of mind, by his fire-side
305 Rebuild it to his liking. I have thought
Of Thee, thy learning, gorgeous eloquence,
And all the strength and plumage of thy Youth,
Thy subtile speculations, toils abstruse
Among the Schoolmen, and platonic forms
310 Of wild ideal pageantry,[4] shaped out

8. STC's *long exile* from Ottery St. Mary, his Devonshire birthplace, had begun in 1782, the
year after his father's death, when he was enrolled at Christ's Hospital, London, where the
pupils wore blue uniforms (hence *liveried*, line 276). Lines 275–90 include allusions to STC's
Sonnet IV: To the River Otter, Frost at Midnight, and *Dejection: An Ode*. WW refers to this
period of STC's life again in 8.605–10. *native Stream* (line 282): the River Otter in
Devonshire.
9. STC matriculated at Jesus College, Cambridge, in October 1791. *resigned / My rights*: WW left
St. John's College, Cambridge, in January 1791, his BA without honors disqualifying him from
election to a college fellowship.
1. Pronounced as one syllable.
2. Despite an academically successful first year, STC left Cambridge without a degree in
December 1794 after having become a Unitarian, run up large debts, briefly enrolled in the
cavalry under an alias, befriended Robert Southey (with whom he formed a plan to emigrate
to Pennsylvania and set up a communal farm), and become engaged to Sara Fricker. When
WW first met him, STC was living precariously in Bristol, writing and lecturing on political
subjects.
3. Always, ever.
4. A generalized reference to STC's prodigious philosophical reading, which WW understands as
a substitute for a lack of interaction with nature (lines 312–14). *Schoolmen*: medieval scholas-
tic philosophers; *platonic forms*: in Plato's philosophy, eternal and immutable forms or ideas in
which the general qualities of things we experience (e.g., roundness, similarity, beauty, good-
ness, etc.) somehow participate.

From things well matched, or ill, and words for things,
The self-created sustenance of a mind
Debarred from Nature's living images,
Compelled to be a life unto itself,
315   And unrelentingly possessed by thirst
Of greatness, love, and beauty. Not alone,
Ah! surely not in singleness of heart
Should I have seen the light of evening fade
Upon the silent Cam, if we had met,
320   Even at that early time: I needs must hope,
Must feel, must trust, that my maturer age,
And temperature less willing to be moved,
My calmer habits, and more steady voice
Would with an influence benign, have soothed
325   Or chased away the airy wretchedness
That battened on thy youth. But thou hast trod,
In watchful meditation thou hast trod
A march of glory, which doth put to shame
These vain regrets: health suffers in thee; else
330   Such grief for Thee would be the weakest thought
That ever harboured in the breast of Man.
      A passing word erewhile did lightly touch
On wanderings of my own; and now to these
My Poem leads me with an easier mind.
335   The employments of three winters when I wore
A Student's Gown have been already told,
Or shadowed forth, as far as there is need.
When the third summer[5] brought its liberty
A Fellow Student and myself, he, too,
340   A Mountaineer, together sallied forth
And, Staff in hand, on foot pursued our way
Towards the distant Alps. An open slight
Of College cares and study was the scheme,[6]
Nor entertained without concern for those
345   To whom my worldly interests were dear:

5. I.e., of 1790, the last summer vacation of WW's undergraduate years. From July to October of
that year, without having told any of his family of his plans, WW undertook a walking tour
through France, Switzerland, and the Rhineland—a total of some 2000 miles on foot and
another 820 by boat—with his friend Robert Jones (see Biographical and Topographical Glos-
sary), a native of mountainous north Wales. For details of their itinerary, see *Chrono: EY*, 97–
116; Donald Hayden's *Wordsworth's Walking Tour of 1790*; and WW's own account of September
1790 to DW (*WL*, 1:32–38).
6. In the margin STC has written "14" in pencil by line 343, the fourteenth line on the page of the
MS, and a vertical line by lines 343–45, signaling his comments on these lines on a blank page
following book 6 (see illustration on p. 258): "p. 133 l. 14–16. to *me* were obscure, and *now*
appear rather *awkwardly* expressed. I should wish to trace the classical use of the word 'Con-
cern.' These are passages, which it is so difficult & fretsome to correct; because, if once amiss,
no after genial moment can be pressed into the dull service of amending them. Yet I venture to
propose, thinking dilation better than awkwardness—'A disregard / Of college objects was our
schemes, say rather, / A mere Slight of the studies and the cares / Expected from us, we too
being then / Just at the close of our noviciate: / Nor was it formed by me without some fears, /
And some uneasy forethought of the pain, / The Censures, and ill-omening of these, / To whom
my worldly Interests were dear—.'" In his 1818–20 revisions WW altered and expanded lines
343–45 as follows: "The scheme implied / An open slight of academic cares / At a most urgent
season (for we then / Were near the close of our Noviatiate) / Nor was it, I acknowledge, framed
by me / Without uneasy forethought of the pain, / The censure, and ill-omening of those / To
whom our worldly interests were dear" (*Prel 1805* [CW], 2:101).

But Nature then was sovereign in my heart,
And mighty forms seizing a youthful Fancy
Had given a charter to irregular hopes.
In any age, without an impulse sent
350 From work of Nations and their goings-on,
I should have been possessed by like desire:
But 'twas a time when Europe was rejoiced,
France standing on the top of golden hours,[7]
And human nature seeming born again.
355 Bound, as I said, to the Alps, it was our lot
To land at Calais on the very Eve
Of that great federal Day;[8] and there we saw
In a mean City, and among a few,
How bright a face is worn when joy of one
360 Is joy of tens of millions. Southward thence
We took our way direct through Hamlets, Towns,
Gaudy with reliques of that Festival,
Flowers left to wither on triumphal Arcs
And window Garlands. On the public roads,
365 And once three days successively, through paths
By which our toilsome journey was abridged
Among sequestered villages we walked,
And found benevolence and blessedness
Spread like a fragrance, every where, like Spring
370 That leaves no corner of the land untouched.
Where Elms, for many and many a league, in files,
With their thin umbrage,[9] on the stately roads
Of that great Kingdom, rustled o'er our heads,
For ever near us as we paced along,
375 'Twas sweet at such a time, with such delights
On every side, in prime of youthful strength
To feed a Poet's tender melancholy
And fond conceit of sadness, to the noise
And gentle undulation which they made.
380 Unhoused, beneath the Evening Star we saw
Dances of Liberty, and in late hours
Of darkness, dances in the open air.
Among the vine-clad Hills of Burgundy
Upon the bosom of the gentle Soane
385 We glided forward with the flowing Stream:
Swift Rhone,[1] thou wert the wings on which we cut

7. A recollection of Shakespeare's Sonnet 16, line 5: "Now stand you on the top of golden hours." Compare 10.989–1000.
8. July 13, 1790, the day before the first anniversary of the fall of the Bastille and "the eve of the day when the king [Louis XVI] was to swear fidelity to the new constitution" ("Autobiographical Memoranda," in *Prose*, 3:373).
9. Shade, especially that cast by trees (from Latin *umbra*, "shadow").
1. WW and Jones were traveling down the Saône River towards Lyon, in central eastern France, where the Rhone River merges with it. In the margin STC has written "5" by line 386, signaling his comments on a blank page of the MS following book 6: "135. l. 5. 'we *cut*.' May 'cut' be used neutrally in pure language? Is [i.e., If] so, tis right & the best; if not 'we flew' or 'we rush'd.'" In his 1818–20 revisions WW retained the verb *cut* but made it transitive by giving it an object in an added line: "A lofty passage with majestic ease."

Between thy lofty rocks! Enchanting show
Those woods, and farms, and orchards did present,
And single Cottages, and lurking Towns,
390 Reach after reach, procession without end
Of deep and stately Vales. A lonely Pair
Of Englishmen we were, and sailed along
Clustered together with a merry Crowd
Of those emancipated, with a host
395 Of Travellers, chiefly Delegates, returning
From the great Spousals newly solemnized
At their Chief City in the sight of Heaven.
Like bees they swarmed, gaudy, and gay as bees;
Some vapoured[2] in the unruliness of joy
400 And flourished with their swords, as if to fight
The saucy air. In this blithe Company
We landed, took with them our evening Meal,
Guests welcome almost as the Angels were
To Abraham of old.[3] The Supper done,
405 With flowering cups elate, and happy thoughts,
We rose at signal giv'n,[4] and formed a ring
And hand in hand danced round and round the Board:
All hearts were open, every tongue was loud
With amity and glee: we bore a name
410 Honoured in France, the name of Englishmen,
And hospitably did they give us hail
As their forerunners in a glorious course,[5]
And round and round the board they[6] danced again.
With this same Throng our voyage we pursued
415 At early dawn; the Monastery Bells
Made a sweet jingling in our youthful ears:
The rapid River flowing without noise,
And every Spire we saw among the rocks
Spake with a sense of peace, at intervals
420 Touching the heart amid the boisterous Crew
With which we were environed. Having parted
From this glad Rout, the Convent of Chartreuse
Received us two days afterwards, and there
We rested in an awful Solitude;[7]
425 Thence onward to the Country of the Swiss.

---

2. Talked grandiloquently; boasted or blustered.
3. A reference to Genesis 18.1–15, in which God appears to Abraham as three men (not angels) who, after being received hospitably, tell him that his wife Sarah will bear a child.
4. A quotation from *Paradise Lost* 1.776.
5. A reference to England's so-called Glorious Revolution of 1688–89, in which the Roman Catholic King James II was deposed and replaced by the jointly reigning Protestants Mary Stuart and her husband William of Orange.
6. The alternative reading "we" was inserted into MS B (but not MS A) at an indeterminable stage in what appears to be MW's hand. In *Prel 1850* WW did adopt the pronoun "we."
7. Awe-inspiring; *Chartreuse*: the Grande Chartreuse, a monastery of the Carthusian order of monks, located in the Chartreuse Mountains north of the city of Grenoble (also referred to in 8.410). Carthusians pass most of their time in silence and avoid contact with the outside world. WW and Jones stayed at the monastery on August 4 and 5 before proceeding north to Lake Geneva.

'Tis not my present purpose to retrace
That variegated journey step by step;
A march it was of military speed,
And earth did change her images and forms
430 Before us, fast as clouds are changed in Heaven.
Day after day, up early and down late,
From vale to vale, from hill to hill we went,
From Province on to Province did we pass,
Keen Hunters in a chace of fourteen weeks
435 Eager as birds of prey, or as a Ship
Upon the stretch when winds are blowing fair.
Sweet coverts did we cross of pastoral life,
Enticing Vallies, greeted them and left
Too soon, while yet the very flash and gleam
440 Of salutation were not passed away.
Oh! sorrow for the Youth who could have seen
Unchastened, unsubdued, unawed, unraised
To patriarchal dignity of mind,
And pure simplicity of wish and will,
445 Those sanctified abodes of peaceful Man.
My heart leaped up when first I did look down[8]
On that which was first seen of those deep haunts,
A green recess, an aboriginal vale
Quiet,[9] and lorded over and possessed
450 By naked huts, wood-built, and sown like tents
Or Indian cabins over the fresh lawns,
And by the river side. That day we first
Beheld the summit of Mont Blanc,[1] and grieved
To have a soulless image on the eye
455 Which had usurped upon a living thought
That never more could be: the wond'rous Vale
Of Chamouny did on the following dawn,
With its dumb cataracts and streams of ice,
A motionless array of mighty waves,
460 Five rivers broad and vast, make rich amends
And reconciled us to realities.
There small birds warble from the leafy trees,
The Eagle soareth in the element;
There doth the Reaper bind the yellow sheaf,
465 The Maiden spread the hay-cock in the sun,
While Winter like a tamed lion walks

8. In the margin STC has written "13" in ink by this line, signaling his comment on a blank leaf
   of the manuscript following book 6: "137. l. 13. leap'd *up*—look'd down / leap'd high?—or
   rather O!. my heart leap'd when first &c—." In his 1818–20 revisions WW altered the begin-
   ning of the line to "How leap'd my heart."
9. Evidently the Trient Valley in Switzerland, lying between Martigny and Chamonix (Hayden,
   Wordsworth's Walking Tour, 33–35). DW records that WW returned to this valley on his Conti-
   nental tour with her and MW in 1820: "how much more interesting did the spot become when
   he told me was it the same dell, that *'aboriginal vale,'* that *'green recess'* so often mentioned by
   him—the first of the kind that he had passed through in Switzerland" (*DWJ*, 2:280).
1. The highest mountain in western Europe (15,782 feet), southeast of the Chamonix Valley (lines
   456–61) on the modern-day border between France and Italy.

Descending from the mountains to make sport[2]
Among the cottages by beds of flowers.
            Whate'er in this wide circuit we beheld,
470   Or heard, was fitted to our unripe state
Of intellect and heart. By simple strains
Of feeling, the pure breath of real life,
We were not left untouched. With such a book
Before our eyes we could not chuse but read
475   A frequent lesson of <u>sound tenderness,</u>
The universal reason of mankind,
The truth of Young and Old. Nor, side by side
Pacing, two brother Pilgrims, or alone
Each with his humour, could we fail to abound
480   (Craft this which hath been hinted at before)
In dreams and fictions pensively composed,
Dejection taken up for pleasure's sake
And guided sympathies; the willow wreath,[3]
Even among those solitudes sublime,
485   And sober posies of funereal flowers
Culled from the gardens of the Lady Sorrow
Did sweeten many a meditative hour.
            Yet still in me, mingling with these delights
Was something of stern mood, an <u>underthirst</u>
490   <u>Of vigour,</u> never utterly asleep.
Far different dejection once was mine,
A deep and genuine sadness then I felt:
The circumstances I will here relate
Even as they were. Upturning with a Band
495   Of Travellers, from the Valais we had clomb[4]
Along the road that leads to Italy;
A length of hours making of these our Guides
Did we advance, and having reached an Inn[5]
Among the mountains, we together ate
500   Our noon's repast, from which the Travellers rose,
Leaving us at the Board. Erelong we followed,
Descending by the beaten road that led
Right to a rivulet's edge, and there broke off.
The only track now visible was one

2. In the margin STC has written "7" in ink by this line, signaling his comment on a blank leaf in the manuscript following book 6: "138. l. 17. This line I would omit; as it clearly carries a the [*sic*] metaphor of the Lion, & yet is contradictory to the idea of a '*tamed*' Lion, / 'to make sport' &c is here at once the proof his having been tamed, & the object of his 'descending from the mountains'—which appear incompatible." In his 1818–20 revisions WW altered and expanded lines 466–67: "While Winter like a Lion that had issued / In threats and anger from his darksome cave / Among the mountains, to a gentler mood / Is won as he descends, and maketh sport" (*Prel 1805* [CW], 2:106).
3. A traditional symbol of grief, especially for unrequited or lost love.
4. Climbed. On August 17 WW and Jones met a group of mule drivers on their way up to the Simplon Pass (altitude 6588 feet) in the Swiss canton of Valais, lunched at an *Inn* (line 498), and then, resuming their hike on their own, lost their way.
5. MS B here omits a line from the equivalent passage in MS A: "Did we advance, and having reach'd an Inn / A seasonable halting-place, an Inn." WW subsequently revised these lines in MS A to remove the repetition of "Inn": "And reached a seasonable halting-place / Where we together ate our noon's repast" (*Prel 1805* [CW], 2:668).

505 Upon the further side, right opposite,
    And up a lofty Mountain. This we took
    After a little scruple,[6] and short pause,
    And climbed with eagerness, though not, at length,
    Without surprise and some anxiety
510 On finding that we did not overtake
    Our Comrades gone before. By fortunate chance,
    While every moment now encreased our doubts,
    A Peasant met us, and from him we learned
    That to the place which had perplexed us first
515 We must descend, and there should find the road
    Which in the stony channel of the Stream
    Lay a few steps, and then along its banks;[7]
    And further, that thenceforward all our course
    Was downwards, with the current of that Stream.
520 Hard of belief we questioned him again,
    And all the answers which the Man returned
    To our enquiries in their sense and substance,
    Translated by the feelings which we had,
    Ended in this, that we had crossed the Alps.[8]
525   Imagination! lifting up itself
    Before the very eye and progress of my Song[9]
    Like an unfathered vapour; here that Power,
    In all the might of its endowments, came
    Athwart me; I was lost as in a cloud,
530 Halted without a struggle to break through
    And now recovering, to my Soul I say
    I recognise thy glory; in such strength
    Of usurpation, in such visitings
    Of awful promise, when the light of sense
535 Goes out in flashes that have shewn to us
    The invisible world, doth Greatness make abode,
    There harbours[1] whether we be Young or Old.
    Our destiny, our nature, and our home
    Is with infinitude and only there,
540 With hope it is, hope that can never die,
    Effort, and expectation, and desire,
    And something evermore about to be.
    The mind beneath such banners militant
    Thinks not of spoils, trophies, nor of aught

---

6. Hesitation.
7. After having been directed to their intended path, WW and Jones descended through the Gondo Ravine, along the Doveria River, to the village of Gondo, where they spent the night.
8. WW originally planned to follow this line with an epic simile referring to caves and expressing his sense of anti-climax at the discovery of having crossed the Alps, but by the autumn of 1804 decided to apply the simile to his first experience of London (see 8.711–27). Compare WW's exaltation of the imagination in 13.66–83 (the ascent of Mt. Snowdon).
9. Eye . . . Song: WW's zeugma (a figure in which one word refers to two or more other words in the sentence, though applying in sense to only one of them) may have been inspired by Shakespeare, Much Ado about Nothing 4.1.229 ("the eye and prospect of my soul"), or King John 2.1.208 ("the eye and prospect of your town"). WW uses a similar phrase in 7.725.
1. Revised in pencil in MS B from the original reading "habour."

545 That may attest its prowess, blest in thoughts[2]
That are their own perfection and reward,
Strong in itself, and in the access of joy
Which hides it like the overflowing Nile.[3]
        The dull and heavy slackening which ensued
550 Upon those tidings by the Peasant given
Was soon dislodged; downwards we hurried fast.
And entered with the road which we had missed
Into a narrow chasm: the brook and road
Were fellow-travellers in this gloomy Pass,
555 And with them did we journey several hours
At a slow step. The immeasurable height
Of woods decaying, never to be decayed,
The stationary blasts of water-falls,
And every where along the hollow rent[4]
560 Winds thwarting winds, bewildered and forlorn,
The torrents shooting from the clear blue sky,
The rocks that muttered close upon our ears,
Black drizzling crags that spake by the way-side
As if a voice were in them, the sick sight
565 And giddy prospect of the raving stream,
The unfettered clouds, and region of the Heavens,
Tumult and peace, the darkness and the light
Were all like workings of one mind, the features
Of the same face, blossoms upon one tree,
570 Characters[5] of the great Apocalypse,
The types and symbols of Eternity,
Of first and last, and mist, and without end.[6]
        That night our lodging was an Alpine House,
An Inn, or Hospital, as they are named,
575 Standing in that same valley by itself
And close upon the confluence of two Streams,
A dreary Mansion, large beyond all need,
With high and spacious rooms, deafened and stunned
By noise of waters, making innocent sleep

2. STC comments on lines 544–45 on a blank leaf in the manuscript following book 6: "141. l. 3. 4.—*aught*: *thoughts*—was a hitch to my ear—
    ? Seeks for no trophies, struggles for no spoils / That may attest &c."
In his 1818–20 revisions WW adopted STC's suggestion for line 544.
3. STC comments on this line, "D[itt]*o*. l. 7.—Was it by mere caprice or a beginning of an impulse to alter, from having looked over the latter half of this Book for the purpose of correcting, which I employed myself on for the ~~purpose~~ deadening of a too strong feeling, which the personal Passages, so exquisitely beautiful, had excited—that I wished this faultless Line to stand
        'Spread o'er it, like the fertilizing Nile.'—?
        For fear, it should be so, I will leave off. Ὕστερον ἀδιον ασω."
The Greek phrase, a variant of which STC included in his prefatory note to *Kubla Khan* (NCC, 181), means "I shall sing something sweeter later." WW did not alter line 548.
4. Gorge.
5. Letters (in keeping with the metaphor of the book of nature, line 473).
6. A near-quotation of *Paradise Lost* 5.165, in which Adam and Eve praise the Creator. WW later quoted lines 553–72 with the date 1799 (although they were actually composed in 1804) in his pamphlet *Kendal and Windermere Railway* (1845), naming their source as "a MS. poem in which I attempted to describe the impression made upon my mind by the descent towards Italy along the Simplon before the new military road had taken place of the old muleteer track with its primitive simplicities" (*Prose*, 3:353). He reprinted the lines, again with the date 1799 but adding the title *The Simplon Pass*, in his *Poems* of 1845.

580 Lie melancholy among weary bones.[7]
          Uprisen betimes, our journey we renewed
     Led by the Stream, 'ere noon-day magnified
     Into a lordly River,[8] broad and deep,
     Dimpling along in silent majesty,
585 With mountains for its neighbours, and in view
     Of distant mountains, and their snowy tops,
     And thus proceeding to Locarno's Lake,
     Fit resting place for such a Visitant.
          —Locarno, spreading out in width like Heaven,
590 And Como, thou, a treasure by the earth
     Kept to itself, a darling bosomed up
     In Abyssinian privacy,[9] I spake
     Of thee, thy chestnut woods, and garden plots
     Of Indian corn, tended by dark-eyed Maids,
595 Thy lofty steeps, and pathways roofed with vines,
     Winding from house to house, from town to town,
     Sole link that binds them to each other, walks
     League after league, and cloistral avenues
     Where silence is, if music be not there:
600 While yet a Youth, undisciplined in Verse,
     Through fond ambition of my heart, I told
     Your praises;[1] nor can I approach you now
     Ungreeted by a more melodious Song,
     Where tones of learned Art and Nature mixed
605 May frame enduring language. Like a breeze
     Of sunbeam over your domain I passed
     In motion without pause; but ye have left
     Your beauty with me, and impassioned sight
     Of colours and of forms, whose power is sweet
610 And gracious, almost might I dare to say,
     As virtue is, or goodness, sweet as love
     Or the remembrance of a noble deed,
     Or gentlest visitations of pure thought
     When God, the giver of all joy, is thanked
615 Religiously, in the silent blessedness,
     Sweet as this last itself; for such it[2] is.
          Through those delightful pathways we advanced
     Two days, and still in presence of the Lake
     Which, winding up among the Alps, now changed
620 Slowly its lovely countenance, and put on

7. *Innocent sleep*: a phrase from Shakespeare, *Macbeth* 2.2.33. In 1820 the Wordsworths passed the eight-storey stone *Spittal* (hospice) in Gondo where WW and Jones had overnighted uncomfortably thirty years earlier, but DW could not persuade her brother to reenter it (*DWJ*, 2:258–59).
8. The Toce, which empties into Lake Maggiore (*Locarno's Lake*, line 587) in the Duchy of Milan (modern-day Italy), which WW and Jones reached on August 19. They seem to have traveled east ca. 22 miles from the southern end of Lake Maggiore to the town of Como, at the southern end of Lake Como.
9. Abyssinia (modern-day Ethiopia) was known in WW's day for being inaccessible to foreigners, but WW is doubtless also recalling its description in *Paradise Lost* as "by som[e] suppos'd / True Paradise" (4.281–82).
1. I.e., in *Descriptive Sketches* (1793), lines 80–161, composed when WW was 21 or 22 years old.
2. I.e., beauty's *power* (line 609).

A sterner character. The second night,
In eagerness, and by report[3] misled
Of those Italian clocks that speak the time
In fashion different from ours, we rose
625 By moonshine, doubting not that day was near,[4]
And that, meanwhile, coasting the Water's edge
As hitherto, and with as plain a track
To be our guide, we might behold the scene
In its most deep repose.—We left the Town
630 Of Gravedona with this hope; but soon
Were lost, bewildered among woods immense,
Where, having wandered for a while, we stopped
And on a rock sat down to wait for day,
An open place it was, and overlooked
635 From high, the sullen water underneath,
On which a dull red image of the moon
Lay bedded, changing oftentimes its form
Like an uneasy snake: long time we sate,
For scarcely more than one hour of the night,
640 Such was our error, had been gone when we
Renewed our journey. On the rock we lay
And wished to sleep but could not for the stings
Of insects, which with noise like that of noon
Filled all the woods; the cry of unknown birds,
645 The mountains, more by darkness visible[5]
And their own size than any outward light,
The breathless wilderness of clouds, the clock
That told with unintelligible voice
The widely-parted hours, the noise of streams
650 And sometimes rustling motions nigh at hand
Which did not leave us free from personal fear,
And lastly the withdrawing Moon, that set
Before us while she yet was high in heaven,
These were our food, and such a summer night
655 Did to that pair of golden days succeed,
With now and then a doze and snatch of sleep,
On Como's Banks, the same delicious Lake.
    But here I must break off, and quit at once,
Though loth, the record of these wanderings;
660 A theme which may seduce me else beyond
All reasonable bounds. Let this alone
Be mentioned as a parting word, that not
In hollow exultation, dealing forth
Hyperboles of praise comparative,
665 Not rich one moment to be poor for ever,

3. The sound.
4. WW and Jones were presumably staying in Gravedona or in Domaso, on the western side of
   Lake Como, when they were misled by the church bells (which would have sounded first the
   quarter-hours and then the hours, e.g., a total of four times for 1:45, six for 2:00) and set out
   before daylight, probably on August 22 (Hayden, *Wordsworth's Walking Tour*, 62–64).
5. *Darkness visible*: a phrase from *Paradise Lost* 1.63. The mountains were sufficiently large that
   their very darkness made them stand out more (against the moonlight).

Not prostrate, overborn, as if the mind
Itself were nothing, a mean pensioner[6]
On outward forms, did we in presence stand
Of that magnificent region. On the front
670 Of this whole Song is written that my heart
Must in such temple needs have offered up
A different worship. Finally whate'er
I saw, or heard, or felt was but a stream
That flowed into a kindred stream, a gale
675 That helped me forwards, did administer
To grandeur and to tenderness, to the one
Directly, but to tender thoughts by means
Less often instantaneous in effect,
Conducted me to these along a path
680 Which in the main was more circuitous.
            Oh! most beloved Friend, a glorious time,
A happy time that was; triumphant looks
Were then the common language of all eyes
As if awaked from sleep, the Nations hailed
685 Their great expectancy:[7] the fife of War
Was then a spirit-stirring sound indeed,
A Blackbird's whistle in a vernal grove.
We left the Swiss exulting in the fate
Of their near Neighbours, and when shortening fast
690 Our pilgrimage, nor distant far from home,
We crossed the Brabant Armies on the fret[8]
For battle in the cause of Liberty.
A Stripling, scarcely of the household then
Of social life,[9] I looked upon these things
695 As from a distance, heard, and saw, and felt,
Was touched, but with no intimate concern;
I seemed to move among them as a bird
Moves through the air, or as a fish pursues
Its business, in its proper[1] element,
700 I needed not that joy, I did not need
Such help; the ever-living Universe,
And independent spirit of pure youth
Were with me at that season, and delight
Was in all places spread around my steps
705 As constant as the grass upon the fields.

6. I.e., drawing support from external impressions but returning nothing (imaginatively) for them.
7. I.e., of political change inaugurated by the French Revolution.
8. Belgian republican soldiers waiting anxiously to engage the Austrian army, which had been sent to suppress the republic declared in October 1789 in the south Netherlands (then an Austrian possession). By December 1790 the republican forces were routed and Austrian rule restored. WW and Jones, who had traveled north through Switzerland (mid-August to September 21) and then by boat on the Rhine River from Basel to Cologne (September 22–28), must have crossed Belgium on their way to the English Channel, but nothing certain is known of their movements between September 29 and their return to Cambridge by late October. *near Neighbours* (line 689): the French.
9. I.e., hardly yet an adult.
1. Own (from French *propre*).

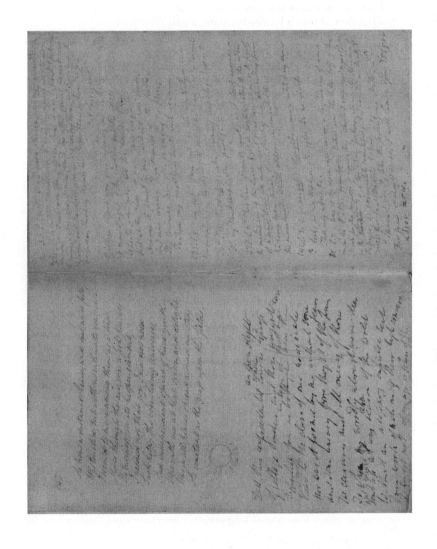

Book Seventh

RESIDENCE IN LONDON

Five years are vanished since I first poured out,
Saluted by that animating breeze,
Which met me issuing from the City's Walls,
A glad preamble to this Verse:[1] I sang
5 Aloud in Dythyrambic[2] fervour, deep
But short-lived transport, like a torrent sent
Out of the bowels of a bursting cloud
Down Sca'fell, or Blencathara's rugged sides,[3]
A water-spout from Heaven. But 'twas not long
10 Ere the interrupted stream broke forth once more
And flowed awhile in strength, then stopped for years,
Not heard again until a little space
Before last primrose-time.[4] Beloved Friend,
The assurances then given unto myself
15 Which did beguile me of some heavy thoughts
At thy departure to a foreign Land
Have failed; for slowly doth this work advance.[5]
Through the whole summer have I been at rest,
Partly from voluntary holiday
20 And part through outward hindrance.[6] But I heard
After the hour of sunset yester even,
Sitting within doors betwixt light and dark,
A voice that stirred me. 'Twas a little Band,
A Quire[7] of Redbreasts, gathered somewhere near
25 My threshold, Minstrels from the distant woods
And dells, sent in by Winter to bespeak
For the old Man a welcome, to announce
With preparation artful and benign,
Yea, the most gentle music of the year,
30 That their rough Lord had left the surly North,[8]
And hath begun his journey. A delight

---

1. Writing these lines in the autumn of 1804 (probably October), WW refers to his composition of 1.1–54 in November 1799. *City's Walls:* see note on 1.6–8.
2. Wild, irregular (from *dithyramb*, an ancient Greek choral hymn sung to honor Dionysus or Bacchus).
3. Scafell and Blencathra, mountains in the Lake District.
4. Although slightly misleading in implying that composition of the *glad preamble* (*short-lived transport*, line 6) preceded that of *Prel 1799* (*flowed awhile in strength*, line 11), lines 4–13 accord with the evidence (for which see *Chrono: MY*, 11–15, 628–55) that WW did little substantial work on *The Prelude* between roughly December 1801 and January 1804 (*a little space / Before last primrose-time*, i.e., shortly before early spring).
5. After having assured himself that he could finish *The Prelude* in five books for STC to take with him to Malta, WW composed some 1500 lines of the poem between ca. January 14 and ca. March 12, 1804. But probably between March 6 and ca. March 12, just before or during the preparation of the MS that was to be sent to STC, WW decided to extend the poem beyond five books. By March 18 a fair copy of books 1–5 as well as of WW's shorter poems (now designated MS M or DC 44) had been sent, in several packets, to STC in London (*Chrono: MY*, 248, 254–56).
6. WW's *holiday* from work on *The Prelude* seems to have lasted from mid-June to early October 1804, during which time he had frequent visitors and his daughter Dora was born (August 16).
7. Choir.
8. *PPrel* notes that line 30 may have been modeled on James Thomson's *Spring* (1728), lines 11–12: "And see where surly Winter passes off / Far to the North, and calls his ruffian Blasts."

At this unthought-of greeting, unawares
Smote me, a sweetness of the coming time,
And listening, I half whispered, we will be,
35 Ye heartsome Choristers, ye and I will be
Brethren, and in the hearing of bleak winds
Will chaunt together. And, thereafter, walking
By later twilight on the hills, I saw
A Glow-worm from beneath a dusky shade
40 Or canopy of the[9] yet unwithered fern
Clear shining, like a Hermit's taper seen
Through a thick forest: silence touched me here
No less than sound had done before; the Child
Of Summer, lingering, shining by itself,
45 The voiceless Worm on the unfrequented hills
Seemed sent on the same errand with the Quire
Of Winter that had warbled at my door,
And the whole year seemed tenderness and love.
      The last Night's genial feeling overflowed
50 Upon this morning, and my favorite grove,[1]
Now tossing its dark boughs in sun and wind,
Spreads through me a commotion like its own,
Something that fits me for the Poet's task
Which we will now resume with chearful hope,
55 Nor checked by aught of tamer argument
That lies before us, needful to be told.
      Returned from that excursion, soon I bade
Farewell for ever to the private Bowers
Of gownèd Students,[2] quitted these no more
60 To enter them, and pitched my vagrant tent,
A casual dweller and at large, among
The unfenced regions of society.[3]
      Yet undetermined to what plan of life
I should adhere, and seeming thence to have
65 A little space of intermediate time
Loose and at all full command, to London first
I turned, if not in calmness, nevertheless
In no disturbance of excessive hope,
At ease from all ambition personal,
70 Frugal as there was need, and though self-willed,
Yet temperate and reserved, and wholly free
From dangerous passions. 'Twas at least two years
Before this season when I first beheld
That mighty place, a transient visitant;
75 And it pleased me my abode to fix[4]

9. Erased in MS B, as in MS A, probably in the 1818–20 stage of revision (see *Prel 1805* [CW], 686).
1. A grove of fir trees in Ladywood, a half-mile from Dove Cottage, dear to WW because his brother John had regularly walked there during his stay at Dove Cottage in January–September 1800.
2. By late October 1790 WW returned to Cambridge from his Continental walking tour with Robert Jones (recounted in 6.338–705), and in January 1791 he was awarded a BA.
3. In contrast to his literally and figuratively enclosed Cambridge college.
4. *Prel 1805* (CW) notes that WW here conflates three periods of residence in London: early 1791, ca. December 1792–mid-1793, and ca. February–August 1795. *first beheld* (line 73): Schneider, 63, and Reed (*Chrono: EY*, 81) conjecture that WW first visited London in late summer 1788.

Single in the wide waste, to have a house
It was enough, what matter for a home,
That owned me, living chearfully abroad
With fancy on the stir from day to day,
80 And all my young affections[5] out of doors.
        There was a time, when whatsoe'er is feigned
Of airy Palaces and Gardens built
By Genii of Romance, or hath in grave
Authentic History been set forth of Rome,
85 Alcairo, Babylon, or Persepolis,
Or given upon report by Pilgrim Friars
Of golden Cities, ten months' journey deep
Among Tartarean[6] wilds, fell short, far short,
Of that which I in simpleness believed
90 And thought of London, held me by a chain
Less strong of wonder and obscure delight.
I know not that herein I shot beyond
The common mark of childhood: but I well
Remember that among our flock of Boys
95 Was one, a Cripple from the birth, whom chance
Summoned from School to London, fortunate
And envied Traveller![7] and when he returned
After short absence, and I first set eyes
Upon his person, verily, though strange
100 The thing may seem, I was not wholly free
From disappointment to behold the same
Appearance, the same body, not to find
Some change, some beams of glory brought away
From that new region. Much I questioned him,
105 And every word he uttered, on my ears
Fell flatter than a cagèd Parrot's note
That answers unexpectedly awry,
And mocks the Prompter's listening. Marvellous things
My fancy had shaped forth of sights and shows,
110 Processions, Equipages, Lords and Dukes,
The King and the King's Palace, and not last
Or least, heaven bless him! the renowned Lord Mayor,[8]
Dreams hardly less intense than those which wrought
A change of purpose in young Whittington
115 When he in friendlessness, a drooping Boy
Sate on a Stone, and heard the bells speak out

5. Feelings, emotions; *abroad*: away from his family.
6. Infernal; *Alcairo* (line 85): i.e., Memphis, an ancient Egyptian city on the Nile, site of the Sphinx; *Babylon*: ancient Mesopotamian city famed for its "hanging gardens"; *Persepolis*: capital of the ancient Persian empire, sacked by Alexander the Great's army in 331 B.C.E.; *report by Pilgrim Friars* (line 86): probably a reference to Samuel Purchas, *Purchas His Pilgrimage* (1613), of which WW owned a copy of the third edition (1617; *Reading 1800–15*, no. 327) and from which STC drew the opening lines of *Kubla Khan* (see *NCC*, 180 and n. 4).
7. Probably Philip Braithwaite, a fellow lodger with WW at Ann Tyson's house in Hawkshead and later a schoolmaster (Thompson, 39–46).
8. Evidently a generic reference to the Lord Mayor's Show, an elaborate procession in early November in which the annually elected Lord Mayor of London travels by coach to the Royal Courts of Justice to swear allegiance to the Crown; *Equipages*: ceremonious displays, or perhaps more specifically carriages and horses.

Articulate music.[9] Above all, one thought
Baffled my understanding, how men lived
Even next-door neighbours, as we say, yet still
120   Strangers, and knowing not each other's names.
Oh! wondrous powers of words, how sweet they are
According to the meaning which they bring,
Vauxhall and Ranleagh,[1] I then had heard
Of your green groves, and wilderness of lamps,
125   Your gorgeous Ladies, fairy cataracts,
And pageant fire-works; nor must we forget
Those other wonders, different in kind,
Though scarcely less illustrious in degree,
The River proudly bridged, the giddy top
130   And whispering Gallery of St Paul's, the Tombs
Of Westminster, the Giants of Guildhall,
Bedlam and the two figures at its Gates,[2]
Streets without end, and Churches numberless,
Statues with flowery Gardens in vast Squares,
135   The Monument, and Armoury of the Tower.[3]
          These fond imaginations of themselves
Had long before given way in season due,
Leaving a throng of others in their stead;
And now I looked upon the real scene,
140   Familiarly perused it day by day
With keen and lively pleasure, even there
Where disappointment was the strongest, pleased
Through courteous self-submission, as a tax
Paid to the object by prescriptive[4] right,
145   A thing that ought to be. Shall I give way,
Copying the impression of the memory,
Though things remembered idly do half seem
The work of fancy, shall I, as the mood
Inclines me, here describe, for pastime's sake,
150   Some portion of that motley imagery,

9. According to a seventeenth-century legend, the young Dick Whittington, despairing of fame and fortune in London, was about to abandon the city when he heard the bells of St. Mary-le-Bow seeming to say to him "Turn again Whittington, Lord Mayor of London," whereupon he remained in London and was eventually elected Lord Mayor. A stone at the foot of Highgate Hill, north London, marks the spot where he supposedly heard the bells. The historical Richard Whittington (ca. 1350–1423) was a wealthy mercer and moneylender who served four times as Lord Mayor.
1. Vauxhall, on the south side of the Thames, and Ranelagh, on the north side, were fashionable public gardens in eighteenth-century London, sites of musical entertainment, fireworks, and balls.
2. Bedlam . . . Gates: popular name of the Bethlem Royal Hospital, a famous insane asylum founded in the thirteenth century and located from 1675 to 1815 in Moorfields, east London. Above its gates were two stone statues, representing Melancholy and Raving Madness, by the Danish-born sculptor Caius Gabriel Cibber (1630–1670); they are preserved in the museum of the current Bethlem Royal Hospital in southeast London. Whispering Gallery: balcony beneath the cupola of St. Paul's Cathedral, in which a whisper can be heard on the opposite side of the gallery, 102 feet away; Tombs / Of Westminster: i.e., of Westminster Abbey; Giants of Guildhall: limewood statues representing the legendary giants Gog and Magog in the Guildhall, the historic (and now mostly ceremonial) center of London's civic government.
3. The collection of royal armor in the Tower of London. Monument: a stone column (202 feet high) designed by Sir Christopher Wren and built in 1671–77 to commemorate London's Great Fire of 1666.
4. Established, customary.

A vivid pleasure of my Youth, and now
Among the lonely places that I love,
A frequent day-dream for my riper mind.[5]
—And first the look and aspect of the place,
155 The broad high-way appearance, as it strikes
On Strangers of all ages, the quick dance
Of colours, lights and forms, the Babel din,
The endless stream of Men, and moving things,
From hour to hour the illimitable walk
160 Still among Streets with clouds and sky above,
The wealth, the bustle and the eagerness,
The glittering Chariots[6] with their pampered Steeds,
Stalls, Barrows, Porters; midway in the Street
The Scavenger,[7] who begs with hat in hand,
165 The labouring Hackney Coaches, the rash speed
Of Coaches travelling far,[8] whirled on with horn
Loud blowing, and the sturdy Drayman's Team
Ascending from some Alley of the Thames
And striking right across the crowded Strand
170 Till the fore Horse veer round with punctual[9] skill:
Here, there, and every where a weary Throng,
The Comers and the Goers face to face,
Face after face, the string of dazzling Wares,
Shop after shop, with[1] Symbols, blazoned Names,
175 And all the Trademan's honours overhead;
Here, fronts of houses like a title page
With letters huge inscribed from top to toe;
Stationed above the door like guardian Saints,
There, allegoric shapes, female or male;
180 Or physiognomies[2] of real men,
Land Warriors, Kings, or Admirals of the Sea,
Boyle, Shakespear, Newton or the attractive head
Of some Scotch Doctor,[3] famous in his day.
      Meanwhile, the roar continues, till at length,
185 Escaped as from an enemy, we turn
Abruptly into some sequestered nook
Still as a sheltered place when winds blow loud.
At leisure thence, through tracts of thin resort[4]

5. Though framed as a rhetorical question, this sentence ends with a period rather than a question mark in both MSS B and A.
6. Private carriages.
7. Street-sweeper.
8. Intercity coaches, such as the mail coaches; *Hackney Coaches*: carriages for hire within London, with seats for six people.
9. Exact, precise (an archaic usage). *Drayman's Team*: horses pulling a dray (a low-sided cart used especially for transporting beer barrels); *Strand*: street running along the north side of the Thames, linking the City of London to Westminster.
1. Inserted by MW in both MSS B and A.
2. Faces.
3. Altered in 1818–20 to "Quack-Doctor." WW probably means James Graham (1745–1794), a charismatic confidence man who set up a "Temple of Health" in London in 1780 and attracted a large following with his claims to cure sexual disorders by magnetism, electricity, and other means. WW had satirized him in his *Imitation of Juvenal* (1796). *Boyle*: Robert Boyle (1627–1691), distinguished chemist and founding member of the Royal Society.
4. Less frequented parts of the city.

And sights and sounds that come at intervals
190 We take our way: a raree-show⁵ is here
With children gathered round, another Street
Presents a company of dancing Dogs,
Or Dromedary, with an antic⁶ pair
Of Monkies on his back, a minstrel Band
195 Of Savoyards, or single or⁷ alone,
An English Ballard-singer. Private Courts
Gloomy as Coffins, and unsightly Lanes
Thrilled by some female Vender's scream, belike
The very shrillest of all London Cries,⁸
200 May then entangle us a while,⁹
Conducted through those labyrinths unawares
To privileged regions and inviolate,
Where from their airy lodges studious Lawyers
Look out on waters, walks, and gardens green.¹
205   Then back into the throng until we reach,
Following the tide that slackens by degrees,
Some half-frequented scene, where wider Streets
Bring straggling breezes of suburban air:
Here files of ballads dangle from dead walls,²
210 Advertisements of giant size, from high
Press forward in all colours on the sight,
These bold in conscious merit, lower down
That fronted with a most imposing word
Is, peradventure, one in masquerade.³
215 As on the broadening Causeway we advance,
Behold a Face turned up towards us, strong
In lineaments, and red with overtoil;
'Tis one, perhaps, already met elsewhere,
A travelling Cripple, by the trunk cut short,
220 And stumping with his arms:⁴ in Sailor's garb,
Another lies at length beside a range
Of written characters, with chalk inscribed
Upon the smooth flat stones: the Nurse is here

5. A portable peepshow in a box, typically with cardboard or wood cutout scenes placed in front of colored glass lighted from behind by a candle or gas lamp.
6. Grotesque, ludicrous.
7. or . . . or: either . . . or; Savoyards: itinerant minstrel bands from the Savoy region in southeastern France.
8. "The proclamation of wares to be sold in the streets" (OED); Thrilled: penetrated, pierced (an obsolescent figurative sense).
9. A hypometric line, extended in Prel 1850 to "May then entangle our impatient steps" (Prel 1850 [CW], 142).
1. A reference to the Inns of Court, four institutions—each with its own buildings and grounds—responsible for the training and professional conduct of barristers (courtroom lawyers) in England and Wales. WW stayed with his friend Basil Montagu at Lincoln's Inn in early 1795 (Chrono: EY, 138, 163).
2. Walls without windows or doors, providing sellers of broadside ballads space to display their merchandise.
3. I.e., a poster that does not reveal openly what it is advertising. In a draft (MS X, DC MS 47) WW identified the imposing word (in the double sense of impressive and deceitful) opening the advertisement as "Inviting" (Prel 1805 [CW], 2:324).
4. Probably Samuel Horsey, commonly called the "King of the Beggars," a legless beggar who frequented central London for several decades in the late eighteenth and early nineteenth centuries and about whom Charles Lamb wrote in his essay "A Complaint of the Decay of Beggars in the Metropolis" (1822).

The Bachelor that loves to sun himself,
225 The military Idler, and the Dame
     That field-ward takes her walk in decency.[5]
          Now homeward, through the thickening hubub where
     See, among less distinguishable Shapes,[6]
     The Italian with his Frame of Images[7]
230 Upon his head, with basket at his waist
     The Jew, the stately and slow-moving Turk
     With freight of slippers piled beneath his arm.
     Briefly, we find, if tired of random sights,
     And haply to that search our thoughts should turn,
235 Among the crowd, conspicuous less or more,
     As we proceed, all specimens of Man
     Through all the colours which the sun bestows,
     And every character of form and face,
     The Swede, the Russian; from the genial south
240 The Frenchman and the Spaniard; from remote
     America the hunter Indian; Moors,
     Malays, Lascars,[8] the Tartar and Chinese,
     And Negro Ladies in white muslin gowns.
          At leisure let us view from day to day,
245 As they present themselves, the Spectacles
     Within doors, troops of wild Beasts, birds and beasts
     Of every nature from all Climes convened
     And, next to these, those mimic sights that ape
     The absolute presence of reality,
250 Expressing, as in a mirror, sea and land,
     And what earth is, and what she hath to shew;
     I do not here allude to subtlest craft,
     By means refined attaining purest ends,[9]
     But imitations fondly made in plain
255 Confession of Man's weakness and his loves,
     Whether the Painter, fashioning a work
     To Nature's circumambient[1] scenery,
     And with his greedy pencil[2] taking in
     A whole horizon on all sides, with power
260 Like that of Angels or commissioned[3] Spirits,
     Plant us upon some lofty Pinnacle,
     Or in a Ship on Waters, with a world
     Of life, and life-like mockery, to East,

5. With modesty, propriety; *field-ward*: toward the countryside.
6. Allusions to *Paradise Lost*: the "universal hubbub wild" of Chaos (2.951) and the figure of Death "that shape had none / Distinguishable in member, joint, or limb" (2.667–68).
7. Box of statuettes (presumably of saints).
8. East Indian sailors (or, if WW is using the word more loosely, simply people from India).
9. "Imaginative art creatively reforming, not merely copying, materials of the external world" (*Prel 1805* [CW], 1:200n). WW is instead referring to arts such as panorama-painting (lines 256–64) and model-building (lines 265–79), which do seek to copy faithfully the external world.
1. Surrounding.
2. Paintbrush (the primary meaning of *pencil* in the eighteenth century).
3. Charged with specific tasks. PPrel notes a reference to Satan's placement of Christ upon a pinnacle of the Temple in Jerusalem (see Matthew 4.5, Luke 4.9, and Milton's *Paradise Regained* 4.541–50).

To West, beneath, behind us, and before;[4]
265 Or more mechanic Artist represent
By scale exact, in Model, wood or clay,
From shading colours also borrowing help,[5]
Some miniature of famous spots and things,
Domestic, or the boast of foreign Realms,
270 The Firth of Forth,[6] and Edinburgh throned
On Crags, fit Empress of that morning Land;
Saint Peter's Church, or more aspiring aim,
In microscopic vision, Rome itself
Or else perhaps some rural haunt, the Falls
275 Of Tivoli[7]
And high upon the Steep that mouldering Fane,
The Temple of the Sybil, every tree
Through all the landscape, tuft, stone, scratch minute,
And every Cottage lurking in the rocks,
280 All that the Traveller sees when he is there.
       Add to these exhibitions mute and still
Others of wider scope, where living men,
Music, and shifting pantomimic scenes
Together join their multifarious aid
285 To heighten the allurement. Need I fear
To mention by its name, as in degree
Lowest of these, and humblest in attempt,
Yet richly graced, with honours of its own
Half-rural Sadler's Wells.[8] Though at this time
290 Intolerant, as is the way of Youth
Unless itself be pleased, I more than once
Here took my seat, and maugre[9] frequent fits
Of irksomeness, with ample recompense
Saw Singers, Rope-dancers, Giants and Dwarfs,
295 Clowns, Conjurors, Posture-masters, Harlequins,[1]
Amid the uproar of the rabblement,
Perform their feats. Nor was it mean delight
To watch crude nature work in untaught minds,
To note the laws and progress of belief;

4. Immensely popular from the mid 1790s to the late 1850s, panoramas were large-scale scenes painted on cylindrical surfaces and designed to be viewed from the center of the cylinder. The first purpose-built panorama building, containing a view of London by Robert Barker (1739–1806), opened in Leicester Square in 1794 and was some ninety feet in diameter.
5. Exhibitions of architectural and topographical models became popular in London in the late seventeenth century and remained so well into the nineteenth century.
6. The estuary of the River Forth in eastern Scotland, flowing into the North Sea. Edinburgh is situated on the south side of the Firth.
7. A waterfall on the Aniene River in the town of Tivoli, eighteen miles east of Rome. Above the falls stand the remains of a Roman temple possibly dedicated to the Tiburtine Sybil (line 277), an oracular nymph in Roman legend. In both MSS B and A, line 275 was originally left unfinished and probably not completed until the 1818–20 stage of revision, when lines 274 and 276 were also altered: "Or haply some choice rural haunt, the Falls / Of Tivoli, and high upon that steep, / The Sybil's mouldering Temple! every tree" (Prel 1805 [CW], 2:121).
8. A musical theater built in 1683 (and rebuilt in 1765) in Islington, then a northeastern suburb of London.
9. Pronounced máwg-er, meaning "in spite of" (a word already becoming archaic in the late eighteenth century, from the French malgré).
1. Clowns (traditionally, colorfully costumed mute characters in pantomimes); Posture-masters: contortionists or acrobats.

300   Though obstinate in this way, yet on that
     How willingly we travel, and how far!
     To have, for instance, brought upon the scene
     The Champion Jack the Giant-killer,[2] lo!
     He dons his Coat of Darkness; on the stage
305   Walks and atchieves his wonders, from the eye
     Of living mortal safe as is the moon
     "Hid in her vacant interlunar Cave,"[3]
     Delusion bold! and faith must needs be coy;[4]
     How is it wrought? His garb is black, the word
310   *Invisible* flames forth upon his Chest.
           Nor was it unamusing here to view
     Those samples as of the ancient Comedy
     And Thespian times,[5] dramas of living Men
     And recent things, yet warm with life, a Sea-fight,
315   Shipwreck, or some domestic incident,
     The fame of which is scattered through the Land;
     Such as, of late, this daring Brotherhood
     Set forth, too holy theme for such a place,
     And, doubtless, treated with irreverence,
320   Albeit with the very best of skill,
     I mean, O distant Friend! a Story drawn
     From our own ground, the Maid of Buttermere,
     And how the Spoiler came, "a bold bad Man"[6]
     To God unfaithful, Children, Wife, and Home,
325   And wooed the artless daughter of the Hills,
     And wedded her, in cruel mockery
     Of love and marriage bonds.[7] O Friend! I speak
     With tender recollection of that time
     When first we saw the Maiden, then a name
330   By us unheard of, in her cottage Inn
     Were welcomed and attended on by her,
     Both stricken with one feeling of delight,
     An admiration if her modest mien
     And carriage, marked by unexampled grace.[8]

2. See the note on 5.365–67.
3. A quotation of Milton's *Samson Agonistes* (1671), line 89.
4. An awkward interruption, omitted in *Prel 1850*. The meaning seems to be that "faith *in* the delusion—the audience's credulity—shows its modesty in the quiet acceptance of the trick" (*NCPrel*).
5. The age of the Greek tragedian Thespis (sixth century B.C.E.); *here* (line 311): at Sadler's Wells.
6. Quoted from a description of the deceitful magician Archimago in Edmund Spenser's *Faerie Queene* (1590–96) 1.1.37.
7. Charles Dibdin's verse melodrama *Edward and Susan, or The Beauty of Buttermere*, performed by the *daring Brotherhood* (line 317) of Sadler's Wells in April–June 1803 and described by Mary Lamb in a letter of July 9, 1803, to DW (*CLL*, 2:117). The drama was based on the notorious story of Mary Robinson (1778–1837), a Buttermere innkeeper's daughter celebrated for her beauty, who in October 1802 had been tricked by one John Hatfield, posing as an aristocratic Scottish member of parliament, into a bigamous marriage with him. STC published an article in the *Morning Post* about the socially improbable marriage (October 11, 1802), as a result of which Hatfield's imposture was exposed. Tried in Carlisle, Scotland, for forgery, Hatfield was convicted and sentenced to death on August 16, 1803. WW, DW, and STC were in Carlisle on that day, and STC visited Hatfield in jail (*DWJ*, 1:196). Hatfield was hanged on September 3, and Mary Robinson eventually remarried (see Donald Reiman, "The Beauty of Buttermere as Fact and Romantic Symbol").
8. WW and STC may have encountered Robinson when they visited Buttermere on November 11, 1799 (*CL*, 1:544), and STC definitely did so when he had tea at her inn on August 1, 1802 (*CL*, 2:835, 846).

335   Not unfamiliarly we since that time
       Have seen her, her discretion have observed,
       Her just opinions, female modesty,
       Her patience and retiredness of mind
       Unsoiled by commendation, and the excess
340   Of public notice. This memorial Verse
       Comes from the Poet's heart, and is her due.
       For we were nursed, as almost might be said,
       On the same mountains, Children at one time
       Must haply often the self-same day
345   Have from our several dwellings gone abroad
       To gather Daffodils on Coker's Stream.[9]
              These last words uttered, to my argument
       I was returning, when, with sundry Forms
       Mingled, that in the way which I must tread
350   Before me stand, thy image rose again,
       Mary of Buttermere! She lives in peace
       Upon the spot where she was born and reared;
       Without contamination does she live
       In quietness, without anxiety:
355   Beside the mountain Chapel sleeps in earth
       Her new-born Infant;[1] fearless as a lamb
       That thither comes from some unsheltered place
       To rest beneath the little rock-like pile
       When storms are blowing. Happy are they both,
360   Mother and Child. These feelings, in themselves
       Trite, do yet scarcely seem so when I think
       Of those ingenuous moments of our youth
       Ere yet by use we have learned to slight the crimes
       And sorrows of the world. Those days are now
365   My theme, and 'mid the numerous scenes which they
       Have left behind them, foremost I am crossed
       Here by remembrance of two figures, one
       A rosy Babe, who for a twelvemonth's space
       Perhaps had been of age to deal about
370   Articulate prattle,[2] Child as beautiful
       As ever sate upon a Mother's knee;
       The other was the Parent of that Babe,
       But on the Mother's cheek the tints were false,
       A painted bloom. 'Twas at a Theatre
375   That I beheld this Pair; the Boy had been[3]
       The pride and pleasure of all lookers-on
       In whatsoever place; but seemed in this
       A sort of Alien scattered from the clouds.
       Of lusty vigour, more than infantine,

9. The River Cocker flows north from Buttermere to WW's birthplace, Cockermouth. As *PPrel*
   notes, WW's identification with Robinson alludes to Milton's *Lycidas*, line 23: "For we were
   nursed upon the self-same hill". *Several*: separate.
1. *NCPrel* suggests that WW may have had privileged local knowledge, but Mary Robinson is not
   recorded as having had a baby by Hatfield.
2. I.e., for about a year had been able to make himself understood.
3. Would have been.

380   He was in limbs; in face, a Cottage rose
       Just three parts blown; a Cottage Child, but ne'er
       Saw I, by Cottage or elsewhere, a Babe
       By Nature's gifts so honoured. Upon a Board
       Whence an attendant of the Theatre
385   Served out refreshments, had this Child been placed
       And there he sate environed with a ring
       Of chance Spectators, chiefly dissolute Men
       And shameless Women, treated[4] and caressed,
       Ate, drank, and with the fruit and glasses played,
390   While oaths, indecent speech, and ribaldry
       Were rife about him as are songs of birds
       In spring-time after showers. The Mother too
       Was present! but of her I know no more
       Than hath been said, and scarcely at this time
395   Do I remember her. But I behold
       The lovely Boy, as I beheld him then,
       Among the wretched and the falsely gay,
       Like one of those who walked with hair unsinged
       Amid the fiery furnace.[5] He hath since
400   Appeared to me oft-times as if embalmed
       By Nature, through some special privilege
       Stopped at the growth he had, destined to live,
       To be, to have been, come and go a Child
       And nothing more, no partner in the years
405   That bear us forward to distress and guilt,
       Pain and abasement, beauty in such excess
       Adorned him in that miserable place.
       So have I thought of him a thousand times,
       And seldom otherwise. But he perhaps,
410   Mary! may now have lived till he could look
       With envy on thy nameless Babe that sleeps
       Beside the mountain Chapel undisturbed.
                  It was but little more than three short years
       Before the season which I speak of now
415   When first,[6] a Traveller from our pastoral hills,
       Southward two hundred miles I had advanced,
       And for the first time in my life did hear
       The voice of Woman utter blasphemy,
       Saw Woman as she is to open shame
420   Abandoned, and the pride of public vice.
       Full surely from the bottom of my heart
       I shuddered; but the pain was almost lost,
       Absorbed and buried, in the immensity
       Of the effect: a barrier seemed at once
425   Thrown in, that from humanity divorced

4. Given treats.
5. Shadrach, Meshach, and Abednego, condemned by the Babylonian King Nebuchadnezzar to
   be burnt alive for refusing to worship a golden image, emerged from the furnace unharmed and
   without "an hair of their head singed" (Daniel 3.12–27).
6. I.e., in October 1787, when WW traveled south to begin his studies at Cambridge, three years
   before his first period of residence in London.

The human Form, splitting the race of Man
In twain, yet leaving the same outward shape.
Distress of mind ensued upon this sight
And ardent meditation: afterwards
430 A milder sadness on such spectacles
Attended; thought, commiseration, grief
For the individual, and the overthrow
Of her soul's beauty: farther at that time
Than this I was but seldom led; in truth
435 The sorrow of the passion[7] stopped me here.
      I quit this painful theme; enough is said
To shew what thoughts must often have been mine
At[8] Theatres, which then were my delight,
A yearning made more strong by obstacles
440 Which slender funds imposed. Life then was new,
The sense was easily pleased, the lustres,[9] lights,
The carving and the gilding, paint and glare,
And all the mean upholstery of the place
Wanted not animation in my sight:
445 Far less the living Figures on the Stage,
Solemn or gay: whether some beauteous Dame
Advanced in radiance through a deep recess
Of thick entangled forest, like the Moon
Opening the clouds; or sovereign King, announced
450 With flourishing Trumpets came in full-blown State
Of the World's greatness, winding round with Train
Of Courtiers, Banners, and a length of Guards;
Or Captive led in abject weeds, and jingling
His slender manacles: or romping Girl
455 Bounced, leapt, and pawed the air; or mumbling Sire,
A scare-crow pattern of old Age, patched up
Of all the tatters of infirmity,
All loosely put together, hobbled in,
Stumping upon a Cane, with which he smites,
460 From time to time, the solid boards, and makes them
Prate[1] somewhat loudly of the whereabout
Of one so overloaded with his years.
But what of this! the laugh, the grin, grimace
And all the antics and buffoonery,
465 The least of them not lost, were all received
With charitable pleasure. Through the night
Between the show, and many-headed mass
Of the Spectators, and each little nook
That had its fray or brawl, how eagerly,
470 And with what flashes, as it were, the mind

7. Feeling, emotion.
8. Altered at an uncertain stage, possibly in MW's hand, to "In."
9. Chandeliers, or prismatic glass pendants hung from chandeliers to enhance their illumination.
1. Talk, chatter. An allusion to Shakespeare, *Macbeth* 2.1.58: "The very stones prate of my whereabout."

Turned this way, that way, sportive and alert
And watchful as a Kitten when at play,
While winds are blowing round her, among grass
And rustling leaves.[2] Enchanting age, and sweet!
475   Romantic almost, looked at through a space,
How small, of intervening years. For then,
Though surely no mean progress had been made
In meditations holy and sublime,
Yet something of a girlish child-like gloss
480   Of novelty survived for scenes like these;
Pleasure that had been handed down from times
When, at a Country Play-house, having caught
In summer, through the fractured wall, a glimpse
Of day-light, at the thought of where I was
485   I gladdened more than if I had beheld
Before me some bright Cavern of Romance,
Or than we do when on our beds we lie
At night, in warmth, when rains are beating hard.[3]
        The matter which detains me now will seem
490   To many neither dignified enough
Nor arduous, and is, doubtless, in itself
Humble and low, yet not to be despised
By those who have observed the curious props
By which the perishable hours of life
495   Rest on each other, and the world of thought
Exists and is sustained.[4] More lofty Themes,
Such as, at least, do wear a prouder face
Might here be spoken of: but when I think
Of these I feel the imaginative Power
500   Languish within me: even then it slept
When, wrought upon by tragic sufferings,
The heart was full; amid my sobs and tears
It slept, even in the season of my youth:
For though I was most passionately moved,
505   And yielded to the changes of the scene
With most obsequious feeling, yet all this
Passed not beyond the suburbs[5] of the mind.
If aught there were of real grandeur here
'Twas only then when gross realities,
510   The incarnation of the Spirits that moved
Amid the Poets' beauteous world called forth,
With that distinctness which a contrast gives
Or opposition, made me recognise

2. NCPrel notes the similarity in imagery between lines 269–74 and WW's description of a play-
ful cat in his poem *Kitten and the Falling Leaves*, also composed in autumn 1804 (see *P2V*
[CW], 93–97).
3. An image repeated from 4.76–77.
4. Lines 492–96 were originally composed as part of *The Ruined Cottage* in February–March
1798, but in *The Prelude* WW has substituted *props* (line 493) for the earlier "links" (compare
his use of the word *props* in 2.219, 294).
5. Perhaps an echo of Shakespeare, *Julius Caesar* 2.1.285–86: "Dwell I but in the suburbs / Of
your good pleasure?" *Obsequious*: obedient.

As by a glimpse, the things which I had shaped
515   And not yet shaped, had seen, and scarcely seen,
Had felt and thought of, in my solitude.[6]
        Pass we from entertainments that are such
Professedly to others titled higher,[7]
Yet in the estimate of youth, at least,
520   More near akin to these than names imply,
I mean the brawls of Lawyers in their Courts
Before the ermined[8] Judge, or that great Stage
Where Senators, tongue-favored Men, perform,
Admired and envied. Oh! the beating heart,
525   When one among the prime of these rose up,
One, of whose name from Childhood we had heard
Familiarly,[9] a household term, like those
The Bedfords, Glocesters, Saliburys of old,
Which the fifth Harry talks of.[1] Silence! hush!
530   This is no trifler, no short-flighted Wit;
Nor stammerer of a minute, painfully
Delivered. No! the Orator hath yoked
The Hours, like young Aurora, to his Car;[2]
Oh! Presence of delight, can patience e'er
535   Grow weary of attending on a track
That kindles with such glory? Marvellous!
The enchantment spreads, and rises; all are rapt
Astonished; like a Hero in Romance
He winds away his never-ending horn;[3]
540   Words follow words, sense seems to follow sense;
What memory and what logic! till the Sense,
Transcendant, superhuman as it is,
Grows tedious even in a young Man's ear.[4]
        These are grave follies: other public shows
545   The Capital City teems with, of a kind
More light, and where but in the holy Church?
There have I seen a comely Bachelor,
Fresh from a toilette of two hours, ascend

---

6. *NCPrel* paraphrases lines 508–16: "I.e., he was deeply moved only when the imaginative world of the poet (Shakespeare, no doubt ° ° °) enabled him to identify things half-pictured or half-articulated within his own mind. The 'gross realities' of stage presentation draw attention to the spiritual qualities of Shakespeare's imagination through the very clumsiness with which they embody, 'incarnate,' his ideal world."
7. Of a higher reputation.
8. A reference to the ermine-tipped robes worn by High Court judges in England.
9. William Pitt the Younger (1759–1806), prime minister (hence *prime*, line 525) for all but three years from 1783 to 1806.
1. Shakespeare, *Henry V* 4.3.51–54: "Then shall our names / Familiar in his mouth as household words, / Harry the King, Bedford and Exeter, Warwick and Talbot, Salisbury and Gloucester, / Be in their flowing cups freshly rememb'red." DW had read the play to WW on May 8, 1802 (*DWJ*, 1:145).
2. Aurora, the Roman goddess of the dawn, commonly depicted crossing the sky in a chariot (*Car*), sometimes accompanied by the Horae (*Hours*). The point of the simile is that Pitt, in contrast to a *stammerer of a minute* (line 531), is capable of speaking at great length.
3. Perhaps a facetious allusion to Milton's description of the humming sound made by a dor-beetle as it flies: "What time the gray-fly winds her sultry horn" (*Lycidas*, line 28).
4. In 1832, in a particularly striking illustration of his rejection of his youthful political sympathies, WW inserted after line 543 a verse paragraph praising Edmund Burke (1729–1797), who had strongly condemned the French Revolution in his *Reflections on the Revolution in France* (1790).

The Pulpit, with seraphic glance look up,
550   And, in a tone elaborately low
Beginning, lead his voice through many a maze,[5]
A minuet course; and winding up his mouth,
From time to time, into an orifice
Most delicate, a lurking eyelet, small
555   And only not invisible, again
Open it out, diffusing thence a smile
Of rapt irradiation exquisite.[6]
Meanwhile the Evangelists, Isaiah, Job,
Moses, and he who penned the other day
560   The Death of Abel, Shakespear, Doctor Young
And Ossian (doubt not, 'tis the naked truth)
Summoned from streamy Morven, each an all
Must in their turn lend ornament and flowers
To entwine the Crook of eloquence with which
565   This pretty Shepherd, pride of all the Plains,
Leads up and down his captivated Flock.[7]
          I glance but at a few conspicuous marks,
Leaving ten thousand others that do each,
In Hall or Court, Conventicle[8] or Shop,
570   In public Room or private, Park or Street,
With fondness reared on his own Pedestal,[9]
Look out for admiration. Folly, vice,
Extravagance in gesture, mien, and dress,
And all the strife of singularity,[1]
575   Lies to the ear, and lies to every sense,
Of these, and of the living shapes they wear
There is no end. Such Candidates for regard,[2]
Although well pleased to be where they were found,
I did not hunt after, or greatly prize,
580   Nor made unto myself a secret boast
Of reading them with quick and curious eye;
But as a common produce, things that are
Today, tomorrow will be, took of them
Such willing note as, on some errand bound
585   Of pleasure or of love, some Traveller might,

5. An echo of Milton, *L'Allegro*, line 142: "The melting voice through mazes running."
6. WW's satire of vain, theatrical preachers is probably modeled on William Cowper's in *The Task*
(1785) 2.430–54.
7. In WW's metaphor, the preacher's eloquence is a shepherd's crook entwined with the *flowers* of
quotations from literature popular in the eighteenth century: the Swiss writer Salomon Gess-
ner's prose epic *Der Tod Abels* (1758), translated into English as *The Death of Abel* (1761) and
the model for STC's *Wanderings of Cain* (composed 1797, published 1828), begun as a collab-
orative project with WW (see the headnote to *LB*, above, and *NCC*, 211–17); Edward Young's
nine-book poem *Night Thoughts on Life, Death, and Immortality* (1742–45), to which WW
refers in his note on line 107 of *Tintern Abbey*; and James Macpherson's versions of epics (e.g.,
Fingal, 1762, and *Temora*, 1763) set in western Scotland (*Morven*) and purportedly translated
from the Scots Gaelic of an ancient bard named Ossian.
8. Meeting-place, in particular a place of worship for Protestant Dissenters from the Church of
England.
9. The revision of this line in *Prel 1850* clarifies the meaning: "Each fondly reared on his own
Pedestal" (*Prel 1850* [CW], 153).
1. Peculiarity, eccentricity.
2. I.e., people and things to be observed.

Among a thousand other images,
Of sea-shells that bestud the sandy beach,
Or daisies swarming through the fields in June.
        But foolishness, and madness in parade,[3]
590 Though most at home in this their dear domain,
Are scattered every where, no rarities
Even to the rudest novice of the Schools.
O Friend! one feeling was there which belonged
To this great City by exclusive right:
595 How often in the overflowing Streets
Have I gone forwards with the Crowd and said
Unto myself, the face of every one
That passes by me is a mystery.[4]
Thus have I looked, nor ceased to look, oppressed
600 By thoughts of what, and whither, when and how
Until the shapes before my eyes became
A second-sight procession, such as glides
Over still mountains,[5] or appears in dreams;
And all the ballast of familiar life,
605 The present, and the past, hope, fear, all stays
All laws of acting, thinking, speaking Man
Went from me, neither knowing me, nor known.[6]
And once, far travelled in such mood, beyond
The reach of common indications, lost
610 Amid the moving pageant, 'twas my chance
Abruptly to be smitten with the view
Of a blind Beggar, who, with upright face
Stood propped against a Wall, upon his Chest
Wearing a written paper, to explain
615 The Story of the Man and who he was;
My mind did at this spectacle turn round
As with the might of waters, and it seemed
To me that in this Label was a type
Or emblem of the utmost that we know
620 Both of ourselves, and of the universe;
And on the shape of this unmoving Man,
His fixèd face, and sightless eye, I looked
As if admonished from another world.[7]
        Though reared upon the base of outward things,
625 These chiefly are such structures as the mind
Builds for itself. Scenes different there are,
Full formed, which take, with small internal help,
Possession of the faculties, the peace

3. On display.
4. *PPrel* notes the contrast here to WW's experience of Hawkshead, in which "The face of every neighbour whom I met / Was as a volume to me" (4.58–59).
5. A reference to Lake District legends of spectral horsemen, about which WW had written in *An Evening Walk* (1793), lines 183–88.
6. As *PPrel* notes, an echo of Job 7.10: "He shall no more return to his house, neither shall his place know him any more."
7. Compare the leech gatherer in *Resolution and Independence*, whom WW describes as "like a Man from some far region sent, / To give me human strength, and strong astonishment" (lines 118–19).

Of night, for instance, the solemnity
630 Of nature's intermediate hours of rest,
When the great tide of human life stands still,
The business of the day to come unborn,
Of that gone by, locked up as in the grave;
The calmness, beauty of the spectacle,
635 Sky, stillness, moonshine, empty streets, and sounds
Unfrequent as in desarts:[8] at late hours
Of winter evenings when unwholesome rains
Are falling hard, with people yet astir,
The feeble salutation from the Voice
640 Of some unhappy Woman,[9] now and then
Heard as we pass, when no one looks about,
Nothing is listened to. But these I fear
Are falsly catalogued, things that are, are not
Even as we give them welcome, or assist,
645 Are prompt, or are remiss. What say you then
To times when half the City shall break out
Full of one passion, vengeance, rage, or fear
To executions,[1] to a street on fire,
Mobs, riots, or rejoicings? From those sights
650 Take one, an annual Festival, the Fair
Holden where Martyrs suffered in past time,
And named of Saint Bartholomew;[2] there see
A work that's finished to our hands,[3] that lays,
If any spectacle on earth can do,
655 The whole creative powers of Man asleep.
For once the Muse's help will we implore,
And she shall lodge us, wafted on her wings,
Above the press and danger of the Crowd,
Upon some Show-man's platform: what a hell
660 For eyes and ears! what anarchy and din
Barbarian and infernal! 'tis a dream
Monstrous in colour, motion, shape, sight, sound.
Below, the open space, through every nook
Of the wide area, twinkles, is alive
665 With heads; the midway region and above
Is thronged with staring pictures, and huge scrolls,
Dumb proclamations of the prodigies,
And chattering Monkeys dangling from their poles,
And Children whirling in their roundabouts,[4]

8. NCPrel notes the similarity of WW's response to London here to that in his sonnet *Composed upon Westminster Bridge*, p. 402 below.
9. A prostitute soliciting.
1. Public hangings, which attracted large crowds, were conducted outside Newgate Prison in central London until 1868.
2. Bartholomew Fair, a fair held annually (until its suppression in 1855) for two weeks (later reduced to four days) from September 3 at the Smithfield Market, east London, where over 200 Protestant martyrs had been burned alive during the reign of Mary Tudor (1553–58). WW and DW attended the fair with Charles Lamb on September 7, 1802, and WW may have attended it alone in 1791 and 1798 (*Chrono: MY*, 192).
3. Ready-made.
4. Merry-go-rounds.

670 With those that stretch the neck, and strain the eyes,
And crack the voice in rivalship, the crowd
Inviting, with buffoons against buffoons
Grimacing, writhing, screaming, him who grinds
The hurdy-gurdy, at the fiddle weaves,
675 Rattles the salt-box,[5] thumps the kettle-drum,
And him who at the trumpet puffs his cheeks,
The silver-collared Negro with his timbrel,[6]
Equestrians, Tumblers, Women, Girls and Boys,
Blue-breeched, pink-vested, and with towering plumes.
680 —All moveables of wonder from all parts
Are here, Albinos, painted Indians, Dwarfs,
The Horse of knowledge, and the learned Pig,[7]
The Stone-eater, the Man that swallows fire,
Giants, Ventriloquists, the Invisible Girl,
685 The Bust that speaks, and moves its goggling eyes,
The Wax-work, Clock-work, all the marvellous craft
Of modern Merlins,[8] wild Beasts, Puppet Shews,
All out-o'-th'-way, far-fetched, perverted things,
All freaks of Nature, all Promethean[9] thoughts
690 Of Man, his dullness, madness, and their feats,
All jumbled up together to make up
This Parliament of Monsters: tents and booths,
Meanwhile, as if the whole were one vast Mill,[1]
Are vomitting, receiving, on all sides
695 Men, Women, three year's Children, Babes in arms.
       Oh! blank confusion, and a type not false
Of what the mighty City is itself
To all except a Straggler here and there,
To the whole Flock of its inhabitants;
700 An undistinguishable world to Men,
The slaves unrespited[2] of low pursuits,
Living amid the same perpetual flow
Of trivial objects, melted and reduced
To one identity, by differences
705 That have no law, no meaning, and no end,[3]
Oppression under which even highest minds

5. A wooden box normally used for storing salt but popular with street musicians; *hurdy-gurdy*: a stringed instrument sounded by the rotation of a rosined wheel.
6. Tambourine.
7. Animals that performed tricks were a popular London entertainment, horses trained to answer numerical questions with sequential hoof-stamping (or defecation) being regularly exhibited from the late sixteenth century, and the first *learned Pig*, which arranged typographical cards into words, in 1785 (see Richard Altick, *The Shows of London* [Cambridge, MA, 1978], 36, 40–42).
8. Fortune-tellers (from the name of the soothsayer in Arthurian legend); *Wax-work*: exhibitions of wax figures (the most famous of which, Madame Tussaud's, toured Britain and Ireland from 1803 to 1835 before being established in London, where it remains a popular tourist attraction); *Clock-work*: mechanical figures wound up like clocks or moved by continuous rotation of a handle.
9. Daring, reckless (from Prometheus, the god who in Greek mythology formed humanity out of clay and was punished by Zeus for stealing fire from the gods and giving it to humanity). Lines 688–89 echo Milton's description of Hell in *Paradise Lost* 2.624–26: "where ° ° ° Nature breeds, / Perverse, all monstrous, all prodigious things, / Abominable, inutterable, and worse."
1. I.e., factory.
2. Stressed on the second syllable. The meaning is "unresting."
3. Lines 701–705 were originally drafted for *Michael* in 1800 (see *LB* [CW], 329), and were omitted from *Prel 1850*.

Must labour, whence the strongest are not free!
But though the Picture weary out the eye,
By nature an unmanageable sight,
710 It is not wholly so to him who looks
In steadiness, who hath among least things
An under sense of greatest, sees the parts
As parts, but with a feeling of the whole.
This of all acquisitions first awaits
715 On sundry and most widely-different modes
Of education: nor with least delight
On that through which I passed. Attention comes,
And comprehensiveness, and memory,
From early converse with the works of God
720 Among all regions: chiefly where appear
Most obviously simplicity and power.
By influence habitual to the mind
The mountain's outline and its steady form
Gives a pure grandeur; and its presence shapes
725 The measure and the prospect of the soul
To majesty;[4] such virtue have the forms
Perennial of the ancient hills; nor less,
The changeful language of their countenances
Gives movement to the thoughts, and multitude,
730 With order and relation.[5] This, if still,
As hitherto, with freedom I may speak,
And the same perfect openness of mind,
Not violating any just restraint,
As I would hope, of real modesty,
735 This did I feel in that vast receptacle:
The Spirit of Nature was upon me here;
The soul of Beauty and enduring life
Was present as a habit, and diffused
Through meagre lines and colours, and the press
740 Of self-destroying, transitory things,
Composure and ennobling harmony.

Book Eighth

RETROSPECT. LOVE OF NATURE LEADING TO LOVE OF MANKIND

What sounds are those, Helvellyn,[1] which are heard
Up to thy summit? Through the depth of air
Ascending, as if distance had the power
To make the sounds more audible: what Crowd
5   Is yon assembled in the gay green field?
Crowd seems it, solitary Hill! to thee,
Though but a little Family of Men,

---

4. I.e., early experience of natural phenomena helps shape the human soul; *measure . . . prospect*:
See the note on 6.526.
5. Lines 722–30 are drawn from the conclusion to a fragment originally composed in ca. March
1798 in connection with *The Ruined Cottage*. See the note on 2.322–41.
1. See Biographical and Topographical Glossary.

Twice twenty, with their Children and their Wives,
And here and there a Stranger interspersed.
10   It is a summer Festival, a Fair,
Such as, on this side now, and now on that,
Repeated through his tributary Vales
Helvellyn, in the silence of his rest,
Sees annually, if storms be not abroad
15   And mists have left him an unshrouded head.[2]
Delightful day it is for all who dwell
In this secluded Glen, and eagerly
They give it welcome. Long ere heat of noon
Behold the cattle are driven down; the sheep
20   That have for traffic been culled out are penned
In cotes that stand together on the Plain
Ranged side by side; the chaffering[3] is begun.
The Heifer lows uneasy at the voice
Of a new Master, bleat the Flocks aloud;
25   Booths are there none; a Stall or two is here,
A lame Man, or a blind, the one to beg,
The other to make music; hither, too,
From afar, with Basket slung upon her arm
Of Hawker's wares, books, pictures, combs and pins;
30   Some agèd Woman finds her way again,
Year after year a punctual Visitant!
The Show-man with his Freight upon his Back,
And once, perchance, in lapse of many years,
Prouder Itinerant, Mountebank, or He
35   Whose Wonders in a covered Wain[4] lie hid.
But One is here, the loveliest of them all,
Some sweet Lass of the Valley, looking out
For gains, and who that sees her would not buy?
Fruits of her Father's Orchard, apples, pears,
40   (On that day only to such office stooping)
She carries in her Basket, and walks round
Among the crowd half-pleased with, half-ashamed
Of her new calling, blushing restlessly.
The Children now are rich, the old Man now
45   Is generous; so gaiety prevails
Which all partake of, Young and Old. Immense
Is the Recess, the circumambient World
Magnificent, by which they are embraced.
They move about upon the soft green field:
50   How little They, they and their doings seem,
Their herds and flocks about them, they themselves

2. Compare DW's description of the annual Grasmere fair in her journal entry of September 2, 1800: "There seemed very few people and very few stalls, yet I believe there were many cakes and much beer sold. * * * It was a lovely moonlight night. We talked much about a house on Helvellyn. The moonlight shone only upon the village. It did not eclipse the village lights, and the sound of dancing and merriment came along the still air" (*DWJ*, 1:58–59).
3. Bargaining, haggling; *traffic*: sale; *cotes*: sheds built for harboring small animals, particularly sheep.
4. Wagon; *Mountebank*: a traveling quack doctor.

And all which they can further or obstruct!
Through utter weakness pitiably dear,
As tender Infants are: and yet how great!
55   For all things serve them, them the morning-light
Loves as it glistens on the silent rocks,
And them the silent Rocks which now from high
Look down upon them; the reposing Clouds,
The lurking Brooks from their invisible haunts,
60   And old Helvellyn, conscious of the stir,
And the blue sky that roofs their calm abode.[5]
            With deep devotion, Nature, did I feel
In that great City[6] what I owed to thee,
High thoughts of God and Man, and love of Man,
65   Triumphant over all those loathsome sights
Of wretchedness and vice; a watchful eye,
Which, with the outside of our human life
Not satisfied, must read the inner mind:
For I already had been taught to love
70   My Fellow-beings, to such habits trained
Among the woods and mountains, where I found
In thee a gracious Guide, to lead me forth
Beyond the bosom of my Family,
My Friends and youthful Playmates.[7] 'Twas thy power
75   That raised the first complacency[8] in me,
And noticeable kindliness of heart,
Love human to the Creature in himself
As he appeared, a Stranger in my path,
Before my eyes a Brother of this world;
80   Thou first didst with those motions of delight
Inspire me.—I remember, far from home
Once having strayed, while yet a very Child,
I saw a sight, and with what joy and love!
It was a day of exhalations,[9] spread
85   Upon the mountains, mists and steam-like fogs
Redounding every where, not vehement,[1]
But calm and mild, gentle and beautiful,
With gleams of sunshine on the eyelet spots
And loopholes of the hills, wherever seen,
90   Hidden by quiet process, and as soon
Unfolded, to be huddled up again:
Along a narrow Valley and profound

5. *PPrel* suggests that lines 55–61 draw on James Thomson's *Spring* (1728), lines 887–91: "For
   you the roving Spirit of the Wind / Blows Spring abroad; for you the teeming Clouds / Descend
   in gladsome Plenty o'er the World; / And the Sun sheds his kindest Rays for you, / Ye Flower of
   human Race!"
6. London (described in the preceding book).
7. As *NCPrel* notes, although most of book 8 was composed before book 7 (an early version of
   book 8 is preserved in MS Y of ca. October 1804), the account of Grasmere Fair in lines 1–61
   was composed after the completion of book 7 and offers a deliberate contrast to the account of
   Bartholomew Fair in 7.649–95.
8. Tranquil pleasure, satisfaction (without the negative connotation of self-satisfaction).
9. WW's meaning is explained in the next line.
1. Rapid, intense; *Redounding*: arising (a now-obsolete sense).

I journeyed, when, aloft above my head,
Emerging from the silvery vapours, lo!
95 A Shepherd and his Dog! in open day;
Girt round with mists they stood, and looked about
From that enclosure small, inhabitants
Of an aerial Island floating on,
As seemed, with that Abode in which they were,
100 A little pendant area of grey rocks,
By the soft wind breathed forward. With delight
As bland almost, one Evening I beheld,
And at as early age (the spectacle
Is common, but by me was then first seen)
105 A Shepherd in the bottom of a Vale
Towards the centre standing, who with voice,
And hand waved to and fro, as need required,
Gave signal to his Dog, thus teaching him
To chace along the mazes of steep crags
110 The Flock he could not see: and so the Brute,
Dear Creature! with a Man's intelligence
Advancing, or retreating on his steps,
Through every pervious strait, to right or left,
Thridded² away unbaffled; while the Flock
115 Fled upwards from the terror of his bark
Through rocks and seams of turf with liquid gold
Irradiate, that deep farewell light by which
The setting sun proclaims the love he bears
To mountain regions.
                            Beauteous the domain
120 Where to the sense of beauty first my heart
Was opened, tract more exquisitely fair
Than is that Paradise of ten thousand Trees,
Or Gehol's famous Gardens, in a Clime
Chosen from widest Empire, for delight
125 Of the Tartarian Dynasty composed;³
(Beyond that mighty Wall, not fabulous,
China's stupendous mound!)⁴ by patient skill
Of myriads, and boon Nature's lavish help:
Scene linked to scene, an ever growing change,
130 Soft, grand, or gay! with Palaces and Domes
Of Pleasure spangled over, shady Dells
For Eastern Monasteries, sunny Mounds

2. Threaded (an archaic form of the past tense); *pervious strait*: passable narrow space.
3. WW refers to the diplomat Lord Macartney's description, quoted in John Barrow's *Travels in China* (1804), of the gardens at the summer palace of the Chinese emperor Qianlong (1711–1799) in Zhe-hol (*Gehol*) in Tartary: "The Emperor having been informed that, in the course of our travels in China we had shewn a strong desire of seeing every thing curious and interesting, was pleased to give directions to the first minister to shew us his park or garden at Gehol. It is called in Chinese *Van-shoo-yuen*, or Paradise of ten thousand (or innumerable) trees" (126). Lines 119–45 generally recall Milton's description of Eden in *Paradise Lost* 4.208–47, and the *Domes / Of Pleasure* (lines 130–31) particularly recall STC's *Kubla Khan*, lines 2 and 35 (NCC, 182–83).
4. I.e., the Great Wall of China, which Barrow describes as "a mound of earth cased on each side with bricks or stone" (333).

With Temples crested, Bridges, Gondolas,
Rocks, Dens, and Groves of foliage taught to melt
135 Into each other their obsequious hues
Going and gone again, in subtile chace[5]
Too fine to be pursued; or standing forth
In no discordant opposition, strong
And gorgeous, as the colours side by side
140 Bedded among the plumes of Tropic Birds;
And mountains over all embracing all;
And all the landscape endlessly enriched
With waters running, falling, or asleep.
But lovelier far than this the Paradise
145 Where I was reared; in Nature's primitive gifts
Favored no less, and more to every sense
Delicious, seeing that the sun and sky,
The elements and seasons in their change
Do find their dearest Fellow-labourer there,
150 The heart of Man; a district on all sides,
The fragrance breathing of humanity,
Man free, man working for himself, with choice
Of time, and place, and object; by his wants,
His comforts, native occupations, cares;
155 Conducted on to individual ends
Or social, and still followed by a train[6]
Unwooed, unthought-of even, simplicity
And beauty, and inevitable grace.[7]
Yea, doubtless, at an age when but a glimpse
160 Of those resplendent Gardens, with their frame[8]
Imperial, and elaborate ornaments,
Would to a Child be transport[9] over-great,
When but a half-hour's roam through such a place
Would leave behind a dance of images
165 That shall break in upon his sleep for weeks;
Even then the common haunts of the green earth
With the ordinary human interests
Which they embosom, all without regard
As both may seem, are fastening on the heart
170 Insensibly, each with the other's help,
So that we love, not knowing that we love,
And feel, not knowing whence our feeling comes.
Such league have these two principles[1] of joy
In our affections. I have singled out
175 Some moments, the earliest that I could, in which

---

5. I.e., in a delicate mixture (*subtile*, an older spelling of "subtle" still used in WW's time); *obse-
quious*: compliant, obedient.
6. Succession.
7. WW here omits 236 lines from his draft in MS Y, for which see *Prel 1805* (CW), 2:378–88. In
the omitted passage he had contrasted human life unfavorably with nature.
8. Layout.
9. Joy.
1. Sources, causes. They are *the common haunts of the green earth* (line 166) and *ordinary human
interests* (line 167).

Their several currents blended into one,
Weak yet, and gathering imperceptibly,
Flowed in by gushes. My first human love,
As hath been mentioned, did incline to those
180   Whose occupations and concerns were most
Illustrated[2] by Nature and adorned,
And Shepherds were the Men who pleased me first.
Not such as in Arcadian Fastnesses
Sequestered, handed down among themselves,
185   So ancient Poets sing, the golden Age;[3]
Nor such, a second Race, allied to these,
As Shakespear in the wood of Arden placed
Where Phœbe sighed for the false Ganymede,
Or there where Florizel and Perdita
190   Together danced, Queen of the feast and King;
Nor such as Spenser fabled.[4] True it is
That I had heard, what he perhaps had seen,
Of Maids at sun-rise bringing in from far
Their May-bush,[5] and, along the Streets, in flocks,
195   Parading with a Song of taunting rhymes,
Aimed at the Laggards slumbering within doors,
Had also heard from those who yet remembered
Tales of the May-pole dance, and flowers that decked
The Posts and the Kirk-pillars,[6] and of Youths
200   That, each one with his Maid, at break of day
By annual custom issued forth in troops
To drink the waters of some favorite Well
And hang it round with Garlands. This, alas,
Was but a dream; the times had scattered all
205   These lighter graces, and the rural ways
And manners, which it was my chance to see
In childhood, were severe and unadorned,
The unluxuriant produce of a life
Intent on little but substantial needs,
210   Yet beautiful, and beauty that was felt.
But images of danger and distress,
And suffering, these took deepest hold of me,
Man suffering among awful Powers and Forms:
Of this I heard and saw enough to make
215   The imagination restless; nor was free

2. Stressed on the second and fourth syllables.
3. I.e., not the shepherds of Greek and Latin pastoral poetry, set in Arcadia, an idealized region of rural contentment (*Arcadian Fastnesses*).
4. WW also dissociates himself from the idealized pastoral of Edmund Spenser's *Shepheardes Calendar* (1579) and Shakespeare's plays: in *As You Like It*, the shepherdess Phoebe falls in love with *the false Ganymede*, Rosalind disguised as a man; in *The Winter's Tale*, Florizel and Perdita are not only the "king" and "queen" of the sheep-shearing feast but the heirs to the thrones of Bohemia and Sicily.
5. WW refers to traditional May Day celebrations in which young women assembled in the early morning to go into the woods to cut off and bring home branches of hawthorn (*May-bush*).
6. External columns of churches. WW recalls the May Eclogue of Spenser's *Shepheardes Calendar*, lines 11–14: "And home they hasten the postes to dight [adorn], / And all the Kirke pillours eare day light, / With Hawthorne buds, and swete Eglantine, / And girlonds of roses and Sopps [pieces of bread] in wine."

Myself from frequent perils, nor were tales
Wanting, the tragedies of former times,
Or hazards and escapes, which in my walks
I carried with me among crags and woods
220   And mountains: and of these may here be told
One, as recorded by my Household Dame.[7]
       At the first falling of autumnal snow
A Shepherd and his Son one day went forth
(Thus did the Matron's Tale begin) to seek
225   A Straggler of their Flock. They both had ranged
Upon this service the preceding day
All over their own pastures and beyond,
And now, at sun-rise sallying out again
Renewed their search, begun where from Dove-crag,
230   Ill home for bird so gentle, they looked down
On Deep-dale Head, and Brother's-water, named
From those two Brothers that were drowned therein,
Thence, northward, having passed by Arthur's Seat,
To Fairfield's highest summit; on the right
235   Leaving St Sunday's Pike, to Grisdale Tarn
They shot, and over that cloud-loving hill
Seat Sandal, a fond lover of the clouds;
Thence up Helvellyn, a superior Mount
With prospect underneath of Striding-edge,
240   And Grisdale's houseless Vale, along the brink
Of Russet Cove, and those two other Coves,
[Huge skeletons of crags, which from the trunk
Of old Helvellyn spread their arms abroad,
And make a stormy harbour for the winds.[8]
245   Far went those Shepherds in their devious quest,
From mountain ridges peeping as they passed
Down into every Glen: at length the Boy
Said, "Father with your leave I will go back,
And range the ground which we have searched before."
250   So speaking, southward down the hill the Lad
Sprang like a gust of wind, crying aloud,
"I know where I shall find him." "For take note,"
Said here my grey-haired Dame, "that tho' the storm
Drive one of these poor Creatures miles and miles,
255   If he can crawl he will return again
To his own hills, the spots where, when a Lamb,
He learned to pasture at his Mother's side."
After so long a labour, suddenly
Bethinking him of this, the Boy[9]

7. Ann Tyson, WW's landlady in Hawkshead. The *Matron's Tale* of lines 222–311 was composed
originally for *Michael* in October–December 1800, and revised slightly for inclusion here in
October 1804. WW removed the passage in his 1818–20 revisions of *The Prelude*.
8. The area referred to in lines 229–44 is a range of mountains and valleys northeast of Grasmere
(*Russet Cove* is an error for Ruthwaite Cove). In MS B the leaf (pp. 191–92) containing lines
242–94 was excised during the revisions of 1818–20, when the Matron's Tale was omitted from
the poem. The missing lines, in brackets, are printed here from MS A.
9. An octosyllabic line retained from the draft in MS Y (*Prel 1805* [CW] 2:393).

260   Pursued his way towards a brook whose course
Was through that unfenced tract of mountain-ground
Which to his Father's little Farm belonged,
The home and ancient Birth-right of their Flock.
Down the deep channel of the Stream he went,
265   Prying through every nook: meanwhile the rain
Began to fall upon the mountain tops,
Thick storm and heavy which for three hours' space
Abated not; and all that time the Boy
Was busy in his search until at length
270   He spied the Sheep upon a plot of grass,
An Island in the Brook. It was a place
Remote and deep, piled round with rocks where foot
Of man or beast was seldom used to tread;
But now, when every where the summer grass
275   Had failed, this one Adventurer, hunger-pressed,
Had left his Fellows, and made his way alone
To the green plot of pasture in the Brook.
Before the Boy knew well what he had seen
He leapt upon the Island with proud heart
280   And with a Prophet's joy. Immediately
The Sheep sprang forward to the further Shore
And was borne headlong by the roaring flood.
At this the Boy looked round him, and his heart
Fainted with fear; thrice did he turn his face
285   To either brink; nor could he summon up
The courage that was needful to leap back
Cross the tempestuous torrent; so he stood,
A Prisoner on the Island, not without
More than one thought of death and his last hour.
290   Meanwhile the Father had returned alone
To his own house; and now at the approach
Of evening he went forth to meet his Son,
Conjecturing vainly for what cause the Boy
Had stayed so long. The Shepherd took his way]
295   Up his own mountain grounds, where as he walked
Along the Steep that overhung the Brook,
He seemed to hear a voice, which was again
Repeated, like the whistling of a kite.[1]
At this, not knowing why, as oftentimes
300   Long afterwards he has been heard to say,
Down to the Brook he went, and tracked its course
Upwards among th' o'erhanging rocks; nor thus
Had he gone far, ere he espied the Boy
Where on that little plot of ground he stood
305   Right in the middle of the roaring Stream,
Now stronger every moment and more fierce.
The sight was such as no one could have seen

---

1. A fork-tailed bird of prey once common in England.

Without distress and fear. The Shepherd heard
The outcry of his Son, he stretched his Staff
310 Towards him, bade him leap, which word scarce said
The Boy was safe within his Father's arms.
          Smooth life had Flock and Shepherd in old time
Long Springs and tepid Winters on the banks
Of delicate Galesus; and no less
315 Those scattered along Adrea's myrtle Shores.[2]
Smooth life the Herdsman and his snow-white Herd,
To Triumphs and to sacrificial rites
Devoted, on the inviolable Stream
Of rich Clitumnus, and the Goatherd lived
320 As sweetly underneath the pleasant brows
Of cool Lucretilis, where the Pipe was heard
Of Pan, the invisible God thrilling the rocks
With tutelary music, from all harm
The Fold[3] protecting. I myself, mature
325 In manhood then, have seen a pastoral Tract
Like one of these where Fancy might run wild,
Though under skies less generous and serene;
Yet there, as for herself, had Nature framed
A Pleasure-ground, diffused a fair expanse
330 Of level Pasture, islanded with Groves
And banked with woody risings; but the plain
Endless, here opening widely out, and there
Shut up in lesser lakes or beds of lawn
And intricate recesses, creek or bay
335 Sheltered within a shelter, where at large
The Shepherd strays, a rolling hut his home:[4]
Thither he comes with spring-time, there abides
All summer; and at sunrise ye may hear
His flute or flagelet[5] resounding far;
340 There's not a Nook or Hold of that vast Space,
Nor Strait where passage is, but it shall have
In turn its Visitant, telling there his hours
In unlaborious pleasure, with no task
More toilsome than to carve a beechen bowl
345 For Spring or Fountain, which the Traveller finds
When through the region he pursues at will
His devious course. A glimpse of such sweet life
I saw, when from the melancholy Walls

2. The Adriatic coast of Italy. *Galesus:* a river in Apulia, southern Italy, famed in antiquity for the sheep raised on its banks and praised by Horace in *Odes* 2.6 (of which WW had written an imitation in 1794; see *Early Poems and Fragments, 1785–1797* [CW], 760–67).
3. Flock of sheep. *Clitumnus* (line 318): a river in Umbria, central Italy, celebrated in antiquity for the clearness of its water and for the whiteness of the cattle that pastured on its banks, on account of which the bulls were sacrificed on triumphal occasions (lines 316–18 derive from Virgil, *Georgics* 2.146–48); *Lucretilis . . . tutelary music* (lines 318–23): a reference to Horace's *Ode* 1.17.1–4 and 10, in which Faunus is identified with the pipe-playing Pan, whose *tutelary music* protects the sheep;
4. A small cabin on wheels in which the shepherd can sleep near his flock.
5. A small wind instrument like a recorder (now spelled *flageolet*).

Of Goslar, once Imperial![6] I renewed
350 My daily walk along that chearful Plain,
Which, reaching to her Gates, spreads East and West
And Northwards, from beneath the mountainous verge
Of the Hercynian Forest.[7] Yet hail to You,
Your rocks and precipices, ye that seize
355 The heart with firmer grasp! your snows and streams
Ungovernable, and your terrifying winds
That howled so dismally when I have been
Companionless among your solitudes.
There 'tis the Shepherd's task the winter long
360 To wait upon the storms: of their approach
Sagacious,[8] from the height he drives his Flock
Down into sheltering coves, and feeds them there
Through the hard time, long as the storm is locked,
(So do they phrase it) bearing from the stalls
365 A toilsome burthen[9] up the craggy ways,
To strew it on the snow. And when the Spring
Looks out, and all the mountains dance with Lambs,
He through the enclosures, won from the steep Waste,[1]
And through the lower Heights hath gone his rounds;
370 And when the Flock with warmer weather climbs
Higher and higher, him his office leads
To range among them, through the hills dispersed,
And watch their goings, whatsoever track
Each Wanderer chuses for itself; a work
375 That lasts the summer through. He quits his home
At day-spring, and no sooner doth the sun
Begin to strike him with a fire-like heat
Than he lies down upon some shining place
And breakfasts with his Dog: when he hath stayed,
380 As for the most he doth, beyond his time
He springs up with a bound, and then away!
Ascending fast with his long Pole in hand,
Or winding in and out among the crags.
What need to follow him through what he does
385 Or sees in his day's march? He feels himself
In those vast regions where his service is
A Freeman; wedded to his life of hope
And hazard, and hard labour interchanged
With that majestic indolence so dear
390 To native Man.[2] A rambling School-boy, thus

6. See the Biographical and Topographical Glossary. In the Fenwick note to *Lines written in Germany* (a poem first published in *LB 1800*), WW recalled that the town "retains vestiges of its ancient splendour" and that he walked its ramparts daily, composing poetry.
7. Harz Forest (WW uses the Latinate form of the name). On February 27, 1799, DW wrote to STC that she and WW had walked along the edge of the Harz Forest, in the western range of the Harz Mountains, as they traveled south from Goslar to Ostrode, Herberg, and Scharzfeld (*WL*, 1:250–53).
8. Acutely aware (a now-obsolete sense of *sagacious*).
9. I.e., of hay.
1. Mountainside land cleared for pasturing and fenced in.
2. I.e., human nature.

Have I beheld him, without knowing why
Have felt his presence in his own domain
As of a Lord and Master; or a Power
Or Genius,[3] under Nature, under God
395 Presiding; and severest solitudes
Seemed more commanding oft when he was there.
Seeking the raven's nest, and suddenly
Surprized with vapours, or on rainy days
When I have angled up the lonely brooks
400 Mine eyes have glanced upon him, few steps off,
In size a Giant, stalking through the fog,
His Sheep like Greenland Bears:[4] at other times,
When round some shady promontory turning,
His Form hath flashed upon me, glorified
405 By the deep radiance of the setting sun:
Or him have I descried in distant sky,
A solitary object and sublime,
Above all height! like an aerial Cross,
As it is stationed on some spiry Rock
410 Of the Chartreuse,[5] for worship. Thus was Man
Ennobled outwardly before mine eyes,
And thus my heart at first was introduced
To an unconscious love and reverence
Of human nature; hence the human form
415 To me was like an index of delight,
Of grace and honour, power and worthiness.
Meanwhile this Creature, spiritual almost
As those of Books, but more exalted far,
Far more of an imaginative form,
420 Was not a Corin of the groves, who lives
For his own fancies, or to dance by the hour
In coronal, with Phillis in the midst,
But for the purposes of kind,[6] a Man
With the most common, Husband, Father; learned,
425 Could teach, admonish, suffered with the rest
From vice and folly, wretchedness and fear:
Of this I little saw, cared less for it,
But something must have felt.
                                  Call ye these appearances[7]
Which I beheld of Shepherds in my Youth,
430 This sanctity of nature given to Man

3. Tutelary spirit.
4. In lines 397–402 WW recalls James Thomson's description of the optical effects of fog in *Autumn* (1730), lines 725–27, from *The Seasons*: "Seen thro' the turbid Air, beyond the Life, / Objects appear; and, wilder'd, o'er the Waste / The Shepherd stalks gigantic. ° ° °" *Raven's nest* (line 397): See above, 1.336–53.
5. See the note on 6.421–24. In *Descriptive Sketches* (1793), line 70, WW mentioned "angels planted on the aëreal rock" of the Chartreuse Mountains, and in a note explained that he was referring to "crosses seen on the tops of the spiry rocks of the Chartreuse" (*Descriptive Sketches* [CW], 46).
6. By nature; *Corin . . . Phillis*: stock pastoral names (Corin is a shepherd in Shakespeare's *As You Like It*, Phillis a shepherdess in Milton's *L'Allegro*); *coronal*: a circle (literally a "wreath" or "garland," hence a word suited to the pastoral theme of this passage).
7. A hypermetrical line, unaltered through all WW's revisions of *The Prelude*.

A shadow, a delusion, ye who are fed
By the dead letter, not the spirit of things,[8]
Whose truth is not a fashion or a shape
Instinct with vital functions, but a Block
435 Or waxen image which yourselves have made,
And ye adore. But blessèd be the God
Of Nature and of Man that this was so,
That Men did at the first present themselves
Before my untaught eyes thus purified,
440 Removed, and at a distance that was fit.
And so we all of us in some degree
Are led to knowledge, whence so-ever led,
And howsoever; were it otherwise,
And we found evil fast as we find good
445 In our first years, or think that it is found,
How could the innocent heart bear up and live!
But doubly fortunate my lot; not here
Alone, that something of a better life
Perhaps was round me than it is the privilege
450 Of most to move in, but that first I looked
At Man through objects that were great and fair,
First communed[9] with him by their help. And thus
Was founded a sure safeguard and defence
Against the weight of meanness, selfish cares,
455 Coarse manners, vulgar passions that beat in
On all sides from the ordinary world
In which we traffic. Starting from this point,
I had my face towards the truth, began
With an advantage; furnished with that kind
460 Of prepossession without which the soul
Receives no knowledge that can bring forth good,
No genuine insight ever comes to her:
Happy in this, that I with nature walked,
Not having a too early intercourse
465 With the deformities of crowded life,
And those ensuing laughters and contempts
Self-pleasing, which if we would wish to think
With admiration and respect of man,
Will not permit us; but pursue the mind
470 That to devotion willingly would be raised
Into the Temple and the Temple's heart.
          Yet do not deem, my Friend, though thus I speak
Of Man as having taken in my mind
A place thus early which might almost seem
475 Preeminent, that this was really so.
Nature herself was at this unripe time
But secondary to my own[1] pursuits,

8. An allusion to 2 Corinthians 3.6: "the letter killeth, but the spirit giveth life."
9. Stressed on the first syllabus.
1. This word, present in the base-text of MS A, is inserted by MW in MS B, presumably having
   been inadvertently omitted in the initial copying.

And animal activities and all
Their trivial pleasures: and long afterwards
480 When those had died away and Nature did
For her own sake become my joy, even then
And upwards through late youth, until not less
Than three and twenty summers had been told
Was man in my affections and regards
485 Subordinate to her;[2] her awful forms
And viewless agencies: a passion she!
A rapture often, and immediate joy,
Ever at hand: he distant, but a grace
Occasional, an accidental thought,
490 His hour being not yet come.[3] Far less had then
The inferior Creatures, beast or bird, attuned
My spirit to that gentleness of love,
Won from those minute obeisances
Of tenderness which I may number now
495 With my first blessings. Nevertheless on these
The light of beauty did not fall in vain,
Or grandeur circumfuse them to no end.[4]
     Why should I speak of Tillers of the soil?
The Ploughman and his Team; or Men and Boys
500 In festive summer busy with the rake,
Old Men, and ruddy Maids, and Little-ones
All out together, and in sun and shade
Dispersed among the hay-grounds alder-fringed,
The Quarry-man, far heard! that blasts the rocks,
505 The Fishermen in pairs, the one to row
And one to drop the Net, plying their Trade
"Mid tossing Lakes, and tumbling Boats,"[5] and winds
Whistling; the Miner, melancholy Man!
That works by taper light, while all the hills
510 Are shining with the glory of the day.
     But when that first poetic Faculty
Of plain imagination and severe,
No longer a mute Influence of the soul,
An Element of the Nature's inner self,
515 Began to have some promptings to put on
A visible shape, and to the works of art,
The notions and the images of books
Did knowingly conform itself, by these

2. Compare 13.236–40 and *Tintern Abbey*, lines 72–75: "For nature then / (The coarser pleasures of my boyish days, / And their glad animal movements all gone by,) / To me was all in all." In *Prel 1850* WW altered *three and twenty summers* (line 483) to "two and twenty summers," thus identifying the shift in his affections towards humanity with his time in France in 1792 (*Prel 1850* [CW], 169).
3. An allusion to John 2.4, in which Jesus says to Mary, "Woman, what have I to do with thee? mine hour is not yet come."
4. Lines 498–510 were omitted in *Prel 1850*.
5. As NCPrel notes, the quotation is from *My dear and only Love*, a poem by James Graham, 1st Marquess of Montrose (1612–1650), which WW may have encountered in the anthology *A Choice Collection of Comic and Serious Scots Poems* (Edinburgh, 1706–11), 3:111 (*Reading 1800–15*, no. 184). The phrase "whistling Wind" appears in the same stanza of the poem.

Enflamed, and proud of that her new delight,
520 There came among those shapes of human life
A wilfulness of fancy and conceit
Which gave them new importance to the mind;[6]
And Nature and her objects beautified
These fictions, as in some sort in their turn
525 They burnished her. From touch of this new power
Nothing was safe; the Elder-tree that grew
Beside the well-known Charnel-house[7] had then
A dismal look; the Yew-tree had its Ghost
That took its station there for ornament:
530 Then common death was none, common mishap,
But matter for this humour every-where,
The tragic, super-tragic, else left short.[8]
Then, if a Widow staggering with the blow
Of her distress was known to have made her way
535 To the cold grave in which her Husband slept
One night, or haply more than one, through pain
Of half-insensate impotence of mind
The fact was caught at greedily, and there
She was a Visitant the whole year through,
540 Wetting the turf with never-ending tears,
And all the storms of Heaven must beat on her.
          Through wild obliquities could I pursue
Among all objects of the fields and groves
These cravings: when the Fox-glove, one by one,
545 Upwards through every stage of its tall stem
Had shed its bells, and stood by the way-side
Dismantled, with a single one perhaps,
Left at the ladder's top, with which the Plant
Appeared to stoop, as slender blades of grass
550 Tipped with a bead of rain or dew, behold!
If such a sight were seen, would Fancy bring
Some Vagrant thither with her Babes, and seat her
Upon the turf beneath the stately flower
Drooping in sympathy, and making so
555 A melancholy Crest above the head
Of the lorn[9] Creature, while her Little-ones,
All unconcerned with her unhappy plight,
Were sporting with the purple cups that lay
Scattered upon the ground.[1]
                    There was a Copse,
560 An upright bank of wood and woody rock
That opposite our rural Dwelling stood
In which a sparkling patch of diamond light

---

6. WW distinguishes "wilful fancy" from imagination in lines 583–86 below.
7. A building or shed in which disinterred bones were stored so that graves could be reused.
8. I.e., the mind was dissatisfied unless it regarded the tragic as *super-tragic*.
9. Forlorn (a contraction used into the nineteenth century).
1. The fancied scene of lines 591–99 recalls that described in WW's *An Evening Walk* (1793),
lines 241–300 (*An Evening Walk* [CW], 60, 62).

Was in bright weather duly to be seen
On summer afternoons within the wood
565 At the same place. 'Twas doubtless nothing more
Than a black rock, which, wet with constant springs,
Glistered far seen from out its lurking-place
As soon as ever the declining sun
Had smitten it. Beside our Cottage hearth,
570 Sitting with open door, a hundred times
Upon this lustre have I gazed, that seemed
To have some meaning which I could not find;
And now it was a burnished shield, I fancied,
Suspended over a Knight's Tomb, who lay
575 Inglorious, buried in a dusky wood;
An entrance now into some magic cave
Or Palace for a Fair of the rock;
Nor would I, though not certain whence the cause
Of the effulgence, thither have repaired
580 Without a precious bribe, and day by day
And month by month I saw the spectacle,
Nor ever once have visited the spot
Unto this hour. Thus sometimes were the shapes
Of wilful lunacy grafted upon feelings
585 Of the imagination and they rose
In worth accordingly.[2] My present Theme
Is to retrace the way that led me on
Through Nature to the love of Human kind;
Nor could I with such object overlook
590 The influence of this Power which turned itself
Instinctively to human passions, things
Least understood; of this adulterate[3] Power,
For so it may be called, and without wrong,
When with that first compared. Yet in the midst
595 Of these vagaries, with an eye so rich
As mine was, through the chance, on me not wasted
Of having been brought up in such a grand
And lovely region, I had forms distinct
To steady me; these thoughts did oft revolve
600 About some centre palpable which at once
Incited them to motion, and controlled,[4]
And whatsoever shape the fit might take,
And whencesoever it might come, I still
At all times had a real solid world
605 Of images about me; did not pine
As one in cities bred might do, as Thou,

2. WW here recalls the distinction between imagination ("the faculty which produces impressive
   effects out of simple elements") and fancy ("the power by which pleasure and surprize are
   excited by the sudden varieties of situation and by accumulated imagery") in his note to *The
   Thorn* in *LB 1800* (above, p. 38). He returns to the distinction in 13.289–94 and in the Preface
   to *P 1815*.
3. Mixed, impure (because the fancy makes arbitrary associations and connections).
4. That is, the sight of the natural objects (like that of the *black rock* in line 566) controlled as
   well as incited the fancy, because WW always recognized the objects to be real.

Beloved Friend! hast told me that thou didst,
Great Spirit as thou art, in endless dreams
Of sickliness, disjoining, joining things
610   Without the light of knowledge.[5] Where the harm
If, when the Woodman languished with disease
From sleeping night by night among the woods
Within his sod-built Cabin, Indian-wise,
I called the pangs of disappointed love
615   And all the long Etcetera of such thought
To help him to his grave. Meanwhile the Man,
If not already from the woods retired
To die at home, was haply, as I knew,
Pining alone among the gentle airs,
620   Birds, running Streams, and Hills so beautiful
On golden evenings, while the charcoal Pile
Breathed up its smoke, an image of his ghost
Or spirit, that was soon to take its flight.
          There came a time of greater dignity
625   Which had been gradually prepared, and now
Rushed in as if on wings, the time in which
The pulse of Being every where was felt,
When all the several frames of things, like stars
Through every magnitude distinguishable,
630   Were half confounded in each other's blaze,
One galaxy of life and joy.[6] Then rose
Man, inwardly contemplated, and present
In my own being, to a loftier height;
As of all visible natures crown;[7] and first
635   In capability of feeling what
Was to be felt; in being wrapt away
By the divine effect of power and love,
As more than any thing we know instinct
With Godhead, and by reason and by will
640   Acknowledging dependency sublime.
          [Erelong transported hence as in a dream][8]
I found myself begirt with temporal shapes
Of vice and folly thrust upon my view,
Objects of sport, and ridicule, and scorn,
645   Manners and characters discriminate,
And little busy passions that eclipsed,
As well they might, the impersonated thought,
The idea or abstraction of the Kind.[9]
An Idler among academic Bowers
650   Such was my new condition, as at large

5. A reference to STC's urban schooling at Christ's Hospital, as in 6.275–84 and 305–16.
6. Compare the passage in which WW describes his recognition of "one Presence, and the Life / Of the great whole" (3.121–67).
7. In *Prel 1850* WW added here the clause "though born / Of dust, and Kindred to the worm" (*Prel 1850* [CW], 173).
8. Space for this line was left in MSS B and A and the line itself inserted in MS A, probably during the 1818–20 revisions.
9. Human nature.

Hath been set forth:[1] yet here the vulgar light
Of present actual superficial life,
Gleaming through colouring of other times,
Old usages and local privileges,
655 Thereby was softened, almost solemnized,
And rendered apt and pleasing to the view;
This notwithstanding, being brought more near,
As I was now, to guilt and wretchedness,
I trembled, thought of human life at times
660 With an indefinite terror and dismay
Such as the storms and angry elements
Had bred in me, but gloomier far, a dim
Analogy to uproar and misrule,
Disquiet, danger, and obscurity.
665 ——It might be told (but wherefore speak of things
Common to all?) that seeing, I essayed
To give relief, began to deem myself
A moral agent, judging between good
And evil, not as for the mind's delight
670 But for her safety, one who was to *act*,
As sometimes, to the best of my weak means,
I did, by human sympathy impelled;
And through dislike and most offensive pain
Was to the truth conducted; of this faith
675 Never forsaken, that by acting well
And understanding, I should learn to love,
The end[2] of life and every thing we know.
          Preceptress stern, that didst instruct me next,
London! to thee I willingly return.
680 Erewhile my Verse played only with the flowers
Enwrought upon thy mantle,[3] satisfied
With this amusement, and a simple look
Of childlike inquisition, now and then
Cast upwards on thine eye to puzzle out
685 Some inner meanings, which might harbour there.
Yet did I not give way to this light mood
Wholly beguiled, as one incapable
Of higher things, and ignorant that high things
Were round me. Never shall I forget the hour,
690 The moment rather say, when having thridded
The labyrinth of suburban Villages
At length I did unto myself first seem
To enter the great City.[4] On the Roof
Of an itinerant Vehicle[5] I sate
695 With vulgar Men about me, vulgar forms

1. In book 3.
2. Purpose, goal.
3. A recollection of Milton's *Lycidas*, lines 104–105, in which the River Cam (which flows through Cambridge) is personified as having "a Mantle hairy, and [a] Bonnet sedge [i.e., filled with grass], / Inwrought with figures dim."
4. On the date of WW's first visit to London, see the note to 7.72–77.
5. Presumably a stagecoach.

Of houses, pavement, streets, of men and things,
Mean shapes on every side: but at the time
When to myself it fairly might be said,
The very moment that I seemed to know
700 The threshold now is overpassed, Great God!
That aught external to the living mind
Should have such mighty sway! yet so it was
A weight of Ages did at once descend
Upon my heart, no thought embodied, no
705 Distinct remembrances; but weight and power
Power growing with the weight: alas! I feel
That I am trifling: 'twas a moment's pause,
All that took place within me came and went
As in a moment, and I only now
710 Remember that it was a thing divine.
            As when a Traveller hath from open day
With torches passed into some Vault of Earth,
The Grotto of Antiparos, or the Den
Of Yordas[6] among Craven's mountain tracts,
715 He looks and sees the Cavern spread and grow,
Widening itself on all sides, sees, or thinks
He sees,[7] erelong, the roof above his head,
Which instantly unsettles and recedes
Substance and shadow, light and darkness, all
720 Commingled, making up a canopy
Of Shapes and Forms, and Tendencies to shape
That shift and vanish, change and interchange
Like Spectres, ferment quiet, and sublime;
Which, after short space, works less and less
725 Till every effort, every motion gone,
The scene before him lies in perfect view,
Exposed and lifeless as a written book.[8]
But let him pause awhile, and look again
And a new quickening shall succeed, at first
730 Beginning timidly, then creeping fast
Through all which he beholds: the senseless mass
In its projections, wrinkles, cavities,
Through all its surface, with all colours streaming,
Like a magician's airy pageant, parts,

6. *Den of Yordas*: a limestone cave in the Craven district of north Yorkshire, visited by WW and
his brother John sometime between May 19 and June 5, 1800 (*Chrono: MY*, 63; *WL*, 1:298).
Grotto of Antiparos: a cavern noted for its stalactites on the Greek island of Antiparos in the
Aegean Sea.
7. *Sees . . . sees*: WW translates *Aeneid* 6.454 ("aut videt aut vidisse putat"), a phrase doubly
appropriate because Virgil himself uses it within a simile and in connection with Aeneas's
encounter with Dido in the underworld. It was also appropriated by Milton in *Paradise Lost*
1.783–84 ("sees, / Or dreams he sees").
8. The epic simile of lines 711–27 was originally drafted between February and early April 1804
to convey WW's sense of anticlimax after having crossed the Alps in August 1790 (see 6.511–
24 and, for the draft in MS WW, *Prel 1805* [CW], 2:255–57). He then briefly, probably in
April–May 1804, considered using the simile as part of an introductory section of book 7 (see
MS X in *Prel 1805* [CW], 2:318), before deciding, no later than the autumn of 1804, to use it
here.

735 Unites, embodying every where some pressure[9]
　　Or image recognised or new, some type
　　Or picture of the world, forests and lakes,
　　Ships, Rivers, Towers, the Warrior clad in Mail,
　　The prancing Steed, the Pilgrim with his Staff,
740 The mitred Bishop and the thronèd King,
　　A Spectacle to which there is no end.
　　　　　No otherwise had I at first been moved
　　With such a swell of feeling followed soon
　　By a blank sense of greatness passed away
745 And afterwards continued to be moved
　　In presence of that vast Metropolis,
　　The Fountain of my Country's destiny
　　And of the destiny of Earth itself,
　　That great Emporium, Chronicle at once
750 And Burial-place of passions and their home
　　Imperial, and chief living residence.
　　　　　With strong Sensations teeming as it did
　　Of past and present, such a place must needs
　　Have pleased me in those times; I sought not then
755 Knowledge, but craved for power, and power I found
　　In all things; nothing had a circumscribed
　　And narrow influence; but all objects, being
　　Themselves capacious, also[1] found in me
　　Capaciousness and amplitude of mind:
760 Such is the strength and glory of our Youth.
　　The Human-nature unto which I felt
　　That I belonged, and which I loved and reverenced
　　Was not a punctual[2] Presence, but a Spirit
　　Living in time and space, and far diffused.
765 In this my joy, in this my dignity
　　Consisted: the external universe,
　　By striking upon what is found within,
　　Had given me this conception, with the help
　　Of Books, and what they picture and record.
770 　　　'Tis true the History of my native Land
　　With those of Greece compared and popular Rome,[3]
　　Events not lovely nor magnanimous,
　　But harsh and unaffecting in themselves
　　And in our high-wrought modern narratives
775 Stript of their[4] harmonizing soul, the life
　　Of manners and familiar incidents,

9. Impression, imprint. *PPrel* notes a recollection of *Hamlet* 3.2.22–24: "to show * * * the very age and body of the time his form and pressure." *Airy pageant*: an allusion to Shakespeare, *The Tempest* 4.1.155, suggesting a parallel between the "insubstantial pageant" created by Prospero's magic and the spectacle of London.
1. This word was inserted in pencil by MW.
2. Restricted to a particular time or place (as at 10.17).
3. The Roman Republic (as opposed to the Roman Empire, which succeeded the Republic). WW is comparing British history unfavorably with that of ancient Greece and Rome, although the verb "compared" is only implied.
4. Refers to *Events* (line 772).

Had never much delighted me. And less
Than other minds I had been used to owe
The pleasure which I found in place or thing
780   To extrinsic, transitory accidents,
To records or traditions: but a sense
Of what had been here done, and suffered here
Through ages, and was doing, suffering still
Weighed with me, could support the test of thought,
785   Was like the enduring majesty and power
Of independent nature; and not seldom
Even individual remembrances,
By working on the shapes before my eyes,
Became like vital functions of the soul:
790   And out of what had been, what was, the place
Was thronged with impregnations, like those wilds
In which my early feelings had been nursed
And naked valleys, full of caverns, rocks
And audible seclusions, dashing lakes,
795   Echoes and Waterfalls, and pointed crags
That into music touch the passing wind.
          Thus here Imagination also found
An element that pleased her, tried her strength,
Among new objects, simplified, arranged,
800   Impregnated my knowledge, made it live,
And the result was elevating thoughts
Of human Nature. Neither guilt nor vice,
Debasement of the body, or the mind,
Nor all the misery forced upon my sight
805   Which was not lightly passed, but often scanned
Most feelingly, could overthrow my trust
In what we may become, induce belief
That I was ignorant, had been falsely taught,
A Solitary, who with vain conceits
810   Had been inspired, and walked about in dreams.
When from that rueful prospect, overcast
And in eclipse, my meditations turned,
Lo! every thing that was indeed divine
Retained its purity inviolate
815   And unencroached upon, nay, seemed brighter far
For this deep shade in counterview, this gloom
Of opposition, such as shewed itself
To the eyes of Adam, yet in Paradise,
Though fallen from bliss, when "in the East he saw
820   Darkness ere day's mid course, and morning light
More orient in the western cloud, that drew
O'er the blue firmament a radiant white,
Descending slow, with something heavenly fraught."[5]

---

5. Laden, burdened; *orient*: bright, but also eastern. The quotation, with slight variants, is from
   Paradise Lost 11.203–207: dawn is darkened in the east by a cloud while a white light, radiating
   from a troop of cherubim under the command of the archangel Michael, appears in the west.
   The opening quotation mark is omitted in MSS B and A.

Add also that among the multitudes
825 Of that great City oftentimes was seen
Affectingly set forth, more than elsewhere
Is possible, the unity of Man,
One spirit over ignorance and vice
Predominant in good and evil hearts,
830 One sense for moral judgements, as one eye
For the sun's light. When strongly breathed upon
By this sensation, whencesoe'er it comes
By union or communion doth the soul
Rejoice as in her highest joy: for there,
835 There chiefly hath she feeling whence she is,
And, passing through all Nature rests with God.
⁣   And is not, too, that vast Abiding-place
Of human Creatures, turn where'er we may,
Profusely sown with individual sights
840 Of courage, and integrity, and truth,
And tenderness, which here set off by foil
Appears more touching.⁶ In the tender scenes
Chiefly was my delight; and one of these
Never will be forgotten. 'Twas a Man
845 Whom I saw sitting in an open Square
Close to the iron paling that fenced in
The spacious Grass-plot: on the corner-stone
Of the low wall in which the pales were fixed
Sate this one Man, and with a sickly Babe
850 Upon his knee, whom he had hither brought
For sunshine, and to breathe the fresher air.
Of those who passed and me who looked at him
He took no note; but in his brawny Arms
(The Artificer was to the elbow bare
855 And from his work this moment had been stolen)
He held the Child, and bending over it,
As if he were afraid both of the sun
And of the air which he had come to seek,
He eyed it with unutterable love.⁷
860 ⁣   Thus from an early age, O Friend!
My thoughts had been attracted more and more
By slow gradations towards human kind
And to the good and ill of human life:
Nature had led me on, and now I seemed
865 To travel independent of her help,
As if I had forgotten her; but no,
My Fellow-beings still were unto me
Far less than she was, though the scale of love
Were filling fast, 'twas light, as yet, compared
870 With that in which her mighty objects lay.

---

6. Tenderness stands out conspicuously (*set off by foil*) in London because of its rarity.
7. In *Prel 1850* WW transferred lines 837–59 to book 7, where they became lines 598–625 (*Prel 1850* [CW], 153–54).

Book Ninth

As oftentimes a River, it might seem,
Yielding in part to old remembrances,
Part sway'd by fear to tread on onward road
That leads direct to devouring sea,
5 Turns, and will measure back his course, far back
Towards the very regions which he cross'd
In his first outset; so have we long time
Made motions retrograde, in like pursuit
Detained.[1] But now we start afresh; I feel
10 An impulse to precipitate[2] my Verse,
Fair greetings to this shapeless eagerness
Whene'er it comes, needful in work so long,
Thrice needful to the argument[3] which now
Awaits us; oh! how much unlike the past!
15 One which, though bright the promise, will be found
Ere far we shall advance, ungenial, hard
To treat of, and forbidding in itself.
      Free as a colt, at pasture on the hills
I ranged at large through the Metropolis
20 Month after month. Obscurely did I live,
Not courting the society of Men
By literature, or elegance, or rank
Distinguished; in the midst of things, it seemed,
Looking as if from a distance on the world
25 That moved about me; yet insensibly
False preconceptions were corrected thus
And errors of fancy rectified,
Alike with reference to men and things,
And sometimes from each quarter were poured in
30 Novel imaginations and profound.
A year thus spent,[4] this field (with small regret
Save only for the Book-stalls in the streets,
Wild produce, hedge-row fruit, on all sides hung
To tempt the sauntering [traveller] aside)[5]
35 I quitted, and betook myself to France,
Led chiefly by a personal wish
To speak the language more familiarly,

1. Lines 1–9 form the poem's second epic simile referring to water (see 4.248–69 for the first). *PPrel* notes a recollection of William Cowper's *The Task* (1785) 3.1–14: "As one who long in thickets and in brakes / Entangled, winds now this way and that / His devious course uncertain * * * So I, designing other themes, * * * Have rambled wide."
2. Hasten.
3. Theme, subject.
4. In fact WW's extended stay in London in 1791 lasted about four months, probably from late January to late May, with another stay of about three weeks in November (*Chrono: EY*, 117, 122).
5. Line 34 originally read "To lure the sauntering traveller from his track)" in MSS B and A. MW's substitutions of *tempt* and *aside* incorporate WW's penciled alterations to MS A (*Prel 1805* [CW] 2:785–86). The word "traveller," deleted in MS B and a blank space left in its place, is supplied from MS A.

With which intent I chose for my abode
A City on the Borders of the Loire.[6]
40   Through Paris lay my readiest path and there
I sojourned a few days, and visited
In haste each spot of old and recent fame,
The latter chiefly, from the Field of Mars
Down to the Suburbs of St. Anthony,
45 And from Mont Martyr southward, to the Dome
Of Genevieve.[7] In both her clamorous Halls,
The National Synod and the Jacobins,[8]
I saw the revolutionary Power
Toss like a Ship at anchor, rocked by storms;
50 The Arcades I traversed in the Palace huge
Of Orleans,[9] coasted round and round the line
Of Tavern, Brothel, Gaming-house, and Shop,
Great rendezvous of worst and best, the walk
Of all who had a purpose, or had not:
55 I stared and listened with a stranger's ears
To Hawkers and Haranguers, hubbub wild![1]
And hissing Factionists with ardent eyes,
In knots, or pairs, or single, ant-like swarms
Of Builders and Subverters, every face
60 That hope or apprehension could put on,
Joy, anger, and vexation in the midst
Of gaiety and dissolute idleness.
Where silent Zephirs sported with the dust
Of the Bastile,[2] I sate in the open sun,
65 And from the rubbish gathered up a stone
And pocketed the relick in the guise

6. On December 6, 1791 (WL, 1:68), WW reached Orléans, a city on the Loire River in north-central France, about 81 miles southwest of Paris. In a letter of December 7, DW explained that her brother's aim was to become proficient enough in French to qualify "for the office of travelling Companion to some young Gentleman if he can get recommended" (WL, 1:66).
7. Echoing Milton, Paradise Lost 11.386 ("City of old or modern Fame"), WW lists Parisian sites associated with the Revolution. Field of Mars: Champ de Mars, a field (at the northwest end of which the Eiffel Tower now stands) in which the first anniversary of the storming of the Bastille was celebrated and Louis XVI swore loyalty to the new constitution on July 14, 1790, and the National Guard opened fire on republican demonstrators on July 17, 1791, killing dozens; Suburbs of St. Anthony: a working-class quarter in eastern Paris; Mont Martyr: Montmartre, a northern suburb of Paris (incorporated into the city in 1860) and the site of a Benedictine abbey that was destroyed in 1792; Genevieve: the eighteenth-century church of Sainte-Geneviève in the Latin Quarter, renamed the Panthéon and transformed into a secular mausoleum for "great men" of France in 1791 (when the remains of Voltaire and the revolutionary orator Honoré de Mirabeau were moved there).
8. The Society for the Friends of the Constitution, formed in 1789 and quartered in the Dominican monastery of St. Jacques on the Rue Saint-Honoré. Created in order to influence the drafting of a new constitution, the society grew increasingly powerful and militant until it was suppressed in November 1794. National Synod: the Legislative Assembly, created in October 1791 as a successor to the Constituent Assembly and disbanded in September 1792. WW reported to his brother Richard on December 19, 1791, that he had visited "the national assembly, introduced by a member" (WL, 1:71).
9. The fashionable arcades of shops and cafés built in 1781–84 by Philippe d'Orléans in his renovation of the family's vast Parisian residence, the Palais-Royal. WW refers to these arcades, a popular meeting-place, again in 10.83–88.
1. A phrase from Paradise Lost 2.951, where it refers to the sounds encountered by Satan in Chaos (see also 7.227 above).
2. The Bastille, a medieval prison-fortress and arsenal—and symbol of royal authority—in eastern Paris, the storming of which on July 14, 1789, marked the beginning of the French Revolution. By the end of 1789 the fortress had been demolished. Zephirs: zephyrs, mild winds.

Of an Enthusiast, yet, in honest truth,
Though not without some strong incumbences;
And glad (could living man be otherwise?)
70   I looked for something which I could not find,
Affecting more emotion than I felt,
For 'tis most certain that the utmost force
Of all these various objects, which may shew
The temper of my mind as then it was,
75   Seemed less to recompense the Traveller's pains,
Less moved me, gave me less delight than did
A single picture merely, hunted out
Among other sights, the Magdaline of le Brun,[3]
A Beauty exquisitely wrought, fair face
80   And rueful, with its ever-flowing tears.
      But hence to my more permanent residence[4]
I hasten: there by novelties in speech,
Domestic manners, customs, gestures, looks,
And all the attire of country life,
85   Attention was at first engrossed, and thus,
Amused and satisfied, I scarcely felt
The shock of these concussions, unconcerned,
Tranquil, almost, and careless as a flower
Glassed in a Green-house, or a Parlour shrub
90   When every bush and tree, the country through,
Is shaking to the roots; indifference this
Which may seem strange; but I was unprepared
With needful knowledge, had abruptly passed
Into a theatre, of which the stage
95   Was busy with an action far advanced.
Like others I had read, and eagerly
Sometimes, the master Pamphlets of the day;[5]
Nor wanted such half-insight as grew wild
Upon that meagre soil, helped by Talk
100 And Public News; but having never chanced
To see a regular Chronicle which might shew
(If any such indeed existed then)
Whence the main Organs of the public Power
Had sprung, their transmigrations when and how
105 Accomplished, giving thus unto events
A form and body, all things were to me
Loose and disjointed, and the affections left

---

3. *The Repentant Magdalene*, painted by Charles Le Brun (1616–1690) for the Carmelite convent of Paris, where it was a tourist attraction until its confiscation by the Revolutionary government in the summer of 1792. The painting depicts a tearful Mary Magdalene, having cast her jewelry on the ground, drawing a blue robe around her shoulders and looking imploringly towards heaven.
4. Orléans, where WW resided for perhaps two months before relocating to Blois early in 1792.
5. The catalogue of the auction of WW's library in 1859 records "Pamphlets and Ephemera— French; a bundle" without further identification (*OxPrel*). But WW may be referring to Edmund Burke's *Reflections on the Revolution in France* (1790) and critical replies to it like Mary Wollstonecraft's *Vindication of the Rights of Men* (1790), James Mackintosh's *Vindiciae Gallicae* (1791), and Thomas Paine's *Rights of Man*, part 1 (1791). See *Reading 1770–99*, nos. 41(ii), 164, 194(ii), and 267(i).

Without a vital interest. At that time,
Moreover, the first storm was overblown,
110 And the strong hand of outward violence
Locked up in quiet.[6] For myself, I fear
(Now in connection with so great a theme)
To speak (as I must be compelled to do)
Of one so unimportant: a short time
115 I loitered, and frequented night by night
Routs,[7] card-tables, the formal haunts of Men,
Whom in the City privilege of birth
Sequestered from the rest, societies
Where through punctilios of elegance
120 And deeper causes, all discourse, alike
Of good and evil in the time, was shunned
With studious care: but 'twas not long ere this
Proved tedious, and I gradually withdrew
Into a noisier world; and thus did soon
125 Become a Patriot;[8] and my heart was all
Given to the People, and my love was theirs.
    A knot of military Officers[9]
That to a Regiment appertained which then
Was stationed in the City were the chief
130 Of my associates: some of these wore Swords
Which had been seasoned in the Wars,[1] and all
Were men well born, at least laid claim to such
Distinction, as the Chivalry of France.
In age and temper differing, they had yet
135 One spirit ruling in them all, alike
(Save only one hereafter to be named)
Were bent upon undoing what was done:[2]
This was their rest, and only hope, therewith
No fear had they of bad becoming worse,
140 For worst to them was come, nor would have stirred,
Or deemed it worth a moment's thought to stir
In any thing, save only as the act
Looked thitherward. One, reckoning by years,
Was in the prime of manhood, and erewhile

6. WW's time in Orléans and Blois coincided with a period of relative political calm between the massacre of republicans on the Champ de Mars (see the note on line 46 above) and that of the royal bodyguards, the Swiss Guards, by members of a newly formed Paris Commune in August 1792.
7. Parties.
8. Republican.
9. Written originally as "Offices," then corrected in pencil at an uncertain date (it is correct in MS A).
1. Presumably the American War of Independence, in which French forces supported the American army (1778–83).
2. Lodging with a group of cavalry officers in Orléans, WW wrote his brother Richard on December 19, 1791, "I had imagined that there were some people of wealth and circumstance favorers of the Revolution, but here there is not one to be found" (WL 1:69–70). A majority of the officers in the early Revolutionary army were royalists, and nearly 6,000—over half the officer corps—emigrated in the six months following the "Flight to Varennes" on June 21, 1791, when the king was forcibly returned to Paris after having been caught trying to escape to a royalist citadel near the Luxembourg border (Doyle, 156). The only one republican officer was Michel Beaupuy, whom WW met later in Blois (see lines 294–347 below).

145 He had sate Lord in many tender hearts,
     Though heedless of such honours now, and changed:
     His temper was quite mastered by the time,
     And they had blighted him, had eat away
     The beauty of his person, doing wrong
150 Alike to body and to mind: his port,[3]
     Which once had been erect and open, now
     Was stooping and contracted, and a face
     By nature lovely in itself, expressed
     As much as any that was ever seen,
155 A ravage out of season, made by thoughts
     Unhealthy and vexatious. At the hour,
     The most important of each day, in which
     The public News was read, the fever came
     A punctual visitant, to shake this Man,
160 Disarmed his voice, and fanned his yellow cheek
     Into a thousand colours; while he read,
     Or mused, his sword was haunted by his touch
     Continually, like an uneasy place
     In his own body. 'Twas in truth an hour
165 Of universal ferment; mildest men
     Were agitated, and commotions, strife
     Of passion and opinion filled the walls
     Of peaceful houses with unquiet sounds.
     The soil of common life was at that time
170 Too hot to tread upon: oft said I then,
     And not then only, "what a mockery this
     Of history, the past, and that to come!
     Now do I feel how I have been deceived,
     Reading of Nations and their works, in faith,
175 Faith given to vanity and emptiness;
     Oh! laughter for the Page that would reflect
     To future times the face of what now is!"[4]
     The Land all swarmed with passion, like a Plain
     Devoured by locusts, Carra, Gorsas,[5] add
180 A hundred other names, forgotten now,
     Nor to be heard of more, yet were they Powers
     Like earthquakes, shocks repeated every day,
     And felt through every nook of town and field.
          The Men already spoken of as chief
185 Of my Associates were prepared for flight
     To augment the band of Emigrants in Arms

3. Carriage, bearing (from the French *porter*, "carry, bear").
4. "The historian's 'page' would bring ridicule upon itself by attempting to describe the complexities of the contemporary situation" (*PPrel*).
5. Jean-Louis Carra (1743–1793) and Antoine-Joseph Gorsas (1752–1793), journalists and radical Girondin (antimonarchist) members of the National Convention, both guillotined during a purge of the Girondists, who opposed the centralization of power in Paris. According to Thomas Carlyle, WW claimed in 1840 to have witnessed Gorsas's execution on October 7, 1793 (*Reminiscences*, ed. K. J. Fielding and Ian Campbell [Oxford, 1997], 405); but there is no independent evidence that WW returned to France in that year, after France had declared war on Britain. It is possible that WW met Gorsas in Paris in late 1791 or autumn 1792 (Nicholas Roe, *Wordsworth and Coleridge*, 40–41).

Upon the Borders of the [Rhine],[6] and leagued
With foreign Foes mustered for instant war.
This was their undisguised intent, and they
190 Were waiting with the whole of their desires
The moment to depart.
                An Englishman,
Born in a Land, the name of which appeared
To licence some unruliness of mind,
A Stranger, with Youth's further privilege,
195 And that indulgence which a half-learned speech
Wins from the courteous, I who had been else
Shunned and not tolerated freely lived
With these Defenders of the Crown, and talked
And heard their notions, nor did they disdain
200 The wish to bring me over to their cause.
        But though untaught by thinking or by books
To reason well of polity or law
And nice distinctions, then on every tongue,
Of natural rights and civil, and to acts
205 Of nations, and their passing interests,
(I speak comparing these with other things)
Almost indifferent, even the Historian's Tale
Prizing but little otherwise than I prized
Tales of the Poets, as it made my heart
210 Beat high and filled my fancy with fair forms,
Old Heroes and their sufferings and their deeds;
Yet in the regal Sceptre and the pomp
Of Orders and Degrees I nothing found
Then, or had ever, even in crudest youth,
215 That dazzled me; but rather what my soul
Mourned for or loathed, beholding that the best
Ruled not, and feeling that they ought to rule.
        For, born in a poor District,[7] and which yet
Retaineth more of ancient homeliness,
220 Manners erect, and frank simplicity
Than any other nook of English Land,
It was my fortune scarcely to have seen
Through the whole tenor of my School-day time
The face of one, who, whether Boy or Man,
225 Was vested with attention or respect
Through claims of wealth or blood; nor was it least
Of many debts which afterwards I owed
To Cambridge, and an academic life
That something there was holden up to view

---

6. In both MSS B and A the original reading, "Loire," was corrected in pencil at an uncertain date to "Rhine." Many of the *émigré* officers joined Louis XVI's brother Charles d'Artois and the Prince de Condé in the German Rhineland to plan a counterrevolutionary invasion of France. On August 27, 1791, encouraged by the *émigrés*, Austria and Prussia vaguely threatened punishment if the French royal family were harmed (the Declaration of Pillnitz); and on April 20, 1792, France declared war on Austria.
7. As *PPrel* notes, WW's own early childhood was not impoverished since his father was the agent to a wealthy landowner, the Earl of Lonsdale.

230   Of a Republic, where all stood thus far
        Upon equal ground, that they were brothers all
        In honour, as of one community,
        Scholars and Gentlemen, where furthermore
        Distinction lay open to all that came,
235   And wealth and titles were in less esteem
        Than talents and successful industry.[8]
        Add unto this, subservience from the first
        To God and Nature's single sovereignty,
        Familiar presences of awful Power
240   And fellowship with venerable books
        To sanction[9] the proud workings of the soul,
        And mountain liberty. It could not be
        But that one tutored thus, who had been formed
        To thought and moral feeling in the way
245   This Story hath described, should look with awe
        Upon the faculties of Man, receive
        Gladly the highest promises, and hail
        As best the government of equal rights
        And individual worth. And hence, O Friend!
250   If at the first great out-break I rejoiced
        Less than might well befit my youth, the cause
        In part lay here, that unto me the events
        Seemed nothing out of nature's certain course,
        A gift that rather had come late than soon.
255   No wonder then if advocates like these
        Whom I have mentioned, at this riper day
        Were impotent to make my hopes put on
        The shape of theirs, my understanding bend
        In honour to their honour, zeal which yet
260   Had slumbered, now in opposition burst
        Forth like a Polar Summer; every word
        They uttered was a dart by counter-winds
        Blown back upon themselves, their reason seemed
        Confusion-struck by a higher power
265   Than human understanding, their discourse
        Maimed, spiritless, and in their weakness strong
        I triumphed.
                        Meantime, day by day the roads
        (While I consorted with these Royalists)
        Were crowded with the bravest Youth of France
270   And all the promptest of her Spirits, linked
        In gallant Soldiership, and posting on
        To meet the War upon her Frontier bounds.[1]
        Yet at this very moment do tears start

---

8. WW greatly exaggerates the egalitarianism of eighteenth-century Cambridge: as a scholarship-student (see the note on 3.50) he was given inferior quarters in his college and had to wear a different gown from the "fellow-commoner" and aristocratic undergraduates, whose wealth and social status effectively exempted them from studying (Schneider, 22–23).
9. Confirm.
1. WW refers to volunteers traveling east to the Rhineland to serve in the depleted French army after the declaration of war against Austria (see the note on line 187 above).

Into mine eyes; I do not say weep,
275 I wept not then, but tears have dimmed my sight
In memory of the farewells of that time,
Domestic severings, female fortitude
At dearest separation, patriot love
And self-devotion, and terrestrial hope
280 Encouraged with a martyr's confidence;[2]
Even files of Strangers merely seen but once
And for a moment, men from far with sound
Of music, martial tunes, and banners spread
Entering the City, here and there a face
285 Or person singled out among the rest,
Yet still a Stranger and beloved as such,
Even by these passing spectacles my heart
Was oftentimes uplifted, and they seemed
Like arguments from Heaven that 'twas a cause
290 Good, and which no one could stand up against
Who was not lost, abandoned, selfish, proud,
Mean, miserable, wilfully depraved,
Hater perverse of equity and truth.
       Among that band of Officers was one
295 Already hinted at, of moral mold,[3]
A Patriot, thence rejected by the rest
And with an oriental loathing spurned,
As of a different Cast. A meeker Man
Than this lived never, or a more benign,
300 Meek, though enthusiastic to the height
Of highest expectation. Injuries
Made him more gracious, and his nature then
Did breathe its sweetness out most sensibly[4]
As aromatic flowers on an Alpine turf
305 When foot hath crushed them. He through the events
Of that great change wandered in perfect faith
As through a Book, an old Romance or Tale
Of Fairy,[5] or some dream of actions wrought
Behind the summer clouds. By birth he ranked
310 With the most noble, but unto the poor
Among mankind he was in service bound
As by some tie invisible, oaths professed
To a religious Order. Man he loved
As man; and to the mean and the obscure
315 And all the homely in their homely works
Transferred a courtesy, which had no air

2. I.e., with a confidence comparable to that of a Christian martyr, although in support of worldly hopes. *self-devotion*: individuals' devotion to the revolutionary cause.
3. Characterized by his adherence to a moral ideal. This was Michel Beaupuy (see Biographical and Topographical Glossary), who was not one of the cavalry officers WW lodged with in Orléans but rather the commandant of an army regiment garrisoned in Blois, to which WW, following Annette Vallon (see Glossary), moved in early 1792. WW may have first met Beaupuy at a meeting of the revolutionary club *Les Amis de la Constitution* (Roe, *Wordsworth and Coleridge*, 49–51).
4. Perceptibly.
5. Such as Edmund Spenser's *Faerie Queene* (1590–96); see also lines 457–64 below.

Of condescension, but did rather seem
A passion and a gallantry, like that
Which he, a Soldier, in his idler day
320 Had payed to Woman; somewhat vain he was,
Or seemed so, yet it was not vanity
But fondness, and a kind of radiant joy
That covered him about when he was bent
On works of love or freedom, or revolved
325 Complacently[6] the progress of a cause
Whereof he was a part; yet this was meek
And placid, and took nothing from the Man
That was delightful: oft in solitude
With him did I discourse about the end
330 Of civil government, and its wisest forms,
Of ancient prejudice, and chartered rights,
Allegiance, faith, and laws by time matured,
Custom and habit, novelty and change,
Of self-respect and virtue in the Few
335 For patrimonial honour set apart
And ignorance in the labouring Multitude.
For he, an upright Man and tolerant,
Balanced these contemplations in his mind
And I, who at that time was scarcely dipped
340 Into the turmoil, had a sounder judgement
Than afterwards, carried about me yet
With less alloy to its integrity
The experience of past ages, as through help
Of Books and common life it makes its way
345 To youthful minds, by objects over near
Not pressed upon, nor dazzled or misled
By struggling with the crowd for present ends.
          But though not deaf and obstinate to find
Error without apology on the side
350 Of those who were against us, more delight
We took, and let this freely be confessed,
In painting to ourselves the miseries
Of royal Courts, and that voluptuous life
Unfeeling, where the Man who is of soul
355 The meanest thrives the most, where dignity,
True personal dignity, abideth not,
A light and cruel world, cut off from all
The natural inlets of just sentiment,
From lowly sympathy, and chastening truth,
360 When good and evil never have the name,
That which they ought to have; but wrong prevails
And vice at home. We added dearest themes,
Man and his noble nature, as it is
The gift of God and lies in his own power,
365 His blind desires and steady faculties

6. *revolved* / *Complacently*: considered with pleasure.

Capable of clear truth, the one to break
Bondage, the other to build liberty
On firm foundations, making social life,
Through knowledge spreading and imperishable,
370 As just in regulation, and as pure
As individual in the wise and good.
We summoned up the honorable deeds
Of ancient Story,[7] thought of each bright spot
That could be found in all recorded time
375 Of truth preserved, and error passed away,
Of single Spirits that catch the flame from Heaven
And how the multitude of men will feed
And fan each other, thought of Sects, how keen
They are to put the appropriate nature on,
380 Triumphant over every obstacle
Of custom, language, country, love and hate,
And what they do, and suffer for their creed,
How far they travel, and how long endure,
How quickly mighty Nations have been formed
385 From least beginnings, how, together locked
By new opinions, scattered tribes have made
One body spreading wide as clouds in heaven.
To aspirations then of our own minds
Did we appeal; and finally beheld
390 A living confirmation of the whole
Before us in a People risen up
Fresh as the morning Star: elate we looked
Upon their virtues, saw in rudest men
Self-sacrifice the firmest, generous love
395 And continence[8] of mind, and sense of right
Uppermost in the midst of fiercest strife.
        Oh! sweet it is in academic Groves
Or such retirement, Friend! as we have known
Among the mountains, by our Rotha's Stream,
400 Greta or Derwent,[9] or some nameless Rill
To ruminate with interchange of talk
On [rational][1] liberty, and hope in Man,
Justice and peace: but far more sweet such toil,
Toil say I, for it leads to thoughts abstruse,
405 If Nature then be standing on the brink
Of some great trial, and we hear the voice
Of One devoted, one whom circumstance
Hath called upon to embody his deep sense
In action, give it outwardly a shape,

7. History.
8. Self-restraint; *rudest* (line 393): least educated.
9. Rivers in the Lake District that were particularly dear to WW and STC: the Rothay in Gras-
   mere, the Greta in Keswick (where STC's family lived), and the Derwent (which flowed past
   WW's birthplace, and after which STC named his third son) in Cockermouth (see also
   1.274–307).
1. The reading in MSS B and A is "national," but in both cases it has been corrected in pencil to
   "rational" (the reading from the earlier MS Y).

410 And that of benediction to the world:
     Then doubt is not, and truth is more than truth,
     A hope it is and a desire, a creed
     Of zeal by an authority divine
     Sanctioned of danger, difficulty or death.
415 Such conversation under Attic[2] shades
     Did Dion hold with Plato, ripened thus
     For a Deliverer's glorious task, and such,
     He, on that ministry already bound,
     Held with Eudemus and Timonides,
420 Surrounded by Adventurers in Arms
     When those two Vessels with their daring Freight
     For the Sicilian Tyrant's overthrow
     Sailed [from] Zacynthus, philosophic war
     Led by Philosophers. With harder fate
425 Though like ambition such was he, O Friend!
     Of whom I speak, of Beaupuis (let the Name
     Stand near the worthiest of antiquity)
     Fashioned his life, and many a long discourse
     With like persuasion honored we maintained,
430 He on his part accoutred for the worst.
     He perished fighting in supreme command
     Upon the Borders of the unhappy Loire
     For Liberty, against deluded Men,
     His Fellow-countrymen,[3] and yet most blessed
435 In this, that he the fate of later times
     Lived not to see, nor what we now behold
     Who have as ardent hearts as he had then.
          Along that very Loire, with Festivals
     Resounding at all hours, and innocent yet
440 Of civil slaughter, was our frequent walk
     Or in wide Forests of the neighbourhood,
     High woods and over-arched with open space
     On every side,[4] and footing many a mile
     Inwoven roots and moss smooth as the sea,
445 A solemn region. Often in such place
     From earnest dialogues I slipped in thought
     And let remembrance steal to other times
     When Hermits from their sheds and caves forth-strayed,

2. Greek. Lines 415–24 draw on the Greek biographer Plutarch's *Life of Dion* in Sir Thomas North's translation (1579; *Reading 1800–15*, no. 321[i]): exiled from his native Syracuse, in southeastern Sicily, by its ruler Dionysius the Younger, Dion, a disciple of Plato, was assisted by the philosophers Eudemus and Timonides in plotting to overthrow Dionysius after the failure of Plato's efforts at mediation. Sailing from the Ionian island of Zycanthus with a small mercenary force, Dion invaded Sicily and captured Syracuse in 357 B.C.E., but was himself assassinated four years later; Dionysius resumed power in 346 B.C.E. See also 10.946–50. In line 423 the original reading in MSS B and A, "for," was corrected to "from" by WW in pencil during his 1818–20 revisions.
3. WW is mistaken: although Beaupuy (promoted to the rank of general) was twice wounded in 1793 while leading the suppression of a royalist rebellion in the Vendée region of the Loire valley in western France, he was transferred to the Rhineland the following year and killed in battle against the Austrian army near Freiburg im Breisgau on October 19, 1796 (Paul Huot, *Des Vosges au Rhin* [Paris, 1866], 287).
4. An echo of *Paradise Lost* 9.1106–1107: "a Pillard shade / High overarcht, and echoing Walks between."

       Walked by themselves, so met in shades like these,
450 And if a devious Traveller was heard
       Approaching from a distance, as might chance,
       With speed and echoes loud of trampling hoofs
       From the hard floor reverberated, then
       It was Angelica thundering through the woods
455 Upon her palfrey, or that gentler Maid,
       Erminia,[5] fugitive as fair as She.
       Sometimes I saw, methought, a pair of Knights
       Joust underneath the trees, that, as in storm,
       Did rock above their heads: anon the din
460 Of boisterous merriment and music's roar,
       With sudden Proclamation! burst from haunt
       Of Satyrs in some viewless glade, with dance
       Rejoicing o'er a Female in the midst,
       A mortal Beauty their unhappy Thrall;[6]
465 The width of those huge Forests, unto me
       A novel scene, did often in this way
       Master my fancy, while I wandered on
       With that revered Companion. And sometimes
       When to a Convent in a meadow green
470 By a brook side we came, a roofless Pile
       And not by reverential touch of Time
       Dismantled, but by violence abrupt,
       In spite of those heart-bracing colloquies,
       In spite of real fervour, and of that
475 Less genuine and wrought up within myself
       I could not but bewail a wrong so harsh,
       And for the matin bell to sound no more
       Grieved, and the evening Taper, and the Cross
       High on the topmost Pinnacle, a sign
480 Admonitory, by the Traveller
       First seen above the woods.[7]
                     And when my Friend
       Pointed upon occasion to the Site
       Of Romarentin, home of ancient Kings,
       To the imperial Edifice of Blois
485 Or to that rural Castle, name now slipped
       From my remembrance, where a Lady lodged
       By the first Francis wooed, and bound to him
       In chains of mutual passion; from the Tower,

5. A Saracen princess who flees the Crusader knight Tancredi on horseback in Torquato Tasso's *Gerusalemme liberata* (1581) 7.1–22; *Angelica*: a virgin princess who flees the enamored knight Rinaldo on a white horse in Ludovico Ariosto's *Orlando furioso* (1532) 1.7, a stanza WW had translated in 1802 (P2V [CW], 596).
6. WW probably has in mind Spenser's *Faerie Queene* 1.6.7–13, in which the maiden Una is rescued by satyrs from the knight Sansloy, or 3.10.43–44, in which the young Hellenore, abandoned by her seducer Paridell, dances with satyrs in a forest.
7. Many French monasteries had closed since the 1760s, but in November 1789 the National Assembly nationalized the property of the Catholic Church, and in February 1790 it dissolved all monasteries and convents except those engaged in educational or charitable work (Doyle, 136–37). In lines 53–79 of *Descriptive Sketches*, composed probably in France, WW lamented the expulsion of the monks from the Grande Chartreuse (see 6.422–24) in October 1792 after a five-month occupation by French soldiers (*Descriptive Sketches* [CW], 42, 44, 46).

As a Tradition of the Country tells,
490 Practised to commune with her Royal Knight
By cressets and love-beacons, intercourse
'Twixt her high-seated Residence and his
Far off at Chambord on the Plain beneath.⁸
Even here, though less than with the peaceful House
495 Religious, 'mid these frequent monuments
Of Kings, their vices or their better deeds,
Imagination, potent to enflame
At times with virtuous wrath and noble scorn,
Did also often mitigate the force
500 Of civic prejudice, the bigotry,
So call it, of a youthful Patriot's mind,
And on these spots with many gleams I looked
Of chivalrous delight. Yet not the less
Hatred of absolute rule, where will of One
505 Is law for all, and of that barren pride
In those who, by immunities unjust
Betwixt the Sovereign and the People stand,
His helpers and not theirs, laid stronger hold
Daily upon me, mixed with pity too,
510 And love; for where hope is there love will be
For the⁹ abject multitude. And when we chanced
One day to meet a hunger-bitten Girl
Who crept along, fitting her languid self
Unto a Heifer's motion, by a cord
515 Tied to her arm, and picking thus from the lane
Its sustenance,¹ while the Girl with her two hands
Was busy knitting, in a heartless² mood
Of solitude, and at the sight my Friend
In agitation said, "'Tis against that
520 Which we are fighting," I with him believed
Devoutly that a Spirit was abroad
Which could not be withstood, that poverty,
At least like this, would in a little time
Be found no more, that we should see the earth
525 Unthwarted in her wish to recompense
The industrious, and the lowly Child of Toil,
All institutes for ever blotted out
That legalized exclusion, empty pomp
Abolished, sensual state and cruel power
530 Whether by edict of the one or few,

8. Lines 481–93 refer to sites in or near Blois associated with the French king François I (1494–1547). *Site / of Romarentin*: partly demolished fifteenth-century château in the village of Romorantin, the home of François's mother; *Edifice of Blois*: the 564-room Château de Blois (built thirteenth to seventeenth centuries) in the city center; *rural Castle . . . Chambord*: possibly the Château de Muides (today Château du Marais), home of François's mistress the Comtesse de Thoury (d. 1530) near his grand sixteenth-century hunting lodge of Chambord, if the story is not altogether fanciful; *cressets*: torches.
9. This word was inserted in pencil by MW, presumably to accord with MS A.
1. *And picking . . . sustenance*: a grammatically awkward shift in antecedent from the girl to the heifer.
2. Despondent.

And finally, as the sum and crown of all,
Should see the People having a strong hand
In making their own Laws, whence better days
To all mankind. But, these things set apart,
535 Was not the single confidence enough
To animate the mind that ever turned
A thought to human welfare, that henceforth
Captivity by mandate without law[3]
Should cease, and open occasion lead
540 To sentence in the hearing of the world
And open punishment, if not the air
Be free to breathe in, and the heart of Man
Dread nothing. Having touched this argument
I shall not, as my purpose was, take note
545 Of other matters, which detained us oft
In thought or conversation, public acts,
And public persons, and the emotions wrought
Within our minds by the ever-varying wind
Of Record and Report which day by day
550 Swept over us: but I will here instead
Draw from obscurity a tragic Tale,[4]
Not in its spirit singular indeed
But haply worth memorial, as I heard
The events related by my patriot Friend
555 And others who had borne a part therein.
          Oh! happy time of youthful Lovers! thus
My Story may begin, Oh! balmy time
In which a Love-knot[5] on a Lady's brow
Was fairer than the fairest Star in heaven!
560 To such inheritance of blessedness
Young Vaudracour was brought by years that had
A little over-stepped his stripling prime.
A Town of small repute in the heart of France
Was the Youth's Birth-place: there he vowed his love

---

3. Probably a reference to *lettres de cachet* (literally, "sealed letters"), extrajudicial orders issued by or in the name of the king in the *Ancien Régime* and frequently used to imprison individuals without trial (see also lines 666–67 and 727–28 below). Their use was abolished after the Revolution.
4. The *tragic Tale* of Vaudracour and Julia in lines 556–935 has frequently been interpreted as a covert version of or a substitute for an account of WW's relationship with Annette Vallon, although it has also been interpreted as representing "a doomed revolution against social and political institutions" (Alan Liu, *Wordsworth and the Sense of History*, 376). WW extracted this section and published a revised version of it separately in *The River Duddon* volume (1820) under the title *Vaudracour and Julia* with a prefatory note: "The following was written as an Episode in a work from which its length may perhaps exclude it. The facts are true; no invention as to these has been exercised, as none was intended." In 1832 he removed the section altogether from *The Prelude*, replacing it with a brief summary (*Prel 1850* 9.557–85). Later, in the IF note to *Vaudracour and Julia*, he claimed that the story was "Faithfully narrated, though with the omission of many pathetic circumstances, from the mouth of a French Lady, who had been an eye and ear-witness of all that was done & said." F. M. Todd, "Wordsworth, Helen Maria Williams and France," *Modern Language Review* 43 (1948): 456–64, notes parallels to Williams's story of the elopement of Antoine du Fossé and Monique C. in *Letters Written in France, in the Summer of 1790* (1790), and Liu, 376, notes parallels between Vaudracour and the eponymous protagonist of William Godwin's novel *Caleb Williams* (1794). WW may have derived the name Vaudracour from that of a Lieutenant de Vaudracourt who had served in Beaupuy's battalion in May 1791 (C. L. Shaver, *Times Literary Supplement*, February 21, 1958: 101).
5. A ribbon tied in a distinctive way and worn as a sign of love.

565 To Julia, a bright Maid, from Parents sprung
Not mean in their condition; but with rights
Unhonoured of Nobility, and hence
The Father of the Young Man, who had place
Among that order, spurned the very thought
570 Of such alliance. From their cradles up,
With but a step between their several homes
That Pair had thriven together, year by year,
Friends, Play-mates, Twins in pleasure, after strife
And petty quarrels had grown fond again,
575 Each other's advocate, each other's help,
Nor ever happy if they were apart:
A basis this for deep and solid love,
And endless constancy, and placid truth;
But whatsoever of such treasures might
580 Beneath the outside[6] of their youth have lain
Reserved for mellower years, his present mind
Was under fascination; he beheld
A vision, and he loved the thing he saw.
Arabian fiction never filled the world
585 With half the wonders that were wrought for him;
Earth lived in one great presence of the spring,
Life turned the meanest of her implements
Before his eyes to price above all gold,
The house she dwelt in was a sainted shrine,
590 Her chamber window did surpass in glory
The portals of the East, all paradise
Could by the simple opening of a door
Let itself in upon him, pathways, walks
Swarmed with enchantment till his spirits sunk
595 Beneath the burthen, overblessed[7] for life.
This state was theirs, 'till whether through effect
Of some delirious hour, or that the Youth,
Seeing so many bars betwixt himself
And the dear haven where he wished to be
600 In honorable wedlock with his love
Without a certain knowledge of his own,
Was inwardly prepared to turn aside
From law and custom, and entrust himself
To Nature for a happy end of all,
605 And thus abated of that pure reserve
Congenial to his loyal heart, with which
It would have pleased him to attend the steps
Of Maiden so divinely beautiful
I know not, but reluctantly must add
610 That Julia, yet without the name of Wife
Carried about her for a secret grief
The promise of a Mother. To conceal

---

6. Surface.
7. Blessed beyond endurance.

The threatened shame the Parents of the Maid
Found means to hurry her away by night
615 And unforewarned, that in a distant Town
She might remain shrouded in privacy
Until the Babe was born.[8] When morning came
The Lover thus bereft, stung with his loss
And all uncertain whither he should turn,
620 Chafed like a wild beast in the toils: at length,
Following as his suspicions led, he found
O joy! sure traces of the fugitives,
Pursued them to the Town where they had stopped,
And lastly to the very House itself
625 Which had been chosen for the Maid's retreat.
The sequel may be easily divined:
Walks backwards, forwards, morning, noon and night,
When decency and caution would allow,
And Julia, who, whenever to herself
630 She happened to be left a moment's space,
Was busy at her casement, as a Swallow
About its nest, ere long did thus espy
Her Lover, thence a stolen interview
By night accomplished, with a ladder's help.
635   I pass the raptures of the Pair; such theme
Hath by a hundred Poets been set forth
In more delightful verse than skill of mine
Could fashion, chiefly by that darling Bard
Who told of Juliet and her Romeo,
640 And of the Lark's note heard before its time,
And of the streaks that laced the severing clouds
In the unrelenting East.[9] 'Tis mine to tread
The humbler province of plain History,
And, without choice of circumstance, submissively
645 Relate what I have learned. The Lovers came
To this resolve, with which they parted, pleased
And confident, that Vaudracour should hie
Back to his Father's house, and there employ
Means aptest to obtain a sum of gold,
650 A final portion,[1] even, if that might be,
Which done, together they could then take flight
To some remote and solitary place
Where they might live with no one to behold
Their happiness, or to disturb their love;
655 Immediately, and with this mission charged,

8. In Williams's *Letters*, 129–30, Monique (though now married to Antoine) is moved from Rouen to Caen for the birth of her son to avoid her father-in-law's notice. Annette Vallon, too, was moved by her family from Blois to Orléans for the last three or four months of her pregnancy by WW.
9. *Darling Bard . . . unrelenting East:* An allusion to Shakespeare, *Romeo and Juliet* 3.5.1–8, in which Romeo, having spent the night with Juliet, must leave when the lark's song signals dawn: "It was the lark, the herald of the morn, / No nightingale. Look, love, what envious streaks / Do lace the severing clouds in yonder east."
1. A financial settlement in place of his inheritance.

Home to his Father's House the Youth returned
And there remained a while, without hint given
Of his design; but if a word were dropped
Touching the matter of his passion, still
660 In hearing of his Father, Vaudracour
Persisted openly that nothing less
Than death should make him yield up hope to be
A blessed Husband of the Maid he loved.
            Incensed at such obduracy[2] and slight
665 Of exhortations and remonstrances
The Father threw out threats that by a mandate
Bearing the private signet of the State[3]
He should be baffled in his mad intent,
And that should cure him. From this time the Youth
670 Conceived a terror, and by night or day
Stirred no where without Arms. Soon afterwards
His Parents to their Country Seat withdrew
Upon some feigned occasion; and the Son
Was left with one Attendant in the house.
675 Retiring to his Chamber for the night,
While he was entering at the door, attempts
Were made to seize him by three armed Men,
The instruments of ruffian power; the Youth,
In the first impulse of his rage, laid one
680 Dead at his feet, and to the second gave
A perilous wound, which done, at sight
Of the dead Man he peacefully resigned
His Person to the Law, was lodged in prison,
And wore the fetters of a Criminal.
685   Through three week's space, by means which love
      devised,
The Maid in her seclusion had received
Tidings of Vaudracour, and how he sped
Upon his enterprize. Thereafter came
A silence, half a circle did the moon
690 Complete, and then a whole, and still the same
Silence; a thousand, thousand fears and hopes
Stirred in her mind, thoughts waking, thoughts of sleep
Entangled in each other, and at last
Self-slaughter[4] seemed her only resting-place.
695 So did she fare in her uncertainty.
            At length, by interference of a Friend,
One who had sway at Court, the Youth regained
His liberty, on promise to sit down
Quietly in his Father's house, nor take
700 One step to reunite himself with her
Of whom his Parents disapproved: hard law

2. Here stressed on the second syllable.
3. *Mandate . . . State*: a *lettre de cachet* (see the note on line 538). In Williams's *Letters*, 130–31,
   Antoine's father applies for such a letter in order to have his daughter-in-law confined.
4. Suicide (a term used also in *Hamlet* 1.2.131–32: "that the Everlasting had not fix'd / His canon
   'gainst self-slaughter").

To which he gave consent only because
His freedom else could no wise be procured.
Back to his Father's house he went; remained
705   Eight days, and then his resolution failed;
He fled to Julia, and the words with which
He greeted her were these. "All right is gone,
Gone from me, Thou no longer now art mine,
I thine; a Murderer, Julia, cannot love
710   An innocent Woman; I behold thy face,
I see thee, and my misery is complete."
She could not give him answer; afterwards
She coupled with his Father's name some words
Of vehement indignation; but the Youth
715   Checked her, nor would he hear of this; for thought
Unfilial, or unkind, had never once
Found harbour in his breast. The Lovers thus
United once again together lived
For a few days, which were to Vaudracour
720   Days of dejection, sorrow and remorse
For that ill deed of violence which his hand
Had hastily committed: for the Youth
Was of a loyal spirit, a conscience nice[5]
And over tender for the trial which
725   His fate had called him to. The Father's mind
Meanwhile remained unchanged, and Vaudracour
Learned that a mandate had been newly issued
To arrest him on the spot. Oh pain it was
To part! he could not—and he lingered still
730   To the last moment of his time, and then,
At dead of night with snow upon the ground,
He left the City, and in Villages
The most sequestered of the neighbourhood
Lay hidden for the space of several days
735   Until the horseman bringing back report
That he was nowhere to be found, the search
Was ended. Back returned the ill-fated Youth,
And from the House where Julia lodged (to which
He now found open ingress, having gained
740   The affection of the family, who loved him
Both for his own, and for the Maiden's sake)
One night retiring, he was seized.—But here
A portion of the Tale may well be left
In silence, though my memory could add
745   Much how the Youth, and in short space of time
Was traversed from without,[6] much, too, of thoughts
By which he was employed in solitude
Under privation and restraint, and what
Through dark and shapeless fear of things to come,

5. Fastidious, sensitive.
6. Thwarted by external pressures.

750 And what through strong compunction for the past
He suffered, breaking down in heart and mind.
Such grace, if grace it were, had been vouchsafed,
Or such effect had through the Father's want
Of power, or through his negligence ensued,
755 That Vaudracour was suffered to remain,
Though under guard and without liberty,
In the same City with the unhappy Maid
From whom he was divided. So they fared
Objects of general concern, till, moved
760 With pity for their wrongs, the Magistrate,
The same who had placed the Youth in custody,
By application to the Minister
Obtained his liberty upon condition
That to his Father's House he should return.
765   He left his Prison almost on the eve
Of Julia's travail;[7] she had likewise been
As from the time, indeed, when she had first
Been brought for secresy to this abode,
Though treated with consoling tenderness,
770 Herself a Prisoner, a dejected one,
Filled with a Lover's and a Woman's fears,
And whensoe'er the Mistress of the House
Entered the Room for the last time at night
And Julia with a low and plaintive voice
775 Said, "You are coming then to lock me up,"
The Housewife when these words, always the same,
Were by her Captive languidly pronounced
Could never hear them uttered without tears.
          A day or two before her Child-bed time
780 Was Vaudracour restored to her, and soon
As he might be permitted to return
Into her Chamber after the Child's birth
The Master of the Family begged that all
The household might be summoned, doubting not
785 But that they might receive impressions then
Friendly to human kindness.[8] Vaudracour
(This heard I from one present at the time)
Held up the new-born Infant in his arms
And kissed and blessed, and covered it with tears,
790 Uttering a prayer that he might never be
As wretched as his Father; then he gave
The Child to her who bare it, and she too
Repeated the same prayer, took it again,
And muttering something faintly afterwards
795 He gave the Infant to the Standers-by,
And wept in silence upon Julia's neck.
          Two months did he continue in the House,

---

7. Labor.
8. I.e., stimulating kindness in the beholders.

And often yielded up himself to plans
Of future happiness. "You shall return,
800 Julia," said he, "and to your Father's House
Go with your Child, you have been wretched, yet
It is a Town where both of us were born,
None will reproach you, for our loves are known,
With ornaments the prettiest you shall dress
805 Your Boy, as soon he can run about,
And when he thus is at his play my Father
Will see him from the window, and the Child
Will by his beauty move his Grandsire's heart,
So that it will be softened, and our loves
810 End happily as they began." These gleams
Appeared but seldom, oftener he was seen
Propping a pale and melancholy face
Upon the Mother's bosom, resting thus
His head upon one breast, while from the other
815 The Babe was drawing in its quiet food.
At other times, when he, in silence, long
And fixedly had looked upon her face,
He would exclaim, "Julia, how much thine eyes
Have cost me!" During day-time when the Child
820 Lay in its cradle, by its side he sate,
Not quitting it an instant. The whole Town
In his unmerited misfortunes now
Took part, and if he either at the door
Or window for a moment with his Child
825 Appeared, immediately the Street was thronged
While others frequently without reserve
Passed and repassed before the house to steal
A look at him. Oft at this time he wrote
Requesting, since he knew that the consent
830 Of Julia's Parents never could be gained
To a clandestine marriage, that his Father
Would from the birth-right of an eldest Son
Exclude him, giving but, when this was done,
A sanction to his nuptials: vain request,
835 To which no answer was returned. And now
From her own home the Mother of his Love
Arrived to apprise the Daughter of her fixed
And last resolve, that since all hope to move
The old Man's heart proved vain, she must retire
840 Into a Convent, and be there immured.[9]
Julia was thunderstricken by these words,
And she insisted on a Mother's rights
To take her Child along with her, a grant
Impossible, as she at last perceived;
845 The Persons of the house no sooner heard

---

9. Confined (for the rest of her life). In her *Letters* Williams mentions having met nuns who "had been forced by their parents to take the veil" (119).

Of this decision upon Julia's fate
Than every one was overwhelmed with grief,
Nor could they frame a manner soft enough
To impart the tidings to the Youth; but great
850 Was their astonishment when they beheld him
Receive the news with calm despondency,
Composed and silent, without outward sign
Of even the least emotion; seeing this,
When Julia scattered some upbraiding words
855 Upon his slackness,[1] he thereto returned
No answer, only took the Mother's hand
Who loved him scarcely less than her own Child
And kissed it without seeming to be pressed
By any pain that 'twas the hand of one
860 Whose errand was to part him from his Love
For ever. In the City he remained
A season after Julia had retired
And in the Convent taken up her home,
To the end that he might place his infant Babe
865 With a fit Nurse, which done, beneath the roof
Where now his little One was lodged he passed
The day entire, and scarcely could at length
Tear himself from the cradle to return
Home to his Father's house, in which he dwelt
870 A while, and then came back that he might see
Whether the Babe had gained sufficient strength
To bear removal. He quitted this same Town
For the last time attendant by the side
Of a close chair, a Litter or Sedan[2]
875 In which the Child was carried. To a hill
Which rose at a league's distance from the Town
The Family of the house where he had lodged
[Attended him and from him parted there,][3]
Watching below until he disappeared
880 On the hill top. His eyes he scarcely took,
Through all that journey, from the Chair in which
The Babe was carried; and at every Inn
Or place at which they halted or reposed
Laid him upon his knees, nor would permit
885 The hands of any but himself to dress
The Infant or undress. By one of those
Who bore the Chair these facts at his return
Were told; and in relating them he wept.
This was the manner in which Vaudracour

---

1. I.e., when Julia, seeing this, upbraided him for his slackness.
2. Sedan chair, an enclosed chair carried on poles by two bearers, one in front and the other behind; *attendant*: accompanying; *Litter*: an enclosed (*close*) bed or couch borne on men's shoulders (or an animal's back) and used for transporting the sick.
3. A space for line 878 was left in both MSS B and A but never filled in in MS B. The line supplied here in brackets was inserted into MS A probably during the revisions of 1818–20; the comma after "there" is an editorial addition.

890 Departed with his Infant; and thus reached
     His Father's House, where to the innocent Child
     Admittance was denied. The young Man spake
     No words of indignation or reproof
     But of his Father begged, a last request,
895 That a retreat might be assigned to him,
     A house where in the Country he might dwell
     With such allowance as his wants required,
     And the more lonely that the Mansion was
     'Twould be welcome. To a Lodge that stood
900 Deep in a Forest, with leave given, at the age
     Of four and twenty summers he retired
     And thither took with him his Infant Babe
     And one Domestic for their common needs,
     An aged Woman. It consoled him here
905 To attend upon the Orphan and perform
     The office of a Nurse to his young Child
     Which after a short time by some mistake
     Or indiscretion of the Father died.
     The Tale I follow to its last recess
910 Of suffering or of peace, I know not which;
     Theirs be the blame who caused the woe, not mine.
     From that time forth he never uttered word
     To any living.[4] An Inhabitant
     Of that same Town in which the Pair had left
915 So lively a remembrance of their griefs
     By chance of business coming within reach
     Of his retirement to the spot repaired
     With the intent to visit him. [He reached][5]
     The House, and only found the Matron there
920 Who told him that his pains were thrown away,
     For that her Master never uttered word
     To living soul, not even to her. Behold
     While they were speaking Vaudracour approached,
     But, seeing someone there, just as his hand
925 Was stretched towards the garden gate he shrunk
     And like a shadow glided out of view.
     Shocked at his savage outside from the place
     The Visitor retired.
                         Thus lived the Youth
     Cut off from all intelligence[6] with Man,
930 And shunning even the light of common day,
     Nor could the voice of Freedom which thro' France
     Soon afterwards resounded, public hope,

4. In the published version of *Vaudracour and Julia*, WW altered this sentence to "From this time forth he never shared a smile / With mortal creature" (*Prel 1805* [CW], 1:265)—probably, *OxPrel* suggests, to avoid recalling Iago in *Othello* 5.2.303: "From that time forth I never will speak word."
5. The end of this line was left incomplete in MS B; the two words in brackets are supplied from MS A.
6. Communication.

Or personal memory of his own deep wrongs
Rouze him; but in those solitary shades
935 His days he wasted, an imbecile mind.

Book Tenth

RESIDENCE IN FRANCE AND FRENCH REVOLUTION

It was a beautiful and silent day
That overspread the countenance of earth,
Then fading, with unusual quietness
When from the Loire I parted, and through scenes
5 Of vineyard, orchard, meadow-ground and tilth,
Calm waters, gleams of sun, and breathless trees
Towards the fierce Metropolis turned my steps
Their homeward way to England.[1] From his Throne
The King had fallen;[2] the congregated Host,
10 Dire cloud upon the front of which was written
The tender mercies of the dismal wind
That bore it, on the Plains of Liberty
Had burst innocuously,[3] say more, the swarm
That came elate and jocund, like a Band
15 Of Eastern Hunters, to enfold in ring
Narrowing itself by moments and reduce
To the last punctual spot of their despair,
A race of victims, so they deemed themselves,
Had shrunk from sight of their own task, and fled
20 In terror;[4] desolation and dismay
Remained for them whose fancies had grown rank
With evil expectations, confidence
And perfect triumph to the better cause.
The State, as if to stamp the final seal
25 On her security, and to the world
Shew what she was, a high and fearless soul,
Or rather in a spirit of thanks to those
Who had stirred up her slackening faculties
To a new transition, had assumed with joy
30 The body and the venerable name
Of a Republic:[5] lamentable crimes,

1. WW left Blois for Orléans in September or October 1792, and from there traveled to Paris, where he seems to have remained for several weeks (probably late October to late November) before returning to London (*Chrono: EY*, 135–38).
2. Angered by news of the Brunswick Manifesto of July 25, 1792, in which the allied forces of Austria and Prussia threatened "forever memorable vengeance" against Paris if the French royal family were harmed, crowds attacked the Tuileries Palace on August 10 and massacred the royal bodyguards, the Swiss Guards, while Louis XVI and his family, who had sought refuge in the National Assembly, were imprisoned in the Temple, a medieval Parisian fortress.
3. Led by the Duke of Brunswick, the allied armies (*congregated Host*), whose intentions had been signaled in the Brunswick Manifesto (*upon the front of which . . . bore it*), invaded France on August 19 and quickly captured the towns of Longwy and Verdun, but on September 20 their advanced was stopped by French forces at Verdun (*Dire cloud . . . burst innocuously*), and they retreated to the Rhine.
4. I.e., the allied armies, like hunters closing on their prey, had expected to entrap the French army in a single (*punctual*, as at 8.763) spot, but after being thwarted had *fled / In terror*.
5. On September 22, 1792, the National Convention, which had first sat two days earlier, abolished the monarchy and proclaimed France a republic.

'Tis true, had gone before this hour, the work
Of massacre in which the senseless sword
Was prayed to as a judge; but these were past,
35 Earth free from them for ever, as was thought,
Ephemeral monsters, to be seen but once,
Things that could only shew themselves and die.[6]
        This was the time in which, enflamed with hope,
To Paris I returned. Again I ranged
40 More eagerly than I had done before
Through the wide City, and in progress passed
The Prison where the unhappy Monarch lay
Associate with his Children and his Wife
In bondage, and the Palace lately stormed
45 With roar of canon,[7] and a numerous Host.
I crossed (a blank and empty area then)
The Square of the Carousel, few weeks back
Heaped up with dead and dying,[8] upon these
And other sights looking as doth a Man
50 Upon a Volume whose contents he knows
Are memorable, but from him locked up,
Being written in a tongue he cannot read,
So that he questions the mute leaves with pain
And half upbraids their silence. But that night
55 When on my bed I lay, I was most moved
And felt most deeply in what world I was;
My room was high and lonely, near the roof
Of a large Mansion or Hotel, a spot
That would have pleased me in more quiet times,
60 Nor was it wholly without pleasure then.
With unextinguished taper I kept watch,
Reading at intervals; the fear gone by
Pressed on me almost like a fear to come;
I thought of those September Massacres,
65 Divided from me by a little month,[9]
And felt and touched them, a substantial dread;
The rest was conjured up from tragic fictions
And mournful Calendars of true history,[1]
Remembrances and dim admonishments.

6. WW would have been in Blois or Orléans when he heard of the September Massacres, in which
   crowds of *sansculottes*—i.e., working-class supporters of the Revolution, known by the fact that
   they did not wear the silk knee-breeches, *culottes*, favored by the bourgeoisie—reacting to news
   of the initial French defeat at Verdun (see the note on line 13 above), attacked the Parisian
   prison population, the majority of which consisted of common criminals, and executed between
   1,100 and 1,400 prisoners after summary trials from September 2 to 7 (Doyle, 191–92).
7. Cannon (a variant spelling in use during the eighteenth century). Lines 1–43 are missing from
   MS A. *Prison*: the Temple (see the note on line 9), from which Louis XVI was taken to his exe-
   cution on January 21, 1793, and Marie Antoinette to hers on October 16, 1793. Their son,
   Louis-Charles, remained imprisoned there until his death, at the age of ten, from scrofula on
   June 8, 1795. *Palace*: the Tuileries Palace (see the note on line 9).
8. Place du Carrousel, the square in which the bodies of those killed during the assault on the
   Tuileries Palace on August 10 were piled up to be burned or loaded onto carts for burial.
9. A phrase from *Hamlet* 1.2.147, where Hamlet refers to the period between his father's death
   and his mother's remarriage.
1. *Calendars . . . history*: chronicles.

70   "The horse is taught his manage[2] and the wind
     Of heaven wheels round and treads in his own steps,
     Year follows year, the tide returns again,
     Day follows day, all things have second birth;
     The earthquake is not satisfied at once."
75 And in such way I wrought upon myself
     Until I seemed to hear a voice that cried
     To the whole City, "Sleep no more."[3] To this
     Add comments of a calmer mind, from which
     I could not gather full security,
80 But at the best it seemed a place of fear
     Unfit for the repose of night,
     Defenceless as a wood where tigers roam.
          Betimes next morning to the Palace Walk
     Of Orleans[4] I repaired and entering there
85 Was greeted, among divers other notes,
     By voices of the Hawkers in the crowd
     Bawling, "Denunciation of the crimes
     Of Maximilian Robespierre": the speech
     Which in their hands they carried was the same
90 Which had been recently pronounced the day
     When Robespierre, well knowing for what mark
     Some words of indirect reproof had been
     Intended, rose in hardihood and dared
     The Man who had an ill surmise of him
95 To bring his charge in openness, whereat
     When a dead pause ensued and no one stirred,
     In silence of all present, from his seat
     Louvet walked singly through the avenue
     And took his station in the Tribune,[5] saying,
100 "I, Robespierre, accuse thee!" 'Tis well known
     What was the issue of that charge, and how
     Louvet was left alone without support
     Of his irresolute Friends: but these are things
     Of which I speak only as they were storm
105 Or sunshine to my individual mind,
     No further. Let me then relate that now,
     In some sort seeing with my proper[6] eyes
     That Liberty, and Life and Death would soon,

2. The paces a horse is taught in a riding school (with a possible allusion to Shakespeare's *As You Like It* 1.1.13: "they are taught their manage"). The metaphor may have been suggested to WW by the fact that meetings first of the Constituent Assembly and later of the National Convention were held in a former riding academy, the Salle du Manège (*PPrel*). The passage in quotation marks is WW's imagined address to himself.
3. A quotation from *Macbeth* 2.2.32–33, 38: "Methought I heard a voice cry, 'Sleep no more! / Macbeth does murther sleep.' * * * Still it cried, 'Sleep no more!' to all the house."
4. The arcades of the Palais-Royal, as in 9.50–51.
5. Speaker's rostrum; *avenue*: aisle. On October 29, 1792, Jean-Baptiste Louvet de Couvray (1760–1797), a Girondin member of the National Convention (see the note on 9.179), accused Robespierre (see Biographical and Topographical Glossary) of aspiring to dictatorial power, and the speech was published the next day. Allowed time to prepare a response, Robespierre exonerated himself on November 6, appealing to the principles of the Revolution and excusing its violence as necessary. Thereafter Robespierre consolidated his power and engineered the expulsion of the Girondists from the Convention in May–June 1793.
6. Own (after the French *propre*).

To the remotest corners of the land,
110 Lie in the arbitriment[7] of those who ruled
The capital City; what was struggled for,
And by what Combatants victory must be won;
The indecision on their part whose aim
Seemed best,[8] and the straight-forward path of those
115 Who in attack or in defence alike
Were strong through their impiety, greatly I
Was agitated; yea, I could almost
Have prayed that throughout earth upon all souls
Worthy of liberty, upon every soul
120 Matured to live in plainness and in truth
The gift of tongues[9] might fall, and men arrive
From the four quarters of the winds to do
For France what without help she could not do,
A work of honour; think not that to this
125 I added, work of safety; from such thought
And the least fear about the end of things
I was as far as Angels are from guilt.
        Yet did I grieve, nor only grieved, but thought
Of opposition and of remedies,
130 An insignificant Stranger, and obscure,
Mean as I was, and little graced with powers
Of eloquence even in my native speech,
And all unfit for tumult and intrigue,
Yet would I willingly have taken up
135 A service at this time for cause so great,
However dangerous. Inly I revolved[1]
How much the destiny of man had still
Hung upon single persons, that there was,
Transcendent to all local patrimony,[2]
140 One Nature as there is one Sun in heaven,
That objects, even as they are great, thereby
Do come within the reach of humblest eyes,
That Man was only weak through his mistrust
And want of hope, where evidence divine
145 Proclaimed to him that hope should be most sure,
That, with desires heroic and firm sense,
A Spirit thoroughly faithful to itself,
Unquenchable, unsleeping, undismayed,
Was as an instinct among Men, a stream
150 That gathered up each petty straggling rill

7. "The power to decide for others; absolute decision, direction, or control" (OED).
8. I.e., the Girondists. OxPrel notes the comparable opinion expressed by STC in his address *Conciones ad Populum* (1795): "The Girondists * * * were men of enlarged views and great literary attainments; but they seem to have been deficient in that vigour and daring activity, which circumstances made necessary" (*Lectures 1795: On Politics and Religion*, ed. Lewis Patton and Peter Mann [Princeton, 1971], 34).
9. As, according to Acts 2:3–4, the Holy Spirit spoke through the Apostles in foreign tongues at Pentecost.
1. Pondered.
2. I.e., not confined by nationality or locality (so that a foreigner might also influence events in France).

And vein of water, glad to be rolled on
In safe obedience, that a mind whose rest
Was where it ought to be, in self-restraint,
In circumspection and simplicity,
155 Fell rarely in entire discomfiture
Below its aim, or met with from without
A treachery that defeated it, or foiled.
——On the other side, I called to mind those truths
Which are the common-places of the Schools,
160 A theme[3] for Boys, too trite even to be felt,
Yet with a revelation's liveliness
In all their comprehensive bearings known
And visible to Philosophers of old,
Men who, to business of the world untrained,
165 Lived in the Shade, and to Harmodius known
And his compeer Aristogiton, known
To Brutus,[4] that tyrannic Power is weak,
Hath neither gratitude, nor faith, nor love,
Nor the support of good or evil men
170 To trust in, that the Godhead which is ours
Can never utterly be charmed or stilled,[5]
That nothing hath a natural right to last
But equity and reason, that all else
Meets foes irreconcilable, and at best
175 Doth live but by variety of disease.
          Well might my wishes be intense, my thoughts
Strong and perturbed, not doubting at that time,
Creed which ten shameful years have not annulled,[6]
But that the virtue of one paramount mind
180 Would have abashed those impious crests,[7] have quelled
Outrage and bloody power, and in despite
Of what the People were through ignorance
And immaturity, and in the teeth
Of desperate opposition from without,
185 Have cleared a passage for just government,
And left a solid birth-right to the State,
Redeemed according to example given
By ancient Lawgivers.
                    In this frame of mind
Reluctantly to England I returned,
190 Compelled by nothing less than absolute want

---

3. Topic for an assigned essay.
4. Marcus Junius Brutus (ca. 85–42 B.C.E.), Roman republican and co-conspirator in the assassination of Julius Caesar, subsequently defeated in battle against Caesar's grandnephew Octavian (who became the first Roman emperor, Augustus). *Harmodius . . . Aristogiton*: Athenian noblemen executed after their failed attempt to kill the tyrant Hippias in 514 B.C.E., but celebrated as heroes after the expulsion of Hippias from Athens in 510.
5. Subdued or destroyed.
6. WW deleted line 178 during his revisions of 1818–20. The *shameful years* encompassed the Terror under Robespierre (1793–94), the rise of Napoleon to supreme power (1796–99), and the war against Britain (from 1793).
7. The Jacobins. WW takes the metaphor of plumed helmets from the seraph Abdiel's rebuke to Satan in *Paradise Lost* 6.188: "This greeting on thy impious Crest receive."

Or funds for my support, else,[8] well assured
That I both was and must be of small worth,
No better than an alien in the Land,
I doubtless should have made a common cause
195 With some who perished, haply perished too,[9]
A poor mistaken and bewildered offering,
Should to the breast of Nature have gone back
With all my resolutions, all my hopes,
A Poet only to myself, to Men
200 Useless, and even, belovèd Friend! a soul
To thee unknown.[1]
                    When to my native Land
(After a whole year's absence) I returned,
I found the air yet busy with the stir
Of a contention which had been raised up
205 Against the Traffickers in[2] Negro blood,
An effort which, though baffled, nevertheless
Had called back old forgotten principles
Dismissed from service, had diffused some truths
And more of virtuous feeling through the heart
210 Of the English People. And no few of those
So numerous (little less in verity
Than a whole Nation crying with one voice)
Who had been crossed in this their just intent
And righteous hope, thereby were well prepared
215 To let that journey sleep awhile and join
Whatever other Caravan appeared
To travel forwards towards Liberty
With more success. For me that strife[3] had ne'er
Fastened on my affections, nor did now
220 Its unsuccessful issue much excite
My sorrow, having laid this faith to heart,
That if France prospered good Men would not long
Pay fruitless worship to humanity,
And this most rotten branch of human shame,
225 Object, as seemed, of a superfluous pains,
Would fall together with its parent tree.
        Such was my then belief, that there was one,
And only one, solicitude for all;

8. Because otherwise. WW revised this blunt assertion substantially in *Prel 1850*: "Dragged by a chain of harsh necessity, / So seemed it,—now I thankfully acknowledge, / Forced by the gracious providence of Heaven— / To England I returned" (*Prel 1850* [CW], 202).
9. The Girondists, with whom WW sympathized, were expelled from the Convention in May–June 1793, and twenty-one Girondin deputies were guillotined in Paris on October 31, while others committed suicide or were executed in the provinces (Doyle, 253).
1. I.e., had he stayed in France, WW would not have met STC (as in fact he did in 1795). *A Poet only to myself*: WW had published only his sonnet *On Seeing Miss Helen Maria Williams Weep at a Tale of Distress* by 1792; his first two volumes of poetry, *An Evening Walk* and *Descriptive Sketches*, were published in late January 1793, within two months of his return to England from France.
2. Corrected by MW in pencil from "on," but without the deletion of the original word. A bill to abolish the slave trade gradually throughout the British empire had been passed by the House of Commons on April 2, 1792, but was blocked by the House of Lords. A similar bill was finally passed by both houses of parliament in February 1807 (see WW's *Sonnet, to Thomas Clarkson*, addressed to the founder of the Society for Effecting the Abolition of the Slave Trade).
3. The abolitionist cause.

And now the strength of Britain was put forth
230   In league with the confederated Host,[4]
Not in my single self alone I found,
But in the minds of all ingenuous Youth,
Change and subversion from this hour. No shock
Given to my moral nature had I known
235   Down to that very moment; neither lapse
Nor turn of sentiment that might be named
A revolution save at this one time,
All else was progress on the self-same path
On which with a diversity of pace
240   I had been travelling; this a stride at once
Into another region.[5] True it is
'Twas not concealed with what ungracious eyes
Our native Rulers from the very first
Had looked upon regenerated France,[6]
245   Nor had I doubted that this day would come;
But in such contemplation I had thought
Of general interests only, beyond this
Had never[7] once foretasted the event.
Now had I other business, for I felt
250   The ravage of this most unnatural strife
In my own heart: there lay it like a weight
At enmity with all the tenderest springs
Of my enjoyments. I, who with the breeze
Had played, a green leaf on the blessed tree
255   Of my belovèd Country; nor had wished
For happier fortune than to wither there,
Now from my pleasant station[8] was cut off
And tossed about in whirlwinds. I rejoiced,
Yes, afterwards, truth painful to record!
260   Exulted in the triumph of my soul
When Englishmen by thousands were o'erthrown,
Left without glory on the Field, or driven,
Brave hearts, to shameful flight.[9] It was a grief,

---

4. France declared war on Britain and the Dutch Republic on February 1, 1793, and Britain responded by joining a military alliance (the "First Coalition") with Austria, Prussia, Spain, Portugal, and the Dutch Republic, and sending an army to Flanders to battle the French. When WW composed these lines in 1804, Britain was still at war with France and would remain so for another decade.
5. Whereas the French Revolution itself "[s]eemed nothing out of nature's certain course" to WW (9.253), Britain's entry into the war against France did seem to him a *revolution* (line 237).
6. In fact the English response to the French Revolution was initially largely positive, and the hostility of Edmund Burke's *Reflections on the Revolution in France* (1790) began to be more widely echoed only after 1791, when the immensely high sales of Thomas Paine's *Rights of Man* (1791–92) and the formation of numerous "corresponding societies" dedicated to political reform suggested popular support for republicanism in Britain. In May and December 1792 the government issued proclamations aimed at suppressing radical publications.
7. This word, needed for the sense and meter, was inserted in pencil in MS B.
8. Position, viewpoint. Once the war had begun WW was also cut off from Annette Vallon and their daughter, Caroline (born December 15, 1792), whom WW would see for the first time in Calais in 1802, during the Peace of Amiens, an eleven-month hiatus in the war.
9. WW is probably referring to the Battle of Hondschoote, northern France, on September 6–8, 1793, in which British forces under the Duke of York were outflanked and forced to retreat, or to the Battle of Toulon, September 18–December 18, 1793, in which French Revolutionary forces led by Napoléon Bonaparte (then an artillery officer) suppressed a royalist rebellion and forced the evacuation of the British forces that had been supporting the royalists.

Grief call it not, 'twas any thing but that,
265 A conflict of sensations without name,
Of which he only who may love the sight
Of a Village Steeple as I do can judge,
When in the Congregation, bending all
To their great Father,[1] prayers were offered up
270 Or praises for our Country's Victories,
And 'mid the simple worshippers, perchance,
I only, like an uninvited Guest,
Whom no one owned sate silent, shall I add,
Fed on the day of vengeance yet to come?
275 Oh! much have they to account for, who could tear
By violence at one decisive rent
From the best Youth in England their dear pride,
Their joy in England; this too, at a time
In which worst losses easily might wear
280 The best of names, when patriotic love
Did of itself in modesty give way
Like the Precursor when the Deity
Is come whose Harbinger he is, a time
In which apostacy from ancient faith
285 Seemed but conversion to a higher creed,
Withal, a season dangerous and wild,
A time in which Experience would have plucked
Flowers out of any hedge, to make thereof
A Chaplet,[2] in contempt of his grey locks.[3]
290   Ere yet the Fleet of Britain had gone forth
On this unworthy service, whereunto
The unhappy counsel of a few weak Men
Had doomed it, I beheld the Vessels lie,
A brood of gallant Creatures, on the deep
295 I saw them in their rest, a sojourner
Through a whole month of calm and glassy days
In that delightful Island[4] which protects
Their place of convocation; there I heard
Each evening, walking by the still sea-shore,
300 A monitory sound which never failed,
The sunset Canon. When the Orb went down
In the tranquility of Nature, came
That voice, ill requiem! seldom heard by me
Without a spirit overcast, a deep

1. An echo of STC's *Rime of the Ancyent Marinere*, lines 639–40 (published in *LB* 1798): "And all together pray, / While each to his great father bends."
2. A wreath for the head.
3. *NCPrel* paraphrases WW's "four remarkably cryptic points" in lines 278–89 as follows: (1) "defeats of the French—and thus of republicanism in England and elsewhere—could be described as English victories" (lines 278–80), (2) "the true love of one's country gives way to the falsely patriotic wish for victory, as John the Baptist gives place to Christ" (lines 280–83), (3) "Rejection of earlier true belief could thus seem [falsely] to be conversion to a higher faith" (lines 283–85), (4) "'Experience' ° ° ° would at this time have adopted any disguise, however inappropriate, so as to lay claim to political innocence" (lines 286–89).
4. The Isle of Wight, where WW stayed with his Hawkshead friend William Calvert in the summer of 1793 and saw the British fleet in the waters off Portsmouth, preparing for war.

305 Imagination, thought of woes to come,
And sorrow for mankind, and pain of heart.
          In France, the Men who for their desperate ends
Had plucked up mercy by the roots were glad
Of this new enemy. Tyrants, strong before
310 In devilish pleas,[5] were ten times stronger now,
And thus beset with Foes on every side
The goaded Land waxed mad; the crimes of few
Spread into madness of the many, blasts
From hell came sanctified like airs from heaven;[6]
315 The sternness of the Just, the faith of those
Who doubted not that Providence had times
Of anger and of vengeance, theirs[7] who throned
The human understanding paramount
And made of that their God,[8] the hopes of those
320 Who were content to barter short-lived pangs
For a paradise of ages, the blind rage
Of insolent tempers, the light vanity
Of intermeddlers, steady purposes
Of the suspicious, slips of the indiscreet,
325 And all the accidents of life, were pressed
Into one service, busy with one work;
The Senate was heart-stricken, not a voice
Uplifted, none to oppose or mitigate:[9]
Domestic carnage now filled all the year
330 With Feast-days; the old Man from the chimney-nook,
The Maiden from the bosom of her Love,
The Mother from the cradle of her Babe,
The Warrior from the field, all perished,
Friends, enemies, of all parties, ages, ranks,
335 Head after head, and never heads enough
For those who bade them fall: they found their joy,
They made it, ever thirsty, as a Child,
If light desires of innocent little Ones
May with such heinous appetites be matched,
340 Having a toy, a windmill, though the air
Do of itself blow fresh, and makes the vane
Spin in his eyesight, he is not content,
But with the play-thing at arm's length he sets
His front against the blast, and runs amain

5. An allusion to *Paradise Lost* 4.393–94, implicitly comparing Robespierre to Satan: "So spake the Fiend, and with necessitie, / The Tyrants plea, excus'd his devlish deeds."
6. An allusion to *Hamlet* 1.4.41: "Bring with thee airs from heaven, or blasts from hell."
7. Referring to *those* in line 315.
8. A reference to the French Revolutionary government's de-Christianizing activities, such as the renaming of Notre Dame Cathedral the Temple of Reason on November 10, 1793, by the radical materialist Pierre-Gaspard Chaumette, president of the Paris Commune, who was opposed by Robespierre and executed on April 13, 1794. Robespierre inaugurated a Festival of the Supreme Being on June 8, 1794, which was effectively ended by Robespierre's own execution on July 28.
9. On June 2, 1793, surrounded by some 80,000 *sansculottes* (see the note on line 37) with 100 cannon, the National Convention acceded to the protestors' demand to approve the arrest of the Girondin deputies.

To make it whirl the faster.[1]
345   In the depth
Of these enormities, even thinking minds
Forgot at seasons whence they had their being,
Forgot that such a sound was ever heard
As Liberty upon earth; yet all beneath
350 Her innocent authority was wrought,
Nor could have been, without her blessèd name.
The illustrious Wife of Roland, in the hour
Of her composure, felt that agony
And gave it vent in her last words.[2] O Friend!
355 It was a lamentable time for man
Whether a hope had e'er been his or not,
A woeful time for them whose hopes did still
Outlast the shock; most woeful for those few,
They had the deepest feeling of the grief,
360 Who still were flattered,[3] and had trust in man.
Meanwhile, the Invaders fared as they deserved;
The Herculean Common-wealth had put forth her arms
And throttled with an infant Godhead's might
The snakes about her cradle:[4] that was well
365 And as it should be, yet no cure for those
Whose souls were sick with pain of what would be
Hereafter brought in charge against mankind.
Most melancholy at that time, O Friend!
Were my day thoughts, my dreams were miserable,
370 Through months, through years, long after the last beat
Of those atrocities (I speak bare truth,
As if to thee alone in private talk)
I scarcely had one night of quiet sleep,
Such ghastly visions had I of despair
375 And tyranny and implements of death,
And long orations which in dreams I pleaded
Before unjust Tribunals, with a voice
Labouring, a brain confounded, and a sense
Of treachery and desertion in the place
380 The holiest that I knew of, my own soul.[5]
      When I began at first, in early Youth,

1. In this extraordinary comparison of the guillotine to a toy windmill, WW refers to the "Great Terror," during which 1,515 people were executed between June 10, 1794, when the Revolutionary Tribunal in Paris was given exclusive jurisdiction over political trials and defendants were denied the right to have legal representation and call witnesses, and July 27, when Robespierre's arrest was ordered by the National Convention (Doyle, 275).
2. Manon (Jeanne Marie) Roland (née Phlipon, 1754–1793), known as Madame Roland, a cofounder of the Girondin faction in 1792, was imprisoned on June 1, 1793, and executed on November 8. Passing the statue of Liberty in the Place de la Révolution on her way to the guillotine, she is said to have exclaimed, "O Liberty, what crimes are committed in your name!"
3. Groundlessly hopeful.
4. In 1794, having earlier repelled the Duke of Brunswick's forces and suppressed the rebellion in the Vendée (see the notes on line 13 above and on 9.434), the French Revolutionary army occupied Belgium, southern Holland, and the Rhineland. In classical myth, the infant Hercules (Greek Heracles), the son of the god Jupiter (Zeus) and the mortal Alcmene, strangles two serpents sent by Jupiter's wife Juno (Hera) to kill him.
5. WW "in his nightmares is a victim of the Terror, and falsely accused, yet cannot wholly absolve himself from collusion in the violence" (PPrel).

To yield myself to Nature, when that strong
And holy passion overcame me first,
Neither day nor night, evening or morn
385 Were free from the oppression: but Great God!
Who send'st thyself into this breathing world
Through Nature and through every kind of life,
And mak'st Man what he is, Creature divine
In single or in social eminence
390 Above all these raised infinite ascents
When reason, which enables him to be,
Is not sequestered, what a change is here![6]
How different ritual for this after worship,
What countenance to promote this second love.[7]
395 That first was service but to things which lie
At rest, within the bosom of thy will:
Therefore to serve was high beatitude;
The tumult was a gladness, and the fear
Ennobling, venerable; sleep secure,
400 And waking thoughts more rich than happiest dreams.
      But as the ancient Prophets were enflamed[8]
Nor wanted consolations of their own
And majesty of mind, when they denounced
On Towns and Cities, wallowing in the abyss
405 Of their offences, punishment to come;
Or saw like other men with bodily eyes
Before them in some desolated place
The consummation of the wrath of Heaven;
So did some portion of that spirit fall
410 On me to uphold me through those evil times,
And in their rage and dog-day heat I found
Something to glory in, as just and fit,
And in the order of sublimest laws;
And even if that were not, amid the awe
415 Of unintelligible chastisement,
I felt a kind of sympathy with power,
Motions raised up within me, nevertheless,
Which had relationship to highest things.
Wild blasts of music thus did find their way
420 Into the midst of terrible events,
So that worst tempests might be listened to:
Then was the truth received into my heart
That under heaviest sorrow earth can bring,
Griefs bitterest of ourselves or of our Kind,
425 If from the affliction somewhere do not grow
Honour which could not else have been, a faith,
An elevation, and a sanctity,
If new strength be not given, or old restored,

---

6. An echo of *Romeo and Juliet* 2.3.64–66: "Holy Saint Francis, what a change is here! / Is Rosa-
line, that thou didst love so dear, / So soon forsaken?" (*Prel 1805* [CW]).
7. Love of humanity, as distinguished from love of nature; *countenance*: appearance of favor.
8. Inspired.

The blame is ours not Nature's. When a taunt
430 Was taken up by Scoffers in their pride,
Saying, "behold the harvest which we reap
From popular Government and Equality,"
I saw that it was neither these, nor aught
Of wild belief engrafted on their names
435 By false philosophy, that caused the woe,
But that it was a reservoir of guilt
And ignorance, filled up from age to age,
That could no longer hold its loathsome charge,[9]
But burst and spread in deluge through the Land.
440   And as the desart hath green spots, the sea
Small islands in the midst of stormy waves,
So that disastrous period did not want
Such sprinklings of all human excellence
As were a joy to hear of. Yet (nor less
445 For those bright spots, those fair examples given
Of fortitude, and energy, and love,
And human nature faithful to itself
Under worst trials) was I impelled to think
Of the glad time when first I traversed France,
450 A youthful Pilgrim, above all remembered
The day when through an Arch that spanned the Street,
A rainbow made of garish ornaments,
Triumphal pomp for Liberty confirmed,
We walked, a pair of weary Travellers,
455 Along the town of Arras, place from which
Issued that Robespierre, who afterwards
Wielded the sceptre of the Atheist crew.[1]
When the calamity spread far and wide,
And this same City, which had even appeared
460 To outrun the rest in exultation, groaned
Under the vengeance of her cruel Son,
As Lear reproached the winds,[2] I could almost
Have quarreled with that blameless spectacle
For being yet an image in my mind
465 To mock me under such a strange reverse.
          O Friend! few happier moments have been mine
Through my whole life than that when first I heard
That this foul Tribe of Moloch was o'erthrown,[3]
And their chief Regent levelled with the dust.

9. Contents, burden.
1. Milton's phrase for the fallen angels, the word *atheist* used in the sense of "impious" (*Paradise Lost* 6.370). Although he rejected Christianity, Robespierre did not deny the existence of God. WW and Robert Jones (see Biographical and Topographical Glossary) had spent the night of July 16, 1790—two days after the first anniversary of the storming of the Bastille (see 6.360–70)—in Arras, a city in northern France and the birthplace of Robespierre, who practiced law there before being elected to the Estates-General in 1788, and later to the National Assembly, as a deputy for the Artois province.
2. *King Lear* 3.2.16–20: "I tax you not, you elements, with unkindness * * *. Then let fall / Your horrible pleasure. / Here I stand your slave."
3. An allusion to one of the fallen angels named in *Paradise Lost* 1.392–93: "First Moloch, horrid King besmearch'd with blood / Of human sacrifice."

470   The day was one which haply[4] may deserve
     A separate chronicle. Having gone abroad
     From a small Village where I tarried then,
     To the same far-secluded privacy
     I was returning. Over the smooth Sands
475   Of Leven's ample Æstuary lay
     My journey,[5] and beneath a genial sun,
     With distant prospect among gleams of sky
     And clouds, and intermingled mountain tops
     In one inseparable glory clad,
480   Creatures of one etherial substance, met
     In Consistory, like a diadem
     Or crown of burning Seraphs, as they sit
     In the Empyrean.[6] Underneath this show
     Lay, as I knew, the nest of pastoral Vales
485   Among whose happy fields I had grown up
     From childhood. On the fulgent[7] spectacle,
     Which neither changed, nor stirred, nor passed away,
     I gazed, and with a fancy more alive
     On this account, that I had chanced to find
490   That morning, ranging through the church yard graves
     Of Cartmel's rural Town, the place in which
     An honoured Teacher of my youth was laid.[8]
     While we were School-boys he had died among us
     And was borne hither, as I knew, to rest
495   With his own Family. A plain Stone, inscribed
     With name, date, office, pointed out the spot,
     To which a slip of verses was subjoined,
     (By his desire, as afterwards I learned)
     A fragment from the Elegy of Gray.[9]
500   A week, or little less, before his death
     He had[1] said to me, "my head will soon lie low,"
     And when I saw the turf that covered him,

4. Perhaps (from *by hap*, meaning "by chance").
5. The tidal sands of Morecambe Bay, into which the River Leven flows eight miles south from Windermere, provided a shortcut between the Cartmel and Furness Peninsulas of Cumbria (formerly Lancashire), as mentioned also below in lines 515–29. WW had been visiting cousins in Rampside, a village at the south end of the Furness Peninsula, when he learned, probably on August 20 or 21, 1794, of Robespierre's execution (*Chrono: EY*, 157–58).
6. In classical cosmology, the highest heavenly sphere, made of fire (and in Christian cosmology, as in *Paradise Lost* 3.57–58, the abode of God and the angels); *etherial substance*: a quotation from *Paradise Lost* 6.330; *Consistory*: council (as in Milton's *Paradise Regained* 1.42); *Seraphs*: in medieval Christian theology, angels of the highest of nine orders (recalling Milton's *At a Solemn Music*, line 10: "Where the bright Seraphim in burning row").
7. Resplendent, brightly shining.
8. William Taylor (1754–1786), the headmaster of Hawkshead Grammar School from 1781 to 1786, was buried in the graveyard of the priory church in Cartmel, a village on the Cartmel Peninsula.
9. The tombstone is inscribed with the last four lines (with variants) of Thomas Gray's *Elegy Written in a Country Churchyard* (1751): "His merits, stranger, seek not to disclose, / Or draw his Frailties from their dread abode; / There they alike in trembling Hope repose / The Bosom of his Father and his God" (*OxPrel*).
1. This word was inserted in pencil by MW. *PPrel* notes that WW had incorporated Taylor's words to him in a ballad he composed in March 1787, when he was sixteen, *And Will You Leave Me Thus Alone*, lines 41–44: "Heav'n told me once—but I was blind / My head would soon lie low / —A rose within our Garden blew / Amid December's snow" (*Early Poems and Fragments* [CW], 388).

After the lapse of full eight years,[2] those words,
With sound of voice and countenance of the Man
505 Came back upon me; so that some few tears
Fell from me in my own despite. And now,
Thus travelling smoothly o'er the level Sands,
I thought with pleasure of the Verses graven
Upon his Tomb-stone, saying to myself,
510 He loved the Poets, and if now alive
Would have loved me, as one not destitute
Of promise, nor belying the kind hope
Which he had formed when I, at his command,
Began to spin, at first, my toilsome Song.[3]
515 Without me and within, as I advanced,
All that I saw, or felt, or communed with
Was gentleness and peace. Upon a small
And rocky Island near, a fragment stood
(Itself like a sea rock) of what had been
520 A Romish Chapel,[4] where in ancient times
Masses were said at the hour which suited those
Who crossed the Sands with ebb of morning tide:
Not far from this still Ruin all the Plain
Was spotted with a variegated crowd
525 Of Coaches, Wains,[5] and Travellers, horse and foot,
Wading, beneath the conduct of their Guide
In loose procession through the shallow Stream
Of inland water: the great Sea, meanwhile,
Was at safe distance far retired.[6] I paused,
530 Unwilling to proceed, the scene appeared
So gay and chearful, when a Traveller
Chancing to pass, I carelessly enquired
If any news were stirring: he replied
In the familiar language of the day
535 That "*Robespierre was dead.*" Nor was a doubt,
On further question, left within my mind
But that the tidings were substantial truth,
That He and his Supporters all were fallen.[7]
         Great was my glee of spirit, great my joy
540 In vengeance, and eternal justice, thus
Made manifest. "Come now ye golden times,"
Said I, forth-breathing on those open Sands
A hymn of Triumph, "as the morning comes

2. That is, between Taylor's death in 1786 and WW's visit to his grave in 1794.
3. WW's earliest poems were exercises set by Taylor (*Prose*, 3:372; *Chrono: EY*, 298–301); the
texts are available in *Early Poems and Fragments* (CW).
4. The remains (no longer extant) of a Catholic chapel built in the fourteenth century by the
monks of Furness Priory on an island in Morecambe Bay.
5. Wagons.
6. WW describes travelers fording the Leven estuary with guides as they cross the sands of More-
cambe Bay at low tide.
7. Robespierre's death was first reported in England in the *Times* on August 16, 1794 (*NCPrel*).
He and over eighty associates, including Louis de Saint-Just and Georges Auguste Couthon—
also members of the powerful Committee of Public Safety—had been guillotined on July 29–
30; *familiar* (line 534): plain.

Out of the bosom of the night, come Ye:
545 Thus far our trust is verified; behold!
They who with clumsy desperation brought
A river of blood, and preached that nothing else
Could cleanse the Augean Stable, by the might
Of their own Helper have been swept away;
550 Their madness is declared and visible;
Elsewhere will safety[8] now be sought, and Earth
March firmly towards righteousness and peace."
Then schemes I framed more calmly, when and how
The madding Factions might be tranquillized,
555 And, though through hardships manifold and long,
The mighty renovation would proceed:
Thus, interrupted by uneasy bursts
Of exultation, I pursued my way
Along that very Shore which I had skimmed
560 In former times, when, spurring from the Vale
Of Nightshade and St Mary's mouldering Fane
And the Stone Abbot, after circuit made
In wantonness of heart, a joyous Crew
Of School-boys, hastening to their distant home,
565 Along the margin of the moonlight Sea,
We beat with thundering hoofs the level Sand.[9]
From this time forth, in France, as is well known,
Authority put on a milder face,[1]
Yet every thing was wanting that might give
570 Courage to those who looked for good by light
Of rational experience, good I mean
At hand, and in the spirit of past aims.
The same belief I nevertheless retained;
The language of the Senate and the acts
575 And public measures of the Government,
Though both of heartless omen,[2] had not power
To daunt me; in the People was my trust
And in the virtues which mine eyes had seen,
And to the ultimate repose of things
580 I looked with unabated confidence;
I knew that wound external could not take

8. Alludes to the Committee of Public Safety, which was deprived of most of its authority on August 11, 1794. A river (line 547): changed from the plural "Rivers" of MS A, and retained as a singular thereafter; Augean Stable: that is, Robespierre unleashed a river of blood in the name of purifying France, just as, in classical myth, Hercules diverted the rivers Alpheus and Peneus in order to cleanse the stables of King Augeas of thirty years' accumulation of dung (the fifth of the twelve labors demanded of Hercules as expiation for killing his children); Helper: the guillotine. Invented by a committee of the National Assembly (including Dr. Joseph-Ignace Guillotin, after whom it was named) as an efficient and "humane" instrument of decapitation, the guillotine was first used in 1792 and last used in 1977, after which capital punishment was abolished in France.
9. Lines 558–66 refer back to 2.99–144, line 566 repeating 2.144 verbatim. In Prel 1850 WW divided book 10 into two books, the new book 11 beginning after line 566.
1. The Great Terror initiated by Robespierre ended almost immediately after his execution, and only forty-six people were guillotined in Paris from August to December of that year (Doyle, 282).
2. Discouraging.

Life from the young Republic, that new Foes
Would only follow in the path of shame
Their brethren, and her triumphs be in the end
585 Great, universal, irresistible.
This faith, which was an object in my mind
Of passionate intuition, had effect
Not small in dazzling me; for thus, through zeal,
Such victory I confounded in my thoughts
590 With one far higher and more difficult,
Triumphs of unambitious peace at home
And noiseless fortitude.³ Beholding still
Resistance strong as heretofore, I thought
That what was in⁴ degree the same was likewise
595 The same in quality, that as the worse
Of the two spirits then at strife remained
Untired, the better surely would preserve
The heart that first had rouzed him,⁵ never dreamt
That transmigration could be undergone,
600 A fall of being suffered, and of hope
By creature⁶ that appeared to have received
Entire conviction what a great ascent
Had been accomplished, what high faculties
It had been called to. Youth maintains, I knew,
605 In all conditions of society,
Communion more direct and intimate
With Nature and the inner strength she has,
And hence, ofttimes, no less, with Reason, too,
Than Age or Manhood, even. To Nature then
610 Power had reverted; habit, custom, law,
Had left an interregnum's open space⁷
For her to stir about in, uncontroled.
The warmest judgements and the most untaught
Found in events which every day brought forth
615 Enough to sanction them, and far, far more
To shake the authority of canons drawn
From ordinary practice. I could see
How Babel-like the employment was of those
Who, by the recent Deluge stupefied,
620 With their whole souls went culling from the day
Its petty promises to build a tower

3. That is, WW continued to hope that the goals of the French Revolution would be accomplished and lead to peaceful reform in Britain.
4. This word was inserted in ink by MW.
5. That is, WW recalls imagining that France's continued resistance in battle against Britain and its allies (the worse / Of the two spirits) after the Terror demonstrated a commitment to the original principles of the Revolution, and that France (the better spirit) would maintain that commitment so long as its enemies were tireless.
6. The French Republic, which WW now (in 1804, after Napoleon's coronation as emperor, referred to in lines 928–40 below) regards as having changed in character after the Terror.
7. The period after Robespierre's death (or, if WW means the phrase more generally, since the beginning of the French Revolution), when Nature, or feeling, to which youth feels most closely connected, had replaced habit, custom, law as the basis for political judgment.

For their own safety;[8] laughed at gravest heads,
Who, watching in their hate of France for signs
Of her disasters,[9] if the stream of rumour
625 Brought with it one green branch, conceited[1] thence
That not a single tree was left alive
In all her forests. How could I believe
That wisdom could in any shape come near
Men clinging to delusions so insane?
630 And thus, experience proving that no few
Of my opinions had been just, I took
Like credit to myself where less was due,
And thought that other motions were as sound,
Yea could not but be right, because I saw
That foolish Men opposed them.
635   To a strain
More animated I might here give way
And tell, since juvenile errors are my theme,
What in those days through Britain was performed
To turn all judgments out of their right course;
640 But this is passion over near ourselves,[2]
Reality too close and too intense,
And mingled up with something in my mind
Of scorn and condemnations personal,
That would profane the sanctity of verse.
645 Our Shepherds (this say merely) at that time
Thirsted to make the guardian Crook of Law
A tool of Murder; they who ruled the State,
Though with such awful proof before their eyes
That he who would sow death, reaps death, or worse,
650 And can reap nothing better, child-like, longed
To imitate, not wise enough to avoid,
Giants in their impiety alone,
But, in their weapons and their warfare base
As vermin working out of reach, they leagued
655 Their strength perfidiously, to undermine
Justice, and make an end of Liberty.[3]
            But from these bitter truths I must return
To my own History. It hath been told[4]
That I was led to take an eager part
660 In arguments of civil polity
Abruptly, and indeed before my time:

8. That is, those who, frightened by the Terror, sought for signs of improvement in the French situation were acting as futilely as those who built the Tower of Babel in the hope of reaching heaven (Genesis 11.3–9).
9. The subject of the verb *laughed* is *I*, the poet himself.
1. Conceived (a now-obsolete usage). *Prel 1805* (CW) notes that the references to *Deluge* (line 619) and *one green branch* suggest an ironic allusion to Genesis 8:6–12.
2. Too personal to be described with propriety.
3. That is, the British government (*Our Shepherds*, line 645), seeking to imitate the repressiveness of Robespierre's regime, undermined justice and liberty, although not by open violence but covertly, like rats hiding in the walls (*vermin working out of reach*). WW himself, while living in Alfoxden, had been watched by a government spy in August 1797 (Gill, 127–28).
4. In 9.294–543. WW again recalls his state of mind in 1791–92.

I had approached, like other Youth, the Shield
Of human nature from the golden side[5]
And would have fought even to the death to attest
665 The quality of the metal which I saw.
What there is best in individual Man,
Of wise in passion, and sublime in power,
What there is strong and pure in household love,
Benevolent in small societies,
670 And great in large ones also, when called forth
By great occasions, these were things of which
I something knew, yet even these themselves,
Felt deeply,[6] were not thoroughly understood
By Reason; nay far from it, they were yet,
675 As cause was given me afterwards to learn,
Not proof against the injuries of the day,
Lodged only at the Sanctuary's door,
Not safe within its bosom.[7] Thus prepared,
And with such general insight into evil,
680 And of the bounds which sever it from good,
As books and common intercourse with life
Must needs have given (to the noviciate[8] mind,
When the world travels in a beaten road,
Guide faithful as is needed), I began
685 To think with fervour upon management
Of Nations, what it is and ought to be,
And how their worth depended on their Laws
And on the Constitution of the State.[9]
        Oh! pleasant exercise of hope and joy!
690 For great were the auxiliars[1] which then stood
Upon our side, we who were strong in love!
Bliss was it in that dawn to be alive,
But to be young was very heaven: oh! times,
In which the meagre, stale, forbidding ways
695 Of custom, law, and statute took at once
The attraction of a Country in Romance;
When Reason seemed the most to assert her rights
When most intent on making of herself
A prime Enchanter to assist the work

5. *Shield . . . golden side*: WW alludes to a fable (told in the *Moralities* of "Sir Harry Beaumont," i.e., Joseph Spence, 1753) in which two knights, approaching from opposite directions a shield that is gold on one side and silver on the other, dispute which metal the shield is made of until a third knight arrives to settle the argument. Lines 662–65 (line 662 shortened to "the shield") and 689–727 were published with minor variants in STC's periodical *The Friend* on October 26, 1809, in the second part of an essay "On the Errors of Party Spirit," where he quotes the passages (identified as Wordsworth's) in connection with his assertion, "Many there were, young Men of the loftiest minds, yea the prime stuff out of which manly Wisdom and practicable Greatness is to be formed, who had appropriated their hopes and the ardour of their souls to Mankind at large, to the wide expanse of national Interests, which then seemed fermenting in the French Republic" (*Friend*, 2:147).
6. I.e., although felt deeply.
7. A reference to the immunity, under medieval law, of fugitives and debtors from arrest within a church.
8. Inexperienced (from *novice*, a candidate for admission to a religious order).
9. Compare the conversations with Michel Beaupuy reported in 9.328–36.
1. Allies, helpers.

700 Which then was going forwards in her name.
    Not favoured spots alone, but the whole earth
    The beauty wore of promise, that which sets,
    To take an image which was felt, no doubt,
    Among the bowers of paradise itself,
705 The budding rose above the rose full blown.
    What temper[2] at the prospect did not wake
    To happiness unthought-of? The inert
    Were rouzed, and lively natures rapt away.[3]
    They who had fed their childhood upon dreams,
710 The Playfellows of Fancy, who had made
    All powers of swiftness, subtilty, and strength
    Their ministers, used to stir in lordly wise
    Among the grandest objects of the sense
    And deal with whatsoever they found there
715 As if they had within[4] some lurking right
    To wield it: they too, who, of gentle mood,
    Had watched all gentle motions, and to these
    Had fitted their own thoughts, schemers more mild,
    And in the region of their peaceful selves,[5]
720 Did now find helpers to their hearts' desire,
    And stuff at hand, plastic as they could wish,
    Were called upon to exercise their skill,
    Not in Utopia, subterraneous fields,
    Or some secreted Island, Heaven knows where,
725 But in the very world which is the world
    Of all of us, the place on which, in the end,
    We find our happiness, or not at all.[6]
        Why should I not confess that earth was then
    To me what an inheritance new-fallen
730 Seems, when the first time visited, to one
    Who thither comes to find in it his home?
    He walks about and looks upon the place
    With cordial transport, moulds it, and remoulds,
    And is half-pleased with things that are amiss,
735 'Twill be such joy to see them disappear.
        An active partisan, I thus convoked[7]
    From every object pleasant circumstance

---

2. Temperament.
3. Enraptured.
4. This word was inserted in pencil by MW.
5. In *The Friend* WW inserted a line, retained in subsequent reprintings (see the next note): "Now was it that both found, the Meek and Lofty."
6. In lines 723–27 WW recalls lines 47–55 of his Prospectus to *The Recluse*, composed in 1800 and published in the Preface to *Exc* (p. 445 below). WW published lines 689–727 as a separate poem, under the title *The French Revolution, as It Appeared to Enthusiasts at Its Commencement*, in *P 1815* and collections thereafter. A footnote explained that the lines were "from the unpublished poem of which some account is given in the Preface to the Excursion." Printing them in *The Friend* in 1809, STC introduced them as follows: "My honoured Friend has permitted me to give a value and relief to the Present Essay, by a quotation from one of his unpublished Poems ° ° °. I trust there are many of my Readers of the same Age with myself, who will throw themselves back into the state of thought and feeling, in which they were when France was reported to have solemnized her first sacrifice of error and prejudice on the bloodless altar of Freedom, by an Oath of Peace and Good-will to all Mankind" (*Friend*, 2:147).
7. Summoned.

To suit my ends; I moved among mankind
With genial feelings still predominant;
740 When erring, erring on the better part,
And in the kinder spirit; placable,
Indulgent oft-times to the worst desires,
As, on one side, not uninformed that men
See as it hath been taught them, and that time
745 Gives rights to error: on the other hand
That throwing off oppression must be work
As well of licence as of liberty;[8]
And above all, for this was more than all,
Not caring if the wind did now and then
750 Blow keen upon an eminence that gave
Prospect so large into futurity, happy,[9]
In brief, a child of nature, as at first,
Diffusing only those affections wider
That from the cradle had grown up with me,
755 And losing, in no other way than light
Is lost in light, the weak in the more strong.
          In the main outline, such it might be said
Was my condition, till with open war
Britain opposed the Liberties of France:[1]
760 This threw me first out of the pale of love,
Soured, and corrupted upwards to the source
My sentiments, was not,[2] as hitherto,
A swallowing up of lesser things in great,
But change of them into their opposites,
765 And thus a way was opened for mistakes
And false conclusions of the intellect
As gross in their degree, and in their kind
Far, far more dangerous. What had been a pride
Was now a shame; my likings and my loves
770 Ran in new channels, leaving old ones dry,
And thus a blow which in maturer age
Would but have touched the judgement, struck more deep
Into sensations near the heart: meantime,
As from the first, wild theories were afloat,[3]
775 Unto the subtleties of which, at least,
I had but lent a careless ear, assured
Of this, that time would soon set all things right,

8. A distinction made by Milton in, e.g., his Sonnet 12, lines 11–14: "Licence they mean when they cry libertie; / For who loves that [liberty], must first be wise and good; / But from that mark how far they roave we see / For all this wast of wealth, and loss of blood."
9. This hypermetrical word, present in both MSS B and A, is also crossed out in pencil in both, and was deleted permanently in WW's 1818–20 revisions. In his *Letter to the Bishop of Llandaff*, written in 1793 but not published in his lifetime, WW ridiculed the bishop, "[a]t a period big with the fate of the human race," for attaching "so much attention to the personal sufferings of the late royal martyr" (*Prose*, 1:32).
1. France declared war on Britain on February 1, 1793, and Britain declared war on France ten days later.
2. I.e., there was not.
3. *OxPrel* asserts that by *wild theories* WW means the political philosophy of William Godwin, whose *Enquiry concerning Political Justice* was published in February 1793. WW does refer to Godwin below, lines 805–29.

Prove that the multitude had been oppressed,
And would be so no more.
                            But when events
780 Brought less encouragement, and unto these
The immediate proof of principles no more
Could be entrusted, while the events themselves,
Worn out in greatness and in novelty,
Less occupied the mind, and sentiments
785 Could through my understanding's natural growth
No longer justify themselves through faith
Of inward consciousness, and hope that laid
Its hand upon its object; evidence
Safer, of universal application, such
790 As could not be impeached was sought elsewhere.
        And now, become Oppressors in their turn,
Frenchmen had changed a war of self-defence
For one of conquest, losing sight of all
Which they had struggled for; and mounted up
795 Openly in the view of earth and heaven
The scale of Liberty.[4] I read her doom,
Vexed inly somewhat, it is true, and sore,
But not dismayed, nor taking to the shame
Of a false Prophet; but, rouzed up I stuck
800 More firmly to old tenets, and to prove
Their temper, strained them more, and thus in heat
Of contest did opinions every day
Grow into consequence[5] till round my mind
They clung, as if they were the life of it.
805   This was the time when all things tended fast
To depravation; the Philosophy
That promised to abstract the hopes of man
Out of his feelings, to be fixed thenceforth
For ever in a purer element,
810 Found ready welcome.[6] Tempting region that
For Zeal to enter and refresh herself,
Where passions had the privilege to work,
And never hear the sound of their own names:[7]
But, speaking more in charity, the dream

4. In 1793 the French Revolutionary army was expelled from Belgium and busied with suppressed rebellions in France itself; but in 1794 it went on the offensive, reoccupying Belgium and the Rhineland and launching invasions against northern Spain and Piedmont (northwestern Italy). By the end of the following year, having occupied Holland and secured peace from Prussia and Spain, France could devote its military efforts solely to conquest. WW's metaphor of Liberty being weighed in the balance (scale) recalls the golden scales hung in the heavens by God in Paradise Lost 4.996–1005 and by Zeus in Homer's Iliad 8.66–77.
5. Assume the status of facts prove / Their temper (lines 800–801): test their strength.
6. A reference to Godwin's Enquiry concerning Political Justice, which opposed all forms of government force and argued that individuals can be motivated solely by reason to act benevolently towards others. The work's mixture of utilitarianism, individualism, rationalism, and optimism was well received in English radical circles in the early 1790s, including WW, who met Godwin at least nine times between February and August 1795 (Chrono: EY, 164–66, 182–83). But as the war between France and Britain continued, Godwin was increasingly attacked in the press. In lines 814–29 WW offers a mocking summary of Godwin's philosophy.
7. That is, Godwin's claims for the power of reason were themselves emotional rather than rational.

815 Was flattering to the young ingenuous mind
Pleased with extremes, and not the least with that
Which makes the human Reason's naked self
The object of its fervour: what delight!
How glorious! in self-knowledge and self-rule
820 To look through all the frailties of the world
And, with a resolute mastery shaking off
The accidents of nature, time, and place
That make up the weak being of the past,
Build social freedom on its only basis,
825 The freedom of the individual mind,
Which, to the blind restraint of general laws
Superior, magisterially adopts
One guide, the light of circumstances, flashed
Upon an independent intellect.[8]
830   For howsoe'er unsettled, never once
Had I thought ill of human kind, or been
Indifferent to its welfare; but, enflamed
With thirst of a secure intelligence
And sick of other passion, I pursued
835 A higher nature, wished that man should start
Out of the worm-like state in which he is,
And spread abroad the wings of Liberty,
Lord of himself in undisturbed delight.[9]
A noble aspiration, yet I feel[1]
840 The aspiration, but with other thoughts
And happier; for I was perplexed, and sought
To accomplish the transition by such means
As did not lie in nature, sacrificed
The exactness of a comprehensive mind
845 To scrupulous and microscopic views
That furnished out materials for a work
Of false imagination, placed beyond
The limits of experience and of truth.
    Enough, no doubt, the advocates themselves
850 Of ancient institutions had performed
To bring disgrace upon their very names,[2]
Disgrace of which custom and written law
And sundry moral sentiments, as props
And emanations of these institutes,
855 Too justly bore a part. A veil had been

---

8. Lines 825–29 are adapted from WW's tragedy *The Borderers* (composed 1796–97, published 1842) 3.5.31–35, in which the manipulative Rivers, whose "reason is almost exclusively employed in justifying his past enormities and in enabling him to commit new ones" (as WW explains in his Preface), congratulates the impressionable Mortimer for having (as Rivers mistakenly believes) murdered the elderly baron Herbert: "You have obeyed the only law that wisdom / Can ever recognize: the immediate law / Flashed from the light of circumstances / Upon an independent intellect" (*The Borderers* [CW], 210).
9. Lines 835–38 recall Edmund Spenser's *Muiopotmos: or the Fate of the Butterfly* (1590), lines 209–11: "What more felicitie can fall to creature, / Than to enjoy delight with libertie, / And to be Lord of all the workes of Nature."
1. I still feel.
2. The names of the institutions.

Uplifted; why deceive ourselves? 'Twas so,
'Twas even so, and sorrow for the Man
Who either had not eyes wherewith to see,
Or seeing hath forgotten. Let this pass;
860   Suffice it that a shock had then been given
To old opinions, and minds of all men
Had felt it; that my mind was both let loose,
Let loose and goaded.[3] After what hath been
Already said of patriotic love,
865   And hinted at in other sentiments,
We need not linger long upon this theme.
This only may be said, that from the first
Having two natures in me, joy the one,
The other melancholy, and withal
870   A happy man, and therefore bold to look
On painful things, slow, somewhat, too, and stern
In temperament, I took the knife in hand
And, stopping not at parts less sensitive,
Endeavoured with my best of skill to probe
875   The living body of society
Even to the heart: I pushed without remorse
My speculations forward; yea, set foot
On Nature's holiest places. Time may come
When some dramatic story may afford
880   Shapes livelier to convey to thee, my Friend,
What then I learned or think I learned of truth
And the errors into which I was betrayed
By present objects, and by reasonings false
From the beginning,[4] inasmuch as drawn
885   Out of a heart which had been turned aside
From nature by external accidents,
And which was thus confounded more and more,
Misguiding and misguided. Thus I fared,
Dragging all passions, notions, shapes of faith
890   Like culprits to the bar, suspiciously
Calling the mind to establish in plain day
Her titles[5] and her honours, now believing,
Now disbelieving, endlessly perplexed
With impulse, motive, right and wrong, the ground
895   Of moral obligation, what the rule
And what the sanction, till, demanding proof
And seeking it in every thing, I lost
All feeling of conviction, and, in fine,[6]
Sick, wearied out with contrarieties,
900   Yielded up moral questions in despair,

---

3. That is, *let loose* by the French Revolution from *old opinions* and *goaded* by it to form new ones.
4. Possibly, as *NCPrel* suggests, an anticipation of *The Excursion* (the narrative section of the projected *Recluse*), in books 3 and 4 of which the Solitary, dejected by the failure of the French Revolution and disappointed in his hopes for humanity, finds solace in communion with nature and the powers of the imagination.
5. Credentials. The simile is of passions and ideas being questioned like the defendant in a trial.
6. In the end.

And for my future studies, as the sole
Employment of the enquiring faculty,
Turned towards mathematics,[7] and their clear
And solid evidence.—Ah! then it was
905 That Thou, most precious Friend! about this time
First known to me, didst lend a living help
To regulate my Soul, and then it was
That the belovèd Woman[8] in whose sight
Those days were passed, now speaking in a voice
910 Of sudden admonition like a brook
That does but cross a lonely road, and now
Seen, heard, and felt, and caught at every turn,
Companion never lost through many a league,
Maintained for me a saving intercourse
915 With my true self; for, though impaired and changed
Much, as it seemed, I was no further changed
Than as a clouded, not a waning moon:[9]
She in the midst of all preserved me still
A Poet, made me seek beneath that name
920 My office upon earth, and nowhere else;
And lastly,[1] Nature's self, by human love
Assisted, through the weary labyrinth
Conducted me again to open day,
Revived the feelings of my earlier life,
925 Gave me that strength and knowledge full of peace,
Enlarged and never more to be disturbed,
Which through the steps of our degeneracy,
All degradation of this age, hath still
Upheld me, and upholds me at this day
930 In the catastrophe (for so they[2] dream,
And nothing less) when finally, to close
And rivet up the gains of France, a Pope
Is summoned in to crown an Emperor;
This last opprobrium, when we see the dog
935 Returning to his vomit,[3] when the sun
That rose in splendor, was alive, and moved
In exultation among living clouds,

7. Compare the reference to "Poetry and Geometric truth, / The knowledge that endures" (5.64–65). PPrel suggests that WW does not mean mathematics specifically, but more generally the "independent world / Created out of pure Intelligence" (6.186–87). NCPrel speculates that the intellectual crisis to which WW refers in lines 889–904 occurred in spring 1796, when he was reading the second edition of Godwin's Political Justice (see WL, 1:170).
8. DW, who moved with WW to Racedown, Dorset, on ca. September 26, 1795. Although WW must have met STC by that date, they were not in regular contact before June 1797. In his 1818–20 revisions WW omitted the apostrophe to STC in lines 904–907.
9. Compare Tintern Abbey, lines 116–22.
1. Referring back to then it was in line 904, i.e., the time of the intellectual crisis WW has been recalling.
2. Napoleon's supporters; catastrophe: dramatic conclusion (the etymological sense of the word).
3. An image from 2 Peter 2.22. WW refers to the fact that the abolition of the French monarchy in 1792 was succeeded by Napoleon's declaring himself Emperor of the French in May 1804. Napoleon, whose army had invaded Rome in 1798, summoned Pope Pius VII to Paris in November for a coronation modeled after those of the medieval Holy Roman Emperors. But at the ceremony itself, on December 4 (possibly after WW had composed these lines of The Prelude), Napoleon took the crown from the pope's hands and crowned himself.

Hath put his function and his glory off,
And, turned into a gewgaw, a machine,
940 Sets like an opera phantom.[4]
                            Thus, O Friend!
Through times of honour, and through times of shame
Have I descended, tracing faithfully
The workings of a youthful mind, beneath
The breath of great events, its hopes no less
945 Than universal, and its boundless love;[5]
A Story destined for thy ear, who now
Among the basest, and the lowest fallen
Of all the race of men, dost make abode
Where Etna looketh down on Syracuse,
950 The City of Timoleon.[6] Living God!
How are the Mighty prostrated![7] they first,
They first of all that breathe should have awaked
When the great voice was heard out of the tombs
Of ancient Heroes. If for France I have grieved
955 Who, in the judgment of no few, hath been
A trifler only, in her proudest day
Have been distressed to think of what she once
Promised, now is, a far more sober cause
Thine eyes must see of sorrow, in a Land
960 Strewed with the wreck of loftiest years,[8] a Land
Glorious indeed, substantially renowned
Of simple virtue once, and manly praise,
Now without one memorial hope, not even
A hope to be deferred; for that would serve
965 To chear the heart in such entire decay.
          But indignation works where hope is not,
And Thou, O Friend! wilt be refreshed. There is
One great Society alone on earth,
The noble Living and the noble Dead:[9]
970 Thy consolation shall be there, and Time

4. Mechanical sun in a stage set; *gewgaw*: "a gawdy trifle, plaything, or ornament" (*OED*).
5. WW did read the completed *Prelude* aloud to STC in early January 1807 (*Chrono: MY*, 345).
6. In August 1804 the Wordsworths received word of STC's intention to visit Sicily, and they had no further reports of his whereabouts until February 1805 (*WL*, 1:498, 521n). When WW composed these lines, he could therefore imagine that STC was *now* (line 946) on the island. In fact STC was there from August 10 to November 7, 1804, mostly in or near Syracuse. *Etna*: Mount Etna (ca. 11,000 feet), on the eastern side of Sicily, Europe's highest active volcano (which STC climbed twice); *Timoleon*: Corinthian general (d. ca. 337 B.C.E.) who deposed the tyrant Dionysius the Younger (on whom see also 9.415–24) from Syracuse in 343 B.C.E., established a new constitution, and oversaw the city's regeneration. (Although WW would not have known it, STC lodged at an estate on the site of Timoleon's villa outside Syracuse: see CN, 2:2915.) WW contrasts ancient with modern Sicily, which from 1735 to 1860 was ruled by the Neapolitan branch of the Spanish royal family, the Bourbons (the king from 1759 to 1825 being Ferdinand III). On December 12, 1804, STC wrote his wife, "of Sicily in general all is exaggerated grossly except the abominableness of the Government, & the vice & abject wretchedness of the people" (*CL*, 2:1157).
7. An adaptation of David's lament for Saul and Jonathan in 2 Samuel 1.19: "how are the mighty fallen!"
8. *PPrel* notes a recollection of William Cowper's *The Task* (1785) 2.75–77: "Alas for Sicily! rude fragments now / Lie scatter'd where the shapely column stood. / Her palaces are dust."
9. An assertion repeated in *The Convention of Cintra* (1809), WW's published denunciation of the agreement of August 1808 whereby the defeated French forces were permitted to evacuate

And Nature shall before thee spread in store
Imperishable thoughts, the place itself
Be conscious of thy presence, and the dull
Sirocco[1] air of its degeneracy
975　Turn as thou mov'st into a healthful breeze
To cherish and invigorate thy frame.
　　　Thine be those motions strong and sanative,[2]
A ladder for thy Spirit to reascend
To health and joy and pure contentedness:
980　To me the grief confined, that Thou art gone
From this last spot of earth where Freedom now
Stands single in her only Sanctuary,[3]
A lonely Wanderer, art gone, by pain
Compelled and sickness, at this latter day,
985　This heavy time of change[4] for all mankind;
I feel for Thee, must utter what I feel;
The sympathies, erewhile, in part discharged,
Gather afresh, and will have vent again;
My own delights do scarcely seem to me
990　My own delights, the lordly Alps themselves,
Those rosy Peaks from which the Morning looks
Abroad on many Nations, are not now,
Since thy migration and departure, Friend,
The gladsome image in my memory
995　Which they were used to be; to kindred scenes,
On errand, at a time how different!
Thou takest[5] thy way, carrying a heart more ripe
For all divine enjoyment, with the soul
Which Nature gives to Poets, now by thought
1000　Matured, and in the summer of its strength.
Oh! wrap him in your Shades, ye Giant Woods,
On Etna's side, and thou, O flowery Vale
Of Enna![6] is there not some nook of thine,

---

from Portugal without interference from the victorious British forces: "There is a spiritual community binding together the living and the dead; the good, the brave and the wise, of all ages. We would not be rejected from that community; and therefore do we hope" (*Prose*, 1:339). This idea of community may be derived from Edmund Burke's definition of society as "a partnership not only between those who are living, but between those who are living, those who are dead, and those who are to be born" (*Reflections on the Revolution in France* [London, 1790], 144).
1. Hot wind blowing from North Africa over the Mediterranean, here a metaphor for Sicily's *degeneracy* under the Bourbon dynasty.
2. Healing, curative. A reference, as in 6.249–50, to STC's hope of recovering his health in the Mediterranean.
3. I.e., Britain, which from May 1803 to April 1805 conducted the war against Napoleonic France without allies.
4. Art gone . . . change: WW incorporates quotations from Milton's elegy *Lycidas*, line 37: "But O the heavy change, now thou art gon[e]."
5. Pronounced as one syllable. WW contrasts the European political climate of 1804 with the hopeful one he had experienced during his walking tour of 1790, "a time when Europe was rejoiced, / France standing on the top of golden hours, / And human nature seeming born again" (6.352–54).
6. Province in central Sicily where, in classical myth (e.g., Ovid, *Metamorphoses* 5.385–408), the goddess Proserpina is abducted by the god Pluto, ruler of the underworld. WW's phrase recalls *Paradise Lost* 4.268–71: "Not that faire field / Of Enna, where Proserpin gathering flours / Her self a fairer Floure by gloomie Dis [Pluto] / Was gatherd."

From the first play-time of the infant earth,
1005   Kept sacred to restorative delight?
                    Child of the mountains, among Shepherds reared,
        Even from my earliest school-day time, I loved
        To dream of Sicily; and now a strong[7]
        And vital promise wafted from that Land
1010   Comes o'er my heart: there's not a single name
        Of note belonging to that honoured Isle,
        Philosopher or Bard, Empedocles
        Or Archimedes,[8] deep and tranquil Soul,
        That is not like a comfort to my grief.
1015   And O Theocritus! so far have some
        Prevailed among the Powers of heaven and earth
        By force of graces which were theirs, that they
        Have had, as thou reportest, miracles
        Wrought for them in old time; yea, not unmoved
1020   When thinking of my own belovèd Friend,
        I hear thee tell how bees with honey fed
        Divine Comates, by his tyrant Lord
        Within a Chest imprisoned impiously,
        How with their honey from the fields they came
1025   And fed him there, alive from month to month
        Because the Goatherd, blessèd Man! had lips
        Wet with the Muse's Nectar.[9]
                            Thus I soothe
        The pensive moments by this calm fire-side[1]
        And find a thousand fancied images
1030   That chear the thoughts of those I love, and mine:
        Our prayers have been accepted: Thou wilt stand,[2]
        Not as an Exile but a Visitant
        On Etna's top; by pastoral Arethuse[3]
        (Or if that Fountain be indeed no more,
1035   Then near some other Spring, which by the name

---

7. This word is written over an erased word, no longer legible but presumably "sweet" as in MS A. In line 1009, *vital* is also written over an erased word, possibly "gladsome" as in MS A.
8. WW recalls distinguished figures from Sicily's time as a Greek colony (ca. 735 to 241 B.C.E.): *Empedocles* (ca. 492–423 B.C.E.), philosopher from Acragas (modern Agrigento) who formulated the classical theory of the four elements (earth, water, fire, and air) and is popularly supposed to have jumped into the crater of Mt. Etna; *Archimedes* (ca. 287–ca. 212 B.C.E.), mathematician and inventor from Syracuse who created the science of hydrostatics.
9. WW summarizes the story of the goatherd Comates from the *Idylls* 7.78–85 of the Syracusan pastoral poet Theocritus (early third century B.C.E.).
1. I.e., at Dove Cottage.
2. Possibly an allusion to the statement attributed to Archimedes (with reference to the action of a lever), "Give me a place to stand, and I shall move the earth," or more likely to STC's motto "He hath stood," a pun on the meaning of his initials in (ungrammatical) Greek (see NCC, 136 n. 1, 226 n. 3).
3. Arethusa, a spring on the island of Ortygia in Syracuse, into which, in classical myth (e.g., Ovid's *Metamorphoses* 5.572–641), the nymph of the same name was said to have been transformed in her unsuccessful attempt to flee the river god Alpheus, who flowed under the sea to be united with her. Both Virgil (*Eclogues* 10.1–5) and Milton (*Lycidas*, line 85) invoke Arethusa as a muse, and STC refers to the myth of Alpheus in *Kubla Khan* (composed 1797 or 1798), lines 3–5: "Where ALPH, the sacred river, ran / Through caverns measureless to man / Down to a sunless sea" (NCC, 182).

Thou gratulatest, willingly deceived)
Shalt linger as a gladsome Votary,[4]
And not a Captive, pining for his home.

Book Eleventh

IMAGINATION, HOW IMPAIRED AND RESTORED

Long time hath man's unhappiness and guilt
Detained us; with what dismal sights beset
For the outward view, and inwardly oppressed
With sorrow, disappointment, vexing thoughts,
5 Confusion of the judgment, zeal decayed,
And lastly, utter loss of hope itself,
And things to hope for. Not with these began
Our Song, and not with these our Song must end.[1]
Ye motions of delight that through the fields
10 Stir gently, breezes and soft airs that breathe
The breath of paradise, and find your way
To the recesses of the soul! Ye Brooks
Muttering along the stones, a busy noise
By day, a quiet one in silent night,
15 And you, Ye Groves, whose ministry it is
To interpose the covert of your shades,
Even as a sleep, betwixt the heart of man
And the uneasy world, 'twixt man himself,
Not seldom, and his own unquiet heart,
20 Oh! that I had a music, and a voice,
Harmonious as your own, that I might tell
What ye have done for me. The morning shines,
Nor heedeth Man's perverseness; Spring returns,
I saw the Spring return when I was dead
25 To deeper hope;[2] yet had I joy for her,
And welcomed her benevolence, rejoiced
In common with the Children of her love,
Plants, insects, beast in field, and bird in bower.
So neither were complacency nor peace,
30 Nor tender yearnings wanting for my good
Through those distracted times;[3] in Nature still

4. Devotee, worshipper; *gratulatest*: greet, salute. In MSS B and A the closing parenthesis is placed at the end of line 1034, but the clause in lines 1035–36 is grammatically dependent on line 1034 and should therefore be included within the parenthesis. STC observed women washing clothes in the fountain in October 1804 (*Shorter Works and Fragments*, ed. H. J. Jackson and J. R. de J. Jackson [Princeton, 1995], 145–46), and it now flows into a small pond created in 1843.
1. An allusion to *The Idiot Boy* in *LB*, lines 445–46: "And with the owls began my song, / And with the owls must end." WW may also be alluding to a personal loss: on February 11, 1805, he was informed that his brother John (see Biographical and Topographical Glossary) had drowned at sea. Further work on *The Prelude* was interrupted until ca. late April, when he composed books 11 and 12 (*Chrono: MY*, 289; *Prel 1805* [CW], xi). In the first draft, MS Z, the book began with what became line 42 (*Prel 1805* [CW], 2:438).
2. A recollection of *Paradise Lost* 3.41–42: "Thus with the Year / Seasons return, but not to me return / Day, or the sweet approach of Ev'n or Morn."
3. Of WW's intellectual crisis described in 10.889–904 (i.e., possibly spring 1796); *complacency*: satisfaction.

      Glorying, I found a counterpoise in her,
      Which, when the spirit of evil was at height
      Maintained for me a secret happiness.
35 Her I resorted to, and loved so much
      I seemed to love as much as heretofore;
      And yet this passion, fervent as it was,
      Had suffered change; how could there fail to be
      Some change, if merely hence, that years of life
40 Were going on, and with them loss or gain
      Inevitable, sure alternative.
            This History, my Friend! hath chiefly told
      Of intellectual power, from stage to stage
      Advancing, hand in hand with love and joy,
45 And of imagination teaching truth
      Until that natural graciousness of mind
      Gave way to over-pressure of the times
      And their disastrous issues. What availed,
      When Spells forbade the Voyager to land,
50 The fragrance which did ever and anon
      Give notice of the Shore, from arbours breathed
      Of blessèd sentiment and fearless love?
      What did such sweet remembrances avail,
      Perfidious then, as seemed, what served they then?
55 My business was upon the barren seas,
      My errand was to sail to other coasts:[4]
      Shall I avow that I had hope to see,
      I mean that future times would surely see
      The Man to come parted as by a gulph
60 From him who had been, that I could no more
      Trust the elevation which had made me one
      With the great Family that here and there
      Is scattered through the abyss of ages past,
      Sage, Patriot, Lover,[5] Hero; for it seemed
65 That their best virtues were not free from taint
      Of something false and weak which could not stand
      The open eye of Reason. Then I said,
      Go to the Poets; they will speak to thee
      More perfectly of purer creatures, yet
70 If Reason be nobility in man,
      Can aught be more ignoble than the man
      Whom they describe, would fasten if they may
      Upon our love by sympathies of truth.
            Thus strangely did I war against myself;
75 A Bigot to a new Idolatry[6]

---

4. I.e., the claims of *blessèd sentiment and fearless love* seemed *perfidious* to WW when he was enchanted (*Spells*, line 49) by Godwin's philosophy (see the note on 10.810), which, however, he now regards as *barren*. The imagery of lines 48–56 recalls that of *Paradise Lost* 4.156–65, where Satan's delight in the scents of Eden is compared to that of sailors in the wind-blown "Odours from the spicie shoare / Of Araby the blest."
5. Revised in *Prel 1850* to "Warrior, Patriot."
6. Godwinian rationalism, implicitly compared here to Roman Catholicism (but note also the use of the word "Idols" in line 127 below).

Did like a Monk who hath forsworn the world
Zealously labour to cut off my heart
From all the sources of her former strength,
And, as by simple waving of a wand,
80   The wizard instantaneously dissolves
Palace or grove,[7] even so did I unsoul
As readily by syllogistic words,
Some charm of Logic ever within reach,
Those mysteries of passion which have made
85   And shall continue evermore to make
(In spite of all that Reason hath performed,
And shall perform, to exalt and to refine)
One brotherhood of all the human race
Through all the habitations of past years
90   And those to come; and hence an emptiness
Fell on the Historian's page, and even on that
Of Poets, pregnant with more absolute truth,[8]
The works of both withered in my esteem,
Their sentence was, I thought, pronounced, their rights
95   Seemed mortal, and their empire passed away.
              What then remained in such eclipse? what light
To guide or chear? The laws of things which lie
Beyond the reach of human will or power;
The life of nature by the God of love
100 Inspired, celestial presence ever pure;
These left, the soul of Youth must needs be rich,
Whatever else be lost, and these were mine,
Not a deaf echo, merely, of the thought,
Bewildered recollections, solitary,
105 But living sounds. Yet in despite of this,
This feeling, which howe'er impaired or damped,
Yet having been once born can never die.
'Tis true that Earth with all its appanage[9]
Of elements and organs, storm and sunshine,
110 With its pure forms and colours, pomp of clouds,
Rivers and mountains, objects among which
It might be thought that no dislike or blame,
No sense of weakness or infirmity
Or aught amiss could possibly have come,
115 Yea, even the visible universe was scanned
With something of a kindred spirit,[1] fell
Beneath the domination of a taste
Less elevated, which did in my mind
With its more noble influence interfere,
120 Its animation, and its deeper sway.

7. As Prospero makes the masque of classical goddesses disappear abruptly in Shakespeare's *The Tempest* 4.1.148–56.
8. WW recalls here Aristotle's description, referred to in the Preface to *LB* 1802 (see p. 86 above), of poetry as more philosophical than history.
9. A "natural or necessary * * * accompaniment, endowment" (*OED*). The pronoun *its* in lines 108 and 110 in MS B seems to be an authorial revision of "her" in MS A (*Prel 1805* [CW], 1:297n).
1. To the rationalism described in lines 74–90.

          There comes (if need be now to speak of this
          After such long detail of our mistakes),
          There comes a time when Reason, not the grand
          And simple Reason,[2] but that humbler power
125 Which carries on its no inglorious work
          By logic and minute analysis
          Is of all Idols[3] that which pleases most
          The growing mind. A Trifler would he be
          Who on the obvious benefits should dwell
130 That rise out of this process; but to speak
          Of all the narrow estimates of things
          Which hence originate were a worthy theme
          For philosophic Verse.[4] Suffice it here
          To hint that danger cannot but attend
135 Upon a Function rather proud to be
          The enemy of falshood than the friend
          Of truth, to sit in judgment than to feel.
               Oh! soul of Nature excellent and fair
          That didst rejoice with me, with whom I too
140 Rejoiced, through early youth before the winds
          And powerful waters, and in lights and shades
          That marched and countermarched about the hills
          In glorious apparition, now all eye
          And now all ear, but ever with the heart
145 Employed, and the majestic intellect,
          Oh! soul of Nature, that dost overflow
          With passion and with life, what feeble men
          Walk on this earth! how feeble have I been
          When thou wert in thy strength. Nor this thro' stroke
150 Of human suffering, such as justifies
          Remissness and inaptitude of mind,
          But through presumption,[5] even in pleasure pleased
          Unworthily, disliking here, and there
          Liking, by rules of mimic art transferred
155 To things above all art. But more, for this,[6]
          Although a strong infection of the age,
          Was never much my habit, giving way
          To a comparison of scene with scene,
          Bent overmuch on superficial things,
160 Pampering myself with meagre novelties
          Of colour or proportion, to the moods
          Of time or season to the moral power

2. *Grand / And simple Reason*: compare "reason in her most exalted mood" in 13.170.
3. Compare the reference to Godwinian rationalism as *Idolatry* in line 75 above, as well as the parenthetical concession to Reason in lines 86–87.
4. That is, *The Recluse*.
5. Presumptuousness, arrogance.
6. That is, the *disliking* and *liking* referred to in lines 153–54. The *infection* referred to in the following line is a purely aesthetic appreciation of nature, as in the fashionable eighteenth-century theory of the picturesque, which valued such qualities in landscape as variety, irregularity, and rusticity. One of the leading theorists of the picturesque was William Gilpin (1724–1800), whose *Observations on the River Wye* WW and DW may have used on their walk through the Wye valley in 1798 (see the note on line 19 of *Tintern Abbey*).

The affections, and the spirit of the place
Less sensible.[7] Nor only did the love
165 Of sitting thus in judgment interrupt
My deeper feelings, but another cause
More subtle and less easily explained
That almost seems inherent to the Creature,
Sensuous and intellectual as he is,
170 A twofold Frame of body, and of mind;
The state to which I now allude was one
In which the eye was master of the heart,
When that which is in every stage of life
The most despotic of our senses gained
175 Such strength in me as often held my mind
In absolute dominion. Gladly here,
Entering upon abstruser argument,
Would I endeavour to unfold the means
Which Nature studiously employs to thwart
180 This tyranny, summons all the senses each
To counteract the other and themselves,
And makes them all, and the objects with which all
Are conversant, subservient in their turn
To the great ends of Liberty and Power.
185 But this is matter for another Song;[8]
Here only let me add that my delights,
Such as they were, were sought insatiably,
Though 'twas a transport of the outward sense,
Not of the mind, vivid but not profound,
190 Yet was I often greedy in the chace,
And roamed from hill to hill, from rock to rock,
Still craving combinations of new forms,
New pleasure, wider empire for the sight,
Proud of its own en[dow]ments,[9] and rejoiced
195 To lay the inner faculties asleep.
         Amid the turns and counter-turns, the strife
And various trials of our complex being,
As we grow up, such thraldom of that sense
Seems hard to shun: and yet I knew a Maid,[1]
200 Who, young as I was then, conversed with things
In higher style; from appetites like these
She, gentle Visitant! as well she might,
Was wholly free; far less did critic rules
Or barren intermeddling subtilties
205 Perplex her mind; but wise as Women are

---

7. Sensitive, responsive.
8. *The Recluse*. WW omitted this line in *Prel 1850*, when it was clear that he would not complete *The Recluse*.
9. MS B has "enjoyments," almost certainly in error and "probably an inadvertent anticipation of 'rejoiced,'" as *Prel 1805* [CW] suggests. The word was altered in 1818–20 to "endowments," in accordance with the original reading in MS A. WW describes in lines 186–94 the same state of mind that he had described in *Tintern Abbey*, lines 68–74.
1. Mary Hutchinson (as in 6.233–36), whom WW had known since childhood and married in 1802. Like WW, she was born in 1770 (*young as I was then*).

When genial circumstance hath favored them,[2]
She welcomed what was given, and craved no more.
Whatever scene was present to her eyes,
That was the best, to that she was attuned
210 Through her humility and lowliness,
And through a perfect happiness of soul
Whose variegated feelings were in this
Sisters, that they were each some new delight:
For she was Nature's inmate.[3] Her the birds
215 And every flower she met with, could they but
Have known her, would have loved. Methought such
Of sweetness did her presence breathe around
That all the trees, and all the silent hills
And every thing she looked on should have had
220 An intimation how she bore herself
Towards them and to all creatures. God delights
In such a being; for her common thoughts
Are piety, her life is blessedness.
　　　　Even like this Maid, before I was called forth
225 From the retirement of my native hills,
I loved whate'er I saw;[4] nor lightly loved,
But fervently, did never dream of aught
More fair, more grand, more exquisitely framed
Than those few nooks to which my happy feet
230 Were limited. I had not at that time
Lived long enough, nor in the least survived
The first diviner influence of this world
As it appears to unaccustomed eyes;
I worshipped then among the depths of things
235 As my soul bade me: could I then take part
In aught but admiration, or be pleased
With any thing but humbleness and love?
I felt, and nothing else; I did not judge,
I never thought of judging, with the gift
240 Of all this glory filled and satisfied.
And afterwards, when through the gorgeous Alps
Roaming, I carried with me the same heart:
In truth, this degradation,[5] howsoe'er
Induced, effect in whatsoe'er degree
245 Of custom, that prepares such wantonness
As makes the greatest things give way to least,
Of any other cause that hath been named,

2. Good fortune; *Perplex her mind*: an allusion to WW's own poem *The Tables Turned* in *LB 1798*, lines 26–28: "Our meddling intellect / Misshapes the beauteous forms of things; / —We murder to dissect."
3. Companion, fellow dweller. In lines 214–21 WW adapts lines originally applied to his sister in the fragment *I would not strike a flower* (composed between October 6 and December 28, 1798), lines 25–31: "For she is Nature's inmate, and her heart / Is everywhere * * * And blessed are your days / That such delights are yours" (*LB* [CW], 313; and see also the source note on *Nutting*, p. 130 above).
4. That is, when WW left the Lake District for Cambridge in October 1787, aged seventeen.
5. Of the imagination, as described in lines 148–95 above; *Roaming*: in the summer of 1790; see 6.338–705.

Or lastly, aggravated by the times,[6]
Which with their passionate sounds might often make
250 The milder minstrelsies of rural scenes
Inaudible, was transient; I had felt
Too forcibly, too early in my life
Visitings of imaginative[7] power
For this to last: I shook the habit off
255 Entirely and for ever, and again
In Nature's presence stood, as I stand now,
A sensitive, and a creative Soul.
        There are in our existence spots of time,
Which with distinct preeminence retain
260 A renovating[8] Virtue, whence, depressed
By false opinion and contentious thought,
Or aught of heavier or more deadly weight,
In trivial occupations and the round
Of ordinary intercourse, our minds
265 Are nourished and invisibly repaired,
A virtue, by which pleasure is enhanced,
That penetrates, enables us to mount
When high, more high, and lifts us up when fallen.[9]
This efficacious spirit chiefly lurks
270 Among those passages of life in which
We have had deepest feeling that the mind
Is lord and master, and that outward sense
Is but the obedient servant of her will.
Such moments worthy of all gratitude
275 Are scattered every where, taking their date
From our first childhood; in our childhood even
Perhaps are most conspicuous. Life with me,
As far as memory can look back, is full
Of this beneficent influence. At a time
280 When scarcely (I was then not six years old)
My hand could hold a bridle, with proud hopes
I mounted, and we rode towards the hills:
We were a pair of Horsemen; honest James[1]
Was with me, my encourager and guide.
285 We had not travelled long ere some mischance
Disjoined me from my Comrade, and through fear
Dismounting, down the rough and stony Moor
I led my Horse, and stumbling on, at length

6. I.e., by the political events recounted in books 9 and 10.
7. MW originally wrote "the" before this word, then crossed out the definite article, in accordance with the reading in MS A.
8. Replacing "vivifying" (an alternative reading in MS A, incorporated as a correction in MS B), which in turn had replaced "fructifying" in *Prel 1799* 1.290. WW retained "renovating" in *Prel 1850*.
9. Lines 256–65 and 274–76 are incorporated with revisions from the original "spots of time" passage in *Prel 1799* 1.288–96. As NCPrel notes, the emphasis on the mind as *lord and master* (line 272) is an important addition to the new version.
1. Identified in *Prel 1850* as "An ancient Servant of my Father's House" (*Prel 1850* [CW] 239), "but not improbably a servant of his maternal grandparents, the Cooksons, in Penrith, where the events here recounted took place" (*Prel 1805* [CW]). Lines 279–316 are incorporated with revisions from *Prel 1799* 1.296–327.

Came to [a] bottom, where in former times
290   A Murderer had been hung in iron chains.[2]
The Gibbet mast was mouldered down, the bones
And iron case were gone, but on the turf
Hard by, soon after that fell[3] deed was wrought,
Some unknown hand had carved the Murderer's name.
295   The monumental[4] writing was engraven
In times long past, and still, from year to year,
By superstition of the neighbourhood
The grass is cleared away; and to this hour
The letters are all fresh and visible.[5]
300   Faltering, and ignorant where I was, at length
I chanced to espy those characters inscribed
On the green sod: forthwith I left the spot
And, reascending the bare common, saw
A naked Pool that lay beneath the hills,
305   The Beacon on the summit,[6] and more near
A Girl who bore a pitcher on her head
And seemed with difficult steps to force her way
Against the blowing mind. It was, in truth,
An ordinary sight; but I should need
310   Colours and words that are unknown to man
To paint the visionary dreariness
Which, while I looked all round for my lost Guide,
Did at that time invest the naked Pool,
The Beacon on the lonely Eminence,
315   The Woman, and her garments vexed and tossed
By the strong wind. When in a blessèd season
With those two dear Ones,[7] to my heart so dear,
When in the blessèd time of early love,
Long afterwards, I roamed about
320   In daily presence of this very scene;
Upon the naked pool and dreary crags,
And on the melancholy Beacon, fell
The spirit of pleasure, and youth's golden gleam;[8]
And think ye not with radiance more divine

2. If the story is true, the scene would have been the Cowdrake Quarry (ca. one mile east of the Penrith Beacon mentioned in line 305), where Thomas Nicholson was hanged on August 31, 1767, for the murder of Thomas Parker on November 18, 1766 (OxPrel). But NCPrel and Gill, 16, propose that WW conflates Nicholson's execution with that of the serial poisoner Thomas Lancaster, whose body was left to rot in 1672 in a gibbet adjacent to a small pond called the Priest Pot, ca. 1,000 feet southeast of Hawkshead and 500 feet north of Esthwaite Water. WW refers to this latter site in his Unpublished Tour of the Lake District: "Part of the Irons & some of the wood work remained in my memory" (Prose, 2:333). [a]: the indefinite article, present in MS A, was omitted in MS B, presumably inadvertently; bottom: valley, low-lying land.
3. Fierce, cruel.
4. Memorial.
5. Whether WW actually saw the letters cut in the turf or is remembering local legend is open to question; he does not refer to them in the corresponding passage in Prel 1799 1.310–13. J. Walker's History of Penrith (1858) reports that the letters were the murdered man's initials, although the murderer's initials would be more plausible (OxPrel, NCPrel).
6. Penrith Beacon, previously mentioned in 6.242.
7. DW and Mary Hutchinson, as in 6.208–45. In Prel 1850 WW altered the line to "Of early love, the loved One at my side" (Prel 1850 [CW], 241).
8. This line is repeated almost verbatim from 6.245.

325 From these remembrances, and from the power
    They left behind? So feeling comes in aid
    Of feeling, and diversity of strength
    Attends us, if but once we have been strong.
    Oh! mystery of Man, from what a depth
330 Proceed thy honours! I am lost, but see
    In simple childhood something of the base
    On which thy greatness stands, but this I feel,
    That from thyself it is that thou must give,
    Else never canst receive.⁹ The days gone by
335 Come back upon me from the dawn almost
    Of life: the hiding-places of my power
    Seem open; I approach, and then they close;
    I see by glimpses now; when age comes on
    May scarcely see at all; and I would give
340 While yet we may, as far as words can give,
    A substance and a life to what I feel;
    I would enshrine the spirit of the past
    For future restoration. Yet another
    Of these, to me, affecting incidents
    With which we will conclude.
345   One Christmas-time,
    The day before the Holidays began,
    Feverish, and tired, and restless, I went forth
    Into the fields, impatient for the sight
    Of those two Horses which should bear us home,
350 My Brothers and myself.¹ There was a Crag,²
    An Eminence, which from the meeting-point
    Of two high-ways ascending, overlooked
    At least a long half-mile of those two roads,
    By each of which the expected Steeds might come,
355 The choice uncertain. Thither I repaired
    Up to the highest summit: 'twas a day
    Stormy, and rough, and wild, and on the grass
    I sate, half-sheltered by a naked wall:
    Upon my right hand was a single sheep,
360 A [whistling]³ hawthorn on my left, and there,
    With those Companions at my side, I watched,
    Straining my eyes intensely, as the mist
    Gave intermitting prospect of the wood
    And plain beneath. Ere I to School returned
365 That dreary time, ere I had been ten days

9. *That from . . . receive:* An allusion to STC's *Dejection: An Ode*, lines 46–47 (quoted from the version printed in the *Morning Post*, October 4, 1802): "O EDMUND! we receive but what we give, / And in *our* life alone does Nature live." This poem, a response to WW's Intimations Ode, was first published in the *Morning Post* on WW's wedding day (and STC's own ninth wedding anniversary).
1. The day was perhaps December 19, 1783 (*Chrono: EY,* 58). WW was thirteen at the time, and his brothers Richard (1768–1816) and John (1772–1805) attended the Hawkshead Grammar School with him. Lines 346–89 are incorporated with minor revisions from *Prel 1799* 1.330–74.
2. Perhaps a ridge near Borwick Lodge, a mile-and-a-half north of Hawkshead.
3. A blank was left at this point in MS B; the adjective is supplied from MS A.

A Dweller in my Father's House, he died,
And I and my two Brothers,[4] Orphans then,
Followed his Body to the Grave. The event
With all the sorrow which it brought appeared
370   A chastisement; and when I called to mind
That day so lately passed, when from the crag
I looked in such anxiety of hope,
With trite reflections of morality,
Yet in the deepest passion, I bowed low
375   To God, who thus corrected my desires:
And afterwards the wind and sleety rain
And all the business[5] of the elements,
The single sheep and the one blasted tree,
And the bleak music of that old stone wall,
380   The noise of wood and water, and the mist
Which on the line of each of those two Roads
Advanced in such indisputable[6] shapes,
All these were spectacles and sounds to which
I often would repair, and thence would drink
385   As at a fountain: and I do not doubt
That in this later time, when storm and rain
Beat on my roof at midnight, or by day
When I am in the woods, unknown to me
The workings of my spirit thence are brought.
390   Thou wilt not languish here, O Friend! for whom
I travel in these dim uncertain ways;
Thou wilt assist me, as a Pilgrim gone
In quest of highest truth. Behold me then
Once more in Nature's presence thus restored,
395   Or otherwise,[7] and strengthened once again
(With memory left of what had been escaped)
To habits of devoutest sympathy.

Book Twelfth

SAME SUBJECT (CONTINUED)

From Nature doth emotion come, and moods
Of calmness equally are Nature's gift,
This is her glory; these two attributes
Are sister horns[1] that constitute her strength;
5   This twofold influence is the sun and shower
Of all her bounties, both in origin

---

4. Richard and John. The youngest brother, Christopher (1774–1846), was in Penrith during the funeral of their father (*WL*, 2:185), who had died on December 30, 1783. Their mother had died five years earlier (see 5.256–58).
5. Activity.
6. Stressed on the second syllable. The line alludes to Hamlet's address to his father's ghost: "Thou com'st in such a questionable shape / That I will speak to thee" (*Hamlet* 1.4.43–44).
7. *Thus . . . otherwise*: i.e., restored by this means or by another.
1. *Prel 1805* (CW) suggests a sense cited by the *OED* from Biblical and related contexts: "An emblem of power and might; a means of defence or resistance." Line 5 may also recall the horned rays in Habakkuk 3.4: "And his [God's] brightness was as the light; he had horns coming out of his hand: and there was the hiding of his power."

And end alike benignant. Hence it is,
That Genius, which exists by interchange
Of peace and excitation,[2] finds in her
10 His best and purest Friend, from her receives
That energy by which he seeks the truth,
Is rouzed, aspires, grasps, struggles, wishes, craves
From her that happy stillness of the mind
Which fits him to receive it when unsought.
15   Such benefit may souls of humblest frame
Partake of, each in their degree: 'tis mine
To speak of what myself have known and felt,
Sweet task! for words find easy way, inspired
By gratitude and confidence in truth.
20 Long time, in search of knowledge desperate,
I was benighted, heart and mind; but now[3]
On all sides day began to reappear,
And it was proved indeed that not in vain
I had been taught to reverence a Power[4]
25 That is the very quality and shape
And image of right reason,[5] that matures
Her processes by steady laws, gives birth
To no impatient or fallacious hopes,
No heat of passion or excessive zeal,
30 No vain conceits, provokes to no quick turns
Of self-applauding intellect, but lifts
The Being into magnanimity,[6]
Holds up before the mind, intoxicate
With present objects and the busy dance
35 Of things that pass away, a temperate shew
Of objects that endure, and by this course
Disposes her, when over-fondly set
On leaving her incumbrances behind,
To seek in Man, and in the frame of life
40 Social and individual, what there is
Desirable, affecting, good or fair
Of kindred permanence, the gifts divine
And universal, the pervading grace
That hath been, is, and shall be. Above all
45 Did nature bring again that wiser mood
More deeply reestablished in my soul,
Which, seeing little worthy or sublime
In what we blazon with the pompous names
Of power and action, early tutored me
50 To look with feelings of fraternal love

2. Stimulation, encouragement (a now-archaic sense in use into the nineteenth century).
3. I.e., after the crisis (possibly of spring 1796) described in 10.889–904.
4. Nature.
5. Presumably, "reason in her most exalted mood," identified with "clearest insight, amplitude of mind" in 13.169–70. The term "right reason" is used in Stoic philosophy to designate the order of nature, and in Christian theology and ethics to designate an innate faculty of moral judgment (as in *Paradise Lost* 6.41–43 and 12.83–85).
6. Literally, greatness of soul.

Upon those unassuming things that hold
A silent station in this beauteous world.
    Thus moderated, thus composed, I found
Once more in Man an object of delight,
55 Of pure imagination, and of love;
And, as the horizon of my mind enlarged,
Again I took the intellectual eye
For my instructor, studious more to see
Great Truths than touch and handle little ones,
60 Knowledge was given accordingly: my trust
Was firmer in the feelings which had stood
The test of such a trial; clearer far
My sense of what was excellent and right;
The promise of the present time retired
65 Into its true proportion; sanguine[7] schemes,
Ambitious virtues pleased me less; I sought
For good in the familiar face of life
And built thereon my hopes of good to come.[8]
    With settling judgments now of what would last
70 And what would disappear, prepared to find
Ambition, folly, madness, in the men
Who thrust themselves upon this passive world
As rulers of the world, to see in these,
Even when the public welfare is their aim;
75 Plans without thought, or bottomed[9] on false thought
And false philosophy: having brought to test
Of solid life and true result the Books
Of modern Statists, and thereby perceived
The utter hollowness of what we name
80 The wealth of Nations,[1] where alone that wealth
Is lodged and how encreased, and having gained
A more judicious knowledge of what makes
The dignity of individual Man,
Of Man, no composition of the thought,
85 Abstraction, shadow, image, but the man
Of whom we read, the man whom we behold
With our own eyes; I could not but inquire,
Not with less interest than heretofore,
But greater, though in a spirit more subdued,
90 Why is this glorious Creature to be found
One only in ten thousand? What one is,
Why may not many be? What bars are thrown
By nature in the way of such a hope?
Our animal wants, and the necessities
95 Which they impose, are these the obstacles?

---

7. Hopeful, confident.
8. *I sought . . . to come:* WW draws a contrast with his earlier Godwinian hopes, as summarized
   in ll.57–60.
9. Based, founded (a now-obsolete sense).
1. A general allusion to Adam Smith's *Inquiry into the Nature and Causes of the Wealth of Nations*
   (1776), a defense of free-market economies; *Statists:* political philosophers.

If not, then others vanish into air.
Such meditations bred an anxious wish
To ascertain how much of real worth
And genuine knowledge, and true power of mind
100 Did at this day exist in those who lived
By bodily labour, labour far exceeding[2]
Their due proportion, under all the weight
Of that injustice which upon ourselves
By composition of society
105 Ourselves entail. To frame such estimate
I chiefly looked (what need to look beyond?)
Among the natural abodes of men,
Fields with their rural works, recalled to mind
My earliest notices,[3] with these compared
110 The observations of my later youth
Continued downwards to that very day.
        For time had never been in which the throes
And mighty hopes of Nations, and the stir
And tumult of the world, to me could yield,
115 How far soe'er transported and possessed,
Full measure of content; but still I craved
An intermixture of distinct regards[4]
And truths of individual sympathy
Nearer ourselves. Such often might be gleaned
120 From that great City, else it must have been
A heart-depressing wilderness indeed,
Full soon to me a wearisome abode;
But much was wanting; therefore did I turn
To you, ye Pathways, and ye lonely Roads,
125 Sought you enriched with every thing I prized,
With human kindness, and with Nature's joy.
        Oh! next to one dear state of bliss vouchsafed
Alas! to few in this untoward[5] world,
The bliss of walking daily in Life's prime
130 Through field or forest with the Maid we love,
While yet our hearts are young, while yet we breathe
Nothing but happiness, living in some place,
Deep Vale, or any where, the home of both,
From which it would be misery to stir;
135 Oh! next to such enjoyment of our youth,
In my esteem, next to such dear delight
Was that of wandering on from day to day
Where I could meditate in peace, and find
The knowledge which I loved, and teach the sound

2. A hypermetric line, altered in *Prel 1850* to "By bodily toil, labour exceeding far" (*Prel 1850* [CW], 247).
3. Observations (of society).
4. Sights or experiences. That is, WW could not comprehend national and international events without some connection or reference to local, individual experience. Lines 112–277 derive from the conclusion of MS Y (composed ca. October 1804), following the draft of what became most of book 8 (see *Prel 1805* [CW], 2:413–20).
5. Unfortunate, vexatious.

140 Of Poet's music to strange fields and groves,
Converse with Men, where if we meet a face
We almost meet a friend; on naked Moors
With long, long ways before, by Cottage bench,
Or Well-spring, where the weary Traveller rests.
145   Few sights more please me than a public road:
'Tis my delight,[6] such object hath had power
O'er my imagination since the dawn
Of childhood, when its disappearing line,
Seen daily afar off on one bare steep[7]
150 Beyond the limits which my feet had trod,[8]
Was like a guide into eternity,
At least to things unknown, and without bound.
Even something of the grandeur which invests
The Mariner who sails the roaring sea
155 Through storm and darkness, early in my mind
Surrounded, too, the Wanderers of the Earth,
Grandeur as much, and loveliness far more:
Awed have I been by strolling Bedlamites,[9]
From many other uncouth Vagrants, passed
160 In fear, have walked with quicker step; but why
Take note of this? When I began to enquire,
To watch and question those I met, and held
Familiar talk with them, the lonely roads
Were schools to me in which I daily read
165 With most delight the passions of mankind,
There saw into the depth of human souls,
Souls that appear to have no depth at all
To vulgar eyes. And now, convinced at heart
How little that to which alone we give
170 The name of education hath to do
With real feeling and just sense, how vain
A correspondence with the talking world
Proves to the most, and called to make good search
If man's estate, by doom of Nature yoked
175 With toil, is therefore yoked with ignorance;
If virtue be indeed so hard to rear,
And intellectual strength so rare a boon,
I prized such walks still more; for there I found
Hope to my hope, and to my pleasure peace,
180 And steadiness, and healing, and repose
To every angry passion. There I heard

6. Lines 145–46 are a revision of the version in MS A: "I love a public road: few sights there are / That please me more * * *."
7. *Prel 1805* (CW) suggests that this word was MW's mistaken attempt to correct MS A's obviously incorrect "sleep." The draft of this line in MS Z (probably of early 1805) has the reading "slope" (*Prel 1805* [CW], 2:458). The line was expanded in *Prel 1850*: "One daily present to my eyes, that crossed / The naked summit of a far-off hill" (*Prel 1850* [CW], 248–49).
8. Identified in *OxPrel* as the road, which as a child WW could see from the garden of his house in Cockermouth, leading over Watch or Hay Hill to the village of Isel, three miles northeast of Cockermouth.
9. Madmen (a word derived from Bedlam, the popular name of the London insane asylum, on which see the note on 6.132).

From mouths of lowly men, and of obscure,
A tale of honour; sounds in unison
With loftiest promises of good and fair.
185   There are who think that strong affections, love
Known by whatever name, is falsely deemed
A gift, to use a term which they would use,
Of vulgar Nature, that its growth requires
Retirement, leisure, language purified
190 By manners thoughtful and elaborate,
That whoso feels such passion in excess
Must live within the very light and air
Of elegances that are made by Man.[1]
True is it, where oppression worse than death
195 Salutes the Being at his birth, where grace
Of culture hath been utterly unknown,
And labour in excess, and poverty
From day to day preoccupy the ground
Of the affections, and to Nature's self
200 Oppose a deeper nature, there indeed
Love cannot be; nor does it easily thrive
In cities, where the human heart is sick,
And the eye feeds it not, and cannot feed:
Thus far, no further, is that inference[2] good.
205   Yes, in those wanderings deeply did I feel
How we mislead each other, above all
How Books mislead us, looking for their fame
To judgments of the wealthy few, who see
By artificial lights, how they debase
210 The many for the pleasure of those Few,
Effeminately level down the truth
To certain general notions for the sake
Of being understood at once, or else
Through want of better knowledge in the men
215 Who frame them, flattering thus our self-conceit
With pictures that ambitiously set forth
The differences, the outside marks by which
Society has parted man from man,
Neglectful of the universal heart.[3]
220   Here, calling up to mind what then I saw,
A youthful traveller, and see daily now
Before me in my rural neighbourhood,
Here might I pause and bend in reverence
To Nature, and the power of human minds,

---

1. Lines 185–204, like the "Matron's Tale" in 8.222–311, were composed originally for *Michael* in October–December 1800, and revised for inclusion here.
2. I.e., of lines 185–93, that love requires cultivation.
3. *PPrel* notes the similar sentiment expressed in WW's letter of June 7, 1802, to John Wilson, an undergraduate at Glasgow University: "People in our rank of life are perpetually falling into one sad mistake, namely, that of supposing that human nature and the persons they associate with are one and the same thing. Whom do we generally associate with? Gentlemen, persons of fortune, professional men, ladies, persons who can afford to buy * * * books of half a guinea price * * *. These persons are, it is true, a part of human nature, but we err lamentably if we suppose them to be fair representatives of the vast mass of human existence" (*WL* 1:355).

225   To Men, as they are Men within themselves.
     How oft high service is performed within
     When all the external man is rude in shew,
     Not like a temple rich with pomp and gold
     But a mere mountain Chapel such as shields
230   Its simple worshippers from sun and shower.
     Of these, said I, shall be my song, of these,
     If future years mature me for the task,
     Will I record the praises, making Verse
     Deal boldly with substantial things, in truth
235   And sanctity of passion, speak of these
     That justice may be done, obeisance paid
     Where it is due: thus haply shall I teach,
     Inspire, through unadulterated[4] ears
     Pour rapture, tenderness, and hope, my theme
240   No other than the very heart of man
     As found among the best of those who live
     Not unexalted by religious hope,
     Not uninformed by books, good books, though few,
     In Nature's presence: thence may I select
245   Sorrow that is not sorrow, but delight,
     And miserable love that is not pain
     To hear of, for the glory that redounds
     Therefrom to human-kind and what we are.
     Be mine to follow with no timid step
250   Where knowledge leads me; it shall be my pride
     That I have dared to tread this holy ground,
     Speaking no dream, but things oracular,
     Matter not lightly to be heard by those
     Who to the letter of the outward promise
255   Do read the invisible soul,[5] by men adroit
     In speech and for communion with the world
     Accomplished, minds whose faculties are then
     Most active when they are most eloquent,
     And elevated most when most admired.[6]
260   Men may be found of other mold than these
     Who are their own upholders, to themselves
     Encouragement,[7] and energy, and will,
     Expressing liveliest thoughts in lively words
     As native passion dictates. Others, too,
265   There are among the walks of homely life
     Still higher, men for contemplation framed,
     Shy, and unpractised in the strife of phrase,
     Meek men, whose very souls perhaps would sink
     Beneath them, summoned to such intercourse:

4. Uncorrupted.
5. I.e., those who judge the inner qualities of others by their outward appearance.
6. Lines 231–59 recall WW's poetic manifesto in the Prospectus to *The Recluse* (composed in 1800 and published with *The Excursion* [see p. 444, below] in 1814).
7. Compare the "visitings / Of the Upholder, of the tranquil Soul / Which underneath all passion lives secure" in 3.115–17.

270 Theirs is the language of the heavens, the power,
The thought, the image, and the silent joy;
Words are but under-agents in their souls;
When they are grasping with their greatest strength
They do not breathe among them:[8] this I speak
275 In gratitude to God, who feeds our hearts
For his own service, knoweth, loveth us,
When we are unregarded by the world.[9]
        Also about this time did I receive
Convictions still more strong than heretofore
280 Not only that the inner frame is good,
And graciously composed, but that no less
Nature through all conditions hath a power
To consecrate, if we have eyes to see,
The outside of her creatures, and to breathe
285 Grandeur upon the very humblest face
Of human life. I felt that the array
Of outward circumstance and visible form
Is to the pleasure of the human mind
What passion makes it, that meanwhile the forms
290 Of nature have a passion in themselves
That intermingles with those works of man
To which she summons him, although the works
Be mean, have nothing lofty of their own;
And that the genius of the Poet hence
295 May boldly take his way among mankind
Wherever Nature leads, that he hath stood
By Nature's side among the Men of old,
And so shall stand for ever. Dearest Friend,
Forgive me if I say that I, who long
300 Had harboured reverentially a thought
That Poets, even as Prophets, each with each
Connected in a mighty scheme of truth,
Have, each for his peculiar dower,[1] a sense
By which he is enabled to perceive
305 Something unseen before: forgive me, Friend,
If I, the meanest of this Band, had hope
That unto me had also been vouchsafed
An influx,[2] that in some sort I possessed
A privilege, and that a work of mine,
310 Proceeding from the depth of untaught things,
Enduring and creative, might become

8. The antecedent is *Words* (line 272). That is, the world of the *Meek men* (line 268) is not a verbal one. NCPrel suggests that WW was thinking of (among others) his brother John, who was to drown a few months after these lines were composed.
9. Lines 223–77 were first published separately as the conclusion to the Postscript of WW's volume *Yarrow Revisited and Other Poems* (1835), in which he introduced the passage as "extracted from his MSS. written above thirty years ago: it turns upon the individual dignity which humbleness of social condition does not preclude, but frequently promotes" (*Prose*, 3:258).
1. Endowment, talent.
2. Inspiration (recalling the etymological sense of *influence*, "flow in," from the Latin *influere*).

A power like one of Nature's.[3] To such mood
Once above all, a Traveller at that time
Upon the plain of Sarum, was I raised;
315   There on the pastoral Downs[4] without a track
To guide me, or along the bare white roads
Lengthening in solitude their dreary line,
While through those vestiges of ancient times
I ranged, and by the solitude o'ercome,
320   I had a reverie and saw the past,
Saw multitudes of men, and here and there
A single Briton in his wolf-skin vest
With shield and stone axe stride across the Wold;[5]
The voice of spears was heard, the rattling spear
325   Shaken by arms of mighty bone, in strength
Long mouldered of barbaric majesty.
I called upon the darkness; and it took,
A midnight darkness seemed to come and take
All objects from my sight; and lo! again
330   The desart visible by dismal flames!
It is the sacrificial Altar, fed
With living men, how deep the groans,[6] the voice
Of those in the gigantic wicker thrills
Throughout the region far and near, pervades
335   The monumental hillocks;[7] and the pomp
Is for both worlds, the living and the dead.
At other moments, for through that wide waste
Three summer days I roamed, when 'twas my chance
To have before me on the downy Plain
340   Lines, circles, mounts, a mystery of shapes
Such as in many quarters yet survive,
With intricate profusion figuring o'er
The untilled ground, the work, as some divine,[8]
Of infant science, imitative forms
345   By which the Druids covertly expressed
Their knowledge of the heavens, and imaged forth
The constellations, I was gently charmed,

---

3. Compare WW's expressed hope in 6.67–69 of leaving behind a poetic "monument."
4. Treeless chalk hills, used for grazing sheep; *plain of Sarum*: Salisbury Plain (*Sarum* being the medieval Latin name for Salisbury), an area of ca. 300 square miles in central southern England, in which Stonehenge is located and which WW crossed on foot and alone ca. late July or early August 1793 on his way from the Isle of Wight (see 10.290–301) to Wales, where he was to stay with his friend Robert Jones (*Chrono: EY*, 165). Lines 315–53 derive generally from lines 172–89 of WW's poem *Salisbury Plain*, composed in 1793–94 (see *The Salisbury Plain Poems* [CW], 26–27).
5. Plain (a poetic word).
6. *It is . . . groans*: a passage taken verbatim from *Salisbury Plain*, lines 184–85.
7. Neolithic barrows (burial mounds), of which there are dozens in Salisbury Plain; *gigantic wicker*: a wicker effigy of human shape in which the Druids, an ancient Celtic priestly class, were claimed by Roman writers like Julius Caesar (*Gallic Wars* 6.16) to burn people in ritual sacrifice (also mentioned in *Salisbury Plain*, lines 424–32). In a notebook of 1796–97 (DC MS 12, fol. 49) WW listed nine references to Druids (eight in classical authors and one in the English Renaissance poet Michael Drayton). The source of his information about Druids for *Salisbury Plain* may have been Aylett Sammes's *Britannia Antiqua Illustrata: or, The Antiquities of Ancient Britain, Derived from the Phoenicians* (London, 1676), 103–105 (*The Salisbury Plain Poems* [CW], 35n).
8. Conjecture.

Albeit with an antiquarian's dream,
And saw the bearded Teachers, with white wands
350 Uplifted, pointing to the starry Sky
Alternately, and Plain below, while breath
Of music seemed to guide them, and the Waste
Was cheared with stillness and a pleasant sound.
      This for the past, and things that may be viewed
355 Or fancied in the obscurities of time.
Nor is it,[9] Friend, unknown to thee, at least
Thyself delighted, Thou for my delight
Hast said, perusing some imperfect verse
Which in that lonesome journey was composed,
360 That also I must then have exercised
Upon the vulgar forms of present things
And actual world of our familiar days
A higher power, have caught from them a tone,
An image, and a character, by books
365 Not hitherto reflected.[1] Call we this
But a persuasion taken up by Thee
In friendship: yet the mind is to herself
Witness and judge, and I remember well
That in life's every-day appearances
370 I seemed about this period to have sight
Of a new world, a world, too, that was fit
To be transmitted and made visible
To other eyes, as having for its base
That whence our dignity originates,
375 That which both gives it being and maintains
A balance, an ennobling interchange
Of action from within and from without,
The excellence, pure spirit, and best power
Both of the object seen, and eye that sees.[2]

9. Presumably referring, like *This* in line 354, to the *antiquarian's dream* described in lines 337–53.
1. WW refers to STC's reaction to *Salisbury Plain*, the original version of which was drafted probably between late July and September 1793 and completed by May 23, 1794 (*Chrono: EY*, 25). Evidently STC heard WW read this version of the poem in Bristol in August or September 1795 (*Chrono: EY*, 167), and he read and commented on the manuscript of the revised and expanded version of September–November 1795, *Adventures on Salisbury Plain*, in March 1796 (*Chrono: EY*, 179). STC was unable to publish *Adventures*, as he hoped, in his short-lived periodical *The Watchman* (see *The Salisbury Plain Poems* [CW], 7–8), and it remained unpublished—apart from the sections extracted from it and published in *LB* as *The Female Vagrant*—until 1842, when it appeared in further revised form as *Guilt and Sorrow*. In *BL*, chap. 4, STC recalled his reaction to WW's reading (without mentioning his own commentary on the manuscript of *Adventures*): "I shall hardly forget the sudden effect produced on my mind, by his recitation of a manuscript poem, which still remains unpublished * * *. There was here, no mark of strained thought, or forced diction, no crowd or turbulence of imagery; and * * * manly reflection, and human associations had given both variety, and an additional interest to natural objects" (*NCC*, 414 and n. 4).
2. *Prel 1805* (CW) clarifies the syntax of lines 373–79: the clauses beginning *That whence* and *That which* (lines 374 and 375) as well as the nouns *excellence, spirit,* and *power* in line 378 all refer back to *its base* in line 373.

Book Thirteenth

CONCLUSION

In one of these excursions, travelling then
Through Wales on foot, and with a youthful Friend,
I left Bethkelet's huts at couching-time,
And westward took my way to see the sun
5   Rise from the top of Snowdon.[1] Having reached
The Cottage at the Mountain's foot, we there
Rouzed up the Shepherd, who by ancient right
Of office is the Stranger's usual Guide,
And after short refreshment sallied forth.
10   —It was a Summer's night, a close warm night,
Wan, dull, and glaring,[2] with a dripping mist
Low-hung and thick that covered all the sky,
Half threatening storm and rain; but on we went
Unchecked, being full of heart, and having faith
15   In our tried Pilot.[3] Little could we see,
Hemmed round on every side with fog and damp,
And, after ordinary Travellers' chat
With our Conductor, silently we sunk
Each into commerce with his private thoughts:
20   Thus did we breast the ascent, and by myself
Was nothing either seen or heard the while
Which took me from my musings, save that once
The Shepherd's Cur[4] did to his own great joy
Unearth a Hedgehog in the mountain crags
25   Round which he made a barking turbulent.
This small adventure, for even such it seemed
In that wild place and at the dead of night,
Being over and forgotten, on we wound
In silence as before. With forehead bent
30   Earthward, as if in opposition set
Against an enemy, I panted up
With eager pace, and no less eager thoughts.
Thus might we wear perhaps an hour away,
Ascending at loose distance each from each,
35   And I, as chanced, the foremost of the Band,
When at my feet the ground appeared to brighten,
And with a step or two seemed brighter still,

1. The highest mountain in Wales (3,560 feet); *youthful Friend*: Robert Jones (see Biographical and Topographical Glossary), with whom WW made his walking tour of north Wales in June–August 1791; *Bethkelet's*: Beddgelert, a small village in northwest Wales, near Mount Snowdon; *couching-time*: bedtime. Probably between January and March 1804 WW composed this account of his ascent of Mount Snowdon (lines 1–65) as the opening of the last book of the provisional five-book *Prelude* (for a transcription of the draft in MS W see *Prel 1805* [CW], 2:284–86).
2. Probably WW's variant of the northern English dialect word *glarry* or *glaurie*, meaning "clammy," "sticky," or "rainy" (*NCPrel*).
3. Guide.
4. Dog (a word formerly used particularly for a shepherd's dog).

Nor had I time to ask the cause of this,
For instantly a Light upon the turf
40 Fell like a flash. I looked about and lo!
The Moon stood naked in the Heavens, at height
Immense above my head, and on the shore
I found myself of a huge sea of mist,
Which meek and silent rested at my feet.
45 A hundred hills their dusky backs upheaved
All over this still Ocean,⁵ and beyond,
Far, far beyond the vapours shot themselves
In headlands, tongues, and promontory shapes
Into the Sea, the real Sea, that seemed
50 To dwindle and give up its majesty,
Usurped upon as far as sight could reach.
Meanwhile the Moon looked down upon this shew
In single glory, and we stood, the mist
Touching our very feet: and from the shore
55 At distance not the third part of a mile
Was a blue chasm, a fracture in the vapour,
A deep and gloomy breathing-place through which
Mounted the roar of waters, torrents, streams
Innumerable, roaring with one voice.⁶
60 The universal Spectacle throughout
Was shaped for admiration and delight,
Grand in itself alone, but in that breach
Through which the homeless voice of waters rose,
That dark deep thorough-fare, had Nature lodged
65 The Soul, the Imagination of the whole.
          A meditation rose in me that night
Upon the lonely mountain when the scene
Had passed away,⁷ and it appeared to me
The perfect image of a mighty Mind,
70 Of one that feeds upon infinity,
That is exalted by an under-presence,
The sense of God, or whatsoe'er is dim
Or vast in its own being, above all
One function of such mind had Nature there

5. A hundred . . . Ocean: an allusion to the creation of the earth in Paradise Lost 7.285–87: "Immediately the Mountains huge appeer / Emergent, and thir broad bare backs upheave / Into the Clouds."
6. Some of the details in lines 45–59 derive from lines 494–506 of WW's Descriptive Sketches (1793), where, however, they are set in the Alps and the time of day is morning (see Descriptive Sketches [CW], 86, 88). That scene, in turn, shares some details of the misty cliff scene in James Beattie's poem The Minstrel (1771) 1.21, a stanza quoted in James Clarke's Survey of the Lakes of Cumberland, Westmorland, and Lancashire (London, 1787), 73 (Reading 1770–99, no. 55; Reading 1800–15, no. 102.ii). Referring to Skiddaw, a mountain (3,053 feet) in the northern Lake District, Clarke observes that "every sound is much more distinctly heard" on the mountain when there is fog or mist in the surrounding valley. WW's breathing-place (line 57) may also recall line 18 of STC's Kubla Khan (composed in 1797 or 1798): "As if this earth in fast thick pants were breathing" (NCC, 182).
7. When . . . away: Compare 6.525–49, where WW's apostrophe to imagination follows his account of having crossed the Alps with Robert Jones: in neither case is the reflection on imagination presented as coinciding with the sight that inspired it.

75 Exhibited by putting forth in midst
    [Of][8] circumstance most awful and sublime,
    That domination which she oftentimes
    Exerts upon the outward face of things,
    So moulds them, and endues, abstracts, combines,
80 Or by abrupt and unhabitual influence
    Doth make one object so impress itself
    Upon all others, and pervade them so,
    That even the grossest minds must see and hear
    And cannot chuse but feel. The Power which these
85 Acknowledge, when thus moved, which Nature thus
    Thrusts forth upon the senses, is the express
    Resemblance, in the fullness of its strength
    Made visible, a genuine Counterpart
    And Brother of the glorious faculty
90 Which higher minds bear with them as their own;
    This is the very spirit in which they deal
    With all the objects of the universe.
    They from their native selves can send abroad
    Like transformation, for themselves create
95 A like existence, and, whene'er it is
    Created for them, catch it by an instinct;[9]
    Them the enduring and the transient both
    Serve to exalt; they build up greatest things
    From least suggestions,[1] ever on the watch,
100 Willing to work and to be wrought upon,
    They need not extraordinary calls[2]
    To rouze them, in a world of life they live,
    By sensible impressions not enthralled,
    But quickened, rouzed, and made thereby more fit
105 To hold communion with the invisible world.
    Such minds are truly from the Deity;
    For they are Powers; and hence the highest bliss
    That can be known is theirs, the consciousness
    Of whom they are habitually infused
110 Through every image,[3] and through every thought,
    And all impressions: hence religion, faith,
    And endless occupation for the soul,

8. The reading in MS B partly incorporates the penciled alteration in MS A of the original read-
   ing "and that / With" to "in midst / Of." The substitution of "Of" for "With" was presumably
   overlooked when MS B was copied from MS A, assuming that the substitution preceded the
   copying (*Prel 1805* [CW], 1:315, 2:967, 998). MS W contains drafts of lines 1–65, 77–94, and
   later lines of what was originally conceived as the final book of the five-book *Prelude* (see *Prel
   1805* [CW], 2:284–88); but it does not contain a draft of lines 66–76, which must have been
   composed later, in spring 1805, after WW had decided to expand the poem.
9. Compare WW's description of the "infant Babe" whose mind, "as an agent of the one great
   mind, / Creates, creator and receiver both" (2.272–73).
1. In his note to *The Thorn* in *LB 1800* WW defined imagination as "the faculty which produces
   impressive effects out of simple elements."
2. Stimuli. *Prel 1805* (CW) notes an echo of Milton's *Samson Agonistes*, lines 1382–83: "Some
   rouzing notions in me which dispose / To something extraordinary my thoughts." In the Preface
   to *LB 1800* WW insisted that "the human mind is capable of excitement without the applica-
   tion of gross and violent stimulants" (p. 80 above).
3. Impression, experience.

Whether discursive or intuitive,[4]
Hence sovereignty within and peace at will,
115 Emotion which best foresight need not fear
Most worthy then of trust when most intense,
Hence chearfulness in every act of life,
Hence truth in moral judgements and delight
That fails not in the external universe.
120   Oh who is he that hath his whole life long
Preserved, enlarged, this freedom in himself.
For this alone is genuine Liberty.
Witness, ye Solitudes! where I received
My earliest visitations, careless then
125 Of what was given me, and which now I roam
A meditative, oft a suffering Man,
And yet, I trust, with undiminished powers,[5]
Witness, whatever falls[6] my better mind,
Revolving with the accidents of life,
130 May have sustained, that, howsoe'er misled,
I never in the quest of right and wrong
Did tamper with myself from private aims;[7]
Nor was in any of my hopes the dupe
Of selfish passions; nor did wilfully
135 Yield ever to [mean cares and low pursuits;][8]
But rather did with jealousy[9] shrink back
From every combination that might aid
The tendency, too potent in itself,
Of habit to enslave the mind, I mean
140 Oppress it by the laws of vulgar sense,
And substitute a universe of death,[1]
The falsest of all worlds, in place of that
Which is divine and true. To fear and love,
To love as first and chief, for there fear ends,
145 Be this ascribed; to early intercourse
In presence of sublime and lovely Forms,
With the adverse principles of pain and joy,
Evil, as one[2] is rashly named by those
Who know not what they say. From love, for here

---

4. An allusion to a distinction made in *Paradise Lost* 5.487–90, where the archangel Raphael tells Adam, "reason is her [the soul's] being, / Discursive, or Intuitive; discourse / Is oftest yours, the latter most is ours [the angels']." The distinction was significant to STC, who was to quote this passage from *Paradise Lost* in chapter 10 of *BL* in connection with his own distinction between reason and understanding (NCC, 450).
5. WW had recently completed the Intimations Ode when he composed these lines, probably in March 1804 (see *Prel 1805* [CW], 2:295 for the draft in MS W). As NCPrel notes, later in MS W (in lines revised as 11.336–37) he expressed the anxiety that "the very fountains of my powers / Seem open I approach & then they close" (*Prel 1805* [CW], 2:303).
6. Adversities, lapses.
7. WW clarified his meaning in *Prel 1850*: "Never did I, in quest of right and wrong, / Tamper with conscience from a private aim" (*Prel 1850* [CW], 262).
8. The conclusion of the line, left blank in MS B, is supplied from MS A.
9. I.e., "vigilance in guarding a possession from loss or damage" (OED).
1. A quotation from *Paradise Lost* 2.622–23: "A Universe of death, which God by curse / Created evil, for evil only good." See also lines 130–31 of the Intimations Ode.
2. I.e., pain; *pain and joy*: i.e., in WW's childhood, as recorded in 1.308–309: "I grew up / Fostered alike by beauty and by fear."

150   Do we begin and end,[3] all grandeur comes,
     All truth and beauty, from pervading love,
     That gone, we are as dust. Behold the fields
     In balmy spring-time, full of rising flowers
     And blissful creatures; see that Pair, the Lamb
155   And the Lamb's Mother, and their tender ways
     Shall touch thee to the heart: in some green bower
     Rest, and be not alone, but have thou there
     The One who is thy choice of all the world;
     There linger, lulled, and lost, and rapt away,
160   Be happy to thy fill: thou callst this love
     And so it is; but there is higher love
     Than this, a love that comes into the heart
     With awe and a diffusive[4] sentiment;
     Thy love is human merely; this proceeds
165   More from the brooding Soul, and is divine.
          This love more intellectual cannot be
     Without Imagination, which in truth
     Is but another name for absolute strength
     And clearest insight, amplitude of mind,
170   And reason in her most exalted mood.[5]
     This faculty hath been the moving Soul
     Of our long labour: we have traced the stream
     From darkness, and the very place of birth
     In its blind cavern, whence is faintly heard
175   The sound of waters, followed it to light
     And open day, accompanied its course
     Among the ways of Nature; afterwards
     Lost sight of it bewildered and engulphed,
     Then given it greeting, as it rose once more
180   With strength, reflecting in its solemn breast
     The works of man, and face of human life;
     And lastly, from its progress have we drawn
     The feeling of life endless,[6] the one thought
     By which we live, Infinity and God.
185   Imagination having been our theme,

---

3. A clause omitted in *Prel 1850*: "By love subsists / All lasting grandeur, by pervading love" (*Prel 1850* [CW], 262).
4. Perhaps in the sense of "dispensing or shedding widely or bountifully" (*OED*). NCPrel suggests a parallel with *Tintern Abbey*, lines 28–29: "sensations sweet, / Felt in the blood, and felt along the heart." Someone—possibly STC—has written a "C" in the margin in pencil against lines 161–62, indicating a suggested revision that is written on the upper margin of p. 334 (fol. 179v) of MS B: "Both these delights the mild & passionate / And rightly so." In his 1818–20 revisions WW altered these lines to "Rightly bestow'st that name on both delights, / The mild and passionate" (*Prel 1805* [CW], 2:225).
5. Compare the "highest reason in a soul sublime," identified with passion in 5.39–40, and "the grand / And simple Reason" referred to in 11.123–24.
6. Compare WW's reflections on "the faith that looks through death" in the Intimations Ode, lines 182–89, and his "supposition of *another* and a *better* world" in a letter of March 12, 1805, concerning his brother John's death (*WL*, 1:556). The image of the partly subterranean river recalls "ALPH, the sacred river" in STC's *Kubla Khan*, lines 3–5 and 25–28. The use of rivers as figures for WW's intellectual development is recurrent in *The Prelude*: see also 1.274–88, 3.10–12, 3.39–55, and 6.672–80. In 9.1–9 he compares the course of the poem's narrative to a river (and see also 4.248–69).

So also hath that intellectual love,
For they are each in each, and cannot stand
Dividually.[7]—Here must thou be, O Man!
Strength to thyself; no Helper hast thou here;
190 Here keepest thou thy individual state,
No other can divide with thee this work,
No secondary hand can intervene
To fashion this ability;[8] 'tis thine,
The prime and vital principle is thine
195 In the recesses of thy nature, far
From any reach of outward fellowship,
Else 'tis not thine at all.[9]—But joy to him,
Oh! joy to him who here hath sown, hath laid
Here the foundations of his future years!
200 For all that friendship, all that love can do,
All that a darling countenance can look
Or dear voice utter to complete the Man,
Perfect him, made imperfect in himself,
All shall be his: and he whose soul hath risen
205 Up to the height of feeling intellect
Shall want no humbler tenderness, his heart
Be tender as a nursing Mother's heart,
Of female softness[1] shall his life be full,
Of little loves and delicate desires,[2]
210 Mild interests and gentlest sympathies.
           Child of my Parents! Sister of my Soul!
Elsewhere[3] have strains of gratitude been breathed
To thee for all thy early tenderness
Which I from thee imbibed. And true it is
215 That later seasons owed to thee no less;
For spite of the sweet influence and the touch
Of other kindred hands that opened out
The springs of tender thought in infancy,
And spite of all which singly I had watched
220 Of elegance, and each minuter charm
In nature or in life, still to the last,
Even to the very going-out of youth,

7. Separately (Milton uses the adjective *dividual* twice in *Paradise Lost*, at 7.382 and 12.85).
8. For *intellectual love* (line 186).
9. Lines 188–97, addressed to humanity, recall, as at 11.333–34, lines 46–47 of STC's *Dejection: An Ode* (in the *Morning Post* version of October 4, 1802): "we receive but what we give, / And in *our* life alone does Nature live." The reference to *joy* in lines 197–99 also recalls two passages in STC's poem, at lines 65–72 and 129–39, the latter addressed to WW himself (disguised under the name Edmund): "Joy lifts the spirit, joy attunes thy voice, / To thee do all things live from pole to pole, / Their life the eddying of thy living soul!" (133–35).
1. Compare the "female service" that the eponymous shepherd of *Michael* does, rocking his son Luke's "cradle with a woman's gentle hand" (lines 162–68).
2. An echo of Shakespeare, *Much Ado about Nothing* 1.1.303: "soft and delicate desires." The line also recalls line 18 of WW's own poem *The Sparrow's Nest* (composed in 1802), an oblique tribute to DW: "humble cares, and delicate fears" (P2V [CW], 213). WW's revision in *Prel 1850* made the connection with the earlier poem explicit: "Of humble cares and delicate desires" (*Prel 1850* [CW], 264). DW is addressed directly in lines 211–68 below.
3. See, e.g., 6.210–18 and 10.907–20 as well as *Tintern Abbey*, lines 116–22, *The Sparrow's Nest*, and *To a Butterfly* (P2V [CW], 203–204).

The period[4] which our Story now hath reached,
I too exclusively esteemed that love,
225 And sought that beauty, which, as Milton sings,
Hath terror in it.[5] Thou didst soften down
This over-sternness: but for thee, sweet Friend,
My soul, too reckless of mild grace, had been
Far longer what by Nature it was framed,
230 Longer retained its countenance severe,
A rock with torrents roaring, with the clouds
Familiar, and a favorite of the Stars:
But thou didst plant its crevices with flowers,
Hang it with shrubs that twinkle in the breeze,
235 And teach the little birds to build their nests
And warble in its chambers. At a time
When Nature, destined to remain so long
Foremost in my affections, had fallen back
Into a second place,[6] well pleased to be
240 A hand-maid to a nobler than herself,
When every day brought with it some new sense
Of exquisite regard for common things,
And all the earth was budding with these gifts
Of more refined humanity, thy breath,
245 Dear Sister, was a kind of gentler spring
That went before my steps.[7] With such a theme,
Coleridge! with this my argument, of thee
Shall I be silent? O most loving Soul!
Placed on this earth to love and understand,
250 And from thy presence shed the light of love,
Shall I be mute ere thou be spoken of?
Thy gentle Spirit to my heart of hearts
Did also find its way; and thus the life
Of all things and the mighty unity
255 In all which we behold, and feel, and are,
Admitted more habitually a mild
Interposition, and closelier gathering thoughts
Of man and his concerns,[8] such as become
A human Creature, be he who he may,
260 Poet, or destined to an humbler name;
And so the deep enthusiastic joy,

---

4. WW evidently refers to the time of intellectual and moral crisis recounted in 10.889–94, possibly spring 1796; *going-out*: end.
5. *Paradise Lost* 9.490–92 (lines spoken by Satan of Eve): "She fair, divinely fair, fit Love for Gods, / Not terrible, though terror be in Love, / And Beautie."
6. *At a time . . . second place*: i.e., the period between WW's crisis (see the note on line 223) and his departure with DW from Alfoxden in July 1798. Compare 8.476–85, and *Tintern Abbey*, lines 73–86, in which WW refers similarly to his passage from an unreflective childhood love of nature to a mature one informed by the "still, sad music of humanity" (line 91).
7. In *Prel 1850* WW inserted here a nine-line tribute to MW: "Thereafter came / One, whom with thee [DW] friendship had early paired; / She came, no more a Phantom to adorn, / A moment, but an inmate of the heart * * *" (*Prel 1850* [CW], 265–66).
8. Lines 256–58 credit STC with WW's becoming more accustomed (*more habitually*) to allow human concerns to impinge (*a mild / Interposition*) upon his thoughts. *and thus . . . and are* (lines 253–55): The phrasing recalls that of *Tintern Abbey*, lines 48–50: "With an eye made quiet by the power / Of harmony * * * / We see into the life of things."

The rapture of the Hallelujah sent
From all that breathes and is, was chastened, stemmed,
And balanced, by a Reason which indeed
265   Is Reason; duty and pathetic[9] truth;
And God and Man divided, as they ought,
Between them the great system of the world
Where Man is sphered, and which God animates.
                    And now, O Friend![1] this History is brought
270   To its appointed close: the discipline
And consummation[2] of the Poet's mind
In every thing that stood most prominent
Have faithfully been pictured; we have reached
The time (which was our object from the first)
275   When we may, not presumptuously, I hope,
Suppose my powers so far confirmed, and such
My knowledge as to make me capable
Of building up a work that should endure,[3]
Yet much hath been omitted, as need was,
280   Of Books how much![4] and even of the other wealth
Which is collected among woods and fields,
Far more: for Nature's secondary grace,
That outward illustration[5] which is hers,
Hath hitherto been barely touched upon,
285   The charm more superficial, and yet sweet,
Which from her works finds way, contemplated[6]
As they hold forth a genuine counterpart
And softening mirror of the moral world.
                    Yes, having tracked the main essential Power,
290   Imagination, up her way sublime,
In turn might Fancy also be pursued
Through all her transmigrations, till she too
Was purified, had learned to ply her craft
By judgment steadied.[7] Then might we return
295   And in the Rivers and the Groves behold
Another face; might hear them from all sides
Calling upon the more instructed mind
To link their images with subtle skill

9. "Pertaining or relating to the passions or emotions of the mind" (*OED*).
1. STC.
2. Perfection, culmination in development.
3. Compare 1.124–274, where WW elaborates his poetic ambitions, and 6.64–69, where he
   expresses the "daring thought, that [he] might leave / Some monument behind."
4. See book 5 for WW's consideration of the influence of his reading on his intellectual
   development.
5. Of the *moral world* (line 288).
6. Stressed on the second syllable (the more common pronunciation until the end of the nine-
   teenth century).
7. See WW's Note on *The Thorn* in *LB 1800* (p. 38 above) for his earlier distinction between
   imagination and fancy, echoed in *The Prelude* 8.586. In letters of September 10, 1802, to Wil-
   liam Sotheby and of January 15, 1804, to Richard Sharp—the latter in the context of praising
   WW as "the first & greatest philosophical Poet"—STC distinguished imagination as a "*modify-
   ing*, and *co-adunating* [i.e., unifying] Faculty" from fancy as an "aggregating Faculty" (*CL*,
   2:865–66, 1034). In *BL*, esp. chaps. 4 and 13 (NCC, 416–20, 449, 488–89), STC elaborated
   the distinction further in response to WW's own formulation of it in the Preface to *P 1815* (see
   below, pp. 511–18).

Sometimes, and by elaborate research
300 With forms and definite appearances
Of human life, presenting them sometimes
To the involuntary sympathy
Of our internal being, satisfied
And soothed with a conception of delight
305 Where meditation cannot come, which thought
Could never heighten. Above all, how much
Still nearer to ourselves is overlooked
In human nature and that marvellous world
As studied first in my own heart, and then
310 In life, among the passions of mankind
And qualities commixed, and modified
By the infinite varieties and shades
Of individual character. Herein
It was for me (this justice bids me say)
315 No useless preparation to have been
The pupil of a public School,[8] and forced
In hardy independence to stand up
Among conflicting passions and the shock
Of various tempers, to endure and note
320 What was not understood, though known to be:
Among the mysteries of love and hate,
Honour and shame, looking to right and left,
Unchecked by innocence too delicate
And moral notions too intolerant,
325 Sympathies too contracted. Hence, when called
To take a station among men, the step
Was easier, the transition more secure,
More profitable also; for the mind
Learns from such timely exercise to keep
330 In wholesome separation the two natures,
The one that feels, the other that observes.
　　　　Let one word more of personal circumstance,
Not needless, as it seems, be added here.
Since I withdrew unwillingly from France,[9]
335 The Story hath demanded less regard
To time and place; and where I lived and how
Hath been no longer scrupulously marked.
Three years, until a permanent abode
Received me with that Sister of my heart
340 Who ought by rights the dearest to have been
Conspicuous through this biographic Verse,
Star seldom utterly concealed from view,
I led an undomestic Wanderer's life.
In London chiefly was my home; and thence
345 Excursively,[1] as personal friendships, chance

8. Hawkshead Grammar School, which as a "free school" was nominally open to all qualified male pupils, regardless of wealth, hence *public*.
9. On WW's departure from France late in 1792, see 10.188–91.
1. Erratically. WW refers to the period from December 1792 to September 1795.

Or inclination led, or slender means
Gave leave, I roamed about from place to place,
Tarrying in pleasant nooks, wherever found
Through England or through Wales.² A Youth (he bore
350 The name of Calvert;³ it shall live if words
Of mine can give it life) without respect
To prejudice or custom, having hope
That I had some endowments by which good
Might be promoted, in his last decay,
355 From his own Family withdrawing part
Of no redundant Patrimony, did
By a Bequest sufficient for my needs
Enable me to pause for choice, and walk
At large and unrestrained, nor damped too soon
360 By mortal cares. Himself no Poet, yet
Far less a common Spirit of the world,
He deemed that my pursuits and labours lay
Apart from all that leads to wealth, or even
Perhaps to necessary maintenance
365 Without some hazard to the finer sense,
He cleared a passage for me, and the stream
Flowed in the bent of Nature.
                                            Having now
Told what best merits mention, further pains
Our present labour seems not to require,
370 And I have other tasks.⁴ Call back to mind
The mood in which this Poem was begun,
O Friend! the termination of my course
Is nearer now, much nearer; yet even then
In that distraction and intense desire
375 I said unto the life which I had lived,
Where art thou?⁵ Hear I not a voice from thee
Which 'tis reproach to hear? Anon I rose
As if on wings, and saw beneath me stretched
Vast prospect of the world which I had been,⁶
380 And was; and hence this Song, which like a Lark
I have protracted, in the unwearied Heavens
Singing, and often with more plaintive voice
Attempered to the sorrows of the Earth;
Yet centring all in love, and in the end

2. See the note on line 5 above.
3. In lines 349–67 WW pays tribute to the younger brother of his Hawkshead friend William Calvert (see the note on 10.298), Raisley Calvert (see Biographical and Topographical Glossary), who died in January 1795, bequeathing WW £900 to enable him to devote himself fully to poetry (WL, 1:126–27, 133–34, 546). See also WW's sonnet To the Memory of Raisley Calvert (p. 404 below).
4. A reference to the philosophical section of The Recluse.
5. A reference to the self-reproach of 1.274–79, composed between ca. October 6, 1798, and ca. June 5, 1800 (Chrono: EY, 31), as well as an allusion to Genesis 3.9, in which God asks Adam, "Where art thou?" before reproaching him for eating the apple.
6. An allusion to Paradise Lost 5.86–89, in which Eve recalls to Adam her dream of seeing "[t]he Earth outstretcht immense, a prospect wide / And various."

385 All gratulant[7] if rightly understood.
        Whether to me shall be allotted life,
    And with life power, to accomplish aught of worth
    Sufficient to excuse me in Men's sight
    For having given this Record of myself
390 Is all uncertain:[8] but, belovèd Friend!
    When looking back, thou seest in clearer view
    Than any sweetest sight of yesterday
    That summer when on Quantock's grassy Hills
    Far ranging, and among the sylvan Coombs[9]
395 Thou in delicious words with happy heart
    Didst speak the Vision of that Ancient Man,
    The bright-eyed Mariner, and rueful woes
    Didst utter of the Lady Christabel;[1]
    And I, associate in such labour, walked
400 Murmuring of Him who, joyous hap! was found,
    After the perils of his moonlight ride
    Near the loud Waterfall; or her[2] who sate
    In misery near the miserable Thorn;
    When thou dost to that Summer turn thy thoughts,
405 And hast before thee all which then we were,
    To thee, in memory of that happiness
    It will be known, by thee at least, my Friend,
    Felt, that the history of a Poet's mind
    Is labour not unworthy of regard.
410 To thee the work shall justify itself.
        The last and later portions of this Gift
    Which I for Thee design have been prepared
    In times which have from those wherein we first
    Together wantoned in wild Poesy,
415 Differed thus far, that they have been, O Friend!
    Times of much sorrow, of a private grief
    Keen and enduring,[3] which the frame of mind
    That in this meditative History
    Hath been described more deeply makes me feel,

7. Expressing pleasure or joy.
8. On March 6, 1804, WW informed Thomas De Quincey of *The Prelude*, "This Poem will not be published these many years, and never during my lifetime, till I have finished a larger and more important work [*The Recluse*] to which it is tributary" (*WL*, 1:454).
9. Wooded hollows among the hills; *That summer*: actually mid-July 1797 to ca. June 25, 1798, when WW and DW lived in Alfoxden, Somerset (see Biographical and Topographical Glossary), four miles from STC's cottage in Nether Stowey, and WW planned *The Recluse* (*WL*, 1:212); *Quantock's grassy Hills*: the range of heathland hills over which WW and STC walked on their visits to each other in 1797–98.
1. WW refers to two poems STC composed in Somerset in 1797–98, *The Rime of the Ancient Mariner* (printed as the first poem in *LB 1798*) and part 1 of *Christabel* (part 2 was composed in August 1800, after STC had moved to Keswick in the Lake District). *Christabel* was originally intended for *LB 1800*, but was excluded (and WW's own *Michael* substituted for it), according to STC's report, because of its length and the fact that it seemed to contradict the collection's purpose of determining "how far those passions, which alone give any value to extraordinary Incidents, were capable of interesting, in & for themselves, in the incidents of common Life" (*CL*, 1:631). The poem remained unpublished until 1816.
2. Martha Ray in *The Thorn*. WW alludes self-mockingly to Martha Ray's refrain, "Oh misery! oh misery! / Oh woe is me! oh misery!" *Him* (line 400): Johnny Foy in *The Idiot Boy*.
3. I.e., the drowning of WW's brother John (see Biographical and Topographical Glossary) in February 1805.

420 Yet likewise hath enabled me to bear
    More firmly; and a comfort now, a hope,
    One of the dearest which this life can give,
    Is mine; that Thou art near, and wilt be soon
    Restored to us in renovated health:
425 When after the first mingling of our tears,
    'Mong other consolations, we may find
    Some pleasure from this Offering of my love.[4]
        Oh! yet a few short years of useful life,
    And all will be complete, thy race be run,[5]
430 Thy monument of glory will be raised,
    Then, though too weak to tread the ways of truth,
    This age fall back to old idolatry,
    Though Men return to servitude as fast
    As the tide ebbs, to ignominy and shame
435 By Nations sink together, we shall still
    Find solace in the knowledge which we have,
    Blessed with true happiness if we may be
    United helpers forward of a day
    Of firmer trust, joint labourers in the work
440 (Should Providence such grace to us vouchsafe)
    Of their redemption, surely yet to come.
    Prophets of Nature, we to them will speak
    A lasting inspiration, sanctified
    By reason and by truth: what we have loved
445 Others will love; and we may teach them how,
    Instruct them how the mind of Man becomes
    A thousand times more beautiful than the earth
    On which he dwells, above this Frame of things
    (Which 'mid all revolutions in the hopes
450 And fears of Men doth still remain unchanged)
    In beauty exalted, as it is itself
    Of substance and of fabric more divine.[6]

                                            June 1805

Emendations

Emended readings are given before the brackets, the original MS readings
after. As indicated in the headnote, emendations derived from MS A (as tran-
scribed in *Prel 1805* [CW], 2:587–993) are omitted from this list.

4. When WW completed *The Prelude* in May 1805 (*Chrono: MY*, 15), STC had been abroad for
   just over a year, and he did not return to England until August 1806. After traveling to the Lake
   District in October 1806, he separated from his wife in December and joined WW, MW, DW,
   and Sara Hutchinson at the home of Sir George Beaumont (see Biographical and Topographi-
   cal Glossary) in Coleorton, Leicestershire, in the English Midlands, where he stayed until
   mid-April. Over a series of evenings ending on January 7, 1807, WW read *The Prelude* aloud to
   the household, including STC, who recorded his immediate response in *To William Words-
   worth* (reprinted in Nineteenth-Century Responses below).
5. *PPrel* notes an allusion to Milton's *Samson Agonistes*, lines 597–98: "My race of glory run, and
   race of shame, / And I shall shortly be with them that rest."
6. Compare WW's declaration, in lines 40–41 of the Prospectus to *The Recluse*: "the Mind of
   Man, / My haunt, and the main region of my Song" (p. 445 below).

1.32: river] river,
1.78: couched,] couch'd
1.162: lack] lack,
1.185: tales] tales.
1.202: Did] Did,
1.220: banks,] banks
1.261: ambition] ambition,
1.263: again,] again
1.281: Birth-place,] Birth-place
1.315: frost] frost,
1.520: felt,] felt
2.42: know] know,
2.139: air,] air
2.283: heart,] heart
2.422: all] all,
2.448: Yours:] Your's:
3.266: old,] old
3.312: stopped,] stopp'd;
3.487: Scholar":] Scholar:
3.589: thoughts.] thoughts
3.654: seen,] seen
4.35: garden] garden,
4.40: Brook,] Brook;
4.105: sea,] sea;
4.150: lay,] lay;
4.212: like),] like)
4.299: truth,] truth;
4.310: note,] note
4.337: grounds] grounds,
4.429: flight;] flight
4.445: indifference,] indifference
4.446: words] words,
4.473: He] He,
4.488: tired."] tired.
5.100: look] look,
5.163: hand,] hand
5.465: upleaping] upleaping,
5.507: abroad,] abroad
5.601: wonder,] wonder
5.618: Nature] Nature,
6.48: tell,] tell
6.113: knowledge] knowledge,
6.149: own.] own,
6.299: times] times,
6.307: Youth,] Youth
6.407: Board:] Board
    [1818–20 revision]
6.416: ears:] ears
    [1818–20 revision]
6.432: went,] went
6.523: had,] had;
6.589: Heaven,] Heaven
6.646: size] size,
6.680: circuitous.] circuitous
6.681: time,] time
7.1: out,] out

7.34: whispered,] whisper'd
7.47: door,] door
7.84: Rome,] Rome
7.129: top] top,
7.149: sake,] sake
7.171: Throng,] Throng
7.211: sight,] sight
7.263: East,] East
7.307: Cave,] Cave
7.310: *Invisible*] Invisible
7.348: when,] when
7.409: perhaps,] perhaps
7.412: undisturbed.] undisturb'd
7.475: space,] space
7.488: hard.] hard
7.519: youth,] youth
7.540: sense;] sense
7.627: help,] help
7.687: Shews,] Shews
8.150: sides,] sides
8.157: Unwooed,] Unwoo'd
8.203: alas,] alas
8.207: childhood,] childhood
8.232: therein,] therein
8.249: before."] before"
8.251: aloud,] aloud
8.252: note,"] note,
8.263: Flock.] Flock
8.267: hours'] hour's
8.332: Endless,] Endless;
8.418: Books,] Books;
8.424: common,] common;
8.440: fit.] fit
8.477: pursuits,] pursuits
8.522: mind;] mind
8.566: springs,] springs
8.708: me] me,
8.712: Earth,] Earth
8.714: tracts,] tracts;
8.799: arranged,] arranged
8.819: "in] in
8.858: seek,] seek
9.4: sea,] sea
9.47: Jacobins,] Jacobins
9.82: speech,] speech
9.101: shew] shew,
9.113: speak] speak,
9.214: youth,] youth
9.299: benign,] benign
9.337: tolerant,] tolerant
9.419: Timonides,] Timonides
9.440: slaughter,] slaughter
9.498: scorn,] scorn
9.546: acts,] acts
9.619: turn,] turn
9.626: divined:] divined

9.628: allow,] allow
9.668: intent,] intent
9.723: spirit,] spirit
9.752: vouchsafed,]
  vouchsafed
9.754: ensued,] ensued
9.755: remain,] remain
9.756: liberty,] liberty
9.775: up,"] up"
9.793: again,] again
9.800: House] House,
9.847: grief,] grief
9.853: this,] this
9.855: slackness,] slackness
9.863: home,] home
9.897: required,] required
10.17: despair,] despair
10.18: themselves,] themselves
10.26: soul,] soul
10.32: true,] true
10.38: which,] which
10.41: City,] City
10.44: bondage,] bondage;
10.45: Host.] Host
10.47: Carousel,] Carousel
10.51: up,] up
10.52: read,] read
10.59: times,] times
10.65: month,] month
10.74: once."] once"
10.79: security,] security
10.81: night,] night
10.87–88: "Denunciation . . .
  Robespierre"] *Denunciation . . .*
  Robespierre
10.99: saying,] saying
10.100: thee!" 'Tis] thee"! "Tis
10.106: now,] now
10.112: won;] won,
10.125: added,] added
10.154: simplicity,] simplicity
10.201: Land] Land,
10.202: returned,] return'd
10.206: effort which,]
  effort, which
10.244: France,] France
10.245: come;] come
10.247: only,] only
10.263: grief,] grief
10.267: judge,] judge
10.273: add,] add
10.296: days] days,
10.300: failed,] fail'd
10.330: chimney-nook,]
  chimney-nook
10.337: thirsty,] thirsty

10.367: mankind.] mankind;
10.381: Youth,] Youth
10.383: first,] first
10.393: worship,] worship
10.394: love.] love
10.405: come;] come
10.408: Heaven;] Heaven,
10.428: restored,] restored
10.438: charge,] charge;
10.451: day] day,
10.487: away,] away
10.508: Verses] Verses,
10.567: France,] France
10.573: I] I,
10.594: same] same,
10.612: in,] in
10.680: good,] good
10.682: given (to] given; to
10.684: needed),] needed,
10.716: it:] it,   [1818–20
  revision]   who,] who
10.720: hearts'] heart's
10.724: where,] where;
10.726: end,] end
10.734: amiss,] amiss
10.742: desires,] desires
10.743: As,] As   side,] side
10.763: great,] great;
10.774: afloat,] afloat
10.784: sentiments] sentiments,
10.809: element,] element
10.811: herself,] herself
10.815: mind] mind,
10.823: past,] past
10.838: delight.] delight,
10.856: so,] so
10.861: opinions,] opinions;
10.865: sentiments,] sentiments
10.866: theme.] theme
10.868: one,] one
10.873: And,] And
10.898: and, in fine,] and in fine
10.905: Thou,] Thou
10.920: else;] else,
10.925: strength] strength,
10.934: opprobrium,] opprobrium
10.937: clouds,] clouds
10.966: not,] not
10.1020: Friend,] Friend
10.1034: more,] more)
10.1036: deceived)] deceived,
11.5: decayed,] decay'd
11.8: Song,] Song;
11.34: happiness.] happiness;
11.70: man,] man
11.79: wand,] wand

11.81: so] so,
11.82: words,] words
11.94: was, I thought,] was
    I thought
11.103: thought,] thought
11.122: mistakes),] mistakes,)
11.133: Verse. Suffice] Verse;
    suffice
11.143: apparition,] apparition;
11.144: ear,] ear;
11.189: profound,] profound
11.201: style;] style,
11.203: free;] free,
11.226: loved,] lov'd
11.237: love?] love;
11.238: judge,] judge
11.293: wrought,] wrought
11.355: repaired] repair'd,
11.366: died,] died
11.391: ways;] ways
12.21: now] now,
12.38: behind,] behind
12.51: things] things,
12.66: less;] less
12.89: subdued,] subdued
12.91: is,] is
12.96: not,] not;
12.114: world,] world
12.115: possessed,] possessed
12.150: trod,] trod
12.161: enquire,] enquire
12.177: boon,] boon
12.182: obscure,] obscure
12.210: Few,] Few
12.220: saw,] saw
12.230: shower.] shower

12.231: these,] these
12.331: Altar,] Alter,
12.343: divine,] divine
12.363: tone,] tone
12.375: maintains] maintains,
13.13: rain;] [MS indecipherable]
13.44: silent] silent,
13.64: thorough-fare,]
    thorough-fare
13.79: combines,] combines
13.82: so,] so
13.96: instinct;] [MS
    indecipherable]
13.112: soul,] soul
13.114: will,] will
13.116: intense,] intense
13.117: life,] life
13.189: here;] here
13.197: him,] him
13.218: infancy,] infancy
13.221: last,] last
13.250: love,] love
13.306: all,] all
13.310: life,] life
13.320: understood,] understood
13.334: France,] France
13.347: place,] place
13.369: require,] require
13.398: Christabel;] Christabel
13.410: itself.] itself
13.411: last] last,
13.419: described] described,
13.421: hope,] hope
13.431: though] though,
13.439: work] work,

From POEMS, IN TWO VOLUMES
(1807)

In 1805 the last edition of *Lyrical Ballads* was published and Wordsworth finished composing the thirteen-book *Prelude*. Between late December of that year and late March of the next, Dorothy and Mary Wordsworth made a collection of fair-copy manuscripts of shorter poems that William had written since 1800. The arrangement of the sonnets marked "the beginning of Wordsworth's efforts to arrange poems in small groups to shape a larger context" (*P2V* [CW], 6). On June 15, 1806, he informed the publisher John Taylor of his interest in publishing a new collection of his poetry and sought Taylor's advice in negotiating with T. N. Longman, who had published the second to fourth editions of *Lyrical Ballads* and was evidently prepared to offer Wordsworth only £40 for the new publication (*P2V* [CW], 11). By November 24, Dorothy could report to her friend Catherine Clarkson that "Wm is going to publish *two* smaller volumes and is to have 100 Guineas [i.e., £105] for 1,000 Copies" (*WL*, 2:104; see also Owen, "Costs, Sales, and Profits," 95).

In preparing the manuscript for the printer (a complicated process involving the poet himself, his sister, his wife, and Coleridge, as described in detail by Jared Curtis in his Introduction to *P2V* [CW]), Wordsworth began a practice he was to maintain in his subsequent collections of poetry, arranging the poems in separately titled sections: "The Orchard Pathway," "Poems Composed during a Tour, Chiefly on Foot," "Miscellaneous Sonnets," and "Sonnets Dedicated to Liberty" in volume 1, "Poems Written during a Tour in Scotland," "Moods of My Own Mind," "The Blind Highland Boy; with Other Poems," and the Intimations Ode (standing alone with its own title page) in volume 2. As Wordsworth explained to Lady Beaumont on May 21, 1807, the poems within a group gain meaning by being read in relation to one another: "if individually they want weight, perhaps, as a Body, they may not be so deficient * * * these Sonnets [on liberty], while they each fix the attention upon some important sentiment separately considered, do at the same time collectively make a Poem on the subject of civil Liberty and national independence" (*WL*, 2:147). The collection is particularly noteworthy for its two sections of 47 sonnets—of over 500 Wordsworth was to publish—which Stuart Curran describes as representing "the most significant recasting of the form since Milton" (see pp. 672–78 below).

The publisher or printer evidently confused the first section title for that of the entire collection, because the book was advertised before publication as "the Orchard Pathway, a collection of poems, with other Miscellaneous Poems" (*P2V* [CW], 26). When the volumes were published, sometime between April 28 and May 8, 1807, the title was correctly printed as *Poems, in Two Volumes*— the title Wordsworth had originally intended for *LB 1800*—while the title and motto of the first section were omitted altogether, whether accidentally or at the author's request or for reasons of printing economy when Wordsworth's Advertisement was canceled. Presumably Wordsworth insisted at the last minute on withdrawing the Advertisement, which alludes to his stalled progress on *The Recluse*. But while it did not appear in print, the

Advertisement survives in the manuscript sent to the printer and is tran-
scribed here from the photograph in *P2V* (CW), 540:

> The short Poems, of which these Volumes consist, were chiefly composed
> to refresh my mind during the progress of a work of length and labour, in
> which I have for some time been engaged; and to furnish me with employ-
> ment when I had not resolution to apply myself to that work, or hope that I
> should proceed with it successfully. Having already, in the Volumes enti-
> tled Lyrical Ballads, offered to the world a considerable collection of short
> poems, I did not wish to add these to the number, till after the completion
> and publication of my larger work; but, as I cannot even guess when this
> will be, and as several of these Poems have been circulated in manuscript,
> I thought it better to send them forth at once. They were composed with
> much pleasure to my own mind, & I build upon that remembrance a hope
> that they may afford profitable pleasure to many readers.

Had the Advertisement been published, it might have served contemporary
readers to explain the Latin epigraph printed on the title pages of both volumes
of *P2V*, lines 8–9 of the *Culex* [*Gnat*], a poem formerly attributed to Virgil:
"Posterius graviore sono tibi Musa loquetur / Nostra: dabunt cum securos mihi
tempora fructus" [Hereafter our Muse will speak to you more gravely, when
the seasons yield me their fruits with ease]. Alternatively, Wordsworth may
have conceived the epigraph as a kind of substitute for the Advertisement. In
any event, he sought to promote *Poems, in Two Volumes* by referring on its title
page to his previous collection: "by William Wordsworth, Author of *The Lyri-
cal Ballads.*"

Although it contained many of the poems for which Wordsworth is now
best known (such as *Resolution and Independence, I wandered lonely as a
Cloud, Elegiac Stanzas*, the Intimations Ode, and the sonnets *Composed
upon Westminster Bridge* and *The world is too much with us*), *Poems, in Two
Volumes* was not a commercial success, at least in comparison with *Lyrical
Ballads*: seven years after publication, 230 of the 1000 copies printed remained
unsold (Owen, "Costs, Sales, and Profits," 96). Nor was it well received by con-
temporary reviewers, several of whom, including the nineteen-year-old Lord
Byron, compared *P2V* unfavorably to *Lyrical Ballads* (see *CH*, 169–70, 177–
78, 186–87). In the *Edinburgh Review* (October 1807), resuming the line of
criticism he had begun five years earlier, Francis Jeffrey faulted Wordsworth's
diction, versification, choice of subjects, and especially his connection of
lofty sentiments to lowly "objects and incidents." Only for the sonnets did Jef-
frey reserve some praise (*CH*, 189, 200).

Modern criticism has tended to focus on individual poems within *P2V*,
although Alan Jones's volume *Wordsworth: The 1807 Poems* gathers some
nineteenth-century and twentieth-century assessments of *P2V* as a whole;
and Stuart Curran's "'Multum in Parvo'" addresses the collection as such. In
the Modern Criticism section of this Norton Critical Edition, the sonnets
are discussed by Stuart Curran, *Resolution and Independence* by Michael
O'Neill, the *Ode to Duty* and *Elegiac Stanzas* by Geoffrey Hartman, and the
Intimations Ode by both Hartman and Steven Knapp (and see also the sepa-
rate headnote to the *Ode*).

As with *Lyrical Ballads*, Wordsworth made textual revisions while the
printing proceeded, or in the proofs (which do not survive), and a total of
three leaves in the two volumes were canceled and replaced—changes for
which the publisher charged Wordsworth (*P2V* [CW], 32–33; *Cornell*, no.
19). For the printing complications created by Wordsworth's revisions of the
Ode to Duty, see the first note on that poem. The poems included here from
P2V follow the original edition in text and order, and the classification of the
poems in *P 1815* is indicated in the notes.

POEMS,

IN

TWO VOLUMES,

BY

WILLIAM WORDSWORTH,

AUTHOR OF

THE LYRICAL BALLADS.

Posterius graviore sono tibi Musa loquetur
Nostra: dabunt cum securos mihi tempora fructus.

VOL. I.

LONDON:

PRINTED FOR LONGMAN, HURST, REES, AND ORME,
PATERNOSTER-ROW.

1807.

TO THE DAISY †

In youth from rock to rock I went,
From hill to hill, in discontent
Of pleasure high and turbulent,
            Most pleas'd when most uneasy;
5   But now my own delights I make,
My thirst at every rill can slake,
And gladly Nature's love partake
            Of thee, sweet Daisy!

When soothed a while by milder airs,
10   Thee Winter in the garland wears
That thinly shades his few grey hairs;
            Spring cannot shun thee;
Whole summer fields are thine by right;
And Autumn, melancholy Wight![1]
15   Doth in thy crimson head delight
            When rains are on thee.

In shoals and bands, a morrice train,
Thou greet'st the Traveller in the lane;

---

† *P 1815*: Poems of the Fancy. Composed perhaps between April 16 and July 8, 1802 (*Chrono: MY*, 161). WW's note (printed at the end of *P2V*, vol. 1): "This Poem, and two others to the same Flower, which the Reader will find in the second Volume, were written in the year 1802; which is mentioned, because in some of the ideas, though not in [the] manner in which those ideas are connected, and likewise even in some of the expressions, they bear a striking resemblance to a Poem (lately published) of Mr. Montgomery, entitled, a Field Flower. This being said, Mr. Montgomery will not think any apology due to him; I cannot however help addressing him in the words of the Father of English Poets.

> Though it happe me to rehersin [repeat]—
> That ye han [have] in your freshe songis saied,
> Forberith me, and beth [be] not ill apaied [contented],
> Sith [since] that ye se I doe it in the honour
> Of Love, and eke [also] in service of the Flour [flower]."

WW quotes Chaucer's *Legend of Good Women* (1372–84), lines 78–82 (omitting "eft", "again," at the end of line 78), from Robert Anderson's anthology *The Works of the British Poets* (Edinburgh, 1792–1807), 1:415. The poem to which he refers, by James Montgomery (1771–1854), is *A Field Flower; on Finding One in Full Bloom on Christmas Day*, published in *The Wanderer of Switzerland, and Other Poems* (London, 1806), 151–53. Montgomery's poem in quatrains celebrates the hardiness of daisies. In *P 1815* WW added, as an epigraph, lines 366–78 of George Wither's Eclogue 4 from *The Shepherds Hunting* (1615), explaining in a footnote that "Her" in line 1 refers to "His Muse" (*P 1815*, 1:235).

> Her divine skill taught me this,
> That from everything I saw
> I could some instruction draw,
> And raise pleasure to the height
> Through the meanest object's sight.
> By the murmur of a spring,
> Or the least bough's rustelling;
> By a Daisy whose leaves spread
> Shut when Titan goes to bed;
> Or a shady bush or tree;
> She could more infuse in me
> Than all Nature's beauties can
> In some other wiser man.

1. Living thing (a now-archaic word).

If welcome once thou count'st it gain;
20   Thou art not daunted,
Nor car'st if thou be set at naught;
And oft alone in nooks remote[2]
We meet thee, like a pleasant thought,
      When such are wanted.

25 Be Violets in their secret mews
The flowers the wanton Zephyrs[3] chuse;
Proud be the Rose, with rains and dews
      Her head impearling;
Thou liv'st with less ambitious aim,
30 Yet hast not gone without thy fame;
Thou art indeed by many a claim
      The Poet's darling.

If to a rock from rains he fly,
Or, some bright day of April sky,
35 Imprison'd by hot sunshine lie
      Near the green holly,
And wearily at length should fare;
He need but look about, and there
Thou art! a Friend at hand, to scare
40   His melancholy.

A hundred times, by rock or bower,
Ere thus I have lain couch'd an hour,
Have I derived from thy sweet power
      Some apprehension;
45 Some steady love; some brief delight;
Some memory that had taken flight;
Some chime of fancy wrong or right;
      Or stray invention.

If stately passions in me burn,
50 And one chance look to Thee should turn,
I drink out of an humbler urn
      A lowlier pleasure;
The homely sympathy that heeds
The common life, our nature breeds;
55 A wisdom fitted to the needs
      Of hearts at leisure.

When, smitten by the morning ray,
I see thee rise alert and gay,
Then, chearful Flower! my spirits play
60   With kindred motion:

2. "In northern dialects pronounced to rhyme with 'nought' and 'thought'" (P2V [CW], 403).
3. Breezes; *secret mews*: possibly an echo of Edmund Spenser's *Faerie Queene* (1590–96) 2.7.19:
"But safe I have them kept in secret mew [i.e., hiding-place], / From hevens sight, and powre of
al which them poursew" (P2V [CW], 403).

At dusk, I've seldom mark'd thee press
The ground, as if in thankfulness,
Without some feeling, more or less,
  Of true devotion.

65 And all day long I number yet,
All seasons through, another debt,[4]
Which I wherever thou art met,
  To thee am owing;
An instinct call it, a blind sense;
70 A happy, genial influence,
Coming one knows not how nor whence,
  Nor whither going.

Child of the Year! that round dost run
Thy course, bold lover of the sun,
75 And chearful when the day's begun
  As morning Leveret,
Thou long the Poet's praise shalt gain;[5]
Thou wilt be more belov'd by men
In times to come; thou not in vain
80   Art Nature's Favorite.

LOUISA[†]

I met Louisa in the shade;
And, having seen that lovely Maid,
Why should I fear to say
That she is ruddy, fleet, and strong;
5 And down the rocks can leap along,
Like rivulets in May?

And she hath smiles to earth unknown;
Smiles, that with motion of their own
Do spread, and sink, and rise;
10 That come and go with endless play,
And ever, as they pass away,
Are hidden in her eyes.

She loves her fire, her Cottage-home;
Yet o'er the moorland will she roam
15 In weather rough and bleak;

4. The comma after *through* in line 66 was added by WW in *P 1815*; the comma after *thankfulness* in line 62 is an editorial emendation (following *P2V* [CW]) demanded by the sense.
5. WW's note in *P 1815* and later editions: "See, in Chaucer and the elder Poets, the honours formerly paid to this flower." *Leveret*: a young hare.
† *P 1815*: Poems founded on the Affections. Composed perhaps between January 23 and 27, 1802, certainly by February 9 (*Chrono: MY*, 26). Henry Crabb Robinson identified Louisa with MW's sister Joanna Hutchinson, but she has also been identified with DW (see *P2V* [CW], 403–404, 421). The poem was originally intended to be included in volume 2 of *LB 1802*, but it was omitted from that volume and published for the first time in *P2V*.

And when against the wind she strains,
Oh! might I kiss the mountain rains
That sparkle on her cheek.

Take all that's mine "beneath the moon,"[1]
20   If I with her but half a noon
May sit beneath the walls
Of some old cave, or mossy nook,
When up she winds along the brook,
To hunt the waterfalls.

She was a Phantom of delight[†]

She was a Phantom of delight
When first she gleam'd upon my sight;
A lovely Apparition, sent
To be a moment's ornament;
5   Her eyes as stars of Twilight fair;
Like Twilight's, too, her dusky hair;
But all things else about her drawn
From May-time and the chearful Dawn;
A dancing Shape, an Image gay,
10   To haunt, to startle, and way-lay.

I saw her upon nearer view,
A Spirit, yet a Woman too!
Her household motions light and free,
And steps of virgin liberty;
15   A countenance in which did meet
Sweet records, promises as sweet;
A Creature not too bright or good
For human nature's daily food;
For transient sorrows, simple wiles,
20   Praise, blame, love, kisses, tears, and smiles.

And now I see with eye serene
The very pulse of the machine;[1]
A Being breathing thoughtful breath;
A Traveller betwixt life and death;
25   The reason firm, the temperate will,

---

1. A quotation from Shakespeare's *King Lear* 4.6.26. A variant, "beneath the visiting moon," appears in *Antony and Cleopatra* 4.15.68. In his copy of *P2V*, James Dykes Campbell (1838–1895; STC's first biographer) recorded the original version of line 23 intended for *LB 1802*: "When she goes barefoot up the brook" (*P2V* [CW], 70).
† P 1815: Poems of the Imagination. Composed probably between October 14, 1803, and March 6, 1804 (*Chrono: MY*, 35). IF note: "1804 Town End [i.e., Dove Cottage]. The germ of this poem was four lines composed as a part of the verses on the Highland Girl. Though beginning in this way, it was written from my heart as is sufficiently obvious." In the first of his "Lake Reminiscences" (1839), Thomas De Quincey insisted that "these exquisite lines were dedicated to Mrs Wordsworth; were understood to describe her" (*Works*, gen. ed. Grevel Lindop [London, 2000–2003], 11:51); and in his *Memoirs of William Wordsworth* (London, 1851), 2:306, the poet's nephew Christopher reported WW's confirmation that the poem was about "his dear wife."
1. "Applied to the human and animal frame as a combination of several parts" (*OED* sense 4c).

Endurance, foresight, strength and skill;
A perfect Woman; nobly plann'd,
To warn, to comfort, and command;
And yet a Spirit still, and bright
30   With something of an angel light.

TO THE SMALL CELANDINE†

Pansies, Lilies, Kingcups, Daisies,
Let them live upon their praises;
Long as there's a sun that sets
Primroses will have their glory;
5   Long as there are Violets,
They will have a place in story:
There's a flower that shall be mine,
'Tis the little Celandine.

Eyes of some men travel far
10   For the finding of a star;
Up and down the heavens they go,
Men that keep a mighty rout!
I'm as great as they, I trow,
Since the day I found thee out,
15   Little flower!—I'll make a stir
Like a great Astronomer.

Modest, yet withal an Elf
Bold, and lavish of thyself,
Since we needs must first have met
20   I have seen thee, high and low,
Thirty years or more, and yet
'Twas a face I did not know;
Thou hast now, go where I may,
Fifty greetings in a day.

25   Ere a leaf is on a bush,
In the time before the Thrush
Has a thought about its nest,
Thou wilt come with half a call,
Spreading out thy glossy breast
30   Like a careless Prodigal;
Telling tales about the sun,
When we've little warmth, or none.

† *P 1815*: Poems of the Imagination. Composed probably on April 30–May 1, 1802 (*Chrono: MY*, 28). WW's note in *P2V*: "Common Pilewort." The lesser celandine or pilewort is a perennial plant with heart-shaped leaves and a yellow flower. From the IF note: "It is remarkable that this flower, coming out so early in the Spring as it does, and so bright & beautiful, & in such profusion should not have been noticed earlier in English verse. What adds much to the interest that attends it is its habit of shutting itself up & opening out according to the degree of light & temperature of the air."

Poets, vain men in their mood!
Travel with the multitude;
35 Never heed them; I aver
That they all are wanton Wooers;
But the thrifty Cottager,
Who stirs little out of doors,
Joys to spy thee near her home,
40 Spring is coming, Thou art come!¹

Comfort have thou of thy merit,
Kindly, unassuming Spirit!
Careless of thy neighbourhood,
Thou dost shew thy pleasant face
45 On the moor, and in the wood,
In the lane—there's not a place,
Howsoever mean it be,
But 'tis good enough for thee.

Ill befal the yellow Flowers,
50 Children of the flaring hours!
Buttercups, that will be seen,
Whether we will see or no;
Others, too, of lofty mien;
They have done as worldlings do,
55 Taken praise that should be thine,
Little, humble Celandine!

Prophet of delight and mirth,
Scorn'd and slighted upon earth!
Herald of a mighty band,
60 Of a joyous train ensuing,
Singing at my heart's command,
In the lanes my thoughts pursuing,
I will sing, as doth behove,
Hymns in praise of what I love!

TO THE SAME FLOWER†

Pleasures newly found are sweet
When they lie about our feet:
February last my heart
First at sight of thee was glad;
5 All unheard of as thou art,
Thou must needs, I think, have had,

---

1. In editions of his *Poetical Works* from 1836 to 1845, WW inserted the following stanza between lines 40 and 41: "Drawn by what peculiar spell, / By what charm for sight or smell, / Do those wingèd dim-eyed creatures, / Labourers sent from waxen cells, / Settle on thy brilliant features, / In neglect of buds and bells / Opening daily at thy side, / By the season multiplied?" (P2V [CW], 81). In the *Poems* of 1845 he transferred the stanza to between lines 40 and 41 of *To the Same Flower*.
† P 1815: Poems of the Fancy. Composed probably on May 1, 1802 (*Chrono: MY*, 28).

Celandine! and long ago,
Praise of which I nothing know.

I have not a doubt but he,
10   Whosoe'er the man might be,
Who the first with pointed rays,
(Workman worthy to be sainted)
Set the Sign-board[1] in a blaze,
When the risen sun he painted,
15   Took the fancy from a glance
At thy glittering countenance.

Soon as gentle breezes bring
News of winter's vanishing,
And the children build their bowers,
20   Sticking 'kerchief-plots of mold
All about with full-blown flowers,
Thick as sheep in shepherd's fold!
With the proudest Thou art there,
Mantling in the tiny square.

25   Often have I sigh'd to measure
By myself a lonely pleasure,
Sigh'd to think, I read a book
Only read perhaps by me;
Yet I long could overlook
30   Thy bright coronet and Thee,
And thy arch and wily ways,
And thy store of other praise.

Blithe of heart, from week to week
Thou dost play at hide-and-seek;
35   While the patient Primrose sits
Like a Beggar in the cold,
Thou, a Flower of wiser wits,
Slipp'st into thy shelter'd hold;
Bright as any of the train
40   When ye all are out again.[2]

Thou art not beyond the moon,
But a thing "beneath our shoon;"
Let, as old Magellen[3] did,
Others roam about the sea;

---

1. The sign of a shop, inn, or other business.
2. In his *Poems* of 1845 WW transferred to between lines 40 and 41 the stanza that he had previously inserted into *To the Small Celandine*: see the note on line 40 of that poem.
3. Ferdinand Magellan (ca. 1480–1521), Portuguese explorer whose expedition of 1519–22 was the first to sail from the Atlantic Ocean to the Pacific and across the Pacific. In *MP 1820* WW altered lines 43–45 to "Let, with bold adventr'ous skill, / Others thrid the polar sea; / Rear a pyramid who will," and in his *Poetical Works* of 1827 he altered them again: "Let the bold Adventurer thrid / In his bark the polar sea; / Rear who will a pyramid." "*Beneath our shoon*": not a quotation from but an allusion to Milton's *Comus* (1634), lines 634–35: "the dull swayn / treads on it [i.e., "a bright golden flowre"] daily with his clouted shoon [studded shoes]."

45 Build who will a pyramid;
   Praise it is enough for me,
   If there be but three or four
   Who will love my little Flower.

To H. C.,

SIX YEARS OLD[†]

O Thou! whose fancies from afar are brought;
Who of thy words dost make a mock apparel,
And fittest to unutterable thought
The breeze-like motion and the self-born carol;
5 Thou Faery Voyager! that dost float
In such clear water, that thy Boat
May rather seem
To brood on air than on an earthly stream;[1]
Suspended in a stream as clear as sky,
10 Where earth and heaven do make one imagery;
O blessed Vision! happy Child!
That art so exquisitely wild,
I think of thee with many fears
For what may be thy lot in future years.

15 I thought of times when Pain might be thy guest,
Lord of thy house and hospitality;
And grief, uneasy Lover! never rest
But when she sate within the touch of thee.
Oh! too industrious folly!
20 Oh! vain and causeless melancholy!
Nature will either end thee quite;
Or, lengthening out thy season of delight,
Preserve for thee, by individual right,
A young Lamb's heart among the full-grown flocks.
25 What hast Thou to do with sorrow,
Or the injuries of tomorrow?
Thou art a Dew-drop, which the morn brings forth,

† P 1815: Poems referring to Childhood. Composed possibly between March 27 and ca. June 17, 1802; completed almost certainly by March 6, 1804 (*Chrono: MY*, 26, 156, 180–81 n. 55). In a letter of October 14, 1803, STC quoted from line 12 while describing his eldest son Hartley (1796–1849), the H. C. of the title: "Hartley is what he always was—a strange strange Boy— '*exquisitely wild*'! An utter Visionary! like the Moon among thin Clouds, he moves in a circle of Light of his own making—he alone, in a Light of his own" (*CL*, 2:1014). Compare with this poem lines 85–131 of the Intimations Ode (pp. 436–37 below).

1. WW's note on lines 6–8 (printed at the end of vol. 1 of *P2V*, omitted in *P 1815* and thereafter): "See Carver's Description of his Situation upon one of the Lakes of America." WW refers to Jonathan Carver, *Travels through the Interior Parts of North America* (London, 1778), 132–33: "The water [of Lake Superior] in general appeared to lie on a bed of rocks. When it was calm, and the sun shone bright, I could sit in my canoe, where the depth was upwards of six fathoms, and plainly see huge piles of stone at the bottom * * *. The water at this time was as pure and transparent as air; and my canoe seemed as if it hung suspended in that element. It was impossible to look attentively through this limpid medium at the rocks below, without finding, before many minutes were elapsed, your head swim, and your eyes were no longer able to behold the dazzling scene."

Not doom'd to jostle with unkindly shocks;[2]
Or to be trail'd along the soiling earth;
30 A Gem that glitters while it lives,
And no forewarning gives;
But, at the touch of wrong, without a strife
Slips in a moment out of life.

Among all lovely things my Love had been[†]

Among all lovely things my Love had been;
Had noted well the stars, all flowers that grew
About her home; but she had never seen
A Glow-worm, never one, and this I knew.

5   While riding near her home one stormy night
A single Glow-worm did I chance to espy;
I gave a fervent welcome to the sight,
And from my Horse I leapt; great joy had I.

Upon a leaf the Glow-worm did I lay,
10 To bear it with me through the stormy night:
And, as before, it shone without dismay;
Albeit putting forth a fainter light.

When to the Dwelling of my Love I came,
I went into the Orchard quietly;
15 And left the Glow-worm, blessing it by name,
Laid safely by itself, beneath a Tree.

The whole next day, I hoped, and hoped with fear;
At night the Glow-worm shone beneath the Tree:
I led my Lucy to the spot, "Look here!"
20 Oh! joy it was for her, and joy for me!

I travell'd among unknown Men[†]

I travell'd among unknown Men,
In Lands beyond the Sea;
Nor England! did I know till then
What love I bore to thee.

2. In P 1815 WW revised line 28 to "Not framed to undergo unkindly shocks," and in 1827 he
revised it again: "Ill fitted to sustain unkindly shocks."
† Composed on April 12, 1802, and copied into a letter of April 16 to STC (*Chrono: MY*, 27, 160;
WL, 1:347–48). In the letter WW reported, "The incident of this Poem took place about seven
years ago [i.e., at Racedown, Dorset] between Dorothy and me." The poem was ridiculed by
reviewers of *P2V* (e.g., in the *Beau Monde* of October 1807, reprinted in *CH*, 183) and by Richard
Mant (1776–1848) in his *Simpliciad; A Satirico-Didactic Poem* (1808), lines 94–97: "Poets, who
fix their visionary sight / On Sparrow's eggs in prospect of delight, / With fervent welcome greet
the glow-worm's flame, / Put it to bed and bless it by its name." WW never reprinted the poem.
† P 1815: Poems of the Affections. Composed probably ca. April 29, 1801, when WW included a
draft of the poem in a letter to Mary Hutchinson, who made a fair copy in a set of *LB 1800*

5   'Tis past, that melancholy dream!
     Nor will I quit thy shore
     A second time; for still I seem
     To love thee more and more.

     Among thy mountains did I feel
10   The joy of my desire;
     And She I cherish'd turn'd her wheel
     Beside an English fire.

     Thy mornings shew'd—thy nights conceal'd
     The bowers where Lucy play'd;
15   And thine is, too, the last green field
     Which Lucy's eyes survey'd!

ODE TO DUTY[†]

     Stern Daughter of the Voice of God![1]
     O Duty! if that name thou love
     Who art a Light to guide, a Rod
     To check the erring, and reprove;
5   Thou who art victory and law
     When empty terrors overawe;
     From vain temptations dost set free;
     From strife and from despair; a glorious ministry.

     There are who ask not if thine eye
10   Be on them; who, in love and truth,
     Where no misgiving is, rely
     Upon the genial sense of youth:

(*Chrono: MY*, 21; *WL*, 1:333; *P2V* [CW], xxxii). Originally intended for inclusion in *LB 1802* after *A slumber did my spirit seal* (see *P2V* [CW], 407), but in fact first published in *P2V*. On the so-called "Lucy poems" see the first note on *Strange fits of passion I have known* (p. 113 above).
† *P 1815*: Poems proceeding from Sentiment and Reflection. Drafted (apart from the first stanza) probably early in 1804, the first stanza added probably between late March 1804 and early December 1806 (*Chrono: MY*, 36, 247). WW revised the poem considerably in proof and again after printing of the volume had begun, necessitating the replacement of two leaves (the original printed version, which omits the first stanza and begins "There are who tread a blameless way," is reprinted in *P2V* [CW], 109–10). *P2V* (CW), 32, conjectures that STC was involved in the final arrangement of the poem and may even have written the first stanza. IF note: "This ode, written 1805, is on the model of Gray's Ode to Adversity which is copied from Horace's Ode to Fortune—Many & many a time have I been twitted by my wife and sister for having forgotten this dedication of myself to the stern law-giver. Transgressor indeed I have been, from hour to hour, from day to day; I would fain hope however, not more flagrantly nor in a worse way than most of my tuneful brethren. But these last words are in a wrong strain. We should be rigorous to ourselves, & forbearing if not indulgent to others, & if we make comparisons at all it ought to be with those who have morally excelled us." Thomas Gray's *Ode to Adversity* (1753), itself possibly modeled on Horace's *Ode* 1.35, concludes with a request to the personified Adversity, "Teach me to love and to forgive, / Exact my own defects to scan, / What others are, to feel, and know myself a Man" (lines 46–48).
    In 1836 WW added an epigraph adapted from the description of the man of "perfect virtue" in the *Moral Epistles* 120.10 of the Roman writer Seneca the Younger (ca. 4 B.C.E.—65 C.E.): "Jam non consilio bonus, sed more eo perductus, ut non tantum recte facere possim, sed nisi recte facere non possim" [Now I am not deliberately good, but from habit I have been led not only to be able to act rightly, but to be unable to act other than rightly]. For an interpretation of the ode, see the excerpt from Geoffrey Hartman's *Wordsworth's Poetry 1787–1814* reprinted below (pp. 724–29).
1. An allusion to Milton's *Paradise Lost* 9.653, in which Eve describes God's prohibition against eating the apple as "Sole Daughter of his voice."

Glad Hearts! without reproach or blot;
Who do thy work, and know it not:
15   May joy be theirs while life shall last!
And Thou, if they should totter, teach them to stand fast!

Serene will be our days and bright,
And happy will our nature be,
When love is an unerring light,
20   And joy its own security.
And bless'd are they who in the main
This faith, even now, do entertain:
Live in the spirit of this creed;
Yet find that other strength, according to their need.

25   I, loving freedom, and untried;
No sport of every random gust,
Yet being to myself a guide,
Too blindly have reposed my trust:
Resolved that nothing e'er should press
30   Upon my present happiness,
I shoved unwelcome tasks away;[2]
But thee I now would serve more strictly, if I may.

Through no disturbance of my soul,
Or strong compunction in me wrought,
35   I supplicate for thy controul;
But in the quietness of thought:
Me this uncharter'd freedom tires;
I feel the weight of chance desires:[3]
My hopes no more must change their name,
40   I long for a repose which ever is the same.

Yet not the less would I throughout
Still act according to the voice
Of my own wish; and feel past doubt
That my submissiveness was choice:
45   Not seeking in the school of pride
For "precepts over dignified,"[4]
Denial and restraint I prize
No farther than they breed a second Will more wise.

Stern Lawgiver! yet thou dost wear
50   The Godhead's most benignant grace;
Nor know we any thing so fair
As is the smile upon thy face;

---

2. Perhaps an echo of Milton's *Lycidas*, line 118: "And shove away the worthy bidden guest."
3. Compare WW's reference to "the weight of too much liberty" in the *Prefatory Sonnet* (*Nuns fret not*), line 13 (p. 402 below).
4. WW quotes approximately from the Dedication (to parliament) of Milton's treatise *The Doctrine and Discipline of Divorce* (1643), in which he rejects as "empty and overdignifi'd precepts" the Mosaic law, or Torah, prescribed in Exodus, Leviticus, Numbers, and Deuteronomy.

Flowers laugh before thee on their beds;
And Fragrance in thy footing treads;
55 Thou dost preserve the Stars from wrong;
And the most ancient Heavens through Thee are fresh
    and strong.[5]

To humbler functions, awful Power!
I call thee: I myself commend
Unto thy guidance from this hour;
60 Oh! let my weakness have an end!
Give unto me, made lowly wise,[6]
The spirit of self-sacrifice;
The confidence of reason[7] give;
And in the light of truth thy Bondman let me live!

From Poems composed during
a tour, chiefly on foot

1.

BEGGARS[†]

She had a tall Man's height, or more;
No bonnet screen'd her from the heat;
A long drab-colour'd Cloak she wore,
A Mantle reaching to her feet:

5. *P2V* (CW) notes that WW refers to lines 55–56, before proceeding to quote lines 57–64, in his "Reply to 'Mathesis,'" a letter contributed to STC's periodical *The Friend* (December 14, 1809, and January 9, 1810) and advocating the moral self-education of youth: "in his [WW's] character of Philosophical Poet, having thought of Morality as implying in its essence voluntary obedience, and producing the effect of order, he transfers, in the transport of imagination, the law of Moral to physical Natures, and, having contemplated, through the medium of that order, all modes of existence as subservient to one spirit, concludes his address to the power of Duty in the following words" (*Prose*, 2:24).
6. A quotation from Raphael's warning to Adam in *Paradise Lost* 8.173–74: "be lowlie wise: / Think onely what concernes thee and thy being."
7. As *P2V* (CW) notes, a phrase from Samuel Johnson's *Life of Addison* (1771), para. 166: "Truth * * * sometimes steps forth in the confidence of reason." How familiar WW was with Johnson's *Lives of the Poets* at this time is not certain, however (see *Reading 1800–15*, no. 230.iii).
† *P 1815*: Poems of the Imagination. Composed March 13–14, 1802 (*Chrono: MY*, 26), and printed as the first of the five poems in this section of *P2V*, which was given its own title page. WW revised the poem extensively and repeatedly from 1827 onwards (see the critical apparatus in *P2V* [CW], 113–15). IF note: "Town-End. 1802. Met & described by me to my Sister near the Quarry at the head of Rydal Lake—a place still a chosen resort of vagrants travelling with their families." DW recorded the incident in her diary on June 10, 1800: "On Tuesday, May 27th, a very tall woman * * * called at the door. She had on a very long brown cloak and a very white cap without bonnet; her face was excessively brown, but it had plainly once been fair. She led a little bare-footed child about 2 years old by the hand, and said her husband who was a tinker was gone before with the other children. I gave her a piece of bread. Afterwards on my road to Ambleside * * * I saw two boys before me, one about 10, the other about 8 years old, at play chasing a butterfly. They were wild figures, not very ragged, but without shoes and stockings; the hat of the elder was wreathed round with yellow flowers, the younger whose hat was only a rimless crown, had stuck it round with laurel leaves. They continued at play till I drew very near, and then they addressed me with the begging cant and the whining voice of sorrow. I said 'I served your mother this morning.' (The Boys were so like the woman who had called at the door that I could not be mistaken.) 'O!' says the elder, 'you could not serve my mother for she's dead, and my father's on at the next town—he's a potter.' I persisted in my assertion, and that I would give them nothing. Says the elder, 'Come, let's away,' and away they flew like lightning" (*DWJ*, 1:47). In 1808 WW told Henry Crabb Robinson (see Biographical and Topographical Glossary) that the poem's purpose was "the power of physical beauty & the charm of health & vigour in childhood even in a state of the greatest moral depravity" (*HCR*, 1:53).

5   What other dress she had I could not know;
           Only she wore a Cap that was as white as snow.

           In all my walks, through field or town,
           Such Figure had I never seen:
           Her face was of Egyptian brown:
10   Fit person was she for a Queen,
           To head those ancient Amazonian files:[1]
Or ruling Bandit's Wife, among the Grecian Isles.

           Before me begging did she stand,
           Pouring out sorrows like a sea;
15   Grief after grief:—on English Land
           Such woes I knew could never be;
           And yet a boon I gave her; for the Creature
Was beautiful to see; a Weed of glorious feature![2]

           I left her, and pursued my way;
20   And soon before me did espy
           A pair of little Boys at play,
           Chasing a crimson butterfly;
           The Taller follow'd with his hat in hand,
Wreath'd round with yellow flow'rs, the gayest of the land.

25   The Other wore a rimless crown,
           With leaves of laurel stuck about:
           And they both follow'd up and down,
           Each whooping with a merry shout;
           Two Brothers seem'd they, eight and ten years old;
30   And like that Woman's face as gold is like to gold.[3]

           They bolted on me thus, and lo!
           Each ready with a plaintive whine;
           Said I, "Not half an hour ago
           Your Mother has had alms of mine."
35   "That cannot be," one answer'd, "She is dead."
"Nay but I gave her pence, and she will buy you bread."

           "She has been dead, Sir, many a day."
           "Sweet Boys, you're telling me a lie;
           "It was your Mother, as I say—"
40   And in the twinkling of an eye,
           "Come, come!" cried one; and, without more ado,
Off to some other play they both together flew.

---

1. Rows of the legendary female warriors of ancient Scythia.
2. *Weed of glorious feature*: a quotation from Edmund Spenser's *Muiopotmos: or The Fate of the Butterflie* (1590), line 213.
3. In *MP 1820* WW altered lines 29–30: "In their fraternal features I could trace / Unquestionable lines of that wild Suppliant's face."

5.

RESOLUTION AND INDEPENDENCE†

There was a roaring in the wind all night;
The rain came heavily and fell in floods;
But now the sun is rising calm and bright;
The birds are singing in the distant woods;
5   Over his own sweet voice the Stock-dove broods;[1]
The Jay makes answer as the Magpie chatters;
And all the air is fill'd with pleasant noise of waters.

All things that love the sun are out of doors;
The sky rejoices in the morning's birth;
10   The grass is bright with rain drops; on the moors
The Hare is running races in her mirth;
And with her feet she from the plashy[2] earth
Raises a mist; which, glittering in the sun,
Runs with her all the way, wherever she doth run.

† *P 1815*: Poems of the Imagination. Drafted May 3–7, 1802 (*Chrono: MY*, 28), with the title *The Leech-gatherer* and sent to Sara and Mary Hutchinson (see *P2V* [CW], 316–23 for the text of Sara's transcript). Responding to Sara's objections to that original version, WW explained: "I describe myself as having been exalted to the highest pitch of delight by the joyousness and beauty of Nature and then as depressed, even in the midst of those beautiful objects, to the lowest dejection and despair. A young Poet in the midst of the happiness of Nature is described as overwhelmed by the thought of the miserable reverses which have befallen the happiest of all men, viz Poets—I think of this till I am so deeply impressed by it, that I consider the manner in which I was rescued from my dejection and despair almost as an interposition of Providence. ∗ ∗ ∗ I then describe him, whether ill or well is not for me to judge with perfect confidence, but this I can *confidently* affirm, that, though I believe God has given me a strong imagination, I cannot conceive a figure more impressive than that of an old Man like this, the survivor of a Wife and ten children, travelling alone among the mountains and all lonely places, carrying with him his own fortitude, and the necessities which an unjust state of society has entailed upon him" (*WL*, 1:366–67). A much-revised version of the poem (with the published title and omitting reference to the leech-gatherer's family) was copied for the printer in November 1806, WW intending that it should form the first poem of a section with the general title "Resolution and Independence"; but he then changed his mind and placed the poem at the end of the present section (*P2V* [CW], 123).
   In the IF note WW recalled, "This Old Man I met a few hundred yards from my cottage at Town-End, Grasmere; & the account of him is taken from his own mouth. I was in the state of feeling described in the beginning of the poem, while crossing over Barton Fell from Mr. Clarkson's [i.e., the abolitionist Thomas Clarkson (1760–1846)] at the foot of Ulswater, towards Askam [i.e., at the northern end of Ullswater, ca. 12 miles northeast of Grasmere]. The image of the hare I then observed on a ridge of the fell." DW recorded the incident in her journal on October 3, 1800: "we met an old man almost double. He had on a coat, thrown over his shoulders, above his waistcoat and coat. Under this he carried a bundle, and had an apron on and a night-cap. ∗ ∗ ∗ He had dark eyes and a long nose. John [Wordsworth] ∗ ∗ ∗ took him for a Jew. He was of Scotch parents, but had been born in the army. He had had a wife, and 'a good woman, and it pleased God to bless us with ten children.' ∗ ∗ ∗ His trade was to gather leeches, but now leeches are scarce, and he had not strength for it. He lived by begging, and was making his way to Carlisle [near the Scottish border], where he should buy a few godly books to sell. ∗ ∗ ∗ He had been hurt in driving a cart, his leg broke, his body driven over, his skull fractured" (*DWJ*, 1:63). On September 10, 1816, Henry Crabb Robinson recorded WW as telling him that "he did actually meet [the leech-gatherer] near Grasmere, except that he gave to his poetic character powers of mind which his original did not possess" (*Diary, Reminiscences, and Correspondence*, ed. Thomas Sadler, 3rd ed. [London, 1872], 1:278). For a discussion of "the poem's consciousness of itself as a poem," see the excerpt from Michael O'Neill's *Romanticism and the Self-Conscious Poem* reprinted below (pp. 716–21). On the verse form, see the note on line 43.
1. WW quoted this line in the Preface to *P 1815* in order to illustrate how "the affections are called in by the imagination to assist in marking the manner in which the bird reiterates and prolongs her soft note" (p. 513 below).
2. Marshy, full of small pools or puddles.

15 I was a Traveller then upon the moor;
   I saw the Hare that rac'd about with joy;
   I heard the woods, and distant waters, roar;
   Or heard them not, as happy as a Boy:
   The pleasant season did my heart employ:
20 My old remembrances went from me wholly;
   And all the ways of men, so vain and melancholy.

   But, as it sometimes chanceth, from the might
   Of joy in minds that can no farther go,
   As high as we have mounted in delight
25 In our dejection do we sink as low,
   To me that morning did it happen so;
   And fears, and fancies, thick upon me came;
   Dim sadness, & blind thoughts I knew not nor could name.

   I heard the Sky-lark singing in the sky;
30 And I bethought me of the playful Hare:
   Even such a happy Child of earth am I;
   Even as these blissful Creatures do I fare;
   Far from the world I walk, and from all care;
   But there may come another day to me,
35 Solitude, pain of heart, distress, and poverty.

   My whole life I have liv'd in pleasant thought,
   As if life's business were a summer mood;
   As if all needful things would come unsought
   To genial faith, still rich in genial good;
40 But how can He expect that others should
   Build for him, sow for him, and at his call
   Love him, who for himself will take no heed at all!

   I thought of Chatterton,[3] the marvellous Boy,
   The sleepless Soul that perish'd in its pride;
45 Of Him[4] who walk'd in glory and in joy
   Behind his plough, upon the mountain-side:
   By our own spirits are we deified;
   We Poets in our youth begin in gladness;
   But thereof comes in the end despondency and madness.[5]

3. Thomas Chatterton (1752–1770), who died of an arsenic overdose at age seventeen, composed pseudo-antique poetry that purported to be by a fifteenth-century monk called Thomas Rowley. WW's verse form, a variant of rhyme royal (*ababbcc*) with a hexameter final line in each stanza, is adopted from Chatterton's *Excelent Balade of Charitie* (1770).
4. Robert Burns (see Biographical and Topographical Glossary), whose short life was marked by financial difficulties and ill health. See also the *Address to the Sons of Burns* below (pp. 415–16).
5. As *P2V* (CW) point out, WW's phrasing in lines 48–49 recalls stanza 35 of his "translation" of *The Cuckoo and the Nightingale*, a poem attributed in WW's time to Chaucer but now to Sir John Clanvowe (d. 1391) or his son Thomas (d. 1410): "For thereof come all contraries to gladness; / thence sickness comes, and overwhelming sadness, / Mistrust and jealousy, despite, debate, / Dishonour, shame, envy importunate, / Pride, anger, mischief, poverty, and madness" (*Translations of Chaucer and Virgil* [CW], 50).

50　Now, whether it were by peculiar grace,
　　A leading from above, a something given,
　　Yet it befel, that, in this lonely place,
　　When up and down my fancy thus was driven,
　　And I with these untoward thoughts had striven,[6]
55　I saw a Man before me unawares:
　　The oldest Man he seem'd that ever wore grey hairs.

　　My course I stopped as soon as I espied
　　The Old Man in that naked wilderness:
　　Close by a Pond, upon the further side,
60　He stood alone: a minute's space I guess
　　I watch'd him, he continuing motionless:
　　To the Pool's further margin then I drew;
　　He being all the while before me full in view.[7]

　　As a huge Stone is sometimes seen to lie
65　Couch'd on the bald top of an eminence;
　　Wonder to all who do the same espy
　　By what means it could thither come, and whence;
　　So that it seems a thing endued with sense:
　　Like a Sea-beast crawl'd forth, which on a shelf
70　Of rock or sand reposeth, there to sun itself.

　　Such seem'd this Man, not all alive nor dead,
　　Nor all asleep; in his extreme old age:[8]
　　His body was bent double, feet and head
　　Coming together in their pilgrimage;
75　As if some dire constraint of pain, or rage
　　Of sickness felt by him in times long past,
　　A more than human weight upon his frame had cast.

　　Himself he propp'd, his body, limbs, and face,
　　Upon a long grey Staff of shaven wood:
80　And, still as I drew near with gentle pace,
　　Beside the little pond or moorish flood[9]
　　Motionless as a Cloud the Old Man stood;
　　That heareth not the loud winds when they call;
　　And moveth altogether, if it move at all.

85　At length, himself unsettling, he the Pond
　　Stirred with his Staff, and fixedly did look
　　Upon the muddy water, which he conn'd,

6. In *MP 1820* WW altered lines 53–54 to "When I with these untoward thoughts had striven, / Beside a Pool bare to the eye of Heaven."
7. In *BL* STC juxtaposed lines 59–63 and 80–84 to illustrate what he considered WW's "*disharmony* in style" (*NCC*, 525–26). In *MP 1820* WW omitted the stanza containing lines 57–63 altogether.
8. In the Preface to *P 1815* WW quoted lines 64–72 and 82–84 to illustrate "the conferring, the abstracting, and the modifying powers of the Imagination" (p. 514 below).
9. In *MP 1820* WW altered this line to "Upon the margin of that Moorish flood."

As if he had been reading in a book:
And now such freedom as I could I took;[1]
90 And, drawing to his side, to him did say,
"This morning gives us promise of a glorious day."

A gentle answer did the Old Man make,
In courteous speech which forth he slowly drew:
And him with further words I thus bespake,
95 "What kind of work is that which you pursue![2]
This is a lonesome place for one like you."
He answer'd me with pleasure and surprize;
And there was, while he spake, a fire about his eyes.

His words came feebly, from a feeble chest,
100 Yet each in solemn order follow'd each,
With something of a lofty utterance drest;
Choice word, and measured phrase; above the reach
Of ordinary men; a stately speech!
Such as grave Livers do in Scotland use,
105 Religious men, who give to God and Man their dues.

He told me that he to this pond had come
To gather Leeches, being old and poor:
Employment hazardous and wearisome!
And he had many hardships to endure:
110 From Pond to Pond he roam'd, from moor to moor,
Housing, with God's good help, by choice or chance:
And in this way he gain'd an honest maintenance.

The Old Man still stood talking by my side;
But now his voice to me was like a stream
115 Scarce heard; nor word from word could I divide;
And the whole Body of the man did seem
Like one whom I had met with in a dream;
Or like a Man from some far region sent;
To give me human strength, and strong admonishment.

120 My former thoughts return'd: the fear that kills;
The hope that is unwilling to be fed;
Cold, pain, and labour, and all fleshly ills;
And mighty Poets in their misery dead.
And now, not knowing[3] what the Old Man had said,
125 My question eagerly did I renew,
"How is it that you live, and what is it you do?"

He with a smile did then his words repeat;
And said, that, gathering Leeches, far and wide

1. In *MP 1820* WW altered this line to "And now a stranger's privilege I took."
2. In *MP 1820* WW altered this line to "What occupation do you there pursue?"
3. Altered in *P 1815* to "But now, perplex'd by." In *MP 1820* WW altered the entire line to "Perplexed, and longing to be comforted."

He travelled; stirring thus about his feet
130 The waters of the Ponds where they abide.
"Once I could meet with them on every side;
But they have dwindled long by slow decay;
Yet still I persevere, and find them where I may."

While he was talking thus, the lonely place,
135 The Old Man's shape, and speech, all troubled me:
In my mind's eye I seem'd to see him pace
About the weary moors continually,
Wandering about alone and silently.
While I these thoughts within myself pursued,
140 He, having made a pause, the same discourse renewed.

And soon with this he other matter blended,
Chearfully uttered, with demeanour kind,
But stately in the main; and, when he ended,
I could have laugh'd myself to scorn, to find
145 In that decrepit Man so firm a mind.
"God," said I, "be my help and stay secure;
I'll think of the Leech-gatherer on the lonely moor."

From SONNETS[†]

PREFATORY SONNET[‡]

Nuns fret not at their Convent's narrow room;
And Hermits are contented with their Cells;
And Students with their pensive Citadels:
Maids at the Wheel,[1] the Weaver at his Loom,
5 Sit blithe and happy; Bees that soar for bloom,
High as the highest Peak of Furness Fells,[2]
Will murmur by the hour in Foxglove bells:
In truth, the prison, unto which we doom
Ourselves, no prison is: and hence to me,
10 In sundry moods, 'twas pastime to be bound
Within the Sonnet's scanty plot of ground:

---

† This is the first of the two sections of sonnets with which vol. 1 of *P2V* concludes. In his IF note on this section WW explained how his interest in the sonnet form was stimulated: "In the cottage of Town-End, one afternoon, in 1801, my Sister read to me the Sonnets of Milton. I had long been well acquainted with them, but I was particularly struck on that occasion with the dignified simplicity and majestic harmony that runs through most of them—in character so totally different from the Italian, and still more so from Shakespeare's fine Sonnets. I took fire, if I may be allowed to say so, and produced three sonnets the same afternoon, the first I ever wrote, except an irregular one at School. Of these three the only one I distinctly remember is, "*I grieved for Bonaparte* &c." One was never written down; the third, which was I believe preserved, I cannot particularise." WW misremembered the date, which *DWJ*, 1:149, gives as May 21, 1802; and *P2V* (CW), 409, notes that he had actually composed at least five sonnets before that date, one of which (*Written in very early Youth*) was published in *P2V*. On WW's use of the sonnet, see the excerpt from Stuart Curran's *Poetic Form and British Romanticism* reprinted below (pp. 672–78).
‡ *P 1815*: Miscellaneous Sonnets. Composed perhaps in late 1802 (*Chrono: MY*, 32).
1. I.e., spinning-wheel.
2. The hills and mountains of the Furness peninsula in the southwestern part of the Lake District. The *highest Peak* of the Furness Fells is Coniston Old Man (2,634 feet).

Pleas'd if some Souls (for such there needs must be)
Who have felt the weight of too much liberty,
Should find short solace there, as I have found.

From Miscellaneous Sonnets

9.

TO THE RIVER DUDDON[†]

petrarchan sonnet

O mountain Stream! the Shepherd and his Cot
Are privileg'd Inmates of deep solitude:
Nor would the nicest Anchorite[1] exclude
A Field or two of brighter green, or Plot
5   Of tillage-ground, that seemeth like a spot
Of stationary sunshine: thou hast view'd
These only, Duddon! with their paths renew'd
By fits and starts, yet this contents thee not.
Thee hath some awful Spirit impell'd to leave,
10   Utterly to desert, the haunts of men,
Though simple thy Companions were and few;
And through[2] this wilderness a passage cleave
Attended but by thy own Voice, save when
The Clouds and Fowls of the air thy way pursue.

14.

COMPOSED UPON

WESTMINSTER BRIDGE,

Sept. 3, 1803[†]

Earth has not any thing to shew more fair:
Dull would he be of soul who could pass by
A sight so touching in its majesty:
This City now doth like a garment wear

---

† P 1815: Miscellaneous Sonnets. Composed possibly between September 27 and October 1804 (*Chrono: MY*, 38). On the River Duddon see the Topographical and Biographical Glossary. WW later devoted a sonnet sequence to the river, published in *The River Duddon: A Series of Sonnets; Vaudracour and Julia; and Other Poems* (1820).
1. The strictest recluse.
2. The reading in *P2V* is "though," a printer's error corrected in *P 1815*.
† P 1815: Miscellaneous Sonnets. Begun perhaps on July 31, 1802, and completed probably on September 3, 1802. IF note: "composed on the roof of a coach, on my way to France, Sepbr. 1802." Compare DW's description of the scene: "After various troubles and disasters, we left London on Saturday morning at 1/2-past 5 or 6, the 31st of July (I have forgot which). We mounted the Dover Coach at Charing Cross [in London]. It was a beautiful morning. The City, St. Paul's, with the River [Thames] and a multitude of little boats, made a most beautiful sight as we crossed Westminster Bridge. The houses were not yet overhung by their cloud of smoke, and they were spread out endlessly, yet the sun shone so brightly, with such a fierce light, that there was even something like the purity of one of nature's own grand spectacles" (*DWJ*, 1:172–73). WW and DW were traveling to Calais to see Annette and Caroline Vallon (see Biographical and Topographical Glossary), during the (temporary) cessation of hostilities between France and Britain, negotiated in May 1802. WW did not correct the year given in the title until 1838.

5   The beauty of the morning; silent, bare,
    Ships, towers, domes, theatres, and temples lie
    Open unto the fields, and to the sky;
    All bright and glittering in the smokeless air.
    Never did sun more beautifully steep
10   In his first splendor valley, rock, or hill;
    Ne'er saw I, never felt, a calm so deep!
    The river glideth at his own sweet will:
    Dear God! the very houses seem asleep;
    And all that mighty heart is lying still!

15.[†] *delightful*

    "Beloved Vale!" I said, "when I shall con[1]
    Those many records of my childish years,
    Remembrance of myself and of my peers
    Will press me down: to think of what is gone
5   Will be an awful thought, if life have one."
    But, when into the Vale I came, no fears
    Distress'd me; I look'd round, I shed no tears;
    Deep thought, or awful vision, I had none.
    By thousand petty fancies I was cross'd,
10   To see the Trees, which I had thought so tall,   *he grew up—*
    Mere dwarfs; the Brooks so narrow, Fields so small. *things looked smaller now*
    A Juggler's Balls old Time about him toss'd;
    I looked, I stared, I smiled, I laughed; and all
    The weight of sadness was in wonder lost.

positive anxesis

18.[†]

    The world is too much with us; late and soon,
    Getting and spending, we lay waste our powers:
    Little we see in nature that is ours;
    We have given our hearts away, a sordid boon!
5   This Sea that bares her bosom to the moon;
    The Winds that will be howling at all hours
    And are up-gathered now like sleeping flowers;
    For this, for every thing, we are out of tune;
    It moves us not[1]—Great God! I'd rather be
10   A Pagan suckled in a creed outworn;
    So might I, standing on this pleasant lea,

---

† *P 1815*: Miscellaneous Sonnets. Composed probably between May 21 and late 1802 (*Chrono: MY*, 30).
1. Study, peruse; *Vale*: probably Esthwaite Vale, the valley in which Hawkshead is situated.
† *P 1815*: Miscellaneous Sonnets. Composed probably between May 21, 1802, and March 6, 1804 (*Chrono: MY*, 29).
1. In *P 1815* WW inserted a period before the dash (partly recovering the punctuation of the manuscript sent to the printer, which had a period without a dash).

Have glimpses that would make me less forlorn;[2]
Have sight of Proteus coming from the sea;
Or hear old Triton[3] blow his wreathed horn.

19.†

It is a beauteous Evening, calm and free;
The holy time is quiet as a Nun
Breathless with adoration; the broad sun
Is sinking down in its tranquillity;
5 The gentleness of heaven is on the Sea:
Listen! the mighty Being is awake
And doth with his eternal motion make
A sound like thunder—everlastingly.
Dear Child![1] dear Girl! that walkest with me here,
10 If thou appear'st untouch'd by solemn thought,
Thy nature is not therefore less divine:
Thou liest in Abraham's bosom all the year;[2]
And worshipp'st at the Temple's inner shrine,[3]
God being with thee when we know it not.

20.

TO THE MEMORY
OF
RAISLEY CALVERT†

Calvert! it must not be unheard by them
Who may respect my name that I to thee

---

2. The semicolon after the word is an editorial emendation after WW's correction in *P 1815*, restoring the reading of the printer's manuscript. In some copies of P2V the line ends with a colon, in others with no punctuation mark (*P2V* [CW], 150). *pleasant lea*: a phrase from Edmund Spenser's *Colin Clouts Come Home Again* (1595), line 283, a *lea* being a tract of open ground.
3. In Greek mythology, the son of Poseidon and Amphitrite (the god and goddess respectively of the sea), who blows through a twisted conch shell to raise or calm the waves; *Proteus*: in Greek mythology, a shape-changing sea god (WW perhaps recalling Milton's *Paradise Lost* 3.603–604: "call up unbound / In various shapes old Proteus from the Sea").
† *P 1815*: Miscellaneous Sonnets. IF note: "This was composed on the beach near Calais in the autumn of 1802." WW probably composed the sonnet between August 1 and 29, 1802 (*Chrono: MY*, 31), when he and DW were in Calais to meet Annette Vallon and her daughter by WW, Caroline (see Biographical and Topographical Glossary), before his marriage to Mary Hutchinson. It was the first time WW had seen Caroline, now aged nine. In her journal DW recorded, "The weather was very hot. We walked by the seashore almost every evening with Annette and Caroline, or Wm. and I alone" (*DWJ*, 1:174).
1. Caroline Vallon.
2. WW alludes to Luke 16.22: "And it came to pass, that the beggar died, and was carried by the angels into Abraham's bosom." In the parable of the beggar Lazarus and the rich man (Luke 16.19–31), the fortunes of the two in life are reversed in death, Lazarus being taken to heaven and the rich man sent to hell.
3. A figurative reference to the ancient Israelite Temple built by Solomon in Jerusalem, the innermost room of which, the Holy of Holies, entered by the high priest only on Yom Kippur, contained the Ark of the Covenant, a symbol of God's presence (see 1 Kings 6).
† *P 1815*: Miscellaneous Sonnets. Composed probably between May 21, 1802, and March 6, 1804 (*Chrono: MY*, 29). On Calvert, who died of tuberculosis in January 1795, leaving WW a bequest of £900, see the Biographical and Topographical Glossary and *The Prelude* 13.349–67.

Ow'd many years of early liberty.
This care was thine when sickness did condemn
5 Thy youth to hopeless wasting, root and stem:
That I, if frugal and severe, might stray
Where'er I liked; and finally array
My temples with the Muse's diadem.
Hence, if in freedom I have lov'd the truth,
10 If there be aught of pure, or good, or great,
In my past verse; or shall be, in the lays
Of higher mood,[1] which now I meditate,
It gladdens me, O worthy, short-lived Youth!
To think how much of this will be thy praise.

From Sonnets Dedicated to Liberty[†]

1.

COMPOSED BY THE

SEA-SIDE, near CALAIS,

August, 1802[‡]

Fair Star of Evening, Splendor of the West,
Star of my Country! on the horizon's brink
Thou hangest, stooping, as might seem, to sink
On England's bosom; yet well pleas'd to rest,
5 Meanwhile, and be to her a glorious crest
Conspicuous to the Nations. Thou, I think,
Should'st be my Country's emblem; and should'st wink,
Bright Star! with laughter on her banners, drest
In thy fresh beauty. There! that dusky spot
10 Beneath thee, it is England; there it lies.
Blessings be on you both! one hope, one lot,
One life, one glory! I, with many a fear
For my dear Country, many heartfelt sighs,
Among Men who do not love her linger here.

1. An echo of Milton's *Lycidas* (1637), line 87: "That strain I heard was of a higher mood."
† On May 21, 1807, WW wrote Lady Beaumont about this section of *P2V*, "I would boldly say at once, that these Sonnets, while they each fix the attention upon some important sentiment separately considered, do at the same time collectively make a Poem on the subject of civil Liberty and national independence, which, either for simplicity of style or grandeur of moral sentiment, is, alas! likely to have few parallels in the Poetry of the present day" (*WL*, 2:147).
‡ *P 1815*: Sonnets dedicated to Liberty. Composed probably between August 1 and 29, 1802 (*Chrono: MY*, 31). See the first note on *It is a beauteous Evening, calm and free* for the circumstances of WW's visit to Calais in August 1802. In her journal DW observed, "we had delightful walks after the heat of the day was passed away—seeing far off the coast of England like a cloud crested with Dover Castle, which was built like the summit of the cloud—the evening star and the glory of the sky" (*DWJ*, 1:174).

2.

C A L A I S,

August, 1802[†]

Is it a Reed that's shaken by the wind,
Or what is it that ye go forth to see?[1]
Lords, Lawyers, Statesmen, Squires of low degree,
Men known, and men unknown, Sick, Lame, and Blind,
5   Post forward all, like Creatures of one kind,
With first-fruit offerings[2] crowd to bend the knee
In France, before the new-born Majesty.
'Tis ever thus. Ye Men of prostrate mind!
A seemly reverence may be paid to power;
10 But that's a loyal virtue, never sown
In haste, nor springing with a transient shower:
When truth, when sense, when liberty were flown
What hardship had it been to wait an hour?
Shame on you, feeble Heads, to slavery prone!

4.[†]

I griev'd for Buonaparte, with a vain
And an unthinking grief! the vital blood
Of that Man's mind what can it be? What food
Fed his first hopes? What knowledge could He gain?[1]
5   'Tis not in battles that from youth we train
The Governor who must be wise and good,
And temper with the sternness of the brain
Thoughts motherly, and meek as womanhood.
Wisdom doth live with children round her knees:
10 Books, leisure, perfect freedom, and the talk
Man holds with week-day man in the hourly walk
Of the mind's business: these are the degrees
By which true Sway doth mount; this is the stalk
True Power doth grow on; and her rights are these.

---

† P 1815: Sonnets dedicated to Liberty. Composed probably between August 1 and 29, 1802 (*Chrono: MY*, 31); first published in the *Morning Post*, January 13, 1803.
1. An ironic allusion to Matthew 11.7: "And as they departed, Jesus began to say unto the multitudes concerning John [the Baptist], What went ye out into the wilderness to see? A reed shaken with the wind?"
2. Religious offerings of the first produce of a harvest, here referring metaphorically to France's devotion to Napoleon (see Biographical and Topographical Glossary), whose appointment as Consul for Life was confirmed by plebiscite on August 16, 1802. In the *Morning Post* line 8 read, "Thus fares it ever. Men of prostrate mind!"
† P 1815: Sonnets dedicated to Liberty. Composed probably on May 21, 1802 (*Chrono: MY*, 29); first published in the *Morning Post*, September 16, 1802 (and reprinted January 29, 1803). In P 1815 WW added the date 1801 as the title.
1. In P 1815 WW altered lines 2–4 to "And an unthinking grief! for, who aspires / To genuine greatness but from just desires. / And knowledge such as *He* could never gain?"

5.

CALAIS,

August 15th, 1802[†]

Festivals have I seen that were not names:
This is young Buonaparte's natal day;
And his is henceforth an established sway,
Consul for life.[1] With worship France proclaims
5   Her approbation, and with pomps and games.
Heaven grant that other Cities may be gay!
Calais is not: and I have bent my way
To the Sea-coast, noting that each man frames
His business as he likes. Another time
10 That was, when I was here long years ago:[2]
The senselessness of joy was then sublime!
Happy is he, who, caring not for Pope,
Consul, or King, can sound[3] himself to know
The destiny of Man, and live in hope.

8.

TO TOUSSAINT L'OUVERTURE[†]

Toussaint, the most unhappy Man of Men!
Whether the rural Milk-maid by her Cow
Sing in thy hearing, or thou liest now
Alone in some deep dungeon's earless den,[1]
5 O miserable chieftain! where and when
Wilt thou find patience? Yet die not; do thou

---

† *P 1815*: Sonnets dedicated to Liberty. Composed probably on August 15, 1802 (*Chrono: MY*, 32); first published in the *Morning Post*, February 26, 1803.
1. See the note on line 6 of *Calais, August, 1802. Buonaparte's natal day*: Napoleon was born on August 15, 1769.
2. A reference to WW's arrival in Calais with his friend Robert Jones on July 13, 1790, at the beginning of their walking tour through France, Switzerland, and the Rhineland: see *The Prelude* 6.349–60.
3. Consult.
† *P 1815*: Sonnets dedicated to Liberty. Composed probably between August 1 and 29, 1802 (*Chrono: MY*, 31); first published in the *Morning Post*, February 2, 1803 (signed W. L. D.). François-Dominique Toussaint Louverture (1743–1803), born a slave in Saint-Domingue, a French colony in the western half of the island of Hispaniola (modern Haiti), was a leader of a revolt in 1791–93 that compelled the French to emancipate the colony's slaves. Joining the French army in 1794, he conducted a campaign against occupying Spanish and British troops in Hispaniola, and by 1798 had become the most powerful military commander in the colony. Leading, against the wishes of the French government, an invasion of the neighboring Spanish colony of Santo Domingo (modern Dominican Republic) in 1801, he quickly assumed control of the entire island and promulgated a new constitution, confirming the abolition of slavery and making himself the governor for life. In early 1802 Napoleon sent an expedition to restore French authority, and Toussaint Louverture was arrested and deported to France, arriving in July. On August 25, possibly after WW had written the sonnet, Toussaint Louverture was imprisoned in the castle Fort-de-Joux, in the Jura Mountains, and on April 7, 1803, he was to die there.
1. In *P 1815* WW altered lines 2–4 to "Whether the all-cheering sun be free to shed / His beams around thee, or thou rest thy head / Pillowed in some dark dungeon's noisome den," and in *MP 1820* he altered them again: "Whether the whistling Rustic tend his plough / Within thy hearing, or Thou liest now / Beside some deep dungeon's earless den."

Wear rather in thy bonds a chearful brow:
Though fallen Thyself, never to rise again,
Live, and take comfort. Thou hast left behind[2]
10 Powers that will work for thee; air, earth, and skies;
There's not a breathing of the common wind
That will forget thee; thou hast great allies;
Thy friends are exultations, agonies,
And love, and Man's unconquerable mind.[3]

12.

THOUGHT OF A BRITON

ON THE

SUBJUGATION OF SWITZERLAND[†]

Two Voices are there; one is of the Sea,
One of the Mountains; each a mighty Voice:
In both from age to age Thou didst rejoice,
They were thy chosen Music, Liberty!
5 There came a Tyrant, and with holy glee
Thou fought'st against Him;[1] but hast vainly striven;
Thou from thy Alpine Holds at length art driven,
Where not a torrent murmurs heard by thee.
Of one deep bliss thine ear hath been bereft:
10 Then cleave, O cleave to that which still is left!
For, high-soul'd Maid, what sorrow would it be
That mountain Floods should thunder as before,
And Ocean bellow from his rocky shore,
And neither awful Voice be heard by thee!

2. In the *Morning Post* lines 6–9 read, "* * * be thou / Life to thyself in death; with cheerful brow / Live, loving death, not let one thought in ten / Be painful to thee. * * *"
3. A phrase from Thomas Gray's ode *The Progress of Poesy* (1757), line 65 (*P2V* [CW], 413).
† *P 1815*: Sonnets dedicated to Liberty. Composed probably between October 30, 1806, and late February 1807 (*Chrono: MY*, 43); reprinted by STC in his periodical *The Friend*, October 26, 1809, as "one of the noblest Sonnets in our Language, and the happiest comment on the line of Milton [*L'Allegro*, line 36]—'The *mountain* Nymph, sweet Liberty'" (*The Friend*, 2:233). From the IF note: "This was composed while pacing to and fro between the Hall of Coleorton [see Biographical and Topographical Glossary], then rebuilding, & the principal Farm-house of the Estate, in which we lived for 9 or 10 months." WW himself described the sonnet in 1808 as the best he had written (*WL*, 2:265), and he told Henry Crabb Robinson, "were it generally admired it would evince an elevation of mind an[d] a strength & purity [of] fancy which we have not yet witnessed" (*HCR*, 1:53). In March 1798 the French army had invaded Switzerland and imposed a central government on the previously autonomous Swiss cantons, and Swiss independence from France was not fully restored until after Napoleon's defeat in 1815, although resistance from the Swiss and counter-attacks by Austrian and Russian forces had compelled Napoleon to negotiate an Act of Mediation, reestablishing the Swiss Confederation, in 1803.
1. Napoleon.

13.

WRITTEN IN LONDON,

September, 1802[†]

O Friend! I know not which way I must look
For comfort, being, as I am, opprest,
To think that now our Life is only drest
For shew; mean handywork of craftsman, cook,
5   Or groom! We must run glittering like a Brook
In the open sunshine, or we are unblest:
The wealthiest man among us is the best:
No grandeur now in nature or in book
Delights us. Rapine, avarice,[1] expence,
10   This is idolatry; and these we adore:
Plain living and high thinking are no more:
The homely beauty of the good old cause
Is gone; our peace, our fearful innocence,
And pure religion breathing household laws.

14.

LONDON,

1802[†]

Milton! thou should'st be living at this hour:
England hath need of thee: she is a fen
Of stagnant waters: altar, sword and pen,
Fireside, the heroic wealth of hall and bower,
5   Have forfeited their ancient English dower
Of inward happiness. We are selfish men;
Oh! raise us up, return to us again;
And give us manners, virtue, freedom, power.
Thy soul was like a Star and dwelt apart:
10   Thou hadst a voice whose sound was like the sea;
Pure as the naked heavens, majestic, free,

† P 1815: Sonnets dedicated to Liberty. Composed probably by September 22, 1802 (*Chrono: MY*, 32). IF note: "This was written immediately after my return from France to London, when I could not but be struck, as here described, with the vanity and parade of our own country, especially in great towns and cities as contrasted with the quiet, and I may say the desolation, that the revolution had produced in France. This must be borne in mind, or else the reader may think that in this & the succeeding sonnets I have exaggerated the mischief engendered & fostered among us by undisturbed wealth."

1. Possibly an echo of Milton's Sonnet 15 (*On the Lord General Fairfax*), lines 13–14: "In vain doth Valour bleed / While Avarice, & Rapine share the land." *Good old cause* (line 12): popular name for the republican cause in the English Civil War (1642–51).

† P 1815: Sonnets dedicated to Liberty. Composed probably by September 22, 1802 (*Chrono: MY*, 32). In November 1802 WW informed an unidentified correspondent, "Milton's Sonnets * * * I think manly and dignified compositions, distinguished by simplicity and unity of object and aim, and undisfigured by false or vicious ornaments. They are in several places incorrect, and sometimes uncouth in language, and, perhaps, in some, inharmonious; yet, upon the whole, I think the music exceedingly well suited to its end, that is, it has an energetic and varied flow of sound crowding into narrow room more of the combined effect of rhyme and blank verse than can be done by any other kind of verse I know of" (*WL*, 1:379).

So didst thou travel on life's common way,
In chearful godliness; and yet thy heart
The lowliest duties on itself[1] did lay.

18.

October, 1803[†]

One might believe that natural miseries
Had blasted France, and made of it a land
Unfit for Men; and that in one great Band
Her Sons were bursting forth, to dwell at ease.
5 But 'tis a chosen soil, where sun and breeze
Shed gentle favors; rural works are there;
And ordinary business without care;
Spot rich in all things that can soothe and please!
How piteous then that there should be such dearth
10 Of knowledge; that whole myriads should unite
To work against themselves such fell despite:[1]
Should come in phrenzy and in drunken mirth,
Impatient to put out the only light
Of Liberty that yet remains on Earth!

20.

October, 1803[†]

These times touch money'd Worldlings[1] with dismay:
Even rich men, brave by nature, taint the air
With words of apprehension and despair:
While tens of thousands, thinking on the affray,
5 Men unto whom sufficient for the day
And minds not stinted or untill'd are given,
Sound, healthy Children of the God of Heaven,
Are cheerful as the rising Sun in May.
What do we gather hence but firmer faith
10 That every gift of noble origin
Is breathed upon by Hope's perpetual breath;
That virtue and the faculties within
Are vital, and that riches are akin
To fear, to change, to cowardice, and death!

1. Altered in *MP 1820* to "herself."
† *P 1815*: Sonnets dedicated to Liberty. Composed probably between October 14, 1803, and early January 1804 (*Chrono: MY*, 36). Shortly after the resumption of war between Britain and France in May 1803, Napoleon established a camp in Boulogne, on France's northern coast, to prepare a force to invade England. Financed by the sale of France's North American territories to the United States (the Louisiana Purchase) in 1803, preparations continued until 1805, when the plan was abandoned. This sonnet and the next two were written when the French invasion was expected imminently.
1. Cruel punishment.
† *P 1815*: Sonnets dedicated to Liberty. On the date of composition and political context, see the source note to Sonnet 18.
1. Worldly, pleasure-seeking people.

22.

October, 1803†

When, looking on the present face of things,
I see one Man,¹ of Men the meanest too!
Rais'd up to sway the World, to do, undo,
With mighty Nations for his Underlings,
5   The great events with which old story rings
Seem vain and hollow; I find nothing great;
Nothing is left which I can venerate;
So that almost a doubt within me springs
Of Providence, such emptiness at length
10   Seems at the heart of all things. But, great God!
I measure back the steps which I have trod,
And tremble, seeing, as I do, the strength
Of such poor Instruments, with thoughts sublime
I tremble at the sorrow of the time.

From Poems Written during a Tour in Scotland†
2.
THE SOLITARY REAPER‡

Behold her, single in the field,
Yon solitary Highland Lass!
Reaping and singing by herself;
Stop here, or gently pass!
5   Alone she cuts, and binds the grain,

† P 1815: Sonnets dedicated to Liberty. On the date of composition and political context, see note 1 to Sonnet 18.
1. Napoleon.
† From the IF note: "Mr. Coleridge, my Sister & myself started together from Town End to make a tour in Scotland—August [15, 1803]. Poor Coleridge was at that time in bad spirits, & somewhat too much in love with his own dejection, and he departed from us, as is recorded in my Sister's Journal, soon after we left Loch Lomond." From August 15 to September 25, 1803, WW and DW toured Scotland, accompanied by STC until August 29, when he went his own way. They travelled north through Dumfries and Glasgow to Ballachulish, and south from Blair Athol through Stirling, Edinburgh, Lasswade (where they visited Walter Scott on September 17), and Melrose. For details of their itinerary, see DW's *Recollections of a Tour Made in Scotland A.D. 1803* (*DWJ*, 1:191–430), *Chrono: MY*, 221–37, and Donald Hayden's *Wordsworth's Travels in Scotland*. All four poems selected here from this section of P2V were composed well after the tour.
‡ P 1815: Poems of the Imagination. Composed probably on November 5, 1805 (*Chrono: MY*, 45); copied into letters of November 7 to Lady Beaumont and of December 15 to Thomas Clarkson (*WL*, 639, 654–55). WW's note (printed at the end of vol. 2 of P2V): "This Poem was suggested by a beautiful sentence in a MS Tour in Scotland written by a Friend, the last line being taken from it *verbatim*." The friend is identified in WW's letters (*WL*, 1:638–39 and 652, 2:104) as Thomas Wilkinson, whose *Tours to the British Mountains* (London, 1824) circulated in manuscript for years before being published. The published version of the passage to which WW refers is on p. 12: "Passed a female who was reaping alone: she sung in Erse [the dialect of Gaelic spoken in the Scottish Highlands] as she bended over her sickle; the sweetest human voice I ever heard: her strains were tenderly melancholy, and felt delicious, long after they were heard no more." DW noted in her *Recollections* (September 13, 1803), "It was not uncommon in the more lonely parts of the Highlands to see a *single* person so employed" (*DWJ*, 1:380). For discussion of the poem's versification, see Susan Wolfson's article "Wordsworth's Craft" reprinted below (pp. 582–92).

And sings a melancholy strain;
O listen! for the Vale profound
Is overflowing with the sound.

No Nightingale did ever chaunt
10   So sweetly to reposing bands
Of Travellers in some shady haunt,
Among Arabian Sands:
No sweeter voice was ever heard
In spring-time from the Cuckoo-bird,
15   Breaking the silence of the seas
Among the farthest Hebrides.[1]

Will no one tell me what she sings?
Perhaps the plaintive numbers flow
For old, unhappy, far-off things,
20   And battles long ago:
Or is it some more humble lay,
Familiar matter of today?
Some natural sorrow, loss, or pain,
That has been, and may be again!

25   Whate'er the theme, the Maiden sung
As if her song could have no ending;
I saw her singing at her work,
And o'er the sickle bending;
I listen'd till I had my fill:[2]
30   And, as I mounted up the hill,
.The music in my heart I bore,
Long after it was heard no more.

The Black girl who sang gospel at my high school conurt—
3. *she was amazing.*

STEPPING WESTWARD[†]

While my Fellow-traveller and I were walking by the side of Loch Ket-
terine [i.e., Katrine], one fine evening after sun-set, in our road to a Hut
where in the course of our Tour we had been hospitably entertained
some weeks before, we met, in one of the loneliest parts of that solitary
region, two well dressed Women, one of whom said to us, by way of
greeting, "What you are stepping westward ?"

---

1. An archipelago off the west coast of Scotland, the *farthest* islands of which are in the group
called the Outer Hebrides or Western Isles. In 1827 WW altered line 13 to "Such thrilling
voice was never heard."
2. *Till I had my fill*: altered in *MP 1820* to "motionless and still."
† *P 1815*: Poems of the Imagination. Composed probably on June 3, 1805 (*Chrono: MY*, 40).
DW's report in her *Recollections* for September 11, 1803, corresponds closely to WW's in his
headnote: "The sun had been set for some time, when, being within a quarter of a mile of the
ferryman's hut, our path having led us close to the shore of the calm lake, we met two neatly
dressed women, without hats, who had probably been taking their Sunday evening's walk. One
of them said to us in a friendly, soft tone of voice, 'What! you are stepping westward?' I cannot
describe how affecting this simple expression was in that remote place, with the western sky in
front, *yet* glowing with the departed sun. Wm. wrote the following poem long after, in remem-
brance of his feelings and mine" (*DWJ*, 1:367).

    "*What you are stepping westward?*"—"*Yea.*"
    —'Twould be a wildish destiny,
    If we, who thus together roam
    In a strange Land, and far from home,
5 Were in this place the guests of Chance:
    Yet who would stop, or fear to advance,
    Though home or shelter he had none,
    With such a Sky to lead him on?

    The dewy ground was dark and cold;
10 Behind, all gloomy to behold;
    . And stepping westward seem'd to be
    A kind of *heavenly* destiny;
    I liked the greeting; 'twas a sound
    Of something without place or bound;
15 And seem'd to give me spiritual right.
    To travel through that region bright.

    The voice was soft, and she who spake
    Was walking by her native Lake:
    The salutation had to me
20 The very sound of courtesy;
    Its power was felt; and while my eye
    Was fixed upon the glowing sky,
    The echo of the voice enwrought
    A human sweetness with the thought
25 Of travelling through the world that lay
    Before me in my endless way.

6.

TO A HIGHLAND GIRL

(At Invermeyde, upon Loch Lomend.)†

    Sweet Highland Girl, a very shower
    Of beauty is thy earthly dower!
    Twice seven consenting years have shed
    Their utmost bounty on thy head:
5 And these gray Rocks; this household Lawn;
    These Trees, a veil just half withdrawn;

† P 1815: Poems of the Imagination. Composed probably between October 14, 1803, and March 6, 1804 (*Chrono: MY*, 35). Inversnaid is a village near the north end of the eastern bank of Loch Lomond, a large lake straddling the geological boundary between the Scottish Lowlands and Highlands. IF note: "This delightful creature & her demeanour are particularly described in my Sister's Journal. The sort of prophecy with which the verses conclude has through God's goodness been realized, and now, approaching the close of my 73rd year I have a most vivid remembrance of her and the beautiful objects with which she was surrounded. ° ° ° In illustration of this class of poems I have scarcely anything to say beyond what is anticipated in my Sister's faithful and admirable Journal." On August 26, 1803, WW, DW, and STC lodged with a Highland family, of whom DW recorded, "The children could not speak a word of English: they were very shy at first; but after I had caressed the eldest, and given her a red leather purse, with which she was delighted, she took hold of my hand and hung about me, changing her side-long looks for pretty smiles" (*DWJ*, 1:266–67).

This fall of water, that doth make
A murmur near the silent Lake;
This little Bay, a quiet Road
10   That holds in shelter thy Abode;
In truth together ye do seem
Like something fashion'd in a dream;
Such Forms as from their covert peep
When earthly cares are laid asleep!
15   Yet, dream and vision as thou art,
I bless thee with a human heart:
God shield thee to thy latest years!
I neither know thee nor thy peers;
And yet my eyes are fill'd with tears.

20   With earnest feeling I shall pray
For thee when I am far away:
For never saw I mien, or face,
In which more plainly I could trace
Benignity and home-bred sense
25   Ripening in perfect innocence.
Here, scatter'd like a random seed,
Remote from men, Thou dost not need
The embarrass'd look of shy distress,
And maidenly shamefacedness:
30   Thou wear'st upon thy forehead clear
The freedom of a Mountaineer.
A face with gladness overspread!
Sweet looks, by human kindness bred!
And seemliness complete, that sways
35   Thy courtesies, about thee plays;
With no restraint, but such as springs
From quick and eager visitings
Of thoughts, that lie beyond the reach
Of thy few words of English speech:
40   A bondage sweetly brook'd, a strife
That gives thy gestures grace and life!
So have I, not unmov'd in mind,
Seen birds of tempest-loving kind,
Thus beating up against the wind.

45   What hand but would a garland cull
For thee who art so beautiful?
O happy pleasure! here to dwell
Beside thee in some heathy dell;
Adopt your homely ways and dress.
50   A Shepherd, thou a Shepherdess!
But I could frame a wish for thee
More like a grave reality:
Thou art to me but as a wave
Of the wild sea; and I would have
55   Some claim upon thee, if I could,

Though but of common neighbourhood.
What joy to hear thee, and to see!
Thy elder Brother I would be,
Thy Father, any thing to thee!

60 Now thanks to Heaven! that of its grace
Hath led me to this lonely place.
Joy have I had; and going hence
I bear away my recompence.
In spots like these it is we prize
65 Our Memory, feel that she hath eyes:
Then, why should I be loth to stir?
I feel this place was made for her;
To give new pleasure like the past,
Continued long as life shall last.
70 Nor am I loth, though pleased at heart,
Sweet Highland Girl! from Thee to part;
For I, methinks, till I grow old,
As fair before me shall behold,
As I do now, the Cabin small,
75 The Lake, the Bay, the Waterfall;
And Thee, the Spirit of them all!

8.

ADDRESS
TO THE SONS OF BURNS
after visiting their Father's Grave
(August 14th, 1803)†

Ye now are panting up life's hill!
'Tis twilight time of good and ill,
And more than common strength and skill
    Must ye display
5 If ye would give the better will
        Its lawful sway.

Strong bodied if ye be to bear
Intemperance with less harm, beware!

† *P 1815*: Poems proceeding from Sentiment and Reflection. Composed probably between early September 1805 and February 21, 1806 (*Chrono: MY*, 40). In *P 1815* WW omitted the word *Address* from the title; in 1827 he added a new opening stanza, inserted three new stanzas between lines 18 and 19, and made extensive further revisions (reproduced in the critical apparatus of *P2V* [CW], 196–97). On Robert Burns see the Biographical and Topographical Glossary, *Resolution and Independence*, lines 45–46, and "A Letter to a Friend of Robert Burns" of 1816 (*Prose*, 3:115–29). WW and DW visited Burns's house and grave in Dumfries on the morning of August 18, 1803: "We talked of Coleridge's children and family *** and our [i.e., WW's and MW's] own new-born son John *** while the grave of Burns's son, which we had just seen by the side of his father, and some stories heard at Dumfries respecting the dangers his surviving children were exposed to, filled us with melancholy concern, which had a kind of anxious connexion with ourselves" (*DWJ*, 1:202; see also *CN*, 1:1434).

But if your Father's wit ye share,
          Then, then indeed,
10 Ye Sons of Burns! for watchful care
          There will be need.[1]

For honest men delight will take
To shew you favor for his sake,
15 Will flatter you; and Fool and Rake[2]
          Your steps pursue:
And of your Father's name will make
          A snare for you.

Let no mean hope your souls enslave;
20 Be independent, generous, brave!
Your Father such example gave,
          And such revere!
But be admonish'd by his Grave,
          And think, and fear!

Fish have nets;
fleas have traps;
and men have
flatterers.

Worldly glory; lust

Consider
your
ways

populist
patriot

Don't drink

From Moods of My Own Mind[†]
1.

TO A BUTTERFLY[‡]

mental
comfort?

Stay near me—do not take thy flight! a
A little longer stay in sight! a
Much converse do I find in Thee, b
Historian of my Infancy! b
5 Float near me; do not yet depart! c
Dead times revive in thee: b
Thou bring'st, gay Creature as thou art! c
A solemn image to my heart, c
My Father's Family! b

a symbol
that conjures
a memory

10 Oh! pleasant, pleasant were the days, d
The time, when in our childish plays d
My Sister Emmeline and I e
Together chaced the Butterfly! e
A very hunter did I rush f
15 Upon the prey:—with leaps and springs g

---

1. WW omitted lines 7–12 in *MP 1820*, then restored them in 1827.
2. In *MP 1820* WW revised lines 13–15 to "For their beloved Poet's sake, / Even honest men delight will take / To flatter you; and Fool and Rake."
† On May 21, 1807, WW wrote Lady Beaumont about this section of *P2V*, "turn to the 'Moods of my own Mind.' There is scarcely a Poem here of above thirty Lines, and very trifling these poems will appear to many; but, omitting to speak of them individually, do they not, taken collectively, fix the attention upon a subject eminently poetical, viz., the interest which objects in nature derive from the predominance of certain affections more or less permanent, more or less capable of salutary renewal in the mind of the being contemplating these objects? This is poetic, and essentially poetic, and why? because it is creative" (*WL*, 2:147).
‡ *P 1815*: Poems referring to Childhood. Composed March 14, 1802 (*Chrono: MY*, 26; *DWJ*, 1:123). From the IF note: "My Sister and I were parted immediately after the death of our Mother who died in 1778, both being very young."

I follow'd on from brake to bush;
But She, God love her! feared to brush
The dust from off its wings.

Nice ending

3.[†]

O Nightingale! thou surely art
A Creature of a fiery heart—[1]
These notes of thine they pierce, and pierce;
Tumultuous harmony and fierce!
5   Thou sing'st as if the God of wine
Had help'd thee to a Valentine;[2]
A song in mockery and despite
Of shades, and dews, and silent Night,
And steady bliss, and all the Loves
10   Now sleeping in these peaceful groves!

pagan ideals

A poet is one who walks at night talking to himself.

I heard a Stockdove[3] sing or say
His homely tale, this very day.
His voice was buried among trees,
Yet to be come at by the breeze:[4]
15   He did not cease; but coo'd—and coo'd;
And somewhat pensively he woo'd:
He sang of love with quiet blending,
Slow to begin, and never ending;
Of serious faith, and inward glee;
20   That was the Song, the Song for me!

Wordsworth ideals

Sing without ceasing.

May this be my life.

How can I sing forever?

4.[†]

My heart leaps up when I behold
A Rainbow in the sky:[1]

Windmills, trains, airplanes, B-ball, skating, health — my childhood obsessions. I loved to move. I also loved the Scripture.

[†] *P 1815*: Poems of the Imagination. Composed probably between early February and early April 1807 (*Chrono: MY*, 44). In his *Guide through the District of the Lakes* WW noted that "[i]t is not often that the nightingale resorts to these vales" (*Prose*, 2:228).

1. A phrase from Shakespeare's *Henry VI*, part 3, 1.4.87, WW's use of which was ridiculed in Richard Mant's *Simpliciad* (see the note on *Among all lovely things my Love had been*), lines 247–48: "And yours the fiery nightingale's, that sings / With skirmish and capricious passagings." WW replaced the phrase *a fiery* with the word "ebullient" in *P 1815*, but afterwards restored the original reading and retained it in subsequent editions.

2. Mate.

3. A wild pigeon.

4. In the Preface to *P 1815* WW quoted lines 13–14, observing that the verb *buried* is "a metaphor expressing the love of *seclusion* by which this Bird is marked; and characterising its note as not partaking of the shrill and the piercing, and therefore more easily deadened by the intervening shade" (p. 513 below).

[†] *P 1815*: Poems referring to Childhood. Composed probably on March 26, 1802 (*Chrono: MY*, 27). STC reprinted the poem in *The Friend*, August 10, 1809, with the prefatory remark, "Men are ungrateful to others only when they have ceased to look back on their former selves with joy and tenderness. They exist in fragments. * * * A contemporary poet has exprest and illustrated this sentiment with equal fineness of thought and tenderness of feeling" (*Friend*, 2:41). In *P 1815* WW printed the poem first in vol. 1 and used lines 7–9 (which STC had printed in italics for emphasis) as an epigraph to the Intimations Ode.

1. In Genesis 9.12–17 the rainbow is the sign of God's postdiluvian covenant with all living creatures not to destroy the earth.

"They exist in fragments." — Coleridge on men

How can I be a better man based on what I did in my childhood?

418   WORDSWORTH'S POETRY AND PROSE

anaphora

So was it when my life began;   past
So is it now I am a Man;   present
5 So be it when I shall grow old,   future
    Or let me die!
The Child is Father of the Man;
And I could wish my days to be
Bound each to each by natural piety.

Children need a
lot of sunshine. They
should grow up
outside.

What is natural piety? a reverence
for nature?

7.†

I wandered lonely as a Cloud
That floats on high o'er Vales and Hills,
When all at once I saw a crowd
A host of dancing Daffodills;
5 Along the Lake, beneath the trees,
Ten thousand dancing[1] in the breeze.

The waves beside them danced, but they
Outdid the sparkling waves in glee:—
A Poet could not but be gay
10 In such a laughing[2] company:
I gaz'd—and gaz'd—but little thought
What wealth the shew to me had brought:

For oft when on my couch I lie
In vacant or in pensive mood,
15 They flash upon that inward eye[3]
Which is the bliss of solitude,
And then my heart with pleasure fills,
And dances with the Daffodils.[4]

---

† P 1815: Poems of the Imagination. Composed probably between late March 1804 and early
  1807 (*Chrono: MY*, 37). WW had instructed the printer of *P2V* to place this poem sixth in the
  series, between *Written in March* and *Who fancied what a pretty sight*, but the printer, probably
  for reasons of economy, in fact placed it seventh between *The Small Celandine* and *Who fan-
  cied what a pretty sight* (see *P2V* [CW], 28–29, 207). IF note: "The two best lines [identified in
  pencil in the MS as lines 15–16] in it are by Mary. The daffodils grew & still grow on the mar-
  gin of Ulswater & probably may be seen to this day as beautiful in the month of March nodding
  their golden heads beside the dancing & foaming waves." DW recorded on April 15, 1802,
  "there was a long belt of them along the shore [of Ullswater], about the breadth of a country
  turnpike road. I never saw daffodils so beautiful. They grew among the mossy stones about and
  about them; some rested their heads upon these stones as on a pillow for weariness; and the
  rest tossed and reeled and danced, and seemed as if they verily laughed with the wind, that
  blew upon them over the lake; they looked ever so gay, so glancing, ever changing" (*DWJ*,
  1:131).
1. Altered in *P 1815* to "golden"; *Ten thousand*: altered in *P 1815* to "Fluttering and." WW
   defended the precision of the description in lines 5–8 in a letter of February 1808 to Sir George
   Beaumont (*WL*, 2:194–95). After line 6 WW inserted an additional stanza in *P 1815*: "Continu-
   ous as the stars that shine / And twinkle on the milky way, / They stretched in never-ending
   line / Along the margin of a bay: / Ten thousand saw I at a glance, / Tossing their heads in
   sprightly dance."
2. Altered in *P 1815* to "jocund."
3. In *P 1815* WW added a footnote (not subsequently reprinted) to this line: "The subject of these
   Stanzas is rather an elementary feeling and simple impression (approaching to the nature of an
   ocular spectrum) upon the imaginative faculty, than an *exertion* of it. * * *"
4. In *BL* STC contrasted lines 15–16 with 17–18 (i.e., lines 21–22 and 23–24 of the 1815 text): "It
   is a well known fact, that bright colours in motion both make and leave the strongest impres-
   sion on the eye. Nothing is more likely too, than that a vivid image * * * may become the link of

10.

GIPSIES[†]

Yet are they here?—the same unbroken knot
Of human Beings, in the self-same spot!
   Men, Women, Children, yea the frame
   Of the whole Spectacle the same!
5 Only their fire seems bolder, yielding light:
Now deep and red, the colouring of night;
   That on their Gipsy-faces falls, – *good*
   Their bed of straw and blanket-walls.
—Twelve hours, twelve bounteous hours, are gone while I
10 Have been a Traveller under open sky,
   Much witnessing of change and chear,
   Yet as I left I find them here![1]

The weary Sun betook himself to rest.
—Then issued Vesper[2] from the fulgent West,
15   Outshining like a visible God
   The glorious path in which he trod.
And now, ascending, after one dark hour,
(And one night's diminution of her power,) – *good*
   Behold the mighty Moon! this way
20   She looks as if at them—but they
Regard not her:—oh better wrong and strife
Better vain deeds or evil than such life![3] – *False*
   The silent Heavens have goings on;
   The stars have tasks—but these have none.[4]

Vow. Mixed up.

---

association in recalling the feelings and images that had accompanied the original impression. But if we describe this in such lines, as [15–16,] in what words shall we describe the joy of retrospection, when the images * * * pass before that conscience which is indeed the *inward* eye * * *? Assuredly we seem to sink most abruptly, not to say burlesquely, and almost in a *medly* from this couplet to [lines 17–18]" (NCC, 532–33).

† P 1815: Poems of the Imagination. Composed ca. but not before February 26, 1807 (*Chrono: MY*, 44). IF note: "Composed at Coleorton, 1807. I had observed them as here described near Castle Donnington on my way to & from Derby." In *BL* STC criticized the poem as an example of "*mental* bombast" (i.e., "thoughts and images too great for the subject"), a "fault of which none but a man of genius is capable" (NCC, 532–34).

1. The stanza break was omitted in *MP 1820* and subsequent editions.
2. Hesperus, the evening star (a poetical usage).
3. In *MP 1820* WW altered line 22 to "(By nature transient) than such torpid life!"
4. William Hazlitt (see Biographical and Topographical Glossary) criticized lines 23–24 in a note to his essay "On Manner" (1817): "Mr Wordsworth * * * had made an attack on a set of gipsies for having done nothing in four and twenty hours. * * * And why should they, if they were comfortable where they were? We did not expect this turn from Mr Wordsworth, whom we had considered as the prince of poetical idlers, and patron of the philosophy of indolence" (*Selected Writings*, ed. Duncan Wu [London, 1998], 2:46n). In *MP 1820* WW added four lines to the end of the poem: "Yet, witness all that stirs in heaven and earth! / In scorn I speak not;—they are not what their birth / And breeding suffers them to be; / Wild outcasts of society!" In 1827 he altered lines 23–24 to "Life which the very stars reprove / As on their silent tasks they move!" On October 24, 1828, he explained to Barron Field that the phrase *goings on* in line 23 had been unsatisfactory and that "the concluding apologia should be cancelled" (*WL*, 3:645), but he did not thereafter omit lines 25–28.

12.
TO A BUTTERFLY†

[handwritten margin notes: Common meter / a / a / b / b / c / c / confine]

[handwritten margin note top right: Time in Nature.]

I've watch'd you now a full half hour,
Self-pois'd upon that yellow flower;
And, little Butterfly! indeed
I know not if you sleep, or feed.
5   How motionless! not frozen seas
More motionless! and then
What joy awaits you, when the breeze
Hath found you out among the trees,
And calls you forth again!

10   This plot of Orchard-ground is ours;
My trees they are, my Sister's flowers;
Stop here whenever you are weary,
And rest as in a sanctuary!
Come often to us, fear no wrong;
15   Sit near us on the bough!
We'll talk of sunshine and of song;
And summer days, when we were young,
Sweet childish days, that were as long
As twenty days are now!

[handwritten margin note left of stanza: Wordsworth write a poem to a butterfly — and it's really good. The butterfly is his Muse. Nature is his Muse.]

[handwritten note right: A-1 line]

[handwritten note: deep.]

From The Blind Highland Boy;
with other poems

THE BLIND HIGHLAND BOY
(A Tale told by the Fire-side)†

Now we are tired of boisterous joy,
We've romp'd enough, my little Boy!
Jane hangs her head upon my breast,
And you shall bring your Stool and rest,
5   This corner is your own.

There! take your seat, and let me see
That you can listen quietly;

---

† *P 1815:* Poems founded on the Affections. Composed on April 20, 1802 (*Chrono: MY,* 28; *DWJ,* 1:135).
† *P 1815:* Poems referring to Childhood. Composed probably between March 1804 and March 1806 (*Chrono: MY,* 37). WW's note (printed at the end of vol. 2 of *P2V*): "The incident upon which this Poem is founded was related to me by an eye witness." IF note: "The story was told me by George Mack[e]reth for many years parish-clerk of Grasmere. He had been an eye-witness of the occurrence. The vessel in reality was a washing-tub, which the little fellow had met with on the shore of the loch." In *P 1815* WW substituted the following note: "It is recorded in Dampier's Voyages that a Boy, the Son of a Captain of a Man of War, seated himself in a Turtle-shell and floated in it from the shore to his Father's Ship, which lay at anchor at the distance of half a mile. Upon the suggestion of a Friend, I have substituted such a Shell for that less elegant vessel in which my blind voyager did actually intrust himself to the dangerous current of Loch Levin, as was related to me by an Eye-witness." See the note on line 115 on WW's adoption of STC's suggestion. Loch Leven is a sea inlet on the west coast of Scotland.

And as I promised I will tell
That strange adventure which befel
10   A poor blind Highland Boy.

A *Highland* Boy!—why call him so?
Because, my Darlings, ye must know,
In land where many a mountain towers,
Far higher hills than these of ours!
15   He from his birth had liv'd.

He ne'er had seen one earthly sight;
The sun, the day; the stars, the night;
Or tree, or butterfly, or flower,
Or fish in stream, or bird in bower,
20   Or woman, man, or child.

And yet he neither drooped nor pined,
Nor had a melancholy mind;
For God took pity on the Boy,
And was his friend; and gave him joy
25   Of which we nothing know.

His Mother, too, no doubt, above
Her other Children him did love:
For, was she here, or was she there,
She thought of him with constant care,
30   And more than Mother's love.

And proud she was of heart, when clad
In crimson stockings, tartan plaid,
And bonnet with a feather gay,
To Kirk he on the sabbath day
35   Went hand in hand with her.

A Dog, too, had he; not for need,
But one to play with and to feed;
Which would have led him, if bereft
Of company or friends, and left
40   Without a better guide.

And then the bagpipes he could blow;
And thus from house to house would go,
And all were pleas'd to hear and see;
For none made sweeter melody
45   Than did the poor blind Boy.

Yet he had many a restless dream;
Both when he heard the Eagles scream,
And when he heard the torrents roar,
And heard the water beat the shore
50   Near which their Cottage stood.

Beside a lake their Cottage stood,
Not small like ours, a peaceful flood;
But one of mighty size, and strange;
That, rough or smooth, is full of change,
55   And stirring in its bed.

For to this Lake, by night and day,
The great Sea-water finds its way
Through long, long windings of the hills;
And drinks up all the pretty rills
60   And rivers large and strong:

Then hurries back the road it came—
Returns, on errand still the same;
This did it when the earth was new;
And this for evermore will do,
65   As long as earth shall last.

And, with the coming of the Tide,
Come Boats and Ships, that sweetly ride,
Between the woods and lofty rocks;
And to the Shepherds with their Flocks
70   Brings[1] tales of distant Lands.

And of those tales, whate'er they were,
The blind Boy always had his share;
Whether of mighty Towns, or Vales
With warmer suns and softer gales,
75   Or wonders of the Deep.

Yet more it pleased him, more it stirr'd,
When from the water-side he heard
The shouting, and the jolly cheers,
The bustle of the mariners
80   In stillness or in storm.

But what do his desires avail?
For He must never handle sail;
Nor mount the mast, nor row, nor float
In Sailor's ship or Fisher's boat
85   Upon the rocking waves.

His Mother often thought, and said,
What sin would be upon her head
If she should suffer this: "My Son,
Whate'er you do, leave this undone;
90   The danger is so great."

---

1. A grammatical error (since the subject of the verb is *Boats and Ships*) present in the MSS of the
poem but corrected to "Bring" in *P 1815*.

Thus lived he by Loch Levin's side
Still sounding with the sending tide,
And heard the billows leap and dance,
Without a shadow of mischance,
95   Till he was ten years old.

When one day (and now mark me well,
You² soon shall know how this befel)
He's in a vessel of his own,
On the swift water hurrying down
100   Towards the mighty Sea.

In such a vessel ne'er before³
Did human Creature leave the shore:
If this or that way he should stir,
Woe to the poor blind Mariner!
105   For death will be his doom.

Strong is the current; but be mild,
Ye waves, and spare the helpless Child!
If ye in anger fret or chafe,
A Bee-hive would be ship as safe
110   As that in which he sails.⁴

But say, what was it? Thought of fear!
Well may ye tremble when ye hear!
—A Household Tub, like one of those
Which women use to wash their clothes,
115   This carried the blind Boy.⁵

2. Altered to "Ye" in *P 1815*.
3. Altered to "never more" in *P 1815*.
4. In *P 1815* WW omitted lines 106–110.
5. In 1808 STC commented in his notebook, "I almost fear, that the alteration would excite sur-prize and uneasy contempt in Verbidegno's mind towards one less loved, at least: but had I written the sweet Tale of the Blind Highland Boy, I would have substituted for the washing Tub, and the awkward Stanza in which it is specified the image suggested in the following Lines from [William] Dampier's Travels [i.e., *A Collection of Voyages* (1729)], Vol. I p. 105–106: 'I heard of a monstrous green Turtle once taken at the Port Royal in the Bay of Campeachy, that was four feet deep from the back to the belly, and the belly six feet broad. Captⁿ Roch's Son, of about 9 or 10 years of age, went in it as in a boat, on board his Father's Ship, about a quarter of a mile from the Shore.' * * * Why might not some Mariners have left this Shell on the shore of Loch Levin for a while, about to have it transported inland for a curiosity; & the blind boy have found it. Would not the incident be in equal keeping with that of the child, as well as the image & *tone* of romantic uncommonness" (CN, 3:3240). "Verbidegno" was STC's mock-Italian version of WW's name (from *verbi*, "words," and *degno*, "worth"). In *P 1815* WW replaced lines 111–15 with the following new stanzas:

But say what bears him?—Ye have seen
The Indian's Bow, his arrows keen,
Rare beasts, and birds with plummage bright
Gifts which, for wonder or delight,
5   Are brought in ships from far.

Such gifts had those sea-faring men
Spread round that Haven in the glen;
Each hut, perchance, might have its own,
And to the Boy they all were known,
10   He knew and prized them all.

Close to the water he had found
This Vessel, push'd it from dry ground,
Went into it; and, without dread,
Following the fancies in his head,
120   He paddled up and down.[6]

A while he stood upon his feet;
He felt the motion—took his seat;
And dallied thus, till from the shore
The tide retreating more and more
125   Had suck'd, and suck'd him in.

And there he is in face of Heaven!
How rapidly the Child is driven!
The fourth part of a mile I ween
He thus had gone, ere he was seen
130   By any human eye.

But when he was first seen, oh me!
What shrieking and what misery!
For many saw; among the rest
His Mother, she who loved him best,
135   She saw her poor blind Boy.

But for the Child, the sightless Boy,
It is the triumph of his joy!
The bravest Traveller in balloon,
Mounting as if to reach the moon,
140   Was never half so bless'd.

And let him, let him go his way,
Alone, and innocent, and gay!
For, if good Angels love to wait
On the forlorn unfortunate,
145   This Child will take no harm.

But now the passionate lament,
Which from the crowd on shore was sent,

And one, the rarest, was a Shell
Which he, poor Child, had studied well;
The Shell of a green Turtle, thin
And hollow;—you might sit therein,
15   It was so wide and deep.

'Twas even the largest of its kind,
Large, thin, and light as birch-tree rind,
So light a Shell that it would swim,
And gaily lift its fearless brim
20   Above the tossing waves.

WW revised the lines further in *MP 1820* (see *P2V* [CW], 225).
6. In *P 1815* WW revised lines 116–20: "And with the happy burden hied, / And pushed it from Loch Levin's side,— / Stepped into it; and, without dread, / Following the fancies in his head, / He paddled up and down."

The cries which broke from old and young
In Gaelic, or the English tongue;
150   Are stifled—all is still.

And quickly with a silent crow
A Boat is ready to pursue;
And from the shore their course they take,
And swiftly down the running Lake
155   They follow the blind Boy.[7]

With sound the least that can be made
They follow, more and more afraid,
More cautious as they draw more near;
But in his darkness he can hear,
160   And guesses their intent.

"*Lei-gha—Lei-gha*"—then did he cry
"*Lei-gha—Lei-gha*"—most eagerly;[8]
Thus did he cry, and thus did pray,
And what he meant was, "Keep away,
165   And leave me to myself!"

Alas! and when he felt their hands——
You've often heard of magic Wands,
That with a motion overthrow
A palace of the proudest shew,
170   Or melt it into air.

So all his dreams, that inward light
With which his soul had shone so bright,
All vanish'd,—'twas a heartfelt cross
To him, a heavy, bitter loss,
175   As he had ever known.

But hark! a gratulating voice
With which the very hills rejoice:
'Tis from the crowd, who tremblingly

7. In *P 1815* WW added two stanzas after line 155:

                     But soon they move with softer pace,
                     So have ye seen the fowler chase
                     On Grasmere's clear unruffled breast
                     A Youngling of the wild-duck's nest
        5   With deftly-lifted oar.

                     Or as the wily Sailors crept
                     To seize (while on the Deep it slept)
                     The hapless Creature which did dwell
                     Erewhile within the dancing Shell,
       10   They steal upon their prey.

8. Substituted for the originally drafted "Lega lega" evidently on the advice of Walter Scott, whose assistance WW had sought on January 20, 1807, in identifying the Erse word repeated to WW by the eyewitness to the event and "signifying—'beware,' keep away, let me alone" (*WL*, 2:123–24).

Had watch'd the event, and now can see
180   That he is safe at last.

And then, when he was brought to land,
Full sure they were a happy band,
Which gathering round did on the banks
Of that great Water give God thanks,
185   And welcom'd the poor Child.

And in the general joy of heart
The blind Boy's little Dog took part;
He leapt about, and oft did kiss
His master's hands in sign of bliss,
190   With sound like lamentation.

But most of all, his Mother dear,
She who had fainted with her fear,
Rejoiced when waking she espies
The Child; when she can trust her eyes,
195   And touches the blind Boy.

She led him home, and wept amain,
When he was in the house again:
Tears flow'd in torrents from her eyes,
She could not blame him, or chastise:
200   She was too happy far.

Thus, after he had fondly braved
The perilous Deep, the Boy was saved;
And, though his fancies had been wild,
Yet he was pleased, and reconciled
205   To live in peace on shore.[9]

THE GREEN LINNET[†]

The May is come again;—how sweet
To sit upon my Ochard-seat!
And Birds and Flowers once more to greet,
          My last year's Friends together:
5   My thoughts they all by turns employ;
A whispering Leaf is now my joy,

9. In *P 1815* WW added a stanza after line 205: "And in the lonely Highland Dell / Still do they
keep the Turtle shell; / And long the Story will repeat / Of the blind Boy's adventurous feat, /
And how he was preserved."
† *P 1815*: Poems of the Fancy. Composed perhaps between April 16 and July 8, 1802 (*Chrono:
MY*, 27). From the IF note: "composed in Town End Orchard where the Bird was often seen as
here described." The linnet is a songbird common in England.

And then a Bird will be the toy
　　That doth my fancy tether.[1]

　　One have I mark'd, the happiest Guest
10　In all this covert of the blest:
　　Hail to Thee, far above the rest
　　　　In joy of voice and pinion,
　　Thou, Linnet! in thy green array,
　　Presiding Spirit here to-day,
15　Dost lead the revels of the May,
　　　　And this is thy dominion.

　　While Birds, and Butterflies, and Flowers
　　Make all one Band of Paramours,
　　Thou, ranging up and down the bowers,
20　　　Art sole in thy employment;
　　A Life, a Presence like the Air,
　　Scattering thy gladness without care,
　　Too bless'd with any one to pair,
　　　　Thyself thy own enjoyment.

25　Upon yon tuft of hazel trees,
　　That twinkle to the gusty breeze,
　　Behold him perch'd in ecstasies,
　　　　Yet seeming still to hover;
　　There! where the flutter of his wings
30　Upon his back and body flings
　　Shadows and sunny glimmerings,
　　　　That cover him all over.

　　While thus before my eyes he gleams,
　　A Brother of the Leaves he seems;
35　When in a moment forth he teems
　　　　His little song in gushes:
　　As if it pleas'd him to disdain
　　And mock the Form which he did feign,[2]
　　While he was dancing with the train
40　　　Of Leaves among the bushes.

---

1. In *P 1815* WW revised the first stanza:

> Beneath these fruit-tree boughs that shed
> Their snow-white blossoms on my head,
> With brightest sunshine round me spread
> 　　Of spring's unclouded weather,
> In this sequestered nook how sweet
> To sit upon my Orchard-seat!
> And Flowers and Birds once more to greet,
> 　　My last year's Friends together.

2. In *MP 1820* WW altered this line to "The voiceless Form he chose to feign."

SONNET,

TO THOMAS CLARKSON,

On the final passing of the Bill for the Abolition
of the Slave Trade, March, 1807[†]

Clarkson! it was an obstinate Hill to climb;
How toilsome, nay how dire it was, by Thee
Is known,—by none, perhaps, so feelingly;
But Thou, who, starting in thy fervent prime,
5   Didst first lead forth this pilgrimage sublime,
Hast heard the constant Voice its charge repeat,
Which, out of thy young heart's oracular seat,
First roused thee.—O true yoke-fellow of Time
With unabating effort, see, the palm
10 Is won, and by all Nations shall be worn!
The bloody Writing is for ever torn,
And Thou henceforth shalt have a good Man's calm,
A great Man's happiness; thy zeal shall find
Repose at length, firm Friend of human kind!

A COMPLAINT [†]

There is a change—and I am poor;
Your Love hath been, nor long ago,
A Fountain at my fond Heart's door,
Whose only business was to flow;
5   And flow it did; not taking heed
Of its own bounty, or my need.

What happy moments did I count!
Bless'd was I then all bliss above![1]
Now, for this consecrated Fount
10 Of murmuring, sparkling, living love,
What have I? shall I dare to tell?
A comfortless, and hidden WELL.

---

† *P 1815*: Sonnets dedicated to Liberty. Composed probably on March, 26, 1807, or shortly after (*Chrono: MY*, 44). Thomas Clarkson (1760–1846), a cofounder of the Society for Effecting the Abolition of the Slave Trade in 1787, moved for the sake of his health to Pooley Bridge on the eastern end of Ullswater in 1794 and was a close friend of the Wordsworths from 1800. In 1804 he became active in the revived abolitionist cause and moved away from the Lake District. In February 1807 a bill prohibiting the slave trade (though not slavery itself) throughout the British Empire was finally passed by both houses of parliament. See also *The Prelude* 10.201–26.

† *P 1815*: Poems founded on the Affections. Composed probably between October 30, and December, 1806 (*Chrono: MY*, 43). IF note: "Suggested by a change in the manners of a friend. Town-End 1806." The friend would have been STC, who, in ill health and determined to separate from his wife, stayed with the Wordsworths at Coleorton from December 21, 1806 to mid-April 1807 (*Chrono: MY*, 343–51; Gill, 255–58).

1. Line 8 draws on the first line of WW's translation of the lyric *Quanto mai felici siete* by the Italian poet and librettist Pietro Metastasio (Pietro Trapassi, 1698–1782): "Oh! bless all bliss above" (see *P2V* [CW], 592–93).

A Well of love—it may be deep—
I trust it is, and never dry:
15 What matter? if the Waters sleep
In silence and obscurity.
—Such change, and at the very door
Of my fond Heart, hath made me poor.

LINES,

Composed at GRASMERE, during a walk, one Evening, after a stormy
day, the Author having just read in a Newspaper that the dissolution of
MR. Fox was hourly expected[†]

Loud is the Vale! the Voice is up
With which she speaks when storms are gone,
A mighty Unison of streams!
Of all her Voices, One!

5 Loud is the Vale;—this inland Depth
In peace is roaring like the Sea;
Yon Star upon the mountain-top
Is listening quietly.

Sad was I, ev'n to pain depress'd,
10 Importunate and heavy load![1]
The Comforter hath found me here,
Upon this lonely road;

And many thousands now are sad,
Wait the fulfilment of their fear;
15 For He must die who is their Stay,
Their Glory disappear.

A Power is passing from the earth
To breathless Nature's dark abyss;
But when the Mighty pass away
20 What is it more than this,

That Man, who is from God sent forth,
Doth yet again to God return?—
Such ebb and flow must ever be,
Then wherefore should we mourn?

---

† P 1815: Epitaphs and Elegiac Poems. Composed probably in early September 1806 (*Chrono:*
MY, 43). Charles James Fox, the leader of the Whigs, died on September 13, 1806, after
months of serious illness. On WW's estimation of Fox, see the headnote to *LB 1800* (p. 73).
1. WW's note (printed at the end of vol. 2 of *P2V*): "'*Importuna e grave salma.*' Michael Angelo."
WW translated this sonnet by the sculptor and poet Michelangelo Buonarroti (1475–1564) in
ca. 1805 (see *Rid of a vexing and heavy load* in *P2V* [CW], 535) and revised his translation on
January 19, 1840 (see *At Florence—From M. Angelo* in *Sonnet Series and Itinerary Poems,*
1820–1845 [CW], 780).

ELEGIAC STANZAS,

Suggested by a Picture of PEELE CASTLE, in a Storm,

painted

BY SIR GEORGE BEAUMONT[†]

I was thy Neighbour once, thou rugged Pile!
Four summer weeks I dwelt in sight of thee:
I saw thee every day; and all the while
Thy Form was sleeping on a glassy sea.

5 So pure the sky, so quiet was the air!
So like, so very like, was day to day!
Whene'er[1] I look'd, thy Image still was there;
It trembled, but it never pass'd away.

How perfect was the calm! it seem'd no sleep;
10 No mood, which season takes away, or brings:
I could have fancied that the mighty Deep
Was even the gentlest of all gentle Things.

Ah! THEN, if mine had been the Painter's hand,
To express what then I saw; and add the gleam,
15 The light that never was, on sea or land,
The consecration, and the Poet's dream;[2]

I would have planted thee, thou hoary Pile!
Amid a world how different from this!
Beside a sea that could not cease to smile;
20 On tranquil land, beneath a sky of bliss:

Thou shouldst have seem'd a treasure-house, a mine
Of peaceful years; a chronicle of heaven:—
Of all the sunbeams that did ever shine
The very sweetest had to thee been given.[3]

---

† P 1815: Epitaphs and Elegiac Poems. Composed probably between ca. May 20 and June 27, 1806 (*Chrono: MY*, 43), Beaumont (see Biographical and Topographical Glossary) acknowledging receipt of the poem on June 29 (*Chrono: MY*, 321 n. 23). IF note: "Sir George Beaumont painted two pictures of this subject one of which he gave to Mrs. Wordsworth saying she ought to have it: but Lady B[eaumont] interfered & after Sir George's death she gave it to Sir Uvedale Price [(1747–1829), author of *An Essay on the Picturesque* (1794)] in whose house at Foxley I have seen it—rather grudgingly I own." WW would have seen the ruined fourteenth-century Piel Castle, on Piel Island in the mouth of the harbor of Barrow-in-Furness, when he was staying with cousins in Rampside in August–September 1794 (*Chrono: EY*, 157–58). He may have seen one or both versions of Beaumont's oil painting *A Storm: Peele Castle*, depicting a boat sailing past the castle in a storm, at the Royal Academy of Arts in London on May 2, 1806 (*Chrono: MY*, 321). An engraving of the painting was used as the frontispiece to vol. 2 of *P 1815*, and one version is now in the Wordsworth Museum, Grasmere.
1. The reading in *P2V* is "When'er," a printer's error corrected in *P 1815*.
2. In *MP 1820* WW altered lines 15–16 to "The lustre, known to neither sea nor land, / But borrowed from the youthful Poet's dream." Encouraged by his friend Barron Field, WW restored the *P2V* version of the lines in 1832 (*P2V* [CW], 267, 428).
3. WW omitted this stanza in *MP 1820*.

25 A Picture had it been of lasting ease,
   Elysian[4] quiet, without toil or strife;
   No motion but the moving tide, a breeze,
   Or merely silent Nature's breathing life.

   Such, in the fond delusion of my heart,
30 Such Picture would I at that time have made:
   And seen the soul of truth in every part;
   A faith, a trust, that could not be betray'd.

   So once it would have been,—'tis so no more;
   I have submitted to a new controul:
35 A power is gone, which nothing can restore;
   A deep distress hath humaniz'd my Soul.[5]

   Not for a moment could I now behold
   A smiling sea and be what I have been:
   The feeling of my loss will ne'er be old;
40 This, which I know, I speak with mind serene.

   Then, Beaumont, Friend! who would have been the Friend,
   If he had lived, of Him whom I deplore,[6]
   This Work of thine I blame not, but commend;
   This sea in anger, and that dismal shore.

45 Oh 'tis a passionate Work!—yet wise and well;
   Well chosen is the spirit that is here;
   That Hulk which labours in the deadly swell,
   This rueful sky, this pageantry of fear!

   And this huge Castle, standing here sublime,
50 I love to see the look with which it braves,
   Cased in the unfeeling armour of old time,
   The light'ning, the fierce wind, and trampling waves.

   Farewell, farewell the Heart that lives alone,
   Hous'd in a dream, at distance from the Kind![7]
55 Such happiness, wherever it be known,
   Is to be pitied; for 'tis surely blind.

   But welcome fortitude, and patient chear,
   And frequent sights of what is to be borne![8]

4. Blessed (from Elysium, the abode of the blessed dead in Greek mythology).
5. A reference to the drowning of WW's brother John (see Biographical and Topographical Glossary) on February 5, 1805, when the ship under his command, the *Earl of Abergavenny*, was wrecked off the south coast of England. Declining the offer of a seaside cottage in 1808, WW wrote, "since the loss of my dear Brother, we have all had such painful and melancholy thoughts connected with the ocean that nothing but a paramount necessity could make us live near it" (*WL*, 2:212).
6. Lament; *Him*: John Wordsworth.
7. Humanity.
8. Printed "born" in *P2V*, an error corrected in 1827.

Such sights, or worse, as are before me here.—
60   Not without hope we suffer and we mourn.[9]

Ode [Intimations of Immortality]

The precise chronology of the poem's composition is uncertain and involves a complex poetic interaction with Coleridge. From the outset, however, Wordsworth seems to have conceived the poem as an ode. On March 27, 1802, Dorothy Wordsworth recorded, "At breakfast William wrote part of an ode" (*DWJ*, 1:128), probably some or all of stanzas 1–4 (lines 1–57); and the next day he visited Coleridge. On April 4 Coleridge began the first version of *Dejection: An Ode*, which responds to the questions in lines 56–57 of Wordsworth's ode (see *NCC*, 153–54, 155 n. 1). The revised version of *Dejection* was published in the *Morning Post* on October 4, Wordsworth's wedding day and Coleridge's own wedding anniversary. Meanwhile Wordsworth had resumed work on his ode, probably composing some of stanzas 5–8 (lines 58–131) on June 17, 1802 (*DWJ*, 1:159). He apparently completed the last seven stanzas only in early 1804, but the poem must have been finished by ca. March 6, when Mary copied it into a manuscript for Coleridge to take to Malta (see the photograph and transcription in *P2V* [*CW*], 360–73). The *Ode* was published with its own title page in *P2V*, its placement as the final poem in the collection emphasizing its importance. In *P 1815* the poem, uniquely unclassified, was again placed at the end of volume 2, but with the expanded title *Ode: Intimations of Immortality from Recollections of Early Childhood* and a different epigraph. Though it is commonly known as the "Intimations Ode" or "Immortality Ode," its original title in *P2V* was simply *Ode*.

Reviewing *P2V* in the *Edinburgh Review* (October 1807), Francis Jeffrey complained that the *Ode* (from which he quoted lines 51–57 and 132–70) was "the most illegible and unintelligible part of the publication" (*CH*, 199; and see *WL*, 2:162 for Wordsworth's reaction). In an unsigned review in the *Eclectic* (January 1808), John Montgomery objected to the poem on religious grounds: "The Poet assumes the doctrine of pre-existence, (*a doctrine which religion knows not, and the philosophy of the mind abjures*) and intimates that the happiness of childhood is the reminiscence of blessedness in a former state" (*CH*, 213). Such complaints may have induced Wordsworth later to provide two unusually substantial commentaries on the *Ode*, the first in a letter of January 1815 to Catherine Clarkson: "This poem rests entirely upon two recollections of childhood, one that of a splendour in the objects of sense which is passed away, and the other an indisposition to bend to the law of death as applying to our own particular case. A Reader who has not a vivid recollection of these feelings having existed in his mind in childhood cannot understand that poem" (*WL*, 3:189). The second comment, concerned with stanzas 5–11, was the long note Wordsworth dictated to Isabella Fenwick in 1843 (the space between square brackets indicating a space left blank in the manuscript):

> This was composed during my residence at Town-End, Grasmere, two years at least passed between the writing of the four first stanzas & the remaining part. To the attentive & competent reader the whole sufficiently explains itself, but there may be no harm in adverting here to particular feelings or *experiences* of my own mind on which the structure of the poem partly rests. Nothing was more difficult for me in childhood than to admit the notion of death as a state applicable to my own being.

9. Edward Wilson, *Review of English Studies* n.s. 43 (1992): 75–80, notes an echo in line 60 of 1 Thessalonians 4.13: "But I would not have you to be ignorant, brethren, concerning them which are asleep, that ye sorrow not, even as others which have no hope."

I have said elsewhere "a simple child that lightly draws its breath and feels its life in every limb, what should it know of death?" [*We are seven*, lines 1–4] but it was not so much from [ ] of animal vivacity that *my* difficulty came as from a sense of the indomitableness of the spirit within me. I used to brood over the stories of Enoch & Elijah & almost to persuade myself that whatever might become of others I s[houl]d be translated in something of the same way to heaven. With a feeling congenial to this I was often unable to think of external things as having external existence & I communed with all that I saw as something not apart from but inherent in my own immaterial nature. Many times while going to school have I grasped at a wall or tree to recall myself from this abyss of idealism to the reality. At that time I was afraid of such processes. In later periods of life I have deplored, as we have all reason to do, a subjugation of an opposite character & have rejoiced over the remembrances, as is expressed in the lines "obstinate questionings &c." To that dreamlike vividness & splendour which invest objects of sight in childhood every one, I believe, if he would look back, could bear testimony, & I need not dwell upon it here—but having in the Poem regarded it as presumptive evidence of a prior state of existence, I think it right to protest against a conclusion which has given pain to some good & pious persons that I meant to inculcate such a belief. It is far too shadowy a notion to be recommended to faith as more than an element in our instincts of immortality. But let us bear in mind that, tho' the idea is not advanced in revelation, there is nothing there to contradict it, & the fall of Man presents an analogy in its favor. Accordingly, a preexistent state has entered into the popular creeds of many nations, and among all persons acquainted with classic literature is known as an ingredient in Platonic philosophy. Archimedes said that he could move the world if he had a point whereon to rest his machine. Who has not felt the same aspirations as regards the world of his own mind? Having to wield some of its elements when I was impelled to write this Poem on the "Immortality of the soul" I took hold of the notion of preexistence as having sufficient foundation in humanity for authorizing me to make for my purpose the best use of it I could as a Poet.

Although long admired as Wordsworth's finest ode, and one of his most important lyric poems generally, the *Ode* presents considerable difficulties of interpretation. The earliest extended critical discussion of it, conducted in *Notes and Queries* in 1889–90, concerned the possible meaning of line 28 (see Gene Ruoff in the *Wordsworth Circle* 12 [1981]: 45–51). Modern criticism has focused largely on the ode's thematic structure, its conceptions of memory and immortality, and its relation to other works of Wordsworth and Coleridge. It is widely agreed that the poem has a tripartite structure, corresponding to a greater or lesser degree with the division of classical odes into a strophe, antistrophe, and epode: stanzas 1–4 lament a loss of joy and vision in adulthood; stanzas 5–8 (or 5–7) intimate the soul's immortality by reference to childhood reminiscences of existence before physical life; and the final stanzas propose the function (consoling or otherwise) of the mature "philosophic mind." For analyses of its structure, see Florence Marsh, "Wordsworth's *Ode*: Obstinate Questionings"; and Jared Curtis, *Wordsworth's Experiments with Tradition*, chap. 7. Rejecting Lionel Trilling's influential argument (in "Wordsworth's 'Ode: Intimations of Immortality'") that the poem questions the existence of a distinct poetic faculty, Helen Vendler maintains that it "represents the power of the acquisition of metaphor" ("Lionel Trilling and the Immortality Ode," 84). Frances Ferguson analyzes the poem's insistent questioning of memory, logic, and metaphysics "as indices to the mind's ability to confer value" (*Wordsworth: Language as Counter-Spirit*, 96–125), while

Marjorie Levinson interprets the *Ode* as an allegory of Wordsworth's disillusionment with the French Revolution and his compensatory appeal to a non-rational spirituality (*Wordsworth's Great Period Poems*, 80–100). Paul Magnuson (*Coleridge and Wordsworth*, 278–89) and Lucy Newlyn (*Coleridge, Wordsworth, and the Language of Allusion*, 147–59) explore the poem's dialogue with Coleridge, Newlyn focusing on the role of Hartley Coleridge. Paul Fry identifies it with other irregular Pindaric odes as an expression of uncertainties (*The Poet's Calling in the English Ode*, chap. 6). The winter 1981 issue of the *Wordsworth Circle* contains essays on the *Ode* by critics of various perspectives. Of the criticism reprinted in this edition, the excerpt from Geoffrey Hartman's *Wordsworth's Poetry, 1787–1814* examines the patterns of "flux and reflux" in the *Ode* (pp. 721–24 below), while Steven Knapp's essay analyzes its "partial or ambiguous allegorization of natural agents" (pp. 732–37 below).

ODE

Paulò majora canamus[1]

There was a time when meadow, grove, and stream,
The earth, and every common sight,
    To me did seem
    Apparell'd in celestial light,
5 The glory and the freshness of a dream.
It is not now as it has been of yore;—[2]
    Turn wheresoe'er I may,
      By night or day,
The things which I have seen I now can see no more.

10   The Rainbow comes and goes,
      And lovely is the Rose,
      The Moon doth with delight
    Look round her when the heavens are bare;
      Waters on a starry night
15   Are beautiful and fair;
    The sunshine is a glorious birth;
    But yet I know, where'er I go,
That there hath pass'd away a glory from the earth.

    Now, while the Birds thus sing a joyous song,
20   And while the young Lambs bound

---

1. From Virgil's *Eclogue* 4.1: "Let us sing somewhat more loftily." On the prophecy announced in the eclogue, see n. 2 on the Appendix of *LB 1802* (p. 159). WW replaced this epigraph in *P 1815* with lines 7–9 of *My heart leaps up when I behold*: "The Child is Father of the Man; / And I could wish my days to be / Bound each to each by natural piety." On the significance of the substitution, see Peter Manning, "Wordsworth's Intimations Ode and Its Epigraphs," *Journal of English and German Philology* 82 (1982): 526–40.
2. Lines 1–6 recall lines 9–16 of *The Mad Monk*, published pseudonymously in the *Morning Post* on October 13, 1800, and attributed variously to WW and STC (see *LB* [CW], 802–4, on the problems of attribution): "There was a time when earth, and sea, and skies, / The bright green vale and forest's dark recess, / When all things lay before my eyes, / In steady loveliness. / But now I feel on earth's uneasy scene / Such motions as will never cease! / I only ask for peace— / Then wherefore must I know, that such a time has been?" (*LB* [CW], 804–805).

As to the tabor's³ sound,
To me alone there came a thought of grief:
A timely utterance gave that thought relief,
     And I again am strong.
25 The Cataracts blow their trumpets from the steep,
No more shall grief of mine the season wrong;
I hear the Echoes through the mountains throng,
The Winds come to me from the fields of sleep,
          And all the earth is gay,
30   Land and sea
     Give themselves up to jollity,
          And with the heart of May
     Doth every Beast keep holiday,
          Thou Child of Joy
35 Shout round me, let me hear thy shouts, thou happy Shepherd Boy!

Ye blessed Creatures, I have heard the call
     Ye to each other make; I see
The heavens laugh with you in your jubilee;
     My heart is at your festival,
40   My head hath its coronal,⁴
The fullness of your bliss, I feel—I feel it all.
          Oh evil day! if I were sullen
          While the Earth herself is adorning,
               This sweet May-morning,
45   And the Children are pulling,
               On every side,
          In a thousand vallies far and wide,
     Fresh flowers; while the sun shines warm,
And the Babe leaps up on his mother's arm:—
50   I hear, I hear, with joy I hear!
     —But there's a Tree, of many one,
A single Field⁵ which I have look'd upon,
Both of them speak of something that is gone:
          The Pansy at my feet
55   Doth the same tale repeat:
Whither is fled the visionary gleam?
Where is it now, the glory and the dream?

Our birth is but a sleep and a forgetting:
The Soul that rises with us, our life's Star,
60   Hath had elsewhere its setting,
               And cometh from afar:
          Not in entire forgetfulness,
          And not in utter nakedness,
But trailing clouds of glory do we come
65   From God, who is our home:
Heaven lies about us in our infancy!

3. Drum's.
4. The phrasing in lines 36–40 is similar to that of *The Idle Shepherd-Boys*, lines 27–30.
5. *A Tree . . . single Field*: an image that recurs in *The Prelude* 4.76–83 and 6.90–109.

Shades of the prison-house begin to close
      Upon the growing Boy,
But He beholds the light, and whence it flows,
70   He sees it in his joy;
The Youth, who daily farther from the East
    Must travel, still is Nature's Priest,
      And by the vision splendid
      Is on his way attended;
75 At length the Man perceives it die away,
And fade into the light of common day.

Earth fills her lap with pleasures of her own;
Yearnings she hath in her own natural kind,
And, even with something of a Mother's mind,
80   And no unworthy aim,
    The homely Nurse doth all she can
To make her Foster-child, her Inmate Man,
    Forget the glories he hath known,
And that imperial palace whence he came.[6]

85 Behold the Child among his new-born blisses,
A four year's Darling of a pigmy size!
See, where mid work of his own hand he lies,
Fretted by sallies of his Mother's kisses,
With light upon him from his Father's eyes![7]
90 See, at his feet, some little plan or chart,
Some fragment from his dream of human life,
Shap'd by himself with newly-learned art;
    A wedding or a festival,
    A mourning or a funeral;
95   And this hath now his heart,
    And unto this he frames his song:
    Then will he fit his tongue
To dialogues of business, love, or strife;
    But it will not be long
100   Ere this be thrown aside,
    And with new joy and pride
The little Actor cons another part,
Filling from time to time his "humourous[8] stage"
With all the Persons, down to palsied Age,
105 That Life brings with her in her Equipage;
    As if his whole vocation
    Were endless imitation.

6. Contrast with lines 77–84 the forgetting of nature's "playthings" in *The Prelude* 5.346–49.
7. WW would have been thinking particularly of STC's son Hartley (on whom see *To H. C.* above), who was actually six in 1802 (WW corrected the age in *P 1815*). Compare with lines 85–89 STC's *Christabel* (composed 1798–1800 and originally intended for *LB 1800*), lines 644–49: "A little child, a limber elf, / Singing, dancing to itself, / A fairy thing with red round cheeks / That always finds, and never seeks, / Makes such a vision to the sight / As fills a father's eyes with light" (*NCC*, 179).
8. Fanciful, whimsical (*OED* sense 3). The quotation is from line 1 of Samuel Daniel's dedicatory sonnet to Fulke Greville in *Musophilus* (1599), which WW read in November 1801 (*Reading 1800–15*, no. 125.i).

Thou, whose exterior semblance doth belie
      Thy Soul's immensity;
110 Thou best Philosopher, who yet dost keep
Thy heritage, thou Eye among the blind,
That, deaf and silent, read'st the eternal deep,
Haunted for ever by the eternal mind,—
      Mighty Prophet! Seer blest!
115   On whom those truths do rest,
Which we are toiling all our lives to find;[9]
Thou, over whom thy Immortality
Broods like the Day, a Master o'er a Slave,
A Presence which is not to be put by;[1]
120   To whom the grave
Is but a lonely bed without the sense or sight
      Of day or the warm light,
A place of thought where we in waiting lie;[2]
Thou little Child, yet glorious in the might
125 Of untam'd pleasures, on thy Being's height,[3]
Why with such earnest pains dost thou provoke
The Years to bring the inevitable yoke,
Thus blindly with thy blessedness at strife?
Full soon thy Soul shall have her earthly freight,
130 And custom lie upon thee with a weight,
Heavy as frost, and deep almost as life![4]

      O joy! that in our embers
      Is something that doth live,
      That nature yet remembers
135   What was so fugitive!
The thought of our past years in me doth breed
Perpetual benedictions: not indeed
For that which is most worthy to be blest;

---

9. In *MP 1820* WW inserted a new line after line 116: "In darkness lost, the darkness of the grave."

1. Compare WW's insistence in his "Essay upon Epitaphs," first published in STC's periodical *The Friend* on February 22, 1810, concerning "an intimation or assurance within us, that some part of our nature is imperishable": "If we look back upon the days of childhood, we shall find that the time is not in remembrance when, with respect to our individual Being, the mind was without this assurance" (p. 497 below). For his part STC thought the assurance of an afterlife a more urgent matter, remarking in his notebook, "concerning Pre-existence men in general have neither care or belief" (*CN*, 3:3701).

2. WW omitted lines 120–23 in *MP 1820* after STC in *BL*, noting the connection between this poem and *We are seven*, had objected to "the frightful notion of lying *awake* in his grave! The analogy between death and sleep is too simple, too natural, to render so horrid a belief possible for children" (*NCC*, 535). But evidently it was not horrid to WW, whom DW records on April 29, 1802, as lying next to her in a trench and thinking "that it would be sweet thus to lie so in the grave, to hear the *peaceful* sounds of the earth, and just to know that our dear friends were near" (*DWJ*, 1:139–40). WW later explained, as recorded in his nephew Christopher's *Memoirs of William Wordsworth* (London, 1851), 2:486, "In my Ode on the 'Intimations of Immortality in Childhood,' I do not profess to give a literal representation of the state of the affections and of the moral being in childhood. I record my own feelings at that time—my absolute spirituality, my 'all-soulness,' if I may so speak. At that time I could not believe that I should lie down quietly in the grave, and that my body would moulder into dust."

3. WW altered line 125 in *P 1815* to "Of heaven-born freedom, on thy Being's height."

4. Compare WW's observation in *The Prelude* 13.138–43 of the "tendency, too potent in itself, / Of habit to enslave the mind ° ° ° And substitute a universe of death, / The falsest of all worlds, in place of that / Which is divine and true."

        Delight and liberty, the simple creed
140   Of Childhood, whether fluttering or at rest,
        With new-born hope for ever in his breast:—[5]
                Not for these I raise
                The song of thanks and praise;
                But for those obstinate questionings
145   Of sense and outward things,
                Fallings from us, vanishings;
                Blank misgivings of a Creature
        Moving about in worlds not realiz'd,[6]
        High instincts, before which our mortal Nature
150   Did tremble like a guilty Thing surpriz'd:
                But for those first affections,
                Those shadowy recollections,
                        Which, be they what they may,
        Are yet the fountain light of all our day,
155   Are, yet a master light of all our seeing;
                Uphold us, cherish us, and make[7]
        Our noisy years seem moments in the being
        Of the eternal Silence:[8] truths that wake,
                        To perish never;
160   Which neither listlessness, nor mad endeavour,
                        Nor Man nor Boy,
        Nor all that is at enmity with joy,
        Can utterly abolish or destroy![9]
                Hence, in a season of calm weather,
165   Though inland far we be,
        Our Souls have sight of that immortal sea
                        Which brought us hither,[1]
                Can in a moment travel thither,
        And see the Children sport upon the shore,
170   And hear the mighty waters rolling evermore.

        Then, sing ye Birds, sing, sing a joyous song!
                And let the young Lambs bound
                As to the tabor's sound!
        We in thought will join your throng,
175   Ye that pipe and ye that play,

5. In *P 1815* WW altered this line to "new-fledged hope still fluttering."
6. WW's friend R. P. Graves later reported to Christopher Wordsworth, "I remember Mr. Words-
   worth saying that, at a particular stage of his mental progress, he used to be so frequently rapt
   into an unreal transcendental world of idea that the external world seemed no longer to exist in
   relation to him, and he had to re-convince himself of its existence *by clasping a tree * * *.* I could
   not help connecting this fact with that obscure passage [lines 144–48] in his great Ode on the
   'Intimations of Immortality'" (*Memoirs*, 2:480). See also the IF note quoted in the headnote.
7. In *P 1815* WW altered this line to "Uphold us—cherish—and have power to make."
8. Compare WW's *Stanzas on the Power of Sound* (composed 1828–34, published 1835), lines
   217–18: "O Silence! are Man's noisy years / No more than moments of thy life?" (*Last Poems,
   1821–1850* [CW], 123).
9. An echo of Milton, *Paradise Lost* 2.92–93: "More destroy'd then thus / We should be quite
   abolisht and expire."
1. *In a season . . . hither*: In his second "Essay upon Epitaphs" (composed 1810) WW uses similar
   imagery to express a nearly opposite thought: "how apt, in a series of calm weather, we are to
   forget that rain and storms have been, and will return, to interrupt any scheme of business of
   pleasure which our minds are occupied in arranging" (*Prose*, 2:63).

Ye that through your hearts to day
Feel the gladness of the May!
What though the radiance which was once so bright
Be now for ever taken from my sight,
180   Though nothing can bring back the hour
Of splendour in the grass, of glory in the flower;
        We will grieve not, rather find
        Strength in what remains behind,
        In the primal sympathy
185   Which having been must ever be,
        In the soothing thoughts that spring
        Out of human suffering,
        In the faith that looks through death,
In years that bring the philosophic mind.[2]

190 And oh ye Fountains, Meadows, Hills, and Groves,
Think not of any severing of our loves!
Yet in my heart of hearts I feel your might;
I only have relinquish'd one delight
To live beneath your more habitual sway.
195 I love the Brooks which down their channels fret,
Even more than when I tripp'd lightly as they;
The innocent brightness of a new-born Day
        Is lovely yet;
The Clouds that gather round the setting sun
200 Do take a sober colouring from an eye
That hath kept watch o'er man's mortality;
Another race hath been, and other palms are won.
Thanks to the human heart by which we live,
Thanks to its tenderness, its joys, and fears,
205 To me the meanest flower[3] that blows can give
Thoughts that do often lie too deep for tears.

2. A phrase from Oliver Goldsmith, *The Traveller, or a Prospect of Society* (revised version, 1765), lines 39–40: "Say, should the philosophic mind disdain / That good, which makes each humbler bosome vain?" (Moorman, 2:24n).
3. An echo of Thomas Gray, *Ode on the Pleasure Arising from Vicissitude* (1775), line 45: "The meanest flowret of the vale."

From THE EXCURSION (1814) *with* THE RUINED COTTAGE (1799)

The Ruined Cottage was begun in the spring of 1797 as the story, recounted by the Pedlar (i.e., peddler, an itinerant seller of tools and other small wares), of the decline of Margaret and her husband, the late inhabitants of a now-ruined cottage, into poverty and illness. While perhaps drawing on the image, in Robert Southey's poem *Joan of Arc* (1796) 7.320–31, of a distraught mother vainly awaiting the return of her soldier husband from battle, Wordsworth's poem would also have reflected his direct observation of rural poverty around Racedown, Dorset, in 1795–97 (see *WL*, 1:154, 162), poverty exacerbated by the bad harvest of 1794 and extremely harsh winter of 1794–95. But between January and March 1798, having meanwhile relocated to Alfoxden and begun the collaboration with Coleridge that would produce *Lyrical Ballads*, Wordsworth more than doubled the poem's length by adding an account of the Pedlar's life, education, and philosophical ideas. As Jonathan Wordsworth notes, "Where the original anticipates *Michael*, the additions belong rather with *The Prelude*" (*The Music of Humanity*, xiii); and indeed Wordsworth did incorporate some of this material into *Prel 1805* 2.322–41 and 7.492–96, 722–30. In the expanded version Margaret's story becomes the occasion for the Pedlar's moral reflections: "But we have known that there is often found in mournful thoughts * * * A power to virtue friendly" (lines 286–88 of MS B [1798] and 227–29 of MS D [1799]).

On March 6, 1798, the day that Dorothy finished transcribing the revised *Ruined Cottage*, William wrote James Tobin (who had visited Alfoxden in September), "I have written 1300 lines of a poem in which I contrive to convey most of the knowledge of which I am possessed. My object is to give pictures of Nature, Man, and Society. Indeed I know not any thing which will not come within the scope of my plan" (*WL*, 1:212; see also 454 and 518). What exactly constituted the "1300 lines" is uncertain, but it must have included the *The Ruined Cottage*, which was now to form part of a large philosophical poem in blank verse whose title Wordsworth revealed to his friend James Losh on March 11: "*The Recluse or views of Nature, Man, and Society*" (*WL*, 1:214). In September 1799 Coleridge assured Wordsworth that the poem would be of service "to those, who, in consequence of the complete failure of the French Revolution, have thrown up all hopes of the amelioration of mankind, and are sinking into an almost epicurean selfishness" (*CL*, 1:527). The project was to preoccupy Wordsworth for the next fifteen years, and to an extent haunt him thereafter, although he never completed the poem as such. In December 1824, Dorothy informed Henry Crabb Robinson that her brother "has not yet looked at *The Recluse*; he seems to feel the task so weighty that he shrinks from beginning with it" (*WL*, 4:292).

Critics have often maintained that the project, conceived with Coleridge in 1797–98, was more reflective of his temperament and interests than of Wordsworth's own (see, e.g., Jonathan Wordsworth, *The Borders of Vision*, 340–77; Gill, 145–47; Duncan Wu, *Wordsworth: An Inner Life*, 301, 314). To be sure, Coleridge repeatedly encouraged Wordsworth to write the poem (e.g., CL, 1:538, 575), and as late as 1815 (when he dictated the *Biographia Literaria*) he was still expressing hopes for its realization: Wordsworth, he insisted, "is capable of producing * * * the FIRST GENUINE PHILOSOPHIC POEM" (NCC, 544). It was also Coleridge who, expressing his disappointment that *The Excursion* was not the poem he was expecting, instructed Wordsworth himself on May 30, 1815, what *The Recluse* was supposed to contain:

> Of course, I expected the Colors, Music, imaginative Life, and Passion of *Poetry*; but the matter and arrangement of *Philosophy* * * * I supposed you first to have meditated the faculties of Man in the abstract, in their correspondence with his Sphere of action, and first, in the Feeling, Touch, and Taste, then in the Eye, & last in the Ear * * * and demonstrating that the Senses were living growths and developements of the Mind & Spirit in a much juster as well as higher sense, than the mind can be said to be formed by the Senses—. Next, I understood that you would take the Human Race in the concrete * * * and not disguising the sore evils, under which the whole Creation groans, to point out however a manifest Scheme of Redemption from this Slavery, of Reconciliation from this Enmity with Nature * * * and to conclude by a grand didactic swell on the necessary identity of a true Philosophy with true Religion * * * Such or something like this was the Plan, I had supposed that you were engaged on—. (CL, 4:575)

Since Coleridge's letter betrays his own philosophical and theological concerns of the 1810s, it should not be taken as a precise recollection of what he and Wordsworth had discussed almost seventeen years earlier. But it is probable (as Gill, 145, suggests) that the project foundered on its very inclusiveness, as conveyed in Wordsworth's letter to James Tobin quoted above. Highly conscious of Milton's example in *Paradise Lost*, Wordsworth must have remained committed to *The Recluse* for so long, if increasingly notionally, because he thought that only such a comprehensive and elevated theme was fully appropriate to the "beauteous Fabric" of the epic poetry to which he aspired (*Prel 1805* 1.229).

Faced, in March 1798, with the more immediate challenge of financing his planned travel to Germany with his sister and Coleridge, Wordsworth allowed Coleridge to offer *The Ruined Cottage* to Joseph Cottle for publication; but the poem was not published (see the headnote to *LB 1798*). Between February and November 1799 Wordsworth returned to *The Ruined Cottage*, removing the history of the Pedlar's intellectual development (which he developed into an independent poem, *The Pedlar*, in 1802). This version of the poem, in 538 lines, was the last to be called *The Ruined Cottage*: between December 21, 1803, and March 18, 1804, Wordsworth recombined the 1799 *Ruined Cottage* and 1802 *Pedlar* under the latter title (*RC* [CW], xi). Meanwhile, in early 1800 he had begun composing part 1, book 1, of *The Recluse* proper, *Home at Grasmere*, only to abandon it within the year (*Home at Grasmere* [CW], 13). Having completed the thirteen-book *Prelude* in 1805, he resumed and finished *Home at Grasmere* the following year (though he never published it). In 1808 he composed another "philosophical" section of *The Recluse*, *The Tuft of Primroses*. But his principal work towards *The Recluse*, from either September 1806 or December 1809 to May 1814 (*Exc* [CW], 426–28), involved the narrative of part 2, which he published in August 1814 in an expensive quarto edition of 447 pages under the title *The Excursion; Being a Portion of The Recluse, A Poem* (a smaller, cheaper octavo edition followed six years later).

Structured as a conversation among four principal speakers—the Poet, the Wanderer (formerly the Pedlar), the Solitary, and the Pastor—the poem is divided into nine books, of which Book 1 incorporates (with revisions) the combined *The Ruined Cottage* and *Pedlar* from 1804. In Geoffrey Hartman's summary, "emphasis is shifted * * * from the individual fates that are charactered, to the more comprehensive question of how man can face death or mutability and remain uninjured" (*Wordsworth's Poetry, 1787–1814*, 299). In the Preface Wordsworth explained the poem's place in *The Recluse*, included a "Prospectus" extracted from *Home at Grasmere*, and referred to a "long finished" biographical and "preparatory Poem" (i.e., *Prel 1805*) as the "Antichapel" to *The Recluse*. That he mentioned *The Recluse* so prominently, not least on the title page, indicates that in 1814 he still considered it a realizable project. When he reprinted *The Excursion* in 1836, recognizing that he would not complete what Dorothy had described in 1805 as "the Task of his life" (*WL*, 1:576), Wordsworth omitted the poem's earlier subtitle.

In his long IF note on *The Excursion*, the poet identified with the Pedlar and acknowledged "that the character I have represented in his person is chiefly an idea of what I fancied my own character might have become in his circumstances," that is, without the benefits of a grammar school and university education. "All that relates to Margaret & the ruined cottage &c," he added, "was taken from observations made in the South West of England & certainly it would require more than seven leagued boots to stretch in one morning from a common in Somersetshire or Dorsetshire, to the heights of Furness Fells [in the Lake District] & the deep vallies they embosom. For thus dealing with space I need make, I trust, no apology; but my friends may be amused by the truth."

John Keats considered *The Excursion* was one of "three things to rejoice at in this Age" (*Letters of John Keats*, ed. Hyder Rollins [Cambridge, MA, 1958], 1:203—the other two were William Hazlitt's critical taste and Benjamin Robert Haydon's paintings, on which see Wordsworth's *To R. B. Haydon*). But Keats's high estimation of the poem was not widely shared by contemporaries. Percy and Mary Shelley were "much disappointed" with the poem (see the first note on Percy's *To Wordsworth* in Nineteenth-Century Responses), and Lord Byron ridiculed in it his own epic-length poem, *Don Juan* (1819–23), as a "drowsy frowsy poem, call'd the 'Excursion,' / Writ in a manner which is my aversion" (3.94). Most of the reviewers were little kinder, although Charles Lamb reviewed the poem favorably in the *Quarterly* of October 1814 (*CH*, 404–15). Francis Jeffrey notoriously began his critique in the *Edinburgh Review* (November 1814), "This will never do," and proceeded to characterize the poem as "a tissue of moral and devotional ravings" founded on "a few very simple and familiar ideas" accompanied by "long words, long sentences, and unwieldy phrases" (*CH*, 382, 385). The longest and most thoughtful review, by Hazlitt, appeared in three issues of the *Examiner* between August and October 1814 and assessed *The Excursion* as "a philosophical pastoral poem * * * not so much a description of natural objects, as of the feelings associated with him, not an account of the manners of rural life, but the result of the Poet's reflections on it" (*CH*, 369–70). In contrast to Jeffery, Hazlitt pronounced the poet's ideas "subtle and profound," but objected to his making "pedlars and ploughmen his heroes and interpreters of his sentiments" (*CH*, 377).

Modern critics have tended to concur with nineteenth-century reviewers in finding *The Excursion* ponderous and dull, but a number of studies have sought to reassess the poem either in relation to *The Recluse* project or *sui generis*: examples include the articles assembled in the spring 1978 issue of the *Wordsworth Circle*, Jonathan Wordsworth's *The Borders of Vision*, Kenneth Johnston's *Wordsworth and "The Recluse,"* Duncan Wu's *Wordsworth: An Inner Life*, and Sally Bushell's *Re-reading "The Excursion."* The "Prospectus" is discussed in M. H. Abrams's *Natural Supernaturalism*, 19–32, and the representation of Margaret is the focus of Karen Swann's essay excerpted here under Modern Criticism. Unlike *The Excursion* itself, however, the earlier form of its first book, *The Ruined Cottage*, has been appreciated as one of Wordsworth's major poems since Jonathan Wordsworth, himself a forceful advocate of its value, first published the 1799 version (MS D) in his *Music of Humanity*. Recent criticism on the poem includes Jonathan Barron and Kenneth Johnston, "'A Power to Virtue Friendly,'" on the Pedlar's character; and Stephen Gill, *Wordsworth's Revisitings*, chap. 2, on Wordsworth's revisions of the poem. To facilitate comparison of *The Ruined Cottage*, in the final recension to bear that title—centered on the story of Margaret—with its transformation in book 1 of *The Excursion*, the "reading text" of MS D, reproduced from *RC* (CW), is here printed on verso pages facing the corresponding passages of *The Excursion*, reproduced from the first edition of 1814. The Preface to *The Excursion* and the "Essay on Epitaphs" are also printed from the first edition.

From The Excursion, Being a Portion of The Recluse, A Poem

PREFACE

THE Title-page announces that this is only a Portion of a Poem; and the Reader must be here apprized that it belongs to the second part of a long and laborious Work, which is to consist of three parts.[1]—The Author will candidly acknowledge that, if the first of these had been completed, and in such a manner as to satisfy his own mind, he should have preferred the natural order of publication, and have given that to the World first; but, as the second division of the Work was designed to refer more to passing events,[2] and to an existing state of things, than the others were meant to do, more continuous exertion was naturally bestowed upon it, and greater progress made here than in the rest of the Poem; and as this part does not depend upon the preceding, to a degree which will materially injure its own peculiar interest, the Author, complying with the earnest entreaties of some valued Friends,[3] presents the following Pages to the Public.

It may be proper to state whence the Poem, of which The Excursion is a part, derives its Title of THE RECLUSE.—Several years ago, when the Author retired to his native Mountains,[4] with the hope of being enabled to construct a literary Work that might live, it was a reasonable thing that he should take a review of his own Mind, and examine how far Nature and Education had qualified him for such employment. As subsidiary to this preparation, he undertook to record, in Verse, the origin and progress of his own powers, as far as he was acquainted with them. That Work, addressed to a dear Friend,[5] most distinguished for his knowledge

1. I.e., of *The Recluse* proper. The first part was to incorporate *Home at Grasmere* (composed 1800 and 1806), possibly *The Tuft of Primroses* (composed 1808), and other materials never written; the second part was *The Excursion* itself; and the third part was never written.
2. Notably the French Revolution, on which the Solitary reflects in *Exc* 3.718–842.
3. Possibly Sir George and Lady Beaumont (see Biographical and Topographical Glossary).
4. In fact WW conceived the scheme of *The Recluse* in discussion with STC in Somerset in 1798 (see the headnote), before he moved to Grasmere in December 1799.
5. I.e., *The Prelude*, which remained untitled in WW's lifetime and was known in the family as "the poem to Coleridge."

and genius, and to whom the Author's Intellect is deeply indebted, has been long finished; and the result of the investigation which gave rise to it was a determination to compose a philosophical Poem, containing views of Man, Nature, and Society; and to be entitled, The Recluse; as having for its principal subject the sensations and opinions of a Poet living in retirement.—The preparatory Poem is biographical, and conducts the history of the Author's mind to the point when he was emboldened to hope that his faculties were sufficiently matured for entering upon the arduous labour which he had proposed to himself; and the two Works[6] have the same kind of relation to each other, if he may so express himself, as the Anti-chapel has to the body of a gothic Church. Continuing this allusion, he may be permitted to add, that his minor Pieces, which have been long before the Public, when they shall be properly arranged, will be found by the attentive Reader to have such connection with the main Work as may give them claim to be likened to the little Cells, Oratories, and sepulchral Recesses, ordinarily included in those Edifices.

The Author would not have deemed himself justified in saying, upon this occasion, so much of performances either unfinished, or unpublished, if he had not thought that the labour bestowed by him upon what he has heretofore and now laid before the Public, entitled him to candid attention for such a statement as he thinks necessary to throw light upon his endeavours to please, and he would hope, to benefit his countrymen.—Nothing further need be added, than that the first and third parts of the Recluse will consist chiefly of meditations in the Author's own Person; and that in the intermediate part (The Excursion) the intervention of Characters speaking is employed, and something of a dramatic form adopted.

It is not the Author's intention formally to announce a system: it was more animating to him to proceed in a different course; and if he shall succeed in conveying to the mind clear thoughts, lively images, and strong feelings, the Reader will have no difficulty in extracting the system for himself. And in the mean time the following passage, taken from the conclusion of the first Book of the Recluse,[7] may be acceptable as a kind of *Prospectus* of the design and scope of the whole Poem.

> *On Man, on Nature, and on Human Life*
> *Musing in Solitude, I oft perceive*
> *Fair trains of imagery before me rise,*
> *Accompanied by feelings of delight*
> 5 *Pure, or with no unpleasing sadness mixed;*
> *And I am conscious of affecting thoughts*
> *And dear remembrances, whose presence soothes*
> *Or elevates the Mind,[8] intent to weigh*
> *The good and evil of our mortal state.*
> 10 *—To these emotions, whencesoe'er they come,*
> *Whether from breath of outward circumstance,*
> *Or from the Soul—an impulse to herself,*

6. *The Prelude* and *The Recluse.*
7. The "Prospectus" is extracted from the conclusion of *Home at Grasmere* (for transcriptions of early drafts see *Home at Grasmere* [CW], 265–67, 395–403), a poem that WW, intending to incorporate it into *The Recluse*, never published. WW used variants of the phrase "Nature, Man, and Society" frequently in WW's descriptions of *The Recluse* project (see the headnote).
8. *Whose presence . . . mind*: Compare *Tintern Abbey*, lines 26–31, and *The Prelude* 1.618–26.

I would give utterance in numerous Verse.[9]
—Of Truth, of Grandeur, Beauty, Love, and Hope—
15 And melancholy Fear subdued by Faith;
Of blessed consolations in distress;
Of moral strength, and intellectual power;
Of joy in widest commonalty spread;
Of the individual Mind that keeps her own
20 Inviolate retirement, subject there
To Conscience only, and the law supreme
Of that Intelligence which governs all;
I sing:—"fit audience let me find though few!"[1]

So prayed, more gaining than he asked, the Bard,
25 Holiest of Men.—Urania,[2] I shall need
Thy guidance, or a greater Muse, if such
Descend to earth or dwell in highest heaven!
For I must tread on shadowy ground, must sink
Deep—and, aloft ascending, breathe in worlds
30 To which the heaven of heavens[3] is but a veil.
All strength—all terror, single or in bands,
That ever was put forth in personal form;
Jehovah—with his thunder, and the choir
Of shouting Angels, and the empyreal thrones,[4]
35 I pass them, unalarmed. Not Chaos, not
The darkest pit of lowest Erebus,[5]
Nor aught of blinder vacancy—scooped out
By help of dreams, can breed such fear and awe
As fall upon us often when we look
40 Into our Minds, into the Mind of Man,
My haunt, and the main region of my Song.[6]
—Beauty—a living Presence of the earth,
Surpassing the most fair ideal Forms
Which craft of delicate Spirits hath composed
45 From earth's materials—waits upon my steps;
Pitches her tents before me as I move,
An hourly neighbour. Paradise, and groves
Elysian, Fortunate Fields—like those of old
Sought in the Atlantic Main,[7] why should they be
50 A history only of departed things,
Or a mere fiction of what never was?
For the discerning intellect of Man,
When wedded to this goodly universe
In love and holy passion, shall find these
55 A simple produce of the common day.

---

9. A phrase from Milton, *Paradise Lost* 5.150.
1. *Paradise Lost* 7.31: "fit audience find, though few."
2. The muse of astronomy in Greek mythology, also invoked by Milton in *Paradise Lost* 7.30–31.
3. A phrase from *Paradise Lost* 7.13 and 553.
4. A phrase from *Paradise Lost* 2.430; *shouting Angels*: perhaps alluding to *Paradise Lost* 2.520, where it is the fallen angels who make a "deafning shout."
5. In ancient Greek literature a place of darkness and passage between earth and Hades, but in *Paradise Lost* 2.883 a name for the whole of Hell. WW's use of Miltonic rhetoric here throws into relief the fact that his epic subject is neither biblical nor cosmic but human.
6. Compare WW's exaltation of "the mind of Man" in *The Prelude* 13.444–52.
7. Ocean (a poetic usage).

    —I, long before the blissful hour arrives,
    Would chaunt, in lonely peace, the spousal verse
    Of this great consummation:—and, by words
    Which speak of nothing more than what we are,
60 *Would I arouse the sensual from their sleep*
    Of Death, and win the vacant and the vain
    To noble raptures; while my voice proclaims
    How exquisitely the individual Mind
    (And the progressive powers perhaps no less
65 *Of the whole species) to the external World*
    Is fitted:—and how exquisitely, too,
    Theme this but little heard of among Men,
    The external World is fitted to the Mind;[8]
    And the creation (by no lower name
70 *Can it be called) which they with blended might*
    Accomplish:—this is our high argument.
    —Such grateful haunts foregoing, if I oft
    Must turn elsewhere—to travel near the tribes
    And fellowships of men, and see ill sights
75 *Of madding passions mutually inflamed;*
    Must hear Humanity in fields and groves
    Pipe solitary anguish; or must hang
    Brooding above the fierce confederate storm
    Of sorrow, barricadoed evermore[9]
80 *Within the walls of Cities; may these sounds*
    Have their authentic comment,—that, even these
    Hearing, I be not downcast or forlorn!
    —Come thou prophetic Spirit, that inspir'st
85 *The human Soul*[1] *of universal earth,*
    Dreaming on things to come; and dost possess
    A metropolitan Temple in the hearts
    Of mighty Poets;[2] *upon me bestow*
    A gift of genuine insight; that my Song
    With star-like virtue in its place may shine;
90 *Shedding benignant influence,—and secure,*
    Itself, from all malevolent effect
    Of those mutations that extend their sway
    Throughout the nether sphere![3]*—And if with this*
    I mix more lowly matter; with the thing
95 *Contemplated, describe the Mind and Man*
    Contemplating; and who, and what he was,

8. *How exquisitely . . . fitted to the Mind*: In an 1802 addition to the Preface to *LB*, WW argued that the poet "considers man and nature as essentially adapted to each other, and the mind of man as naturally the mirror of the fairest and most interesting qualities of nature" (pp. 87–88 above). See also *Tintern Abbey*, lines 106–108, and *The Prelude* 8.757–59. In his copy of *Exc* William Blake annotated this passage disapprovingly: "You shall not bring me down to believe such fitting & fitted I know better & Please your Lordship" (*The Complete Poetry and Prose of William Blake*, ed. David Erdman, 2nd ed. [Berkeley, 1982], 667).
9. An echo of *Paradise Lost* 8.241: "barricado'd strong" (referring to the gates of Hell).
1. *Come thou . . . human Soul*: WW's note (printed at the end of the volume): "Not mine own fears, nor the prophetic Soul / Of the wide world dreaming on things to come. *Shakespeare's Sonnets* [no. 107, lines 1–2]."
2. A phrase WW used also in *Resolution and Independence*, line 123: "And mighty Poets in their misery dead."
3. In lines 90–93 WW echoes *Paradise Lost* 7.375 ("Shedding sweet influence") and 10.660–62 (on the postlapsarian alignment of the planets).

The transitory Being that beheld
This Vision,—when and where, and how he lived;—
Be not this labour useless. If such theme
100 *May sort with highest objects, then, dread Power,*
Whose gracious favour is the primal source
Of all illumination, may my Life
Express the image of a better time,
More wise desires, and simpler manners;—nurse
105 *My Heart in genuine freedom:—all pure thoughts*
Be with me;—so shall thy unfailing love
Guide, and support, and cheer me to the end!"

THE RUINED COTTAGE (1799)
1st PART

'Twas summer and the sun was mounted high.
Along the south the uplands feebly glared
Through a pale steam, and all the northern downs
[4] In clearer air ascending shewed far off
Their surfaces with shadows dappled o'er   5
Of deep embattled clouds:[1] far as the sight
Could reach those many shadows lay in spots
Determined and unmoved, with steady beams
Of clear and pleasant sunshine interposed;
[10] Pleasant to him who on the soft cool moss   10
Extends his careless limbs beside the root
Of some huge oak whose aged branches make
A twilight of their own, a dewy shade
Where the wren warbles while the dreaming man,
[15] Half-conscious of that soothing melody,   15
With side-long eye looks out upon the scene,
By those impending branches made more soft,
More soft and distant.[2] Other lot was mine.
[21] Across a bare wide Common I had toiled
With languid feet which by the slipp'ry ground   20

---

1. Lines 1–7 are a blank-verse adaptation of a passage in rhyming couplets from *An Evening Walk* (1793), lines 53–56, and revisions WW made to that passage in 1794 (see *An Evening Walk* [CW], 34).
2. A model for WW's *dreaming Man* in line 10–18 may have been the philosopher who observes the world's afflictions with serene detachment in Lucretius's *De rerum natura* (first century B.C.E.) 2.1–19, a work WW is known to have read by 1794 (*Reading 1770–99*, no. 160.ii, *Reading 1800–15*, no. AI12; *Exc* [CW], 376).

From The Excursion (1814)

BOOK FIRST[1]

THE WANDERER

'Twas summer, and the sun had mounted high:
Southward, the landscape indistinctly glared
Through a pale steam; but all the northern downs,
In clearest air ascending, shew'd far off
5   A surface dappled o'er with shadows, flung
From many a brooding cloud; far as the sight
Could reach, those many shadows lay in spots
Determined and unmoved, with steady beams
Of bright and pleasant sunshine interposed.
10   Pleasant to him who on the soft cool moss
Extends his careless limbs along the front
Of some huge cave, whose rocky ceiling casts
A twilight of its own, an ample shade,
Where the wren warbles; while the dreaming Man,
15   Half conscious of the soothing melody,
With side-long eye looks out upon the scene,
By that impending covert made more soft,
More low and distant! Other lot was mine;
Yet with good hope that soon I should obtain
20   As grateful resting-place, and livelier joy.

---

1. WW's summary of book 1, printed after the Preface in *Exc* (1814): "A summer forenoon—The Author reaches a ruined Cottage upon a Common, and there meets with a revered Friend, the Wanderer, of whom he gives an account—The Wanderer while resting under the shade of the Trees that surround the Cottage relates the History of its last Inhabitant."

Were baffled still, and when I stretched myself
On the brown earth my limbs from very heat
Could find no rest nor my weak arm disperse
The insect host which gathered round my face
And joined their murmurs to the tedious noise   25
Of seeds of bursting gorse that crackled round.
I rose and turned towards a group of trees
Which midway in that level stood alone,
And thither come at length, beneath a shade
Of clustering elms that sprang from the same root   30
I found a ruined house, four naked[3] walls
[31]   That stared upon each other. I looked round
And near the door I saw an aged Man,
Alone, and stretched upon the cottage bench;
[37]   An iron-pointed staff lay at his side.   35
With instantaneous joy I recognized
That pride of nature and of lowly life,
The venerable Armytage, a friend
As dear to me as is the setting sun.
                    Two days before   40
We had been fellow-travellers. I knew
That he was in this neighbourhood and now
Delighted found him here in the cool shade.
He lay, his pack of rustic merchandize[4]

Wordsworth's old men

dignity

3. A revision of "clay" in MS B (*RC* [CW], 44).
4. Goods sold to country people.

Across a bare wide Common I was toiling[2]
With languid feet, which by the slippery ground
Were baffled; nor could my weak arm disperse
The host of insects gathering round my face,
25 And ever with me as I paced along.

     Upon that open level stood a Grove,
The wished-for Port to which my steps were bound.
Thither I came, and there—amid the gloom
Spread by a brotherhood of lofty elms—
30 Appeared a roofless Hut; four naked walls
That stared upon each other! I looked round,
And to my wish and to my hope espied
Him whom I sought; a Man of reverend age,
But stout and hale, for travel unimpaired.
35 There was he seen upon the Cottage bench,
Recumbent in the shade, as if asleep;
An iron-pointed staff lay at his side.[3]

2. WW preserves from RC his description of the landscape of Salisbury Plain, despite relocating
the scene of the events to the Lake District in Exc; see the headnote.
3. The Pedlar of RC having retired (see lines 466–68 below) and become a Wanderer in Exc, he
no longer has a "pack of rustic merchandize" (RC, line 44).

Him had I marked the day before—alone
And in the middle of the public way
40 Stationed, as if to rest himself, with face
Turned tow'rds the sun then setting, while that staff
Afforded to his Figure, as he stood,
Detained for contemplation or repose,
Graceful support; the countenance of the Man
45 Was hidden from my view, and he himself
Unrecognized; but, stricken by the sight,
With slacken'd footsteps I advanced, and soon
A glad congratulation we exchanged
At such unthought-of meeting.—For the night
50 We parted, nothing willingly; and now
He by appointment waited for me here,
Beneath the shelter of these clustering elms.[4]

*   *   *

4. The long section omitted here, in which the poet recounts the education and character of the
Pedlar, whom he declares to have known since childhood, derives from material that WW
composed in 1798 and included in MS B of RC but then omitted from MS D, treating it as
material for a separate poem, *The Pedlar* (1801–1802), before reuniting it with Margaret's story
in MS E (1803–1804) under the title *The Pedlar*. The account of the Wanderer's childhood
closely resembles that of WW's own in *The Prelude*. For texts of the different versions of this
section, see RC (CW), 44 and 46 (MS B), 384–412 (MS E), and *Exc* (CW), 50–61.

Pillowing his head—I guess he had no thought   45
Of his way-wandering life. His eyes were shut;
The shadows of the breezy elms above
Dappled his face. With thirsty heat oppress'd
[476] At length I hailed him, glad to see his hat
Bedewed with water-drops, as if the brim   50
Had newly scoop'd a running stream. He rose
And pointing to a sun-flower bade me climb
The [   ] wall where that same gaudy flower
[485] Looked out upon the road. It was a plot
Of garden-ground, now wild, its matted weeds   55
Marked with the steps of those whom as they pass'd,
The goose-berry trees that shot in long lank slips,
Or currants hanging from their leafless stems
[490] In scanty strings, had tempted to o'erleap
The broken wall. Within that cheerless spot,   60
Where two tall hedgerows of thick willow boughs
[493] Joined in a damp cold nook, I found a well
Half-choked [with willow flowers and weeds.][5]
I slaked my thirst and to the shady bench

5. DW left a gap in the MS, and WW penciled in the phrase in brackets (RC [CW], 49).

So was He[5] framed; and such his course of life
Who now, with no Appendage but a Staff,
The prized memorial of relinquish'd toils,
Upon that Cottage bench reposed his limbs,
470　Screened from the sun. Supine the Wanderer lay,
His eyes as if in drowsiness half shut,
The shadows of the breezy elms above
Dappling his face. He had not heard my steps
As I approached; and near him did I stand
475　Unnotic'd in the shade, some minutes' space.
At length I hailed him, seeing that his hat
Was moist with water-drops, as if the brim
Had newly scooped a running stream. He rose,
And ere the pleasant greeting that ensued
480　Was ended, "'Tis," said I, "a burning day;
My lips are parched with thirst, but you, I guess,
Have somewhere found relief." He, at the word,
Pointing towards a sweet-briar,[6] bade me climb
The fence hard by, where that aspiring shrub
485　Looked out upon the road. It was a plot
Of garden-ground run wild, its matted weeds
Marked with the steps of those, whom, as they pass'd,
The gooseberry trees that shot in long lank slips,
Or currants hanging from their leafless stems
490　In scanty strings, had tempted to o'erleap
The broken wall. I looked around, and there,
Where two tall hedge-rows of thick alder boughs
Joined in a cold damp nook, espied a Well
Shrouded with willow-flowers and plumy fern.
495　My thirst I slaked, and from the chearless spot
Withdrawing, straightway to the shade returned
Where sate the Old Man on the Cottage bench;

5. The Wanderer.
6. Eglantine, a species of rose.

Returned, and while I stood unbonneted   65
To catch the motion of the cooler air
The old Man said, "I see around me here
[502]   Things which you cannot see: we die, my Friend,
Nor we alone, but that which each man loved
And prized in his peculiar nook of earth   70
[505]   Dies with him or is changed, and very soon
Even of the good is no memorial left.
The Poets in their elegies and songs
Lamenting the departed call the groves,
They call upon the hills and streams to mourn,   75

Orpheus

[510]   And senseless rocks, nor idly; for they speak
In these their invocations with a voice
Obedient to the strong creative power
Of human passion. Sympathies there are
More tranquil, yet perhaps of kindred birth,   80
[515]   That steal upon the meditative mind
And grow with thought. Beside yon spring I stood
And eyed its waters till we seemed to feel
One sadness, they and I. For them a bond
Of brotherhood is broken: time has been   85
[520]   When every day the touch of human hand
Disturbed their stillness, and they ministered
To human comfort. When I stooped to drink,
A spider's web hung to the water's edge,
And on the wet and slimy foot-stone lay   90
[525]   The useless fragment of a wooden bowl;[6]
It moved my very heart. The day has been

6. Compare lines 88–91 with *An Evening Walk*, lines 255–56: "For hope's deserted well why wistful look? / Chok'd is the pathway, and the pitcher broke" (*An Evening Walk* [CW], 62). The image of pitcher alludes openly, and that of the wooden bowl obliquely, to Ecclesiastes 12.6–7: "Or ever * * * the pitcher be broken at the fountain, or the wheel broken at the cistern. Then shall the dust return to the earth as it was: and the spirit shall return unto God who have it."

And, while, beside him, with uncovered head,
I yet was standing, freely to respire,
500 And cool my temples in the fanning air,
Thus did he speak. "I see around me here
Things which you cannot see: we die, my Friend,
Nor we alone, but that which each man loved
And prized in his peculiar nook of earth
505 Dies with him, or is changed; and very soon
Even of the good is no memorial left.
—The Poets, in their elegies and songs
Lamenting the departed, call the groves,
They call upon the hills and streams to mourn,
510 And senseless rocks; nor idly; for they speak,
In these their invocations, with a voice
Obedient to the strong creative power
Of human passion. Sympathies there are
More tranquil, yet perhaps of kindred birth,
515 That steal upon the meditative mind,
And grow with thought. Beside yon Spring I stood,
And eyed its waters till we seemed to feel
One sadness, they and I. For them a bond
Of brotherhood is broken: time has been
520 When, every day, the touch of human hand
Dislodged the natural sleep that binds them up
In mortal stillness; and they minister'd
To human comfort. As I stooped to drink,
Upon the slimy foot-stone I espied
525 The useless fragment of a wooden bowl,
Green with the moss of years; a pensive sight
That moved my heart!—recalling former days

When I could never pass this road but she
Who lived within these walls, when I appeared,
[530] A daughter's welcome gave me, and I loved her   95
As my own child. O Sir! the good die first,
And they whose hearts are dry as summer dust
Burn to the socket. Many a passenger
Has blessed poor Margaret for her gentle looks
[535] When she upheld the cool refreshment drawn   100
From that forsaken spring, and no one came
But he was welcome, no one went away
[538] But that it seemed she loved him. She is dead,
The worm is on her cheek, and this poor hut,
Stripp'd of its outward garb of houshold flowers,   105
Of rose and sweet-briar, offers to the wind
A cold bare wall whose earthy top is tricked
With weeds and the rank spear-grass.[7] She is dead,
And nettles rot and adders sun themselves
Where we have sate together while she nurs'd   110
Her infant at her breast. The unshod Colt,
The wandring heifer and the Potter's ass,
Find shelter now within the chimney-wall
Where I have seen her evening hearth-stone blaze
And through the window spread upon the road   115
Its chearful light.—You will forgive me, Sir,
But often on this cottage do I muse
As on a picture, till my wiser mind
Sinks, yielding to the foolishness of grief.

7. *This poor hut . . . spear-grass:* possibly a recollection of Oliver Goldsmith, *The Deserted Village* (1770), lines 47–48: "Sunk are thy bowers in shapeless ruins all, / And the long grass o'ertops the mouldering wall"; *tricked:* decked.

When I could never pass that road but She
Who lived within these walls, at my approach,
530   A Daughter's welcome gave me; and I loved her
As my own child. O Sir! the good die first,
And they whose hearts are dry as summer dust
Burn to the socket. Many a Passenger
Hath blessed poor Margaret for her gentle looks,
535   When she upheld the cool refreshment drawn
From that forsaken Spring; and no one came
But he was welcome; no one went away
But that it seemed she loved him. She is dead,
The light extinguished of her lonely Hut,
540   The Hut itself abandoned to decay,
And She forgotten in the quiet grave!

        "I speak," continued he, "of One whose stock
Of virtues bloom'd beneath this lowly roof.
She was a Woman of a steady mind,
545   Tender and deep in her excess of love,
Not speaking much, pleased rather with the joy
Of her own thoughts: by some especial care
Her temper had been framed, as if to make
A Being—who by adding love to peace
550   Might live on earth a life of happiness.
Her wedded Partner lacked not on his side
The humble worth that satisfied her heart:
Frugal, affectionate, sober, and withal
Keenly industrious. She with pride would tell

She had a husband, an industrious man,   120
Sober and steady; I have heard her say
That he was up and busy at his loom
In summer ere the mower's scythe had swept
[557]   The dewy grass, and in the early spring
Ere the last star had vanished. They who pass'd   125
At evening, from behind the garden-fence
[560]   Might hear his busy spade, which he would ply
After his daily work till the day-light
Was gone and every leaf and flower were lost
In the dark hedges. So they pass'd their days   130
In peace and comfort, and two pretty babes
[565]   Were their best hope next to the God in Heaven.
—You may remember, now some ten years gone,
Two blighting seasons when the fields were left
With half a harvest. It pleased heaven to add   135
[570]   A worse affliction in the plague of war:
A happy land was stricken to the heart;
'Twas a sad time of sorrow and distress:⁸
A wanderer among the cottages,
I with my pack of winter raiment saw   140
The hardships of that season: many rich
[575]   Sunk down as in a dream among the poor,
And of the poor did many cease to be,
And their place knew them not.⁹ Meanwhile, abridg'd
Of daily comforts, gladly reconciled   145
To numerous self-denials, Margaret
[580]   Went struggling on through those calamitous years
With chearful hope: but ere the second autumn
A fever seized her husband. In disease
He lingered long, and when his strength returned   150
[585]   He found the little he had stored¹ to meet
The hour of accident or crippling age
Was all consumed. As I have said, 'twas now
A time of trouble; shoals² of artisans

8. When WW began composing *The Ruined Cottage* in 1797, the bad harvests and food riots of
1794–95 (when the price of wheat nearly doubled) were a very recent memory and the war with
France was into its fifth year. See also the first note on *The Old Cumberland Beggar* (p. 133
above). WW's reference to *ten years gone* (line 133) suggests, however, that he is placing the
events recounted by the Pedlar at the time of the American War of Independence (1775–82). In
his IF note on *Exc* WW remarked, "I was born too late to have a distinct remembrance of the
origin of the American war, but the state in wh. I represent Robert's mind to be I had frequent
opportunities of observing at the commencement of our rupture with France in [17]93."
9. This phrase echoes Milton, *Paradise Lost* 7.144 ("whom thir place knows here no more"), which
in turn echoes Job 7.10 ("He shall return no more to his house, neither shall his place know
him any more") and Psalm 103.16 ("For the wind passeth over it, and it is gone; and the place
thereof shall know it no more").
1. Money he had saved.
2. Crowds.

555 That he was often seated at his loom,
In summer, ere the Mower was abroad
Among the dewy grass,—in early spring,
Ere the last Star had vanished.—They who passed
At evening, from behind the garden fence
560 Might hear his busy spade, which he would ply,
After his daily work, until the light
Had failed, and every leaf and flower were lost
In the dark hedges. So their days were spent
In peace and comfort; and a pretty Boy
565 Was their best hope,—next to the God in Heaven.

    Not twenty years ago,[7] but you I think
Can scarcely bear it now in mind, there came
Two blighting seasons when the fields were left
With half a harvest. It pleased heaven to add
570 A worse affliction in the plague of war;
This happy Land was stricken to the heart!
A Wanderer then among the Cottages
I, with my freight of winter raiment, saw
The hardships of that season; many rich
575 Sank down, as in a dream, among the poor;
And of the poor did many cease to be
And their place knew them not. Meanwhile abridg'd
Of daily comforts, gladly reconciled
To numerous self-denials, Margaret
580 Went struggling on through those calamitous years
With chearful hope: but ere the second autumn
Her life's true Help-mate on a sick-bed lay,

---

7. The "ten years" of *RC*, line 133, are doubled in *Exc.*

[590] Were from their daily labour turned away   155
To hang for bread on parish charity,[3]
They and their wives and children—happier far
Could they have lived as do the little birds
[595] That peck along the hedges or the kite
That makes her dwelling in the mountain rocks.   160
Ill fared it now with Robert, he who dwelt
In this poor cottage; at his door he stood
And whistled many a snatch of merry tunes
[600] That had no mirth in them, or with his knife
Carved uncouth figures on the heads of sticks,   165
Then idly sought about through every nook
Of house or garden any casual task
Of use or ornament, and with a strange,
[605] Amusing but uneasy novelty
He blended where he might the various tasks   170
Of summer, autumn, winter, and of spring.
But this endured not; his good-humour soon
Became a weight in which no pleasure was,
[610] And poverty brought on a petted mood
And a sore temper: day by day he drooped,   175
And he would leave his home, and to the town
Without an errand would he turn his steps
Or wander here and there among the fields.
[615] One while he would speak lightly of his babes
And with a cruel tongue: at other times   180
He played with them wild freaks of merriment:
And 'twas a piteous thing to see the looks
Of the poor innocent children. 'Every smile,'
[620] Said Margaret to me here beneath these trees,

3. To depend on the local parish for "outdoor relief" (food or money given to the poor in their homes). See also the note on line 173 of *The Old Cumberland Beggar*.

Smitten with perilous fever. In disease
He lingered long; and when his strength return'd,
585 He found the little he had stored, to meet
The hour of accident or crippling age,
Was all consumed. Two children had they now,
One newly born. As I have said, it was
A time of trouble; shoals of Artisans
590 Were from their daily labour turn'd adrift
To seek their bread from public charity,
They, and their wives and children—happier far
Could they have lived as do the little birds
That peck along the hedges, or the Kite
595 That makes his dwelling on the mountain Rocks!

A sad reverse it was for Him[8] who long
Had filled with plenty, and possessed in peace,
This lonely Cottage. At his door he stood,
And whistled many a snatch of merry tunes
600 That had no mirth in them; or with his knife
Carved uncouth figures on the heads of sticks—
Then, not less idly, sought, through every nook
In house or garden, any casual work
Of use or ornament; and with a strange,
605 Amusing, yet uneasy novelty,
He blended, where he might, the various tasks
Of summer, autumn, winter, and of spring.
But this endured not; his good humour soon
Became a weight in which no pleasure was:
610 And poverty brought on a petted mood
And a sore temper: day by day he drooped,
And he would leave his work—and to the Town,
Without an errand, would direct his steps,
Or wander here and there among the fields.
615 One while he would speak lightly of his Babes,

---

8. The name of Margaret's husband, revealed at this point in *RC*, is revealed only at line 881 in *Exc.*

'Made my heart bleed.'" At this the old Man paus'd   185
And looking up to those enormous elms
He said, "'Tis now the hour of deepest noon.
At this still season of repose and peace,
[625]   This hour when all things which are not at rest
Are chearful, while this multitude of flies   190
Fills all the air with happy melody,
Why should a tear be in an old man's eye?
Why should we thus with an untoward mind
[630]   And in the weakness of humanity
From natural wisdom turn our hearts away,   195
To natural comfort shut our eyes and ears,
And feeding on disquiet thus disturb
The calm of Nature with our restless thoughts?"

END OF THE FIRST PART

And with a cruel tongue: at other times
He toss'd them with a false unnatural joy:
And 'twas a rueful thing to see the looks
Of the poor innocent children. "Every smile,"
620 Said Margaret to me, here beneath these trees,
"Made my heart bleed."
                          At this the Wanderer paused;
And, looking up to those enormous Elms,
He said, "'Tis now the hour of deepest noon.—
At this still season of repose and peace,
625 This hour, when all things which are not at rest
Are chearful; while this multitude of flies
Is filling all the air with melody;
Why should a tear be in an Old Man's eye?
Why should we thus, with an untoward mind,
630 And in the weakness of humanity,
From natural wisdom turn our hearts away,
To natural comfort shut our eyes and ears,
And, feeding on disquiet, thus disturb
The calm of nature with our restless thoughts?"

———————

Second Part

[635] He spake with somewhat of a solemn tone:
But when he ended there was in his face   200
Such easy chearfulness, a look so mild
That for a little time it stole away
All recollection, and that simple tale
[640] Passed from my mind like a forgotten sound.
A while on trivial things we held discourse,   205
To me soon tasteless.[4] In my own despite
I thought of that poor woman as of one
Whom I had known and loved. He had rehearsed
[645] Her homely tale with such familiar power,
With such a[n active][5] countenance, an eye   210
So busy, that the things of which he spake
Seemed present, and, attention now relaxed,
There was a heartfelt chillness in my veins.
[650] I rose, and turning from that breezy shade
Went out into the open air and stood   215
To drink the comfort of the warmer sun.
Long time I had not stayed ere, looking round
Upon that tranquil ruin, I returned
[655] And begged of the old man that for my sake
He would resume his story. He replied,   220
"It were a wantonness[6] and would demand
Severe reproof, if we were men whose hearts
Could hold vain dalliance with the misery
[660] Even of the dead, contented thence to draw

4. Tedious, insipid.
5. WW penciled the word into a gap left in the MS by DW.
6. Extravagance, self-indulgence.

635 He spake with somewhat of a solemn tone:
     But, when he ended, there was in his face
     Such easy chearfulness, a look so mild,
     That for a little time it stole away
     All recollection, and that simple Tale
640 Passed from my mind like a forgotten sound.
     A while on trivial things we held discourse,
     To me soon tasteless. In my own despite
     I thought of that poor Woman as of one
     Whom I had known and loved. He had rehearsed
645 Her homely Tale with such familiar power,
     With such an active countenance, an eye
     So busy, that the things of which he spake
     Seemed present; and, attention now relax'd,
     There was a heart-felt chillness in my veins.—
650 I rose; and, turning from the breezy shade,
     Went forth into the open air, and stood
     To drink the comfort of the warmer sun.
     Long time I had not staid, ere, looking round
     Upon that tranquil Ruin, I return'd,
655 And begged of the Old Man that, for my sake,
     He would resume his story.—
                                    He replied,
     "It were a wantonness, and would demand
     Severe reproof, if we were Men whose hearts
     Could hold vain dalliance with the misery
660 Even of the dead; contented thence to draw

A momentary pleasure never marked   225
By reason, barren of all future good.
But we have known that there is often found
In mournful thoughts, and always might be found,
[665]   A power to virtue friendly; were't not so,
I am a dreamer among men, indeed   230
An idle dreamer. 'Tis a common tale,
By moving accidents[7] uncharactered,
A tale of silent suffering, hardly clothed
[670]   In bodily form, and to the grosser sense
But ill adapted, scarcely palpable[8]   235
To him who does not think. But at your bidding
I will proceed.
                        While thus it fared with them
To whom this cottage till that hapless year
Had been a blessed home, it was my chance
To travel in a country far remote.   240
[675]   And glad I was when, halting by yon gate
That leads from the green lane, again I saw
These lofty elm-trees. Long I did not rest:
With many pleasant thoughts I cheer'd my way
O'er the flat common. At the door arrived,   245
[680]   I knocked, and when I entered with the hope
Of usual greeting, Margaret looked at me
A little while, then turned her head away
Speechless, and sitting down upon a chair
Wept bitterly. I wist[9] not what to do   250
[685]   Or how to speak to her. Poor wretch! at last
She rose from off her seat—and then, oh Sir!
I cannot tell how she pronounced my name:
With fervent love, and with a face of grief
Unutterably helpless, and a look   255

7. A phrase WW used also in *Hart-leap Well*, line 97 ("The moving accident is not my trade"), probably appropriating it from Shakespeare's *Othello* 1.3.135 ("Of moving accidents by flood and field").
8. Comprehensible. The Pedlar's description in lines 231–37 reflects WW's own distaste for sensationalist literature (see the Preface to *LB 1800*, p. 81 above).
9. Knew (a "pseudo-archaism" according to the *OED*).

A momentary pleasure, never marked
By reason, barren of all future good.
But we have known that there is often found
In mournful thoughts, and always might be found,
665 A power to virtue friendly; were't not so,
I am a Dreamer among men, indeed
An idle Dreamer! 'Tis a common Tale,
An ordinary sorrow of Man's life,
A tale of silent suffering, hardly clothed
670 In bodily form.—But, without further bidding,
I will proceed.—
                    While thus it fared with them,
To whom this Cottage, till those hapless years,
Had been a blessed home, it was my chance
To travel in a Country far remote.
675 And glad I was, when, halting by yon gate
That leads from the green lane, once more I saw
These lofty elm-trees. Long I did not rest:
With many pleasant thoughts I chear'd my way
O'er the flat Common.—Having reached the door
680 I knock'd,—and, when I entered with the hope
Of usual greeting, Margaret looked at me
A little while; then turn'd her head away
Speechless,—and sitting down upon a chair
Wept bitterly. I wist not what to do,
685 Or how to speak to her. Poor Wretch! at last
She rose from off her seat, and then,—O Sir!
I cannot *tell* how she pronounced my name.—
With fervent love, and with a face of grief
Unutterably helpless, and a look

[690]   That seem'd to cling upon me, she enquir'd
        If I had seen her husband. As she spake
        A strange surprize and fear came to my heart,
        Nor had I power to answer ere she told
        That he had disappeared—just two months gone.   260
[695]   He left his house; two wretched days had passed,
        And on the third by the first break of light,
        Within her casement full in view she saw
        A purse[1] of gold. 'I trembled at the sight,'
        Said Margaret, 'for I knew it was his hand   265
[705]   That placed it there, and on that very day
        By one, a stranger, from my husband sent,
        The tidings came that he had joined a troop
[710]   Of soldiers going to a distant land.[2]
        He left me thus—Poor Man! he had not heart   270
        To take a farewell of me, and he feared
        That I should follow with my babes, and sink
        Beneath the misery of a soldier's life.'[3]
[715]   This tale did Margaret tell with many tears:

1. Money from the substantial "bounty" paid to men enlisting in the army (£7 12s. 6d. by 1803, and subsequently raised as the war with France continued).
2. Presumably America, if Robert enlisted at the time of the American rebellion.
3. Margaret's story contrasts with that of *The Female Vagrant*, who follows her enlisted husband to America and after his death returns to England, where she is reduced to begging.

690   That seemed to cling upon me, she enquired
        If I had seen her Husband. As she spake
        A strange surprize and fear came to my heart,
        Nor had I power to answer ere she told
        That he had disappear'd—not two months gone.
695   He left his House: two wretched days had pass'd,
        And on the third, as wistfully she rais'd
        Her head from off her pillow, to look forth,
        Like one in trouble, for returning light,
        Within her chamber-casement she espied
700   A folded paper, lying as if placed
        To meet her waking eyes. This tremblingly
        She open'd—found no writing, but therein
        Pieces of money carefully enclosed,
        Silver and gold.—"I shuddered at the sight,"
705   Said Margaret, "for I knew it was his hand
        Which placed it there: and ere that day was ended,
        That long and anxious day! I learned from One
        Sent hither by my Husband to impart
        The heavy news,—that he had joined a Troop
710   Of Soldiers, going to a distant Land.
        —He left me thus—he could not gather heart
        To take a farewell of me; for he fear'd
        That I should follow with my Babes, and sink
        Beneath the misery of that wandering Life."

715   This Tale did Margaret tell with many tears:

And when she ended I had little power   275
To give her comfort, and was glad to take
Such words of hope from her own mouth as serv'd
To cheer us both: but long we had not talked
[720] Ere we built up a pile of better thoughts,
And with a brighter eye she looked around   280
As if she had been shedding tears of joy.
We parted. It was then the early spring;
I left her busy with her garden tools;
[725] And well remember, o'er that fence she looked,
And while I paced along the foot-way path   285
Called out, and sent a blessing after me
With tender chearfulness and with a voice
That seemed the very sound of happy thoughts.
[730]   I roved o'er many a hill and many a dale
With this my weary load, in heat and cold,   290
Through many a wood, and many an open ground,
In sunshine or in shade, in wet or fair,
Now blithe, now drooping, as it might befal,
[735] My best companions now the driving winds
And now the 'trotting brooks'⁴ and whispering trees   295
And now the music of my own sad steps,
With many a short-lived thought that pass'd between
And disappeared. I came this way again
[740] Towards the wane of summer, when the wheat
Was yellow, and the soft and bladed grass⁵   300
Sprang up afresh and o'er the hay-field spread
Its tender green. When I had reached the door
I found that she was absent. In the shade
[745] Where now we sit I waited her return.
Her cottage in its outward look appeared   305
As chearful as before; in any shew
Of neatness little changed, but that I thought
The honeysuckle crowded round the door
And from the wall hung down in heavier wreathes,
And knots of worthless stone-crop started out   310
Along the window's edge, and grew like weeds

---

4. A phrase adapted from Robert Burns's *To W. S[impso]n, Ochiltree* (1786), line 87: "Adown some trottin burn's meander [i.e., bustling stream's windings]."
5. A phrase from Shakespeare, *A Midsummer Night's Dream* 1.1.211: "Decking with liquid pearl the bladed grass."

And when she ended I had little power
To give her comfort, and was glad to take
Such words of hope from her own mouth as served
To chear us both:—but long we had not talked
720   Ere we built up a pile of better thoughts,
And with a brighter eye she look'd around
As if she had been shedding tears of joy.
We parted.—'Twas the time of early spring;
I left her busy with her garden tools;
725   And well remember, o'er that fence she looked,
And, while I paced along the foot-way path,
Called out, and sent a blessing after me,
With tender chearfulness; and with a voice
That seem'd the very sound of happy thoughts.

730   I roved o'er many a hill and many a dale,
With my accustomed load; in heat and cold,
Through many a wood, and many an open ground,
In sunshine and in shade, in wet and fair,
Drooping, or blithe of heart, as might befal;
735   My best companions now the driving winds,
And now the "trotting brooks" and whispering trees,
And now the music of my own sad steps,
With many a short-lived thought that pass'd between,
And disappeared.—I journey'd back this way
740   Towards the wane of Summer; when the wheat
Was yellow; and the soft and bladed grass
Springing afresh had o'er the hay-field spread
Its tender verdure. At the door arrived,
I found that she was absent. In the shade,
745   Where now we sit, I waited her return.

Against the lower panes. I turned aside
[753]   And stroll'd into her garden.—It was chang'd:
The unprofitable bindweed spread his bells
From side to side and with unwieldy wreaths   315
Had dragg'd the rose from its sustaining wall
And bent it down to earth; the border-tufts—
Daisy and thrift and lowly camomile
And thyme—had straggled out into the paths
Which they were used to deck. Ere this an hour   320
[765]   Was wasted. Back I turned my restless steps,
And as I walked before the door it chanced
A stranger passed, and guessing whom I sought
He said that she was used to ramble far.
The sun was sinking in the west, and now   325
[770]   I sate with sad impatience. From within
Her solitary infant cried aloud.
[775]   The spot though fair seemed very desolate,
The longer I remained more desolate.

Her Cottage, then a chearful Object, wore
Its customary look,—only, I thought,
The honeysuckle, crowding round the porch,
Hung down in heavier tufts: and that bright weed,
750 The yellow stone-crop, suffered to take root
Along the window's edge, profusely grew,
Blinding the lower panes. I turned aside,
And strolled into her garden. It appeared
To lag behind the season, and had lost
755 Its pride of neatness. From the border lines
Composed of daisy and resplendent thrift,
Flowers straggling forth had on those paths encroached
Which they were used to deck:—Carnations, once
Prized for surpassing beauty, and no less
760 For the peculiar pains they had required,
Declined their languid heads—without support.
The cumbrous bind-weed, with its wreaths and bells,
Had twined about her two small rows of pease,
And dragged them to the earth.—Ere this an hour
765 Was wasted.—Back I turned my restless steps,
And, as I walked before the door, it chanced
A Stranger passed; and, guessing whom I sought,
He said that she was used to ramble far.—
The sun was sinking in the west; and now
770 I sate with sad impatience. From within
Her solitary Infant cried aloud;
Then, like a blast that dies away self-stilled,
The voice was silent. From the bench I rose;
But neither could divert nor soothe my thoughts.
775 The spot, though fair, was very desolate—
The longer I remained more desolate.

And, looking round, I saw the corner-stones,   330
Till then unmark'd, on either side the door
With dull red stains discoloured and stuck o'er
[780] With tufts and hairs of wool,[6] as if the sheep
That feed upon the commons thither came
Familiarly and found a couching-place   335
Even at her threshold.—The house-clock struck eight;
[785] I turned and saw her distant a few steps.
Her face was pale and thin, her figure too
Was chang'd. As she unlocked the door she said,
'It grieves me you have waited here so long,   340
But in good truth I've wandered much of late
[790] And sometimes, to my shame I speak, have need
Of my best prayers to bring me back again.'
While on the board[7] she spread our evening meal
She told me she had lost her elder child,   345
That he for months had been a serving-boy

6. WW probably draws in lines 330–33 on an observation in DW's journal for February 4, 1798:
"The moss rubbed from the pailings by the sheep, that leave locks of wool, and the red marks
[i.e., paint branding] with which they are spotted, upon the wood" (*DWJ*, 1:7).
7. Table.

And, looking round, I saw the corner stones,
Till then unnotic'd, on either side the door
With dull red stains discolour'd, and stuck o'er
780 With tufts and hairs of wool, as if the Sheep,
That fed upon the Common, thither came
Familiarly; and found a couching-place
Even at her threshold. Deeper shadows fell
From these tall elms;—the Cottage-clock struck eight;—
785 I turned, and saw her distant a few steps.
Her face was pale and thin, her figure too
Was changed. As she unlocked the door, she said,
"It grieves me you have waited here so long,
But, in good truth, I've wandered much of late,
790 And, sometimes,—to my shame I speak, have need
Of my best prayers to bring me back again."
While on the board she spread our evening meal
She told me,—interrupting not the work
Which gave employment to her listless hands,
795 That she had parted with her elder Child;

Apprenticed by the parish. 'I perceive
[798] You look at me, and you have cause. Today
I have been travelling far, and many days
[800] About the fields I wander, knowing this   350
Only, that what I seek I cannot find.
And so I waste my time: for I am changed;
And to myself,' said she, 'have done much wrong,
And to this helpless infant. I have slept
[805] Weeping, and weeping I have waked; my tears   355
Have flow'd as if my body were not such
As others are, and I could never die.
But I am now in mind and in my heart
More easy, and I hope,' said she, 'that heaven
[810] Will give me patience to endure the things   360
Which I behold at home.' It would have grieved
Your very heart to see her. Sir, I feel
The story linger in my heart. I fear
'Tis long and tedious, but my spirit clings
[815] To that poor woman: so familiarly   365
Do I perceive her manner, and her look
And presence, and so deeply do I feel
Her goodness, that not seldom in my walks
A momentary trance comes over me;

To a kind Master on a distant farm
Now happily apprenticed—"I perceive
You look at me, and you have cause; to-day
I have been travelling far; and many days
800   About the fields I wander, knowing this
Only, that what I seek I cannot find.
And so I waste my time: for I am changed;
And to myself, said she, have done much wrong
And to this helpless Infant. I have slept
805   Weeping, and weeping I have waked; my tears
Have flowed as if my body were not such
As others are; and I could never die.
But I am now in mind and in my heart
More easy; and I hope," said she, "that heaven
810   Will give me patience to endure the things
Which I behold at home." It would have grieved
Your very soul to see her; Sir, I feel
The story linger in my heart: I fear
'Tis long and tedious; but my spirit clings
815   To that poor Woman:—so familiarly
Do I perceive her manner, and her look,
And presence, and so deeply do I feel
Her goodness, that, not seldom, in my walks

[820]   And to myself I seem to muse on one   370
        By sorrow laid asleep or borne away,
        A human being destined to awake
        To human life, or something very near
        To human life, when he shall come again
[825]   For whom she suffered. Sir, it would have griev'd   375
        Your very soul to see her: evermore
        Her eye-lids droop'd, her eyes were downward cast;
        And when she at her table gave me food
        She did not look at me. Her voice was low,
[830]   Her body was subdued. In every act   380
        Pertaining to her house-affairs appeared
        The careless stillness which a thinking mind
        Gives to an idle matter—still she sighed,
[835]   But yet no motion of the breast was seen,
        No heaving of the heart. While by the fire   385
        We sate together, sighs came on my ear;
[838]   I knew not how, and hardly whence they came.
        I took my staff, and when I kissed her babe

A momentary trance comes over me;
820 And to myself I seem to muse on One
By sorrow laid asleep;—or borne away,
A human being destined to awake
To human life, or something very near
To human life, when he shall come again
825 For whom she suffered. Yes, it would have grieved
Your very soul to see her: evermore
Her eyelids drooped, her eyes were downward cast;
And, when she at her table gave me food,
She did not look at me. Her voice was low,
830 Her body was subdued. In every act
Pertaining to her house affairs, appeared
The careless stillness of a thinking mind
Self-occupied; to which all outward things
Are like an idle matter. Still she sighed,
835 But yet no motion of the breast was seen,
No heaving of the heart. While by the fire
We sate together, sighs came on my ear,
I knew not how, and hardly whence they came.

Ere my departure to her care I gave,
840 For her Son's use, some tokens of regard,

[845]   The tears stood in her eyes I left her then
        With the best hope and comfort I could give;   390
        She thanked me for my will, but for my hope
        It seemed she did not thank me.
                                        I returned
        And took my rounds along this road again
[850]   Ere on its sunny bank the primrose flower
        Had chronicled the earliest day of spring.   395
        I found her sad and drooping; she had learn'd
        No tidings of her husband: if he lived
        She knew not that he lived; if he were dead
[855]   She knew not he was dead. She seemed the same
        In person [   ] appearance, but her house   400
        Bespoke a sleepy hand of negligence;
[858]   The floor was neither dry nor neat, the hearth
        Was comfortless [   ],⁸
        The windows too were dim, and her few books,
        Which, one upon the other, heretofore   405
[862]   Had been piled up against the corner-panes
        In seemly order, now with straggling leaves

8. The remainder of this line is missing in the MS.

Which with a look of welcome She received;
And I exhorted her to have her trust
In God's good love, and seek his help by prayer.
I took my staff, and when I kissed her babe
845   The tears stood in her eyes. I left her then
With the best hope and comfort I could give;
She thanked me for my wish;—but for my hope
Methought she did not thank me.
                             I returned,
And took my rounds along this road again
850   Ere on its sunny bank the primrose flower
Peeped forth, to give an earnest of the Spring.
I found her sad and drooping; she had learned
No tidings of her Husband; if he lived
She knew not that he lived; if he were dead
855   She knew not he was dead. She seem'd the same
In person and appearance; but her House
Bespake a sleepy hand of negligence.
The floor was neither dry nor neat, the hearth
Was comfortless, and her small lot of books,
860   Which, in the Cottage window, heretofore
Had been piled up against the corner panes
In seemly order, now, with straggling leaves

Lay scattered here and there, open or shut
As they had chanced to fall. Her infant babe
[865]   Had from its mother caught the trick[9] of grief   410
And sighed among its playthings. Once again
I turned towards the garden-gate and saw
More plainly still that poverty and grief
Were now come nearer to her: the earth was hard,
With weeds defaced and knots of withered grass;   415
[870]   No ridges there appeared of clear black mould,
No winter greenness; of her herbs and flowers
It seemed the better part were gnawed away
Or trampled on the earth; a chain of straw
[875]   Which had been twisted round the tender stem   420
Of a young apple-tree lay at its root;
The bark was nibbled round by truant sheep.
Margaret stood near, her infant in her arms,
And seeing that my eye was on the tree
[880]   She said, 'I fear it will be dead and gone   425
Ere Robert come again.' Towards the house
Together we returned, and she inquired
If I had any hope. But for her Babe
And for her little friendless Boy, she said,
[885]   She had no wish to live, that she must die   430

9. "A particular habit, way, or mode of acting" (OED).

Lay scattered here and there, open or shut,
As they had chanced to fall. Her Infant Babe
865 Had from its Mother caught the trick of grief,
And sighed among its playthings. Once again
I turned towards the garden gate, and saw,
More plainly still, that poverty and grief
Were now come nearer to her: weeds defaced
870 The harden'd soil, and knots of wither'd grass;
No ridges there appeared of clear black mold,
No winter greenness; of her herbs and flowers,
It seemed the better part were gnawed away
Or trampled into earth; a chain of straw,
875 Which had been twined about the slender stem
Of a young apple-tree, lay at its root;
The bark was nibbled round by truant Sheep.
—Margaret stood near, her Infant in her arms,
And, noting that my eye was on the tree,
880 She said, "I fear it will be dead and gone
Ere Robert come again," Towards the House
Together we returned; and she enquired
If I had any hope:—but for her Babe
And for her little orphan Boy, she said,
885 She had no wish to live, that she must die

Of sorrow. Yet I saw the idle loom
Still in its place. His sunday garments hung
Upon the self-same nail, his very staff
Stood undisturbed behind the door. And when
I passed this way beaten by Autumn winds   435
[891]   She told me that her little babe was dead
And she was left alone. That very time,
I yet remember, through the miry lane
She walked with me a mile, when the bare trees
Trickled with foggy damps, and in such sort   440
[901]   That any heart had ached to hear her begg'd
That wheresoe'er I went I still would ask
For him whom she had lost. We parted then,
Our final parting, for from that time forth
[905]   Did many seasons pass ere I returned   445
Into this tract¹ again.
                              Five tedious years
She lingered in unquiet widowhood,
A wife and widow. Needs must it have been

1. Area, region.

Of sorrow. Yet I saw the idle loom
Still in its place; his Sunday garments hung
Upon the self-same nail; his very staff
Stood undisturbed behind the door. And when,
890 In bleak December, I retraced this way,
She told me that her little Babe was dead,
And she was left alone. She now, released
From her maternal cares, had taken up
The employment common through these Wilds, and gain'd
895 By spinning hemp a pittance for herself;
And for this end had hired a neighbour's Boy
To give her needful help. That very time
Most willingly she put her work aside,
And walked with me along the miry road
900 Heedless how far; and, in such piteous sort
That any heart had ached to hear her, begged
That, wheresoe'er I went, I still would ask
For him whom she had lost. We parted then,
Our final parting; for from that time forth
905 Did many seasons pass ere I return'd
Into this tract again.
                              Nine tedious years;
From their first separation, nine long years,

[910] A sore heart-wasting. I have heard, my friend,
       That in that broken arbour she would sit   450
       The idle length of half a sabbath day—
       There, where you see the toadstool's lazy head—
       And when a dog passed by she still would quit
       The shade and look abroad. On this old Bench
[915] For hours she sate, and evermore her eye   455
       Was busy in the distance, shaping things
       Which made her heart beat quick. Seest thou that path?
       (The green-sward now has broken its grey line)
       There to and fro she paced through many a day
[920] Of the warm summer, from a belt of flax   460
       That girt her waist spinning the long-drawn thread
       With backward steps.²—Yet ever as there passed
       A man whose garments shewed the Soldier's red,
       Or crippled Mendicant³ in Sailor's garb,
[925] The little child who sate to turn the wheel   465
       Ceased from his toil, and she with faltering voice,
       Expecting still to learn her husband's fate,
       Made many a fond⁴ inquiry; and when they
[928] Whose presence gave no comfort were gone by,

2. Bridgport, Dorset, near Racedown (where WW and DW lived in 1795–97), was a center for producing twine for fishing nets and lines. One end of a long fiber of flax or hemp was attached to a rotating hook and the remainder wound around the waist of the spinner, who walked backwards from and towards the hook, releasing the fiber, while the hook was turned to twist the strands together (RC [CW], 70).
3. Beggar. Soldier's red: From the late seventeenth century to the end of the nineteenth, most regiments of the British army wore red coats.
4. Tender.

She lingered in unquiet widowhood;
A Wife and Widow. Needs must it have been
910 A sore heart-wasting! I have heard, my Friend,
That in yon arbour oftentimes she sate
Alone, through half the vacant Sabbath-day,
And if a dog passed by she still would quit
The shade, and look abroad. On this old Bench
915 For hours she sate; and evermore her eye
Was busy in the distance, shaping things
That made her heart beat quick. You see that path,
Now faint,—the grass has crept o'er its grey line;
There, to and fro, she paced through many a day
920 Of the warm summer, from a belt of hemp
That girt her waist, spinning the long drawn thread
With backward steps. Yet ever as there pass'd
A man whose garments shewed the Soldiers red,
Or crippled Mendicant in Sailor's garb,
925 The little Child who sate to turn the wheel
Ceas'd from his task; and she with faultering voice
Made many a fond enquiry; and when they,
Whose presence gave no comfort, were gone by,
Her heart was still more sad. And by yon gate,

Her heart was still more sad. And by yon gate   470
[930] Which bars the traveller's road she often stood
And when a stranger horseman came, the latch
Would lift, and in his face look wistfully,
Most happy if from aught discovered there
Of tender feeling she might dare repeat   475
[935] The same sad question. Meanwhile her poor hut
Sunk to decay, for he was gone whose hand
At the first nippings of October frost
Closed up each chink and with fresh bands of straw
Chequered the green-grown thatch. And so she lived   480
[940] Through the long winter, reckless and alone,
Till this reft house by frost, and thaw, and rain
Was sapped; and when she slept the nightly damps
Did chill her breast, and in the stormy day
[945] Her tattered clothes were ruffled by the wind   485
Even at the side of her own fire. Yet still
She loved this wretched spot, nor would for worlds
Have parted hence; and still that length of road
And this rude bench one torturing hope endeared,
Fast rooted at her heart, and here, my friend,   490
[950] In sickness she remained, and here she died,
Last human tenant of these ruined walls."[5]

---

5. In MS B the poem ends at this point, although in the same manuscript WW drafted—and canceled—three attempts at a more optimistic conclusion (see RC [CW], 259–61), which he later revised and incorporated into MS D. In his IF note WW recalled that the section corresponding to lines 446–92 was the earliest written of the poem, although he seems to have been mistaken in assigning their composition to 1795 rather than 1797 (RC [CW], 3–4). STC quoted an early version of lines 445–92 in a letter of June 10, 1797 (CL, 1:327).

930   That bars the Traveller's road, she often stood,
      And when a stranger Horseman came the latch
      Would lift, and in his face look wistfully;
      Most happy, if, from aught discovered there
      Of tender feeling, she might dare repeat
935   The same sad question. Meanwhile her poor Hut
      Sank to decay: for he was gone—whose hand,
      At the first nipping of October frost,
      Closed up each chink, and with fresh bands of straw
      Chequered the green-grown thatch. And so she lived
940   Through the long winter, reckless and alone;
      Until her House by frost, and thaw, and rain,
      Was sapped; and while she slept the nightly damps
      Did chill her breast; and in the stormy day
      Her tattered clothes were ruffled by the wind;
945   Even at the side of her own fire. Yet still
      She loved this wretched spot, nor would for worlds
      Have parted hence; and still that length of road,
      And this rude bench, one torturing hope endeared,
      Fast rooted at her heart: and here, my Friend,
950   In sickness she remained; and here she died,
      Last human Tenant of these ruined Walls."

        The old Man ceased: he saw that I was mov'd;
        From that low Bench, rising instinctively,
        I turned aside in weakness, nor had power   495
[955]   To thank him for the tale which he had told.
        I stood, and leaning o'er the garden-gate
        Reviewed that Woman's suff'rings, and it seemed
        To comfort me while with a brother's love
        I blessed her in the impotence of grief.   500
[960]   At length [   ] the [   ]⁶
        Fondly, and traced with milder interest
        That secret spirit of humanity
        Which, 'mid the calm oblivious tendencies
        Of nature, 'mid her plants, her weeds, and flowers,   505
[965]   And silent overgrowings, still survived,
        The old man, seeing this, resumed and said,
        "My Friend, enough to sorrow have you given,
        The purposes of wisdom ask no more;
        Be wise and chearful, and no longer read   510
[970]   The forms of things with an unworthy eye.
        She sleeps in the calm earth, and peace is here.
        I well remember that those very plumes,
        Those weeds, and the high spear-grass on that wall,

6. The bracketed spaces indicate erased words that were not replaced in the MS: "upon" after
length, and "hut I fix'd my eyes" after *the* (RC [CW], 73).

The Old Man ceased: he saw that I was moved;
From that low Bench, rising instinctively
I turn'd aside in weakness, nor had power
955   To thank him for the Tale which he had told.
I stood, and leaning o'er the Garden wall,
Reviewed that Woman's sufferings; and it seemed
To comfort me while with a Brother's love
I bless'd her—in the impotence of grief.
960   At length towards the Cottage I returned
Fondly,—and traced, with interest more mild,
That secret spirit of humanity
Which, mid the calm oblivious tendencies
Of Nature, mid her plants, and weeds, and flowers,
965   And silent overgrowings, still survived.
The Old Man, noting this, resumed, and said,
"My Friend! enough to sorrow you have given,
The purposes of wisdom ask no more;
Be wise and chearful; and no longer read[9]
970   The forms of things with an unworthy eye.
She sleeps in the calm earth, and peace is here.
I well remember that those very plumes,
Those weeds, and the high spear-grass on that wall,

---

9. In 1845 WW replaced line 969 with six lines of explicitly Christian consolation: "No more
would she have craved as due to One / Who, in her worst distress, had ofttimes felt / The
unbounded might of prayer * * *" (*Exc* [CW], 75).

By mist and silent rain-drops silver'd o'er,   515
[975]   As once I passed did to my heart convey
So still an image of tranquillity,
So calm and still, and looked so beautiful
Amid the uneasy thoughts which filled my mind,
That what we feel of sorrow and despair   520
[980]   From ruin and from change, and all the grief
The passing shews of being leave behind,
Appeared an idle dream that could not live
Where meditation was. I turned away
And walked along my road in happiness."   525
[985]   He ceased. By this the sun declining shot
A slant and mellow radiance which began
To fall upon us where beneath the trees
We sate on that low bench, and now we felt,
Admonished thus, the sweet hour coming on.   530
[990]   A linnet warbled from those lofty elms,
A thrush sang loud, and other melodies,
At distance heard, peopled the milder air.
The old man rose and hoisted up his load.
[995]   Together casting then a farewell look   535
Upon those silent walls, we left the shade
And ere the stars were visible attained
A rustic inn, our evening resting-place.

                         THE END

By mist and silent rain-drops silver'd o'er,
975   As once I passed, did to my heart convey
So still an image of tranquillity,
So calm and still, and looked so beautiful
Amid the uneasy thoughts which filled my mind
That what we feel of sorrow and despair
980   From ruin and from change, and all the grief
The passing shews of Being leave behind,
Appeared an idle dream, that could not live
Where meditation was. I turned away
And walked along my road in happiness."

985   He ceased. Ere long the sun declining shot
A slant and mellow radiance, which began
To fall upon us, while beneath the trees
We sate on that low Bench: and now we felt,
Admonished thus, the sweet hour coming on.
990   A linnet warbled from those lofty elms,
A thrush sang loud, and other melodies,
At distance heard, peopled the milder air.
The Old Man rose, and, with a sprightly mien
Of hopeful preparation, grasped his Staff:
995   Together casting then a farewell look
Upon those silent walls, we left the Shade;
And, ere the Stars were visible, had reached
A Village Inn,—our Evening resting-place.

END OF THE FIRST BOOK

ESSAY UPON EPITAPHS[†]

It needs scarcely be said, that an Epitaph presupposes a Monument, upon which, it is to be engraven. Almost all Nations have wished that certain external signs should point out the places where their Dead are interred. Among savage Tribes unacquainted with Letters, this has mostly been done either by rude stones placed near the Graves, or by Mounds of earth raised over them. This custom proceeded obviously from a twofold desire; first, to guard the remains of the deceased from irreverent approach or from savage violation; and, secondly, to preserve their memory. "Never any," says Cambden, "neglected burial but some savage Nations; as the Bactrians which cast their dead to the dogs; some varlet Philosophers, as Diogenes, who desired to be devoured of fishes; some dissolute Courtiers, as Mecænas,[1] who was wont to say, Non tumulum curo; sepelit natura relictos.

> I'm careless of a Grave:—Nature her dead will save."[2]

As soon as Nations had learned the use of letters, Epitaphs were inscribed upon these Monuments; in order that their intention might be more surely and adequately fulfilled. I have derived Monuments and Epitaphs from two sources of feeling: but these do in fact resolve themselves into one. The invention of Epitaphs, Weever, in his discourse of funeral Monuments, says rightly, "proceeded from the presage or fore-feeling of Immortality, implanted in all men naturally, and is referred to the Scholars of Linus the Theban Poet, who flourished about the year of the World two thousand seven hundred; who first bewailed this Linus their Master, when he was slain, in doleful verses then called of him Œlina, afterwards Epitaphia, for that they were first sung at burials, after engraved upon the Sepulchres."[3]

---

† According to his IF note on his epitaphs and elegiac poems, WW wrote this essay while translating epitaphs by the Italian poet Gabriello Chiabrera (1552–1638). Six of the eight translations were published in three issues of STC's periodical *The Friend* between December 28, 1809, and February 22, 1810, and the last issue included this essay. WW "did not intend it to be published now," DW wrote Lady Beaumont on February 28, "but Coleridge was in such bad spirits that when the time came he was utterly unprovided" with material (*WL*, 1:391). In the same letter DW noted that her brother had "written two more Essays on the same subject, which will appear when there is need"; but *The Friend* ceased publication on March 15 and WW never published the second and third essays (they were first published in 1876). Reprinting the essay as a note on *Exc* 5.984 ("And whence that tribute [to the dead]? wherefore these regards?"), WW omitted two introductory paragraphs that had appeared in the earlier version (for which see *Prose*, 2:49, or *Friend*, 2:335–36) and incorporated various corrections. In accordance with the general policy of printing texts as they appeared in volumes published by WW, the text here follows that in the first edition of *Exc*. In the first half of the essay, on the sense of the immortality of the soul, WW returns to a subject addressed in the Intimations Ode, while in the second half, on the common language and sympathetic feeling to be cultivated in epitaphs, he recalls the poetic principles elaborated in the Preface to *LB 1800* and *LB 1802*.

1. Maecenas (70–8 B.C.E.), Roman poet and patron, whose wish (reported by Seneca, *Epistulae* 92.35) may be translated more literally, "I do not care about a tomb; nature buries the remains"; *Bactrians*: in antiquity, inhabitants of the Persian region of Bactria, in which Zoroastrianism was the dominant religion; *Diogenes*: Greek Cynic philosopher (ca. 412/403–ca. 324/321 B.C.E.).
2. WW quotes William Camden's *Remains concerning Britain* (1605) as quoted in John Weever's *Ancient Funerall Monuments within the United Monarchie of Great-Britain, Ireland, and the Islands Adjacent* (London, 1631), 23 (*Prose*, 2:100–101).
3. Weever, 9. In Greek mythology, Linus, the son of Apollo and a Muse, invented melody and traveled to Thebes, where he was killed with his own lyre by Heracles.

And, verily, without the consciousness of a principle of Immortality in the human soul, Man could never have had awakened in him the desire to live in the remembrance of his fellows; mere love, or the yearning of Kind towards Kind, could not have produced it. The Dog or Horse perishes in the field, or in the stall, by the side of his Companions, and is incapable of anticipating the sorrow with which his surrounding Associates shall bemoan his death, or pine for his loss; he cannot pre-conceive this regret, he can form no thought of it; and therefore cannot possibly have a desire to leave such regret or remembrance behind him. Add to the principle of love, which exists in the inferior animals, the faculty of reason which exists in Man alone; will the conjunction of these account for the desire? Doubtless it is a necessary consequence of this conjunction; yet not I think as a direct result, but only to be come at through an intermediate thought, viz. that of an intimation or assurance within us, that some part of our nature is imperishable. At least the precedence, in order of birth, of one feeling to the other, is unquestionable. If we look back upon the days of childhood, we shall find that the time is not in remembrance when, with respect to our own individual Being, the mind was without this assurance;[4] whereas, the wish to be remembered by our Friends or Kindred after Death, or even in Absence, is, as we shall discover, a sensation that does not form itself till the *social* feelings have been developed, and the Reason has connected itself with a wide range of objects. Forlorn, and cut off from communication with the best part of his nature, must that Man be, who should derive the sense of immortality, as it exists in the mind of a Child, from the same unthinking gaiety or liveliness of animal Spirits with which the Lamb in the meadow, or any other irrational Creature, is endowed; who should ascribe it, in short, to blank ignorance in the Child; to an inability arising from the imperfect state of his faculties to come, in any point of his being, into contact with a notion of Death; or to an unreflecting acquiescence in what had been instilled into him! Has such an unfolder of the mysteries of Nature, though he may have forgotten his former self, ever noticed the early, obstinate, and unappeaseable inquisitiveness of Children upon the subject of origination? This single fact proves outwardly the monstrousness of those suppositions: for, if we had no direct external testimony that the minds of very young Children meditate feelingly upon Death and Immortality, these inquiries, which we all know they are perpetually making concerning the *whence*, do necessarily include correspondent habits of interrogation concerning the *whither*. Origin and tendency are notions inseparably co-relative. Never did a Child stand by the side of a running Stream, pondering within himself what power was the feeder of the perpetual current, from what neverwearied sources the body of water was supplied, but he must have been inevitably propelled to follow this question by another: "towards what abyss is it in progress? what receptacle can contain the mighty influx?" And the spirit of the answer must have been, though the word might be Sea or Ocean, accompanied perhaps with an image gathered from a Map, or from the real object in Nature—these might have been the *letter*, but the *spirit* of the answer must have been *as* inevitably,—a recep-

---

4. Compare stanzas 5–8 of the Intimations Ode on childhood intimations of the immortality of the soul.

tacle without bounds or dimensions;—nothing less than infinity. We may, then, be justified in asserting that the sense of Immortality, if not a co-existent and twin birth with Reason, is among the earliest of her Off-spring: and we may further assert, that from these conjoined, and under their countenance, the human affections are gradually formed and opened out. This is not the place to enter into the recesses of these investigations; but the subject requires me here to make a plain avowal that, for my own part, it is to me inconceivable, that the sympathies of love towards each other, which grow with our growth, could ever attain any new strength, or even preserve the old, after we had received from the outward senses the impression of Death, and were in the habit of having that impression daily renewed and its accompanying feeling brought home to ourselves, and to those we love; if the same were not counter-acted by those communications with our internal Being, which are ante-rior to all these experiences, and with which revelation coincides, and has through that coincidence alone (for otherwise it could not possess it) a power to affect us. I confess, with me the conviction is absolute, that, if the impression and sense of Death were not thus counterbalanced, such a hollowness would pervade the whole system of things, such a want of correspondence and consistency, a disproportion so astounding betwixt means and ends, that there could be no repose, no joy. Were we to grow up unfostered by this genial warmth, a frost would chill the spirit, so penetrating and powerful, that there could be no motions of the life of love; and infinitely less could we have any wish to be remembered after we had passed away from a world in which each man had moved about like a shadow.—If, then, in a Creature endowed with the faculties of foresight and reason, the social affections could not have unfolded themselves uncounte-nanced by the faith that Man is an immortal being; and if, consequently, neither could the individual dying have had a desire to survive in the remembrance of his fellows, nor on their side could they have felt a wish to preserve for future times vestiges of the departed; it follows, as a final infer-ence, that without the belief in Immortality, wherein these several desires originate, neither monuments nor epitaphs, in affectionate or laudatory commemoration of the Deceased, could have existed in the world.

Simonides, it is related, upon landing in a strange Country, found the Corse of an unknown person, lying by the Sea-side; he buried it, and was honoured throughout Greece for the piety of that Act.[5] Another ancient Philosopher, chancing to fix his eyes upon a dead Body, regarded the same with slight, if not with contempt; saying, "see the Shell of the flown Bird!"[6] But it is not to be supposed that the moral and tender-hearted Simonides was incapable of the lofty movements of thought, to which that other Sage gave way at the moment while his soul was intent only upon the indestruc-tible being; nor, on the other hand, that he, in whose sight a lifeless human Body was of no more value than the worthless Shell from which the living

5. Simonides (ca. 556–ca. 469 B.C.E.), Greek lyric poet. WW's source of the story is either Vale-rius Maximus's *Facta et dicta memorabilia* [Memorable Deeds and Sayings] 1.7(externa).3, a work of which there were two copies in WW's library at Rydal Mount (*Reading 1800–15*, no. 406), or Cicero's *De divinatione* [On Divination] 1.56.27 (*Prose*, 2:101–102). WW also versified the story in a sonnet, *I find it written of SIMONIDES*, published in the *Morning Post*, October 10, 1803 (see *Poems, 1800–1807* [CW], 583–84).
6. The philosopher meant may be Heraclitus (mid-sixth century B.C.E.), who is supposed to have declared corpses more worthless than dung (frag. 96).

fowl had departed, would not, in a different mood of mind, have been affected by those earthly considerations which had incited the philosophic Poet to the performance of that pious duty. And with regard to this latter, we may be assured that, if he had been destitute of the capability of communing with the more exalted thoughts that appertain to human Nature, he would have cared no more for the Corse of the Stranger than for the dead body of a Seal or Porpoise which might have been cast up by the Waves. We respect the corporeal frame of Man, not merely because it is the habitation of a rational, but of an immortal Soul. Each of these Sages was in Sympathy with the best feelings of our Nature; feelings which, though they seem opposite to each other, have another and a finer connection than that of contrast.—It is a connection formed through the subtle progress by which, both in the natural and the moral world, qualities pass insensibly into their contraries, and things revolve upon each other. As, in sailing upon the orb of this Planet, a voyage, towards the regions where the sun sets, conducts gradually to the quarter where we have been accustomed to behold it come forth at its rising; and, in like manner, a voyage towards the east, the birth-place in our imagination of the morning, leads finally to the quarter where the Sun is last seen when he departs from our eyes; so, the contemplative Soul, travelling in the direction of mortality, advances to the Country of everlasting Life; and, in like manner, may she continue to explore those cheerful tracts, till she is brought back, for her advantage and benefit, to the land of transitory things—of sorrow and of tears.

On a midway point, therefore, which commands the thoughts and feelings of the two Sages whom we have represented in contrast, does the Author of that species of composition, the Laws of which it is our present purpose to explain, take his stand. Accordingly, recurring to the twofold desire of guarding the Remains of the deceased and preserving their memory, it may be said, that a sepulchral Monument is a tribute to a Man as a human Being; and that an Epitaph, (in the ordinary meaning attached to the word) includes this general feeling and something more; and is a record to preserve the memory of the dead, as a tribute due to his individual worth, for a satisfaction to the sorrowing hearts of the Survivors, and for the common benefit of the living: which record is to be accomplished, not in a general manner, but, where it can, in *close connection with the bodily remains of the deceased*: and these, it may be added, among the modern Nations of Europe are deposited within, or contiguous to their places of worship. In ancient times, as is well known, it was the custom to bury the dead beyond the Walls of Towns and Cities; and among the Greeks and Romans they were frequently interred by the way-sides.

I could here pause with pleasure, and invite the Reader to indulge with me in contemplation of the advantages which must have attended such a practice. I could ruminate upon the beauty which the Monuments, thus placed, must have borrowed from the surrounding images of Nature— from the trees, the wild flowers, from a stream running perhaps within sight or hearing, from the beaten road stretching its weary length hard by. Many tender similitudes must these objects have presented to the mind of the Traveller, leaning upon one of the Tombs, or reposing in the coolness of its shade, whether he had halted from weariness or in compliance with the invitation, "Pause Traveller!" so often found upon the Monuments. And to its Epitaph also must have been supplied strong appeals to visible appearances or immediate impressions, lively and affecting analogies of Life as a Journey—Death as a Sleep overcoming the tired Wayfarer—of Misfortune as a Storm that falls suddenly upon him—of Beauty as a Flower that passeth away, or of innocent pleasure as one that may be gathered—of Virtue that standeth firm as a Rock against the beating Waves;—of Hope "undermined insensibly like the Poplar by the side of the River that has fed it,"[7] or blasted in a moment like a Pine-tree by the stroke of lightening upon the Mountain top—of admonitions and heart-stirring remembrances, like a refreshing Breeze that comes without warning, or the taste of the waters of an unexpected Fountain. These, and similar suggestions must have given, formerly, to the language of the senseless stone a voice enforced and endeared by the benignity of that Nature, with which it was in unison.—We, in modern times, have lost much of these advantages: and they are but in a small degree counterbalanced to the Inhabitants of large Towns and Cities, by the custom of depositing the Dead within, or contiguous to, their places of worship; however splendid or imposing may be the appearances of those Edifices, or however interesting or salutary the recollections associated with them. Even were it not true that Tombs lose their monitory virtue when thus obtruded upon the notice of Men occupied with the cares of the World, and too often sullied and defiled by those cares, yet still, when Death is in our thoughts, nothing can make amends for the want of the soothing influences of Nature, and for the absence of those types of renovation and decay, which the fields and woods offer to the notice of the serious and contemplative mind. To feel the force of this sentiment, let a man only compare in imagination the unsightly manner in which our Monuments are crowded together in the busy, noisy, unclean, and almost grassless Church-yard of a large Town, with the still seclusion of a Turkish Cemetery, in some remote place; and yet further sanctified by the Grove of Cypress in which it is embosomed. Thoughts in the same temper as these have already been expressed with true sensibility by an ingenuous Poet of the present day. The subject of his Poem is "All Saints Church, Derby:" he has been deploring the forbidding and unseemly appearance of its burial-ground, and uttering a wish, that in past times the practice had been adopted of interring the Inhabitants of large Towns in the Country.—

> Then in some rural, calm, sequestered spot,
> Where healing Nature her benignant look
> Ne'er changes, save at that lorn season, when,
> With tresses drooping o'er her sable stole,
> She yearly mourns the mortal doom of man,
> Her noblest work, (so Israel's virgins erst,
> With annual moan upon the mountains wept
> Their fairest gone) there in that rural scene,
> So placid, so congenial to the wish
> The Christian feels, of peaceful rest within
> The silent grave, I would have stray'd:
> . . . .
> —wandered forth, where the cold dew of heaven

7. Source unidentified.

Lay on the humbler graves around, what time
The pale moon gazed upon the turfy mounds,
Pensive, as though like me, in lonely muse,
'Twere brooding on the Dead inhum'd beneath.
There, while with him, the holy Man of Uz,
O'er human destiny I sympathiz'd,
Counting the long, long periods prophecy
Decrees to roll, ere the great day arrives
Of resurrection, oft the blue-eyed Spring
Had met me with her blossoms, as the Dove
Of old, return'd with olive leaf, to cheer
The Patriarch mourning o'er a world destroy'd:
And I would bless her visit; for to me
'Tis sweet to trace the consonance that links
As one, the works of Nature and the word
Of God.——

                                    JOHN EDWARDS.[8]

A Village Church-yard, lying as it does in the lap of Nature, may indeed be most favourably contrasted with that of a Town of crowded Population; and Sepulture therein combines many of the best tendencies which belong to the mode practised by the Ancients, with others peculiar to itself. The sensations of pious cheerfulness, which attend the celebration of the Sabbath-day in rural places, are profitably chastised by the sight of the Graves of Kindred and Friends, gathered together in that general Home towards which the thoughtful yet happy Spectators themselves are journeying. Hence a Parish Church, in the stillness of the Country, is a visible centre of a community of the living and the dead; a point to which are habitually referred the nearest concerns of both.

As, then, both in Cities and in Villages, the Dead are deposited in close connection with our places of worship, with us the composition of an Epitaph naturally turns still more than among the Nations of Antiquity, upon the most serious and solemn affections of the human mind; upon departed Worth—upon personal or social Sorrow and Admiration—upon Religion individual and social—upon Time, and upon Eternity. Accordingly it suffices, in ordinary cases, to secure a composition of this kind from censure, that it contains nothing that shall shock or be inconsistent with this spirit. But, to entitle an Epitaph to praise, more than this is necessary. It ought to contain some Thought or Feeling belonging to the mortal or immortal part of our Nature touchingly expressed; and if that be done, however general or even trite the sentiment may be, every man of pure mind will read the words with pleasure and gratitude. A Husband bewails a Wife; a Parent breathes a sigh of disappointed hope over a lost Child; a Son utters a sentiment of filial reverence for a departed Father or Mother; a Friend perhaps inscribes an encomium recording the companionable qualities, or the solid virtues, of the Tenant of the Grave, whose departure has left a sadness upon his memory. This, and a pious admonition to the Living, and a humble expression of Christian confidence in Immortality, is the language of a thousand Church-yards; and it does not

---

8. From John Edwards, *All Saints' Church, Derby* (Derby, 1805), 40–41. Edwards (b. ca. 1772) was a friend of STC and a subscriber to *The Friend* (*Friend*, 2:341 n. 1, 426).

often happen that any thing, in a greater degree discriminate or appropri-
ate to the Dead or to the Living, is to be found in them. This want of
discrimination has been ascribed by Dr. Johnson, in his Essay upon the
Epitaphs of Pope, to two causes; first, the scantiness of the Objects of
human praise; and, secondly, the want of variety in the Characters of Men;
or to use his own words, "to the fact, that the greater part of Mankind have
no Character at all."[9] Such language may be holden without blame among
the generalities of common conversation; but does not become a Critic and
a Moralist speaking seriously upon a serious Subject. The objects of admi-
ration in Human Nature are not scanty but abundant; and every Man has
a Character of his own, to the eye that has skill to perceive it. The real
cause of the acknowledged want of discrimination in sepulchral memorials
is this: That to analyse the Characters of others, especially of those whom
we love, is not a common or natural employment of Men at any time. We
are not anxious unerringly to understand the constitution of the Minds of
those who have soothed, who have cheered, who have supported us: with
whom we have been long and daily pleased or delighted. The affections are
their own justification. The Light of Love in our Hearts is a satisfactory
evidence that there is a body of worth in the minds of our friends or kin-
dred, whence that Light has proceeded. We shrink from the thought of
placing their merits and defects to be weighed against each other in the
nice balance of pure intellect: nor do we find much temptation to detect
the shades by which a good quality or virtue is discriminated in them from
an excellence known by the same general name as it exists in the mind of
another; and, least of all, do we incline to these refinements when under
the pressure of Sorrow, Admiration, or Regret, or when actuated by any
of those feelings which incite men to prolong the memory of their Friends
and Kindred, by records placed in the bosom of the all-uniting and equal-
izing Receptacle of the Dead.

The first requisite, then, in an Epitaph is, that it should speak, in a
tone which shall sink into the heart, the general language of humanity as
connected with the subject of Death—the source from which an Epitaph
proceeds; of death and of life, To be born and to die are the two points in
which all men feel themselves to be in absolute coincidence. This general
language may be uttered so strikingly as to entitle an Epitaph to high
praise; yet it cannot lay claim to the highest unless other excellencies
be superadded. Passing through all intermediate steps, we will attempt to
determine at once what these excellencies are, and wherein consists the
perfection of this species of composition. It will be found to lie in a due
proportion of the common or universal feeling of humanity to sensations
excited by a distinct and clear conception, conveyed to the Reader's mind,
of the Individual, whose death is deplored and whose memory is to be
preserved; at least of his character as, after death, it appeared to those

9. WW quotes from the examination of Alexander Pope's epitaphs which Samuel Johnson
appended to his biography of Pope in *The Lives of the English Poets* (1779–81), paragraph 415:
"for the greater part of mankind of *have no characters at all*, have little that distinguishes them
from others equally good or bad, and therefore nothing can be said of them which may not be
applied with equal propriety to a thousand more" (*The Lives of the Most Eminent English Poets*,
ed. Roger Lonsdale [Oxford, 2006], 4:88). Johnson was himself adapting line 2 of Pope's *Epis-
tle to a Lady* (1735): "Most Women have no Characters at all." According to his nephew Chris-
topher, WW unaware when he wrote his essay of Johnson's own "Essay on Epitaphs," published
in the *Gentleman's Magazine* in September 1740 (*Prose*, 2:103).

who loved him and lament his loss. The general sympathy ought to be quickened, provoked, and diversified, by particular thoughts, actions, images,—circumstances of age, occupation, manner of life, prosperity which the Deceased had known, or adversity to which he had been subject; and these ought to be bound together and solemnized into one harmony by the general sympathy. The two powers should temper, restrain, and exalt each other. The Reader ought to know who and what the Man was whom he is called upon to think of with interest. A distinct conception should be given (implicitly where it can, rather than explicitly) of the Individual lamented. But the Writer of an Epitaph is not an Anatomist who dissects the internal frame of the mind; he is not even a Painter who executes a portrait at leisure and in entire tranquillity: his delineation, we must remember, is performed by the side of the Grave; and, what is more, the grave of one whom he loves and admires. What purity and brightness is that virtue clothed in, the image of which must no longer bless our living eyes! The character of a deceased Friend or beloved Kinsman is not seen, no—nor ought to be seen, otherwise than as a Tree through a tender haze or a luminous mist,[1] that spiritualizes and beautifies it; that takes away indeed, but only to the end that the parts which are not abstracted may appear more dignified and lovely, may impress and affect the more. Shall we say then that this is not truth, not a faithful image; and that accordingly the purposes of commemoration cannot be answered?—It *is* truth, and of the highest order! for, though doubtless things are not apparent which did exist, yet, the object being looked at through this medium, parts and proportions are brought into distinct view which before had been only imperfectly or unconsciously seen: it is truth hallowed by love—the joint offspring of the worth of the Dead and the affections of the Living!—This may easily be brought to the test. Let one, whose eyes have been sharpened by personal hostility to discover what was amiss in the character of a good man, hear the tidings of his death, and what a change is wrought in a moment!—Enmity melts away; and, as it disappears, unsightliness, disproportion, and deformity, vanish; and, through the influence of commiseration, a harmony of love and beauty succeeds. Bring such a Man to the Tomb-stone on which shall be inscribed an Epitaph on his Adversary, composed in the spirit which we have recommended. Would he turn from it as from an idle tale? Ah! no— the thoughtful look, the sigh, and perhaps the involuntary tear, would testify that it had a sane, a generous, and good meaning; and that on the Writer's mind had remained an impression which was a true abstract of the character of the deceased; that his gifts and graces were remembered in the simplicity in which they ought to be remembered. The composition and quality of the mind of a virtuous man, contemplated by the side of the Grave where his body is mouldering, ought to appear, and be felt as something midway between what he was on Earth walking about with his living frailties, and what he may be presumed to be as a Spirit in Heaven.

It suffices, therefore, that the Trunk and the main Branches of the Worth of the Deceased be boldly and unaffectedly represented. Any further detail, minutely and scrupulously pursued, especially if this be done

---

1. A phrase (as *Prose*, 2:104, notes) from STC's *Dejection: An Ode* (1802), line 62: "This light, this glory, this fair luminous mist" (*NCC*, 156).

with laborious and antithetic discriminations, must inevitably frustrate its own purpose; forcing the passing Spectator to this conclusion,—either that the Dead did not possess the merits ascribed to him, or that they who have raised a monument to his memory and must therefore be supposed to have been closely connected with him, were incapable of perceiving those merits; or at least during the act of composition had lost sight of them; for, the Understanding having been so busy in its petty occupation, how could the heart of the Mourner be other than cold? and in either of these cases, whether the fault be on the part of the buried Person or the Survivors, the Memorial is unaffecting and profitless.

Much better is it to fall short in discrimination than to pursue it too far, or to labour it unfeelingly. For in no place are we so much disposed to dwell upon those points, of nature and condition, wherein all Men resemble each other, as in the Temple where the universal Father is worshipped, or by the side of the Grave which gathers all Human Beings to itself, and "equalizes the lofty and the low."[2] We suffer and we weep with the same heart; we love and are anxious for one another in one spirit; our hopes look to the same quarter; and the virtues by which we are all to be furthered and supported, as patience, meekness, good-will, temperance, and temperate desires, are in an equal degree the concern of us all. Let an Epitaph, then, contain at least these acknowledgments to our common nature; nor let the sense of their importance be sacrificed to a balance of opposite qualities or minute distinctions in individual character; which if they do not, (as will for the most part be the case) when examined, resolve themselves into a trick of words, will, even when they are true and just, for the most part be grievously out of place; for, as it is probable that few only have explored these intricacies of human nature, so can the tracing of them be interesting only to a few. But an Epitaph is not a proud Writing shut up for the studious; it is exposed to all, to the wise and the most ignorant; it is condescending, perspicuous, and lovingly solicits regard; its story and admonitions are brief, that the thoughtless, the busy and indolent, may not be deterred, nor the impatient tired; the stooping Old Man cons the engraven record like a second horn-book;[3]—the Child is proud that he can read it—and the Stranger is introduced by its mediation to the company of a Friend: it is concerning all, and for all:—in the Church-yard it is open to the day; the sun looks down upon the stone, and the rains of Heaven beat against it.

Yet, though the Writer who would excite sympathy is bound in this case more than in any other, to give proof that he himself has been moved, it is to be remembered, that to raise a Monument is a sober and a reflective act; that the inscription which it bears is intended to be permanent and for universal perusal; and that, for this reason, the thoughts and feelings expressed should be permanent also—liberated from that weakness and anguish of sorrow which is in nature transitory, and which with

2. WW adapts line 24 of *There never breathed a man who when his life*, the fourth of his translations from Chiabrera's epitaphs, which had been published in *The Friend* on December 28, 1809: "one poor monument can suffice / To equalize the lofty and the low" (*Shorter Poems, 1807–1820* [CW], 64; *Friend*, 2:248).
3. A device used in schools to teach children to read, consisting of a paper printed with the alphabet, covered by transparent horn, and mounted on a wooden tablet with a handle; *cons*: peruses, studies.

instinctive decency retires from notice.[4] The passions should be subdued, the emotions controlled; strong indeed, but nothing ungovernable or wholly involuntary. Seemliness requires this, and truth requires it also: for how can the Narrator otherwise be trusted? Moreover, a Grave is a tranquillizing object: resignation, in course of time, springs up from it as naturally as the wild flowers, besprinkling the turf with which it may be covered, or gathering round the monument by which it is defended. The very form and substance of the monument which has received the inscription, and the appearance of the letters, testifying with what a slow and laborious hand they must have been engraven, might seem to reproach the Author who had given way upon this occasion to transports of mind, or to quick turns of conflicting passion; though the same might constitute the life and beauty of a funeral Oration or elegiac Poem.

These sensations and judgments, acted upon perhaps unconsciously, have been one of the main causes why Epitaphs so often personate the Deceased, and represent him as speaking from his own Tomb-stone. The departed Mortal is introduced telling you himself that his pains are gone; that a state of rest is come; and he conjures you to weep for him no longer. He admonishes with the voice of one experienced in the vanity of those affections which are confined to earthly objects, and gives a verdict like a superior Being, performing the office of a Judge, who has no temptations to mislead him, and whose decision cannot but be dispassionate. Thus is Death disarmed of its sting, and affliction unsubstantialized. By this tender fiction the Survivors bind themselves to a sedater sorrow, and employ the intervention of the imagination in order that the reason may speak her own language earlier than she would otherwise have been enabled to do. This shadowy interposition also harmoniously unites the two worlds of the Living and the Dead by their appropriate affections. And I may observe, that here we have an additional proof of the propriety with which sepulchral inscriptions were referred to the consciousness of Immortality as their primal source.

I do not speak with a wish to recommend that an Epitaph should be cast in this mould preferably to the still more common one, in which what is said comes from the Survivors directly; but rather to point out how natural those feelings are which have induced men, in all states and ranks of Society, so frequently to adopt this mode. And this I have done chiefly in order that the laws, which ought to govern the composition of the other, may be better understood. This latter mode, namely, that in which the Survivors speak in their own Persons, seems to me upon the whole greatly preferable: as it admits a wider range of notices; and, above all, because, excluding the fiction which is the ground-work of the other, it rests upon a more solid basis.

Enough has been said to convey our notion of a perfect Epitaph; but it must be observed that one is meant which will best answer the *general* ends of that species of composition. According to the course pointed out, the worth of private life, through all varieties of situation and character,

---

4. Compare WW's account, in a letter of May 1, 1805, of his difficulty writing a poem memorializing his brother John: "At first I had a strong impulse to write a poem that should record my Brother's virtues and be worthy of his memory. I began to give vent to my feelings, with this view, but I was overwhelmed by my subject and could not proceed * * *. This work must therefore rest awhile till I am something calmer" (*WL*, 1:586).

will be most honourably and profitably preserved in memory. Nor would the model recommended less suit public Men, in all instances save of those persons who by the greatness of their services in the employments of Peace or War, or by the surpassing excellence of their works in Art, Literature, or Science, have made themselves not only universally known, but have filled the heart of their Country with everlasting gratitude. Yet I must here pause to correct myself. In describing the general tenour of thought which Epitaphs ought to hold, I have omitted to say, that, if it be the *actions* of a Man, or even some *one* conspicuous or beneficial act of local or general utility, which have distinguished him and excited a desire that he should be remembered, then, of course, ought the attention to be directed chiefly to those actions or that act; and such sentiments dwelt upon as naturally arise out of them or it. Having made this necessary distinction I proceed.—The mighty Benefactors of mankind, as they are not only known by the immediate Survivors, but will continue to be known familiarly to latest Posterity, do not stand in need of biographic sketches, in such a place; nor of delineations of character to individualize them. This is already done by their Works, in the Memories of Men. Their naked names, and a grand comprehensive sentiment of civic Gratitude, patriotic Love, or human Admiration; or the utterance of some elementary Principle most essential in the constitution of true Virtue; or an intuition, communicated in adequate words, of the sublimity of intellectual Power,— these are the only tribute which can here be paid—the only offering that upon such an Altar would not be unworthy!

> What needs my Shakespeare for his honoured bones
> The labour of an age in piled stones,
> Or that his hallowed reliques should be hid
> Under a star-y-pointing pyramid?
> Dear Son of Memory, great Heir of Fame,
> What need'st thou such weak witness of thy name?
> Thou in our wonder and astonishment
> Hast built thyself a live-long Monument.
> And so sepulchred, in such pomp dost lie,
> That Kings for such a Tomb would wish to die.[5]

5. WW quotes lines 1–8 and 15–16 of Milton's *On Shakespear*, a poem first published in the Second Folio of Shakespeare's *Works* (1632).

From POEMS (1815)

In assembling his first collected edition—one that would incorporate *Lyrical Ballads* and *Poems, in Two Volumes*, while adding poems written since 1807—Wordsworth confronted the same problem as in *P2V*, namely how best to arrange the poems. In *P2V* the sonnets had been grouped thematically, but the other poems in looser categories. Writing to Coleridge on May 5, 1809, Wordsworth elaborated a thematic organization with eight categories, omitting those of the sonnets (which in the event he retained from *P2V*): "Poems relating to childhood," "fraternal affections," "natural objects and their influence," "Naming of Places," "Poems relating to human life," "social and civic duties," "those relating to Maternal feeling," and "old age" (*Shorter Poems, 1807–1820* [CW], 20–22; WL, 2:334–36). In 1811 Wordsworth began considering another method of organization that would "make more clear [his] intentions in writing them" (WL, 2:471), arranging the poems in three classes, thematic (more specifically, the period of life represented), generic, and psychological: "according to their subjects," "accordingly to the mold in which the composition is cast," and "According to the Powers * * * put forth in the Composition of them" (DC MS 24, qtd. in *Shorter Poems, 1807–1820* [CW], 22). Among the "Powers" specified were fancy and imagination. The following May, discussing his plans for the new collected edition with Henry Crabb Robinson (see Biographical and Topographical Glossary), he evidently emphasized the third of these classes: "Wordsworth purposes * * * arranging the poems with some reference either to the fancy, imagination, reflection, or mere feeling contained in them." In his diary Robinson sought to clarify Wordsworth's "rather obscure account of poetic abstraction": the poet first conceives an object in its "essential nature," and then "reclothes his *idea* in an individual dress which expresses the essential quality, and has also the spirit and life of a sensual object" (*CRB*, 1:89–90). Three years later, in the Preface to *P 1815*, Wordsworth would define imagination more expansively as a creative as well as a modifying power.

Annotating a copy of *P2V* (now in the Yale University Library), Wordsworth sketched out the classifications of poems more or less as they would appear in *P 1815*: "Poems upon Childhood," "Poems of The affections Friendship Love &c," "Poems of the Fancy," "Poems of Imagination," "Poems of Sentiment & Reflection," "Sonnets. Miscellaneous," "[Sonnets] Dedicated to Liberty," "Inscriptions," "Elegiac" (this became "Epitaphs and Elegiac Poems" in fact), "Old Age," and "Final Ode" (i.e., the Intimations Ode) (*Shorter Poems, 1807–1820* [CW], 611–12). To these Wordsworth then added a class of "Juvenile Pieces." One of the reasons for his concern with the arrangement of poems was his conception, explained in the Preface to *The Excursion* and briefly mentioned in the Preface to *P 1815*, of their relation to *The Recluse*: if *The Prelude* was to be the "Anti-chapel" to the "gothic Church" of *The Recluse*, then "his minor Pieces * * * *when they shall be properly arranged*, will be found by the attentive Reader to have such connection with the main Work as may give them claim to be likened to the little Cells, Oratories, and sepulchral Recesses, ordinarily included in those edifices" (emphasis added). Of course, it is questionable whether any arrangement would have assisted contemporaries in appreciating the place of the peripheral elements in a structure of which, by Wordsworth's admission, two-thirds remained to be built. As it is, Wordsworth settled on two distinct methods of classification, one deriving from the content or form of the poems themselves, the other deriving from the psychology of their creation. When, in 1826, Crabb Robinson objected that readers had little interest in the state of mind with which poems were written, Wordsworth responded that such classification is "of slight importance as matter of Reflection, but of great as matter of *feeling* for the Reader by making one Poem smooth the way for another" (*WL*, 4:440).

In connection with his psychological classification, Wordsworth returned in the Preface to *P 1815* to a question that had occupied him earlier in his 1800 note on *The Thorn* and in *The Prelude* 8.586 and 13.289–94, the distinction between the faculties of fancy and imagination. But whereas his definition of fancy, as "the power by which pleasure and surprize are excited by sudden varieties of situation and by accumulated imagery," remained essentially unchanged from 1800 to 1815 (see p. 517 n. 6), that of imagination changed from "the faculty which produces impressive effects out of simple elements" in the note on the *Thorn* to, in the Preface to *P 1815*, a modifying or transformative power whose purpose is "to incite and support the eternal." The revised definition, which assumes the superiority of imagination to fancy, has affinities with the one that Coleridge had developed first in letters of 1802–1804, then in literary lectures of 1808 and 1811–12, and finally in print in a contribution to Robert Southey's *Omniana* in 1812 (from which Wordsworth quotes Coleridge's definition of fancy, albeit to criticize it). Prompted by what likely seemed to him as an appropriation of his own intellectual labor, Coleridge undertook in *Biographia Literaturia* (1817) to distinguish imagination from fancy more fully and in more explicitly philosophical terms, taking issue with Wordsworth's version of the distinction in the Preface to *P 1815*: see p. 514 n. 1 below and *NCC*, 416 and n. 5.

Contemporary reviewers of *P 1815* were more appreciative of Wordsworth's poetic gifts than the reviewers of *P2V* had been: the *British Lady's Magazine* (July 1815), for example, praised Wordsworth for disregarding contemporary fashion and following "the hallowed footsteps of his predecessors" (*CH*, 529), while the *Champion* (June 1815) proclaimed him "the greatest poetical genius of the age" (*CH*, 527). But the reviewers did not share the poet's conviction that his classifications assisted an understanding of the poems. The reviewer in the *Monthly Review* (November 1815), observing that the Wordsworth's Preface "is not remarkable for clearness of idea nor for humility of tone," devoted a paragraph to the question: "we have a poem belonging to the class of 'Fancy,' with no possible distinguishing characteristic from another in the class of 'Imagination'" (*CH*, 558). Indeed most of the reviewers remarked on the aggressively defensive tone of the Preface and especially the "Essay, Supplementary to the Preface" (see *CH*, 529, 533–34, 557–62, 570, 578–79), thus confirming Crabb Robinson's fear that those self-justificatory texts would "afford a triumph to his enemies" (*CRB*, 1:165). Although, according to Robinson, Thomas De Quincey persuaded Wordsworth to omit a "personal attack on [Francis] Jeffrey in his preface to his poems in the new edition" (*CRB*, 1:161)—and in fact Jeffrey is never referred to directly in either the Preface or the Essay—the remarks about contemporary criticism in the Preface and Essay betray, as Robinson observed, Wordsworth's resentment at the thirteen years of abuse to which Jeffrey had subjected him in the pages of the *Edinburgh Review* (*CRB*, 1:165). A year later, in *A Letter to a Friend of Robert Burns*, Wordsworth did attack Jeffrey directly (see the excerpt from Jeffrey in Nineteenth-Century Responses, p. 560 and source note below).

P 1815 was published in an edition of 500 copies, which were sold by 1819–20 (Owen, "Costs, Sales, and Profits," 98). The edition was dedicated "as a lasting memorial of a friendship" to Sir George Beaumont (see Biographical and Topographical Glossary) and included, as frontispieces, engravings of two paintings by Beaumont, an illustration of *Lucy Gray*, lines 13–16, in volume 1 and *A Storm: Peele Castle* in volume 2 (see the first note on *Elegiac Stanzas*). The texts and order of the writings printed here from *P 1815* follow those of the original edition, the classifications of the poems being indicated in the notes.

From PREFACE

* * *

In the Preface to that part of "The Recluse," lately published under the title of "The Excursion," I have alluded to a meditated arrangement of my minor Poems, which should assist the attentive Reader in perceiving their connection with each other, and also their subordination to that Work.[1] I shall here say a few words explanatory of this arrangement, as carried into effect in the present Volumes.

The powers requisite for the production of poetry are, first, those of observation and description, i.e. the ability to observe with accuracy things as they are in themselves, and with fidelity to describe them, unmodified by any passion or feeling existing in the mind of the Describer:[2] whether the things depicted be actually present to the senses, or have a place only in the memory. This power, though indispensable to a Poet, is one which he employs only in submission to necessity, and never for a continuance of time; as its exercise supposes all the higher qualities of the mind to be passive, and in a state of subjection to external objects, much in the same way as the Translator[3] or Engraver ought to be to his Original. 2dly, Sensibility,—which, the more exquisite it is, the wider will be the range of a Poet's perceptions; and the more will he be incited to observe objects, both as they exist in themselves and as re-acted upon by his own mind. (The distinction between poetic and human sensibility has been marked in the character of the Poet delineated in the original preface,[4] before-mentioned). 3rdly, Reflection,—which makes the Poet acquainted with the value of actions, images, thoughts, and feelings; and assists the sensibility in perceiving their connection with each other. 4thly, Imagination and Fancy,—to modify, to create, and to associate. 5thly, Invention,—by which characters are composed out of materials supplied by observation; whether of the Poet's own heart and mind, or of external life and nature; and such incidents and situations produced as are most impressive to the imagination, and most fitted to do justice to the characters, sentiments, and passions, which the Poet undertakes to

1. See the Preface to *Exc* (p. 443 above).
2. In the Preface to *LB 1800* WW had said, "I have at all times endeavoured to look steadily at my subject, consequently I hope it will be found that there is in these Poems little falsehood of description" (p. 82 above).
3. Compare WW's claim in the Preface to *LB 1802*: "it is proper that he should consider himself as in the situation of a translator, who deems himself justified when he substitutes excellences of another kind for those which are unattainable by him" (p. 86 above).
4. WW refers to his assertion in the Preface to *LB 1800* that the true poet must possess "more than usual organic sensibility [and have] also thought long and deeply" (p. 79 above).

illustrate. And, lastly, Judgment,—to decide how and where, and in what degree, each of these faculties ought to be exerted; so that the less shall not be sacrificed to the greater; nor the greater, slighting the less, arrogate, to its own injury, more than its due. By judgment, also, is determined what are the laws and appropriate graces of every species of composition.[5]

*   *   *

It is deducible from the above, that poems, apparently miscellaneous, may with propriety be arranged either with reference to the powers of mind *predominant* in the production of them; or to the mould in which they are cast; or, lastly, to the subjects to which they relate. From each of these considerations, the following Poems have been divided into classes; which, that the work may more obviously correspond with the course of human life, for the sake of exhibiting in it the three requisites of a legitimate whole, a beginning, a middle, and an end,[6] have been also arranged, as far as it was possible, according to an order of time, commencing with Childhood, and terminating with Old Age, Death, and Immortality. My guiding wish was, that the small pieces of which these volumes consist, thus discriminated, might be regarded under a two-fold view; as composing an entire work within themselves, and as adjuncts to the philosophical Poem, "The Recluse." This arrangement has long presented itself habitually to my own mind.[7] Nevertheless, I should have preferred to scatter the contents of these volumes at random, if I had been persuaded that, by the plan adopted, any thing material would be taken from the natural effect of the pieces, individually, on the mind of the unreflecting Reader. I trust there is a sufficient variety in each class to prevent this; while, for him who reads with reflection, the arrangement will serve as a commentary unostentatiously directing his attention to my purposes, both particular and general. But, as I wish to guard against the possibility of misleading by this classification, it is proper first to remind the Reader, that certain poems are placed according to the powers of mind, in the Author's conception, predominant in the production of them; *predominant*, which implies the exertion of other faculties in less degree. Where there is more imagination than fancy in a poem it is placed under the head of imagination, and vice versâ. Both the above Classes might without impropriety have been enlarged from that consisting of "Poems founded on the Affections;" as might this latter from those, and from the class "Proceeding from Sentiment and Reflection." The most striking characteristics of each piece, mutual illustration, variety, and proportion, have governed me throughout.

*   *   *

None of the other Classes, except those of Fancy and Imagination, require any particular notice. But a remark of general application may be

5. In the paragraphs omitted here, WW distinguishes seven "moulds" or genres of poetry: 1) narrative (including epic, historical, romance, and mock-heroic), 2) dramatic (including opera), 3) lyrical (including the hymn, ode, elegy, song, and ballad), 4) idyllium ("descriptive chiefly either of the processes and appearance of external nature * * * or of characters, manners, and sentiments"—e.g., the epitaph, inscription, sonnet, verse epistle, and loco-descriptive poetry), 5) didactic, 6) philosophical satire, and 7) a "composite species" combining the previous three (e.g., Edward Young's *Night Thoughts* [1742–45] and William Cowper's *The Task* [1785]).
6. As *Prose*, 3:41, notes, an Aristotelian principle: "A whole is that which has a beginning, a middle, and an end" (*Poetics* 1450b25–26).
7. See the headnote.

made. All Poets, except the dramatic, have been in the practice of feign-
ing that their works were composed to the music of the harp or lyre: with
what degree of affectation this has been done in modern times, I leave to
the judicious to determine. For my own part, I have not been disposed to
violate probability so far, or to make such a large demand upon the Reader's
charity. Some of these pieces are essentially lyrical; and, therefore, cannot
have their due force without a supposed musical accompaniment; but, in
much the greatest part, as a substitute for the classic lyre or romantic harp,
I require nothing more than an animated or impassioned recitation, adapted
to the subject. Poems, however humble in their kind, if they be good in that
kind, cannot read themselves: the law of long syllable and short must not be
so inflexible—the letter of metre must not be so impassive to the spirit of
versification—as to deprive the Reader of a voluntary power to modulate, in
subordination to the sense, the music of the poem;—in the same manner as
his mind is left at liberty, and even summoned, to act upon its thoughts and
images. But, though the accompaniment of a musical instrument be fre-
quently dispensed with, the true Poet does not therefore abandon his privi-
lege distinct from that of the mere Proseman;

> He murmurs near the running brooks
> A music sweeter than their own.[8]

I come now to the consideration of the words Fancy and Imagination,
as employed in the classification of the following Poems. "A man," says an
intelligent Author, has "imagination," in proportion as he can distinctly
copy in idea the impressions of sense: it is the faculty which *images* within
the mind the phenomena of sensation. A man has fancy in proportion as
he can call up, connect, or associate, at pleasure, those internal images
($\varphi\alpha\nu\tau\alpha\zeta\epsilon\iota\nu$[9] is to cause to appear) so as to complete ideal representations
of absent objects. Imagination is the power of depicting, and fancy of
evoking and combining. The imagination is formed by patient observation;
the fancy by a voluntary activity in shifting the scenery of the mind. The
more accurate the imagination, the more safely may a painter, or a poet,
undertake a delineation, or a description, without the presence of the
objects to be characterized. The more versatile the fancy, the more original
and striking will be the decorations produced.—*British Synonyms dis-
criminated, by W. Taylor.*[1]
Is not this as if a man should undertake to supply an account of a
building, and be so intent upon what he had discovered of the foundation
as to conclude his task without once looking up at the superstructure?
Here, as in other instances throughout the volume, the judicious Author's
mind is enthralled by Etymology; he takes up the original word as his
guide, his conductor, his escort, and too often does not perceive how
soon he becomes its prisoner, without liberty to tread in any path but that
to which it confines him.[2] It is not easy to find out how imagination, thus

8. *A Poet's Epitaph*, lines 39–40.
9. The Greek word *phantazein* (slightly misprinted in *P 1815*) means "to make visible," "to present
   to the eye," "to picture in the mind."
1. WW quotes the first paragraph of the entry "Imagination. Fancy" in William Taylor, *English
   Synonyms Discriminated* (London, 1813), 242.
2. The English word *imagination* derives from the Latin *imaginatio*, "a mental image"; *fancy*,
   originally a contraction of *fantasy*, derives from the Greek *phantasia*, "appearance," "presenta-
   tion (to consciousness)."

explained, differs from distinct remembrance of images; or fancy from quick and vivid recollection of them: each is nothing more than a mode of memory. If the two words bear the above meaning, and no other, what term is left to designate that Faculty of which the Poet is "all compact;"[3] he whose eye glances from earth to heaven, whose spiritual attributes body-forth what his pen is prompt in turning to shape; or what is left to characterise fancy, as insinuating herself into the heart of objects with creative activity?——Imagination, in the sense of the word as giving title to a Class of the following Poems, has no reference to images that are merely a faithful copy, existing in the mind, of absent external objects; but is a word of higher import, denoting operations of the mind upon those objects, and processes of creation or of composition, governed by certain fixed laws. I proceed to illustrate my meaning by instances. A parrot *hangs* from the wires of his cage by his beak or by his claws; or a monkey from the bough of a tree by his paws or his tail. Each creature does so literally and actually. In the first Eclogue of Virgil, the Shepherd, thinking of the time when he is to take leave of his Farm, thus addresses his Goats;

> Non ego vos posthac viridi projectus in antro
> Dumosa *pendere* procul de rape ordebo.

> ——half way up
> Hangs one who gathers samphire,[4]

is the well-known expression of Shakespear, delineating an ordinary image upon the Cliffs of Dover. In these two instances is a slight exertion of the faculty which I denominate imagination, in the use of one word: neither the goats nor the samphire-gatherer do literally hang, as does the parrot or the monkey; but, presenting to the senses something of such an appearance, the mind in its activity, for its own gratification, contemplates them as hanging.

> As when far off at Sea a Fleet descried
> *Hangs* in the clouds, by equinoxial winds
> Close sailing from Bengala or the Isles
> Of Ternate or Tydore, whence Merchants bring
> Their spicy drugs; they on the trading flood
> Through the wide Ethiopian to the Cape
> Ply, stemming nightly toward the Pole: so seem'd
> Far off the flying Fiend.[5]

3. A phrase from Shakespeare, *A Midsummer Night's Dream* 5.1.7–8: "The lunatic, the lover, and the poet / Are of imagination all compact [i.e., composed]." WW proceeds to allude to lines 10–16 of the speech: "The poet's eye, in a fine frenzy rolling, / Doth glance from heaven to earth, from earth to heaven; / And as imagination bodies forth / The forms of things unknown, the poet's pen / Turns them to shapes * * *."
4. Virgil, *Eclogues* 1.76–77 ("No longer shall I, lying down in a verdant grotto, watch you in the distance hanging from a thorn-covered cliff"); Shakespeare, *King Lear* 4.6.14–15 (conflated text). Samphire is an edible plant that grows among rocks on Britain's southern and western coasts. *Prose*, 3:42, notes that the figurative use of the verb *hang* had already been discussed, with reference to the same examples from Virgil and Shakespeare, in an essay attributed in WW's time to Oliver Goldsmith (?1728–1774), "Poetry Distinguished from Other Writing": "There are certain words in every language particularly adapted to Poetical expression; some from the image or idea they convey to the imagination; and some from the effect they have upon the ear" (*Essays and Criticism by Dr. Goldsmith* [London, 1798], 2:190).
5. Milton, *Paradise Lost* 2.636–43.

Here is the full strength of the imagination involved in the word, *hangs*, and exerted upon the whole image: First, the Fleet, an aggregate of many Ships, is represented as one mighty Person, whose track, we know and feel, is upon the waters; but, taking advantage of its appearance to the senses, the Poet dares to represent it as *hanging in the clouds*, both for the gratification of the mind in contemplating the image itself, and in reference to the motion and appearance of the sublime object to which it is compared.

From images of sight we will pass to those of sound:

> Over his own sweet voice the Stock-dove *broods*;[6]

of the same bird,

> His voice was *buried* among trees,
> Yet to be come at by the breeze;
>
> O, Cuckoo! shall I call thee *Bird*,
> Or but a wandering *Voice*?[7]

The Stock-dove is said to *coo*, a sound well imitating the note of the bird; but, by the intervention of the metaphor *broods*, the affections are called in by the imagination to assist in marking the manner in which the Bird reiterates and prolongs her soft note, as if herself delighting to listen to it, and participating of a still and quiet satisfaction, like that which may be supposed inseparable from the continuous process of incubation. "His voice was buried among trees," a metaphor expressing the love of *seclusion* by which this Bird is marked; and characterising its note as not partaking of the shrill and the piercing, and therefore more easily deadened by the intervening shade; yet a note so peculiar, and withal so pleasing, that the breeze, gifted with that love of the sound which the Poet feels, penetrates the shade in which it is entombed, and conveys it to the ear of the listener.

* * *

Thus far of images independent of each other, and immediately endowed by the mind with properties that do not inhere in them, upon an incitement from properties and qualities the existence of which is inherent and obvious. These processes of imagination are carried on either by conferring additional properties upon an object, or abstracting from it some of those which it actually possesses, and thus enabling it to react upon the mind which hath performed the process, like a new existence.[8]

I pass from the Imagination acting upon an individual image to a consideration of the same faculty employed upon images in a conjunction by which they modify each other. The Reader has already had a fine instance before him in the passage quoted from Virgil, where the apparently perilous

6. *Resolution and Independence*, line 5.
7. *O Nightingale! thou surely art*, lines 13–14; *To the Cuckoo* (originally published in *P2V*), lines 3–4. WW proceeds to refer to the stock-dove in *O Nightingale! thou surely art*, line 15: "He did not cease; but coo'd—and coo'd."
8. Compare WW's analogy between nature and the imagination in *The Prelude* 13.77–83: "That domination which she oftentimes / Exerts upon the outward face of things, / So moulds them, and endues, abstracts, combines * * * That even the grossest minds must see and hear." *Prose*, 3:44–45, also notes a parallel to Alexander Gerard's *Essay on Genius* (London, 1774), 29: "Even when it [imagination] exerts itself in the simplest manner, * * * it in some degree displays its creative power. * * * [W]hen it only exhibits simple ideas which have been derived from the senses, it confers something original upon them, by the manner in which it exhibits them."

situation of the Goat, hanging upon the shaggy precipice, is contrasted
with that of the Shepherd, contemplating it from the seclusion of the
Cavern in which he lies stretched at ease and in security. Take these
images separately, and how unaffecting the picture compared with that
produced by their being thus connected with, and opposed to, each other!

> As a huge Stone is sometimes seen to lie
> Couched on the bald top of an eminence,
> Wonder to all who do the same espy
> By what means it could thither come, and whence;
> So that it seems a thing endued with sense,
> Like a Sea-beast crawled forth, which on a shelf
> Of rock or sand reposeth, there to sun himself.
> Such seemed this Man; not all alive or dead,
> Nor all asleep, in his extreme old age.
> Motionless as a cloud the old Man stood,
> That heareth not the loud winds when they call,
> And moveth altogether if it move at all.[9]

In these images, the conferring, the abstracting, and the modifying pow-
ers of the Imagination, immediately and mediately acting, are all brought
into conjunction. The Stone is endowed with something of the power of
life to approximate it to the Sea-beast; and the Sea-beast stripped of some
of its vital qualities to assimilate it to the stone; which intermediate
image is thus treated for the purpose of bringing the original image, that
of the stone, to a nearer resemblance to the figure and condition of the
aged Man; who is divested of so much of the indications of life and motion
as to bring him to the point where the two objects unite and coalesce in
just comparison. After what has been said, the image of the Cloud need
not be commented upon.

Thus far of an endowing or modifying power: but the Imagination also
shapes and *creates*; and how? By innumerable processes; and in none does
it more delight than in that of consolidating numbers into unity, and dis-
solving and separating unity into number,[1]—alternations proceeding from,
and governed by, a sublime consciousness of the soul in her own mighty
and almost divine powers. Recur to the passage already cited from Milton.
When the compact Fleet, as one Person, has been introduced "Sailing from
Bengala," "They," i. e. the "Merchants," representing the Fleet resolved
into a Multitude of Ships, 'ply' their voyage towards the extremities of the
earth: "So" (referring to the word "As" in the commencement) "seemed the
flying Fiend;" the image of his Person acting to recombine the multitude
of Ships into one body,—the point from which the comparison set out.
"So seemed," and to whom seemed? To the heavenly Muse who dictates
the poem,[2] to the eye of the Poet's mind, and to that of the Reader, present

9. *Resolution and Independence*, lines 64–72, 82–84. Henry Crabb Robinson (see Biographical
and Topographical Glossary) recorded in his diary for May 31, 1802, that WW had quoted to
him "the picture of the Old Man in his Leech Gatherer [as *Resolution and Independence* was
originally titled] and the simile of the stone on the eminence as an instance of an imaginative
creation" (*CRB*, 1:90).
1. In attributing a separative power to imagination, WW differs from STC, who in *BL* defines
imagination more restrictively as an "esemplastic" power, i.e., shaping into one: "It dissolves,
diffuses, dissipates, in order to re-create; or where this is rendered impossible, yet still at all
events it struggles to idealize and to unify" (*NCC*, 449, 488). See also the headnote.
2. An allusion to Milton's invocations of his muse in *Paradise Lost*, as in 9.21–23, "my Celestial
Patroness, who deignes / Her nightly visitations unimplor'd, / And dictates to me slumbring."

at one moment in the wide Ethiopian, and the next in the solitudes, then
first broken in upon, of the infernal regions!

Modo me Thebis, modo ponit Athenis.[3]

Hear again this mighty Poet,—speaking of the Messiah going forth to
expel from Heaven the rebellious Angels,

Attended by ten thousand, thousand Saints
He onward came: far off his coming shone,—[4]

the retinue of Saints, and the Person of the Messiah himself, lost almost
and merged in the splendour of that indefinite abstraction, "His coming!"
    As I do not mean here to treat this subject further than to throw some
light upon the present Volumes, and especially upon one division of
them, I shall spare myself and the Reader the trouble of considering the
Imagination as it deals with thoughts and sentiments, as it regulates the
composition of characters,[5] and determines the course of actions: I will
not consider it (more than I have already done by implication) as that
power which, in the language of one of my most esteemed Friends, "draws
all things to one, which makes things animate or inanimate, beings with
their attributes, subjects with their accessaries, take one colour and serve
to one effect."[6] The grand store-house of enthusiastic and meditative
Imagination, of poetical, as contradistinguished from human and dra-
matic Imagination,[7] is the prophetic and lyrical parts of the holy Scrip-
tures, and the works of Milton, to which I cannot forbear to add those of
Spenser. I select these writers in preference to those of ancient Greece
and Rome because the anthropomorphitism of the Pagan religion sub-
jected the minds of the greatest poets in those countries too much to the
bondage of definite form; from which the Hebrews were preserved by
their abhorrence of idolatry. This abhorrence was almost as strong in our
great epic Poet,[8] both from circumstances of his life, and from the con-
stitution of his mind. However imbued the surface might be with classi-
cal literature, he was a Hebrew in soul; and all things tended in him
towards the sublime. Spenser, of a gentler nature, maintained his free-
dom by aid of his allegorical spirit, at one time inciting him to create
persons out of abstractions; and at another, by a superior effort of genius,

---

3. Horace, *Epistles* 2.1.213 (comparing the poet's power to a magician's): "[he] sets me down now
   in Thebes, now in Athens."
4. *Paradise Lost* 6.767–68.
5. WW presumably reserves for imagination a specifically regulative function in the *composition
   of characters*, for at the beginning of the Preface he defines Invention as the power "by which
   characters are composed out of materials supplied by observation."
6. WW's note: "Charles Lamb upon the genius of Hogarth." WW quotes from "On the Genius
   and Character of Hogarth," *The Reflector* 2 (1811): 64, in which Lamb praises William Ho-
   garth's engraving *Gin Lane* (1751). Lamb's sentence begins, "There is more of imagination in
   it—that power which draws all things to one ° ° °."
7. *Prose*, 3:47, suggests that WW's distinction between *enthusiastic Imagination* and *dramatic
   Imagination* derives from the John Dennis's distinction, in *The Grounds of Criticism in Poetry*
   (1704), between "Vulgar Passion ° ° ° which is moved by objects themselves, or by Ideas in the
   ordinary Course of Life," and "Enthusiastick Passion ° ° ° which is moved by the Ideas in Con-
   templation, or the Meditation of things that belong not to common Life" (*The Critical Works*,
   ed. E. N. Hooker [Baltimore, 1939], 1:338). WW mentions Dennis's distinction in a letter of
   January 1815 (*WL*, 3:188), when he is likely to have been writing the Preface. See also *Reading
   1800–15*, no. 133.
8. Milton.

to give the universality and permanence of abstractions to his human beings, by means of attributes and emblems that belong to the highest moral truths and the purest sensations,—of which his character of Una[9] is a glorious example. Of the human and dramatic Imagination the works of Shakespear are an inexhaustible source.

> I tax not you, ye Elements, with unkindness,
> I never gave you Kingdoms, called you Daughters.[1]

And if, bearing in mind the many Poets distinguished by this prime quality, whose names I omit to mention; yet justified by a recollection of the insults which the Ignorant, the Incapable, and the Presumptuous have heaped upon these and my other writings,[2] I may be permitted to anticipate the judgment of posterity upon myself; I shall declare (censurable, I grant, if the notoriety of the fact above stated does not justify me) that I have given, in these unfavourable times, evidence of exertions of this faculty upon its worthiest objects, the external universe, the moral and religious sentiments of Man, his natural affections, and his acquired passions; which have the same ennobling tendency as the productions of men, in this kind, worthy to be holden in undying remembrance.

*   *   *

To the mode in which Fancy has already been characterized as the Power of evoking and combining, or, as my friend Mr. Coleridge has styled it, "the aggregative and associative Power," my objection is only that the definition is too general.[3] To aggregate and to associate, to evoke and to combine, belong as well to the Imagination as to the Fancy; but either the materials evoked and combined are different; or they are brought together under a different law, and for a different purpose. Fancy does not require that the materials which she makes use of should be susceptible of change in their constitution, from her touch; and, where they admit of modification, it is enough for her purpose if it be slight, limited, and evanescent. Directly the reverse of these, are the desires and demands of the Imagination. She recoils from every thing but the plastic, the pliant, and the indefinite. She leaves it to Fancy to describe Queen Mab as coming,

---

9. A princess and representation of religious truth in book 1 of Edmund Spenser's allegorical romance-epic *The Faerie Queene* (1590–96).
1. *King Lear* 3.2.16–17 (conflated text).
2. WW would have been thinking particularly of Francis Jeffrey, who had reviewed both *P2V* and *Exc* severely in the *Edinburgh Review*. In January or February 1815 WW wrote to Daniel Stuart, editor of the *Courier*, to ask that space be given to a series of articles by Thomas De Quincey (see Biographical and Topographical Glossary) "upon the subject of the stupidities, the ignorance, and the dishonesties of the Edinburgh Review; and principally as relates to myself, whom, perhaps you know, the Editor [Jeffrey] has long honored with his abuse" (*WL*, 3:198). (If written, the articles were never published.) On February 27, 1815, DW recommended the Preface and "Essay, Supplementary" to her sister-in-law Priscilla: "You will find that he [WW] speaks in a lofty tone which will no doubt surprise the blind adorers of that ignorant Coxcomb Jeffrey" (*WL*, 3:206).
3. WW quotes STC's definition of *fancy* in "The Soul and its organs of Sense," one of his contributions to Robert Southey's *Omniana, or Horæ Otiosiores* (London, 1812), 2:14. In the same article he defined *imagination* as the "shaping or modifying power." In *BL* STC in turn quoted WW's objection and replied, "if by the power of evoking and combining, Mr. W. means the same as, and no more than, I meant by the aggregative and associative, I continue to deny, that it belongs at all to the imagination; and I am disposed to conjecture, that he has mistaken the co-presence of fancy with imagination for the operation of the latter singly" (*NCC*, 481). See also the headnote.

> In shape no bigger than an agate stone
> On the fore-finger of an Alderman.[4]

Having to speak of stature, she does not tell you that her gigantic Angel was as tall as Pompey's Pillar; much less that he was twelve cubits, or twelve hundred cubits high; or that his dimensions equalled those of Teneriffe or Atlas;[5]—because these, and if they were a million times as high, it would be the same, are bounded: The expression is, "His stature reached, the sky!" the illimitable firmament!—When the Imagination frames a comparison, if it does not strike on the first presentation, a sense of the truth of the likeness, from the moment that it is perceived, grows—and continues to grow—upon the mind; the resemblance depending less upon outline of form and feature than upon expression and effect, less upon casual and outstanding, than upon inherent and internal, properties:—moreover, the images invariably modify each other.—The law under which the processes of Fancy are carried on is as capricious as the accidents of things, and the effects are surprizing, playful, ludicrous, amusing, tender, or pathetic, as the objects happen to be appositely produced or fortunately combined.[6] Fancy depends upon the rapidity and profusion with which she scatters her thoughts and images, trusting that their number, and the felicity with which they are linked together, will make amends for the want of individual value: or she prides herself upon the curious subtilty and the successful elaboration with which she can detect their lurking affinities. If she can win you over to her purpose, and impart to you her feelings, she cares not how unstable or transitory may be her influence, knowing that it will not be out of her power to resume it upon an apt occasion. But the Imagination is conscious of an indestructible dominion;—the Soul may fall away from it, not being able to sustain its grandeur, but, if once felt and acknowledged, by no act of any other faculty of the mind can it be relaxed, impaired, of diminished.—Fancy is given to quicken and to beguile the temporal part of our Nature, Imagination to incite and to support the eternal.—Yet is it not the less true that Fancy, as she is an active, is also, under her own laws and in her own spirit, a creative faculty. In what manner Fancy ambitiously aims at a rivalship with the Imagination, and Imagination stoops to work with the materials of Fancy, might be illustrated from the compositions of all eloquent writers, whether in prose or verse; and chiefly from those of our own Country. Scarcely a page of the impassioned parts of Bishop Taylor's Works can be opened that shall not afford examples.[7]—Referring the Reader to those inestimable Volumes, I will content myself with placing a conceit

---

4. Shakespeare, *Romeo and Juliet* 1.4.56–57 (Mercutio teasing Romeo).
5. WW alludes to the description of Satan in *Paradise Lost* 4.987 (which, however, refers to immobility, not height): "Like Teneriffe or Atlas unremov'd." Teneriffe is the largest of the Canary Islands (with a volcanic peak) off the coast of Morocco, and the Atlas a mountain range in northwestern Africa. *Pompey's Pillar*: a monolithic triumphal column (ca. 88 feet high) built by the Romans in Alexandria in 297 C.E. ; *twelve cubits*: ca. 400 inches (the cubit being an ancient unit of measurement based on the length of a forearm).
6. This account of fancy recalls the definition given in the note to *The Thorn* in *LB 1800*: "the power by which pleasure and surprize are excited by sudden varieties of situation and by accumulated imagery."
7. WW admired the writings of the Anglican cleric and theologian Jeremy Taylor (1613–1667) (*Reading 1800–15*, no. 381), and he read to Henry Crabb Robinson from Taylor's *Dissuasive against Popery* (3rd ed., 1664) on May 13, 1812 (*CRB*, 1:83).

(ascribed to Lord Chesterfield) in contrast with a passage from the Paradise Lost;

> The dews of the evening most carefully shun,
> They are the tears of the sky for the loss of the Sun.[8]

After the transgression of Adam, Milton, with other appearances of sympathizing Nature, thus marks the immediate consequence,

> Sky lowered, and muttering thunder, some sad drops
> Wept at completion of the mortal sin.[9]

The associating link is the same in each instance;—dew or rain, not distinguishable from the liquid substance of tears, are employed as indications of sorrow. A flash of surprize is the effect in the former case, a flash of surprize and nothing more; for the nature of things does not sustain the combination. In the latter, the effects of the act, of which there is this immediate consequence and visible sign, are so momentous that the mind acknowledges the justice and reasonableness of the sympathy in Nature so manifested; and the sky weeps drops of water as if with human eyes, as "Earth had, before, trembled from her entrails, and Nature given a second groan."[1]

✳   ✳   ✳

Finally, I will refer to Cotton's "Ode upon Winter,"[2] an admirable composition though stained with some peculiarities of the age in which he lived, for a general illustration of the characteristics of Fancy. The middle part of this ode contains a most lively description of the entrance of Winter, with his retinue, as "A palsied King," and yet a military Monarch,— advancing for conquest with his Army; the several bodies of which, and their arms and equipments, are described with a rapidity of detail, and a profusion of *fanciful* comparisons, which indicate on the part of the Poet extreme activity of intellect, and a correspondent hurry of delightful feeling. He retires from the Foe into his fortress, where

> a magazine
> Of sovereign juice is cellared in.
> Liquor that will the siege maintain
> Should Phœbus ne'er return again.[3]

✳   ✳   ✳

8. From *Advice to a Lady in Autumn*, verses ascribed to Philip Dormer Stanhope, fourth earl of Chesterfield (1694–1773) in the anonymous *Life of the Late Earl of Chesterfield: or, The Man of the World* (London, 1774), 2:249, WW slightly misquoting the second line: "Those tears of the sky for the loss of the sun."
9. *Paradise Lost* 9.1002–1003.
1. *Paradise Lost* 9.1000–1001. WW proceeds to refer to his own *Address to My Infant Daughter* (composed 1804, published in *P 1815*) as an example of the "interchange" between imagination and fancy.
2. I.e., *Winter* by Charles Cotton (1630–1687), of whose *Poems on Several Occasions* (1689) WW acquired a copy at some point (*Reading 1800–15*, no. 118). Charles Lamb had copied out stanzas 21–52 of *Winter* for WW in a letter of March 5, 1803 (*CLL*, 2:98–102). The phrase *palsied King* is quoted from stanza 28.
3. Quoted from *Winter*, stanza 39. In the conclusion to the Preface, after quoting stanzas 40–49 of *Winter* "as an instance still more happy of Fancy employed in the treatment of feeling," WW expresses his "regret at the necessity of separating my compositions from some beautiful Poems of Mr. Coleridge, with which they have long been associated in publication" (i.e., in *LB*), and adverts to the inclusion of three short poems (which he does not identify) by "a Female Friend" (i.e., DW): they are *Address to a Child*, *The Mother's Return*, and *The Cottager to Her Infant*.

YEW-TREES[†]

THERE is a Yew-tree, pride of Lorton Vale,
Which to this day stands single, in the midst
Of its own darkness, as it stood of yore,
Not loth to furnish weapons for the Bands
5   Of Umfraville or Percy ere they marched
To Scotland's Heaths;[1] or Those that crossed the Sea
And drew their sounding bows at Azincour,
Perhaps at earlier Crecy, or Poictiers.[2]
Of vast circumference and gloom profound
10   This solitary Tree!—a living thing
Produced too slowly ever to decay;
Of form and aspect too magnificent
To be destroyed. But worthier still of note
Are those fraternal Four of Borrowdale,[3]
15   Joined in one solemn and capacious grove;
Huge trunks!—and each particular trunk a growth
Of intertwisted fibres serpentine
Up-coiling, and inveterately convolved,—
Nor uninformed with Phantasy, and looks
20   That threaten the prophane;—a pillared shade,
Upon whose grassless floor of red-brown hue,
By sheddings from the pining umbrage tinged
Perennially—beneath whose sable roof
Of boughs, as if for festal purpose, decked
25   With unrejoicing berries, ghostly Shapes
May meet at noontide—Fear and trembling Hope,

† Classed under "Poems of the Imagination." The earliest version was composed probably at the time of, or shortly after, WW's visit to Lorton, between September 23 and October 5, 1804; it was extensively revised between 1811 and 1814 (P2V [CW], 605). Lorton is a small village four miles southeast of Cockermouth at the northern end of the Vale of Lorton. On May 9, 1815, WW recommended to the poem to Henry Crabb Robinson as "among the best [of the "Poems of the Imagination"] for the imaginative power displayed in them," though Robinson confessed he did "not understand in what [its] excellence consists" (CRB, 1:166). In BL STC quoted lines 13–33 as an example of WW's poetry "most obviously manifesting this faculty" of imagination (NCC, 541–42).
1. WW probably means Robert Umfraville, 8th earl of Angus (ca. 1277–1325), who fought against the Scots at the Battle of Bannockburn (June 24, 1314); and either Henry Percy, 1st Lord Percy (1273–1314), who fought against the Scots under Edward I in the 1290s, or Sir Henry Percy ("Harry Hotspur," 1364–1403), who fought against the Scots in 1385 and again at the Battle of Otterburn (August 5, 1388).
2. Three battles (Agincourt, October 25, 1415; Crécy, August 26, 1345; Poitiers, September 19, 1356), fought with longbows, in the Hundred Years' War (1377–1453), a series of conflicts between England and France.
3. The valley through which the River Derwent runs north into Derwent Water. From the IF note: "These Yew-trees are still standing, but the spread of that at Lorton is much diminished by mutilation. I will here mention that a little way up the hill on the road leading from Rossthwaite to Stonethwaite [at the southern end of the valley] lay the trunk of a yewtree which appeared, as you approached, so vast was it its diameter, like the entrance of a cave & not a small one. Calculating upon what I have observed of the slow growth of this tree in rocky situations, & of its durability, I have often thought that the one I am describing must have been as old as the Christian era. The tree lay in the line of a fence. Great masses of its ruins were strown about, & some had been rolled down the hillside & lay near the road at the bottom. As you approached the tree, you were struck with the number of shrubs & young plants, ashes &c. which had found a bed upon the decayed trunk & grew to no inconsiderable height, forming, as it were, a part of the hedgerow. In no part of England, or of Europe, have I ever seen a yewtree at all approaching this in magnitude, as it must have stood."

Silence and Foresight—Death the Skeleton
And Time the Shadow,—there to celebrate,
As in a natural temple scattered o'er
30   With altars undisturbed of mossy stone,
United worship; or in mute repose
To lie, and listen to the mountain flood
Murmuring from Glaramara's inmost caves.[4]

From ESSAY, SUPPLEMENTARY TO THE PREFACE†

*   *   *

Whither then shall we turn for that union of qualifications which must necessarily exist before the decisions of a critic can be of absolute value? For a mind at once poetical and philosophical; for a critic whose affections are as free and kindly as the spirit of society, and whose understanding is severe as that of dispassionate government? Where are we to look for that initiatory composure of mind which no selfishness can disturb? For a natural sensibility that has been tutored into correctness without losing any thing of its quickness; and for active faculties capable of answering the demands which an Author of original imagination shall make upon them,—associated with a judgment that cannot be duped into admiration by aught that is unworthy of it?—Among those and those only, who, never having suffered their youthful love of poetry to remit much of its force, have applied, to the consideration of the laws of this art, the best power of their understandings. At the same time it must be observed—that, as this Class comprehends the only judgments which are trust-worthy, so does it include the most erroneous and perverse. For to be mis-taught is worse than to be untaught; and no perverseness equals that which is supported by system, no errors are so difficult to root out as those which the understanding has pledged its credit to uphold. In this Class are contained Censors, who, if they be pleased with what is good, are pleased with it only by imperfect glimpses, and upon false principles; who, should they generalize rightly to a certain point, are sure to suffer for it in the end;—who, if they stumble upon a sound rule, are fettered by misapplying it, or by straining it too far; being incapable of perceiving when it ought to yield to one of higher order. In it are found Critics too petulant to be passive to a genuine Poet, and too feeble to grapple with him; Men, who take upon them to report of the course which *he* holds whom they are utterly unable to accompany,—confounded if he turn quick upon the wing, dismayed if he soar steadily into "the region;"[1]—

---

4. Dove Nest Caves in Combe Gill on the northern slope of Glaramara, a mountain in the central Lake District.
† This essay, published at the end of volume 1 of *P 1815* and reprinted thereafter in WW's collected editions, must have been written at the same time as the Preface (probably January 1815), for WW refers to it in the last sentence of the Preface: "what I have further to remark shall be inserted, by way of interlude, at the close of this Volume." Looking over *P 1815* on April 16, 1815, Henry Crabb Robinson confided to his diary, "The supplement to his preface to his preface I wish he had left unwritten, for it will afford a triumph to his enemies. * * * But his manly avowal of his sense of his own poetic merits, I by no means censure."
1. The reference is uncertain, but possibly to Milton, *Paradise Lost* 7.425: "Part loosly wing the Region, part more wise."

Men of palsied imaginations and indurated hearts; in whose minds all healthy action is languid,—who, therefore, feed as the many direct them, or with the many, are greedy after vicious provocatives;—Judges, whose censure is auspicious, and whose praise ominous! In this Class meet together the two extremes of best and worst.

The observations presented in the foregoing series, are of too ungracious a nature to have been made without reluctance; and were it only on this account I would invite the Reader to try them by the test of comprehensive experience. If the number of judges who can be confidently relied upon be in reality so small, it ought to follow that partial notice only, or neglect, perhaps long continued, or attention wholly inadequate to their merits— must have been the fate of most works in the higher departments of poetry; and that, on the other hand, numerous productions have blazed into popularity, and have passed away, leaving scarcely a trace behind them:—it will be, further, found that when Authors have at length raised themselves into general admiration and maintained their ground, errors and prejudices have prevailed concerning their genius and their works, which the few who are conscious of those errors and prejudices would deplore; if they were not recompensed by perceiving that there are select Spirits for whom it is ordained that their fame shall be in the world an existence like that of Virtue, which owes its being to the struggles it makes, and its vigour to the enemies whom it provokes;—a vivacious quality ever doomed to meet with opposition, and still triumphing over it; and, from the nature of its dominion, incapable of being brought to the sad conclusion of Alexander, when he wept that there were no more worlds for him to conquer.[2]

*   *   *

As I do not mean to bring down this retrospect to our own times, it may with propriety be closed at the era of this distinguished event. From the literature of other ages and countries, proofs equally cogent might have been adduced that the opinions announced in the former part of this Essay are founded upon truth. It was not an agreeable office, nor a prudent undertaking, to declare them, but their importance seemed to render it a duty. It may still be asked, where lies the particular relation of what has been said to these Volumes?—The question will be easily answered by the discerning Reader who is old enough to remember the taste that was prevalent when some of these Poems were first published, 17 years ago; who has also observed to what degree the Poetry of this Island has since that period been coloured by them;[3] and who is further aware of the unremitting hostility with which, upon some principle or other, they have

2. A legend deriving from a speech by Alexander recorded by the Roman historian Quintus Curtius Rufus (first or early second century c.e.), *History of Alexander the Great* 9.6.20–22. WW's source is unknown, but *Prose*, 3:86, suggests as possibilities Robert Burton, "Democritus to the Reader" in *The Anatomy of Melancholy* (although the 1621 edition left by Charles Lamb at Allan Bank in 1810 did not yet contain the sentence concerning Alexander); and William Congreve's play *The Way of the World* (1700) 2.1.116 (see *Reading 1800–15*, nos. 76 and 111). In the succeeding section, omitted here, WW surveys poetry from the sixteenth to mid-eighteenth century.
3. *Prose*, 3:101, comments, WW "seems to mean that *Lyrical Ballads* had had a marked influence on English poetry between the 1790s and 1815. It is hard to trace such an influence, nor does Wordsworth appear to record it elsewhere, except in a few specific and trifling cases."

each and all been opposed. A sketch of my own notion of the constitution of Fame, has been given; and, as far as concerns myself, I have cause to be satisfied. The love, the admiration, the indifference, the slight, the aversion, and even the contempt, with which these Poems have been received, knowing, as I do, the source within my own mind, from which they have proceeded, and the labour and pains, which, when labour and pains appeared needful, have been bestowed upon them,—must all, if I think consistently, be received as pledges and tokens, bearing the same general impression though widely different in value;—they are all proofs that for the present time I have not laboured in vain; and afford assurances, more or less authentic, that the products of my industry will endure.[4]

If there be one conclusion more forcibly pressed upon us than another by the review which has been given of the fortunes and fate of Poetical Works, it is this,—that every Author, as far as he is great and at the same time *original*, has had the task of *creating* the taste by which he is to be enjoyed: so has it been, so will it continue to be. This remark was long since made to me by the philosophical Friend for the separation of whose Poems from my own I have previously expressed my regret.[5] The predecessors of an original Genius of a high order will have smoothed the way for all that he has in common with them;—and much he will have in common; but, for what is peculiarly his own, he will be called upon to clear and often to shape his own road:—he will be in the condition of Hannibal among the Alps.[6]

And where lies the real difficulty of creating that taste by which a truly original Poet is to be relished? Is it in breaking the bonds of custom, in overcoming the prejudices of false refinement,[7] and displacing the aversions of inexperience? Or, if he labour for an object which here and elsewhere I have proposed to myself, does it consist in divesting the Reader of the pride that induces him to dwell upon those points wherein Men differ from each other, to the exclusion of those in which all Men are alike, or the same; and in making him ashamed of the vanity that renders him insensible of the appropriate excellence which civil arrangements, less unjust than might appear, and Nature illimitable in her bounty, have conferred on Men who stand below him in the scale of society? Finally, does it lie in establishing that dominion over the spirits of Readers by which they are to be humbled and humanized, in order that they may be purified and exalted?

If these ends are to be attained by the mere communication of *knowledge*, it does *not* lie here.—TASTE, I would remind the Reader, like IMAGINATION, is a word which has been forced to extend its services far beyond

---

4. Compare WW's letter of May 21, 1807, to Lady Beaumont concerning *P2V*: "Trouble not yourself upon their present reception; of what moment is that compared with what I trust is their destiny, to console the afflicted, to * * * [make] the happy happier, to teach the young and the gracious of every age, to see, to think and feel, and therefore to become more actively and securely virtuous. * * * I have expressed my calm confidence that these Poems will live" (*WL*, 2:146, 150).
5. See the last note to the Preface (p. 578 n. 3).
6. The Carthaginian general Hannibal (247–183/182 B.C.E.) invaded Italy by leading an army (including three dozen elephants) across the Alps in 218 B.C.E. (Livy, *History of Rome* 21.30–38).
7. A phrase WW repeats, along with the argument of this paragraph, from the Preface to *LB 1800* (p. 79 above).

the point to which philosophy would have confined them. It is a metaphor, taken from a *passive* sense of the human body, and transferred to things which are in their essence *not* passive,—to intellectual *acts* and *operations*.[8] The word, imagination, has been over-strained, from impulses honourable to mankind, to meet the demands of the faculty which is perhaps the noblest of our nature. In the instance of taste, the process has been reversed; and from the prevalence of dispositions at once injurious and discreditable,—being no other than that selfishness which is the child of apathy,—which, as Nations decline in productive and creative power, makes them value themselves upon a presumed refinement of judging. Poverty of language is the primary cause of the use which we make of the word, imagination;[9] but the word, Taste, has been stretched to the sense which it bears in modern Europe by habits of self-conceit, inducing that inversion in the order of things whereby a passive faculty is made paramount among the faculties conversant with the fine arts. Proportion and congruity, the requisite knowledge being supposed, are subjects upon which taste may be trusted; it is competent to this office;—for in its intercourse with these the mind is *passive*, and is affected painfully or pleasurably as by an instinct.[1] But the profound and the exquisite in feeling, the lofty and universal in thought and imagination; or in ordinary language the pathetic[2] and the sublime;—are neither of them, accurately speaking, objects of a faculty which could ever without a sinking in the spirit of Nations have been designated by the metaphor—*Taste*. And why? Because without the exertion of a co-operating *power* in the mind of the Reader, there can be no adequate sympathy with either of these emotions: without this auxiliar impulse elevated or profound passion cannot exist.

* * * If every great Poet with whose writings men are familiar, in the highest exercise of his genius, before he can be thoroughly enjoyed, has to call forth and to communicate *power*, this service, in a still greater degree, falls upon an original Writer, at his first appearance in the world.—Of genius the only proof is, the act of doing well what is worthy to be done, and what was never done before: Of genius, in the fine arts, the only infallible sign is the widening the sphere of human sensibility, for the delight, honor, and benefit of human nature. Genius is the introduction of a new element into the intellectual universe: or, if that be not allowed, it is the application of powers to objects on which they had not before been exercised, or the employment of them in such a manner as to produce effects hitherto unknown.[3] What is all this but an advance, or a

8. *Prose*, 3:103, notes the comparable argument of Alexander Gerard, *An Essay on Taste* (Edinburgh, 1759), 110: "taste, being a faculty of a derivative kind, implies in its mental exertion mental *actions*, which are strengthened by use and exercise."
9. A thought repeated in *Prel* (1850) 6.593–94 (not present in the 1805 version): "Imagination— here the Power so called / Through sad incompetence and exercise" (*Prel 1850* [CW], 129).
1. *Prose*, 3:103, suggests that WW's argument derives from a distinction, in eighteenth-century aesthetics (e.g., Francis Hutcheson's *Inquiry into the Original of Our Ideas of Beauty and Virtue* [2nd ed., 1726]), between "absolute beauty" (beauty perceived as such without reference to another object) and "comparative beauty" (beauty perceived in objects recognized as imitations of something else).
2. "Producing an effect upon the emotions" (*OED* sense A1).
3. WW here generalizes a thought he had expressed to Henry Crabb Robinson in May 1812: "Speaking of his own poems, Wordsworth said he principally valued them as being *a new power* in the literary world * * * [and] he himself looked to the powers of the mind his poems call forth, and the energies they presuppose and excite, as the standard by which they are to be estimated" (*CRB*, 1:89).

conquest, made by the soul of the Poet? Is it to be supposed that the Reader can make progress of this kind, like an Indian Prince or General—stretched on his Palanquin,[4] and borne by his Slaves? No, he is invigorated and inspirited by his Leader, in order that he may exert himself, for he cannot proceed in quiescence, he cannot be carried like a dead weight. Therefore to create taste is to call forth and bestow power, of which knowledge is the effect; and *there* lies the true difficulty.

* * *

Away, then, with the senseless iteration of the word, *popular,* applied to new works in Poetry, as if there were no test of excellence in this first of the fine arts but that all Men should run after its productions, as if urged by an appetite, or constrained by a spell!—The qualities of writing best fitted for eager reception are either such as startle the world into attention by their audacity and extravagance;[5] or they are chiefly of a superficial kind, lying upon the surfaces of manners; or arising out of a selection and arrangement of incidents, by which the mind is kept upon the stretch of curiosity, and the fancy amused without the trouble of thought. But in every thing which is to send the soul into herself, to be admonished of her weakness or to be made conscious of her power;—wherever life and nature are described as operated upon by the creative or abstracting virtue of the imagination; wherever the instinctive wisdom of antiquity and her heroic passions uniting, in the heart of the Poet, with the meditative wisdom of later ages, have produced that accord of sublimated humanity, which is at once a history of the remote past and a prophetic annunciation of the remotest future, *there*, the Poet must reconcile himself for a season to few and scattered hearers.—Grand thoughts, (and Shakespeare must often have sighed over this truth) as they are most naturally and most fitly conceived in solitude, so can they not be brought forth in the midst of plaudits without some violation of their sanctity. Go to a silent exhibition of the productions of the Sister Art, and be convinced that the qualities which dazzle at first sight, and kindle the admiration of the multitude, are essentially different from those by which permanent influence is secured. Let us not shrink from following up these principles as far as they will carry us, and conclude with observing—that there never has been a period, and perhaps never will be, in which vicious poetry, of some kind or other, has not excited more zealous admiration, and been far more generally read, than good; but this advantage attends the good, that the *individual,* as well as the species, survives from age to age: whereas, of the depraved, though the species be immortal the individual quickly *perishes;* the object of present admiration vanishes, being supplanted by some other as easily produced; which, though no better, brings with it at least the irritation of novelty,—with adaptation, more or less skilful, to the changing humours

4. "A covered litter or conveyance * * * used in India and other Eastern countries, consisting of a large box with wooden shutters like Venetian blinds, carried by four or six (rarely two) men by means of poles projecting before and behind" (*OED*).
5. *Prose,* 3:106, suggests plausibly that WW may have had in mind Lord Byron, whose poems published between 1812 and 1815 had sold tens of thousands of copies. In general WW's criticism here of contemporary literature recalls that in the Preface to *LB 1800.*

of the majority of those who are most at leisure to regard poetical works when they first solicit their attention.

Is it the result of the whole that, in the opinion of the Writer, the judgment of the People is not to be respected? The thought is most injurious; and could the charge be brought against him, he would repel it with indignation. The People have already been justified, and their eulogium pronounced by implication, when it was said, above—that, of *good* Poetry, the *individual*, as well as the species, *survives*. And how does it survive but through the People? what preserves it but their intellect and their wisdom?

> ——Past and future, are the wings
> On whose support, harmoniously conjoined,
> Moves the great Spirit of human knowledge——
>   *MS.*[6]

The voice that issues from this Spirit, is that Vox populi which the Deity inspires.[7] Foolish must he be who can mistake for this a local acclamation, or a transitory outcry—transitory though it be for years, local though from a Nation. Still more lamentable is his error, who can believe that there is any thing of divine infallibility in the clamour of that small though loud portion of the community, ever governed by factitious influence, which, under the name of the PUBLIC, passes itself, upon the unthinking, for the PEOPLE.[8] Towards the Public, the Writer hopes that he feels as much deference as it is intitled to: but to the People, philosophically characterized, and to the embodied spirit of their knowledge, so far as it exists and moves, at the present, faithfully supported by its two wings, the past and the future, his devout respect, his reverence, is due. He offers it willingly and readily; and, this done, takes leave of his Readers, by assuring them—that, if he were not persuaded that the Contents of these Volumes, and the Work to which they are subsidiary, evinced something of the "Vision and the Faculty divine;"[9] and that, both in words and things, they will operate in their degree, to extend the domain of sensibility for the delight, the honor, and the benefit of human nature, notwithstanding the many happy hours which he has employed in their composition, and the manifold comforts and enjoyments they have procured to him, he would not, if a wish could do it, save them from immediate destruction;—from becoming at this moment, to the world, as a thing that had never been.

---

6. *Prel* (1850) 6.449–51 (a passage not present in the 1805 version).
7. WW plays on the proverb (usually used ironically) *vox populi, vox Dei*, "The voice of the people is the voice of God."
8. *PUBLIC . . . PEOPLE*: WW here articulates publicly a distinction he had made privately in letters since 1808 (e.g., *WL*, 2: 145, 194).
9. *Exc* 1.79.

YARROW VISITED
September, 1814[†]

AND is this—Yarrow?—*This* the Stream
Of which my fancy cherish'd,
So faithfully, a waking dream?
An image that hath perish'd!
5 O that some Minstrel's harp were near,
To utter notes of gladness,
And chase this silence from the air,
That fills my heart with sadness!

Yet why?—a silvery current flows
10 With uncontrolled meanderings;
Nor have these eyes by greener hills
Been soothed, in all my wanderings.
And, through her depths, Saint Mary's Lake[1]
Is visibly delighted;
15 For not a feature of those hills
Is in the mirror slighted.

A blue sky bends o'er Yarrow vale,
Save where that pearly whiteness
Is round the rising sun diffused,
20 A tender, hazy brightness;
Mild dawn of promise! that excludes
All profitless dejection;
Though not unwilling here to admit
A pensive recollection.

25 Where was it that the famous Flower
Of Yarrow Vale lay bleeding?
His bed perchance was yon smooth mound
On which the herd is feeding:
And haply from this crystal pool,
30 Now peaceful as the morning,

† Classed under "Poems of the Imagination." Composed in early September 1814, revised
between mid-September and late October (*Chrono: MY*, 52; *Shorter Poems, 1807–1820* [CW],
137). Yarrow Water is a river ca. 30 miles south of Edinburgh in the Borders region of Scot-
land. During their Scottish tour of 1803, WW and DW had decided not to visit the river (*DWJ*,
1:391), and afterwards WW composed *Yarrow Unvisited* (published in *P2V* and reprinted imme-
diately before this poem in *P 1815*), a mock-ballad dramatizing their decision. On September 1,
1814, WW did visit the Yarrow with MW, Sara Hutchinson, and, as he recalled in his IF note,
the poet James Hogg (on whom see *Extempore Effusion upon the Death of James Hogg*, p. 551
below) and Robert Anderson (1750–1807), editor of the anthology *The Works of the British
Poets* (1795–1807), which WW's brother John had given to him (IF note; *Reading 1800–15*, no.
9). WW also told IF, "I seldom read or think of this poem without regretting that my dear Sister
was not of the party, as she would have had so much delight in recalling the time when, travel-
ling together in Scotland, we declined going in search of this celebrated stream, not altogether,
I will frankly confess, for the reasons assigned in the poem [*Yarrow Unvisited*] on the occa-
sion." In that poem the poet's persona agrees not to visit the river in order to preserve the image
of it that he has derived from eighteenth-century ballads set there.
1. St. Mary's Loch, the source of the Yarrow.

The Water-wraith ascended thrice—
And gave his doleful warning.[2]

Delicious is the Lay[3] that sings
The haunts of happy Lovers,
35 The path that leads them to the grove,
The leafy grove that covers:
And Pity sanctifies the verse
That paints, by strength of sorrow,
The unconquerable strength of love;
40 Bear witness, rueful Yarrow!

But thou, that didst appear so fair
To fond imagination,
Dost rival in the light of day
Her delicate creation:
45 Meek loveliness is round thee spread,
A softness still and holy;
The grace of forest charms decayed,
And pastoral melancholy.[4]

That Region left, the Vale unfolds
50 Rich groves of lofty stature,
With Yarrow winding through the pomp
Of cultivated nature;
And, rising from those lofty groves,
Behold a Ruin hoary!
55 The shattered front of Newark's Towers,
Renowned in Border story.[5]

Fair scenes for childhood's opening bloom,
For sportive youth to stray in;
For manhood to enjoy his strength;
60 And age to wear away in!
Yon Cottage seems a bower of bliss;
It promises protection
To studious ease, and generous cares,
And every chaste affection![6]

2. In lines 25–32 WW combines references to two ballads called *The Braes of Yarrow*, one by William Hamilton (1704–1754) and the other by John Logan (1748–1788). In Hamilton's poem a young man is speared to death on the river bank by a rival for the affections of a "bonny bride" (*Poems on Several Occasions* [Edinburgh, 1760], 67–72); in Logan's poem, from which the phrase "the flower of Yarrow" is taken, a young woman learns of her lover's drowning in the river from the appearance of his ghost: "Thrice did the water-wraith ascend, / And gave a doleful groan thro' Yarrow" (*Poems* [London, 1780], 4–7).
3. A short poem intended to be sung.
4. Charles Lamb wrote WW on April 28, 1815, that "no lovelier stanza [than lines 41–48] can be found in the wide world of poetry—yet the poem on the whole seems condemned to have behind it a melancholy of imperfect satisfaction, as you had wronged the feeling with which in what had preceded it [*Yarrow Unvisited*] you had resolved never to visit it" (*CLL*, 3:146–47).
5. Newark Castle, a fifteenth-century ruined castle in the Yarrow Valley and a setting of Walter Scott's popular narrative poem *The Lay of the Last Minstrel* (1805). In September 1831 WW visited the castle with Scott.
6. In *MP 1820* WW altered lines 62–64 to "It promises protection / To all the nestling brood of thoughts / Sustained by chaste affection!"

65 How sweet, on this autumnal day,
The wild wood's fruits to gather,
And on my True-love's[7] forehead plant
A crest of blooming heather!
And what if I enwreathed my own!
70 'Twere no offence to reason;
The sober Hills thus deck their brows
To meet the wintry season.

I see—but not by sight alone,
Lov'd Yarrow, have I won thee;
75 A ray of Fancy still survives—
Her sunshine plays upon thee!
Thy ever-youthful waters keep
A course of lively pleasure;
And gladsome notes my lips can breathe,
80 Accordant to the measure.

The vapours linger round the Heights,
They melt—and soon must vanish;
One hour is theirs', nor more is mine—
Sad thought, which I would banish,
85 But that I know, where'er I go,
Thy genuine image, Yarrow,
Will dwell with me—to heighten joy,
And cheer my mind in sorrow.

Surprized by joy—impatient as the Wind[†]

SURPRIZED by joy—impatient as the Wind
I wished[1] to share the transport—Oh! with whom
But Thee, long[2] buried in the silent Tomb,
That spot which no vicissitude can find?
5 Love, faithful love recalled thee to my mind—
But how could I forget thee?—Through what power,
Even for the least division of an hour,
Have I been so beguiled as to be blind
To my most grievous loss?—That thought's return
10 Was the worst pang that sorrow ever bore,
Save one, one only, when I stood forlorn,
Knowing my heart's best treasure was no more;
That neither present time, nor years unborn
Could to my sight that heavenly face restore.

7. MW, who accompanied WW to Yarrow in 1814.
† Classed under "Miscellaneous Sonnets." Composed probably between 1813 and mid-October 1814 (*Chrono: MY*, 51). IF note: "This was in fact suggested by my daughter Catherine long after her death." Catharine had died suddenly on June 4, 1812, aged four.
1. Altered in *MP 1820* to "turned."
2. Altered in *MP 1820* to "deep."

From THANKSGIVING ODE, JANUARY 18, 1816, WITH OTHER SHORT PIECES (1816)

In May 1809 WW had published the pamphlet *Concerning the Convention of Cintra* to express his passionate disapproval of the agreement of August 30, 1808, whereby French forces, which had been routed by British forces under Sir Arthur Wellesley at Vimeiro, Portugal, were permitted to withdraw unhindered and with all their equipment. In June 1815 Wellesley, now the 1st Duke of Wellington, commanded the army that defeated Napoleon's Imperial French forces at Waterloo, Belgium. After January 18, 1816, a day of national thanksgiving proclaimed to commemorate Napoleon's defeat, Wordsworth composed an ode for the occasion and gathered it in March with eleven "Miscellaneous Piece, referring chiefly to recent public events" into a volume that was published in the late spring (*Shorter Poems, 1807–1820* [CW], 535–36). As he explained to John Scott on March 11, "I could not resist the Temptation of giving vent to my feelings as collected in force upon the morning of the day appointed for a general Thanksgiving. Accordingly, I threw off a sort of irregular Ode upon this subject, which spread to nearly 350 lines" (*WL*, 3:284). In a six-page Advertisement, WW explained the motivations of the volume: "the present publication owes its existence to a patriotism, anxious to exert itself in commemorating that course of action, by which Great Britain has, for some time past, distinguished herself above all other countries." Anticipating that, in the face of the hardships created by almost twenty-two years of war against the French, readers might object to his "exultation, unchecked by these distresses," Wordsworth stated "his own belief that these sufferings will be transitory." He then proceeded to advocate "martial propensities, and an assiduous cultivation of military virtues" as the means of insuring Britain's independence, freedom, and security in the future. "Politically," as Mary Moorman observes, "Wordsworth had now come to a point of no return" (2:292).

Wordsworth's celebration of military power, particularly in lines 279–82 of the *Ode*, did indeed appall some of his contemporaries. In the *Examiner* of February 22, 1818, Leigh Hunt quoted line 282 as evidence of Wordsworth's "strange piety" (122), while Percy Bysshe Shelley satirized the lines bitterly in his *Peter Bell the Third* (composed 1819, published 1840), lines 634–43 (*Shelley's Poetry and Prose*, ed. Donald Reiman and Neil Fraistat [New York, 2001], 361):

> Then Peter wrote odes to the Devil;—
> In one of which he meekly said:—
> "May Carnage and Slaughter,
> Thy niece and thy daughter,
> May Rapine and Famine,

> Thy gorge ever cramming,
> Glut thee with living and dead!

> "May death and damnation,
> And Consternation,
> Flit up from Hell with pure intent!"

Four years later, in canto 8, stanza 9 of *Don Juan*, Lord Byron too quoted Wordsworth by way of condemning his justification of violence in the Thanksgiving Ode:

> "Carnage" (so Wordsworth tells you) "is God's daughter:"
> If *he* speak truth, she is Christ's sister, and
> Just now behaved as in the Holy Land.

To ensure that his meaning was clear, Byron added a note in which he quoted lines 279–82 and commented, "this is perhaps as pretty a pedigree for Murder as ever was found out by Garter King at Arms [i.e., the senior heraldic authority in England and Wales]." But only in 1845, when he divided the ode into two poems, did Wordsworth omit lines 281–82.

The *Ode* volume, in 64 pages, was published in an edition of 500 copies, of which 220 remained unsold by 1834 (Owen, "Costs, Sales, and Profits," 98–99). In a note before the *Ode* WW pointed out, "This Publication may be considered as a sequel to the Author's 'Sonnets, dedicated to Liberty;' it is therefore printed uniform with the two volumes of his Poems [*P 1815*] * * * to admit of their being conveniently bound up together." The two poems included here from the volume are printed from the original edition.

ODE

THE MORNING OF THE DAY APPOINTED FOR A

GENERAL THANKSGIVING

January 18, 1816[†]

HAIL, universal Source of pure delight![1]
Thou that canst shed the bliss of gratitude
On hearts howe'er insensible or rude,

[†] Composed between January 18 and February 25, 1816 (*Shorter Poems, 1807–1820* [CW], 180). See the headnote for the occasion of the poem. WW described it to Robert Southey as not strictly an ode, "but a poem composed or supposed to be composed on the morning of the thanksgiving, uttering the sentiments of an individual upon that occasion. It is a dramatised ejaculation; and this, if anything can, must excuse the irregular frame of the metre" (*WL*, 3:324). In *MP 1820* he placed the poem after the "Sonnets dedicated to Liberty" with its own title page. He revised the poem extensively in 1836 (only the most significant revisions being noted here), and in his 1845 *Poetical Works* divided the ode into two poems, one preserving the original title and the other called *Ode. 1815* (see *Shorter Poems, 1807–1820* [CW], 190–200). IF note: "The first stanza of this Ode was composed almost extempore in front of Rydal Mount before Church-time, on such a morning and precisely with such objects before my eyes as are here described. The view taken of Napoleon's character and proceedings is little in accordance with that taken by some historians and critical philosophers. I am glad & proud of the difference, and trust that this series of poems, infinitely below the subject as they are, will survive to counteract in unsophisticated minds the pernicious and degrading tendency of those views and doctrines that lead to the idolatry of power as power, and in that false splendour to lose sight of its real nature and constitution as it often acts for the gratification of its possessor or without reference to a beneficial end—an infirmity that has characterised men of all ages, classes, & employments since Nimrod became a mighty hunter before the Lord." WW alludes to Genesis 10.9, in which Nimrod, a great-grandson of Noah, is described as "a mighty hunter before the Lord."

1. Line 1 was altered in 1836 to "Hail, orient Conqueror of gloomy Night!"

Whether thy orient visitations smite
5   The haughty towers where monarchs dwell;
Or thou, impartial Sun, with presence bright
Cheer'st the low threshold of the Peasant's cell!
—Not unrejoiced I see thee climb the sky
In naked splendour, clear from mist or haze,
10   Or cloud approaching to divert the rays,
Which even in deepest winter testify
            Thy power and majesty,
Dazzling the vision that presumes to gaze.
—Well does thine aspect usher in this Day;
15   As aptly suits therewith that timid pace,
Framed in subjection to the chains
That bind thee to the path which God ordains
            That thou shalt trace,
Till, with the heavens and earth, thou pass away!
20   Nor less the stillness of these frosty plains,
Their utter stillness,—and the silent grace
Of yon etherial summits white with snow,
Whose tranquil pomp, and spotless purity,
            Report of storms gone by
25   To us who tread below,
Do with the service of this Day accord
—Divinest object, which the uplifted eye
Of mortal man is suffered to behold,
Thou, who upon yon snow-clad Heights hast poured
30   Meek splendour, nor forget'st the humble Vale,
Thou who dost warm Earth's universal mould,—
And for thy bounty wert not unadored
            By pious men of old;
Once more, heart-cheering Sun, I bid thee hail!
35   Bright be thy course to-day, let not this promise fail!

    Mid the deep quiet of this morning hour,
All nature seems to hear me while I speak,—
By feelings urged, that do not vainly seek
Apt language, ready as the tuneful notes
40   That stream in blithe succession from the throats
            Of birds in leafy bower,
Warbling a farewell to a vernal shower.
—There is a radiant but a short-lived flame,
That burns for Poets in the dawning East;—
45   And oft my soul hath kindled at the same,
When the captivity of sleep had ceased;
But he who fixed immovably the frame
Of the round world, and built, by laws as strong,
            A solid refuge for distress,
50   The towers of righteousness;
He knows that from a holier altar came
The quickening spark of this day's sacrifice;
Knows that the source is nobler whence doth rise

The current of this matin song;
55   That deeper far it lies
Than aught dependant on the fickle skies.

Have we not conquered?—By the vengeful sword?
Ah no, by dint of Magnanimity;
That curbed the baser passions, and left free
60   A loyal hand to follow their liege Lord,
Clear-sighted Honour—and his staid Compeers,
Along a track of most unnatural years,
In execution of heroic deeds;
Whose memory, spotless as the crystal beads
65   Of morning dew upon the untrodden meads,
Shall live enrolled above the starry spheres.
—Who to the murmurs of an earthly string
          Of Britain's acts would sing,
          He with enraptured voice will tell
70   Of One whose spirit no reverse could quell;
Of One that mid the failing never failed:
Who paints how Britain struggled and prevailed,
Shall represent her labouring with an eye
          Of circumspect humanity;
75   Shall shew her clothed with strength and skill,
          All martial duties to fulfil;
Firm as a rock in stationary fight;
In motion rapid as the lightning's gleam;
Fierce as a flood-gate bursting in the night
80   To rouse the wicked from their giddy dream—
Woe, woe to all that face her in the field!
Appalled she may not be, and cannot yield.

And thus is missed the sole true glory
          That can belong to human story!
85   At which *they* only shall arrive
          Who through the abyss of weakness dive:
The very humblest are too proud of heart:
And one brief day is rightly set apart
To Him who lifteth up and layeth low;
90   For that Almighty God to whom we owe,
Say not that we have vanquished—but that we survive.

How dreadful the dominion of the impure!
Why should the song he tardy to proclaim
That less than power unbounded could not tame
95   That Soul of Evil—which, from Hell let loose,
Had filled the astonished world with such abuse,
As boundless patience only could endure?
—Wide-wasted regions—cities wrapped in flame—
Who sees, and feels, may lift a streaming eye
100   To Heaven,—who never saw may heave a sigh;
But the foundation of our nature shakes,

And with an infinite pain the spirit aches,
When desolated countries, towns on fire,
     Are but the avowed attire
105 Of warfare waged with desperate mind
Against the life of virtue in mankind;
      Assaulting without ruth
      The citadels of truth;
While the old forest of civility[2]
110 Is doomed to perish, to the last fair tree.

   A crouching purpose—a distracted will—
Opposed to hopes that battened upon soon,
And to desires whose ever-waxing horn
Not all the light of earthily power could fill;
115 Opposed to dark, deep plots of patient skill,
And the celerities of lawless force
Which, spurning God, had flung away remorse—
What could they gain but shadows of redress?
—So bad proceeded propagating worse;
120 And discipline was passion's dire excess.[3]
Widens the fatal web—its lines extend,
And deadlier poisons in the chalice blend—
When will your trials teach you to be wise?
—O prostrate Lands, consult your agonies!

125   No more—the guilt is banished,
   And with the Guilt the Shame is fled,
And with the Guilt and Shame the Woe hath vanished,
Shaking the dust and ashes from her head!
—No more, these lingerings of distress
130 Sully the limpid stream of thankfulness.
    What robe can Gratitude employ[4]
So seemly as the radiant vest of Joy?
What steps so suitable as those that move
In prompt obedience to spontaneous measures
135 Of glory—and felicity—and love,
Surrendering the whole heart to sacred pleasures?

    Land of our fathers! precious unto me
Since the first joys of thinking infancy;[5]

---

2. On August 22, 1836, the poet John Kenyon objected to WW that "the two words 'forest' and 'civility'—both in derivation and in their actual usage—contradict each other." WW accepted the criticism, explaining, "the Forest was intended * * * as a metaphor to express those usages and habits of civilization, which from their antiquity may be compared to a forest whose origin is unknown" (*WL*, 6:293 and n.). In 1836 he replaced lines 109–10 with a quatrain: "While the fair gardens of civility, / By ignorance defaced, / By violence laid waste, / Perish without reprieve for flower or tree."
3. WW's note: "'A discipline the rule whereof is passion.'—LORD BROOK." WW quotes from stanza 7 of *A Treatie of Warres* by Fulke Greville, Baron Brooke (1554–1628). WW had been reading Greville's works in 1809 (*Reading 1800–15*, no. 190.ii).
4. In the 1816 volume the printer mistakenly inserted a stanza break between lines 130 and 131, as WW complained in a letter of January 29, 1816 (*WL*, 3:277–78).
5. In 1836 WW inserted three new lines after line 138: "Loved with a passion since I caught thy praise / A Listener, at or on some patient knee, / With an ear fastened to rude ballad lays—."

When of thy gallant chivalry I read,
140 And hugged the volume on my sleepless bed!
O England!—dearer far than life is dear,
If I forget thy prowess, never more
Be thy ungrateful son allowed to hear
Thy green leaves rustle, or thy torrents roar!
145 But how can *He* be faithless to the past,
Whose soul, intolerant of base decline,
Saw in thy virtue a celestial sign,
That bade him hope, and to his hope cleave fast!
The nations strove with puissance;—at length
150 Wide Europe heaved; impatient to be cast,
    With *all* her living strength,
    With *all* her armed powers,
    Upon the offensive shores.
The trumpet blew a universal blast!
155 But Thou art foremost in the field;—there stand:
Receive the triumph destined to thy Hand!
All States have glorified themselves;—their claims
Are weighed by Providence, in balance even;
And now, in preference to the mightiest names,
160 To Thee the *exterminating sword* is given.
Dread mark of approbation, justly gained!
Exalted office, worthily sustained!

    Imagination, ne'er before content,
    But aye ascending, restless in her pride,
165   From all that man's performance could present,
    Stoops to that closing deed magnificent,
    And with the embrace is satisfied.
    —Fly, ministers of Fame,
Whate'er your means, whatever help ye claim,
170 Bear through the world these tidings of delight
—Hours, Days, and Months, have borne them in the sight
Of mortals, travelling faster than the shower,
    That land-ward stretches from the sea,
    The morning's splendors to devour;[6]
175 But this appearance scattered extacy,—
And heart-sick Europe blessed the healing power.
    —*The shock is given—the Adversaries bleed*—
    Lo, Justice triumphs! Earth is freed!
Such glad assurance suddenly went forth—
180 It pierced the caverns of the sluggish North—
    It found no barrier on the ridge
Of Andes—frozen gulphs became its bridge—
The vast Pacific gladdens with the freight—
Upon the Lakes of Asia 'tis bestowed—
185 The Arabian desert shapes a willing road
    Across her burning breast,

6. In 1836 WW inserted a new line after 174: "In summer's loveliest hour."

For this refreshing incense from the West!
        —Where snakes and lions breed,
Where towns and cities thick as stars appear;
190 Wherever fruits are gathered, and where'er
The upturned soil receives the hopeful seed—
While the Sun rules, and cross the shades of night—
The unwearied arrow hath pursued its flight!
The eyes of good men thankfully give heed,
195   And in its sparkling progress read
How virtue triumphs, from her bondage freed![7]
Tyrants exult to hear of kingdoms won,
And slaves are pleased to learn that mighty feats are done;
Even the proud Realm, from whose distracted borders
200 This messenger of good was launched in air,
France, conquered France amid her wild disorders,
Feels, and hereafter shall the truth declare,
That she too lacks not reason to rejoice,
And utter England's name with sadly-plausive voice.

205   Preserve, O Lord! within our hearts
        The memory of thy favour,
        That else insensibly departs,
        And loses its sweet savour!
Lodge it within us!—As the power of light
210 Lives inexhaustibly in precious gems,
Fixed on the front of Eastern diadems,
So shine our thankfulness for ever bright!
What offering, what transcendant monument
Shall our sincerity to Thee present?
215 —Not work of hands; but trophies that may reach
To highest Heaven—the labour of the soul;
That builds, as thy unerring precepts teach,
Upon the inward victories of each,
Her hope of lasting glory for the whole.
220 —Yet might it well become that City now,
Into whose breast the tides of grandeur flow,
To whom all persecuted men retreat;
If a new temple lift its votive brow
Upon the shore of silver Thames—to greet
225 The peaceful guest advancing from afar?
Bright be the distant fabric, as a star
Fresh risen—and beautiful within!—there meet
Dependance infinite, proportion just;
—A pile that grace approves, and time can trust.[8]

230   But if the valiant of this land
In reverential modesty demand,
That all observance, due to them, be paid

---

7. Line 196 was altered in 1836 to "Of virtue crowned with glory's deathless meed."
8. In 1836 WW inserted a new line after 229: "With his most sacred wealth, heroic dust!"

Where their serene progenitors are laid;
Kings, warriors, high-souled poets, saint-like sages,
235 England's illustrious sons of long, long ages;
Be it not unordained that solemn rites,
Within the circuit of those gothic walls,[9]
Shall be performed at pregnant intervals;
Commemoration holy that unites
240 The living generations with the dead;
       By the deep soul-moving sense
       Of religious eloquence,—
       By visual pomp, and by the tie
       Of sweet and threatening harmony;
245   Soft notes, awful as the omen
       Of destructive tempests coming,
       And escaping from that sadness
       Into elevated gladness;
       While the white-rob'd choir attendant,
250   Under mouldering banners pendant,
Provoke all potent symphonies to raise
       Songs of victory and praise,
For them who bravely stood unhurt—or bled
With medicable wounds, or found their graves
255 Upon the battle field—or under ocean's waves;
Or were conducted home in single state,
And long procession—there to lie,
Where their sons' sons, and all posterity,
Unheard by them, their deeds shall celebrate!

260   Nor will the God of peace and love
       Such martial service disapprove.
       He guides the Pestilence—the cloud
       Of locusts travels on his breath;
       The region that in hope was ploughed
265 His drought consumes, his mildew taints with death;
       He springs the hushed Volcano's mine,
He puts the Earthquake on her still design,[1]
Darkens the sun, hath bade the forest sink,
And, drinking towns and cities, still can drink
270 Cities and towns—'tis Thou—the work is Thine!
—The fierce Tornado sleeps within thy courts—
       He hears the word—he flies—
       And navies perish in their posts;
For Thou art angry with thine enemies!
275   For these, and for our errors,
       And sins that point their terrors,
We bow our heads before Thee, and we laud
And magnify thy name, Almighty God!

9. I.e., of Westminster Abbey in London.
1. This line was admired by Henry Crabb Robinson, who thought that it "deserves to pass into a proverb" (CRB, 1:182).

But thy most dreaded instrument,
280   In working out a pure intent,
         Is Man—arrayed for mutual slaughter,—
         Yea, Carnage is thy daughter![2]
Thou cloth'st the wicked in their dazzling mail,
And by thy just permission[3] they prevail;
285   Thine arm from peril guards the coasts
             Of them who in thy laws delight:
Thy presence turns the scale of doubtful fight,
Tremendous God of battles, Lord of Hosts!

                To THEE—TO THEE—[4]
290 On this appointed Day shall thanks ascend,
     That Thou hast brought our warfare to an end,
     And that we need no further victory!
     Ha! what a ghastly sight for man to see;
     And to the heavenly saints in peace who dwell,
295   For a brief moment, terrible;
     But to thy sovereign penetration fair,
     Before whom all things are, that were,
     All judgments that have been, or e'er shall be,
     Links in the chain of thy tranquillity!
300 Along the bosom of this favoured nation,
     Breathe thou, this day, a vital undulation!
             Let all who do this land inherit
             Be conscious of Thy moving spirit!
     Oh, 'tis a goodly Ordinance,—the sight,
305 Though sprung from bleeding war, is one of pure delight;
     Bless thou the hour, or ere the hour arrive,
     When a whole people shall kneel down in prayer,
     And, at one moment, in one spirit, strive
     With lip and heart to tell their gratitude
310   For thy protecting care,
     Their solemn joy—praising the Eternal Lord
             For tyranny subdued,
     And for the sway of equity renewed,
     For liberty confirmed, and peace restored!

315   But hark—the summons!—down the placid Lake
     Floats the soft cadence of the Church-tower bells;
     Bright shines the Sun, as if his beams might wake
     The tender insects sleeping in their cells;
     Bright shines the Sun—and not a breeze to shake
320 The drops that point the melting icicles:—

2. See the headnote for the poetic responses to lines 279–82 from P. B. Shelley and Lord Byron. When WW republished the *Ode* as two poems in 1845, he included this stanza in *Ode. 1815* but omitted lines 281–82.
3. *by . . . permission*: altered in 1836 to "for thy righteous purpose."
4. In 1836 WW added five new lines before 289: "Forbear:—to Thee— / With fervent thoughts, but in a gentler strain / Of Contemplation, by no sense of wrong, / (Too quick and keen) incited to disdain / Of pity pleading from the heart in vain—." He also inserted a line after 289: "Just God of christianised Humanity."

O, enter now his temple gate!
Inviting words—perchance already flung,
(As the crowd press devoutly down the aisle
Of some old minster's venerable pile)
325   From voices into zealous passion stung,
While the tubed engine feels the inspiring blast,
And has begun—its clouds of sound to cast
                Towards the empyreal Heaven,
                As if the fretted roof were riven.
330   *Us,* humbler ceremonies now await;
But in the bosom with devout respect,
The banner of our joy we will erect,
And strength of love our souls shall elevate:
For to a few collected in his name,
335   Their heavenly Father will incline his ear,
Hallowing himself the service which they frame;—
Awake! the majesty of God revere!
        Go—and with foreheads meekly bowed
Present your prayers—go—and rejoice aloud—
340   The Holy One will hear!
And what mid silence deep, with faith sincere,
Ye, in your low and undisturbed estate,
Shall simply feel and purely meditate
Of warnings—from the unprecedented might,
345   Which, in our time, the impious have disclosed;
And of more arduous duties thence imposed
Upon the future advocates of right;
                Of mysteries revealed,
                And judgments unrepealed,—
350   Of earthly revolution,
                And final retribution,—
        To his omniscience will appear
An offering not unworthy to find place,
On this high DAY of THANKS, before the Throne of Grace!

To R. B. Haydon, Esq.†

HIGH is our calling, Friend!—Creative Art
(Whether the instrument of words she use,
Or pencil pregnant with etherial hues,)
Demands the service of a mind and heart,

† *MP 1820:* Miscellaneous Sonnets. Composed ca. November 30, 1815 (*Shorter Poems, 1807–1820* [CW], 174), sent in a letter to Haydon on December 21 (*WL,* 3:257–59), and first published in the *Examiner* and the *Champion* simultaneously on March 31, 1816. Benjamin Robert Haydon (1786–1846) was an English painter who favored historical and biblical scenes. Although commercially unsuccessful, he was admired by WW. His immense painting *Christ's Entry into Jerusalem* (1815–20) includes portraits of WW and John Keats (see *WL,* 3:577 and n. 1), and his separate 1842 portrait of WW (now in the National Portrait Gallery, London) is one of the best-known representations of the poet. On their troubled relationship in the years after 1815, see Gill, 314. WW was evidently confused about the order of Haydon's initials, and although they were printed correctly in the periodical publications, they remained reversed in WW's own volumes until 1836.

5 Though sensitive, yet, in their weakest part,
   Heroically fashioned—to infuse
   Faith in the whispers of the lonely Muse,
   While the whole world seems adverse to desert:
   And, oh! when Nature sinks, as oft she may,
10 Through long-lived pressure of obscure distress,
   Still to be strenuous for the bright reward,
   And in the soul admit of no decay,—
   Brook no continuance of weak-mindedness:—
   Great is the glory, for the strife is hard!

From THE RIVER DUDDON: A SERIES OF SONNETS: VAUDRACOUR AND JULIA; AND OTHER POEMS (1820)[†]

From The River Duddon: A Series of Sonnets

XXXIII.

CONCLUSION[‡]

Wordsworth loved rivers.

I THOUGHT of Thee, my partner and my guide,
As being past away.—Vain sympathies!
For, *backward*, Duddon! as I cast my eyes,
I see what was, and is, and will abide;
5 Still glides the Stream, and shall for ever glide;[1]
The Form remains, the Function never dies;
While *we*, the brave, the mighty, and the wise,
We Men, who in our morn of youth defied
The elements, must vanish;—be it so!
10 Enough, if something from our hands have power
To live, and act, and <u>serve the future hour;</u>
And if, as tow'rd the silent tomb we go,

---

† The volume, dedicated to WW's brother Christopher, was published with a brief Advertisement: "This Publication, together with 'The Thanksgiving Ode,' Jan. 18, 1816, 'The Tale of Peter Bell,' and 'The Waggoner,' completes the third and last volume of the Author's Miscellaneous Poems." Stephen Gill observes that it "is a poetical miscellany," containing such forms as "a lament, inscriptions, lyric addresses, odes and further sonnets, and a short topographical effusion [*Composed at Cora Linn*]. * * * [I]t is a highly literary showcase of skill in traditional forms, which draws on classical and historical sources" ("Wordsworth and *The River Duddon*," 24–25). It is also very grounded in the Lake District, opening with the sonnet sequence *The River Duddon*, closing with a 108-page prose "Topographical Description of the Lakes," and including 27 pages of notes on the sonnets.

‡ The last of a sequence of thirty-three sonnets "called forth by one of the most beautiful streams of his native country" (as WW expresses it in the volume's dedication), on which WW provides a topographical note to preface the sequence: "The River Duddon rises upon Wrynose Tell, on the confines of Westmorland, Cumberland, and Lancashire; and, serving as a boundary to the two latter counties, for the space of about twenty-five miles, enters the Irish sea, between the isle of Walney and the lordship of Milum." The sequence was composed at intervals from 1802 to 1820, the *Conclusion* (with seven others) between December 1818 and March 1819 (*Sonnet Series and Itinerary Poems, 1820–1845* [CW], 55, 75).

1. Probably an echo of Philip Francis's 1746 translation (of which WW owned the 1807 edition) of Horace's *Epistle* 2.43: "Still glides the river, and will ever glide" (*Sonnet Series and Itinerary Poems* [CW], 109).

Thro' love, thro' hope, and faith's transcendant dower,
We feel that we are greater than we know.[2]

gift

COMPOSED AT CORA LINN,

IN SIGHT OF WALLACE'S TOWER[†]

"—How Wallace fought for Scotland, left the name
Of Wallace to be found, like a wild flower,
All over his dear Country; left the deeds
Of Wallace, like a family of ghosts,
To people the steep rocks and river banks
Her natural sanctuaries, with a local soul
Of independence and stern liberty."   *MS.*

LORD of the Vale! astounding Flood!
The dullest leaf, in this thick wood,
Quakes—conscious of thy power;
The caves reply with hollow moan;
5 And vibrates, to its central stone,
Yon time-cemented Tower!

And yet how fair the rural scene!
For thou, O Clyde, hast ever been
Beneficent as strong;
10 Pleased in refreshing dews to steep
The little trembling flowers that peep
Thy shelving rocks among.

Hence all who love their country, love
To look on thee—delight to rove
15 Where they thy voice can hear;
And, to the patriot-warrior's Shade,
Lord of the vale! to Heroes laid
In dust, that voice is dear!

2. WW's note: "'And I feel that I am happier than I know.'—MILTON. The allusion to the Greek
Poet will be obvious to the classical reader." The quotation is from *Paradise Lost* 8.282. The
allusion, in line 7, is to a line from the *Lament for Bion* by the Hellenistic poet Moschus (sec-
ond century B.C.E.). In 1788 or 1789, while at Cambridge, WW had translated the passage
(lines 99–104) in which the line occurs, and here he echoes his translation closely: "But we the
great the mighty and the wise / Soon as we perish in the hollow earth * * * Slumber a vast inter-
minable sleep" (*Early Poems and Fragments, 1785–1797* [CW], 690; see also *Sonnet Series and
Itinerary Poems* [CW], 109).
† MP 1820: Poems of the Imagination. Composed between July 25, 1814 (when WW visited
Corra Linn with MW and Sara Hutchinson), and ca. early 1820, the earliest version (for which
see *Shorter Poems, 1807–1820* [CW], 126–28) being extensively revised before the poem was
published in the *River Duddon* volume. The epigraph is *The Prelude* 1.216–22 (and see the
note to those lines on the Scottish patriot Sir William Wallace [ca. 1270–1305]). Corra Linn is
the largest of the four Falls of the Clyde on the River Clyde near New Lanark, Scotland. IF
note: "I had seen this celebrated Waterfall twice before [in 1801 and 1803]. But the feelings to
which it had given birth were not expressed till they recurred in presence of the object on this
occasion." *Wallace's Tower*, in fact built a century after Wallace's death, is the ruined Corra
Castle, overlooking the waterfall.

Along thy banks, at dead of night,
20 Sweeps visibly the Wallace Wight;[1]
Or stands, in warlike vest,
Aloft, beneath the moon's pale beam,
A Champion worthy of the Stream,
Yon grey tower's living crest!

25 But clouds and envious darkness hide
A Form not doubtfully descried:—
Their transient mission o'er,
O say to what blind region flee
These Shapes of awful phantasy?
30 To what untrodden shore?

Less than divine command they spurn;
But this we from the mountains learn,
And this the valleys show,
That never will they deign to hold
35 Communion where the heart is cold
To human weal and woe.

The man of abject soul in vain
Shall walk the Marathonian Plain;
Or thrid the shadowy gloom,
40 That still invests the guardian Pass,
Where stood sublime Leonidas,[2]
Devoted to the tomb.

Nor deem that it can aught avail
For such to glide with oar or sail
45 Beneath the piny wood,
Where Tell once drew, by Uri's lake,
His vengeful shafts—prepared to slake
Their thirst in Tyrants' blood![3]

1. Courageous (an archaic usage). WW is probably alluding to Walter Scott's application of the adjective to Wallace in *Marmion: A Tale of Flodden Field* (1808) 2.113, 3.197 (Introd.), 3.25.20, and 6.20.14.
2. King of Sparta, killed in 480 B.C.E. while commanding outmaneuvered Greek forces against the Persians in the pass of Thermopylae. *Marathonian Plain* (line 38): WW refers to the routing of the Persians by the Athenians on the narrow plain of Marathon at the end of the first Persian War (490 B.C.E.).
3. A reference to legend of the fourteenth-century Swiss folk hero William Tell: while being conveyed to a dungeon by boat across Lake Lucerne (*Uri's lake*), a storm arose and Tell, as the strongest man aboard, was given the rudder, allowing him to steer the boat towards a rocky ledge and escape the tyrant Gessler, whom he later assassinated.

ODE,

COMPOSED UPON AN EVENING OF EXTRAORDINARY SPLENDOR AND BEAUTY[†]

I.

HAD this effulgence disappeared
With flying haste, I might have sent
Among the speechless clouds a look
Of blank astonishment;
5 But 'tis endued with power to stay,
And sanctify one closing day,
That frail Mortality may see,
What is?—ah no, but what *can* be!
Time was when field and watery cove
10 With modulated echoes rang,
While choirs of fervent Angels sang
Their vespers in the grove;
Or, ranged like stars along some sovereign height,
Warbled, for heaven above and earth below,
15 Strains suitable to both.—Such holy rite,
Methinks, if audibly repeated now
From hill or valley, could not move
Sublimer transport, purer love,
Than doth this silent spectacle—the gleam—
20 The shadow—and the peace supreme!

II.

No sound is uttered,—but a deep
And solemn harmony pervades
The hollow vale from steep to steep,
And penetrates the glades.
25 Far-distant images draw nigh,
Call'd forth by wond'rous potency
Of beamy radiance, that imbues
Whate'er it strikes, with gem-like hues!
In vision exquisitely clear,
30 Herds range along the mountain side;
And glistening antlers are descried;
And gilded flocks appear.

---

† *MP 1820*: Poems of the Imagination (with the title *Evening Ode*). Begun in the summer of 1817 and revised extensively before publication (see *Shorter Poems, 1807–1820* [CW], 255–57, for the text of the earliest complete draft). WW's note (printed immediately after the poem in the *River Duddon* volume): "The multiplication of mountain-ridges, described, at the commencement of the third stanza of this Ode, as a kind of Jacob's Ladder, leading to Heaven [see Genesis 28.10–19], is produced either by watery vapours, or sunny haze,—in the present instance by the latter cause. See the account of the Lakes at the end of this volume ['Topographical Description of the Lakes']. The reader, who is acquainted with the Author's Ode, intitled, 'Intimations of Immortality, &c.' will recognize the allusion to it [esp. stanzas 1, 2, and 5] that pervades the last stanza of the foregoing Poem." From the IF note: "Felt, & in a great measure composed, upon the little mount in front of our abode at Rydal."

Thine is the tranquil hour, purpureal Eve!
But long as god-like wish, or hope divine,
35 Informs my spirit, ne'er can I believe
That this magnificence is wholly thine!
—From worlds not quickened by the sun
A portion of the gift is won;
An intermingling of Heaven's pomp is spread
40 On ground which British shepherds tread!

III.

And, if there be whom broken ties
Afflict, or injuries assail,
Yon hazy ridges to their eyes,
Present a glorious scale,
45 Climbing suffused with sunny air,
To stop—no record hath told where!
And tempting fancy to ascend,
And with immortal spirits blend!
—Wings at my shoulder seem to play;
50 But, rooted here, I stand and gaze
On those bright steps that heaven-ward raise
Their practicable way.[1]
Come forth, ye drooping old men, look abroad
And see to what fair countries ye are bound!
55 And if some Traveller, weary of his road,
Hath slept since noon-tide on the grassy ground,
Ye Genii![2] to his covert speed;
And wake him with such gentle heed
As may attune his soul to meet the dow'r
60 Bestowed on this transcendent hour!

IV.

Such hues from their celestial Urn
Were wont to stream before my eye,
Where'er it wandered in the morn
Of blissful infancy.
65 This glimpse of glory, why renewed?
Nay, rather speak with gratitude;
For, if a vestige of those gleams
Surviv'd, 'twas only in my dreams.
Dread Power! whom peace and calmness serve
70 No less than Nature's threatening voice,
If aught unworthy be my choice,

1. In *MP 1820* WW added a note: "In the lines 'Wings at my shoulder seem to play,' &c. * * * I am under obligation to the exquisite Picture by Mr. Alstone, now in America. It is pleasant to make this acknowledgement to men of genius, whom I have the honour to rank among my friends." WW refers to *Jacob's Dream* by Washington Allston (1779–1843), a painting showing a sleeping Jacob with rows of angels standing above him. WW must have seen it in the artist's London studio in December 1817; in late 1818 or early 1819 he sent Allston a copy of the poem (*WL*, 3:504–505 and nn.).
2. Local spirits (here meant playfully).

From THEE if I would swerve,
O, let thy grace remind me of the light,
Full early lost and fruitlessly deplored;
75 Which, at this moment, on my waking sight
Appears to shine, by miracle restored!
My soul, though yet confined to earth,
Rejoices in a second birth;
—'Tis past, the visionary splendour fades,
80 And Night approaches with her shades.

ODE.—1817†

BENEATH the concave of an April sky,
When all the fields with freshest green were dight,
Appeared, in presence of that spiritual eye
That aids or supersedes our grosser sight,
5 The form and rich habiliments of One
Whose countenance bore resemblance to the sun,
When it reveals, in evening majesty,
Features half lost amid their own pure light.
Poised in the middle region of the air
10 He hung,—then floated with angelic ease,
Softening that bright effulgence by degrees,
Until he reached a rock, of summit bare,
Where oft the vent'rous Heifer drinks the summer breeze.
Upon the apex of that lofty cone
15 Alighted, there the Stranger stood alone;
Fair as a gorgeous Fabric of the East
Suddenly raised by some Enchanter's power,
Where nothing was; and firm as some old Tower
Of Britain's realm, whose leafy crest
20 Waves high, embellish'd by a gleaming shower!

II.

Beneath the shadow of his purple wings
Rested a golden Harp;—he touch'd the strings;
And, after prelude of unearthly sound
Poured through the echoing hills around,
25 He sang, "No wintry desolations,
Scorching blight, or noxious dew,
Affect my native habitations;
Buried in glory, far beyond the scope
Of man's enquiring gaze, and imaged to his hope

---

† MP 1820: Poems of the Imagination (with the title Ode). Composed in April 1817 and revised
extensively before publication (see Shorter Poems, 1807–1820 [CW], 233–36, for the text of the
earliest complete draft), as well as in later editions, especially from 1836 on (see the apparatus
in Shorter Poems, 1807–1820 [CW], 237–41). In 1827 WW changed the title to Vernal Ode.
From the IF note: "Composed to place in view the immortality of succession where immortality
is denied, as far as we know, to the individual creature."

30 (Alas, how faintly!) in the hue
Profound of night's ethereal blue;
And in the aspect of each radiant orb;—
Some fix'd, some wandering with no timid curb;
But wandering orb and fix'd, to mortal eye,
35 Blended in absolute serenity,
And free from semblance of decline;—
So wills eternal Love with Power divine.

III.

"And what if his presiding breath
Impart a sympathetic motion
40 Unto the gates of life and death,
Throughout the bounds of earth and ocean;
Though all that feeds on nether air,
Howe'er magnificent or fair,
Grows but to perish, and entrust
45 Its ruins to their kindred dust;
Yet, by the Almighty's ever-during care,
Her procreant vigils Nature keeps
Amid the unfathomable deeps;
And saves the peopled fields of earth
50 From dread of emptiness or dearth.
Thus, in their stations, lifting tow'rd the sky
The foliag'd head in cloud-like majesty,
The shadow-casting race of Trees survive:
Thus, in the train of Spring, arrive
55 Sweet Flowers;—what living eye hath viewed
Their myriads?—endlessly renewed,
Wherever strikes the sun's glad ray;
Where'er the joyous waters stray;
Wherever sportive zephyrs bend
60 Their course, or genial showers descend!
Rejoice, O men! the very Angels quit
Their mansions unsusceptible of change,
Amid your pleasant bowers to sit,
And through your sweet vicissitudes to range!"

IV.

65 O, nursed at happy distance from the cares
Of a too-anxious world, mild pastoral Muse!
That, to the sparkling crown Urania wears,
And to her sister Clio's[1] laurel wreath,
Prefer'st a garland cull'd from purple heath,
70 Or blooming thicket moist with morning dews;
Was such bright Spectacle vouchsafed to me?

---

1. The muse of history; *mild pastoral Muse*: Thalia; *Urania*: the muse of astronomy.

And was it granted to the simple ear
Of thy contented Votary
Such melody to hear!
75   *Him* rather suits it, side by side with thee,
Wrapped in a fit of pleasing indolence,
While thy tired lute hangs on the hawthorn tree,
To lie and listen, till o'er-drowsed sense
Sinks, hardly conscious of the influence,
80   To the soft murmur of the vagrant Bee.
—A slender sound! yet hoary Time
Doth, to the *Soul* exalt it with the chime
Of all his years;—a company
Of ages coming, ages gone;
85   Nations from before them sweeping—
Regions in destruction steeping;—
But every awful note in unison
With that faint utterance, which tells
Of treasure sucked from buds and bells,
90   For the pure keeping of those waxen cells;
Where She, a statist prudent to confer
Upon the public weal; a warrior bold,—
Radiant all over with unburnished gold,
And armed with living spear for mortal fight;
95   A cunning forager
That spreads no waste;—a social builder, one
In whom all busy offices unite
With all fine functions that afford delight,
Safe through the winter storm in quiet dwells!

V.

100   And is She brought within the power
Of vision?—o'er this tempting flower
Hovering until the petals stay
Her flight, and take its voice away?
Observe each wing—a tiny van!—
105   The structure of her laden thigh;
How fragile!—yet of ancestry
Mysteriously remote and high;
High as the imperial front of man,
The roseate bloom on woman's cheek;
110   The soaring eagle's curved beak;
The white plumes of the floating swan;
Old as the tyger's paws, the lion's mane
Ere shaken by that mood of stern disdain
At which the desert trembles.—Humming Bee!
115   Thy sting was needless then, perchance unknown;
The seeds of malice were not sown;
All creatures met in peace, from fierceness free,
And no pride blended with their dignity.

—Tears had not broken from their source;
120 Nor anguish strayed from her Tartarian den:[2]
The golden years maintained a course
Not undiversified, though smooth and even;
We were not mocked with glimpse and shadow then;
Bright Seraphs mixed familiarly with men;[3]
125 And earth and stars composed a universal heaven!

2. Tartarus, in Greek mythology the part of the underworld in which the wicked are punished for their misdeeds in life.
3. An allusion to Milton, *Paradise Lost* 9.1–3: "No more of talk where God or Angel Guest / With Man, as with his friend, familiar us'd / To sit indulgent * * *."

From ECCLESIASTICAL SKETCHES (1822)†

MUTABILITY‡

FROM low to high doth dissolution climb,
And sinks from high to low, along a scale
Of awful notes. whose concord shall not fail;
A musical but melancholy chime,
5 Which they can hear who meddle not with crime,
Nor avarice, nor over-anxious care.
Truth fails not; but her outward forms that bear
The longest date do melt like frosty rime,
That in the morning whitened hill and plain
10 And is no more; drop like the tower sublime
Of yesterday, which royalty did wear
Its crown of weeds, but could not even sustain
Some casual shout that broke the silent air,
Or the unimaginable touch of Time.[1]

---

† Published in March 1822, this volume consisted of a sequence of 102 sonnets, divided among
three sections, all of which had been composed between July 14, 1820, and November 24, 1821
(*Sonnet Series and Itinerary Poems, 1820–1845* [CW], 134–35). In a brief Advertisement, WW
explained the sequence's personal and public contexts: "During the month of December, 1820,
I accompanied a much-loved and honoured Friend [Sir George Beaumont] in a walk through
different parts of his Estate, with a view to fix upon the Site of a New Church which he
intended to erect. It was one of the most beautiful mornings of a mild season,—our feelings
were in harmony with the cherishing influences of the scene; and such being our purpose, we
were naturally led to look back upon past events with wonder and gratitude, and on the future
with hope. Not long afterwards, some of the Sonnets which will be found towards the close of
this Series were produced as a private memorial of that morning's occupation. [Second para-
graph:] The Catholic Question, which was agitated in Parliament about that time, kept my
thoughts, in the same course; and it struck me, that certain points in the Ecclesiastical History
of our Country might advantageously be presented to view in Verse. Accordingly I took up the
subject, and what I now offer to the Reader, was the result. * * *" The *Catholic Question*, which
had troubled WW at least since 1809, was whether to repeal the Test and Corporation Act,
which prohibited Roman Catholics from voting, serving in the armed forces, or sitting in Par-
liament. *Ecclesiastical Sketches* is one manifestation of WW's opposition to Catholic emanci-
pation (for his more vehement private expressions, see, e.g., *WL*, 3:108, 540, 544, 566, 4:55,
310–15, 437–48, 358–65, 527–29; also Gill, 361–63). The volume sold poorly, and in fact the
Roman Catholic Relief Bill was eventually passed by Parliament in 1829.
‡ Composed between January 17 and November 24 (probably by March 12), 1821, this is the
sixteenth sonnet in part 3 of the sequence.
1. *Sonnet Series and Itinerary Poems* [CW], 272, suggests that the imagery of lines 10–14 may
have been inspired by John Dyer's *The Ruins of Rome* (1740), lines 38–42: "The Pilgrim oft / At
dead of Night, 'mid his Oraison [prayer] hears / Aghast the Voice of Time, disparting Tow'rs, /
Tumbling all precipitate down dash'd, / Rattling around, loud thundring to the Moon." WW
expressed his admiration of Dyers's poem on several occasions (see *Reading 1800–15*, no. 150).

From POETICAL WORKS (1827)

Scorn not the sonnet[†]

SCORN not the Sonnet; Critic, you have frowned,
Mindless of its just honours;—with this Key
Shakspeare unlocked his heart; the melody
Of this small Lute gave ease to Petrarch's wound;
5 A thousand times this Pipe did Tasso sound;
With it Camöens soothed an Exile's grief;
The Sonnet glittered a gay myrtle leaf
Amid the cypress with which Dante crowned
His visionary brow: a glow-worm Lamp,
10 It cheered mild Spenser, called from Faery-land
To struggle through dark ways; and, when a damp
Fell round the path of Milton, in his hand
The Thing became a trumpet; whence he blew
Soul-animating strains—alas, too few!

---

† Placed, untitled, at the beginning of the second section of "Miscellaneous Sonnets." Composed probably ca. January and no later than April 1827 (*Last Poems, 1821–1850* [CW], 82). IF note: "Composed, almost ex tempore, in a short walk on the western side of Rydal Lake." In the poem WW names celebrated writers of sonnets: Shakespeare, who wrote 154 sonnets; Francesco Petrarca (1304–1374), Italian lyric poet who wrote 317 love sonnets; Torquato Tasso (1544–1595), Italian epic and lyric poet; Luís Vaz de Camões (ca. 1524–1580), Portuguese epic poet sent to the colonies of Goa and Macau on obligatory military service (not exiled); Dante Alighieri (1265–1321), whose early poetry included numerous sonnets; Edmund Spenser (ca. 1552–1599), who wrote a sequence of Petrarchan sonnets called the *Amoretti* (1595); and Milton, who wrote sonnets in English and Italian, though the one WW probably has chiefly in mind here is that on his blindness, *When I consider how my light is spent.*

From POETICAL WORKS (1836–37)

Extempore Effusion upon the Death of James Hogg[†]

WHEN first, descending from the moorlands,
I saw the Stream of Yarrow glide
Along a bare and open valley,
The Ettrick Shepherd was my guide.[1]

5 When last along its banks I wandered,
Through groves that had begun to shed
Their golden leaves upon the pathways,
My steps the border minstrel[2] led.

The mighty Minstrel breathes no longer,
10 Mid mouldering ruins low he lies;
And death upon the braes[3] of Yarrow,
Has closed the Shepherd-poet's eyes:

Nor has the rolling year twice measured,
From sign to sign, its stedfast course,
15 Since every mortal power of Coleridge
Was frozen at its marvellous source;

† Classed under "Epitaphs." Composed between November 21 and December 3, 1835 (*Last Poems, 1821–1850* [CW], 305), and first published in the *Newcastle Journal*, December 2, 1835, and the *Atheneum*, December 12, 1835. An impoverished Scottish writer who had worked as a shepherd until his mid-30s and was widely known as the "Ettrick Shepherd" after his birth-place, Hogg (1770–1835) was the author of the novel *The Private Memoirs and Confessions of a Justified Sinner* (1824), a satire of religious fanaticism, and of the anonymously published *Poetic Mirror* (1816), a collection of poetry that included parodies of WW and STC. In the *Poetical Works* (1836–37) WW included a two-columned note to the poem at the end of vol. 5:

Walter Scott died	21st Sept. 1832.
S. T. Coleridge	25th July, 1834.
Charles Lamb	27th Dec. 1834.
Geo. Crabbe	3rd Feb. 1832.
Felicia Hemans	16th May, 1835.

In his IF note WW added, "These verses were written extempore immediately after reading a notice of the Ettrick Shepherd's death, in the Newcastle Paper to the Editor of wh. I sent a copy for publication. The persons lamented in these verses were all either of my friends or acquaintance."
1. On September 1, 1814, WW had first visited Yarrow Water, in the Scottish Borders region, with Hogg (see the first note to *Yarrow Visited*, p. 526 above). In the IF note WW remarked, "He was undoubtedly a man of original genius, but of coarse manners & low & offensive opinions."
2. Sir Walter Scott, whom WW first met on his Scottish tour of 1803 (see the introductory note on "Poems written during a Tour of Scotland" in *P2V*, p. 411 above). In the lines 9–10 WW refers to Scott's burial on the grounds of the ruined Dryburgh Abbey in the Scottish Borders.
3. Hills (Scottish and northern English dialect). WW also alludes to two eighteenth-century ballads called *The Braes of Yarrow*, on which see *Yarrow Visited*. In line 42 below he summarizes the ballads' subjects.

The 'rapt One, of the godlike forehead,
The heaven-eyed creature sleeps in earth:
And Lamb, the frolic and the gentle,[4]
20   Has vanished from his lonely hearth.

Like clouds that rake the mountain-summits,[5]
Or waves that own no curbing hand,
How fast has brother followed brother,
From sunshine to sunless land!

25   Yet I, whose lids from infant slumbers
Were earlier raised, remain to hear
A timid voice, that asks in whispers,
"Who next will drop and disappear?"

Our haughty life is crowned with darkness,
30   Like London with its own black wreath,
On which with thee, O Crabbe! forth-looking,
I gazed from Hampstead's breezy heath.[6]

As if but yesterday departed,
Thou too art gone before; but why,
35   O'er ripe fruit, seasonably gathered,
Should frail survivors heave a sigh?

Mourn rather for that holy Spirit,
Sweet as the spring, as ocean deep;
For Her[7] who, ere her summer faded,
40   Has sunk into a breathless sleep.

No more of old romantic sorrows,
For slaughtered Youth or love-lorn Maid!
With sharper grief is Yarrow smitten,
And Ettrick mourns with her their Poet dead.
                                   Nov. 1835.

---

4. An allusion to STC's description of Lamb in *This Lime Tree Bower My Prison*, line 28, as "gentle-hearted" (*NCC*, 137). On Lamb see the Biographical and Topographical Glossary. STC's poem was written in 1797, when their friendship with WW was closest.

5. When the poem was published in the *Newcastle Journal* and *Atheneum*, WW included a note on this line: "In the above is an expression borrowed from a Sonnet by Mr. G. Bell, the Author of a small volume of Poems lately published at Penrith. Speaking of [the mountain] Skiddaw, he says, 'Yon dark cloud *rakes* and shrouds its noble brow.' [T]hese Poems, though incorrect often in expression and metre, do honour their unpretending Author; and may be added to the number of proofs daily occurring, that a finer perception of the appearances of Nature is spreading through the humbler Classes of Society" (*Last Poems, 1821–1850* [CW], 470).

6. George Crabbe (1754–1833), author of popular, socially realistic poetry such as *The Village* (1783), *Tales* (1812), and *The Borough* (1810). In his IF note WW recalled being impressed by Crabbe's knowledge of natural history during their walks on Hampstead Heath, then a northern suburb of London where Crabbe paid long annual visits to WW's friend the banker Samuel Hoare.

7. Felicia Hemans (1793–1835), an immensely popular poet with whom WW was on friendly terms. WW's assessment of her (in the IF note on this poem) is quoted in the note on her *To Wordsworth* in Nineteenth-Century Responses (p. 565 below).

From POEMS, CHIEFLY OF EARLY AND LATE YEARS (1842)

Airey-Force Valley†

           ——Not a breath of air
Ruffles the bosom of this leafy glen.
From the brook's margin, wide around, the trees
Are stedfast as the rocks; the brook itself,
5 Old as the hills that feed it from afar,
Doth rather deepen than disturb the calm
Where all things else are still and motionless.
And yet, even now, a little breeze, perchance
Escaped from boisterous winds that rage without,
10 Has entered, by the sturdy oaks unfelt;
But to its gentle touch how sensitive
Is the light ash! that, pendent from the brow
Of yon dim cave, in seeming silence makes
A soft eye-music of slow-waving boughs,
15 Powerful almost as vocal harmony
To stay the wanderer's steps and soothe his thoughts.

† Classed under "Poems of the Imagination" in *Poetical Works* (1845). Composed September 28–29, 1835 (*Last Poems, 1821–1850* [CW], 285). In September 1835 WW had visited the Aira Force Valley (in which the eponymous waterfall is located), on the northern side of Ullswater, with Joshua Watson, a philanthropist and friend of WW's brother Christopher, and Watson's daughter. On October 5, 1825, WW sent Watson a copy of the poem, commenting, "My walk from Lyulph's Tower to Hallsteads was beguiled by throwing into blank verse a description of the Scene which struck Miss Watson and me at the same moment" (*WL*, 6:104).

CRITICISM

Nineteenth-Century Responses

SAMUEL TAYLOR COLERIDGE

To W. Wordsworth[†]

Lines composed for the greater part on the Night, on which he finished
the recitation of his Poem (in thirteen Books) concerning the growth and
history of his own mind. Jan^ry, 1807. Cole-orton, near Ashby de la Zouch.

> O Friend! O Teacher! God's great Gift to me!
> Into my heart have I receiv'd that day
> More than historic, that prophetic Lay,
> Wherein (high theme by Thee first sung aright)
> 5 Of the Foundations and the Building-up
> Of thy own Spirit, thou hast lov'd to tell
> What may be told, to the' understanding mind
> Revealable; and what within the mind
> May rise enkindled. Theme as hard as high!
> 10 Of Smiles spontaneous, and mysterious Fear;
> (The First-born they of Reason, and Twin birth)
> Of Tides obedient to external Force,
> And Currents self-determin'd, as might seem,
> Or by interior Power: of Moments aweful,
> 15 Now in thy hidden Life; and now abroad,

† From late October 1806 to June 10, 1807, the Wordsworth family resided in Hall Farm, a house
lent to them by Sir George Beaumont (see Biographical and Topographical Glossary) in Coleor-
ton, Leicestershire. Shocked by STC's physical decline after his two years abroad in Malta and
Italy, distressed about his unhappy marriage, and anxious for him to resume literary work (WL,
2:86–87), WW and DW encouraged him to spend the winter with them, which he did, arriving
on December 21 and departing in mid-April. In early January WW read aloud the thirteen-
book Prelude (of which STC had previously read only the first five books) in the presence of
STC, DW, MW, and Sara Hutchinson. Afterwards he lent STC the manuscript copied by MW;
C's annotations in book 6 are transcribed in the notes of this Norton Critical Edition. STC's
more immediate response, however, was this poem, transcribed here from the autograph fair
copy in the Wordsworth Trust archive, Grasmere (WLMS 14/7). Reprinted by permission of
the Wordsworth Trust.
  On May 22, 1815, having learned through Lady Beaumont that STC was assembling his
poetic manuscripts, WW sought to discourage him from publishing the poem: "The commen-
dation would be injurious to us both, and my work when it appears, would labour under a great
disadvantage in consequence of such a precursorship of Praise" (WL, 3:238). STC responded
on May 30 that "there is nothing in the Lines as far [as] your Powers are concerned, which I
have not as fully expressed elsewhere" (CL, 4:572); and he did publish a revised version of the
poem in his Sybilline Leaves (1817), but under the title To a Gentleman and omitting lines 28–
31 and 53–61. The title To William Wordsworth was first used in STC's posthumously pub-
lished Poetical Works (1834), still sixteen years before The Prelude was published. On the
biographical context of the poem's publication, see further NCC, 200 n. 1. STC's later critique
in BL of WW's poetry and poetic theory is too extensive and detailed to be included in this sec-
tion, but is cited where relevant in the notes of this Norton Critical Edition, particularly those
to LB.

Mid festive crowds, *thy* Brows too garlanded,
A Brother of the Feast: of Fancies fair,
Hyblæan[1] Murmurs of poetic Thought,
Industrious in its Joy, by lilied Streams
20   Native or outland, Lakes and famous Hills!
Of more than Fancy, of the Hope of Man
Amid the tremor of a Realm aglow—
Where France in all her Towns lay vibrating,
Ev'n as a Bark becalm'd on sultry seas
25   Beneath the voice from Heaven, the bursting crash
Of Heaven's immediate thunder! when no Cloud
Is visible, or Shadow on the Main!
Ah! soon night roll'd on night, and every Cloud
Open'd its eye of Fire: and Hope aloft
30   Now flutter'd, and now toss'd upon the Storm
Floating! Of Hope afflicted, and struck down,
Thence summon'd homeward, homeward to thy Heart,
Oft from the Watch-tower of Man's absolute Self,
With Light unwaning on her eyes, to look
35   Far on—herself a Glory to behold,
The Angel of the Vision! Then (last strain!)
Of *Duty*, chosen Laws controlling[2] choice,
Virtue and Love! An Orphic[3] Tale indeed,
A Tale divine of high and passionate Thoughts
To their own music chaunted!
40   Ah great Bard!
Ere yet that last Swell dying aw'd the Air,
With steadfast ken I view'd thee in the Choir
Of every-enduring Men. The truly Great
Have all one Age, and from one visible space
45   Shed influence:[4] for they, both power and act,
Are permanent, and Time is not with them,.
Save as it worketh for them, they in it.
Nor less a sacred Roll, than those of old,
And to be plac'd, as they, with gradual fame
50   Among the Archives of Mankind, thy Work
Makes audible a linkèd Song of Truth,
Of Truth profound a sweet continuous Song
Not learnt, but native, her own natural notes!
Dear shall it be to every human Heart,

---

1. Honeyed (a poetical usage). Hybla was an ancient Greek colony in southeastern Sicily, famous for its honey.
2. In the right margin of the manuscript, STC, perhaps hoping for WW's advice, proposed possible alternatives to *controlling*: "impelling? directing?" He did not change the word, however, when he later published the poem. *Angel of the Vision*: possibly an allusion to "the great vision of the guarded Mount" in Milton's *Lycidas*, lines 161–63 (where the angel meant is Michael).
3. Oracular, entrancing (referring in a general way to the mystery cults associated with the legendary Greek poet Orpheus, whose music was said to charm wild animals and even trees and rocks). STC printed lines 37–39 in his periodical *The Friend* (December 19, 1809) by way of introducing an extract from *The Prelude*: see the note on *Prelude* 1.431.
4. STC alludes in lines 40–44 to WW's claim in *Prelude* 10.967–73 that "There is / One great Society alone on earth" in which "Time / And Nature shall before thee [STC himself] spread in store / Imperishable thoughts."

To me how more than dearest! Me, on whom
55   Comfort from Thee and Utterance of thy Love
Came with such heights and depths of Harmony,
Such sense of Wings uplifting, that the Storm
Scatter'd and whirl'd me, till my Thoughts became
A bodily Tumult! And thy faithful Hopes,
60   Thy Hopes of me, dear Friend! by me unfelt
Were troublous to me, almost as a Voice
Familiar once and more than musical
To one cast forth, whose hope had seem'd to die,
A wanderer with a worn-out heart,
65   Mid strangers pining with untended wounds!

O Friend! too well thou knowst, of what sad years
The long Suppression had benumm'd my soul,
That even as Life returns upon the Drown'd,
The' unusual Joy awoke a throng of Pains—
70   Keen Pangs of Love, awakening, as a Babe,
Turbulent, with an outcry in the Heart:
And Fears self-will'd, that shunn'd the eye of Hope,
And Hope, that would not know itself from Fear:
Sense of pass'd Youth, and Manhood come in vain;
75   And all, which I had cull'd in Wood-walks wild,
And all, which patient Toil had rear'd, and all,
Commune with Thee had open'd out, but Flowers
Strew'd on my Corse, and borne upon my Bier,
In the same Coffin, for the self-same Grave![5]

80   —That way no more! and ill beseems it me,
Who came a Welcomer in Herald's Guise
Singing of Glory and Futurity,
To wander back on such unhealthful Road
Plucking the Poisons of Self-harm! and ill
85   Such Intertwine beseems triumphal wreaths
Strew'd before thy Advancing! Thou too, Friend!
O injure not the memory of that Hour
Of thy Communion with my nobler mind
By pity or grief, already felt too long!
90   Nor let my words import more blame than need.
The Tumult rose and ceas'd: for Peace is nigh
Where Wisdom's Voice has found a list'ning Heart.
Amid the howl of more than wintry Storms
The Halcyon[6] hears the voice of vernal Hours,
Already on the Wing!
95   Eve following eve,
Dear tranquil Time, when the sweet sense of Home

5. STC included lines 70–79 in chapter 10 of *BL* with reference to his "deficiency in self-controul, and the neglect of concentering [his] powers to the realization of some permanent work" (*NCC*, 460–61).
6. In Greek legend, a bird that calmed the sea and wind at the winter solstice so that it could breed in a nest floating on the water.

> Becomes most sweet! hours for their own sake hail'd,
> And more desir'd, more precious, for thy Song!
> In silence listn'ning, like a devout Child,
> 100 My Soul lay passive, by thy various strain
> Driven as in surges now, beneath the stars,
> With momentary Stars of my own Birth,
> Fair constellated Foam[7] still darting off
> Into the darkness! now a tranquil Sea
> 105 Outspread and bright, yet swelling to the Morn!
>
> And when, o Friend! my Comforter! my Guide![8]
> Strong in thyself and powerful to give strength!
> Thy long sustained Law finally close,
> And thy deep Voice had ceas'd—/ yet thou thyself
> 110 Wert still before mine eyes, and round us both
> That happy Vision of beloved Faces!
> All, whom I deepliest love, in one room all!
> Scarce conscious and yet conscious of its Close,
> I sate, my Being blended in one thought,
> 115 (Thought was it? or aspiration? or Resolve?)
> Absorb'd, yet hanging still upon the sound:
> And when I rose, I found myself in Prayer!
>   S. T. Coleridge.

FRANCIS JEFFREY

From the Edinburgh Review[†]

* * * It is the great misfortune of Mr. Wordsworth * * * that he is exceedingly apt to make choice of subjects which are not only unfit in themselves to excite any serious emotion, but naturally present themselves to ordinary minds as altogether ridiculous; and, consequently, to revolt and disgust his readers by an appearance of paltry affectation, or incomprehensible conceit. We have the greatest respect for the genius of Mr.

7. In the published version of the poem, STC added a footnote quoting a passage from his own *Friend* of November 23, 1809, in which he describes his voyage with the Wordsworths off the coast of Cuxhaven, northeastern Germany, in September 1798: "A beautiful white cloud of Foam at momentary intervals coursed by the side of the Vessel with a Roar * * * and every now and then light detachments of this cloud-like foam darted off from the vessel's side" (*NCC*, 203 n. 1).

8. The comma after *when* is an editorial substitution for STC's opening parenthesis, which has no corresponding closing parenthesis in the manuscript.

† From an unsigned review of John Wilson's *The Isle of the Palms, and Other Poems* in the *Edinburgh Review* 19 (February 1812): 374–75. The reviewer, Francis Jeffrey (1773–1850), trained in Edinburgh as a lawyer and later active as a judge and Whig member of parliament, co-founded the *Edinburgh Review* with Sidney Scott in 1802 and edited the journal until 1829. Although he admired other poets of the time, such as Lord Byron and John Keats, he was consistently unsympathetic to WW's poetry, famously beginning his review of *The Excursion* with the sentence, "This will never do" (see *CH*, 381–404); and he was responsible for designating WW, STC, and Robert Southey the "Lake Poets." The remarks reprinted here appear in a review of a book by the Tory poet and journalist John Wilson (1785–1854), a sometime friend of WW and STC who later criticized both in his contributions to *Blackwood's Edinburgh Magazine* (founded in 1817). For his part, WW concluded his *Letter to a Friend of Robert Burns* (1816) with a scathing attack on Jeffrey, whom he compared to Robespierre and Napoleon: "as often as a work of original genius comes before him, [he] avails himself of that opportunity to re-proclaim to the world the narrow range of his own comprehension" (*Prose*, 3:126–29).

Wordsworth, and the most sincere veneration for all we have heard of his character; but it is impossible to contemplate the injury he has done to his reputation by this poor ambition of originality, without a mixed sensation of provocation and regret. We are willing to take it for granted, that the spades and the eggs, and the tubs which he commemorates, actually suggested to him all the emotions and reflexions of which he has chosen to make them the vehicles; but they surely are not the only objects which have suggested similar emotions; and we cannot understand why the circumstance of their being quite unfit to suggest them to any other person, should have recommended them as their best accompaniments in an address to the public. We do not want Mr. Wordsworth to write like Pope or Prior,[1] nor to dedicate his muse to subjects which he does not himself think interesting. We are prepared, on the contrary, to listen with a far deeper delight to the songs of his mountain solitude, and to gaze on his mellow pictures of simple happiness and affection, and his lofty sketches of human worth and energy; and we only beg, that we may have these nobler elements of his poetry, without the debasement of childish language, mean incidents, and incongruous images. * * *

WILLIAM HAZLITT

From On the Living Poets[†]

* * *

Mr. Wordsworth is the most original poet now living. He is the reverse of Walter Scott in his defects and excellences. He has nearly all that the other wants, and wants all that the other possesses. His poetry is not external, but internal; it does not depend upon tradition, or story, or old song; he furnishes it from his own mind, and is his own subject. He is the poet of mere sentiment. Of many of the Lyrical Ballads, it is not possible to speak in terms of too high praise, such as Hartleap Well, the Banks of the Wye [i.e., *Tintern Abbey*], Poor Susan, parts of the Leech-gatherer, the lines to a Cuckoo, to a Daisy, the Complaint, several of the Sonnets, and a hundred others of inconceivable beauty, of perfect originality, and pathos. They open a finer and deeper vein of thought and feeling than any poet in modern times has done, or attempted. He has produced a deeper impression, and on a smaller circle, than any other of his contemporaries. His powers have been mistaken by the age, nor does he exactly understand them himself. He cannot form a whole. He has not the constructive faculty. He can give only the fine tones of thought, drawn from his mind by accident or nature, like the sounds drawn from the Æolian harp by the wandering gale.—He is totally deficient in all the machinery

---

1. The poets Alexander Pope (1688–1744) and Matthew Prior (1664–1721).
† On Hazlitt (1778–1830) see the Biographical and Topographical Glossary. Notwithstanding his personal and political differences with WW, Hazlitt's criticism of WW's poetry is measured and respectful. His best-known assessment of WW is in the *The Spirit of Age* (1825); but much of what Hazlitt writes there about, e.g., the poet's originality, celebration of "household truths," preference for plain diction and hostility to classical references, and excessive self-centeredness, repeats points already made in his lecture "On the Living Poets" of March 3, 1818, subsequently published in *Lectures on the English Poets* (London, 1818), 309–24. The present selection (omitting Hazlitt's quotation of the whole of *Hart-leap Well*) is reprinted from the first edition.

of poetry. His *Excursion*, taken as a whole, notwithstanding the noble materials thrown away in it, is a proof of this. The line labours, the sentiment moves slow, but the poem stands stock-still. The reader makes no way from the first line to the last. It is more than any thing in the world like Robinson Crusoe's boat, which would have been an excellent good boat, and would have carried him to the other side of the globe, but that he could not get it out of the sand where it stuck fast. I did what little I could to help to launch it at the time, but it would not do.[1] I am not, however, one of those who laugh at the attempts or failures of men of genius. It is not my way to cry "Long life to the conqueror." Success and desert are not with me synonymous terms; and the less Mr. Wordsworth's general merits have been understood, the more necessary is it to insist upon them. This is not the place to repeat what I have already said on the subject. The reader may turn to it in the Round Table. I do not think, however, there is any thing in the larger poem equal to many of the detached pieces in the Lyrical Ballads. * * *

Mr. Wordsworth is at the head of that which has been denominated the Lake school of poetry; a school which, with all my respect for it, I do not think sacred from criticism or exempt from faults, of some of which faults I shall speak with becoming frankness; for I do not see that the liberty of the press ought to be shackled, or freedom of speech curtailed, to screen either its revolutionary or renegado extravagances. This school of poetry had its origin in the French revolution, or rather in those sentiments and opinions which produced that revolution; and which sentiments and opinions were indirectly imported into this country in translations from the German about that period. Our poetical literature had towards the close of the last century, degenerated into the most trite, insipid, and mechanical of all things, in the hands of the followers of Pope and the old French school of poetry. It wanted something to stir it up, and it found that something in the principles and events of the French revolution. From the impulse it thus received, it rose at once from the most servile imitation and tamest common-place, to the utmost pitch of singularity and paradox. The change in the belles-lettres was as complete, and to many persons as startling, as the change in politics, with which it went hand in hand. There was a mighty ferment in the heads of statesmen and poets, kings and people. According to the prevailing notions, all was to be natural and new. Nothing that was established was to be tolerated. All the common-place figures of poetry, tropes, allegories, personifications, with the whole heathen mythology, were instantly discarded; a classical allusion was considered as a piece of antiquated foppery; capital letters were no more allowed in print, than letters-patent of nobility were permitted in real life; kings and queens were dethroned from their rank and station in legitimate tragedy or epic poetry, as they were decapitated elsewhere; rhyme was looked upon as a relic of the feudal system, and regular metre was abolished along with regular government. Authority and fashion, elegance or arrangement, were hooted out of countenance, as ped-

---

1. An ironic allusion to the first sentence of Francis Jeffrey's review of *The Excursion*, on which see the source note on p. 560. Hazlitt published his own critical review of WW's poem in the *Examiner* on August 21 and 28, 1814, and included a revised version of it (adding the comment that "an intense intellectual egotism swallows up everything" in the poem) in his book *The Round Table* (1817). See also the headnote to *The Excursion*, p. 442 above.

antry and prejudice. Every one did that which was good in his own eyes. The object was to reduce all things to an absolute level; and a singularly affected and outrageous simplicity prevailed in dress and manners, in style and sentiment. A striking effect produced where it was least expected, something new and original, no matter whether good, bad, or indifferent, whether mean or lofty, extravagant or childish, was all that was aimed at, or considered as compatible with sound philosophy and an age of reason. The licentiousness grew extreme: Coryate's Crudities[2] were nothing to it. The world was to be turned topsy-turvy; and poetry, by the good will of our Adam-wits, was to share its fate and begin *de novo* [anew]. It was a time of promise, a renewal of the world and of letters; and the Deucalions, who were to perform this feat of regeneration, were the present poet-laureat[3] and the authors of the Lyrical Ballads. The Germans, who made heroes of robbers, and honest women of cast-off mistresses, had already exhausted the extravagant and marvellous in sentiment and situation: our native writers adopted a wonderful simplicity of style and matter. The paradox they set out with was, that all things are by nature equally fit subjects for poetry; or that if there is any preference to be given, those that are the meanest and most unpromising are the best, as they leave the greatest scope for the unbounded stores of thought and fancy in the writer's own mind. Poetry had with them "neither buttress nor coigne of vantage to make its pendant bed and procreant cradle." It was not "born so high: its aiery buildeth in the cedar's top, and dallies with the wind, and scorns the sun."[4] It grew like a mushroom out of the ground; or was hidden in it like a truffle, which it required a particular sagacity and industry to find out and dig up. They founded the new school on a principle of sheer humanity, on pure nature void of art. It could not be said of these sweeping reformers and dictators in the republic of letters, that "in their train walked crowns and crownets; that realms and islands, like plates, dropt from their pockets:" but they were surrounded, in company with the Muses, by a mixed rabble of idle apprentices and Botany Bay convicts, female vagrants, gipsies, meek daughters in the family of Christ, of ideot boys and mad mothers, and after them "owls and night-ravens flew." They scorned "degrees, priority, and place, insisture, course, proportion, season, form, office, and custom in all line of order:"[5]—the distinctions of birth, the vicissitudes of fortune, did not enter into their abstracted, lofty, and levelling calculation of human nature. He who was more than man, with them was none. They claimed kindred only with the commonest of the people: peasants, pedlars, and village-barbers, were their oracles and bosom friends. Their poetry, in the extreme to which it professedly tended, and was in effect carried, levels all distinctions of nature and society; has "no figures nor no fantasies," which the prejudices of superstition or the customs of the world draw in the brains of men; "no trivial fond records" of all that has existed in the history of

2. *Coryates Crudities, Hastily Gobbled up in Five Months Travels* (1611), an account of the travels of Thomas Coryate (ca. 1577–1617) through western Europe.
3. Robert Southey (see Biographical and Topographical Glossary); *Deucalions*: in Greek mythology, Deucalion is a son of Prometheus who with his father builds an ark to survive a flood created by Zeus to punish the Pelasgians for offering him a sacrificed boy.
4. Hazlitt quotes Shakespeare, *Macbeth* 1.6.7–8, and *Richard III* 1.3.262–64.
5. Hazlitt quotes Shakespeare, *Antony and Clepoatra* 5.2.91–92, *Titus Andronicus* 2.3.97, and *Troilus and Cressida* 1.3.86–88.

past ages; it has no adventitious pride, pomp, or circumstance, to set it
off; "the marshal's truncheon, nor the judge's robe;" neither tradition,
reverence, nor ceremony, "that to great ones 'longs:"[6] it breaks in pieces
the golden images of poetry, and defaces its armorial bearings, to melt
them down in the mould of common humanity or of its own upstart
self-sufficiency. They took the same method in their new-fangled "metre
ballad-mongering" scheme, which Rousseau did in his prose paradoxes—of
exciting attention by reversing the established standards of opinion and
estimation in the world. They were for bringing poetry back to its primi-
tive simplicity and state of nature, as he was for bringing society back to
the savage state: so that the only thing remarkable left in the world by
this change, would be the persons who had produced it. A thorough adept
in this school of poetry and philanthropy is jealous of all excellence but
his own. He does not even like to share his reputation with his subject;
for he would have it all proceed from his own power and originality of
mind. Such a one is slow to admire any thing that is admirable; feels no
interest in what is most interesting to others, no grandeur in any thing
grand, no beauty in any thing beautiful. He tolerates only what he him-
self creates; he sympathizes only with what can enter into no competition
with him, with "the bare trees and mountains bare, and grass in the
green field." He sees nothing but himself and the universe. He hates all
greatness and all pretensions to it, whether well or ill-founded. His ego-
tism is in some respects a madness; for he scorns even the admiration of
himself, thinking it a presumption in any one to suppose that he has taste
or sense enough to understand him. He hates all science and all art; he
hates chemistry, he hates conchology; he hates Voltaire; he hates Sir Isaac
Newton; he hates wisdom; he hates wit; he hates metaphysics, which he
says are unintelligible, and yet he would be thought to understand them;
he hates prose; he hates all poetry but his own; he hates the dialogues in
Shakspeare; he hates music, dancing, and painting; he hates Rubens, he
hates Rembrandt; he hates Raphael, he hates Titian; he hates Vandyke;
he hates the antique; he hates the Apollo Belvidere; he hates the Venus
of Medicis.[7] This is the reason that so few people take an interest in his
writings, because he takes an interest in nothing that others do!—The
effect has been perceived as something odd; but the cause or principle
has never been distinctly traced to its source before, as far as I know.

*   *   *

6. Hazlitt quotes Shakespeare, *Julius Caesar* 2.1.231, *Hamlet* 1.5.99, and *Measure for Measure*
   2.2.59, 61. In the following sentence he quotes *1 Henry IV* 3.1.128.
7. Hazlitt lists famous artists and artworks: Peter Paul Rubens (1577–1640) and Anthony van
   Dyke (1599–1641), Flemish painters; Rembrandt van Rijn (1606–1669), Dutch painter and
   engraver; Raphael (Raffaello Sanzio, 1483–1520) and Titian (Tiziano Vecellio, ca. 1488/90–
   1576), Italian painters; the *Apollo Belvedere* (in the Vatican Museum) and the *Venus de' Medici*
   (in the Uffizi Gallery, Florence), classical statues widely considered at the time to epitomize
   male and female beauty, respectively.

PERCY BYSSHE SHELLEY

To Wordsworth[†]

Poet of Nature, thou hast wept to know
That things depart which never may return:
Childhood and youth, friendship and love's first glow,
Have fled like sweet dreams, leaving thee to mourn.
5 These common woes I feel. One loss is mine
Which thou too feel'st, yet I alone deplore.
Thou wert as a lone star,[1] whose light did shine
On some frail bark in winter's midnight roar:
Thou hast like to a rock-built refuge stood
10 Above the blind and battling multitude:
In honoured poverty thy voice did weave
Songs consecrate to truth and liberty,—[2]
Deserting these, thou leavest me to grieve,
Thus having been, that thou shouldst cease to be.

FELICIA HEMANS

To Wordsworth[‡]

THINE is a strain to read among the hills,
The old and full of voices;—by the source
Of some free stream, whose gladdening presence fills
The solitude with sound; for in its course

---

† The English poet Shelley (1792–1822), who became well acquainted with WW's friend Robert Southey (see Biographical and Topographical Glossary) between November 1812 and January 1813 but never met WW himself, published this sonnet, which deplores WW's growing political conservatism, in his collection *Alastor; or, The Spirit of Solitude* (1816), from which the text is taken. Shelley's reaction to WW's *Excursion* was recorded by his future wife Mary in her journal on September 14, 1814: "Shelley * * * brings home Wordsworths Excursion of which we read a part—much disappointed—He is a slave" (*Journals*, ed. Paula Feldman and Diana Scott-Kilvert [Oxford, 1987], 1:25). On April 22, 1815, the couple "look[ed] over" WW's *Poems*, published that year (*Journals*, 1:76).

1. An allusion to WW's sonnet *London, 1802* (p. 409 above), line 9: "Thy [Milton's] soul was like a Star and dwelt apart."

2. Visiting Keswick (where Southey lived) in the Lake District in December 1811, Shelley claimed to have heard that "Wordsworth * * * yet retains the integrity of his independence, but his poverty is such that he is frequently obliged to beg for a shirt to his back" (*Letters*, ed. Frederick Jones [Oxford, 1964], 1:208–209). WW's *P2V* (1807) included a section of "Sonnets Dedicated to Liberty."

‡ The most widely read woman poet in Britain and the United States in the nineteenth century, and perhaps second only to Lord Byron in popularity in England between 1820 and 1835, Hemans (1793–1835) supported herself, her mother, and her five sons with her writing after her husband left her in 1818. The present poem was first published under the title *To the Author of The Excursion and the Lyrical Ballads* in the *Literary Magnet* of April 1826, and was reprinted with slight changes in Hemans's volume *The Records of Woman: With Other Poems* (1828). The latter version is reprinted here. WW was the first and Hemans the second poet whose poetry was reviewed by the *Literary Magnet* in its "Living Poets of England" series (both in 1826). Hemans's poem reflects her effort to affiliate herself publicly with WW, whose poetic reputation was rising in the 1820s. In July 1830 she spent a fortnight with the Wordsworths at Rydal Mount, and she dedicated her *Scenes and Hymns of Life* (1834) to WW. After her death WW told Isabella Fenwick, "there was much sympathy between us & if opportunity had allowed me to see more of her I should have loved & valued her accordingly. As it is, I remember her with true affection for her amiable qualities" (IF note to *Extempore Effusion upon the Death of James Hogg*).

5   Even such is thy deep song, that seems a part
    Of those high scenes, a fountain from their heart.

    Or its calm spirit fitly may be taken
        To the still breast, in sunny garden-bowers,
    Where vernal winds each tree's low tones awaken,
10   And bud and bell with changes mark the hours.
    There let thy thoughts be with me, while the day
    Sinks with a golden and serene decay.

    Or by some hearth where happy faces meet,
        When night hath hush'd the woods, with all their birds,
15 There, from some gentle voice, that lay were sweet
        As antique music, link'd with household words.
    While, in pleased murmurs, woman's lip might move,
    And the rais'd eye of childhood shine in love.

    Or where the shadows of dark solemn yews
20   Brood silently o'er some lone burial-ground,
    Thy verse hath power that brightly might diffuse
    A breath, a kindling, as of spring, around;
    From its own glow of hope and courage high,
    And steadfast faith's victorious constancy.

25 True bard, and holy!—thou art ev'n as one
        Who, by some secret gift of soul or eye,
    In every spot beneath the smiling sun,
        Sees where the springs of living waters lie:
    Unseen awhile they sleep—till, touch'd by thee,
30 Bright healthful waves flow forth to each glad wanderer free.

THOMAS DE QUINCEY

From On Wordsworth's Poetry[†]

* * * Now, amongst all works that have illustrated our own age, none can more deserve an earnest notice than those of the Laureate; and on some grounds, peculiar to themselves, none so much. Their merit in fact is not only supreme but unique; not only supreme in their general class, but unique as in a class of their own. And there is a challenge of a separate nature to the curiosity of the readers, in the remarkable contrast between the first stage of Wordsworth's acceptation with the public and that

† On De Quincey (1785–1859) see the Biographical and Topographical Glossary. His earlier essays on WW, written as parts of his "Lake Reminiscences" and "Autobiography" for *Tait's Edinburgh Magazine* in 1839 and 1840, contained indiscreet biographical anecdotes and reflected the deterioration of De Quincey's personal relationship with the Wordsworth family after 1815. But this essay, first published in *Tait's* in September 1845, is De Quincey's most sustained assessment of WW's poetry. The text is excerpted from the critical edition by Frederick Burwick in vol. 15 of *The Works of Thomas De Quincey* (London: Pickering, 2003), 223–42. A long discussion of *The Excursion* (of which De Quincey is severely critical) has been omitted, as have the author's footnotes (with one exception). Reprinted by permission.

which he enjoys at present. One original obstacle to the favourable impression of the Wordsworthian poetry, and an obstacle purely self-created, was his theory of poetic diction. The diction itself, without the theory, was of less consequence; for the mass of readers would have been too blind or too careless to notice it. But the preface to the second edition of his Poems, [i.e. *Lyrical Ballads*] (2 vols. 1799–1800,) compelled them to notice it. Nothing more injudicious was ever done by man. An unpopular truth would, at any rate, have been a bad inauguration, for what, on *other* accounts, the author had announced as 'an experiment.' His poetry was already an experiment as regarded the quality of the subjects selected, and as regarded the mode of treating them. That was surely trial enough for the reader's untrained sensibilities, without the unpopular truth besides, as to the diction. But, in the mean time, this truth, besides being unpopular, was also, in part, false: it was true and it was *not* true. And it was not true in a double way. Stating broadly, and allowing it to be taken for his meaning, that the diction of ordinary life, in his own words, 'the very language of man,' was the proper diction for poetry, the writer meant no such thing; for only a *part* of this diction, according to his own subsequent restriction, was available for such a use. And, secondly, as his own subsequent practice showed, even this part was available only for peculiar classes of poetry. In his own exquisite 'Laodamia,' in his Sonnets, in his 'Excursion,' few are his obligations to the idiomatic language of life, as distinguished from that of books, or of prescriptive usage. Coleridge remarked, justly, that 'The Excursion' bristles beyond most poems with what are called 'dictionary' words; that is, polysyllabic words of Latin or Greek origin. And so it must ever be, in meditative poetry upon solemn philosophic themes. The gamut of ideas needs a corresponding gamut of expressions; the scale of the thinking, which ranges through *every* key, exacts, for the artist, an unlimited command over the entire scale of the instrument which he employs. * * *

But a blunder, more perhaps from thoughtlessness and careless reading, than from malice on the part of the professional critics, ought to have roused Wordsworth into a firmer feeling of the entire question. These critics had fancied that, in Wordsworth's estimate, whatsoever was plebeian was also poetically just in diction; not as though the impassioned phrase were sometimes the vernacular phrase, but as though the vernacular phrase were universally the impassioned. They naturally went on to suggest, as a corollary, which Wordsworth could not refuse, that Dryden and Pope must be translated into the flash diction of prisons and the slang of streets, before they could be regarded as poetically costumed. Now, so far as these critics were concerned, the answer would have been—simply to say, that much in the poets mentioned, but especially of the racy Dryden, actually is in that vernacular diction for which Wordsworth contended; and, for the other part, which is *not*, frequently it *does* require the very purgation, (if *that* were possible,) which the critics were presuming to be so absurd. In Pope, and sometimes in Dryden, there is much of the unfeeling and the prescriptive slang which Wordsworth denounced. During the eighty years between 1680 and 1740, grew up that scrofulous taint in our diction, which was denounced by Wordsworth as technically 'poetic language;' and, if Dryden and Pope were less infected than others, this was merely because their understandings were finer. Much there is in both poets, as regards diction, which *does* require correction. And if, *so* far, the critics should resist Wordsworth's principle of reform, not he but they, would have been found the patrons of deformity. This course would soon have turned the tables upon the critics. For the poets, or the class of poets, whom they unwisely selected as models, susceptible of no correction, happen to be those who chiefly require it. But *their* foolish selection ought not to have intercepted or clouded the question when put in another shape, since in this shape it opens into a very troublesome dilemma. Spenser, Shakespere, the Bible of 1610, and Milton—how say you, William Wordsworth,—are these right and true as to diction, or are they not? If you say—they *are*; Then what is it that you are proposing to change? What room for a revolution?

*   *   *

Passing from the diction of Wordsworth's poetry to its matter, the least plausible objection ever brought against it, was that of Mr. Hazlitt: 'One would suppose,' he said, 'from the tenor of his subjects, that on this earth there was neither marrying nor giving in marriage.' But as well might it be said of Aristophanes:[1] 'One would suppose, that in Athens no such thing had been known as sorrow and weeping.' Or Wordsworth himself might say reproachfully to some of Mr. Hazlitt's more favoured poets: 'Judging by *your* themes, a man must believe that there is no such thing on our planet as fighting and kicking.' * * * Surely, if every man finds his powers limited, every man would do well to respect this silent admonition of nature, by not travelling out of his appointed walk, through any coxcombry of sporting a spurious versatility. And in this view, what Mr. Hazlitt made the reproach of the poet, is amongst the first of his praises. But there is another reason why Wordsworth could not meddle with festal raptures like the glory of a wedding-day. These raptures are not only too brief, but (which is worse) they tend downwards: even for a long as they last, they do not move upon an ascending scale. And even *that* is not their worst fault: they do not diffuse or communicate themselves: the wretches chiefly interested in a marriage are so selfish, that they keep all the rapture to themselves. Mere joy, that does not linger and reproduce itself in reverberations or mirrors, is not fitted for poetry. What would the sun be itself, if it were a mere blank orb of fire that did not multiply its splendours through millions of rays refracted and reflected; or if its glory were not endlessly caught, splintered, and thrown back by atmospheric repercussions?

There is, besides, a still subtler reason, (and one that ought not to have escaped the acuteness of Mr. Hazlitt,) why the muse of Wordsworth could not glorify a wedding festival. Poems no longer than a sonnet he *might* derive from such an impulse: and one such poem of his there really is. But whosoever looks searchingly into the characteristic genius of Wordsworth, will see that he does not willingly deal with a passion in its direct aspect, or presenting an unmodified contour, but in forms more complex and oblique, and when passing under the shadow of some secondary passion. Joy, for instance, that wells up from constitutional sources, joy that is ebullient from youth to age and cannot cease to sparkle, he yet exhibits

1. Athenian comic dramatist (ca. 460/450–ca. 386 B.C.E.).

in the person of Matthew,[2] the village schoolmaster, as touched and over-gloomed by memories of sorrow. In the poem of 'We are Seven,' which brings into day for the first time a profound fact in the abysses of human nature, namely, that the mind of an infant cannot admit the idea of death, any more than the fountain of light can comprehend the aboriginal darkness, * * * the little mountaineer, who furnishes the text for this lovely strain, she whose fulness of life could not brook the gloomy faith in a grave, is yet (for the effect upon the reader) brought into connexion with the reflex shadows of the grave: and if she herself has *not*, the reader *has*, the gloom of that contemplation obliquely irradiated, and raised in relief upon his imagination, even by her. Death and its sunny antipole are forced into connexion.

* * *

At length, as the eighteenth century was winding up its accounts, forth stepped William Wordsworth, of whom, as a reader of all pages in nature, it may be said that, if we except Dampier, the admirable buccaneer, and some few professional naturalists, he first and he last looked at natural objects with the eye that neither will be dazzled from without nor cheated by preconceptions from within. Most men look at nature in the hurry of a confusion that distinguishes nothing: *their* error is from without. Pope, again, and many who live in towns, make such blunders as that of supposing the moon to tip with silver the hills *behind* which she is rising, not by erroneous use of their eyes, (for they use them not at all,) but by inveterate preconceptions. Scarcely has there been a poet with what could be called a learned eye, or an eye *extensively* learned, before Wordsworth. Much affectation there has been of that sort since *his* rise, and at all times much counterfeit enthusiasm: but the sum of the matter is this, that Wordsworth had his passion for nature fixed in his blood;—it was a necessity, like that of the mulberry-leaf to the silk-worm; and through his commerce with nature did he live and breathe. Hence it was, viz, from the *truth* of his love, that his knowledge grew; whilst most others, being merely hypocrites in their love, have turned out merely *charlatans* in their knowledge. This chapter, therefore, of *sky* scenery may be said to have been revivified amongst the resources of poetry by Wordsworth— rekindled, if not absolutely kindled. * * *

As another of those natural appearances which must have haunted men's eyes since the Flood, but yet had never forced itself into *conscious* notice until arrested by Wordsworth, I may notice an effect of *iteration* daily exhibited in the habits of cattle:

> The cattle are grazing,
> Their heads never raising;
> There are forty feeding like one.[3]

Now, merely as a *fact*, and if it were nothing more, this characteristic appearance in the habits of cows, when all repeat the action of each, ought not to have been overlooked by those who profess themselves engaged in holding up a mirror to nature. But the fact has also a profound meaning as a hieroglyphic. In all animals which live under the protection

2. De Quincey's note: "See the exquisite poems, so little understood by the common-place reader, of *The Two April Mornings* and *The Fountain*."
3. *Written in March* (1807), lines 8–10.

of man a life of peace and quietness, but do not share in his labours or in his pleasures, what we regard is the species, and not the individual. * * *

A volume might be filled with such glimpses of novelty as Wordsworth has first laid bare, even to the apprehension of the *senses*. For the *understanding*, when moving in the same track of human sensibilities, he has done only not so much. How often (to give an instance or two) must the human heart have felt that there are sorrows which descend far below the region in which tears gather; and yet who has ever given utterance to this feeling until Wordsworth came with his immortal line—

> Thoughts that do often lie too deep for tears?[4]

This sentiment, and others that might be adduced, (such as 'The child is father of the man,') have even passed into the popular mind, and are often quoted by those who know *not* whom they are quoting. Magnificent, again, is the sentiment, and yet an echo to one which lurks amongst all hearts, in relation to the frailty of merely human schemes for working good, which so often droop and collapse through the unsteadiness of human energies,—

> ——foundations must be laid
> In Heaven.[5]

How? Foundations laid in realms that are *above*? But *that* is at war with physics;—foundations must be laid *below*. Yes; and even so the poet throws the mind yet more forcibly on the hyperphysical character—on the grandeur transcending all physics—of those shadowy foundations which alone are enduring.

But the great distinction of Wordsworth, and the pledge of his increasing popularity, is the extent of his sympathy with what is *really* permanent in human feelings, and also the depth of this sympathy. Young and Cowper, the two earlier leaders in the province of meditative poetry, are too circumscribed in the range of their sympathies, too exclusive, and oftentimes not sufficiently profound. Both these poets manifested the quality of their strength by the quality of their public reception. Popular in some degree from the first, they entered upon the inheritance of their fame almost at once. Far different was the fate of Wordsworth; for, in poetry of this class, which appeals to what lies deepest in man, in proportion to the native power of the poet, and his fitness for permanent life, is the strength of resistance in the public taste. Whatever is too original will be hated at the first. It must slowly mould a public for itself; and the resistance of the early thoughtless judgments must be overcome by a counter resistance to itself, in a better audience slowly mustering against the first. Forty and seven years it is since William Wordsworth first appeared as an author. Twenty of those years he was the scoff of the world, and his poetry a bye-word of scorn. Since then, and more than once, senates have rung with acclamations to the echo of his name. Now at this moment, whilst we are talking about him, he has entered upon his seventy sixth year. For himself, according to the course of nature, he cannot be far from his setting; but his poetry is but now clearing the clouds

4. Intimations Ode, line 203.
5. *Malham Cove* (1819), lines 10–11.

that gathered about its rising. Meditative poetry is perhaps that which will finally maintain most power upon generations more thoughtful; and in this department, at least, there is little competition to be apprehended by Wordsworth from any thing that has appeared since the death of Shakespere.

RALPH WALDO EMERSON

From English Traits[†]

* * *

On the 28th August I went to Rydal Mount to pay my respects to Mr. Wordsworth. His daughters called in their father, a plain, elderly, white-haired man, not pre-possessing, and disfigured by green goggles. He sat down, and talked with great simplicity. He had just returned from a journey. His health was good, but he had broken a tooth by a fall, when walking with two lawyers, and had said, that he was glad it did not happen forty years ago; whereupon they had praised his philosophy.

He had much to say of America, the more that it gave occasion for his favourite topic—that society is being enlightened by a superficial tuition [i.e., instruction], out of all proportion to its being restrained by moral culture. Schools do no good. Tuition is not education. He thinks more of the education of circumstances than of tuition. 'Tis not question whether there are offences of which the law takes cognizance, but whether there are offences of which the law does not take cognizance. Sin is what he fears, and how society is to escape without gravest mischief from this source—? He has even said what seemed a paradox, that they needed a civil war in America, to teach the necessity of knitting the social ties stronger. "There may be," he said, "in America, some vulgarity in manner, but that's not important. That comes of the pioneer state of things. But I fear they are too much given to the making of money; and, secondly, to politics; that they make political distinction the end, and not the means. And I fear they lack a class of men of leisure—in short, of gentlemen—to give a tone of honour to the community. I am told that things are boasted of in the second class of society there, which, in England,—God knows, are done in England every day,—but would never be spoken of. In America I wish to know not how many churches or schools, but what newspapers? My friend Colonel Hamilton,[1] at the foot of the hill, who was a year in America, assures me that the newspapers are atrocious, and accuse members of Congress of stealing spoons!" He was against taking off the tax on newspapers in England, which the reformers represent as a tax upon knowledge, for this reason, that they would be inundated with base prints. He said, he talked on political aspects, for he wished to impress on me and all good Americans to cultivate the moral, the conservative,

---

† On his first trip to England in 1833, the American Transcendentalist essayist, philosopher, and poet Emerson (1803–1882) met WW, then aged sixty-three, at Rydal Mount. The text is taken from the first British edition of Emerson's *English Traits* (London, 1856), 10–13, in which the account of his visit to WW concludes the first chapter.

1. Thomas Hamilton (1782–1842), Scottish novelist and travel writer, author of *Men and Manners in America* (2 vols., 1833).

&c. &c., and never to call into action the physical strength of the people, as had just now been done in England in the Reform Bill,—a thing prophesied by Delolme.[2] He alluded once or twice to his conversation with Dr. Channing,[3] who had recently visited him (laying his hand on a particular chair in which the Doctor had sat).

The conversation turned on books. Lucretius[4] he esteems a far higher poet than Virgil: not in his system, which is nothing, but in his power of illustration. Faith is necessary to explain anything;, and to reconcile the foreknowledge of God with human evil. Of Cousin[5] (whose lectures we had all been reading in Boston) he knew only the name.

I inquired if he had read Carlyle's[6] critical articles and translations. He said, he thought him sometimes insane. He proceeded to abuse Goethe's "Wilhelm Meister" heartily. It was full of all manner of fornication. It was like the crossing of flies in the air. He had never gone farther than the first part; so disgusted was he that he threw the book across the room. I deprecated this wrath, and said what I could for the better parts of the book; and he courteously promised to look at it again. Carlyle, he said, wrote most obscurely. He was clever and deep, but he defied the sympathies of everybody. Even Mr. Coleridge wrote more clearly, though he had always wished Coleridge would write more to be understood. He led me out into his garden, and showed me the gravel walk in which thousands of his lines were composed. His eyes are much inflamed. This is no loss, except for reading, because he never writes prose, and of poetry he carries even hundreds of lines in his head before writing them. He had just returned from a visit to Staffa, and within three days had made three sonnets on Fingal's Cave,[7] and was composing a fourth, when he was called in to see me. He said, "If you are interested in my verses, perhaps you will like to hear these lines." I gladly assented; and he recollected himself for a few moments, and then stood forth and repeated, one after the other, the three entire sonnets with great animation. I fancied the second and third more beautiful than his poems are wont to be. The third is addressed to the flowers, which, he said, especially the ox-eye daisy, are very abundant on the top of the rock. The second alludes to the name of the cave, which is "Cave of Music;" the first to the circumstance of its being visited by the promiscuous company of the steamboat.

This recitation was so unlooked for and surprising—he, the old Wordsworth, standing apart, and reciting to me in a garden-walk, like a schoolboy declaiming—that I at first was near to laugh; but recollecting myself,

2. Jean Louis Delome (1740–1806), Swiss constitutional theorist who lived in political exile in England for over two decades and published *The Constitution of England* (1772).
3. William Ellery Channing (1780–1842), American Unitarian clergyman and abolitionist writer who had met WW in England in July 1822 (see *WL*, 4:606 and n.).
4. Titus Lucretius Carus (ca. 95–ca. 55 B.C.E.), Roman Epicurean poet, author of *De rerum natura* [*On the Nature of Things*] in six books (see *Reading 1770–99*, no. 160).
5. Victor Cousin (1792–1867), French philosopher, the English translation of whose *Introduction to the History of Philosophy* was published in Boston in 1832.
6. Thomas Carlyle (1795–1881), Scottish author, historian, and translator of *Wilhelm Meister's Apprenticeship* (3 vols., 1824) by the German writer Johann Wolfgang Goethe (1749–1832). The first book of Goethe's novel (originally published in 1795–96) is concerned with the eponymous protagonist's unfounded belief that his beloved Marianne is unfaithful to him.
7. A cave on the coast of the uninhabited island of Staffa in the Scottish Inner Hebrides. The sonnets by WW to which Emerson refers are *We saw, but surely, in the motley crowd*, *Thanks for the lesson of this Spot—fit school*, *Ye shadowy Beings, that have rights and claims*, and (the one addressed to the Flowers) *Flowers on the Top of the Pillars at the Entrance of the Cave.*

that I had come thus far to see a poet, and he was chanting poems to me, I saw that he was right and I was wrong, and gladly gave myself up to hear. I told him how much the few printed extracts had quickened the desire to possess his unpublished poems. He replied, he never was in haste to publish; partly, because he corrected a good deal, and every alteration is ungraciously received after printing; but what he had written would be printed, whether he lived or died. I said, "Tintern Abbey" appeared to be the favourite poem with the public, but more contemplative readers preferred the first books of the "Excursion," and the "Sonnets." He said, "Yes, they are better." He preferred such of his poems as touched the affections to any others; for whatever is didactic,—what theories of society, and so on,—might perish quickly; but whatever combined a truth with an affection was κτῆμα ες αει,[8] good to-day and good for ever. * * *

When I prepared to depart, he said he wished to show me what a common person in England could do, and he led me into the enclosure of his clerk, a young man to whom he had given this slip of ground, which was laid out, or its natural capabilities shown, with much taste. He then said he would show me a better way towards the inn; and he walked a good part of a mile, talking, and ever and anon stopping short to impress the word or the verse, and finally parted from me with great kindness, and returned across the fields.

Wordsworth honoured himself by his simple adherence to truth, and was very willing not to shine; but he surprised by the hard limits of his thought. To judge from a single conversation, he made the impression of a narrow and very English mind; of one who paid for his rare elevation by general tameness and conformity. Off his own beat, his opinions were of no value. It is not very rare to find persons loving sympathy and ease, who expiate their departure from the common, in one direction, by their conformity in every other.

JOHN STUART MILL

From Autobiography[†]

* * *

My education, I thought, had failed to create these feelings in sufficient strength to resist the dissolving influence of analysis, while the whole course of my intellectual cultivation had made precocious and premature analysis the inveterate habit of my mind. I was thus, as I said to myself, left stranded at the commencement of my voyage, with a well-equipped

8. Emerson paraphrases the Greek phrase from *The Peloponnesian War* 1.22.4 by the historian Thucydides (ca. 460/55–ca. 400 B.C.E.). A more accurate translation is "a possession for ever."
† A utilitarian philosopher, economist, and advocate of individual liberty (particularly women's rights), Mill (1806–1873) was one of the most important contributors to nineteenth-century English social and political theory. Rigorously educated from the age of three by his father, a Scottish philosopher, in Greek, Latin, mathematics, logic, economics, history, the natural sciences, and poetry, Mill suffered a mental breakdown when he was twenty. His posthumously published *Autobiography* (first drafted in 1853–54 and revised in the 1860s) describes his depression of 1826–27 and its gradual dissipation, which he attributed in part to his reading of Wordsworth's poetry. The present excerpt is from the *Autobiography*, 2nd ed. (London, 1873), 138–39, 146–49.

ship and a rudder, but no sail; without any real desire for the ends which
I had been so carefully fitted out to work for: no delight in virtue, or the
general good, but also just as little in anything else. The fountains of van-
ity and ambition seemed to have dried up within me, as completely as
those of benevolence. I had had (as I reflected) some gratification of van-
ity at too early an age: I had obtained some distinction, and felt myself of
some importance, before the desire of distinction and of importance had
grown into a passion: and little as it was which I had attained, yet having
been attained too early, like all pleasures enjoyed too soon, it had made
me *blasé* and indifferent to the pursuit. Thus neither selfish nor unselfish
pleasures were pleasures to me. And there seemed no power in nature
sufficient to begin the formation of my character anew, and create in a
mind now irretrievably analytic, fresh associations of pleasure with any
of the objects of human desire.

*   *   *

This state of my thoughts and feelings made the fact of my reading
Wordsworth for the first time (in the autumn of 1828), an important
event in my life. I took up the collection of his poems from curiosity, with
no expectation of mental relief from it, though I had before resorted to
poetry with that hope. In the worst period of my depression, I had read
through the whole of Byron[1] (then new to me), to try whether a poet,
whose peculiar department was supposed to be that of the intenser feel-
ings, could rouse any feeling in me. As might be expected, I got no good
from this reading, but the reverse. The poet's state of mind was too like
my own. His was the lament of a man who had worn out all pleasures, and
who seemed to think that life, to all who possess the good things of it,
must necessarily be the vapid, uninteresting thing which I found it. His
Harold and Manfred had the same burden on them which I had; and I was
not in a frame of mind to desire any comfort from the vehement sensual
passion of his Giaours, or the sullenness of his Laras. But while Byron was
exactly what did not suit my condition, Wordsworth was exactly what did.
I had looked into the Excursion two or three years before, and found little
in it; and I should probably have found as little, had I read it at this time.
But the miscellaneous poems, in the two-volume edition of 1815 (to which
little of value was added in the latter part of the author's life), proved to be
the precise thing for my mental wants at that particular juncture.

In the first place, these poems addressed themselves powerfully to one
of the strongest of my pleasurable susceptibilities, the love of rural objects
and natural scenery; to which I had been indebted not only for much of
the pleasure of my life, but quite recently for relief from one of my longest
relapses into depression. In this power of rural beauty over me, there was
a foundation laid for taking pleasure in Wordsworth's poetry; the more
so, as his scenery lies mostly among mountains, which, owing to my early
Pyrenean excursion, were my ideal of natural beauty. But Wordsworth
would never have had any great effect on me, if he had merely placed
before me beautiful pictures of natural scenery. Scott does this still bet-

---

1. Lord Byron (1788–1824), the most popular English poet of the early nineteenth century. Mill
proceeds to refer to Byron's *Childe Harold's Pilgrimage* (1812, 1818, 1819), a narrative poem in
four cantos, and *Manfred* (1817), a closet drama in three acts.

ter than Wordsworth, and a very second-rate landscape does it more effectually than any poet. What made Wordsworth's poems a medicine for my state of mind, was that they expressed, not mere outward beauty, but states of feeling, and of thought coloured by feeling, under the excitement of beauty. They seemed to be the very culture of the feelings, which I was in quest of. In them I seemed to draw from a source of inward joy, of sympathetic and imaginative pleasure, which could be shared in by all human beings; which had no connexion with struggle or imperfection, but would be made richer by every improvement in the physical or social condition of mankind. From them I seemed to learn what would be the perennial sources of happiness, when all the greater evils of life shall have been removed. And I felt myself at once better and happier as I came under their influence. There have certainly been, even in our own age, greater poets than Wordsworth; but poetry of deeper and loftier feeling could not have done for me at that time what his did. I needed to be made to feel that there was real, permanent happiness in tranquil contemplation. Wordsworth taught me this, not only without turning away from, but with a greatly increased interest in the common feelings and common destiny of human beings. And the delight which these poems gave me, proved that with culture of this sort, there was nothing to dread from the most confirmed habit of analysis. At the conclusion of the Poems came the famous Ode, falsely called Platonic, "Intimations of Immortality:" in which, along with more than his usual sweetness of melody and rhythm, and along with the two passages of grand imagery but bad philosophy so often quoted, I found that he too had had similar experience to mine; that he also had felt that the first freshness of youthful enjoyment of life was not lasting; but that he had sought for compensation, and found it, in the way in which he was now teaching me to find it. The result was that I gradually, but completely, emerged from my habitual depression, and was never again subject to it. I long continued to value Wordsworth less according to his intrinsic merits, than by the measure of what he had done for me. Compared with the greatest poets, he may be said to be the poet of unpoetical natures, possessed of quiet and contemplative tastes. But unpoetical natures are precisely those which require poetic cultivation. This cultivation Wordsworth is much more fitted to give, than poets who are intrinsically far more poets than he.

* * *

MATTHEW ARNOLD

From Preface *to* The Poems of Wordsworth[†]

* * *

Wordsworth has been in his grave for some thirty years, and certainly his lovers and admirers cannot flatter themselves that this great and steady light of glory as yet shines over him. He is not fully recognised at home;

---

† A poet, influential literary and social critic, and educational reformer, Arnold (1822–1888) first published this essay as the preface to his selection of *The Poems of Wordsworth* (London, 1879), reprinting it in his *Essays in Criticism, Second Series* (1888). It is excerpted here from the first printing.

he is not recognised at all abroad. Yet I firmly believe that the poetical performance of Wordsworth is, after that of Shakspeare and Milton, of which all the world now recognises the worth, undoubtedly the most considerable in our language from the Elizabethan age to the present time. Chaucer is anterior; and on other grounds, too, he cannot well be brought into the comparison. But taking the roll of our chief poetical names, besides Shakspeare and Milton, from the age of Elizabeth downwards, and going through it,—Spenser, Dryden, Pope, Gray, Goldsmith, Cowper, Burns, Coleridge, Scott, Campbell, Moore, Byron, Shelley, Keats (I mention those only who are dead),—I think it certain that Wordsworth's name deserves to stand, and will finally stand, above them all. Several of the poets named have gifts and excellences which Wordsworth has not. But taking the performance of each as a whole, I say that Wordsworth seems to me to have left a body of poetical work superior in power, in interest, in the qualities which give enduring freshness, to that which any one of the others has left.

*　　*　　*

This is a high claim to make for Wordsworth. But if it is a just claim, if Wordsworth's place among the poets who have appeared in the last two or three centuries is after Shakspeare, Molière, Milton, Goethe, indeed, but before all the rest, then in time Wordsworth will have his due. We shall recognise him in his place, as we recognise Shakspeare and Milton; and not only we ourselves shall recognise him, but he will be recognised by Europe also. Meanwhile, those who recognise him already may do well, perhaps, to ask themselves whether there are not in the case of Wordsworth certain special obstacles which hinder or delay his due recognition by others, and whether these obstacles are not in some measure removable.

The *Excursion* and the *Prelude*, his poems of greatest bulk, are by no means Wordsworth's best work. His best work is in his shorter pieces, and many indeed are there of these which are of first-rate excellence. But in his seven volumes the pieces of high merit are mingled with a mass of pieces very inferior to them; so inferior to them that it seems wonderful how the same poet should have produced both. Shakspeare frequently has lines and passages in a strain quite false, and which are entirely unworthy of him. But one can imagine his smiling if one could meet him in the Elysian Fields and tell him so; smiling and replying that he knew it perfectly well himself, and what did it matter? But with Wordsworth the case is different. Work altogether inferior, work quite uninspired, flat and dull, is produced by him with evident unconsciousness of its defects, and he presents it to us with the same faith and seriousness as his best work. Now a drama or an epic fill the mind, and one does not look beyond them; but in a collection of short pieces the impression made by one piece requires to be continued and sustained by the piece following. In reading Wordsworth the impression made by one of his fine pieces is too often dulled and spoiled by a very inferior piece coming after it.

Wordsworth composed verses during a space of some sixty years; and it is no exaggeration to say that within one single decade of those years, between 1798 and 1808, almost all his really first-rate work was produced. A mass of inferior work remains, work done before and after this golden prime, imbedding the first-rate work and clogging it, obstructing our approach to it, chilling, not unfrequently, the high-wrought mood with which we leave it. To be recognised far and wide as a great poet, to be possible and receivable as a classic, Wordsworth needs to be relieved of a great deal of the poetical baggage which now encumbers him. To administer this relief is indispensable, unless he is to continue to be a poet for the few only, a poet valued far below his real worth by the world.

There is another thing. Wordsworth classified his poems not according to any commonly received plan of arrangement, but according to a scheme of mental physiology. He has poems of the fancy, poems of the imagination, poems of sentiment and reflexion, and so on.[1] His categories are ingenious but far-fetched, and the result of his employment of them is unsatisfactory. Poems are separated one from another which possess a kinship of subject or of treatment far more vital and deep than the supposed unity of mental origin which was Wordsworth's reason for joining them with others.

The tact of the Greeks in matters of this kind was infallible. We may rely upon it that we shall not improve upon the classification adopted by the Greeks for kinds of poetry; that their categories of epic, dramatic, lyric, and so forth, have a natural propriety, and should be adhered to. It may sometimes seem doubtful to which of two categories a poem belongs; whether this or that poem is to be called, for instance, narrative or lyric, lyric or elegiac. But there is to be found in every good poem a strain, a predominant note, which determines the poem as belonging to one of these kinds rather than the other; and here is the best proof of the value of the classification, and of the advantage of adhering to it. Wordsworth's poems will never produce their due effect until they are freed from their present artificial arrangement, and grouped more naturally.

Disengaged from the quantity of inferior work which now obscures them, the best poems of Wordsworth, I hear many people say, would indeed stand out in great beauty, but they would prove to be very few in number, scarcely more than half-a-dozen. I maintain, on the other hand, that what strikes me with admiration, what establishes in my opinion Wordsworth's superiority, is the great and ample body of powerful work which remains to him, even after all his inferior work has been cleared away. He gives us so much to rest upon, so much which communicates his spirit and engages ours!

This is of very great importance. If it were a comparison of single pieces, or of three or four pieces, by each poet, I do not say that Wordsworth would stand decisively above Gray, or Burns, or Keats, or Manzoni, or Heine.[2] It is in his ampler body of powerful work that I find his superiority. His good work itself, his work which counts, is not all of it, of course, of equal value. Some kinds of poetry are in themselves lower kinds than others. The ballad kind is a lower kind; the didactic kind, still more, is a lower kind. Poetry of this latter sort, counts, too, sometimes, by its biographical interest partly, not by its poetical interest pure and simple; but then this can only be when the poet producing it has the power and importance of Wordsworth, a power and importance which he assuredly did not establish by such didactic poetry alone. Altogether, it is, I say, by

---

1. Arnold refers to WW's classification of his poems in *P 1815*.
2. Heinrich Heine (1797–1856), German lyric and satirical poet and essayist; *Gray:* Thomas Gray (1716–1771), English lyric poet whose poetic diction WW criticized in the Preface to *LB 1800*; *Burns:* Robert Burns (1759–1796), Scottish poet and lyricist; *Manzoni:* Alessandro Manzoni (1785–1873), Italian poet and novelist.

the great body of powerful and significant work which remains to him, after every reduction and deduction has been made, that Wordsworth's superiority is proved.

To exhibit this body of Wordsworth's best work, to clear away obstructions from around it, and to let it speak for itself, is what every lover of Wordsworth should desire. Until this has been done, Wordsworth, whom we, to whom he is dear, all of us know and feel to be so great a poet, has not had a fair chance before the world. When once it has been done, he will make his way best not by our advocacy of him, but by his own worth and power. We may safely leave him to make his way thus, we who believe that a superior worth and power in poetry finds in mankind a sense responsive to it and disposed at last to recognise it. Yet at the outset, before he has been duly known and recognised, we may do Wordsworth a service, perhaps, by indicating in what his superior power and worth will be found to consist, and in what it will not.

Long ago, in speaking of Homer, I said that the noble and profound application of ideas to life is the most essential part of poetic greatness. I said that a great poet receives his distinctive character of superiority from his application, under the conditions immutably fixed by the laws of poetic beauty and poetic truth, from his application, I say, to his subject, whatever it may be, of the ideas

> On man, on nature, and on human life,

which he has acquired for himself. The line quoted is Wordsworth's own;[3] and his superiority arises from his powerful use, in his best pieces, his powerful application to his subject, of ideas "on man, on nature, and on human life."

*   *   *

Voltaire[4] was right in thinking that the energetic and profound treatment of moral ideas, in this large sense, is what distinguishes the English poetry. He sincerely meant praise, not dispraise or hint of limitation; and they err who suppose that poetic limitation is a necessary consequence of the fact, the fact being granted as Voltaire states it. If what distinguishes the greatest poets is their powerful and profound application of ideas to life, which surely no good critic will deny, then to prefix to the term ideas here the term moral makes hardly any difference, because human life itself is in so preponderating a degree moral.

It is important, therefore, to hold fast to this: that poetry is at bottom a criticism of life; that the greatness of a poet lies in his powerful and beautiful application of ideas to life,—to the question: How to live. Morals are often treated in a narrow and false fashion, they are bound up with systems of thought and belief which have had their day, they are fallen into the hands of pedants and professional dealers, they grow tiresome to some of us. We find attraction, at times, even in a poetry of revolt against them; in a poetry which might take for its motto Omar Kheyam's words: "Let us make up in the tavern for the time which we

3. Arnold quotes the first line of the Prospectus to *The Recluse* (see p. 444 above).
4. Born François-Marie Arouet (1694–1778), Voltaire was a prolific French Enlightenment writer, historian, and philosopher, who became interested in English literature and the British political system during his exile in London (1726–28).

have wasted in the mosque."[5] Or we find attractions in a poetry indifferent to them, in a poetry where the contents may be what they will, but where the form is studied and exquisite. We delude ourselves in either case; and the best cure for our delusion is to let our minds rest upon that great and inexhaustible word *life*, until we learn to enter into its meaning. A poetry of revolt against moral ideas is a poetry of revolt against *life*; a poetry of indifference towards moral ideas is a poetry of indifference towards *life*.

* * *

And when we come across a poet like Wordsworth, who sings,

> Of truth, of grandeur, beauty, love and hope,
> And melancholy fear subdued by faith,
> Of blessed consolations in distress,
> Of moral strength and intellectual power,
> Of joy in widest commonalty spread—[6]

then we have a poet intent on "the best and master thing," and who prosecutes his journey home. We say, for brevity's sake, that he deals with *life*, because he deals with that in which life really consists. This is what Voltaire means to praise in the English poets,—this dealing with what is really life. But always it is the mark of the greatest poets that they deal with it; and to say that the English poets are remarkable for dealing with it, is only another way of saying, what is true, that in poetry the English genius has especially shown its power.

Wordsworth deals with it, and his greatness lies in his dealing with it so powerfully. I have named a number of celebrated poets above all of whom he, in my opinion, deserves to be placed. * * * Where, then, is Wordsworth's superiority? It is here; he deals with more of *life* than they do; he deals with *life*, as a whole, more powerfully.

No Wordsworthian will doubt this. * * * But we must be on our guard against the Wordsworthians, if we want to secure for Wordsworth his due rank as a poet. The Wordsworthians are apt to praise him for the wrong things, and to lay far too much stress upon what they call his philosophy. His poetry is the reality, his philosophy,—so far, at least, as it may put on the form and habit of "a scientific system of thought," and the more that it puts them on,—is the illusion. Perhaps we shall one day learn to make this proposition general, and to say: Poetry is the reality, philosophy the illusion. But in Wordsworth's case, at any rate, we cannot do him justice until we dismiss his formal philosophy.

The *Excursion* abounds with philosophy, and therefore the *Excursion* is to the Wordsworthian what it never can be to the disinterested lover of poetry,—a satisfactory work. * * *

Even the "intimations" of the famous Ode, those corner-stones of the supposed philosophic system of Wordsworth,—the idea of the high instincts and affections coming out in childhood, testifying of a divine home recently left, and fading away as our life proceeds,—this idea, of

5. Arnold paraphrases, from a French translation of 1867, no. 368 of the quatrains (commonly known in English as the *Rubáiyát*) of the Persian poet Omar Khayyám (1048–1131) (*The Complete Prose Works of Matthew Arnold*, ed. R. H. Super [Ann Arbor, MI, 1960–78], 9:343).
6. From the Prospectus to *The Recluse*, lines 14–18.

undeniable beauty as a play of fancy, has itself not the character of poetic truth of the best kind; it has no real solidity. The instinct of delight in Nature and her beauty had no doubt extraordinary strength in Wordsworth himself as a child. But to say that universally this instinct is mighty in childhood, and tends to die away afterwards, is to say what is extremely doubtful. In many people, perhaps with the majority of educated persons, the love of nature is nearly imperceptible at ten years old, but strong and operative at thirty. In general we may say of these high instincts of early childhood, the base of the alleged systematic philosophy of Wordsworth, what Thucydides says of the early achievements of the Greek race:—"It is impossible to speak with certainty of what is so remote; but from all that we can really investigate, I should say that they were no very great things."[7]

* * *

Wordsworth's poetry is great because of the extraordinary power with which Wordsworth feels the joy offered to us in nature, the joy offered to us in the simple primary affections and duties; and because of the extraordinary power with which, in case after case, he shows us this joy, and renders it so as to make us share it.

The source of joy from which he thus draws is the truest and most unfailing source of joy accessible to man. It is also accessible universally. Wordsworth brings us word, therefore, according to his own strong and characteristic line, he brings us word

Of joy in widest commonalty spread.

Here is an immense advantage for a poet. Wordsworth tells of what all seek, and tells of it at its truest and best source, and yet a source where all may go and draw for it.

Nevertheless, we are not to suppose that everything is precious which Wordsworth, standing even at this perennial and beautiful source, may give us. Wordsworthians are apt to talk as if it must be. They will speak with the same reverence of *The Sailor's Mother*, for example, as of *Lucy Gray*. They do their master harm by such lack of discrimination. *Lucy Gray* is a beautiful success; *The Sailor's Mother* is a failure. To give aright what he wishes to give, to interpret and render successfully, is not always within Wordsworth's own command. It is within no poet's command; here is the part of the Muse, the inspiration, the God, the "not ourselves." In Wordsworth's case, the accident, for so it may almost be called, of inspiration, is of peculiar importance. No poet, perhaps, is so evidently filled with a new and sacred energy when the inspiration is upon him; no poet, when it fails him, is so left "weak as is a breaking wave."[8] * * * It might seem that Nature not only gave him the matter for his poem, but wrote his poem for him. He has no style. He was too conversant with Milton not to catch at times his master's manner, and he has fine Miltonic lines; but he has no assured poetic style of his own, like Milton. When he seeks to have a style he falls into ponderosity and pomposity.

* * *

7. Thucydides, *The Peloponnesian War* 1.1.3.
8. From *A Poet's Epitaph*, line 58.

Wordsworth owed much to Burns, and a style of perfect plainness, relying for effect solely on the weight and force of that which with entire fidelity it utters, Burns could show him.

> The poor inhabitant below
> Was quick to learn and wise to know,
> And keenly felt the friendly glow
>   And softer flame;
> But thoughtless follies laid him low
> And stain'd his name.[9]

Every one will be conscious of a likeness here to Wordsworth; and if Wordsworth did great things with this nobly plain manner, we must remember, what indeed he himself would always have been forward to acknowledge, that Burns used it before him.

Still Wordsworth's use of it has something unique and unmatchable. Nature herself seems, I say, to take the pen out of his hand, and to write for him with her own bare, sheer, penetrating power. This arises from two causes: from the profound sincereness with which Wordsworth feels his subject, and also from the profoundly sincere and natural character of his subject itself. He can and will treat such a subject with nothing but the most plain, first-hand, almost austere naturalness. His expression may often be called bald, as, for instance, in the poem of *Resolution and Independence;* but it is bald as the bare mountain tops are bald, with a baldness which is full of grandeur.

Wherever we meet with the successful balance, in Wordsworth, of profound truth of subject with profound truth of execution, he is unique. His best poems are those which most perfectly exhibit this balance. I have a warm admiration for *Laodameia* and for the great *Ode;* but if I am to tell the very truth, I find *Laodameia* not wholly free from something artificial, and the great *Ode* not wholly free from something declamatory. If I had to pick out poems of a kind most perfectly to show Wordsworth's unique power, I should rather choose poems such as *Michael, The Fountain, The Highland Reaper.* And poems with the peculiar and unique beauty which distinguishes these, Wordsworth produced in considerable number; besides very many other poems of which the worth, although not so rare as the worth of these, is still exceedingly high.

On the whole, then, as I said at the beginning, not only is Wordsworth eminent by reason of the goodness of his best work, but he is eminent also by reason of the great body of good work which he has left to us. With the ancients I will not compare him. In many respects the ancients are far above us, and yet there is something that we demand which they can never give. Leaving the ancients, let us come to the poets and poetry of Christendom. Dante, Shakspeare, Molière, Milton, Goethe, are altogether larger and more splendid luminaries in the poetical heaven than Wordsworth. But I know not where else, among the moderns, we are to find his superiors.

*   *   *

9. Robert Burns, *A Bard's Epitaph*, lines 19–24.

Modern Criticism

GENERAL STUDIES

SUSAN J. WOLFSON

From Wordsworth's Craft[†]

Composition and Craft

If you consult 'craft' in a Wordsworth concordance or a database, the report is not often cheering. There is much to do with contrivance, debased art, suspect artfulness: the 'dangerous craft of picking phrases out / From languages that want the living voice / To make of them a nature to the heart' (*Prel.1805* vi 130–2), the 'craft' of 'gilded sympathies' in affected 'dreams and fictions' (vi 481–3), 'the marvellous craft / Of modern Merlins' (vii 686–7), 'the Wizard's craft' ('The Egyptian Maid' 44), modern 'Life' decked out by 'the mean handywork of craftsman' ('London 1802' 4), assassins led by those 'whose craft holds no consent / With aught that breathes the ethereal element' (*Dion* 54–5), the 'craft of age, seducing reason' (*Borderers* 363) or 'the craft / Of a shrewd Counsellor' ('Wars of York and Lancaster' 1–2). About as good as it gets is a rare reverence for 'the painter's true Promethean craft' ('Lines suggested' 24) or the poet's hope that his own 'Imagination' has 'learn'd to ply her craft / By judgement steadied' (*Prel.1805* xiii 290–4). Making rigorous inquisition into Wordsworth and poetic craft might even seem perversity, for he is, legendarily, the antithesis. What care for craft can there be in his praise for 'Poets . . . sown / By Nature; Men endowed with highest gifts, / The vision and the faculty divine, / Yet wanting the accomplishment of Verse' (*The Excursion* i 81–4)—'wanting' signifying no urgent desire but an unimportant, accidental lack?

It was Wordsworth, after all, who prompted Hazlitt's wry lecture on the 'new school' of poetry (1818), a few years after *The Excursion* (1814) and twenty years after the debut of *Lyrical Ballads*. With a principle of 'pure nature void of art', this school (said Hazlitt) had expelled traditions of craft as surely as the French Revolution had expelled the monarchy:

> According to the prevailing notions, all was to be natural and new. Nothing that was established was to be tolerated. [. . .] rhyme was

† From *The Cambridge Companion to Wordsworth,* ed. Stephen Gill (Cambridge: Cambridge University Press, 2003), 108–24. Notes have been edited. Copyright © 2003 Cambridge University Press. Reprinted with the permission of Cambridge University Press.

looked upon as a relic of the feudal system, and regular metre was abolished along with regular government.[1]

This is burlesque, but Hazlitt is taking his cue from such manifestos as the Preface to *Lyrical Ballads*, in which Wordsworth rejected neoclassical tenets to declare that 'all good poetry is the spontaneous overflow of powerful feelings' (*LB* 744). So convinced was the poet of this sweeping equation that he called it back, some pages on, to elaborate:

> I have said that Poetry is the spontaneous overflow of powerful feelings: it takes its origin from emotion recollected in tranquillity: the emotion is contemplated till by a species of reaction the tranquillity gradually disappears, and an emotion, similar to that which was before the subject of contemplation, is gradually produced, and does itself actually exist in the mind. In this mood successful composition generally begins, and in a mood similar to this it is carried on.
>
> (*LB* 756)

No utterance in Wordsworth's critical writing, remarks Stephen Parrish, 'has taken on the historical significance of [this] one' (*The Art of the 'Lyrical Ballads'* (Cambridge: Harvard University Press, 1973), p. 4). If the 'Poet' (as Wordsworth knew) is a crafter by etymology (Greek for *maker*), what sort of poetic 'making' is a 'spontaneous overflow'?

*   *   *

The illusion of poetic passivity under the force of natural inevitability has prompted a critique in recent decades of what might be termed a 'craft of spontaneity', analogous to the insinuation of ideology under the guise of 'organic' origination and value. Anthony Easthope, for one, indicts the Wordsworthian formula with leaving 'unproblematized as aesthetic, formal and natural' the constructedness of 'poetic discourse'.[2] Well before him, Coleridge (collaborator on the first edition of *Lyrical Ballads*) thought the Wordsworthian conception at least contradictory, and so begged to differ. Poetic imagination, he proposes in *Biographia Literaria* (1817), is a balancing act of 'a more than usual state of emotion, with more than usual order; judgement ever awake and steady self-possession, with enthusiasm and feeling profound or vehement' (*BL* ii 17). Yet Wordsworth's own practice (if not always theorizing) has a way of making Coleridge's case (and unmaking Easthope's). Even poems seemingly staged to show how 'emotion recollected in tranquillity' may turn into a 'spontaneous overflow of powerful feelings' give deliberate craft an important role in the drama.

*   *   *

It is with semantically rich craft that Wordsworth shapes the end of the first stanza of another poem in these volumes, 'The Solitary Reaper':

> Alone she cuts, and binds the grain,
> And sings a melancholy strain;
> O listen! for the Vale profound
> Is overflowing with the sound.
>
> (5–8)

1. 'On the Living Poets', *The Complete Works of William Hazlitt*, ed. P. P. Howe (21 vols.; 1930–4), v, pp. 161–2. [See also above, p. 562.]
2. Anthony Easthope, *Poetry as Discourse* (London: Methuen, 1983), p. 23.

The theme is the Wordsworthian myth of poetry, doubled in poet and Maid. To her emotive overflowing (her sound pure song, the import evocatively mysterious), he matches a deftly crafted song. Note how the enjambment (overflowing) of lines 7–8 performs what it describes: 7 halts in a pause of deep silence, then the syntax flows over to 8, where the sound runs softly through the stresses and slips of 'overflowing with the' toward the rhyme. Listen, too, to how beautifully this rhyme has 'sound' echo, as if returning from, 'Vale profound' (how much duller would be 'the sound / Is overflowing the Vale profound'). To the power of this sound, Dorothy Wordsworth could attest: 'There is something inexpressibly soothing to me in the sound of those two Lines', she wrote, listening to and then renewing them with her own echo: 'I often catch myself repeating them' (*WL* i 649–50).

The prototype of this catching is the poem itself. At its conclusion, Wordsworth crafts his lines not only to recall but also to catch its inspiration:

> Whate'er the theme, the Maiden sang
> As if her song could have no ending;
> I saw her singing at her work,
> And o'er the sickle bending;
> I listen'd till I had my fill:
> And, as I mounted up the hill,
> The music in my heart I bore,
> Long after it was heard no more.
>
>   (25–32)

Theme shapes poetry, not only in the lilting measures linking Maiden's song to poet's but also in the semantics of rhyme and non-rhyme. In this craft and subtle art, the poet's rhymes are not of her actions (*work* and *sang* are unrhymed) but his. Murmuring through *sang, song, ending, singing*, the stanza's first rhyme chimes at the falling feminine-measured *bending*, the word literally resounding *ending*, as if to signify how the impression of a song with 'no ending' were to be (and now is) realized in the rhyme of recollection. The 1815 version of the daffodil poem added a stanza that capitalizes on this sense of an ending:

> They stretched in never-ending line
> Along the margin of the bay.

The first line pauses at the verbal margin of 'line', where, without terminal punctuation, it seems to stretch its claims emblematically into the page's open space—an effect that superimposes on the illusion of the flowers' never-ending line their continuation into the poet's open-ended line.[3] Wordsworth's craft at once evokes this suggestion and gives it a poetic correlative.

Ending and *bending* play in the stanza from 'The Solitary Reaper' as similar tropes of poetic craft: *ending* ends the verse line, and *bending* coincides with the bending of the verse line into the poet's listening.

---

3. 'The use of line-endings can be a type or symbol or emblem of what the poet values, as well as the instrument by which his values are expressed', proposes Christopher Ricks (91). For his brilliant discussion of Wordsworth's performance with terms of poetic form, including this instance, see 'A Pure Organic Pleasure from the Lines', in *The Force of Poetry* (1995), pp. 91–116.

Wordsworth intensifies this experiential shift from seeing to pre-poetic listening with the rhyme that rings through *till* / *fill* / *bill* ('I listen'd till I had my fill' is a wonderful little self-listening couplet). He lost this chord when (in 1820) he revised 'till I had my fill' to 'motionless and still', but it was to gain a rich mine in the multiple and interrelated senses of 'still': arrested motion and hushed sound; the counter-pulse (even so) and duration (even yet) in which successful composition begins. In the wake of these vibrations, even as the final lines describe a parting of poet and Maid, the craft of couplets keeps them coupled, and show the shadow of no parting from her. The music 'heard no more' is borne in the 'heart' ('heard' shifted only by a letter) and then, as after-effect and in imagination, reborn in poetic craft.

This textual transformation may be what licensed Wordsworth to place this poem, in 1807, in the subgroup *Poems Written During a Tour in Scotland* and, simultaneously, to append a potentially contradictory note: 'This Poem was suggested by a beautiful sentence in a MS. Tour in Scotland written by a Friend, the last line being taken from it *verbatim*.'[4] retained this note of influence in 1815, even as he assigned the lyric to his own *Poems of the Imagination*. This is the sentence (to which he alludes but stops short of quoting) from his friend's 1789 journal:

> Passed a female who was reaping alone: she sung in Erse as she bended over her sickle; the sweetest human voice I ever heard: her strains were tenderly melancholy, and felt delicious, long after they were heard no more.[5]

Until 1824, when Thomas Wilkinson's *Tours to the British Mountains* was finally published, a general reader had to take Wordsworth's word for his debts and their limit to the last phrase (its perfect iambic tetrameter predicting the poem's measure). When in November 1806 he told Wilkinson, 'your Journal [. . .] is locked up with my manuscripts' (*WL* iii 104), he meant its whereabouts while on loan to him, but the verb 'locked up' uncannily intimates a textual association.

The linked and imported material does not belie Wordsworth's mythology of recollection so much as collate poetic craft with an already textualized memory. Wordsworth has not simply fabricated history (a fiction of 'written during' denying pre-reading and after-writing), nor has he simply lifted and shifted Wilkinson's prose into his rhymes and metres, nor, in a similar textual influence, blithely plucked his sister's journal-prose about the golden daffodils (15 April 1802) for transplant into his own garden of verses. Recollecting these texts in imagination-as-text is the forge of a poetic craft that keeps visible the workmanship exercised to shape 'emotion recollected' into 'successful composition'.

4. *P2V* 415. Peter Manning comments that Wordsworth's placement of the poem in 1807 in the subgroup advertised as 'Written During' belies the craft of recollection by 'presenting as a spontaneous record a subsequent, carefully ordered collection' ('"Will No One Tell Me What She Sings?": "The Solitary Reaper" and the Contexts of Criticism', in *Reading Romantics: Text and Context* (New York and Oxford: Oxford University Press, 1990) p. 258.
5. *P2V* 415. Observing that Wordsworth wrote his poem in 1805, two years after the tour on which he took Wilkinson's *Tours* as a guide, Manning reads the note as an originary rather than an intermediary text—less significant, however, as a verbal source than as a reflection of Wordsworth's composition of the poem within 'a specific historic matrix' (the domestic situations and international events of 1805–7) even as the poem itself, in a mode of polemically conservative nostalgia, invests the reaper 'with the aura of mythic timelessness' (*ibid.* 254–5, 267–8).

Crafted Measures

The slipperiest issue in this success is metre, the radical distinction of verse from conversation or prose. Is poetic metre spontaneous and organic? Or is it supplementary, super-added, even wrought in opposition to, the pulse of spontaneity? As M. H. Abrams remarked (at about the time Wimsatt was worrying the question of emotion as the muse of poetic craft), 'the justification of poetic meter' was 'particularly trouble-some' to Wordsworth, for 'although the natural language of feeling may be broadly rhythmical, the use in poetry of highly regular stress and stanza patterns would seem a matter not of nature, but of artifice and convention' (*The Mirror and the Lamp* (1953; 1958), p. 116). 'I write in metre', Coleridge says with no apology, 'because I am about to use a lan-guage different from that of prose' (*BL* ii 69). His critique in *Biographia* (ch. 18) of the Wordsworthian mythology of composition is particularly tuned to the advent of metre, which he ascribes to a 'balance in the mind effected by that spontaneous effort which strives to hold in check the workings of passion'. Revising Wordsworth's equation of poetry to a spontaneous overflow of passion, Coleridge theorizes a spontaneous countercheck, a 'balance of antagonists [. . .] organized into *metre*' (ii 64). Yet, as we shall see, Wordsworth sometimes agrees, and over the course of his theory (even in the Preface[s] to *Lyrical Ballads*) and his practice, metre plays as a sliding signifier. It shuttles and shifts between nature and culture, passion and restraint, text and intertexture—oppositions which themselves may reverse polarity, depending on the pressure of the moment. Caught in the labyrinth of metre, Wordsworth maps a deeper, more self-conscious commitment to poetic craft than some readers recognize.

The most radical metre is blank verse, 'blank' of rhyme—and thus to some, blank as versecraft. For Wordsworth as for everyone, the romance was the trope of blank-verse 'liberty', and its primer was Milton's note on 'The Verse' of *Paradise Lost*, which announced 'an example set, the first in English, of ancient liberty recovered' from 'the modern bondage of rhyming'. Dr. Johnson worried that such verse was nearly self-cancelling, 'verse only to the eye' (*Life of Milton* (1783)). Coleridge echoed him: when metre—'the sole acknowledged difference' between prose and verse—becomes 'metre to the eye only', the craft of verse, 'even to the most delicate ear', may be 'unrecognisable'. For proof, he prosed part of Words-worth's 'The Brothers' (*Lyrical Ballads* 1800) to show that (save a few phrases) no 'ear *could* suspect, that these sentences were ever printed as metre' (*BL* i 79–80). To interrogators such as Easthope, this effect is culpa-bly crafty: 'pentameter would disavow its own metricality' (74), 'would ren-der poetic discourse transparent' (75), would suppress 'recognition of the work of metric *production*—and so of the poem as constructed artifice' in order to foist the illusion of a 'spontaneously generated *product*' (67).

Yet this critique elides an effect not lost on Wordsworth's contempo-rary, Charles James Fox, then Whig leader in Parliament: the demo-cratizing of blank verse in *Lyrical Ballads*. If we expect Whig politics to pattern Whig poetics, it is a sign of how ingrained conventions of craft were that Fox felt able to complain to Wordsworth about seeing the mea-sure of lofty contemplation in 'Tintern Abbey' deployed for the humble

tales 'Michael' and 'The Brothers': 'I am no great friend to blank verse
for subjects which are to be treated of with simplicity' (Christopher
Wordsworth, *Memoirs of William Wordsworth* (2 vols.; 1851) i 172). Words-
worth's challenge was calculated: he had begun 'Michael' as a pastoral
ballad (*LB* 319–20), a 'low' form, then decided to give the shepherd's story
a claim to blank verse. This is a move that reverses Easthope's claims: far
from disavowing poetic craft, Wordsworth visibly motivates it to confront
what his 1798 'Advertisement' called 'that most dreadful enemy to our
pleasures, our own pre-established codes of decision' (*LB* 739).

*   *   *

   The attachment of passion to versification involves central questions of
poetic origin and agency, ones not easily reduced to critical measures
that discern only mystificatory device. At times, metre seems to matter as
an art that is the antithesis of artifice. A note Wordsworth added in the
1800 *Lyrical Ballads* to one of his most famous poems in blank verse
points this way as it speaks of the 'impassioned [. . .] versification' (*LB*
357). Years later he told this story of its crafting:

> I began it upon leaving Tintern, after crossing the Wye, and con-
> cluded it just as I was entering Bristol in the evening. [. . .] Not a
> line of it was altered, and not any part of written down till I reached
> Bristol. It was published almost immediately after.   (*LB* 357)

A recollection of poetic passion is synonymous with a passion for poetry.
'I have not ventured to call this Poem an Ode', he said in his note of 1800
to 'Lines written a few miles above Tintern Abbey, on Revisiting the Banks
of the Wye during a Tour, July 13, 1798'; but venture he does: 'it was writ-
ten with a hope that in the transitions, and the impassioned music of the
versification would be found the principal requisites of that species of
composition' (*LB* 357). The transitions and the versification are the work-
ings of passion through craft, the verse not just conveying but turning
(Latin *versus: turning*) the feelings—in a form informed almost instinc-
tively (Geoffrey Hartman suggests) by the generic structuring of the ode
through turn and counterturn (*Wordsworth's Poetry, 1787–1814*, 27). It's a
Latin pun Wordsworth liked; see, for example, 'the turnings intricate of
Verse' (*Prel.1805* v 627).
   Yet for all this passion of versification, metre persists as a critical prob-
lem, and does so less for the incidental reason Hazlitt suggests, the poeti-
cal reforms associated with Wordsworth and the 'Lake School', than for
its durable mark of distinction from other modes of language. For liberal
poetics, this effect was an embarrassment both to myths of spontaneous
origination and to any insistence on the common language of poetry,
prose, and conversation—the other big claim of the Preface of 1800, also
in the teeth of neoclassical consensus. In *Elements of Elocution* (1781),
for example, John Walker described prose as 'common, familiar and prac-
tical [in] nature', and verse as 'beautiful, elevated, and ideal [. . .] the
latter as different from the former as the elegant step of a minuet is from
the common motions of walking' (239). Metrical feet are art, not nature,
ideal not familiar, elegant and elevated, not common and pedestrian,
practised and courtly, not just practical: class difference is the elemen-
tary code in this description. So when Wordsworth, theorizing a common

language of common values, raised the question in his Preface to *Lyrical Ballads*—'Is there then, it will be asked, no essential difference between the language of prose and metrical composition?'—and stayed to answer, 'there neither is nor can be any essential difference' (*LB* 749), he knew he was putting his feet in his mouth. In the opening paragraph he referred to his 'experiment' in 'fitting to metrical arrangement a selection of the real language of men in a state of vivid sensation' (*LB* 741) without pausing over the work of 'fitting', as though there were no ultimate contradiction between fit and feel, arranged and real. But a few paragraphs on, the poet (parenthetically) concedes a bit of craft: 'the real language' he has been advertising has actually been 'purified' from 'its real defects, from all lasting and rational causes of dislike or disgust'; a poetic 'real' has replaced the socially 'real' (744).

*   *   *

Fits of Passion

In more than a few lyrical ballads, the efficacy of metre 'in tempering and restraining the passion' that produces poetry (Preface *LB* 755) is under stress. The untitled ballad that opens with the spondee 'Strange fits of passion' is just such a meta-metrical crisis. It recounts what Wordsworth (with another referent) calls a 'fit of imagination' (*LB* 398): a poet is on a nocturnal trek to his beloved's cottage, towards which the moon appeared to descend; as it 'dropp'd' below the roof, he had a vivid sensation that she might be dead. He would convey this fit, as the Preface says, 'fitting [it] to metrical arrangement' (*LB* 741)—a fitting that presumably contrasts 'fits of passion'. But the archaic sense of *fits* as poetic craft (*OED*, 'Fit, fytte': 'A part or section of a poem or song, a canto'), observes Hartman, leaves its sense 'unsettled' (*Wordsworth's Poetry* xix).

From its start, the ballad is haunted by an uncertain relation between psychic and poetic fits. For all its speaker's irony about the shaping fantasies of which the lunatic, the lover, and the poet are compact ('What fond and wayward thoughts will slide / Into a Lover's head—' (25–6)), his ballad cannot defuse a sense that this too-knowing 'will slide' is not just diagnostic, but helplessly predictive. In its present-progressive inception, the poet's confession seems compelled as well as rehearsed:

> Strange fits of passion I have known,
> And I will dare to tell,
> But in the lover's ear alone,
> What once to me befel.
> (1–4)

Is the event at hand extraordinary ('once') or habitual ('fits')?

As metre enters this question, the ballad shimmers into a counter-Preface. Metre may promise to fit passion to 'continual and regular impulses' (*LB* 756) but in this poem its pulsation seems less to restrain than to revive the original compulsion, giving a sensation of a fated sequence, of a consciousness continually possessed:

> Upon the moon I fix'd my eye,
> All over the wide lea;

> My horse trudg'd on, and we drew nigh
> Those paths so dear to me.
>
> And now we reach'd the orchard-plot,
> And, as we climb'd the hill,
> Towards the roof of Lucy's cot
> The moon descended still.
>   (9–16)

A present progressive tense in a draft, 'And now I've reached the orchard-plot' (*LB* 294), predicts the first line's strange-familiar 'I have known', while the punctuated acceleration from *and* to *and* spells a hypnotic (re)possession. Telling his wayward thoughts in an ambiguously situated 'now,' this balladeer is more than recollecting them: he is reliving them. His lines, tightly (almost over-) rhymed, reined into prescribed iambic tetrameter and trimeter, seem as fixed as his moonstruck eye:

> And, all the while, my eyes I kept
> On the descending moon.
>
> My horse mov'd on; hoof after hoof
> He rais'd and never stopp'd:
>   (19–22)

Telling seems to have become another fit of passion, induced by a metrical repetition of the paces that first led helplessly wayward; mania as metre. But are we sure of this pathology, or might there be a metrical plot? Might the metre have been crafted to induce our sympathy with a strange case? To lead us to expect disaster, and thus to endorse the lunatic surmise?

> 'O mercy!' to myself I cried,
> 'If Lucy should be dead!'
>   (27–28)

By this point, we probably think so, too (this climax is an anti-climax).[6]

In this strange fit, metre produces passion even as it fits it out. Sometimes Wordsworth strips his verse to an almost radical metrical punctuation of passion:

> 'O misery! oh misery!
> O woe is me! oh misery!'
>   ('The Thorn' 252–3)
>
> Oh! what's the matter? what's the matter?
> What is't that ails young Harry Gill?
> That evermore his teeth they chatter,
> Chatter, chatter, chatter still.
>   ('Goody Blake, and Harry Gill' 1–4)

---

6. In the key phrase 'Strange fits of passion' Barbara Johnson sees 'Wordsworth's poetic project' summarized: 'poetry is a fit, an outburst, an overflow, of feeling; and poetry is an attempt to fit, to arrange, feeling into form' ('Strange Fits: Poe and Wordsworth on the Nature of Poetic Language,' in *A World of Difference* (Baltimore, Johns Hopkins University Press, 1989) p. 95).

> The owlets hoot, the owlets curr,
> And Johnny's lips they burr, burr, burr.
>   . . .
> 'The cocks did crow to-whoo, to-whoo.'
>   ('The Idiot Boy' 114–15, 460)

'The Idiot Boy' is the lightest case, uttering a little ode to joy in rhyme with nature's sounds. But the others, fraught with that 'undue proportion of pain' for which metre is the recommended antidote (*LB* 755), convey more ambiguous effects. The metrics of 'Goody Blake', 'rather than converting pain into pleasure by reducing excitement to a regular level', Adela Pinch argues, convey anarchy, 'a painful disintegration of a man into a chattering old woman'.[7] As in 'Strange fits', metre is not just mimetic of passion but symptomatic of diseased poetic craft. And more: a betrayal of Wordsworth's hint in the Preface of maintaining a 'manly' style with 'words metrically arranged' (*LB* 755)—no small concern to Coleridge when he described 'Tintern Abbey', a poem by virtue of metre only, as a 'manly reflection' on 'passion and appetite' (*BL* i 79).

Passion intensified by feminine incursion (whether from female suffering or a passion-prone literary culture) saturates the controversial metres of 'The Thorn'. The poem ends with a male balladeer's repetition of, and seeming possession by, a woman's repeated cry, in metrically punctuated sounds: 'O misery! oh misery! / O woe is me! oh misery!' In his ground-breaking reading of this ballad as a manic monologue, Stephen Parrish proposes that the force of Wordsworth's craft is to make us wonder whether the balladeer has heard any woman at all—or whether, in a moment of panic and its aftermath, he has (mis)taken the sound of the wind for her cry (100–1; 105). In all these ballads of passion, Wordsworth crafts the mimetic metres to signal literary as well as natural inspirations. 'O woe is me! oh misery!' has legible textual lineage, as if from a handbook of pathetic expressions. The metrics of chatter in 'Goody Blake, and Harry Gill' not only employ onomatopoeia but draw attention to the device itself.

Commenting on both these ballads in his Preface, Wordsworth argues for a pleasure principle in the alliance of 'elementary' passion and a craft that solicits interest. The effect of metre, he says, depends both on 'the pleasure [. . .] derive[d] from the perception of similitude in dissimilitude' and on 'the blind association of pleasure [. . .] previously received from works of rhyme or metre of the same or similar construction' (*LB* 756, 757). He is willing to guess that even if a poet's words fail to grab a reader—that is, seem 'incommensurate with the passion'—metre may supply the needed measure:

> in the feelings of pleasure which the Reader has been accustomed to connect with metre in general, and in the feeling, whether chearful or melancholy, which he has been accustomed to connect with that particular movement of metre, there will be found something which will greatly contribute to impart passion to the words, and to effect the complex end which the poet proposes to himself.   (*LB* 756)

7. *Strange Fits of Passion: Etymologies of Emotion, Hume to Austen* (Stanford University Press, 1996), pp. 90–1.

In line with this value-added custom, the long note he appended to 'The Thorn' in 1800 explains metre as an antidote to his other risky poetic experiment, 'the repetition of words' in the poem 'not only as symbols of the passion, but as *things*, active and efficient, which are of themselves part of the passion'. For those not 'accustomed to sympathize with men feeling in that manner or using such language', Wordsworth hopes for 'the assistance of Lyrical and rapid Metre'. To the potentially alien(ating) spectacle of how 'superstition acts upon the mind', he 'superadd[s] the charm' of metre (*LB* 351, 754); one *super*-meets another. Likewise, 'Goody Blake, and Harry Gill', he says in the Preface, is 'related in metre' in hopes of 'draw[ing] attention to the truth' of its tale of hysteric possession, aiding its communication to 'many hundreds of people who would never have heard of it' had it not been versed as 'a Ballad, and in a more impressive metre than is usual in Ballads' (*LB* 757).

Yet metre crafted to facilitate a reader's sympathy might be fabricating it, as an immediately preceding remark concedes: 'We see that Pope by the power of verse alone, has contrived to render the plainest common sense interesting, and even frequently to invest it with the appearance of passion' (*LB* 757). Pope's metres seem to manufacture interest, as a mnemonic aid or artifice of investment yielding a dubious return, a contrived appearance. This yoking of contradictory interests—whether metre evokes natural expression or just shams a passion; whether it aids common sympathy or serves a contrived common sense—is sufficiently strained to prompt Wordsworth to revise the Preface in 1802. Reassigning metre to a poetics of estrangement and defamiliarization, he now argues that the 'complex feeling of delight' in poetic pleasure (so described in 1800) involves 'an indistinct perception perpetually renewed of language closely resembling that of real life, and yet, in the circumstance of metre, differing from it so widely' (757). In this difference, metre is effective not because it doesn't interfere with passion, but because it does. Correspondingly, he revises the paragraph about the effect of 'tempering and restraining' passion to say that 'the tendency of metre to divest language in a certain degree of its reality, and thus to throw a sort of half consciousness of unsubstantial existence over the whole composition', makes it easier to endure 'pathetic situations and sentiments' which 'have a greater proportion of pain connected with them' (755). The conscious craft and its derealizing effect are now essential.

The Crafted Poet

Even with this revision, Wordsworth does not ultimately unravel the issue of circular and reciprocal causes and consequences. Its very irresolution keeps the matter active in the meta-poetry of poetic craft. The metrical poetry that became his greatest devotion was his perpetually revised autobiography (later called *The Prelude*), a work whose craft does not just organize recollection but also produces it. In writing as a poet about becoming a poet, Wordsworth stages the autobiographical subject as both constituted and made legible by its affinity for poetic craft.

* * *

Wordsworth's perpetual revisions of this and other poems have had debatable effects on theme and argument, but he was always motivated by a craftsman's attention.[8] Advising an aspiring poet in 1824, he stressed the importance of 'the logical faculty': 'the materials upon which that faculty is exercised in poetry are so subtle, so plastic, so complex, the application of it requires an adroitness which can proceed from nothing but practice'. In this practised craftwork, 'emotion is so far from bestowing' any help (he went on to add) that 'at first it is ever in the way of it' (*WL* iv 546).

This was no late-developing news. Arguing in 1814 with a correspondent about whether 'such thoughts as arise in the progress of composition should be expressed in the first words that offer themselves, as being likely to be most energetic and natural', Wordsworth countered, 'My first expressions I often find detestable; and it is frequently true of second words as of second thoughts, that they are the best' (*WL* iii 179). The poet who became famous for equating the best poetry with a spontaneous overflow of feeling turns out to have had second thoughts about this expression as well.

LUCY NEWLYN

The Public[†]

* * *

'There is little need to advise me against publishing; it is a thing which I dread as much as death itself' (*EY*, 211). So Wordsworth wrote to James Tobin in March 1798, when his public reception was still an unknown quantity—at once the focus for long-term ambitions, and the cause of immediate practical concerns. The comment betrays his sense of a deep implicit connection between emergence into the public sphere and loss of personal identity: a connection felt so strongly that it resembles the threat of extinction. Despite the temporal and discursive gap which intervened between this letter and the composition of *The Prelude*, one might read Wordsworth's bald, prosaic acknowledgement of anxiety as a gloss on the famous passage in *The Prelude*, Book VIII where he likens creative process to a 'ferment quiet and sublime | Which, after a short space, works less and less' (ll. 424–5), until finally 'every effort, every motion gone | The scene before him lies in perfect view | Exposed, and lifeless as a written book' (ll. 725–7).[1] In this later passage, the achievement of finality is revealingly associated with a text that lies open to the gaze of passers-by— its creative vitality drained from it, at the point when it becomes most available to public scrutiny.

At all times in his writing career, Wordsworth disclosed an almost paranoid fear that poets were at the mercy of a hostile reading-public. In

8. See my discussion and relevant bibliography in *Formal Charges: The Shaping of Poetry in British Romanticism* (Stanford: Stanford University Press, 1997).
† From *Reading, Writing, and Romanticism: The Anxiety of Reception* (Oxford: Oxford Univ. Press, 2000), 91–99. Notes have been edited. Reprinted by permission.
1. See *Prelude* (1805), viii, 724–7. For discussions of this passage in terms of Wordsworth's fear of textuality, see Jonathan Wordsworth, *William Wordsworth: The Borders of Vision* (Oxford: Clarendon Press, 1982), 188–9; Mary Jacobus, *Romanticism, Writing and Sexual Difference* (Oxford: Clarendon Press, 1989), 14–16; and Lucy Newlyn, '"Questionable Shape": The Aesthetics of Indeterminacy', in John Beer (ed.), *Questioning Romanticism* (Baltimore: Johns Hopkins University Press, 1995), 226–9.

his critical writings he expressed the belief that he must transform the taste of his readers before he could be understood. His relations with reviewers were edgy and defensive because he construed them as the representatives and arbiters of public taste, whose capriciousness made them less willing to be transformed than were 'the people' themselves. He also saw in reviewers a threat to the privacy and distance of writers, whose personal and domestic lives were open to the gaze of the public— a threat of exposure which is hinted at in 'Star-Gazers' by a figuration of reading as 'prying and poring' to no happy or useful end. A more fearless revisionary poet than Coleridge, he was also subject to graver doubts about his stability as a writing-subject. He saw that the provisionality of literary tradition—its openness to the modifications and revisions of successive generations of reader-writers—made his own work vulnerable to misreading. Furthermore, he had no overarching system of authority on which to rely. While sharing Coleridge's assumptions about the damaging effects of passive reading, he did not believe that the Bible provided a model for reflective understanding. Nor—despite repeated attempts to establish a communitarian basis for acts of reading and interpreting—did he place an equivalent faith in hermeneutic principles of sympathy and community as the means whereby taste might be transformed. His less theorized, more improvisatory position appears by comparison intensely beleaguered. For him, the task of creating 'the taste by which he [was] to be enjoyed' was one of eliciting the reader's trust and cooperation in his literary endeavour—or, as he put it in 1815, of 'establishing that dominion over the spirits of readers by which they are to be humbled and humanised, in order that they may be purified and exalted.[2] In this position of maximum dependency on readers, disguised as maximum power over them, the continuity and coherence of poetic self were all that could be relied on to ensure survival.

Wordsworth's anxieties were intensified by an awareness that, however deeply he identified his own voice with that of the people, his poetry would never be popular. The best-selling authors of this period—Byron, Scott, Bloomfield—had formulas for success that were very different from his own. Wordsworth envied their popularity, but he was also critical of public taste, which he saw as too readily satisfied by narrative stimulants. For this reason, perhaps, Wordsworth's negotiations with his audience showed a mixture of tough-minded pragmatism and vulnerability. Throughout his career, the hope that he might ensure his correct reception involved him in the careful overseeing of how his volumes were produced, advertised, and marketed, as well as in a more theoretical attempt to direct the public's expectations. It was not until the hostile reception of *Poems in Two Volumes* (1807) that he had any genuine cause to feel aggrieved by the reactions of his audience; and yet as early as 1800 the pre-emptive direction of his authorial strategies was visible. The production of *Lyrical Ballads* was seen by him in terms of both commercial viability and the construction of a durable literary identity. Letters to Cottle dictating the shape of the volumes and the appearance of their typeface showed his concern with the minutiae of presentation;[3] while

2. See 'Essay Supplementary to the Preface' (1815), in *Wordsworth Prose*, iii. 80–1.
3. See Gill, 185.

the Preface attempted to frame the volume's critical reception in a semi-apologetic series of directives to the reader. From the beginning, print must be warily supervised if self-image was to be made secure: Wordsworth intervened in both production and reception as a defensive measure.

Defence mechanisms are, however, notorious for eliciting the responses they are designed to pre-empt. Lamb wished the Preface had appeared separately, because it made the ballads look as if they were 'Experiments on the public taste' (Marrs, i. 266–7)—so provoking Jeffrey's labelling of the Lake Poets as a new sect, to which Wordsworth objected.[4] Coleridge, with the benefit of hindsight, observed in Biographia Literaria that the Preface was 'the true origin of the unexampled opposition which Mr Wordsworth's writings have been since doomed to encounter'.[5] There is no doubt that by presenting himself as a theorist Wordsworth laid himself open to attack. Reviewer after reviewer took him to task for the 'system' underlying Lyrical Ballads, and went on holding this against him, even in the reception of much later works. ('Wordsworth is eminently, and as we think, faultily, a systematic writer', wrote a reviewer for the British Critic, as late as 1821.)[6] It is also clear that when his exalted claims for the poet appeared in the expanded Preface to Lyrical Ballads (1802), he further weakened his standing with the reviewers by clothing himself in a grandeur which conflicted with his claim to be 'a man speaking to men'.[7] But although the defensiveness of his prefatorial material appears to have provoked rather than appeased his critics, this was not how Wordsworth himself saw the matter. The earnestness with which he packaged himself for public consumption increased as a result of attacks on Poems in Two Volumes, which he had risked submitting to the public with no theoretical framework. 'It is impossible that any expectations can be lower than mine concerning the immediate effect of this little work upon what is called the Public',[8] he claimed in a letter of May 1807; yet when they were lambasted by Jeffrey his reaction was one of wounded horror. The lesson he chose to learn from this was that the public could be relied on not at all; and that the reception of future volumes must be more tightly controlled than ever.

If hostile reviewers were to discard some of his output as trivial, it was Wordsworth's prerogative to show that underlying principles connected all his works according to a grand predetermined plan: hence the Preface to The Excursion, where his autobiographical poem is described as the 'ante-chapel' to a 'gothic Church', with all the minor pieces comprising its 'little cells, oratories, and sepulchral recesses'.[9] When both Jeffrey and Hazlitt proved resistant to these unifying claims, he retaliated with more: Poems (1815) had both a directive Preface, explaining the volume's internal categorization of poetic faculties, and an 'Essay Supplementary to the

4. Gill, 267.
5. BL (CC) i. 70–1. Coleridge has in mind Francis Jeffrey's reviews in the Edinburgh Review, 1 (1802) and 11 (1807).
6. British Critic, 15 (Feb. 1821), 114.
7. See esp. the passage beginning 'Poetry is the breath and finer spirit of all knowledge' (Wordsworth Prose, i. 141).
8. To Lady Beaumont, May 1807 (WL iii. 145).
9. Wordsworth's Poetical Works, ed. E. De Selincourt (5 vols., Oxford: Clarendon Press, 1949), v. 2. * * *

Preface' proclaiming the poet's immunity to hostile reception. Subsequent volumes were even more monolithic, showing an increasing preoccupation with the coherence and organic unity of poetic self. Revising each poem for its new appearance, Wordsworth placed what Stephen Gill has called an 'inordinate' demand on his readers, who must check every poem for its revisions to keep track of the growth of the poet's mind.[1] Determined as he was to keep his great autobiographical poem in reserve, he used the revisionary process as an alternative means of incorporating his life into his works. Nowhere since Milton's Defences had self-image, or the illusion of a seamless continuity between public and private identities, been so carefully cultivated.[2]

Nor does the parallel with Milton stop there. Wordsworth's abiding concern was with finding a worthy audience; and increasingly the label 'fit though few' had an appropriate resonance, given the exacting nature of his expectations and the extent of his disappointment with the public at large.[3] As early as 1800, he established the imaginative poverty of professional critics by referring to them as 'numerous', claiming that the reader must 'utterly reject' their canon of criticism 'if he wishes to be pleased with these volumes'.[4] Worthy readers were by inference at once enlightened and singular—a position of privilege, as far as Wordsworth was concerned, though not one that always met with gratitude. Crabb Robinson, writing about *The Convention of Cintra* in the *London Review* (1809), contrasted the prose of Burke, who 'being schooled in the House of Commons always laboured to make himself intelligible to the lowest capacity', with that of Wordsworth himself, who wrote 'from the woods and lakes', and seemed 'content to be understood and relished by a few like himself'.[5] A reviewer on the *British Critic*, writing in 1815, took the poet's reclusiveness as a sign that he was out of kilter with his age: 'whose minds are set upon intrigues and fees, business and bustle, places and preferments. . . . To such as these the retired poet cannot speak: they have not learned the alphabet of his language'.[6]

Wordsworth's exclusiveness afforded him little compensation, however, for failing to reach a wider audience: 'remember no poem of mine will ever be popular', he wrote ruefully to George Beaumont, in 1808, '. . . I say not this in modest disparagement of the Poem ['Peter Bell'], but in sorrow for the sickly taste of the Public in verse. The *People* would love the Poem . . . but the *Public* (a very different Being) will never love it' (*MY* i. 194). Even less convincing, as a defensive measure, is his slanted account of literary history in the 'Essay Supplementary' of 1815. Arguing that all great poets except Thomson had been neglected since their first appearance, he traces the unreliability of critical taste through the eighteenth century. Special emphasis is given to the ephemerality of the poetic canon, as established by Johnson, and to Johnson's factual error in claiming that

1. Gill, 367.
2. See Dustin Griffin, *Regaining Paradise: Milton and the Eighteenth Century* (Cambridge: Cambridge University Press, 1986), ch. 2; and Lucy Newlyn, *'Paradise Lost' and the Romantic Reader* (Oxford: Clarendon Press, 1993), 27–8.
3. See Milton's invocation to Urania, *Paradise Lost*, vii. 30–1; echoed by Wordsworth in his 'Prospectus' to *The Recluse*, which was incorporated into 'Home at Grasmere': see ll. 970–2.
4. Preface to *Lyrical Ballads* (1800), in *Wordsworth Prose* i. 128.
5. *London Review* 2/4 (1 Nov. 1809).
6. Review of *The Excursion*, *British Critic*, 3 (May 1815), 451.

Milton was a popular poet during his lifetime. Using the 'slow progress of Milton's fame' and the public's 'unremitting hostility' to his own works as 'pledges and proofs' that 'the products of his industry will endure', Wordsworth brought himself into line with his great precursor.[7] True greatness was seen not only to survive initial unpopularity, but to be confirmed and guaranteed by the purblindness of public and critical opinion.

It was a case of special pleading, made more transparent by Wordsworth's wish (as in the earlier letter to Beaumont) to distinguish 'the people' from 'the public', so keeping open the possibility of becoming a popular poet. And it was immediately seized on by hostile reviewers as a mark of arrogance. 'This prophecy is not merely implied', wrote a reviewer in the *Monthly Review*, of Wordsworth's prediction of immortality: 'it is directly and plainly delivered by the prophet himself, of himself, and for his own benefit'.[8] Taking advantage of a perceived disjunction between the poet's lofty ambitions and the lowly tenor of his poems, the reviewer went on: 'We are so thoroughly overwhelmed by the high and mighty tone of this author's prose, that we really must have immediate recourse to his verse, in order to get rid of the painful humiliation and sense of inferiority which he inflicts on his readers'.[9] The jibes which followed were designed to puncture what were seen as inflated claims to grandeur on the poet's part; and the ease with which the reviewer hit his targets proved how readily Wordsworth's defensiveness played into his readers' hands.

*   *   *

In cavalier comments such as 'I care little for the praise of any . . . professional critic, but as it may help me to my pudding',[1] Wordsworth came to sound increasingly like Coleridge, whose pronouncements on the reading-public were notorious for their stentorian moral tone. Writing to Lady Beaumont in May 1807, apprehensive about the reception of *Poems in Two Volumes*, he complained that 'These people in the senseless hurry of their idle lives, do not *read* books, they merely snatch a glance at them that they may talk about them' (*MY* i. 150). Scott complained that Wordsworth did not do enough to conciliate the public by accommodating himself to their taste, and concluded that his friend cared little for what his readers thought of him. But this was impercipient. Wordsworth remained heavily dependent on the reception of his works by leading periodicals, and looked anxiously to the reviews for signs that he was succeeding in his mission to create the taste by which he was enjoyed: 'for those who dip into books in order to give an opinion', he lamented, '. . . for this multitude of unhappy, and misguided, and misguiding beings, an entire regeneration must be produced; and if this be possible, it must be a work *of time*' (*MY* i. 150).

The yearning to be popular nonetheless remained constant throughout his poetic career, and continued, paradoxically, to inform his most unworldly claims to patient aloofness. Accustomed to thinking of himself as undervalued—'we shall never grow rich', wrote Dorothy in August 1816, 'for I now perceive clearly that till my dear Brother is laid in his grave, his writings will not produce any profit' (*MY* ii. 247)—Wordsworth

7. 'Essay Supplementary to the Preface' (1815), in *Wordsworth Prose*, iii, esp. 70–84.
8. *Monthly Review*, 78 (Nov. 1815), 229.
9. Ibid. 230.
1. Quoted in Gill, 165.

went on courting recognition while appearing to accept neglect. 'We want no pensions or reversions for our heirs, and no monuments by public or private Subscription' he wrote proudly to Southey in April 1830: 'We shall have a monument in our works if they survive and if they do not we should not deserve it' (*LY* iii. 566). Well into his later years, after the advent of prosperity and with accolades showering in from all quarters, he adopted the stance of one whose true worth would be known only hereafter. '[I]f it be of God—it must stand' (*MY* ii. 181) has a quiet self-justifying confidence that is again reminiscent of Milton, the poet with whom he consistently strove to identify himself. In review after review during the 1820's and onwards, Milton's name was coupled with his own, as though in obedience to his prophecy.

Even the awareness that he must look to posterity for lasting fame was bound up with the pragmatics of reception. The poet who campaigned concertedly to extend the duration of copyright, and thus to ensure that his family benefited after his death by his growing reputation, can hardly be said to have desensitized himself to public opinion. Equating poetic identity with private property, he strove to keep his in the family, thereby guaranteeing that the select few by whom he was genuinely appreciated in his lifetime would stand to gain, when his true worth finally came to be acknowledged by the fickle many. And by the same token, his strategy of deferring *The Prelude*'s publication until after his death was an act of poetic and economic 'husbandry'. In Erickson's words, its purpose was 'to give his heirs the strongest possible claim on his literary estate for as long as possible'. Wordsworth 'had come to feel that he had triumphed over his critics . . . by living long enough to enjoy the financial fruits of his poetic labor and to give his heirs the posthumous benefit of the returns from his collected works for another forty two years'.[2]

Wordsworth's anxiety with respect to contemporary neglect was always heavily disguised as a trust in future generations of readers. Writing to Sergeant Talfourd, in his 1838 petition to the House of Commons, he explained that the Bill for perpetual copyright had for its main object 'to relieve men of letters from the thraldom of being forced to court the living generation, to aid them in rising above degraded taste and slavish prejudice'.[3] Just as his obsessive habits of poetic revision were evidence of a poet who 'had difficulty in thinking of any work, even published work, as a final statement';[4] so his policy of deferral with respect to successful reception was an attempt to postpone for as long as possible the day of final judgement. By the same token, if publication was metaphorically associated in Wordsworth's imagination with the finality of death, then by a curious twist of logic, death itself became a moment of 'publication', when the poet relinquished self-possession. At a time when to think of the end of copyright was to think of the end of life, its extension became, in Susan Eilenberg's metaphor, a species of 'life-insurance', signifying the need to fix and ensure the durability of poetic self. Perhaps fearing

2. *The Economy of Literary Form,: English Literature and the Industrialisation of Publishing, 1800–1850* (Baltimore: Johns Hopkins University Press, 1996), 67–8.
3. *Wordsworth Prose*, iii. 319. This sentence appears in the 'Appendix' to the Reports of the Select Committee of the House of Commons.
4. Stephen Gill, '"Affinities Preserved": Poetic Self-Reference in Wordsworth', *Studies in Romanticism*, 24 (1985), 535. 'He let nothing go', Gill claims: 'Of all the great poets he surely practices the most frugal imaginative husbandry' (ibid. 533).

that, in the process of becoming more widely read after his death, his own identity might be dispersed or lost, Wordsworth addressed the government

> as if it had jurisdiction over the border between the dead and the living and could repair by legal means the damage death wreaks upon human bonds . . . In seeking a way round the limitation on copyright the poet sought to pronounce from beyond the grave a controversion of his own mortality.[5]

*   *   *

STEPHEN GILL
Wordsworth's Poems: Textual Considerations[†]

Wordsworth made two memorable observations about textual issues and they are both unequivocal. "A correct text is the first object of an editor," he told Sir Walter Scott (November 7, 1805: *WL*, 1:642). To would-be anthologist Alexander Dyce he declared, "You know what importance I attach to following strictly the last Copy of the text of an Author" (ca. April 19, 1830: *WL*, 5:236). No modern editor will quibble with the first of these statements. The second, though, which at first glance looks straightforward, actually carries quite a freight of difficulties concerning both principle and practice. This brief note considers what they are and how they came about.

Wordsworth's career was a very long one. The first poem published under his name, *An Evening Walk*, appeared in 1793; the final collected volumes of the now–Poet Laureate were in the press at his death in 1850. To appreciate why modern editors are still troubled by textual issues, it is necessary to have some idea of what Wordsworth's compositional and publishing practices were over this long span.

Wordsworth made a niche for himself in the early nineteenth century marketplace with little volumes of recently composed verse, *Lyrical Ballads* (1798; 1800; 1802; 1805) and *Poems, in Two Volumes* (1807). What established him as a major presence was a monumental quarto in 1814, *The Excursion*, and a first Collected Works the following year. The latter in particular drew attention to its importance by classifying the gathering of lyric poetry according to a system of the poet's own devising. From now on until his death the pattern remained the same. New publications would be issued at intervals, some presenting work that had remained in manuscript for years, others collecting together recent composition. Thus *The White Doe of Rylstone* in 1815 was followed by *Thanksgiving Ode* (1816), *Peter Bell* (1819), *The River Duddon* (1820), *Memorials of a Tour on the Continent 1820* (1822), and so on until the final discrete offering, *Poems, Chiefly of Early and Late Years*, in 1842.

Throughout the second part of his writing lifetime, Wordsworth was also consolidating what he had begun with the *Poems* of 1815, that is, he complemented the publication of new verse by issuing at regular intervals

---

5. *Strange Power of Speech: Wordsworth, Coleridge, and Literary Possession* (Oxford: Oxford University Press, 1992), 196.
† Written for this Norton Critical Edition.

multi-volume Collected Poetical Works. The procession is a stately one of handsomely produced sets—1820, 1827, 1832, 1836—until the last decade of Wordsworth's life, when his publisher sought to capitalize on the poet's growing fame by issuing numerous reprintings of the multi-volume editions as well as a single volume Collected Works. In 1849–50 appeared a new edition, a six-volume *Poetical Works of William Wordsworth*. It was the last one in Wordsworth's lifetime and it was seen through the press, at least notionally, by him. It is the text and format of this edition, "the last Copy of the text," that must constitute the final authority.

As the final authority, however, it has enormous drawbacks. The first and most obvious one is that the 1849–50 collection, though in six volumes, did not include all of Wordsworth's poetry. *The Prelude* had been kept back for posthumous publication, so it was not included. The first book of *The Recluse*, entitled *Home at Grasmere*, now regarded as a key text, was not included. Interesting juvenilia, some poems dropped from the canon, other poems not published for unknown reasons—none of these appeared in the final authorized edition.

As an editorial problem, this is in fact more apparent than real. It is clear that Wordsworth "authorized" the publication of *The Prelude*. He prepared a final text well before his death and on many occasions affirmed his intention that the poem should be issued posthumously. No modern editor need have any qualms about including *The Prelude* in the Wordsworth canon (though which text of this multi-version poem ought to be preferred is also a matter for debate). All other material not authorized for publication by the poet simply needs to be acknowledged as such and either presented separately from the main body of the canonical poems as supplementary or identified in notes as being poetry not included in the final lifetime edition. With such a procedure no reader will be misled and the views of the poet about "the last Copy of the text of an Author" will have been respected.

The second problem is much more complex. Wordsworth published a great many poems in a considerable number of volumes—between 1793 and 1850 there were fifteen new volumes of verse and from 1815 onwards nine collected editions (these counts exclude reprint editions, selections, pamphlets, American, and other unauthorized editions). Although they were of course determined by commercial considerations, these publications were all important to Wordsworth as artist. As the great twentieth-century editor Ernest de Selincourt observed, "It is probable that no poet ever paid more meticulous or prolonged attention to his text than Wordsworth."[1] He was rarely, perhaps one might say never, willing to regard a poem as "finished." Each plan for a new publication was taken as an opportunity to review the evolving corpus. Poems that had been carefully worked over for their first appearance were revised for their next appearance in a Collected Works. Then, in all likelihood, they were revised further for the next Collected Works. And then for the one after that. Details of wording might be tinkered with; occasionally whole stanzas might be changed, removed or added; a poem might have its structural identity altered and a new title provided; poems might be moved about within the

1. Preface to *The Poetical Works of William Wordsworth*, ed. Ernest de Selincourt, vol. 1 (Oxford, 1940), p. v.

overall classification set out in 1815; a poem might be dropped from the canon altogether. Detailed evidence, some of it amusing, much of it astonishing, is laid out in Stephen Gill, *Wordsworth's Revisitings* (2011). The process of revision was compulsive and comprehensive and tremendously important to Wordsworth. It terminated only with his death.

The implications of Wordsworth's continual attention to the text of his poems are considerable. The edition of 1849–50 embodies the final version of poems that in some cases had been in print for half a century. Their shifting identities may have been marked by only slight changes over the years, sometimes no more than adjustments to punctuation or the variation of an epithet or adverb. In some cases, on the other hand, the revisions substantially modified the original poem overall. Take, for example, changes to Book 1 of *The Excursion* in 1845. Attentive readers (the phrase is Wordsworth's) who had known the poem since its first appearance in 1814 might have been struck by how explicitly in revision the reconciling wisdom offered by the Wanderer had been given a Christian base. Slight or substantial, revisions authorized for the final edition both embody the same fact—that this edition is authorized by an elderly man, many of whose best poems date back to his 20s and 30s, and that it appeared in political, social and personal circumstances differing very markedly from those in which his earlier work had originated and appeared.

With effort, attentive readers could, of course, trace the progress of a text over the years by comparison of one version with the most recently published one, and, amazingly, Wordsworth did have such admirers. His faithful friend, Henry Crabb Robinson, was one such, but even Robinson, as he perused the new collection *Poems, Chiefly of Early and Late Years* in 1842, would not have been able to detect that *Guilt and Sorrow; or, Incidents Upon Salisbury Plain* was not quite what it seemed. Wordsworth presented it as a poem of early years, a reflection of his appalled response to the outbreak of war between Great Britain and France in 1793: it was in fact a reworking of the two poems he did write then so substantial that one is justified in thinking of it not as a poem of "early" years at all. Since the earlier poems, however, *Salisbury Plain* and *Adventures on Salisbury Plain*, had remained in manuscript, their development into what was finally authorized as *Guilt and Sorrow* was untraceable.

Two other lesser considerations remain to be touched on briefly. The first is a matter of fact. In 1815 Wordsworth classified his lyric poems, not in order of date of composition or of publication, but "with reference to the powers of mind *predominant* in the production of them." As he explained in a Preface, his "guiding wish was, that the small pieces of which these volumes consist, thus discriminated, might be regarded under a two-fold view; as composing an entire work within themselves, and as adjuncts to the philosophical Poem, *The Recluse*" (above, p. 510). As the corpus of poems evolved, the categories were developed and rearranged, but the principle remained intact, its form finalized in the edition of 1849–50. Wordsworth was confident that the arrangement would "unostentatiously" direct the attention of readers "to [his] purposes, both particular and general." Readers might question the appropriateness of "unostentatiously" applied to a comprehensive and prescriptive classification system, but they will certainly be aware of one aspect of it: it makes chronological study of the poems very difficult. To examine the progress of this or that aspect of Wordsworth's art one would have to unpick his classification using other research materials. The ordering of the poems from 1815 on was designed to frustrate chronological study, but since historically based, chronologically inflected discussion is what most Wordsworth scholars and critics deal in, editors nowadays for the most part acknowledge and then ignore his classification.

The second consideration introduces, at last, the question of evaluative literary judgment—not which text is correct but which version of a poem is the best. Adherence on grounds of bibliographical principle either to the first published text, or to the last, does not allow for the possibility that with this or that poem neither is to be preferred. Editors will of course want to be bibliographically scrupulous and consistent, but readers may wonder whether it is always the case that the text of the final authorized edition presents the poems in their finest state, that is, in their finest state as works of poetic art. Might it be that, for example, *Elegiac Stanzas Suggested by a Picture of Peele Castle* is most impressive as a poem in the version published in the 1827 *Collected Poetical Works*, rather than that of its first appearance in 1807 or its last in 1849–50?

This note has raised the most important issues which face any editor of Wordsworth. There are many more aspects of the subject which deserve attention. Fuller discussion of them, and of the points already discussed, will be found in Stephen Gill, "Wordsworth's Poems: The Question of Text," in Robert Brinkley and Keith Hanley (eds.), *Romantic Revisions* (1992), 43–63; and in Zachary Leader, *Revision and Romantic Authorship* (1996), 19–77, a strongly argued critique of dominant current editorial practice.

STUDIES OF INDIVIDUAL COLLECTIONS OR WORKS

NEIL FRAISTAT

From The "Field" of *Lyrical Ballads* (1798)[†]

[1]

Critical opinion about *Lyrical Ballads* (1798) is nowhere more divided than over the issue of its coherence as a collection.[1] Arguments for the unity of the volume must contend with three important objections voiced by critics. First, the financial need occasioned by Wordsworth and

---

[†] From *The Poem and the Book: Interpreting Collections of Romantic Poetry* (Chapel Hill: Univ. of North Carolina Press, 1985), 49–53, 69–78. Notes have been edited. Copyright © 1985 by the University of North Carolina Press. Used by permission of the publisher.
1. Until quite recently, most scholars agreed with Emile Legouis's opinion that *Lyrical Ballads* (1798) is a "somewhat random and incongruous assemblage." See "Some Remarks on the Composition of the *Lyrical Ballads* of 1798" (1962), p. 3. Even Ruth Cohen, who has read the 1800 edition as a coherent structure, calls the 1798 edition a "scattered and random selection . . . which, we must remember, had been published quickly under the pressure of financial need." See "The 1800 Ordering of *Lyrical Ballads*" (1976), p. 33. Opposing such views are R. L. Brett and Alun R. Jones, who insist "that it is as a *body* of poetry that *Lyrical Ballads* first influenced the course of English poetry and that it is as a body of poetry that it should be studied." See "*Lyrical Ballads*" (1988), p. x. Stephen Prickett, in his short but suggestive "*The Lyrical Ballads*" (1975), argues that the 1798 volume possesses an organic unity in which each poem "changes the nature of the

Coleridge's impending trip to Germany forced them to rush *Lyrical Ballads* through the press—resulting in a volume that "represents a considerable degree of compromise, expediency, and chance."[2] Second, doubts have arisen that a single plan was carefully adhered to during the creation of the volume, despite later statements made by each poet to the contrary.[3] And third, there is what John Jordan terms "the spread of the volume itself."[4]

Sufficient evidence exists, however, to counter these objections. Although *Lyrical Ballads* was in some ways a hasty production, it was produced by two formidable poets—both of whom, as we have seen, showed an unusual concern for the unity and ordering of their poetic works. Wordsworth's self-proclaimed distaste for miscellaneous poems "jumbled together at random" was matched by what Max Schulz calls Coleridge's "abiding concern for the design of a thing."[5] It is, in fact, hard to imagine that their lifelong care for the organization of their volumes did not manifest itself in 1798, however quickly *Lyrical Ballads* was assembled.[6] Indeed, while the poems were going through the press, Wordsworth traveled to Bristol several times to supervise the printing. On one of his last trips, he brought "Lines Written a Few Miles above Tintern Abbey, on Revisiting the Banks of the Wye during a Tour, July 13, 1798." And though often referred to as an afterthought to *Lyrical Ballads*, "Tintern Abbey" more probably stems from Wordsworth's sense that a fit conclusion was needed for the volume.[7]

whole, and therefore of all the other parts" (p. 28). Yet to the detriment of his thesis, Prickett concerns himself primarily with five poems scattered throughout. James Averill, who has published the best discussion of the book's coherence to date, finds that although *Lyrical Ballads* "is not a seamless work, it is stitched together in workmanlike fashion." See "Shape of *Lyrical Ballads*" (1981), p. 402. Although Averill's consideration of *Lyrical Ballads* as an "odal volume" highlights spatial contiguity among the poems and my own focus is on the thematic and verbal resonances running throughout the whole, I believe our points of view are generally compatible.

2. See Jacobus, *Tradition and Experiment*, p. 4.
3. For the seminal statement of this viewpoint, see Mark Reed's carefully argued "'Plan' of The *Lyrical Ballads*" (1965).
4. Jordan, *Why "The Lyrical Ballads"?* (1976) p. 38.
5. For Wordsworth's comment, see De Selincourt, *Poetical Works of William Wordsworth*, 1:x. For Coleridge, see Schulz, *The Poetic Voices of Coleridge*, p. 23.
6. Averill convincingly demonstrates that both poets cared from the start about the details and arrangement of their volumes. See "Shape of *Lyrical Ballads*," pp. 388–90. He concludes, "There is no reason to think that a book put together by two such poets would be more random or structurally unconsidered than those each put together on his own" (p. 390). Wordsworth and Coleridge's concern for the format of *Lyrical Ballads* is apparent in Coleridge's letter to Cottle on 4 June 1798; see Griggs, *Collected Letters of Samuel Taylor Coleridge*, 1:412.
7. In a similar way, Wordsworth wrote "Michael" specifically to conclude the 1800 edition. He informs Cottle on 23 December 1800: "By the same post I send you two other sheets containing a poem entitled, *Michael*. This poem contains 493 or 4 lines. If it be sufficient to fill the volume to 205 pages or upwards, printing it at 18 lines, or never more than 19 in a page as was done in the first Edition of Lyrical Ballads you will print this poem immediately after the *Poems on the Naming of Places* and consider it as, (with the two or three Notes adjoined) finishing the work. If it does not fill up so much space as to make the volume 205 pages you must not print immediately the Poem of Michael, as I wish it to conclude the volume. If what I have sent does not make the vol: amount to 205 pages let me know immediately *how many* pages it amounts to, and I will send you something to insert between Michael and the Poems on the *Naming of Places*." See De Selincourt and Shaver, *Letters of William and Dorothy Wordsworth: The Early Years*, p. 307. Wordsworth apparently felt that "Tintern Abbey" was in its proper place, for it remains the closing poem in the first volume of the 1800 edition, though he shifted the order of several others. For the reordering of this edition, see Cohen, "The 1800 Ordering of *Lyrical Ballads*," and James Scoggins, *Imagination and Fancy* (1966), pp. 27–38. Jared Curtis, in his recent edition of Wordsworth's *Poems, in Two Volumes* (1807), remarks that the Intimations Ode was deliberately chosen to close the 1807 collection "just as 'Tintern Abbey' was placed to conclude *Lyrical Ballads* in 1798" (p. 22).

In 1843, when Wordsworth told Isabella Fenwick that the "Ancient Mariner" was the seed from which the collection grew, he noted that *Lyrical Ballads* "was to consist as Mr. Coleridge has told the world, of Poems chiefly on natural subjects taken from common life but looked at, as much as might be, through an imaginative medium."[8] But Mr. Coleridge had, in fact, given a somewhat different set of particulars. The *Biographia* suggests that *Lyrical Ballads* was planned to consist of poetry of "two sorts," with each poet contributing only one type of poem.[9] The following passage is well known but worth quoting at length:

> . . . it was agreed, that my endeavours should be directed to persons and characters supernatural, or at least romantic; yet so as to transfer from our outward nature a human interest and a semblance of truth sufficient to procure for these shadows of imagination that willing suspension of disbelief for the moment, which constitutes poetic faith. Mr. Wordsworth, on the other hand, was to propose to himself as his object, to give the charm of novelty to things of every day, and to excite a feeling analogous to the supernatural, by awakening the mind's attention from the lethargy of custom, and directing it to the loveliness and the wonders of the world before us. (*BL*, 2:6)

Coleridge recounts here that, while he would link the extraordinary world with the ordinary, Wordsworth was to link the ordinary world with the extraordinary. From this a blending would result: the natural and supernatural worlds would become coextensive. Although the poems of *Lyrical Ballads* would be of "two sorts," they would exist as a vital imaginative body, presenting unity in multeity.

If true, much of what Coleridge suggests—as he himself notes in the *Biographia*—changed before *Lyrical Ballads* passed through the press. Neither poet seems to have worked according to any clear division of labor: Wordsworth wrote "Goody Blake and Harry Gill" and "The Thorn," which, as John Jordan has argued, "depend on a belief in the supernatural," even "if they have psychological explanations";[1] and Coleridge produced "The Nightingale," "The Foster-Mother's Tale," and "The Dungeon"—all very much centered in the natural world. Nor was there any discernible attempt to balance the number of contributions from each poet: Wordsworth wrote nineteen of the twenty-three poems in the collection. Such discrepancies, coupled with the difference between the recollections of the two poets, have led most critics to justifiable doubts that *Lyrical Ballads* was created from a precisely articulated aesthetic plan. Yet however divergent the comments later made by Wordsworth and Coleridge about the plan of the volume, it is clear from the Advertisement of 1798 and the preface of 1800 that both poets thought the volume had a purpose and a plan.

Thus, if "compromise, expediency, and chance" played a role in the formation of *Lyrical Ballads*, it is equally certain that the desire for a

---

8. See Owen, *Wordsworth and Coleridge: "Lyrical Ballads" 1798* (1967), p. 136 (hereafter all quotations from the poems of and notes to the 1798 edition will be cited in the text as Owen).
9. John Shawcross, *Biographia Literaria* (1907), 2:5.
1. Jordan, *Why "The Lyrical Ballads"?*, p. 12.

harmonized and unified collection played a role as well.[2] Coleridge seems to have just such a conception in mind when he tries to interest Cottle in publishing the 1798 edition by comparing the whole to an ode, with individual poems that "are as stanzas, good relatively rather than absolutely."[3] With his deft analogy, Coleridge shifts Cottle's attention away from what has been characterized in an earlier chapter as the "inner" meaning of the poems to their "outer" meaning as a group. Like the reader alert to what Coleridge called "that Impetuousity of Transition, and that Precipitation of Fancy and Feeling, which are the *essential* excellencies of the sublimer Ode" (*LC*, 1:289), Cottle is asked to see beyond the apparent incongruities of style and subject among the poems of *Lyrical Ballads* to their essential likeness.[4] As informed readers of the collection, we are similarly charged.

To be sure, Coleridge's comparison of *Lyrical Ballads* to an ode is both richly suggestive and somewhat limited. The "spread of the volume" indicates that there was probably no elaborate design for the positioning or even the selection of every poem. We should not expect, nor will we find, the sequentiality or coherence of a single long poem among the poems in the book. Yet, in its pairing of such poems as "Expostulation and Reply" with "The Tables Turned" and "Anecdote for Fathers" with "We Are Seven," in its use of "Ancient Mariner" and "Tintern Abbey" as framework poems and "The Thorn" as a centerpiece, in its thematically integrated though not always spatially juxtaposed clusters of poems, *Lyrical Ballads* does show signs of significant organization. Not only are local transitions made between a few sets of poems, but, as we shall see, a larger system of resonant effects operates throughout the volume.

Wordsworth and Coleridge further promoted the unity of *Lyrical Ballads* by publishing it anonymously, as the work of a single poet.[5] To consider the effectiveness of such a strategy we must unlearn most of what

2. Jordan in *Why "The Lyrical Ballads"*? argues persuasively that this desire is responsible for the omission from the volume of "Lewti," a poem incongruous with the others in style and concerns (p. 43). For a more detailed discussion of the publication of *Lyrical Ballads* (1798), see Jordan, pp. 33–52. For bibliographical details of the issue containing "Lewti," see Foxon, "The Printing of *Lyrical Ballads*, 1798."

3. This letter * * * was written to Cottle on 28 May 1798. Coleridge has introduced some confusion by referring here to "the volumes" of 1798. See Owen, "*Lyrical Ballads*" 1798, p. xiii, for a possible explanation of his reference. Parrish, in *Art of "The Lyrical Ballads*," believes that Coleridge claimed the collection was like an ode in order to placate Cottle's fears "that the contents of the volume would not be homogeneous" (p. 40). Even if this were so, however, it would not necessarily negate the truth of Coleridge's statement or indicate that he was being insincere. Indeed, such an observation is characteristic of Coleridge. Some thirty-five years later, for instance, Coleridge remarks that Shakespeare's "extraordinary sonnets form, in fact a poem of so many stanzas of fourteen lines each." See H. N. Coleridge, *Table Talk* (entry for 14 May 1833) (1835), 1:93.

4. I would agree with Averill, who in "Shape of *Lyrical Ballads*" understands Coleridge as implying that the volume "read correctly becomes a single poem" (pp. 390–91). Whereas Averill is more interested in the overall structure than in the theme of such a "poem," theories about the "theme" of *Lyrical Ballads* abound and are produced even by those who do not fully believe in the unity of the volume. For instance, John Danby in *The Simple Wordsworth* (1963) argues that *Lyrical Ballads* is devoted mainly to pointing out "the dislocation between man and nature" (p. 130). Albert Gérard, in *English Romantic Poetry* (1968), writes that the major concern in *Lyrical Ballads* is "the evil present in the human condition" (p. 185). In *Why "The Lyrical Ballads"*?, Jordan suggests that perhaps "the turns on gratitude (and ingratitude)—familiar, neighborly, tribal, social—are close to the 'theme' of the 1798 *Lyrical Ballads*" (p. 185). My own sense of the volume comes closest to that of Paul Sheats, who finds in "The *Lyrical Ballads*" (1975) that the whole is fundamentally concerned with the "liberation of the reader from his own 'pre-established codes of decision'" (p. 133).

5. Jordan comments, "Probably Wordsworth and Coleridge were chiefly interested in keeping their names off the title page, particularly *two* names." See *Why "The Lyrical Ballads"*?, p. 43.

we know about the volume and see it through the eyes of a contemporary ignorant of its dual authorship. Such a reader has only the evidence of the volume to guide him, and this evidence is purposely misleading. Twice in the Advertisement, reference is made to the "author" of the volume. This fictive persona, apparently responsible for all of the poems in *Lyrical Ballads*, is the objective embodiment of a poetic friendship which Thomas McFarland aptly characterizes as "nothing less than a symbiosis, a development of attitude so dialogical and intertwined that in some instances not even the participants themselves could discern their respective contributions."[6]

Not until the preface of 1800 did Wordsworth disavow in public the existence of this fictive Coleridge-Wordsworth. Yet even there he states that Coleridge's poems would never have been joined to his own had not he believed that "the poems of my Friend would in a great measure have the same tendency as my own, and that, though there would be found a difference, there would be found no discordance in the colours of our style; as our opinions on the subject of poetry do almost entirely coincide" (Owen, pp. 153–54). From this almost entire coincidence of the two poets' opinions about poetry arose the amalgam "poet" of the Advertisement.

Stephen Parrish has shown that *Lyrical Ballads* is in many ways a dramatic work. The appreciative reader is tempted to look behind the scenes to discover the dramatist. This impulse is perhaps what prompts William Heath to comment that the placement of "Tintern Abbey" at the end of the volume "seems designed to answer that reader who asks, justifiably, what consciousness operates behind the voice singing in most of these ballads, and why he should attend to it."[7] As Heath implies, the poems of *Lyrical Ballads* reflect the unity of their "author's" poetic style and thoughts. To discover the shape of the world presented by the volume is to disclose the shape of his consciousness. In other words, each poem of the volume contributes to the larger perceptual "field" created by the collection as a whole.

If in both language and subject *Lyrical Ballads* (1798) sets an agenda for the well-known debate about poetry that Wordsworth joined more openly in 1800, at an even more fundamental level the volume is concerned with exploring the proper role of the poet himself. Paul Sheats has claimed that the narrators of both "Simon Lee" and "The Idiot Boy" function "in the same way as the pedlar."[8] However, no one has yet recognized the number of resemblances between the Pedlar, renamed the Wanderer in *The Excursion*, and the "author" of *Lyrical Ballads*—particularly in the breadth of their minds. The "author" of *Lyrical Ballads*, for instance, is capable of producing poetry ranging from the abstruse "Ancient Mariner" to the contemplative "Tintern Abbey" to the more folkish "Goody Blake and Harry Gill." Likewise, the narrator of *The Excursion* tells us that the Wanderer "often touched / Abstrusest matter, reasoning of the

---

6. McFarland, *Romanticism and the Forms of Ruin* (1981), p. 57. McFarland's entire first chapter closely examines the symbiosis between Wordsworth and Coleridge, pp. 56–103. See also Parrish, *Art of "The Lyrical Ballads,"* pp. 34–79.
7. Parrish, of course, discusses the dramatic nature of *Lyrical Ballads* throughout *Art of "The Lyrical Ballads."* For Heath, see *Wordsworth and Coleridge* (1970), p. 36.
8. See Sheats, "The *Lyrical Ballads*," p. 140.

mind / Turned inward; or at my request would sing / Old songs, the product of his native hills" (*PW*, 1:64–67).[9]

*   *   *

[III]

"I pass, like night, from land to land," the Ancient Mariner tells the Wedding Guest (l. 619). The darkness of the Mariner's night filters throughout *Lyrical Ballads*. Character after character discovers the inadequacy of a human society based upon sterile preconceptions and close-mindedness and is subsequently cast adrift in a type of death-in-life. Alienation of this kind is generally expressed in the volume by motion of two sorts: the cramped near-paralysis of the prisoner or the aimless wandering of the outcast.

Albert of "The Foster-Mother's Tale," the second poem of the volume, is both a prisoner and a wanderer.[1] During his youth, Albert's immense learning convinces him of the falsity of his society's codes of decision. His subsequent "heretical and lawless talk" (l. 55) causes him to be cast into a dungeon. Imprisoned by the forces of an old and sterile world, Albert fittingly escapes to the "new world" of America (l. 76), where he "all alone, set sail by moonlight / Up a great river . . . / And ne'er was heard of more" (ll. 78–80). What we know of the Albert of *Osorio* is irrelevant here. More to the point is his function in *Lyrical Ballads*, where, of all the many prisoners and wanderers, Albert is the only character really to escape from his world. The Foster-Mother tells Maria that it is supposed that Albert "lived and died among the savage men" (l. 81). Ironically, though, the men of the old world are more truly savages. The openness of a landscape in which one can set sail alone "Upon a great river, great as any sea" (l. 79) promises much in contrast to the "hole" into which Albert is cast by the civilized men of his society.

Yet Albert's wanderings in the new, unstructured world of America represent a type of liberation unavailable to the other characters of the volume. Maria properly characterizes his story as a "sweet tale / Such as would lull a listening child to sleep" (ll. 68–69). The true prisoners in the poem are Maria and the Foster-Mother, for whom there is no escape. Indeed, even the Female Vagrant, who attempts such an escape, can find no liberation in the wartorn America she visits as the wife of a soldier. That America is merely a new world structured upon the same life-denying principles of the old. Her tale, like that of most of the other characters in *Lyrical Ballads*, is anything but "sweet." For these characters are confronted by a world in which only the child or the idiot can feel completely at home.

9. Unless otherwise designated, all quotations from Wordsworth's poetry other than the *Lyrical Ballads* are taken from De Selincourt and Darbishire, *Poetical Works of William Wordsworth* (hereafter cited in the text as *PW*). All quotations from Coleridge's poems, other than those in *Lyrical Ballads*, are from E. H. Coleridge, *Complete Poetical Works of Samuel Taylor Coleridge* (1912).
1. Coleridge seems to have conceived of "The Ancient Mariner" and "The Foster-Mother's Tale" as companion poems. Although Wordsworth separates the two in 1800, Coleridge re-pairs them as the first and second poems, respectively, in *Sibylline Leaves*. In "Shape of *Lyrical Ballads*," Averill notes that the first sixteen lines of "The Foster-Mother's Tale" seem to refer the reader back to the "Ancient Mariner" and that these lines were dropped in 1800 when the two poems were no longer juxtaposed (p. 398). One might add that they were restored in *Sibylline Leaves*.

The dungeon into which Albert is thrown in "The Foster-Mother's Tale" first objectifies in *Lyrical Ballads* the dungeon grate through which the sun seems to peer at the Ancient Mariner. But the dungeon grate materializes again in both "The Convict" (poem #22) and "The Dungeon" (poem #14). Indeed, the narrator of "The Convict" himself peers "through the glimmering grate, / That outcast of pity [to] behold" (ll. 11–12). In the extremity of his alienation, the Ancient Mariner's heart becomes as "dry as dust." And we are told that on the "woful day" when Martha Ray of "The Thorn" (poem #12) is abandoned by her lover, "A cruel, cruel fire . . . / Into her bones was sent. / It dried her body like a cinder / And almost turn'd her brain to tinder" (ll. 128–32). We are thus well prepared to understand the dire alienation of the convict, whose "bones are consumed, and his life-blood is dried, / With wishes the past to undo" (ll. 21–22). Estranged from even himself, in grief "self-consumed" (l. 29), the convict is also the "Poor victim" (l. 45) of a society that chooses to alienate him further by confining him to what in "The Dungeon" is called an "uncomforted / And friendless solitude" (ll. 12–13).

"Have I not reason to lament / What man has made of man?" (ll. 23–24), concludes the narrator of "Lines Written in Early Spring." This question serves as a fit preface to the group of poems that immediately follow it, consisting of "The Thorn," "The Last of the Flock," and "The Dungeon." Indeed, "The Dungeon" begins by indignantly echoing, "And this place our forefathers made for man!" (l. 1). As if he were not already vulnerable enough to the forces of an alien world that defeats his understanding, man insists on structuring society upon principles that violate community. "The Last of the Flock" (poem #13) and "The Complaint of the Forsaken Indian Woman" (poem #21), poems that border "The Dungeon" and "The Convict," respectively, examine other "outcasts of pity" imprisoned by the structures that people create for one another.

Both the Shepherd of "The Last of the Flock" and the Indian Woman of "The Complaint of the Forsaken Indian Woman" are forsaken by their society.[2] Refused aid from his parish in "a time of need" (l. 42), the Shepherd is forced to sell his sheep, one by one. For the Shepherd, however, each sale is prophetic of all that stands between himself and complete nakedness:[3]

> To see the end of all my gains,
> The pretty flock which I had reared
> With all my care and pains,
> To see it melt like snow away!
> For me it was a woeful day. (ll. 56–60)

Like the "woful day" on which Martha Ray is forever alienated from her world, this woeful day leaves the Shepherd permanently estranged from his surroundings: "No peace, no comfort could I find, / No ease, within doors or without, / . . . / Oft-times I thought to run away" (ll. 75–76, 79). Obsessed by his loss, the Shepherd can find no further meaning in his

---

2. These two poems are, in fact, grouped together in 1800 as the fifth and fourth poems, respectively, of the first volume.
3. This point is made by Hartman in his convincing discussion of "The Last of the Flock" in *Wordsworth's Poetry*, p. 144.

family or in life itself: "And now I care not if we die, / And perish all of poverty" (ll. 39–40).

Such a mental contraction dooms the Shepherd to be the prisoner of his own closed mind, "a jarring and dissonant thing / Amid this general dance and minstrelsy" (ll. 25–26), as the succeeding poem, "The Dungeon," phrases it. And it is as such that the narrator of "The Last of the Flock" first encounters him: "I have not often seen / A healthy man, a man full grown / Weep in the public roads alone" (ll. 2–4). If, then, the Shepherd is a victim of his own failure of vision, this failure would not be possible without the existence of an economic system that first encourages him to value his life in terms of his property and then abandons him to face his losses unaided. In a society in which each member is taught to look after his own interests, the welfare of others is of little importance.

"The Complaint of the Forsaken Indian Woman" poignantly restates the theme of "The Last of the Flock." Here, a woman overcome by sickness is abandoned by her companions: "Alas! you might have dragged me on / Another day, a single one!" (ll. 21–22). Her child given to "A woman who was not thy mother" (l. 32), the forsaken Indian Woman is "For ever left alone" (l. 59). As an "outcast of pity," trapped within the double prison of the structures of her society and a diseased body, the Indian Woman expresses more than the Shepherd's mere indifference to life: "Before I see another day / Oh let my body die away!" (ll. 1–2). Her plight reveals that one can be betrayed by internal as well as external forces. For the body can become as great a prison as any created by man for man. Certainly this is the case with Simon Lee.

Like the Shepherd, Simon Lee is a victim of poverty; like the forsaken Indian Woman, he is also a victim of his own body; and like both, he faces unaided a source of immedicable pain. Once a man "so full of glee" (l. 18), Simon is trapped by the passage of time in much the same way as Matthew, another "man of glee" ("The Fountain," l. 20), who appears in Lyrical Ballads (1800). Both men suffer because they can no longer be what they once were. Though their losses through time have been great— Matthew survives his family and Simon is the "sole survivor" (l. 24) of the inhabitants of Ivor Hall—each "Mourns less for what age takes away / Than what it leaves behind" ("The Fountain," ll. 35–36). And for Simon Lee time has left poverty, an infirm body, and a haunting sense of the past. This helps to explain why Simon's spirit seems so imprisoned by his broken body, in marked contrast to the old man in "Old Man Travelling," whose "bending figure" (l. 5) is the home for a mind "by nature led / To peace so perfect" (ll. 12–13).

Troubled in mind and infirm of body, Simon, "the poorest of the poor" (l. 60), is forced to work, "though weak, / —The weakest in the village" (ll. 39–40). Alone, Simon Lee can do little to combat an assault from within and without that has inevitable results: "Few months of life has he in store, / . . . / For still, the more he works, the more / His poor old ancles swell" (ll. 65, 67–68). Thus, the substance of the tale "the gentle reader" is to find in "Simon Lee" concerns not only the "burthen weighty" of time but also, as in "The Last of the Flock" and "The Complaint," the way in which the alienation of one human being from another is ultimately fatal for each. In fact, Lyrical Ballads contains two striking examples of the suicidal state of mind responsible for this alienation.

Through the course of his alienation, the Ancient Mariner learns the importance of community. His departing words to the Wedding Guest memorably state this knowledge: "He prayeth best who loveth best, / All things both great and small" (ll. 647–48). To participate in a state of mind that would make aliens of other living things is to make oneself an alien, cut off completely from community. Although it is the third poem of the volume, "Lines Left upon a Seat in a Yew-tree" is the first written by Wordsworth, and it stands as his preliminary statement of the ethic of "Ancient Mariner." Contempt or disdain for others, as the youth in the "Yew-tree" discovers, is ultimately suicidal.

Because his talents are neglected by the world, the youth "with rash disdain" (l. 19) turns away from his fellow beings "And with the food of pride sustained his soul / In solitude" (ll. 20–21). Just as Blake's Urizen is always pictured in circumscribed space, the similarly solipsistic youth of the "Yew-tree" sits surrounded by the yew tree he has "taught" to encircle him (l. 10). And as he sits, the youth gazes upon the barren rocks before him, in which he finds an "emblem of his own unfruitful life" (l. 29). The youth cannot long survive upon "the food of pride." He dies completely isolated, proof that "The man, whose eye / Is ever on himself, doth look on one, / The least of nature's works" (ll. 51–53). Rephrasing the Mariner's recognition of the importance of community, the narrator of the "Yew-tree" comments: "he, who feels contempt / For any living thing, hath faculties / Which he has never used" (ll. 48–50).

These faculties also remain unused by Harry Gill, a man who vows to take vengeance on "Old Goody Blake" because she takes sticks from his hedge for firewood "when her old bones . . . [are] cold and chill" (l. 62). The delight Harry Gill takes in seizing this poor woman is indicative of the coldness of his heart, a coldness that is soon to become his ontological condition. For in response to Goody Blake's prayer, "O may he never more be warm!" (l. 100), Harry turns away from her "icy-cold," and "all who see him say 'tis plain, / That, live as long as he may, / He never will be warm again" (ll. 118–20). Those in *Lyrical Ballads* who feel contempt for others live suicidal lives, self-exiled into the "icy-cold" imprisonment of their own solipsism.

On the other hand, those characters in the volume who attempt to love others are not usually successful. The Ancient Mariner's tale, testifying to the divorce between the mind and the world, begins a noncontiguous group of poems concerned with marriage but ending in radical divorce. If the Wedding Guest is prevented from celebrating the marriage of a bride who is "Red as a rose" (l. 38), it is because there is a force in his world that can turn this red into the scarlet associated with the abandoned Martha Ray. The abandoned brides and brides-to-be of the *Lyrical Ballads* find themselves lonely, desperate wanderers. Indeed, the Mariner's powerful lament for his isolation is to echo throughout the marriage group: "Alone, alone, all all alone / Alone on the wide wide Sea" (ll. 224–25). This striking repetition of the "al" sound is to reappear in "The Female Vagrant" (poem #5) with much the same effect.

The Female Vagrant suffers increasing degrees of isolation, beginning with her first estrangement from her society, when she and her father are evicted forcibly from their home: "All but the bed where his old body lay, / All, all was seized, and weeping side by side, / We sought a home where we uninjured might abide" (ll. 52–54). The Female Vagrant's alienation is marked, like the Mariner's, by an inability to pray: "I could not pray:— through tears that fell in showers, / Glimmer'd our dear-loved home, alas! no longer ours!" (ll. 62–63).[4] Left homeless, she speaks to her lover "of marriage and our marriage day" (l. 70). Yet even though they soon marry, marriage is only a temporary solution to the Female Vagrant's homelessness. Destitution shortly forces her family to America where "All perished—all, in one remorseless year, / Husband and children! . . . / . . . all perished" (ll. 131–33). With all ties to humanity severed, she returns to England with only one desire: to "shun the spot where man might come" (l. 171).

Yet the Female Vagrant, again like the Mariner, finds a still moment of joy at sea, where the "heavenly silence" that "did the waves invest" brings "a joy to . . . [her] despair" (ll. 142, 144). Even so, she is forced to recognize the painful contrast between this moment of joy and the constant despair that reawaits her on land:

> Some mighty gulph of separation past,
> I seemed transported to another world:—
> A thought resigned with pain, when from the mast
> The impatient mariner the sail unfurl'd,
> And whistling, called the wind that hardly curled
> The silent sea. (ll. 163–68)

The "impatient mariner" is part of a world that refuses to remain motionless. Forced from stillness by the inexorable movement of the ship homeward, the Female Vagrant feels just as inexorably doomed to homelessness: "From the sweet thoughts of home, / And from all hope I was forever hurled" (ll. 168–69). Indeed, she returns to her "own countrée" an alien, "homeless near a thousand homes" (l. 179). A prisoner of "that perpetual weight which on her spirit lay" (l. 270), she has been as the poem closes "Three years a wanderer" (l. 262) across the English countryside.

Whereas marriage is useless as a remedy for alienation, it sometimes serves as a cause. Such is the case with both the Mad Mother and Martha Ray. Originally from "far . . . over the main" (l. 4), the Mad Mother is literally an alien to her surroundings. And this alienation is compounded by her marriage: though the Mad Mother can tell her child, "I am thy father's wedded wife" (l. 72), she must also painfully admit, "Thy father cares not for my breast" (l. 61). Abandoned by her husband, the Mad Mother becomes a homeless wanderer with only her child between her faltering mind and the radical loneliness that leads to insanity: "She has a baby on her arm, / Or else she were alone" (ll. 5–6).

---

4. However similar in effect, their alienation differs significantly in cause. That is, the Female Vagrant, unlike the Mariner, is a victim of unjust political and social conditions. Indeed, as originally conceived in 1795, the Female Vagrant's story was an overt attack on contemporary oppression of the poor, with which Wordsworth linked other injustices, such as England's entry into war against France. See Gill, *Salisbury Plain Poems* (1975), p. 5. As presented in 1798, "The Female Vagrant" retains much of its force as a protest against social oppression and war. Its attack on wealthy landowners and enclosure, in particular, make it one of the most overtly political poems of *Lyrical Ballads*, though one might argue that, even so, it is more a psychological or ontological study than a political one. Beginning with *Lyrical Ballads* (1802), and throughout subsequent revisions, Wordsworth muted the political elements of the poem. For the changing states of the manuscript, see Gill's edition.

Martha Ray, however, has nothing to shield her from such loneliness; she is even suspected of murdering her newborn child. Because she is betrayed by "unthinking" Stephen Hill, Martha Ray's wedding day becomes the "woful day" when she is forever alienated from her world. Like the Mad Mother, Martha, it is said, "was with child, and she was mad" (l. 139)—yet "in her womb the infant wrought / About its mother's heart, and brought / Her senses back again" (ll. 150–52). Martha, of course, can gain no lasting comfort from her child, if she ever actually was pregnant and did indeed give birth. Instead, like the Ancient Mariner she becomes an obsessive-compulsive, moving perpetually between her hut and the mountaintop, who in her "exceeding pain" is heard endlessly to repeat: "Oh misery! oh misery! / O woe is me! oh misery!" (ll. 252–53).

The characters of the marriage group, like those in the cluster of poems about imprisonment, are isolated aliens in their world, obsessed by their losses, helpless before the mystery at the heart of existence. Nor does there seem to be a way for them to reconnect with others. If, as we have seen, questions are a necessary step to this end, often a character's most earnest questions are left unanswered. Indeed, the volume insists that unanswered questions are an inevitable condition of human life. For words themselves are powerless to bridge completely the gap between the mind and the surrounding world.

While defending his use of tautology to Isabella Fenwick, Wordsworth says:

> . . . now every man must know that an attempt is rarely made to communicate impassioned feelings without something of an accompanying consciousness of the inadequateness of our own powers, or the deficiencies of language. During such efforts there will be a craving in the mind, and as long as it is unsatisfied the Speaker will cling to the same words, or words of the same character. (Owen, p. 140)

The inadequacy of words paradoxically leads to the mind's obsession with these same words. In a similar way, the mind's inability to comprehend certain aspects of its world can lead to obsession with these aspects. Thus, repetition, another characteristic of the traditional ballad, is also used often in *Lyrical Ballads* to depict obsession. For instance, the narrator's inability in "Anecdote for Fathers" (poem #9) to understand young Edward's preference of Kilve to Liswyn farm results in his fixation on the same question: "And five times did I say to him, / Why? Edward, tell me why?" (ll. 47–48). Likewise, the narrator of "We Are Seven" (poem #10), unable to understand the young girl's view of death, is obsessed with the desire to make her understand the logic of his arithmetic. His many subtractions of two from seven end in this last futile repetition: "But they are dead; those two are dead! / Their spirits are in heaven!" (ll. 65–66). Mystery and obsession, then, are two related forces in *Lyrical Ballads*. It is therefore unsurprising that "The Thorn," the poem in the volume that deals most directly with mystery, is the poem most filled with the questions of its narrator and the obsessions of its characters.

"The Thorn," moreover, gathers together the thematic strands of the preceding poems, which, in addition to mystery and obsession, include alienation, homelessness, and human suffering. Placed twelfth of twenty-three

poems, "The Thorn" is itself composed of twenty-three stanzas, and at its
mid-point—thus at the very center of the book—is the stanza concerning
Martha Ray's aborted marriage plans and her attendant madness.[5] Here
the reader reaches the heart of the darkness within *Lyrical Ballads*.

* * *

MARY JACOBUS

From Tradition and Experiment in Wordsworth's "Lyrical Ballads" 1798[†]

'It is supposed, that by the act of writing in verse an Author makes a for-
mal engagement that he will gratify certain known habits of association',
wrote Wordsworth in the 1800 'Preface' to *Lyrical Ballads*.[1] The chal-
lenge of the 1798 volume lay in its refusal to fulfil audience expecta-
tions—in particular, expectations about the ballad. His readers were not
only required to find 'A tale in every thing' ('Simon Lee', 1. 76), but forced
to look critically at the fashion for supernatural and pseudo-antiquarian
balladry which had reached its peak during the mid-1790s. Along with
many of their contemporaries, Wordsworth and Coleridge tried their
hand at this by-product of the ballad revival. Both were influenced by the
German poet, Gottfried Bürger, whose ballads appeared in translation
during the 1790s and offered a striking model for their own up-dating
of traditional themes and techniques. But where Coleridge accepted the
supernatural, Wordsworth reacted against it. Although Bürger undoubt-
edly attracted him for a time, the uncongenial values of the supernatural
ballad led him to create a new kind of ballad emphasizing the importance
of the everyday, of feeling rather than situation. The questions Wordsworth
asks—what is a story? What makes an adventure? What part does the mind
play in creating both?—culminate in the open anti-supernaturalism of
Peter Bell. Rooted as it is in an ephemeral fashion, the ballad experiment
offers the most illuminating example of Wordsworth's self-defining rela-
tion to his literary context. Nowhere is his contemporaneity more marked,
and nowhere is his divergence more individual.

I. The Literary Ballad

Wordsworth's famous claim for Percy's *Reliques*—that English poetry
'has been absolutely redeemed by it'—goes with a generous acknowledge-
ment of his own debt:

> I do not think that there is an able writer in verse of the present day
> who would not be proud to acknowledge his obligations to the Rel-
> iques; I know that it is so with my friends; and, for myself, I am
> happy in this occasion to make a public avowal of my own.[2]

5. I am grateful to Joseph Wittreich for bringing the stanzaic patterning of "The Thorn" to my
   attention.
† From *Tradition and Experiment in Wordsworth's "Lyrical Ballads" 1798* (Oxford: Clarendon
   Press, 1976), 209–17, 233–50. Notes have been edited. Reprinted by permission.
1. *Prose Works*, i. 122.
2. 'Essay, Supplementary to the Preface', 1815 (*Prose Works*, iii. 78).

Behind this 'public avowal' lies the full weight of the ballad revival. In 1800, when he invoked 'The Babes in the Wood' in support of his own poetic theories, Wordsworth still felt the need to caution the reader against 'a mode of false criticism which has been applied to Poetry in which the language closely resembles that of life and nature.'[3] But he could rely on his reader knowing Addison's defence of the ballad, a hundred years before. However apologetically, the *Spectator* papers had made a case for 'The Babes in the Wood' which might almost have been made by Blair or Wordsworth himself:

> This Song is a plain simple Copy of Nature, destitute of all the Helps and Ornaments of Art. The Tale of it is a pretty Tragical Story, and pleases for no other Reason, but because it is a Copy of Nature. There is even a despicable Simplicity in the Verse; and yet, because the Sentiments appear genuine and unaffected, they are able to move the Mind of the most polite Reader with inward Meltings of Humanity and Compassion.[4]

Percy too bases his claims for the ballad on qualities bound up with its lack of sophistication:

> In a polished age, like the present, I am sensible that many of these reliques of antiquity will require great allowances to be made for them. Yet have they, for the most part, a pleasing simplicity, and many artless graces, which in the opinion of no mean critics have been thought to compensate for the want of higher beauties, and if they do not dazzle the imagination, are frequently found to interest the heart.[5]

Increasingly, to say that the traditional ballad 'interests the heart' is to say that it expresses all that is most lasting and important in human feeling. The ballad collections which follow Percy are prefaced in terms that grow less defensive as they gain in critical sophistication. Pinkerton, for instance, in the introduction to his *Scottish Tragic Ballads* of 1781, shares Blair's assumptions about the origins of poetry ('the original language of men in an infant state of society'), and again the ballad-makers' power to move is linked directly with their lack of literary pretension: 'Their mode of expression was simple and genuine. They of consequence touched the passions truly and effectively.'[6] Like Blair's primitive bards, they appealed with special directness to 'the passions and the ear', and because 'The passions of men have been and will be the same through all ages',[7] their writing is held to have the same timeless validity as that of Homer, Shakespeare, and Ossian. With these credentials, the ballad was bound to have important connotations for Wordsworth in 1798.

Yet the traditional ballad seems to have had little direct influence on Wordsworth's experiment. Of all the poems written during spring 1798, only 'The Mad Mother' (and, less certainly, 'The Thorn') owes anything to a traditional source.[8] Wordsworth's purchase of the *Reliques* did not

---

3. 1800 'Preface' (*Prose Works*, i. 152).
4. *Spectator*, No. lxxxv (7 June 1711), ed. D. F. Bond, i. 362–3.
5. *Reliques of Ancient English Poetry* (1765), i. x.
6. 'Dissertation I', *Scottish Tragic Ballads*, pp. x, xvii.
7. Ibid., p. xvii.
8. See p. 621 below.

take place until his arrival in Germany later the same year,[9] and it is tempting to think that he returned to Percy by way of imitators like Bürger; certainly 'Lucy Gray', composed during his Goslar stay,[1] owes more to the style of the 'justly admired' stanza of 'The Babes in the Wood' later cited in the 1800 'Preface' ('These pretty Babes with hand in hand/ Went wandering up and down . . .')[2] than do any of the ballads of 1798:

> The storm came on before its time,
> She wander'd up and down,
> And many a hill did Lucy climb
> But never reached the Town.   (ll. 29–32)

The colloquial vigour and flamboyance of Wordsworth's ballad experiment has no real counterpart in the traditional ballad. Nor does it help to invoke the popular broadside. All one has to go on are the later references to street ballads in *The Prelude*—the 'English Ballad-singer' and 'files of ballads' in the London streets[3]—and a pious hope expressed to Wrangham ten years after the event:

> I have so much felt the influence of these straggling papers, that I have many a time wished that I had talents to produce songs, poems, and little histories, that might circulate among other good things in this way, supplanting partly the bad; flowers and useful herbs to take place of weeds. Indeed some of the Poems which I have published were composed not without a hope that at some time or other they might answer this purpose.[4]

Wordsworth had been anticipated in his hope by the missionary efforts of Hannah More; but unlike hers, the ballads of 1798 can never have been seriously intended for an unsophisticated audience. Only 'Goody Blake, and Harry Gill' ('one of the rudest of this collection')[5] is at all reminiscent of broadside—and even here Wordsworth is far closer to Hannah More's imitations in the *Cheap Repository* series than to the genuine broadside. His originality lay in approaching the imitation ballad from a startlingly anti-literary direction. The effect is quite distinct from the literary ballads of his contemporaries, but the impulse—revitalizing, sophisticated, and self-conscious—is the same.

*   *   *

> The moving accident is not my trade,
> To freeze the blood I have no ready arts . . .
> ('Hart-Leap Well', ll. 97–8)

By 1800, Wordsworth's meditative values were firmly established as the basis of his ballad experiment. Bürger's 'Der wilde Jäger', a story of violence punished by violence, becomes 'Hart-Leap Well', a tale of silent suffering in which nature conspires to obliterate human pride in the chase and to mourn the death of the hunted hart.[6] In 1798, Wordsworth

9. See *DWJ* i. 31.
1. See Reed, p. 256 and n.
2. *Prose Works*, i. 154.
3. See *Prelude*, vii. 195–6, 209.
4. 5 June 1808; *MY* i. 248.
5. 1800 'Preface' (*Prose Works*, i. 150).
6. See Geoffrey Hartman, *PQ* xlvii (1968), 55–68.

had responded more straightforwardly to Bürger's *"Tra ra la"'*, but already his own ballads were designed to supply the 'manners connected with the permanent objects of nature and partaking of the simplicity of those objects'[7] which he found lacking in the supernatural ballad. Wordsworth's experiment produced some of his most provocative redefinitions. The ballad-reader's expectations are aroused, disappointed—and redirected towards what were for Wordsworth more significant aspects of human experience. His achievement is to adapt the ballad to portraying precisely those states and feelings least susceptible to narrative presentation. At the same time, he forces us to reassess the importance of the everyday. While the supernatural ignores the ordinary world, the mind can transform it, and in one way or another all the ballads of 1798 concern the workings of the imagination. 'Goody Blake, and Harry Gill' shows the power of imagination to enforce humane values. 'The Thorn' reveals what the imagination can make of a suggestive group of objects in a landscape, and its difficulty in apprehending the obscure and inarticulate suffering associated with them. 'The Idiot Boy' burlesques the ballad of supernatural adventure in order to establish new priorities—the feelings and experiences which irradiate the everyday. Written within a few weeks of one another, these ballads show Wordsworth challenging the genre he has adopted—insisting first on writing with a definite 'purpose', then on questioning the very basis of narrative convention, and finally subverting it altogether. The result is a genre capable not simply of expressing Wordsworth's vision, but of modifying and extending the reader's; offered 'Suck stores as silent thought can bring', we are shown how to 'find / A tale in everything' ('Simon Lee', ll. 74, 75–6). The ballads of 1798 are not only technically exhilarating in their own right, but among Wordsworth's most effective statements about the aims and functions of his poetry.

I. 'Goody Blake, and Harry Gill'

Wordsworth's comments on 'Goody Blake, and Harry Gill' in the 1800 'Preface' anticipate Coleridge's later remarks about 'The Three Graves':

> I wished to draw attention to the truth that the power of the human imagination is sufficient to produce such changes even in our physical nature as might almost appear miraculous. The truth is an important one; the fact (for it is a *fact*) is a valuable illustration of it.[8]

The first of the ballads of spring 1798 grows out of the interest in morbid psychology reflected in Parts III and IV of 'The Three Graves'. Like Coleridge, Wordsworth had been reading Hearne, and a case-history from a contemporary scientific work provides the '*fact*' on which he insists. In early March, he had written to Cottle 'merely to request (which I have very particular reasons for doing) that you would contrive to send me Dr Darwin's Zoönomia *by the first carrier*'.[9] By mid-March, Dorothy writes to Cottle: 'We have received the books for which we are much

---

7. *WL*, i. 255.
8. *Prose Works*, i. 150.
9. *WL*, i. 199 (for the date of Wordsworth's letter, see Reed, p. 224n.). Coleridge had met Darwin in 1796 (see *CL* i. 177) and probably knew *Zoönomia* before 1798; see *The Notebooks of Samuel Taylor Coleridge*, ed. Kathleen Coburn, i. 188n.

obliged to you. They have already completely answered the purpose for which William wrote for them.'[1] It is easy to see why this episode from Darwin's *Zoönomia; or, the Laws of Organic Life* (1794–6) captured Wordsworth's interest; like the opening sections of 'The Three Graves', it centres on a curse-scene, vivid enough in its own right to offset Darwin's flat reporting:

> I received good information of the truth of the following case which was published a few years ago in the newspapers. A young farmer in Warwickshire, finding his hedges broke, and the sticks carried away during a frosty season, determined to watch for the thief. He lay many cold hours under a hay-stack, and at length an old woman, like a witch in a play, approached, and began to pull up the hedge; he waited till she had tied up her bottle of sticks, and was carrying them off, that he might convict her of the theft, and then springing from his concealment, he seized his prey with violent threats. After some altercation, in which her load was left upon the ground, she kneeled upon her bottle of sticks, and raising her arms to heaven beneath the bright moon then at the full, spoke to the farmer already shivering with cold, 'Heaven grant, that thou never mayest know again the blessing to be warm.' He complained of cold all the next day, and wore an upper coat, and in a few days another, and in a fortnight took to his bed, always saying nothing made him warm, he covered himself with very many blankets, and had a seive over his face, as he lay; and from this one insane idea he kept his bed over twenty years for fear of the cold air, till at length he died.[2]

The circumstantial detail and sudden, casual impressiveness of Darwin's account provided the basis for the central scene of 'Goody Blake, and Harry Gill' almost as they stand. The supernatural may be rationalized, but the small drama retains its power.

What is new in Wordsworth's ballad is a moral context in which to view the confrontation. His version does more than draw attention to the power of the mind over the body; it depicts the imagination as an agent of moral justice. Unlike the innocent trio in 'The Three Graves', Harry suffers because he has been insensible to the suffering of another. Southey's complaint that 'Goody Blake, and Harry Gill' might 'promote the popular superstition of witchcraft'[3] is beside the point, since the poem really concerns hardship. Darwin's 'old woman, like a witch in a play' becomes Goody Blake, living alone in the poorest of counties, and unable to afford local fuel prices ('in that country coals are dear, / For they come far by wind and tide', ll. 31–42).[4] In this context, Harry's policing activities are a form of persecution, and Darwin's empty metaphor ('he seized his prey') is transformed into the stalking and ambush of an unsuspecting victim:

> And fiercely by the arm he took her,
> And by the arm he held her fast,
> And fiercely by the arm he shook her,

1. *c.*12 March; *WL*, i. 214–15 (for the date, see *CL*, i. 399n.).
2. *Zoönomia* (2 vols., London, 1794–6), ii (1796), 359.
3. *Critical Review*, xxiv. 200. Cf. Southey's own version of the theme in 'The Witch.'
4. In 1795, Dorothy wrote from Racedown that 'The peasants are miserably poor; their cottages are shapeless structures . . . of wood and clay—indeed they are not at all beyond what might be expected in savage life' (*WL*, i. 162).

> And cried, 'I've caught you then at last!'
> Then Goody, who had nothing said,
> Her bundle from her lap let fall;
> And kneeling on the sticks, she pray'd
> To God that is the judge of all. (ll. 89–96)

In Darwin's version, the old woman's curse had merely been the last word in an altercation, but Goody's prayer has the authentic speech rhythms of desperation, and her appeal 'To God that is the judge of all' challenges the property values which for Harry had transcended humanity:

> She pray'd, her wither'd hand uprearing,
> While Harry held her by the arm—
> 'God! who art never out of hearing,
> 'O may he never more be warm!'
> The cold, cold moon above her head,
> Thus on her knees did Goody pray,
> Young Harry heard what she had said,
> And icy-cold he turned away. (ll. 97–104)

The old hand is withered; yet upreared beneath 'The cold, cold moon', it has an eery authority: 'Young Harry heard what she had said . . .' At the start, Harry is an incomprehensible grotesque, his compulsive activity mirrored in the jigging rhythms and jangling onomatopoeia:

> Oh! what's the matter? what's the matter?
> What is't that ails young Harry Gill?
> That evermore his teeth they chatter,
> Chatter, chatter, chatter still. (ll. 1–4)

By the end, the spectacle has taken on cautionary meaning, and Harry's disquiet is as much that of guilt as unbalance: 'Yet still his jaws and teeth they clatter, / Like a loose casement in the wind' (ll. 115–16). The answer to our opening question, 'what's the matter? what's the matter?', lies in the central encounter—unobtrusively yet effectively rewritten to yield Wordsworth's humanitarian lesson: 'Now think, ye farmers all, I pray, / Of Goody Blake and Harry Gill' (ll. 127–8).

The political implications of 'Goody Blake, and Harry Gill' were not lost on Dr. Burney: 'if all the poor are to help themselves, and supply their wants from the possessions of their neighbours, what imaginary wants and real anarchy would it not create?'[5] Wordsworth has subverted a genre which his contemporaries were accustomed to think of as educating the poor not only in virtue, but in acceptance of the status quo. His models would have been the propagandist ballad-tracts of Hannah More's *Cheap Repository* rather than the popular broadside. The prospectus for the *Cheap Repository for Publications on Religious and Moral Subjects*, issued in 1795, anticipates Wordsworth's later reference to his own didactic intentions in writing ballads ('flowers and useful herbs to take place of weeds'):[6]

> THE immediate object of this Institution is the circulation of religious and useful Knowledge, as an antidote to the poison continually

5. *Monthly Review*, xxix (June 1799), 207.
6. *WL*, ii. 248.

flowing through the channel of those licentious publications which
are vended about our cities, towns, and villages . . .

WHEN it is considered what vast multitudes there are whose read-
ing is in a great measure confined to these corrupt performances . . .
it must be obvious that it is become a point of no small consequence
to correct so great an evil, which is not likely to be done effectually
without condescending to supply tracts equally cheap, and adapted
in like manner to the capacity of the common people. And since the
poison which is to be counteracted is but too palatable, it is the more
material to endeavour that the antidote shall be made pleasant also:
a variety of harmless allurements will be used, in order to invite a
perusal . . .

BEING well aware that sermons, catechisms, and other grave and
religious Tracts may be had from some existing societies, it is not
intended to furnish in general from this Institution the same kind of
didactic pieces. Instructive and entertaining Stories, Lives, Deaths,
remarkable Dispensations of Providence, and moral Ballads will
form a considerable part of the intended publications . . . [7]

Hannah More's prospectus was printed and available, like her tracts, in
Bath—the area where her missionary efforts were concentrated.[8] Words-
worth might well have seen the version printed in the *Monthly Magazine*
for January 1797, and he can hardly have avoided coming into contact
with the tracts themselves. By early 1796, over two million ballads and
tales had been sold, whether to 'the common people' or to their would-be
benefactors.[9] 'We shall prefer what is striking, to what is merely didactic',
affirmed the 'Plan' in the *Monthly Magazine;*[1] and temperance, industry,
or industrial calm, are preached in the guise of eye-catching stories with
energetic rhythms and catchy phrasing. In *The Riot: or, Half a loaf is bet-
ter than no bread* (1795), one worker argues another out of machine-
breaking ('I'd rather be hungry than hang'd, I protest');[2] in the same year,
Patient Joe, or, the Newcastle Collier was rewarded for keeping out of
trouble by miraculous escape from a pit disaster. Other self-explanatory
titles do their best to promote honesty among the working classes—*The
Roguish Miller; or, Nothing got by cheating* (1795), and *The Hampshire
Tragedy; shewing how a servant maid first robbed her master, and was after-
wards struck dead for telling a lie. A True Story* (1796). Probably the best
known of all was Hannah More's temperance tract, *The Carpenter; Or,
the Danger of evil company* (1795), narrating a family man's fall from
prosperity to drunken poverty; and in its sturdy ballad rhythms—

> THERE was a young West-country man,
> A Carpenter by trade;
> A skilful wheelwright too was he,
> And few such Waggons made.

7. Prospectus, *Cheap Repository for Publications on Religious and Moral Subjects* (Bath, 1795). p. [1].
8. See M. G. Jones, *Hannah More* (Cambridge, 1952), pp. 125–71, for an account of these
   activities.
9. See G. H. Spinney, 'Cheap Repository Tracts: Hazard and Marshall Edition', *Library*, 4th ser. xx
   (1939–40), 295–340, for the origin and history of the project and for the dating of individual
   ballads.
1. *Monthly Magazine*, iii (January 1797), 14.
2. *The Riot* was said to have checked an actual riot near Bath; see William Roberts, *Memoirs of
   the Life and Correspondence of Mrs. Hannah More* (4 vols., London, 1834), ii. 386.

—one can see where Wordsworth learned his cautionary presentation of Harry Gill ('before' and 'after'):

> Young Harry was a lusty drover,
> And who so stout of limb as he?
> His cheeks were red as ruddy clover,
> His voice was like the voice of three. (ll. 17–20)

Hannah More's aim, to combine popular appeal with 'religious and useful Knowledge', is matched by Wordsworth's claim for his poems, 'that each of them has a worthy *purpose*'.[3] The important difference is that where Hannah More wished to edify the semi-literate, Wordsworth was asking his literate readers to think about their own code.

The 1800 'Preface' calls 'Goody Blake, and Harry Gill' 'one of the rudest of this collection,' justifying its popular presentation in terms of the 'truth' about the workings of the imagination which it conveys ('I have the satisfaction of knowing that it has been communicated to many hundreds of people who would never have heard of it, had it not been narrated as a Ballad, and in a more impressive metre than is usual in Ballads').[4] But the flamboyance of Wordsworth's writing has behind it a literary impulse as well as a popularizing one. It is surely Bürger's ' "*Tra ra la*" ' which lies behind the onomatopoeic verve and grotesqueness of the opening and closing stanzas of 'Goody Blake, and Harry Gill'. Wordsworth's knowledge of German would have been rudimentary at this stage; he went to Germany in the autumn of 1798 specifically 'to acquire the German language', and only then did he purchase Bürger's *Gedichte* in the original.[5] But it was in March—the month when he was at work on 'Goody Blake, and Harry Gill', 'The Thorn', and probably 'The Idiot Boy—that the German trip was mooted, and anyone whose interest had been sufficiently aroused by Taylor's account of Bürger in the *Monthly Magazine* had only to turn to one of the translations of 'Lenore' which included the original text.[6] Taylor's praise of 'popular forms of expression, caught by the listening artist from the voice of agitated nature' applies equally to Wordsworth's ballads.[7] Both poets create highly-wrought effects on the basis of a vigorous spoken idiom. As Taylor observes of Bürger, 'the interjection [is] his favourite part of speech', and 'Lenore' is intensified by the rousing cries that reappear in 'The Idiot Boy' (' "Holla, Holla!" '), by exclamations of horror—'Ha sieh! ha sieh! im Augenblick, / Huhu! ein grässlich Wunder!'—or by moments when conventional narrative breaks down under sheer pressure of excitement: 'Und hurre hurre, hop hop hop! / Ging's fort in sausendem Galopp . . .' The onomatopoeic sound effects which were felt to defy translation ('Und horch! und horch! den Pfortenring / Ganz lose, leise, klinglingling!') go with a deliberate cultivation of the

---

3. 1800 'Preface' (*Prose Works*, i. 124).
4. *Prose Works*, i. 150.
5. See *WL*, i. 213, and *DWJ* i. 31. For a brief discussion of Wordsworth's acquaintance with German literature before the Goslar period, see L. A. Willoughby, 'Wordsworth and Germany', *German Studies Presented to Professor H. G. Fiedler* (Oxford, 1938), pp. 438–42.
6. Spencer and Stanley had both incorporated texts of the German. In reading the original, Wordsworth would have had Coleridge's beginner's knowledge of German to help him, as well as the German grammar and dictionary Coleridge owned; see W. W. Beyer, 'Coleridge's Early Knowledge of German', *MP* lii (1954–5). 192–200, and *CL*, i. 435.
7. See *Monthly Magazine*, i (March 1796), 118

grotesque; the transformation of ghostly rider into skeleton, for instance, is dwelt on with ghoulish relish: 'Zum Schädel, ohne Zopf und Schopf, / Zum nackten Schädel ward sein Kopf . . .'[8] 'Yet still his jaws and teeth they clatter' ('Goody Blake, and Harry Gill', 1. 115) has the same outlandishness. This unexpected convergence of English didacticism and German sensationalism in 'Goody Blake, and Harry Gill' is to prove the point of departure for Wordsworth's ballad experiment.

II. 'The Thorn'

Within a matter of days, Wordsworth went on to experiment much more radically with the spirited 'manner of relating' which he admired in Bürger. He seems to have begun without any thought of writing a ballad. The Fenwick Note recalls that the poem 'Arose out of my observing, on the ridge of Quantock Hill, on a stormy day a thorn which I had often passed in calm and bright weather without noticing it,'[9] and Dorothy's *Journal* confirms that on 19 March 'William wrote some lines describing a stunted thorn'.[1] The lines themselves survive in the Alfoxden Notebook:

> A summit where the stormy gale
> Sweeps through the clouds from vale to vale
> A thorn there is which like a stone
> With jagged lychens is oergrown
> A thorny [sic] that wants is [sic] thorny points
> A toothless thorn with knotted joints
> Not higher than a two years child.
> It stands upon that spot so wild
> Of leaves it has repaired its loss
> With heavy tufts of dark green moss
> Which from the ground a plenteous crop
> Creeps upward to its very top
> To bury it for ever-more.[2]

Wordsworth's description is immediately followed by 'A Whirl-Blast from behind the Hill'—another attempt to capture a transient weather-effect among the Quantocks—and has the air of an impressionistic jotting made for its own sake. Asked, as he asks himself at the end of 'A Whirl-Blast', 'This long description why endite?', Wordsworth might well have replied with equal inconsequentiality ('Because it was a pleasant sight').[3] But the Fenwick Note goes on, 'I said to myself, "Cannot I by some invention do as much to make this Thorn prominently an impressive object as the storm has made it to my eyes at this moment". I began the poem accordingly and composed it with great rapidity.'[4] In his 'invention', the thorn, already 'Not

8. Quotations are from the parallel text in Spencer's *Leonora. Translated from the German.*
9. I.F. note to 'The Thorn' (*PW* ii. 511).
1. *DWJ* i. 13.
2. DC MS. 14: *PW* ii. 240 app. crit. Cf. 'the lonely thorn . . . with top cut sheer' at the start of Crowe's local poem, *Lewesdon Hill*, and the 'aged Thorn', a symbol of oppressed worth, in Cottle's *Malvern Hills*—the latter returned to Cottle only a week before Wordsworth wrote his own description (see *EY*, p. 214): 'How bent its matted head, by the bleak wind / That in one current comes . . .' (ll. 41–2).
3. Ibid.: *PW* ii. 128 app. crit. For the date of 'A Whirl-Blast', see *DWJ* i. 12–13, and Reed, pp. 227–8n.
4. *PW* ii. 511. De Selincourt prints 'permanently' for 'prominently'.

higher than a two years child', forms the starting-point for a tale of seduction, infanticide, and madness.

The commonest of all literary associations for a thorn tree were illegitimate birth and child-murder. In Langhorne's *Country Justice*, it is under a thorn that the pitying robber finds the body of an unmarried mother with her new-born child ('Seest Thou afar yon solitary Thorn, / Whose aged *Limbs* the Heath's wild Winds have torn?');[5] and in Richard Merry's *Pains of Memory* (1796), a remorseful seducer recalls: 'There on the chilly grass the babe was born, / Beneath that bending solitary thorn . . .'[6] The Scots ballad known as 'The Cruel Mother' shows how traditional the association would have been:

> AND there she's lean'd her back to a thorn,
>   Oh, and alas-a-day! Oh, and alas-a-day!
> And there she has her baby born,
>   Ten thousand times good night, and be wi' thee.
>
> She has houked a grave ayont the sun,
>   Oh, and alas-a-day! Oh, and alas-a-day!
> And there she has buried the sweet babe in,
>   Ten thousand times good night, and be wi' thee.
>
> And she's gane back to her father's ha',
>   Oh, and alas-a-day! Oh, and alas-a-day!
> She's counted the leelest maid o' them a',
>   Ten thousand times good night and be wi' thee.
>
> ✻   ✻   ✻   ✻   ✻   ✻   ✻   ✻   ✻   ✻   ✻   ✻   ✻   ✻   ✻
>
> O look not sae sweet my bonny babe,
>   Oh, and alas-a-day! Oh, and alas-a-day!
> Gin ze smyle sae ze'll smyle me dead;
>   Ten thousand times good night and be wi' thee.[7]

One would like to think that the torment of the final stanza comes through in Martha's cry of misery. But although Wordsworth must have known 'The Cruel Mother',[8] there were other and more immediate associations. Already in spring 1797, the haunted bower, gibbet, pond, and grave of Bürger's 'Des Pfarrers Tochter von Taubenhain' had become the haunted graves and thorn of 'The Three Graves'. With 'The Three Graves' once more in mind when Coleridge took it up during the spring of 1798, Wordsworth turned to Bürger for the 'invention' he needed.

Like 'The Thorn', 'Des Pfarrers Tochter von Taubenhain' ('The Lass of Fair Wone', as it became in Taylor's translation) focuses on a spot haunted by past suffering and guilt. 'The parson's bower of yew' is the scene of an infanticide about which Bürger is prepared to be explicit as Wordsworth is not:

---

5. *The Country Justice*, ii (1775), p. 24.
6. *The Pains of Memory* (London, 1796), p. 13.
7. *Ancient and Modern Scottish Songs, Heroic Ballads, etc.*, ed. David Herd (and edn., 2 vols., Edinburgh, 1776), ii. 237–8.
8. It was included by Wordsworth in a common-place book (see *PW* ii. 514), but R. S. Woof, 'The Literary Relations of Wordsworth and Coleridge, 1795–1803' (Doctoral Dissertation, Toronto, 1959), pp. 228–39, argued convincingly for a date of post-1800 for this entry.

> There rending pains and darting throes
> Assail'd her shuddering frame;
> And from her womb a lovely boy,
> With wail and weeping came.
>
> Forth from her hair a silver pin
> With hasty hand she drew,
> And prest against its tender heart,
> And the sweet babe she slew.
>
> Erst when the act of blood was done,
> Her soul its guilt abhorr'd:
> 'My Jesus! what has been my deed?
> Have mercy on me, Lord!'
>
> With bloody nails, beside the pond,
> Its shallow grave she tore:
> 'There rest in God; there shame and want
> Thou can'st not suffer more:
>
> Me vengeance waits. My poor, poor child,
> Thy wound shall bleed afresh,
> When ravens from the gallows tear
> Thy mother's mould'ring flesh.'[9]

The blend of horror and piety is characteristic—and, as Wordsworth would surely have recognized, disingenuous. For all his pious sentiments, Bürger forces us to dwell on the sensational facts (the murdered infant, the mother's bloody nails, the mouldering flesh on the gibbet), and his interest in the mother's guilt leaves no room for her suffering. Pity is ousted by vicarious interest in violence and pain. Wordsworth plays down the gothicism of his source by transferring it to an everyday setting. The haunted 'pond of toads' and the 'barren grave, / Three spans in length' which figure in Bürger's opening stanzas become part of the Quantock landscape—'a little muddy pond' and a moss-covered mound:

> And to the left, three yards beyond,
> You see a little muddy pond
> Of water, never dry;
> I've measured it from side to side:
> 'Tis three feet long, and two feet wide.
>
> And close beside this aged thorn,
> There is a fresh and lovely sight,
> A beauteous heap, a hill of moss,
> Just half a foot in height. (ll. 29–37)[1]

---

9. *Monthly Magazine*, i (April 1796), 224.
1. * * * The pond itself was not an invention (see *DWJ* i. 16); but Wordsworth's prettified grave-mound, with its 'mossy network' and 'cups, the darlings of the eye, / So deep is their vermil-ion dye' (ll. 43–4) may recollect the 'fronds of studded moss . . . Begemm'd with scarlet shields, and cups of gold' in Charlotte Smith's 'Apostrophe to an Old Tree', from *Elegiac Sonnets, and Other Poems* (1797), p. 50.

The pond is resolutely prosaic; the mound, no longer a barren grave, is 'fresh and lovely'; and the gibbet, emblem of guilt, has been replaced by the thorn, symbol of suffering. Most important of all, the skull that seems to eye the grave below becomes a living woman. For the supernatural haunting of Bürger's poem, Wordsworth substitutes something more substantial, and also something that requires a less superficial response— the grief and unbalance of a human being bound to the spot by its tragic associations.

Wordsworth's adaptation of 'The Lass of Fair Wone' raises precisely those questions which his source had evaded. 'The Thorn' is a poem not just about suffering, but about the difficulty of comprehending it, which had been so effectively evoked in *The Borderers*:

> Action is transitory, a step, a blow—
> The motion of a muscle—this way or that,
> 'Tis done—and in the after vacancy
> We wonder at ourselves like men betray'd.
> Suffering is permanent, obscure and dark,
> And has the nature of infinity.[2]

To some extent *The Borderers* had explored as well as stated this central tragic opposition, and in doing so anticipated the study of compulsive behaviour into which Wordsworth converted the spectral hauntings of 'The Lass of Fair Wone'. The woman circling the grave of her illegitimate child in the moonlight is alone in the midst of a village community; like Martha's, her suffering remains obscure, uncomprehended, viewed from a distance by the curious villagers. She is both enigmatic ('no one ever heard her voice'), and surrounded by hearsay: 'in the church-yard sod her feet have worn / A hollow ring; they say it is knee-deep—'.[3] Martha too—similarly isolated, similarly spied upon—becomes a focus, for local curiosity:

> 'Now wherefore thus, by day and night,
> 'In rain, in tempest, and in snow,
> 'Thus to the dreary mountain-top
> 'Does this poor woman go?
> 'And why sits she beside the thorn
> 'When the blue day-light's in the sky,
> 'Or when the whirlwind's on the hill,
> 'Or frosty air is keen and still,
> 'And wherefore does she cry?—
> 'Oh wherefore? wherefore? tell me why
> 'Does she repeat that doleful cry?'   (ll. 78–88)

No one knows whether a living child was born to Martha, and no one can separate her cries of grief from their supernatural accretions:

> For many a time and oft were heard
> Cries coming from the mountain-head,
> Some plainly living voices were,
> And others, I've heard many swear,
> Were voices of the dead . . .   (ll. 170–44)

2. *The Borderers*, MS. B: *PW* i. 188, ll. 1539–44.
3. Ibid.: *PW* i. 143, ll. 388, 394–5.

Cut off from the human world, Martha has the mad mother's fellowship
with nature: 'And she is known to every star, / And every wind that
blows . . .' (ll. 69–70). We come face to face with her only once, in a vivid
scene which releases the poem's underlying implications. When the nar-
rator stumbles on her huddled figure, during a sudden storm, he sees for
the first time the reality of her suffering:

> I looked around, I thought I saw
> A jutting crag, and off I ran,
> Head-foremost, through the driving rain,
> The shelter of the crag to gain,
> And, as I am a man,
> Instead of jutting crag, I found
> A woman seated on the ground.
>
> I did not speak—I saw her face,
> Her face it was enough for me;
> I turned about and heard her cry,
> 'O misery! O misery!'   (ll. 192–202)

Martha is revealed to the narrator as a fellow human being ('And, as I am
a *man* . . .'), but at this moment of direct contact, the inevitability of her
isolation is most strongly felt. The narrator's instinctive flight—'I saw her
face, / Her face it was enough for me'—suggests the difficulty of con-
fronting, still less entering into, misery such as hers.

'The character of the loquacious narrator will sufficiently shew itself
in the course of the story', wrote Wordsworth in the 1798 'Advertisement'.[4]
This telescope-bearing retailer of local gossip and superstition provides
the basis for Wordsworth's experimental narrative. Bürger's device of
question and answer becomes an extended display of uncertainty. Woman,
thorn, pond, and mound are the fixed points round which the poem
revolves; we return to them again and again, yet are never able to clarify
their connections or significance. The narrator is as mystified as his ques-
tioner: '"Now wherefore thus . . . ?"', 'I cannot tell; I wish I could . . .';
'"But wherefore . . . ?"' 'Nay rack your brain—'tis all in vain . . .' The sen-
sationalism of 'The Lass of Fair Wone' becomes lurid conjecture, neither
confirmed nor denied:

> 'But what's the thorn? and what's the pond?
> 'And what's the hill of moss to her?
> 'And what's the creeping breeze that comes
> 'The little pond to stir?'
> I cannot tell; but some will say
> She hanged her baby on the tree,
> Some say she drowned it in the pond,
> Which is a little step beyond,
> But all and each agree,
> The little babe was buried there,
> Beneath that hill of moss so fair.   (ll. 210–20)

---

4. *Prose Works*, i. 117.

'The Thorn' successfully undermines the convention of an omniscient and objective narrator. Bürger gives us the crude facts: Wordsworth filters and distorts them through the imagination of his story-teller. A story, he implies, is not so simple a concept as Bürger had assumed; nor are facts so important in themselves—it is 'the feeling therein developed' that gives them their true significance. The villagers are rebuked by the quaking grave-mound during their quest for circumstantial evidence of Martha's guilt ('And for the little infant's bones / With spades they would have sought', ll. 234–5). And if their question should be left unasked and unanswered, so our questions too are unanswerable: how can we ever know what the thorn means to Martha? Not that her feelings alone ('"O misery! O misery!"') give the poem its hold on the imagination. The narrator colours the story he tells by his own involvement with it, and the mingled facts and conjectures take their life from the play of his mind.

In 1800, Wordsworth replied to Southey's damning verdict on 'The Thorn' ('he who personates tiresome loquacity, becomes tiresome himself')[5] with an elaborate defence of his narrative method. The note provides an illuminating account of what he had hoped to achieve by his use of the story-teller whose character he describes in such incongruous detail:

> The character which I have here introduced speaking is sufficiently common. The Reader will perhaps have a general notion of it, if he has ever known a man, a Captain of a small trading vessel, for example, who being past the middle age of life, had retired upon an annuity or small independent income to some village or country town of which he was not a native, or in which he had not been accustomed to live. Such men, having little to do, become credulous and talkative from indolence; and from the same cause, and other predisposing causes by which it is probable that such men may have been affected, they are prone to superstition. On which account it appeared to me proper to select a character like this to exhibit some of the general laws by which superstition acts upon the mind.[6]

The last sentence of what Jeffrey calls 'this very peculiar description'[7] reveals Wordsworth's purpose in telling his story as he does. 'The Thorn' is not a dramatic monologue designed to be read for what it reveals about the mind of a hypothetical sea-captain.[8] But nor is it a poem concerned solely with the elusive nature of Martha's suffering. Its narrative method reflects Wordsworth's interest in the interplay between the two—in the imaginative processes by which the simple elements of Martha's tragedy take on their sombre impressiveness. The note continues:

> Superstitious men are almost always men of slow faculties and deep feelings; their minds are not loose, but adhesive; they have a reasonable share of imagination, by which word I mean the faculty which

5. *Critical Review*, xxiv. 200.
6. *PW* ii. 512.
7. For Jeffrey's parody of Wordsworth's defensive circumstantiality—'"Of this piece the reader will necessarily form a very erroneous judgement, unless he is apprised, that it was written by a pale man in a green coat,—sitting cross-legged on an oaken stool,—with a scratch on his nose, and a spelling dictionary on the table"'—see the *Edinburgh Review*, xii (April 1808), 137.
8. The reverse is persuasively argued by S. M. Parrish in '"The Thorn": Wordsworth's Dramatic Monologue', *ELH* xxiv (1957), 153–63 (*The Art of the Lyrical Ballads*, pp. 97–112).

produces impressive effects out of simple elements; but they are utterly destitute of fancy, the power by which pleasure and surprise are excited by sudden varieties of situation and by accumulated imagery.[9]

Wordsworth's story-teller lacks the skills of the sophisticated narrator ('the power by which pleasure and surprise are excited'). But, like the stormy weather which had transformed the thorn in Wordsworth's original glimpse, his mind 'produces impressive effects out of simple elements'; and it is this that he has in common with the poet himself.

The 1800 'Preface' deals with the theory of Wordsworth's experiment: his note on 'The Thorn' goes into some of the problems that faced him in putting it into practice. The technical difficulty of substituting feeling for action in a primarily narrative genre is matched by that of conveying a simple narrator's imaginative involvement with his story:

> I had two objects to attain; first, to represent a picture which should not be unimpressive, yet consistent with the character that should describe it; secondly, while I adhered to the style in which such persons describe, to take care that words, which in their minds are impregnated with passion, should likewise convey passion to Readers who are not accustomed to sympathize with men feeling in that manner or using such language. It seemed to me that this might be done by calling in the assistance of Lyrical and rapid Metre. It was necessary that the Poem, to be natural, should in reality move slowly; yet I hoped, that, by the aid of the metre, to those who should at all enter into the spirit of the Poem, it would appear to move quickly.[1]

Wordsworth's solution—his use of a fast-moving ballad stanza—allowed him to create the illusion of progress while continuing to dwell on Martha's unchanging misery. It also licensed him to draw on the rhythms and repetitions of actual speech. His defence of 'tautology' in 'The Thorn' contains his most central statement about 'the language of passion':

> Words, a Poet's words more particularly, ought to be weighed in the balance of feeling, and not measured by the space which they occupy upon paper. For the Reader cannot be too often reminded that Poetry is passion: it is the history or science of feelings: now every man must know that an attempt is rarely made to communicate impassioned feelings without something of an accompanying consciousness of the inadequateness of our own powers, or the deficiencies of language. During such efforts there will be a craving in the mind, and as long as it is unsatisfied the Speaker will cling to the same words, or words of the same character.[2]

The sea-captain's rambling ineptitude as a story-teller intensifies, rather than weakening, the effect of his tale. His conventional shortcomings become strengths—at once a token of his involvement and a means of involving the reader. When Wordsworth wrote of 'the interest which the mind attaches to words, not only as symbols of the passion, but as *things,*

9. *PW* ii. 512.
1. *PW* ii. 512–13.
2. *PW* ii. 513.

active and efficient, which are of themselves part of the passion',[3] he was invoking the expressive, behaviourist theory of language used by Joseph Priestley to explain the effect of figurative speech—'scarce considered and attended to as *words*, but . . . viewed in the same light as *attitudes, gestures,* and *looks,* which are infinitely more expressive of *sentiments* and *feelings* than words can possibly be'.[4] The Thorn' enacts the narrator's own fascination with Martha's dimly perceived tragedy, drawing on the processes of communication to mirror those of the imagination. Just as Martha's refrain-like cry becomes cumulatively expressive, so the narrator's garrulousness ends by communicating the incommunicable—'Suffering is permanent, obscure and dark, / And has the nature of infinity.'[5]

* * *

JAMES C. McKUSICK

[*Lyrical Ballads* and the Natural World][†]

William Wordsworth's name is ineluctably associated with the English Lake District, the place where he spent his childhood and adolescence, and to which he returned on a permanent basis in December 1799. Settling into Dove Cottage, Grasmere, with his sister Dorothy, Wordsworth determined to make his home and his poetic career among the lakes and mountains that had first awakened and nourished his childhood imagination. His is a poetry of place, rooted not only in a concrete awareness of geographic location, but also in the significance that attaches to particular places as a result of childhood memory.[1]

Wordsworth's great autobiographical poem, *The Prelude,* provides a narrative account of his intellectual and spiritual development, and its depiction of his childhood in the Lake District has shaped much of what modern readers understand about his rootedness there. However, *The Prelude* was not published until 1850, and it remained a closely guarded manuscript during Wordsworth's lifetime, known only to a small circle of his family and friends. To his contemporaries, Wordsworth was known through the developing canon of his published poetry, starting with two relatively obscure works published in 1793: *An Evening Walk* and *Descriptive Sketches.* With the publication of *Lyrical Ballads* (first published in 1798, with revised editions appearing in 1800 and 1802), and continuing through *The Excursion* (1814) and *Collected Poems* (1815), his international reputation as a poet was assured. Throughout the nineteenth century, Wordsworth was known to readers on both sides of the Atlantic as the most prominent of the "Lake Poets," and the deep-rooted affiliation of his writing with that particular place was further confirmed by the publication of his *Guide to the Lakes,* the best known and most frequently republished of Wordsworth's writings during his lifetime.

3. *PW* ii. 513.
4. *A Course of Lectures on Oratory and Criticism* (London, 1777), p. 77.
5. *The Borderers,* MS. B: *PW* i. 188, ll. 1543–4.
† From *Green Writing: Romanticism and Ecology* (Basingstoke: Macmillan, 2000), 53–65. Reprinted by permission.
1. For a more detailed study of these local affiliations, see David McCracken, *Wordsworth and the Lake District: A Guide to the Poems and their Places* (Oxford: Oxford University Press, 1985).

In recent decades, however, the grounding of Wordsworth's poetry in a specific locale, and his reputation as a nature poet, has been called into question. Each generation of literary critics, from the New Critics through the post-Structuralists, has discovered new ways of reading Wordsworth's poetry through the lens of its own theoretical preoccupations. Although the continuing exegesis of his work has certainly led to a more thorough understanding of his multifaceted complexity, both as person and as poet, nevertheless something of the radical and elemental simplicity of his poetry has been lost in the process. Accordingly, this essay will examine some fundamental questions about the meaning of Wordsworth's poetry as it emerges from the lived experience of dwelling in the English Lake District.

The Place of Poetry

William Wordsworth was born on April 7, 1770, at Cockermouth in Cumberland, and his earliest childhood memories (as he recounted them in *The Prelude*) were of the sound of the river Derwent, whose murmurs "from his alder shades and rocky falls . . . sent a voice / That flowed along my dreams" (book 1, lines 272–74).[2] It is perhaps significant that his first memories are of sounds, a speaking-forth of the landscape directly into the "dreams" of the infant, making him an engaged participant in the world that surrounds him, not merely a detached observer. This sense of participation is more concretely evoked in Wordsworth's description of bathing in the river Derwent and sporting along its banks as a five-year-old boy (book 1, lines 291–98). The "voice" of the river speaks out to the child as a companion, or imaginary playmate, in a tone both comforting and mysterious.

The childhood experience of nature was not always so pleasant or reassuring to Wordsworth. *The Prelude* records several occasions when the presence of the natural world appeared ominous and foreboding, most notably the boat-stealing episode, which climaxes in the sudden, terrifying apparition of "a huge peak, black and huge, / As if with voluntary power instinct" (book 1, lines 378–79), and the episode of the drowned man, whose decomposing body suddenly bursts above the surface of the lake "with his ghastly face, a spectre shape / Of terror" (book 5, lines 450–51). The immanence of death, and the sudden eruption of fear into a seemingly placid landscape, is a theme frequently encountered in Wordsworth's description of his childhood. Surely the death of both parents during his childhood had something to do with Wordsworth's sense of fear and foreboding in the natural world; his mother died when he was only eight years old, and his siblings were subsequently dispersed to live with various relatives, marking the end of Wordsworth's very close childhood relationship with his beloved sister Dorothy. His father's death occurred in 1783, when William was thirteen years old. A painful sense of loss and exile pervades much of Wordsworth's autobiographical writing, and his childhood sense of joyful immediacy and participation in the

2. William Wordsworth, *The Prelude*, ed. Ernest de Selincourt (London: Oxford University Press, 1928). Subsequent citations of *The Prelude* refer to the 1850 edition of this poem by book and line number.

natural world is balanced elsewhere by darker tonalities, and even a morbid fascination with death.

In a note that he dictated to Isabella Fenwick in 1843, Wordsworth looks back on his childhood awareness of the natural world. He recalls his morbid fascination with death, and the obstinate denial of his own mortality, in a remarkably candid free-associative commentary:

> Nothing was more difficult for me in childhood than to admit the notion of death as a state applicable to my own being. . . . But it was not so much from [feelings] of animal vivacity that *my* difficulty came as from a sense of the indomitableness of the spirit within me. I used to brood over the stories of Enoch and Elijah, and almost to persuade myself that, whatever might become of others, I should be translated, in something of the same way, to heaven. (*Poetical Works,* 4:463)

The child's stubborn denial of death, and his aspiration to a "heavenly" state of complete disembodiment, contrasts sharply with his infantile sense of total bodily immersion in the flow of the river Derwent. Wordsworth goes on to describe how the entire visible world threatened to vanish into an "abyss of idealism" at certain moments of his childhood:

> With a feeling congenial to this, I was often unable to think of external things as having external existence, and I communed with all that I saw as something not apart from, but inherent in, my own immaterial nature. Many times while going to school have I grasped at a wall or tree to recall myself from this abyss of idealism to the reality. At that time I was afraid of such processes. (*Poetical Works,* 4:463)

The modality of visual imagery is part of the problem of "immateriality" that Wordsworth recalls here; it is only through the immediacy of touch—the rough stones of a wall, or the furrowed bark of a tree—that the child can be returned to the presence of the world around him. His fear of being lost in an "abyss of idealism" is akin to the problem of pure subjectivity posed by the philosophical idealism of George Berkeley (1685–1753): if objects have no existence beyond our perception of them, then how can anything be known to exist outside of ourselves? Bishop Berkeley's answer—that God sees everything and thereby guarantees its existence—is unsatisfying to the young Wordsworth, who was coming of age in a secular society where such faith was eroding before the onslaught of Humean skepticism. Only the immediacy of touch, or (as we have seen) the pervasive sound of a natural voice, can recall the child to the "reality" of his existence in a physical body, in a material world.

* * *

Wordsworth's early poetry, particularly his *Descriptive Sketches*, is weakened by an essentially empirical mode of presentation, with its relentless bifurcation of subject and object. In these early poems of picturesque description, the poet himself is merely a detached observer, not a participant in the scenes that he describes. With the advent of Wordsworth's mature poetic voice, however, that stance of touristic detachment is superseded by poems that dramatize the involvement of the speaker in the places and events that he describes. Particularly in the *Lyrical Ballads*, Wordsworth achieves a sense of participation that enables the reader, as well, to become vicariously invested in the world of the poem. Wordsworth's contributions to *Lyrical Ballads* are not "nature poems," if that term is taken to denote the precise and detailed description of natural objects. Wordsworth's best poems are neither descriptive nor minutely detailed. Rather, they evoke a dynamic world through the vivid sensory imagery of its beholding by an engaged participant. It is a poetry of unmediated experience, not of detached description.[3]

A telling manifesto for this new kind of poetry is "Expostulation and Reply," first published in *Lyrical Ballads* and undoubtedly one of the most familiar poems in the Wordsworth canon. Its very familiarity, however, makes it difficult for us to notice the radical nature of its departure from the prevailing norms of its culture. The first stanzas are spoken in the voice of a schoolmaster, "Matthew," chiding a wayward student:

> "Why William, on that old grey stone,
> "Thus for the length of half a day,
> "Why William, sit you thus alone
> "And dream your time away?" (lines 1–4)[4]

Although this question is evidently intended to be merely rhetorical, a way of rebuking the lazy student for his alleged waste of time, "William" responds as if it were seriously intended to evoke a response. This response is telling, in part, for what it does not say. It does not engage the schoolmaster in a debate concerning the relative merits of books written by "dead men," nor does it defend the value of "looking round" on Mother Earth. To engage the question in those terms would be to concede the validity of the worldview they entail, in which books are the main repositories of knowledge, and sight is the primary modality of perception.

Instead, "William" proposes that there are other ways of knowing, and various non-visual modalities of perception:

> "The eye it cannot chuse but see,
> "We cannot bid the ear be still;
> "Our bodies feel, where'er they be,
> "Against, or with our will." (lines 17–20)

In many ways, this stanza is a *non sequitur*. It bluntly declares that the senses affect us directly and immediately, without the intervention of our conscious will. Such a declaration should not be regarded as merely an assertion of empirical reality, however, since the content of sensory perception may be other than what "science" teaches us. If science is the accumulated knowledge of humankind, as conveyed by books, then the repudiation of book-learning may also connote the rejection of secular humanism as a way of knowing. Since the advent of Renaissance humanism, book-learning (and the fetishization of the printed book as an object of acquisition, textual analysis, and marginal commentary) has impeded our contact with other ways of knowing, ways that precede humanism in the order of history and of experience. Humanism impedes our coming to

3. On this topic see Geoffrey H. Hartman, *The Unmediated Vision: An Interpretation of Wordsworth, Hopkins, Rilke, and Valéry* (New Haven, CT: Yale University Press, 1954). The phenomenological approach developed in Hartman's earlier work has strong affinities with the methodology of eco-criticism, especially in its concern for the epistemology of perception.
4. All citations from *Lyrical Ballads* refer to the text of the first edition (London, 1798) by title and line number.

know ourselves as participants in a living world, a world that we inhabit not only as knowing subjects, but also as organic beings, "mere animals" engaged in the daily tasks of eating, breathing, sleeping, and dreaming.

"William" develops some of these implications in the following stanza:

> "Nor less I deem that there are powers,
> "Which of themselves our minds impress,
> "That we can feed this mind of ours,
> "In a wise passiveness." (lines 21–24)

What are these "powers" that impress the mind, regardless of our volition? The poem does not say. Indeed, it leaves the nature of these "powers" deliberately imprecise, and the reader is left to ponder whether these "powers" are meant to be the sort of invisible presences that Immanuel Kant calls the *Ding an sich*—the unknowable object that stands at the source of our perceptions—or whether Wordsworth intends something even more uncanny, such as the pagan nature-spirits that inhabit the world of Coleridge's Ancient Mariner. By its very imprecision, this stanza implies a critique of more precise ways of knowing, including those embodied in the "books" that allegedly contain all that is known, and worth knowing, in heaven and earth. The student's dreamlike states of awareness, by contrast, are utterly inscrutable, and perhaps finally inexplicable by means of the rational method of scientific inquiry. Such uncanny "powers" can only be approached indirectly and experientially, by a "wise passiveness."

"William" addresses his interlocutor with a further question concerning this state of "wise passiveness":

> "Think you, mid all this mighty sum
> "Of things forever speaking,
> "That nothing of itself will come,
> "But we must still be seeking?" (lines 25–28)

The answer to this rhetorical question is rather less evident than most readers would suppose. It both echoes and gently caricatures the Protestant work ethic of the schoolmaster, who evidently is in the habit of encouraging his students to engage in an active "seeking" of knowledge. The student inquires whether such active "seeking" is really the best way to attain knowledge, especially if the natural world is conceived as a "mighty sum / Of things forever speaking." If things speak directly to us, then we need not seek them out. Yet the tone of this question is hardly self-assured; it implies an openness to experience without predicating what the actual content of that experience may be. It is a meditation on the possibility of conversational exchange with the things that surround us, not a prescription for the results of rational inquiry.

The theme of conversation is further developed in the poem's last stanza, which serves to remind the schoolmaster—and the reader as well—that the most significant conversations occur when we are "alone":

> "—Then ask not wherefore, here, alone,
> "Conversing as I may,
> "I sit upon this old grey stone
> "And dream my time away." (lines 29–32)

The premise that one may "converse" with natural objects, in the absence of any human interlocutor, makes sense only if one accepts the profoundly anti-humanistic implications of this poem. To the daydreaming student, the "old grey stone" provides more engaging companionship than even the most learned and articulate schoolmaster. The tone of the poem is not hostile to humankind—indeed, it addresses "Matthew" as "my good friend"—but it poses a serious question, and implies a serious critique, of the rational, scientific, and humanistic ways of knowing. Like the courtly denizens of Shakespeare's Forest of Arden, "William" renounces the discourse of erudition, and instead discovers "books in the babbling brooks, and sermons in stones."

"Expostulation and Reply" is a remarkably successful poem because it allows both sides of the argument to be heard. If the schoolteacher is made to appear a stern taskmaster, the student is also presented as somewhat defensive and dogmatic in his rejection of book-learning; the poem enables the reader to ponder the limitations of both positions while allowing each to speak for itself. The next poem in *Lyrical Ballads*, entitled "The Tables Turned," addresses some of the same themes, and is even more radically experimental in form. It explores whether a "conversation" is possible between the human mind and the objects of the natural world, and it calls into question the objectivity of our conventional ways of knowing.

The poem's first stanza is addressed to a "friend" who is stubbornly attached to book-learning; this addressee is presumably the schoolteacher "Matthew" of the previous poem. The most significant interlocutors of this poem, however, are the personified presences of the sun, who casts "his first sweet evening yellow" upon the surrounding fields, and the "woodland linnet," whose sweet music conveys more wisdom than is found in any book. The transforming light of the sunset enables the poet to perceive something other than the cold, hard objects of Newtonian science, and the songs of the woodland birds similarly convey something more worthwhile and engaging than mere determinate knowledge. The critique of book-learning is most explicitly conveyed in the poem's penultimate stanza:

> Sweet is the lore which nature brings;
> Our meddling intellect
> Misshapes the beauteous forms of things;
> —We murder to dissect. (lines 25–28)

The "lore" of nature is something other than the factual knowledge obtained by the "meddling intellect," and this poem is vehement in its rejection of such knowledge, especially if it is procured through the death-dealing methods of eighteenth-century natural history, a science that was mainly concerned with the dissection and anatomical description of individual specimens, not with the study of living creatures in their native habitat.

The final stanza of "The Tables Turned" dismisses both "science" and "art," exhorting the reader to engage in a very different kind of seeing and knowing:

> Enough of science and of art;
> Close up those barren leaves;
> Come forth, and bring with you a heart
> That watches and receives. (lines 29–32)

The "barren leaves" of books are implicitly contrasted with the more fecund leaves of the "long green fields"; and the outrageously mixed metaphor of a "heart / That watches" provides another indication of just how far beyond conventional epistemology this poem is prepared to go. As a radical credo of ecological awareness, this poem may seem preachy and even dogmatic in some of its pronouncements; yet its brash assertiveness bespeaks a willingness to run stylistic risks in the service of a larger and more comprehensive vision of human possibility. This poem turns the tables upon the entire Western tradition of scientific knowledge, and it proposes a new role for humankind among the speaking presences of the natural world. The place of poetry, and the task of the poet, is thus inherently dialogical; the poet must seek to engage those inhuman voices in conversation, at some risk to his own sense of identity, self-confidence, and stylistic decorum. To judge by the early reviews, *Lyrical Ballads* broke many rules of good taste, and transgressed against numerous tenets of conventional wisdom.

Departure and Return

Many of the poems in *Lyrical Ballads* are shaped by an underlying narrative of departure and return. This narrative pattern is decisively established by the first poem in the collection, "The Rime of the Ancyent Marinere," whose protagonist sets forth from his native land on a voyage of exploration, returning home after many adventures a changed man. This narrative pattern, whose literary analogues go at least as far back as *The Odyssey,* repeats itself in Wordsworth's poem "The Female Vagrant," which describes how its protagonist lived happily in her rural cottage until she was thrown out into the wider world and carried off to America aboard a British naval vessel. She finally returns home to England, bereft of her family and broken in spirit. A more light-hearted instance of this pattern of departure and return occurs in "The Idiot Boy," which tells how Betty Foy sends her son, Johnny, on horseback into the night to fetch a doctor for her sick neighbor, Susan Gale. Instead of carrying out his appointed mission, however, Johnny wanders aimlessly in the dark forest until, by good luck, the horse brings him safely home. Once again, the wanderer returns home deeply changed by his experience; but in Johnny's case, these changes are entirely beneficial, and even cathartic for the local village community. Susan Gale is miraculously cured of her illness, Betty Foy discovers how deeply she loves her son, and Johnny brings home vivid memories of a strange moonlit forest lurking just beyond the boundaries of the known and familiar world.

In all three of these poems, the resonances of "home" are developed through a series of contrasts with the wild, remote, and often terrifying places encountered on the outward journey. * * * So too, in "The Female Vagrant," the protagonist recollects her childhood in a cottage by the river Derwent in terms that evidently idealize that experience, presumably as a result of the misery that has occurred since her departure:

> Can I forget what charms did once adorn
> My garden, stored with pease, and mint, and thyme,
> And rose and lilly for the sabbath morn?

> The sabbath bells, and their delightful chime;
> The gambols and wild freaks at shearing time;
> My hen's rich nest through long grass scarce espied;
> The cowslip-gathering at May's dewy prime;
> The swans, that, when I sought the water-side,
> From far to meet me came, spreading their snowy pride.
>   (lines 19–27)

This catalog of remembered sensations, olfactory and auditory as well as visual, reveals how the concept of "home" is ordinarily constructed after one has left it behind; notably absent are any jarring or discordant elements that would lend this imagery the facticity of an actual experience. The concept of "home" tends toward the merely nostalgic in this poem, and the archaic metrical form of the Spenserian stanza also gives this passage a remote, unreal, even mythic quality. Composed in 1793, this is among the earliest works ever published by Wordsworth, and it lacks the precision of imagery and the direct vernacular mode of expression that characterize most of his other contributions to *Lyrical Ballads*. The inverted word order, "From far to meet me came," exemplifies precisely the sort of stilted phraseology that Coleridge would later deplore in the Preface to his "Sheet of Sonnets" (1796); indeed, during their period of close collaboration on *Lyrical Ballads,* Wordsworth may well have learned from Coleridge how to avoid the pitfalls of conventional sonneteers: "their inverted sentences, their quaint phrases, and incongruous mixture of obsolete and spenserian words."[5]

Yet there is good reason to scrutinize the depiction of "home" in "The Female Vagrant," because it does reveal a great deal about Wordsworth's fundamental attitudes and beliefs about the best way of life in a rural community. The stanza just cited describes a broad range of domesticated plants in the speaker's garden, including edible peas, aromatic herbs, and ornamental flowers. She is surrounded by a great variety of tame and wild animals, including the frolicking sheep whose fleece provides a commodity for the local market, the free-ranging hen whose eggs provide daily sustenance, and the wild swans who provide nothing more tangible than friendly companionship. Subsequent stanzas describe how she is accompanied to market by her faithful dog, while her father remains at home to tend their beehives, and a "red-breast known for years" conveys a friendly greeting by pecking at her casement window. Their basic subsistence is further eked out by her father's catching fish in a nearby lake; in a note to the poem, Wordsworth describes how "several of the Lakes in the north of England are let out to different Fishermen, in parcels marked out by imaginary lines drawn from rock to rock" (*Lyrical Ballads,* 72n). These "imaginary lines" define an individual's right to take fish from a lake that is the common property of the local village. The most notable feature of the lifestyle depicted in this poem is its reliance on multiple modes of subsistence—vegetable gardening, poultry-farming, sheep-raising, bee-keeping, and fishing—which all contribute

---

5. The Preface to Coleridge's *Sheet of Sonnets* (1796) advocates a poetic style in harmony with nature: "those Sonnets appear to me the most exquisite, in which moral Sentiments, Affections, or Feelings, are deduced from, and associated with, the scenery of Nature. . . . They create a sweet and indissoluble union between the intellectual and the material world" (Coleridge, *Poetical Works,* vol. 2, 1139). Such a style might well be termed "Green Writing."

to the foodstuffs and market commodities produced by this father-and-daughter family unit.

The subsistence mode of agriculture described in this poem appears to be entirely sustainable in the long term, and in fact such a mode of production, based on a widely varied set of crops rotated annually, eked out by fishing, livestock grazing, and the seasonal gathering of nuts, berries, and firewood from village common areas, had persisted relatively unchanged throughout rural England since the Middle Ages.[6] To be sure, such a mode of existence was far from being the relaxed and idyllic way of life depicted in "The Female Vagrant," particularly in years of drought, pestilence, or crop failure; as previously noted, there is certainly an idealized pastoral quality in the way Wordsworth describes it. Nevertheless, because it was based on a widely variable set of foodstuffs and commodities, such a subsistence lifestyle was intrinsically more sustainable and resilient than more modern methods of agriculture, which typically rely upon the intensive cultivation of a single crop, year after year, and provide very little recourse in the event of crop failure. As a mode of subsistence, polyculture is inherently more sustainable than monoculture, and it certainly provides a more varied and interesting way of life to the individual farmer. However "unreal" such a lifestyle may appear to the modern reader, we may safely assume that it is, on the whole, accurately drawn from Wordsworth's own memories of rural life as he observed it during his childhood on the banks of the river Derwent. Further instances of Wordsworth's personal knowledge of traditional modes of rural subsistence may be adduced from his poem "Nutting," which portrays the guilty pleasures of nut-gathering in the woods, and *The Prelude,* which describes how the young Wordsworth clambered out on cliffs to gather eggs from birds' nests (book 1, lines 327–39).

During the eighteenth century, the traditional methods of subsistence agriculture were gradually being supplanted by more capital-intensive modes of production, and the common areas upon which the local farmers relied for their seasonal grazing and gathering activities were increasingly being withdrawn for exclusive private use by the process of enclosure. These modernizing tendencies in rural areas were greatly accelerated during the 1790s with the advent of the Napoleonic Wars, which drove up the prices of agricultural commodities and made the intensive production of market crops a highly profitable endeavor. In "The Female Vagrant," Wordsworth describes how the incursion of a wealthy landowner, who purchases and encloses all of the surrounding properties, eventually drives out the poem's protagonist and her father from their hereditary lands. This wealthy intruder erects "a mansion proud our woods among" (line 39), and by denying access to these local woods, while also withdrawing the right to fish in local waters, he ultimately succeeds in evicting the father and daughter from their humble cottage. Evidently their traditional rights of access to the lake, woods, and other common

6. For a thoughtful discussion of Wordsworth's poetry in the context of contemporary agricultural practices, see Kenneth MacLean, *Agrarian Age: A Background for Wordsworth* (New Haven, CT: Yale University Press, 1950). MacLean provides useful information on Wordsworth's opposition to the enclosure of common lands in Grasmere, citing a local informant: "It was all along of him [Wordsworth] that Grasmere folks have their Common open. Ye may ga now reet up to sky over Grisedale, wi'out laying leg to fence, and all through him" (21).

areas were not respected by the wealthy intruder, who took "no joy . . . [to] stray / Through pastures not his own" (lines 41–42). Since these common rights are generally matters of local tradition rather than law, the father and daughter have no legal recourse when their rights are usurped by their wealthy neighbor. They are thrown out of their ancestral home and into a wider world of suffering and death.[7]

"The Female Vagrant" is the most overtly political of any of the poems published in Lyrical Ballads, and its harsh criticism of wealthy landowners is integral to a larger set of political concerns, which also include a critique of British military adventurism and a deep solicitude for the plight of homeless wanderers. Although these political views are generally regarded as a fairly typical articulation of the ideology of the French Revolution and the Rights of Man, they might also be understood as emerging from a deeper set of beliefs and concerns that remained crucially important to Wordsworth throughout his entire career, even after his youthful enthusiasm for revolutionary politics had been discarded in favor of a more conservative political stance. Despite these changes in his political orientation, Wordsworth remained consistent in his opposition to what we might term the military-industrial complex, especially as it affected the traditional ways of life in rural England. * * * Wordsworth consistently opposed the "development" and "improvement" of rural landscapes, and he remained a staunch defender of sustainable agricultural methods, traditional rural architecture, and all of England's open, scenic, and wild areas, especially in the Lake District. Wordsworth was truly ahead of his time, and radically innovative in his concern for the preservation of traditional rural ways of life, and in his defense of the poor, the homeless, and all the wild creatures that dwell beyond the pale, outside the conventional boundaries of human civilization. In his persistent engagement with these issues, Wordsworth foreshadows some of the most vital concerns of the modern environmental movement.

*   *   *

NICHOLAS ROE

The Politics of "Tintern Abbey"[†]

The composition of 'Tintern Abbey' in July 1798 focuses more gradual changes in Wordsworth during that summer. The poem is Wordsworth's most impressive celebration of those moments when 'We see into the life of things', but it was also his last expression of belief in the One Life itself. 'Tintern Abbey' is a coda to the months of mutual influence and

---

7. A similar act of usurpation occurs in "Goody Blake, and Harry Gill," another poem from Lyrical Ballads (1798). In this narrative poem, which Wordsworth based on an actual incident, the wealthy landowner Harry Gill catches Goody Blake gathering sticks from his hedge for firewood. Although such stick-gathering was customarily permitted on common lands, Harry seizes the poor old woman and threatens her with "vengeance" for her crime. Just as in "The Female Vagrant," the traditional common rights of local inhabitants have been criminalized as acts of "trespass" as a consequence of the enclosure of common lands. (Harry's hedge marks the boundary of his private enclosure.)

† From Wordsworth and Coleridge: The Radical Years (Oxford: Clarendon Press, 1988), 268–75. Reprinted by permission.

creativity Wordsworth had shared with Dorothy and Coleridge since mid-1797, when most of the *Lyrical Ballads* were written. But Wordsworth's concern with the restorative power of memory in 'Tintern Abbey' also foreshadows the poetry he would write at Goslar the following winter, which would form the germ of *The Prelude*.

The transitional movement of 'Tintern Abbey' appears in a reticent acknowledgement of uncertainty that serves to qualify Wordsworth's repeated claims to faith. It emerges most obviously in the conditional mood of many lines, for example in the following:

> such, perhaps,
> As may have had no trivial influence
> (ll. 32–3)

and:

> Nor less, I trust,
> To them I may have owed another gift
> (ll. 36–7)

and, later on:

> other gifts
> Have followed, for such loss, I would believe
> Abundant recompence.
> (ll. 87–9)

Throughout 'Tintern Abbey' Wordsworth's thanks for the 'other gifts' of nature and memory appear in a context of personal loss, 'changed, no doubt, from what [he] was' (l. 67), and an awareness of quotidian 'solitude, or fear, or pain, or grief' (l. 144) that had informed Coleridge's 'Fears in Solitude'. While 'Tintern Abbey' is a hymn to the One Life in nature 'and in the mind of man', it also articulates a sombre elegiac voice in 'The still, sad music of humanity' and 'all | The dreary intercourse of daily life' (ll. 92, 132.). That joyless mean of existence is the shadow that falls between Wordsworth's intimated doubt—'If this | Be but a vain belief' (ll. 50–1)—and his countering affirmation, 'How oft, in spirit, have I turned to thee | O sylvan Wye' (ll. 56–7). Similarly, his claim that

> Nature never did betray
> The heart that loved her
> (ll. 123–4)

—is modified by its implied recollection of other and earlier betrayals, even in the prayer of 'chearful faith' with which the poem concludes.

Wordsworth's poetry of 'chearful faith' in 'Tintern Abbey' is complicated by, and derives its power from, a lasting awareness of insecurity that issues in the poem's characteristic idiom of assertion and simultaneous reservation. One immediate reason for this was, perhaps, Wordsworth's incipient doubt about the adequacy of One Life to his own spiritual experience—even as he gave that vision of a living universe its fullest and most beautiful expression. But more fundamentally, and in a longer perspective, 'Tintern Abbey' represents a moment of transition that quietly re-enacts the more violent oscillations of his political and philosophic opinions in earlier years. This intersection of a meditative philosophic

poem with the revolutionary experience of the decade is the key to under-
standing 'Tintern Abbey' as Wordsworth's reply to 'Fears in Solitude' and,
beyond that, its identity with *The Recluse*.

 Wordsworth's and Dorothy's walking tour from Bristol up the Wye val-
ley and back took four days, from 10 to 13 July 1798. Before setting off
they both visited James Losh at Bath on 8 July, Losh noting in his diary
'Miss Wordsworth and Wordsworth . . . at Dinner Do. Tea & Supper' (LD
iii). On the following day Losh continues, 'The Wordsworth's all night
and at Breakfast. Walk with them', which suggests that he may have
accompanied his guests towards Bristol, from where on 10 July the Words-
worths continued together over the Severn to Chepstow and the Wye,
then on to Tintern. What did Wordsworth and Losh talk about on those
two days at Bath? The conversation must have turned on the forthcoming
Lyrical Ballads and projected trip to Germany; a little earlier in the year
Losh had noted 'were there any place to go to emigration would be a pru-
dent thing for literary men and the friends of freedom' (LD iii). But if this
much is a reasonable conjecture, they doubtless also touched on political
affairs, mutual acquaintances, and shared experiences following their
coincidence at Paris six years before in autumn 1792. As Wordsworth
parted from Losh in July 1798 it seems highly likely that politics, poetry,
his recent past and immediate future would have been much on his
mind. On the evening of 10 July, perhaps, he arrived at Tintern and then
or shortly afterwards began to compose his poem (Reed, pp. 33, 243).

 The opening lines of 'Tintern Abbey' anchor the whole upon Words-
worth's earlier visit to the Wye 'five years' previously. At that particular
moment Wordsworth's belief had been

> That if France prospered good men would not long
> Pay fruitless worship to humanity

(P. x. 222–3)

—a hope that he had recently vindicated against the death of Louis and
the September Massacres in *A Letter to the Bishop of Llandaff*. Days
before he walked up the Wye to Tintern, though, Wordsworth had
watched the British fleet arming in the Solent for war with France—a
sight that gave him additional cause for doubt. He described the scene in
his fragmentary poem 'At the Isle of Wight', and some curious echoes of
this poem are heard at the beginning of 'Tintern Abbey':

> How sweet to walk along the woody steep
> When all the summer seas are charmed to sleep;
> While on the distant sands the tide retires
> Its last faint murmur on the ear expires;
> 5 The setting sun [ ] his growing round
> On the low promontory—purple bound
> For many a league a line of gold extends,
> Now lessened half his glancing disc de[scends]
> The watry sands athwart the ? [ ]
> 10 Flush [ ] sudden [ ] not [ ]
> While anchored vessels scattered far [ ]
> Darken with shadowy hulks [ ]

> O'er earth o'er air and ocean [   ]
> Tranquillity extends her [   ]
> But hark from yon proud fleet in peal profound
> 16 Thunders the sunset cannon; at the sound
> The star of life appears to set in blood,
> And ocean shudders in offended mood,
> Deepening with moral gloom his angry flood.
>
> (*PW* i. 307–8)

The first four lines of this fragment seem to be recollected, five years later, in the 'steep and lofty cliffs' of 'Tintern Abbey'; in the 'sweet inland murmur' of the River Wye and, at the end of the poem, once again in 'these steep woods and lofty cliffs'. But in recalling the fragment of 1793 these verbal echoes also identify changes in Wordsworth himself. In the earlier poem the tranquillity of evening is shattered by the cannon, the 'gold' and 'purple' sunset is transformed in Wordsworth's eyes to a sky of 'blood', and his 'Evening Voluntary' concludes as a war requiem for France. In 'Tintern Abbey', of course, there is no violent dislocation of feeling, but the landscape and natural scenery are comparably stylized and subordinate to the poet's mood. Wordsworth's quirky footnote—'The river is not affected by the tides a few miles above Tintern'—establishes the distance of the open sea and, by implication, the disturbance of his former self as well.

Although it is not superficially apparent, Wordsworth's reposeful landscape in the first paragraph of 'Tintern Abbey' reminds of the misgivings and betrayal he had endured five years before, and is valued precisely because of that memory of former unease. His isolation then enhances present joy in Dorothy's companionship, his 'dear, dear Friend'. It also defines the antiphonal relation of 'Tintern Abbey' to 'Fears in Solitude' by which Wordsworth answers Coleridge's dejection with a subdued reminder of a comparable experience in his own past, asserting visionary insight and

> that blessed mood,
> In which the burthen of the mystery,
> In which the heavy and the weary weight
> Of all this unintelligible world
> Is lighten'd
>
> (ll. 38–42)

—against his own awareness or revolutionary failure, and Coleridge's despair:

> —O my God!
> It is indeed a melancholy thing,
> And weighs upon the heart, that he must think
> What uproar and what strife may now be stirring
> This way or that way o'er these silent hills . . .

While Wordsworth's recollection of 1793 differentiates his present self in 1798, it also lends urgency to the admitted possibility that his beliefs now may ultimately turn out to be 'vain' as his former confidence in France had proved. That tremor of anxiety is amplified elsewhere in 'Tintern Abbey', where the poem touches deeper memories and associations in the subtitled date, 'July 13, 1798'[1] This was very likely the day on which Wordsworth completed his poem on returning to Bristol. It was also the eighth anniversary of the day Wordsworth first set foot in France in 1790, along with Robert Jones whom he was intending to visit in North Wales when he walked past Tintern in 1793. The date therefore had a personal significance for Wordsworth that served to connect Tintern and France; moreover, the day was also celebrated in the revolutionary calendar as the eve before Bastille day, the anniversary of the Revolution itself.

Wordsworth had witnessed the ceremony of *Fédération* on 14 July twice. In 1790 he was an interested visitor, and told Dorothy that 'the whole nation was mad with joy, in consequence of the revolution' (*EY*, p. 36). Two years later he had joined the *Fête* at Blois as a patriot himself, and would have heard Grégoire—a man of philosophy and humanity'—declare that 'The present augurs well for the future. Soon we shall witness the liberation of all humankind. Everything confirms that the coming revolution . . . will inaugurate the federation of all mankind!' The subtitle of 'Tintern Abbey' inevitably recalls Wordsworth's own experience of revolution at these two moments in 1790 and 1792. It also invokes the millenarian optimism of those early years in Grégoire's prophecy, but defers 'the coming revolution' once again until tomorrow: a 14 July perpetually postponed. No longer identified with revolutionary action or progress, human regeneration has become the prerogative of the individual mind in communion with nature and, introspectively, with itself. It was precisely this reconciliation of revolutionary idealism with subjective experience that Coleridge was unable to sustain after spring 1798, and which defines Wordsworth's identity as poet of *The Prelude* over the next seven years.

In 'Tintern Abbey', as later in *The Prelude*, the fructifying treason of memory 'augurs well' for times to come, enabling Wordsworth to confront human suffering and vicissitude with a redeeming continuity:

> While here I stand, not only with the sense
> Of present pleasure, but with pleasing thoughts
> That in this moment there is life and food
> For future years . . .
>
> (ll. 63–6)

The lines immediately following are the imaginative axis of the whole poem: 'And so I dare to hope,' Wordsworth writes,

> Though changed, no doubt, from what I was, when first
> I came among these hills . . .

His recognition of future possibility and simultaneous acknowledgement of erosion, of change, draw upon the past to construe hope in despite of loss. Unlike Coleridge in 'France, an Ode' or 'Fears in Solitude', Wordsworth's 'dare to hope' embraced the crisis of a generation left without 'light | To guide or chear', turning the experience of defeat to 'food | For future years'. By reflecting wider anxieties within the horizons of per-

---

1. For a brief discussion of revolutionary associations of 13 July, among them the death of Marat, see J. R. Watson 'A Note on the Date in the Title of *Tintern Abbey*', *TWC* x (Autumn 1979), 379–80. See also K. R. Johnston, 'The Politics of *Tintern Abbey*', *TWC* xiv (Winter 1983), 6–14, and R. A. Brinkley, 'Vagrant and Hermit: Milton and the Politics of *Tintern Abbey*', *TWC* xvi (Summer 1985), 126–33.

sonal experience at this moment in mid-1798, Wordsworth had already fulfilled Coleridge's 1799 idea of *The Recluse* as a poem of philosophic restitution for the collapse of the Revolution in France and the associated demise of reform at home. The whole fabric of 'Tintern Abbey'—language, mood, philosophic bias—is grounded in Wordsworth's radical years. It expresses the redemptive wish that he had shared with Coleridge and other friends of liberty, in his pleased recognition of nature as

> The guide, the guardian of [his] heart, and soul
> Of all [his] moral being
>
> (ll. 111–2)

—and it gives thanks for Dorothy's healing presence since Racedown days in maintaining this 'saving intercourse' with nature and his true self. 'Tintern Abbey' does all of these things, but in the context of a lasting vulnerability—'And so I dare to hope'—that was the common legacy of revolution to Wordsworth, Coleridge, and their contemporaries. Wordsworth's consciousness of human weakness and fallibility,

> The still, sad music of humanity,
> Not harsh nor grating, though of ample power
> To chasten and subdue

—was the hardest lesson of revolution, but for Wordsworth it proved most fruitful. More than the aspiration he felt with his generation,

> —a time when Europe was rejoiced,
> France standing on the top of golden hours,
> And human nature seeming born again

—it was failure that made Wordsworth a poet.

ANDREW M. COOPER

[Writing and Identity in *Tintern Abbey*]†

* * *

Arguably, the impetus for Wordsworth's greatest poetry is his fear that by internalizing nature, his supposed source of inspiration, he is generating an opaque self-consciousness that only screens him from her. It is ostensibly the actual process of composing the poem that remarries the poet with nature and allays his fear of separation, at least for the nonce. The question Shelley poses is: since Wordsworth's doubts concern the tendency of poetry to appropriate the external world, trapping the poet in a self-enclosed realm of surrogate representations, how can he expect to solve this problem by writing yet more poetry?[1] Assuming the new poem supplies the poet a means of self-transformation, how can he be sure it is a positive one? If the poet *is* altered by his writing, then his perception

---

† From *Doubt and Identity in Romantic Poetry* (New Haven: Yale University Press, 1988), 158–60. Reprinted by permission of Yale University Press.
1. Cf. James K. Chandler's remarks on the factitiousness of the ostensibly spontaneous, meditative form of Wordsworth's and Coleridge's "conversation" poems, in "Romantic Allusiveness," *Critical Inquiry* 8 (1982):461.

will also be altered; where then is the guarantee that the inspiration he
thinks he has recovered isn't really a delusion? The question gains force
from the fact that so many of the epiphanies in *The Prelude* spring from
relatively banal cognitive confusions, such as the boy's failure to take
parallax into account when noticing a crag's apparent change in position
as he moves away from it (the rowboat episode in Book I, 373–85), or his
dizziness from playfully spinning in circles (the end of the ice-skating
episode eighty lines later). The successful poem itself guarantees the
authenticity of the poet's inspiration, Wordsworth might plausibly reply.
And yet Wordsworth's much-honored later career as a Burkean spokes-
man for the Establishment was a standing example to Shelley of how
inferior verse can "succeed" in the world by succumbing to the same
mundane criteria it ought to transform.

"Tintern Abbey" explores these problems. The poet begins by depicting
a scene whose actual referent turns out to be his own mind immediately
engaged in contemplation:

> Five years have past; five summers, with the length
> Of five long winters! and again I hear
> These waters, rolling from their mountain-springs
> With a soft inland murmur.—Once again
> Do I behold these steep and lofty cliffs,
> That on a wild secluded scene impress
> Thoughts of more deep seclusion; and connect
> The landscape with the quiet of the sky.   [1–8]

Even if the mountain springs are not a domestic version of the Nile, com-
pared in *The Prelude* to the imagination "Poured from his fount of Abys-
sinian clouds / To fertilize the whole Egyptian plain" (VI, 615–16), clearly
we are invited to see the poet's sense of refreshment as arising from a
renewed flow of inspiration after five years of urban drought. The ensu-
ing image of cliffs that "impress / *Thoughts* of more deep seclusion," gent-
ling the wild sublimity of the landscape and harmonizing it with the
quiet sky, shows that Wordsworth is recomposing the scene like a painter.
The "blending, fusing power" (*BL* 2:150) of his imagination emerges more
forcibly in the "plots of cottage-ground . . . Which . . . *lose themselves* 'Mid
groves and copses," and in the "hedge-rows, *hardly hedge-rows*, little lines
/ Of sportive wood run wild"—signs of habitation no sooner discerned
than they dissolve before our eyes, merging with the surrounding green-
ery. These authorial interventions reach their climax, ending all possibil-
ity of objective description, with the picturesque vision of

>   wreaths of smoke
> Sent up, in silence, from among the trees!
> With some uncertain notice, as might seem
> Of vagrant dwellers in the houseless woods,
> Or of some Hermit's cave, where by his fire
> The Hermit sits alone.   [17–22]

As the full stop of the exclamation mark indicates, the "notice" is the
poet's own, grown "uncertain" because he has taken his eye off the actual
external scene in order to reimagine it through his description. Poetry's
usurpation of that scene becomes explicit with the image of the Hermit,

a patent fiction whose sole reason for appearing in the well-populated valley is, as Richard J. Onorato and others have pointed out,[2] that he personifies the poet's now fully objectified "thoughts of more deep seclusion."

Moreover, the closing address to Dorothy, intended to resolve the doubt that such imaginative projection might be deluded, in fact only reawakens it. Wordsworth's argument is that, since the younger Dorothy views the scene the same way as he did five years ago, his present realization of "something far more deeply interfused" will be repeated in her when she likewise revisits the scene, perhaps sometime after he is dead. Nevertheless, if Dorothy upon her return will experience the same problematic self-consciousness as Wordsworth now does, one wonders whether he has solved his present difficulties or merely fobbed them off on her (and Dorothy, unlike Wordsworth, has no younger sibling whom she can address in turn). This disquieting possibility reflects a basic contradiction in Wordsworth's argument. He is implying that Dorothy's present experience includes him standing beside her as a part of the landscape, analogously to the way his own present experience contains an objectified image of himself during *his* first visit, namely the factitious Hermit; yet such fraternal companionship is precisely what makes Dorothy's experience *unlike* Wordsworth's first visit, which, as the image of the Hermit goes to show, he made alone. The basis for Wordsworth's assertion of their identity is that he can catch in her voice "The language of my former heart, and read / My former pleasures in . . . thy wild eyes" (116–19). His knowledge depends, in other words, on his interpreting Dorothy's responses in terms of his youthful self—a process of representation no less usurping of its object than was his perplexed survey of the valley which needed to be resolved in the first place.

The cause of Wordsworth's difficulty is of course that writing, instead of transcribing thought, can displace it by generating an immediacy of its own. Observes Coleridge:

> If one thought leads to another, so often does it blot out another. This I find when having lain musing on my sofa, a number of interesting thoughts having suggested themselves, I conquer my bodily indolence, and rise to record them in these books, alas! my only confidants. The first thought leads me on indeed to new ones; but nothing but the faint memory of having had these remains of the other, which had been even more interesting to me. . . . my thoughts crowd each other to death.[3]

Contrary to Wordsworth's confident assumptions, writing here produces not self-unity but a dreamlike, schizoid split between Coleridge the indolent but alert freethinker and Coleridge the writer, whose dutiful effort at the physical activity of composition only adds to his inertia by stymieing him mentally. Elsewhere Coleridge finds it utterly "opposite to nature and the fact to talk of the 'one moment' of Hume, of our whole being an

2. Richard J. Onorato, *The Character of the Poet: Wordsworth in "The Prelude"* (Princeton: Princeton University Press, 1971), pp. 45–47. See also L. J. Swingle, "Wordsworth's 'Picture of the Mind,'" in *Images of Romanticism: Verbal and Visual Affinities*, ed. Karl Kroeber and William Walling (New Haven: Yale Univ. Press, 1978), pp. 86–88.
3. Coleridge, "Anima Poetae," from *The Portable Coleridge*, ed. I. A. Richards (New York: Viking, 1950), pp. 314–15.

aggregate of successive single sensations";[4] but the above passage suggests just such a discontinuity. The flux of associative thought being too rapid and turbulent for cogent representation, the self, swept forward within a narrow envelope of recent recollections, remains forever incomplete because it is unable to objectify its private musings within the concrete world of action.

* * *

MARK JONES

From The Lucy Poems[†]

* * *

There appear to be two main aspects of the aesthetic motivation for devising and/or keeping the 'Lucy' grouping: the enhancement of 'A slumber' and the 'discovery' of narrative. I consider the former here, and the latter in the next section. Because of the grouping, Sykes Davies notes, 'A slumber' 'acquired a prominence in the whole body of Wordsworth's work which it had not previously enjoyed, and which it has never since lost' (151). Though he barely documents this observation, if anything he understates the degree to which 'A slumber' has been 'made' by the editorial grouping.[1] De Vere and Swinburne, both writing after Arnold and to a large extent responding to his views on Wordsworth, both praise 'A slumber' extravagantly. Swinburne, it is true, does not explicitly mention the grouping, but the extreme economy of expression for which he praises 'A slumber' is arguably the function of the grouping, which makes it possible to understand more than the poem itself says.

> in a lesser lyric than this [i.e., than 'Ode to Duty'] we find the same spontaneous and sublime perfection of inspired workmanship. None but a poet of the first order could have written the eight lines in which the unforeseeing security of a charmed and confident happiness is opposed to the desolate certitude of unforeseen bereavement by a single touch of contrast, a single note of comparison, as profound in its simplicity as the deepest wellspring of human emotion or remembrance itself. No elaboration of elegiac lament could possibly convey that sense of absolute and actual truth, of a sorrow set to music of its own making,—a sorrow hardly yet wakened out of wonder into sense of its own reality,—which is impressed at once and for ever on the spirit of any reader, at any age, by those eight faultless and incomparable verses. (776)

By the turn of the century, 'A slumber' was receiving a significant share of critical attention. Josephine Miles indicates its centrality by the mid-twentieth century, observing that it is quoted in three out of seven essays

4. Coleridge, *Notebooks*, ed. Kathleen Coburn, 3 vols. (New York: Pantheon, 1957), 2, entry 2370.
† From *The "Lucy Poems": A Case Study in Literary Knowledge* (Toronto: University of Toronto Press, 1995), 72–87, 275–79. Notes have been edited. Reprinted by permission of the author.
1. 'She dwelt' was by far the most popular of the 'Lucy Poems' throughout the nineteenth century, 'A slumber' the least or second least. While 'She dwelt' remains popular, 'A slumber' now draws most attention by far. A crude tally I've made of the pre-Arnoldian judgments ranks the poems as follows (counting positives, negatives, and parodies): 'She dwelt' (11–2–4), 'Three years' (6–0–0), 'Strange fits' (3–0–0), 'I travelled' (2–0–0), and 'A slumber' (3–2–0).

in a critical collection (*Wordsworth: Centenary Essays*, ed. Gilbert Dunklin [1951]) where no other 'Lucy Poem' is mentioned (Miles 128). In 1959 David Ferry finds 'A slumber' 'at the powerful center of this poet's art' (76), but Miles' doubts are worth considering: 'These are of course the terms, this the poetry, of our own era, and therefore the selection of it may reflect us primarily' (128). And as the rest of Ferry's statement suggests, it is not solely modern tastes but also the Victorian grouping that makes 'A slumber' central. Having just read 'She dwelt' and 'Three years,' he says: 'All this brings us to the lyric which is at the powerful center . . .'

The power of 'A slumber' in this context is more than an accidental effect of the editorial grouping. The grouping makes it, as Powell suggests, a sequel, and something always accrues to sequels from the lead. The other 'Lucy Poems' are, arguably, as good alone as in the group: we don't need 'She dwelt' to appreciate 'Three years,' or 'Strange fits' to understand 'I travelled.' This is not to say that the grouping does not subtly transmute them also. But the spareness of 'A slumber' and its want of a Lucy put it at once outside the 'Lucy Poems' grouping and at its centre. * * * The 'Lucy Poems' grouping is, in its effects, the Victorians' most important interpretive achievement with these poems, but *as* an interpretation it is unusual. In one sense, it is unusually mediatory: in its falsification of Wordsworth's text it seems an egregious case of interpretation's displacement of its original; and in presenting the 'Lucy Poems' as a textual sequence it imposes, as we shall see, sequential readings. In another sense, however, the grouping seems like the least imposing of interpretations: without explicitly dictating the meaning of the poems, it merely suggests their interrelatedness. To a considerable extent, I think that the grouping owes its endurance to this ambiguity: however useful in rendering the poems more definite, it does not *seem* officious or dictatorial, and thus it escapes the internal censors of its inheritors. One can take or leave a conventional interpretation, such as Sykes Davies' alternative reading of 'A slumber' as a description of mystical trance. By contrast, the 'Lucy Poems' grouping both facilitates and demands subsequent participation. It imposes more order while seeming to impose less, or none at all.

Tales of Lucy: The Narratization of Lyric

Piecing the 'Lucy Poems' together in 1871, Oliphant remarked 'what a consistent story they tell.' Besides clarifying and enhancing 'A slumber,' the nineteenth-century grouping imposed closure by narratizing lyric. In arguing this, I do not mean to claim that the poems *are* lyric in an objective and absolute sense, but on the contrary that they appear as lyrics in some settings, as narrative in others; what I call the 'narratization of lyric' is a transmutation of appearances, not essences. As Adena Rosmarin has argued, generic categorization is not a matter of fitting contingent works to essential categories, but of 'expedient error' with heuristic or 'explanatory power': we wilfully view works as instances of various kinds for the sake of posing certain expectations and/or highlighting certain qualities.[2] It is tempting to suppose that Wordsworth was himself concerned with this dynamic, since the interpretive problems presented by the 'Lucy

2. *The Power of Genre* (1985) 20, 25. Rosmarin borrows 'expedient error' from Hans Vaihinger.

Poems' derive from their generically liminal dispositions, both as parts/
wholes and as 'lyrical ballads.' In other words, our modern theoretical
dubiety as to the objectivity and stability of genres, typified by Rosmarin's
powerful analysis, and our correlative self-consciousness in using them to
'describe' works, seem to derive from, and are certainly aggravated by,
romanticism's flagrant crossings of genre;[3] conversely, the decisions within
practical criticism that the 'Lucy Poems' *are* one kind of thing or another
appears as the repression or containment of such romantic indecision and
of the 'crisis' it brings. In their crossing of part and whole, lyric and ballad,
the 'Lucy Poems' constitute another case of those Wordsworthian 'border-
ers' which generally have two opposite but correlative effects: they make
you self-conscious regarding the taxonomic principles you ordinarily
employ without thinking, but they may also goad you to suppress this dis-
abling self-consciousness through summary invocation of those same
principles. In this case, the historical decision has favoured narrative.[4]

*   *   *

That most of the 'Lucy Poems' first appeared in *Lyrical Ballads* might be
taken to suggest that they are simply half-narrative, but 'lyrical ballad' may
also suggest a departure *from* ballad *toward* lyric. In considering the debts
of the 'Lucy Poems' to the traditional ballads of Percy's *Reliques*, Herbert
Hartman observes 'the unsuitability of Wordsworth's genius for the strict
ballad form and spirit,' and cites the poetry's own disclaimer: 'The moving
accident is not my trade' (136).[5] In a similar spirit, pointing out that
the 'ballad revival' was an event of the eighteenth century and not of the
romantic period, Karl Kroeber argues that 'the Romantics put the ballad to
the service of lyricism': 'The evolution of Romantic lyricism is, in some
measure at least, the gradual transformation of simple narrative structure
as the basis of lyric organization into a discontinuous, non-narrative struc-
ture' which was 'demanded by the poets' efforts to express that which is not
objective.'[6] Kroeber is not referring specifically to *Lyrical Ballads*, but he
could be; both in its animus against 'frantic novels, sickly and stupid Ger-
man Tragedies, and deluges of idle and extravagant stories in verse,' and in
its famous specification of the point of Wordsworth's own poetry—the

---

3. Jameson argues that 'literary production has in modern times ceaselessly and systematically
   undermined . . . generic restrictions,' and that writing *within* genres is now 'subliterary' (*The
   Political Unconscious* [1981], 106–7). The crossings of genres in the 'Lucy Poems,' as in 'lyrical
   ballad' generally, can only alter whatever genres are crossed and deteriorate their distinctive-
   ness in the long run, thus evincing their conventionality. When it has to be pointed out to us
   that 'lyrical ballad' is contradictory, or that it was in Wordsworth's day, this is in no small part
   because *Lyrical Ballads* has actually made lyric and ballad compatible—and thus effaced the
   conditions for appreciating its own originality. See also Rosmarin 35, on the value of breaking
   genres; Herbert Lindenberger, *On Wordsworth's Prelude* (1963), 13–15; and Stuart Curran,
   Poetic Form and British Romanticism (1986), especially 182.
4. So far as I know, Geoffrey Hartman was first to dwell on the importance of 'borderers' in Words-
   worth (*WP*, esp. 158f, ch. 6, and 224–6). But I am obliged to an anonymous press reader who notes
   Charles G. D. Roberts' observation of 1892: 'Wordsworth's peculiar province is that border-land
   wherein Nature and the heart of Man act and react upon each other. His vision is occupied not so
   much with Nature as with the relations between Nature and his inmost self' (Roberts 274–5).
5. Citing 'Hart-Leap Well,' line 97 (*PW* 2:252).
6. *Romantic Narrative Art* (1960), 51, 58. Kroeber has recently developed his historical thesis in 'Nar-
   rative and De-Narrativized Art,' suggesting that romanticism flirts with de-narratization and ulti-
   mately re-embraces narrative: only with modernism is the 'decision *against* narrative' made firm
   (see especially 215–16). On a romantic retreat from narrative, see also Susan Wolfson, 'Keats's
   Isabella' (1985); and Alan Liu, *Wordsworth* (1989), 75–87. In an argument that anticipates my own,
   Tilottama Rajan views the 'Lucy poems' as 'the lyricisation of the beautiful soul' (88) and Shelley's
   'Alastor' as its re-narratization ('The Web of Human Things' [1994], especially 87–8, 104).

feeling therein developed gives importance to the action and situation, and not the action and situation to the feeling'—Wordsworth's Preface speaks of a retreat from narrative (Owen 74, 73). The notion of de-narratized ballad fits the 'Lucy Poems' in particular, and from this standpoint their editorial-interpretive renarratization appears curiously retrograde.

Individually, the 'Lucy Poems' can be read to bear out this non- or even anti-narrative characterization. It is suggestive that while 'Lucy Gray' is more aptly called 'lyrical *ballad*' than any of the canonical poems, those who 'eviscerate' it to create a 'Lucy Poem' essentially cut out the narrative elements to leave the lyric.[7] Of the five canonical poems, 'Strange fits' comes closest to ballad, yet even its narrative qualities seem to belong to anti-narrative or parody. * * * The poem's superficially balladic form thus emphasizes the inapplicability of received ways of telling to a radically subjective message. Though the plodding transit between the lyrical first and last stanzas develops some narrative expectation, even this turns out to be spurious, for the climactic event—'At once, the bright moon dropped'—is, objectively taken, too preposterous to be believed. One makes sense of the moon's fall only by internalizing it, as a trick of the eye, which is to explain it away. Only once the poem's narrative tension has been defused does it manifest the real event, the appearance of 'wayward thoughts.' Our experience in reading this poem is thus likely to follow a pattern of disappointment and mild surprise such as Wordsworth described once in 'There was a Boy,' and again, according to De Quincey, in personal conversation:

> I have remarked [says Wordsworth], from my earliest days, that, if under any circumstances, the attention is energetically braced up to an act of steady observation, or of steady expectation, then, if this intense condition of vigilance should suddenly relax, at that moment any beautiful, any impressive visual object, or collection of objects, falling upon the eye, is carried to the heart with a power not known under other circumstances. (*Recollections* 160)

Rather than an expectation that builds to a conclusion, this is a pattern of baffled expectation *and* unlooked-for mental event. Simply to occur is an inward thought's mode of happening: it is not narrative but lyric.

In all of the 'Lucy Poems,' thoughts and 'feelings' are more important than objective events or 'actions,' specific points in time more than temporal process. The poems specialize in points where temporal and emotional perspectives are reversed. If we approach 'She dwelt'—to take only one more example—as a story, we find that it is over before it has begun. It is not only that Lucy 'is dead before we so much as hear of her,' as Oliphant remarks (*Literary History* 1:307), though that is important. The tone of the poem's beginning is not narrative but descriptive, or more specifically pre-narrative. Like 'There was a monster who lived under a hill,' 'She dwelt among the untrodden ways' implies that a story is about to be told. By line 9, 'She lived unknown, and few could know,' the tone is still pre-narrative; there is no suggestion that Lucy has died until the next

---

7. See Eric Robertson, *Wordsworthshire* (1911) 151; G.M. Harper, *John Morley and other Essays* (1920) 129–30; John Jones, *The Egotistical Sublime* (1954) 72–3.

line, 'When Lucy ceased to be,' declares everything to be over. Now it turns out (and this may be why the first edition italicized *'liv'd'*) that 'dwelt' and 'lived' *were* narrations of an action, the beginning, middle, and end of Lucy's life. Lucy seems to begin the poem alive and to end up in her 'grave,' yet her death never arises; we discover her having-died.

* * *

How the poems can 'tell their own tale' despite a variable sequence scarcely constitutes a problem for the early commentators, for the very presumption of an objective biographical referent makes it natural that the poems should disguise as much as they reveal: as in allegory, some obscurity is expected. Once reference is presumed, contradictions, confusions, and even the dearth of evidence may *be* evidence that a 'history' (Myers 34) has been hidden or disguised. Modern psychobiography makes the same assumptions but then scrutinizes the text as, by definition, the only clue to the repressed referent.[8] In early criticism, referential assumptions more commonly produce identification-studies, which largely bypass the text (it won't tell the truth anyway) in search for the referent, literally dead-ending in the *corpus delicti*. Biographical critics name various originals for Lucy,[9] especially Dorothy,[1] but seldom bother to articulate the poetic 'story,' which has importance only as scaffolding, as an opening assumption.

The project of identifying Lucy belongs predominantly to the early twentieth century, but that, I suspect, is less because we have evolved beyond the 'vulgar curiosity' of these critics than it is because they exhausted the candidates for Lucy. In any case, I shall also use later examples which tend to be more fully elaborated. In 1926, Anton Bertram can simply demand: 'Is it not as clear as day that the Lucy Poems are a revelation of the actual past?' (480). In a biographical study of 1953, H. M. Margoliouth argues that the 'hitherto mysterious' 'Lucy Poems' refer primarily to Mary Hutchinson's younger sister Margaret ('Peggy'), who died of consumption in 1796, and secondarily to Mary herself (51–3, 58). Margoliouth's most substantial evidence is that the poems are written after Peggy's death. Therefore his argument relies on the poems no more than

8. The best examples of psychobiographical criticism are the arguments of Frederick Bateson and Richard Matlack and various essays by Geoffrey Hartman, especially 'The Interpreter's Freud' (*Easy Pieces* [1985], 137–54). Psychobiography is not, of course, wholly distinct from simple efforts to identify Lucy. Donald Reiman's 'The Poetry of Familiarity' (1978), informative as to William's and Dorothy's relations, lies somewhere between: it invokes Freud and in some ways follows Bateson, but generally rests content with identification rather than dwell on the text's repressive and refractive qualities. 'Strange fits,' Reiman claims, 'certainly refers to Dorothy as Lucy,' and 'the five so-called "Lucy poems" were written about the same imagined death of Dorothy' (156; but see also 157–8).
9. In 1934, Herbert Hartman listed previous identifications for Lucy: Dorothy, Mary, 'Annette Vallon, "Lucy Gray," some ideal maiden, an adopted gipsy child, or the unknown object of a "real experience of youthful love and bewildering grief"—to these has been added "Li'le Hartley" Coleridge' (137–38). Hartman gives sources for most of these.
1. One can make a fair case for this view. I hesitate to mention Coleridge's comment of 1799, since he was speaking solely of 'A slumber' when we don't know that the poems were associated. For a balanced account, see Mary Moorman, 1:423–6. Since Dorothy is important to most psychoanalytic approaches to the poems, it is not surprising that Bateson (*Wordsworth* [1954], 151–3) and Matlack make strong cases for the identification. The hardest evidence is that Wordsworth uses 'Lucy' (1) in 'Among all lovely things,' and told Coleridge that 'The incident of this Poem took place about seven years ago between Dorothy and me' (letter of 16 April 1802, *Letters* 1:348), and (2) in an early draft of 'Nutting' (DC MS. 16, *PW* 2:504–6), and that 'Other fragments of "Nutting" . . . demonstrate conclusively that the "Beloved Friend" of the poem is Dorothy' (Bateson 152). Now that Butler and Green have made these fragments available, it is plain that the evidence is hardly 'conclusive.'

on other texts such as letters, and it illustrates how the assumption of an objective story can work to justify a certain inattention to the poetry's version, especially where there are conflicting details.

* * *

The search for Lucy's bones is an illuminating because both extreme and graphic version of the 'referential fallacy,' and it was, with the rise of formalist analysis, castigated as such.[2] As befits a 'fallacy,' one is inclined to regard it simply as a critical naïveté, and to locate its essential failure not in the inability to prove a specific objective referent, but in the more basic failure to consider what *that* could prove. It seems to turn on a fundamental error as to genre, on a mistaking of the fictional for the factual. Yet there is an important sense in which this has also been an 'expedient error,' a canny simplification facilitating interpretive mastery. In calling the poems 'hitherto mysterious,' Margoliouth implies that his biographical identification dispels their mystery; Harris proposes his as 'a solution of a literary problem of long standing,' and envisions himself as holding 'the key in the lock: presently we shall be able to turn it' (5, 11). The lock-and-key is an image both of revelation and of closure. In taking the poetry's speaker(s) for Wordsworth, in ignoring its fictionality or 'literariness,' and in conceiving it as a lock or puzzle with a single definitive solution, such approaches reduce its manifold indeterminacy to one empirical question – 'Who was this Lucy?' (Harris 3)—which *might* be answered decisively. But these simplifications and pretensions to closure are, it seems to me, more to be doubted than the referential assumption on which they are based. For as Richard Matlack cogently argues in resurrecting the question 'Who was Lucy?' for purposes of psychobiography, 'The charge of irrelevance cannot be made categorically. Issues are relevant or irrelevant with respect to contexts of preoccupation, not a priori' (46). The important matter is what critical practice an assumption of reference serves.[3] Hence, though the referential assumptions of the identification-readings have been in disgrace in recent years, I think it would be mistaken to dismiss them altogether.

* * *

Abandoning the quest for a biographical Lucy inevitably entails a greater emphasis on poetic form—and hence, I will argue, a drastic reconception of her 'story'—but it also initiated other attempts at solution, such as the production of 'literary' originals. In dismissing biographical inquiries, Garrod merely displaces the quest for origins, citing poems by Thomas Tickell, Baron George Lyttelton, Edward Moore, Thomas Chatterton, and especially Samuel Rogers (90–1); Herbert Hartman, whose essay on 'Wordsworth's "Lucy"' (1934) is equally important, approves these remarks and adds William Collins to the possible influences (138, 141). Harold Bloom's reformative theory of poetic influence responds to the tendency of literary source-hunting to degenerate into

---

2. For early dismissals of reference, see the discussion of Winchester and Garrod, below. Geoffrey Durrant speaks for many later critics in pronouncing Lucy's identity 'irrelevant' ('Zeno's Arrow' [1969] 60)

3. Matlack's project is not, however, entirely distinct from identifications. While the identification of Lucy and Dorothy generates psychobiographical readings, it is designed also to 'dispel the mystery of [the poems'] genesis' (46).

something much like biographical source-hunting; in so far as either activity simply assumes the explanatory virtue of the 'source' or 'referent,' it becomes sterile. But just as the identification of Lucy with biographical originals can, in the hands of a sufficiently dialectical psychobiographical method, encourage rather than foreclose inquiry, so literary precedents may prove useful in the grasp of a sufficiently dialectical understanding of poetic development. However subject to dead-ending, the increasing attention to these sources in the early twentieth century is an important facet of the shift not just toward formalist analysis, but also toward the dialectical literary history espoused by formalism.[4]

The rejection of biographical identifications has equally profound implications for the reading of Lucy's 'story' in that she is henceforth assumed to be more fictional than real. Now the poems generate Lucy, not the other way around; now she is symbolic and significant, not primarily an existential signified; now her 'story' is the centre of interest, no longer a background assumption posited to be forgotten. But while this story remains as cryptic as ever, now the old ways of explaining-away its obscurity—by invoking the poet's 'reserve,' by revering his privacy, by diverting attention to objective physical referents—are no longer available. Formalism makes it necessary to read Lucy's story to the letter.

The 'Lucy Poems' criticism continues to be shaped by this invitation or challenge to narrative reading, as I illustrate by using three modern commentaries. In *The Heart's Events* (1976), Patricia Ball attempts to articulate the Lucy narrative:

> Do the Lucy poems . . . tell a story? It is possible to summarise them so that they do. The speaker of the poems loved a girl of grace and beauty called Lucy, who lived in a secluded country spot and occupied herself with the usual domestic employments. He used to visit her frequently at her cottage, his horse knowing the path there without any guidance. The love affair was happy, the lovers trusted each other, Lucy being ready to tease him for his moods. Despite being momentarily visited by inexplicable fears that she might die, the lover is shocked when that event occurs, and his view of his native place, and the earth in general, remains deeply affected by it. (10)

Ball is hardly uncritical of this way of telling the 'story' and proceeds well beyond it. But her formulation clarifies the nature of the problem: though certain details are drawn from most of the poems, the plot, such as it is, must be developed out of 'Strange fits.' There is not much room for narrative after Lucy dies in 'She dwelt,' the next poem in Ball's sequence. As Ball notes (11), she must draw on the cancelled stanza of 'Strange fits' to flesh the story out; as she does not note, the statement that the lover is 'momentarily visited by inexplicable fears' jibes with 'Strange fits,' but maybe not with 'A slumber' ('I had no human fears'). But the central problem is the obvious deficiency in narrative interest, or plot. If the poems imply a story, it is hard to pretend that that is their point. 'Such a bald account,' Ball com-

<hr/>

4. Formalist literary history is 'dialectical' in that it explains literary development as reaction against 'source' or predecessor forms, but also as their subsumption, as in parody or 'foregrounding.' Geoffrey Hartman's comparative discussion of 'Lucy Poems' by Wordsworth and by Lyttelton ('Beyond Formalism' [1966]) is exemplary. But the majority of source studies of the 'Lucy Poems' fail to make such use of them: that 'sources' are so often listed in footnotes and appendices, the cul-de-sacs of scholarship, may indicate how little we understand about putting them to use.

ments, 'is an obvious way of demonstrating that theirs is a lyric vitality. None the less, that lyricism does depend upon the narrative or historical framework, slight though it is' (10). This states in a nutshell the difficulty of narrative readings, but it characteristically understates the debt of this 'narrative or historical framework' to Victorian interpretation and editing, and fathers it on Wordsworth. Ball acknowledges the poems' ambiguous status in the authorial text of 1850: 'they are neither one poem broken into five parts,' she says, 'nor are they five independent poems' (10). But her unquestioning assumption that there are five and that 'A slumber' is one of them (17–18) and her misleading statement that Wordsworth 'regarded their being placed in a certain sequence as important' (10) evince the Victorian influence; surely 'sequence' is a leading term for poems that are not all contiguous in any Wordsworth edition.

Ball's answer to a lyric 'sequence' that seems not 'to deal . . . with the sequence of facts' (13) is to construe it as an internal narrative, or 'inner history' (6) of 'the heart's events.' This strategy is characteristic of modern readings, though the procedures for narratizing the inner history vary. Ball's procedure is to consider each poem in 'sequence,' tracing the speaker's psychic development. But her description of the poems as 'an imaginative effort . . . to articulate an extended process of inner shock' (9) glimpses the irreconcilability of the poems' lyric form and sequential exegesis. When Ball charts this psychic progress, the result is less than compelling: in 'I travelled,' 'the sense of exploring an emotional situation is strongly advanced'; this poem 'finds a more oblique way of approaching the fact of Lucy's death'; 'The "difference" has been more precisely plotted.' In 'Three years,' 'nature and Lucy are brought together far less literally to aid Wordsworth's continuing attempt to find ways of representing adequately what Lucy was' (14–15). Ball's reliance on comparatives shows the strain imposed by the editorial sequence. One could reorder the poems and still argue the same thing, which is to say that 'the extended process of inner shock' is being read into rather than out of them. The 'Lucy Poems' are, frankly, short on plot, whether we take their 'events' to be objective or subjective; sequential readings are therefore inherently dutiful, compelled rather than compelling. Why consider all five, even if we have nothing new to say about 'Strange fits,' and 'I travelled' only waylays the argument? The grouping exerts its pressure.

The majority of critics do not consider all five poems; one might add that the best criticism does not. But the pressure toward narrative reading remains: any grouping still encourages it, while the poems themselves act as obstacles. One interesting solution is to seize this very difficulty as one's advantage, and emphasize the story's non-narrativity as its genius. This paradoxical strategy is implicit in Oliphant's account of Lucy's 'story, which is no story' (*Literary History* 1:307), but it is best elaborated by James Averill:

> Elegy, particularly as Wordsworth practices it, is suspended between narrative and lyric. . . . The 'Lucy' poems, particularly, act as appendices to tragedy. The story they tell us by glimpses is familiar both in life and literature, but the remarkable feature of the poems is what is absent from them. After reading the four 'Lucy' poems in *Lyrical Ballads* (1800), the reader knows little about such rudimentary facts

as who the lovers were, where they lived, who their families were, let
alone what specifically their relationship was or what happened to
the girl. Our expectations of a conventional love-found-love-lost nar-
rative would be to learn some such details. It is as if Wordsworth set
out to write a tragic story without plot or even characters, to achieve
the sympathetic response by centering on the bare fact of death and
on the survivor's reaction to it. In place of moving accidents, there is
the drama of consciousness: for the excitement of the death, we are
asked to substitute an uncanny premonition in 'Strange Fits of Pas-
sion' or the ironically pathetic vulnerability of having been 'without
human fears' in 'A Slumber Did My Spirit Seal.' (*Wordsworth* 207–8)

Averill draws an interesting parallel between 'Wordsworth's desire to
internalize the action of narrative poetry' and the practice of Henry James.
He compares Wordsworth's statement that 'incidents are among the low-
est allurements of poetry' (*Letters* 1:234) and James's 'What is character
but the determination of incident? What is incident but the illustration of
character?' (Averill 208–10). While the 'internal narrative' reading is not
new with Averill, he evinces the credibility of this genre by reading sev-
eral *Lyrical Ballads*, not just the 'Lucy Poems,' into it. But the paradoxical
bent of his reading is evident in that the 'Lucy Poems' become its corner-
stones precisely because they are *least* like narrative of all Wordsworth's
'narrative' poems. Despite Averill's recourse only to the 'four' in *Lyrical
Ballads*, his treatment of them as narrative owes as much as Ball's to the
Victorian tradition; the one point he does not have to demonstrate is the
crucial one that they are narrative in the first place. 'It is as if Wordsworth
set out to write a tragic story without plot or even characters': it is as if
Wordsworth set out to write lyric. Like modern readings that marvel at
the 'elision' of Lucy in 'A slumber' (see note 38 above), Averill's might be
described as presenting an apple as an extraordinary orange. Discussions
of 'A slumber' as being about Lucy without mentioning her, and of the
grouping as a narrative 'without plot,' are fundamentally similar in that
they defamiliarize the works, presenting them as what they evidently are
not. It may seem equally illegitimate for me to declare what they are and
are not, yet I think Averill's presentation of them as narrative is interest-
ing and educative precisely to the degree that his presumed genre is
askew. As Rosmarin points out, if genre criticism makes 'the edifying
mistake of classification' (22), 'what the critic seeks is not a "fit" but the
most suggestive "misfit"' (45). But rather than invent his own misfit,
Averill exploits the 'edifying mistake' imposed by the Victorian editors.[5]

In construing the 'Lucy Poems' as internal narrative, both Ball and
Averill associate them with later developments in internal narrative,
which Wordsworth is supposed to have anticipated or influenced. Ball
asserts that 'the Lucy poems are Wordsworth's *In Memoriam*' (19), and
she uses them to introduce a book-length study of Victorian poetry. Aver-
ill argues that '[i]n opposing character and incident, Wordsworth antici-
pates the Victorian discrimination between novels of plot and of

---

5. Rosmarin's phrase suggests that all classifying is mistake, while her useful comments on wilful
   errors of classification (21–2, 45) imply that some mistakes are greater—or more 'edifying'—
   than others. 'What makes a genre "good,"' she argues, 'is its power to make the literary text
   "good"' (49). Classification, she suggests, is a way of imposing comparisons between dissimilar
   objects—in Averill's case, between lyrics and narratives.

character,' citing 'Austen, Trollope, James, Woolf, and Forster' (*Words-worth* 209). Informed by the editorial grouping but ignoring its historical constitution, these arguments effect a subtle but significant historical reversal. Subjective as the 'Lucy Poems' are, their appearance as subjective *narrative* is largely due to Victorian decisions and probably would not have been recognized in Wordsworth's broken and shifting lyrical orderings. It is possible to see the 'Lucy Poems' as anticipating *In Memoriam* (1850) by fifty years only by forgetting that *In Memoriam* preceded Palgrave's serialization of them by eleven years, or that Oliphant's serialization (1871) explicitly invokes *Maud* (1855) as a model. Here Tennyson is merely synecdoche for the broader development at mid-century of lyrical series as media for subjective narrative—a development the 'Lucy Poems' do not so much anticipate as get caught up in. Other works of the period— Poe's 'The Poetic Principle' (1850), Whitman's *Leaves of Grass* (1855), and even the narratization of painting[6]—suggest a widespread interest in lyrical series. Understandably, Poe is sometimes taken to mark a movement away from narrative poetry, but in holding that *Paradise Lost* can be 'regarded as poetical, only . . . as a series of minor poems,' and on the other hand that 'a poem may be improperly brief' (71–3), he justifies precisely the lyrical series then being, or soon to be, developed by his contemporaries, including the anthologists. Implicit in the disjunctive serial form is the discontinuous narrative of subjectivity.[7] Not that this development can be ascribed merely to the accidents of formal mutation: the strain both to produce and to accept it may best be seen in the fate of a work that Clifford Siskin (*Historicity* 114–24) treats as yet another arrangement of famous Wordsworth lyrics—*The Prelude*. That *The Prelude* appeared in the same year as Poe's essay and Tennyson's *In Memoriam* is not entirely coincidental, if one considers that one cause for its delay was Wordsworth's own inability fully to endorse the art he himself was producing: a thoroughly subjective art in a narrative, that is public, mode. If it is easy now to 'recognize' the 'Lucy Poems' as early instances of 'internal narrative,' this category was not fully viable when they were *first* composed.

*   *   *

THOMAS PFAU

[Traumatic History and Lyric Awakening in *Michael*][†]

*   *   *

The ballad form typically revolves around a moment of interpretive crisis, which, however local, incidental, or even apocryphal, may be considered as a symptom of deep-seated historical antagonisms. In Wordsworth's

---

6. As Mario Praz remarks, between 1830 and 1860 English painting, with its emphasis on subject, on the moral to be inculcated, the story to be told, was almost a branch of literature' (*The Hero in Eclipse* 28).
7. As Wellek notes, Poe's theory 'has influenced all subsequent theories of the short story' (*History* 3:161).
† From *Romantic Moods: Paranoia, Trauma, and Melancholy, 1794–1840* (Baltimore, John Hopkins University Press, 2005) 192–207. Notes have been edited and renumbered. © 2005 The Johns Hopkins University Press. Reprinted with permission of The Johns Hopkins University Press.

Lyrical Ballads, for example, tensions at the level of economic and regional history are repeatedly reproduced as the formal enigma of a lyric voice bordering on the unintelligible. As the last poem in the 1800 edition of *Lyrical Ballads*, however, "Michael" struggles and ultimately breaks with the constraints that the genre imposed on Wordsworth. If earlier ballads seem exemplary in their allegiance to anonymous, incidental folk knowledge, their contingent and ephemeral world ultimately interferes with Wordsworth's professional ambitions. Exasperated and positively stimulated into action by Coleridge's failure to complete "Christabel"—which had been slated to be the closing piece in the 1800 *Lyrical Ballads*—Wordsworth conceives of and identifies "Michael" as "A Pastoral Poem." More than most poems in that collection, "Michael" appears as a formal hybrid, combining elements of the credal poetry deriving from a particular strain of the ballad with those of pastoral and elegiac writing. Formally, "Michael" completes and reflexively sublates (in the Hegelian sense) the project of *Lyrical Ballads*. For it takes as its proper object the limitations of the ballad form by dramatizing, at the level of action, its protagonist's precarious transition from the self-enclosed world of local (balladic) knowledge into the unbounded world of agrarian capitalism and its myriad connections with urban commerce and speculation. As we shall see, the historical valence and the limitations of the ballad genre are themselves at the very heart of the story told by Wordsworth's "Michael." Rather than constituting an evasion of history—which new historicism has rather schematically construed as an evasion of referentiality—the symbolic overdetermination at work *in* "Michael" and the explicit generic marking *of* "Michael" as "A Pastoral Poem" strongly suggest that some kind of awakening is imminent. In their own ways, both the author of *Lyrical Ballads* and his protagonist are about to awaken from the rhetorical and epistemological limitations of the ballad genre. At an authorial and professional level, Wordsworth is about to reflect (and thereby transcend) the apparent incommensurability of the ballad genre with his literary and cultural ambitions as these take shape around 1800. Simultaneously, his characters appear increasingly restless (e.g., Leonard in "The Brothers") within the manifestly closed system of social cognition associated with the ballad (e.g., "low and rustic life," "slow feelings," and "simple and unelaborated expressions"). Subjectivity in these late ballads is no longer embedded *in* and identified with its rustic setting; rather it is *haunted* by the incipient recognition of this world as palpably anachronistic ("Simon Lee" and "Hart-Leap Well") and suffused with disquieting markers of sexual guilt and death (Lucy and Matthew poems).

It is in this context that I invoke Freud's conception of "trauma," whose distinctive symptomatic feature of "repetition compulsion" is said to respond to a past so catastrophic at the time of its original occurrence as to have precluded its conscious assimilation by the subject. As a result, an enigmatic past continues to trace the conscious history of its subject with an oblique insistence for which "haunting" seems just the right word. Subjected thus to an inscrutable (because never consciously experienced) causality, the subject is obliged, in Freud's words, "to *repeat* the . . . material as a contemporary experience instead of . . . *remembering* it as something belonging to the past," and he or she typically does so with "unwished-for exactitude" (1920, 18). As Cathy Caruth has recently argued, Freud's theory of trauma allows us "to recognize the possibility of a history that is no longer straightforwardly referential (that is, no longer based on simple models of experience and reference)"; the formal eloquence of literature may itself be taken as a "parable of trauma" and, indeed, as "a parable of psychoanalytic theory itself as it listens to a voice that it cannot fully know but to which it nonetheless bears witness" (Caruth 1996, 11, 9). Caruth's argument amounts to a new prescription for close, scrupulous reading of the literary text, and for an insistent listening to literature's characteristic tonal mix of vocal urgency and textual reticence, a dynamic of which the hybrid genre of the ballad is a particularly striking manifestation. I concur that to approach the text as "an address that remains enigmatic yet demands a listening and a response" may indeed allow "*history* . . . [to] arise where *immediate understanding* may not" (ibid., 11; emphasis in original). Like Freud's controversial account of the origin of Judaism and a distinct community of the Jewish people—for which his conception of trauma is marshaled as an analogy—Wordsworth's "Michael" remembers the disintegration of a seemingly timeless familial, economic, and spiritual order. Its story tells of the protagonist's "traumatic departure" (ibid., 15) from his phantasmagorical order of time and place. Exodus here is realized as a narrative of progressive disillusionment that continues to point back at an instance of catastrophic *méconnaissance* in the protagonist's past. As will be seen, the world of "Michael" is the kind of place where "history can be grasped only in the very inaccessibility of its occurrence" (ibid., 18).

Like his yet humbler literary and social counterpart in the 1798 *Lyrical Ballads*, Simon Lee, Wordsworth's Michael is a survivor; and like the stubborn huntsman, Michael is presented in such a way as to make us doubt that he ever fully comprehends the "accident" that he has survived. Indeed, it is only with considerable unease that we embark on our analytic quest for a knowledge that we suspect has continued to elude Wordsworth's archetypal protagonist. For right from its beginning, the poem stages our belated initiation into Michael's world with such scriptural concision as to make us shrink from obtruding with the discursive, secular agenda of "critical" reading. To persist, we feel, is to perpetrate an almost sacrilegious disturbance of the past. For the symbolic order of this "history / Homely and rude" (line 35) seems to conspire against all analytic interest and against the potential disruption of a tacit covenant between text and reader. The story of Michael, who survives the traumatic disintegration of a world of which he believed himself to be a permanent inhabitant, is designed to compel and chasten us. It does so by hinting, subtly yet persistently, at a profound connection between the psychological enigma of survival and the ethical burden of remembering. Clearly, readers are invited to premise their critical response to "Michael" on the terms so insistently furnished by the poem itself: its biblical imagery, the rhetoric of intergenerational covenant, and the opposition between country and city—itself embedded in what Geoffrey Hartman has called "an immemorial covenant between man and the land" (Hartman 1971, 265). Hartman was also among the first to view the poem's rustic idyll as besieged by the growing forces of industrialization, though he preferred to consign that threat to the periphery of the poem's ostensibly autonomous affective order. For him "Michael" is "Pastoral in the most genuine sense," a text whose "care of nature" and "of the human" has only been "heightened by the spirit of the time" (262).

More recent historicist criticism has questioned what Hartman, with critical empathy, identifies as the poem's opening mandate to the reader: namely, to separate the wheat from the chaff by discriminating sharply between spiritual and economic, familial and social, past and present matter: in short, to divide the essential (human) from the contingent (historical).[1] Where Hartman appraises Wordsworthian symbolism as the embodiment of an inalienable spiritual "knowledge" (in ways that deconstructive readings a decade later were no longer prepared to), the first exponents of a revived romantic historicism have tended to view aesthetic form as the possibly unconscious evasion of a latent social knowledge. To some extent my reading of "Michael" is aimed at a (dialectical) reconciliation of these views. As I mean to argue, what we typically subsume under the category of aesthetic form cannot but *produce* knowledge, though that knowledge (as Freud was to observe) may indeed be achieved only by the subject's persistent attempts to evade it or, at least, to evade being dominated by it. The particular narrative and symbolic organization that gives a poem like "Michael" its unmistakable character—its "form"—may thus be understood to break down a traumatic knowledge that not merely slumbers beneath the symbolic surface of Wordsworthian narrative but also conditioned the text's formal production and eventual reception. Such knowledge, at once overwhelming and inescapable, is processed at several levels in the poem, ranging from the characterization of Michael himself to the text's symbolic predetermination of the reader's performance. In what, we ask, does this knowledge consist, and why must the poem stage its experience as a dialectical process in which the formal defenses against the knowledge in question effectively turn out to be the instruments for its critical realization?

Just when the Wordsworthian still life of agrarian self-sufficiency seems complete—a pastel of "endless industry" and familial bliss realized in a cottage that "as it chanc'd . . . on rising ground / Stood single"—the balance suddenly tilts:

> Long before the time
> Of which I speak, the Shepherd had been bound
> In surety for his Brother's Son, a man
> Of an industrious life and ample means,
> But unforeseen misfortunes suddenly
> Had press'd upon him, and old Michael now
> Was summon'd to discharge the forfeiture,
> A grievous penalty, but little less
> Than half his substance.
>   (WORDSWORTH 1992a, 260, LINES 219–27)

---

1. See readings of "Michael" by [David] Simpson 1987, [Marjorie] Levinson 1986, [Susan] Eilenberg, and [Mark] Schoenfield. Levinson's account is arguably the most astute and comprehensive in its configuration of the spiritual, economic, and aesthetic dimensions of "Michael." Commenting specifically on the opening of "Michael," Levinson remarks how "this narrator, self-designated a poet, does not merely symbolize or stand in for Luke; he is Luke, reincarnated and sublimated, as it were. The reader is induced to share the narrator's vision of himself as the Son who will perpetuate Michael's line—disseminate the story and finish the sheepfold in finer tone, with language instead of stones" (74).

The shock of these disclosures is about more than economic contingencies; for Michael's seemingly incidental financial reversals also impress on us how the "hidden valley" (line 8) with its archetypal streams, its rocks and "common air" (line 66) is affiliated with the intricate and hazardous urban world of manufacture, trade, and credit-based speculation. Rather than rounding off the scene of pastoral containment with a tribute to the values of consanguinity and kinship loyalties, the family connections so belatedly and abruptly introduced into the narrative effectively reposition Michael as an unwitting participant in a historically distinctive phase of England's evolving political economy.

This recognition, at once inescapable and unbearable for Michael, warrants more precise elaboration. To begin with, Michael's embrace of agrarian self-sufficiency runs counter to the declining share of agriculture within Britain's overall national economy. As Eric Hobsbawm remarks, by 1800, agriculture "occupied no more than a third of the population and provided about the same fraction of the national income." At the same time, Michael's vision of permanent independence as a freeholder highlights the amphiboly of the terms "soil" and "landed interest" in late-eighteenth-century Britain. For another reason for the "prominence of agriculture was that the 'landed interest' dominated British politics and social life. To belong to the upper classes meant to own an estate and a 'seat.'"[2] In Wordsworth's pastoral, Michael's dominant fantasy of land-ownership seems to rest on the reverse conclusion, namely, that to own land will elevate one's social position. At the same time, Michael's tenacious commitment to this fantasy of landownership and permanent social accreditation as a freeholder also echoes a siege mentality that was beginning to spread among the agrarian producers toward the end of the century. For by then agricultural improvements were rapidly expanding productivity and thus squeezing the profits of an excessively large agrarian sector. Seen against the background of a "growing surplus of the rural poor," Wordsworth's Michael, though sensible of changes wrought in the local economy, remains unable to conceptualize their macroeconomic causes. Many of the rural poor, Michael being quite typical in this respect, thus proved "slow to abandon the life of their ancestors, the life ordained by God and fate, the only life traditional communities know or can conceive."[3]

Michael suddenly experiences the complex effects of what Adam Smith had already analyzed as a deep-structural process, "a revolution of the greatest importance to the public happiness" that was gradually brought about by "the silent and insensible operation of . . . commerce and manufactures" (1976 [1776] [vol. 1, bk. 3, chap. 4], 440). This revolution not only accounts for the gradual decline in feudal landownership and the simultaneous transmutation of landed wealth into mobile capital. It also ensured that an attachment to the older, feudal notions of inalienable property relations—underwritten not by distant markets but by consanguinity, "connections," and local knowledge—would sooner or later become a costly illusion. Smith's analyses deserve close attention, for they suggest that effective management of small estates, a skill so abundantly displayed by

2. Hobsbawm 1968, 97.
3. Hobsbawm 1968, 99.

the industrious Michael, is also an economically self-defeating proposition: "A small proprietor . . . who knows every part of his little territory, who views it with the affection which property, especially small property, naturally inspires, and who upon that account takes pleasure not only in cultivating but in adorning it, is generally of all improvers the most industrious, the most intelligent, and the most successful." At the same time, however, "the law of primogeniture, and perpetuities of different kinds" remain a powerful reality. Consequently, Smith concludes, there is at any given point in time only a very limited quantity of land available for acquisition, "so that what is sold always sells at a monopoly price. The rent never pays the interest of the purchase-money, and is besides burdened with repairs and other occasional charges." In characteristically dispassionate language, Smith thus concludes that "to purchase land is everywhere in Europe a most unprofitable employment of small capital" (ibid., 441) and, even where it does not lead to ruin, will forever consign its proprietor to economic and social marginality. A writer for the *Commercial and Agricultural Magazine* put the case rather more bluntly: "A wicked, cross-grained, petty farmer is like the sow in his yard, almost an insulated individual, who has no communication with, and therefore, no reverence for the opinion of the world."[4] Put in more genteel terms, this dismal portrait has been echoed by many contemporary historians. Remarking on the declining price of basic food costs that had resulted from increased agricultural productivity, Roy Porter sees such developments as a major factor in the growing rates of bankruptcy experienced by families that had farmed their lands for generations. His characterization of the pressures felt by late-eighteenth-century small farmers could well serve as a plot summary for Wordsworth's "Michael." "Minor gentry and freeholders unable to diversify felt the pinch most. Many farmers went out of business, otherwise got into debt . . . rents fell into arrears, or had to be lowered, some farms became tenantless, and incomes in the landed sector stagnated or dropped" (Porter, 203–4).

By 1800, the cult of "improvement" had largely faded, but Smith's 1776 analyses of small freeholders' habitual overestimating of the value of landed property (and so subscribing to an illusion bound to undermine their economic base) remained valid. The "distressful tidings" that suddenly reach Michael's ear cannot, then, be written off as mere contingencies. Rather, they confront Michael with the traumatic recognition that his lifelong pursuit of agrarian self-sufficiency has, literally, been a bad investment of his only capital—many decades of arduous physical labor.[5] At the same time, the deceptive simplicity of a life spent plowing patrimonial fields and shearing flocks of sheep under the "Clipping Tree" has effectively prevented Michael from recognizing that, although he has sought to fortify his life against the impingements of urban commerce and speculation by his labor, he has involved himself in much larger and infinitely more complex economic realities. Michael's life illustrates what

---

4. Quoted in [E.P.] Thompson [*The Making of the English Working Class*] 1966, 219.
5. In dramatizing the tension between the illusory time of Michael's lived history and the recognition of that history as an illusion—as merely "empty," chronological time—the poem anticipates a figure of thought that was to be fully articulated in the philosophy of the later Schelling. * * *

Pierre Bourdieu calls the "homogeneity of habitus," an "immanent law, *lex insita,* laid down in each agent by his earliest upbringing, which is the precondition . . . for the co-ordination of practices" (Bourdieu 80–81). Like the Lacanian unconscious, the "objective intention" of such a habitus resembles the structure of a complex language that conditions the "actions," "works," and "conscious intentions" (ibid., 79) of individuals and, for that very reason, falls outside the range of subjective understanding. Consequently, Bourdieu insists, one must safeguard against "all forms of the occasionalist illusion which consists in directly relating practices to properties inscribed in [a given] situation." In truth, "interpersonal relations are never, except in appearance, *individual-to-individual* relationships and . . . the truth of the interaction is never entirely contained in the interaction" (ibid., 81). The latter point is especially germane to Wordsworth's poem. For in choosing to underwrite his nephew's economic ventures in the city, Michael characteristically and dangerously confuses familial and economic motives by assisting the extended family with a show of financial support. What may have been a gesture of loyalty, however, also amounts, however unwittingly, to a risky investment of the very returns yielded by decades of unalienated labor. As Michael now finds, the risk extends all the way to his very "substance."

With the day of Luke's departure drawing near, Michael offers his son a revealing account of his long and inconclusive march to economic independence:

> 'tis a long time to look back, my Son,
> And see so little gain from sixty years.
> These fields were burthen'd when they came to me,
> 'Till I was forty years of age, not more
> Than half of my inheritance was mine.
> I toil'd and toil'd; God bless'd me in my work
> And 'till these three weeks past the land was free.
> (WORDSWORTH 1992a, 265, LINES 382–88)

Even now, that is, Michael cannot acknowledge that the land was only ever "free" in a highly conditional sense. Nor does he seem fully conscious of the fact that the imperiled status of "half his substance" is the result of his own vicarious involvement in a market economy whose financial logic continues to elude him. This structural illusion or "blind love" (line 78) at the heart of Michael's conception of property, and his consequent incapacity to recognize that his entire adult life has been predicated on that very illusion, leads to a series of peculiar decisions that effectively repeat the original *méconnaissance.*[6] Begotten late and, it seems, groomed strictly for the role of the heir to whom Michael could bequeath his landed property, Luke constitutes in his father's imaginary a repetition of his own life: "from the Boy there came / Feelings and emanations / . . . / that the Old Man's Heart seem'd born again" (lines 210–14).

6. The poem's diction is itself effectively an encryption of the fundamentally ambivalent status of the land; thus Michael tells Luke that he wishes to bequeath his land "free as the wind / That passes over it." For a reading of the multiple ambiguities in these lines, see Levinson 1986, 70.

Now, following the discovery of his land's impending seizure by distant creditors—and, along with it, the traumatic shock of having to recognize his entire economic and familial history as a prolonged illusion—Michael chooses to put up Luke as collateral for what was to be his landed inheritance. In so entrusting his son to yet "another kinsman" in the city—who once again is presumed to be "a prosperous man / Thriving in trade" (lines 259–60)—Michael uncannily repeats the very act that had led to his present insolvency. Lest we miss the point, Wordsworth interpolates Isabel's daydream of one Richard Bateman, who "with a Basket on his arm" was sent to London and, having been successfully apprenticed, grew "wondrous rich" and returned to adorn the chapel of his birthplace with "marble" floors (lines 266–80). Isabel's generic reverie ("These thoughts and many others of like sort / Pass'd quickly through the mind of Isabel" [lines 281–82]), so evocative of connections between capitalism and romance, only stages at a more transparent level what, at bottom, are also Michael's defensive illusions. The circular pattern continues as Michael, prior to Luke's departure, rededicates himself to initiating his son into a life that will essentially repeat Michael's own, as well as the lives of his ancestors: "I wish'd that thou should'st live the life they liv'd," he tells Luke, and he affirms the intergenerational covenant by noting that "herein / I but repay a gift which I myself / Receiv'd at others' hands" (lines 381, 372–74).

Finally, there is the "Sheep-fold" itself, so programmatically hailed as "An emblem of the life thy Fathers liv'd," as "anchor" and "shield," a wall devised both to contain the property within and to keep at bay the entropic world without. Indeed, the sheepfold is at once the very heart of Michael's illusion *and* the object that will precipitate his awakening to the illusory character of his economic and familial "habitus." For as an attempt at enclosure, the wall intimates the land's implicit status as a form of capital rather than as inalienable "soil." At the same time, Michael's preoccupation with enclosing his patrimonial field constitutes the objective expression of a deeply personal and genealogical covenant between himself, his son, and what he considers to be an immutable nature. The ambivalent status of the sheepfold—at once material evidence of the encroaching capitalist forms of agrarian production and symbolic evidence of an anti-modern, defensive mode of being—exemplifies what Anthony Giddens has described as the modern disjunction of space and place:

> In pre-modern societies, space and place largely coincide, since the spatial dimensions of social life are, for most of the population, and in most respects, dominated by "presence"—by localised activities. . . . The advent of modernity increasingly tears space away from place by fostering relations between "absent" others, locationally distant from any given situation of face-to-face interaction. In conditions of modernity, place becomes increasingly *phantasmagorical:* that is to say, locales are thoroughly penetrated by and shaped in terms of social influences quite distant from them. What structures the locale is not simply that which is present on the scene; the "visible form" of the locale conceals the distanciated relations which determine its nature. (Giddens, [*The Consequences of Modernity* (1990)], 18–19)

Like all *phantasmata*, however, the sheepfold—as well as the elaborate archetypal world of Michael's household and the "hidden valley" to which it stands in synecdochic relation—constitutes no mere illusion. For even as it throws into relief Michael's devotion to labor and an intergenerational covenant, the sheepfold also facilitates the reader's gradual awakening to the protagonist's inescapable modernity. For as the narrative progresses, readers become more acutely conscious of the disjunction of space from place described by Giddens. Rather than functioning as an intact symbol, that is, the sheepfold progressively unveils and so demystifies its architect's overinvestment in a homespun, defensive symbolism. Furthermore, when considered as the summa of the entire collection of *Lyrical Ballads,* the crisis of the sheepfold—namely, that soil and land no longer coincide with the space in which property relations constitute themselves—also throws into relief the preceding ballads' apparent overinvestment in oral and folk culture. In short, the crisis of Michael the protagonist is also expressive of limitations intrinsic to the ballad genre and, hence, of the relative modernity of the romantic lyric.[7]

* * *

KAREN SWANN

From Suffering and Sensation in *The Ruined Cottage*[†]

Chancing on a haunted ruin, an overheated youth meets an old man who sees things that others cannot see and who tells him the story of a suffering woman—a tale that raises the dead and makes the youth's blood run cold. This is the plot of Wordsworth's *Ruined Cottage,* which, critics agree, is expressly not the sort of narrative my summary would evoke. The peddler himself makes this point, in a speech often taken to be Wordsworth's ventriloquistic defense of his own project:

> It were a wantonness, and would demand
> Severe reproof, if we were men whose hearts
> Could hold vain dalliance with the misery
> Even of the dead, contented thence to draw
> A momentary pleasure never marked
> By reason, barren of all future good.
> But we have known that there is often found
> In mournful thoughts, and always might be found,
> A power to virtue friendly; were't not so,
> I am a dreamer among men—indeed
> An idle dreamer. 'Tis a common tale,
> By moving accidents uncharactered,
> A tale of silent suffering, hardly clothed

---

7. "[T]ruly modern poetry is a poetry that has become aware of the incessant conflict that opposes a self, still engaged in the daylight world of reality, of representation, and of life, to what Yeats calls the soul," Paul de Man writes in "Lyric and Modernity" (de Man 1983, 171). "Translated into terms of poetic diction, this implies that modern poetry uses an imagery that is both symbol and allegory, that represents objects in nature but is actually taken from purely literary sources."

† From *PMLA* 106 (1991): 83–95. Notes have been remembered. Reprinted by permission of the Modern Language Society of America.

> In bodily form, and to the grosser sense
> But ill adapted, scarcely palpable
> To him who does not think.   (280–95)[1]

Already informing this poetic defense is a distinction that becomes central to Wordsworth's 1800 Preface to *Lyrical Ballads*—between, on the one hand, a degraded sensational literature that wantonly dallies with misery for the delight of grosser sense and, on the other, the scarcely palpable, yet powerfully antidotal, charms of the new poetry of suffering.

The peddler's tale would translate a woman's local and insupportable misery into food for virtuous thought. Critics have tended to cast Wordsworth's project in similar terms, without, however, necessarily agreeing on the value of such a translation. In the past the poem has been widely celebrated as a controlled, dispassionate response to human suffering; more recently, though, Jerome McGann has criticized its "displacement" of attention from the historical determinants of Margaret's pain—the costly American war, the decline of small farming and the cottage industry in England, the system of impressment, and so on—onto her exemplary, idealized figure and the moral education of the reader (81–85). For McGann this displacement underpins the "grand illusion" of Romanticism, "the idea that poetry, or even consciousness, can set one free of the ruins of history and culture" (91). I do not want to contest McGann's account of Wordsworth's use of the rural poor; but I do want to point out that to characterize Wordsworth's poetry of the late 1790s as either "transcending" or "suppressing" history and culture (or even as holding out this possibility for poetry) is to overlook the work's obvious engagement with one particular social field, the literary marketplace. Hearing the Preface's polemic in the peddler's speech reminds us that as an experiment with genre the poem sharply and directly confronts a public taste for sensational literature—a taste that by 1800 had become for Wordsworth the locus of a host of displaced anxieties about modernity and, indeed, the very sign of "the ruins of history and culture."

Furthermore, the peddler's equivocal definition of his own project—it "*were* a wantonness," it "*would* demand," "*if* we were men"—hints that *The Ruined Cottage* may be more complexly situated with respect to the public taste than has previously been acknowledged. In the pages that follow I use *The Ruined Cottage* to explore Wordsworth's powerful and uneasy collusion with the nascent mass culture of the late 1790s. I begin by considering the technical innovations that distinguish Wordsworth's poetry of suffering from the popular fiction his poems habitually engage: his use of a mediating narrative consciousness to interpose distance between the reader and the narrative of suffering—thus encouraging a meditative rather than a stimulated response to painful events—and his invention of a "technical apparatus," or complex narrative frame, that would throw attention to narrative acts themselves and thus invite the public to reflect on its own investments in sensationalism. I propose that each of these innovations borrows from the tactics, and produces the effects, of the literature Wordsworth expressly challenges—that the ped-

---

1. Unless otherwise specified, all quotations from *The Ruined Cottage* are taken from the reading text of ms. B in Butler and are identified by line numbers. Butler is also the source of quotations from *The Pedlar* and "Incipient Madness."

dler's often celebrated distance from the story of the abandoned woman is purchased through gothic technique and that the apparatus Wordsworth develops to regulate untoward responses to representations itself elicits a fascinated response. Finally I suggest that the technical innovations in *The Ruined Cottage* allow Wordsworth to deploy a popular, feminine narrative machinery without becoming identified with a popular audience. Intended to appeal to an already constructed public of extravagantly passionate, feminized readers, his narrative apparatus simultaneously creates the readers-to-be of high Romantic poetry—an audience whose pleasure it is to exist at a small distance from the captivated feminine heart.

I

Margaret stems as much from literature as from life, and most immediately from the hosts of abandoned and suffering women who people sensational fiction and monthly-magazine poetry of the late eighteenth century (J. Wordsworth 50–67; Jacobus 159–72; Averill; Mayo). But critics agree in seeing a difference between these stock figures and the heroine of *The Ruined Cottage* (or its later avatars), a difference that for many hinges on the distance between the peddler and Margaret. For these readers the peddler's objectivity and self-control allow him to function as a screen that accurately represents Margaret's suffering while tempering our potentially morbid or wanton responses to it (Manning 207; Sheats 139, 150).

Yet the peddler's distance from Margaret must be purchased, and the price, I would argue, is a sensationalizing of the abandoned woman. If when telling the story of Margaret the peddler seems to maintain mobility and equanimity in the face of loss, in his role within the story he is at first overinvolved with his subject, his orbits influenced by her comings and goings. Recalling his first visit to the cottage after learning of Robert's departure, he dwells on an unsettling experience of abandonment. Margaret is not at home when he arrives, so he sits down to wait where "now" he and his auditor sit. But she has taken to wandering far, as he later discovers. Her desertion of home effects his domestication, the shrinking of his "rounds" to a constricted circling. For an hour he wastes out his abandonment ("Ere this an hour / Was wasted") with "impatience," restlessly pacing to and fro ("back I turned / My restless steps"), increasingly feeling the "desolation" of the spot, at one point conjuring a stranger who brings him word of "whom [he] sought" ("And as I walked before the door it chanced / A stranger passed, and guessing whom I sought / He said that she was used to wander far") (361–87).

Abandonment can befall anyone.[2] Perhaps a recognition of this sort informs the peddler's subsequent distancing of Margaret, who reappears, apparitionlike, at the stroke of the hour, as a "changed" and wasted figure:

> The church-clock struck eight;
> I turn'd and saw her distant a few steps.

---

2. See Wolfson 106–07 for a related claim that the peddler's vigilance against overnear responses to suffering is prompted by the intensity of his identification with Margaret.

> Her face was pale and thin, her figure too
> Was changed.   (394–97)

Earlier, alone in the garden, the peddler had been measuring the "change" in Margaret's circumstances (362–72); now, Margaret decisively crystallizes and contains change in her vitiated body. Yet this body becomes a fresh enigma. Margaret herself first casts her change as an uncanny, dehumanizing difference:

> "I am changed,
> And to myself," said she, "have done much wrong,
> And to this helpless infant. I have slept
> Weeping, and weeping I have waked; my tears
> Have flowed as if my body were not such
> As others are, and I could never die.["]   (405–10)

Changed to an ever-wasting, emblematic body, Margaret fascinates and eludes the peddler's powerful eye, which "look[s] deep into the shades of difference / As they lie hid in all exterior forms" (95–96) but finds itself strangely impotent to penetrate this "subdued" figure and its "trick of grief" (419, 449):

> still she sighed,
> But yet no motion of the breast was seen,
> No heaving of the heart. While by the fire
> We sate together, sighs came on my ear;
> I knew not how and hardly whence they came.
>   (422–26)

Margaret returns as a ghost of her former self. Arguably, the peddler's account of her mechanically going through the motions is an accurately observed representation of her suffering. But one might equally argue that his narrative works to transform her human body into an eerily inspirited simulacrum of a body—or, in more tendentious words, into a gothic spirit.[3] Abstractedness continues to shadow Margaret, until, at the end of the tale, she lingers on the peddler's eye as an unquiet thing:

> I have heard, my Friend,
> That in that broken arbour she would sit
> The idle length of half a sabbath day,
> There—where you see the toadstool's lazy head—
> And when a dog passed by she still would quit
> The shade and look abroad. On this old Bench
> For hours she sate, and evermore her eye
> Was busy in the distance, shaping things
> Which made her heart beat quick. Seest thou that path?
> (The greensward now has broken its grey line)
> There, to and fro she paced through many a day
> Of the warm summer, from a belt of flax
> That girt her waist spinning the long-drawn thread
> With backward steps.   (485–98)

---

3. In this context see Jacobus's description of Margaret as a "hinterland" character who exists between the human and the nonhuman (177).

This detailed portrait is often and justly hailed for the way it lends concreteness and naturalness to the stock figure of the abandoned woman. Yet a reader attentive to the drift of the peddler's successive portraits of Margaret can also see, in this portrait of Margaret as human bobbin, the final turn of a reductive narrative machinery.

*   *   *

As other readers have shown, one need not enlist Freud when teasing out the poem's fascination with the mother; one need only go to Wordsworth's "Incipient Madness," originally drafted as part of *The Ruined Cottage* (Manning 197–201; Schapiro 124–25). I quote its opening lines:

> I cross'd the dreary moor
> In the clear moonlight; when I reached the hut
> I enter'd in, but all was still and dark—
> Only within the ruin I beheld
> At a small distance, on the dusky ground,
> A broken pane which glitter'd in the moon
> And seemed akin to life. There is a mood,
> A settled temper of the heart, when grief,
> Become an instinct, fastening on all things
> That promise food, doth like a sucking babe
> Create it where it is not. From this time
> I found my sickly heart had tied itself
> Even to this speck of glass. It could produce
> A feeling as of absence [   ]
> [   ] on the moment when my sight
> Should feed on it again. Many a long month
> Confirm'd this strange incontinence. . . .
>
>   (1–17)

Margaret is here reduced to vanishing: her to and fro, her shaping eye, her eerily lifelike sighing resolve into the merest pulse or glitter of a speck of glass, one in a chain of revenants that grief, "like a sucking babe" and possibly in a constant reenactment of that early loss, creates to compensate for abandonment.

Reading the peddler's treatment of Margaret through this fragment at the gothic limits of *The Ruined Cottage* suggests that there is method, and a poetic value, to his bouts of incipient madness, to those moments when his untoward investments in the tale seem to threaten its collapse into the poetry of sensation. For the speaker's distance from and mastery of his subject—the distance that is often claimed to ensure the difference between the poetry of suffering and the poetry of sensation—is achieved by gothic means, by the depersonalization, mechanization, and ghosting of persons. Yet "Incipient Madness," which with equal justice could have been called "The Mother's Curse," also suggests some of the pitfalls of this use of gothic technique. In psychoanalytic terms, the babe's triumph is also its betrayal into the strange incontinence of desire, into an abandoned and never-satisfied craving for phantasmic signs. In the terms of Wordsworth's 1800 Preface, at the gothic limits of the poem it is the most reduced of Margaret figures—one "changed" to a "speck" without even "bodily form"—that enslaves the observer to sense, betrays him into a craving for representation. In Wordsworth's poem, as in sensational literature itself as popularly construed, the tactical deployment of gothic technique would seem to risk the tactician's captivation by a fascinating technics.

II

* * *

In *The Ruined Cottage* Wordsworth personifies the coordinates of his technical apparatus and then partly dismantles the machine, giving independent causes to the poet's wanderings, the peddler's rounds, and Margaret's restless pacing and shaping. But from the perspective of "Incipient Madness," these efforts to subordinate a captivating technics to the aesthetic discipline of realism are madness full-blown, for they grant autonomy to a figure whose effective life derives from the eye's investment in the material projection of a technical apparatus. This is the delusion into which we fall when praising the reality of Margaret—a delusion that the poem at once fosters and challenges, as, for example, in the peddler's description of his tale:

> 'Tis a common tale,
> By moving accidents uncharactered,
> A tale of silent suffering, hardly clothed
> In bodily form, and to the grosser sense
> But ill adapted, scarcely palpable
> To him who does not think.   (290–95)

In the 1800 Preface Wordsworth distinguishes his characters from personifications of abstract ideas, claiming he "want[s] to keep [his] Reader in the company of flesh and blood" (161)—an odd statement from the creator of the *mutilés* of the *Lyrical Ballads*, that ragtag assortment of knotted joints, withered arms, swollen ankles, and rattling bones. Here, though, the insistence is on the near disembodiment of the tale's human forms. We can take this passage as a ventriloquized assertion of the poem's difference from the literature of sensation, which according to detractors is always too fleshly or too ghostly. But the description of Margaret—who exists throughout the poem as neither flesh nor apparition but abstract person, personified geometric coordinate, sign mysteriously "akin to life"—also identifies her as the irreducible remainder of a fascinating technics that endures through all efforts to gentle or abandon it.

Margaret is the remainder of a representational economy that the poetry of suffering would gentle. But if she figures the ineluctability of representation itself, she also alludes to an enormously popular representation, the abandoned woman. Earlier I proposed that the poem's gendered plot is a secondary construction, that the abstracted figure of Margaret derives, not from the mother, but from a technical apparatus. Yet the question of gender of course remains: why should Wordsworth invoke *this* figure and *this* plot in his poetic study of "every man" captivated by an unmasterable technics? The answer lies not so much in every subject's experience of the maternal, I would argue, as in the particular shape of late-eighteenth-century literary culture, where Wordsworth's was just one among many voices displacing a range of anxieties about the power of representations in a technological age onto a nascent mass public, a public often identified with popular sensational fiction, feminine characters and plots, and a feminine or feminized audience. In *The Ruined Cottage* Wordsworth does not in any simple way deploy a feminine plot to reinforce a social agenda involving the domestication of popular or feminine subjects. Rather, he adopts a familiar narrative machinery because it can function culturally as an allusion to gender and class and particularly to a certain class of feminine readers; and his poetic practices, instead of working consistently to naturalize the social, tend to acknowledge as a technics—as a captivating representational economy— phenomena that socially powerful narratives seek to naturalize. I want to speculate that the intended effect is to challenge the work of ideology, but in a way that returns power to the poet as commercial traveler. This poet has his eye on one social phenomenon, the market, a reading public whose social divisions *The Ruined Cottage* hardens, questions, and exploits by removing the taint of "sensationalism," now understood as a class of fictions, from the popular classless world of the poem and from the class of the poet's idealized readers and yet by capitalizing on a technics with a proven mass appeal.

III

* * *

An admittedly perverse reading of *The Ruined Cottage* through the looking glass might begin with a glance at the telling succession of figures that appear within the cottage's ruined walls. A profitless poet finds therein a companionable form, a peddler, who most agree is an idealized version of the Wordsworthian poet.[4] A teller of traditional tales, a man speaking to men, he creates a "world" from the stuff of life:

> Though poor in outward shew, he was most rich;
> He had a world about him—'twas his own,
> He made it—for it only lived to him
> And to the God who looked into his mind.
>
> (86–89)

This world is most obviously the rural, natural one of *The Ruined Cottage*. But if in his leisure time the peddler is a man speaking to men, he is also a commercial traveler selling his wares to "maids who live . . . / In lonely villages or straggling huts" (45–46). In the light of this professional life, the images nested like Chinese boxes within the *camera* of his mind are provocative, for in Wordsworth's culture they function almost as shorthand allusions to the literary marketplace: a domestic interior and, within its walls, the oddly fascinating character of an abandoned woman and, finally, there where glittering objects are wont to appear, the library of a female reader, which the peddler lingers over on his second visit to Margaret after Robert's departure:

> The windows they were dim, and her few books,
> Which one upon the other heretofore

4. My understanding of these figures as the projections of an apparatus is influenced by Parker, who, in discussing the opening of the poem, examines the (to my mind gothically) overwrought character of the poet, describes hut and peddler as "apparitionlike," and analyzes the peddler as a version of the poet's "dreaming man."

> Had been piled up against the corner panes
> In seemly order, now with straggling leaves
> Lay scattered here and there, open or shut
> As they had chanced to fall.   (443–48)

Outside the leaves are "straggling" too, suggesting the natural world's encroachment on the human (377). Inside, though, the cultural would seem to encroach on the natural—on what is sometimes suggested to be Margaret's particularly close bond to nature and on the felt immediacy of her responses to loss. I meant to trouble these assumptions about Margaret's naturalness by claiming her as the remainder of a fascinating technics. But pausing over this series of culturally overdetermined representations helps us recall that if Margaret figures something excessive in representation itself, she also belongs to a line of charged, often gendered images that represent that excess as the sway popular literature exerts over the reading public.[5] Seen through the glass of *Peter Bell*, Margaret's cottage is the spot where the world the poet emphatically makes reflects the world in which he makes his living, the spot where what Wordsworth calls rustic life—a culture in which all, but particularly the abandoned woman, enjoy a privileged relation to nature—fleetingly betrays its engagement with a literary culture whose excesses are often, but not always, represented and provoked by feminine figures.

That is, in the world of *The Ruined Cottage* as elsewhere, exorbitant effects crystallize around, but do not solely befall, the figure of the woman. Although the poem is set in the country and its events begin ten years in the past, the society the peddler invokes is afflicted by the economic crisis and the attendant alienated aesthetics that Wordsworth associates with modernity. The first stricken is Robert. In a time when "shoals of artisans" are losing work, a "fever" consumes his "stores"; his symptomatic response is a dissociation of sensibility (he "whistled many a snatch of merry tunes / That had no mirth in them" [215–16]), a craving for incident (he takes to wandering), and a love of novelty and ornament ("with his knife [he] / Carved uncouth figures on the heads of sticks" [216–17]).[6] Margaret is next to exhibit symptoms of the urban disease— paleness, constant sighing, a neglect of industry for profitless fantasy. Most damning of all, she has been reading. But what? A humble cottage might well possess the Bible, to which Coleridge attributes the elevated habits of speech and mind Wordsworth found in his statesmen. But Margaret's paleness and sighs, the lassitude and compulsiveness hinted at by her books' disorder, imply other, less wholesome food—fare more like that on which the peddler feasted in his family home. Versed in traditionary tales, he has "small need of books," we are told in *The Pedlar*:

> But greedily he read, and read again
> Whate'er the Minister's old Shelf supplied,

5. For a discussion of the popularity of the abandoned woman in 1798, see Mayo's contention that "bereaved mothers and deserted females were almost a rage" in the magazine literature of the 1790s (496).
6. Simpson locates Wordsworth's depiction of Robert's malaise in the context of the poet's concern about the effects on independent artisans of the decline of England's cottage industry (192–93); I found Simpson's broad argument about Wordsworth's resistance to an ascendant luxury economy helpful to my thinking about the poet's complicated relation to the economy and tastes that condition his own success.

> The life and death of Martyrs who sustain'd
> Intolerable pangs, and here and there
> A straggling volume torn and incomplete
> That left half-told the preternatural tale,
> Romance of Giants, Chronicle of Fiends,
> Profuse in garniture of wooden cuts,
> Strange and uncouth, . . .
>   forms which once seen
> Co[uld never be forgotten.]   (158, 164–74)

Here we may have found not simply the plausible contents of Margaret's library but a plausible vehicle of the disease that circulates through the world of *The Ruined Cottage.* For the language of this description, "straggling" across the drafts of 1798–1800 and from the peddler's childhood home to Margaret's "straggling" hut, marks Robert's "strange" behavior and "uncouth" wood carving and Margaret's "straggling" leaves.[7]

For Wordsworth there is no shame attached to reading the old romances and tales of martyrs. Their hinted circulation here is nonetheless slightly unsettling to the status of the peddler's traditionary tale. What if the peddler's constructions are shaped less by Margaret's life or by his own lived experience than by unforgettable stories of martyrs who "sustain'd / Intolerable pangs" and of "ghostly," "dire" figures of romance? What if Margaret has been reading the same stories and, under their spell, casting a life buffeted by rapacious state economic and foreign policies as a more private tale of suffering, changing herself into the emblematic, eternally weeping figure of the romantic martyr? Possibly all the characters in *The Ruined Cottage* are complicit in the production of a modern Gothic. In the middle of the poem both peddler and poet find themselves agitated, and the peddler breaks off: "Why should we thus . . . [feed] on disquiet?" (251–55). It is at this moment that the poet, already introduced to us as a man prone to sensibility, his blood chilled (271), finds himself sway to a "taste" for more of the same (264–65). Poet's and peddler's shared, muted frisson teasingly suggests that the story of Margaret, told as an antidote to a corrupted modern taste, may also feed that taste. Even more teasingly—in the kind of teasing we associate with postmodernism—the similarity between their responses to Margaret and her own disquiet invites us to wonder whether she herself battens on tales like the story of Margaret—tales perhaps brought to her by the peddler, who circulates with his wares among maids.

A postmodern reading might applaud this narrative exorbitancy as Wordsworth at his most radically self-reflexive. Yet it is also possible to see in this submerged portrait of a community of readers one more circulation of a culture's anxious representation of the effects of certain popular books. We know this representation from Wordsworth's attack on sensational fiction in the 1800 Preface, which raises the specter of a public passionately cleaving to the sensationalized signs an alienated, self-perpetuating technology reproduces (159–60). Wordsworth's linking

---

7. Ferguson points out that this is a landscape littered with books (222). I hope to connect this
    emphasis on reading, which she persuasively elaborates, to Wordsworth's anxieties about the
    market in which he will be read. Wolfson also notes this passage, arguing that the peddler's
    distance can be seen as a defense against potential revivals of an earlier appetite for sensa-
    tional fiction (101).

of this threat to "a multitude of causes unknown to former times," such as urbanization, political upheaval, and the ascendency of a mass media, suggests that popular representations of a dangerous literature gather urgency from less easily focused anxieties about the power of ideologies—the ideas a culture impregnates with passion—in an age of mass communication. Does *The Ruined Cottage* simply reproduce, in its obverse mirror, Wordsworth's and his culture's anxieties about the excessive power of sensational literature? Or is the poem also a self-reflexive study of this idea?

Coming from a different direction, my questions touch on issues raised by recent explorations of the politics of Wordsworth's poetry, work that has frequently focused on his portrayals of women. Addressing the ideological stakes of the poetry of suffering, historicist and feminist critics have been pointing out what should have been obvious—that the distribution of labor in Wordsworth's poetry between those who contemplate suffering and those who suffer, die, or incorporate into a natural order mirrors an unequal distribution of mobility and power within his culture at large. *The Ruined Cottage* is no exception to the general rule, as Margaret Homans and Marlon Ross have persuasively shown. In Wordsworth's poetry, as in his culture, the woman's function is to naturalize ideology, presenting as real what is in fact a widely propagated construction of reality (Homans 20–25; Ross). Thus, paradoxically, the more Wordsworth tries to realize the abandoned woman fully and sympathetically, the more firmly he locates himself on the side of delusion or false consciousness; the poem becomes one more episode in the circulation of received ideas. But what of the self-reflexive Wordsworth, the poet of the apparatus, who habitually undoes the work of realism—who obtrudes poetic machinery, exposes the "natural" body of the suffering woman as a passionately invested sign, hints that the power of the story of Margaret derives from a circulating-library effect? If this is the Wordsworth we see shaping *The Ruined Cottage*, does it follow that his poem should be aligned, not with the recirculation of socially powerful ideas, but with the demystification of ideological effects?

But as we have discovered, it is not always possible to draw the line between a study and a passionate reenactment of fascination, and the figure that obtrudes its mechanism can be the most sensationally seductive of all. The inevitable complicity between the self-reflexive poem and the tastes the work challenges causes Wordsworth anxiety during his labor on *The Ruined Cottage*; perhaps adding to that anxiety is an awareness that the poem achieves its power by exploiting that complicity, through its treatment of the woman. For the poet who reflects on the operation of cultural ideas recognizes that the abandoned woman is not invoked to contain woman's excessive power; rather, the woman extravagantly attached to the signifiers of absence serves to figure, domesticate, and provoke the passions that characterize all relations between subjects and signs. She allows the reader to find "at a small distance"—the distance that only increases fascination—the captivated heart. By reproducing this figure in a way that invites our reflection on it, Wordsworth creates a poem that glitters, that changes in the light, that by turns entices and reproves untoward readerly appetites.

During the decline of the cottage industry and the ascendency of a luxury economy, the poet's stores are the tales of that decline, a fabric

Wordsworth weaves, "alters" and "refits" with the help of numerous femi-
nine hands (Butler 25). That he imagines capturing the market he also
challenges is suggested by *The Ruined Cottage*'s slightly wishful adum-
bration of two possible paths of the peddler's stores: in one a traditionary
tale passes in a kind of literary inheritance from a peddler, a "chosen
son," to *his* chosen son, a masculine poet; in the other a peddler circu-
lates his wares among "maids"—cultural shorthand for all the innocents
who become swept up in passions they thought they were only studying.

*   *   *

Works Cited

Averill, James H. *Wordsworth and the Poetry of Human Suffering.* Ithaca:
Cornell UP, 1980.

Butler, James, ed. The Ruined Cottage *and* The Pedlar. By William
Wordsworth. Ithaca: Cornell UP, 1979.

Coleridge, Samuel Taylor. *The Notebooks of Samuel Taylor Coleridge.* Ed.
Kathleen Coburn. Vol. 3. Bollingen Series 50. Princeton: Princeton
UP, 1973.

Ferguson, Frances. *Wordsworth: Language as Counter-spirit.* New Haven:
Yale UP, 1977.

Homans, Margaret. *Woman Writers and Poetic Identity: Dorothy Words-
worth, Emily Brontë, and Emily Dickinson.* Princeton: Princeton UP,
1980.

Jacobus, Mary. *Tradition and Experiment in Wordsworth's Lyrical Ballads
(1798).* Oxford: Clarendon, 1976.

Manning, Peter J. "Wordsworth, Margaret, and the Pedlar." *Studies in
Romanticism* 15 (1976): 195–220.

Mayo, Robert. "The Contemporaneity of the *Lyrical Ballads.*" *PMLA* 69
(1954): 486–522.

McGann, Jerome J. *The Romantic Ideology: A Critical Investigation.* Chi-
cago: U of Chicago P, 1983.

Owen, W. J. B., ed. *Lyrical Ballads, 1798.* By William Wordsworth. 2nd
ed. Oxford: Oxford UP, 1969.

Parker, Reeve. "'Finer-Distance': The Narrative Art of Wordsworth's 'The
Wanderer.'" *ELH* 39 (1972): 87–111.

Ross, Marlon B. "Naturalizing Gender: Woman's Place in Wordsworth's
Ideological Landscape." *ELH* 53 (1986): 391–410.

Schapiro, Barbara. *The Romantic Mother: Narcissistic Patterns in Roman-
tic Poetry.* Baltimore: Johns Hopkins UP, 1983.

Sheats, Paul D. *The Making of Wordsworth's Poetry, 1785–1798.* Cam-
bridge: Harvard UP, 1973.

Simpson, David. *Wordsworth's Historical Imagination: The Poetry of Dis-
placement.* New York: Methuen, 1987.

Wolfson, Susan J. *The Questioning Presence: Wordsworth, Keats, and the
Interrogative Mode in Romantic Poetry.* Ithaca: Cornell UP, 1986.

Wordsworth, Jonathan. *The Music of Humanity: A Critical Study of Words-
worth's Ruined Cottage.* New York: Harper, 1969.

Wordsworth, William. "Incipient Madness." Butler 468–69.

———. Note to "The Thorn." Owen 138–41.

———. *The Pedlar.* Butler 382–449.

———. *Peter Bell.* Ed. John E. Jordan. Ithaca: Cornell UP, 1985.
———. Preface. Owen 153–79.
———. *The Ruined Cottage.* Butler 42–75.

STUART CURRAN

[Wordsworth's Sonnets][†]

*   *   *

To give Wordsworth his due, he sat by while every bard of his acquaintance was hatching sonnets, thinking the results, or so he recalled much later, "egregiously absurd" (*WLLY*, I, 71). His belated entry into the field is all the more remarkable for its having been deserted by every one of its previous champions. By the end of the first decade of the nineteenth century, shortly after Wordsworth's first sonnets were published, the sonnet had regained the low esteem it had held through most of the eighteenth century, its recent history being held by more than one critic a key to a vitiated public taste:

> Formerly (we speak not of the times of Elizabeth and James) few attempted it, and still fewer succeeded. But the present race of poetasters have made ample amends for this blank in our literature. Attracted by its brevity and supposed facility, and probably not a little dazzled by the meretricious ornament of which it has been found to be susceptible, every rhyming schoolboy and love-sick girl now give their crude effusions to the public under the denomination of sonnets. The press teems with volumes of this description, and unless another Censor shall "sweep the swarm away," in all probability the evil will progressively increase until it become a real disgrace to British Literature.[1]

Against this swarm, or perhaps in Olympian disregard of it, Wordsworth wrote and published his sonnets. The forty-seven "Miscellaneous Sonnets" and "Sonnets Dedicated to Liberty," published in the *Poems, in Two Volumes* of 1807, represent the most significant recasting of the form since Milton.

And yet, when Wordsworth turned to the form in 1802 to begin an involvement that is unparalleled in English literature, however independent of the school of the 1790s he held himself, was it possible for him not to have recalled Coleridge's ventures, whether for his friend's excesses or his limited achievements? This supposition is materially strengthened when it is recognized that virtually all the sonnets printed in the *Poems, in Two Volumes,* already separated into two parts, were transcribed early in 1804 for the notebook that Coleridge was to take with him on his excursion to Malta. One of those sonnets, the thirteenth of the "Sonnets

---

† From *Poetic Form and British Romanticism* (New York: Oxford Univ. Press, 1986), 39–49. © 1986 by Oxford University Press. Notes have been renumbered. Reprinted by permission.
1. *Quarterly Review,* 2 (November 1809), 281–a review by John Hoppner of William Lisle Bowles's *Poems, Never Before Published.* Hoppner appears to echo the complaint of Mary Robinson***, but she directs her criticism at a misuse of the form by novice poets, not to its contents.

Dedicated to Liberty" ("O Friend! I know not which way I must look"), was originally addressed to Coleridge and would have extended the personal frame of reference already established by the partial manuscript of *The Prelude* that was also prepared for the notebook.[2]

Two writings in Coleridge's career as author of sonnets are of particular interest for Wordsworth's later endeavors: the "Sonnets on Eminent Characters" and the "Introduction to the Sonnets." Whatever their lapses in an ultimate scale of value, the "Sonnets on Eminent Characters" stand out from the thousands of sonnets published in the closing decade of the eighteenth century for their creation of a sustained public posture and unified cultural vision. Wordsworth's address to Coleridge in the thirteenth of the "Sonnets Dedicated to Liberty" is more than a gesture of friendship, more even than an echo of Coleridge's addresses to Bowles and Southey: it is as well an implicit acknowledgement of obligation to his example. As for the "Introduction to the Sonnets," Wordsworth clearly would have seen its horizons as parochial, but even where his tones are most stentorian, the sonnets of the *Poems, in Two Volumes* uniformly attain to power out of a self-consciousness intensified by formal enclosure, a highly sophisticated version of the "lonely feeling" that Coleridge saw inherent in the sonnet. As he began his tutelage with the sonnet, Wordsworth stressed the element of confinement, "crowding into narrow room more of the combined effect of rhyme and blank verse than can be done by any other form of verse I know of" (*WLEY*, 379). Many years later, reflecting on his mastery of the form, he elaborated this figure, celebrating the "pervading sense of intense Unity in which the excellence of the Sonnet has always seemed to me mainly to consist. Instead of looking at this composition as a piece of architecture, making a whole out of three parts, I have been much in the habit of preferring the image of an orbicular body,—a sphere,—or a dew-drop" (*WLLY*, II, 604–605). It may be that "'twas pastime to be bound / Within the Sonnet's scanty plot of ground," as Wordsworth testifies in the "Prefatory Sonnet" of the 1807 edition (lines 10–11), but the sense of isolation, of "some lonely feeling," however refined the emotion or privileged the experience, underlies all the great sonnets of Wordsworth's maturity.[3]

* * * The "Sonnets Dedicated to Liberty," beginning with the very first— "Composed by the Sea-side, near Calais, August, 1802" ("Fair Star of Evening, Splendor of the West")—continually surprise the reader either by enforcing immense distances that link nations and cultures or by a sudden reversion to saving particularities like "those Boys that in yon meadow-ground / In white sleev'd shirts are playing by the score" (lines 3–4), which he celebrates in the tenth, "Composed in the Valley, near Dover, On the Day of landing." As the entire sequence of "Sonnets Dedicated to Liberty" suggests, to Wordsworth's mind prospect rightly viewed must become vision. What both sequences also and even more subtly suggest is

2. This notebook, now known as DC MS.44, survives in an incomplete state, but its contents and order have been shrewdly resuscitated in the prefatory matter and Appendix I of Jared Curtis's edition of *Poems, in Two Volumes, and Other Poems, 1800–1807* (Ithaca: Cornell University Press, 1981), cited for reference throughout this discussion.
3. The opening line of the "Prefatory Sonnet," which was written about the same time as the first passage quoted, clearly reflects the same notion. Compare "Nuns fret not at their Convent's narrow room" to the "narrow room" in which the poet crowds his effects.

that "some lonely feeling" is in constant definition, self-contemplating and self-creating on the axis of its visionary extension.

For something like four years Wordsworth contemplated these sonnet sequences, originally as one unit and then split by subject matter into two. Many years later, he recalled the singular episode that spurred his career as a master of the sonnet:

> In the cottage of Town End, one afternoon in 1801 [actually May 1802], my Sister read to me the Sonnets of Milton. I had long been well acquainted with them, but I was particularly struck on that occasion by the dignified simplicity and majestic harmony that runs through most of them,—in character so different from the Italian, and still more so from Shakespeare's fine Sonnets. I took fire, if I may be allowed to say so, and produced three Sonnets the same afternoon, the first I ever wrote except an irregular one at school. Of these three, the only one I distinctly remember is "I grieved for Buonaparté."[4]

In other words, Wordsworth began his enterprise in the attempt to recapture the tone and ethos of the Miltonic sonnet. It was natural enough that he do so, although, notwithstanding Milton's contemporary reputation as the foremost writer of sonnets in English, only Coleridge among his fellow poets had dared so openly to risk the comparison. The careful dating of the "Sonnets Dedicated to Liberty"—the earliest of which (the first) specifies "August, 1802" as the point of composition—testifies to how quickly and thoroughly Wordsworth engaged himself in the attempt to rival, or equal, Milton.

The boldness of the undertaking and the integrity of the achievement alike depend on Wordsworth's unwillingness to fall back on mere imitation. But also the numerous signals that alert the reader to a Miltonic context seem deliberately placed, creating a complex interplay between a generic tradition and a modern sensibility conditioned by past history and past literature. To view the "Miscellaneous Sonnets" from the immediate perspective of the "Sonnets Dedicated to Liberty" is to be aware of an anomaly, or at least a curiosity. Amid the many prospect poems are six sonnets emphasized by being uniquely grouped in triplets and seeming of a wholy different cast from the rest: three "To Sleep" (nos. 5 through 7) and another three "From the Italian of Michelangelo" (nos. 10 through 12). Moreover, were these six poems removed from the sequence, a surprisingly coherent pattern would emerge among the sonnets preceding the last few in which the tone deepens. The two sonnets in which ships are perceived at a distance (nos. 2 and 8) have an obvious corollary in the sonnets in which cloud shapes spur the imagination (nos. 3 and 4): these poems, as it were, surround and condition our response to the sonnets "To Sleep." Likewise, the translations from Michelangelo are surrounded by sonnets linked by their rusticity and their connections with the poet's past, "To the River Duddon" (no. 9) and "Written in very early youth" (no.

---

4. "Note to 'Miscellaneous Sonnets'," 1843, in *WPW*, III, 417. Dorothy's journal entry for 21 May 1802 is more laconic and presumably more accurate: "Wm wrote two sonnets on Buonaparte after I had read Milton's sonnets to him" (*Journals*, ed. Mary Moorman [London: Oxford University Press, 1971], p. 127). There are actually four sonnets among Wordsworth's juvenilia: his very first publication was an unabashed indulgence in sensibility, "Sonnet on Seeing Miss Helen Maria Williams Weep at a Tale of Distress," printed in *The European Magazine*, 40 (1787), 202.

13). Further indication of this pattern is provided by the sonnet of nostal-
gic return, "'Beloved Vale!' I said, 'when I shall con'" (no. 15), which
stands between two poems in which life seems or is suspended, with the
sleeping city of the Westminster Bridge sonnet (no. 14) and the dead child
glimpsed in a dream—sleep once more intruding upon the sequence in
both—in no. 16, "Methought I saw the footsteps of a throne." The inter-
weaving of theme and subject is as apparent as the interconnections are at
first obscure: Wordsworth goes out of his way to indicate that he is prac-
ticing upon the reader, but forces our active intelligence to engage his in
the process of discovery.

* * *

The "Miscellaneous Sonnets" are entirely free of the "cold glitter"
Coleridge associated with Petrarch, but they retain in a remarkable
transformation the "heavy conceits and metaphysical abstractions" of the
Renaissance sonnet tradition. The modes of thought Wordsworth
explores are not the ostensible subject of his sonnets, as they are in the
strictly philosophical elaboration of those he translates from Michelan-
gelo. They are instead implicit, universally felt impulses within the
mind—indeed, the primary means by which we recognize the workings
of the imagination in all its "miscellaneous" guises.[5]

* * *

As usual with Wordsworth at this point in his career, there is nothing
doctrinaire about his employment of a universal rhythm except his asser-
tion of its universal applicability. Even the moral outcry of "The world is
too much with us" (no. 18) traces its lineage to this aesthetic rhythm
whose perversion is everywhere evident: "late and soon, / Getting and
spending, we lay waste our powers" (18.1–2)—powers of imaginative
growth and renewal, connecting singular and universal, the palpable and
ineffable, not to be reduced to materialistic contracts without being
destroyed. The poem does not merely inveigh against such perversions: it
enacts through its intrinsic rhythm the necessary antidote, moving from
the chill moralism of its opening to a pagan remythologizing of the world
with Proteus and Triton envisioned arising from the sea at its end. The
effect is scarcely isolated, but joins with the Westminster Bridge sonnet
and its own surrounding poems—"Lady I the songs of Spring were in the
grove" (no. 17) and "It is a beauteous Evening, calm and free" (no. 19)—in
a reinforced sense of the sublimity attending the internalization of the
rhythm already subtly marked. Each begins in the local and mundane yet
discovers there a locus for the infinite, discovers beyond the fixed and
known—like the ship embarking for an open ocean—an incarnate poten-
tiality. The sonnets virtually explode from their access to power: a sleep-
ing city is discovered to be animated by a "mighty heart" (14.14); a dormant
winter garden is seized by "all the mighty ravishment of Spring" (17.14);
the ocean beside which the poet and innocent child walk is both a "mighty
Being" and "awake" (19.6). The repeated adjective acknowledges dynamic
force underlying all experience. These sonnets testify—but in fact so do

5. That this was Wordsworth's intention in the "Miscellaneous Sonnets" is clear from his com-
ments on the sequence in his letter to Lady Beaumont of 21 May 1807 (*WLMY*, I, 145–151).

all the "Miscellaneous Sonnets"—to Wordsworth's ringing assertion as he recalls crossing the Simplon Pass: "Our destiny, our being's heart and home, / Is with infinitude" (*Prelude*, VI.604–605). However preoccupied with the things of this world, we are continually drawn forth to touch the infinite, reverting, as we must, to solid ground again. The Petrarchan system has been transfigured, its principles discovered to be those not of cosmology but of psychology. Of course, that had always been true, as Coleridge, before denigrating Petrarch, especially ought to have realized.

Wordsworth not only reestablishes the underlying mode of Petrarchan thought within the sonnet, but does so by eschewing the romantic and divine subjects by which that mode was conventionally expressed. If only by example, he suggests the innumerable ways in which the earthly and universal intersect, the infinite capacity of the mind to charge the mundane with spiritual import. The achievement is as brilliant on the one hand as it is vernacularly conceived on the other, the two poles of conception and execution in terms of their art wonderfully recreating the reach between the spiritually charged and the mundane. Yet, there is an even subtler aspect of this achievement, one directly related to the inner dynamics of the form Wordsworth employs. The Petrarchan sonnet, reduced to abstract principle, balances, as the Michelangelo sonnets so clearly demonstrate, here and there, finite and infinite, micro- and macrocosm. The tension existing between these poles empowers Wordsworth's series of "Miscellaneous Sonnets": invariably, octave and sestet turn on some variation of this division. Whatever Coleridge in a momentary lapse of self-recognition may have thought improper about a sonnet's harboring "metaphysical abstractions," Wordsworth shows an extraordinary capacity to conceive the Petrarchan form with the eye of a geometrician, first reducing it to its abstract relations before imagining it anew.

Having become sensitive to the structural intricacies of the "Miscellaneous Sonnets," we should expect of the "Sonnets Dedicated to Liberty" a comparable richness of effect in the Miltonic mode. Unlike the variations on an abstract theme that motivate the earlier series, these sonnets are organized in a narrative sequence; yet, if we try to pursue a simple line of plot through them, we immediately recognize their affinities with the *Lyrical Ballads* and *The Prelude*. For the true narrative is internalized, events serving as markers for the mental and imaginative growth discerned in the narrative voice. As with the "Miscellaneous Sonnets," the prospect sonnet accentuates perspective. Wordsworth, whether deliberately or not, recapitulates the pattern that Bowles had popularized, extending his sonnet sequence as travelogue into a public and political realm, so insistently forcing moral questions to the center of the observing consciousness that it becomes a conscience for its times. In the process, throughout the twenty-six poem sequence that constituted the original "Sonnets Dedicated to Liberty," Wordsworth recaptures the tone and moral grandeur of Milton with an almost unerring touch, one inspired as much by past example as by present urgency. It is small wonder that it could not be sustained when, later, he expanded the series to document the ensuing course of the Napoleonic Wars, for they are only the immediate occasion, not the underlying cause, of this sonnet sequence.

With powerful effect Wordsworth incorporates the mixed emotions of his countrymen into the quandaries of the sequence. Written, except for the last poem, between May 1802 and October 1803 and insisting on this temporal framework through conspicuous dating, the poems reflect the general public ambivalence that, accompanied the Peace of Amiens (25 March 1802 to 18 May 1803). After ten years of war England was financially strapped, physically exhausted, and morally dispirited; and yet, the Peace settled nothing. If anything, it threw into sharp relief the futility of the war abroad and the ignominy of an English state where financial speculation made fortunes for some while others were deprived of what had long been assumed to be constitutional rights. Relief over the cessation of war was antithetically combined with disgust over the means of peace.

Wordsworth supplies no answers but rather confronts directly what in a rigorous analysis might be said to distinguish England from France. The evening star that shines over his homeland as he stands on the Calais beach in the first sonnet is greeted with patriotic emotion: "Fair Star of Evening, Splendor of the West, / Star of my Country!" (1.1–2). Yet, the subtle shift of syntax that follows presages the course of the ensuing sequence: "Thou, I think, / Should'st be my Country's emblem" (1.6–7). By the middle of the sequence the star no longer represents his country, nor is it even perceived as participating in the times, but is set apart in the distant memory of John Milton: "Thy soul was like a Star and dwelt apart" (14.9). As Lee Johnson has perceptively observed, the star of sonnet 1 is portrayed in nuptial terms, that of sonnet 14—"London, 1802"— is conceived elegiacally.[6] In the opening sonnet Wordsworth finds himself isolated in France "with many a fear / For my dear Country, many heartfelt sighs, / Among Men who do not love her" (1.12–14). The sense of separation intensifies as he looks upon Napoleon's election as First Consul with a disgust wholly opposite the jubilation he felt a decade before in witnessing the birth of the Republic. But rather than dissipating upon his return to England, his alienation only increases, as does his fear for his country, now reconceived as "a fen / Of stagnant waters" (14.2–3). "London, 1802," at the center of the sequence, records a nadir of despair. Paradoxically, this most famous of the "Sonnets Dedicated to Liberty" is not the independent statement about the nature of English society it is customarily perceived to be, but a momentary and partial denunciation in the midst of a psychological progression. Indeed, it justifies its crucial point midway through the sequence by serving as a fulcrum from which the demoralized poet allows himself tentatively to assert a sober optimism about the future state of Europe.

* * *

These are public statements, but they are also notably self-reflexive. Infused with the power of his mentor, Wordsworth discovers himself and his vision renewed in the process. The sonnets record the process of their own creation, a coming to vision by discovering the mental preconceptions necessary to utter the Miltonic voice, to write a Miltonic sonnet. No less than the "Miscellaneous Sonnets" are the Miltonic "Sonnets Dedicated to Liberty" psychological in their orientation. What begins as a simple, if extreme, polarization of France and England soon prompts an

6. Lee M. Johnson, *Wordsworth and the Sonnet*, Anglistica 19 (Copenhagen: Rosenkilde and Bagger, 1973), p. 49.

inner division—one between the temptation to despair and the duty to hope, between the issue of the moment and the liberty not subject to time, between the alienated poet and the mentor whom he projects from himself and who speaks for the highest ideals of his culture. Wordsworth creates the greatest of neo-Miltonic sonnet sequences through the profound imagining of what Milton would have required of the poet who would emulate him.

And yet the same might be said of Wordsworth's sense of the more distant Petrarch. And, once we distinguish the styles and characteristic conceptions Wordsworth inherits from the two poets, we should recognize the remarkable extent to which, however distinct the two traditions—the one emphasizing links between the mundane and supernal, the other between individual and cultural values—they share common features that themselves make the two sonnet sequences aspects of one great and revitalizing whole subsuming them within its commanding mental structure. The imaginative rhythm of the "Miscellaneous Sonnets" is in its essential drive the same urge that motivates the "Sonnets Dedicated to Liberty."

* * *

M. H. ABRAMS

The Idea of *The Prelude*†

In this era of constant and drastic experimentation with literary materials and forms, it is easy to overlook the radical novelty of *The Prelude* when it was completed in 1805. The poem amply justified Wordsworth's claim to have demonstrated original genius, which he defined as "the introduction of a new element into the intellectual universe" of which the "infallible sign is the widening the sphere of human sensibility."[1]

The Prelude is a fully developed poetic equivalent of two portentous innovations in prose fiction, of which the earliest examples had appeared in Germany only a decade or so before Wordsworth began writing his poem: the *Bildungsroman* (Wordsworth called *The Prelude* a poem on "the growth of my own mind"[2]) and the *Künstlerroman* (Wordsworth also spoke of it as "a poem on my own poetical education," and it far surpassed all German examples in the detail with which his "history," as he said, was specifically "of a Poet's mind").[3] The whole poem is written as a sustained address to Coleridge—"I speak bare truth / As if alone to thee

† From *Natural Supernaturalism: Tradition and Revolution in Romantic Literature* (New York W. W. Norton & Company, 1971), 74–80. Notes have been renumbered. Copyright © 1971 by W. W. Norton & Company, Inc. Used by permission of W. W. Norton & Company, Inc.
1. "Essay, Supplementary to the Preface of 1815," *Literary Criticism of Wordsworth*, ed. Zall, p. 184. See also *The Prelude*, XII, 298–312. Upon first hearing the complete *Prelude*, Coleridge specified the bold novelty of the "high theme, by thee first sung aright," which is the "foundations and building up / Of a Human Spirit" (*To William Wordsworth*, ll. 4–8).
2. To Beaumont, 25 Dec. 1804, *Letters: The Early Years*, p. 518; and the Isabella Fenwick note to *The Norman Boy, Poetical Works*, I, 365.
3. Isabella Fenwick note to *There Was a Boy*, and *The Prelude*, XIII, 408; my italics. K. P. Moritz's *Anton Reiser* was published in 1785, J. J. Heinse's *Ardinghello* in 1789, Goethe's *Wilhelm Meister's Lehrjahre* in 1795–6, and Hölderlin's *Hyperion* in 1797–9. On the later evolution of the novel about the development of the artist, see Maurice Beebe, *Ivory Towers and Sacred Founts* (New York, 1964).

in private talk" (X, 372–3); Coleridge, however, is an auditor *in absentia*, and the solitary author often supplements this form with an interior monologue, or else carries on an extended colloquy with the landscape in which the interlocutors are "my mind" and "the speaking face of earth and heaven" (V, 11–12). The construction of *The Prelude* is radically achronological, starting not at the beginning, but at the end—during Wordsworth's walk to "the Vale that I had chosen" (I, 100), which telescopes the circumstances of two or more occasions but refers primarily to his walk to the Vale of Grasmere, that "hermitage" (I, 115) where he has taken up residence at that stage of his life with which the poem concludes.[4] During this walk an outer breeze, "the sweet breath of Heaven," evokes within the poet "a corresponding mild creative breeze," a prophetic *spiritus* or inspiration which assures him of his poetic mission and, though it is fitful, eventually leads to his undertaking *The Prelude* itself; in the course of the poem, at times of imaginative dryness, the revivifying wind recurs in the role of a poetic leitmotif.[5]

Wordsworth does not tell his life as a simple narrative in past time but as the present remembrance of things past, in which forms and sensations "throw back our life" (I, 660–1) and evoke the former self which coexists with the altered present self in a multiple awareness that Wordsworth calls "two consciousnesses." There is a wide "vacancy" between the I now and the I then,

> Which yet have such self-presence in my mind
> That, sometimes, when I think of them, I seem
> Two consciousnesses, conscious of myself
> And of some other Being.
>
> (II, 27–33)

The poet is aware of the near impossibility of disengaging "the naked recollection of that time" from the intrusions of "after-meditation" (III, 644–8). In a fine and subtle figure for the interdiffusion of the two consciousnesses, he describes himself as one bending from a drifting boat on a still water, perplexed to distinguish actual objects at the bottom of the lake from surface reflections of the environing scene, from the tricks and refractions of the water currents, and from his own intrusive but inescapable image (that is, his present awareness).[6] Thus "incumbent o'er the surface of past time" the poet, seeking the elements of continuity between his two disparate selves, conducts a persistent exploration of the nature

---

4. The opening "preamble" to *The Prelude* has, on no valid evidence, been widely attributed to Wordsworth's walk from Bristol to Racedown in September, 1795. John Finch, however, presents convincing evidence that the chief prototype in Wordsworth's life was his walk to Grasmere in the fall of 1799; see his essay, "Wordsworth's Two-Handed Engine," *Bicentenary Wordsworth Studies, in Memory of John Alban Finch*, ed. Jonathan Wordsworth worth (Ithaca, N.Y.; 1970). It is probable, as de Selincourt and Darbishire suggest (*The Prelude*, p. 512), that Wordsworth deliberately telescoped aspects of his arrival at Racedown with his later walk to Grasmere Vale in order to make the induction to *The Prelude* the typological instance of a change of venue which signifies a new stage in his spiritual history. Mary Lynn Woolley deals with Wordsworth's fusion of separate places and incidents into a single typical valley, in "Wordsworth's Symbolic Vale as It Functions in *The Prelude*," *Studies in Romanticism*, VII (1968), 176–89. See also Mark L. Reed, *Wordsworth, The Chronology of the Early Years* (Cambridge, Mass., 1967), pp. 30, 170–1. That *The Prelude* concludes in time with Wordsworth's residence at Grasmere is indicated in XIII, 338–9.
5. E.g., *The Prelude*, VII, 1–56; XI, 1–12.
6. IV, 247–64. See also the early MS JJ, *The Prelude*, p. 641, on the "visible scene" of "recollected hours," "islands in the unnavigable depth / Of our departed time."

and significance of memory, of his power to sustain freshness of sensa-
tion and his "first creative sensibility" against the deadening effect of
habit and analysis, and of manifestations of the enduring and the eternal
within the realm of change and time.[7] Only intermittently does the nar-
rative order coincide with the order of actual occurrence. Instead Words-
worth proceeds by sometimes bewildering ellipses, fusions, and as he
says, "motions retrograde" in time (IX, 8).

Scholars have long been aware that it is perilous to rely on the factual
validity of *The Prelude*, and in consequence Wordsworth has been
charged with intellectual uncertainty, artistic ineptitude, bad memory, or
even bad faith. The poem has suffered because we know so much about
the process of its composition between 1798 and 1805—its evolution
from a constituent part to a "tail-piece" to a "portico" of *The Recluse*, and
Wordsworth's late decision to add to the beginning and end of the poem
the excluded middle: his experiences in London and in France.[8] A work
is to be judged, however, as a finished and free-standing product; and in
The Prelude as it emerged after six years of working and reworking, the
major alterations and dislocations of the events of Wordsworth's life are
imposed deliberately, in order that the design inherent in that life, which
has become apparent only to his mature awareness, may stand revealed
as a principle which was invisibly operative from the beginning. A super-
vising idea, in other words, controls Wordsworth's account and shapes it
into a structure in which the protagonist is put forward as one who has
been elected to play a special role in a providential plot. As Wordsworth
said in the opening passage, which represents him after he has reached
maturity: in response to the quickening outer breeze

> to the open fields I told
> A prophecy: poetic numbers came
> Spontaneously, and cloth'd in priestly robe
> My spirit, thus singled out, as it might seem,
> For holy services.   (I, 59–63)

Hence in this history of a poet's mind the poet is indeed the "transitory
Being," William Wordsworth, but he is also the exemplary poet-prophet
who has been singled out, in a time "of hopes o'erthrown . . . of derelic-
tion and dismay," to bring mankind tidings of comfort and joy; as Words-
worth put it in one version of the Prospectus,

> that my verse may live and be
> Even as a light hung up in heaven to chear
> Mankind in times to come.[9]

---

7. In a passage in *The Friend* (Essay V, 10 Aug. 1809) Coleridge described the ability of men
"to contemplate the past in the present" so as to produce that "continuity in their self-
consciousness" without which "they exist in fragments." He cited Wordsworth's *My Heart
Leaps Up* to illustrate the concept; *The Friend*, ed. Barbara E. Rooke (2 vols.; London, 1969), I,
40. Herbert Lindenberger, *On Wordsworth's "Prelude"* (Princeton, 1963), chap. V, has empha-
sized Wordsworth's "time-consciousness," and identified *The Prelude* as an ancestor of modern
"time-books."
8. A detailed account of the evolution of *The Prelude*, both in its overall scheme and its constitu-
ent passages, is to be found in John Finch, *Wordsworth, Coleridge, and "The Recluse," 1789–
1814*, doctoral thesis (Cornell University, 1964) chaps. IV, VI.
9. MS B, *Poetical Works*, V, 339; for the age of dereliction and dismay see *The Prelude*, II,
448–57.

The spaciousness of his chosen form allows Wordsworth to introduce some of the clutter and contingency of ordinary experience. In accordance with his controlling idea, however, he selects for extended treatment only those of his actions and experiences which are significant for his evolution toward an inherent end,[1] and organizes his life around an event which he regards as the spiritual crisis not of himself only, but of his generation: that shattering of the fierce loyalties and inordinate hopes for mankind which the liberal English—and European—intellectuals had invested in the French Revolution.

> Not in my single self alone I found,
> But in the minds of all ingenuous Youth,
> Change and subversion from this hour.
> (X, 232–4)

The Prelude, correspondingly, is ordered in three stages. There is a process of mental development which, although at times suspended, remains a continuum;[2] this process is violently broken by a crisis of apathy and despair; but the mind then recovers an integrity which, despite admitted losses, is represented as a level higher than the initial unity, in that the mature mind possesses powers, together with an added range, depth, and sensitivity of awareness, which are the products of the critical experiences it has undergone. The discovery of this fact resolves a central problem which has been implicit throughout *The Prelude*—the problem of how to justify the human experience of pain and loss and suffering; he is now able to recognize that his life is "in the end / All gratulant if rightly understood" (XIII, 384–5).

The narrative is punctuated with recurrent illuminations, or "spots of time," and is climaxed by two major revelations. The first of these is Wordsworth's discovery of precisely what he has been born to be and to do. At Cambridge he had reached a stage of life, "an eminence," in which he had felt that he was "a chosen Son" (III, 82 ff., 169), and on a walk home from a dance during a summer dawn he had experienced an illumination that he should be, "else sinning greatly / A dedicated Spirit" (IV, 343–4); but for what chosen, or to what dedicated, had not been specified. Now, however, the recovery from the crisis of despair after his commitment to the French Revolution comprises the insight that his destiny is not one of engagement with what is blazoned "with the pompous names/ Of power and action" in "the stir/ And tumult of the world," but one of withdrawal from the world of action so that he may meditate in solitude: his role in life requires not involvement, but detachment.[3] And that role is to be one of the "Poets, even as Prophets," each of whom is endowed with the power "to perceive / Something unseen before," and so to write a new kind of poetry in a new poetic style. "Of these, said I, shall be my Song; of these . . . / Will I record the praises": the ordinary world of lowly, suffering men and of commonplace or trivial things transformed

---

1. *The Prelude*, XIII, 269–79: Though "much hath been omitted, as need was," the "discipline / And consummation of the Poet's mind / In everything that stood most prominent / Have faithfully been pictured."
2. In the deviations from its true line of development at Cambridge, for example, "the mind / Drooped not; but there into herself returning / With prompt rebound seemed fresh as heretofore" (1850 ed., III, 95–8).
3. *The Prelude*, XII, 44–76, 112–16. Cf. *Home at Grasmere*, ll.664–752.

into "a new world . . . fit / To be transmitted," of dignity, love, and heroic grandeur (XII, 220–379). Wordsworth's crisis, then, involved what we now call a crisis of identity, which was resolved in the discovery of "my office upon earth" (X, 921). And since the specification of this office entails the definition, in the twelfth book, of the particular innovations in poetic subjects, style, and values toward which his life had been implicitly oriented, *The Prelude* is a poem which incorporates the discovery of its own *ars poetica*.

His second revelation he achieves on a mountain top. The occasion is the ascent of Mount Snowdon, which Wordsworth, in accordance with his controlling idea, excerpts from its chronological position in his life in 1791, before the crucial experience of France, and describes in the concluding book of *The Prelude*.[4] As he breaks through the cover of clouds the light of the moon "upon the turf / Fell like a flash," and he sees the total scene as "the perfect image of a mighty Mind" in its free and continuously creative reciprocation with its milieu, "Willing to work and to be wrought upon" and so to "create / A like existence" (XIII, 36–119). What has been revealed to Wordsworth in this symbolic landscape is the grand locus of *The Recluse* which he announced in the Prospectus, "The Mind of Man— / My haunt, and the main region of my song," as well as the "high argument" of that poem, the union between the mind and the external world and the resulting "creation . . . which they with blended might / Accomplish." The event which Wordsworth selects for the climactic revelation in *The Prelude*, then, is precisely the moment of the achievement of "this Vision" by "the transitory Being" whose life he had, in the Prospectus, undertaken to describe as an integral part of *The Recluse*.

In the course of *The Prelude* Wordsworth repeatedly drops the clue that his work has been designed to round back to its point of departure. "Not with these began / Our Song, and not with these our Song must end," he had cried after the crisis of France, invoking the "breezes and soft airs" that had blown in the "glad preamble" to his poem (XI, 1 ff. and VII, 1 ff.). As he nears the end of the song, he says that his self-discovery constitutes a religious conclusion ("The rapture of the Hallelujah sent / From all that breathes and is") which is at the same time, as he had planned from the outset, an artistic beginning:

> And now, O Friend; this history is brought
> To its appointed close: the discipline
> And consummation of the Poet's mind.
> . . . we have reach'd
> The time (which was our object from the first)
> When we may, not presumptuously, I hope,
>   Suppose my powers so far confirmed, and such
> My knowledge, as to make me capable
> Of building up a work that should endure.
>   (XIII, 261–78)

---

4. On the date of Wordsworth's ascent of Snowdon see Raymond Dexter Havens, *The Mind of a Poet* (2 vols.; Baltimore, 1941), II, 607–8. Wordsworth deleted from *The Prelude* the apologetic acknowledgment in MS W that "I must premise that several years / Are overleap'd to reach this incident" (*Prelude*, p. 478).

That work, of course, is *The Recluse*, for which *The Prelude* was designed to serve as "portico . . . part of the same building." *The Prelude*, then, is an involuted poem which is about its own genesis—a prelude to itself. Its structural end is its own beginning; and its temporal beginning, as I have pointed out, is Wordsworth's entrance upon the stage of his life at which it ends. The conclusion goes on to specify the circular shape of the whole. Wordsworth there asks Coleridge to "Call back to mind / The mood in which this Poem was begun." At that time,

> I rose
> As if on wings, and saw beneath me stretch'd
> Vast prospect of the world which I had been
> And was; and hence this Song, which like a lark
> I have protracted . . .
>
> (XIII, 370–81)

This song, describing the prospect of his life which had been made visible to him at the opening of *The Prelude*, is *The Prelude* whose composition he is even now concluding.[5]

PAUL DE MAN

[The Boy of Winander][†]

*   *   *

There is a short poem by Wordsworth that was written toward the end of 1798 during his stay in Goslar, and that the poet always granted a particular significance. He sent it to his friend Coleridge, collected it in the 1800 volume of the *Lyrical Ballads*, put it at the head of the "Poems of the Imagination"—the most important section of his poetic works—and finally made a place for it in the fifth book of his great autobiographical poem *The Prelude*, the first version of which dates from 1805 but which was published only posthumously in a version that was considerably— and infelicitously—revised by the author. These thirty-three lines suffice for Wordsworth to provide us with a first approach to the problem that we seek to understand.

The poem leads us at first into an apparently idyllic world in which nature and consciousness correspond with the reassuring symmetry of voice and echo:

5. It is surprising that the *Prelude* should sometimes be said—even by admirers who express insightful things about its component parts—to be formless and aggregative in the whole and to end in a perfunctory conclusion in which nothing is concluded. Wordsworth was one of the great masters of complex poetic structure. *Tintern Abbey*, for example—in which the conclusion (anticipating his sister's future memories of the present time) turns back upon itself to assimilate the elements of the entire poem, until it closes by echoing the opening description— has a circular structure which is similar to that of *The Prelude* and, on its smaller scale, equally intricate. Moreover, as Wordsworth told Miss Fenwick, *Tintern Abbey* was composed in its entirety before a word was committed to paper. In contrast to the economy of the lyric, the capaciousness of an epic-length autobiography permits, and requires, excursions and details which mask its architectonics; but there is no reason to think that Wordsworth's shaping skill deserted him when, at the height of his powers, he worked and reworked this "ante-chapel" to the great "gothic church" that was to be his monument as a poet.
† From *The Rhetoric of Romanticism* (New York: Columbia University Press, 1984), 50–55. Copyright © 1984 Columbia University Press. Reprinted with permission of the publisher.

> There was a Boy, ye knew him well, ye Cliffs
> And Islands of Winander! many a time
> At evening, when the stars had just begun
> To move along the edges of the hills,
> Rising or setting, would he stand alone
> Beneath the trees, or by the glimmering Lake,
> And there, with fingers interwoven, both hands
> Press'd closely, palm to palm, and to his mouth
> Uplifted, he, as through an instrument,
> Blew mimic hootings to the silent owls
> That they might answer him. —And they would shout
> Across the watery Vale, and shout again,
> Responsive to his call, with quivering peals,
> And long halloos, and screams, and echoes loud
> Redoubled and redoubled; concourse wild
> Of mirth and jocund din! . . .

> (V.389–404)[1]

Readers of Wordsworth know the charm of this world, the gentle constancy of which is expressed in words like "responsive" or "interwoven." The analogical correspondence between man and nature is so perfect that one passes from one to the other without difficulty or conflict, in a dialogue full of echo and joyful exchange. The significance in Wordsworth's thought of this unity filled with analogy is well-known; one finds frequent evidence of it in his poetic as well as his critical works, as, for example, in the oft-cited explanation in the 1800 Preface to the *Lyrical Ballads:* "[the poet] considers man and nature as essentially adapted to each other, and the mind of man as naturally the mirror of the fairest and most interesting properties of nature."[2] Criticism, meanwhile, has especially emphasized this somewhat pantheistic and Schellingesque aspect of Wordsworth, so much so that even the most recent investigations hesitate to go beyond it. And yet we sense, even in this poem, how another dimension opens up and replaces this illusory analogy. For when, in the continuation of the poem, the voice of the birds becomes silent and that of the mountain streams takes its place, the reassuring stability of the beginning disappears and gives way to the precarious adjective "uncertain" that is added to the key word "Heaven":

> . . . the visible scene
> Would enter unawares into his mind
> With all its solemn imagery, its rocks,
> Its woods, and that *uncertain* Heaven, receiv'd
> Into the bosom of the steady Lake.

> (V.409–13)

This tone of uncertainty may already be noted in an earlier passage of the poem where, in lines 18 and 19, one finds the unusual expression

---

1. Wordsworth, *The Prelude*, Ernest de Selincourt, ed.; rev. ed., Helen Darbishire, ed. (Oxford: Clarendon, 1959). All citations are from the 1805 manuscript unless otherwise indicated, and are henceforth cited in the text by volume and line nos. only.
2. Wordsworth and Coleridge, *Lyrical Ballads 1798*, W. J. B. Owen, ed., 2d ed. (Oxford: Oxford University Press, 1969), p. 167.

"... *hung* / Listening ..." when one would have expected "... *stood* / Listening ...":

> Then sometimes, in that silence, while he *hung*
> Listening, a gentle shock of mild surprise
> Has carried far into his heart the voice
> Of mountain torrents; ...
>
> (V.406–9)

It is as if at the very moment that the corresponding echo is lost, the solid ground of a world in which nature and consciousness are "interwoven" slips out from under one's feet and leaves us hovering between heaven and earth. But the word "hung" in "... *hung* / Listening ..." concerns us for other reasons as well. Wordsworth chose it in the second, 1815, Preface to the *Lyrical Ballads* (in examples that he borrowed from Virgil and Milton) in order to illustrate the moment in which the lower form of poetic imagination—"fancy"—transforms itself into true visionary "imagination."[3] While "fancy" depends upon a relationship between mind and nature, "imagination" is defined by the power of its language precisely not to remain imitatively and repetitively true to sense perception. This language is empowered to produce appearances "for the gratification of the mind in contemplating the image itself." The transition from perception to imagination implies a growing boldness of language which distances itself more and more from the norm. In contrast to the language of imagination, the "jocund din" and "mimic hootings" of the beginning appear flat and mechanical. But at the same time an element of anxiety is introduced into the poem.

We may better understand the essence of this anxiety if we observe that the same verb "to hang" reappears in the second part of the poem (typographically separated from the first by a space), and that it represents the thematic connection between the two apparently free-standing halves. When Wordsworth tells us in the most unadorned manner that the boy died, we expect the discreet lament of an elegy or the formal reserve of an epitaph. Instead we note the ardent and—for Wordsworth—typical poetry of an ode to a specific and privileged place, a poetry the earnestness of which stands in profound contrast to the overflowing joy of the earlier world of echoes:

> This Boy was taken from his Mates, and died
> In childhood, ere he was full ten years old.
> —Fair are the woods, and beauteous is the spot,
> The Vale where he was born; the Churchyard *hangs*
> Upon a Slope above the Village School,
> And there, along that bank, when I have pass'd
> At evening, I believe that oftentimes
> A full half-hour together I have stood
> Mute—looking at the Grave in which he lies.
>
> (V.414–22)

With this, the origin of the anxiety is disclosed to us. There is a hidden but indubitable connection between the loss of the sense of correspondence

3. *The Prose Works of William Wordsworth*, W. J. B. Owen and Jane Worthington Smyser, eds. (Oxford: Clarendon, 1974), 3:32.

and the experience of death. The boy's surprise at standing perplexed before the sudden silence of nature was an anticipatory announcement of his death, a movement of his consciousness passing beyond the deceptive constancy of a world of correspondences into a world in which our mind knows itself to be in an endlessly precarious state of suspension: above an earth, the stability of which it cannot participate in, and beneath a heaven that has rejected it. The only hope is that the precariousness will be fully and wholly understood through the mediation of poetic language, and that thereby the fall into death will be every bit as gentle as that of the "uncertain Heaven, receiv'd / Into the bosom of the steady Lake."

Thus, in Wordsworth's poetic world there seem to be two tendencies that are separated by the instant of transition from the one to the other. This sequence—the transformation of an echo language into a language of the imagination by way of the mediation of a poetic understanding of mutability—is a reappearing theme in this poet. In the second book of *The Prelude*, in a passage that probably dates from shortly after "There was a boy . . . ," there is a similar scene that plays itself out in a related setting. In a somewhat too conspicuous inn, built on the site of a simple hut "more worthy of a poet's love," the young Wordsworth and his friends play in the noisy manner of children, and their voices echo back from the hills. As in "There was a boy . . . ," this noisy pleasure suddenly gives way to the delicate melody of a solitary flute:

> But ere the fall
> Of night, when in our pinnace we return'd
> Over the dusky Lake, and to the beach
> Of some small Island steer'd our course with one,
> The Minstrel of our troop, and left him there,
> And row'd off gently, while he blew his flute
> Alone upon the rock; Oh! then the calm
> And dead still water lay upon my mind
> Even with a weight of pleasure, and the sky
> Never before so beautiful, sank down
> Into my heart, and held me like a dream.
>   (II.170–80)

Even more strongly than the ending of "There was a boy . . . ," these lines testify to the fine mixture of anxiety and consenting submission with which consciousness admits mortality. The contrast between the two worlds is always the same: a lively, pleasurably entertaining but destructive world strikes up against a reflective and silent world that stands nearer to an authentic understanding of our situation, the threatened beauty of which, however, is necessarily brittle. The essential moment above all other poetic moments is that of the transition from one world to the other. The poet's language takes its impetus from this meeting place: it illuminates this mid-point from which it glimpses its inauthentic past in the light of the precarious knowledge of its future.

*   *   *

ALAN LIU

From Wordsworth: The History in "Imagination"†

* * *

The readings we now have of the Simplon Pass episode, among which Geoffrey Hartman's is in the vanguard,[1] are so powerful that the episode has become one of a handful of paradigms capable by itself of representing the poet's work. I seek in this essay to re-imagine Wordsworth's 1790 trip and *The Prelude*'s insertion of Imagination into that trip. To do so, I will begin and end within the framework of contemporary "touring" experience. * * * A tour is designed to make sense only of a passage, not of a goal. If an exploration were a sentence, its goal would be the last word. But in a tour, the real goal is the sense of the sentence's overall completion, a sense that cannot appear within the sentence but only on the plane of the grammar framing sentences. From a viewpoint within a tour, therefore, any sense of completion posited at the terminus can only appear as a gap.

In Hartman's reading, Wordsworth's "self" forms in this gap as a denial of nature's sourcehood balanced dialectically against restitution to nature. Holding fast to the tour model with its worldly concerns, as opposed to Hartman's model of the mystic pilgrimage,[2] I offer a reformulation, which, if formally only an addition, ultimately declares something quite different about what we believe the self to be. It seems to me that the "self" arises in a three-body problem: history, nature, self. In *The Prelude*—as in the nineteenth century with its historicist and evolutionist concerns generally—history is the base upon which the issue of nature's sourcehood is worked out. *The Prelude* organizes the 1790 tour so that "nature" is precipitated in book 6 only as a temporary denial of the "history" behind any tour, and the goal of the denial—not contravened until the purge of books 9–10—is to carve the "self" out of history. The theory of denial is "Imagination."

What is "history," whose detail for Wordsworth is the French Revolution? Let me simply gesture for the moment. Something must rush into the gap discovered on a tour with a determined goal, something whose essence will be a sourcehood *elsewhere*. Such is a preliminary, ad hoc definition of history at its contact point with experience: a sense, not yet formulated into idea, that the completion of the present depends perpetually

† From *ELH* 51 (1984): 505–48. Notes have been edited. © 1984 The Johns Hopkins University Press. Reprinted with permission of The Johns Hopkins University Press.

1. *Wordsworth's Poetry, 1787–1814*, with the essay "Retrospect 1971" (New Haven: Yale Univ. Press, 1975). My discussion in the following paragraphs bases itself on the book as a whole, but with special reference to "Synopsis: The Via Naturaliter Negativa," 31–69.

   I should also mention Thomas Weiskel's work, which, through its phrasing of the Imagination in Simplon Pass as "amnesia," "resistance," and "rejection," has particularly guided my description of Imagination as "denial" (*The Romantic Sublime: Studies in the Structure and Psychology of Transcendence* [Baltimore: Johns Hopkins Univ. Press, 1976], 202–03).

2. Hartman's description of the poet's "turn" of mind at Simplon Pass models itself on a Pauline or Augustinian "mystic" conversion (33) whose external manifestation as "pilgrimage" is directly contrasted to the experience of the "revolutionary" in 1790 France (56). My insistence upon "turn" as worldly "tour" implies in part that being a "pilgrim" in 1790 does not distinguish Wordsworth from the thousands of French *fédérés* journeying to and from the Fête of Federation; cf. Mona Ozouf, "La Fédération en prend son caractère singulier d'être plus et mains qu'un pèlerinage" (*La fête révolutionnaire, 1789–1799* [Paris: Gallimard, 1976], 71).

upon something beyond—whether that force of beyond will ultimately be thought as Hegelian "Geist" (anchored in a future sense) or the later Wordsworthian "realities" of people, nation, and church (rooted in the past). We might think here of the anthem of historical sourcehood in book 8 of *The Prelude:*

> Great God!
> That aught *external* to the living mind
> Should have such mighty sway! yet so it was
> A weight of Ages did at once descend
> Upon my heart; no thought embodied, no
> Distinct remembrances; but weight and power,
> Power growing with the weight.
>
> (700–706)

A full rethinking of Hartman's "apocalyptic" Imagination will finally require sketching the specifically Wordsworthian, as opposed to Hegelian process of "embodying" the sense of history in thought. A bare paraphrase of Hartman's argument might run as follows: in the beginning, there is a radical of consciousness whose very condition of being is its effort to emerge as self-consciousness. Emergence involves a dialectic between "apocalypse," in which the self moves toward imaginative independence from nature, and "humanization," in which the self restores nature to primacy through the "myth" that nature guided mind beyond itself in the first place. The final outcome is "humanized imagination," reached by 1805 in the Simplon Pass and Snowdon episodes: a consciousness aware of self as the "borderer" subsuming both the powers of mind and nature. Such imagination may be called "humanized" because nature is the common medium through which mind allies itself to everyday human existence.[3]

Yet, of course, such a bare reading of Hartman misses his book's very pulse: the tremendous pathos with which it watches over, as if over a dead body, the empiricist component in the dialectic of self—the return to nature. Hartman is never more moving than when describing this return, and it soon becomes clear that his dialectic was never a balance but a master-slave relation of apocalypse to humanization in which the traitorous slave binds the master. For Hartman, nature is Wordsworth's tragic flaw and the return to nature his Prometheus bound. Apocalyptic imagination appears in a cloak of connotation—"apocalyptic vigor" and bravery in the face of "dangers," for example[4]—dramatizing its heroic priority as the origin of phenomena. By contrast, humanizing nature is "pedantically faithful," an "avoidance of apocalypse," an "evaded recognition," an effort to "retard" or "beguile," a "displacement," and a "flight" by which Wordsworth "dooms himself."[5] If apocalypse is phenomenal, in other words, humanization can only be epiphenomenal "myth," "superstition," or "illusion."[6]

*   *   *

3. Hartman, esp. 140.
4. Hartman, 61, xiii.
5. Hartman, 39, 61, 61, 147, 147, 257, 293–94, 187. Examples of such terminology could be multiplied.
6. Hartman, 135, 330, 330.

With this dynamo powering his method, Hartman cannot avoid viewing Wordsworth's return to nature as tragic—not unless the poetry after c. 1805 is made to vanish. Wordsworth's Snowdon-consciousness is aware of itself as the totality of the mind-nature dialectic and so measures up to Hegel's epiphanic Absolute Knowledge. But the "late" poetry after this peak from c. 1805 to the 1814 *Excursion* then appears a fall because post-self-consciousness is unimaginable in the Hegelian method. It is the tragedy of post-self-consciousness that casts its long shadow over the early corpus.

This essay bases itself on a reverse or empiricist dialectic by which the power of Hartman's reading can be extended integrally into the whole corpus. The consciousness Wordsworth sketches in *The Prelude* of 1805 is merely the beginning of a counter-dialectic by which such polarizations as "self vs. nature" are eliminated on all fronts in order to render being back to certain logocentric identities (people, nation, church). Conceiving these identities not as posterior syntheses but as presences prior to factionalization, Wordsworth uses them ultimately to transmit the logos back to a reimagined—or perhaps, actively *un*imagined—reality.[7] In Wordsworth's mature view, it seems to me, consciousness is not the terminus of phenomena because it is also not the origin. The origin lies in historical phenomena, even though that sourcehood is empty at conception and must be invested by mind before it can be seen at last—whether as people, nation, church, or some other container—as originary. Though Wordsworth's poetry moves in a field of absence that repays dialectical and deconstructive study, his mind is finally one of the most non-dialectical and reconstructive we know. He turns back the Hegelian movement toward philosophy so that mind literally, rather than mentally, "turns" or "tours" in the world. Dialectic and factionalization become unthought through Wordsworth's version of the Lukácsian novel, or form adjusting self-consciousness to reality:[8] all those later Memorial Tours and Itinerary poems where he remembers that the philosophy of mind is historical being.

The Motive of Description: The 1790 Letter

It will be useful first to view Wordsworth's 1790 trip as much as possible from the perspective of 1790 itself. After shipping to Calais on July 13,

---

7. David Simpson's excellent recent work, *Wordsworth and the Figurings of the Real* (Atlantic Highlands, NJ: Humanities Press, 1982) is consonant with the overall view of Wordsworth I offer. The "sense of history," as I try to sketch it, involves the discovery of a confusion in referentiality that can be developed in Simpson's terms. First there is an insertion of "elsewhereness" or denied originality into the "present" cognate with the discovery of "figuration" and of the self as maker of figures. Then there is what I have called Wordsworth's empiricist "counterideology": the effort to organize figures into the "Real." Simpson also sustains a fruitful comparison of the English Romantics with Hegel and other Continental thinkers.

8. A particularly fruitful exercise is to read Hartman together with Georg Lukács's *The Theory of the Novel: A Historico-Philosophical Essay on the Forms of Great Epic Literature*, trans. Anna Bostock (Cambridge: MIT Press, 1971). E.g., 54:

> Only when a subject, far removed from all life and from the empirical which is necessarily posited together with life, becomes enthroned in the pure heights of essence, when it has become nothing but the carrier of the transcendental synthesis, can it contain all the conditions for totality within its own structure and transform its own limitations into the frontiers of the world. But such a subject cannot write an epic: the epic *is* life, immanence, the empirical.

Wordsworth could not write *The Recluse*, we can speculate, because he did not know that it had to be a novel, the second home of epic; Wordsworth's real *Recluse* is to be found in the substitute novel of his tours.

Wordsworth and Robert Jones spent the summer walking through France, Switzerland, the Savoy, and upper Italy along a route with three segments: 1790-a, a beeline south through France to St. Vallier highlighted by a boat trip on the Saône (July 13 to August 1); 1790-b, a winding, looping, and at times back-tracking passage from St. Vallier through the Savoy, Switzerland, and Italy back up to Basel (August 1 to September 21); and 1790-c, a beeline by boat up the Rhine to Cologne and then home (September 22 to sometime in October).[9] The vertical legs of the tour—each straightforward, each undertaken partly by boat, and each immersed in the sights of Liberty (the celebrations of the French *fédérés* and preparations of the Belgian Republican armies, respectively)—flank the divagations of 1790-b as if between facing mirrors.

* * *

It is difficult, however, to discover the real logic of connection in description. The elusiveness of such logic is illustrated in the sketch of the "variegated journey" quoted from *The Prelude* earlier. Wordsworth glosses over vague predication—the connective motion sketched by "went" and "pass"—with a cloud of adverbial prepositional phrases that are themselves vague ("From vale to vale . . .") but so conventional that the reader merely assumes the kind of motion meant. The underlying logic of a tour is always unrecoverable behind the conventional, behind modifiers that narrate the relationship between any two point-scenes according to a ready-made plot. With astonishing frequency in the letter, as in the sentence, "My Spirits have been kept in a perpetual hurry of delight by the almost uninterrupted succession of sublime and beautiful objects . . . ," Wordsworth adopts the most conventional "modifier" of all locodescriptive tourist experience: a logic of aesthetic movement (as in, "I am moved") expressible in the formula, "sublimity" ← ("delight") → "beauty." As in Denham's "Cooper's Hill," movement between scenes of the sublime and beautiful transforms into a convention of affective movement, "delight."[1] One moves from the mountain to the river in a trajectory that is pleasure.

* * *

We might sum up by saying that a tour is motivated by desire for some special *significance* (whether conceived as meaning or feeling) missing at home: a sense of eventfulness whose site is inherently "out there," other, or elsewhere and so from the first adapted to the form of "convention." Convention is the sense of a meaningfulness described by someone prior and other, a significance whose mere redescription in any itinerary will result in a feeling of complete eventfulness.

---

9. I am aided in grasping the details and total shape of the 1790 trip by Raymond Dexter Havens, *The Mind of a Poet: The Prelude, A Commentary* (Baltimore: Johns Hopkins Press, 1941), 2:418ff; Mary Moorman, *William Wordsworth, A Biography: The Early Years, 1770–1803* (Oxford: Clarendon, 1957), 128–49; and Mark L. Reed, *Wordsworth: The Chronology of the Early Years, 1770–1799* (Cambridge: Harvard Univ. Press, 1967), 97–115. Havens (420ff) includes useful maps of the trip.
1. Describing "the steepe horrid roughness of the Wood" or "the gentle calmness of the flood," Denham observes, "Such huge extreams when Nature doth unite, / Wonder from thence results, from thence delight" (*The Poetical Works of Sir John Denham*, ed. Theodore Howard Banks, Jr. (New Haven: Yale Univ. Press, 1928), 79.

When Wordsworth models 1790-b as if it simply mirrors -a or -c, then, he follows convention, the form of a tour's meaning. Like Bruce, however, he also wants 1790-b to localize a "goal" in a particular segment of the tour rather than on the plane of the tour's overall completion. But since a tour's real goal of convention can never be focused adequately on a segment (conventional expressions of ecstasy at any Alp or Niagara thus show the thinness of conventionality), the stopgap of convention begins to hollow out in Switzerland. In Wordsworth's 1790 letter, the gap between Alpine point-scenes becomes increasingly difficult to fill with modifiers premising behind aesthetic cliché a meaningfulness, a sense of motivated connection, to be acquired merely by redescribing the scene. And as the gaps become ever more insistent, ever more empty of motivated connection, there begins to come to view the fundamental under-motivation of the 1790 tour. Wordsworth, after all, had no good reason to leave England and the chance of a fellowship[2] behind—an embarrassing circumstance that his letter deals with by emphasizing how practical he has been (how much money he has *not* spent) and by apologizing to his Uncle William ("I should be sorry if I have offended him") (*WL* 1:32, 37). What can fill the gap in motivation in lieu of the conventional?

Observe the gap in "pleasure" between lower and upper Lake Geneva in the following passage, a space of desire that conventional aesthetics will not explain and that demands "amends," a sort of scenic version of "apology" to Uncle William:

> The lower part of the lake did not afford us a pleasure equal to what might have been expected from its celebrity. This was owing partly to its width, and partly to the weather, which was one of those hot glaring days in which all distant objects are veiled in a species of bright obscurity. But the higher part of the lake made us ample amends, 'tis true we had the same disagreeable weather but the banks of the water are infinitely more picturesque, and as it is much narrower, the landscape suffered proportionally less from that pale steam which before almost entirely hid the opposite shore.
>
> (*WL* 1:33)

We recognize here the two-point model of touring in which description, after a strenuous effort, finally orders the point-scenes as a hierarchy of "low" to "high," as a structure with an innate motive for forward momentum. First there is a "lower" point of view felt as insignificant: the goal does not match its celebrated description. Then, after a gap, a "higher" point of view repeats the former in a key of greater significance. In the interstice is an ill-defined, ambivalent medium of signification apparent only as a confusion of sensation: a "hot glare," "veil," or "bright obscurity." Considered one way, this obscurity projects Wordsworth's difficulty in description, his lack of aesthetic cliché with which to explain the difference/sameness between lower and upper lakes. We almost hear a sigh of relief when, in the last sentence, he resumes the conventional with the word, "picturesque." Considered another way, "bright obscurity" attests to dependence on an *alternate* resource of convention even more banal: talking about the "weather." "Bright obscurity" is an atmospherics or ambience,

2. The 1790 letter mentions that Wordsworth had acquainted Uncle William "with my having given up all thoughts of a fellowship . . ." (*WL* 1:37).

something in the air "out there" in which connection can still be posited as commonly understood.

Following the description of Lake Geneva is a more immense "bright obscurity." Wordsworth cloaks the sights later to be monumentalized in book 6 of *The Prelude* within inexpressibility *topoi* and other clichés of circumvention:

> we left our bundles and struck over the mountains to Chamouny to visit the glaciers of Savoy. You have undoubtedly heard of these celebrated s[c]enes, but if you have not read of them any description which I have here room to give you must be altogether inadequate. . . . At Brig we quitted the Valais and passed the Alps at the Semplon [sic] in order to visit part of Italy. The impressions of three hours of our walk among the Alps will never be effaced.
>
> (WL 1:33)

Wordsworth says to Dorothy: only *if* you know the description of the Chamounix could I describe it to you. Description only gestures toward a pleasure of description "out there," hanging in air between brother and sister. Just so, when he says that the impressions of the Simplon Pass "will never be effaced," it is unclear what impressions were etched in the first place; impressiveness also hangs in air, in a pleasure of convention.

*   *   *

The conclusion to be reached so far, then, is that history in a tour ornaments nature in order to limn nature's participation in the true, background signified: conventionality or civilization. But something is missing in the picture. If we compare a locodescriptive or prospect *paysage moralisé* such as Denham's "Cooper's Hill" or Pope's "Windsor Forest" with Wordsworth's tour, we notice a striking contrast. History in "Cooper's Hill" and "Windsor Forest" decorates nature, but points toward the background signified of civilization so unambiguously that it is as if natural landscape itself were the ornament. In a Wordsworthian tour, the arrow of signification from historical ornament toward the background is curiously blunted: historical markers point nowhere and decorate nature to no purpose.

In order to explain the deflection, Wordsworth's tour should be unfolded into three planes instead of two: history marks the background, nature stands in the *middle* ground, and the real foreground stages the tourist himself or the "I" of description. * * * If "Nature" now meant the outdoors specifically, the outdoors was only a setting in which the ancient, universal nature could reappear as the individual. Extending such an analysis, I suggest that in the threefold "painting" of a tour, the middle ground of nature is merely a mediation within the real antithesis of the time between background historical convention and foreground self. Nature, the boundary, is the real mark in the painting. The historical signifier seems to point to no background signified because an interposed veil of nature—really only an idea or mark of naturalness—deflects the arrow of signification so that it points invisibly to the foreground self, which thus originates as if from nowhere, or from nature itself. A tourist in Wordsworth's mould is a historical man who, as soon as he spots scenery, thinks himself primitive and original.

* * * Wordsworth takes care to round out his 1790 letter with homage to social and historical action in France during "*l'année heureuse.*" Landscape is supposed to be the foreground ("Among the more awful scenes of the Alps, I had not a thought of man . . . ," *EY*, 34). Historical background is the supplemental "delight" or ornamental "interest":

> But I must remind you that we crossed it at the time when the whole nation was mad with joy, in consequence of the revolution. It was a most interesting period to be in France, and we had many delightful scenes where the interest of the picture was owing solely to this cause.
>
> (WL 1:36)

But I suggest that the letter's perspective should be read in reverse: it is history in 1790 that is the sufficient motive and nature the real supplement or mark. The slightly "mad" truancy of 1790 (the letter mentions those who thought the trip "mad and impracticable" [*WL* 1:37]) is sanctioned not so much by nature as by the fact that now "a whole nation was mad with joy." History, whose very icon is the Federation, or convention, of a nation, is the common convention of meaningfulness from which the individual with shortcomings in specific motives, in "selfhood," can differentiate himself only by using a province of history—the history of aesthetic taste—to mark a boundary in the middle ground. Only through a flourish of nature can Wordsworth's tourist "I" then appear on the foreground as an "original" denying history and conventionality. An aesthetic tour through France in 1790, after all, is not the same as a tour at other times. Wordworth's core statement is this: "in 1790, Federation and political spirit is 'in the air' as everyone else's motivation, but I am individual enough to view it all as a matter of aesthetics"—thus the complacent "egotism" at his letter's end when he spotlights himself in the foreground as the final object of aesthetics. While everyone else may be a *sanscullotte*, he and Jones have the originality to be gypsies at the center of a genre- or subject-painting:

> Our appearance is singular, and we have often observed that, in passing thro' a village, we have excited a general smile. Our coats which we had made light on purpose for our journey are of the same piece; and our manner of bearing our bundles, which is upon our heads, with each an oak stick in our hands, contributes not a little to that general curiosity which we seem to excite. But I find I have again relapsed into Egotism. . . .
>
> (WL 1:37)

The Ego dresses as a "natural" to mark himself off from the historical.

In order to study self-demarcation further, we need to shift at this point from 1790 to the later perspective of book 6 of *The Prelude*.[3] Book 6's description of the 1790 tour, read in its own context, is a sustained effort to deny history by asserting nature as the separating mark constitutive of the "egotistical" self. Let me add another figure for Wordsworth's nature in its role as deflective mediation: "mirror" as opposed to lens. Book

---

3. A full study would here study at least *Descriptive Sketches* among the poetry of the intervening years.

6's goal is to prevent the self from looking through the mark of nature, as through a lens, to underlying history.

*   *   *

Book 6's creation of a mirror denying history occurs in two phases. Instigating the first is a moment of insecurity in the balance between nature and history. Wordsworth begins describing his 1790 trip by confessing his younger self's undermotivation, and then immediately compensates with the main motive, "Nature":

> An open slight
> Of College cares and study was the scheme,
> Nor entertain'd without concern for those
> To whom my worldly interests were dear:
> But Nature then was sovereign in my heart,
> And mighty forms seizing a youthful Fancy
> Had given a charter to irregular hopes.
> (342–48)

But there is a curious flicker in the main motive, a double- or perspective-picture. By a conceit carried in diction—"sovereign," "seizing," "charter"—Wordsworth already allows history to infiltrate the very core of nature. Nature is the ground, but the figure—the Revolution—tends to usurp the status of the ground with the same hidden *virtù* by which the trick-image of death in Holbein's *The Ambassadors* seizes every viewer. Book 6 then compounds the danger by declaring the supplemental motive, history, with such enthusiasm that the Revolution's ornamental gilding threatens to distract the eye entirely:

> In any age, without an impulse sent
> From work of Nations, and their goings-on,
> I should have been possessed by like desire:
> But 'twas a time when Europe was rejoiced,
> France standing on the top of golden hours,
> And human nature seeming born again.
> Bound, as I said, to the Alps, it was our lot
> To land at Calais on the very eve
> Of that great federal Day. . . .
> (349–57)

The implication is that idleness, a perennial concern in Wordsworth's poetry,[4] has the best excuse it will ever have at this time when history supplements scenic holiday with the "work" of nations. History's background helps nature license personal holiday so nicely, indeed, that Wordsworth's oddly passive phrasing of desire ("I should have been possessed by like desire") culminates in the thesis of agency by lottery: "it was our lot / To land" at a particular time in history. The undermotivation with which the 1790 tour begins in book 6 thus incites overmotivation, a double sufficiency of natural and historical motive only precariously organized so that history is subordinate. If history is "work," after all, desire for nature must be indolence.

---

4. See Jeffrey Baker, *Time and Mind in Wordsworth's Poetry* (Detroit: Wayne State Univ. Press, 1980), 113–43.

It is now that book 6 launches its first defense against history, its initial use of nature as a condensation/displacement by which overmotivation can seem to mirror the self rather than transmit the historical whole: the great set-piece describing the ambience of the Fête of Federation. To appreciate the vanity of this piece, we need to recover with some precision the ambience of 1790. Wordsworth and Jones spent the actual day of Federation, July 14, on the road to Ardres, and so did not reach the site of the nearest large fête in Arras until the 16th. They then passed belatedly through the sites of other major fêtes in the department capitals of Troyes, Dijon, and Lyons. In one sense, it did not matter that they missed the celebration of significant fêtes. Secondary celebrations in thousands of smaller towns and villages promulgated the spirit of the larger ones in Paris and the local capitals, and preliminary celebrations such as the Federation of the Pas-de-Calais, Nord, and Somme at Lille in June, as well as subsequent holidays such as the July 18 *Fête Exécutée à la Mémoire de la Fédération Générale* at Champs Elysées, further dispersed Federation Day in time. Altogether, the Federation was a month-long background of celebration to be encountered anywhere. "Southward thence / We took our way direct through Hamlets, Towns, / Gaudy with reliques of that Festival" (360–62), Wordsworth says, and adds that on the boat trip to Lyons, he met "a host / Of Travellers, chiefly Delegates, returning / From the great Spousals newly solemniz'd / At their chief City in the sight of Heaven" (6: 394–97).

But in another sense the young poet must have been at a crucial distance from the spirit of the fêtes. It is significant that his French at the time was far from fluent.[5] We have to be aware of two different views of Federation Day: that of the French themselves, whose architectural, sculptural, visual, pantomimic, and ritual representations of confederation were conventionalized by verbal meaning—by words inscribing ritual in time—and that of Wordsworth, whose access primarily, or only, to the panorama of ritual, "reliques," and the physical behavior of *fédérés* resulted in the need for surrogate verbalization.

We can begin to approximate the French view by noting that the Fête of Federation occurred at a time when the new machinery of state, though already largely operative, hung in suspension between the verbal principles stated by the 1789 Declaration of Rights and the verbal codification still to be enacted in the 1791 Constitution.[6] The hollow between declaration and enactment, the gap in the Revolution's own "description," was the space of oath—the Oath of Federation—and the pithiness of the Oath (epitomized in Louis XVI's one sentence) was such that it had to be supplemented immediately by non-verbal representations—by forms of ritual that were actually all the oath had of substance. * * *

If this labyrinth of visual and ritual representations provided the Oath with substance, it in return received from verbalization the convention of directed form, of a single, motivated flow of prophecy renouncing the past and pointing toward the future. The Declaration, Oath, and Consititution

---

5. During his second trip to France in 1791–92, Wordsworth wrote his brother, Richard: "I am not yet able to speak french with decent accuracy but must of course improve very rapidly" (December 19, 1791; *WL* 1:70).
6. Ronald Paulson has recently studied the representational structure of contemporary British reactions to the Revolution in his *Representations of Revolution (1789–1820)* (New Haven: Yale Univ. Press, 1983).

were the official seals of a massive under-narrative of popular verbaliza-
tion whose epic was the encyclopedic lists of grievances collected for the
Estates General in 1789 and whose episodes were such actions as "the
Fall of the Bastille" collectively described in newspapers, pamphlets,
memoirs, and gossip. It was the task of the under-narrative to make sure
that the meaning carried in ritual or pantomime would read, destruction
→ construction, rather than the reverse. Put another way, it was the task
of the under-narrative to *historicize* visual representation.

The fête on the Paris Champs-de-Mars is a telling example of such his-
toricism. In her fine study, Mona Ozouf suggests that Revolutionary fêtes
situated themselves on "open" amphitheatres and other panoramic spaces
designed to project openness to nature, to a new social decorum of frater-
nity, and—most generally, perhaps—to new meaning.[7] The key point is
that open space for meaning, especially in an urban center such as Paris,
could only be created by destruction of the old. Nature could not be
introduced into a metropolis without displacing something artificial; a
fraternal social decorum could not be achieved without tearing down the
divisive etiquette of aristocratic fêtes; and old symbols could not be writ-
ten over until erased. Generally, the symbolic actions of the Revolution
thus took place either in angry dislocation from traditional sites of mean-
ing (to such peripheral spaces as a Tennis Court, for example) or in vio-
lent erasures of meaning on such old sites as the Bastille. * * *

How to make something constructive out of violent excavation? Just as
contemporary paintings of patriots planting Liberty Trees depended upon
a left-to-right convention of "reading" to specify that the Tree, held at a
diagonal, is being planted and not uprooted,[8] so the digging at the
Champs-de-Mars required convention-making verbalization, epitomized
by the popular song, to show that destructive excavation ("humbling")
merely prophesies construction ("raising up"). So, too, the "excavation" of
the body politic at Versailles on October 5 required its own verbalizations
showing that violent evacuation was really a filling, a reunion in which the
King filled the emptiness in Paris. Marat spoke of the event in these terms:

> It is a source of great rejoicing for the good people of Paris to have
> their King in their midst once again. His presence will very quickly
> do much to change the outward appearance of things, and the poor
> will no longer die of starvation.[9]

It was as if the nation experienced a hunger, an evacuation at its center,
that the kidnapping of the King magically filled (the filling was then to be
emptied again, of course, in the 1791 flight to Varennes completing this
diptych of representation).

As Burke knew, no enactment is complete without such propaganda,
or historicizing description, accompanying the very spade-work of action.
Once excavation had created the amphitheatre at the Champs-de-Mars,
there arose at the center a large, pyramidal altar—the podium for the
nation's ultimate piece of propaganda or descriptive convention enlisting

7. I abbreviate considerably the conclusions in Ozouf's chapter, "La fête et l'espace," 149–87.
8. See the reproduction on the cover of Burke's *Reflections* (O'Brien's edition) of *The Tree of Free-
   dom, 1789 (Musée Carnavalet).*
9. Albert Soboul, *The French Revolution, 1787–1799* . . . , trans. Alan Forrest and Colin Jones
   (New York: Random House, 1975), 157.

the Fête in a historical process of construction. On this altar, on July 14, the Bishop of Autun (Talleyrand), surrounded by hundreds of white-robed priests, said mass preparatory to the King's Oath. Thus despite the fact that the Fête built itself on undermining the Bastille, on emptying Versailles, and on evacuating religion itself, and despite even the ill omen of unrelenting rain that day, the verbalization peaking in the Bishop's blessing made a totally conventional, but profoundly historical, promise that the explosion of energy seen everywhere in visual form and symbolic action pointed forward to the millenium rather than backward to hell. The blessing transformed the famous rain from ill omen to covenant, a sign of fertility prophesying something like that ultimate celebration of fraternity and nature-become-religion in the Champs-de-Mars: the 1794 fête devoted to the "Supreme Being and Nature." At that fête, the altar became an actual "mountain" complete with grottoes modelled after Claude Lorrain's *Sermon on the Mount*.[1]

* * *

Now we can turn to the alternative verbalization of book 6 by which Wordsworth takes to an extreme his younger self's aestheticization of revolution: georgic—the genre closely associated in the eighteenth century with locodescription and the tour but not yet realized in the 1790 letter (even though Wordsworth studied Virgil's *Georgics* closely—particularly the third and fourth—at Cambridge soon before the 1790 trip).[2] In lines 355–425, he describes the Revolution as merely a season in vegetable landscape, a "benevolence and blessedness . . . like Spring" that flowers as a rustic Mayday or perhaps harvest-festival among "the vine-clad Hills of Burgundy." In this world, the "reliques" of the fête—"Flowers left to wither on triumphal Arcs, / And window-Garlands"—are not so much garnishes as integral parts of the landscape of growth and decay. Here the very roads along which the young traveler walks appear only as files of "Elms . . . With their thin umbrage." "Enchanting" were "Those woods, and farms, and orchards . . . ," exclaims the poet-as-*agricola*. In the spirit of the fourth *Georgic*, Wordsworth then inserts within agrarian landscape a simile comparing the *fédérés* to "bees" that "swarm'd, gaudy and gay. . . ." Finally, book 6's set-piece reaches its climax in descriptions of *Carmagnol* dances that now, however, appear merely a country dance. "We rose at signal given, and form'd a ring / And, hand in hand, danced round and round," Wordsworth says, and seems so taken with this image of rustic revolution that he repeats it: ". . . round, and round the board they danced again."

Two "snapshots" from the *Georgics*: a) a plowman working in the field at the end of the first *Georgic* suddenly turns up rusting armor and heroic bones in his fields;[3] b) Virgil himself, digging for the story behind the

---

1. Ozouf, plates 6–7, juxtaposes the "mountain" with Claude's painting.
2. Ben Ross Schneider Jr., *Wordsworth's Cambridge Education* (Cambridge: Cambridge Univ. Press, 1957), 165–66. Schneider notes Wordsworth's particular attention to the description of beehive society in the fourth *Georgic*.
3. Paulson remarks with regard to Constable in his *Literary Landscape: Turner and Constable* (New Haven: Yale Univ. Press, 1982), 131: "It is well . . . to remember the political dimension of the georgic poem: the symbol of regeneration becomes the rusted sword of the soldier's rotting corpse turned up by the plough, and civil war always casts a shadow over harvest."
   My understanding of the historical implications of georgic is greatly enriched by L. P. Wilkinson, *The Georgics of Virgil: A Critical Survey* (Cambridge Univ. Press, 1969).

spontaneous generation of "bees" in the fourth, suddenly turns up an entire epyllion, or contained epic, buried in his narrative. Keeping in mind the historical milieu so profoundly in the background of Virgil's work, I offer this preliminary understanding of georgic based on these snapshots: georgic is the supreme mediational form by which to bury history in nature, epic in pastoral. Like the tour mode, it is the form in which history turns into the background, the manure, for landscape. Through georgic, Wordsworth is able, at least at first glance, to make the entire under-narrative of the Revolution sink into unbroken invisibility. In a sense, the young traveler he depicts walks through a landscape that is natural only because it is prehistorical; the possibility of history has not yet evolved. Contemporary engravings depict Liberty pointedly as a woman carrying a broken yoke;[4] if France was "georgic" in 1790, after all, such fertility harvested the mass destruction of the agrarian Great Fear of 1789. But in his georgic, Wordsworth appreciates joy without the haunt of historical fear, the yoke of rustic labor without the jagged edge of break with past oppression.

The purpose of the mirror of georgic nature is to hide history in order, finally, to reflect the self. At the beginning of his "vanity," Wordsworth recounts "How bright a face is worn when joy of one / Is joy of tens of millions" (359–60). In the mirror of nature, this proportion is reversed: history's "tens of millions" focus to foreground the poet's "joy of one." Halfway through the set-piece, external observation of vegetable process thus deflects momentarily into self-absorption:

> 'Twas sweet at such a time, with such delights
> On every side, in prime of youthful strength,
> To feed a Poet's tender melancholy
> And fond conceit of sadness. . . .
>
> (375–78)

The tour's original undermotivation becomes "melancholy," the convention in locodescription framing the subjective self. Subjectivity then steps even more vainly into the foreground when Wordsworth elevates his younger self above the celebrating *fédérés*:

> In this blithe Company
> We landed, took with them our evening Meal,
> Guests welcome almost as the Angels were
> To Abraham of old.
>
> (401–404)

As in Genesis 18:1–15, where angels prophesy the birth of Isaac to Abraham, the blessed tourist steps momentarily out of history altogether in prophetic anticipation of his own self, of an "Isaac" that then appears as the *deus ex machina* of the whole set-piece. What is the specific point of rustic festivity and dancing? Says Wordsworth,

> . . . All hearts were open, every tongue was loud
> With amity and glee; we bore a name
> Honour'd in France, the name of Englishmen,

---

4. See the illustration in Henderson, 314.

And hospitably did they give us Hail
As their forerunners in a glorious course,
And round, and round the board they danced again.
(408–413)

Suddenly, the Revolution "hails" the English poet at the focus of its circle.

Such is book 6's first mirror screening background history from view. Yet, despite its gorgeous polish, the mirror is inadequate because of a basic undecidability in georgic making it at all times, and especially in Wordsworth's time, just as likely to exhume history as bury it. The genres of the tour work and the georgic, which the Preface of 1815 will call "Idyllic" and "Didactic," respectively, are alike problematic because they tend to fall between the three "master" genres of Narrative, Drama, or Lyric composing Wordsworth's and literary history's trinity, on the one hand, and true servant genres with clearly-defined formal traits (such as Ode as opposed to Elegy), on the other.[5] The generic field in any age, I suggest, distributes itself between master and servant genres with some unstable mediator always filling the role played by tour and georgic in Wordsworth's time. Tour and georgic are preeminently mixed genres in which the stability of "genre" as a convention is always threatening to come apart under the pressure of the times. Tour and georgic in the late eighteenth and early nineteenth centuries are the pressure points where the entire generic field is beginning to rearrange around the massive intrusion of specifically historical reality and the form jury-rigged to "imitate" it: the novel. In the era soon to produce a novelist like Scott, history became *the* subject of mimesis, and the georgic world of nature projected in book 6 of *The Prelude* can only bury history out of sight provisionally. There are, after all, those protruding "bones" in the soil, which, because Gothic romance is denied to georgic as an escape valve, cannot be easily covered. Too much energy of repression must be expended to keep the georgic mirror from turning transparent. If Wordsworth's simile likening the *fédérés* to "bees" alludes to the *Georgics*, after all, it certainly also points to the epic use of "bees" in Homer and in Virgil himself, as well as to the brilliant "problem georgic" at the close of book 1 of *Paradise Lost*, where Satanic history threatens to swarm into the pastoral tranquillity of the "belated peasant."

The climactic, second phase of book 6's defense against history then begins at Mont Blanc precisely upon the discovery that georgic is transparent. The demands Wordsworth makes at this point upon georgic to bury history create such tension in the convention that the epic pole first seems to disappear entirely to leave an exaggerated insistence upon pastoral. The Mont Blanc episode begins as a fond, georgic look homeward to pastoral: "Sweet coverts did we cross of pastoral life, / Enticing Vallies . . ." (6:437–38). But like Milton's "belated peasant," the young traveler suddenly experiences a near-eruption of the demonic into the harvest-world: the peak of Mont Blanc discovers itself as a gap in georgic fertility, as a "soulless image . . . Which had usurp'd upon a living

5. For a study of the formation and transformation of genre hierarchies, see Alistair Fowler, *Kinds of Literature: An Introduction to the Theory of Genres and Modes* (Cambridge: Harvard Univ. Press, 1982), esp. 213–34.

thought" (452–5). There is some strange devil of history, I suggest, behind "usurpation" that the poet-as-*agricola* would rather not see. The whiteness at Mont Blanc—like that in *The White Doe of Rylstone*—is the space in which history can ghost into the present; it is not no-meaning but a panic of too much possible meaning. Whiteness is the page for a possible epic whose stern mood must either be recognized or thwarted. For the time being, the whiteness at Mont Blanc—protruding like a heroic bone—is simply ploughed under again. In an "amends" reproducing that at Lake Geneva in the 1790 letter, Wordsworth returns to the world of fertility in the Vale of Chamounix by means of a suspiciously hyperbolical pastoral:

> There small birds warble from the leafy trees,
> The Eagle soareth in the element;
> There doth the Reaper bind the yellow sheaf,
> The Maiden spread the haycock in the sun,
> While Winter like a tamed Lion walks
> Descending from the mountain to make sport
> Among the cottages by beds of flowers.
> (462–68)

Not a trace of grimness does the "Reaper" seem to betray. But notice the suppression of narrative necessary to screen grimness. Arranged around the hinge of the "Reaper" are two diptychs: the "small birds" with the "Eagle," and the "Maiden" with the "Lion" of winter. There is a muted story of predation here, of some spoliation or usurpation in the area of Chamounix that the 1805 book 6 (still without the Convent of Chartreuse excursus) must prettify.

It is the near-eruption of history at Mont Blanc that provokes the climactic veiling at Simplon Pass. It will be useful to retain Hartman's labelling of the sequence: 6a, the ascent ("Yet still in me, mingling with these delights / Was something of stern mood . . . ," 488–524); 6b, the halt ("Imagination! lifting up itself . . . ," 525–48); and 6c, the descent through Gondo Gorge ("The dull and heavy slackening that ensued . . . ," 549–80). Ascent and descent form the paradigmatic "two points" of the tour, and the halt is the "gap." So much work has been done on the sequence that I will offer only a schematic of 6a and c in order to move quickly to 6b. 6a is a trajectory of serial repetition guided at the end by the "Peasant," or holdover *agricola* from the georgic universe. More specifically, 6a pictures an implicit struggle between the vectors of the horizontal and vertical. The horizontal, intoned in the tedious diction of "A length of hours," "Ere long we follow'd," and "at length," is the progress of pure repetition, of one foot after another without describable motive. The vertical, heard in the verbs of "we had clomb," "the Travellers rose," and "climb'd with eagerness," is the vector of significance and motivation. Disappointment, first sounded in Wordsworth's and Jones's request that the Peasant *repeat* his message, but fully realized only in the descent pictured by 6c, arrives upon the discovery that vertically is itself simply a disguised form of flat repetition: "downwards we hurried fast," 6c begins in its record of descent chiastically opposed to ascent. "Downwards" merely repeats without meaningful connection the previously upward "climb." 6c, indeed, is a microcosm of the disconnected repetition disappointing Wordsworth so gravely. Gondo Gorge appears as a landscape of binary points separated by oxymoronic divide: "The immeasurable height / Of woods decaying, never to be decay'd . . . Winds thwarting winds . . . Tumult and peace, the darkness and the light. . . ."

What radical of motivation can connect the "two points" whose disconnection images the undermotivation of the whole tour? Here we reach the goal of this essay, Wordsworth's addition of 6b and the "bright obscurity" of the "Imagination":

> Imagination! lifting up itself
> Before the eye and progress of my Song
> Like an unfather'd vapour; here that Power,
> In all the might of its endowments, came
> Athwart me; I was lost as in a cloud,
> Halted, without a struggle to break through.
> And now recovering, to my Soul I say
> I recognise thy glory; in such strength
> Of usurpation, in such visitings
> Of awful promise, when the light of sense
> Goes out in flashes that have shewn to us
> The invisible world, doth Greatness make abode,
> There harbours whether we be young or old.
> Our destiny, our nature, and our home
> Is with infinitude, and only there;
> With hope it is, hope that can never die,
> Effort, and expectation, and desire,
> And something evermore about to be.
> The mind beneath such banners militant
> Thinks not of spoils or trophies, nor of aught
> That may attest its prowess, blest in thoughts
> That are their own perfection and reward,
> Strong in itself, and in the access of joy
> Which hides it like the overflowing Nile.
>   (6:525–48)

Here is the great mirror of the "imaginary" into which Wordsworth looks to reflect upon his "self." The process of this reflection is complex and sums up the entire pathway of deflection I have sketched so far. Crucial is the passage's initial flicker from first person singular ("I was lost," "I say," and "I recognise") to first person plural ("shewn to us," "whether we be young or old," "Our destiny, our nature, and our home") and then to the impersonal ("its prowess," "Strong in itself," "hides it"). Looking outwards, the "I" perceives "we's" and "our's" that are the pronouns of convention and collectivity. "We" and "our" are signifiers of background that, given a chance, would point directly into the history heard with such frightening force and precision in the vocabulary of 6b as a whole: "Power . . . all the might of its endowments . . . struggle to break through . . . glory . . . strength / Of usurpation . . . Greatness . . . banners militant . . . spoils or trophies . . . prowess . . . Strong in itself." But there is a deflection here, and the arrow or signification bends, in an extraordinary sentence, to point perpetually "there" into a historically ungrounded "being" we might call "objectified subjectivity":

> Our destiny, our nature, and our home
> Is with infinitude, and only there;
> With hope it is, hope that can never die,
> Effort, and expectation, and desire,
> And something evermore about to be.

The perpetual "out there" of such desired "being" is propped up, we notice, upon reference to external "nature" as pure figure. The "I" comes to see "nature" as if in quotes: "*like* the overflowing Nile." Anointing itself with a figure of externality as groundless in origin as the Nile itself, which in the 1850 poem pours from a "fount of Abyssinian clouds," the "I" thus comes into the majesty of objectivity seemingly without any further need for the mediation of the most human approach to objectivity: collectivity. History is denied, and the "I" engenders itself autogenetically as the very crown of what I have called objectified subjectivity: a mind knowing itself only in the impersonal—"Strong in *itself*." The "I," in sum, looks into the background of collective history, deflects upon nature's polish of objectivity, and at last sees itself reflected as the awesome, historically free personality of "*The* mind."

Imagination and Napoleon

But book 6 cannot be read wholly on its own. Let me now open the aperture completely to view Simplon Pass in the overall context of *The Prelude* and 1804, when book 6 and much of the following poem was composed. In this context, it becomes important to stare fixedly into, and *through*, the mirror of the Imagination. In the construction of the total *Prelude* in 1804, I believe, Wordsworth deliberately inserted background signifiers of historicity in the Imagination passage as avenues toward an order of the "symbolic" to be activated with the realization that the "self" must enroll—literally, enlist in the Grasmere Volunteers[6]—in a collective system authorized from some source "elsewhere" than the self, in the Nile that is history.[7] Specifically, book 6 and the Imagination passage look forward to the direct concern of books 9 and 10 with the agon of history. Wordsworth probably composed most of books 9 and 10 immediately after finishing 6 in late April, 1804; and possibly all three books dealing with France were composed in a single manuscript.[8] In the movement of the total poem, 6b's denial of history really acts like a tocsin warning the reader that the "nature" and "self" thus far imagined are insecure until the poem confronts history's sourcehood.

What is in the mirror of Imagination in 1804? MS. WW shows that Wordsworth originally inserted what is now 8:711–27—the first part of the simile of the cave—between 6a and 6b.[9] 6b is like the cave because it is a

6. As Wordsworth did in 1803 (Moorman, 602–03).
7. Barbara T. Gates studies Wordsworth's use of "rivers" as images of history in "Wordsworth and the Course of History," *Research Studies* 44 (1976): 199–207. Gates, partly under the guidance of R. G. Collingwood, also speaks of the "historical imagination" in "The Prelude and the Development of Wordsworth's Historical Imagination," *Études Anglaises* 30 (1977): 169–78, but her approach is to make historical imagination a secondary faculty in addition to "apocalyptic imagination."
8. *The Prelude: 1799, 1805, 1850*, ed. Jonathan Wordsworth, M. H. Abrams, and Stephen Gill (New York: W. W. Norton, 1979), 519.
9. *The Prelude: 1799, 1805, 1850*, 216n.

flat surface with a through-the-looking-glass effect. The more we look, the more we are pulled through its plane into an interior, self-motivated reality: "Shapes and Forms and Tendencies to Shape" that create an entire world within the cave of nature. 6b cavitates the mirror of nature, I suggest, to show the protruding bones of the historical world of 1804. Specifically, I believe that if we look into the cave, we will see through the self in the foreground, through even the nature in the middle ground, to a frightening skeleton in the background: whatever else it is, Imagination is the haunt of Napoleon (the great Bone of the time). More precisely, if Imagination is a mirror, the mirror is of magistrates and shows a canny double for uncanny Napoleon; it simultaneously negates and subsumes Napoleon in an effort, anticipatory of books 9 and 10, to purge tyranny from the world so that "nature" can inaugurate true freedom.

We need to be careful here with degrees of certainty. What I propose is a ladder of certainty: no one piece of evidence in the following presentation leads absolutely to the conclusion that Napoleon stands in the background of 6b, but the sum, I believe, has plausibility; and such plausibility in the specific thesis will be sufficient to carry the general thesis that 6b cannot but be deliberately charged with history. I highlight the most telling specifics in italics, but I also include supplementary suggestions based on circumstances and sometimes wordplay that would appear far-fetched in normal times. * * *

1) 18–19 *Brumaire*. In 1799 Napoleon returned unexpectedly to France from his Egyptian campaign, reached Paris on October 16 with massive popular support, and took control of the Directory in the *coup d'état* of 18–19 *Brumaire* (November 9–10).[1] *The Annual Register* (years 1758–92, 1794–96, 1800, 1802–1811, and 1814–20 were in Wordsworth's Rydal Mount library)[2] banners the world's astonishment at this advent as if from nowhere, choosing a style of language—"in defiance of reason . . . not any one . . . could have imagined"—that we will need to consider later:

> Whether we contemplate the great affairs of nations in a political or military point of view, the return of Buonaparte to France . . . is the grand and leading event in the history of 1800. . . . Who could have believed that a simple sub-lieutenant of artillery, a stranger to France, by name and by birth, was destined to govern this great empire, and to give the law, in a manner, to all the continent, in defiance of reason . . . ? There is not any one in the world who could have imagined the possibility of an event so extraordinary.[3]

"*Brumaire*" is the month of "mists" in the vividly imagined Revolutionary calendar, and Napoleon's takeover climaxed in his famous personal appearance before the hostile Council of Five Hundred at St. Cloud. In the world's eye, we might say, Napoleon burst upon the scene as a kind of "vapour" or cloud, an upstart and illegitimate spirit. 6b begins with

1. Contemporary accounts of Napoleon and the Napoleonic years will be cited when used; I have also benefited from modern accounts, the two most helpful for my purposes being M. J. Sydenham, *The First French Republic, 1792–1804* (London: B. T. Batsford, 1974) and David Chandler, *The Campaigns of Napoleon* (New York: Macmillan, 1966).
2. Chester L. Shaver and Alice C. Shaver, 9.
3. *The Annual Register, or a View of the History, Politics, and Literature for the Year 1800* (London: W. Otridge, 1801), 66.

a *coup d'état* of Imagination retracing something like the spirit of 18–19 *Brumaire*: an "unfather'd vapour" starts up in defiance of all expectation, comes with "Power" upon a poet who, like France in 1799, was "Halted without a struggle to break through," and changes the regime with such "strength / Of usurpation" that the astonished poet, like France before Napoleon's renewed spectacles of state,[4] must say, "I recognise thy glory." Such recognition of "glory"—the great instance of "bright obscurity"— merely makes official what the poet had unconsciously, in an analogy to French popular support for Napoleon, depended upon all along.

Anchoring the reading of Imagination as *coup d'état* is Wordsworth's strong use of the figure, "usurpation," a use prepared for in the chronicle of Mont Blanc. Usurpation in book 6 is a figure backed up by allusion to *Macbeth*, the poem's preferred exemplar of the usurper. Just after describing the descent through Gondo Gorge, Wordsworth describes "innocent Sleep" lying "melancholy among weary bones" (6:579–80; *Macbeth* 2.2.36). In one sense, the allusion points ahead in the poem, and backward in time, to book 10 and the night in 1792 when the poet heard a voice in the Paris hotel quoting the regicide Macbeth: "Sleep no more" (10:77; *Macbeth*, 2.2.35). Since book 10 moves on immediately to the confrontation between Robespierre and Louvet, we can guess that Wordsworth's Macbeth, in the context of 1792, figures Robespierre (whom 10:458–62 also represents as an offspring of Lear). But in another sense, the allusion to *Macbeth* in book 6 with its addition of the image of "bones" points to Old Boney: *in the context of the years immediately preceding 1804, "usurper" cannot refer to anyone other than Napoleon*. After 18–19 *Brumaire*, "usurper" was applied to Bonaparte in English parliamentary speeches, pamphlets, and newspapers with the consistency of a technical term and irrespective of party affiliation or sympathy with French republicanism. Whether he was thought merely to epitomize republicanism or to break with it, the premise was that Napoleon was a usurper.[5] * * *

2) Marengo and Aboukir. Completing the *coup* is the "battle," and, indeed, campaign of Imagination. A *Swiss mountain pass in 1804 was first and foremost a military site*: the avenue of the "modern Hannibal," as Coleridge will later describe Napoleon's forces.[6] It is even more suggestive that 6b inscribes within the literal setting of the Swiss Alps the figure of the Nile, and so folds into Simplon Pass the two most crucial scenes of battle in the Napoleonic wars prior to Trafalgar in 1805: Switzerland (together with northern Italy) and Egypt. The Alpine region, Wordsworth's model of political independence, was the ground of Napoleon's most brilliant successes, and the mouth of the Nile that of his only major defeat to date. The lamination of the two is interpretive: if 6b begins with *coup d'état*, such illegality becomes progressively transformed until, by the end, Wordsworth has purged tyranny from Imagination in the flow of the Nile.

* * *

4. Beginning with the pageantry of Napoleon's symbolic move to the Tuileries on February 19, 1800 (Sydenham, 235).
5. On political differences in British attitudes toward Napoleon after the usurpation, see F. J. MacCunn, *The Contemporary English View of Napoleon* (London: G. Bell, 1914).
6. Coleridge, 2:138.

In the context of 1804, then, any imagination of an Alpine pass would remember the military "genius" of Bonaparte. It seems natural that Wordsworth's halt "without a struggle to break through" at the beginning of 6b should lead to the "banners militant" toward the close. The martial air of 6b, indeed, fairly trumpets itself. If we read in the spirit of the banners, Wordsworth's "visitings / Of awful promise, when the light of sense / Goes out in flashes that have shewn to us / The invisible world" hint the violence of artillery. Even Wordsworth's great rallying speech has a military ring:

> Our destiny, our nature, and our home
> Is with infinitude, and only there;
> With hope it is, hope that can never die,
> Effort, and expectation, and desire,
> And something evermore about to be.

Whatever else it is, this speech—in its very cadence—is a double of Napoleon's widely publicized rallying speeches to his armies. After the 1796 breakthrough in the Maritime Alps, for example, *The Annual Register* quotes Bonaparte addressing his troops:

> You have precipitated yourselves, like a torrent, from the heights of the Appennines. You have routed and dispersed all who have opposed your progress. . . . Yes, soldiers, you have done much; but does there remain nothing more to be done? Though we have known how to vanquish, we have not known how to profit of our victories. . . . Let us depart! we have yet forced marches to make, enemies to subdue, laurels to gather, injuries to revenge.[7]

But the parade of "banners militant," of course, does not conclude the martial review of 6b. Continues Wordsworth:

> The mind beneath such banners militant
> Thinks not of spoils or trophies, nor of aught
> That may attest its prowess, blest in thoughts
> That are their own perfection and reward,
> Strong in itself, and in the access of joy
> Which hides it like the overflowing Nile.

Here, even amid the military anthem, his act of purging Napoleon begins. *Wordsworth's stress in 1804 that the Imagination is its own reward, and eschews spoils and trophies, should be seen to reject precisely Napoleon's famed "spoliations."* * * *

3) The Spirit of Imagination. In sum, Wordsworth in 6b makes a preliminary trial of the method by which history can be cleansed of tyranny so that only the shining "genius" figured by Napoleon will reign. Here we reach the most telling point of correspondence between Wordsworth's Imagination and Napoleon—that of pure spirit. While general British reaction to Bonaparte fluctuated from uncertainty before his "usurpation" in 1800 to enthusiasm during the Peace of Amiens in 1802 and finally to renewed hostility, *one species of reaction was constant if officially inadmissible: admiration of the "genius," "sublimity," and "imagination" represented by Napoleon.* Bonaparte was, as Scott will later call him in his biography,

7. *Annual Register,* 1796 (1800), 91.

the "master-spirit" of the age.[8] *The Annual Register*, for example, consistently admired Napoleon's gifts of mind until its first notes of distrust in the 1802 volume (published in 1803). In its character sketch of 1800, for instance, it discovers Napoleon's youthful "spark of genius," and then marvels at his mature genius: Bonaparte possesses "a firm and undaunted spirit, and a genius penetrating, sublime, and inventive," and "His letters, his speeches, his actions, all proclaimed a sublimity of courage, imagination, and design, beyond the limits of vulgar conception."[9] * * *

Wordsworth and the Sense of History

Recall the diversionary force that Napoleon sent to demonstrate in Simplon Pass. If my presentation has even the barest plausibility, it will appear that Wordsworthian "nature" is precisely such an imaginary antagonist against which the self battles in feint, in a ploy to divert attention from the real battle to be joined between *history* and self. Whatever the outcome of the skirmish, called dialectic, between "nature" and self, history, the real antagonist, is thus momentarily denied so that when it debouches at last, it will be recognized with shock by the feinting mind as the greatest power of the Wordsworthian defile. As envisioned in the framework of the total *Prelude*—where the books of unnatural history then come at the point of climax rather than, as in *Paradise Lost*, of denouement—denial is the threshold of Wordsworth's most truly shocking act of Imagination: the sense of history. The true apocalypse will come when history crosses the zone of "nature" to occupy the self directly, when the sense of history and Imagination thus become one, and "nature," the mediating figure, is no more.

Let me draw back at this point to locate where I have come, and where the tour still leads. In a fine essay, Karl Kroeber recently began with a call to arms: "Despite critical clichés of the 1960s and 1970s, the primary thrust of Romantic art was toward neither apocalypse nor transcendence but toward the representation of reality as historical process."[1] Much as I agree with Kroeber's approach, it seems to me that the divide he makes between the representation of history and the "apocalyptic" imagination of nature championed by Hartman is too deep. The thrust of my reading has been that however strongly the paradigm of book 6 seems to deny history, its projection of "Imagination" divides itself from history only as consciousness from unconsciousness. The "apocalypse" in which the Wordsworthian self declares its independence from nature is the very battle site of repression, the pass in which history is continually erupting from behind nature.

Repression in Simplon Pass, as I have also tried to suggest, is so charged with the stuff of history that it looks forward by design to books 9 and 10 and the full disclosure of history. As I have elsewhere written,[2] books 9

---

8. Sir Walter Scott, *The Life of Napoleon Buonaparte, Emperor of the French, with a Preliminary View of the French Revolution* (Exeter: J. and B. Williams, 1843), 1:216.

9. *Annual Register, 1800* (1801), 11.

1. "Romantic Historicism: The Temporal Sublime," in *Images of Romanticism: Verbal and Visual Affinities*, ed. Karl Kroeber and William Walling (New Haven: Yale Univ. Press, 1978), 149–65.

2. " 'Shapeless Eagerness': The Genre of Revolution in Books 9–10 of *The Prelude*," *Modern Language Quarterly* 43 (1982): 3–28.

and 10 begin precisely by challenging the earlier "tour" view of history, its conventional landscape of "nature," and its assumptions about the security of the self in that landscape. "Through Paris lay my readiest path," Wordsworth says in book 9, initiating the tour mode of description,

> and there
> I sojourn'd a few days, and visited
> In haste each spot of old and recent fame
> The latter chiefly, from the Field of Mars
> Down to the Suburbs of St. Anthony. . . .
>   (9:40–44)

If the Champs-de-Mars in 1790 epitomized the georgic nature Wordsworth expected to harvest from the Revolution, now, after the 1791 "massacre" of radicals on its soil, it lies as fallow as other Revolutionary sites: it is an unnatural place, a blank page in nature awaiting new inscription. Says Wordsworth in book 10 about the barren georgic of Revolution: "a taunt / Was taken up by scoffers in their pride, / Saying, 'behold the harvest which we reap / From popular Government and Equality . . .'" (10:429–32). It is the discovery of history's massacre at the very source of nature's "harvest" that then provokes *The Prelude*'s reimagination of nature on the "spots of time" and finally the peak of Snowdon. On Snowdon, a "bright obscurity" once more veils the earth, "usurping" the "majesty" of reality and guarding the pass with the aid of "the Imagination" standing in the "chasm." But now the glorious obscurity that is Imagination's defense of nature can rest in confident security (13:40–65). "For this alone," says Wordsworth, reflecting on the mind's recovered "Power," "is genuine Liberty . . ." (13:119).

Having taken my argument this far, however, it appears that the exploration of history's sourcehood has just begun. A fuller reading of the Wordsworth corpus would proceed at this point to trace the sense of history from its peaceful veiling on Snowdon into the later works, where Wordsworth progressively restores history to priority as his most inclusive topic, as the "reality" underlying all others. As I suggested earlier, history enters into experience as a sense of "elsewhereness," a chasm in being where presence is in exchange with absence or infinitude. Infinite absence can wear many names, many ideological vestments or "ideas" of history doomed always to be after-the-fact. Originating in a sense of alienated sourcehood that in its very moment of discovery—like the Nile flowing from undiscovered sources—evacuates the notions of "sourcehood" or "origination," an idea of history, it seems, can only emerge with a certain air of unreality. The moment when an individual seeks to explain the reality of history, or first recognizes the existence of a reality in need of historical account, is also the moment when he discovers that he cannot by himself originate a fully sufficient explanation. How, then, to know history as real?

The largest, most capacious theme of Wordsworth's life work, I believe, fits that of the nineteenth century generally: realizing the sense of history as an ideology or philosophy that explains away originating absence. Within the envelope of this theme fit the traditional problems of Wordsworth criticism: time, nature, self, mind. Wordsworth's career begins with "tour" works such as *Descriptive Sketches* (or what might be termed degenerate tour works such as *Salisbury Plain*) and ends, after tracing the line of time, nature, self, and mind, in that remarkable series of tour forms or affiliated works in the later poetry: the many Memorial Tours, the River Duddon sequence, and even *Ecclesiastical Sonnets*. These early and late tour forms are thoroughly historical. The early works strive to dam the gap opened up by historical events, and the later ones to "re-member" the landscape mutilated by history so that it can be walked upon again as reality—to piece the Continent and Britain together again, in other words, after Waterloo. I say "thoroughly historical" rather than "historiographical" because Wordsworth cannot be said to work explicitly in philosophy of history (with the exception of late commentary on contemporary historians).[3] The tours are what he has instead of explicit philosophy.

* * *

SIMON JARVIS

[Infinity in *The Prelude*][†]

* * *

Illimitable Walk

The elevation of the finite to infinite significance has often been thought of as a governing trope of Wordsworth's work. It has then been easy to think that his problem with London—an environment in which he sometimes felt uncomfortable[1]—was that it failed to achieve this elevation; that urban life fixated on the merely finite, contingent or accidental at the expense of loftier or more permanent objects better suited to successful spiritual lift-off. The work on London thus comes to look satirical. From the pure and permanent vantage of Helvellyn or philosophy, a pettier life is to be mocked or denounced. This was certainly what Coleridge wanted, when he was giving an account of Wordsworth's poem in 1832: Wordsworth, recall, was to assume 'a satiric or Juvenalian spirit as he approached the high civilization of cities and towns'.[2] The difficulty, though, is that many precisely of the most striking lines in Wordsworth's account of his experience in London do not fit this, and indeed that broader features of its articulation and placement do not support it.

It is clear from the start of Wordsworth's account of his London experience that the difficulty of register which has so often confronted modern poets attempting to write about cities—which is at bottom a difficulty of register consequent upon attempting to write poetry about modern experience itself—persists for him too. Wordsworth gives a history of his own advances and setbacks in writing the poem to Coleridge. He

---

3. Such as the poems in the *Memorials of a Tour in Italy, 1837* on Niebuhr and the three 1842 poems titled "In Allusion to Various Recent Histories and Notices of the French Revolution."

† From *Wordsworth's Philosophic Song* (Cambridge: Cambridge University Press, 2007), 137–47. Notes have been edited. Copyright © 2006 Simon Jarvis. Reprinted with the permission of Cambridge University Press.

1. But not always. 'I begin to wish much to be in town; cataracts and mountains, are good occasional society, but they will not do for constant companions.' Wordsworth to William Mathews, 7. xi. 1794, *EY*, p. 136.

2. S. T. Coleridge, *Table talk recorded by Henry Nelson Coleridge (and John Taylor Coleridge)*, ed. Carl Woodring (2 vols., Princeton: Princeton University Press, 1990), vol. I, pp. 307–8 (21 July 1832).

announces that he is now ready to continue in terms which make it clear
that special difficulties pertain to rendering urban experience in verse:
'we will now resume with chearful hope, / Nor check'd by aught of tamer
argument / Which lies before us, needful to be told' (vii. 54–6). He starts
again; but he has to start again twice. London has fallen below his fan-
cies of it twice. In childhood a friend of his had gone to London and had,
to Wordsworth's astonishment, returned looking and sounding much the
same as when he left. Although as a man he no longer expected to find a
golden citadel, other fond imaginations had taken its place.

> These fond imaginations, of themselves,
> Had long before given way, in season due,
> Leaving a throng of others in their stead;
> And now I look'd upon the real scene,
> Familiarly perused it day by day
> With keen and lively pleasure, even there
> Where disappointment was the strongest, pleased
> Through courteous self-submission, as a tax
> Paid to the object by prescriptive right,
> A thing that ought to be. Shall I give way,
> Copying the impression of the memory,
> (Though things remember'd idly do half seem
> The work of Fancy) shall I as the mood
> Inclines me, here describe, for pastime's sake,
> Some portion of that motley imagery,
> A vivid pleasure of my youth, and now,
> Among the lonely places that I love,
> A frequent day-dream for my riper mind.
> —And first . . .
>
> (vii. 145–54)

The difficulties which Wordsworth had in getting the poem to start in
the first place afflict him again. Just as he has initially sidled into the
poem by asking himself whether all his youthful intimations of grandeur
were really only building up to this failure to write, and then by failing to
answer the question and instead starting to talk about what those youth-
ful intimations of grandeur were, so here another logical slippage allows
him to start writing about London. 'Shall I . . .' proposes a question mark
which never arrives. After this he simply does get under way, tellingly,
with a connective: '—And first, . . .' The leap appears decisionistic rather
than decisive, in the sense that it is made for the very purpose of obviat-
ing the anxiety of blockage. The difficulty of thinking the apparently idi-
otically contingent minutenesses of one's own experience fit to write a
poem about, a difficulty which, after Wordsworth, it has become hard
even to think of as a difficulty, was, fatefully, broken through at the start
of the poem; but here it apparently has to be broken through, and in a
similar way, all over again. It is as though going to the city makes us feel
with renewed defeat that our own silly singularity can carry no general
weight. That Wordsworth does feel anxious about this emerges from the
apologetic nature of this passage: from the quite unconvincing sugges-
tion that this part of the poem should be thought of as a bit of hobbyism
('for pastime's sake'); from the connection made between idle remembering

and fancy, a connection which implies the opposite connection between involuntary remembering and imagination; and, most of all, from the account of the mingled disappointment and pleasure which Wordsworth says he felt when he arrived. It is hard to enter into this account of 'keen and lively pleasure', because pleasure is not usually thought of as a 'tax', nor felt 'by prescriptive right'. Wordsworth seems to be saying that although he was in fact disappointed he made himself be pleased. We could remove this difficulty by thinking that saying that these pleasures were 'keen and lively' is just a way of being polite. Yet Wordsworth generally has little trouble admitting that youthful pleasures were forced ('The tragic super-tragic, else left short' [viii. 532]). The difficulty therefore needs to be preserved, rather than erased. It gains force in the subtle parataxis which closes the sentence: what is the 'thing that ought to be'? Thematically and primarily, it is the pleasure which Wordsworth feels because he ought to feel it. Yet syntactically and secondarily it may also be the 'object', London itself. London is *a thing that ought to be*, this under sense insinuates. The city perhaps remains in itself an ideality, retains also the shape of a norm rather than becoming a bare fact, even after successive fantasies of it have been chastened. It cannot be seen at once; it never ends. 'There is always something more to see.'

It is, in fact, this 'always more' which hangs over the attempt to 'describe' into which Wordsworth now plunges.

> And first, the look and aspect of the place,
> The broad high-way appearance, as it strikes
> On Strangers of all ages; the quick dance
> Of colours, lights and forms; the Babel din;
> The endless stream of men, and moving things;
> From hour to hour the illimitable walk
> Still among Streets with clouds and sky above; . . .
>
> (vii. 154–60)

It is not hard to see here at least one reason why poets immediately preceding Wordsworth should have found mock a comfortable medium in which to versify the city. Johnson's remark about Thomson's difficulty in organizing *The Seasons*, that '[o]f many appearances subsisting all at once, no rule can be given why one should be mentioned before another'[3] can be felt to apply equally acutely to descriptions of cities, and it reminds us of what is unusual in this passage within the whole poem's frame, that although he is continuing, as throughout, to describe his own memories, yet none the less, to describe one's own memories of the city is to begin to describe the multiplicity of the city itself; so that whereas Wordsworth's accounts of his Lakeland memories are distinguished from picturesque precisely by their lack of interest in any attempt at exhaustive description of what is merely given, he here at once pitches himself or finds himself pitched into a catalogue which, in trying to do more than merely give a list of notable items, he begins at a level of extreme generality. This generality attempts to offer something of the universal phenomenology of the city, its look and aspect in so far as that look and aspect is the same

---

3. R. D. Stock, ed., *Samuel Johnson's Literary Criticism* (Lincoln: University of Nebraska Press, 1974), p. 270.

for all. It is just this which exposes the writing to the guffaw at apparent vacuity which most critics and many readers of Wordsworth's time still had in their repertoire. ('Mr Wordsworth first undertakes to tell his readers "what *look*" the city bore, and also with what "*aspect*" it appeared; and his conclusion is, that it had a 'broad high-way *appearance*".') These first two lines do indeed appear emptied of purchase by the willed arbitrariness of getting started: something must be written, at any rate. The thought drops into a list which continues for the whole passage and recurs often throughout the book. Yet that there really was something Wordsworth wanted to say about the highways appears a few lines later: 'From hour to hour the illimitable walk / Still among Streets with clouds and sky above.' But of course there is nothing about the 'many appearances subsisting at once' of the city which makes them in themselves more or less difficult to describe simultaneously than the appearances of a mountainous region; nor is the city in itself more multiple than such a region. So the illimitability which is referred to here cannot be simply the fact that one could walk forever without coming to an end. That goes for everywhere else too. The implication, rather, as the remainder of the passage suggests, is that the walk is illimitable because one can never in truth *arrive* anywhere, and thus that one can never in fact *go* anywhere either. 'Still among Streets' grasps this in one move: the primary sense, that however far we walk we are still walking among streets, also contains a secondary possibility, that however far we walk we are still, that is, motionless.

> Here, there, and everywhere, a weary Throng!
> The Comers and the Goers face to face,
> Face after face; the string of dazzling Wares,
> Shop after Shop, with Symbols, blazon'd Names,
> And all the Tradesman's honours overhead;
> Here, fronts of houses, like a title-page,
> With letters huge inscribed from top to toe;
> Stationed above the door like guardian Saints,
> There, allegoric shapes, female or male;
> Or physiognomies of real men,
> Land Warriors, Kings, or Admirals of the Sea,
> Boyle, Shakespear, Newton; or the attractive head
> Of some Scotch Doctor, famous in his day.
>   (vii. 171–83)

One of the habitual ways of organizing appearances subsisting all at once in the century preceding Wordsworth was the conveniently arbitrary 'Here . . . there'. These markers gave the pointedness and apparent meaningfulness of spatial apposition to an otherwise too evidently contingent ordering. Wordsworth resorts to this device too, but only after he has already destroyed it with the opening line of this passage. Once 'Here, there, and everywhere' have been forced into a list they no longer bear any organizing power. 'Here' and 'there' are instances of 'everywhere'. The tacit resonance of 'Still among streets', that we walk without being able to arrive anywhere, is developed in these lines. The possible destinations are pointers to something else.

The illimitability of the city raises a problem of knowledge. The scarcely precedented speculation in Wordsworth's writing—that universality, if at all, is to be attained precisely by attention to what seems entirely personal or idiosyncratic—is brought up against difficulties there. In so far as the city is in any way one city, its unity consists not in a place or a series of places but in an ideality which sublates or abolishes any particular place, in *a thing that ought to be*. How is such an ideality to be known? Wordsworth's solution to this problem is abrupt. It repeats the decision which allowed him to begin to write about the city in the first place.

> From those sights
> Take one, an annual Festival, the Fair
> Holden where Martyrs suffer'd in past time,
> And nam'd of Saint Bartholomew; there see
> A work that's finish'd to our hands, that lays,
> If any spectacle on earth can do,
> The whole creative powers of man asleep!
> For once the Muse's aid will we implore,
> And she shall lodge us, wafted on her wings,
> Above the press and danger of the Crowd
> Upon some Show-man's Platform: . . .
>
> (vii. 649–59)

'—And first, . . .'; 'From these sights / Take one . . .' The appeal to the Muse which follows reinforces this decisionism with a poetic *metabasis eis allo genos*, a resolution of a difficulty by a leap into a different order of being.[4] Wordsworth notes the emergency character of this leap: 'For once . . .'[5] 'The Muse' is by this date flightless. But '[f]or once' she is needed, since she allows us to imagine a vantage which we cannot really have. The sudden ascent is all the more conspicuous because Wordsworth's writing is usually so cautious about the kind of knowledge which elevation is supposed to confer over what, either figuratively or literally, is looked down upon. It is from this willed aerial perspective that we can see the production of consumption: 'as if the whole were one vast Mill' (vii. 692). The solution comes at a critical point in the book, because Wordsworth is going on to treat the fair as a model for understanding the whole city:

> O blank confusion! and a type not false
> Of what the mighty City is itself
> To all except a Straggler here and there,
> To the whole swarm of its inhabitants;
> An undistinguishable world to men,
> The slaves unrespited of low pursuits,
> Living amid the same perpetual flow
> Of objects, melted and reduced
> To one identity by differences
> That have no law, no meaning, and no end;
> Oppression under which even highest minds
> Must labour, whence the strongest are not free!
>
> (vii. 696–707)

---

4. See Kant, *Critique of Pure Reason*, p. 494.
5. A point noted by John Plotz, 'The necessary veil: Wordsworth's "Residence in London"', in *The Crowd: British Literature and Public Politics* (Berkeley, Calif.: University of California Press, 2000), pp. 15–42, p. 34. I thank Neil Hertz for drawing my attention to this work.

What constitutes the City as 'itself' is not, as so much poetry of city life would have it, an ungraspable or even infinite plurality, but a single ideality. It is a lived ideality of unchanging self-sameness: the same perpetual flow, one identity. The *rich variety* of city life is usually thought of as lying in its many differences. But here these 'differences' are not opposed to that blank identity. They establish it. This seems not to make sense. How can it be the case that *differences* make this '[a]n undistinguishable world to men'? The writing implies that there might be differences which do have a law, a meaning and an end. For these differences to be distinguishable, we must find a way to stand outside the perpetual flow of illusory plurality—a plurality, for example, of many 'moveables of wonder' (vii. 680). That perpetual flow is the element in which we live and breathe, however 'high' our minds may be. There is no spiritual aristocracy which may stand above it. If there were, the appeal to the Muse would not be needed. Yet it is only from this no-place that the whole view has been delivered. It is this difficulty that the passage immediately comes back to:

> But though the picture weary out the eye,
> By nature an unmanageable sight,
> It is not wholly so to him who looks
> In steadiness, who hath among least things
> An under sense of greatest; sees the parts
> As parts, but with a feeling of the whole.
> (vii. 708–13)

The city is '[b]y nature an unmanageable sight' or 'picture' because it is not really a sight or picture at all. It has only been possible to represent it as such with the Muse's help. We can have no knowledge of the whole, but only 'a feeling of the whole'. More strangely, this feeling of the whole is the opposite of the 'one identity' mentioned before. *This* feeling of the whole requires that we wrest our attention from that abstract unity. It requires that we see the parts as parts; that we feel those differences which really do have a law, a meaning and an end. It is an *under*, not an *over* 'sense of greatest'. What may be hoped for from this under sense is kept carefully limited. It cannot untie anyone from the string of dazzling wares. It forms a rub or botch in that surface seamlessness. The gaze is 'not wholly' blinded by the false whole. It may see something if it look in steadiness.

'Not Wholly So'

The exceptional difficulty of London as an object or illusory-object for verse is confirmed by the recursion to it in the following book. This book is given the indicative title 'Retrospect', but the subtitle, 'Love of Nature leading to love of Mankind', hardly lets us know that we are to return to London. Wordsworth begins the book on a physical vantage-point, Helvellyn, which is implicitly contrasted with the fantasized vantage afforded by the 'Muse' in book 7, as though to recruit from 'fields and their rural works' that steadiness which he has just invoked. Whereas in the earlier book Wordsworth became continually anxious that his subject matter was too tame, asking himself whether he needed to fear mentioning a place name as humble as Sadler's Wells in verse, and thus indicating that he did fear to do it (as one might even today fear to mention Cricklewood or Finchley Road); whereas he concedes there that his matter is likely to 'seem / To many neither dignified enough nor arduous'; here, by contrast, the difficulty is to attempt again first to give an adequate sense of the grandeur which he experienced in entering London and then to give an adequate sense of the blankness he felt when that grandeur had almost at once passed away:

<blockquote>
On the Roof
Of an itinerant Vehicle I sate
With vulgar men about me, vulgar forms
Of houses, pavement, streets, of men and things,
Mean shapes on every side; but at the time
When to myself it fairly might be said,
The very moment that I seem'd to know,
The threshold now is overpass'd—Great God!
That aught external to the living mind
Should have such mighty sway! yet so it was—
A weight of Ages did at once descend
Upon my heart, no thought embodied, no
Distinct remembrances; but weight and power,
Power, growing with the weight: alas! I feel
That I am trifling: 'twas a moment's pause,
All that took place within me, came and went
As in a moment, and I only now
Remember that it was a thing divine.
(viii. 693–710)
</blockquote>

The experience of entering the city was so powerful that he remembers almost nothing about it. Now he feels that he is trifling, not because the matter is too light for his grander verse, but because his verse is too mundane or too restricted to seize the grandeur of his experience of the city;— and yet not, in truth, of his experience of the city, but his experience of the ideality of the city. For this weight of ages descends not at the sight of a picture, but at the point when he seemed to know, when to himself it fairly might be said, that he was now in the city. We might expect to be given some idea of the sensory cues which allowed him to say this to himself, but he draws attention to the fact that he has no distinct remembrances to offer at all. The experience of weight and power arises from an encounter with an ideality of the city: 'a thing that ought to be'.

Wordsworth's own chiasmic play on 'weight' and 'power' strikes him as empty, and so he embarks on an extended simile which is intended to make clearer in what way this was 'a thing divine':

<blockquote>
As when a traveller hath from open day
With torches pass'd into some Vault of Earth,
The Grotto of Antiparos, or the Den
Of Yordas among Craven's mountain tracts;
He looks and sees the Cavern spread and grow,
Widening itself on all sides, sees, or thinks
He sees, erelong, the roof above his head,
Which instantly unsettles and recedes
Substances and shadow, light and darkness, all
</blockquote>

Commingled, making up a Canopy
Of Shapes and Forms, and Tendencies to Shape,
That shift and vanish, change and interchange
Like Spectres, ferment quiet, and sublime;
Which, after a short space, works less and less
Till every effort, every motion gone,
The scene before him lies in perfect view,
Exposed and lifeless as a written book.
But let him pause awhile, and look again
And a new quickening shall succeed, at first
Beginning timidly, then creeping fast
Through all which he beholds: the senseless mass
In its projections, wrinkles, cavities,
Through all its surface, with all colours streaming,
Like a magician's airy pageant, parts,
Unites, embodying everywhere some pressure
Or image, recognis'd or new, some type
Or picture of the world; forests and lakes,
Ships, rivers, towers, the Warrior clad in Mail,
The prancing Steed, the Pilgrim with his Staff,
The mitred Bishop and the throned King,
A Spectacle to which there is no end.
    No otherwise had I at first been mov'd
With such a swell of feeling follow'd soon
By a blank sense of greatness pass'd away
And afterwards continued to be mov'd
In presence of that vast Metropolis,
The Fountain of my Country's destiny
And of the destiny of Earth itself,
That great Emporium, Chronicle at once
And Burial-place of passions and their home
Imperial, and chief living residence.

                                        (viii. 711–51)

This simile is the unmasking of an unmasking. Its shape is important. By
the time readers reach 'Exposed and lifeless as a written book' they may be
ready for 'So' to reply to 'As', for the relevance of this vehicle to the tenor,
the entry into London, to be delivered. What follows instead is a second
look at the vehicle: 'But let him pause a while . . .' The cave at first provides
an unusual kind of sublimity, one which follows not from the grandeur or
fearfulness of the object, nor from any attempt, and failure, to provide an
intuition to reason, but simply from the attempt and failure to see what is
there, a 'ferment *quiet*, and sublime'. This recedes as the traveller does
see what is there, and arrives at a kind of dead letter of perception.[6] The
second cathexis which follows appears at first to be a rebirth of the power
just lost. Yet its shape is quite different. The roof now offers a world of
representations. It is a surface in which the traveller can if he wants see

6. A good deal has at some times turned on the figure of the dead letter in Wordsworth's writing;
   it will be discussed in more detail in a later chapter of the book. I shall suggest that there is a
   materialist current in Wordsworth's writing, but that instead of being a materialism of ultimate
   literalness, such as Paul de Man finds in Kant's *Critique of Judgement* ('Phenomenality and
   materiality in Kant', in *Aesthetic ideology*, ed. Andrzej Warminski (Minneapolis and London:
   University of Minnesota Press, 1996) pp. 70–90), it is a current which runs in opposition to the
   phenomenalization of soul and world in modern philosophy.

infinitely many representations. It is 'A Spectacle to which there is no end.' This second attempt repeats the illimitable character of the city. 'There is always something more to see.'

Its strangeness hinges on the imagined dead letter. The book is lifeless, like any book, yet it can be read. But what we do when we read a book is not really to bring it back to life. The scene is a train of spirits which appear animated but are not alive. This strangeness persists into the tenor, which after this delay now arrives. Wordsworth's initial sense of sublimity (not, however, as in the cave, a sense of sublimity prompted by an appearance, but rather a sense prompted by his own act of understanding) is replaced by a 'blank' disappointment, the city as a dead letter; and this in turn is replaced by a long or endless period in which he 'continued to be mov'd': moved, that is, not by what he may now solidly perceive as a reality, but by the illimitable train of spirits of urban life. The simile is the unmasking of an unmasking in the sense that it does not take us from illusion to reality, but from appearance to appearance: to the recognition that the city, as city, is infinite appearance, 'A Spectacle to which there is no end.'

Although this passage is legitimately read as a compensation for the critical treatment in book 7 (a reading which is most trenchantly put by Mary Jacobus when she argues that 'The Cave of Yordas saves the city from satire and gives it back to romance'[7])—and although, indeed, Wordsworth himself thinks of it (viii. 678–85) as a more serious attempt to return to a subject which was only played with or puzzled at there—its fundamental thoughts and feelings are of a piece with the earlier treatment's equivocality. As Thomas Pfau remarks, the simile 'gradually reattaches itself to that ambivalent heart of civilization, London, whose semiotic and perceptual entropy it was meant to counterbalance'.[8] The concluding lines of the passage, with their breathless conjunctive linking of opposites, indicate this equivocality: 'Chronicle at once / And Burial-place of passions and their home / Imperial, and chief living residence.' Burial-place *and* living residence. This gathering of the *personae* of distinction or vocation ('the' warrior, 'the' pilgrim, 'the' bishop) was not accidentally a meeting of spirits, of the living dead. The city's living-dead character is awesome. It is for the poet to feel that awe, but also to look steadily through and beyond it. He is to feel the power of those spirits without worshipping them: 'not wholly so'.

* * *

MICHAEL O'NEILL

[Self-Consciousness in *Resolution and Independence*][†]

In 'Resolution and Independence' the poem's consciousness of itself as a poem is central to its achievement. This consciousness is shown by a

7. Mary Jacobus, *Romanticism, Writing, and Sexual Difference: Essays on* The Prelude (Oxford: Clarendon Press, 1989), p. 111.
8. Thomas Pfau, *Wordsworth's Profession: Form, Class, and the Logic of Early Romantic Cultural Production* (Stanford, Calif.: Stanford University Press, 1997), p. 370.
† From *Romanticism and the Self-Conscious Poem* (Oxford: Clarendon Press, 1997), 37–45. Notes have been renumbered. Reprinted by permission.

characteristic feature of Wordsworthian and Romantic poetry: the poem's gradual, indirect, compelling shaping of itself into a journey. A central figure in that journey is figurativeness itself: relatively straightforward at the beginning, metaphor and its workings grow increasingly self-exploratory as the poem progresses. Even the opening's straightforwardness is deceptive. The poem does not simply move from happiness to depression before recovery as a result of the encounter with the Leech-gatherer. The opening's 'now' is conscious of a previously troubled 'then', as is hinted by the initial lines: 'There was a roaring in the wind all night; | The rain came heavily and fell in floods, | But now the sun is rising calm and bright' (1–3). In this poem, unlike 'Ode: Intimations of Immortality', 'There was . . .' is not a formulation that looks back to some lost glory; rather, it intimates the unstable happiness of the present. This happiness, lithely conveyed through the lines about the hare in stanza 2, should not be underplayed; here, indeed, the poem's use of the present tense results in an epiphanic syntax. The hare in all its exuberant vigour springs forth from these lines:

> The Hare is running races in her mirth;
> And with her feet she from the plashy earth
> Raises a mist; which, glittering in the sun,
> Runs with her all the way, wherever she doth run.
>
> (11–14)

These lines suggest that happiness, in this poem, consists in an imaginative sympathy with fellow-creatures. But if the 'mist' that the hare 'Raises' is wholly natural, it hints at the imagination's aura-bestowing powers; certainly the imagination choreographs the verbal dance performed by plashy earth and glittering mist. In this recognition lie the seeds of subsequent disquiet. For the poet wishes to understand his happiness as a recovery of boyish lack of self-consciousness: 'I heard the woods, and distant waters, roar, | Or heard them not, as happy as a Boy' (17–18). That comparison points up the distance between the poet as adult and as boy, as does the later, more insistent, 'I bethought me of the playful Hare: | Even such a happy Child of earth am I' (30–1). In the former lines the desired lack of consciousness is asserted self-consciously; in the latter the poet's primitivism—his sense of himself as 'a happy Child of earth'— betrays the same kinds of fear as Keats's assertions of the word 'happy' in stanza 3 of 'Ode on a Grecian Urn'. The poet has already retreated into the past tense; 'that morning', he confesses, 'fear, and fancies, thick upon me came; | Dim sadness, and blind thoughts I knew not nor could name' (26, 27–8). That past tense concedes that the vision of the hare could not last; at the same time, it consigns to the past the 'sadness' which the reader experiences in the present. But the only refuge from 'untoward thoughts' (54) of the 'despondency and madness' (49) that a wryly feminine rhyme sees as the lot of poets is the creative transformation of such thoughts attempted by the poem's second half.

Because the notion (often simplified) of the autonomous self has been under attack in recent criticism of the Romantics, appreciative analysis of the play of inwardness and self-exploration in Wordsworth's poetry has been unusefully vetoed. Thus Richard Bourke sees 'Resolution and Independence' as showing poetry's tendency to operate by means of exclusion and restriction; he writes: 'The act of restriction through which the poetic figure comes into its own cancels the act of inclusion which remains the reputed purpose of literary design.'[1] This hostile judgement has its own misdirected acuteness. If, as Bourke does, one reads the poem in the light of the universalist axioms of the Preface to *Lyrical Ballads*, the poet's wish to 'include' may seem to be undone by his poem's self-concern. Certainly the line, 'Over his own sweet voice the Stock-dove broods' (5), is descriptive of the poem itself, which broods over its own voice. In his 'Preface to the Edition of 1815' Wordsworth singles out this line to show how the imagination operates:

> by the intervention of the metaphor *broods*, the affections are called in by the imagination to assist in marking the manner in which the bird reiterates and prolongs her soft note, as if herself delighting to listen to it, and participating of a still and quiet satisfaction, like that which may be supposed inseparable from the continuous process of incubation.[2]

His own poem 'broods' over itself in a secondary sense of the word: that is, it builds into its development worried anxiety about the function of a poet. In doing so, Wordsworth, arguably, points up a gap between his highly 'metaphoric' way of writing and a 'language near to the real language of men'.[3] 'Resolution and Independence' serves for the critic in Wordsworth as a test-case of the imagination's activity. The famous stanza (64–70) just after the old man has entered the poem almost deconstructs such activity as it runs in slow-motion 'the conferring, the abstracting, and the modifying powers of the Imagination'.[4] 'As a huge Stone . . .' (64); 'So that it seems . . .' (68); 'Like a Sea-beast . . .' (69); (and at the start of the next stanza) 'Such seemed this Man . . .'(71): the largely monosyllabic diction and clearly signposted comparisons work less to evoke the old man than to indicate the poet at work. However, the writing is neither still-born nor laboured. Its 'modifying' phrases and movements engage the reader in the drama of sense-making staged in the poem: sense-making that is cautiously and intricately aware of its own processes, and reluctant to claim decisive success. The passage is prepared for by the lines, 'My course I stopped as soon as I espied | The Old Man in that naked wilderness' (57–8). When the Leech-gatherer is made the object of a series of likenesses, the poem's course, too, is 'stopped' before it continues in its one foot forwards, two feet sideways manner. The passage's would-be clinching 'Such *seemed* this Man' is noteworthy for its evasive verb. Wordsworth's claim that 'the two objects unite and coalesce in just comparison' over-simplifies the effect of a fine, risk-taking passage.[5]

'Resolution and Independence' marks a point at which latent tensions at work in the Preface to *Lyrical Ballads* manifest themselves. One such tension is the pull between what Chapter 5 calls 'self- and other-awareness'. In the Preface Wordsworth suggests that a movement between the two

1. Richard Bourke, *Romantic Discourse and Political Modernity: Wordsworth, The Intellectual and Cultural Critique* (New York: St. Martin's Press, 1993), 239.
2. *Prose Works*, iii. 32.
3. 'Preface to *Lyrical Ballads* (1800)', *Prose Works*, i. 150.
4. 'Preface to the Edition of 1815', *Prose Works*, iii. 33.
5. 'Preface to the Edition of 1815', *Prose Works*.

forms of awareness is inevitable; after the poet has 'thought long and deeply' he will 'discover what is really important to men'.[6] But 'Resolution and Independence' is brought up against the difficulty of any such discovery. At the same time, the questioning of and imagining generated by the Leech-gatherer reinstates other-awareness, though the 'other' is now a mystery rather than an equivalent to the 'self'. Stephen Gill argues that the poem 'testifies to Wordsworth's capacity to seize on something outside himself, however trivial the material'.[7] Wordsworth's double operation in the poem—moving 'outside himself' while examining his imagination at work—is underestimated by Bourke's reading.

Bourke is right to point out that Wordsworth emphasizes the Leech-gatherer's 'courteous speech' (93) and 'lofty utterance' (101), thus elevating his language 'above the reach | Of ordinary men' (102–3).[8] But, throughout the poem, Wordsworth is shaping intuitions on the margins of language. He is able in this poem to use the idea of language as ornament— the old man's 'words' (99) are 'With something of a lofty utterance drest' (101)—because it is what the Leech-gatherer is, rather than what he says, which is of first importance. What he says matters less for its almost banal content than for what it suggests (first) about the old man's self-sufficiency and capacity to endure, and (second) about Wordsworth's own ability to transform experience imaginatively. Words do not incarnate meaning in the Leech-gatherer's case; rather, they act as enigmatic signs towards barely graspable significance. Sternly rebuking Sara Hutchinson for not sufficiently admiring the poem in its first version, Wordsworth writes in a letter of 14 June 1802:

> A person reading this poem with feelings like mine will have been awed and controlled, expecting almost something spiritual or supernatural—What is brought forward? 'A lonely place, a Pond', 'by which an old man *was*, far from all house or home'—not stood or sat, but '*was*'—the figure presented in the most naked simplicity possible.[9]

Subsequently Wordsworth revised lines 55–6 to read 'I saw a Man before me unawares: | The oldest Man he seemed that ever wore grey hairs'. The change indicates loss of confidence that the effect he had aimed at in the phrase 'by which an old man was' was being communicated. In the revised lines the ambiguously suggestive 'unawares' leaves the reader unsure whether any lack of awareness was the poet's or the old man's. That unsureness brings about an acute awareness of unawareness, making the reader debate the value of unawareness; it might be the poet's soon-to-be-rebuked unawareness (because self-pityingly engrossed by his 'untoward thoughts', 54); it might be the old man's sublimely indifferent unawareness. The writing, in the revised version, substitutes a tangled self-consciousness for the more insistent mimicry of 'naked simplicity' attempted by the original version.

6. 'Preface to *Lyrical Ballads* (1800)', *Prose Works*, i. 126.
7. Stephen Gill, *William Wordsworth: A Life* (Oxford: Clarendon Press, 1989), 201.
8. Bourke, *Romantic Discourse*, 238.
9. Letter quoted from McMaster (ed.), *William Wordsworth: A Critical Anthology*, 86. For a facsimile and transcription of the poem with the reading Wordsworth gives in his letter, see *'Poems, in Two Volumes' and Other Poems, 1800–1807*, ed. Jared Curtis (Ithaca, NY: Cornell University Press, 1983), 318–19.

In answer to Bourke, then, it is necessary to say that Wordsworth is not trying (and failing) to make his words reinforce a predetermined egalitarian politics. Instead, he seeks to record an experience which brings out yet tests to the limit his poetic resources. In the recording of that testing, however, lies the poem's success. For it is Wordsworth who creates the dialogic effects which allow poet and reader to explore different perspectives in a way that supports Bourke's best insight, that 'Resolution and Independence continually draws attention to itself, to its particular evolution and status.'[1] It does so in a fashion that prevents its resolution from being too resolved and suggests the troubling nature of poetic independence. The poem shows that it can, if it chooses, absorb the Leechgatherer within a visionary mode in the stanzas starting 'The Old Man still stood talking by my side' (113) and 'While he was talking thus, the lonely place' (134). But in both cases the Leech-gatherer's talk leads the poet into a 'troubled' (135) reverie. In the first stanza Wordsworth continues, 'But now his voice to me was like a stream | Scarce heard; nor word from word could I divide' (114–15). Incapacity to hear properly is bound up with the renewed finding of imaginative power. Transforming the old man's speech into a natural force, one that is continuous and hardly audible, the simile illustrates the poet's discovery that loneliness and uncanniness stir his imagination: this discovery both passes into and covertly contends with the notion of moral efficacy, 'strong admonishment' (119), embodied in the figure of the Leech-gatherer.

In fact, the Old Man's effect, despite the heartened gestures of the final stanza, is less moral than imaginative. Because he sets going the poet's imagination, he can be said to 'admonish' Wordsworth not to despair imaginatively, not to dwell on the chilling exempla of 'mighty Poets in their misery dead' (123). Again, the second stanza mentioned above (134–40) gives quickened access to the hiding-places of the poet's power and a sense of the poet's bewilderment at the visionary seeings of his 'mind's eye' (136): 'In my mind's eye I seemed to see him pace | About the weary moors continually, | Wandering about alone and silently' (136–8). Borrowed from Chatterton's 'An Excelente Balade of Charitie', the stanza form—rhyme royal with a final alexandrine—is used well by Wordsworth here (as elsewhere in the poem). Its central b rhymes 'wander' 'continually' in and out of one another, much as the Old Man's 'shape, and speech' trouble the poet's imagination. The transference of 'weary' from human wanderer to natural environment in the phrase 'weary moors' displays the 'conferring, the abstracting, and the modifying powers of the Imagination'. A weariness, not far removed from visionary dreariness, is experienced as a state in which human being and natural scene participate. The lines give access to an inner dimension in which time is experienced as a never-ending, haunting continuum. 'Silently' does much to suggest this inner dimension glimpsed by the poem, as though its words were negotiating with the state that prompts them into being. One might wish to adapt to these lines Arnold's famous comment on lines 19–21 of Tennyson's 'Ulysses': 'It is no blame to their rhythm, which belongs to another order of movement than Homer's, but it is true that these three

---

1. Bourke, Romantic Discourse, 229.

lines by themselves take up nearly as much time as a whole book of the *Iliad*.[2] Tennyson's lines read: 'Yet all experience is an arch wherethrough | Gleams that untravelled world, whose margin fades | For ever and for ever when I move' (19–21).[3]

For Wordsworth and Tennyson 'experience' is as much a question of the present-tense travelling through the lines as an extra-textual reality; the reader is caught up in a labyrinth of sound and syntax, temporarily denied recourse to narrative goals. Even when the stanza under discussion in 'Resolution and Independence' snaps out of reverie in the crisply deployed final couplet of the stanza, there is still a sense in which the preceding imaginative 'trouble' goes on. Wordsworth's resolution in the final stanza is obliquely but powerfully related to the imaginative independence reaffirmed, in however 'troubling' a manner, in the previous stanza. The confident future tense of 'I'll think of the Leech-gatherer on the lonely moor' (147) has at the back of its mind the ongoing present implied by 'continually' (137).

GEOFFREY HARTMAN

From 1801–1807: The Major Lyrics[†]

* * *

The Intimations Ode

Once more, to the poet of the Intimations Ode, a thought of grief comes on a fine spring morning. And, again as in "Resolution and Independence," instead of saying immediately it was this or that which grieved him, Wordsworth goes on to think aloud, as if thinking and grief had now an intimate link, and the one would always issue, at some point, in the other. This time, however, the recognition that restores him is elusive. There is no Leech-gatherer: it is all a dialogue of the soul with itself in the presence of nature. The joy must spring from deep within thought; the consolation perhaps from the very grief he feels. We sense the constant possibility of reversal even more than in "Resolution and Independence."

The irregular rhythms, a privilege of the ode form, work independently of specific stanza or stage of argument to express the flux and reflux of a mind for which reversal is no longer simply the structure of experience but its own structure, its very *style* of thought. Wordsworth does mention in the third stanza a "timely utterance" which gave him relief, but what happened is kept vague, and the event, in any case, could not have been determining, since the grief returns in the next stanza. There is, finally, again encouraged by the ode (the sublimest of the lyric genres), a larger pattern of flux and reflux: even though each stanza tends to mingle rising and falling rhythms, stanzas III and IV are, as it were, a "Counter-turn" to stanzas I and II, while stanza V is a kind of epode or "stand" in which the passion seems to level out into a new generalization or withdrawal from

2. Matthew Arnold, 'On Translating Homer', quoted in *The Poems of Tennyson*, ed. Christopher Ricks (London: Longmans, 1969), 563.
3. Quoted from *The Poems of Tennyson*, ed. Ricks.
† From *Wordsworth's Poetry 1787–1814* (New Haven: Yale University Press, 1964), 273–88. Notes have been edited and renumbered. Reprinted by permission of the author.

personal immediacy.[1] Related to this larger pattern is the Ode's admixture of reflection, question, invocation, petition, and praise, which approaches the Psalms in sublimity, and also recalls the confessional style of St. Augustine.

The subject of the Ode, Lionel Trilling has said, is growing up. Yet though it is true that the subject is conceived, except for the organizing myth, in naturalistic terms, Wordsworth's high style and the religious intensity of his emotions must be considered. There is a Hebrew prayer which praises God's mercy in restoring the soul every morning to its body, even as He restores it to the dead. Some of the terror of discontinuity behind the gratitude of this prayer is also in Wordsworth's Ode. The poet fears a decay of his "genial" responses to nature, and he fears that this decay has affected his powers of renovation. Growing up is not enough; the development of abstract sympathies is not enough; these must be linked, else they cannot be actualized, to the renewal of earlier feelings, to *joy* in nature.[2] It is easy to gain the world and to lose one's soul.

This deeper concern with renewal explains why Wordsworth is so affected by what appears to be a very little thing: a wrong echo. On this May morning, his heart responds with a thought of grief instead of equal gaiety. All other creatures have the proper harmonic echo, the immediate internal response to nature's influence. The young lambs bound "As to the tabor's sound"—there is no tabor, but Wordsworth sees their joy as a responsive joy. He calls them and the other participants in nature's jubilee "blessed Creatures": "And God created . . . every living creature that moveth . . . and God saw that it was good. And God blessed them, saying, Be fruitful and multiply." God responded to them, God *recognized* them, but the poet's heart is dull. We remember the opening of "Resolution and Independence," where everything echoes and responds: the Jay to the Magpie, the Stockdove to its own call, and even the glittering mist to the hare wherever the latter runs.

That Wordsworth should take a momentary grief as an omen questioning his power to be renewed, to be 'naturally' renewed, is typical of his spiritual state at this time. *The Prelude* also begins with a failed response (overcome more lightly), and the fear that his "genial spirits" might be decaying was already quietly expressed in the meditations of "Tintern Abbey." We have to do with a recurrent, not an unusual, fear. The Ode, in fact, begins with a general statement, and only then proceeds to mention the particular moment which perhaps was the occasion of that generality.[3] Each failure of joy, each feeling of indifference or alienation, newly accuses the poet. Much later in his life, when he seems to be more resigned to what he here still resists, and an "Evening of Extraordinary Splendour" surprises him, he will querulously demand: "This glimpse of

1. My comment, because of the complexity of the transitions, is only roughly correct. St. vi, for example, is a subtle counter-turn to st. v; so that, in a sense, there is no "stand." (The edition of 1807, by the way, has no stanza numberings.) "The ode was intended for such readers only as had been accustomed to watch the flux and reflux of their inmost nature, to venture at times into the twilight realms of consciousness, and to feel a deep interest in modes of inmost being" (Coleridge, *Biographia Literaria* ch. 22).
2. Coleridge, in his dialogue with the Intimations Ode, uses "joy" to mean the feeling that enables or accompanies a living, regenerative contact with nature (see the Dejection Ode).
3. The supposition that the first two stanzas are the "utterance" mentioned in st. iii is strongly supported by E. D. Hirsch, *Wordsworth and Schelling* (1960), pp. 150–51. Cf. H. M. Margoliouth, *Wordsworth and Coleridge* (1953), p. 101.

glory, why renewed?"[4] But in the Ode he rises to an answering vigor of imagination.

There is first the "timely utterance" which frees him for other utterances:

> The Cataracts blow their trumpets from the steep,
> No more shall grief of mine the season wrong.

The second verse is surely the inner call by which, in this restored continuum of inner and outer events, he replies to the cataracts. It is followed by a movement like the Psalmist's "Awake the dawn," when he accepts the fact that the initiative is with him, and indicates his readiness to join "in thought" what others may still feel at heart. "Thou Child of Joy / Shout round me, let me hear thy shouts . . ." "Then, sing ye Birds, sing, sing a joyous song." There are, finally, those "intimations of immortality" which remind him of actual continuities and permanent points of relation with the Nature he has known.

These affirmative movements are interrupted, of course, by renewed questionings and qualifications (extending even into imagery and rhythm), so that the continuity of the Ode is as precarious as the "natural piety" which is its subject. But though this precariousness is just—the Ode is prayer as well as celebration—one contradiction seems not to have been expressed clearly enough by Wordsworth, which may perhaps explain why so many have felt the Ode to be confused, or not completely unified. There are, if we look closely, two quite different "intimations of immortality." Whereas one implies the mortality of nature:

> questionings
> Of sense and outward things,
> Fallings from us, vanishings;
> Blank misgivings of a Creature
> Moving about in worlds not realiz'd . . .

the other implies its immortality:

> the primal sympathy
> Which having been must ever be.

In stanza IX especially, when Wordsworth says that his thanksgivings are less for the visionary gleam than for the visionary dreariness, and goes on to describe the latter as:

> those first affections,
> Those shadowy recollections,
> Which, be they what they may,
> Are yet the fountain light of all our day,
> Are yet a master light of all our seeing;

it is hard to follow him. He seems to be willfully confusing moments of darkness and fear in which nature seemed alien to the child with moments of splendor and beauty which first developed the child's affections and drew them to nature in a more intimate way.

---

4. *PW*, 4, 12. *Evening Voluntaries*, IX (composed 1817).

The confusion is willful, I think, and may be resolved; but not by the Ode alone. It needs an understanding of Wordsworth's conception of the progress of the soul. Wordsworth shares with St. Augustine the knowledge of a personal mercy which is part of a mercy to mankind. Both have been rescued 'unto life'; but life for Wordsworth is the freeing of his soul from solipsism. Before the child is naturalized, and sporadically at later times, its soul moves in another world than "nature," or if in nature, then one that is colored by a sublime and terrible imagination. The soul's eventual turning to nature is therefore a real conversion, and proof of self-transcending transcending powers. Man's growth into humanity is founded on this conversion. A child is an "Alien scatter'd from the Clouds," but the strength which its imagination exhibits in going out of itself and blending with a lesser nature is the source of all further strength: it is for Wordsworth *the* act of re-generation.[5] Every step in growing up is but an extension of this constitutive sympathy. The mature man, therefore, bases his faith in self-transcendence on the ease or unconsciousness with which the apocalyptic imagination turned in childhood toward life. Then the crisis was to go from self-love (unconscious) to love of nature, and now it is to go from self-love (conscious) to love of man. Each transition is precarious; but the second cannot occur without the first, and the first is the sign that the second is possible. "The Child is the father of the Man."

By the time the poet understands nature's role, only intimations of his unself-conscious powers of relationship remain. The nature to which he appeals in his great envoi:

> And oh ye Fountains, Meadows, Hills, and Groves,
> Think not of any severing of our loves!

is dying to him; and the perilous progress of the Ode comes from Wordsworth's resistance to this appearance of death. I say "appearance," because, were nature really lost to him, the excursive or self-renewing vigor of his soul might be impugned. Wordsworth cannot give up nature without giving up his faith in renovation. The whole issue turns on faith and hope.

"Ode to Duty"

The "Ode to Duty" is more in need of interpretation than the other poems so far considered. This is not only because it has failed to attract devoted attention, but also for an intrinsic reason. Wordsworth is speaking in the Ode in his "character of philosophical poet";[6] and our immediate difficulty with it stems from a diction of generality, not to say vagueness, which its "philosophical" character seems to have imposed. What identity, first of all, do we give the Duty to which Wordsworth desires to submit? It cannot be only conscience, since he says approvingly that it is in the quietness of thought he supplicates, undisturbed in soul or by compunction. Nor can it be only obedience to the dictate of positive

---

5. The ancient Natura, as in the fertile Chaos of Spenser's Garden of Adonis (*Faerie Queene*, Bk. III, canto VI), clothes the soul with a "first being" sufficient to let it enter the changeable world. But Wordsworth's Nature gives the soul its "second being," which is more essential insofar as it lays the ground for all further second being or rebirth.
6. Grosart, *Prose Works of Wordsworth* (1876), I, 326. From Wordsworth's "Answer to the Letter of Mathetes" published in *The Friend* in 1809.

or divine law, even though the Miltonic personification which opens the Ode, and the description of Duty as lawgiver in the first and seventh stanzas, must be considered. But this (the sterner demand) is at once qualified:

> Stern Daughter of the Voice of God!
> O Duty! if that name thou love . . .

> Stern Lawgiver! yet thou dost wear
> The Godhead's most benignant grace . . .

Wordsworth, no doubt, is asking for a guide stricter than conscience or consciousness; even the regular form of the Ode, Horatian rather than pseudo-Pindaric, indicates his wish to escape the eternal flux of the inner life. Yet the chief emotion expressed by him, and expressed movingly, is for a *self-devoted* dedication,[7] and this eliminates the possibility that Duty's compulsion could stem from authority or the dictate of external law. Duty is "stern" only in the sense that she is, or could be, a "great Task-master"[8] for Wordsworth.

This leaves us with the rather simple idea that Duty is conscientiousness: due attention to the world and its cares. As Wordsworth will say many years later: "The education of man, and above all of a Christian, is the education of *duty*, which is most forcibly taught by the business and concerns of life."[9] This meaning of Duty at first escapes us because the poet's style of address is so high. Yet his elevated style has surely the same intent as certain stanzas to the daisy, also in the 1807 volume, although these are more playful.[1] Just as he exalts the humble daisy, he here dignifies the simple duties imposed by life, or those "lowliest duties" which his heart, like Milton's, accepts to lay upon itself.[2] It is, most probably, the image of Milton in Wordsworth's mind, rather than an abstract ethics, which determined his conception of Duty.

The Milton referred to is the poet of the great political and personal sonnets as well as the visionary of *Paradise Lost*. Between 1802 and 1804 Wordsworth wrote a volley of sonnets, many of them "Dedicated to Liberty" and mingling the personal and the prophetic strains. We know that the first impulse to these was given by a rereading of Milton in May 1802: previously Wordsworth had eschewed the sonnet form. We remember also what the poet had written to Lamb in 1801, about Milton and the "Union of Tenderness and Imagination." Milton's sonnets were confirmatory evidence of a great spirit, of a visionary spirit, submitting his imagination to daily and historical event. Here was a man whose soul dwelt apart like a star, yet with an ideal of service that informed both poetry

---

7. I use Protesilaus' phrase in Laodamia (st. VIII) to suggest an analogy.
8. See Milton's sonnet "How soon hath Time," and cf. "Ode to Duty," st. IV: "I shov'd unwelcome tasks away."
9. Grosart, *I*, 349. From a letter of 1830 to the Rev. Dr. Wordsworth. Earlier proof that this is the sense of duty intended by Wordsworth may be drawn from his first reasoned classification of his poems, in a letter to Coleridge in May 1809. The "Ode to Duty" is there classed among a group of poems "relating to the social and civic duties, chiefly interesting to the imagination through the understanding, and not to the understanding through the imagination, as the political sonnets" etc. (*Middle Years*, *I*, 308–09).
1. There are three poems to the daisy in the 1807 collection. *The Simpliciad* objected to his giving the daisy a "function apostolical," but the last stanza of the opening poem of Vol. 1, "Child of the Year!" etc., is a good example of wantoning high style.
2. "Milton! thou should'st be living at this hour" (composed 1802, published 1807).

and life. This ideal was maintained despite blindness and despite adversity. The presence of Milton in the "Ode to Duty" is confirmed by its allusions to his writings. There is the opening line, there is a direct quotation from a prose tract in the sixth stanza, and in the last a patent echo of Raphael's warning that Adam should keep his imagination on earth and cultivate his garden: "Be lowly wise; / Think only what concerns thee and thy being."

In "Resolution and Independence," whose title, in relation to the Ode, speaks for itself, Wordsworth had already broached the subject of Duty in this sense of planning, sowing, building, loving. They are, strangely enough, selfish cares, which arise when our unconscious faith in nature diminishes, and we realize to what extent our futures and those of the "kind" depend on the individual person. To this point Wordsworth had come in 1802, with or without Milton; and in the Ode of 1804 the same problem is once more resumed. Stanzas II and III in acknowledge that there are those who continue to rely on the "genial sense of youth" (they are still deified by their own spirits), but that Wordsworth himself, and perhaps everyone at some time, needs the additional security of a self-determined rather than instinctive involvement in the things of this world. The Ode's true subject is, once again, the humanization of the spirit.

Like Collins in "To Manners" or Gray in "To Adversity" (Wordsworth acknowledges the latter as his pattern) the poet goes out to meet the inevitable, accepts the necessity for transcending a previous mode of being, and calls up his calling. There is strength in this attitude, but also the pathos that a man should come to need a bond stronger than nature to keep his spirit with nature. The "empty terrors" and "vain temptations" which the first stanza mentions abstractly are those of the autonomous imagination: they are apocalyptic fears and gratuitous desires. The poet's later confession, "Me this uncharter'd freedom tires; / feel the weight of chance desires;" reveals more cogently the personal circumstance, but is no clearer. Wordsworth expects the reader to infer the particular experience from the generalizing (or biblical) expressions, which is good Neoclassical procedure: in this Wordsworth *has* changed. He no longer conveys the impression of speaking "from the depth of untaught things" but deals out what everyone should know, perhaps too well.

The bond stronger than nature Wordsworth calls duty and also reason. It is by no means opposed to nature but supports nature's earlier agency. Explicitly discussing in his *Answer to Mathetes* (1809) the stage of life in which youth passes into manhood, he admits that the "sacred light of childhood" cannot be more than a remembrance to the maturing man. He then continues in a passage of unusual clarity: "He [the youth] may, notwithstanding, be remanded to nature, and with trustworthy hopes, founded less upon his sentient than upon his intellectual being; to nature, as leading back insensibly to the society of reason, but to reason and will, as leading back to the wisdom of nature. A re-union, in this order accomplished, will bring reformation and timely support; and the two powers of reason and nature, thus reciprocally teacher and taught, may advance together in a track to which there is no limit."[3] Reason, here, is not a radically new source of strength—not discontinuous with the older faith in

3. Grosart, *I*, 318.

nature—but it does involve a methodic or ceremonial *prise de conscience;* and it is this which the "Ode to Duty" exhibits. The Ode moves us, if at all, by its dignified self-consciousness, by the invented ceremonial of the self giving the self away, and to a power it has called for that purpose: "I call thee: I myself commend . . . thy Bondman let me live!" Byron's *Manfred* will not better this tone, although he resists all the powers he summons.

Thus Wordsworth's "awful Power" of Duty is simply the inner strength of voluntarily dedicating oneself to the household bonds of life. Take away the idea of voluntary obedience, substitute for it a decision to rely on external authority, and you make nonsense of Wordsworth as you do of Milton. In Psalm 19, which moves structurally from the glory of nature to the light of "the law," both testimonies are praised because they renew the heart: "The law of the Lord is perfect, converting the soul: the testimony of the Lord is sure, making wise the simple." The emphasis remains on the inner man. Wordsworth remembered another verse of Psalm 19 in his beautiful lines on Duty in the seventh stanza:

> Thou dost preserve the Stars from wrong;
> And the most ancient Heavens through Thee are fresh and strong.

Compare the Psalmist's description of the sun as a "bridegroom coming out of his chamber, and [who] rejoiceth as a strong man to run his race." The stars too are preserved and the heavens renewed by the virtue of voluntary obedience. Even if such lines, as Wordsworth admitted, transfer "in the transport of imagination, the law of moral to physical natures,"[4] this does not dispute the truth they suggest but indicates the changed mode of its venue, which is no longer as if directly from nature but from nature via the resolved or meditative soul. Yet the weakness of the Ode remains: the style in which it talks about Duty makes us suspect a virtue that does not arise from human nature, or which transcends it.

I should not be understood to say that there is no change in Wordsworth between 1798 and 1804, between:

> Some silent laws our hearts may make,
> Which they shall long obey;[5]

and his address to the "Stern Lawgiver." The only question is what kind of change there is. In 1804, obviously, it is not the heart alone which makes these laws, and they are by no means silently made. But the views held respectively in 1798 and 1804 are still reconcilable, for laws are made in both cases (resolutions might be a preciser word) and they are made freely by the person unto himself. That they are "silent" in one case and rather vocal in the other ("Stern Daughter of the Voice of God . . .") is to be explained by the greater need in 1804 of a formal act of will, since nature, though disclosing to man his powers for relationship, binds only to herself, whereas Wordsworth is now concerned with a formal self-surrender "to labours by which his livelihood is to be earned or his social

---

4. Grosart, *1,* 326. Coleridge understood perfectly this conception of Duty, after hearing *The Prelude* recited: "Then (last strain) / Of Duty, chosen Laws controlling choice." (1807, "To William Wordsworth").
5. "It is the first mild day of March" (*Lyrical Ballads*).

duties performed." Still, in both cases, the "act of obedience [is] to a moral law established by himself."[6]

Where then is the change? Primarily in the style, where it appears to be. Let us characterize that style more closely on the basis of the two Odes. It has already been said that there is a certain vague or perhaps "philosophical" generality in some of Wordsworth's expressions, and which might be attributed to his subject or to the genre of the Sublime Ode.[7] The heightening, actually, is due to the genre which is consciously chosen to revalue the subject: childhood and practical duties are not traditional themes for elevated treatment. Unfortunately, when Wordsworth calls Duty a "Stern Lawgiver," the serious parody can be overlooked: only a close and puzzled reading shows that he means his determination to take common household duties as seriously as if they were indeed divine law. The ordinary reader of 1807 (and of today) would surely think that the Duty referred to is a 'sublime' personification of the moral law as it expresses itself in outward code or inward conscience. And it is quite possible that in his desire for a greater affiliation with the poets of the past or with the present public formed by them, Wordsworth slipped into a conflation of an original thought and the traditional perspective from which he wanted only the style.

Symptoms of a generalizing diction already appear in the Intimations Ode. The phrase "timely utterance" has confuted a generation of interpreters. Why did the poet not specify of what nature, other than timely, the utterance was? He is keeping the experience at a certain level of generality. He does not specify, for the same reason, the content of the "thought of grief." Though he begins his Ode with a specific sentiment, it is still expressed in very general terms, and we learn nothing about the conditions in which it arose except that the season was spring. It happens that "timely utterance" is a well-chosen phrase, for it emphasizes the restoration of a natural cycle, and the whole vital necessity of being drawn out of oneself. Yet like many other expressions it skirts vagueness. "Fields of sleep" is another difficulty in the same stanza: what does it stand for? The West? The west wind that awakens nature yet recalls the region nearest the setting sun? A mingling of the themes of birth and death would not be inappropriate, but again one is uncertain as to whether the phrase has real mystery or is a periphrasis avoiding a more specific term.

The change of style, then, is due to a poet consciously fashioning his own diction of generality. If it is asked why Wordsworth modifies his style in this way, and runs the risk of falling back into Poetic Diction, the answer is that he thinks of himself as entering a new stage of life, in which his mission is to propagate his knowledge, and draw closer to his kind. There is no change of heart, but there is a self-conscious attempt to assume that *his* truths are also *general* truths, or will be accepted as such in time, so that certain intimate features of his experience should not obtrude. His mission is to reveal the multifariousness and curious depth of that which binds man to man and man to nature, and not that which separates them. "In spite of difference of soil and climate, of language and

---

6. Grosart, *1*, 326.
7. That there is a vagueness in Wordsworth's conception and imagery is argued by Cleanth Brooks, *Well Wrought Urn* (1947), ch. 7.

manners, of laws and customs; in spite of things silently gone out of mind; and things violently destroyed; the poet binds together by passion and knowledge the vast empire of human society, as it is spread over the earth, and over all time."[8] Wordsworth, in beginning to look on his thoughts as representative, tends to confuse, as Coleridge remarked, self-established convictions with generally accepted truths.[9] This, ironically enough, would be an evasion of self-consciousness in the very poem that ceremonially affirms the self in order to limit it.

"Peele Castle"

When we read in Wordsworth's poem on his brother's death, "A deep distress hath humaniz'd my Soul," and remember what he had said in a less personal but hardly less tragic context, "By our own spirits are we deified," the question arises again what his attitude is toward this relentless humanizing of imagination. And although the man who speaks to us is standing on lowly ground, conscious of his solitary and individual state, we are reminded of a vaster and truly epic theme, which his destiny as a whole presents. For here is Adam given his sights of death, or Gilgamesh confronted with his mortality. It is the same perplexed or rebellious or finally consenting response.

"Peele Castle" not only urges the poet's consent to mortality but seems already to confirm it. Wordsworth admits, speaking now in his own person, radical loss and absolute change: "A power is gone, which nothing can restore." For the first time also he does not talk of recompense until the last line, which in its brevity and isolation is like the inscription on a tomb. If in the "Ode to Duty" he still deifies his own spirit in the very act of voluntary submission, here the blow has fallen and has made what he thought a sacrifice an irreversible doom.

Yet the energy with which Wordsworth accepts loss, his direct unequivocal affirmation of it—there are no mixed rhythms, no qualifications as in the Intimations Ode—and his conscious sympathy with the pictured storm, amount to almost an *amor fati* and reveal how much of power is left. We are obliged to ask what has been lost (he says "*a* power") and what it is that remains, so clear and unimpregnable in him. I think the answer to the first part of that question is definitely not his faith in nature. It is quite true that nature led him on, to a conception that proved false; but it is clearly his own soul which betrayed him through the "fond delusion" that nature is more than it can be. A distinction between the roles played respectively by nature and the soul in this betrayal may seem niggling, but the contrast is, after all, between a past and a present *conception* (picture). While the first few stanzas describe nature directly, the next five mention the picturing response of a mind that would have added *its* light ("the light that never was")[1] to nature and so perpetuated an experience in trust and hope. Although the heart goes *with* nature in this perpetuation (it extends the image from day to eternity instead of from day to day) it also goes *beyond* nature in its desire for steadfastness. By changing to the

---

8. Preface (1802) to *Lyrical Ballads*.
9. Letter to Lady Beaumont, April 3, 1815 (Harper, *Wordsworth*, p. 528).
1. It did in fact add its light to nature. The conditional tense indicates a potentiality then exercised, but not consciously, and not in the form of an actual painting.

conditional mood when the mental representation is described ("Ah! THEN if mine had been the Painter's hand . . ."), Wordsworth tells us quite precisely what is lost: this kind of potentiality, this capacity for generous error and noble illusion, which made life correspond to the heart's desire. The sea from now on could smile and smile and still be thought a villain. True steadfastness is only in "fortitude, and patient chear."

"Peele Castle," therefore, repeats in an open and personal way the thought of radical loss haunting the Lucy and Matthew Poems. It is not epochal in Wordsworth's growth except in the manner of a grammatical period: the delusion, like a sentence, has run its course, and must be formally concluded. The last part of the poem, beginning with the address to Beaumont and ending with the "Farewell" and "Welcome" (faint echoes of Collins), ritually signals the poet's entry into a new mode of life. But if the implication of these imperatives is different from those addressed to Dorothy at the end of "Tintern Abbey" ("Therefore let the moon / Shine on thee in thy solitary walk; / And let the misty mountain winds be free / To blow against thee") their mood is comparable. Both evoke the 'meeting soul' which goes out to whatever demand realizes it.

This also partially answers the question what in Wordsworth resists and is clarified by loss. In terms of the two contrasting states of mind and the image dominating each, the answer is simple: the rugged castle resists, the "dread watch-tower of man's absolute self," in Coleridge's memorable phrase.[2] That a more lucid self-consciousness has been attained is suggested by the unusual progression, in the poem, from milder to sterner nature, as well as by the very structure of the poem. The structure of "Peele Castle," with one significant difference presently to be mentioned, is that of 'X' revisited: the poet confronts a previous stage of life and comes to a new consciousness of human destiny.

The character of this consciousness is brought out on comparing "Peele Castle" and "Tintern Abbey." Both look back (revisit) approximately the same stage of life but from a vantage point differing by seven years. Since the experience reviewed is almost identical, we can measure the difference in the poet who reviews it. The summer of 1793 (revisited in "Tintern Abbey") and that of 1794 ("Peele Castle") were equally important for the recovery of Wordsworth's faith in nature or natural process. His description of Peele Castle stresses the continuity of day with day and of each thing with its neighbor:

> So pure the sky, so quiet was the air!
> So like, so very like, was day to day!
> Whene'er I look'd, thy Image still was there;
> It trembled, but it never pass'd away.

It is all a balm shed on the wounds of time. And, by "Tintern Abbey," Wordsworth's faith in natural continuity has become so strong that he can already associate loss with humanization (he hears "The still, sad music of humanity"). His sensibility is being transformed, not radically weakened. He believes, moreover, that his former self may be revived or continued by his sister. The long coda in which he expresses this belief

2. It is also tempting to bring in Burke's theory of the sublime ("And this huge Castle, standing here sublime . . .") since the contrast turns on feelings of beauty replaced by feelings of sublimity.

owes something to Coleridge's habit of accepting separation from joy as long as he can think of participating in the joy of other persons.[3] But with John's death in 1805 that imaginative kind of hope becomes too painful. The poet in fact concenters himself against the temptation of hope. He does not even return, in "Peele Castle," to the original site: he accepts his loss and is not tempted to try his soul. "Not for a moment could I now behold / A smiling sea and be what I have been." This modification in the structure of the poem of revisit indicates that an irreversible stage has been attained. There is no nostalgia for a previous mode of being except in the last, lingering "Farewell," and in the elegiac return of certain sounds and words. Wordsworth's new strength is in not dallying with the hope that his soul may revive once more toward the past. He faces only to future in the assured consciousness that, if he cannot bear the divine glimpses which the past offers, he can sustain the human sorrows to come.[4]

"Peele Castle" itself shows no diminution of imaginative vigor. Like Milton's Nativity Ode, it is an envoi which displays what may be forfeit and takes from it a dying splendor. An eloquent modulation of tenses moves us through the past and a response to nature then possible, to the present which kills this possibility, and finally to Beaumont's picture which allows a new, though intellectually prompted, empathy. There is, in other words, not only a generous constatation of what was and could have been, but also a demonstration of the resolute mind in the act of embracing what is and will be. Nothing is denied by the poet: a lost magnanimity is fully acknowledged, and a present imagination given a new image to enjoy.

Yet Wordsworth's implied program is perilously close to renouncing everything that could engage the imagination. First, the challenge of past modes of being. Next, the possibility of surmise itself, especially concerning a sympathetic nature, one that participates in the growth and destiny of the human soul. Wordsworth does not deny the notion, here or elsewhere; but he is even more cautious about it than Milton, who used it in "Lycidas" to provide a frail if imaginative moment of comfort. Perhaps he is afraid of returning to the "spot" in his mind that still wounds him, the drowning of his brother, its irreversibility, and the feeble wishfulness of every notion of supernatural-natural sympathy. This should not have affected all imaginings, but it does. Every self-transcending hope or fancy turns back into a pang of loss. "O do not Thou too fondly brood," he writes in further elegiac verses on his brother, "On any earthly hope, however pure!"[5] This lesson he will urge in *The Excursion*, where excessive hope is revealed as a form of violence against nature, a form of the apocalyptic imagination.

There is a final restraint to be mentioned. Whereas Milton, after enjoying the surmise of nature's sympathy, spurns it for a transcendent

3. The first poem which Coleridge patterns on this structure of separation and vicarious participation is "This Lime-Tree Bower, My Prison," which stems from 1797 and so anticipates "Tintern Abbey." The most pathetic instance of it is his verse letter to Sara Hutchinson, later the Dejection Ode. See Griggs, *Collected Letters*, 2, 790–98.
4. Moreover, by the time of "Peele Castle," Wordsworth has finished *The Prelude* and faced the challenge of the past: "I said unto the life which I had lived / Where art thou? Hear I not a voice from thee / Which 'tis reproach to hear?" (*Prelude* XIV. 377–79). His program now is to be haunted no longer by childhood and adolescence. There is no desire to be cut off from them (as in 1793) but also none to enter again that area of trial.
5. *PW*, 4, 265. See also the preceding poem "To the Daisy." Both poems, though composed in 1805, were not published till much later.

consolation, which is Lycidas' redemption, Wordsworth will not engage imaginatively even in that. A poetry of statement—"Not without hope we suffer and we mourn"—is the most he will allow. His letters after John's death do show him turning toward the idea of another world,[6] but in "Peele Castle" the consolation is purely human. If he has religious thoughts (I have just quoted the only verse which tends that way) he does not tap them; he is yet strong enough in himself. There may come a time for them, but it has not come. Nor will Wordsworth allow his imagination to dwell seriously on post-existence even after he has found the doctrine necessary, except in "Laodamia" where the Classical background liberates him.

*   *   *

STEVEN KNAPP

Quasi-Personification in the *Intimations Ode*[†]

The foregoing argument may help to explain both the (temporary) popularity of sublime personification and the relative failure of its *deliberate* practice. (The stress on "deliberate" is crucial here: personifications in Milton, Spenser, and Virgil were produced without the benefit of eighteenth-century notions of the sublime.) Powerfully concentrated—but also harmlessly enclosed—in the reflexive space of its own allegorical agency, the sublime personification was an ideal answer to the Enlightenment's ambivalence toward alien belief and archaic literature. But the very combination of qualities that makes the figure an ideal solution to a theoretical paradox—the desire for simultaneous identification with and dissociation from an image of "fanatical" power—at the same time deprives it of all but a momentary illusion of success. Both the attractive power and the overt fictionality of the personification derive from its "absorption" in its own allegorical meaning.[1] Yet fictionality within a poem is a relative effect; it depends on the isolation of the fictional agent from those other agents, including the poetic speaker, with which its fictionality is implicitly contrasted. The poet who fails or refuses to insulate the personification from contact with less overtly fictional agents invites the leveling effect deplored by critics of Milton's Sin and Death, while the poet who succeeds must give up the illusion of a genuinely threatening encounter. If the former replaces the sublime with allegory proper, the latter collapses into rhetorical posturing. The relative inadequacy of twentieth-century accounts of eighteenth-century sublime poetry may reflect the difficulty in deciding when a given poem has succumbed to which danger, as well as the frequent suspicion that it has managed to fall prey to both. This splitting apart of the sublime into its antithetical components may be

---

6. *Early Letters* (1935), p. 460.

† From *Personification and the Sublime: Milton to Coleridge* (Cambridge, MA: Harvard University Press, 1985), 98–106. Reprinted by permission of the publisher. Copyright © 1985 by the President and Fellows of Harvard College.

1. Long after being struck by the self-absorption of personified abstractions, I encountered Michael Fried's fascinating study *Absorption and Theatricality: Painting and Beholder in the Age of Diderot* (Berkeley: University of California Press, 1980). While the points of contact between Fried's argument and this one are too complex and numerous to record here, his book confirms my sense of the importance of self-enclosed agency in eighteenth-century art in various media.

exactly the effect cultivated by an antisublime performance such as *The Dunciad*, with its vertiginous oscillation between depictions of genuine fanatic self-absorption and of calculating hypocrisy. If a poet like Collins avoids such oscillation, he does so partly by signalling his awareness of how close that danger lies.[2]

It may be that major poetry could not be written in the sublime personifying mode, at least until the submergence of poetic ambivalence in its explicit eighteenth-century form. An alternative to the practical antinomies of sublime personification was devised by Wordsworth, who replaced the formal personifications of the eighteenth century with such quasi-allegorical but ostensibly natural figures as the Leech-Gatherer, the Discharged Soldier, the Blind Beggar, and the Philosopher-Child in the "Intimations Ode."[3] The preternatural self-enclosure of such figures comes closest to the abstract and formal reflexiveness of sublime personification in the encounter with the Blind Beggar, whose identity is wholly absorbed by the inscription he literally wears around his neck:

> . . .'twas my chance
> Abruptly to be smitten with the view
> Of a blind beggar, who, with upright face,
> Stood propped against a wall, upon his chest
> Wearing a written paper, to explain
> The story of the man, and who he was.
> My mind did at this spectacle turn round
> As with the might of waters, and it seemed
> To me that in this label was a type
> Or emblem of the utmost that we know
> Both of ourselves and of the universe,
> And on the shape of this unmoving man,
> His fixèd face and sightless eyes, I looked
> As if admonished from another world.[4]

By partially naturalizing the role that an eighteenth-century poet would unhesitatingly have assigned to a fully allegorical agent, Wordsworth allows his sublime figures to inhabit the same narrative or discursive space as the poet himself. Yet the resulting loss of an urbane and skeptical distance from such images of fanatical self-absorption disturbed even Coleridge, whose notorious attack on the eighth stanza of the "Intimations Ode" can be viewed as a refusal to accept Wordsworth's

2. On the relation of sublime personification to Pope's *Dunciad*, see John E. Sitter, "Mother, Memory, Muse and Poetry after Pope," *ELH*, 44 (1977), 312–336. The proximity of the sublime to satire is intriguingly discussed by Thomas Weiskel in *The Romantic Sublime: Studies in the Structure and Psychology of Transcendence* (Baltimore: Johns Hopkins University Press, 1976), pp. 19–20. For an attempt to reconcile Augustan satire and post-Augustan sublime poetry under a broader notion of urbane discourse, see Marshall Brown, "The Urbane Sublime," *ELH*, 45 (1978), 236–254.
3. Jonathan Wordsworth gathers these figures together under the inevitable generic title of "borderers." See his lecture "William Wordsworth, 1770–1969," *Proceedings of the British Academy*, 55 (1969), 211–228; see also his *William Wordsworth: The Borders of Vision* (Oxford: Clarendon, 1982).
4. *The Prelude: 1799, 1805, 1850*, ed. Jonathan Wordsworth, M. H. Abrams, and Stephen Gill (New York: Norton, 1979), p. 260; 1805 version, VII.610–623. All quotations of *The Prelude* are from this edition and are given hereafter in the text by year, book, and line. For a full reading of the Blind Beggar passage and its context in the London episode, see Neil Hertz, "The Notion of Blockage in the Literature of the Sublime," in *Psychoanalysis and the Question of the Text, Selected Papers from the English Institute, 1976–77*, ed. Geoffrey H. Hartman (Baltimore: Johns Hopkins University Press, 1978), pp. 79–84.

ambiguous naturalization of allegory. As the last example in his list of
Wordsworth's "characteristic defects," Coleridge gives the following lines
from the poet's apostrophe to the emblematic Child:

> Thou best philosopher who yet dost keep
> Thy heritage! Thou eye among the blind,
> That, deaf and silent, read'st the eternal deep,
> Haunted for ever by the Eternal Mind—
> Mighty Prophet! Seer blest!
> On whom those truths do rest,
> Which we are toiling all our lives to find!
> Thou, over whom thy immortality
> Broods like the day, a master o'er the slave,
> A presence that is not to be put by.[5]

The general defect these lines are meant to exemplify is "an approxima-
tion to what might be called *mental* bombast, as distinguished from ver-
bal: for, as in the latter there is a disproportion of the expressions to the
thoughts, so in this there is a disproportion of thought to the circumstance
and occasion" (*BL* [*CC*], II, 136). In the case of this stanza, however, the
"disproportion" takes the particularly interesting form of a dislocation of
consciousness. Coleridge can make no literal sense of imputing *that* sort
of consciousness to *that* sort of agent: "In what sense is a child of that age
a *philosopher?* In what sense does he *read* 'the eternal deep'? In what sense
is he declared to be '*for ever haunted*' by the Supreme Being? or so inspired
as to deserve the splendid titles of a *mighty prophet, a blessed seer?* By
reflection? by knowledge? by conscious intuition? or by *any* form or modi-
fication of consciousness?" (*BL* [*CC*], II, 138). But an attempt to read the
passage without imputing such consciousness to the Child proves equally
futile, for "if these mysterious gifts, faculties, and operations, are *not*
accompanied with consciousness; who *else* is conscious of them? or how
can it be called the child, if it be no part of the child's conscious being?"
Coleridge nevertheless experiments with two figurative readings. Perhaps
the imputation of sublime consciousness to the Child only stands for the
pantheist claim that every individual existence partakes of universal
Spirit; but in that case the Child's "magnificent attributes" would be
"equally suitable to a *bee,* or a *dog,* or a *field of corn* . . . The omnipresent
Spirit works equally in *them,* as in the child; and the child is equally
unconscious of it as they." The second figurative reading is suggested by
four lines that Wordsworth later omitted but that originally followed
immediately after the passage quoted above:

> To whom the grave
> Is but a lonely bed without the sense or sight
> Of day or the warm light,
> A place of thought where we in waiting lie.

5. *BL* [*CC*], II, 138. I quote Wordsworth's passage as it appears in Coleridge's text; subsequent
references to these lines are based on the standard text in *PWW,* IV, 282.
    My treatment of Coleridge's critique of this passage ignores the complexities of Coleridge's
personal ambivalences both toward Wordsworth and toward philosophical children. But see
Thomas McFarland, "Wordsworth's Best Philosopher," *Wordsworth Circle,* 13 (1982), 64–68,
for the intriguing thesis that Wordsworth modeled his apostrophe to the Child on Coleridge's
manner of praising the intellect of his own infant son Hartley.

"Surely," Coleridge remarks, "it cannot be that this wonder-rousing apostrophe is but a comment on the little poem of 'We are seven?'" Such a reading would translate the Child's consciousness of immortality into the mere incapacity of imagining death, an incapacity he would share with "all finite beings alike, of whatever age, and however educated or uneducated." In short, Coleridge concludes, Wordsworth's apostrophe has only the force of every specious paradox: "Thus it is with splendid paradoxes in general. If the words are taken in the common sense, they convey an absurdity; and if, in contempt of dictionaries and custom, they are so interpreted as to avoid the absurdity, the meaning dwindles into some bald truism. Thus you must at once understand the words *contrary* to their common import, in order to arrive at any *sense*; and *according* to their common import, if you are to receive from them any feeling of *sublimity* or *admiration*" (*BL* [*CC*], II, 139–141).

*   *   *

In personification, then, self-consciousness is imputed to a figurative agent. But what happens when self-consciousness is *figuratively* imputed to a *natural* agent, as in the case of Wordsworth's Child?[6] The imputation of an unnatural mode or degree of consciousness has the effect of isolating the agent from its natural context and thus of moving it closer to the condition of a personification—without, however, assigning it a clear allegorical identity. It seems impossible to read the Child as a personification of, say, immortality, or even of childhood. But the Child's self-consciousness, precisely because it lacks both natural explanation and rhetorical justification, produces an effect of isolated self-enclosure analogous to the stylized reflexiveness of explicit allegory.

There is much in the stanza to suggest that the Child is in fact a modified version of an eighteenth-century sublime personification. The structure of the apostrophe itself, beginning with the first two lines (omitted by Coleridge)—"Thou, whose exterior semblance doth belie / Thy Soul's immensity"—depends on the formulaic repetition of an emphatic "Thou," followed three times by a relative clause:

> Thou, whose exterior semblance doth belie . . .
> Thou best Philosopher, who yet dost keep . . .
> Thou, over whom thy Immortality
> Broods . . .

The sheer formality and insistent recurrence of this device already give the stanza an extravagant rhetorical heightening, especially after the rather awkward comedy of the preceding stanza. The formula itself is specifically reminiscent of Collins. Of the twelve poems in *Odes on Several Descriptive and Allegoric Subjects,* five begin with exactly this device: the odes to Pity ("O Thou, the Friend of Man assign'd"), to Simplicity ("O Thou by *Nature* taught"), to Mercy ("O Thou, who sit'st a smiling Bride"), to Peace ("O Thou, who bad'st thy Turtles bear"), and, most strikingly, to Fear:

6. In a different context, Frances Ferguson writes evocatively on the effect of personifying what are already persons; see *Wordsworth: Language as Counter-Spirit* (New Haven: Yale University Press, 1977), pp. 26–28.

> Thou, to whom the World unknown
> With all its shadowy Shapes is shown;
> Who see'st appall'd th' unreal Scene
> While Fancy lifts the Veil between . . . [7]

Here the stylistic parallel is reinforced by a thematic one: both Wordsworth and Collins apostrophize an agent who is absorbed in the perception of a vision concealed from the poet himself.

The allegorical suggestions of this possible echo of Collins are further supported by the Child's reflexive brooding, as well as his participation in an emblematic tableau:

> Thou, over whom thy Immortality
> Broods like the Day, a Master o'er a Slave . . .

Coleridge objects in passing to the impropriety "of making a 'master *brood* o'er a slave,' or the *day* brood *at all*" (*BL* [*CC*], II, 138); whatever the precise sense of these lines, they suggest at least a tendency toward a dramatic grouping of personified abstractions. In fact, however, the opacity of these metaphors—the impossibility of translating them into a literal argument despite the strong impression that they ought to be so translated, or of actually visualizing the tableau they suggest—precisely this double opacity thwarts their full allegorization. The semantic and tonal ambiguity of "broods" (benevolently nurtures or moodily contemplates?) is not clarified but rather repeated by the crossed allegorical signals of the simile likening Immorality first to the day, then to a taskmaster. Allegorical tendencies are further hindered by the implied identification of the Child with the poet's own recollected infancy. A thorough allegorization of the Child—as a personification, for instance, of our desire for immortality—would have the indirect consequence of allegorizing the poet himself, and thus of converting the entire ode into an allegorical vision in the mode of a medieval dream-poem. (Wordsworth's own much later remarks on the poem do nothing to resolve the ambiguity; they assert both that the consciousness of immortality was a literal memory of the poet's own past, and that the Child's recollection of pre-existence was a merely figurative device for treating what Wordsworth now ponderously calls "the 'Immortality of the Soul,'" *PWW*, IV, 463–464.)

Wordsworth's partial or ambiguous allegorization of natural agents prevents the confident sorting out of literal and figurative intentions. In the context of the present argument it is hard not to view this effect as a lyric or discursive equivalent to the narrative mixing of literal and figurative agents that so disturbed eighteenth-century readers of *Paradise Lost*. The mixing of agents in Milton may reflect a pre-Enlightenment indifference to the maintenance of empirical consistency, but there is some evidence that Wordsworth may have deliberately cultivated the same effect as an essential token of the (for him) central tradition of the Hebraic imagination, consisting chiefly of Milton, Spenser, and the Bible. Rather than simply repudiating all allegory, as the well-known attack on "poetic diction" might suggest, Wordsworth viewed indefinite allegory as a kind of Protestant

---

7. *The Works of William Collins*, ed. Richard Wendorf and Charles Ryskamp (Oxford: Clarendon, 1979), pp. 25, 29, 35, 46, 27.

antidote to the tyranny of sensuous form. "The grand storehouses of enthusiastic and meditative Imagination," he wrote in the 1815 Preface,

> of poetical, as contradistinguished from human and dramatic Imagination, are the prophetic and lyrical parts of the Holy Scriptures, and the works of Milton; to which I cannot forbear to add those of Spenser. I select these writers in preference to those of ancient Greece and Rome, because the anthropomorphitism of the Pagan religion subjected the minds of the greatest poets in those countries too much to the bondage of definite form; from which the Hebrews were preserved by their abhorrence of idolatry. This abhorrence was almost as strong in our great epic Poet, both from circumstances of his life, and from the constitution of his mind. However imbued the surface might be with classical literature, he was a Hebrew in soul; and all things tended in him towards the sublime. (*Prose*, III, 34–35)

The contrast between Hebrew sublimity and classical beauty is of course utterly commonplace; similar remarks by Coleridge and Kant have been quoted in earlier chapters. Equally ordinary is the alignment of Milton on the Hebraic side. But Wordsworth goes on, more surprisingly, to include Spenserian allegory in the same opposition to idolatry. Most telling of all is Wordsworth's observation that Spenser practiced two modes of allegory, the personification of abstractions and what I have been calling the "allegorization" of ostensibly natural agents.[8] Wordsworth's special endorsement of the latter reads like a description of his own emblematic figures: "Spenser, of a gentler nature, maintained his freedom by aid of his allegorical spirit, at one time inciting him to create persons out of abstractions; and, at another, by a superior effort of genius, to give the universality and permanence of abstractions to his human beings, by means of attributes and emblems that belong to the highest moral truths and the purest sensations,—of which his character of Una is a glorious example" (*Prose*, III, 35).[9]

It would be a mistake to cite such remarks as evidence of a genuine return to Renaissance attitudes. Wordsworth shares with the eighteenth century an interest in the general phenomenon of personification, apart from questions of its specific usage, that would have baffled Milton or Spenser. But by endorsing the coexistence and exchangeability of literal and figurative agents in Spenserian allegory, Wordsworth signals the distance between his own poetics and the eighteenth-century interest in such static, formally isolated figures as Mallet's Ruin. Though sometimes equally static—even to the point of ominous fixation—Wordsworth's figures are deprived of the full allegorical formality that would locate them in a sharply delineated figurative space. It is precisely the dislocating power of allegory that he admires. In general, and to Coleridge's frequent distress, Wordsworth seems to have been less involved in the poetic ambivalence that drove Coleridge to seek a reconciling medium between the literal and the figurative, and that inspired the eighteenth-century interest in self-absorbed but overtly fictional agents.

---

8. From this perspective, Ferguson's plausible claim (*Wordsworth*, p. 27) that Wordsworth equated "most personifications" with idolatry needs qualifying.
9. Cf. Wordsworth's call, in the first "Essay upon Epitaphs" (1810), for a "spiritualizing" abstractness in representations of the deceased (*PrW*, I, 56–59).

William Wordsworth: A Chronology

1770   Born at Cockermouth, Cumberland, second son of John Words-
        worth, law-agent to Sir James Lowther (later Lord Lonsdale), and
        Ann Wordsworth (April 7).
1771   Dorothy Wordsworth born (December 25).
1776   Attends Gilbanks' school, Penrith; starts studying Latin (April–
        October).
1778   Ann Wordsworth dies (ca. March 8).
1779   Attends Hawkshead Free Grammar School (until June 1787).
1783   John Wordsworth dies (December 30). Richard Wordsworth, a
        cousin, and Christopher Cookson, an uncle, assume responsibil-
        ity for the children.
1784   Composes first verses (September or October).
1787   *Sonnet, on Seeing Miss Helen Maria Williams Weep at a Tale of
        Distress*, Wordsworth's first published poem, appears in the *Euro-
        pean Magazine* (March). Enters St. John's College, Cambridge
        (October).
1788   Begins composing *An Evening Walk* (summer).
1790   Walking tour with Robert Jones through France, Switzerland,
        and the Rhineland (July 10–October).
1791   Takes final examinations at Cambridge, receives BA (January).
        Visits London (January–May); visits Robert Jones in Wales (late
        May–September), climbs Mt. Snowdon (see *Prelude* 13.1–84).
        Travels to Paris with £40 from his cousin Richard (late Novem-
        ber), then to Orléans (December); becomes acquainted with
        Dufour and Vallon families.
        Composes *Descriptive Sketches* (probably December–late 1792).
1792   Travels to Blois (perhaps February); befriends Michel Beaupuy
        (see *Prelude* 9.294–347) and has love affair with Annette Vallon.
        Louis XVI deposed (August 10).
        Returns to Orléans (September or October); departs for Paris
        in need of money (ca. late October). Returns to England (late
        November or December).
        Anne-Caroline Wordsworth, daughter of Wordsworth and
        Annette Vallon, born in Orléans (December 15).
1793   Publishes *An Evening Walk* and *Descriptive Sketches* (January
        29).
        France declares war on Britain (February 1).
        Writes but does not publish his "Letter to the Bishop of Llan-
        daff" (early spring). Walking tour of Salisbury Plain and Wales
        (late summer): visits Stonehenge and Tintern Abbey. Begins com-
        posing *Salisbury Plain*.

1794 Reunited with Dorothy in Halifax, Yorkshire (February 17); travels with her to Lake District (April). Nurses Raisley Calvert in Keswick (October–December).

1795 Calvert dies, leaving Wordsworth a £900 legacy (ca. January 9). In London, sees William Godwin frequently (February–August). Meets Robert Southey and Coleridge in Bristol (between late August and late September).
      Moves with Dorothy to Racedown, Dorset (late September). Revises *Salisbury Plain*.

1796 Moral crisis (possibly spring; see *The Prelude*, 10.888–904, 11.24–120). In correspondence with Coleridge. Begins *The Borderers* (autumn).

1797 Completes *The Borderers*, begins *The Ruined Cottage* (spring). Moves with Dorothy to Alfoxden Farm, Somerset, to be nearer Coleridge (July). Visits from John Thelwall, Basil Montagu, and Joseph Cottle (July). Government spy reports on visitors to Alfoxden (August).
      Walking tour with Dorothy and Coleridge (November); plans composition of *The Rime of the Ancient Mariner* and *Lyrical Ballads* with Coleridge.

1798 Plans *The Recluse*. Composes sections of *The Ruined Cottage*, *The Old Cumberland Beggar* (probably January–April), poems for *Lyrical Ballads* (spring), and *Peter Bell* (April–May).
      Visit from William Hazlitt (May–June). Visits Tintern Abbey and Wye River valley with Dorothy; composes *Tintern Abbey* (July).
      Publishes *Lyrical Ballads* (September).
      Travels to Germany with Dorothy and Coleridge (September). Spends autumn and winter with Dorothy in Goslar, composing the first version of *The Prelude*, *Ruth*, and the "Lucy poems" (October–February 1799).

1799 Develops plan of *The Prelude*.
      Returns to England with Dorothy (late April). In Sockburn-on-Tees, sorting out financial matters and revising *The Borderers* and *The Old Cumberland Beggar* (ca. late April–December). Walking tour with Coleridge (November). Moves to Dove Cottage, Grasmere, with Dorothy (late December).

1800 Begins *Home at Grasmere* (March); plans second edition of *Lyrical Ballads* with Coleridge and composes new poems for it (April–December).
      Coleridge family moves into Greta Hall, Keswick (June).

1801 Publishes the second edition of *Lyrical Ballads* (January, but dated 1800 on the title page).
      Frequent visits from Mary Hutchinson.

1802 Composes *The Leech Gatherer* (May; published in 1807 as *Resolution and Independence*).
      Publishes the third edition of *Lyrical Ballads* (June).
      Visits Annette Vallon and daughter Caroline with Dorothy in Calais during the Peace of Amiens (August 1–29).
      Marries Mary Hutchinson (October 4).

1803 Son John born (June 18).

Walking tour of Scotland with Dorothy and Coleridge (mid-August–late September). Meets Walter Scott (September).

1804 Enlarges *The Prelude* from five-book plan. Communicates plan of *The Recluse* to Thomas De Quincey (March).

Daughter Dora born (August 16).

1805 Learns that his brother John (b. 1772) has drowned in the wreck of *The Earl of Abergavenny* (February 11).

Completes *The Prelude* (not yet so titled) in thirteen books (May). Publishes the fourth edition of *Lyrical Ballads* (October 9).

1806 In London, meeting literary and political figures (April–May).

Son Thomas born (June 15).

At the Beaumonts' house in Coleorton, Leicestershire (late October–June 10, 1807); visit from Coleridge (late December–February 1807).

1807 Reads *The Prelude* to Coleridge (early January).

Publishes *Poems, in Two Volumes* (May 8) to unfavorable reviews. Begins composing *The White Doe of Rylstone* (October).

1808 Assists Coleridge with his periodical *The Friend* (April–May).

Moves to Allan Bank, Grasmere (May). Daughter Catharine born (September 6).

Visit from De Quincey (November).

1810 Contributes "Essay upon Epitaphs" to *The Friend* (February); works on *The Excursion* (spring).

Son William born (May 12).

Makes unflattering comments about Coleridge to Basil Montague, precipitating two-year break with Coleridge (September 23).

1812 Partial reconciliation with Coleridge effected by Henry Crabb Robinson (May).

Catharine dies suddenly (June 4); Thomas dies of pneumonia (December 1).

1813 Works on *The Excursion* (January–February.)

Appointed Distributor of Stamps (a position in the revenue service) for Westmorland (April). Moves to Rydal Mount, Rydal, his final home (May).

1814 Revises *The Excursion* (February).

Tours Scotland with Mary and Sara Hutchinson (July–early September).

Publishes *The Excursion* (early August) to unfavorable reviews. Writes the preface and "Essay, Supplementary to the Preface" for a collection of his poems (November).

1815 Publishes *Poems* in two volumes (April).

Visits London, meeting Scott and Crabb Robinson (May–June). Publishes *The White Doe of Rylstone* (June).

1816 Composes *Thanksgiving Ode* (January).

Daughter Caroline marries Jean-Baptiste Baudouin in Paris (February 28).

1817 Reads the criticisms of his poetry and poetic theory in Coleridge's *Biographia Literaria* (September). Has strained exchanges with Coleridge at dinner parties in London (December 27 and 30).

WILLIAM WORDSWORTH: A CHRONOLOGY

Meets John Keats at Charles Lamb's "Immortal Dinner" (December 28).

1818 Two visits from Keats in London (January 3 and 5).

Propagandizes in Westmorland on behalf of the Tory party before the general election (March–November).

Composes sonnets about the River Duddon (autumn).

1819 Publishes *Peter Bell* (ca. April 22) and *The Waggoner* (late May).

1820 Publishes *The River Duddon* (April).

Tours Belgium, the Rhineland, Switzerland, northern Italy, and France with Mary, Dorothy, and others (July–November), Crabb Robinson joining the party in Switzerland (August 16). Meets Annette Vallon and Caroline Baudouin in Paris (early October).

Publishes *Poems* in four volumes (late September).

1822 Publishes *Ecclesiastical Sketches* (February) and the first separate edition of *A Description of the Scenery of the Lakes* (April 16).

1823 Suffers from trachoma; abandons a planned trip with Mary to Belgium, Holland, and France (May).

Translates books 1 and 2 of Virgil's *Aeneid* (autumn).

1828 Tours Belgium, the Rhineland, and Holland with Dora and Coleridge (May 22–August 6).

1829 Tours Ireland with John Marshall, a longtime acquaintance (September).

1830 Visit from the poet Felicia Hemans (June). Visits Coleridge in Highgate (December).

1831 Attends meetings of opponents to parliamentary reform (March).

Begins revising *The Prelude* (December).

1833 Visit from Ralph Waldo Emerson (August 28).

1834 Learns that Coleridge died on July 25 (July 27).

Dora seriously ill (November–December).

1835 Dorothy seriously ill (June). Sara Hutchinson dies (June 24).

1837 Publishes first American edition of his poetical works.

Tours France, Italy, Austria, and Germany with Crabb Robinson (March–July), seeing Annette and Caroline for the last time in Paris (March) and visiting Keats's friend Joseph Severn in Rome (May 6).

1838 Receives honorary degree from the new University of Durham (July 21).

1839 Makes final revisions of *The Prelude* (March).

1840 Visit from the Queen Dowager (July).

1841 Dora marries Edward Quillinan after a long engagement (May 11).

1843 Accepts offer of the Poet Laureateship (April 4).

1847 Dora dies of tuberculosis (July 9).

1850 Suffers attack of pleurisy (March). Dies April 23. Buried in Grasmere (April 27).

Mary gives *The Prelude* its title and arranges for its publication (May). *The Prelude* (fourteen-book version) published (July.)

Biographical and Topographical Glossary

People and Places

Alfoxden (now Alfoxton Park Hotel), four miles from Coleridge's cottage in Nether Stowey, the Somerset farmhouse rented by William and Dorothy Wordsworth from June 1797 to June 1798, during the planning and composition of *Lyrical Ballads*.

Allan Bank, house in Grasmere occupied by the Wordsworth household from 1808 to 1811, after Dove Cottage had become too small for William and Mary's growing family.

Sir George Beaumont (1753–1827), patron of the arts, art collector, and amateur landscape painter, who befriended Wordsworth soon after being introduced to him by Coleridge in 1803. His gifts to Wordsworth included drawings and a deed to property in the Lake District, and their friendship lasted until Beaumont's death. He was the dedicatee of Wordsworth's *Poems* (1815).

Michel Beaupuy (Armand-Michel Beauchartie de Beaupuy) (1755–1796), of noble birth but strongly supportive of the French Revolution, a French army officer whom Wordsworth befriended in Blois in 1792 and celebrated in the *Prelude* 9.294–347; killed in battle against the Austrians near Freiburg im Breisgau on October 19, 1796.

Robert Burns (1759–1796), Scottish poet and sometime farmer, whose poetry WW admired; author of *Poems, Chiefly in the Scottish Dialect* (1786), contributor to *The Scots Musical Museum* (1787–1803), and lyricist of *Auld Lang Syne* and some 200 other songs.

Raisley Calvert (1773–1795), younger brother of Wordsworth's Hawkshead friend William Calvert; resolved to share some of his inheritance with Wordsworth to free the poet from the need for other employment; tended by Wordsworth from October through December 1794, died of tuberculosis in Keswick on ca. January 9, 1795, leaving Wordsworth a bequest of £900.

Cockermouth, Cumbria (formerly Cumberland), the village in which Wordsworth was born and lived until his mother's death in 1778. His birthplace is now a museum, Wordsworth House.

Coleorton, Leicestershire, the village in which Sir George Beaumont built his house, Coleorton Hall, in 1804–1808, and in which the Wordsworths resided in a house (Hall Farm) lent to them by Beaumont, from late October 1806 to June 10, 1807. Here Coleridge, who visited from December 21 to mid-April, heard and read the thirteen-book *Prelude* for the first time (see his *To W. Wordsworth* in the Nineteenth-Century Responses).

Samuel Taylor Coleridge (1772–1834), poet and critic, addressee of *The Prelude*; met Wordsworth in 1795 and subsequently became his close friend and collaborator on *Lyrical Ballads* (1798), traveling to Germany with William and Dorothy in 1798; lived in the Lake District, 1800–1804, traveled to Malta in 1804 with a manuscript of books 1–5 of *The Prelude*, and separated from his wife upon returning to England in 1806; heard and read the complete thirteen-book *Prelude* in January 1807, composing in response his poem *To W. Wordsworth*. In 1810 a series of misunderstandings led to a two-year rupture in his friendship with Wordsworth, which never regained its former closeness, although they toured the Rhineland together with Dora Wordsworth in 1828. Coleridge's criticisms in *Biographia Literaria* (1817) prompted Wordsworth to revise some of his poems from *Lyrical Ballads*.

Thomas De Quincey (1785–1859), essayist and journalist, friend of Wordsworth and Coleridge from 1807; lived with the Wordsworths at Allan Bank from October 1808 to February 1809 and occupied Dove Cottage for a dozen years thereafter, but became increasingly estranged from them after 1815. An opium addict like Coleridge, he recounted his experience of opium use in *Confessions of an English Opium-Eater* (1822), and from the 1830s published a series of unflattering reminiscences of Wordsworth and Coleridge.

Derwent, a river in the northwestern part of the Lake District, flowing north from Styhead Tarn through the Borrowdale valley, Derwent Water, and Bassenthwaite Lake, where it turns west before flowing through Cockermouth, directly behind Wordsworth's birthplace, and thence into the Irish Sea at Workington.

Dove Cottage, the small seventeenth-century stone cottage in Grasmere rented by William and Dorothy Wordsworth from 1799 to 1808 (with Mary Wordsworth and Sara Hutchinson joining the household in 1802), and by De Quincey from 1809 to 1835 (though no longer as a residence from 1820). Purchased by the newly formed Wordsworth Trust in 1890, the cottage was opened as a museum, which it remains.

Duddon, a river in the southwestern part of the Lake District, flowing fifteen miles south from its source in the Wrynose Pass (1,289 feet) down to the Irish Sea through the sandy Duddon Estuary; celebrated in Wordsworth's sonnet sequence *The River Duddon*.

Isabella Fenwick (1783–1856), a close friend of the Wordsworths, particularly William and Dora, from the 1830s. Staying at Rydal Mount in the winter of 1842–43, she persuaded William to dictate a series of informative notes (now called the Fenwick Notes) on his published poems.

Goslar, one of the seats of the Holy Roman Emperors in the Middle Ages, a town in Lower Saxony, Germany, where William and Dorothy Wordsworth resided from October 6, 1798, to ca. February 23, 1799, during the coldest recorded winter of the century, and where William began composing *The Prelude*.

Grasmere, Cumbria (formerly Westmorland), a village located immediately north of the lake of the same name. William and Dorothy Wordsworth lived here from 1799 to 1813 (with the Hutchinson sisters from 1802).

Hawkshead, Cumbria (formerly Lancashire), a village located just north of Esthwaite Water, important as a market town from the sixteenth to the nineteenth century. From 1779 to 1787 Wordsworth attended the **Hawkshead Grammar School** (founded in 1585 by Edwin Sandys, archbishop of York; now a museum), which enjoyed a national reputation for its instruction in classics and mathematics, and he lodged with **Ann Tyson** (1713–1796), whom he recalled affectionately in *The Prelude*, book 4.

William Hazlitt (1778–1830), literary and art critic, essayist, lecturer, and painter; befriended Coleridge and Wordsworth in Somerset in 1798, but alienated them during a visit to the Lake District in 1803 and in later years severely criticized both (as well as Robert Southey) for having abandoned their youthful political radicalism.

Helvellyn, the third-highest mountain (3,118 feet) in the Lake District and England, located ca. five miles north of Grasmere. Wordsworth climbed the mountain many times, once (in 1805) in the company of the writer Walter Scott and the chemist Humphry Davy. One of the best-known portraits of Wordsworth is Benjamin Robert Haydon's painting *Wordsworth on Helvellyn* (1842; National Portrait Gallery, London).

Sara Hutchinson (1775–1835), Wordsworth's sister-in-law from 1802 and the object of Coleridge's unrequited love for many years after their first meeting in 1799, although her contact with him effectively ended in 1810; never married and lived mostly with the Wordsworths.

Robert Jones (1769–1835), from Llangynhafal in north Wales, one of Wordsworth's closest friends, whom he met at St. John's College, Cambridge, and with whom he traveled through France, Switzerland, and the Rhineland in 1790 and climbed Mt. Snowdon in Wales in 1791; dedicatee of Wordsworth's *Descriptive Sketches* (1793).

Lake District, the mostly rural region (ca. 885 square miles) of mountains and lakes in northwest England in which Wordsworth was born, spent his childhood, and lived most of his adult life after 1799. It is now situated administratively within Cumbria, a county created in 1974 out of the historical counties of Cumberland and Westmorland and part of Lancashire. The central, most heavily touristed part of the district has been a national park since 1951.

Charles Lamb (1775–1835), essayist, poet, critic; worked as a clerk for the East India Company and cared for his sister Mary, who killed their mother in 1796 in a bout of insanity; author of *Essays of Elia* (1823), co-author (with Mary) of *Tales from Shakespeare* (1807). Introduced to the Wordsworths by Coleridge in 1797, he remained friends with them for the rest of his life.

Napoleon (Napoléon Bonaparte) (1769–1821), Corsican-born soldier and politician, emperor of France (as Napoleon I, 1804–15); joined the French Revolutionary army in 1792, commanding it in Italy in 1796; led an unsuccessful campaign in Egypt in 1798; become First Consul in 1799, Consul for Life in 1802, and emperor in 1804, by which time he controlled much of western Europe. After a disastrous assault on Russia (1812) he was defeated at Leipzig (1813) and forced into exile on Elba (1814), but he returned to France in 1815 (the "Hundred Days") and raised another army; was defeated at the Battle of Waterloo and exiled permanently to the Atlantic island of St. Helena.

Nether Stowey, Somerset, the village thirty miles southwest of Bristol where the Coleridge family lived from 1796 to 1799.

Racedown Lodge, near Crewkerne, Dorset, the house lent to William and Dorothy Wordsworth from September 1795 to June 1797.

Basil Montagu (1770–1851), lawyer and legal reformer, with whom Wordsworth lodged in London in 1795, and whose infant son he and Dorothy cared for at Racedown and Alfoxden, the mother having died in childbirth. In October 1810 Montagu precipitated an eighteen-month estrangement between Coleridge and Wordsworth by repeating Wordsworth's warnings to him about Coleridge's use of opium and alcohol.

Rydal Mount, in Rydal, Cumbria (formerly Westmorland), a mile-and-a-half southeast of Grasmere, Wordsworth's rented home from 1813 until his death.

Maximilien Robespierre (1758–1794), French lawyer and radical Revolutionary politician, renowned as for his rhetoric powers; elected to the Estates General in 1798 and subsequently a member of the National

Assembly, Constituent Assembly, and National Convention, in the last
of which he advocated the execution of Louis XVI. Elected to the Com-
mittee of Public Safety in 1793, he guided and justified the so-called
Reign of Terror of 1793–94, ruthlessly purging political opponents until
the Convention ordered his arrest on July 27, 1794; he was executed the
following day after a failed suicide attempt.

Henry Crabb Robinson (1775–1867), lawyer, journalist, and diarist;
acquaintance of numerous English and German writers. A friend of
both Wordsworth and Coleridge from 1810, he helped reconcile them
in 1812 and traveled with Wordsworth on the European continent in
1820 and 1837.

Robert Southey (1774–1843), poet, biographer, and essayist; Wordsworth's pre-
decessor as Poet Laureate, 1813–43; friend of Wordsworth and Coleridge,
and popularly identified with them as the "Lake Poets." Coleridge's brother-
in-law from 1795, Southey moved his family to Keswick in 1801 to share
a house with the Coleridges, and he oversaw the education of the Coleridge
children after their parents' separation.

Ann Tyson: see **Hawkshead**.

Annette (Marie Anne) Vallon (1766–1841), a French royalist from Blois
whom Wordsworth met probably in Orléans in December 1791 and with
whom he had a romantic relationship in Blois in 1792. Their daughter,
Anne-Caroline (1792–1862), was born in Orléans on December 15,
after Wordsworth had returned to England to raise money from his fam-
ily; and, owing to the outbreak of war between France and Britain in
1793, he did not see her until 1802, when he and Dorothy spent August
with Annette and Caroline in Calais during the short-lived Peace of
Amiens. They met again in Paris in 1820 and 1837. Wordsworth sent
Caroline annual payments of £30 from 1816, when she married, until
1834, and a lump-sum of £400 in 1835. Annette never married, but
adopted the surname Williams after Caroline's birth.

Windermere, the largest lake in the Lake District, ca. eleven miles long
(north–south) and just under a mile wide (east–west) at its widest point,
with eighteen islands, the largest of which, Belle Isle, was the site of a medi-
eval manor house.

Dora (Dorothy) Wordsworth (1804–1847), William's eldest daughter with
Mary and one of his amanuenses; toured the Low Countries and Rhine-
land with her father and Coleridge in 1828; married Edward Quillinan
in 1841; died of tuberculosis in 1847.

Dorothy Wordsworth (1771–1855), William's devoted sister and amanuen-
sis, raised separately from him after their mother's death (1778) but
occasionally reunited with him from 1787 to 1794; lived permanently
with William from 1795, traveling to Germany with him and Coleridge
in 1798. She was an invalid from 1835, suffering from progressive
dementia. Author of posthumously published *Journals* and *Recollections
of a Tour Made in Scotland*; contributor to William's *Guide to the Lakes*
(1810).

John Wordsworth (1772–1805), William's brother, who went to sea in 1788
in the service of the East India Company; drowned when the ship under
his command, the *Earl of Abergavenny*, was wrecked on a sandbar off the
south coast of England.

Mary Wordsworth, née Hutchinson (1770–1859), Sara Hutchinson's older
sister and a childhood friend of Dorothy Wordsworth. Courted by both
John and William Wordsworth, she married William in October 1802.

Northern English Topographical Words

beck: a brook or stream (e.g., John's Beck)

cove: a steep-sided recess in a mountain-side

fell: a mountain or hill (e.g., Rydal Fell)

force: a waterfall (e.g., Dungeon Ghyll Force)

gill (or ghyll): a steep, narrow valley, typically wooded, through which a stream flows (e.g., Greenhead Gill)

holme (or holm): island (e.g., Lady Holme)

howe: a hill or mound

mere: a lake or pond (e.g., Grasmere)

raise: a cairn or pile of stones (e.g., Dunmail Raise)

rill: a small stream

tarn: a mountain lake or pool occupying a corrie, or circular hollow formed by the melting of a glacier (e.g., Easedale Tarn)

thwaite: a piece of land cleared from a forest for residential or agricultural use (a word usually incorporated into place-names, e.g., Applethwaite)

water: a lake (e.g., Coniston Water)

Selected Bibliography

• indicates works included or excerpted in this Norton Critical Edition.

First Publications in Books of Wordsworth's Major Poetry and Prose

An Evening Walk: An Epistle, in Verse; Addressed to a Young Lady, from the Lakes of the North of England. London, 1793. Facsimile reprint, Oxford, 1989.

Descriptive Sketches in Verse, Taken during a Pedestrian Tour in the Italian, Grison, Swiss, and Savoyard Alps. London, 1793.

Lyrical Ballads, with a Few Other Poems. London, 1798. Facsimile reprint, Oxford, 1990. Published anonymously, with four poems by Coleridge.

Lyrical Ballads, with Other Poems. 2 vols. London, 1800. Facsimile reprint, Poole, 1997. Published under Wordsworth's name, but retaining Coleridge's poems.

Lyrical Ballads, with Pastoral and Other Poems. 2 vols. London, 1802. Revised edition, 1805.

Poems, in Two Volumes. 2 vols. London, 1807. Facsimile reprint, Poole, 1997.

The Excursion, Being a Portion of The Recluse: A Poem. London, 1814. Facsimile reprint, Oxford, 1991.

Poems by William Wordsworth. 2 vols. London, 1815. Facsimile reprint, Oxford, 1989.

The White Doe of Rylstone; or The Fate of the Nortons, A Poem. London, 1815.

Thanksgiving Ode, January 18, 1816, with Other Short Pieces, Chiefly Referring to Recent Public Events. London, 1816.

Peter Bell: A Tale in Verse. London, 1819. Facsimile reprint, Oxford, 1992.

The Waggoner: A Poem, to which Are Added Sonnets. London, 1819.

The Miscellaneous Poems of William Wordsworth. 4 vols. London, 1820.

The River Duddon: A Series of Sonnets; Vaudracour and Julia; and Other Poems, to which Is Annexed, A Topographical Description of the Country of the Lakes in the North of England. London, 1820.

A Description of the Scenery of the Lakes in the North of England: Third Edition (Now First Published Separately) with Additions, and Illustrative Remarks on the Alps. London, 1822. Facsimile reprint, Oxford, 1991. Revised edition (with the title *A Guide through the District of the Lakes in the North of England*), Kendal, 1835.

Ecclesiastical Sketches. London, 1822.

The Poetical Works of William Wordsworth. 4 vols. Boston, 1824. First American collected edition.

The Poetical Works of William Wordsworth: A New Edition. 4 vols. London, 1832. Revised editions (in 6 vols.), London, 1836–37; 1840; 1841; 1843.

Yarrow Revisited, and Other Poems. London, 1835.

Poems, Chiefly of Early and Late Years; including The Borderers, A Tragedy. London, 1842.

The Poetical Works of William Wordsworth, DCL, Poet Laureate: A New Edition. 6 vols. London, 1849–50. The final collected edition published in Wordsworth's lifetime.

The Prelude, or Growth of a Poet's Mind; An Autobiographical Poem. London, 1850. Facsimile reprint, Oxford, 1993. Published posthumously.

Critical Editions and Textual Studies

Butler, James. "Wordsworth, Cottle, and the *Lyrical Ballads*: Five Letters, 1797–1800." *Journal of English and German Philology* 75 (1976): 139–53.

The Cornell Wordsworth. Gen. ed. Stephen Maxfield Parrish. 23 vols. Ithaca, NY, 1975–2007: Early Poems and Fragments, 1785–1797, ed. Carol Landon and Jared Curtis (1997); An Evening Walk, ed. James Averill (1984); Descriptive Sketches, ed. Eric Birdsall with Paul Zall (1984); The Salisbury Plain Poems, ed. Stephen Gill (1975); The Borderers, ed. Robert Osborn (1982); The Ruined Cottage and The Pedlar, ed. James Butler (1979); Lyrical Ballads, and Other Poems, 1797–1800, ed. James Butler and Karen Green (1992); Peter Bell, ed. John Jordan (1985); The Prelude, 1798–1799, ed. Stephen Parrish (1977); Home at Grasmere, ed. Beth Darlington (1977); The Thirteen-Book Prelude, ed. Mark Reed (2 vols., 1991); Poems in Two Volumes, and Other Poems, 1800–1807, ed. Jared Curtis (1983); Benjamin the Waggoner, ed. Paul Betz (1981); The Tuft of Primroses, with Other Late Poems for The Recluse, ed. Joseph Kishel (1986); The White Doe of Rylstone, ed. Kristine Dugas (1988); Translations of Chaucer and Virgil, ed. Bruce Graver (1998); Shorter Poems, 1807–1820, ed. Carl Ketchum (1989); Sonnet Series and Itinerary Poems, 1820–1845, ed. Geoffrey Jackson (2004); Last Poems, 1821–1850, ed. Jared Curtis with Apryl Lea Denny-Ferris and Jillian Heydt-Stevenson (1999); The Fourteen-Book Prelude, ed. W. J. B. Owen (1991); The Excursion, ed. Sally Bushell, James Butler, and Michael Jaye (2007). The standard critical edition.
The Fenwick Notes of William Wordsworth. Ed. Jared Curtis. London, 1993. Rev. ed. (e-book), 2007.
Finch, John Alban. "Wordsworth's Two-Handed Engine." In Bicentenary Wordsworth Studies. Ed. Wordsworth and Darlington (see below). 1–13.
The Five-Book Prelude. Ed. Duncan Wu. London, 1997.
Gill, Stephen. "Wordsworth's Poems: The Question of Text." Review of English Studies n.s. 34 (1983): 172–90. Rev. in Romantic Revisions. Ed. Robert Brinkley and Keith Hanley. Cambridge, 1992. 43–63.
Leader, Zachary. "Wordsworth, Revision, and Personal Identity." ELH 60 (1993): 651–83. Reprinted in Leader's Revision and Romantic Authorship. Oxford, 1996. 21–77.
The Letters of William and Dorothy Wordsworth. Revised edition. Ed. Chester L. Shaver, Mary Moorman, and Alan G. Hill. 8 vols. Oxford, 1967–93.
The Love Letters of William and Mary Wordsworth. Ed. Beth Darlington. Ithaca, N.Y., 1981.
Lyrical Ballads: An Electronic Scholarly Edition. Ed. Bruce Graver and Ron Tetreault. 2003. Hosted on the Romantic Circles website. An online edition with photographic reproductions and edited texts of the 1798, 1800, 1802, and 1805 editions of LB, permitting simultaneous comparison of different versions of the texts.
Owen, W. J. B. "Costs, Sales, and Profits of Longman's Editions of Wordsworth." The Library 5th ser. 4 (1957): 93–107.
Parrish, Stephen. "The Editor as Archeologist." Kentucky Review 4 (1983): 3–14.
———. "Foreword." In The Salisbury Plain Poems. Ed. Stephen Gill. Ithaca, NY, 1975. ix–xiii. A brief statement of the editorial principles of The Cornell Wordsworth.
———. "The Whig Interpretation of Literature." Text 4 (1988): 343–50.
———. "The Worst of Wordsworth." The Wordsworth Circle 7 (1976): 89–91.
The Poetical Works of William Wordsworth. Ed. Ernest de Selincourt and Helen Darbishire. 5 vols. Oxford, 1940–49. Revised edition, 1952–59.
The Prelude [1805 and 1850]. Ed. Ernest de Selincourt, rev. Helen Darbishire. Oxford, 1959.
The Prelude, 1799, 1805, 1850. Ed. Jonathan Wordsworth, M. H. Abrams, and Stephen Gill. Norton Critical Edition; New York, 1979.
The Prelude: The Four Texts (1798, 1799, 1805, 1850). Ed. Jonathan Wordsworth. Harmondsworth, 1995.
The Prose Works of William Wordsworth. Ed. W. J. B. Owen and Jane Worthington Smyser. 3 vols. Oxford, 1974. The standard edition, with variant readings and commentary.
Reed, Mark. "The First Title Page of Lyrical Ballads, 1798." Studies in Bibliography 51 (1998): 230–40.
Reiman, Donald. "The Cornell Wordsworth and the Norton Prelude." In Romantic Texts and Contexts. Columbia, MO, 1987. 130–55.
Stillinger, Jack. "Textual Primitivism and the Editing of Wordsworth." Studies in Romanticism 28 (1989): 3–28.
Wordsworth, Jonathan. "The Five-Book Prelude of Early Spring 1804." Journal of English and Germanic Philology 76 (1977): 1–25.
———. "Revision as Making: The Prelude and Its Peers." In Romantic Revisions. Ed. Robert Brinkley and Keith Hanley. Cambridge, 1992. 103–35.

————, and Stephen Gill. "The Two-Part Prelude of 1798–99." *Journal of English and Germanic Philology* 72 (1973): 503–25.
Wu, Duncan. "Editing Intentions." *Essays in Criticism* 41 (1991): 1–10.

Bibliographies and Reference Works

Cooper, Lane. *A Concordance to the Poems of William Wordsworth.* London, 1911. Reprinted New York, 1965; Temecula, CA, 1992.
Hanley, Keith. *An Annotated Critical Bibliography of William Wordsworth.* Hemel Hemstead, 1995. Primary and secondary sources.
————. "William Wordsworth." In *The Cambridge Bibliography of English Literature.* Ed. Joanne Shattock. 3rd ed. Vol. 4. Cambridge, 1999. 492–510. A comprehensive listing of primary sources and very selective listing of secondary sources.
Healey, George Harris. *The Cornell Wordsworth Collection: A Catalogue of Books and Manuscripts.* Ithaca, NY, 1957.
Jones, Mark, and Karl Kroeber. *Wordsworth Scholarship and Criticism, 1973–1984: An Annotated Bibliography, with Selected Criticism, 1809–1972.* New York, 1985.
Kroeber, Karl. "William Wordsworth." In *The English Romantic Poets: A Review of Research and Criticism.* Ed. Frank Jordan. 4th ed. New York, 1985. 255–339. A survey of criticism up to about 1982.
McCracken, David. *Wordsworth and the Lake District: A Guide to the Poems and Their Places.* Oxford, 1984.
McFahern, Patricia, and Thomas Beckwith. *A Complete Concordance to the "Lyrical Ballads" of Samuel Taylor Coleridge and William Wordsworth, 1798 and 1800 Editions.* New York, 1987.
Pinion, F. B. *A Wordsworth Chronology.* Basingstoke, 1988.
Reed, Mark L. *A Bibliography of William Wordsworth 1787–1930.* 2 vols. Cambridge, MA, 2013.
————. *Wordsworth: The Chronology of the Early Years, 1770–1799.* Cambridge, MA, 1967. Includes details of the composition of poems.
————. *Wordsworth: The Chronology of the Middle Years, 1800–1815.* Cambridge, MA, 1975. Includes a chronological list of compositions and publications.
Roe, Nicholas. "William Wordsworth" In *Literature of the Romantic Period.* Ed. Michael O'Neill. Oxford, 1998. 45–64. A survey of criticism up to the mid-1990s.
Shaver, Chester L., and Alice C. Shaver. *Wordsworth's Library: A Catalogue.* New York, 1979.
Wu, Duncan. *Wordsworth's Reading, 1770–1799.* Cambridge, 1993. An alphabetical list of books and periodicals Wordsworth read or is likely to have read up to 1799.
————. *Wordsworth's Reading, 1800–1815.* Cambridge, 1995.

Biographical Works

Barker, Juliet. *William Wordsworth: A Life.* Oxford, 2000.
De Quincey, Thomas. "Lake Reminiscences, from 1807 to 1830 [nos. 1–5]." *The Works of Thomas De Quincey.* Ed. Julian North. Vol. 11. London, 2003. 40–140. A series of indiscreet portraits of the Wordsworths, originally published in *Tait's* in 1839 and republished by De Quincey (with numerous omissions) in 1854.
Gill, Stephen. *William Wordsworth: A Life.* Oxford, 1989.
Hayden, Donald. *Wordsworth's Travels in Scotland.* Tulsa, OK, 1985.
————. *Wordsworth's Walking Tour of 1790.* Tulsa, OK, 1983.
Johnston, Kenneth. *The Hidden Wordsworth: Poet, Lover, Rebel, Spy.* New York, 1998.
Moorman, Mary. *Wordsworth, A Biography: The Early Years, 1770–1803.* Oxford, 1957.
————. *Wordsworth, A Biography: The Later Years, 1803–1850.* Oxford, 1965.
Mullan, John, Chris Hart, and Peter Swaab, eds. *Lives of the Great Romantics I: Shelley, Byron and Wordsworth by Their Contemporaries.* Vol. 3. London, 1996. Reprints of reminiscences by contemporaries.
Newlyn, Lucy. *William and Dorothy Wordsworth.* Oxford, 2013.
Robinson, Henry Crabb. *The Correspondence of Henry Crabb Robinson with the Wordsworth Circle.* Ed. Edith J. Morley. 2 vols. Oxford, 1927.
————. *On Books and Their Writers.* Ed. Edith J. Morley. 3 vols. London, 1938.
Schneider, Ben Ross, Jr. *Wordsworth's Cambridge Education.* Cambridge, 1957.

Sisman, Adam. *The Friendship: Wordsworth and Coleridge*. London, 2006.
Thompson, T. W. *Wordsworth's Hawkshead*. Ed. Robert Woof. London, 1970.
Wordsworth, Christopher. *Memoirs of William Wordsworth*. 2 vols. London, 1851. The earliest biography, by the poet's nephew.
Wordsworth, Dorothy. *The Grasmere Journals*. Ed. Pamela Woof. Oxford, 1991.
———. *The Journals of Dorothy Wordsworth*. Ed. Ernest de Selincourt. 2 vols. London, 1941.
———. *Journals of Dorothy Wordsworth: The Alfoxden Journal 1798 [and] The Grasmere Journals 1800–1803*. Ed. Mary Moorman. 2nd ed. London, 1971.
Wordsworth, Mary. *The Letters of Mary Wordsworth*. Ed. Mary Burton. Oxford, 1958.
Wu, Duncan. *Wordsworth: An Inner Life*. Oxford, 2001.

Criticism

Collections of Essays

Gill, Stephen, ed. *The Cambridge Companion to Wordsworth*. Cambridge, 2003. Introductory essays on various aspects of Wordsworth's work, with an annotated guide to further reading.
———, ed. *"The Prelude": A Casebook*. Oxford, 2006.
Gravil, Richard, and Daniel Robinson, eds.. *The Oxford Handbook of William Wordsworth*. Oxford, 2014.
Johnston, Kenneth, and Gene Ruoff, eds. *The Age of William Wordsworth: Critical Essays on the Romantic Tradition*. New Brunswick, NJ, 1987.
Jones, Alun, ed. *Wordsworth: The 1807 Poems*. Houndmills, 1990.
Pace, Joel, and Matthew Scott, eds. *Wordsworth in American Literary Culture*. Basingstoke, 2005.
Reiman, Donald, ed. *The Romantics Reviewed, Part A: The Lake Poets*. 2 vols. New York, 1972. Reprints of reviews by Wordsworth's contemporaries.
Trott, Nicola, and Seamus Perry, eds. *1800: The New "Lyrical Ballads."* Basingstoke, 2001. Essays focused on the second edition of *Lyrical Ballads*.
Woof, Robert, ed. *William Wordsworth: The Critical Heritage*. Vol. 1 [all published]. London, 2001. Criticism of various kinds (in reviews, letters, journals, etc.) from 1793 to 1820.
Wordsworth, Jonathan, and Beth Darlington, eds. *Bicentenary Wordsworth Studies in Memory of John Alban Finch*. Ithaca, N.Y., 1970.

General Studies

• Abrams, M. H. *Natural Supernaturalism: Tradition and Revolution in Romantic Literature*. New York, 1971.
———. "Wordsworth and Coleridge on Diction and Figures." In *The Correspondent Breeze: Essays on English Romanticism*. New York, 1984. 3–24.
Averill, James. "Wordsworth and Natural Science." *Journal of English and Germanic Philology* 77 (1978): 232–46.
Bate, Jonathan. *Romantic Ecology: Wordsworth and the Environmental Tradition*. London, 1991.
Beer, John. *Wordsworth and the Human Heart*. London, 1977.
———. *Wordsworth in Time*. London, 1978.
Bewell, Alan. *Wordsworth and the Enlightenment: Nature, Man, and Society in the Experimental Poetry*. New Haven, 1989.
Bloom, Harold. "William Wordsworth." In *The Visionary Company: A Reading of English Romantic Poetry*. 2nd ed. Ithaca, NY, 1971. 120–93.
Brown, Marshall. "Wordsworth's Old Gray Stone." In *Preromanticism*. Stanford, 1991. 301–61.
Chandler, James. *Wordsworth's Second Nature: A Study of the Poetry and Politics*. Chicago, 1984.
Clancey, Richard. *Wordsworth's Classical Undersong: Education, Rhetoric, and Poetic Truth*. Basingstoke, 2000.
Collings, David. *Wordsworthian Errancies: The Poetics of Cultural Dismemberment*. Baltimore, 1994.
• Curran, Stuart. *Poetic Form and British Romanticism*. New York, 1988.

Eilenberg, Susan. *Strange Power of Speech: Wordsworth, Coleridge, and Literary Posses-sion.* Oxford, 1992.

Engell, James. "Wordsworth." In *The Creative Imagination: Enlightenment to Roman-ticism.* Cambridge, MA, 1981. 265–76.

Ferguson, Frances. *Wordsworth: Language as Counter-Spirit.* New Haven, 1977.

Fry, Paul. *Wordsworth and the Poetry of What We Are.* New Haven, 2008.

Fulford, Tim. "Wordsworth: The Politics of Landscape." In *Landscape, Liberty and Authority: Poetry, Criticism and Politics from Thomson to Wordsworth.* Cambridge, 1996. 157–213.

Galperin, William. *Revision and Authority in Wordsworth: The Interpretation of a Career.* Philadelphia, 1989.

Gill, Stephen. *Wordsworth and the Victorians.* Oxford, 1998.

———. *Wordsworth's Revisitings.* Oxford, 2011.

Gravil, Richard. *Wordsworth's Bardic Vocation, 1787–1842.* Basingstoke, 2003.

Griffin, Robert. *Wordsworth's Pope.* Cambridge, 1995.

Hamilton, Ross. "'The Science of Feelings': Wordsworth's Experimental Poetry." In Charles Mahoney, ed. *A Companion to Romantic Poetry.* Chichester, 2011. 393–411.

• Hartman, Geoffrey. *Wordsworth's Poetry, 1787–1814.* New Haven, 1964.

———. *The Unremarkable Wordsworth.* London, 1987.

Jarvis, Robin. *Wordsworth, Milton, and the Theory of Poetic Relations.* Basingstoke, 1991.

• Jarvis, Simon. *Wordsworth's Philosophic Song.* Cambridge, 2007.

Kelley, Theresa. *Wordsworth's Revisionary Aesthetics.* Cambridge, 1988.

Langan, Celeste. *Romantic Vagrancy: Wordsworth and the Simulation of Freedom.* Cambridge, 1995.

Liu, Alan. *Wordsworth: The Sense of History.* Stanford, 1989.

McFarland, Thomas. *Romanticism and the Forms of Ruin: Wordsworth, Coleridge, and Modalities of Fragmentation.* Princeton, 1981.

———. *William Wordsworth: Intensity and Achievement.* Oxford, 1992.

• McKusick, James. "Wordsworth's Home at Grasmere." In *Green Writing: Romanticism and Ecology.* Basingstoke, 2000. 53–76.

Modiano, Raimonda. "Coleridge and Wordsworth: The Ethics of Gift Exchange and Literary Ownership." *The Wordsworth Circle* 20 (1989): 113–20.

Newlyn, Lucy. *Coleridge, Wordsworth, and the Language of Allusion.* Oxford, 1986.

———. *"Paradise Lost" and the Romantic Reader.* Oxford, 1994.

• ———. *Reading, Writing, and Romanticism: The Anxiety of Reception.* Oxford, 2001.

Owen, W. J. B. *Wordsworth as Critic.* Oxford, 1969.

Page, Judith. *Wordsworth and the Cultivation of Women.* Berkeley, 1994.

Perkins, David. *Wordsworth and the Poetry of Sincerity.* Cambridge, MA, 1964.

Pfau, Thomas. *Wordsworth's Profession: Form, Class, and the Logic of Early Romantic Cultural Production.* Stanford, 1997.

Piper, H. W. *The Active Universe: Pantheism and the Concept of Imagination in the English Romantic Poets.* London, 1962.

Plotz, Judith. "More Clouds than Glories: Wordsworth and the Sequestered Child." In *Romanticism and the Vocation of Childhood.* Basingstoke, 2011. 41–86.

Potkay, Adam. "The Joys of Doing and of Being: Wordsworth and His Victorian Legacy." *The Story of Joy: From the Bible to Late Romanticism.* Cambridge, 2007. 121–38.

———. *Wordsworth's Ethics.* Baltimore, 2012.

Rader, Melvin. *Wordsworth: A Philosophical Approach.* Oxford, 1967.

• Roe, Nicholas. *Wordsworth and Coleridge: The Radical Years.* Oxford, 1988.

———. *The Politics of Nature: Wordsworth and Some Contemporaries.* London, 1992.

Rzepka, Charles. *The Self as Mind: Vision and Identity in Wordsworth, Coleridge, and Keats.* Cambridge, MA, 1986.

Sheats, Paul. *The Making of Wordsworth's Poetry, 1785–1798.* Cambridge, MA, 1973.

Simpson, David. *Wordsworth and the Figurings of the Real.* London, 1982.

———. *Wordsworth, Commodification and Social Concern: The Poetics of Modernity.* Cambridge, 2009.

———. *Wordsworth's Historical Imagination: The Poetry of Displacement.* London, 1987.

Stafford, Fiona. "Lakes or Oceans?" In *Local Attachments: The Province of Poetry.* Oxford, 2010. 65–95.

Stein, Edward. *Wordsworth's Art of Allusion.* University Park, PA, 1988.

Weiskel, Thomas. *The Romantic Sublime: Studies in the Structure and Psychology of Transcendence.* Baltimore, 1976.

Wiley, Michael. *Romantic Geography: Wordsworth and Anglo-European Spaces.* Houndmills, 1998.

Wlecke, Albert. *Wordsworth and the Sublime: An Essay on Romantic Self-Consciousness.* Berkeley, 1973.

Wolfson, Susan. *The Questioning Presence: Wordsworth, Keats, and the Interrogative Mode.* Ithaca, NY, 1986.

• ———. "Wordsworth's Craft." In *The Cambridge Companion to William Wordsworth.* Cambridge, 2003. 108–24.

Woodring, Carl. *Politics in English Romantic Poetry.* Cambridge, MA, 1970.

Wordsworth, Jonathan. *William Wordsworth: The Borders of Vision.* Oxford, 1982.

Wyatt, John. *Wordsworth and the Geologists.* Cambridge, 1995.

Studies of Particular Collections or Poems

Aarslef, Hans. "Wordsworth, Language, and Romanticism." *Essays in Criticism* 30 (1980): 215–26.

Abrams, M. H. "Structure and Style in the Greater Romantic Lyric." In *The Correspondent Breeze: Essays on English Romanticism.* New York, 1984. 76–108.

———. "Two Roads to Wordsworth." In *The Correspondent Breeze,* 145–57.

Barron, Jonathan, and Kenneth Johnston. "'A Power to Virtue Friendly': The Pedlar's Guilt in *The Ruined Cottage.*" In *Romantic Revisions.* Ed. Robert Brinkely and Keith Hanley. Cambridge, 1992. 64–86.

Bialostosky, D. H. *Making Tales: The Poetics of Wordsworth's Narrative Experiments.* Chicago, 1984.

Bromwich, David. *Disowned by Memory: Wordsworth's Poetry of the 1790s.* Chicago, 1998.

• Cooper, Andrew M. "Nothing Exists but as It Is Perceived." In *Doubt and Identity in Romantic Poetry.* New Haven, 1988. 150–64.

Curran, Stuart. "Multum in Parvo: Wordsworth's *Poems of 1807.*" In *Poems in Their Place: The Intertextuality and Order of Poetic Collections.* Ed. Neil Fraistat. Chapel Hill, NC, 1986. 234–53.

Curtis, Jared. *Wordsworth's Experiments with Tradition: The Lyric Poems of 1802.* Ithaca, NY, 1971.

Duff, David. "Paratextual Dilemmas: Wordsworth's 'The Brothers' and the Problem of Generic Labelling." *Romanticism* 6 (2000): 234–61.

• Fraistat, Neil. "The 'Field' of *Lyrical Ballads.*" In *The Poem and the Book: Interpreting Collections of Romantic Poetry.* Chapel Hill, NC, 1985. 47–94.

Fry, Paul. "Wordsworth's Severe Intimations." In *The Poet's Calling in the English Ode.* New Haven, 1980. 133–61.

Gamer, Michael. "Producing *Lyrical Ballads* 1798 and 1800." In *Romanticism and the Gothic.* Cambridge, 2000. 90–126.

Gill, Stephen. "Wordsworth and *The River Duddon.*" *Essays in Criticism* 57 (2007): 22–41.

Graver, Bruce. "Wordsworth's Georgic Pastoral." *European Romantic Review* 1 (1991): 119–34.

Gravil, Richard. "*Tintern Abbey* and The System of Nature." *Romanticism* 6 (2000): 35–54.

• Jacobus, Mary. *Tradition and Experiment in Wordsworth's "Lyrical Ballads" (1798).* Oxford, 1976.

Johnson, Lee. *Wordsworth and the Sonnet.* Copenhagen, 1973.

Johnston, Kenneth. *Wordsworth and "The Recluse."* New Haven, 1984.

• Jones, Mark. *The Lucy Poems: A Case Study in Literary Knowledge.* Toronto, 1988.

• Knapp, Steven. "Quasi-Personification in the Intimations Ode." In *Personification and the Sublime: Milton to Coleridge.* Cambridge, MA, 1985. 98–106.

Kroeber, Karl. "Wordsworth: The Personal Epic." In *Romantic Narrative Art.* Madison, 1960. 78–112.

Langbaum, Robert. "Wordsworth's Lyrical Characterizations." *Studies in Romanticism* 21 (1982): 319–39.

Levinson, Marjorie. *Wordsworth's Great Period Poems: Four Essays.* Cambridge, 1986.

McFarland, Thomas. "Wordsworth on Man, of Nature, and on Human Life." *Studies in Romanticism* 21 (1982): 601–18.

———. "Wordsworth's Best Philosopher." *The Wordsworth Circle* 13 (1982): 59–68.

McGann, Jerome. "Wordsworth and the Ideology of Romantic Poems." *The Romantic Ideology: A Critical Investigation.* Chicago, 1983. 81–92.

Magnuson, Paul. *Coleridge and Wordsworth: A Lyrical Dialogue.* Princeton, 1988.

Manning, Peter. *Reading Romantics: Text and Context.* New York, 1990.
Marsh, Florence. "Wordsworth's *Ode*: Obstinate Questionings." *Studies in Romanticism* 5 (1966): 219–30.
Mayo, Robert. "The Contemporaneity of the Lyrical Ballads." *PMLA* 69 (1954): 486–522.
• O'Neill, Michael. "Wordsworth." In *Romanticism and the Self-Conscious Poem.* Oxford, 1997. 25–61.
Parrish, Stephen Maxfield. "*Michael* and the Pastoral Ballad." In *Bicentenary Wordsworth Studies.* Ed. Wordsworth and Darlington (see above). 50–75.
———. *The Art of "Lyrical Ballads."* Cambridge, MA, 1973.
Patterson, Annibel. "Wordsworth's Georgic: Genre and Structure in *The Excursion.*" *The Wordsworth Circle* 9 (1978): 75–82.
• Pfau, Thomas. "'Long before the time of which I speak': Traumatic History and Lyric Awakenings." In *Romantic Moods: Paranoia, Trauma, Melancholy, 1790–1840.* Baltimore, 2005. 192–201.
Ross, Marlon. "Naturalizing Gender: Women's Place in Wordsworth's Ideological Landscape." *ELH* 53 (1986): 391–410.
Ruoff, Gene. *Wordsworth and Coleridge: The Making of the Major Lyrics, 1802–1804.* New Brunswick, NJ, 1989.
Rzepka, Charles. "Pictures of the Mind: Iron and Charcoal, 'Ouzy' Tides and 'Vagrant Dwellers' at Tintern, 1798." *Studies in Romanticism* 42 (2003): 155–85.
Sharp, Michele Turner. "Re-Membering the Real, Dis(re)membering the Dead: Wordsworth's 'Essays upon Epitaphs.'" *Studies in Romanticism* 34 (1995): 273–92.
Sharrock, Roger. "The Chemist and the Poet: Sir Humphry Davy and the Preface to *Lyrical Ballads.*" *Notes and Records of the Royal Society of London* 17 (1962): 57–76.
Stafford, Fiona. "Plain Living and Ungarnish'd Stories: Wordsworth and the Survival of Pastoral." *Review of English Studies* n.s. 59 (2007): 118–33.
• Swann, Karen. "Suffering and Sensation in *The Ruined Cottage.*" *PMLA* 106 (1991): 83–95.
Taylor, Anya. "Religions Reading of the Immortality Ode." *Studies in English Literature* 26 (1986): 633–54.
Trilling, Lionel. "Wordsworth's 'Ode: Intimations of Immortality." *English Institute Annual 1941* (1942): 1–28. Reprinted in Trilling's *The Liberal Imagination.* New York, 1950. 125–54.
Vendler, Helen. "Lionel Trilling and the Immortality Ode." *Salmagundi* 41 (1978): 66–86.
Wordsworth, Jonathan. *The Music of Humanity: A Critical Study of Wordsworth's "Ruined Cottage."* London, 1969.

Studies of The Prelude

Abrams, M. H. "*The Prelude* as a Portrait of the Artist." In *Bicentenary Wordsworth Studies.* Ed. Wordsworth and Darlington. (see above). 180–237.
Arac, Jonathan. "Bounding Lines: *The Prelude* and Critical Revision." *Boundary 2* 7.3 (1979): 31–48.
Bahti, Timothy. "Figures of Interpretation, the Interpretation of Figures: A Reading of Wordsworth's 'Dream of the Arab' [in book 5]." *Studies in Romanticism* 18 (1979): 601–27.
Bishop, Jonathan. "Wordsworth and the Spots of Time." *ELH* 26 (1959): 45–65.
Boyd, David. "Wordsworth as Satirist: Book VII of *The Prelude.*" *Studies in English Literature* 13 (1973): 617–31.
Chase, Cynthia. "Accidents of Disfiguration." In *Decomposing Figures: Rhetorical Readings in the Romantic Tradition.* Baltimore, 1986, 13–32.
• de Man, Paul. "Wordsworth and Hölderlin," In *The Rhetoric of Romanticism.* New York, 1984. 47–65.
Erskine-Hill, Howard. *Poetry of Opposition and Revolution: Dryden to Wordsworth.* Oxford, 1996.
Gill, Stephen. *William Wordsworth: "The Prelude."* Cambridge, 1991.
Jacobus, Mary. *Romanticism, Writing and Sexual Difference: Essays on "The Prelude."* Oxford, 1989.
Lindenberger, Herbert. *On Wordsworth's "Prelude."* Princeton, 1963.
• Liu, Alan. "Wordsworth: The History in 'Imagination.'" *ELH* 51 (1984): 505–48.
McConnell, Frank. *The Confessional Imagination: A Reading of Wordsworth's "Prelude."* Baltimore, 1974.

Mellor, Anne K. "Writing the Self/Self Writing: William Wordsworth's *Prelude* / Dorothy Wordsworth's *Journals*." In *Romanticism and Gender*. New York, 1993. 145–70.

Miller, J. Hillis. "The Stone and the Shell: The Problem of Poetic Form in Wordsworth's Dream of the Arab." In *Mouvements premiers: Études critiques offertes à Georges Poulet*. Paris, 1972. 125–47.

Onorato, Richard. *The Character of the Poet: Wordsworth in "The Prelude."* Princeton, 1971.

Reiman, Donald. "The Beauty of Buttermere as Fact and Romantic Symbol." In *Romantic Texts and Contexts*. Columbia, MO, 1987. 216–47.

Index of Poem Titles and First Lines

Titles (italic) supplied by the editor from first lines are given in brackets. First lines (including those used as titles) are alphabetized by their first word, even if it is an article.